MW00379021

1001 MIDNIGHTS

1001 MIDNIGHTS

The Aficionado's Guide to Mystery and Detective Fiction

by BILL PRONZINI and MARCIA MULLER

Arbor House
New York

Published in the United States of America by Arbor House Publishing Company and in Canada by Fitzhenry & Whiteside Ltd.

Manufactured in the United States of America

10 9 8 7 6 5 4 3 2 1

Library of Congress Cataloging in Publication Data

Pronzini, Bill.
1001 midnights.

Bibliography: p.
1. Detective and mystery stories—Book reviews.
I. Muller, Marcia. II. Title. III. Title: One thousand and one midnights.
PN3448.D4P76 1986 809.3'872 85-30817
ISBN: 0-87795-622-7

ACKNOWLEDGMENTS

The editors would like to offer their thanks to the contributors who helped make 1001 Midnights *a reality; and to Bruce Taylor of the San Francisco Mystery Bookstore for his generous assistance.*

CONTENTS

1001 MIDNIGHTS

INTRODUCTION

1001 Midnights is a labor of love.

We are not only writers of crime fiction, but aficionados, collectors, and students of this form of popular literature; and as such, it occurred to us that a book of in-depth reviews of various detective, suspense, and espionage novels and short-story collections would make a valuable addition to the growing body of reference works on the genre. Only one other book of this sort exists—*A Catalogue of Crime* by Jacques Barzun and Wendell Hertig Taylor, published in 1971—but that volume is much different in concept and intent, and does not offer, as this one does, extensive plot synopses or as comprehensive a cross section of criminous story types.

The purpose of *1001 Midnights* is to provide other aficionados, students, and collectors, as well as casual and new readers, with a reference guide to one thousand and one individual titles; to additional works by their authors; and to books of a similar type (whodunit, thriller, police procedural, etc.) by other writers. Every major author in the field, beginning with Edgar Allan Poe, and every major work up to and including books published in 1985, are covered in these pages. Thus, *1001 Midnights* also offers a broad overview of the genre, from its origins to the present, that is informative to those familiar with the genre and to those coming to it for the first time.

Each review gives some general commentary on the author's body of work and how the particular title relates to it. In the case of writers who have a large and diverse canon, we have included at least one title featuring each different story type and/or series character. In addition to critical evaluation, each review contains a brief plot synopsis (*without giving away major plot points or endings*), unusual information pertaining to the work or the author, and a short list of other noteworthy and representative titles. Owing to space limitations, publication data is confined to the first American edition (or British if no U.S. edition exists), with the exception of those instances where the book has been reissued under a different title; the reader may wish to consult other reference works to determine if any edition is currently in print. (A bibliography of references we ourselves have used can be found in the Appendix.) Some of the books reviewed are long out of print, of course, but the interested reader can, with a little diligent effort, find copies in libraries and secondhand bookshops, or through one of the many mail-order dealers who specialize in crime fiction.

All reviewed titles have been broadly classified as to type by letter code, for easy reference. In addition, certain books have been provided with one or two asterisks, for the reasons defined below.

A	Action and Adventure
AD	Amateur Detective
C	Comedy
CS	Classic Sleuth
E	Espionage
H	Historical
O	Paperback Original
PI	Private Eye
PP	Police Procedural
PS	Psychological Suspense
R	Romantic Suspense
SS	Short Story Collection
T	Thriller
W	Whodunit
*	Titles that are especially good or interesting, or that represent a particularly notable series or body of work
**	Cornerstone work in the field

In some cases, multiple coding has been necessary. For example, a paperback original that features an amateur detective and is also humorous would be designated thus: (O/AD/C).

Because of the scope of this guide and our own limitations and personal prejudices, we did not review every single one of the 1001 entries ourselves. In the interest of fairness, we asked other writers and aficionados who are particularly knowledgeable about certain authors and/or types of books to contribute their expertise, thus resulting in reviews that are more informed than they would have been if we had done them entirely ourselves, and the data on particular authors and their work is considerably more detailed. It should be noted that because the mystery community is a small and close-knit one, we and other contributors have, inevitably, reviewed works of friends and acquaintances (and in our case, each other's books). But at all times each of us has made every effort to be impartial; if anything, we feel we have been more exacting with the work of those we know personally.

Each entry is signed with the reviewer's initials, including those written by the two of us. In those cases where we as editors have added significant amounts of information to an entry, or other contributors have added significant amounts, two sets of initials appear. The list of contributors is as follows (biographical data on each is available in the Appendix):

T.B.	Thomas Baird
R.E.B.	Robert E. Briney
M.A.C.	Max Allan Collins
B.C.	Bill Crider
N.D.	Newell Dunlap
S.D.	Susan Dunlap
B.F.	Betty Francis
E.G.	Ed Gorman
E.D.H.	Edward D. Hoch
K.K.H.	Karol Kay Hope
M.J.	Mark Johnson
G.K.	George Kelley
M.L.	Marvin Lachman
J.L.	John Lutz
K.L.M.	Kathleen L. Maio
B.N.M.	Barry N. Malzberg
K.M.	Kate Mattes
E.N.	Ellen Nehr
F.M.N.	Francis M. Nevins
R.J.R.	Robert J. Randisi
A.S.	Art Scott
C.S.	Charles Shibuk
J.S.	Julie Smith
T.S.	Toni Symons
B.T.	Bruce Taylor
J.L.T.	James L. Traylor

Even with such an impressive list of contributors to aid in the decision-making process, the sheer volume of criminous novels and collections published over the past 140 years made the question of which books and authors to review a difficult one. We have attempted to include at least one work by every author past and present who has made any sort of impact on the field, as well as books by promising newcomers. In the case of major authors, several entries have been included. Individual titles were selected for many reasons: that they possess outstanding plots, unusual backgrounds, interesting characters; that they are of historical importance; that they were the bases for well-known films or television shows; that they have languished in undeserved obscurity, or, on the other hand, that they have received what we feel is unwarranted attention; or simply that they might be of interest to contemporary readers.

Because *1001 Midnights* is intended as a celebration of the genre, all but a small percentage of the reviews are favorable in nature. Those that are not stress a book's positive points as well as its negative ones. (The converse is also true: Negative aspects of good novels are also mentioned.) Unfavorably reviewed books have been included because they are by important, popular, or collectable authors, or because they have historical significance, or because they are so hilariously bad that they are worth reading as entertaining "alternative classics."

The two of us, along with our contributors, have exhaustively checked the accuracy of all facts, references, and pertinent dates. However, it is inevitable that in a volume of this size and scope a few (we hope *very* few) minor errors will have slipped by undetected. We beg your indulgence in advance for these—and would in fact be grateful if, should you spot one, you would let us know about it so that it may be corrected in future editions.

If *1001 Midnights* gives you the impetus to seek out and read just one of the titles reviewed herein, we will be pleased. And if it introduces you to many new writers, many new books, then *you* will have made this labor of love a rousing success.

—*Bill Pronzini and Marcia Muller*

San Francisco, California
February 1985

Mystery and Detective Writers A to Z

Aarons, Edward S. *Assignment—Angelina.* Greenwich, Conn.: Fawcett Gold Medal, 1958. (O/E)

Like many writers from the period 1920–50, Edward S. Aarons began his career in the pulp magazines. He also wrote three mystery novels in the late Thirties, and several more in the late Forties. But it wasn't until the paperback-original boom of the early 1950s that he achieved major success and recognition, with his "Assignment" series of espionage novels featuring the action-packed adventures of CIA agent Sam Durrell.

Along with exotic locales across the globe, violence is the main ingredient of the Durrell series; a great deal of blood is spilled in a great many different ways, both by Durrell and the various villains he encounters. *Assignment—Angelina* is typical. It begins (rather irresistibly) with the cold-blooded murders of four men in four different sections of the country: a filling-station owner in Arizona, a building contractor in Indiana, an advertising copywriter in New York, and a fisherman in Louisiana. We know from the first who is responsible—a trio named Mark, Corbin, and Slago—but we don't know why. Durrell's search for the answer leads him to a beautiful woman named Angelina, who may or may not be an ally, and into the usual muddle of James Bondian political intrigue. It also leads him from Washington to the bayous of Louisiana (where Durrell is right at home; he is part Cajun) to New York City and ultimately to a mountaintop in the rugged Poconos where the slam-bang finale takes place.

Despite all the violence and melodrama, this and other Durrell novels are compulsive reading. Aarons was an accomplished writer, with excellent descriptive abilities (particularly in depicting the various locales of his stories) and an expert sense of narrative pacing.

A total of forty Sam Durrell books were produced by Aarons from 1955 to 1975, among the more noteworthy of which are *Assignment to Disaster* (1955), *Assignment—Stella Marni* (1957), *Assignment—School for Spies* (1966), and *Assignment—Sumatra* (1974). After his death in 1975, a number of additional Durrell novels appeared by Will B. Aarons, said to be his son. Two of Aarons's nonseries books, *Escape to Love* (1952) and *Girl on the Run* (1954), are good examples of the paperback-original suspense novels of the early 1950s. A 1948 hardcover, *Nightmare,* is notable for its high level of tension and drama. Aarons also published numerous novels under the pseudonym of Edward Ronns, among them *Terror in the Town* (1947), *Gift of Death* (1948), and *Catspaw Ordeal* (1950); most of these were later reprinted in paperback under his own name.

(*B.P.*)

Abbot, Anthony. *About the Murder of the Clergyman's Mistress.* New York: Covici Friede, 1931. (CS)

Fulton Oursler is best remembered as a magazine editor, for *Liberty* in the 1930s and *Reader's Digest* in the late Forties, and as the author of the religioso blockbuster *The Greatest Story Ever Told* (1949). But in younger days he also contributed to the mystery genre, using the by-line Anthony Abbot for eight detective novels starring New York City police commissioner Thatcher Colt.

The format of the first six is clearly borrowed from S. S. Van Dine's (q.v.) Philo Vance series. Each title falls into a rigid *About the Murder of* pattern; Colt is portrayed as a wealthy mandarin intellectual; his cases are narrated and signed by his faithful male secretary; his familiars include a stupid district attorney, a crusty medical examiner, and a dignified butler; the novels tend to begin with a body found under bizarre circumstances, with strange clues pointing to a host of suspects; the investigation is punctuated by conferences at which, in the spirit of Socratic debate, the detectives offer alternative reconstructions of the crime; and a second murder usually takes place about two-thirds of the way through the book. Like those of the young Ellery Queen, Abbot's variations on the Van Dine framework are better written and characterized and somewhat livelier than the Philo Vance books themselves, although Abbot unfortunately followed Van Dine in declining to play fair with the reader.

The second and perhaps best in the Thatcher Colt series was *About the Murder of the Clergyman's Mistress,* which like many Van Dine novels was based on a famous true crime. In this version of the Hall-Mills case of the 1920s, the bodies of a respected Episcopal minister and of a beautiful singer in his choir are found floating down the East River in a rowboat. Colt quickly takes over personal command of the investigation, with a huge assortment of peculiar clues—nine dumbbells, a bloody-pawed cat, a Chinese sumach leaf, a bag of dulse—implicating various members of the minister's and the singer's households. Staying in full control of a stupendously complex plot, Abbot also treats us to vivid glimpses of early-1930s New York and to a sardonic portrait of the WASP clergy.

Most of the Thatcher Colt novels are cut from the same pattern, including *About the Murder of Geraldine Foster* (1930), which launched the series; *About the Murder of the Circus Queen* (1932), with its background of a circus playing Madison Square Garden; and *About the Murder of a Startled Lady* (1935), with its intimations of the occult. The last two Anthony Abbot titles, *The Creeps* (1939) and *The Shudders* (1943), lack Van Dine elements and are believed to have been ghosted by another writer.

(*F.M.N.*)

Adams, Cleve F. *Shady Lady.* New York: Ace, 1955. (O/PI)

Adams is one of mystery fiction's shadow figures. Born in 1895, he began selling to pulp mystery magazines in the mid-1930s, broke into hardcover novels at the end of the decade, and wrote most of his novels in a burst of creativity (and of recycling earlier pulp tales) during World War II. In all these respects, his career paralleled that of Raymond Chandler (q.v.). But unlike Chandler, Adams is today largely forgotten, even though he forged his own distinctive image of the private detective.

The Adams eye is a sort of prose incarnation of Humphrey Bogart that predates Bogey's movie detectives, but with more stress on the brutality and cynicism and less on the sentimental heart. He has a capacity for long, brooding silences, sudden ribald laughter, mad fury, and aloof arrogance. His features are wolfish and satanic and he often slaps women around during his maniacal fits of rage. He's a racist, a fascist, and a hypocrite, but a tender ballad brings tears to his eyes. In one word, he's an oaf, deliberately drawn by Adams so as to pull the rug out from under Chandler's romantic image of the PI as a contemporary knight.

Most of Adams's novels depend on a stock company of recurring characters, mannerisms, scenes, plot elements, even tag lines of description and dialogue. He was an expert at borrowing story lines from Dashiell Hammett (q.v.), rewriting *Red Harvest* three times and *The Glass Key* twice. But even when he coasted on the most familiar gambits in hard-boiled literature, he showed a genius for juggling diverse groups of shady characters, each with his or her own greedy objective.

Right after Christmas 1949, Adams died of a heart attack. His pulp-writer buddies Robert Leslie Bellem and W. T. Ballard (qq.v.) helped out his widow by finishing his last novel. One version, entitled *Too Fair to Die,* appeared in the March 1951 issue of *Two Complete Detective Books* magazine, and four years later Ace Books published a more polished draft as the paperback original *Shady Lady.* It turned out to be the finest work of Adams's career.

Like many of his earlier novels, among the best of which are *Sabotage* (1940), *Decoy* (1941), and *Up Jumped the Devil* (1943), *Shady Lady* stars a shamus named Rex McBride. In this adventure he trails a missing embezzler's girlfriend from Los Angeles to the mining metropolis of Copper Hill, Montana, arriving just in time to become involved in a vicious gubernatorial primary, a love affair with two sisters, and a string of murders. The plot is plagued with loose ends like many Adams efforts, but the book is so overflowingly rich in character sketches and powerful understated scenes that one is compelled to believe either that Bellem and Ballard contributed huge amounts to the manuscript or that, had he lived longer, Adams might have developed into a talent of near-Chandleresque dimensions. The electoral contest provides a marvelous setting for Adams's ghoulish cynicism about American politics.

In his seminal essay "The Simple Art of Murder," Chandler argued that the PI novel requires a knightly hero to redeem the corrupt milieu. Adams disagreed violently, and in his world the protagonist is not a hero and no less corrupt than anyone else, just tougher and luckier. Repulsive the Adams eye may be, but he's frighteningly hard to forget.

(*F.M.N.*)

*Adams, Samuel Hopkins. *Average Jones.* Indianapolis: Bobbs-Merrill, 1911. (SS)

Samuel Hopkins Adams was a popular author during the first four decades of this century, mainly for his folksy (and noncriminous) "Grandfather Stories." *Average Jones* is one of his few mystery books—a collection of short stories about a different kind of sleuth; Ellery Queen included it on the Queen's Quorum list of the 106 most important books of short crime fiction published between 1845 and 1950.

Average Jones is just that, an average young man named Jones—average, that is, except for the fact that he has inherited some $10 million. Bored with his unproductive existence since leaving college, he decides to undertake a hobby that soon becomes a full-time profession: an advertising "Advisor" who specializes in ferreting out swindles and following up peculiar personal ads in the New York metropolitan area newspapers. His eleven cases include the attempted murder of a mayoral candidate by the unlikely combination of a trombone and an easy chair ("The B-Flat Trombone"); the location of the missing son of a medical quack and the masterful foiling of a lost-gold-mine swindle in the Mexican desert ("Open Trail"); and the enigma of a man who claims to have been born in Ancient Rome 2000 years ago ("The Man Who Spoke Latin").

Jones is an engaging and truly unusual detective, and his adventures are clever, suspenseful, amusing, and well plotted; they have lost none of their charm and readability over the past seventy-five years, despite changing standards in crime fiction.

Adams also wrote two interesting mystery novels, both featuring "impossible" crimes: *The Mystery* (1907), in collaboration with Stewart Edward White, which offers a possible solution to the "Mary Celeste" puzzle; and *The Flying Death* (1908), which deals with two murders apparently committed by a giant prehistoric bird.

(*B.P.*)

Adler, Warren. *Trans-Siberian Express.* New York: Putnam's, 1977. (E/A)

One of crime fiction's most popular subgenres is the tale of mystery and intrigue set on board a fast-moving train. For more than a century, authors from Poe to Christie to Warren Adler have perpetrated all sorts of mayhem on the world's railways—highballing freights and crack passenger specials in this country, the fabled Orient Express, and now the Trans-Siberian Express that spans two continents on its 6000-mile route across Russia to the Sea of Japan.

Dr. Alex Cousins, a Russian-speaking American cancer specialist, has been sent to Moscow on a secret mission by the president of the United States. The mission: to prolong for seven weeks (for unspecified reasons) the life of Viktor Dimitrov, secretary-general of the politburo, who is dying of leukemia. Cousins has done his duty, and now that he is ready to leave Russia, Dimitrov urges him to take the Trans-Siberian Express instead of flying—a "gift," Dimitrov says, the train being one of legendary Victorian grandeur and the scenery being magnificent. Cousins agrees, but with reservations that turn out to be more than warranted. First he meets and becomes romantically involved with Russian beauty Anna Petrovna; then he finds himself enmeshed in a politically motivated conspiracy, trapped on board the train with KGB agents watching his every move. His only chance for escape is to seek help from his fellow passengers, but at least some of them are not who they seem to be. . . .

This is a rousing novel of international intrigue and adventure, populated by sharply drawn characters; the Trans-Siberian Express, in fact, is so realistically depicted that it becomes a character in its own right. Adler's prose tends toward the undistinguished, but his evocation of the Russian scene and the scope and drama of his story more than make up for any deficiencies.

Warren Adler is the author of a number of other contemporary thrillers, among them *The Casanova Embrace* (1978) and *Natural Enemies* (1979). (*B.P.*)

Aird, Catherine. *A Most Contagious Game.* New York: Doubleday Crime Club, 1967. (AD)

Catherine Aird excels at portraying the English countryside's village life with all its petty prejudices, the gentry and near-gentry, and the castles and ruins that dot the landscape. Her series sleuth, Inspector C. S. Sloan, deals with them in the fond yet frustrated manner of a native. Sloan is competent yet low-key, a good foil for the oddities of the suspects. His associates, Superintendent Leeyes, who views each case from the perspective of whatever night-school course he is taking, and Constable Crosby, whose only skill is fast driving, are rather forced and the least believable characters in the series.

Aird's best work is outside the Sloan series. *A Most Contagious Game* gives us Thomas and Dora Harding, a couple portrayed with such fine strokes that they seem to have been taken whole from real life. At fifty-two, Thomas Harding has worked himself into a heart attack and subsequent retirement to an oddly restored Elizabethan country house. He is frustrated by the limitations his health imposes, and he is bored. Dora vacillates between encouraging his diversions and fearing he will bring another attack upon himself. The concerns of this couple and their interplay give the book a very solid base. But add to that Harding's diversion—in tracking down the peculiarities of the remodeling of his house, he finds a secret compartment, a priest's hole, and in it a 150-year-old skeleton. Another body, this time of a young woman, is found, and Harding's search for both killers leads him to the guilty secrets of villagers past and present.

Additional Aird titles are *The Stately Home Murder* (1970), *Parting Breath* (1977), *Passing Strange* (1981), and *Harm's Way* (1984), all of which feature Inspector Sloan. Aird has also written a play and several works of nonfiction.

(*S.D.*)

Albrand, Martha. *Manhattan North.* New York: Coward, McCann, 1971. (AD)

The cover of the paperback edition of this novel hails its author as "the mistress of romantic intrigue." This is a blatant case of mislabeling, probably in an effort to take advantage of the great popularity of Gothic suspense novels in the early Seventies; and fans of that genre who bought this novel on the basis of the cover line must have been sorely disappointed. Albrand's work is suspenseful, but in a realistic, contemporary fashion. She deals with political and other problems of current concern (and in *Manhattan North* she is a good bit ahead of the times, writing of subjects that are frankly controversial), and her settings and characters are reflective of the world as we know it. True, she generally incorporates a love interest in her stories, but this does not always end on a happily-ever-after note.

Manhattan North begins with the fatal stabbing of Supreme Court Justice Clark Jamison Butworth, who has been found in a snowbank in Central Park. The killing of Butworth, a close adviser to the president, prompts the formation of a committee to "investigate the effect of violence on the judiciary and terror as a measure of influencing judicial decisions." Tad Wood, a young liberal lawyer, is asked to organize it, and facts soon emerge that begin to disturb him: The police investigation into Butworth's death is being soft-pedaled, apparently on orders from the administration; there are irregularities about the death, such as the fact that Butworth was disguised in a wig and goatee at the time he was murdered. Tad digs deeper, makes the acquaintance of Butworth's daughter, and is on the scene to help her when she is attacked by a burglar. Or *was* it a simple case of burglary?

As Tad investigates, his personal life also plagues him. His godfather's daughter, Lindy, has been sent abroad quite suddenly, and he receives an urgent plea from her for help. A psychic he has consulted about the Butworth case turns up dead, an apparent suicide.

This is an engrossing novel that takes a hard look at some of the stickiest issues confronting contemporary society. Albrand's early work also concerned itself with current issues, such as her two novels of the wartime Dutch Underground, *No Surrender* (1942) and *Without Orders* (1943). A later novel, *A Call from Austria* (1963), takes up the theme of escaped Nazi war criminals, and *Zurich AZ/900* (1974) is a novel of international medical intrigue.

(*M.M.*)

Aldyne, Nathan. *Slate.* New York: Villard Books, 1984. (AD)

This is the third in a series of novels featuring gay bartender Dan Valentine and his straight friend Clarisse Lovelace. As the story opens, Dan is in the hospital recovering from a bout of double pneumonia; Clarisse is just starting law school. The two embark on a new venture at the urging of Clarisse's uncle Noah—co-ownership of a gay bar in Boston's South End. The building, originally owned by Noah, is across from the District D police station and houses an odd mixture of tenants—including a lesbian couple (one is a swimming pool repair specialist, the other a call girl) who are allowed to stay, and a family of sixteen Gypsies that Clarisse evicts single-handedly. Also present on the first floor next to the bar is Mr. Fred's Tease 'n' Tint hairstyling establishment.

As one might expect from such an odd starting lineup, events do not proceed smoothly. The bar and apartments above (where Clarisse and Dan propose to live) are a shambles. Fortunately, Dan's new lover, Linc, is a carpenter of some creativity; with any luck, the bar, to be named Slate, will open for New Year's.

Enter Sweeney Drysdale II, columnist for BAR (*Boston Area Reporter*—a free newssheet on Boston's bars). Sweeney's column "makes bars . . . and breaks bars," in his words. And he is determined to break Slate. Determined, that is, until he turns up dead in Clarisse's bed on the evening Mr. Fred of hairstyling fame gives a little "do" to welcome his new neighbors.

Events proceed against this zany background. Clarisse and Dan and sidekicks investigate with aplomb. But there's a problem with this novel: It simply lacks substance. Not once are we allowed inside anyone's head to find out what the character feels or why he is the way he is. There are gimmicks aplenty; everyone's terribly eccentric and witty—and shallow. One can't help but compare *Slate* with the sensitive, richly detailed novels of Joseph Hansen (q.v.), which depict gay life with realism and understanding. Against them, the Aldyne books don't stack up; they're like clever reproductions compared to the real thing.

The previous books in this series are *Vermilion* (1980) and *Cobalt* (1982).

(*M.M.*)

*Alexander, David. *Hangman's Dozen.* New York: Roy, 1961. (SS)

David Alexander is an underrated writer, in part at least because he had an idiosyncratic, sometimes self-consciously poetic and mannered style that some readers find off-putting. But his work has undeniable power, and his novels featuring sporting newspaperman Bart Hardin are superior portraits of New York's Broadway and Times Square in the 1950s. His plots, too, are unusual and compelling, as are his offbeat, colorful characters.

Alexander was an even better short-story writer than novelist—certainly his prose was leaner and less eccentric in his short fiction—and the thirteen stories in *Hangman's Dozen* are his best. "The Man Who Went to Taltavul's" (which won a prize in one of Ellery Queen's annual contests) and "Something in the Air" are excellent historical tales with startling twists at the end. "The Other Ones" is a chilling fantasy about some of the murderous inhabitants of hell. "The Gentlest of Brothers" is about a priest. "Run from the Snakes" concerns a wet-brain, an alcoholic so far gone that he no longer even knows who he is. "Face of Evil" is a procedural about a cop named Romano, who appears in many of Alexander's novels. "Love Will Find a Way" deals with three mountain climbers trapped by an avalanche and by their own passions in Switzerland, and the extraordinary crime perpetrated by two of them. The best of the hangman's dozen is "Uncle Tom," a devastating indictment of bigotry and racial injustice in the South—a story Alexander was unable to sell to any magazine in the Forties and Fifties.

This is a heterogeneous collection, illustrating the range and depth of the author's talent.

(*B.P.*)

*Alexander, David. *The Madhouse in Washington Square.* Philadelphia: Lippincott, 1958. (T)

The Madhouse in Washington Square is a tavern frequented by a regular group of social misfits, one of whom is John Cossack, "a painter of barber poles . . . a barroom porter, a manufacturer of bombs, and something of a philosopher." It is Cossack who finds failed writer Carley Dane beaten to death in Dane's Greenwich Village cold-water flat. Any number of people had reason to kill the despicable writer, including most of the habitués of the Madhouse. Cossack doesn't wish to see any of these people, his friends, behind bars. Besides, reporting the murder will interfere with preparations for his grand and compassionate scheme to blow up the tavern with one of his homemade bombs, thus putting its largely unhappy patrons—himself included—out of their collective misery.

As Cossack's scheme unfolds (and as circumstances force him to reluctantly assume the role of sleuth), Alexander introduces the reader to each habitué: Manley Ferguson, a frustrated artist; Helen Landers, a model who, when in her cups, suffers an overwhelming urge to do an impromptu striptease; wasted Peter Dotter, once rich and now a hopeless and pitiful alcoholic; Major Trevor, eighty-year-old veteran of the Boer War and World War I, who supports himself by playing small character roles on the stage and on television; bitter old Martha Appleby, whose driving force for close to twenty years has been her hatred of Carley Dane. Other suspects include Bruno Madegliani, owner of the Madhouse, who loathes and mistrusts his customers and whose secret passion is to find the long-lost idol of his youth, a champion cyclist named the Great Goldoni; Penny Caldwell, a sensitive young poet who fancies herself another Emily Dickinson; and George Dabney Sturgis, a recently discharged soldier who came to New York just to meet Dane and received a rude welcome. Events set in motion in each of these characters' lives during this crucial day are neatly resolved in the final pages; and Cossack reveals the identity of Dane's murderer. As for his bomb . . . well, you'll have to read the novel to find out whether or not the climax is literally an explosive one.

In *A Catalogue of Crime,* Barzun and Taylor called *The Madhouse in Washington Square* "close to unreadable"; Barzun and Taylor obviously have no patience with eccentric prose styles and no empathy for eccentric characters. The fact is, the novel is not only readable but quite moving, owing in large part to David Alexander's ability to sympathetically portray individuals whose lives and actions are far beyond the limits of rational human behavior. His treatment of these misfits is compassionate and gently humorous—and *Madhouse* is a kind of poignant tribute to all misfits, everywhere.

Alexander's other nonseries novels are *Murder Points a Finger* (1953) and *Pennies from Hell* (1960). The latter, a tale of menace and persecution reminiscent of Hugo's *Les Misérables,* is particularly good.

(*M.M./B.P.*)

Alexander, David. *Paint the Town Black.* New York: Random House, 1954. (AD)

Bart Hardin, managing editor of the *Broadway Times,* is in urgent need of $500. On the recommendation of an old friend, television commentator Mike Ainslie, he applies for a press-agent job with the Latin American Trade Alliance. Hired for the position, Hardin returns to his apartment over Bromberg's Flea Circus and finds Ainslie's tortured body in front of his fireplace. Hardin's problems are compounded by the fact that he must break the news to Ainslie's wife, Dorothy, with whom he is in love. The newspaperman's personal involvement with both the murder and the trade alliance—which urgently wants to recover a fake pre-Columbian jug that Ainslie reportedly had in his possession prior to his death—leads him into encounters with a strange curio-shop owner, a psychologist who collects art, a strongman named Andes, and a chinless man with a penchant for sadism.

Hardin is an engaging character: a denizen of Broadway who sports embroidered vests and a cynicism that is undermined by his ability (which he would term a flaw) to care deeply—be it for a murdered friend or his old blind dog. David Alexander's portrayal of the people of Broadway gives full rein to their eccentricities, but stops short of being unbelievable. The plot is intricate, and all elements tie off neatly at the conclusion.

Other notable Bart Hardin titles are *Terror on Broadway* (1954), *Die, Little Goose* (1956), *Shoot a Sitting Duck* (1957), *Dead, Man, Dead* (1959). Alexander also created two other series of two books each. The first features the detective duo of Tommy Twotoes, an eccentric penguin fancier, and private eye Terry Rooke (*Most Men Don't Kill* and *Murder in Black and White,* 1951); the second stars Broadway lawyer Marty Land, who also appears in the Hardin series (*The Death of Daddy-O,* 1960, and *Bloodstain,* 1961).

(*M.M.*)

Allbeury, Ted. *Shadow of Shadows.* New York: Scribner's, 1982. (E)

Ted Allbeury started writing espionage novels in the early 1970s. He specializes in realism and the sense of desolation evident in the best contemporary British spy fiction. What makes Allbeury's novels so authentic is his background: He served with British counterintelligence during World War II. In each of the dozen espionage novels he has written so far, Allbeury creates characters and plots so convincing that the reader can't help but be caught in his webs of suspense.

In Allbeury's best book to date, *Shadow of Shadows,* the game is a battle of wits between Colonel Anatoli Mikhailovich Petrov, a KGB defector, and British Intelligence's James Lawler. Petrov has been supplying valuable information—identities of double agents, locations of "safe houses," and more—until suddenly he stops talking. Lawler's mission is to find out who or what silenced Petrov and to convince him to resume supplying the vital information to British Intelligence.

Allbeury's novelistic skills are apparent in the relationship between the two spies—one Russian, one British—who find they have more in common with each other than they do with the spymasters who control them. The relationship grows despite Petrov's suspicion that Lawler's real mission may be to discover his secrets and then to liquidate him.

With this novel and *The Other Side of Silence* (1981), Ted Allbeury has written espionage classics.

(*G.K.*)

*Allingham, Margery. *Death of a Ghost.* New York: Doubleday Crime Club, 1934. (CS)

Margery Allingham was one of the three major Englishwomen mystery writers of the "Golden Age of Detective Fiction"—the other two, of course, being Agatha Christie and Dorothy L. Sayers (qq.v.). High literary quality marks her books, some of which have been compared to mainstream novels. Her plots are varied and interesting, portraying such subcultures of the time as the publishing industry, high-fashion houses, the world of the theater, and the life of the aesthete. Allingham's plots are not based on razor-sharp surprises, as Christie's are, but rather are known for their eccentricity. Unlike Sayers, Allingham produced a literate story without precious excesses, without intellectual showing off. Her characters are human, if upper-class, and even the minor ones are fully drawn.

Allingham's consummate creation is the suave sleuth Albert Campion. He comes with a mysterious background of royalty, or at least nobility, but he is "an amateur who never used his real name and title." Campion confronts international criminal conspiracies, greedy friends and relations, overweening egos turned to madness, and spy threats against his beloved England. Ultimately, though, Allingham's best books depend on the investigation and deduction of human motives and psychology for their solutions. Very early tales present Albert Campion as the action-adventurer, popular at that time. In *Death of a Ghost,* he becomes more the suave dilettante who senses the subtle psychology in suspense situations. Campion is notable for having no outstanding eccentricities (in contrast to many other Golden Age detectives). He has a vacant face with horn-rimmed spectacles that give him "owlish gravity"; a sign of deep emotion is his taking off his glasses.

In this novel the plot concerns an odd will left by an artist who died years before. The artist, John Lafcadio, considered himself the foremost painter of his age. He left behind a tangled ménage of wife, Belle; family; and sycophants. The will provides that each year a painting be taken from a secret cache and exhibited at an exclusive art show in order to maintain Lafcadio's artistic immortality. During the current exhibit, the lights fail, and when they're turned back on, another painter is found a corpse. A short time later, another minor member of the ménage is also killed.

Campion wades through the art group's murky crosscurrents of emotion and suspicion, exploring alibis and evasions. The police are represented by Inspector Stanislaus Oates, "the shrewdest and at the same time most kindly member of the Yard." Official and amateur come to agree on the killer, but getting the proof means Campion must face a final, ingenious attempt on his own life.

(*T.B.*)

Allingham, Margery. *Mr. Campion and Others.* London: William Heinemann, 1939. (CS/SS)

In this short-story collection, we find Albert Campion at his most vacant, his most Peter Wimsey-ish. The police call him "our Society expert"—he circulates in all the aristocratic circles. In almost all the stories, he has a damsel in distress turning to him in his well-known role as Universal Uncle. He finds that he must straighten the course of true love because of some incredibly stupid action on a girl's part, and he is dismayed to be considered so trustworthy because he is "so old" (over thirty). When not dealing with the youngsters, he must rescue a female of the older generation (he seems to have a species of aunt similar to Bertie Wooster's). The stories are light, with only one killing, and nearly half concern jewel robberies. Allingham's world is cozy and safe, a world where confidence tricks and the theft of jewels have the power to shock. Each of the stories has a lot of incident packed into it. Particularly good are "The Hat Trick," "The Longer View," and "Safe as Houses."

The first edition of this book contained five tales that Albert Campion did not appear in. The paperback edition that one can find now has been rearranged and substituted so that all thirteen stories feature Campion.

(*T.B.*)

Allingham, Margery. *Traitor's Purse.* New York: Doubleday Crime Club, 1941. (CS)

England is at war. The country is threatened by a catastrophic stroke, and time is desperately short. All lines of investigation have gone slack, and only one man knows the enormity of the situation. Only one man has the faintest clue to the heart of the conspiracy. As the story opens, Albert Campion awakes in a hospital bed with total amnesia from a blow to the head.

Hearing himself described as the killer of a policeman, he recklessly escapes and heads for the Bridge Institute, a research organization that is "a living brain factory." The Masters of Bridge are a hereditary group who are the governors of the Institute, and Sir Henry Bull is one of the Senior Masters. When the secretary to the masters is killed, the police question Campion, who was the last man to see him alive.

Campion's investigations are invested with the psychology of paranoia. He walks a tightrope, of sifting clues while trying to reestablish his memory. Stanislaus Oates, head of the CID, has disappeared, and Campion can't confide his memory loss to his love interest, Amanda, because of her trust in him. The only really practical help that comes his way is from his man, Magersfontein Lugg, who recognizes what a blow to the head can do and protects Campion from the police manhunt and from the gang of criminals on his track. The search for the traitor weaves through the criminal conspiracy and the institute itself (and by extension into the government) and leads into the cavernous heart of Nag's Head, the rocky headland that looms over the town of Bridge. Many characters appear, disappear, and reappear throughout the saga, including friends and relations; the policemen Oates, Yeo, and Luke; and the spymaster L.C. Corkran.

This story is Campion's trial by fire—afterward he is a changed man. Later in his career, he has less to do and becomes a sort of consultant. After Allingham's death, her husband continued the Campion adventures in three more novels. One novel that has received much critical approval, *The Tiger in the Smoke* (1952), in some ways seems overdrawn and overwritten. Other recommended titles by Allingham are *Mystery Mile* (1930), *Look to the Lady* (1931), *Sweet Danger* (1933), and *More Work for the Undertaker* (1948). Inducements to read them include the memorable names of characters, both major and minor, and of the various settings. And if you're a fan of that Golden Age staple, a proper plan or map of the scene, these provide cartographic delight.

(*T.B.*)

Alverson, Charles. *Goodey's Last Stand.* Boston: Houghton Mifflin, 1975. (PI)

Joe Goodey's career as a private investigator is launched when he mistakes the mayor's cousin for a gunman and shoots him, an error that forces his resignation from the San Francisco Police Department. His boss, Chief of Detectives Ralph Lehman, promises to wangle Goodey a PI's license as soon as emotions cool, and Goodey takes off—for Mexico, he thinks—stopping at a seaside motel just over the county line. But by the next morning, Lehman tracks Goodey down and forces him to take his first case, dangling the promise of an immediate license.

A stripper named Tina D'Oro—whom Goodey knew slightly but San

Francisco mayor Sanford F. Kolchick knew altogether too well—has been stabbed to death, and the mayor wants the homicide cleared up quickly without involving his name or risking his reelection. Goodey begins by studying Tina's diary, which has been stashed in the safe of Deputy Chief of Police Bruno Kolchick (by no coincidence, the mayor's brother), but finds little to go on. "You could pick up more gossip on a bus ticket," Goodey concludes.

Goodey's investigation takes him to the strip clubs of North Beach; into the back alleys of Chinatown; to the offices of a plastic surgeon who claims to have "created" Tina's body; to the posh home of the mayor himself (who inexplicably lives outside the city in Marin County across the Bay); and even, for a while, to jail. Along the way he finds a Chinese girl asleep in his bed, a dead man on his stair landing—and his true calling as a private eye.

This book is rich in San Francisco background and colorful characters, and includes a nice ongoing bit about Goodey's Chinese landlord, but Goodey's wisecracking manner and lone-wolf posture make him virtually indistinguishable from scores of other stereotypical fictional private eyes.

Goodey has appeared in one other adventure, *Not Sleeping, Just Dead* (1977).

(*M.M.*)

*Ambler, Eric. *A Coffin for Dimitrios.* New York: Knopf, 1939. (T)

Eric Ambler has long been known as a master of international intrigue. His novels typically involve a more or less ordinary protagonist who has blundered into some sinister situation and has become enmeshed in it against his will. He must then extricate himself by appearing to take part in the intrigue, often as a reluctant agent for the authorities. Ambler's narrative style is straightforward and economical; his plots, whether simple or complex, are suspenseful; his action scenes are high points in the books.

A Coffin for Dimitrios is the story of a man with an obsession. Charles Latimer, a writer of detective novels, is on holiday in Istanbul when he meets Turkish Secret Police colonel Haki; Haki admires Latimer's work and, like many policemen, has an idea for a novel, which he thinks Latimer should write. The idea is old-hat, but the story Haki tells Latimer as an aside—about the criminal Dimitrios Makropoulis—fascinates the writer. Dimitrios, who has been fished out of the Bosphorus, dead of a knife wound, has been involved in murder, an assassination plot, pimping, and drug trafficking; now he lies in the morgue, and Latimer impulsively asks to view the body.

The viewing affects Latimer powerfully, and he becomes determined to trace the life of Dimitrios. His search takes him to Smyrna, Athens, Sofia, Geneva, and Paris. It reveals more facets of Dimitrios's life than the police dossiers hold, and it throws Latimer into the company of a mysterious man named Peters who seems very interested in the fact that the writer saw Dimitrios's body in the morgue. So interested, in fact, that he aids the investigation, and Latimer finds himself in a situation stranger and more dangerous than any in his own detective stories.

This is an intriguing and suspenseful novel with an ironic twist at the end that causes us to reflect on how little we really learn from life's experiences. More or less faithful to it is the moody 1944 film version starring Zachary Scott, Sydney Greenstreet, and Peter Lorre, which appeared under the original British title of the novel, *The Mask of Dimitrios*. The film's screenplay was authored by another mystery writer, Frank Gruber (q.v.).

Charles Latimer reappears in one other novel, *The Intercom Conspiracy* (1969).

(*M.M.*)

Ambler, Eric. *Doctor Frigo*. New York: Atheneum, 1974. (T)

As the narrator of this novel, Ernesto Castillo, tells us, "In supermarket French the word *frigo* is used to mean not only refrigerator or freezer but also, a shade contemptuously, frozen meat." And "Dr. Frigo" is the nickname by which Castillo is called at the hospital where he works on the small island of St. Paulles-Alizés, in the French Antilles. Castillo, son of the assassinated dictator of a Central American republic, keeps to himself, close to no one but gallery owner Elizabeth Martens. Even in his relationship with Elizabeth, there is a sense of distance; she is an eccentric, a distant relation of the Austrian Hapsburgs, and tends to intellectualize current happenings in terms of the Thirty Years War.

When Castillo is called to the prefecture one morning, he is puzzled; and he is further surprised to find that Commissaire Gillon wishes to talk about Manuel Villegas, nominal head of the exiled Democratic Socialist party of Castillo's homeland, now residing on the island for reasons of health. Villegas has dismissed his doctor and wishes Castillo, whom he knew as a boy, to attend him. Gillon strongly advises the doctor to do so—and to report what he learns about a possible coup being planned for the Central American republic. Castillo complies reluctantly; he wants nothing to do with the politics of his native country—or, as some people, including his own mother, have suggested, with a plan to avenge his father's murder. And as he is drawn deeper into a web of intrigue, Castillo must come to terms with both the events of the distant past and his immediate present.

Although a bit on the talky side, this is a powerful novel showing a man who is torn between his heritage and the new life he has built for himself, between his basic humanitarian instincts and his desire to preserve his protective facade.

(*M.M.*)

*Ambler, Eric. *The Light of Day.* New York: Knopf, 1963. (T)

This Edgar-winning novel is the story of Arthur Simpson, a roguish con man, petty thief, and sometime pornographer who, as the novel opens, is driving a car-for-hire in Athens. He makes his first mistake when he attempts to rob his client of some traveler's checks and is caught; the man is no ordinary tourist, but an accomplished criminal, and he quickly blackmails Simpson into driving a Lincoln Continental to Istanbul. Simpson's second and third mistakes are not searching the car thoroughly and not having a valid passport. (He is half English, half Egyptian, and the problem of his citizenship is a thread that runs through the narrative.)

The border authorities search the Lincoln and discover weapons inside the doors. When Simpson finally admits how he was coerced into driving the car into Turkey, the Turkish police in turn coerce him into getting at the source of the weapons smuggling. Simpson delivers the car, finagles himself a job as guide for the three men and one woman to whom it seems to belong, then spends several tense days trying to find out what they have planned. As it turns out, all plans go awry—Simpson's, the authorities', and the smugglers'. Soon Simpson finds himself enlisted on *both* sides, in an even worse predicament than he could ever have imagined.

This novel is Ambler at his best, full as it is of double-dealings and harrowing scenes. Arthur Simpson is a likable rogue and a finely drawn character. The reader can get a second glimpse of him in *Dirty Story* (1967).

A film of this novel, called *Topkapi,* was made in 1964; starring Melina Mercouri, Maximilian Schell, and Peter Ustinov, it is colorful and entertaining and contains riveting scenes during which viewers who are afraid of heights would be well advised to keep their eyes shut. A paperback edition of the novel, also published that year, bears the same title as the film.

Ambler carries out his theme of an innocent man caught up in a web of deceit and intrigue in other novels, notably *Background to Danger* (1937), *Cause for Alarm* (1939), and *Epitaph for a Spy* (1952).

(*M.M.*)

Anderson, James. *The Affair of the Blood-Stained Egg Cosy.* New York: McKay, 1975. (W)

This exercise in nostalgia circa 1935 has everything: an earl, his countess, and their scatterbrained daughter; a stately home with a secret passageway; and a weekend house party consisting of every type of guest found in Golden Age literature. There is a contingent of representatives of an unnamed grand duchy, summoned to a secret government meeting conducted by the earl's brother; an uninvited foreign adventuress; the school friend of the scatterbrained daughter; a multimillionaire gun collector from Texas who wants to see the earl's fabulous collection; and the Texan's wife, who wears a million-dollar diamond necklace.

When murder is done and the necklace disappears, Detective Inspector Wilkins, one of the most laconic police officers in all of detective fiction, arrives. A scorecard is almost necessary to keep track of who-was-where-with-whom-and-why. Fortunately, the author has provided a list of characters and a map showing the location of the fifteen bedrooms in the mansion to assist the reader during the convoluted, two-chapter conclusion. All of the action takes place in three days and nights, and there are frequent interruptions as the characters eat meals, take strolls on the grounds, and make a grand tour of the house.

A second book, *The Affair of the Mutilated Mink Coat* (1981), stars the same main characters at yet another house party.

(*E.N.*)

Anderson, Poul. *Murder Bound.* New York: Macmillan, 1962. (PI)

A celebrated writer of fantasy and science fiction for more than thirty-five years, Poul Anderson produced three mystery novels (and a handful of short stories) in the 1950s and 1960s featuring Trygve Yamamura, a half Norwegian, half Japanese/Hawaiian judo expert, samurai-sword connoisseur, and private investigator. *Murder Bound* is the last and in some ways best of the three—an eerie tale of murder and menace spiced with elements of the supernatural.

On board the Norwegian freighter *Valborg* bound for San Francisco, a Nazi fugitive named Benrud is discovered masquerading as chief steward. Benrud, armed with a red fire ax, vanishes during the struggle to capture him. He is presumed drowned, and yet doubts linger in the minds of the *Valborg*'s crew and only passenger, mathematician Conrad Lauring. Those doubts prove prophetic: Later, in San Francisco, Lauring finds himself haunted by a faceless form—a man who whistles the Horst Wessel song, who drips seaweed, who carries a red fire ax. Is it the specter of one who died at sea, what the superstitious Norwegian sailors call a *draug?* Or is Benrud still alive and bent on further crimes? Trygve Yamamura is called in to investigate and sleuths his way to the truth in "a truly chilling climax in the ill-lit hold of the *Valborg,* when natural and seemingly supernatural forces meet and lock in deadly embrace."

Yamamura is much more a cerebral detective than a man of action, so the pace here tends to be rather slow. He is also rather colorless and sketchily drawn, despite his ethnic heritage and skills, and tends to hold some curious (and unappetizing), political and sociological opinions. Still, *Murder Bound* is entertaining, primarily because it is rich in the smell of sea and fog, and the flavor of Norse legends.

Anderson's other two Trygve Yamamura novels are *Perish by the Sword* (1959), which deals with a stolen samurai sword; and *Murder in Black Letter* (1960), which is concerned with a valuable pre-Renaissance manuscript on witchcraft and the murder of a history professor at the University of California.

(*B.P.*)

Anthony, David. *The Midnight Lady and the Mourning Man.* Indianapolis: Bobbs-Merrill, 1969. (PP/T)

The greatest strength of David Anthony's (William Dale Smith's) first novel is the protagonist, Morgan Butler, a Korean War veteran who suffered a breakdown. Upon recovering, he worked briefly for a San Francisco detective agency. At the opening of this story, he is half-owner of an Ohio farm, and because he occasionally feels the need for some action, he keeps his hand in the detective business, taking jobs that are a little outside the law. Often the jobs aren't as lucrative or successful as his clients might wish them to be, since Butler is a man of sensitivity and conscience—good at what he does, but incapable of betraying a well-developed moral code. In this novel he helps a former marine buddy who saved his life—Quartz Willinger, constable in the small college town of Jordan City, Ohio, who is laid up with an on-the-job injury and trusts no one but Butler to hold down the fort during his convalescence.

Tapes that three local college students under psychological counseling made and left with their therapist have been stolen. Butler narrows the focus of the thief down to the tapes of one student, Natalie Claybourne, but before he can find the reason the tape was taken, she is murdered in her dormitory room. Butler must contend with numerous men who may or may not have been her lovers; her wealthy father, who gives phony-sounding stories about why he seems more interested in recovering the tape than in his daughter's killing; and a lady who begins to awaken feelings in Butler that he had considered gone for good.

Anthony's portrayal of a college town and its bohemian denizens is excellent; there is a section in which Butler relates how he copes with campus "spring madness" that any student or former student will immediately recognize. Although the solution is a little predictable and the story somewhat drawn out, this is nonetheless a novel you won't want to put down. (A film version, *The Midnight Man,* starring Burt Lancaster was made in 1974. In it, Butler is transformed into a paroled murderer and night watchman turned detective.)

David Anthony's other books featuring Morgan Butler are *Blood on a Harvest Moon* (1972) and *The Long Hard Cure* (1979). He has also written *The Organization* (1970) and *Stud Game* (1978).

(*M.M.*)

Anthony, Evelyn. *The Tamarind Seed.* New York: Coward, McCann, 1971. (RS)

Evelyn Anthony's novels are a cross between romantic suspense, espionage, and thriller. Romance is the most important element; her main characters are drawn together by immense physical and emotional attraction, often under circumstances of danger and stress. Exotic locales, international events, and political intrigue round out her successful formula.

The Tamarind Seed (made into a film in 1974 with Julie Andrews and Omar Sharif) opens with the arrival of Judith Farrow at Seaways Airport in Barbados. Judith, a young widow who is assistant to the director of the International Secretariat at the United Nations, is getting away from it all—mostly from the memory of a shattered love affair with a high-placed and very married British diplomat. Within days she forms a friendship with a man staying at her hotel, but this time Judith resists romantic involvement: The man is Feodor Sverdlov, a Russian diplomat, most likely a spy, and also married, to a physician who has remained in the USSR.

Upon their return to New York, Judith and Sverdlov continue to see each other, but things are not simple for them. Judith, a British subject, is visited by members of her country's intelligence establishment, warning her to steer clear of Sverdlov. And Sverdlov returns to find his male secretary mysteriously absent; his wife's petition for divorce follows. When Judith delivers a frightening message from one of his colleagues, he fears for his life, and he defects to the British. But doing that means involving Judith in a desperate and dangerous scheme.

This could be standard romance fare, except for Anthony's strong characterization and skillful use of multiple viewpoint. Her backgrounds are well researched, and her grasp of international affairs keeps an otherwise typical love story moving along at a fast pace.

Other noteworthy novels by Anthony are *The Rendezvous* (1983), which deals with Nazi war criminals; *The Assassin* (1970), concerning a Russian assassination plot during an American election; *The Malaspiga Exit* (1974), about international art thievery; and *The Defector* (1981), another novel about torn loyalties to one's country.

(*M.M.*)

Ard, William. *Hell Is a City.* New York: Rinehart, 1955. (PI)

In the early 1950s, when our political and cultural life was dominated by Senator Joe McCarthy and HUAC, and our crime fiction by the bloody exploits of Mike Hammer, a young man named William Ard joined the handful of hard-boiled writers—among them Ross Macdonald (q.v.), Thomas B. Dewey (q.v.), and William Campbell Gault (q.v.)—who carried on the legitimate private-eye tradition of Hammett and Chandler. In Ard's world the PI stands for personal and political decency, a clear line is drawn between dramatically justified violence and gratuitous brutality, and sex is seen as a restoration of oneself and caring for another. Anthony Boucher, the dean of mystery critics, praised Ard over and over for his "deft blend of hardness with human warmth and quiet humor," for turning out "masterpiece(s) of compressed narration . . . backed with action and vigor, written with style and individuality."

Hell Is a City, seventh of Ard's nine novels about private eye Timothy Dane, is the most powerful and exciting of his novels. Dane is pitted against the corrupt forces of law and order in a nightmare New York where the mayor, the police commissioner, and most of the officials are allied with the mobs and determined to hang on to their power in the coming mayoral election. When a young Latino shoots a Brooklyn vice cop who was about to rape the boy's sister, the municipal bosses use their puppets in the news media to portray the case as the cold-blooded murder of a heroic officer, and put out word to shoot on sight whoever might contradict the party line. Brought into the picture by a crusading newspaper editor, Dane finds himself in the classic *roman noir* situation: knowing the truth no one else will believe; threatened on all sides by killers with badges and without; hounded through city streets dark with something more than night.

With its sharply drawn characters, pulsating pace, and terrifying premise, this book could easily have been a masterpiece, were it not for its grotesquely bad denouement, perhaps the first televised criminal trial scene in fiction, where all is set to rights in record time and in an impossibly silly manner. In a later Dane-less novel, *As Bad as I Am* (1959), Ard reworked the same story line to a better effect but without the raw, nightmarish tension of *Hell Is a City.*

Ard was far from a model of all the literary virtues. He wrote quickly and revised too little, and his style, though readable and efficient, lacks the hauntingly quotable quality of Chandler and Ross Macdonald. His plots tend to fall apart under scrutiny and he recycled certain names again and again so that his novels contain small armies of characters named Stix Larsen and Barney Glines. But his best books—among which are *The Diary* (1952), *.38* (1952), *Cry Scandal* (1956), and the paperback original *Club 17* (1957), published under his pseudonym, Ben Kerr—are miracles of storytelling economy in which Ard's special brand of tenderness is integrated with the standard elements of mean-streets fiction. His death from cancer in 1960 at age thirty-seven silenced one of the most distinctive voices in the history of the private-eye novel.

(*F.M.N.*)

*Arden, William. *A Dark Power.* New York: Dodd, Mead, 1968. (PI)

During the same years he was writing the Dan Fortune private-eye novels under his Michael Collins (q.v.) by-line, Dennis Lynds took on the pseudonym William Arden and launched another series, this one dealing with industrial spy and PI-in-spite-of-himself Kane Jackson. The five Jackson novels are written in a spare, unadorned third-person style reminiscent of Dashiell Hammett's, and their protagonist is very much the hard-bitten operative, without the leavening of compassion one finds in other Lynds detectives, like Dan Fortune or Paul Shaw. Most of the Jackson exploits are distinguished by their setting in the jungle of high-level capitalism, principally in the chemical, metallurgical, and pharmaceutical industries where Lynds worked as a trade-publications editor before turning to fiction.

In *A Dark Power,* first and freshest of the series, Jackson is hired by a New Jersey pharmaceutical combine to recover a missing sample of a drug potentially worth millions. The trail leads through the mazes of interoffice love affairs and power struggles, and several corpses are strewn along the path. Although Lynds tends to get lost in his own plot labyrinths, this time he keeps the story line under firm control, meshing counterplots with fine precision, skillfully portraying people trapped by their own drives, and capping the action with a double surprise climax. Jackson reaches the truth by clever guesswork rather than reasoning, but this is the only weakness in one of the best PI novels of the Sixties.

Of the four later Jackson exploits, the most interesting is *Die to a Distant Drum* (1972), which, like Lynds's novels as by Mark Sadler (q.v.), takes as background the turmoil of the Vietnam era. Jackson poses as a revolutionary bomb-maker and joins a Weatherman faction in order to infiltrate a chemical plant and bring out certain evidence of industrial piracy. The result, as usual with Lynds under whatever by-line, is a fine and thoughtful thriller.

(*F.M.N.*)

*Armstrong, Charlotte. *The Balloon Man.* New York: Coward, McCann, 1968. (T)

In her twenty-six-year career, Charlotte Armstrong published dozens of novels and short stories as well as plays and screenplays. Her series detective, MacDougal Duff, appears in only the first three novels; Armstrong is better known for her later works, which combine suspenseful plots with a sensitive depiction of ordinary American people whose moral character is severely tested by extraordinary circumstances. Armstrong's heroes and heroines are normal people with considerable inner resources upon which they call to extricate themselves from dangerous situations that they are in through no fault of their own. The author does not flinch from dealing with such thorny moral issues as the abuse of power by the wealthy, the failure of parents to take responsibility for their offspring, and man's free will; and she has been known to stand firmly on the side of the underdog. These philosophical issues in no way detract from the suspense of her stories, which is always considerable.

As shown by *The Balloon Man,* Armstrong likes young women with guts. The heroine, wife of a rich-boy-turned-drug-addict, sees her husband throw their young son against the kitchen wall, breaking his leg in a fit of drug-induced hallucination. The down-to-earth young mother leaves quickly, with her son, never to return, knowing her husband's drug problem is beyond her help. She figures his rich family will take care of him; they've always hated her anyway, low-class street girl that she is.

The husband's father, however, won't let it go at that and displays an almost insane resentment of her. He's determined to get custody of his grandson, and while the heroine waits in a boardinghouse near the hospital until her son is well enough to take back east, the father-in-law bribes an unsavory school pal of his son's to take a room in the boardinghouse and do all that's necessary to prove her an unfit mother.

What follows is a delightful picture of the lives of the boarders and the inner workings of greed and evil that will stop at nothing to separate a child from its mother. A wonderful celebration of good old American grit. And, we might add, wit.

(*K.K.H.*)

Armstrong, Charlotte. *The Gift Shop.* New York: Coward, McCann, 1967. (T)

The Gift Shop is a classic example of Armstrong's talent and view of the world. Here we have an unassuming, lower-middle-class American girl who is putting herself through college by clerking in an airport gift shop. Her life is ruffled by little more than her boss's occasional temper tantrum. Enter the rich, good-looking bachelor—the youngest of three professionally successful sons who are sources of pride and solace to the patriarch who fathered them. The almost unbelievable hero (are there really such soulful rich young men in the world today?) is hot on the trail of an old school chum who has disappeared under suspicious circumstances (last seen in the gift shop) while researching the whereabouts of the young man's sister, whose existence has just been revealed to the family. And the circumstances of this revelation—a demand that the oldest son, governor of the state, stay the execution of an internationally known crime figure in exchange for the sister's life—are sinister indeed.

The adventure that the gift-shop clerk becomes embroiled in is refreshingly humane; and in the course of it, the bachelor overcomes the girl's resistance to arrogant rich young men. The romance does not proceed without difficulty, however; like many of Armstrong's heroines, she is the self-sufficient kind and not prone to stroking the male ego. This is high adventure, the stuff about which any righter-of-wrongs dreams. It is almost unbelievable, but the author has a way of making us feel it would happen to any one of us, any day now.

Other excellent Charlotte Armstrong titles are *Catch-as-Catch-Can* (1952), *The Better to Eat You* (1954), *A Dram of Poison* (winner of the Edgar for Best Novel of 1956), *The Turret Room* (1965), and *The Protégé* (1970). The best of her fine short stories can be found in the collections *The Albatross* (1957) and *I See You* (1966).

(*K.K.H.*)

Arnold, Margot. *Exit Actors, Dying*. New York: Playboy Press, 1979. (AD/O)

This paperback original is the first of the adventures of Penelope Spring, American anthropologist, and Toby Glendower, Welsh archaeologist. We meet the pair in Turkey on sabbatical from Oxford. The action begins when Penny is seated in an amphitheater and sees a body lying on the grassy stage below. By the time she returns with the police, however, the body has disappeared.

Next, a member of a film crew staying at the same hotel as the academicians turns up missing. Toby finds the man's purloined body, and he and Penny decide to investigate. (Toby has a less-than-altruistic reason: He needs to be back in England in ten days, but the police won't let him leave until the murder is solved.) Using talents developed over the years in their academic specialties, the two middle-aged professors become involved with the personnel of the motion-picture crew and their dependents, as well as study the Turkish countryside, to uncover the criminal and his motives. This is a nice portrayal of two endearing characters and their warm, nonsexual relationship.

Among Arnold's other paperback originals are *The Cape Cod Caper* (1980), *Zadok's Treasure (1980), and Lament for a Lady Laird* (1982). These allow the reader to explore the cranberry bogs of Massachusetts, an archaeological dig in Israel, and a Scottish estate.

(*E.N.*)

Arrighi, Mel. *Alter Ego.* New York: St. Martin's, 1983. (AD/C)

Hank Mercer is a New York mystery writer, author of such modest best sellers as *Death Is My Bedmate* and *Kill Me Tender.* Biff Deegen is Hank's series sleuth, a hard-boiled private eye patterned after Mike Hammer. Hank is tired of Biff and Biff's uncouth style; he wants to scrap him and begin a new series about an erudite, tasteful detective named Amos Frisby. His editor, Norman Wagstaff, is of course opposed to the idea—vehemently. But to placate Hank, who after all is one of his top authors, he agrees over lunch to the following bargain: If Hank can solve a real-life mystery, using Frisby's methods of deduction, *then* he can trade Biff in for Amos. What precipitates this bargain—and what starts Hank off on his all-too-real mystery—is a matchbook dropped on their lunch table by a well-dressed woman, containing the scrawled words "Help me."

The mystery involves a valuable statue called *The Etruscan Dancer,* some urbane crooks, some not so urbane crooks, sexy Marisa Winfield, a poker game, a daring rescue accomplished by Hank using methods better suited to the Human Fly, a chase through the Lexington Avenue subway—and, as it were, the *pièce de résistance:* Biff Deegen. Biff, you see, steps out of the pages of his own books to become a character in Hank's real-life mystery. He doesn't *really* come to life, of course; he is merely an anthropomorphized figment of Hank's overworked imagination, his creator's alter ego. But that doesn't stop him from becoming Hank's detective "partner," sneering at the likes of Amos Frisby and appearing at tense moments to advise Hank on the finer points of physical combat ("Kick him in the balls!").

This amusing and affectionate spoof of both genres seems to have been intended as the first of a series—it is billed on the dust jacket as "A Hank & Biff Mystery"—but so far no second book has appeared. Arrighi's other criminous novels are much more serious in tone; these include such first-rate titles as *Freak-Out* (1968), *The Hatchet Man* (1975), *Turkish White* (1977), and the Hitchcockian thriller *Delphine* (1981), and *Manhattan Gothic* (1985). (*B.P.*)

Ashe, Gordon. *A Nest of Traitors.* New York: Holt, 1970. (PP)

Gordon Ashe is a pseudonym of John Creasey (q.v.), an amazingly prolific British writer who had to his credit some 560 novels published under more than twenty names. *A Nest of Traitors* continues the adventures of Patrick Dawlish and "The Crime Haters," one of his most popular series. A revered British war hero and onetime independent crime fighter, Dawlish is now deputy assistant commissioner of the Metropolitan Police, London, specializing in crimes of international significance. He is also the acknowledged leader of a loosely knit group of crime fighters, the membership representing every major police force in the world.

In this case, Dawlish must alert various international investigative agencies to a widespread passport-fraud scheme that could wreak havoc on immigration and passport control throughout the world. As Dawlish's investigation continues, passport control turns out to be the tip of the iceberg; a select group of the world's most powerful men are on their way to seizing control over each government, major industry, banking system, and society on the planet. By the time Dawlish discovers this master plot, the organization—known as "the Authority"—has almost succeeded, and Dawlish is the one person standing between a free world and its complete domination by this small but vicious group of immensely wealthy megalomaniacs.

Unfortunately, Dawlish is just too perfect; and the Authority is too powerful to really be vulnerable to the heroic antics of what Ashe would have us believe is the last honorable man in the world. Farfetched, but a good book to read yourself to sleep with.

Patrick Dawlish appears in all the Gordon Ashe novels except *The Man Who Stayed Alive* (1955) and *No Need to Die* (1956). Representative titles are *Death on Demand* (1939), *Murder Too Late* (1947), *Elope to Death* (1959), *A Clutch of Coppers* (1969), and *A Blast of Trumpets* (1975).

(*K.K.H.*)

Asimov, Isaac. *Tales of the Black Widowers.* New York: Doubleday, 1974. (SS)

Until the early 1970s, Isaac Asimov was best known to whodunit devotees as the writer who virtually invented the science-fiction mystery. In his novels *The Caves of Steel* (1954) and *The Naked Sun* (1957) and in the short stories collected as *Asimov's Mysteries* (1968), he masterfully bridged the gap between the two genres and proved that genuine detective fiction could be set in the future as well as in the present or past.

Although he had previously written one contemporary mystery novel, *The Death Dealers* (1958), Asimov's best-known crime fiction of the nonfuturistic sort is the long series of Black Widowers tales that debuted in *Ellery Queen's Mystery Magazine* in 1972 and is still going strong today after four hardcover collections' worth of stories. The Black Widowers are five middle-aged professional men—Avalon the patent lawyer, Trumbull the cryptographer, Rubin the writer, Drake the chemist, and Gonzalo the artist—who meet once a month for dinner at an exclusive New York club. Each month one member brings a guest and that guest brings a problem, sometimes but by no means always criminal in nature. The narration of the dilemma is interrupted frequently by cross-examination and highbrow cross-talk among the Widowers, who like Asimov himself are inordinately fond of puns. After each of the five club members has tried to solve the conundrum and failed, a solution—invariably on target—is proposed by Henry, the ancient and unobtrusive waiter who has been serving dinner and drinks throughout the dialogue. Everyone then goes home both intellectually and gastronomically satisfied.

The Black Widowers stories stand or fall on the quality of the puzzles and their resolutions. Characterization and setting are minimal, and too many of the tales are either unfair to the reader or wildly incredible. But the occasional gems are clever indeed, and those who share Asimov's fondness for oddball facts, logical probing, and the spectacle of cultivated men scoring intellectual points off one another will delight in even the weaker links in the chain. The four collections published to date are *Tales of the Black Widowers* (1974), *More Tales of the Black Widowers* (1976), *Casebook of the Black Widowers* (1980), and *Banquets of the Black Widowers* (1984). Asimovians might also look into the author's book-fair whodunit, *Murder at the ABA* (1976), and his short-story collection *The Union Club Mysteries* (1983).

(*F.M.N.*)

Atlee, Philip. *The Green Wound.* Greenwich, Conn.: Fawcett Gold Medal, 1963. (E)

Joseph Liam Gall's first appearance in print was as a free-lance soldier of fortune embroiled in a Burmese civil war in *Pagoda* (1951), a hardcover adventure novel published under James Atlee Phillips's full name. A dozen years later, writing as Philip Atlee, the author revived Gall, made him a disillusioned contract killer for the CIA, and put him through more than twenty paperback spy thrillers, of which the first and best was *The Green Wound.*

The crime writer with whom Phillips seems to have the most in common is Raymond Chandler (q.v.). Both men use a cinematically vivid first-person style (although Phillips avoids the profusions of metaphor and simile that make Chandler so easy to parody) and eschew careful plotting in favor of strong individual scenes and memorable moments. Almost all the Joe Gall novels suffer from near-chaotic structure, but Phillips's finest scenes are so fresh and alive that, as Chandler said of Dashiell Hammett's (q.v.), they seem never to have been written before.

Phillips's treatment of his main character is a brilliant study in schizophrenia. On one level Gall is the stoic code hero of the Hemingway tradition, and on another he stems from Ian Fleming's (q.v.) James Bond, the professional killer for his government, the larger-than-life secret agent forever besting villains of the mythological-monster sort. In the conventional patriotic thriller of this type, we are never allowed to doubt that whatever our side does is right because we are by definition the good guys. Phillips at his best subverts this nonsense and approaches the insight of John Le Carré (q.v.) that perhaps at bottom We and They are mirror images of each other.

Witness, for instance, the story line of *The Green Wound.* Gall is paid a huge sum by his former bosses at the CIA to come out of idyllic semiretirement in an Ozark castle, infiltrate a quiet Texas community, and frustrate a plot to ruin the politically connected millionaire who runs the city. From his vantage point as manager of the local country club, Gall dispassionately observes the viciousness of the ruling class and the institutionalized racism that keeps the blacks in a shantytown on the wrong side of the railroad tracks. In due course Gall learns that the blacks have secretly organized, with the help of federal civil-rights enforcers, to register to vote at the last possible minute and then oust the white politicians at the polls. On Election Day a bloody race war erupts, leaving the city in flames. Later Gall pursues the instigator of the revolt, a horribly disfigured black veteran who was used by army doctors as an experimental animal and is aching for revenge on the entire power structure. The action swings from Mexico to Texas to New Orleans to the Caribbean and back again, but Phillips never resolves the tension between Gall the good soldier and Gall the man who knows he's on the wrong side. This tension, rather than its considerable virtues as an action thriller, is what makes *The Green Wound* one of the finest spy novels ever written by an American.

In most of the later Galls, Phillips downplays or eliminates the structural schizophrenia, and the lesser exploits overstress local color and exotic settings—Sweden, Tahiti, Thailand, Haiti, British Columbia, Korea, and elsewhere—at the expense of story and action. But even the weaker Phillips novels are usually redeemed by several powerful individual scenes that stick in the memory long after the book as a whole is forgotten.

(*F.M.N.*)

Avallone, Michael. *The Case of the Violent Virgin.* New York: Ace, 1957. (Published back to back with *The Case of the Bouncing Betty,* also by Avallone.) (O/PI)

Michael Avallone, who has dubbed himself "The Fastest Typewriter in the East" and "King of the Paperbacks," has published more than 200 novels over the past four decades, some thirty of which feature private eye Ed Noon. On the one hand, Noon is your standard hard-boiled, wisecracking snoop with a taste for copious bloodletting and a Spillane-type hatred of Communists, dissidents, counterculture types, pacifists, militant blacks, militant women, and anyone or anything else of a liberal or civilized cant. On the other hand, he is a distinctly if eccentrically drawn character whose passions include baseball, old movies, and dumb jokes, and who gets himself mixed up with some of the most improbable individuals ever committed to paper.

The gold-toothed, beret-wearing villain in *The Case of the Violent Vir-*

gin, for instance—a guy named Dean, who, like Ed Noon, is on the trail of a six-foot marble statue called the *Violent Virgin,* "The Number One Nude," not to mention one of the world's most precious stones, the "Blue Green." Dean is a very well-spoken fellow; at one point in the narrative, he says to Noon, "Your precipitous exodus from serene sanctuary propels me toward Brobdingnagian measures. Spider and I mourn for your misdemeanors but your palpitating perignations [sic] induce no termination of our grief." Spider, who is Dean's accomplice in crime, is not nearly so well spoken; *he* says things like "Okay, Dad. Make the parley with them. But fast. This choo-choo could get too hot for us."

The "choo-choo" he is referring to is the *Mainliner,* which travels from New York's Grand Central Station to Chicago. Noon is on it because he has been hired to bodyguard a woman named Opal Trace (who doesn't speak her words, she "carols" and "musicales" them). And what a train ride it is, chockablock full of a mixed-up mish-mash of double-dealing, multiple murder, vicious dogs, shoot-outs, a bomb explosion, and, to cap things off, a rousing derailment. None of it makes much sense—but then, one doesn't read Avallone looking for sense.

What one *does* read Avallone for, primarily, is his lurid, bizarre, and often hilarious prose style. Noonisms—as his better similes, metaphors, and descriptive passages have come to be called—abound in *The Case of the Violent Virgin;* there are more to the chapter, in fact, than in just about any other Ed Noon adventure. A sample: "Her hips were beautifully arched and her breasts were like proud flags waving triumphantly. She carried them high and mighty." And: "I flung a quick glance through the soot-stained windows. A mountain range and a dark night sky peppered with salty-looking stars winked at me."

Similar "palpitating perignations" can be found in such other Avallone spectaculars as *The Tall Dolores* (1953); *The Voodoo Murders* (1957); *The Crazy Mixed-Up Corpse* (1957); *Meanwhile Back at the Morgue* (1960), in which you will find the immortal line "The next day dawned bright and clear on my empty stomach"; and *Shoot It Again, Sam!* (1972).

(*B.P.*)

Babcock, Dwight V. *A Homicide for Hannah.* New York: Knopf, 1941. (AD)

Dwight V. Babcock was a prolific contributor to the pulps in the 1930s, and among the best of the writers developed by Joseph T. "Cap" Shaw, *Black Mask*'s editor from 1926–1936 and the guiding force in the development of the type of fiction he called "hard, brittle . . . a full employment of the function of dialogue, and authenticity in characterization and action." In 1944, after publishing two of his three mystery novels, Babcock went to work for Universal Studios, for which he scripted numerous films; he also did promotion work for Disney's *The Great Locomotive Chase* and worked on other Disney productions. The heroine of all three of his novels, Hannah Van Doren, has an angelic appearance that would lend itself to a Disney movie; this innocent facade, however, is at great odds with her connoisseur's passion for murder and mayhem. Not for nothing is she known as "Homicide Hannah, the Gorgeous Ghoul"—even though her interest is purely professional (she writes for *True Crime Cases* magazine) and her background made that interest inevitable (her father was an L.A. homicide cop).

In this, Hannah's first adventure, she teams with Joe Kirby, an out-of-work custom-car salesman, to solve the murder of Steve Wurtzel, a gambling buddy of Joe's who turns up knifed in his (Kirby's) apartment on Christmas Day. The situation is further complicated by two facts: one, on Christmas Eve Kirby rescued a beaten (and very naked) young woman from an alley and gave her shelter, but she has now disappeared; and two, in her place is Wurtzel's corpse *and* a Christmas present left by Kirby's wealthy girlfriend, Veronica Smith ("Miss Gotrocks"), whom he is afraid committed the murder.

When Hannah learns of these events, she reacts as if Joe has given *her* a Christmas present: a homicide for Hannah. She and Joe chase all over Hollywood and environs, bucking heads with, among others: wisecracking reporters, hardboiled cops, the idle (and not so idle) rich, a man with a face that looks like a skeleton, frequenters of the track at Santa Anita (where Veronica's horse, Princess Pat, is running on opening day), and a chemist who works for a firm that manufactures "Protexu," a patented sanitary toilet seat cover.

Babcock's style here is less hardboiled than in his *Black Mask* and other pulp work: there is plenty of breezy humor to go along with the fast action, and some delightful glimpses into the mad social whirl of Hollywood just prior to World War II. Hannah is a lively and irrepressible character—and as it turns out, a very good detective. *A Homicide for Hannah* is good fun from start to finish.

Hannah's other two adventures are *The Gorgeous Ghoul* (1941), in which she and Joe set out to collect a fat reward by returning a missing college boy to his family and in so doing run afoul of murder, a crazy inventor with the instincts of a Peeping Tom, and a *very* unusual matriarch named Sybil; and *Hannah Says Foul Play!* (1946), in which Hannah and Joe travel to Palm Springs during its annual western-days celebration and become mixed up in the murder of a Hollywood gossip columnist. The latter title was published only in digest paperback form, as part of the Avon Murder Mystery Monthly series. Babcock's only other novel is a collaboration with fellow pulp writer Day Keene (q.v.)—*Chautauqua* (1960), a mainstream historical with strong suspense elements, published under the joint by-line of Day Keene and Dwight Vincent.

(*B.P./M.M.*)

Babson, Marian. *The Cruise of a Deathtime.* New York: Walker, 1984. (T)

Marian Babson's novels are peopled with memorable characters. Often they are out-and-out eccentrics, and some may seem downright stereotypical, but they are developed with light humor and affection; Babson is an author who clearly cares about her characters, and because she does, the reader generally does, too. The plots in which these characters are enmeshed are solidly constructed, and the author often fools the reader by allowing him to misinterpret or (wrongly) accept at face value a single fact that later is disproved. Babson is adept at weaving background material into her stories so that we come away from each novel with some interesting new knowledge of an industry or a particular setting.

The setting for *The Cruise of a Deathtime* is the ship *Empress Josephine* on a ten-day voyage to Nhumbala, Africa. On board are the staff, both American and Nhumbalan; the Ordways, a couple who won this cruise of a lifetime by allowing themselves to be humiliated on a television quiz show week after week; Mrs. Anson-Pryce, who is journeying to Africa to check up on her diamond mines; the inscrutable von Schreibers, who remind many of escaped Nazis; D. D. Smithers, quickly nicknamed D-and-D (for "drunk and disorderly") by the staff; and, as the author points up in her prologue, "a supply of coffins, some of which might be needed during the long voyage."

Of course, the coffins *are* needed. And if the author indulges in a tendency to litter the landscape (or promenade deck) with corpses, the reason for the merciless slaughter is well developed. What at first seem like suicides and accidents are quickly revealed to be connected. As passengers and crew alike die in ingenious—and often bizarre—ways, the tension mounts, and the reader will look upon even his most favorite characters with a jaundiced and suspicious eye.

This is an entertaining and suspenseful mystery. Occasionally, however, one has the uneasy feeling that Babson, like so many other authors, does not treat death with the seriousness it merits.

(*M.M.*)

Babson, Marian. *Murder, Murder, Little Star.* New York: Walker, 1980. (W)

A number of the most unlikable characters you'll ever hope to meet are assembled on a London movie set, and real-life drama begins to unfold in front of the uninitiated eyes of Frances Armitage, chaperone to the American child star, Twinkle. Frances is new to the world of films, having been hired only days before to watch over the temperamental (no, actually she's a brat) ten-year-old. But she learns quickly about the unpleasantness and eccentricities of movie people: Morris Moskva, the scriptwriter, who handles his fear of flying by traveling sedated; Laurenda Tilling, Twinkle's mother, who seems to have a very unmaternal resentment of her daughter; Cecile Savoy, *grande dame* of the British stage, who is so insecure she feels threatened by the child she is to costar with; Cecile's nephew Julian, who adopts the guise of youthful suitor to bolster his aunt's ego; Dick Brouder, the exacting director who is the only one who can control Twinkle; Mr. Herkimer ("Herkie"), the producer who hates actresses and wishes he'd gone into the rag trade like his uncles; and Herkie's profit-minded partner, Tor Torrington.

With such a cast of characters, it is no wonder that paranoia arises and Twinkle becomes convinced someone is trying to kill her. This paranoia is eventually proved to have a basis in fact, but before anything sinister actually happens (not until over 100 pages), we are forced to watch these largely unpleasant characters strut and posture, engage in petty game-playing, and verbally and physically attack one another until we hate them as much as Herkie hates actresses. There's a lot of good background on the film industry, both British and American, and Babson's plotting is as solid as ever, but that doesn't make up for the fact that we simply can't care for most of these people. Notable exceptions are Frances Armitage herself, who has escaped dull widowhood and a condescending daughter-in-law to make an adventurous new start in life; and Herkie, a melancholy man who takes wistful pride in the fact that by having had eight wives ("not counting the ones I married twice"), he has outdone Henry VIII.

Other notable novels by this popular author are *The Lord Mayor of Death* (1979), *The Twelve Deaths of Christmas* (1980), *Line Up for Murder* (1981), *A Fool for Murder* (1984), and *Death Swap* (1985). A number of her earlier novels have not yet been published in the United States.

(*M.M.*)

Bagby, George. *Country and Fatal.* New York: Doubleday Crime Club, 1980. (AD/PP)

George Bagby (a pseudonym of Aaron Marc Stein, q.v.) began writing mysteries more than forty years ago, and his formula for suspense hasn't changed much since. The murder cases in which Inspector Schmidt, chief of New York City Homicide, shows his masterful skills of detection are narrated by the author's fictional namesake, George Bagby. Originally Bagby was depicted as a writer assigned to do a book on Schmidt. As the series progresses, the relationship between the two men becomes closer.

In *Country and Fatal,* Bagby's agent has talked him into ghost-writing the autobiography of a famous country-and-western singer, Shadrach McGee, loved throughout the world for his songs of bad women, bad drink, and the inevitable bad jail cell. McGee and company are on tour in New York City, but Bagby can't quite get started with the project; every time he tries to keep a date with what turns out to be the meanest man in the world, someone tries to kill him. Who is trying to keep this book from being written? Why?

Halfway through *Country and Fatal,* the astute reader ought to know. Bagby is great at setting out the puzzle, and since you won't spend much time empathizing with his one-dimensional characters, you should solve the case before Schmitty does. Nonetheless, this story has a quality that keeps one reading.

Among the more than forty other novels about Schmitty and Bagby are *Murder at the Piano* (1935), *Dead on Arrival* (1946), *A Dirty Way to Die* (1955), *Dirty Pool* (1966), *Innocent Bystander* (1976), and *A Question of Quarry* (1981).

(*K.K.H.*)

*Bagley, Desmond. *Flyaway.* New York: Doubleday, 1979. (A)

Picking the best Desmond Bagley high-adventure novel is difficult because they are of uniformly high quality; most critics agree that in the past ten years, Bagley has surpassed the old masters such as Hammond Innes and Alistair MacLean (qq.v.) with such expert novels as *The Vivero Letter* (1968), set in the remote Mexican jungle; *The Snow Tiger* (1974), a tale of an avalanche in the mountains of New Zealand's South Island; and *The Enemy* (1978), which deals with computer technology. Bagley's novels mix carefully researched background detail with a great deal of action and momentum, involving his reader thoroughly in his adventurous plots.

Flyaway may be Bagley's finest work, a slight cut above the others. When Paul Billson disappears into the Sahara Desert, aircraft-industry security chief Max Stafford departs London for Africa to track Billson down. Max learns that Billson, whose father was a legendary flier some decades ago, intends to clear the Billson name; the public still believes Billson's father deliberately vanished over the Sahara so his wife could collect a fortune in insurance benefits. Max catches up with Billson—after much difficulty—but then both men find themselves hunted by forces intent on protecting the secret of Billson Sr.'s disappearance.

This novel is superior high adventure; Bagley's attention to technical detail and his evocation of the desert milieu are impeccable. Bagley drew upon personal experience in the aircraft industry for this novel, which gives it added substance and credibility.

(*G.K./M.M.*)

Bailey, H. C. *Mr. Fortune Objects.* New York: Doubleday Crime Club, 1935. (CS/SS)

One of the most popular of British Golden Age sleuths is H. C. Bailey's Reginald Fortune. Reggie is a doctor whose deductive abilities and refusal to take the facts at face value make him an invaluable asset to Scotland Yard's CID, and he is often called in as scientific adviser on particularly difficult cases. Fortune, whose plump appearance and fondness for gourmet foods belie his dogged devotion to the pursuit of justice, appears in ten novels and fourteen short-story collections.

Mr. Fortune Objects contains six stories (aptly termed "objections" because Reggie persists in taking exception to the obvious solution to each of the cases presented to him). In "The Broken Toad," he investigates the mysterious poisoning of suburban Police Constable Mills, the circumstances of which are "rare and bafflin' " and the solution to which is sure to surprise the reader. "The Three Bears" takes us into the art world, exposing its hypocrisies and affectations, as well as its murderous passions. And in "The Yellow Slugs," Fortune probes into the reasons a young boy attempted to drown his sister, reasons that he thinks are not as simple as the boy claims. "The Little Finger" deals with arson, jewel theft, bloodstains, and a missing digit. "The Angel's Eye" is an entertaining house-party mystery. And "The Long Dinner" concerns a missing painter and a menu that makes gourmand Reggie's mouth water.

Fortune, his boss Lomas, Superintendent Bell, and Inspector Underwood have delighted readers for years. The Reggie Fortune stories are soundly plotted and their logic is impeccable. One might complain of the weak development of secondary characters and somewhat pretentious dialogue, but all in all these remain good light reading.

The better of the Reggie Fortune novels are *Shadow on the Wall* (1934), *The Bishop's Crime* (1941), and *The Life Sentence* (1946). Particularly good among the short-story collections are *Mr. Fortune Explains* (1931) and *The Best of Mr. Fortune* (1943).

Bailey's other series character, lawyer Joshua Clunk, "a champion of the weak and oppressed," is considerably less interesting—perhaps because he appears only in novels and Bailey was a much better writer of short stories than a novelist. The ten Clunk books—among them *The Red Castle Mystery* (1932), *Nobody's Vineyard* (1942), *The Wrong Man* (1945)—are well plotted but are written in a much more turgid style than the Reggie Fortune series. Anyone who can wade through an entire novel bulging with such passages as the following from *Nobody's Vineyard* is a truly dedicated mystery reader.

> *That would be a mad humility, and you're neither humble nor mad. Amen. So be it. Praise God for all. Why then, what is it that*

you fly from? The job and the job masters. Even as I. You from His Highness the Town Clerk and the Circumlocution Office and the Mayor and Aldermen and Councillors. I from a misbegotten Editor, poor fish, and the slavery of cooking stories of tripe and the plague of fools who want to be in them or kept out of them.

(*M.M./B.P.*)

*Ball, John. *In the Heat of the Night.* New York: Harper, 1965. (PP)

John Ball is best known for his series of novels about Virgil Tibbs, black homicide specialist with the Pasadena, California, Police Department. While Tibbs was preceded by Ed Lacy's Toussaint Moore in *Room to Swing* (1957, q.v.), he is the first fully realized black series character. This first Tibbs novel is a strong start, in which the author explores racial conflict far from his hero's usual beat, in the Deep South.

Wells is a sleepy little Carolina town where nothing much happens; so sleepy, in fact, that some prominent citizens have planned a music festival in hopes of attracting badly needed tourist dollars. Then, on a steamy August night, the conductor hired for the festival is found murdered, and Police Chief Bill Gillespie and Officer Sam Wood have more of a case than they can handle. Help comes unexpectedly when Wood detains a black man passing through town, and the man turns out to be Virgil Tibbs.

Wells is a typical small town with typical southern racial prejudice, and its lawmen are no exception. Grudgingly they accept Tibbs's aid, prompted by the urgings of the man who had planned the music festival. And as Tibbs quietly and methodically pursues his investigation, working against the handicap of his racial background, the lawmen each come, in their way, to respect him and acknowledge his exceptional ability. In the final confrontation with the killer, Tibbs turns his race to an advantage—proving that what one man considers a handicap can be another's blessing. This is an engrossing novel with a powerful premise, but it leaves us wishing we had really gotten inside Virgil Tibbs's mind and viewed the case through the eyes of the book's most interesting character.

In the Heat of the Night was made into a 1967 film starring Sidney Poitier and Rod Steiger. Other novels featuring Tibbs are *The Cool Cottontail* (1966), *Johnny Get Your Gun* (1969), *Five Pieces of Jade* (1972), *The Eyes of Buddha* (1976), and *Then Came Violence* (1980).

(*M.M.*)

Ball, John. *Mark One: The Dummy.* Boston: Little, Brown, 1974. (AD)

Espionage writer Edwin Nesbitt is frequently confused with his fictional character Mark Day; both fans and critics are always drawing parallels between the author and his superhero secret agent. Thus it comes as no surprise when, while in Berlin visiting his German publishers, Nesbitt becomes embroiled in an adventure worthy of Mark Day himself.

It begins when Nesbitt returns to his hotel from a press conference and finds a stranger searching his luggage. Trying to think what Day would do under the circumstances, Nesbitt slips into a sort of trance—represented throughout the book by italicized segments that read like a bad spy novel—and attacks the man. Then, without ascertaining whether the intruder is dead or not, he disposes of him—in, of all places, the hotel elevator—and with unconcern that would be believable in a secret agent but is hardly credible in a writer, he sets about his business of researching the city for an upcoming title in his series. Trouble continues to follow Nesbitt, to Vienna, Prague, Istanbul, and eventually India. Improbable events—such as meeting the namesake of another of his fictional creations, Celestine Van Damm—continue to plague him. And he continues to slip into his authorial trance, indulging in very unwriterlike actions.

While all of this adds up to an interesting premise, the whole is not believable, and the character of Edwin Nesbitt comes off as wooden as Nesbitt's own creation. The book lacks the strength of Ball's novels about Virgil Tibbs (namely, the deep characterization of a man who lives in conflict between two cultures) and demonstrates that the police procedural is John Ball's real forte. His talents with the police procedural are further evidenced by his novels featuring Whitewater, Washington police chief Jack Tallon, who first appears in *Police Chief* (1977) and more recently in *Trouble for Tallon* (1981) and *Chief Tallon and the S.O.R.* (1984).

(*M.M.*)

Ballard, W. T. *Say Yes to Murder.* New York: Putnam's, 1942. (PI/T) (Reprinted as *The Demise of a Louse* as by John Shepherd, Belmont, 1962)

W. T. Ballard was one of Joe Shaw's second wave of *Black Mask* boys. His first *Black Mask* story, "A Little Different," appeared in September 1933. It featured Bill Lennox, troubleshooter for the fictitious General Consolidated Studios. (Ballard himself had worked for First National Studios in the early 1930s.)

Lennox was one of the most popular series characters in *Black Mask,* and appeared in twenty-seven stories between 1933 and 1942. He's not a PI exactly, but he has that same hard-boiled ethos; his exploits have an appealing understated sense of immediacy.

After writing short stories for about ten years, Ballard published *Say Yes to Murder,* the first of four Bill Lennox novels, and set the standard for the Hollywood murder mystery. Ballard's gift for this type of story is his careful depiction of scene and his emphasis on character in a subgenre that usually does not rely on such realism. Ballard invented a cast of characters that later became almost clichés of the movie industry. Sol Spurck, the crusty head of General Consolidated Studios; Nancy Hobbs, Lennox's long-suffering girlfriend; and cops named Spellman and Stobert who are not quite as condescending toward Lennox as the typical cops of the hard-boiled detective novel.

In *Say Yes to Murder,* Lennox investigates the murder of Leon Heyworth, a drunken actor whom Lennox finds stabbed and lying under the bed of actress Jean Jeffries, granddaughter of Lennox's old friend Mary Morris. Faithful to Spurck and the studio, Lennox, with the help of Jake Hertz, a studio minion, and an empty piano box, moves the body from Jean's apartment, attempting to keep Mary Morris's name out of the papers.

Along with a superior sense of timing and scene, Ballard's novel shows great intricacy in plotting. Here the vital clue to the solution of the mystery is identity. All the characters are in show business, with consequent multiple personas. Lennox's primary task is wading through the maze of personalities. Ballard presents the murder as a problem of separating illusion from reality, a method quite effective in focusing Hollywood's artificiality.

Noted critic James Sandoe praised Lennox because "he doesn't have to flex his biceps to prove that he's strong." *Say Yes to Murder* is a consistently rewarding hard-boiled novel.

The other three Bill Lennox novels are also excellent: *Murder Can't Stop* (1946), *Dealing Out Death* (1948), and the paperback original *Lights, Camera, Murder* (1960, as by John Shepherd). Ballard was a close friend of fellow pulp writer Norbert Davis (q.v.) and coauthored one novel with him, *Murder Picks the Jury* (1947), under the joint pseudonym Harrison Hunt. (*J.L.T.*)

Ballard, W. T. *Murder Las Vegas Style.* New York: Tower, 1967. (O/PI)

After the demise of the pulps in the early 1950s, W. T. Ballard found a career as a prolific creator of paperback-original novels, both mysteries and westerns. His mysteries appeared under his own name, as well as the names Neil MacNeil and P. D. Ballard, and he even wrote at least one novel in the Nick Carter series. Many of Ballard's novels were set in Las Vegas, including three in a series featuring Detective Lieutenant Max Hunter.

Murder Las Vegas Style is a private-eye novel featuring Mark Foran, who finds himself involved in what at first appears to be a murder/suicide. The question of an inheritance is involved, depending on which of the victims died first, and as Foran digs into the case, though he seems to be making little progress, there are three serious attempts on his life, along with two more murders. The characters include hoods, beautiful women, millionaires, and cops, all of whom are convincingly sketched. The plotting is as convoluted as one could wish, although matters appear simple on the surface. Surprisingly, Ballard avoids the casinos for the most part and instead does an admirable job of giving a fine picture of the "other side" of Las Vegas, the desert.

For more of Ballard's Las Vegas, see his "straight" novel, *Chance Ellson* (1958), and the books in the Hunter series, including *Pretty Miss Murder* (1961).

(*B.C.*)

Ballinger, Bill S. *The Chinese Mask.* New York: New American Library (Signet), 1965. (E/A)

Bill S. Ballinger wrote some thirty mystery, suspense, and espionage novels (as well as two films and over 150 teleplays) during his thirty-year career, many with unusual plots and construction. His first two novels feature private eye Barr Breed; his only other series character, hero of five paperback originals published during 1965 and 1966, is CIA agent Joaquin Hawks—multilingual, half Spanish and half Nez Perce Indian, and virile as they come.

All five of the Hawks novels are set in the exotic Far East, in such locales as Communist China, Bangkok, Saigon, Angkor Wat, Laos, and Indonesia. They are as much spirited adventure stories as espionage novels, with graphically depicted backgrounds and plenty of harrowing jungle chases and narrow escapes. In *The Chinese Mask,* the first of the series, Hawks is assigned to rescue three Western scientists, all of whom have been working on a "psycho-gas that can paralyze the will and nerve of entire armies" and all of whom have been kidnapped from Berlin by the Red Chinese. Hawks crosses the Bamboo Curtain disguised as a member of a traveling Russian circus troop, infiltrates the headquarters of the Red Chinese Army in Peking, and eventually plucks the scientists out of an "impenetrable" prison fortress and leads them to safety—all in clever and exciting fashion.

This and the other four Hawks novels—*The Spy in Bangkok* (1965), *The Spy in the Jungle* (1965), *The Spy at Angkor Wat* (1966), and *The Spy in the Java Sea* (1966)—are enjoyable escapist reading and, in the bargain, offer accurate political, sociologic, and geographic portraits of their various locales in the mid-1960s.

(*B.P.*)

Ballinger, Bill S. *Portrait in Smoke.* New York: Harper, 1950. (PS/T)

Ballinger pioneered a new novelistic approach in the mystery field, one that he utilized in several novels: first-person narration told from the point of view of a professional or amateur detective, alternating with third-person narration involving one or more of the other characters in the story. This enabled him to tell two different yet parallel stories that intersect at or near the end, thereby heightening suspense throughout.

Portrait in Smoke is the first of his split-narration novels, and the book that firmly established his name in the mystery field. The first-person narrator is Danny April, the new owner of a small-time collection agency in Chicago, who finds in the agency files an old photograph of one Krassy Almauniski, a local beauty queen, and falls so in love with her image that he is compelled to track her down. Interwoven with the details of his increasingly puzzling and sinister search, which leads him from the stockyard slums to a modeling school and the Chicago opera, is the third-person chronicle of Krassy's life after winning the *Stockyard Weekly News* beauty contest—an account that is anything but a Cinderella story.

The dust jacket blurb says that *Portrait in Smoke* has "depth and power, unusual suspense, brilliant irony, hard-boiled wit, one of the most fascinating heroines in current fiction, and a whiplash ending." It isn't *that* good, but it is a first-rate crime novel that deserves attention from the contemporary reader. Whether it is Ballinger's best split-narration novel is debatable; some aficionados of his work prefer *The Wife of the Red-Haired Man* (1957), which has a more complex plot and a more dazzling surprise at the end. Also good are *The Tooth and the Nail* (1955) and *The Longest Second* (1957); the latter title has one of the most frightening first chapters in all of suspense fiction. In addition to the many novels under his own name, Ballinger also wrote two under pseudonyms: *The Black, Black Hearse* (1955), as by Frederic Freyer; and *The Doom-Maker* (1959), as by B. X. Sanborn.

(B.P.)

Bandy, Franklin. *Deceit and Deadly Lies.* New York: Charter, 1978. (O/T)

Kevin MacInnes is known as the "Lie King." A specialist with the Psychological Stress Evaluator (lie detector), he makes a living by taking voice readings of people and assessing their truthfulness. For a handsome fee, he will aid any client—governmental or private—in a situation where getting at the truth is paramount; and the fee goes to support his elegant but enigmatic mistress, Vanessa.

One of the subjects MacInnes is asked to evaluate is brought to him by a New York assistant district attorney; the client is a cabby who claims to have overheard two men talking about an assassination plot, something "really big." The man apparently is telling the truth, and MacInnes, spurred by a combination of patriotism (he is a former army officer) and curiosity, aids the authorities by embarking on a search for one of the men described—a search that nearly costs him his lover and his life.

MacInnes is interesting, and so is his work. In the course of the novel, he aids a businessman in making a low bid on a tract of land (and suffers sleepless nights when the seller kills himself); rigs a voice test in such a way as to prove a battered wife accidentally killed her husband (he knows she is really guilty, and he loses sleep over that, too); helps a wealthy Mexican family find where the killer of their young son has hidden his body; and bugs a bedroom conversation between himself and his mistress to evaluate whether she really loves him. The uncertain relationship with Vanessa is a thread through the story, as are MacInnes's fears about misusing his skills.

For all its merits, this novel could stand to be about 100 pages shorter. It is padded with Harold Robbins–like descriptions of expensive clothing, hotels, gourmet meals, and brand names of liquors and wines. There is also a gratuitous side trip into MacInnes's attempt to cure a temporary bout of impotence with a call girl, which causes us to lose track of the main focus of the narrative—finding out who is to be assassinated and stopping the killers. But on the whole, it's a good rainy day book for those who like their settings luxurious and their characters sophisticated, if a trifle stereotypical.

This novel won the MWA Edgar for Best Paperback Original of 1978. In addition, Franklin Bandy has written *The Blackstock Affair* (1980) and *The Farewell Party* (1980).

(*M.M.*)

Banks, Oliver. *The Rembrandt Panel.* Boston: Little, Brown, 1980. (PI)

Boston art dealer Sammy Weinstock and "runner" Harry Giardino seem to have little in common. Weinstock is reputable and knowledgeable, with a shop on Charles Street at the foot of Beacon Hill. Giardino is one of those characters who hang around on the fringes of the art world, buying up works here and there, peddling them to dealers, always waiting for a big score. However, when both are murdered in a particularly brutal and sadistic manner, Homicide men O'Rourke and Callahan sense a connection. Unable to find what it is, they accept the help of international art detective Amos Hatcher, who is taking time off from a seemingly dead-end case in Europe. Hatcher joins forces with the murdered dealer's assistant, Sheila Woods, and in searching the shop they find an old and rare frame, minus its painting, with fingerprints on it that definitely link the two victims. With this discovery, the two (now lovers) start on a trail that takes them from Boston to Amsterdam to Zürich to Cape Cod—and eventually to a missing Rembrandt, a linking of Hatcher's two cases, and a cold-blooded killer.

This is an excellent novel, packed with information about art and the people who make their livings from it. The characterization is uniformly good, especially the established relationship between O'Rourke and Callahan (which is full of humorous camaraderie) and the growing one between

Hatcher and Woods. This, plus the vivid depiction of the somewhat seedy side of Beacon Hill and the various foreign settings, does a great deal to make up for the fact that the plot moves slowly. We know all along who the killer is and what his motivations are, but nonetheless the story sustains our interest on the way to a satisfying conclusion.

Banks's second novel, *The Caravaggio Obsession,* which also has an art background, was published in 1984.

(*M.M.*)

Bannister, Jo. *Striving with Gods.* New York: Doubleday Crime Club, 1984. (AD)

New to the mystery-reading public, Jo Bannister has produced an excellent medical thriller in *Striving with Gods.* Her heroine, Clio Rees, is a physician turned mystery writer who makes a further transformation to amateur detective when her dearest friend dies. Clio's friend, a gay man named Luke, was found dead with a young boy in an apparent suicide pact. Clio doesn't buy the police scenario, and uncovers evidence of a double murder and cover-up. Dr. Rees further finds a medical conspiracy behind the murder.

Bannister's novel is more thriller than mystery. And Clio is more avenging fury than detective. Early on it becomes clear to Rees and the reader who the prime villain is. The greatest mystery is whether Clio will be able to bring the malefactors to justice and avenge her friend before she, too, falls victim. Despite our faith in a happy ending, Bannister does a good job of sustaining the suspense. The murderous confrontations are dramatic, though an extended chase scene goes on a bit long.

But it is the character of Clio Rees and her first-person narration that are the making of *Striving with Gods.* There is a wry quality to her voice that nicely balances the more melodramatic aspects of the plot. She is by no means the omnipotent and omniscient detective. She is a caring, fallible woman. She is also strong and resolute and totally devoid of the feminine failings of the mystery-Gothic heroine. She has, in fact, all the makings of a series sleuth. If only Jo Bannister will oblige.

(K.L.M.)

Bardin, John Franklin. *The Deadly Percheron.* New York: Dodd, Mead, 1946. (PS)

New York psychiatrist George Matthews is visited by a young man named Jacob Blunt who wears flowers in his hair, gives away quarters to people on the street, and fears he is losing his mind—all because of the manipulation of three-foot-tall "leprechauns." Matthews doesn't believe in the leprechauns, of course, but neither does he believe Blunt is anything but sane. He agrees to accompany the young man to meet one of the gnomes, Eustace, who looks suspiciously like a midget and who insists that Blunt now start giving away horses instead of quarters, beginning with a Percheron to the star of a hit Broadway show. The star turns up murdered, the man the police arrest as Jacob Blunt turns out to be an imposter, and an attempt is made on Matthews's life in a subway station. At which point matters *really* become bizarre. Matthews wakes up in a mental hospital some six months later, suffering from partial amnesia and with a hideous scar disfiguring his face. It is only after he adopts an entirely new identity that he is able to effect a release from the hospital and to begin, torturously, to piece his life back together and seek out the truth about the strange events surrounding Jacob Blunt, the leprechauns, and the deadly Percheron.

A most unusual and ingeniously constructed mystery—up to a point. Suspense is high throughout, and there are some forcefully written scenes. But the book's weaknesses far outweigh its strengths. Other scenes and much of the plot strain credulity to the breaking point, the characterization is weak (Matthews isn't very likable, for one), the dialogue is stilted, and the explanation behind all the bizarre happenings is downright silly. All in all, *The Deadly Percheron* is a vaguely irritating and unsatisfying novel.

Bardin has his admirers, who praise the hallucinatory quality of this and such other mysteries as *The Last of Philip Banter* (1947), *Devil Take the Blue-Tail Fly* (1948), *Purloining Tiny* (1978), and four published under the pseudonyms Gregory Tree and Douglas Ashe. But he is definitely an acquired taste, like olives and rutabagas.

(*B.P.*)

Barnard, Robert. *Blood Brotherhood.* New York: Walker, 1978. (AD)

Robert Barnard's element is exposing the underside of the pompous and the powerful, be they royalty, clergy, academics, or pillars of the community. The unique thing about his books is not how witty they are (though that in itself makes them worth reading) but that each one is very different. (Indeed, *Death in a Cold Climate,* 1980, is not humorous; its intriguing quality is its setting in the north of Norway, where Barnard once taught English.)

Blood Brotherhood takes the reader into the cloistered Anglican community of St. Botolph's, where an international group of clerics (an American with an unmuted passion for fundraising; an African bishop who has occasional lurchings into un-Christian tribal customs; assorted Britons; and two Norwegians who, to the horror of the host, turn out to be women) meet to discuss the rarefied matters of the spirit. At a time "when the heather lay like a purple blanket over the moorlands, and a large proportion of the local population were baking uncomfortably and loathing the food on the Costa del Sol," the clerics entertain less than holy thoughts, particularly about the more attractive of the Norwegian women. One of their number is stabbed to death, and the unholy problem is left for the pious group to unravel. Barnard's characters, while created to show various peculiarities—such as the overly hip youth pastor or the television bishop—exist not as stereotypes but as individuals who have grown up into their chosen roles. Entertaining.

(*S.D.*)

Barnard, Robert. *The Case of the Missing Brontë*. New York: Scribner's, 1983. (PP)

This is the third novel featuring Superintendent Perry Trethowen of Scotland Yard. It begins with the detective and his wife returning from a visit to his very peculiar aristocratic family (who are displayed to fine advantage in *Death by Sheer Torture,* 1981). Their car breaks down in a small village, Hutton-Le-Dales, and since they must spend the night there, they do the true British thing—they go to the local pub. No sooner do they settle in than an elderly lady accosts them and announces that she has inherited what appears to be an unpublished manuscript of a novel possibly authored by one of the Brontë sisters. And no sooner do they leave town than the woman is attacked and the manuscript stolen.

Trethowen returns to Hutton-Le-Dales, delighted to be associated with literary matters rather than being thought of only as the policeman with the kinky family—something that happens all too often. His investigations lead him to an unholy preacher (trained in Los Angeles!), the professors of a local last-resort college (here Barnard, a professor himself, is delightfully scathing in his caricatures), and book collectors from two continents, to say nothing of a pair of Norwegian toughs.

Characters in a Barnard book rarely have flattering things to say about each other—and for good reason. Trethowen views humanity with a disdainful eye, which makes for much wary humor. The plot of *The Case of the Missing Brontë* is solid, and the book-collecting background intriguing.

A two-time nominee for an MWA Best Novel Edgar, Barnard has written such other delightful novels as *Death of a Mystery Writer* (1979), *Death of a Literary Widow* (1980), *Death and the Princess* (1982), and *Out of the Blackout* (1985).

(*S.D.*)

Barnes, Linda. *Bitter Finish.* New York: St. Martin's, 1983. (PI)

Michael Spraggue is falling down a flight of steps, the voice of his stunt instructor screaming at him to use his thighs and hips to break the impact of the sharp cement. As the star of Hollywood's latest private-eye melodrama, shooting on location in Boston, Spraggue leaves the car chases to the pros, but the light stunts he likes to do himself. An independently wealthy ex–private investigator turned actor, he's quit the business because he's "mostly dug up dirt everybody would have been better off not knowing." But an emergency phone call summons him back to California's Napa Valley, where Kate Holloway, his not quite ex-lover and longtime business partner in the Holloway Hills Winery, is in jail as a material witness to murder. Kicking and screaming (he really does hate being a private eye), Michael flies to the rescue.

The victim is Holloway Hills' flamboyant Hungarian winemaker—the second in what the papers are calling the "car trunk murders." Kate is notorious in the valley—she's six feet tall, gorgeous, and makes as good a wine as many male vintners—and the not-so-bright deputy sheriff is certain she's a killer as well. Michael seems to be the only person on the scene smart enough to figure out who stashed those cadavers in the trunks of cars, and the deputy sheriff, of course, won't talk to him.

The complicated love situation between Spraggue and Kate is probably the most interesting part of this story, although Barnes does give us a lovely picture of the Napa Valley at harvesttime and lots of detail on the winemaking industry. The action moves well, the clues are nicely hidden, and the reader isn't bored—but neither is the reader glued to the edge of his seat. Spraggue ends up, predictably, all by his lonesome with a crazed killer in a deserted winery at the end of a rarely traveled road. The writing is light, entertaining, and stylistically sound; and hopefully as Linda Barnes matures as a writer, so will Spraggue and company.

Michael Spraggue also appears in *Dead Heat* (1984).

(*K.K.H.*)

Barry, Mike. *The Lone Wolf: Philadelphia Blowup.* New York: Berkley, 1975. (O/A/PS)

The success of Don Pendelton's (q.v.) Executioner series in the early 1970s naturally spawned a host of imitators. Like Mack Bolan, the Executioner, these other rough, tough, and lethal heroes are one-man armies embarked on a personal crusade to destroy the Mafia, the "Communist conspiracy," or similar organizations/ideologies in the name of justice and/or democracy, and by whatever means necessary.

The Lone Wolf series is one such imitation, and on the surface is solidly in the conventional action/slaughter mold. The lone wolf of the title, ex–New York narcotics cop Burt Wulff, embarks on his one-man vendetta against organized drug traffic in the United States when his girlfriend, Marie Calvante, is found dead of an overdose in a Manhattan brownstone. His savage quest carries him through fourteen novels—each one set in a different

U.S. city, each one dealing with a different arm of the vast drug network—and culminates in a bloodbath in the City of Brotherly Love.

But there is much more to this series than meets the casual eye. "Mike Barry" is a pseudonym of Barry N. Malzberg (with Bill Pronzini, q.v.), a writer of no small talent who specializes in plotless, stream-of-consciousness science fiction. Indeed, the Lone Wolf books are essentially plotless, make extensive use of the stream-of-consciousness technique, and are jam-packed with idiosyncratic prose much more suited to a mainstream literary novel than to a paperback paean to violence. ("Hello, death. Pleased to meet you, death. Been with you for a long time, death, waiting in these rooms for your call, and now here you are, old friend, old bastard, and absolutely nothing to do. Have a chair, death. Warm your hands by the fire, pal, rest easy. We'll be together for a long time so don't feel in any hurry to start talking.") And Burt Wulff is anything but your standard macho hero; he is, in fact, a raving lunatic who, by the last three books in the series—*Philadelphia Blowup,* in particular—is knocking off people for the sheer soaring pleasure of it: a serial killer as psychotic as Gilles de Rais or Son of Sam. In this respect, then, his saga is both a mockery and a condemnation of the whole Executioner subgenre.

The Lone Wolf novels are not without their flaws, certainly. They were written rapidly and show it; there are any number of factual and geographic errors, and the lack of cohesive plotting makes for a great deal of repetition. Nevertheless, as amazing hybrids of the literary novel and the potboiler, as a saga of one man's breakdown into psychosis, as an implacable send-up of the Executioner and his ilk, these fourteen books are quite remarkable.

(*B.P.*)

Barth, Richard. *A Ragged Plot.* New York: Dial, 1981. (AD)

Margaret Binton, the Manhattan widow who endeared herself to readers in *The Rag Bag Clan* (1978), solves her second case in this novel of intrigue in the inner city. Margaret, an inquisitive and friendly elderly resident of the Upper West Side, pokes her nose through the fence of a vacant lot on 102nd Street one day. Something suspicious is afoot: An old man is tilling the ground. She continues her observations, befriends Luiz Valdez, and learns he is creating a community vegetable garden with the help of five youthful friends. Margaret volunteers to help and is reluctantly accepted by the others: Peter Muñoz, a sharp-dressing garment-district worker; Cecile, a sullen black activist; Vinnie Tortelli, a young man with a rock-'n'-roll fixation and a record; John Kee, a Korean émigré studying to be a refrigerator repairman; and Jerry Stein, who makes his living hustling pool. And as they are wont to in Margaret's life, strange events suddenly begin to occur.

First Luiz is murdered and Margaret finds his body. Her only clue is the fact that Luiz has noticed something amiss with the cucumber plants. With the help of her friend Bertie, another elderly widow, Margaret digs in the garden and finds a box of diamonds—presumably from the recent armed robbery of a diamond merchant. Once Margaret takes the case to her friends, Lieutenant Morley and Sergeant Schaeffer, her investigation of Luiz's murder and his young helpers begins in earnest.

Margaret Binton is a charming character, full of eccentric habits that have long warmed the hearts of the fans of old-lady sleuths; and her cohorts on the Upper West Side are equally memorable. They do, however, also have a realistic quality not often found in characters of this type. And the novel, while full of light moments, treats the crime of murder with the seriousness it deserves.

The third Margaret Binton novel, *One Dollar Death* (1982), concerns the world of rare-coin collecting. A fourth, *The Condo Kill,* appeared in 1985.

(*M.M.*)

Baxt, George. *The Affair at Royalties.* New York: Macmillan, 1971. (AD)

George Baxt is best known for his Pharaoh Love trilogy—a series of murder mysteries written in the late 1960s and set in the underground of homosexual New York. The books feature a bizarre homosexual black police detective, Pharaoh Love. Another Baxt series features the popular detective duo Sylvia Plotkin and Max Van Larsen, a pair of wacky lovers and sometime partners in crime detection who run across like-minded wackos in the melting pot of New York City.

The Affair at Royalties is no less interesting than the above, although certainly more conservative. A good-looking and brilliant young Englishwoman regains consciousness in what they tell her is her very own bed. She has suffered a total memory loss, nerve-racking in itself; but to make matters worse, she is also the suspect in a brutal murder of which, of course, she has no memory. She can't even remember which of the men at her bedside is her husband, much less if she loves him or not, so she makes eyes at one of them anyway. Unfortunately, he turns out to be the local homicide inspector, and the relationship begins on a rocky note.

As she slowly regains her memory, she finds she is a notorious mystery-story writer. We watch her put her extraordinary analytic mind (and loud mouth) to work solving the mystery of her own amnesia, risking—with true "liberated" woman chutzpah—the possibility that she will, in the process, indict herself for murder.

Good characters, plot, movement, and a particularly nice rendition of what happens when the strong female meets the strong male: Will they destroy each other or fall in love?

Other notable Baxt titles are *A Queer Kind of Death* (1966), with Pharaoh Love; and *"I!" Said the Demon* (1969), with Plotkin and Van Larsen.

(*K.K.H.*)

Bayer, William. *Switch.* New York: Linden Press/Simon & Schuster, 1984. (PP)

Two women from opposite sides of New York City have been murdered, and the head of each is found with the body of the other. One is a prim, repressed schoolteacher; the other a prostitute. There is no evidence that they knew each other or had anything in common.

Detective Frank Janek has the case, and he doesn't think he's dealing with a random, crazy killer. It is not believable, he feels, that the killer took one particular head all the way across town to another particular body, and then returned with the other head, all in a few hours—for no reason.

The day he is given the switched-heads case, Janek falls in love with a woman he meets at the funeral of his old NYPD mentor ("priest," as the cops call it). He soon finds that the woman, Carolyn, is lying to him, and it becomes apparent that all these things—Carolyn, his mentor's death, the switched-heads case—are related in a deadly way.

William Bayer is a New York writer whose work is fed by the pace and tension of the city, and by the anonymity this mass of humanity affords those who would kill. He has written three other novels. One of these, *Peregrine,* about a killer who stalks women in New York City with a deadly falcon, won an MWA Edgar as Best Novel of 1981.

(*M.J.*)

*Becker, Stephen. *The Chinese Bandit.* New York: Random House, 1975. (A)

Stephen Becker is one of the few Americans who can write the novel of suspense and high adventure as well as, if not better than, his counterparts in Great Britain. *The Chinese Bandit* is the first of an outstanding trilogy about the postwar years in the Far East (the other two titles are *The Last Mandarin,* 1979, and *The Blue-Eyed Shan,* 1982) and is so good that it earned Becker accolades as "a modern Dumas."

The bandit of the title is Jake Dodds, a brawling, wenching, semialcoholic marine sergeant, wartime hero, and peacetime bum who finds himself in Peking in 1947 and becomes involved with a wily Chinese black-marketeer named Kao. After Jake nearly kills an American brigadier general in a whorehouse fight, it is Kao who saves him from imprisonment by arranging to smuggle him out of Peking with a camel caravan. Working as a guard and camel-puller, Jake soon finds himself dealing with a progression of traders, nomads, guerrillas, warlords, Japanese deserters, Chinese Communists, Chinese Nationalists, and women good and bad. Not to mention the Gobi Desert, the great snowcapped mountains of Central Asia, and even the legendary *yeti* or Abominable Snowman.

Byzantine plot twists, well-drawn characters, and one of the most graphically detailed of all fictional portraits of postwar China, Mongolia, and Turkestan make this escapist entertainment of the finest sort. But it is even more than that, for Becker writes beautifully and incisively from first-hand knowledge of time and place, giving us keen social and political observations and a work of genuine literary distinction. This is a novel to be read slowly, to be savored, and then to be read again—as are the other two titles in his trilogy.

Becker has also written two contemporary tales of suspense and adventure: *A Covenant with Death* (1964) and *Season of the Stranger* (1966). Under the pseudonym of Steve Dodge, he produced a paperback original with a China setting, *Shanghai Incident* (1955), which was later reissued under his own name. All of these are good, but none is as rich or as memorable as the three later works.

(*B.P.*)

Beechcroft, William. *Position of Ultimate Trust.* New York: Dodd, Mead, 1981. (E/T)

It is the near future, and President Burton Beech sits in the White House. He's a low-key sort of president, tagged by the press with the nickname "Bland Burton." Like any president, Beech has enemies, some of them dangerous. But none more dangerous than superpatriot Senator Carleton Rambeau, who plans to save the country by assassinating Beech so that the hawkish vice president can ascend to the presidency and deal effectively with creeping communism.

The problem is that six tourists on an airboat ride in south Florida's swampland see something they shouldn't, though at the time they don't realize it. Rambeau's cohort Admiral Sturdevant, head of the CIA C Section, immediately dispatches expert hit man Hubbard to dispose of the witnesses before they understand the implications of what they glimpsed. And Rambeau takes it upon himself to assign his own assassin, Agency foul-up Roy Franke, already in Florida to oversee the assassination attempt, to eliminate two of the witnesses.

For Hubbard, though he is pressed for time, this begins as an easy assignment. It becomes less easy when he begins stalking middle-aged Justin Clifford, who is honeymooning with his young wife, Lexie. The Cliffords prove to be tougher and more resourceful than Hubbard anticipated.

While Hubbard, Franke, and the marked-for-death tourists play their dangerous game, Franke's fellow conspirators, Ada and Hoyt, wait on a boat hidden in the swamp. Hoyt is a powerful but simple sort who makes no secret about his lust for Ada, who finds him repugnant.

There is plenty of suspense here—in Washington, D.C., along the highways and beaches of Florida, and on the boat secluded in the simmering Everglades. The style is detailed, slick, and fast-paced, all done in believable fashion. A highly entertaining political thriller.

(J.L.)

Beeding, Francis. *Death Walks in Eastrepps.* New York: Mystery League, 1931. (PP)

At one time *Death Walks in Eastrepps* was regarded as one of the ten greatest detective novels. Well, even mystery critics can make a slip once in a while. This book is quite competent, it rises above the humdrum, but the writing does not contain the verve to make it a classic.

A serial murderer terrorizes the seaside resort village of Eastrepps in Norfolk. The local police, led by Inspector Protheroe and Sergeant Ruddock, search for a brutal homicidal maniac. As the bodies count up to six, Chief Inspector Wilkins of Scotland Yard is called in. The relationships between the East Anglian residents, the individual policemen, and the press are explored. The tangled motives and alibis are sorted out. Public pressure mounts, and results in a false arrest. Then strong police work brings a man unjustly to trial. The woman in his life endeavors to clear his name while the courtroom drama heats up. This is a complex story, full of surprises.

Francis Beeding is the collaborative pseudonym of two English literary men, John Leslie Palmer and Hilary Adam St. George Saunders. Together they wrote thirty-one criminous novels, about half of them spy stories featuring Secret Service agent Colonel Alastair Granby; among the tales are *The Six Proud Walkers* (1928), *Hell Let Loose* (1937), and *The Twelve Disguises* (1942). They also wrote *The House of Dr. Edwardes* (1927), which Alfred Hitchcock transformed into his 1945 Gregory Peck/Ingrid Bergman film, *Spellbound.*

(T.B.)

Bell, Josephine. *Curtain Call for a Corpse.* New York: Macmillan, 1965. (AD)

Josephine Bell (whose real name is Doris Bell Ball) has practiced two professions. She began her career as a physician in the 1920s, when it was an unusual field for a woman. Since 1937 she has practiced a trade more expected of British gentlewomen—the writing of mystery and suspense stories.

In recent years, Bell has specialized in nonseries suspense stories, but she started her writing career with a series of classic mysteries starring David

Wintringham. Her amateur sleuth is, appropriately enough, a doctor. His police counterpart is Inspector Mitchell, who does not always appreciate Dr. Wintringham's interference.

Wintringham's fifth case takes him to the Denbury (boys' prep) School, where he is conveniently related to the headmaster and one of the students. Half-term weekend traditionally features both a father-son cricket match and a theatrical performance. This year's performance of *Twelfth Night* by a third-rate touring company becomes highly memorable when an ill-tempered actor collapses with a bashed skull as the curtain falls.

Wintringham, who attends the dying actor, becomes even more interested in the case when it is discovered that members of the school's staff may also have had reasons for wanting the victim dead. There is plenty of detecting to go around. Mitchell, Wintringham, and an enthusiastic band of young students all have a share of collecting clues and interviewing suspects. The result is a nicely complex investigation, punctuated by a cricket match and climaxing in a classic gathering of the suspects and confrontation with the murderer.

(*K.L.M.*)

Bell, Josephine. *Death in Retirement.* New York: Macmillan, 1956. (PS)

Dr. Olive Clayton is less than pleased when her niece, who has lived with her at Brambles Cottage since her retirement, announces that she will soon be leaving her to be married. When her efforts to discourage or delay Gillian's marital plans fail, Dr. Clayton reluctantly agrees to advertise for a married couple to share expenses and chores, and so allow her to remain in her home. She ends up with the Weavers, a seemingly quiet (if somewhat "common") couple with a nervous little dog in tow.

It soon becomes apparent that it is not just the dog that's nervous. Dr. Clayton's part-time cleaning woman and gardener both refuse to deal with the Weavers, and quit. More and more, the couple's actions seem abnormal. When their dog dies of poisoning, husband and wife accuse each other of attempting to murder his/her mate, or possibly Dr. Clayton. And soon thereafter Mrs. Weaver's strangulation murder is immediately followed by the gas-inhalation death of Mr. Weaver.

As the shady pasts of the Weavers unfold, everyone seems willing to accept the deaths as a murder/suicide. All except a police inspector and a small-town reporter. The plot continues to reveal dark mysteries of the past, centering on the fascinating character of the retired missionary physician, Olive Clayton.

The characterization in *Death in Retirement* is first-rate, from Dr. Clayton (not your average sweet little old lady, to be sure) to two progressively educated children whose troublemaking ways create more difficulties than they have bargained for. The plot has enough detection and plot twists to satisfy classic mystery fans, as well as those readers who prefer the unusual in suspense.

(*K.L.M.*)

Bell, Josephine. *Treachery in Type.* New York: Walker, 1980. (PS)

In Bell's fortieth crime novel, Anita Armstrong, widowed British novelist of former best-seller renown, is forced by declining income to begin writing again. Her idea for a historical romance is cautiously encouraged by her former publishers, and to help in the typing of the manuscript, she engages a secretary named Judy Smith. At the urging of her unscrupulous boyfriend, Chris, Judy steals the manuscript, changes key words, names, and the ending—and submits it to a publisher as her own.

Anita is off in Italy polishing her final draft, quite unaware that Judy's version of the novel has been published and is enjoying a great deal of literary and financial success. Judy's publisher—who is aware that she couldn't have written the book but is keeping quiet about it for obvious and not-so-obvious reasons—gives a party for his author in the small coastal town where she lives. Through a series of events, Chris is drowned after the party, and Judy then tries to escape on the boat she has bought with her royalties. Her father, who is extremely proud of his daughter and totally unaware of the hoax, is on board; a storm is brewing; there is a quarrel between the two of them; and it all evolves into an engrossing and satisfying adventure.

This contemporary tale is one of Bell's best novels and very different from her standard fare. The book is actually a story within a story, beginning with Anita Armstrong, switching to Judy Smith, and taking up Anita's part again at the end. Although this construction seems somewhat odd, it works in keeping the reader's attention.

Among Bell's earlier works, *Death at the Medical Board* (1964) and *A Murder on the Merry-Go-Round* (1965) are highly recommended, especially for their excellent backgrounds and assortments of devious characters. Her later novels include *The Trouble in Hunter Ward* (1976) and *Stroke of Death* (1977).

(*E.N.*)

Bellem, Robert Leslie. *Dan Turner, Hollywood Detective.* Bowling Green, Ohio: Bowling Green University Popular Press, 1983. (PI/C/SS)

Anyone whose sense of humor leans toward the ribald, the outrageous, the utterly absurd is liable to find himself convulsed by the antics and colloquialisms of Dan Turner, Robert Leslie Bellem's immortal "private skulk," who fought, shot, wenched, and wisecracked his way to the solutions of hundreds of pulp-magazine cases from 1934 to 1950. The list of Bellem admirers is long and distinguished and includes humorist S. J. Perelman, who in a *New Yorker* essay titled "Somewhere a Roscoe . . ." called Turner "the apotheosis of all private detectives" and said he was "out of Ma Barker by Dashiell Hammett's Sam Spade."

Although Bellem wrote a handful of novels, none features Dan Turner. Turner, in fact, appeared only in a few scattered anthologies until the publication of this collection of seven of his vintage cases from *Hollywood Detective, Spicy Detective, Speed Detective,* and *Private Detective Stories.* All are set in Hollywood, most deal with the (highly romanticized and inaccurately portrayed) film community, and all are wild, woolly, quite terrible, and very funny. "Drunk, Disorderly and Dead," for instance, contains such typical Bellem lines as "A hulking lug in chauffeur's uniform . . . barged out of the limousine's tonneau and planted his oversize brogan on my running board. He had an improvised handkerchief mask over the lower section of his pan and a blue-barreled automatic in his duke. He said: 'Freeze, snoop, or I'll perforate you like a canceled check.' " And from "Dump the Jackpot": "A thunderous bellow flashed from Dave Donaldson's service .38, full at the prop man's elly-bay. Welch gasped like a leaky flue, hugged his punctured tripes, and slowly doubled over, fell flat on his smeller."

This delightfully wacky collection also contains an introduction, headnotes, and a biographical sketch of Bellem by John Wooley.

Bellem's novels, for the most part, are forgettable. The only exception is his first, *Blue Murder* (1938), which features a Dan Turner–like private eye named Duke Pizzatello and contains some of the same slangy, campy mangling of the English language.

(*B.P.*)

****Bentley, E. C. *Trent's Last Case.* London: Thomas Nelson, 1913. (Originally published in the U.S. under the title *The Woman in Black.*) (CS)**

One of the true cornerstones in the development of the modern detective novel, *Trent's Last Case* has received high praise for more than seventy years. G. K. Chesterton (to whom the book was dedicated) called it "the finest detective story of modern times," while Ellery Queen praised it as "the first great modern detective novel." Later critics have tempered their praise somewhat, and Dilys Winn's *Murder Ink* even lists the book in its Hall of Infamy among the ten worst mysteries of all time.

But there can be no doubt as to the book's importance, especially in the character of detective Philip Trent. Before Bentley's creation of Trent, fictional detectives had always been of the infallible, virtually superhuman type exemplified by C. Auguste Dupin and Sherlock Holmes. English artist Philip Trent, investigating the murder of a wealthy American financier for a London newspaper, represents the birth of naturalism in the detective story. He falls in love with the victim's widow (the woman in black of the original American title), who is the chief suspect in the case, and he is far from infallible as a detective.

Bentley wrote the book as something of an exposure of detective stories, a reaction against the artificial plots and sterile characters of his predecessors. But despite Trent's fallibility, his detective work is skillful. The ending, with its surprise twists, is eminently satisfying. Though slow-paced by modern standards, the book has a graceful prose and quiet humor that have stood up well with the passage of time. Mystery readers were not to see anything remotely like *Trent's Last Case* until Agatha Christie's initial appearance with *The Mysterious Affair at Styles* in 1920.

Happily, Philip Trent's last case wasn't really his last, though E. C. Bentley waited twenty-three years before producing a sequel, *Trent's Own Case,* written in collaboration with H. Warner Allen. This time Trent himself is the chief suspect in a murder case, and if the book falls short of its predecessor, it is still a skillful and attractive novel. Bentley followed it with thirteen short stories about Trent, written mainly for the *Strand* magazine, twelve of which were collected in *Trent Intervenes* (1938), a classic volume of anthology favorites. A final thriller, *Elephant's Work* (1950), is more in the style of John Buchan (q.v.) and is less successful.

(*E.D.H.*)

Berkeley, Anthony. *The Poisoned Chocolates Case.* New York: Doubleday Crime Club, 1929. (AD)

Anthony Berkeley (a pseudonym for A. B. Cox, who also wrote as Francis Iles, q.v.) had an excellent ability to characterize, as is demonstrated in this novel in which the members of London's Crime Club—a carefully chosen group of armchair detectives—match wits to solve the murder of Mrs. Graham Bendix. Mrs. Bendix died after eating poisoned chocolates that were apparently intended for Sir Eustace Pennefather, dissolute member of the aristocracy whom many had reason to kill. The police have found no solution to the problem of who sent the chocolates to Sir Eustace (who seems to have innocently passed them on to Mrs. Bendix), and Roger Sheringham, somewhat pompous founder of the Crime Club, has volunteered the assistance of his learned members. Although Detective Inspector Farrar of Scotland Yard appears to think this an idle amusement, nonetheless he agrees to brief the club on the case.

The members—each characterized in all his or her eccentricities—agree to present their solutions on different nights. And it is no surprise when suspicion falls on one of their number. As theories and evidence pile up, the facts of the case unfold, and the cumulative work of the members—each of whom has his own particular sphere of knowledge, each of whom is certain of the correctness of his solution—leads to the logical but surprising conclusion.

This is a talky novel, with little action or movement. But it should appeal to those who like the combination of good characterization and armchair detection.

Other novels featuring the learned Roger Sheringham include *The Layton Court Mystery* (1929), *The Second Shot* (1931), *Jumping Jenny* (1933), and *Panic Party* (1934).

(*M.M.*)

Berrow, Norman. *The Footprints of Satan.* London: Ward Lock, 1950. (W)

One morning the inhabitants of the English village of Winchingham awaken to find a single line of hoofprints that begin in the middle of the road, in a carpeting of virgin snow, and then lead through gardens, over walls and hedges, through a locked summerhouse and pavilion, across a steep roof inaccessible to humans, to finally end by an old tree from which a man is hanging by the neck. Superstitious terror grips the village: Many believe the devil is responsible. (There is actual historical precedent for such a belief: On the night of February 8, 1855, a similar trail of cloven hoofprints appeared in and around a number of towns in the south of Devon, and no earthly explanation for them was ever discovered.)

The trail and the dead man are not the work of Satan, of course, but that of a very clever murderer. Berrow's development and unraveling of the apparently inexplicable is likewise ingenious, and he builds considerable suspense before his series sleuth, Detective Inspector Lancelot Carolus Smith, finally solves the mystery.

Only one of Berrow's twenty novels—a revised and updated version of the 1940 book *The Ghost House* (1979)—was published in the United States, perhaps because of their numerous flaws: talkiness and overwriting, a colorless Mr. Smith, and some dubious use of English slang (Berrow was a New Zealander). *The Footprints of Satan,* however, his best and most baffling novel, deserves to have been reprinted here—and still should be for the amusement of contemporary readers.

Other of his books worth reading include *The Three Tiers of Fantasy* (1947) and *The Bishop's Sword* (1948), each of which contains no fewer than three neatly worked out "impossible crimes"; and *It Howls at Night* (1937), a nonseries book set in Spain, which has a werewolf theme.

(*B.P.*)

*Biggers, Earl Derr. *The Black Camel.* Indianapolis: Bobbs-Merrill, 1929. (PP)

Although Inspector Charlie Chan of the Honolulu Police Department is a household name throughout the world, he appears in only six novels. The great number of films, radio plays, and comic strips inspired by Chan are proof of the compelling quality of Earl Derr Biggers's creation. However, these offshoots do not do credit to Chan's character. In them, he becomes a stereotypical Chinese, mouthing ridiculous platitudes and doing more than his fair share of bowing and scraping.

To anyone familiar with Chan only from the Thirties' and Forties' B movies, Biggers's novels will come as a refreshing surprise. In them, Chan is portrayed as an amiable, wise man, given to philosophic contemplation. He is an individual in whom the characteristics of the East and the West are delicately blended, and often Biggers uses this cultural mix in his plotting, allowing his detective to discern clues that either an Occidental or Oriental investigator would not. Chan's character is one of considerable depth—a welcome period departure from sinister Orientals such as Sax Rohmer's (q.v.) Dr. Fu Manchu. Unfortunately, Biggers's secondary characters tend to be less interesting, especially his melodramatic and overly romantic young men and women.

A sense of place is another aspect of fiction at which Biggers excelled. *The Black Camel* is set in the Honolulu of the Twenties—a city much different from the one we know today. Waikiki is a quiet beach community where trade winds "mumble at the curtains," a place where flowers bloom unmolested, and the trip into the city itself is a long journey by streetcar.

When movie queen Shelah Fane rents a house on the beach, she expects a restful sojourn, but complications in the form of an ardent shipboard suitor, a disturbing session with her trusted fortune-teller, and fear of a secret in her past arise to disrupt it. When Shelah is found murdered, Chan is called in. The star has left a letter for the fortune-teller, which could perhaps provide the vital key, but before Chan can read it, the lights in the house go out and it is snatched from him. Without this clue, the detective must sort through the conflicting stories of the murdered woman's suitor, secretary, costar, fortune-teller, tourist guide, butler, and a beachcomber—all of whom seem to have had ulterior motives where the film star was concerned.

An entertaining novel, with suspects galore, and a surprise ending.

(*M.M.*)

Biggers, Earl Derr. *Keeper of the Keys.* Indianapolis: Bobbs-Merrill, 1932. (PP)

In this novel, Charlie Chan is far from his normal beat, on a train steaming through the High Sierra toward Truckee, Nevada, not far from

Reno. But the event precipitating this journey after a professional visit to San Francisco—an urgent summons—and its culmination—deception and murder—are nothing new to the inspector.

The reason for Chan's journey is a gathering called by Dudley Ward of Reno. And the person the gathering concerns is Ward's former wife, opera star Ellen Landini. The participants, with the exception of Chan, are two additional ex-husbands of Landini—Dr. Frederic Swan and John Ryder—and her soon-to-be-divorced spouse, opera conductor Luis Romano. Ward holds a formal dinner party and explains his reason for calling them all here: He has learned that Landini bore him a son many years before, a child whose existence and identity she has concealed from him. Ward is determined to find the child—who by now must be a young man—and asks the men for their assistance. Surely Landini mentioned something to them . . . ? The others, while willing to help, can add little to what Ward already knows. Landini has kept her secret well.

Ward, however, is not content to drop his probing, and he announces that Landini has also been invited to the gathering. With her appearance, long-dormant passions begin to ignite. And when the diva is found shot to death in Ward's study, Chan has not only the husbands, present and former, to suspect, but also Landini's much younger fiancé, Hugh Beaton, and Hugh's sister, Leslie. An entertaining novel, reminiscent of the English country-house type of mystery.

(*M.M.*)

Biggers, Earl Derr. *The House Without a Key*. Indianapolis: Bobbs-Merrill, 1925. (PP)

In this first of the Chan novels, we are introduced to the Winterslip family of Waikiki Beach. There are the two feuding brothers, Dan and Amos, who have built a fence between their houses that neither will cross. Miss Minerva is from the Boston branch of the family but shares her cousins' love of the islands—so much so that her six-week visit has extended to ten months. The family is alarmed and has sent a policeman—Minerva's nephew, John Quincy Winterslip—to fetch her back. John Quincy has also been enlisted to watch over Dan's daughter Barbara on board ship as she returns from college on the mainland.

By the time Minerva returns from a beautifully described native luau and finds Dan murdered underneath his mosquito netting, the reader is not surprised. And when Charlie Chan finally comes on the scene, it is a definite relief. Suspicions center upon several characters: Arlene Compton, a former chorus girl and rumored "self-made widow" who was Dan's kept woman; her gigolo-type friend, Stephen Leatherbee; Jim Egan, proprietor of the genteelly decaying Reef and Palm Hotel. As the case progresses, there are nice counterpoints: between Chan and John Quincy Winterslip, the East-

West type of investigator versus the proper but inexperienced Bostonian; and between Barbara Winterslip and Egan's daughter Carlota Maria, the girl who has everything versus the devoted daughter of the poor suspect.

Although the plot is tedious at times and some of the characters are downright stereotypical, Chan is his engaging self from the first.

The other Charlie Chan novels, *The Chinese Parrot* (1927), *Behind That Curtain* (1928), and *Charlie Chan Carries On* (1930), are also excellent.

(*M.M.*)

Black, Gavin. *A Time for Pirates.* New York: Harper, 1971. (A)

There is a riot in Kuala Lumpur, Malaysia—young Malays demonstrating against the Chinese merchants—and Paul Harris is caught in the middle of it. His car is destroyed and he makes his escape on foot, in the process rescuing another stranded European, the young blond wife of a geologist. This geologist, as it turns out, works for an unscrupulous Chinese corporation that Harris suspects of secret oil exploration. Harris loves Malaysia, is concerned about the environment and all that, but figures *someone* is going to develop the oil, so he might as well have a hand in it. With backing from a Japanese firm, he sets about forming a company to beat out the Chinese.

So begins a very readable and rather involved story of conflicting business and political interests, with money, power, and terrorism used to back the various interests (Harris himself is subjected to a couple of physical attacks and attempted kidnappings, plus an attempt on his life). The blonde? Well, she becomes an enigmatic figure, usually appearing whenever a kidnapping is in the offing. This is also a story of races—Malays, Chinese, Japanese, Indians, and Europeans—coming together, seldom in harmony.

Gavin Black (a pseudonym of Oswald Wynd) was born in the Orient and most of his novels take place in the Far East—Malaysia and Singapore in particular. Other books featuring Paul Harris include *Suddenly, at Singapore* (1961), *A Wind of Death* (1967), and *The Golden Cockatrice* (1975).

(*N.D.*)

Black, Lionel. *A Healthy Way to Die.* New York: Avon, 1979. (O/AD)

It's a long way from London's stock exchange to Goresdene, a plush fat-farm where Kate Theobold, reporter for the *Daily Post,* has been sent for a week of torturous exercises and dieting, which is supposed to result in an article about the spa, its clients, routines, and results. Instead, her newspaper gets the *real* inside story when Kate discovers the body of a much-disliked tycoon hanging by the cord of his dressing gown from a water pipe. (She calls the police, her editor, and her husband, Henry, a solicitor.) All the residents of the fat-farm—and some of the employees—are in some way connected with Antrobus, the dead financier, who also had a financial interest in the spa. Kate delves into his background (with Henry's assistance), using her newspaper's files and resources. She also continues her health regimen, delineated in excruciating detail from diet to hot baths, until the final summing-up.

An independent young woman (although happily married to Henry), Kate manages to find corpses in all sorts of places. In *The Penny Murders* (1979), for example, she and Henry become involved when a coin collection is stolen and its owner murdered in a fortresslike London house. Black has a light touch with dialogue in these and Kate's other cases—*Swinging Murder* (1969), *Death Has Green Fingers* (1971), and *Death by Hoax* (1978). He also does his background research thoroughly, and provides plots both devious and complex.

Black's nonseries books include such thrillers as *Ransom for a Nude* (1972), *Arafat Is Next!* (1975), and *The Foursome* (1978).

(*E.N.*)

Blackstock, Charity. *Dewey Death*. London: William Heinemann, 1956. (R)

Charity (a.k.a. Lee) Blackstock's first mystery remains one of the best library mysteries ever published. For London's Inter-Libraries Despatch Association, the biggest scandal had always been the frequent and imaginative typos (e.g., "Law of Tarts") by the typing pool on request forms. That is, until the evil-minded office busybody, Mrs. Warren, is found with her neck broken, spilling out of a book sack.

Despite the investigation led by a Scotland Yard detective, and a second murder, *Dewey Death* cannot be classified as a classic detective story. It isn't even a puzzling mystery. Readers, along with various characters, become increasingly aware of the murderer's identity. This does not, however, lessen the suspense or interest of Blackstock's novel, which is a masterful mixture of romantic fantasy and harsh realism.

With a good deal of humor, the author weaves her suspense plot well through the interplay of day-to-day office life. The heroine (like Blackstock under another pseudonym) is an author of historical romances. When she becomes smitten with a dashing co-worker, she soon learns just how dangerous and disruptive a swashbuckling antihero can be in real life.

Like traditional whodunit writers, Blackstock studies the effects of murder on a small, insular community. But her library locale and her unusual characters are portrayed with a depth unequaled by most of her contemporaries.

Charity Blackstock created several other excellent suspense novels—*The Woman in the Woods* (1958) and *The Foggy, Foggy Dew* (1959) are good examples—before turning to romance fiction more than a decade ago.

(*K.L.M.*)

Blake, Nicholas. *The Beast Must Die.* New York: Harper, 1938. (CS)

British Poet Laureate (1968–72) and novelist Cecil Day Lewis, writing as Nicholas Blake, published a score of popular detective and suspense novels from 1935 to 1968, all but four of which feature an urbane amateur sleuth named Nigel Strangeways. For the most part, the Blake novels are fair-play deductive mysteries in the classic mold and are chock-full of literary references and involved digressions, which makes for rather slow pacing. But they are also full of well-drawn characters and unusual incidents, and offer a wide variety of settings and information on such diverse topics as sailing, academia, the British publishing industry, and the cold war.

The Beast Must Die is considered by some to be Blake's finest work and a crime-fiction classic. When the young son of mystery novelist Felix Cairnes (a.k.a. Felix Lane) is killed by a hit-and-run driver, Lane, who doted on the boy, vows to track down and kill the man responsible. A trail of clues leads him to a film star named Lena Lawson, who was a passenger in the death car, and finally to its driver, George Rafferty, the obnoxious part owner of a Gloucestershire garage. Lane insinuates himself into Rafferty's household as Lena's new lover, and makes preparations to exact his revenge via a sailing "accident." But things don't quite go as he (or the reader) anticipates. And when murder finally does strike, it does so in a wholly unexpected fashion.

The plot is tricky and ingeniously constructed: the first third is told first-person in the form of Felix Lane's diary; there is a brief middle section, called "Set Piece on a River," which is done third-person from Lane's point of view; and the last half is a straightforward, third-person narrative that introduces Nigel Strangeways (and his wife, Georgia, and Inspector Blount of Scotland Yard) and follows Strangeways as he unravels a tangled web of hatreds and unpleasantries. Blake builds the suspense nicely in the first half, makes good use of a subplot involving Lane's affection for Rafferty's own son, Phil, and even spices his narrative with a little sex—an unusual ingredient for mystery novels during the Golden Age.

But *The Beast Must Die* also has its share of flaws. The manner in which Lane tracks down Rafferty—and the ease with which he is able to meet and seduce a popular actress—seem both convenient and contrived; once

Strangeways (who is something of a colorless and priggish sort, at least in this novel) arrives on the scene, the narrative becomes talky and slow, diluting suspense; a physical attack on Strangeways is poorly motivated; and the final revelations, intended as a stunning surprise, are neither stunning nor particularly surprising.

This is a good novel, certainly, one worth reading—but it's not a mystery classic.

A film version of *The Beast Must Die* was produced in France in 1969 under the title *This Man Must Die.* Directed by Claude Chabrol, it is faithful to the novel except in one major (and curious) point: It excludes Nigel Strangeways completely and tells the tale as a straightforward thriller.

(*B.P.*)

Blake, Nicholas. *End of Chapter.* New York: Harper, 1957. (CS)

The London publishing firm of Wenham & Geraldine has always been a conservative one, but now they are about to become embroiled in a scandal—a libel suit that could cost them both money and reputation. No one can prevent the suit from being filed, but something must be done to ensure that the unfortunate circumstances that prompted it will never happen again.

Nigel Strangeways is summoned by the firm's partners, who explain the problem of the memoirs of General Richard Thoresby: When the general's manuscript was received, it contained passages that libeled Thoresby's rival, Major General Sir Charles Blair-Chatterley. After some argument, the author agreed to delete them, and did so. However, before the manuscript was delivered to the printer, someone reinstated the passages. The book has been withdrawn, but the damage has already been done. Strangeways agrees to investigate, under the guise that he has been hired by the firm to do some specialized reading.

The cast of characters Strangeways encounters includes Stephen Protheroe, the author of one great poem, who has withdrawn into the obscurity of his editorial office for twenty-five years; Millicent Miles, writer of torrid romances, who is currently using the office next to Stephen's to write her steamy memoirs; Herbert Bates, the production manager, who has been forced into early retirement after many years with the firm; General Thoresby himself; and Cyprian Gleed, the ne'er-do-well son of Miss Miles. Any of these people—plus a number of less important employees—had the opportunity and motive to alter the proofs. But by the time Strangeways has delved deeper into the situation, murder has been done, and the motive turns out to be more complex than any he has imagined.

This is a well-plotted novel and a good depiction of the publishing world, but it moves very slowly, and Nigel Strangeways fails to come alive in contrast to the other characters—some of whom are extremely memorable. Blake has an irritating habit of making cryptic forecasts such as "He could not know that one of the questions he had asked this morning would lead directly to a murder." Without these, perhaps the suspense would be greater; as it is, *End of Chapter* contains few surprises.

Strangeways's other investigations include the wonderfully titled *The Smiler with the Knife* (1939); *The Corpse in the Snowman* (1941); *Minute for Murder* (1947), which Barzun and Taylor term Blake's "masterpiece"; and *The Worm of Death* (1961). The best of Blake's nonseries crime novels is probably *A Penknife in My Heart* (1959).

(*M.M.*)

Blanc, Suzanne. *The Green Stone.* New York: Harper, 1961. (PP)

The green stone is an emerald worth $1200, a fortune in the Mexican town of San Luis. It draws three strangers inexorably together, and it changes the lives of all three. Inspector Menendes, viewed with suspicion both because he is an educated Indian and because he is a policeman (presumed to be brutal and corrupt), must find the stolen gem in order to validate himself. Jessie Prewitt, the little North American *señora* who accidentally comes into possession of the stone, must deal not only with increasing danger but also with refocusing her life after the sudden end of her marriage. And Luis Perez, who has lifted himself from poverty by creating a job as the town guide, sees the emerald as the means to security, the escape from the ever-present threat of poverty in a society where one misstep is a tumble into destitution, and where there is no second chance.

The unfolding of the plot is simple. Three Indians from a village near San Luis murder a tourist couple to steal their money and, incidentally, the emerald ring. Clues vanish. Inspector Menendes is left with nothing to go on but his own intuition and his knowledge of the area where villagers scorn the Indians, Indians remain silent, both groups see the North Americans as legitimate sources of money, and everyone fears the police.

Suzanne Blanc's strength is her sharp depiction of life in San Luis and of her characters as each struggles and changes. *The Green Stone* is a hauntingly sensitive novel.

Two of Blanc's other novels are also set in Mexico: *The Yellow Villa* (1964) and *The Rose Window* (1967); a third, *The Sea Troll* (1969), takes place on board ship.

(*S.D.*)

Bleeck, Oliver. *The Brass Go-Between.* New York: Morrow, 1969. (A)

Ross Thomas (q.v.) uses the pseudonym Oliver Bleeck for his entertaining Philip St. Ives books. These are fast-paced stories with first-person narration, reminiscent of many private-detective novels. But St. Ives is not a detective, he is a professional go-between—that is, he acts as an intermediary between such parties as kidnappers and the kidnap victim's family, insurance companies and thieves, etc. He has built a reputation in this strange profession and people on both sides of the law seem to trust him.

In *The Brass Go-Between,* the first book of the series, he is dealing with the Coulter Museum in Washington, D.C., attempting to recover a huge brass shield that has been stolen from the museum's Pan-African collection. But there is more to the shield than meets the eye. Not only is it historically priceless, it is also a magnificent work of art. Add to this the fact that at least two opposing African nations claim rightful ownership and it becomes obvious many people would like to discover the whereabouts of the shield.

Naturally, all this complicates St. Ives's job as he encounters many of the interested parties along the way: Winfield Spencer, a rich and reclusive art collector; and Conception Mbwato, a giant emissary from the African nation of Komporeen, to name but two.

This and the other Oliver Bleeck titles—*Protocol for a Kidnapping* (1971), *The Procane Chronicle* (1972), *The Highbinders* (1974), and *No Questions Asked* (1976)—are distinguished for their crisp dialogue, unusual backgrounds, and understated sense of irony. Qualities, of course, that Thomas also infuses into his novels published under his own name.

(*N.D.*)

Bloch, Robert. *The King of Terrors.* New York: Mysterious Press, 1977. (SS)

Robert Bloch has long been recognized as the patriarch of macabre fiction writers, having made his first professional sale half a century ago (to *Weird Tales* in 1934, at the tender age of seventeen). But he has also written extensively in the criminous field, with several novels, hundreds of short stories, and five major collections.

The King of Terrors, subtitled "Tales of Madness and Death," collects the best of his many short works on the theme of psychopathology. "Throughout man's history," Bloch says in his introduction, "I suppose death was the King of Terrors. The ultimate threat to our egos is the thought of their extinction. Now we have recently come to learn that mental illness can also destroy the ego, rob us of our self-awareness and, thus, identity. In a word—*living* death, the King of Terrors' tortured twin."

That tortured twin makes for some truly fearful and fear-filled tales. "The Real Bad Friend," for instance, which covers some of the same psychopathological ground as Bloch's classic novel *Psycho* and predates the book by two years; "Water's Edge," a deceptively simple story about an ex-con and a woman's horrifying retribution against him; and a pair of beautifully understated shockers—"Home Away from Home," about a young woman's ill-advised visit to her psychiatrist uncle in a remote section of England, and "Terror in the Night," about a young man's escape from an insane asylum. Not all the stories here are first-rate—Bloch is uneven—but all are enjoyable and the best ones are truly shuddersome.

Bloch's other criminous collections are also recommended. (It should be noted, however, that there is considerable duplication of stories among them.) They are *Terror in the Night and Other Stories* (1958), *Blood Runs Cold* (1961), *Cold Chills* (1977), and *Out of the Mouths of Graves* (1978).

(*B.P.*)

Bloch, Robert. *Psycho II.* New York: Whispers Press, 1982. (PS)

Bloch's 1959 novel *Psycho* had strong impact on the suspense genre, an impact that was greatly enhanced by Alfred Hitchcock's terrifying 1960 film starring Anthony Perkins and Janet Leigh. Norman Bates and the macabre events that transpired at his family's motel are well known to the American public; and there is possibly no more horrifying scene in the history of the American film than the shower scene from that fine movie.

Now, some twenty-three years later, we have a sequel, *Psycho II.* And, as with most sequels, it is a terrible letdown. Unlike its predecessor, which crackled with suspense and shocks, this novel moves dully and predictably toward a climax that leaves us unsatisfied and somewhat annoyed. Bloch's writing is as sharp as ever, and he gives us a fine glimpse into the mind of a psychotic who is functioning in a controlled state; but *Psycho II* proves once again that there is probably no such thing as a good sequel.

When we encounter Norman Bates this time around, he is in the state hospital; Norman, according to his psychiatrist (the novel's hero), Adam Claiborne, isn't cured; his psychosis has been controlled, however, and in the safe environment of the hospital, he gets on better than most patients. Enter a nun, Sister Barbara, who visits patients at the hospital and is interested in Norman Bates. The two are left alone to talk in the library one stormy afternoon; Norman's psychosis surfaces and he kills Sister Barbara. Exit Norman, in the nun's habit.

Norman hops into the convent's van and takes off with another nun who has accompanied Sister Barbara to the hospital. He kills her, indulges in a disgusting necrophilic episode, then picks up a hitchhiker, and later the van is found burned with two charred corpses inside. Everyone presumes Norman dead, except for his psychiatrist. Claiborne begins a quest that takes him to the small town where Norman's first victim's sister and her husband live—and have just been slain. From there he goes to Hollywood, where a motion picture about Norman is to be made, starring a woman who looks remarkably like the first victim, Mary Crane. And as he becomes entangled with the film-production company, more macabre events occur, convincing him that Norman staged his supposed death.

One has only to look at the title of this book to realize it's a simple job of exploitation. Bloch would have done better to leave Norman Bates in the mental hospital. For a far better treatment of this theme, the reader is advised to try Bloch's *Night-World* (1972), which also chronicles an escape from an asylum, but in a gripping and realistic way. Also recommended are *The Scarf* (a 1947 tale of a psychopathic strangler and Bloch's first novel), *The Kidnapper* (1954), and *The Will to Kill* (a 1954 story about a mentally disturbed Korean War veteran).

(*M.M.*)

Blochman, Lawrence G. *Diagnosis: Homicide.* Philadelphia: Lippincott, 1950. (PP/SS)

Although most of his work is (regrettably) long out of print and he is little known among modern readers, Lawrence G. Blochman was an innovative and popular writer for more than four decades. His early novels and short stories had foreign settings, primarily India, where he spent several years in the 1920s as a newspaperman. *Bombay Mail* (1934), his first and probably most accomplished novel, is set on board an Indian train; features one of his many series characters, Inspector Leonidas Prike of the British CID; and is one of the best of that intriguing subgenre, the railway mystery. Two other Prike novels, *Bengal Fire* (1937) and *Red Snow at Darjeeling* (1938), are also good, as is *Blow-Down* (1939), a nonseries suspense/adventure novel set in a sleepy Central American banana port.

Blochman's most notable creations, however, are his numerous short stories (for such magazines as *Collier's* and *Ellery Queen's Mystery Magazine*) and one novel featuring Dr. Daniel Webster Coffee, pathologist of the Pasteur Hospital in mythical Northbank, New York. Coffee was the first pathologist detective in crime fiction, the forefather of TV's "Quincy," and his cases have a uniform sense of realism as a result of Blochman's interest and research in forensic medicine. *Diagnosis: Homicide,* the first of two Dr. Coffee collections, is of sufficient import that Ellery Queen included it as the 106th and final entry on his Queen's Quorum list of most important volumes of detective short stories.

The eight novelettes in this book are what might be called "forensic procedurals." Coffee's chief criminological weapons, as Ellery Queen has pointed out, are modern (circa 1950) laboratory procedures in pathology, chemistry, serology, microscopy, and toxicology. With these—and the help of his assistant, Dr. Motilal Mookerji, on scholarship from Calcutta Medical College, and police lieutenant Max Ritter—the good doctor solves such baffling cases as the death of a woman after an apparently simple appendectomy ("But the Patient Died"); the strange case of a woman who hears a baby crying in the night, even though there is no baby in her house ("The Phantom Cry-Baby"); and the murder of a doctor to cover up one of the oddest rackets in medical (and criminous) history ("Brood of Evil").

The second Dr. Coffee collection, *Clues for Dr. Coffee* (1964), is likewise excellent and worth seeking out. Somewhat less successful is the only novel featuring the pathologist and his sidekicks, *Recipe for Homicide* (1952); Coffee's talents, as Blochman himself seems to have realized, are better suited to the short-story form.

(*B.P.*)

Block, Lawrence. *After the First Death.* New York: Macmillan, 1969. (T/AD)

Lawrence Block is a topflight professional who has written numerous novels featuring extremely diverse characters and situations. His characterization ranges from the grim depths glimpsed in some of his nonseries books and in his series about alcoholic ex-policeman Matthew Scudder, to the lightweight but amusing private eye/writer Chip Harrison, burglar Bernie Rhodenbarr, and spy Evan Tanner. Whether Block is chronicling a deadly search or a playful romp, he is a consummate master of suspense and manages to keep his reader fearing for the safety of—and solidly rooting for—his protagonist until the last page is turned.

The premise of this nonseries novel is the real-life nightmare of awakening hung over and in a strange place, in the presence of a corpse. Alex Penn awakes to find himself in what obviously is a cheap Manhattan hotel room; there is the severely mutilated body of a hooker on the floor next to the bed, and Penn, an alcoholic coming out of a blackout, does not remember what has happened. At this point, however, Block adds a new twist to a shocking but stock situation: Penn has killed in this manner during a previous blackout, and has only recently been paroled from prison.

Determined not to return to prison, Penn escapes from the hotel and hides out from the police. But as he sobers, an image appears to him: that of an arm wielding the murder knife—an arm that is not his. He realizes he isn't guilty of the crime, has indeed been framed. And he concludes that he may very well also have been framed for the first murder.

What follows is a cat-and-mouse investigation in which Penn slips from place to place in New York and environs, showing up to question old friends and enemies who he thinks may have wanted to see him convicted of murder. As he becomes more and more convinced of his innocence, he enlists the aid of a sympathetic hooker (and heroin addict) and begins to gather hard evidence. The outcome of this investigation hinges on a somewhat unlikely coincidence, but it forces a satisfyingly realistic resolution of Penn's quandary. Likewise, his growing involvement with Jackie, the hooker who aids him, is believable and satisfying.

Other Block nonseries novels are *Death Pulls a Double Cross* (1961), *The Girl with the Long Green Heart* (1965), and *The Specialists* (1969).

(*M.M.*)

Block, Lawrence. *Burglars Can't Be Choosers.* New York: Random House, 1977. (AD)

Bernie Rhodenbarr is no ordinary burglar; he is a professional of finesse, charm, and good common sense. At least that is what he tells himself when he enters an apartment on Manhattan's Upper East Side, where he has been commissioned to find a blue leather box—a box he has been advised not to open. Unfortunately, the box isn't where it should be, nor is there anything else of interest, and Bernie is about to depart when the cops arrive. No novice at such problems, he successfully bribes the officers with his advance on the burglary commission, and is about to take his leave once more when one of them turns up a body in the bedroom. The officer has the grace to faint on the Bokhara carpet; the other is distracted; and Bernie flees.

From here on out, Mr. Rhodenbarr is engaged in a flight to keep himself free, and a quest to find out just who attempted to frame him for the murder of entrepreneur J. Francis Flaxford—tenant of the apartment he was set up to burgle. There are a lot of amusing moments, a surprise roommate for Bernie, and a good amount of burglar lore.

Also entertaining are *The Burglar in the Closet* (1978), *The Burglar Who Liked to Quote Kipling* (1979), *The Burglar Who Studied Spinoza* (1980), and *The Burglar Who Painted Like Mondrian* (1983).

(*M.M.*)

*Block, Lawrence. *Eight Million Ways to Die.* New York: Arbor House, 1982. (PI)

Ex–New York policeman Matthew Scudder is not a formally licensed private investigator; he says you could call what he does "hustling for a buck. . . . I do favors for friends." As this novel opens, he is about to take on a favor for a friend of a friend, Kim Dakkinen, a call girl who wants to get out of the business. Kim is afraid to tell her pimp she is leaving, and Scudder's job is to act as go-between.

The job goes altogether too easily.The pimp is an unusual man named Chance, with a secret hideaway in Brooklyn (to which he has admitted no one, although he later takes Scudder there) and an easygoing manner that convinces Scudder he will let Kim go. When she is brutally murdered, Scudder, an alcoholic who has been attending AA for less than two weeks, begins to drink, suffers a blackout, and wakes up in the hospital. After his release, he is contacted by Chance, who insists he did not kill Kim—or have her killed—and asks that Scudder find out who did. Scudder's quest takes him into the apartments of call girls and through the bars of Manhattan and Harlem. He periodically stops in at AA meetings—just listening, refusing to speak when his turn comes. Teetering on the edge of drunkenness, he crosses and recrosses the city in which there are 8 million ways to die—many of them cataloged from Scudder's obsessive reading of the newspapers—in search of a killer with a motive that is almost impossible to discern.

This novel was nominated for a Mystery Writers of America Edgar and won the Private Eye Writers of America Shamus Award for Best Hardcover Private Eye Novel of 1982. It is grim and powerful and, along with the other Scudder novels—*In the Midst of Death* (1976), *Sins of the Fathers* (1977), *Time to Murder and Create* (1977), and *A Stab in the Dark* (1981)—contains some of Block's finest writing to date.

(*M.M.*)

Bogart, William G. *Hell on Friday.* New York: Jonathan Swift, 1941. (Also published as *Murder Man.* New York: Tech Mysteries, n.d.) (PI)

William G. Bogart was a prolific pulp writer in the Thirties and Forties. His chief claim to fame is that he ghosted a handful of the *Doc Savage* novels that have become so popular in paperback reprint. At his best, he was only a fair novelist; *Hell on Friday* is noteworthy primarily as one of only two mystery novels with a pulp publishing background. (The other is William P. McGivern's (q.v.) *But Death Runs Faster,* published seven years later—a much better mystery novel but lacking the range of pulp lore and true pulpy feel of the Bogart book.)

Hell on Friday's protagonist, private eye Johnny Saxon, is a former "prince of the pulps" who quit writing after three years of phenomenal success because "the business had lost its kick for him [and] his stuff went stale." His partner, Moe Martin, is "the loneliest literary agent in New York"—an emotional sponge who can lose himself in any narrative and therefore is incapable of telling the good from the bad. Saxon is hired by Joe Rogers, head of Rogers Publishing Company, a chain publisher of some twenty-two pulp magazines, to investigate the dubious business practices of a rival publisher, Sam Sontag. Rogers also wants him to help persuade a love-pulpeteer who writes under the name Dulcey Dickens to sign an exclusive contract with his firm. Murder, the appearance of a racketeer named Jasper Ward, the disappearance of Dulcey Dickens, and other complications carry the narrative.

The plot isn't particularly clever or exciting, and the solution holds no real surprises. Still, there is a certain charm to *Hell on Friday* (the title refers obliquely to the fact that Friday was payday for the legion of pulp writers, and often make-up day for the various magazines as well). Saxon and Moe Martin are engaging characters (as is Dulcey Dickens), and the pulp setting is well drawn and packed with details fascinating to anyone with an interest in that vanished era.

Saxon also stars in two other novels by Bogart—*Murder Is Forgetful* (1944) and *The Queen City Murder Case* (1946).

(*B.P.*)

Bonett, John and Emery. *Dead Lion.* New York: Doubleday Crime Club, 1949. (AD)

John and Felicity Carter Coulson (who write under the names John and Emery Bonett) have collaborated in a fruitful mystery career as well as a marriage. Their official joint debut came with the publication of *Dead Lion,* a fine example of the post–World War II British mystery.

Simon Crane comes to Britain to meet his famous uncle—critic, author, and BBC intellectual Cyprian Druse—for the first time. Instead, he finds Druse's body, his head stuck out a window and his neck bloody and broken. It soon becomes clear that many people wished to break Druse's neck: the many authors he destroyed with his vitriolic criticism, and the many women he seduced, humiliated, and abandoned.

When Simon finds himself in love with one of his uncle's embittered conquests, he no longer wishes to play sleuth. Unfortunately, Professor Mandrake does. Mandrake, an anthropologist by trade, had been a BBC colleague of Druse's. More important, he is a natural-born busybody and student of humanity just waiting for a chance to try his hand at detecting. While Simon tries to shield the woman he loves, Mandrake continues to happily meddle, eventually triggering the novel's tragic conclusion.

Dead Lion is an exquisitely crafted classical mystery. But besides providing a satisfying puzzle, like its many Golden Age predecessors, this novel also features three-dimensional, modern characters with psychological quirks and motivations. With small touches, the authors also manage to convey what life was like in England after the war. Theirs is a classic puzzle with new depth and Professor Mandrake as a lovable series sleuth.

The fat, homely professor appears in two other books—*A Banner for Pegasus* (1951) and *No Grave for a Lady* (1959). Later Bonett novels with a

Spanish sleuth and Costa Brava locale are well constructed but lack the charm of the Mandrake mysteries.

(*K.L.M.*)

Bonnamy, Francis. ***The King Is Dead on Queen Street.*** **New York: Duell, 1945. (AD)**

The combination of the Great Intellect and his Loyal Chronicler has been a mainstay of detective fiction since Watson first began keeping records. Academics with plenty of time on their hands to devote to travel and detection have also always been popular. Mix these elements with a colorful wartime setting in Alexandria, Virginia, and eclectic characters who are both native to the area and transient, and you have a perfect recipe for murder.

Peter Shane, former professor and head of the Department of Criminology at the University of Chicago, and his assistant, Bonnamy, are now living in a third-floor apartment in Alexandria while on military assignment. Both are present at a neighborhood party when much-disliked Joe Long, a well-known photographer known as "The King," is found dead—presumably from a fall down the steps of his home. When it is discovered that someone had tied a string across Long's steps, Shane and Bonnamy must attempt to clear their friends and landlady from suspicion, and their investigation focuses on the interrelationships between the party guests, each of whom had an intense reason for wishing to see Long dead. Even the family dogs and the layout of the house do not escape the pair's scrutiny as they study the past histories of this set of oddly associated people.

Francis Bonnamy is a pseudonym for Audrey Boyers Waltz; she wrote seven Shane/Bonnamy novels, taking full advantage of local color and geography of Chicago, Maine, Arizona, and other interesting locales. All loose ends are convincingly tied up at the ends of these humorous books, and the treatment of Shane's detective skills is particularly good. Other noteworthy titles are *Death on a Dude Ranch (1937), which has a Wyoming setting; Dead Reckoning* (1943), which deals with murder in Washington, D.C., and buried pirate treasure on Cape Fear; and *Portrait of the Artist as a Dead Man* (1947), which, like *The King Is Dead on Queen Street,* is set in Alexandria and involves interplay among a group of diverse people in the art world.

(*E.N.*)

Booton, Kage. ***Time Running Out.*** **New York: Doubleday Crime Club, 1968. (PS)**

This is a curious novel in that the characters are unsympathetic and the suspense minimal, yet we feel compelled to keep reading right up to the very end. Perhaps it is because we hope the heroine, Lilianne Krammer, will shape up and stop being a victim, both of others and herself. Perhaps it is because of a presentiment that something awful is going to happen. One out of two isn't bad: Something awful *does* happen, but Lilianne doesn't shape up.

As the story begins, Lilianne has just learned of her husband Carl's appointment to a Department of Defense post in Washington. The daughter of a former senator, now dead by his own hand following a political scandal, Lilianne has dreamed of the glittering social whirl of the capital for all the years she's been exiled in the Pennsylvania suburb where Carl has his electronics firm. Shallow and vain, she can't wait to get back there, certain she will be the center of attention. But Carl shatters all her hopes: The marriage has been deteriorating for some time, and he has no intention of taking her to Washington with him. Lilianne begs and pleads, but Carl is adamant and goes off to Washington without her. In a fit of pique over missing the fun—and being humiliated in front of her friends—Lilianne decides she wants a divorce.

From the moment Lilianne sets foot on the plane to get the quickie Mexican divorce to which Carl has agreed, things begin to deteriorate. The life of a divorcée is not what she had imagined, nor is the second marriage into which she hastily blunders. And when she begins to realize that she has become the victim of a cruel plot, she strikes out in an equally cruel way.

The events of this novel might seem improbable if the character of Lilianne—in all its unlikableness—were not so well developed. And while the ending is downbeat, one feels everyone has gotten what he or she deserved.

Among Booton's other books are *Andrew's Wife* (1964), *The Toy* (1975), and *Who Knows Julie Gordon?* (1980).

(*M.M.*)

Borgenicht, Miriam. *Fall from Grace.* New York: St. Martin's, 1984. (T)

Miriam Borgenicht's novels are highly reflective of the social issues popular at the time of their writing. To these issues she adds the element of fear and its effect upon those experiencing it. Her early heroines were housewives, often educated ones raising small children; later she turned her attention to more radical themes, such as interracial love and marriage; her present-day protagonists are likely to be professional women highly involved with their careers. This latter group are probably her best characters—evidence of a writer who has been rightly called "uneven" growing and getting better as she practices her craft.

Fall from Grace concerns a young nurse's attempt to explain the suicide of her husband, a nationally renowned doctor whom she married just two months previous. Nan Dunlop Gardiner is naturally accused of seducing and marrying William Gardiner for his money, then making his life so miserable that he quickly ended it with a bottle of sleeping pills. Nan is not about to lie down and take this slander, and when the hospital where they both worked asks her to leave, she fights back. Her husband's suicide note said that he had made a big mistake, but Nan knows *she* wasn't it. She is determined to find out what drove the still robust and brilliant physician to end the excitement of their new life together almost before it had begun.

As it turns out, there *are* terrible secrets in her dead husband's past. Broken hearts, mangled bodies, extortion, blackmail, and even murder surface from what had seemed a life built on integrity and compassion. Nan continues to investigate in spite of this, getting help from unexpected sources and betrayal from those she thought her closest allies. In the end, her life and her dead husband's reputation depend on one phone call, which she may or may not be able to steel herself to make.

Though slow-paced and overlong, *Fall from Grace* is rich in the details of the medical world and hospital politics. Those who enjoy medical mysteries will find it compelling.

Notable among Borgenicht's other titles are *A Corpse in Diplomacy* (1949), *Extreme Remedies* (1967), *No Bail for Dalton* (1974), and *False Colors* (1985).

(*K.K.H./M.M.*)

*Borges, Jorge Luis, and Adolfo Bioy-Casares. *Six Problems for Don Isidro Parodi.* Translated from the Spanish by Norman Thomas di Giovanni. New York: Dutton, 1981. (SS/AD)

In 1919, Don Isidro Parodi, a Buenos Aires barber, was falsely sentenced to life in prison for murder. Now, fourteen years later, confined to Cell 273 of the city jail, Don Isidro is "in his forties, sententious and fat"—and he has become a legend. Without stirring from his enforced idleness, he solves the most impenetrable of mysteries by his understanding of human nature and sharp eye for distinguishing what is essential.

The six problems follow a pattern: A visitor to Cell 273 describes the problem; Don Isidro listens, drinks *mate* (which he does not offer to share), and asks a few questions; a few days later the visitor returns, and Don Isidro presents the solution.

In "The Twelve Figures of the World," he employs a simple card trick to show a murder suspect how he was framed. In "The Nights of Goliadkin," a bombastic actor learns how he was used by a dead man to save a valuable diamond. The solution owes a debt to Agatha Christie. "The God of the Bulls" concerns a writer who would compromise a woman's reputation for his own fame; the man is revealed as a pompous ass—but cleared of murder. The other fine stories in this collection are "Free Will and the Commendatore," "Tadio Limaro's Victim," and "Tai An's Long Search."

Borges, one of the most honored writers of his time, and Argentine novelist Bioy-Casares collaborated on the Don Isidro Parodi stories with comic intent, and the tales are filled with satire of writers, actors, religious groups, and the police. For example, one of Don Isidro's clients complains that the Buenos Aires horse races are fixed now "so you can't tell who's going to win anymore." And Don Isidro was convicted of murder not because he was suspected of killing anybody but because a police official owed him a year's rent.

The stories were published in Buenos Aires under the pseudonym H. Bustos Domecq, which was the name of a writer in another fictional collaboration between Borges and Bioy-Casares. As a postscript, the authors included a biography of Bustos Domecq. In the Parodi tales, they say, Bustos Domecq "attempts to combat the cold intellectualism in which Sir Arthur Conan Doyle, Ottolenghi, etc., have immersed this genre. [The stories] are not the filigree of a Byzantine locked in an ivory tower, but are the voice of a true contemporary, who is sensitive to the human pulsebeat and from whose generous pen flows the torrent of his truths."

(*M.J.*)

Boucher, Anthony. *The Case of the Baker Street Irregulars.* New York: Simon & Schuster, 1940. (AD/PP)

Anthony Boucher (William Anthony Parker White) was the fairest and most astute critic the mystery field has ever had; no one better understood crime fiction and those who compose it, and no one wrote about it quite so well. This is due in part, certainly, to Boucher himself being an accomplished writer of mysteries, both fair-play detective novels and short stories.

The Case of the Baker Street Irregulars is his third novel and demonstrates his passionate love for the Sherlock Holmes stories of Sir Arthur Conan Doyle (q.v.). When Metropolis Pictures in Hollywood announces plans to film *The Adventure of the Speckled Band,* its president, F. X. Weinberg, receives a manifesto from that august group of Sherlockians, the Baker Street Irregulars, registering strong protest against the fact that "the delicate and responsible task of transferring this adventure to the screen has been entrusted to the typewriter of Stephen Worth . . . hereinafter to be known as *that rat,* the author of many stupid and illogical mystery novels of the type known as hard-boiled." Metropolis decides to placate the Irregulars, and not coincidentally do itself and its picture some good, by inviting a few of the group to Hollywood to supervise the filming—a masterful publicity stunt that even goes so far as to have the number of the house in which the Irregulars will be staying changed to 221B and a new housekeeper named Mrs. Hudson installed.

Everything goes fine at first. Five Irregulars arrive—an editor, a doctor, a writer, a teacher, a refugee scientist—and it appears that everyone is having a fine time, including the ghost of Sherlock Holmes. But then murder rears its ugly head. And not any simple sort of homicide, either. The clever villain uses such devices as Doyle's Code of the Dancing Men to fuddle and exasperate everyone else involved.

The case is finally solved by the combined efforts of the Irregulars, pretty Maureen O'Breen of Metropolis Pictures' Publicity Department, and Lieutenant Finch of the LAPD. Along the way there are clues galore, plenty of Holmesian scholarship, some sharp characterizations, and a few nice humorous touches. If your taste runs to classic detective stories, and if you are a devotee of Holmes and Watson, you'll have a fine time with *The Case of the Baker Street Irregulars.*

Boucher's other novels are in the same mystery-for-fun vein. They include *The Case of the Seven of Calvary* (1937), which has an academic background (the University of California Berkeley campus) and an engaging armchair detective; *The Case of the Crumpled Knave* (1939), which introduces private detective Fergus O'Breen (Maureen's brother); two more O'Breen investigations, *The Case of the Solid Key* (1941)—a locked-room mystery—and *The Case of the Seven Sneezes* (1942); and *The Marble Forest* (1951), which Boucher coordinated and co-wrote with eleven other members of the northern California chapter of MWA under the pseudonym Theo Durrant, and which was filmed by William Castle in 1958 as *Macabre.*

(*B.P.*)

*Boucher, Anthony. *Exeunt Murderers: The Best Mystery Stories of Anthony Boucher.* Carbondale, Ill.: Southern Illinois University Press, 1983. (SS)

Boucher published some sixty short stories during his thirty-year writing career, about equally divided between mystery/detective and science fiction/fantasy. The twenty-two stories in *Exeunt Murderers* clearly show that he had a fine hand with the form—a finer hand, perhaps, than he had with novels.

Included here are all nine of the Nick Noble stories, Boucher's best series and most inspired work. Noble is an ex-cop who was thrown off the force in disgrace for taking graft, something he resorted to in desperation to pay for an operation his wife needed—an operation that failed and left him a widower. The combination of tragedies turned him into a wino who spends most of his time at a cheap bar called the Chula Negra, drinking rotgut sherry and fending off an invisible fly that keeps pestering him. But even though he is "the lowest and soddenest kind of drunk that even the Skid

Row of Los Angeles can exhibit," he can still deduce with the best, as he proves whenever his friend, Lieutenant MacDonald, brings him cases no one in the department can solve. Dying messages and codes are Noble's specialties. And among his best deductions are those that clear up the murder of a priest in "Screwball Division," the murder of a librarian in "QL 696. C9," and a football mystery in "The Punt and the Pass."

Also included are a pair of cases featuring Sister Ursula, the cloistered nun whom Boucher created for a pair of early novels published under the pseudonym of H. H. Holmes (q.v.). "The Stripper" is the grisly tale of a Jack the Ripper–style murderer on the loose in southern California. "Coffin Corner," like the Nick Noble case mentioned above, has a college-football background.

Boucher's best nonseries stories are here as well: the wonderfully macabre "The Retired Hangman," a much tougher story than was usual with him; "Mystery for Christmas," a story-within-a-story that features Donald Duck and Mickey Mouse; "The Smoke-Filled Locked Room," which combines deduction with some of Boucher's political views; and "The Ultimate Clue," a short-short (again about football) with the ultimate detective-story ending.

An insightful introduction by Francis M. Nevins, Jr. (who coedited the volume with Martin H. Greenberg), rounds out what is surely one of the best and longest-overdue collections to be published in the past several years.

(*B.P.*)

Box, Edgar. *Death in the Fifth Position.* New York: Dutton, 1952. (AD)

George Vidal a mystery writer? Yes indeed, although the mystery in his three detective novels is much inferior to the writing. In the early 1950s, at the end of his first period as a mainstream novelist and the beginning of his career as a writer of live TV drama, Vidal took up the pseudonym of Edgar Box and spent about three weeks turning out a whodunit trilogy whose amateur sleuth is Peter Cutler Sargeant II, a thirtyish, pleasantly pig-faced public-relations consultant and (exclusively hetero) sexual gymnast. Although they're not noteworthy as detective novels, Vidal's guided tours through the worlds of art, politics, and high society entertain royally with countless gleefully sardonic jabs at every target in sight.

The series opens with *Death in the Fifth Position* (1952), in which Peter is retained to provide good PR for the Grand St. Petersburg Ballet. The dance group is feeling the pinch of McCarthyism, courtesy of a right-wing veterans' organization (Motto: "In a true democracy there is no place for a difference of opinion on great issues") incensed at the group's having hired a "Communist" choreographer, Jed Wilbur. At the climax of Wilbur's new ballet, its star is supposed to ascend into the wings in triumph. But on opening night, the wire cable snaps and the prima ballerina falls to her death before the eyes of thousands. Vidal then treats us to many pages of satire about professional dancers and their hangers-on and tedious speculation about homicidal motives, interspersed with two more gruesome deaths, before Peter unveils his surprising but unfair solution.

Death Before Bedtime (1953) finds Peter in Washington as PR adviser to ultraconservative Senator Leander Rhodes and bedmate to Rhodes's nymphomaniac daughter. Rhodes's ambitions to be his party's next presidential candidate come to an abrupt end when he's blown to bits by a gunpowder charge in his fireplace. The investigation, long on speculation and short on substance, is interrupted in its stately progress toward nowhere by (surprise!) another murder, after which Peter uses a mix of guesswork and bluff to expose the guilty party. Once again a lackluster plot is saved by Vidal's mocking gibes at politics, journalism, sex, and society.

In his third and last case, *Death Likes It Hot* (1954), Peter is invited to a weekend house party at a Long Island beachfront mansion and encounters tangled emotions and murder among a cast of ludicrous plutocrats and talentless pseudoartists. Its fairly complex plot, a few deft clues, and a dramatic climax make this the best mystery of the trio, but again it's the pungent satire that brings the book to life.

Clever deductions, fair play with the reader, and the Christie-Queen bag of tricks are not Vidal's strong points. But his mastery of the language permeates even these mysteries that he himself shrugs off as potboilers cranked out for money, and his tone of cynical, good-humored tolerance toward an America populated exclusively by crooks, opportunists, and buffoons is as close to the true spirit of H. L. Mencken as mystery fiction is ever likely to see.

It appears that Vidal had a good time with mysteries, and his pleasure is conveyed to the reader. He must have especially enjoyed himself when he got to write the following, surprisingly accurate, blurb which appeared on the covers of the paperback editions of his three mysteries. "The work that Dr. Kinsey began with statistics, Edgar Box has completed with wit in the mystery novel." Though Spillane and others had already broken down the barriers against writing about sex in the detective story, Vidal went further than anyone else, but he also did it with more humor.

(*F.M.N./M.L.*)

Boyer, Rick. *Billingsgate Shoal.* Boston: Houghton Mifflin, 1982. (W/T)

Rick Boyer won an Edgar for this, his first mystery novel—deserved recognition for a complex suspense novel set in coastal and suburban Massachusetts.

Charles ("Doc") Adams is a medical doctor turned oral surgeon. He is middle-aged, affluent, happily married, and intensely dissatisfied with his life. His depression and insomnia are symptoms of his midlife crisis. The cure is worse than the disease, however, as Doc is thrown headlong into a very violent adventure. It starts with an early-morning sighting of a stranded fishing vessel on the title shoal, continues with the death of a young scuba diver who tries to check out the boat for Adams, and eventually escalates to a kill-or-die confrontation between Doc and the villains.

Billingsgate Shoal has a little bit of everything for everybody. There is hidden treasure, political intrigue, and a murder mystery. There is even a good deal of gore for those who like their thrillers tough and bloody. But it is the believable and very personable voice of Boyer's amateur sleuth that makes even the more outrageous elements of his plot come together in a way that seems realistic and truly suspenseful.

Boyer's second novel, *The Penny Ferry* (1984), a case focusing on present-day evidence of the guilt/innocence of Sacco and Vanzetti, is proof that Boyer's talents are substantial and that Doc Adams has staying power as series sleuth.

(*K.L.M.*)

Boyle, Jack. *Boston Blackie.* Boston: Gregg Press, 1979. (Reprint of 1919 edition published by H.K. Fly, Boston.) (SS)

This is an unusual book in that it consists of previously published short stories put together and revised slightly to resemble chapters in a novel. It is the only Boston Blackie "novel" *or* collection to be published.

The Boston Blackie stories began running in the *American* magazine in 1914; later ones appeared in *Redbook* and *Cosmopolitan.* Although by today's standards they contain overly dramatic language and sentimental plots, they still provide an entertaining insight into popular American fiction of the early 1900s. Included in this reprint edition is a scholarly introduction by Edward D. Hoch, the original illustrations, and still photographs from some of the various Boston Blackie films.

For those unfamiliar with Boyle's Boston Blackie, he was a criminal—primarily a safecracker—and was wanted by many police departments. But he was also a devoted husband, a "university graduate, a scholar, and gentleman." The first half of his nickname derived from his Boston birthplace, the second half from his piercing black eyes.

As interesting as Blackie himself may be, his creator is even more so. Jack Boyle was a San Francisco newspaper editor who became addicted to opium in the legendary dens of Chinatown. This cost him his job, and, unable to get another, he turned to a life of crime—an unsuccessful one, for he was twice arrested and sent to prison, once for forgery and the second time for armed robbery. It was while he was in San Quentin on the robbery conviction that he wrote (and sold) his first Boston Blackie story to *American,* under the pseudonym "6606"—his prison number. Many of the subsequent Blackie stories were to employ drug and prison backgrounds. After his release, Boyle continued his writing career and helped adapt some of his stories for silent films.

Several Blackie silents were made in the 1920s; the first of these, for which Boyle wrote the screenplay, was *The Face in the Fog* (1922) and featured Lionel Barrymore as Blackie. The character underwent a considerable transformation in the series of B talkies that began in 1941 and starred Chester Morris: He became a wise-talking reformed-crook-turned-sleuth with a penchant for dames, danger, and sudden death. The Hollywood incarnation also appeared on the radio and briefly on television in its early years.

(*N.D./B.P.*)

Brackett, Leigh. *No Good from a Corpse.* New York: Coward, McCann, 1944. (PI)

Leigh Brackett is perhaps best known for her science fiction and for her script work on the classic private-eye film *The Big Sleep* (1946); but she also wrote excellent crime fiction (and one very good historical western). Her mysteries tend to be tough-minded and realistic. *No Good from a Corpse,* in fact, can accurately be termed "hard-boiled"—and indeed has been called, by some critics and aficionados, the best traditional private-eye novel written by a woman.

Los Angeles detective Edmond Clive embarks on an angry, vengeful hunt when an old girlfriend, nightclub singer Laurel Dane, is murdered. His quest leads him from Beverly Hills mansions to cheap night spots along the Sunset Strip; from rich playboys (and playgirls) to denizens of the underworld; from threatening telephone calls to a knock on the head to attempts on his life; and from blackmail to several more murders before he finally uncovers the not altogether surprising identity of Laurel's murderer and the truth behind a web of lies and half truths.

Critic Anthony Boucher stated in an introduction to a reissue of this novel in 1964 that Brackett was the one woman who "most successfully captured the authentic Chandleresque male tone." True enough; the tone is *very* Chandleresque, to the point of pastiche. It is as if Miss Brackett deliberately set out to out-Chandler Chandler. About the novel itself, Boucher wrote, "Its ingredients are not startlingly new: it even includes the obligatory night clubs, in which detective-story characters spend so much more time than any other class of people. But the familiar ingredients take on fresh life, partly because Miss Brackett looks at and writes about Los Angeles itself and not its conventionalized fiction image." Also true, pro and con. There is nothing really new in the novel; Brackett covers old ground—and covers it well, even expertly, but the fact remains that Chandler did it first and did it better. Clive is the only memorable character, and he pales alongside Philip Marlowe. With all due respect to Boucher and the book's other boosters, *No Good from a Corpse* is *not* the best traditional private-eye novel written by a woman. That distinction belongs to Dolores Hitchens's *Sleep with Slander* (q.v.).

(*B.P.*)

Brackett, Leigh. *The Tiger Among Us.* New York: Doubleday Crime Club, 1957. (T)

This is Leigh Brackett's best crime novel—a simple, straightforward, consistently gripping, and powerful story of one man's nightmare encounter with random teenage violence. Walter Sherris, an average family man and a white-collar employee of a company in an Ohio mill town, takes a walk along a dark road one night and is brutally beaten by five young "tigers" out looking for thrills. But that is only the beginning of his ordeal. When Sherris is finally released from the hospital, he sets out to do what the police haven't been able to: learn the identities of his attackers and see justice done. It isn't long, however, before he is again the hunted—and his family along with him. For the five boys, continuing their random attacks, have gone too far with another of their victims: They are already murderers and stand ready to kill again. Even if Sherris learns to wear the stripes of the tiger himself, even if he survives this second assault, he knows his life will never be the same.

Fine writing and some genuinely harrowing scenes make *The Tiger Among Us* one of the best of the spate of Fifties novels dealing with juvenile delinquency. In the forcefulness of its message, in fact, it is second only to Evan Hunter's (q.v.) mainstream novel *The Blackboard Jungle.* An effective screen version appeared under the title *13 West Street* in 1962, starring Alan Ladd and Rod Steiger.

Brackett's other crime novels are *An Eye for an Eye* (1957) and *Silent Partner* (1969). She also ghosted a mystery for actor George Sanders, *Stranger at Home* (1946).

(*B.P.*)

Braly, Malcolm. *Shake Him Till He Rattles.* Greenwich, Conn.: Fawcett Gold Medal, 1963. (O/T)

When *On the Yard,* the novel Malcolm Braly based on his years in prison, appeared in 1967, everyone said he was major. But for a major writer, Braly, who was killed in an automobile accident at age fifty-five, is virtually forgotten today. By any standard, however, *Yard* and the three novels he wrote for Gold Medal in the early Sixties are books worth reading, books in many respects as frenetic and confessional as the more literary novels of the era.

Shake Him Till He Rattles concerns Lee Cabiness, a sax player whose only goal is to stay out of prison. Lieutenant Carver of the San Francisco narc squad has other ideas. Braly obviously based Carver on both personal experience and his reading of Dostoevski, for the cop here is almost mythic in his malice and darkness, his repudiation of all human values.

Braly posits the jazz musicians of his book, however, as magic revelers in the human song: "Furg was a child, a vagabond child, a fey and travel-torn minstrel barely suffered in the halls of the minor barons. But, whether they knew it or not, Furg was necessary to them, to breathe into their lives the vital stuff of myth.

Later Braly describes the same world Jack Kerouac earlier set down as "beat." Only Braly saw it differently: "People were coming in. Pink, clean examples of college and social Bohemia, mostly young, roughly thirty per cent gay. He saw Clair moving around. In her white dress with her pale hair she looked chilly. He caught her smile coming and going, like distant sunlight on ice."

The conflict between Cabiness and Carver grows, of course, as the narc makes frustrated moves on his prey, trying to demean and unman him as he closes in. The battle, again, is out of Dostoevski—the perversion of a legal system and its victim. The details, interestingly, remain "beat."

Braly's fiction testifies to the indomitable human spirit of the intelligent loser. There is a wealth of sadness and humor alike in his pages and a kind of quirky defiance. His was the ultimate loneliness, it seemed, belonging as he did to neither world, criminal nor straight. He charted a type of experience seldom seen in crime fiction—the real world of the criminal. A rediscovery of this and Braly's other fine novels—*Felony Tank* (1961), *It's Cold Out There* (1966), and *The Protector* (1979)—is long past due.

(*E.G.*)

*Bramah, Ernest. *Max Carrados.* London: Methuen, 1914. (CS/SS)

For some years it was thought that Ernest Bramah was the pseudonym of some other mystery writer who was doing double duty; or, alternatively, that the pen name represented a group trying its hands at a specialized type of story. Eventually, the author revealed himself (a little bit), and what he revealed was that the pseudonym stood for Ernest Bramah Smith. He was extremely self-effacing; however, details are plentiful about the life and adventures of his greatest creation, Max Carrados, the first and probably the best blind detective in fiction.

Carrados was very much in the Great Detective mold. Even though blind, his personality dominates the stories. He is sophisticated, cynical, and whimsical, and he awes friends, clients, and enemies with feats of subtle brilliance, "seeing" what no blind man can see. Carrados lives at the Turrets in Richmond (just west of London), surrounded by his ménage of secretary, young, brash Annesley Greatorex, and valet, the solemnly decorous Parkinson. He is interested in crimes of originality, and is called upon to solve cases of arson, madness, embezzlement, jewel burglary, a divorce murder, the theft of one of England's greatest relics, a post-office robbery connected with Irish outrages, and to thwart German naval spies. A commentator has said that the setting of these stories is much closer to Raymond Chandler's "mean streets" than to the unreal English country house of Agatha Christie.

The Carrados stories are an Edwardian tour de force, and Ellery Queen called *Max Carrados* "one of the ten best volumes of detective shorts ever written." The eight stories in this collection contain the inevitable meeting between Carrados and disbarred lawyer turned inquiry agent Louis Carlyle, who becomes his "Watson." The tales range from a problem in numismatics (one of Bramah's own little enthusiasms), to train-wrecking tinged with racism, to looting of safe deposits as a result of religious enthusiasm. The problems are logical, the characterizations are excellent, and the backgrounds are exceptional. In the much-anthologized "Tragedy at Brookbend Cottage," a man proposes to remove his wife by the latest scientific methods. Of course, Carrados intervenes, using clues only a blind man can find, and brings the case to its ironic conclusion.

Critics have praised the stories highly, and the two other collections—*The Eyes of Max Carrados* (1923) and *Max Carrados Mysteries* (1927)—are also well worth attention, although the later stories tend to get ponderous and are uneven in quality. The only Max Carrados novel, *The Bravo of London* (1934), proves conclusively that Bramah was a good short-story writer.

(*T.B.*)

Brand, Christianna. *Green for Danger.* New York: Dodd, Mead, 1944. (PP)

Christianna Brand has written mainstream novels, short stories, and juveniles, but she is best known for her detective novels featuring Inspector Cockrill of the Kent, England, County Police. Cockrill (known affectionately as Cockie) is a somewhat eccentric, curmudgeonly fellow—less a character than a catalyst in the cases he solves. He delights in setting up situations that force the murderer's hand, and the murderer's identity usually seems quite obvious to the reader, until Brand introduces a twist designed to delight.

At the beginning of *Green for Danger,* an unlikely group of characters assemble at a military hospital during the blitz of World War II. Each has his reasons for escaping his previous environment; each has expectations of what this assignment will bring. What none of them suspects is that a patient—the postman who, incidentally, delivered their letters saying they were coming to Heron's Park Hospital—will die mysteriously on the operating table, and that all of them will come under Inspector Cockrill's scrutinizing eye as murder suspects.

The characters are numerous, but Brand nonetheless manages to instill unique qualities that enlist the reader's sympathy and create dismay at the revelation of the murderer. The solution is plausible, the motivation well foreshadowed, and the evocation of both the terror and fortitude of those who endured the German bombing is very real indeed.

Inspector Cockrill has also solved such cases as *Heads You Lose* (1941), *Death of Jezebel* (1948), *London Particular* (1952), and *The Three-Cornered Halo* (1957).

(*M.M.*)

Branson, H. C. *The Pricking Thumb.* New York: Simon & Schuster, 1942. (AD)

During his Ann Arbor days, Ross Macdonald (Kenneth Millar) was a close friend of H.C. Branson and an admirer of his work. It is easy to see why. Branson wrote literate, meticulously plotted (but flawed) novels in which the emphasis is on deep-seated conflicts that have their roots in the dark past. Branson's detective, John Bent, like Macdonald's Lew Archer, is less a human being than a vehicle around which to build a narrative, a catalyst to mesh all the elements so that each novel's final statement becomes clear.

In *The Pricking Thumb,* Bent is hired by an acquaintance, Marina Holland, to investigate the disappearance of her stepson, Bob, and the odd behavior of her husband, Gouvion. But when Bent arrives in the small town of New Paget (in an unnamed state, probably Michigan; a sense of place is almost nonexistent), he finds Gouvion dead of an apparently self-inflicted gunshot wound. Also found dead this same night are Marina and Gouvion's doctor, Brian Calvert, under circumstances that suggest the two might have been lovers. It appears to be a case of double homicide perpetrated by Gouvion, who then committed suicide. But there are too many inconsistencies, leading Bent to believe that it is instead a case of triple homicide. His search for the truth takes him along a tangled trail of relationships, old and new hatreds and jealousies, and not a little double-dealing.

There is a good deal of passion among the characters; unfortunately, there is very little in John Bent or in the writing. Bent is a virtual cipher, about whom we know only that he once practiced medicine. "Someone was feeding [one of my patients] arsenic," he says to Marina Holland in the first chapter. "The only way I could cure him was to find out who it was and make them stop, which was a little more difficult than it sounds. At any rate, I ended up with a new profession." The writing, while well crafted, is so detached and emotionless that the reader tends to lose interest.

Had Branson possessed more of Ross Macdonald's talent, had he been able to make Bent more human and sympathetic, had he injected some passion and vividness into his work, he might have become an important figure in the mystery field. As it is, he is chiefly notable not for his work but for his relationship with Kenneth Millar.

Among his other novels, all featuring John Bent, are *I'll Eat You Last* (1941), *Case of the Giant Killer* (1944), and *The Leaden Bubble* (1949).

(*B.P.*)

Brautigan, Richard. *Dreaming of Babylon.* New York: Delacorte, 1977. (PI)

The time is 1942, the place is San Francisco, and a private detective named C. Card is down on his luck. He already has sold everything of value he owns. He owes rent to his landlady, money to all his friends, and various domestic items to all his fellow tenants. Then, amazingly, his luck begins to change with two fortuitous events: (1) His landlady dies, and (2) he gets a client. The trouble is, he has no bullets for his gun and must find some before he meets his client. (What kind of detective goes around with an unloaded gun?)

The search for bullets takes him to the Hall of Justice and to the city morgue, and many a mysterious stranger he meets along the way—a beautiful, crying blonde; a tough, smiling chauffeur; and a lovely, but dead, prostitute, to name but a few. Of course, the bullet search is not aided any by the fact that he keeps slipping into a daydream about ancient Babylon.

This is Richard Brautigan's only criminous novel and, to the average mystery aficionado, the story will seem rambling and plotless, having emerged as it did through the old, capricious byways of the author's mind. It is a story not so much for fans of detective fiction but for fans of Brautigan fiction, for this is the popular poet/novelist who first came to us out of the hippie generation and is responsible for such works of gentle whimsy as *Trout Fishing in America.* Inexplicably, his later novels took on more violent themes. This would include *Dreaming of Babylon,* although, by the standards of modern detective fiction, the book is relatively nonviolent and the author's fanciful comic inventiveness shines through.

(*N.D.*)

Brean, Robert. *Wilders Walk Away.* New York: Morrow, 1948. (AD)

Free-lance magazine writer Reynold Frame comes to the Vermont village of Wilders Lane to do a series of articles on the colonial town and its history. The village's founding family, the Wilders, are a decidedly curious bunch: It is said that no Wilder ever died of old age; they just disappeared. In 1775 patriarch Jonathan Wilder walked down into the cellar of the family house and was never seen again. Another Wilder was a mate on the *Mary Celeste.* Still another vanished from a sandy beach in 1917, in full view of witnesses.

But Wilders "walking away" isn't a phenomenon confined to past history, as Frame soon learns. First young Ellen Wilder and then Aunt Mary also vanish from watched rooms inside the house, while he himself is on the premises.

There is plenty of eerie mystery here, a fine sense of small-town New England life circa 1948, and some fascinating bits and pieces of colonial history woven in. Plus a Revolutionary War treasure, secret passages and hidden rooms, an array of offbeat characters, and of course a love interest for Frame (Constance, one of the few Wilders who does *not* walk away). The solutions to the "impossible" occurrences are well set up, if not particularly ingenious—the trickiest is the sandy-beach disappearance—but that doesn't spoil the book's appeal.

Reynold Frame appears in three other novels—*The Darker the Night* (1949), *Hardly a Man Is Now Alive* (1950), and *The Clock Strikes Thirteen* (1952)—all of which likewise make good use of unusual settings, strange doings, and past crimes. Brean also created another journalist detective, William Deacon, for *The Traces of Brillhart* (1960) and *The Traces of Merilee* (1966).

(*B.P.*)

Breen, Jon L. *The Gathering Place.* New York: Walker, 1984. (W/T)

Well known for a number of years as a critic, short-story writer, and parodist, John Breen turned to the writing of novels in 1983 with *Listen for the Click,* an affectionate parody/pastiche of the classic country-house mystery. *The Gathering Place,* his second novel, is quite different—a bookshop mystery that combines the traditional fair-play whodunit with ghosts and other elements of the paranormal.

When Oscar Vermilion dies of heart failure, his used-book store on Santa Monica Boulevard in Los Angeles, a fixture since 1935 and a gathering place for such literary lights as Nathaniel West and William Faulkner, is in danger of closing for good. But Vermilion's niece, Rachel Hennings, inherits the property, and she has both experience of her own in running a bookshop and a desire to maintain her uncle's legacy. That desire may not be easy to fulfill, however: Not long after her arrival from Arizona, Vermilion's is broken into (although nothing is taken); ghostly manifestations begin to occur in the shop's dusty confines (*something* guides her hand to write F. Scott Fitzgerald's name in a copy of *The Great Gatsby,* a signature that turns out to be authentic); and she is presented with evidence that *The Atlantis Courier,* an early novel by leading Hollywood writer Arlen Kitchener, was actually ghostwritten by a man who was found murdered shortly after Oscar Vermilion's death.

Breen neatly meshes these diverse elements, and a budding romance between Rachel and newspaperman Stu Wellman, into a suspenseful tale that keeps the reader guessing on several fronts. Some may find the supernatural segments of the plot a strain on their credulity; this reviewer and general skeptic had no trouble with them, and in fact found that they add considerable depth and mystery to the story line. Another plus is the bookish lore and information the author weaves throughout the narrative.

One other recommended title by Jon Breen is *Hair of the Sleuthhound* (1982), a collection of some of the best of his short spoofs of distinguished crime writers and their works.

(*B.P.*)

Brett, Michael. *Slit My Throat, Gently.* New York: Pocket Books, 1968. (PI/O)

Michael Brett's series of paperback originals about private eye Pete McGrath were likely intended to provide Pocket Books with a series character to rival Fawcett's Shell Scott, Dell's Mike Shayne, and Signet's various Carter Brown (q.v.) series. McGrath appeared a bit late in the game and apparently failed to find a loyal readership, since only one of the books made it past a single printing. (Sales were probably not helped any by the unattractive photo covers.)

Nevertheless, the McGrath novels are entertaining and adroitly written—satisfying, off-the-rack private-eye yarns that should please most unfussy readers of this sort of thing. One odd note about the series: Brett seems to have been unsure as to what sort of private-eye novel to produce. Some titles, like this one, are straightforward hard-boiled actioners. Others, like *The Flight of the Stiff* (1967), have a strong farcical element, in the manner of Richard S. Prather (q.v.). Pete McGrath never quite came into his own as an identifiable character, though in one respect—his penchant for talking to himself—he probably leads the field.

Here McGrath is hired to find a missing heiress who has run off with a small-time crook and drug addict. Also looking for her—or maybe just for her boyfriend—is a big-time mob boss, who takes drastic measures to get McGrath out of the picture. Corpses with their throats cut start turning up, and McGrath has quite a time of it. Two excellent scenes stand out: McGrath adroitly pumping a shady Atlantic City motel owner by posing as a sleazy divorce detective, and McGrath playing hardball with a junkie prostitute to turn up a lead.

One of the Pete McGrath novels, *Lie a Little, Die a Little* (1968), much changed, was filmed as a moderately pornographic detective spoof, *Cry Uncle,* which attained a modest cult status.

Other enjoyable books in the series: *Kill Him Quickly, It's Raining* (1966), *Dead Upstairs in the Tub* (1967), *Turn Blue, You Murderers* (1967). (*A.S.*)

Brett, Simon. *A Comedian Dies.* New York: Scribner's, 1979. (AD)

Making good use of his background in radio and television, and of his interest in the theater, Simon Brett has created one of the most likable characters among recent series sleuths: Charles Paris, a middle-aged and not very successful radio actor whose vices include drink, women, and stumbling into murder cases that he is forced to solve. The Paris novels are distinguished by solid plotting, well-drawn entertainment-business backgrounds, and a nice interweaving of humor that often borders on spoof.

One of the first things the reader of *A Comedian Dies,* which has a modern British vaudeville background, will notice is that there is a gag at the beginning of each chapter. A gag such as:

> *Feed: I heard on the radio this morning that the police are looking for a man with one eye.*
> *Comic: Typical inefficiency.*

Having discovered this, most readers will no doubt be tempted to flip through the book and read all of the gags immediately, like gulping popcorn. You should refrain from doing this, however. Taken one at a time, every dozen pages or so, each will provoke an amused and tolerant groan; taken all at once, they are sort of like listening to a Bob Hope monologue and may therefore cause severe trauma, if not a sudden desire to take up golf or vote Republican.

On the other hand, the novel itself *is* worth reading all at once. Paris and his estranged wife, Frances, trying once again to mend their marriage, are attending a vaudeville show at the Winter Gardens in Hunstanton, a small English seacoast town. But the show the star performer, comedian Bill Peaky, puts on is not at all what Paris anticipated: Peaky is electrocuted on stage while clutching his electric guitar and microphone. At the inquest, the coroner decides the death was accidental, due to faulty wiring, but Paris has his doubts and starts an investigation of his own. Suspects abound, owing to the fact that Peaky was not a very popular fellow. Paris is something of a bumbler, which only enhances his appeal; and he *does* get to the bottom of things eventually, in spite of the eighteen gags Brett throws at him along the way.

Feed:Do you know, they say that whisky kills more people than bullets.
Comic: Ah well, that's because bullets don't drink.

(*N.D./B.P.*)

Brett, Simon. The Dead Side of the Mike. New York: Scribner's, 1980. (AD)

Between acting jobs (which seems more or less to be the story of his life), Charles Paris takes a job with BBC radio to research and write a program on Swinburne for a new series called "Who Reads Them Now?" Not long afterward, he and another employee find the body of a young female station manager who apparently has committed suicide. But has she really? Matters begin to look decidedly suspicious when an American record producer, with whom the dead woman, Andrea Gower, seems to have been involved, is *also* found dead, an apparent suicide.

Paris extends his investigation from London to New York—his first trip to America—when he is called upon to attend the funeral of his mother-in-law. While there, he picks up important information on the shady record producer (and also learns, somewhat to his surprise, that all Americans are not character actors from soap operas and police thrillers). Back in London, Paris bumbles his way to the solution of the double "suicides"—and barely manages to survive a confrontation with the guilty party.

This is another amusing romp through a segment of the British entertainment industry. Its only flaw, and a minor one it is, is that Brett seems a bit uncomfortable with American dialogue and doesn't quite capture its proper rhythms—an inability a great many other British writers seem also to have been afflicted with.

Paris's other entertaining adventures include *Cast, in Order of Disappearance* (1976), which has a theater background; *So Much Blood* (1977), in which Paris travels to Scotland to attend the Edinburgh Festival; and *Star Trap* (1978), which pits our aging Lothario against a murderer in a hit musical revue.

Simon Brett is also the author of a chilling novel of psychological suspense, *A Shock to the System* (1985).

(*N.D./B.P.*)

Brewer, Gil. *A Killer Is Loose.* Greenwich, Conn.: Fawcett Gold Medal, 1954. (O/T)

In the 1950s and 1960s, Gil Brewer occupied a major stall in the stable of writers of Gold Medal paperback originals, along with John D. MacDonald, Richard S. Prather, and Charles Williams (qq.v.). Brewer's work was uneven but usually interesting and evocative, and quite popular from 1951 to 1958; his first novel, *13 French Street* (1951), sold more than a million copies. Much of his fiction is built around the theme of a man corrupted by an evil, designing woman; but his two best novels, this one and *The Red Scarf,* are departures from that theme.

Set in Florida, as is most of Brewer's fiction, *A Killer Is Loose* is a truly harrowing portrait of a psychotic personality that comes close to rivaling the nightmare portraits in the novels of Jim Thompson (q.v.). It tells the story of Ralph Angers, a deranged surgeon and Korean War veteran obsessed with building a hospital, and his devastating effect on the lives of several citizens. One of those citizens is the narrator, Steve Logan, a down-on-his-luck ex-cop whose wife is about to have a baby and who makes the mistake of saving Angers's life, thus becoming his "pal." As Logan says on page one, by way of prologue, "There was nothing simple about Angers, except maybe the Godlike way he had of doing things."

Brewer maintains a pervading sense of terror and an acute level of tension throughout. The novel is flawed by a slow beginning and a couple of improbable occurrences, as well as by an ending that is a little abrupt—all of which are the probable result of hasty writing (Brewer once said that he wrote most of his early novels in a white heat of seven to ten days). But its strengths far outnumber its weaknesses. Two aspects in particular stand out: One is the curious and frightening relationship that develops between Logan and Angers; the other is a five-page scene in which Angers, with Logan looking on helplessly, forces a scared little girl to play the piano for him—a scene Woolrich might have written and Hitchcock should have filmed.

(*B.P.*)

Brewer, Gil. *The Red Scarf.* New York: Mystery House, 1958. (T)

Motel owner Ray Nichols, hitchhiking home in northern Florida after a futile trip up north to raise capital for his floundering auto court, is given a ride by a bickering and drunken couple named Vivian Rise and Noel Teece.

An accident, the result of Teece's drinking, leaves Teece bloody and unconscious. Unhurt, Nichols finds a suitcase full of money in the car. Vivian, also unhurt, urges that they leave with it together before the police come, saying it belongs to her and offering to pay Nichols for his help. Against his better judgment, he agrees.

It is only later, back home in the town of Lakeview, that Nichols discovers Teece is a courier for an underworld gambling syndicate and that the money really belongs to them. While he struggles with his conscience, several groups begin vying for the loot, including a syndicate man named Wirt Radan, the police—and Teece. Nichols and his wife, Bess, soon become targets, and Brewer leads us through a couple of neat plot turns on the way to a volatile climax.

There is considerable suspense here, some strong characterization, and the various components mesh smoothly. Brewer's prose is leaner and more controlled than in any of his other novels. Anthony Boucher said in the *New York Times* that *The Red Scarf* is the "all-around best Gil Brewer . . . a full-packed story." This reviewer agrees.

Nearly all of Brewer's thirty other novels (all but one of which are paperback originals) are worth reading. Especially good are *And the Girl Screamed* (1956), which has some fine chase sequences; *The Angry Dream* (1957), the second of Brewer's two hardcovers and a tale of hatred out of the past, in a wintry northern setting; and *The Three-Way Split* (1960), a well-done story of charter boats and sunken treasure in a style reminiscent of Hemingway's *To Have and Have Not.*

(*B.P.*)

Brown, Carter. *Lament for a Lousy Lover.* New York: New American Library (Signet), 1960. (PI/O)

The Australian writer Alan G. Yates, a veritable one-man paperback factory, has turned out hundreds of lightweight private-eye and police novels under the Carter Brown pseudonym. The books borrow liberally from the old *Spicy Detective* pulp formula: action, wisecracks, coarse humor, plenty of voluptuous un- and underdressed sexpots.

This one is a bit unusual in that it features two of Brown's regular series characters in one book: Al Wheeler, the skirt-chasing Pine City sheriff's detective; and Mavis Seidlitz, an astonishingly endowed and astoundingly dizzy blonde who somehow manages to find work as a private eye. Their historic meeting was prompted by a suggestion from Anthony Boucher (q.v.), the only mystery critic of consequence to regularly review Brown's paperbacks. As is the case with many of Brown's books, the background is Hollywood. Mavis is on location for the filming of a hit TV western series, hired to keep a couple of feuding starlets apart. The star is murdered (via the ancient wheeze of substituting live bullets for blanks), and Wheeler is assigned to the case. Everybody has a likely motive; another murder ensues; Mavis blunders around like an idiot; Wheeler lusts after the starlets and winds up with Mavis. The first-person narrative alternates between Wheeler and Mavis (Yates/Brown deserves extra credit for successfully managing to provide this burlesque caricature with a semiplausible character voice).

Among the dozens of other Al Wheeler novels are *The Brazen* (1960), *Burden of Guilt* (1970), and *Wheeler Fortune* (1974). Mavis Seidlitz also stars in *None but the Lethal Heart* (1959) and *Tomorrow Is Murder* (1960). Brown's other series characters include L.A. private eye Rick Holman; Randy Roberts, a randy San Francisco lawyer; and Hollywood scriptwriter Larry Baker and his drunken partner, Boris Slivka.

(*A.S.*)

*Brown, Fredric. *The Fabulous Clipjoint.* New York: Dutton, 1947. (PI/T)

Fredric Brown's vision of the world was paradoxical and slightly cockeyed. Things, in his eye, are not always what you might think they are; elements of the bizarre spice the commonplace, and, conversely, elements of the commonplace leaven the bizarre. Madness and sanity are intertwined, so that it is often difficult to tell which is which. The same is true of malevolence and benignity, of tragedy and comedy. Brown seems to have felt that the forces, cosmic or otherwise, that control our lives are at best mischievous and at worst malign, that man has little to say about his own destiny, and that free will is a fallacy. The joke is on us, he seems to be saying on numerous occasions. And it is a joke that all too frequently turns nasty.

Brown employed a deceptively simple, offhand style that allows his fiction to be enjoyed by those interested only in entertainment and also pondered by those interested in the complex themes at its heart. *The Fabulous Clipjoint,* his first novel and the recipient of an Edgar from the Mystery Writers of America, is a good example.

On the one hand, it is a straightforward detective story that introduced the Chicago-based team of private eyes Ed and Am Hunter. Ed, the narrator, is young and idealistic; Ambrose, his uncle and a retired circus performer, is much more pragmatic and somewhat jaded—the voice of experience. When Ed's father, Wally, is shot down in a dark alley, Ed enlists his uncle's help and sets out to find the murderer. Their quest leads them into the seamy underbelly of 1940s society, the world of second-rate criminals, cheap bars, sleazy carnival folk; from a sideshow spieler named Hoagy to a beautiful tramp named Claire Raymond to assorted thugs and tough cops, and finally to a killer.

On the other hand, there are deeper meanings to the narrative—underlying themes of obsession, a young man's bitter and tragic coming of age, and the manipulation of those dark cosmic forces that Brown believed are in control of our lives. The handling of these themes is what makes the novel so grimly powerful. Not Brown's best book, and not for every taste, but unquestionably much more than just another hard-boiled detective tale.

Brown wrote six other Ed and Am Hunter books, none of which, unfortunately, approaches *The Fabulous Clipjoint* in quality. Among them are *The Dead Ringer* (1948); *The Bloody Moonlight* (1949, which has a werewolf theme); *Compliments of a Fiend* (1951); and *Mrs. Murphy's Underpants* (1963).

(*B.P.*)

*Brown, Fredric. *Knock Three-One-Two.* New York: Dutton, 1959. (PS)

Knock Three-One-Two has one of the most compelling (and chilling) opening lines in all of crime fiction: "He had a name, but it doesn't matter: call him *the psycho.*" It is the best of Brown's later novels, and one of his two or three best overall. It is also— in theme, mood, and final message—his most frightening work.

On the surface, *Knock* is a straightforward mystery that interweaves the lives of a maniacal rapist/strangler who preys on women alone at night in their apartments; a liquor salesman named Ray Fleck who is addicted to gambling; a Greek restaurateur, George Mikos, who is in love with Fleck's wife, Ruth; a mentally retarded news vendor named Benny; Dolly Mason, a promiscuous and mercenary beauty operator; and several other characters. But as the opening lines intimate, this is *not* a whodunit: The identity of the psycho is irrelevant to the plot; rather, he is a catalyst, an almost biblical symbol of evil. The suspense Brown creates and sustains here is of the dark and powerful sort perfected by Cornell Woolrich (q.v.), yet uniquely Brown's own in style and handling. It all builds beautifully, inexorably, to a shocking and ironic climax—Brown at his most controlled, dealing with material at its most chaotic.

Equally good are Brown's two other major suspense novels, *The Screaming Mimi* (1949) and *The Far Cry* (1951). *Mimi* is the story of an alcoholic Chicago reporter named Sweeney and his search for both a beautiful woman and a Ripper-style killer; it is also an allegorical retelling of "Beauty and the Beast." *The Far Cry,* set in New Mexico, has been called Brown's tour de force—a fair judgment, for the treatment of its theme of a love/hate obsession is uncommon and its denouement is both horrific and surprisingly bleak for its time.

(*B.P.*)

*Brown, Fredric. *Mostly Murder.* New York: Dutton, 1953. (SS)

Brown wrote excellent short fiction, including dozens of mordant short-shorts—a demanding form at which he proved himself a master. It can be argued, in fact, that except in a half-dozen or so cases, he was a better short-story writer than he was a novelist.

Mostly Murder, his first collection, contains eighteen of his best early stories, from *Ellery Queen's Mystery Magazine* and such pulps as *Black Mask* and *Dime Mystery.* Among them are his masterpiece of psychological horror "Don't Look Behind You," a tour de force in which the *reader* is the intended murder victim; an unusually dark and powerful treatment of the "impossible crime" theme, "The Laughing Butcher"; an ironic little chiller, "Little Apple Hard to Peel"; a Woolrichian tale of terror and suspense, "I'll Cut Your Throat Again, Kathleen"; the wryly humorous "Greatest Poem Ever Written"; and two of his best short-shorts, "Town Wanted" and "Cry Silence." An outstanding collection.

A second gathering of Brown's criminous stories, *The Shaggy Dog and Other Murders* (1963), is likewise first-rate. Also well worth reading are several recent collections: *Homicide Sanitarium* (1984), *Before She Kills* (1984), *Madman's Holiday* (1985), and *The Case of the Dancing Sandwiches* (1985), all limited editions of obscure but entertaining pulp stories; and *Carnival of Crime* (1985), which contains some but not all of his short mysteries, including several from *Mostly Murder,* and a complete checklist of Brown's published works.

(*B.P.*)

Brown, Fredric. *Night of the Jabberwock.* New York: Dutton, 1950. (T)

This entertaining novel, which takes place in one bizarre night, is a perfect example of Fredric Brown's somewhat eccentric view of the world. Doc Stoeger, editor of the Carmel City, Indiana, *Clarion,* sometime philosopher and devotee of the works of Lewis Carroll, has just put the small-town paper to bed. He has a drink in his office, wanders over to Smiley's Tavern for a couple more, and laments the fact that nothing ever happens in Carmel City. What wouldn't he give, Doc says, for just one important story? Then, just as he is about to go home, things start to happen. At first they are mundane: Tuesday's rummage sale is canceled and there is now a nine-inch hole in the front page; a messy divorce story needs to be rewritten because the charges against the husband were not true. But these are nothing like the surprise that visits Doc later at home.

The surprise is a man with the unlikely name of Yehudi Smith, who claims to be a member of a group of Lewis Carroll enthusiasts called the Vorpal Blades (a name taken from *Through the Looking Glass*). Smith invites Doc to a midnight meeting in a haunted house, and Doc is fascinated enough to accept. However, other events intervene: Doc's best friend is injured in an accident and no one can find out what happened; the bank is robbed in a strange way; an escaped lunatic is run to earth; and big-time criminals are on the loose. By the time Doc keeps his appointment with Yehudi Smith and the Vorpal Blades, he has covered and, for various reasons, had to suppress more major stories than most editors do in a year. And when he and Smith go to the haunted house, Doc is embroiled in an Alice-like adventure that leads him not down a rabbit hole or through a looking glass, but to the sheriff's office.

Night of the Jabberwock is definitely not a novel for reformed alcoholics or those with strong principles against the consumption of alcohol. Doc partakes of enough drink so that, in reality, he would have passed out by chapter 3. In spite of that—and the fact that there are enough holes in the plot to drive a liquor truck through—no reader will ever forget this one astonishing night in Carmel City, Indiana.

(*M.M.*)

Browne, Gerald. *11 Harrowhouse.* New York: Arbor House, 1972. (T)

The diamond industry is a fascinating one for readers of suspense novels, and in this story Gerald Browne capitalizes on its mystique by creating The System— a powerful cartel which controls the worldwide diamond market from its headquarters at 11 Harrowhouse Street, London. His hero, known only by the last name of Chesser, is but a small cog in The System's smoothly turning wheel. He keeps his ten-times-yearly appointments to pick up the packets of diamonds The System sells to him, disposes of them in the most expedient and effortless way, and devotes the remainder of his time to his mistress, Maren. Maren, a twenty-five-year-old model, has inherited great wealth from her husband; she is a daredevil, accustomed to luxury, totally indifferent to diamonds, and addicted to the occult. Chesser's life with her should be idyllic, but he and Maren wish to marry, and there is a stricture in her husband's will which forbids her from doing so, under pain of losing her inheritance.

When expatriate American millionaire Clyde Massey contacts Chesser about procuring a diamond large enough and of sufficient quality to become known to the world as The Massey, Chesser is puzzled as to why the eccentric oilman has chosen him. Nevertheless, he goes through the steps to acquire the stone—shocking The System, which regards him as strictly a small-time dealer—and having it cut by a master in Amsterdam. And when the finished stone is stolen from him before he can deliver it to Massey, and Chesser gradually realizes he has become a pawn in a great hoax, he and Maren find themselves drawn into an even greater scheme, which can only wreak havoc on the comfortable lives they have established for themselves.

This is a richly detailed novel, full of interesting diamond industry lore. Those who enjoy large-scale thrillers set in such exotic locales as Paris, the Riviera, the Mediterranean, and the Swiss Alps, and peopled with wealthy and powerful characters will be sure to enjoy Browne's fast-moving story.

Other novels by Browne include *Hazard* (1973) and *19 Purchase Street* (1982).

(*M.M.*)

*Browne, Howard. *The Taste of Ashes.* New York: Simon & Schuster, 1957. (PI)

An early contributor to the Ziff-Davis line of pulps in the 1940s, Howard Browne later became managing editor of several of that Chicago-based publisher's science-fiction and fantasy magazines. He also wrote extensively for radio and early TV, scripting more than 700 dramatic shows for the two media. In 1946 he published his first mystery novel, *Halo in Blood,* under the pseudonym John Evans, and followed it with two more, *Halo for Satan* (1948) and *Halo in Brass* (1949); all three feature Chicago private detective Paul Pine, one of the best of the plethora of tough-guy heroes from that era. Although the Pine novels are solidly in the tradition of Raymond Chandler, they have a complexity and character all their own and are too well crafted to be mere imitations.

The Taste of Ashes is the fourth and (at least as of this writing) final Paul Pine adventure. Browne evidently chose to publish this one under his own name because it is longer, more tightly plotted, and more ambitious than the "Halo" books. Offbeat, violent, exciting, it is the story of Pine's involvement with the lethal Delastone clan: "the Colonel, who wore his hair like the late William Jennings Bryan and was more afraid of scandal than of sudden death; Martha, a member of the sensible-shoe set; the lovely Karen, who owned a temper and a burglar tool; Edwin, who had gone to Heaven, or some place, leaving a monument of horror behind; and Deborah Ellen Frances Thronetree, age seven, an authority on the Bible and Captain Midnight, who was plagued by nightmares." A hood with the wonderful name of Arnie Algebra, a reporter called Ira Groat, and the haunted widow of another private eye are just three of the rich array of other characters Pine encounters on his violent professional (and personal) odyssey.

All three of the John Evans titles are also first-rate. Both *Halo in Blood* and *Halo for Satan* have highly unusual opening situations: In the former,

Pine joins twelve other persons in the burial of a nameless bum; and in the latter, a Chicago bishop is offered a chance to buy a manuscript purportedly in the handwriting of Christ for the staggering sum of $25 million. Browne is also the author, under his own name, of a nonseries novel, *Thin Air* (1954); the sudden, inexplicable disappearance of advertising executive Ames Coryell's wife and his utilization of his ad agency and its methods to track her down form the basis for this tale of suspense. *Thin Air* has received considerable praise, but this reviewer finds it somewhat farfetched and Coryell a less than likable protagonist. Paul Pine is a much better character, and the private-eye novel the true showcase for Browne's talents.

(*B.P.*)

Bruce, Leo. *Case for Three Detectives.* New York: Stokes, 1937. (PP/C)

Case for Three Detectives is at once a locked-room mystery worthy of John Dickson Carr (q.v.) and an affectionate spoof of the Golden Age detectives created by Sayers, Christie, and Chesterton.

When Mary Thurston is found in her bedroom, dead of a slashed throat, during a weekend party at her Sussex country house, it seems to all concerned an impossible, almost supernatural crime: The bedroom door was double-bolted from the inside; there are no secret passages or other such claptrap; the only windows provide no means of entrance or exit; and the knife that did the job is found *outside* the house. The following morning, three of "those indefatigably brilliant private investigators who seem to be always handy when a murder has been committed" begin to arrive. The first is Lord Simon Plimsoll (Lord Peter Wimsey): ". . . the length of his chin, like most other things about him, was excessive," the narrator, Townsend, observes. The second is the Frenchman Amer Picon (Hercule Poirot): "His physique was frail, and topped by a large egg-shaped head, a head so much and so often egg-shaped that I was surprised to find a nose and mouth in it at all, but half-expected its white surface to break and release a chick." And the third is Monsignor Smith (Father Brown), "a small human pudding."

The three famous sleuths sniff around, unearth various clues, and arrive at separate (and elaborate) conclusions, each accusing a different member of the house party as Mary Thurston's slayer. But of course none of them is right. The real solution is provided by Sergeant Beef of the local constabulary, "a big red-faced man of forty-eight or fifty, with a straggling ginger moustache, and a look of rather beery benevolence." Along the way there is a good deal of gentle humor and some sharp observations on the methods of Wimsey, Poirot, and Father Brown. The prose is consistently above average, and the solution to the locked-room murder is both simple and satisfying.

Sergeant Beef is featured in seven other novels by Leo Bruce (a pseudonym of novelist, playwright, poet, and scholar Rupert Croft-Cooke), most of which have been recently reissued here by Academy Chicago in trade paperback. Among them are *Case Without a Corpse* (1937), *Case with Four Clowns* (1939), and *Case with Ropes and Rings* (1940). Each is likewise ingeniously plotted and diverting.

(*B.P.*)

Bruce, Leo. *A Bone and a Hank of Hair.* London: Peter Davies, 1961. (AD)

Croft-Cooke abandoned Sergeant Beef in 1952 and three years later began a second notable series of detective novels, also published under the Leo Bruce by-line, this one featuring Carolus Deene, ex-commando and Senior History Master at Queen's School, Newminster, who solves mysteries as a hobby. Until recently, when Academy Chicago began reprinting these, too, in trade paperback, most of the twenty-three Deene titles were available only in England.

A Bone and a Hank of Hair involves Deene in the strange disappearance of Mrs. Rathbone, Mrs. Rathbone, and Mrs. Rathbone—or are all three the same woman in different guises? Deene's investigation, prompted by relatives of the original Mrs. Rathbone, takes him to an unpleasant home in remote East Kent, some curious parts of London, and an art colony in Cornwall. The jacket blurb says, more or less accurately, "Everywhere he meets bizarre, sometimes richly comic, sometimes sinister characters who bring him at last to the (guaranteed unguessable) conclusion." On hand as usual in this series, in minor roles, are Mrs. Stick, Deene's housekeeper and conscience; and the Gorringers, Deene's headmaster and his (half)witty wife.

Deene and his investigative methods, and Bruce and his blend of sly humor, tricky plotting, and eccentric characters may not be for every taste. But in this and such other adventures as *A Louse for the Hangman* (1958), *Jack on the Gallows Tree* (1960), *Nothing Like Blood* (1962), and *Death in Albert Park* (1964), both perform admirably.

Croft-Cooke also published several worthy criminous novels under his own name, including *Seven Thunders* (1955) and *Paper Albatross* (1968).

(*B.P.*)

*Buchan, John. *The 39 Steps.* Boston: Houghton Mifflin, 1915. (A/E)

One of Alfred Hitchcock's best films was *The 39 Steps,* which he took from John Buchan's excellent adventure/spy novel. While Hitchcock's 1935 film differs in many details and mechanisms from the book, both artists mined the same vein, and it's easy to see what made Hitchcock want to work his transformations on this tale.

The romantic figure of the hero, Richard Hannay, is the perfect early example of the soldier of fortune. He's sound of wind and limb, he's courageous and slightly bored, and he is catapulted by treachery into facing a vast conspiracy that can determine the fate of the world. The writing doesn't contain too much character to clutter up the plot, and there are no female roles in this adventure. (Hitchcock injected character into the story, partly by including female players in the game.) Hannay sets out on the chase, first to hide out from the police, who want him for murder, and also from the German villains who want to stop the secret from getting out. By ruse and disguise, he traverses the well-described wilds of Scotland to stay undercover until the fatal hour. Falling in and out of the clutches of his facile fate, he enlists help as he runs, is chased by airplane, and is captured by his adversaries. This is where James Bond came from.

The Scottish author John Buchan, Baron Tweedsmuir, was also a political official and governor-general of Canada. He wrote many books of history and biography, as well as other adventures, which he called "shockers." The best of the other Hannay books is *Greenmantle* (1916). Another hero, Leithen, is featured in other stories, and Buchan is powerfully descriptive of southern Africa, Europe, and the Middle East.

(*T.B.*)

Burke, J.F. *Location Shots.* New York: Harper, 1974. (PI)

This is the first of three medium-hard-boiled detective novels featuring Sam Kelly, the resident house dick at the Hotel Castlereagh on Seventy-second Street in Manhattan. Kelly is black, bald, and forty—one of the more recent black series detectives in crime fiction. His girlfriend is Madam Bobbie, a voluptuous blonde who lives in the hotel across the square, the Charmain Towers—but her girls do most of their work out of the Castlereagh.

As this book opens, Sam and Madam Bobbie are awakened in her apartment by police sirens. They discover that the street in front of both hotels is full of cops, and Sam goes down to investigate. As it turns out, a woman in room 8A of Kelly's hotel, Anna Jensen, was murdered during the night. Kelly knows for a fact that a friend of his, David Christopher, who lived in 9A, was a "friend" of the dead woman's, but when he goes to 9A, he finds his friend dead as well. At odds with Commander Fuseli, the cop in charge, Sam also finds himself involved with characters indigenous only to New York, as well as talking birds and a search for a manuscript and a tape recording that might lead to the killer.

Burke uses the city of New York so well that it virtually becomes another character in this novel and in the subsequent books in the series. Sam

Kelly is also featured in *Death Trick* (1975) and *Kelly Among the Nightingales* (1979).

(*R.J.R.*)

Burley, W. J. *Wycliffe and the Scapegoat.* New York: Doubleday Crime Club, 1979. (PP)

This story takes place in a clannish seaside English town that observes a rather strange All Hallows' Eve ritual. On a wheel of fire, nine feet in diameter, is burned a life-size effigy—a scapegoat, as it were—and as it burns, the wheel is allowed to roll over a cliff and into the ocean. Thus is evil symbolically cast out for another year. The so-called Fire Festival dates back to Celtic times, but this year's celebration may have been a little different. It develops that the murdered corpse of the town's undertaker was used instead of an effigy. Certainly the undertaker, one Jonathan Riddle, was not a popular man, and the town is full of people who would have liked to see the end of him (including the members of his own family).

Enter Detective Chief Superintendent Wycliffe, who, with his wife, is spending a long weekend near the town. He becomes interested in the case and undertakes his own investigation—a rather routine one, after the colorful dramatics of the Fire Festival. This is a bit of a letdown, although the characters are well drawn enough and the situation interesting enough to hold our interest.

Writing in *Twentieth Century Crime & Mystery Writers,* Carol Cleveland says that Wycliffe is "an unconventional policeman who hates routine and authority, and proceeds about his murder investigations by the gestalt method. He immerses himself in the victim's history and circle of acquaintances until he feels his way to a conclusion." This is the pattern here, and while the method works well enough, Burley's prose is so lacking in flair that it makes the book plodding in tone. The solution, though satisfactory, is not particularly memorable.

Wycliffe appears in a number of other novels, among them *Three-Toed Pussy* (1961), *To Kill a Cat* (1970), *Death in Stanley Street* (1974), and *Wycliffe in Paul's Court* (1980). Burley has also written two novels featuring Henry Pym, a zoology professor and amateur criminologist; these are *A Taste of Power* (1966) and *Death in Willow Pattern* (1970).

(*N.D./B.P.*)

*Burnett, W. R. *High Sierra.* New York: Knopf, 1940. (PS)

"Early in the twentieth century, when Roy Earle was a happy boy on an Indiana farm, he had no idea that at thirty-seven he'd be a pardoned ex-convict driving alone through the Nevada-California desert towards an ambiguous destiny in the Far West."

Thus begins what is, in effect, the biography of Roy Earle, a fictional creation who reflects the lives of several eminent American outlaws of the 1920s and 1930s. The structure and texture of the opening sentence signals the reader that this will be much more than simply a genre piece of tommy guns and molls. Burnett will attempt nothing less than a definitive appraisal of a bandit's life as Earle leaves prison, falls in love, and works toward the robbery that will doom him.

For many, *Sierra* is probably more familiar as the finest of Bogart's films (with the arguable exception of *The Treasure of Sierra Madre*). In the film version, John Huston sought to create a romance, a complex variation on the Robin Hood myth, but Burnett creates a novelistic portrait of Roy Earle that is full of fire and contradiction. Chapter 37 is the key scene in the book. In the space of 3000 words, Roy Earle expounds on himself ("I steal and I admit it"); on his inability to trust ("The biggest rat we had in prison was a preacher who'd gypped his congregation out of the dough he was supposed to build a church with."); and on the failure of the common man to fight for himself ("Why don't all them people who haven't got any dough get together and take the dough? It's a cinch"). He is, throughout the novel, idealistic, naïve, ruthless, and doomed in a way that is almost lyrical. Not unlike Studs Lonigan, Roy Earle becomes sympathetic because his faults, for all their outsize proportion, are human and understandable, and his humility almost Christ-like. "Barmy used to talk to me about earthquakes," Roy says; "he said the old earth just twitched its skin like a dog. We're the fleas, I guess."

Far from the myths created by J. Edgar Hoover's biased attitude toward the criminals of the 1930s, Burnett gives us a sad, sometimes surreal look at a true outlaw. *High Sierra* is filled with every possible kind of feeling, from bleak humor to a pity that becomes Roy Earle's doom. The book's theme of time and fate is worthy of Proust. If you want to know what made the work of "proletariat" America so powerful in the 1930s, all you have to do is pick up this novel.

(*E.G.*)

Burnett, W. R. *Little Caesar.* New York: Knopf, 1929. (PS)

"Mother of God, is this the end of Rico?"

Few movie lines have endured as long and as well as the signature line of Burnett's *Little Caesar* screenplay. He ended the novel on which the movie was based with virtually the same line. Burnett mastered an idiom and rhythm that, while essentially literary, spoke directly to the masses.

Caesar is serious and detailed, charting the rise and fall of a Chicago gangster against a backdrop of political and social turmoil. As in his other great novel, *High Sierra,* Burnett means to treat his headline subject with novelistic scrutiny. In a bittersweet interview given near the end of his life,

Burnett complained that he was often praised for his "plotting," a compliment he refused on the grounds that he never plotted, but let his characters carry the story to its own organic end. To a large degree, Burnett was correct. In some parts, *Little Caesar* is a novel of manners, and the overriding concern is not for the story per se but rather how certain events affect the characters who weave in and out of the book.

Little Caesar is too often used as a bludgeon with which to decimate *The Godfather.* The books should not be compared. Mario Puzo wrote a fine romance, perhaps a novel of the first rank, after all. Burnett, however, wrote a treatise that was part sociology, part character sketch, part comedy and most of all, a naturalistic reflection of the squalid Chicago slums of the time.

Caesar remains fresh, potent, funny, tragic. Rico, its center, like all great characters, eludes final understanding.

The 1930 film version with Edward G. Robinson and Douglas Fairbanks Jr. is likewise a classic. Robinson's portrayal of Rico has often been imitated (by himself as well as others, notably in his role in *Key Largo*) but never surpassed.

Burnett's other major crime novel is *The Asphalt Jungle* (1949), the film version of which—starring Sterling Hayden and Sam Jaffe—has been called "*the* gangster film of the Fifties." Minor but excellent novels are *Dark Hazard* (1933), *The Quick Brown Fox* (1942), and *Vanity Row* (1952). Among Burnett's numerous screenplays are those for *This Gun for Hire* (1941) and the 1955 remake of *High Sierra* starring Jack Palance, *I Died a Thousand Times.*

(*E.G./B.P.*)

Burns, Rex. *Angle of Attack.* New York: Harper, 1979. (PP)

Rex Burns's (Raoul Stephen Schler's) novels featuring Detective Gabriel Wager of the Denver Police Department are notable for their sound grasp of procedure. Unlike the police routine in many novels of this type, the details are made clear without excessive explanation or esoteric jargon. Wager himself is an interesting character, a Chicano—he describes himself as a Hispano—who is at times caught between two cultures: that of his birth, the Hispanic community; and of his work, the police culture. Wager is a thinking man as well as a man of action, and the flaw in the portrayal of his character is that the reader is allowed to see too little of his personal side.

Wager operates in the neighborhood where he grew up, and in *Angle of Attack* he receives a tip from the aging *jefe* of the area that a mob-related homicide Wager has been working on was committed by someone named Frank Covino. Before Wager and his partner, Max Axton, can locate Covino, he is found dead of gunshot wounds. And as their investigation of the victim's life proceeds, they find he was an above-average, hardworking youth with a steady job and a college scholarship, hardly the stuff hit men are made of.

Wager and his partner turn their attention to the dead youth's older brother, now in prison for burglary. The brother is reticent, and before they can dig deeper into what he knows, he, too, is killed, in a prison brawl. Their investigation is further complicated by pressure from the city's Organized Crime Unit, and when the murders are finally resolved, it is in an unorthodox manner—a manner that Wager agonizes over.

Unfortunately, the motivation for this crime comes largely out of left field; there is little if any foreshadowing of it. And the characters, with the exception of Wager, are faceless caricatures of types one might meet in any police procedural. In spite of its interesting setting—Denver—one gets very little sense of place, and the overall effect of the story is one of un-Colorado-like flatness.

Gabe Wager also appeared in *The Alvarez Journal* (1975), winner of an MWA Edgar for Best First Novel; *The Fansworth Score* (1977); and *Speak for the Dead* (1979).

(*M.M.*)

Burton, Miles. *Dark Is the Tunnel.* New York: Doubleday Crime Club, 1936. (CS)

During his thirty-seven-year career, tirelessly prolific British writer Cecil Street published almost as many novels under his Miles Burton pseudonym as he did under his more popular pen name of John Rhode (q.v.). All but two of his sixty-three Burton titles feature the detective team of Inspector Arnold of Scotland Yard and his friend and amateur criminologist Desmond Merrion. These are traditional mysteries with emphasis on deduction rather than police procedure. Emphasis is also on the stories themselves—the mechanics of the puzzle—with the result that Street's characters tend to be sketchily drawn and in many cases two-dimensional. Arnold and Merrion are not exempt; in no book do they come across as much more than puzzle-solving agents, bereft of those human characteristics that make a series sleuth distinctive and memorable. Still, Street's plots are carefully crafted and fairly clued, and offer the reader a variety of settings (many of them English country and seaside locales), as well as interesting backgrounds and themes.

A good example is *Dark Is the Tunnel,* which features that ever-popular mix of murder and trains. The tunnel referred to in the title is a railway tunnel outside London—the two-and-a-half-mile Blackdown Tunnel. It is halfway through the Blackdown that the 5:00 P.M. train from Cannon Street unexpectedly comes to a stop. Apparently someone was working on the line, for the engineer saw a blinking red light, signaling him to stop, and then a green light, signaling him to proceed. But the odd thing is, there had been no report of workers in the tunnel.

Almost simultaneously with the stop, an elderly gentleman named Sir Wilfred Saxonby is found in his locked compartment, dead of a gunshot wound. A suicide? Perhaps, although nothing in his background suggests such a possibility.

Arnold and Merrion follow a tangled skein of motives and of clues that include a pair of wallets, a rhododendron bed, and the movements of a garage repair truck over a thirty-six-hour period, and come up with the solution to the mystery. There is little action along the way, and Street's prose tends to be on the dry and dusty side. But the puzzle is baffling enough to provide armchair detectives with a couple of hours of pleasurable escapist reading.

Other titles in the same vein include the first Arnold and Merrion case, *The Menace on the Downs* (1931); *The Platinum Cat* (1938); *Death Visits Downspring* (1941), a livelier tale than most of the Burtons, in which Arnold and Merrion solve the wartime mystery of the murdered butler and the missing radio station; and *Look Alive* (1950), the last Burton novel to appear in the United States, although twenty-one additional titles were published in England between 1950 and 1960. Two other Burtons of note are *The Secret of High Eldersham* (1930), a tale of witchcraft in which Merrion appears alone; and *The Hardway Diamonds Mystery,* published that same year, which marks Arnold's likewise solo debut.

(B.P./N.D.)

Byrd, Max. *California Thriller.* New York: Bantam, 1981. (O/PI)

California Thriller is the first of three Mike Haller books, and the most noteworthy; it was awarded the Private Eye Writers of America Shamus Award for Best Paperback Novel of 1981. It was the author's first novel.

Mike Haller is a transplanted Boston PI now working out of San Fancisco. Although a viable character, he has been strongly influenced by Robert B. Parker's (q.v.) Boston PI, Spenser. He's as physical, well read, and quick with a wisecrack as Spenser, but where the latter works alone, Haller has an Irish partner who covers his back. He also has a regular lady friend, as does Spenser, and she is Dinah Farrell, who is a psychoanalyst—which, of course, comes in handy now and again.

When one of the country's leading journalists disappears in Sacramento's Central Valley, the man's editor, acting for his wife, hires Mike Haller to find him. With nothing but a two-year-old newspaper clipping to go on, Haller begins retracing the man's steps. He becomes involved with a professor of biochemistry at Berkeley and an ex-cop who has made a fortune in private security work and has his eye on the governor's seat. Before long a young girl turns up dead and Haller becomes convinced that somebody doesn't want the journalist found. When Haller finally finds out what the journalist was on to—politics, murder, and private bacteriological-warfare tests—and gets his hands on some incriminating tapes, he's running for his life and trying to save the lives of thousands.

Byrd's second Mike Haller novel is *Fly Away, Jill* (1981), and the third is *Finders Weepers* (1983).

(*R.J.R.*)

Cain, James M. *Cloud Nine.* New York: Mysterious Press, 1984. (PS)

In the 1930s and 1940s, James M. Cain was the most talked-about writer in America. His novels of that period, like the detective novels of Dashiell Hammett (q.v.) a few years earlier, broke new ground in crime fiction. Until the publication of *The Postman Always Rings Twice* in 1934, sex was a topic handled with kid gloves and almost always peripheral to the central story line; Cain made sex the primary motivating force of his fiction, and presented it to his readers frankly, at times steamily (some of the scenes in *Postman* are downright erotic even by today's standards).

But Cain, of course, was much more than a purveyor of eroticism. His lean, hard-edged prose caused critics to label him a "hard-boiled" writer, but he is much more than that, too. His best works are masterful studies of average people caught up and often destroyed by passion (adultery, incest, hatred, greed, lust). They are also sharp, clear portraits of the times and places in which they were written, especially California in the depression-era Thirties.

Cain's success began to wane in the Fifties and Sixties, however, partly because of a desire to write novels of a different sort from those that had brought him fame, and partly because of a clear erosion of his talents (a seminal fear of all writers) brought about by advancing age. *Cloud Nine* is one of those "different" novels, written in the late 1960s when Cain was seventy-five. It was rejected by his publisher at that time and shelved. Resurrected for publication in 1984, seven years after Cain's death, it was puffed by its publisher as "an important addition in contemporary American literature" and by an advance reviewer as "a minor masterpeice and publishing event of some note." It is none of those things. It is, simply and sadly, a flawed novel of mediocre quality—a pale shadow of his early triumphs.

The novel's basic premise is solid. A teenage girl, Sonya Lang, comes to Maryland real-estate agent Graham Kirby with the news that his nasty half brother, Burwell, has raped her and that she is pregnant as a result. Through a complicated set of circumstances, Graham agrees to marry Sonya, initially for charitable reasons; but he soon falls in love with her. He then discovers that Burwell may be a murderer as well as a rapist, and that another murder may be part of Burwell's future plans. The conflict between Burwell and Graham forms the central tension here, with Sonya as one catalyst and a million dollars in prime real estate as another.

All the elements are present for a classic Cain novel, ones that should combine to keep the reader on tenterhooks, "anxious to find out what happens," as Cain biographer Roy Hoopes says in an Afterword, "but always dreading the ending because of the horror [he senses] would be waiting—'the wish that comes true' that Cain said most of his novels were about." But the elements simply don't mesh. The bulk of the novel is taken up with the relationship (much of it sexual) between Graham and Sonya, to the exclusion of everything else; Burwell doesn't even appear on stage until page 108, and other major plot points are introduced sketchily and/or not developed until the final fifty to sixty pages. Graham is a rather dull and unappealing narrator, not at all one of "those wonderful, seedy, lousy no-goods that you have always understood," as one of Cain's friends described the protagonists of *Postman* and *Double Indemnity.* And the prose is anything but lean and hard-edged. It reads as if Cain, late in life, discovered and became enamoured of commas and clauses, as witness the novel's opening sentence: "I first met her, this girl that I married a few days later, and that the papers have crucified under the pretense of glorification, on a Friday morning in June, on the parking lot by the Patuxent Building, that my office is in."

Not everything about *Cloud Nine* is weak; there are some crisp passages of dialogue reminiscent of vintage Cain, the character of Sonya is well developed, and there is power in the climactic scenes (although none of the existential terror and tragedy of the early books). But on balance, and like the other suspense novels Cain wrote late in life—*The Magician's Wife* (1965), *Rainbow's End* (1975), *The Institute* (1976)—it is minor and disappointing.

(B.P.)

*Cain, James M. *Double Indemnity.* New York: Avon, 1945. (First published in book form in *Three of a Kind.* New York: Knopf, 1943.) (PS/O)

James M. Cain wrote of "the wish that comes true . . . I think my stories have some quality of the opening of a forbidden box, and that it is this rather than violence, sex or any of the things usually cited by way of explanation that gives them the drive so often noted." *Double Indemnity* employs this same technique, already displayed in *The Postman Always Rings Twice* (q.v.), with dazzling ease. Cain, making a quick buck writing a magazine serial in 1936, did not realize it at the time, but he was at the top of his form.

Employing skillful, scalpellike first-person narration, Cain tells his tale of love and murder from the point of view of a lover and murderer.

Insurance man Walter Huff becomes embroiled in a plot to kill a beautiful woman's husband. In addition to the sexual and financial incentives, Phyllis Nirdlinger manages to play upon Huff's boredom and his pride—he knows the insurance game inside and out, and figures with his expertise he can beat it. The husband is murdered, according to Huff's plan, without a hitch. But Huff is dogged by Keyes, a claims agent who *also* knows the insurance game inside and out. Huff begins to realize Phyllis is untrustworthy and just possibly insane, and falls in love with Lola, the daughter of the murdered man by a previous wife, who had very probably been yet another murder victim of Phyllis's.

Double Indemnity is a murder mystery turned inside out: We are forced inside the murderer's skin, only to find it uncomfortably easy to identify with him, and then share his paranoia as the world crumbles piece by piece around him. Huff is a white-collar worker and he's smart—smart enough to sense early on just how major a mistake he's made. His sense of his own frailty and wrongdoing makes him a truly tragic protagonist, as does his sense of loss: "I knew I couldn't have her and never could have her. I couldn't kiss the girl whose father I killed."

Cain liked to explore the workings of businesses, and he never did it better than in *Double Indemnity,* through the characters of Huff and Keyes. But he also gave the pair an understated shared understanding of humanity (an aspect broadened in the widely respected Billy Wilder–directed, Raymond Chandler–scripted film version of 1944). In their final confrontation, Keyes says to Huff (renamed Neff in the film), "This is an awful thing you've done, Neff," and Huff/Neff only says, "I know it." And when Keyes says, "I—kind of liked you, Neff," Huff/Neff says, "I know. Same here."

(*M.A.C.*)

**Cain, James M. *The Postman Always Rings Twice.* New York: Knopf, 1934. (PS)

This brutal little blue-collar love story was a shocking, sexy, "dirty" best seller and set the standard for tough, lean writing. It taught readers (and writers) that dialogue could propel a story by its own steam (and steaminess) with (as Cain himself put it) "a minimum of *he-saids* and *she-replied-laughinglys.*" From its famous first sentence ("They threw me off the hay truck at noon") to its spellbinding final moments on death row, *The Postman Always Rings Twice* moves like a freight train, catching the reader up in a sleazy, unpleasant—and compelling—illicit love affair.

Drifter Frank Chambers finds himself in a roadside eatery called Twin Oaks Tavern (the first of many double images). Nick Papadakis, the friendly

Greek who runs the place, has a wife who "really wasn't any raving beauty, but she had a sulky look to her." Soon Chambers is running the tavern's gas station for the Greek; and by the end of chapter 2, Frank and Cora have made a cuckold of him; by chapter 4 they are attempting Nick's murder. And these are short chapters.

Incredibly, the adulterers engage not just our interest but our sympathy, our collusion. Their lust ("I sunk my teeth into her lips so deep I could feel the blood spurt into my mouth") is contagious, and redeemed by the extravagance of their passion ("I kissed her . . . it was like being in church"). Yet Cain pulls no punches: Their intended murder victim, Nick, is not unsympathetic; Frank genuinely likes Nick, and after Frank and Cora succeed on the second try and kill him, cries genuine tears at his funeral. Frank and Cora—particularly Frank—are so out of control, so much smaller than the web of circumstance and human frailty in which they are caught up, that a strange sort of supportive interest develops for them. Cain feels for these small lovers who are doomed in so big a way. And so do we. When in the aftermath of Nick's murder and the faked auto accident that follows, Cora and Frank indulge in a manic orgy of sadomasochism and passion at the scene of the crime, we are caught up in the moment with them. As Frank says: "Hell could have opened up for me then, and it wouldn't have made any difference. I had to have her, if I hung for it."

Part of the enduring power of *Postman* is its evocation of the depression. Frank and Cora's dream is the American one: They want a business of their own, a family of their own—simple goals that had been made so difficult in hard times. Their greed was small; their aspirations petty. Their love, and their crime, in James Cain's tabloid opera, large.

(*M.A.C.*)

*Cain, James M. *Serenade.* New York: Knopf, 1937. (PS)

Though lesser known than his more famous *The Postman Always Rings Twice* and *Double Indemnity, Serenade* is equally a masterpiece. Most of Cain's best work is of novella length, but *Serenade* is an exception; a wider canvas is required for this more ambitious work with its subject matter that was daring even for Cain.

The operatic undertone of Cain's work comes to the fore here as an opera singer who loses his voice regains it by spending a night of lust and love with a Mexican whore in a deserted church during a thunderstorm. When John Howard Sharp returns to New York City and his singing career, the healing prostitute, Juana, is at his side; but they are soon faced with a threat from the past, the man whose homosexual liaison with Sharp had caused the singer's traumatic loss of voice. In James M. Cain, there can only be one solution to such a situation: murder.

But murder in *Serenade* isn't born of greed and petty self-interest as it is in other Cain novels. The man and woman who share this sexual adventure are admirable and self-sacrificing. Their love is noble, and their tragedy is the deepest, most affecting in all of Cain.

Cain wrote *Serenade* and his two other masterpieces in the 1930s; but his later, lesser (if interesting) works have tended to dilute his reputation. He is easily the peer of Hammett and Chandler, however, neither of whom wrote with Cain's unabashed passion.

Among his better later works are *Past All Dishonor* (1946) and *The Butterfly* (1947); they are, characteristically, in the first person. *Mildred Pierce* (1941) is the best of Cain's third-person works. Several other completed novels are among Cain's papers, and remain unpublished.

(*M.A.C.*)

Cain, Paul. *Fast One.* New York: Doubleday, Doran, 1933. (T)

The hardest of the hard-boiled writers for *Black Mask* in the early 1930s was unquestionably Paul Cain (Peter Ruric). His style, as pulp authority Ron Goulart has noted, at times "becomes as sparse and clipped as that of a McGuffey's Reader." In an afterword to the Southern Illinois reprint edition, critic Irvin Faust says that Cain "hasn't the time or patience for excess baggage. He picks up his literary scalpel and scrapes away conjunctions as if they were bad merchandise . . . He digs into the page with a hard sentence: simple, declarative, exact."

Fast One is Cain's only novel. (He was primarily a screenwriter and is responsible for such films as *One for the Money, Grand Central Murders,* and *Mademoiselle Fifi.*) It was written on a bet and its various sections first appeared in *Black Mask* as five self-contained novelettes prior to book publication. It is unrelentingly grim and stark and brutal, to such an extent that it becomes uncomfortable to read; one begins to feel a kind of breathless despair well before the end. The "hero" is Gerry Kells, a mysterious loner, a criminal who insinuates himself into the Los Angeles underworld and wreaks havoc on its denizens and on others who happen to get in his way. The dust jacket blurb on a 1978 reissue by Southern Illinois University Press says about Kells: "Only the strong prosper in the world of the Depression. Seemingly amoral, Kells does prosper. He strikes to survive, kills without conscience, without time for conscience. But he never becomes a mere killing machine. His integrity, his humanity, abides in a code demanding that he pay for all services: those rendered for him, those rendered against him. He pays with a two-sided coin—loyalty, revenge. He spends money freely, and those who cross him die hard."

Cain knew his Los Angeles and he knew the ways of its Prohibition and post-Prohibition underworld. The portrait he paints of both, and of Gerry Kells, makes *Fast One* an important and compulsively readable novel, despite that feeling of breathless despair it engenders.

The only other book by Cain is *Seven Slayers* (1946), a collection of seven of his other *Black Mask* stories, all of which are in the same tough vein and all of which are excellent samples of pulp writing at its best.

(*B.P.*)

Cameron, Owen. *The Fire Trap.* New York: Simon & Schuster, 1957. (Also published as *The Demon Stirs.*) (PP/PS)

Owen Cameron is one of those talented but unfortunate writers whose work causes a small commotion when first published but for some inexplicable reason is forgotten while lesser writers achieve recognition and a large following. A successful magazine writer, Cameron published seven criminous novels; the last four of these constitute some of the most quietly compelling suspense fiction of the 1950s.

The protagonist of *The Fire Trap* is Deputy Sheriff Jake Brown of the northern California mountain community of Verdi, who is also featured in Cameron's best-known novel, *Catch a Tiger* (1952). Jake's job here is a grim and ugly one: to find out who is responsible for a series of arson fires, the latest of which claimed the lives of two young children. Matters turn even deadlier when an outsider, insurance-claims adjuster Hal Moss, is found shotgunned to death on a back country road. One of the suspects in both crimes is Jake's own father, a surly old loner who has been estranged from Jake for fourteen long, bitter years. Other suspects include Jake's brother, Art; one of his best friends, Floyd Rupert; and a woman with whom he was once involved, Alice Newsom.

"In his stubborn, honest, relentless way," the dust jacket blurb says, "Jake follows his hunches and tracks down his suspicions . . . At every turn [he] is met by his own sense of guilt and frustration—feelings intensified when he realizes that he has unwittingly set the scene for two more murders." It is at terrible personal cost that he eventually arrives at the truth, in a series of climaxes that can only be described as shattering.

This is provocative stuff, told in lean, understated prose that makes it all the more forceful. As is the case with *Catch a Tiger* and two nonseries books, *The Butcher's Wife* (1954) and *The Silent One* (1958), it is a novel that has disturbing things to say about the dark side of human relationships.

(*B.P.*)

Cannell, Dorothy. *The Thin Woman.* New York: St. Martin's, 1984. (AD)

Ellie Simons, heroine of *The Thin Woman,* is one of the most charming fat women you'll ever hope to meet. When confronted by the problem of attending a family reunion in her rotund state, Ellie decides she will present a better image if accompanied by an attractive man. Since there is none in her life, she contacts Eligibility Escorts and is provided with Bentley T. Haskell—a would-be writer who makes a marginal living escorting ladies and composing pornography. During the weekend with her eccentric and rather unpleasant relatives, Ellie begins to feel attracted to Ben and even goes so far as to announce an engagement, which was definitely not in the Eligibility Escorts contract.

Back in London, however, Ben disappears from Ellie's life, only to resurface when her uncle Merlin, who had orchestrated the reunion, dies. Ben agrees to accompany Ellie to the funeral, and at the will reading the couple find they have been named chief beneficiaries—providing they live for six months in the manor house dubbed Merlin's Court and discover the treasure hidden there. These conditions are fascinating to Ellie and Ben, but two additional ones are not: that Ellie lose a total of sixty-three pounds during the time period, and that Ben write a book without a single dirty word.

Ironically, the tasks of weight-losing and clean writing prove, after many initial setbacks, to be the easier chores. The treasure of Merlin's Court eludes them. Greedy and disappointed relatives appear from time to time; strange and frightening accidents plague the household; Ellie's beloved cat is almost murdered.

All of this leads to a resolution that is disappointingly predictable. And Ellie, as she sheds her pounds, becomes a trifle dull, excessively concerned with her appearance, clothes, and her frustrated romance with Ben—leading the reader to the conclusion that perhaps fat people are more interesting than thin ones. All in all, however, this is an entertaining read and a good first novel.

(*M.M.*)

*Canning, Victor. *A Fall from Grace.* New York: Morrow, 1981. (PI/PS)

Beginning with *Polycarp's Progress* in 1935, Victor Canning has written over fifty novels. After World War II, he turned his efforts to espionage fiction, a genre at which he is now acknowledged to be one of the best practitioners.

Fall from Grace, however, is anything but an international thriller. Halfway through this psychological mystery, Canning's main character, private investigator James Helder, is asked how a calm, good-hearted man such as himself got into his somewhat unsavory line of work. Part of Helder's explanation is that he feels himself to be "a sort of gray shape living a gray, humdrum life like so many people. So, to escape from all that, I mix in other and more unorthodox people's lives to add a little crude color to my own."

The unorthodox person Helder is trailing here is the totally amoral John Corbin, about whom Helder observes, "The John Corbins of this world felt compelled to make the occasional obligation to the gods of chance. A little not-too-expensive kindness here, a rare good deed to assuage self-disgust, even at times an isolated self-sacrifice to bring them close to the shriving of some sin."

That really is all this novel is about, but it is enough. Canning gives us an engrossing, incisive study of the world's Corbins, the selfish and impulsive people who charm those close to them and sometimes even themselves, predators with engaging smiles and talent for deception.

This John Corbin lands a job writing the history of the gardens of Illaton Manor, long tended by the family of Corbin's employer, the bishop of Testerburgh. Included in the job are a cabin, extensive research facilities, and circumstances which make it easy to seduce beautiful co-worker Rachel Harrison. Corbin takes advantage of all these conveniences, for a while even convincing himself that he genuinely loves Rachel. But an unexpected opportunity for profitable mischief proves that Corbin's new leaf is only ego-supported self-delusion, a strained hiatus from reality. He enthusiastically reverts to type.

This is a meticulously written, revealing glimpse into the mind of a man who is the serpent in his own Garden of Eden.

Especially good among Canning's early novels are *The Chasm* (1947) and *The House of the Seven Flies* (1952). Other noteworthy titles among his later works include *Firecrest* (1972), *The Rainbird Pattern* (1973), which was the basis for Alfred Hitchcock's last film, *Family Plot,* and *Birds of a Feather* (1985). Also excellent is a collection of four suspense novelettes, *Oasis Nine* (1958).

(*J.L.*)

Carr, A.H.Z. *Finding Maubee.* New York: Putnam's, 1971. (PP)

A.H.Z. Carr's first and only suspense novel (which won the Best First Novel Edgar for 1971) is a police procedural with an unusual setting: the tropical island of St. Caro in the Caribbean. And even for that part of the world, St. Caro is unusual: It can claim to have "the highest rate of illegitimacy and the lowest rate of crime" of all the islands. Illegitimacy on St. Caro carries no special stigma; "outbabies" are usually acknowledged by the fathers. But the young men of this extremely libidinous locale are careful to guard against being saddled with the support of "bushbabies" (those whose paternity is questionable), and thus they keep little black books—sexual diaries.

Dave Maubee's little black book is a thick one, and he has managed to sire "two inbabies, six outbabies, and an undetermined number of bushbabies." It is no wonder he turns to a life of crime—petty theft from tourists—to support these offspring. But when a wealthy tourist, Carl Lattner, is found murdered with a machete at the exclusive Mango Beach Inn, Maubee's boyhood friend, Police Chief Xavier Brooke, is astonished to hear Dave is the prime suspect. It is his little black book, dropped at the crime scene, that points to him.

Xavier, a mainland-educated St. Carovian, begins his investigation amid pressures from both the island's acting governor and a fellow officer who has designs on his job. But despite their insistence on Maubee's guilt, he finds inconsistencies at the scene and among the stories of the resort's high-toned but not always high-principled guests. When he finally sets out to track down the missing Maubee, his search takes him all over the island to the homes of women Maubee has rated "A+" in his book. In his travels, he finds that his old friend's life has taken a surprising new turn, and by the time he apprehends him, he is certain the murder is not as straightforward as it originally seemed.

Carr's characters are well developed and memorable, and the setting he employs is vivid. Issues such as racial strife, Caribbean politics, and obeah (voodoo) form a backdrop for a solid and intelligent procedural. Unfortunately, Carr (who wrote a number of criminous short stories, as well as other, noncriminous books) died shortly after *Finding Maubee*'s publication in 1971, and his Edgar was awarded posthumously. More Xavier Brooke novels would have been enthusiastically welcomed by this reviewer.

(*M.M.*)

*Carr, John Dickson. *The Arabian Nights Murder.* New York: Harper, 1936. (CS/W)

For more than forty-two years, John Dickson Carr was a skilled and enthusiastic player in what he called "the grandest game in the world": the construction of ingeniously plotted murder puzzles, set forth with an illusionist's skill at deception for the bafflement and delight of his readers. Carr, under his own name and especially under the pseudonym Carter Dickson (q.v.), showed a fondness for stories of impossible crime, particularly locked-room murders. He compiled a longer list of variations on this theme than any other writer. Even when no overt "impossibility" is involved, the crimes in Carr's books often have bizarre trappings. Other characteristics are his use of comedy, his fondness for "bad" women, his expert evocation of eerie and threatening atmosphere, the frequent disquisitions on curiosities of history, and his use of the multiple solution—the apparently complete explanation of the crime, which is shown to be flawed and is then replaced by a second (and sometimes a third) solution.

Although Carr was born and educated in the United States (his father was a congressman during the first Wilson administration), he lived for many years in England, and a majority of his books have English settings. He was, however, equally at home on both sides of the Atlantic. He was an officeholder in both the prestigious Detection Club in London and the Mystery Writers of America. From the latter organization he received a special Edgar in 1949 for his biography *The Life of Sir Arthur Conan Doyle,* and again in 1969 in honor of his fortieth anniversary as a mystery writer. In 1962 he received MWA's Grand Master Award. In addition to his books, he wrote several dozen short stories (two of which were award winners in *Ellery Queen's Mystery Magazine*'s annual contests) and many radio plays for the BBC in England and such programs as *Suspense* in the United States. He also reviewed mystery fiction in both *Harper's Magazine* and *EQMM.*

Carr's principal series detective, the bulky and bibulous Dr. Gideon Fell, was introduced in *Hag's Nook* (1933). He is a retired schoolmaster who serves as an unofficial consultant to Scotland Yard. He has at his command a large fund of miscellaneous facts, a formidable analytical mind, and an ability to notice seemingly minute points and make connections between unlikely pieces of information. He is usually on stage for most of a case, stumping around on his two crutch-handled canes, beaming like Old King Cole, asking disconcerting questions, exasperating his friend Superintendent Hadley with his cryptic remarks, and finally gathering the key personnel together for the climactic revelation of the murderer's identity. *The Arabian Nights Murder* is unusual in that Fell appears only in the few pages of the prologue and epilogue. The main text is taken up by the statements of Detective Inspector Carruthers, Assistant Commissioner Armstrong, and Superintendent Hadley, recounting their investigation of the murder of Raymond Penderel, an actor with an unsavory reputation.

Penderel had been found inside an Elizabethan coach in a private museum, stabbed with an ivory dagger taken from a locked case nearby. The body was adorned with a set of ill-fitting false whiskers, and was clutching a cookbook in its arms. Suspects include rich Geoffrey Wade, owner of the museum; his wild daughter and ineffectual son; his prospective son-in-law, soldier of fortune Gregory Mannering; and assorted museum employees. When the three Scotland Yard men have finished their statements, Fell, in pure armchair-detective tradition, picks out just the right combination of overlooked or misinterpreted facts and hands them the solution to the crime.

The book's tour de force of a plot is clothed in Carr's patented combination of atmospheric description, misdirection, action, interesting characters (including the engaging old financial pirate Jeff Wade), and a touch of romance. It is a prime example of Golden Age detection.

(*R.E.B.*)

Carr, John Dickson. *Castle Skull.* New York: Harper, 1931. (CS/W)

Carr's writing career began with a sports column in a local newspaper at the age of fourteen. During his prep-school years at the Hill School, he was already writing locked-room stories and an Oppenheim-style serial. At Haverford College he worked on the college's literary magazine, *The Haverfordian,* and it was here that the first stories about his Parisian magistrate-detective, Henri Bencolin, appeared. When he wrote his first full-fledged mystery novel, it was only natural that he should use Bencolin as his detective. Bencolin's debut in book form was in *It Walks by Night* (1930), and three other books in the series followed within the next two years.

Castle Skull is the second of Bencolin's recorded exploits. The setting is Schloss Schadel, a castle on the Rhine River near the city of Coblenz. The castle had been the home of the world-famous magician Maleger. Some time before the start of the story, Maleger had disappeared from a railway carriage that was under constant observation; his drowned body later turned up in the Rhine. In his will he left Castle Skull jointly to his two friends, the actor Myron Alison and the financier Jérôme D'Aunay. Now Alison has been murdered in spectacular fashion: "The man's vitality was apparently enormous. He had been shot three times in the breast, but he was alive when the murderer poured kerosene on him and ignited it. He actually got to his feet and staggered out in flames across the battlements before he fell." Bencolin, on vacation from his official duties, is persuaded by D'Aunay to investigate Alison's death. He is accompanied on the case by his "Watson," an American writer named Jeff Marle, who narrates the story.

This is the young Carr in full flight: a meticulously constructed formal detective story cloaked in extravagant melodrama and exuberantly macabre trappings, peopled by doom-laden characters. The relative smoothness and restraint of Carr's later work is little in evidence, but there is no denying the power and fascination of the story.

(*R.E.B.*)

*Carr, John Dickson. *The Devil in Velvet.* New York: Harper, 1951. (H/A/W)

Carr's lifelong fascination with history, specifically that of England, shows up in many ways in his books, from casual excursions to important plot elements. His first completed novel, never published and now lost, was a historical romance "with lots of Gadzookses and swordplay." In 1934, using the pseudonym Roger Fairbairn, he published *Devil Kinsmere,* a novel set in the time of Charles II; many years later the book was rewritten and published as *Most Secret* (1964) under Carr's own name. Carr's first novel to merge the detective puzzle with historical construction was *The Bride of Newgate* (1950), well received by both critics and readers.

The second of Carr's historical mysteries, *The Devil in Velvet,* sold better than any of his other novels. Here the detective and historical elements were joined by a third ingredient: the strain of overt fantasy that had cropped up from time to time in his earlier work. Nicholas Fenton, a history professor at Cambridge in the year 1925, makes a deal with the devil to be transported back to the year 1675 in order to solve, and possibly prevent, the murder by poisoning of Lydia, Lady Fenton, the wife of an earlier namesake. Transported back into the body of the earlier Nicholas Fenton, the protagonist finds himself immediately enmeshed in political intrigue: the efforts of Lord Shaftesbury to subvert the monarchy and solidify the power of Parliament. Fenton must also juggle the attentions of two lovely women, Lydia and the mysterious and temperamental Meg York. Eventually he comes to realize that he must do something much more difficult than solving a murder: He must outwit the devil himself in order to save his own life and that of the woman he loves.

Bawdy, turbulent Restoration London is re-created with verve and meticulous attention to historical detail, and the events of the story are viewed with a beguiling combination of twentieth- and seventeenth-century sensibilities.

(*R.E.B.*)

*Carr, John Dickson. *The Three Coffins.* New York: Harper, 1935. (CS/W)

In this Dr. Fell novel, one of the most intricate in the series, the author loses no time in making his intentions clear. In the very first paragraph, two impossible crimes are announced—a locked-room murder and what might be called a "locked-street" murder. The victim in the first crime is Professor Charles Grimaud, a lecturer and writer of independent means, whose habit it is to visit a local pub every evening and hold forth to a fascinated audience on magic, the supernatural, vampirism, the Black Mass, and similar topics. One evening the professor's lecture is interrupted by a man who identifies himself as Pierre Fley, "Illusionist." Although he tries to hide the fact, the professor is terrified by Fley's cryptically threatening remarks. Some days later, Grimaud is in his study at home when a mysterious visitor arrives, forces his way into the room, and locks the door. The door is thereafter under constant observation; the room has no other exits and no hiding places. A shot is heard, and when the door is forced, Grimaud is found alone in the room, dying of a gunshot wound. His visitor has vanished. On that same evening, some distance away, Fley is also shot to death. The crime takes place in the middle of an empty, snow-covered street, with watchers at either end; yet no one sees the murderer, and there are no footprints in the snow.

It quickly develops that Grimaud and Fley shared a deadly secret, with roots going back to turn-of-the-century Hungary. This connection from the past provides the book's title—Fley once told an acquaintance, "Three of us were once buried alive. Only one escaped." When asked how he had escaped, he answered calmly, "I didn't, you see. I was one of the two who did not escape." It also supplies the motive for the crimes. But Fell must delve into more-modern relationships and unravel some subtle trickery in order to explain the apparently impossible circumstances of the crimes and identify the guilty. When the last piece of the puzzle has fallen into place, with an extra twist in the concluding lines of the book, Fell says, "I have committed another crime, Hadley. I have guessed the truth again."

Chapter 17 of the novel has become famous among mystery enthusiasts, and has been reprinted separately. It is "The Locked Room Lecture," in which Fell systematically classifies the principal types of locked-room situation. Other writers—notably Anthony Boucher and Clayton Rawson (qq.v.)—later added to this discussion, and many others have profited from it in constructing their own plot devices. This chapter also contains a comment that has disconcerted more than one reader. When Fell brings the topic of detective fiction into his analysis of impossible situations, he is asked why he does so. " 'Because,' said the doctor frankly, 'we're in a detective story, and we don't fool the reader by pretending we're not. Let's not invent elaborate excuses to drag in a discussion of detective stories. Let's candidly glory in the noblest pursuits possible to characters in a book.' " The device of having a character acknowledge that he *is* a fictional character and comment on the fact has been used more than once in "high" literature. For Carr, it was simply part of playing the game—"the grandest game in the world"—with his readers, and for those readers willing to enter into the spirit of the game, it is a clever and charming touch.

(R.E.B.)

*Carr, John Dickson. *The Third Bullet and Other Stories.* New York: Harper, 1954. (SS/CS/W)

The virtues of Carr's detective novels are present in his short fiction as well. He gets about his work with more directness, and there are fewer atmospheric side trips, but the ingenuity of plot, the sprightly dialogue, and the smooth misdirection are all in evidence. The seven stories in this collection are the cream of his detective short stories.

The title story is actually a long novelette, originally published in England in 1937 and later reprinted in *Ellery Queen's Mystery Magazine,* where all the other stories in the book first appeared. (The book is dedicated to Frederic Dannay, *EQMM*'s founder and editor, "who inspired so many of these stories.") "The Third Bullet" is a fully developed locked-room story, complete with floor plan, false alibis, and a thoroughly detestable villain. In "The Clue of the Red Wig," CID inspector Adam Bell and a delightful interfering reporter, Jacqueline Dubois, investigate the murder of health-and-exercise columnist Hazel Loring, found beaten to death, "half-dressed, in a public garden on a bitter December night."

Three of the stories are locked-room crimes investigated by Dr. Gideon Fell: "The Wrong Problem," "The Proverbial Murder," and "The Locked Room." "The Gentleman from Paris" is an *EQMM* prizewinning story set in Paris in 1849, in which the identity of the detective is of as much interest as the solution to the crime. The remaining story, "The House in Goblin Wood," originally appeared under Carr's pseudonym, Carter Dickson (q.v.), and features Dickson's series detective Sir Henry Merrivale. A girl disappears from a country cottage, all of whose exits are locked or under observation. The story is one of Carr's most ingenious, and also one of his grimmest, in spite of the classic pratfall with which it opens.

This collection is a perfect accompaniment to "The Locked Room Lecture," offering cleverly wrought demonstrations of all of Dr. Fell's analytical points. It also demonstrates the diversity that can exist within one seemingly restrictive category of detective story. And the stories are, above all, immensely readable.

Among the more than fifty books published under the Carr by-line, many are worth special attention. *The Blind Barber* (1934) is a notably smooth blending of grisly murder and all-out farce, as a slasher-type killer is loose on an ocean liner. Dr. Fell is not on board, but acts as an armchair detective in the later chapters. Another of Dr. Fell's cases, *The Crooked Hinge* (1938), has what is probably the most audacious of Carr's plots. *He Who Whispers* (1946) and *Below Suspicion* (1950) expertly mix eerie atmosphere with baffling murders. The latter book features one of Carr's most interesting secondary characters, the barrister Patrick Butler. Among the nonseries books, *The Burning Court* (1937) is the most praiseworthy.

(*R.E.B.*)

Caspary, Vera. *Laura.* Boston: Houghton Mifflin, 1944. (W)

The main strength of Vera Caspary's writing is her depth of characterization; in fact, in many of her mysteries the actual crime takes a back seat to her detailed studies of the persons involved. In this, her first novel, the persona of Laura Hunt, the heroine—initially thought to have been the victim of a brutal murder—is so well described that the reader can visualize her and anticipate her actions and reactions long before she appears on the scene. The other principals—a crime writer and close friend of Laura's, and the investigating officer who finds himself falling in love with his image of her—are likewise drawn in meticulous detail, through the use of their individual narrative voices. (The story is told in sections, each from the viewpoint of one or the other of the main characters.)

The story they tell is basically a simple one. A young "bachelor girl," Laura Hunt, has been shot to death in her apartment in Manhattan's East Sixties. She took the force of the blast in the face, and is virtually unrecognizable except for her attire. Mark McPherson, a police officer with a distinguished record, is assigned to the case and acquires much of his knowledge of Miss Hunt from her friend, a sexually amorphous writer named Waldo Lydecker. There was a fiancé in Miss Hunt's life—an impoverished copywriter from the ad agency where she worked; and an aunt who is quick to complain about the fiancé's shiftlessness—and to use him when convenient. As McPherson delves further into Laura Hunt's life, he becomes entranced with the dead woman, a fascination that Lydecker, who narrates the first section, notices and plays upon.

When McPherson takes up the narrative, we find that Laura is not really dead; she had loaned her apartment to a model frequently used by her agency and gone away to her summer cottage for a few days' contemplation before her impending marriage. McPherson's attention is now focused on the question of who killed the ordinary little model who was temporarily using Laura's apartment, and his suspicions eventually point to Laura herself. The ending, narrated by McPherson, with an intervening section told by Laura, is predictable, but completely satisfying.

Laura was made into a classic suspense film of the same title, starring Dana Andrews, Clifton Webb, and Gene Tierney, and directed by Otto Preminger, in 1944. In another notable novel, *Evvie* (1960), Caspary's characterization of a genuine murder victim is even more sharp and haunting than that of Laura Hunt. And her mastery of the deviant but still socially accepted personality is demonstrated to great effect in *Bedelia* (1945) and *The Man Who Loved His Wife* (1966).

(M.M.)

Caudwell, Sarah. *Thus Was Adonis Murdered.* New York: Scribner's, 1981. (AD)

In her first mystery novel, Sarah Caudwell provides proof that a Victorian epistolary novel, a mystery in the manner of the Golden Age, and a late-twentieth-century sex farce can all be harmoniously combined in one exceptional novel. But then, no less was expected from the child of British author Claud Cockburn and actress Jean Ross (who was Christopher Isherwood's model for Sally Bowles).

Caudwell is a barrister, so it is not surprising that the legal profession features prominently in her story. The central character is Julia Larwood, a gifted barrister who is hopeless with the simple details of daily life. She goes on an art lover's tour of Venice to forget the dunning of the Inland Revenue (her archenemy) and to seduce a beautiful young man or two. Her sexual success (with a taxman, of course!) is quickly followed by disaster: Soon after Julia rises from the bed of her young swain, he is found stabbed to death. Julia, not surprisingly, is arrested.

It is up to her colleagues back at Lincoln's Inn, notably law professor Hillary Tamar, to find the real killer. Narrative and clues are provided by Tamar and supplemented by various letters, especially those of Julia to her barrister friend Selena. The tone is quasi-Victorian, *very* British, and highly amusing. The plot is improbable but skillfully handled. The characters are a delight. All in all, *Thus Was Adonis Murdered* marks a highly impressive debut.

(*K.L.M.*)

Chaber, M. E. *The Splintered Man.* New York: Rinehart, 1955. (E)

Kendall Foster Crossen published more than twenty novels as M. E. Chaber. All but one of these featured Milo March as the first-person narrator and protagonist. At times March functioned in his usual capacity as an insurance investigator, but he often had occasion to work for the State Department or the CIA. There is a certain similarity in many of March's adventures, but Crossen is a writer who perfected his craft, and the Chaber books are fast, smooth, funny in spots, and always entertaining. *The Splintered Man* stands out among them because long before the Beatles were singing about "Lucy in the Sky with Diamonds," Crossen introduced lysergic acid diethylamide (LSD) as a major plot device in an espionage story.

Milo March is called back into the army and sent into East Berlin to find Hermann Gruss, the head of the counterespionage police in West Berlin, who is believed to have defected to the East. Getting into East Berlin is not too hard for March in those days before the Wall. Getting out is something else again, especially when March is caught and given a hefty dose of LSD by a doctor who is experimenting with the drug at a large Russian hospital. The description of the drug's effects on March, while perhaps not clinically accurate by today's standards, is nevertheless convincingly carried off. It is not revealing too much to say that March's inevitable escape from the hospital is accomplished by a little fudging of scientific facts, but the result is still satisfactory.

The cover of the first paperback edition of *The Splintered Man* (Perma Books, 1957) is a collector's dream. March, in his undershorts, cowers in the background while held by two men in uniform. In the foreground are two large, red hands, one holding a red test tube, the other holding a sizable red hypodermic needle. (In the story, March's dose of LSD is administered in a glass of water.)

Milo March's other adventures include *The Gallows Garden* (1958), *Softly in the Night* (1963), *The Flaming Man* (1969), and *Born to Be Hanged* (1973). Crossen also published numerous mystery novels under his own name and such pseudonyms as Christopher Monig, Clay Richards, and Richard Foster.

(*B.C.*)

*Chandler, Raymond. *The Big Sleep.* New York: Knopf, 1939. (PI)

It is difficult to imagine what the modern private-eye story would be like if a forty-five-year-old ex–oil company executive named Raymond Chandler had not begun writing fiction for *Black Mask* in 1933. In his short stories, and definitively in his novels, Chandler took the hard-boiled prototype established by Dashiell Hammet (q.v.), reshaped it to fit his own particular vision and the exigencies of life in southern California, smoothed off its rough edges, and made of it something more than a tale of realism and violence; he broadened it into a vehicle for social commentary, refined it with prose at once cynical and poetic, and elevated the character of the private eye to a mythical status—"down these mean streets a man must go who is not himself mean, who is neither tarnished nor afraid."

Chandler's lean, tough, wisecracking style set the tone for all subsequent private-eye fiction, good and bad. He is certainly the most imitated writer in the genre, and next to Hemingway, perhaps the most imitated writer in the English language. (Howard Browne [q.v.], the creator of PI Paul Pine, once made Chandler laugh at a New York publishing party by introducing himself and saying, "It's an honor to meet you, Mr. Chandler. I've been making a living off your work for years.") Even Ross Macdonald (q.v.), for all *his* refinements of the hard-boiled prototype, and for all his literary intentions, was at the core a Chandler imitator: Lew Archer would not be Lew Archer, indeed might not have been born at all, if Chandler had not created Philip Marlowe.

The Big Sleep, Chandler's first novel, is a blending and expansion of two of his *Black Mask* novelettes, "Killer in the Rain" (January 1935) and "The Curtain" (September 1936)—a process Chandler used twice more, in creating *Farewell, My Lovely* and *The Lady in the Lake,* and which he candidly referred to as "cannibalizing." It is Philip Marlowe's first bow. Marlowe does not appear in any of Chandler's pulp stories, at least not by name; the first-person narrators of "Killer in the Rain" (unnamed) and "The Curtain" (Carmady) are embryonic Marlowes, with many of his attributes. *The Big Sleep* is also Chandler's best-known title, by virtue of the well-made

1944 film version directed by Howard Hawks and starring Humphrey Bogart, Lauren Bacall, and Elisha Cook, Jr.

On one level, this is a complex murder mystery with its fair share of clues and corpses. On another level, it is a serious novel concerned (as is much of Chandler's work) with the corrupting influences of money and power. Marlowe is hired by General Sternwood, an old, paralyzed ex-soldier who made a fortune in oil, to find out why a rare-book dealer named Arthur Gwynn Geiger is holding an IOU signed by Sternwood's youngest daughter, the wild and immoral Carmen, and where a blackmailing gambler named Joe Brody fits into the picture. Marlowe's investigation embroils him with Sternwood's other daughter, Vivian, and her strangely missing husband, Rusty, a former bootlegger; a thriving pornography racket; a gaggle of gangsters, not the least of which is a nasty piece of work named Eddie Mars; hidden vices and family scandals; and several murders. The novel's climax is more ambiguous and satisfying than the film's rather pat one.

The Big Sleep is not Chandler's best work; its plot is convoluted and tends to be confusing, and there are loose ends that are never explained or tied off. Nevertheless, it is still a powerful and riveting novel, packed with fascinating characters and evocatively told. Just one small sample of Chandler's marvelous prose:

> *The air was thick, wet, steamy and larded with the cloying smell of tropical orchids in bloom. The glass walls and roof were heavily misted and big drops of moisture splashed down on the plants. The light had an unreal greenish color, like light filtered through an aquarium tank. The plants filled the place, a forest of them, with nasty meaty leaves and stalks like the newly washed fingers of dead men. They smelled as overpowering as boiling alcohol under a blanket.*

That passage is quintessential Chandler; if it doesn't stir your blood and make you crave more, as it always does for this reviewer, he probably isn't your cup of bourbon.

(*B.P.*)

**Chandler, Raymond. *Farewell, My Lovely*. New York: Knopf, 1940. (PI)

Many critics consider *The Long Goodbye* to be Chandler's finest novel. This one disagrees. That distinction should probably go to *Farewell, My Lovely*—a more tightly plotted, less self-indulgent and overblown book, with characters, scenes, and prose of such artistry that it ranks as not only a cornerstone private-eye novel but a cornerstone work in the genre. Its near-flawless construction is all the more awesome when you consider that like

The Big Sleep, it is a product of "cannibalization": It makes extensive use of "The Man Who Liked Dogs" (*Black Mask,* March 1936); "Try the Girl" (*Black Mask,* January 1937); and "Mandarin's Jade" (*Dime Detective,* November 1937).

Marlowe's client in this case is Moose Malloy, a giant ex-con with a one-track mind: All that matters to him is finding his former girlfriend, Velma, a redhead "cute as lace pants," who disappeared after he was sent to prison. Marlowe is a reluctant detective, his first encounter with Malloy having ended in the wreckage of a bar, Florian's, where Velma once worked and a black bouncer suffering a broken neck; but Malloy won't take no for an answer. As Marlowe's search for Velma develops, "the atmosphere becomes increasingly malevolent and charged with evil." Among the characters he meets are a foppish blackmailer named Lindsay Marriott; a gin-drinking old lady with secrets and a fine new radio; a beautiful blonde with no morals and a rich husband who doesn't give a damn; a Hollywood Indian named Second Planting who has "the shoulders of a blacksmith and the . . . legs of a chimpanzee"; a phony psychic, Jules Amthor; Dr. Sonderborg, who runs a private psychiatric clinic staffed with thugs; Laird Brunette, the tough operator of a gambling ship called the *Royal Crown;* and L.A. and Bay City cops, some of whom are as crooked as a dog's hind leg. The climax, in which Marlowe and Moose Malloy both come face-to-face with the elusive Velma, is a stunner. Like a number of other scenes—especially Marlowe's drugged imprisonment in Sonderborg's clinic, in a room "full of smoke [that] hung straight up in the air, in thin lines, straight up and down like a curtain of small clear beads"—it remains sharp in one's memory long after reading.

Farewell, My Lovely was filmed twice, once in 1944 as *Murder My Sweet,* with Dick Powell as Marlowe, and once in 1975 under its original title, with Robert Mitchum in the starring role. The Powell version is the better of the two, even though Mitchum, aging and slightly seedy, better captures the essence of Marlowe. (Powell isn't bad, though—a surprisingly gritty performance for an actor who began his career as a crooner in Busby Berkley musicals.) Mike Mazurki's portrayal of Moose Malloy in *Murder My Sweet* is more memorable (and credible) than Jack O'Halloran's in *Farewell.* And the *noir* style of the earlier film better captures the flavor of Chandler's work than the arty, full-color remake.

(*B.P.*)

*Chandler, Raymond. *The Lady in the Lake.* New York: Knopf, 1943. (PI)

Even though *The Lady in the Lake* is not Chandler's best novel, it is this reviewer's favorite. It too was "cannibalized" from three pulp novelettes—"Bay City Blues" (*Dime Detective,* November 1937), "The Lady in the

Lake" (*Dime Detective,* January 1939), "No Crime in the Mountains" (*Detective Story,* September 1941)—but it is not as seamless as *The Big Sleep* or *Farewell, My Lovely,* nor as wholly credible. Nevertheless, there is an intangible quality about it, a kind of terrible and perfect inevitability that combines with such tangibles as Chandler's usual fascinating assortment of characters and some unforgettable moments to make it extra satisfying.

The novel opens with Marlowe hired by Derace Kingsley, a foppish perfume company executive, to find his missing wife, Crystal (who he admits he hates and who may or may not have run off with one of his "friends," Chris Lavery). Marlowe follows a tortuous and deadly trail that leads him from L.A. to the beach community of Bay City, to Little Fawn Lake high in the San Bernardino Mountains, to the towns of Puma Point and San Bernardino, and back to both L.A. and Bay City. And it involves him with a doctor named Almore, a tough cop named Degarmo, a half-crippled mountain caretaker, Bill Chess, whose wife is also missing, Kingsley's secretary, Miss Adrienne Fromsett—and the lady in the lake, among other victims. As the dust jacket of the original edition puts it, it is "a most extraordinary case, because . . . Marlowe understands that what is important is not a clue—not the neatly stacked dishes, not the strange telegram . . . but rather the character of [Crystal Kingsley]. When he began to find out what she was like, he took his initial steps into a world of evil, and only then did the idea of what she might have done and what might have been done to her take shape. So it was that not one crime but several were revealed, and a whole series of doors that hid cruel things were suddenly opened.

"Again Chandler proves that he is one of the most brilliant craftsmen in the field, and that his Marlowe is one of the great detectives in fiction."

Amen.

The Lady in the Lake was filmed in 1946, with Robert Montgomery (who also directed) as Marlowe. For its time, it was a radical experiment in filmmaking, in that it is entirely photographed as if through the eyes of Marlowe—a sort of cinematic version of the first-person narrator, with Montgomery himself never seen except in an occasional mirror reflection. The technique doesn't quite work—it, not the story, becomes the focus of attention—but the film is an oddity worth seeing.

(*B.P.*)

*Chandler, Raymond. *The Long Goodbye.* Boston: Houghton Mifflin, 1954. (PI)

The title of this novel is apt. It is a long book and a complex one, and its detractors say they wish Chandler had said goodbye two-thirds of the way through. What these critics fail to understand is that the novel is one of the most realistic looks into the day-to-day life of a private investigator, and the central plot element, that of Philip Marlowe's friendship for the mostly undeserving Terry Lennox, is a compelling unifying element. In it we also see a different side of Marlowe than in Chandler's other novels: the man who is as honorable in his personal relationships as he is in his professional ones.

The story begins when Marlowe first sees Terry Lennox, dissolute man-about-town: he is "drunk in a Rolls-Royce Silver Wraith outside the terrace of the Dancers," a ritzy L.A. nightspot, with a redheaded girl beside him whose blue mink "almost made the Rolls-Royce look like just another automobile." The girl leaves Terry, Good Samaritan Marlowe takes over, and a friendship begins. It is a friendship that Marlowe himself questions, but it persists nonetheless. Marlowe tells Lennox he has a feeling Terry will end up in worse trouble than Marlowe will be able to extricate him from, and in due course this proves true. The redhead, Terry's ex-wife, whom he admittedly married for her money, is murdered in the guesthouse at their Encino spread, and the trouble that Marlowe sensed begins.

Lennox runs to Mexico, and it is reported that he made a written confession and shot himself in his hotel room. But something feels wrong: The Lennox case is being hushed up, and Marlowe begins to wonder if his friend really did kill his ex-wife. A letter that arrives with a "portrait of Madison"—a $5000 bill that Terry had once promised Marlowe—convinces him his suspicions are justified. He tells himself it is over and done with, but he isn't able to forget. The matter plagues him while he is working a case involving an alcoholic writer of best sellers in wealthy Idle Valley (where, he says, "I belonged . . . like a pearl onion on a banana split"). It begins to plague him even more when Sylvia Lennox's sister, Linda Loring, appears and plants additional suspicions in his mind. The suspicions spur him onward, and finally his current case and the Lennox case come together in a shattering climax.

At the end Chandler neatly ties off all the strands of this complicated story, and provides more than a few surprises. An excellent novel with a moving ending.

(*M.M.*)

*Chandler, Raymond. *The Simple Art of Murder.* Boston: Houghton Mifflin, 1950. (SS)

Eleven of the twelve stories in this collection are those that Chandler considered the best of his output for the pulps; the other story, "I'll Be Waiting," was first published in the *Saturday Evening Post* (although Chandler admittedly felt uncomfortable and restricted writing for the slick-magazine medium). Also included here is Chandler's famous and controversial essay on detective fiction, first published in the *Atlantic Monthly,* in which he lauds Hammett and the realistic school of crime writing, and takes a number of shots (some fair, some cheap) at such Golden Age luminaries as Christie, Sayers, and A. A. Milne (qq.v.).

The stories here, as the dust jacket blurb says with typical publishers' overstatement but accurately nonetheless, "hit you as hard as if [Chandler] were driving the last spike on the first continental railroad." "Red Wind," for instance, begins with one of the finest opening paragraphs in the history of the genre:

> *There was a desert wind blowing that night. It was one of those hot dry Santa Anas that come down through the mountain passes and curl your hair and make your nerves jump and your skin itch. On nights like that every booze party ends in a fight. Meek little wives feel the edge of the carving knife and study their husbands' necks. Anything can happen. You can even get a full glass of beer at a cocktail lounge.*

In the original appearance of that story, the private-eye narrator was Johnny Dalmas; here he becomes Philip Marlowe. Similarly, the unnamed narrator in "Finger Man," Carmady in "Goldfish," and Dalmas again in "Trouble Is My Business" are also changed to Marlowe. Johnny Dalmas does get to keep his own name in "Smart-Aleck Kill," no doubt because that novelette is told third-person. And the same is true of Carmady in "Guns at Cyrano's." The only other first-person story in the collection, the lighter-toned and somewhat wacky "Pearls Are a Nuisance," features a much more refined dick named Walter Gage whose antics in search of a string of forty-nine matched pink pearls provide chuckles as well as thrills. Also included are the tough *Black Mask* novelettes "Nevada Gas" and "Spanish Blood," "The King in Yellow" from *Dime Detective,* and "Pick-Up on Noon Street" from *Detective Fiction Weekly.*

All of these stories appear in several other collections, such as the paperback originals *Five Murderers* (1944) and *Finger Man and Other Stories* (1946) and the Tower Books hardcover originals *Red Wind* (1946) and *Spanish Blood* (1946). Next to *The Simple Art of Murder,* the most interesting and important Chandler collection is *Killer in the Rain* (1964), which gathers the eight "cannibalized" stories that were used as the bases for *The Big Sleep, Farewell, My Lovely,* and *The Lady in the Lake.*

(*B.P.*)

*Charteris, Leslie. *The Brighter Buccaneer.* New York: Doubleday Crime Club, 1933. (SS/CS)

Leslie Charteris's long-lived and internationally popular character, the Saint, has appeared in two widely different sorts of tales. In the novels, he is the piratical adventurer and self-appointed executioner, usually involved in melodramatic thrillers with lots of action and political intrigue. The Saint short stories, however, tend to be more jocular and subdued, and often have elements of genuine detection. Charteris has made one particular sort of short story his specialty—the "sting" story, in which Simon Templar out-cons the con men. In doing so, he makes good the losses of the previously fleeced—in line with his reputation as "the Robin Hood of Modern Crime"—and pockets a nice profit for himself in the bargain. Several of the stories in this collection are classics in this genre.

In "The Brain Workers," for instance, Templar adopts his favorite disguise as twittish Sebastian Tombs to outwit one Julian Lamantia, dealer in phony oil stock; in the final story, "The Unusual Ending," Lamantia comes in for another dose of the same (this time he's running a Ponzi scheme). "The Unblemished Bootlegger," a tale of poetic retribution, is noteworthy in that it marks the debut of Peter Quentin, who became one of the Saint's regular accomplices in later stories. "The Appalling Politician" provides a break from the con games. It is a detective story, in which the Saint's long-suffering adversary, Chief Inspector Claude Eustace Teal, calls on Templar to help out with a stolen-treaty problem. In this one, as he often does, Charteris makes use of his fictional alter ego to get off a few witty blasts at pompous British politicians.

The best of all the stories is "The Green Goods Man," in which Templar neatly turns the tables on a counterfeit-money scam artist. It has two truly memorable scenes and a slick double-twist ending.

(*A.S.*)

Charteris, Leslie. *The Saint in New York*. New York: Doubleday Crime Club, 1935. (CS/A)

This novel is perhaps the best of the tales in which Simon Templar adopts the role of Nemesis, dispensing summary justice to criminals. It is one of the grimmest tales in the Saint saga; it is a furiously paced, tightly crafted, wholly satisfactory blood-and-thunder thriller.

Wealthy William Valcross offers the Saint $1 million to avenge the death of his son, who was murdered by a kidnap mob terrorizing New York. The Saint accepts the job, makes up a list of six big-time mobsters to be killed, and announces his intention to clean up the city to the newspapers. In three days of furious action, he makes good on his promise. Along the way he adds another name to his list, the mysterious "Big Fellow," a Moriartyesque mastermind who pulls the strings behind the scenes; and encounters a woman of mystery, Fay Edwards, who saves his life when he's taken for a ride. He also forms an uneasy alliance with John Henry Fernack, chief of New York detectives, who thereafter became a continuing character, reappearing whenever Templar's travels take him to the States.

The episode in which Templar, armed with only a knife and his wits, takes on a houseful of mobsters in order to save a kidnapped girl is as neatly choreographed and exciting an action sequence as is to be found anywhere in Charteris's work. The book concludes with a dramatic surprise ending, in which the Saint learns the identity of the Big Fellow.

The Saint in New York predates by some forty years a paperback landslide of similar one-man-against-the-mob novels written by Don Pendleton (q.v.) and his many imitators. It is unlikely that any have yet equaled this book for excitement; certainly none has come close in style.

Other Saint books of note: *Getaway* (1932), *The Misfortunes of Mr. Teal* (1934) (SS), *Saint Overboard* (1936), *The Happy Highwayman* (1939) (SS), *The Saint in Miami* (1940).

(*A.S.*)

Chase, James Hadley. *No Orchids for Miss Blandish.* New York: Howell Soskin, 1942. (T)

Since the publication of *No Orchids for Miss Blandish,* James Hadley Chase has sold millions of copies of his more than eighty novels. A British writer who uses mostly American characters and settings in his works, Chase has a fast-paced, hard-boiled style perfectly suited to his violent, action-filled novels.

The title character of *Miss Blandish* is a young socialite who is kidnapped by small-time hoods and then kidnapped from them by the members of the Grisson gang, a group based on the notorious Ma Barker and her sons. Ma Grisson's favorite son, Slim, a vicious, perverted killer, takes a special interest in Miss Blandish; so instead of killing her when the ransom is paid, Ma gives her to Slim. She is kept in a narcotic haze by Doc, another of the gang, so that she will submit to Slim's debased desires. Eventually, Miss Blandish's father hires Fenner, a former crime reporter turned private eye, to find his daughter. There is a bloody shoot-out between the gang and the police, but Slim escapes with Miss Blandish. He is finally cornered, but this is not the sort of story in which everyone can live happily ever after.

Chase does a fine job in *Miss Blandish* (even in the revised edition of 1961) of understating the sex and violence, which become more effective than if they had been spelled out. The pace never lags, and the ending is very well handled. *Miss Blandish* is no longer as shocking as its reputation might suggest, but it remains a powerful crime novel.

Chase's novels were well suited to the needs of the early paperback market, and many of them are highly sought after by collectors, as much for their colorful titles and gaudy covers as for their contents. Examples include *Twelve Chinks and a Woman* (Avon, 1952) and *Kiss My Fist!* (Eton, 1952).

(*B.C.*)

Chastain, Thomas. *911.* New York: Mason/Charter, 1976. (PP/T)

Inspector Max Kauffman of the New York Police Department is checking the security on the Macy's Thanksgiving Day Parade when a huge teddy-bear balloon is detonated by a bomb. The incident does not turn out to be an isolated one, and a call to the department's 911 number promises other explosions, one for each of the twelve days of Christmas. A threatening note follows; a truck delivering a Christmas tree to Rockefeller Center explodes; other Christmas trees along Park Avenue are detonated. People begin to die as a result of the bombings, and as day twelve (Christmas Eve) approaches, the entire city seems to be in the clutches of a psychopath.

As the men of the Sixteenth Precinct work to trap the man they call "the Christmas Bomber," there are interwoven scenes depicting the activities of the criminal, as well as the private lives of Kauffman and the Bomb Investigative Unit's John Tynan, all of which makes for a fast-moving thriller in which the bomber's bizarre motivation is tied up with the usually merry Christmas season.

Thomas Chastain has written three other novels featuring Max Kauffman: *Pandora's Box* (1974), *Spanner* (1977), and *High Voltage* (1979). Jake Spanner reappears as the private-eye hero of *Vital Statistics* (1977). Chastain is also the author (with Bill Adler) of *Who Killed the Robbins Family?* (1983), an unfinished novel in which the publisher invites the reader to compose an ending and win a cash prize.

(*M.M.*)

Chaze, Elliot. *Black Wings Has My Angel.* Greenwich, Conn.: Fawcett Gold Medal, 1953. (O/PS)

The reputation of *Black Wings Has My Angel* as the quintessential Gold Medal paperback is deserved. It has everything that made these originals so good: a fast-moving story, sex, and fine descriptive writing.

Escaped con Tim Sunblade (an alias chosen after his jailbreak, "because it smells of the out of doors") is resting up after roughnecking on a drilling rig. In a small hotel in a little fishing village on the Atchafayala, he encounters Virginia, a beautiful prostitute whose $10-a-night fee causes him to guess rightly that she, too, is keeping a low profile; soon he finds she is a high-priced call girl on the run. Virginia seems aloof, even cold, but the two pair off. When Tim tries to ditch her, only to discover she has anticipated him and stolen his money, they reteam and Virginia's passion bubbles to the surface. Camping out in the mountains in Colorado, Tim decides Virginia has what it takes to help him pull off an armored-car job. They move to Denver and set up a respectable front, renting a house, Tim working another hard labor job, as the robbery is meticulously planned, and then carried out.

But Chaze's antihero is too complex to be described simply as amoral; his immoral deeds haunt him in a manner an amoral individual would shrug off. A murder he's committed eats at him as he and Virginia slide into a rich, decadent life-style in New Orleans. Soon Tim is pulled obsessively into his respectable past, for a brief, violent layover in his small hometown, before the couple ride out an even deeper, darker compulsion: to look into a certain abandoned mine shaft, to stare into the darkness that is death.

Gold Medal originals were often James M. Cain (q.v.) pastiches, and Chaze's novel is one of the best—far better than the novels Cain himself was writing at the time. Chaze's bleak social satire—the working and upper classes are shown to be equally venal—helps keep Tim's actions understandable and even sympathetic. The swift, compelling, natural-sounding first-person narration is marked by quietly vivid images ("She was lying on the sleeping bag in the sun, as slim and bare as a sword").

Black Wings Has My Angel (reprinted as *One for My Money,* Berkley, 1962) is an early work, and would seem to promise a major career in the genre for Chaze. But Chaze, a newspaperman, has published novels only occasionally, and not always in the suspense field. In Chaze's recent mystery series about newsman Kiel St. James, the promise of his Gold Medal original is not kept: *Mr. Yesterday* (1984) is haphazardly plotted, an unconvincing structure that collapses upon its interesting characters and well-drawn southern setting.

(*M.A.C.*)

Chernyonok, Mikhail. *Losing Bet.* Translated from the Russian by Antonina W. Bouis. New York: Dial, 1984. (PP)

To many American readers, Martin Cruz Smith's (q.v.) *Gorky Park* was a curiosity—a murder mystery set in Moscow. But since World War II, the mystery has been a popular form in the Soviet Union, and novels by writers such as Vil Vladiminovich Lipatov, the brother team of Arkady and Georgy Alexandrovich Vainer, and Julian Semyonovich Semyonov are widely read. Most of these mysteries would not appeal to Western readers; they are long-winded and parochial. But Mikhail Chernyonok's *Losing Bet* was an excellent choice for translation.

A young woman has fallen—or been pushed—from the balcony of an apartment in Novosibirsk, a city of a million inhabitants in remote western Siberia. Detective Anton Birukov is in charge of the case. The woman, Sanya, is the ex-wife of the apartment's tenant, Yuri Demensky, but he claims he has not seen her for years. In the apartment are found the fingerprints of a well-known professional criminal, Vasya Sipeniatin, but his specialty has always been cunning, not violence. Other suspects include Ovchinnikov, a self-styled ladies' man who borrowed Demensky's apartment for romantic liaisons; Zarvantsev, a talented artist who has "gone commercial"; and Stepnadze, a railroad conductor with a lucrative career on the side, illegal speculation in hard-to-find books.

All had known Sanya, but who had killed her, and what was she doing at Demensky's? As Birukov and his aides methodically track down clues from the bars and theaters of Novosibirsk to the resorts of the Black Sea, they begin to see a conspiracy of bribery and corruption that has led to one murder and will lead to more.

Much of the appeal of *Losing Bet* lies in its incisive but affectionate portrait of working-class Russians at work, play, and love. The police work is without frills. Aside from the interesting structural differences between Soviet and Western police forces, Birukov's crime-solving techniques would seem familiar, and sound, to American readers of police procedurals.

(*M.J.*)

*Chesbro, George. *Shadow of a Broken Man.* New York: Simon & Schuster, 1977. (PI/T)

This is the first Chesbro novel featuring Dr. Robert Fredrickson, a professor of criminology who doubles as a private detective, is a dwarf, and is known to his friends as Mongo. A onetime top circus performer, Mongo possesses some very useful skills for tight situations, among them tumbling and gymnastic ability and a black belt in karate.

While preparing to leave for vacation in Acapulco, Mongo is approached by Mike Foster, who married the widow of famous architect Victor Rafferty. Foster's wife, Elizabeth, happened to see a photograph of a new museum in an architectural magazine, and is convinced that the design is the work of her husband. But Victor died five years ago, and the museum's design is listed as the work of a man named Richard Patern. Victor Rafferty died from a fall into an open smelting furnace, so there was essentially no body to be recovered, and Elizabeth is haunted by the conviction that Rafferty is still alive. Mike Foster's marriage is suffering; he wants Mongo to clear up this matter so he and Elizabeth can get on with their lives.

Mongo assumes there won't be too much complication here, so he postpones his vacation and accepts the case. His first move is to consult professor of design Franklin Manning, resident architectural genius, who flatly tells Mongo that the museum is Rafferty's design, without question. And suddenly Mongo is involved in something much more complex and dangerous than he imagined. Russian and French agents are part of the package, as are U.N. Secretary Rolfe Thaag and more than one victim of Communist brutality.

The writing here is literate and fast-paced, the plot is intricate, the concept is bizarre yet entirely plausible. This is a well-spiced recipe that results in *haute cuisine.*

Chesbro is also the author of *City of Whispering Stone* (1978), *An Affair of Sorcerers* (1979), and *The Beasts of Valhalla* (1985), which likewise feature Mongo.

(*J.L.*)

*Chesterton, G. K. *The Incredulity of Father Brown.* New York: Dodd, Mead, 1926. (SS/CS)

As several critics have observed, the Father Brown stories are small gems to be relished sparingly. If too many are read at one time, the effect is lessened and one might even begin picking holes in their logic. But as detective stories, they are still masterpieces, and the most lasting of all the writing Chesterton produced in his prolific career. Their influence upon later mystery writers—especially John Dickson Carr (q.v.)—was enormous, and Carr's major detective character, Dr. Gideon Fell, was patterned after Chesterton himself.

The Incredulity of Father Brown is not the best of the five Brown collections, but it is unique in that seven of its eight stories contain locked rooms or impossible crimes as a part of their plots. One of these, "The Oracle of the Dog," is perhaps the best of all Father Brown stories, and one of the best detective short stories ever written. The stabbing death of Colonel Druce while alone in a summerhouse whose only entrance is under constant observation, together with a dog that seems to howl at the moment of the colonel's death, sets up a classic situation in which the impossibility of the crime is linked to a seemingly supernatural event. It was a situation to be explored often by Carr and other writers that followed, but their solutions have rarely been as ingenious as the one Chesterton offers here.

The other six impossible-crime stories in the book are "The Arrow of Heaven," in which an American millionaire is killed by an arrow inside a guarded room; "The Miracle of Moon Crescent," featuring the disappearance of a man from a guarded apartment; "The Curse of the Golden Cross," about a curse on defilers of an ancient tomb; "The Dagger with Wings," in which a strange cloaked figure is found dead in unmarked snow; "The Doom of the Darnaways," involving a locked-room poisoning; and "The Ghost of Gideon Wise," wherein Father Brown is confronted with a ghostly appearance. In all, the atmosphere of the inexplicable is brilliantly realized.

(*E.D.H.*)

**Chesterton, G. K. *The Innocence of Father Brown.* New York: Lane, 1911. (SS/CS)

A cornerstone volume, Chesterton's *Innocence of Father Brown* can lay claim to greatness on two counts: It introduced the priest detective whose adventures are still popular three-quarters of a century later, and it contains more classic short stories than almost any other mystery collection before or since.

All twelve of its stories deserve special mention. The opening story, "The Blue Cross," long an anthology and textbook favorite, tells of the first meeting of Father Brown and the master thief Flambeau, who would later become his friend and associate on many cases. "The Secret Garden" has a dual impossibility—the appearance of a beheaded corpse inside a locked and guarded garden, and the disappearance of another man from the same garden. "The Queer Feet" turns upon a brilliant bit of psychology and is a favorite of several critics. "The Flying Stars" involves a diamond theft at a Christmas party, and is Flambeau's last crime. "The Invisible Man" is probably the most famous Father Brown story of all—so famous, in fact, that its solution is known to people who have never read it. Whether Smythe really could have been murdered in his guarded apartment building without anyone seeing the killer is a matter of some dispute, but the story is memorable nonetheless.

"The Honour of Israel Gow" presents Father Brown with a number of bizarre objects, seemingly unrelated. The solution, simple yet startling, reveals a strange sort of honesty rather than a crime. In "The Wrong Shape" a man is stabbed to death with a curved dagger in a locked room, leaving an oddly shaped suicide note. "The Sins of Prince Saradine" is about a murder plot and a duel with rapiers. "The Hammer of God," one of the three or four best Father Brown stories, combines a seemingly superhuman murder beside a great Gothic church with a solution that is simple and satisfying. "The Eye of Apollo" deals with a cult of sun worshipers and a unique murder method. "The Sign of the Broken Sword," perhaps the cleverest and most enjoyable story in the volume, full of paradox and allowing Father Brown to practice some pseudohistorical detection, offers Chesterton's dazzling answer to the question "Where would a wise man hide a body?" The final story, "The Three Tools of Death," is about an apparently brutal murder.

All twelve offer a nice feeling of life in Edwardian England, and if Father Brown lacks the colorful eccentricities of Sherlock Holmes, if his solutions are often more intuition than deduction, this book is still a masterpiece, the single volume by which G. K. Chesterton is most likely to be remembered.

(*E.D.H.*)

Chesterton, G. K. *The Man Who Was Thursday.* New York: Dodd, Mead, 1908. (E/A)

Described by some as a great spy novel and by others as a fine mystery, Chesterton's *Man Who Was Thursday* could more accurately be labeled a religious allegory. It remains the author's best and most popular novel, although its importance in the mystery field is overshadowed by the Father Brown stories.

The book deals with a poet named Syme, an undercover detective, who infiltrates the dangerous Central Anarchist Council in which each revolutionary is named for a day of the week. Though the novel can be read satisfactorily as a chase adventure or even as a political parable of its times, Chesterton's real purpose is a meditation on the nature of religion, full of paradox and wisdom.

Although this was Chesterton's only attempt at the mystery in novel length, his fascination with the detective short story lasted throughout his life. Of special importance are three additional Father Brown collections: *The Wisdom of Father Brown* (1914), *The Secret of Father Brown* (1927), and *The Scandal of Father Brown* (1935), and three collections about other detectives: *The Club of Queer Trades* (1905), *The Man Who Knew Too Much* (1922), and *The Poet and the Lunatics* (1929). The best one-volume selection, containing thirteen stories from the five Father Brown collections and the other three books listed above, is Chesterton's *Selected Stories,* edited by Kingsley Amis (London, 1972). Of lesser importance but still enjoyable for their paradoxes are *Four Faultless Felons* (1930) and *The Paradoxes of Mr. Pond* (1936).

(*E.D.H.*)

Cheyney, Peter. *This Man Is Dangerous.* New York: Coward, McCann, 1938. (W)

Peter Cheyney (1896–1951) never visited the United States in his life and knew next to nothing about Americans, but in the late 1930s be became an instant success in his native England and in Europe, especially France, as a writer of fake-American hard-boiled novels. In *This Man Is Dangerous* and ten subsequent titles, he chronicled the adventures of rootin'-tootin' two-gun-shootin' Lemmy Caution, an indestructible FBI agent who downs liquor by the quart, laughs at bullets flying his way, romances every dame in sight, and blasts away at greasy ethnic-named racketeers and (in the later novels) Nazi spies. Americans, of course, saw these ridiculous exercises for what they were, and only the first few were ever published here.

Certainly no one would read Lemmy Cautions for their plots, which are uniform from book to book—all the nasties double-crossing each other over the McGuffin—nor for their characterizations, which are pure comic strip.

But mystery fans with a taste for lunacy may be attracted by Cheyney's self-created idiom. Lemmy narrates his cases in first person and present tense, a wild-and-crazy stylistic smorgasbord concocted from Grade Z western films, the stories of Ring Lardner and Damon Runyon, eyeball-poppers apparently of Cheyney's own invention (like "He blew the bezuzus" for "He spilled the beans"), and a steady stream of British spellings and locutions.

Nothing but quotation can convey the Cheyney flavor. From *This Man Is Dangerous*:

> *I says good night, and I nods to the boys. I take my hat from the hall an' I walk down the stairs to the street. I'm feeling pretty good because I reckon that muscling in on this racket of Siegella's is going to be a good thing for me, and maybe if I use my brains an' keep my eyes skinned, I can still find some means of double-crossing this wop.*

From *Don't Get Me Wrong* (1939):

> *Me—I am prejudiced. I would rather stick around with a bad-tempered tiger than get on the wrong bias of one of these knife-throwin' palookas; I would rather four-flush a team of wild alligators outa their lunch-pail than try an' tell a Mexican momma that I was tired of her geography an' did not wish to play any more.*

From *Your Deal, My Lovely* (1941):

> *Some mug by the name of Confucius—who was a guy who was supposed to know his vegetables—once issued an edict that any time he saw a sap sittin' around bein' impervious to the weather an' anything else that was goin', an' lookin' like he had been hit in the kisser with a flat-iron, the said sap was sufferin' from woman trouble.*

Lemmy Caution became so popular on the Continent that Eddie Constantine, an American actor, portrayed him in a series of French films. These films were so successful that Jean Luc Godard used Constantine as Caution in his New Wave film *Alphaville*.

Eventually Cheyney launched a second wave of novels, written in a spare ersatz-Hammett style and featuring Slim Callaghan, London's toughest PI. But for those who love pure absurdity, and appreciate the wild stylistic flights of Robert Leslie Bellem and Henry Kane and Richard S. Prather (qq.v.), a treat of comparable dimensions is in store when they tackle the adventures of Lemmy Caution.

(*F.M.N.*)

Cheyney, Peter. *The Stars Are Dark*. New York: Dodd, Mead, 1943. (E)

Cheyney's best work is his series of espionage novels generally referred to as the "Dark Series," of which *The Stars Are Dark* is the second. Here, the breakneck pace of the Caution books is slowed by a genuine interest in character, which makes the story stronger.

Quayle, the master of a British spy ring in World War II, is faced with the task of dealing with a man who has come from Morocco with what he says is important information about German troops there. Is this man what he seems? Quayle puts his agents into action, not hesitating to risk their lives to discover the answer, but it is Quayle who does the most work and takes the most risks. Cheyney does an excellent job of conveying the world of spying, with all its twists and double crosses. No one is what he seems, and everyone knows that; but no one is sure just what anyone else really is. Quayle tells his people no more than they need to know. Readers of John le Carré (q.v.) and William Haggard would recognize Cheyney's world at once.

Not all Cheyney's books with "Dark" in the title belong to his spy series, but another very good one is *Dark Duet* (1942), first published in U.S. paperback as *The Counter Spy Murders* (Avon, 1944). *The Stars Are Dark* was retitled *The London Spy Murders* (Avon, 1944).

(*B.C.*)

*Christie, Agatha. *The ABC Murders*. New York: Dodd, Mead, 1935. (CS)

Agatha Christie has long been acknowledged as the *grande dame* of the Golden Age detective-story writers. Beginning with her moderately successful *The Mysterious Affair at Styles* (1920), Christie built a huge following both in her native England and abroad, and eventually became a household name throughout the literate world. When a reader—be he in London or Buenos Aires—picks up a Christie novel, he knows exactly what he is getting and has full confidence that he is sitting down to a tricky, entertaining, and satisfying mystery.

This enormous reader confidence stems from an effective combination of intricate, ingenious plots and typical, familiar characters and settings. Christie's plots always follow the rules of detective fiction; she plays completely fair with the reader. But Christie was a master at planting clues in unlikely places, dragging red herrings thither and yon, and, like a magician, misdirecting the reader's attention at the exact crucial moment. Her murderers—for all the Christie novels deal with nothing less important than this cardinal sin—are the Least Likely Suspect, the Second Least Likely Suspect, the Person with the Perfect Alibi, the Person with No Apparent Motive. And they are unmasked in marvelous gathering-of-all-suspects scenes where each clue is explained, all loose ends are tied up.

As a counterpoint to these plots, Christie's style is simple (even undistinguished). She relies heavily upon dialogue, and has a good ear for it when dealing with the "upstairs" people who are generally the main characters in her stories: the "downstairs" people fare less well at her hands, and their speech is often stilted or stereotyped.

Christie, however, seldom ventures into the "downstairs" world. Her milieu is the drawing room, the country manor house, the book-lined study, the cozy parlor with a log blazing on the hearth. Like these settings, her characters are refined and tame, comfortable as the slippers in front of the fire—until violent passion rears its ugly head. Not that violence is ever messy or repugnant, though; when murder intrudes, it does so in as bloodless a manner as possible, and its investigation is always conducted as coolly and rationally as circumstances permit. One reason that Christie's works are so immensely satisfying is that we know we will be confronted by nothing really disturbing, frightening, or grim. In short, her books are the ultimate escape reading with a guaranteed surprise at the end.

Christie's best-known sleuths are Hercule Poirot, the Belgian detective who relies on his "little grey cells" to solve the most intricate of crimes; and Miss Jane Marple, the old lady who receives her greatest inspiration while knitting. However, she created a number of other notable characters, among them Tuppence and Tommy Beresford, an amusing pair of detective-agency owners, who appear in such titles as *The Secret Adversary* (1922) and *Postern of Fate* (1973); Superintendent Battle of Scotland Yard, who is featured in *The Secret of Chimneys* (1925), *The Seven Dials Murder* (1929), and others; and the mysterious Harley Quin.

The member of this distinguished cast who stars in *The ABC Murders* is Hercule Poirot. Poirot is considered by many to be Christie's most versatile and appealing detective. The dapper Belgian confesses gleefully to dying his hair, but sees no humor in banter about his prized "pair of moustaches." And yet he has the ability to see himself as others see him and use their misconceptions to make them reveal themselves and their crimes.

A series of alphabetically linked letters are sent to Poirot, taunting him with information about where and when murders will be committed unless he is clever enough to stop them. The aging detective comes out of retirement, he admits, "like a prima donna who makes positively the farewell performance . . . an infinite number of times." Is the murderer a madman who randomly chooses the victim's town by the letter of the alphabet, or is he an extremely clever killer with a master plan? And why has he chosen to force Poirot out of retirement?

These questions plague Poirot's "little grey cells" as the plot thrusts forward and then winds back on itself time and time again. Well into the novel, Christie teases the horrified reader by introducing a coincidence that looks as if it will solve the cases, then snatches it back, dangles another possibility, snatches that one back, too. And so on, until the innovative and surprising conclusion is reached. Poirot is at his most appealing here, and Christie's plotting is at its finest.

(*S.D./M.M.*)

*Christie, Agatha. *And Then There Were None.* New York: Dodd, Mead, 1939. (Also published variously as *Ten Little Niggers* and *Ten Little Indians.*) (T)

Perhaps the most famous of all of Dame Agatha's novels, this is both a masterful cat-and-mouse thriller and a baffling exercise for armchair sleuths—a genuine tour de force. And like all of her best work, it has inspired countless imitations and variations—the ultimate compliment for any crime novel and crime-novel writer.

Ten men and women, none of whom know one another, are either invited or hired to spend a weekend on isolated Indian Island off the Devon coast. Their host is someone calling himself "U. N. Owen" (Unknown), and it soon becomes apparent that he is either a separate individual who is hiding somewhere on the island or that he is one of the ten. Each guest harbors some sort of dark secret or past indiscretion that makes him or her a target for homicide. And one by one, they begin to die in bizarre and frightening ways that loosely coincide with the ten verses of the British nursery rhyme "Ten Little Niggers [Indians]," wherein lies the novel's primary clue. But there is no detective, professional or amateur, here; no one left at all, in fact—except the reader—to explain the murders when the weekend (and the book) draws to a close. Thus *And Then There Were None* is a perfectly apt title.

The effects of the novel are multiple: a gradually mounting sense of terror and suspense that binds reader to chair; a skillful shifting of suspicion from one individual to another, principally through the introduction and manipulation of red herrings; in-depth characterization (not always Christie's long suit); and a surprising denouement that perhaps justifies one critic's judgment of the novel as "the ultimate in whodunits."

And Then There Were None was dramatized by Christie as *Ten Little Niggers,* and was also filmed three times under its U.S. title: in 1945, 1965, and 1975. The first of the three versions, directed by Rene Clair and starring Barry Fitzgerald, Walter Huston, and Louis Hayward, is by far the best and most faithful to the novel—a small classic in its own right.

(*B.P.*)

*Christie, Agatha. *A Caribbean Mystery.* New York: Dodd, Mead, 1965. (CS)

The appeal of Christie's Miss Jane Marple books is their deceptive simplicity. They are quiet, full of thought and conversation, which is seldom interrupted by action. Miss Marple, elderly maiden lady of the village of St. Mary's Mead, is considered an "old dear" or "old pussy" by the other characters. But in her many years of village life she has observed character, and pondered over the failings of her fellow villagers. "So many interesting human problems—giving rise to endless pleasurable speculation." St. Mary's Mead is a microcosm of the larger world outside; and her years of watching events there have honed Miss Marple's perceptive faculties to a fine point.

This novel proves Miss Marple to be as acute while on holiday in the Caribbean as on her home turf. The manager of the Golden Palm Hotel where she is staying resembles a headwaiter from St. Mary's Mead; another guest reminds her of a village barmaid; yet another is like Lady Caroline Wolfe, a local who committed suicide. Thus Miss Marple is able to relate the principles she has evolved in her native village to these new acquaintances.

In this tropical setting, Major Palmgrave (you can tell by his name he's not long for this world) chatters to Miss Marple, retelling his repertoire of tedious tales, including one of a man who killed two wives and escaped. "Do you want to see the picture of a murderer?" he asks. But as he is extracting it from his wallet, he sees someone over Miss Marple's shoulder, turns purple, stuffs the picture back in his wallet—and is dead before the day is over. Only Miss Marple suspects murder. Far from St. Mary's Mead, unaided by her usual friends, but armed with the discovery of similarities to her own villagers and their own—albeit simpler—intrigues, Miss Marple must unearth the truth.

Miss Marple sees her fellow characters as stereotypes—which indeed they are. Christie is as up front about that as she is in laying her clues, reminding her readers they are there, and daring them to outguess her—which, after all, is the fun of a Christie novel.

(*S.D.*)

**Christie, Agatha. *The Murder of Roger Ackroyd.* New York: Dodd, Mead, 1926. (CS/W)

This novel, Hercule Poirot's most signatory case, is the work on which not only Agatha Christie's reputation but that of the mystery of murder and manners, that which might be called the British "high tea school," may be said to rest. Narrated by James Sheppard, trusted family physician and self-appointed confidant to Poirot during his investigation, the novel tracks the events leading up and then subsequent to the murder of Roger Ackroyd, a gentleman of some means and too much knowledge, "an immensely successful manufacturer of (I think) wagon wheels . . . a man of nearly fifty years of age, rubicund of face and genial of manner . . . He is, in fact, the life and soul of our peaceful village of King's Abbot."

King's Abbot is deeply shaken, as well it might be, by the murder of Ackroyd, and the distinguished Belgian detective M. Poirot, now in residence incognito and in retirement in the village, comes in to investigate. As in all fair-play puzzles of detective fiction's Golden Age, Poirot deduces Ackroyd's murderer through the gathering of carefully planted clues, accuses that person, and resolves the tragic case. The murderer's identity is a stunning revelation, however, owing to a narrative device so simultaneously audacious and obvious that it may be said to have altered not only the deductive mystery but the novel form itself. (It is impossible to believe that Vladimir Nabokov did not study this work before composing *Pale Fire.*)

Arguably the finest cerebral detective novel ever published, *The Murder of Roger Ackroyd* is inarguably Christie's finest work. If she had done nothing else, her place in the literature of crime would be secure; if Poirot had done nothing else, his "little grey cells" would have been forever noted. In fact, it is possible that if Christie had written *only* this novel (and perhaps *The ABC Murders* and *And Then There Were None*), her reputation would be much higher than it is (if not the accounting of her estate). But every writer is entitled to be judged by his or her strongest work, and this novel stands alone.

(*B.N.M.*)

*Christie, Agatha. *Murder on the Orient Express.* New York: Dodd, Mead, 1934. (CS)

This is Christie's most imaginative variation on the English house-party mystery: The participants are passengers traveling on the fabled *Orient Express* from Istanbul to Paris; the elements conspire to trap them, but it is a snowstorm in Yugoslavia, rather than the English countryside; the elements that remain constant are the presence of a corpse and that great Belgian detective, M. Hercule Poirot.

The corpse is an American called Ratchett—a man who has approached Poirot, asking him to work for him because he has been receiving death threats. Poirot has turned him down; he senses something evil about Ratchett. And now, with the train trapped in a snowbank, M. Ratchett is dead of stab wounds and the killer is someone on the train. The suspects are the usual Christie contingent: a Hungarian count and countess; a refined British governess with a secret; a British colonel who shares the governess's secret; a stereotypical American matron; an ugly but elegant Russian princess; a "swarthy, menacing" Italian; an American commercial traveler; and the usual assortment of valets, secretaries, and ladies' maids necessary to such a company.

Poirot, at the behest of one of the directors of Compagnie Internationale des Wagons Lits, who is also on the train, sets up in the dining car and goes to work. It soon comes out that the murdered man was a notorious criminal, a particularly vicious kidnapper who has never been punished for his crimes. And it will be no surprise to the Christie fan that all of the passengers seem to have had a personal interest in doing away with this odious person. The reason for the killing is obvious, but the murderer's identity is not; and as Poirot sifts through the evidence, a number of surprises await him—including an audacious (for its time) solution. This entertaining tale, set against a colorful railroading background, is Poirot at his best.

A delightful film version of *Murder on the Orient Express* was made in 1974 with an all-star cast including Albert Finney as Poirot.

The other adventures of Hercule Poirot are equally to be recommended, particularly *The Mysterious Affair at Styles* (1927, Poirot's first case), *The Mystery of the Blue Train* (1928), *Murder on the Orient Express* (1934), *Death on the Nile* (1938), *Mrs. McGinty's Dead* (1952), *Elephants Can Remember* (1972), and *Curtain: Hercule Poirot's Last Case* (1975). What is interesting about this latter book is that Christie cared enough about the little Belgian detective to give him a quiet and dignified death.

(*M.M.*)

*Christie, Agatha. *The Mysterious Mr. Quin.* New York: Dodd, Mead, 1930. (SS)

Christie's most unusual detective is Mr. Harley Quin, who appears in fourteen short stories, most of which are collected in this volume. Quin is indeed a mysterious being, appearing and disappearing at will. And the question his character poses—is he really a supernatural being?—is one that Christie chooses never to answer. The Quin stories are thus mysteries on two levels, and while the more mundane of them, as seen through Mr. Satterthwaite's eyes, are explained, the basic one will always go unresolved. Christie considered these stories her favorites among all her fiction.

In "The Coming of Mr. Quin," we are first introduced to narrator Satterthwaite, "a little bent, dried-up man with a peering face oddly elflike, and an intense and inordinate interest in other people's lives." Satterthwaite is the consummate observer, a man forever watching from the sidelines, and he is a perfect character to chronicle Harley Quin's New Year's Eve arrival at a house party at a fine estate and his subsequent orchestration of a murderous drama. "The Soul of the Croupier" takes both Satterthwaite and Quin to Monte Carlo and onto the fringes of royal society; and in "The Dead Harlequin," Christie deepens the mystery surrounding Harley Quin by implying that he has literally materialized from a painting of himself.

"Harlequin's Lane" is an especially fine story, dealing, as many of these do, with the theme of blighted romance.

The Harley Quin stories are gentle and mannered, as is all of Christie's work, and are sure to appeal to those who relish a touch of ambiguity in their mysteries.

(*M.M.*)

Christie, Agatha. *What Mrs. McGillicuddy Saw!* New York: Dodd, Mead, 1957. (CS)

What Mrs. McGillicuddy saw from the window of her train compartment was a woman being strangled in *her* compartment on a passing train. What she couldn't find out afterward was why no one discovered the body on the train or saw it being removed. And what she couldn't accomplish was getting the police to take her seriously. Old ladies see things, they implied. But Mrs. McGillicuddy's friend, Miss Jane Marple, knew better.

This is a classic Miss Marple novel, with the old lady investigating quietly while orchestrating the moves of others. For Miss Marple (and to a degree, for her creator), people fall into categories. Miss Marple works out her suspicions by associating suspects with people in her village who fall into the same category—and she therefore assumes that people within a particular category will do the same types of deeds for the same reasons. This investigative device comes in handy as she works on the problem of who the woman was and where her body went. By the time the answers to these questions become clear, a whole new, and even more fascinating, question has arisen to replace it.

This is a fast-moving novel, in spite of its basic quietness, and it will keep you turning the pages until you also have the answers Mrs. McGillicuddy seeks. Like many of Christie's novels, it was made into a film: *Murder She Said* (1961), starring Margaret Rutherford (the perfect Miss Marple) and Arthur Kennedy.

Other Jane Marple adventures are *The Body in the Library* (1942), *They Do It with Mirrors* (1952), *A Pocket Full of Rye* (1954), *At Bertram's Hotel* (1966), and *Sleeping Murder* (1976). It is interesting to note that in this last Marple adventure, Christie implied the same gentle exit for her amateur female sleuth as she did for Hercule Poirot—again emphasizing her identification with and her love for her two primary series characters.

(*S.D.*)

*Christopher, John. *The Caves of Night.* New York: Simon & Schuster, 1958. (T)

A British couple, Cynthia and Henry Herrin, arrive in the Austrian village of Frohnberg on their annual holiday. They have been going there for several years, ever since Henry, an amateur speleologist, discovered a new and unexplored chamber—what may be a series of chambers—in a nearby cavern. But things are much different this year. For one thing, a rockfall caused by heavy rains has forced the public closing of the caves; for another, the local *Graf* (nobleman), hedonistic and disillusioned Albrecht, on whose property the entrance lies, has returned to his land after being held prisoner by the Russians for a dozen years; and for a third, flighty young newlyweds Heather and Peter Allen are also staying at the village inn.

Henry persuades the *Graf* to allow him to continue his explorations in the cavern; meanwhile Cynthia and the Allens are entertained by the *Graf*. But Albrecht's interest in Cynthia is more than that of a casual host; and even though she has been a faithful wife for sixteen years, she finds herself fighting a losing battle with her own desires. She and Albrecht have become lovers when, in the company of her husband and the Allens, they venture into the caves to visit Henry's new chamber—a fateful visit that leads to an accidental entrapment of the five. The last half of the novel is their nightmarish struggle for survival, not only against unknown subterranean terrors but against each other and their own passions and weaknesses. And not until the very last sentence is the story's ultimate revelation given to the reader.

This is a superb, low-key novel that begins at a leisurely pace and builds subtly to a high level of tension. The underground scenes are as taut and terrifying as any suspense writing ever committed to paper; the final fifty pages, in fact, are of such a damp-palmed and claustrophobic nature that the reader cannot help but come away from them a little shaken, perhaps with a resolve to leave speleology to others. The writing is well above average, the characterization outstanding, and there is an emotional (and sexual) content seldom found in suspense novels in the 1950s.

Although he is best known for such science-fiction novels as *No Blade of Grass* (1956), John Christopher (Samuel Youd) published five other thrillers that also deserve attention. These are *A Scent of White Poppies* (1959); *The White Voyage* (1960; an Arctic-based chiller); *The Little People* (1967); and *Pendulum* (1968), as by Christopher; and *The Opportunist* (1957), as by Youd.

(*B.P.*)

Clark, Mary Higgins. *Where Are the Children?* New York: Simon & Schuster, 1975. (T)

Mary Higgins Clark has built an impressive career on portraying the plight of menaced children and their parents. Her swift pacing and ability to create an atmosphere of terror enlists the reader quickly on the side of these innocent victims, and even when the identity of the menacer is revealed, we are kept on the edge of our chairs until the victims are delivered from his hands. The building of suspense, in fact, almost makes up for the fact that Clark's characters frequently lack depth and behave in boringly predictable ways.

Where Are the Children? begins with an interesting premise: Nancy Eldredge (née Nancy Harmon), young Cape Cod housewife and mother, was convicted several years before in California of murdering her two children by her first marriage. Her husband committed suicide; her death sentence was overturned on a technicality; the witness needed to retry her disappeared; and Nancy fled to peace and solace on the East Coast. There she met her present husband, Ray, and gave birth to two more children.

The story opens on Nancy's birthday—a day she refuses to acknowledge because it is also the day her first son and daughter died. Ray has decided it is time for Nancy to put the past behind her; but before the family can celebrate, a newspaper article revealing her true identity appears. Then the Eldredge children disappear. Nancy is in shock and suffering from partial amnesia, and suspicion immediately centers on her.

Throughout the story the reader knows exactly where the children are—in the hands of an unnamed madman with a grudge against their mother. And as the action unfolds, it becomes quite obvious who the man is. It takes some unfolding of Nancy's past—under hypnosis—to make her aware of this, however, and once she pieces the fragmented events together, the story rushes to a dramatic but not unexpected climax.

Other thrillers by Clark are *A Stranger Is Watching* (1978), *The Cradle Will Fall* (1980), and *A Cry in the Night* (1982).

(*M.M.*)

Clason, Clyde. *Blind Drifts.* New York: Doubleday Crime Club, 1937. (AD)

Mild-mannered Professor Theocritus Lucius Westborough, an expert on the Roman emperor Heliogabalus, is an amateur sleuth in the classic mold of the Twenties and Thirties: He solves convoluted puzzles through the time-tested Sherlockian methods of keen observation, a storehouse of esoteric knowledge, and deductive reasoning. Westborough—and his creator—specializes in locked-room "miracle problems." Even the best of these offers no challenge to John Dickson Carr (q.v.), but for the most part they are cleverly constructed and well clued. The one in *Blind Drifts* offers a particularly neat and satisfying variation on the theme.

Westborough's home base is Chicago, but here he travels to Colorado to visit a gold mine in which he has inherited 70,000 shares. Not long after his arrival, he finds himself investigating, first, the disappearance of one of the mine's directors, and then the murder of its owner, Mrs. Coranlue Edmonds, known far and wide as a "bearcat on wheels"—a murder by shooting that takes place in front of seven witnesses, in a "blind drift" deep inside the Virgin Queen mine, by a seemingly nonexistent gun.

The plot is twisty and complex, the clues numerous and fairly presented, the motive for Mrs. Edmonds's murder plausible, and the method likewise. The Colorado setting is well depicted, as are the details of the operation and physical makeup of a large gold mine. It is Clason's attention to such detail, more than anything else, that lifts his work above the average puzzle story of the period; you can't read a Westborough novel without learning *something,* and something interesting at that. The one drawback to this and the eight other entries in the series is Clason's sometimes florid, often prolix style. *Blind Drifts* is the only book of his that would not benefit greatly from the excision of ten or fifteen thousand words, and at that it could stand to lose five or six thousand here and there.

The most appealing of Westborough's other cases are *The Death Angel* (1936), set on a Wisconsin country estate called Rumpelstiltzken, where a murder happens in spite of 1542-to-1 odds against it, and a murderer is twice guilty of killing the same man; *The Man from Tibet* (1939), which features a locked-room murder and contains some fascinating background material on the strange customs and rites of Tibet; and *Green Shiver* (1941), which has a Los Angeles setting and another "impossible" plot, the solution to which depends on Westborough's knowledge of Chinese jade.

(*B.P.*)

Cleary, Jon. *Peter's Pence.* New York: Morrow, 1974. (T)

Fergus McBride is the special-projects officer in the Vatican's press-relations bureau. He is also the inside man for a group of IRA extremists who are planning to steal several treasures from the Vatican. The IRA, it seems, is running short of money, and hopes to hold the treasures for ransom.

But then everything begins to go wrong. The date of the theft has to be hurriedly moved up. Then, in tunneling from one underground Vatican room to another, there is a cave-in. The thieves run for their lives, encountering along the way the pope himself. And why not kidnap *him?* He is, after all, the most valued treasure the Vatican has to offer.

McBride, an admirer of the pope, objects to the kidnapping, but he is overruled by his rival within the gang, Seamus Smith—and the growing friction between the two men is yet another problem the gang faces. Despite McBride's objections, the pope (Pope Martin) is hustled out of the Vatican into a stolen police car, taken to a hiding place, and held for 15 million deutsche marks' ransom. Will even Peter's Pence—the annual collection taken in every Catholic church in the world—be enough to cover such a sum?

This is a great idea for a story, especially since the kidnappers are themselves Catholic and suffer varying degrees of guilt over their deed. Despite a tendency to solve several problems by wholesale death, Cleary takes this idea and translates it into a fine, exciting book (an Edgar winner for Best Novel of 1974).

Cleary, whose mainstream novel about his native Australia, *The Sundowners* (1952), was made into an excellent 1960 film with Robert Mitchum and Deborah Kerr, has published a number of other suspense novels set in various parts of the world. *The Pulse of Danger* (1966) has as its background the towering Himalayas; *The Liberators* (1971) is concerned with the Indians of Bolivia; and *Vortex* (1978) takes place in the cyclone country of rural Missouri. Cleary's most recent novels, such as *The Faraway Drums* (1981), have been historical adventure novels in the grand tradition of H. Rider Haggard.

(*N.D.*)

*Clifford, Francis. *Amigo, Amigo.* New York: Coward, McCann, 1973. (A/PS)

Few writers of suspense/adventure novels, British or American, can match Francis Clifford for sheer elemental tension, depth of characterization, and prose of rare smoothness and creative imagery. Clifford's novels are edge-of-the-chair thrillers with global settings—Mexico, Guatemala, England, Ireland, the Eastern Bloc states—and up-to-the-minute plots involving the IRA, espionage activities, the cold war, and random terrorism. But more than that, they are psychological studies of considerable power that adhere to a common theme, as stated by Clifford himself in an interview: "Only during strain—a moral, a physical, or a psychological strain—do you get to know your own character . . . it is only under such circumstances that the right character of a man emerges."

The personal trial by fire of Anthony Lorrimer, a cynical, self-involved, "cold fish" British journalist, begins in Mexico City. About to return to England, he is approached by a man with something to sell—a manuscript purportedly written by Peter Riemeck, a former high-ranking Nazi who was once Heydrich's deputy. This manuscript, according to the salesman, tells not only what happened to those Nazis who fled to South America after the collapse of the Third Reich, but which of them are still alive, their cover identities, and their present whereabouts. Lorrimer isn't about to buy a pig in a poke; he demands proof—and gets it: one name, SS-Oberführer Lutz Kröhl, a former Auschwitz administrator now calling himself Karl Stemmle and living the purgatorial existence of a *curandero*—a dentist and healer—in an isolated village on the rim of a Guatemalan volcano.

Lorrimer goes to Guatemala to meet Kröhl/Stemmle face-to-face: the final proof. After an exhaustive trip by plane, bus, and on foot, he arrives in the village of Navalosa, where he finds Stemmle gone for the day and the German's young, bored, and promiscuous native woman, Mercedes, a willing sexual partner. All along Lorrimer has been wondering: What kind of man is Stemmle? Why would he choose to lead the kind of life he does? When he finally meets the ex-Nazi, he realizes there are no easy answers. It isn't until he and Stemmle and Mercedes find themselves captives of mountain bandits that Lorrimer begins asking those same questions of himself—and learns who the real Anthony Lorrimer is.

Clifford makes the reader feel the heat, the thin air, the frightening desolation of the Guatemalan wilderness; he also makes the reader care about his characters, even the most incidental of them. The *Chicago Tribune* said that *Amigo, Amigo* "takes all superlatives," and that it "will keep you mesmerized." Indeed it will. If you enjoy literate thrillers that really *are* thrillers, don't miss this one.

And don't miss any of Clifford's other suspense novels, especially *The Naked Runner* (1966), a tale of intrigue behind the Iron Curtain that was made into a rather poor 1967 film with Frank Sinatra; *A Wild Justice* (1972), a tale of strife in Ireland told against the backdrop of a bleak Irish winter; and *Goodbye and Amen* (1974), which Ross Macdonald (q.v.) lauded as "an extraordinary thriller about several people of importance who are sequestered with an armed killer in a room of a first-class London hotel. It is intricately and brilliantly constructed, and written with tremendous drive and flair. Not only the ending surprises. There are surprises on nearly every page."

(*B.P.*)

Cody, Liza. *Dupe.* New York: Scribner's, 1981. (PI)

To say that the biggest fault with Liza Cody's first novel is that we don't get to know private eye Anna Lee well enough is testimony to the attractiveness and likableness of her heroine. Anna is a former policewoman in her late twenties, employed by the London private inquiry firm Brierly Security. In a welcome relief from her usual assignments—hunting for missing minors or "scent-counter security"—Anna is assigned to dig into the past of an apparent fatal accident victim, Dierdre Jackson. Dierdre had been estranged from her parents for three years, and her mother wants to know if she was happy in those last years while her father wants information because he suspects Dierdre's car crash was no accident. Representing herself as a friend of the family, Anna traces Dierdre's friends and employers, most of them on the fringes of the film world; and soon she, too, begins to suspect there is more to the young woman's death than a crash on an icy road.

Anna's low-key approach to investigation is refreshing, and she proves herself tough enough when the case requires it. The glimpses we are allowed into Anna's private life—especially those scenes involving her zany and endearing neighbors, Bea and Selwyn Price—are tantalizing. So much so, in fact, that any reader will want to know more about her background, such as what her family was like and why she joined and then left the police force.

An engaging novel with a strong plot, *Dupe* won the John Creasey Award for Britain's Best First Mystery Novel. Cody's second and third novels, also featuring Anna Lee, are *Bad Company* (1982) and *Stalker* (1984).

(*M.M.*)

*Coe, Tucker. *Don't Lie to Me.* New York: Random House, 1972. (PI/PS)

"Tucker Coe" is one of several pseudonyms used by Donald E. Westlake (q.v.). And Mitchell Tobin, the narrator of *Don't Lie to Me* and of four other novels published under the Coe name, is in many ways Westlake's most fascinating creation.

Tobin is an ex–New York City cop who was thrown off the force in disgrace when his partner was shot down while covering for him: Tobin at the time was in bed with a woman named Linda Campbell, another man's wife. Unable to reconcile his guilt, Tobin has withdrawn to the point where little matters in his life except the high wall he is building in the back yard of his Queens home—a continuing project that symbolizes his self-imposed prison and isolation. His forgiving wife Kate and his teen-age son are unable to penetrate those internal walls; no one can, it seems. Occasionally, however, someone from his past or his present manages to persuade him to do this or that "simple" job, thus creating circumstances which force Tobin to utilize his detective's training. The combined result of these cases, as critic Francis M. Nevins has noted, is that Tobin "builds up a store of therapeutic experiences from which he slowly comes to realize that he is not unique in his isolation and guilt, and slowly begins to accept himself and return to the real world."

Don't Lie to Me is the last of the five Tobin novels, the final stage of his mental rehabilitation. He has been given a private investigator's license and is working as a night watchman in Manhattan's Museum of American Graphic Art, and before long Linda Campbell, his former lover, about whom he has ambivalent feelings, reappears in his life. Tobin then discovers the naked body of an unidentified murder victim in one of the museum rooms. Further complications include pressure from hostile cops and from a group of small-time hoodlums with a grudge against Tobin. Against his will, he is forced to pursue his own investigation into the murder, and eventually to reconcile his feelings toward Linda Campbell—and toward himself. The ending is violent, powerful, ironic, and appropriate.

The other four Tobin novels are *Kinds of Love, Kinds of Death* (1966), *Murder Among Children* (1968), *Wax Apple* (1970), and *A Jade in Aries* (1971). It is tempting to say that more Tobin novels would have been welcome, but this is not really the case. Westlake said everything there is to say about Mitch Tobin in these five books, what amounts to a perfect quintology; any additional novels would have seem contrived to capitalize on an established series character.

(*B.P.*)

Coffey, Brian. *Surrounded.* Indianapolis: Bobbs-Merrill, 1974. (T)

Brian Coffey is one of several pseudonyms used by prolific writer Dean R. Koontz (q.v.). During the early 1970s, Koontz wrote a series of three caper novels featuring professional thief Mike Tucker—a more genteel version of Richard Stark's (q.v.) Parker. Tucker's straight job is as an art dealer, but in order to live the wealthy life-style he's accustomed to, he and various other professionals plan and execute occasional big-money heists. Tucker has his principles: He steals only from institutions—banks, insurance companies, department stores—whose losses are fully covered by insurance. And he is good enough so that after fourteen operations in three years, he has never failed.

Surrounded is the middle book in the series, and easily the best of the three. Tucker, along with two men, Frank Meyers and Edgar Bates, plan to rob the posh Oceanview Plaza shopping mall in southern California; the mall includes a bank, a jewelry store, and eighteen other business establishments. The plan is to hit the mall at night, get in and out as quickly as possible, and Tucker has it all worked out perfectly. Except for one thing—a vital piece of information that Meyers, for reasons of his own, has withheld from Tucker.

The result is that an alarm is sounded during the robbery, the police arrive, and Tucker and the others are trapped inside the mall, completely surrounded, with no way out. In a clever variation on the classic locked-room gambit, they manage to hide themselves so that the police aren't able to find them and assume they somehow must have escaped. (The reader isn't told their hiding place until some time afterward, so that you may either match wits with Tucker or share the cops' frustration.)

This is a well-written novel, ingenious and suspenseful. Tucker is no Parker when it comes to toughness, but in the brotherhood of crooks he holds his own. His first caper, *Blood Risk* (1973), is also nicely done: It features another heist that goes sour, that of the biweekly take of a Mafia cell. Here, too, Tucker must improvise to save his own life and those of his partners. The last Tucker novel, *The Wall of Masks* (1975), is less successful: It has a convoluted and rather implausible plot involving Tucker's specialty, art treasures (the Mayan variety), plus some strained humor.

(*B.P./G.K.*)

Cohen, Anthea. *Angel Without Mercy.* New York: Doubleday Crime Club, 1984. (PS)

There have been many stories about lovable rogues and mastermind criminals in suspense fiction over its long history, but a group of novels in which a troubled murderer is the heroine is an unusual event. That is what Anthea Cohen has created in her new "Angel" series. Cohen, a nurse and writer on medical topics for twenty-five years, uses her knowledge of hospital locale and atmosphere to enrich her series.

In *Angel Without Mercy,* Cohen seems to be setting up a classic whodunit—and taking her time about it. She shows us a hateful nurse supervisor named Hughes, and shows us ample evidence of why practically the entire staff of St. Jude's Hospital wants her dead. The reader may become impatient for the murder and the discovery of the body about three-quarters of the way through the book, but Cohen will not be rushed. She is concerned more with the emotional and psychological mystery of human conduct than with a tidy murder puzzle.

Although Cohen allows the reader the chance to reason out the identity of her murderer, she does not feel the need to have the police do the same. Her murderer gets away with it, and lives to return for other deadly adventures in *Angel of Vengeance* (1984) and *Angel of Death* (1985). It is essential to read these novels in order. And it will be interesting to see how Cohen proceeds with her intriguing series.

(*K.L.M.*)

Cohen, Octavus Roy. *Don't Ever Love Me.* New York: Macmillan, 1946. (W)

Octavus Roy Cohen's mysteries are slick and entertaining, smoothly written in a style that no doubt appealed to the readers of the *Saturday Evening Post* and other publications where many of his stories appeared. *Don't Ever Love Me* is a good example of his novel-length work, a light romantic mystery featuring a fairly liberated heroine, at least by the standards of 1946.

Lynn Sheridan, a successful copywriter for a New York advertising firm, is the victim of what seems to be a series of bizarre practical jokes: Someone calls the police to report her murder; someone calls an ambulance service to report that she has been badly hurt; and her escort to the opera is killed by a bullet that passes so close to her that she can hear it buzz by. Naturally all this puts quite a strain on Lynn and her fiancé, Alan Gordon. To say much more about the plot would be unfair, but it involves two more murders and a goodly number of suspects. Cohen manages some adroit misdirection before Gordon, to the astonishment of the homicide detective on the case, manages to figure out just exactly what has been going on. And of course, it's fun to consider the detective's final words on the case in light of today's methods of law enforcement: "The confession is what counts—not how you get it."

Paperback collectors will find the cover of the 1951 Popular Library edition of *Don't Ever Love Me* irresistible, even though the beautiful blonde with the dark eyebrows and the automatic pistol has nothing at all to do with the story.

Jim Hanvey, Detective (1923) is a collection of short stories that demonstrates Cohen's ability in that form. And Cohen came up with the title *Scrambled Yeggs* (1934) years before Richard S. Prather (q.v.).

(*B.C.*)

Cohen, Stanley. *Angel Face.* New York: St. Martin's, 1982. (PP/T)

Angel Face concerns a brutal double murder—not unusual in Manhattan's East Village, but exceptional because the victims are the parents of Stefan Kornienko, a New York police officer. After the deaths, Kornienko is given a week off to tend to personal business, but instead he devotes his time to investigating his parents' killing. The official investigation is being conducted out of a precinct other than Stefan's own, and he is quickly warned to stop his private efforts. Naturally he proceeds anyway. Soon his interest focuses on a fourteen-year-old boy nicknamed "Quick," whose angelic appearance masks what Stefan learns is a truly evil nature; and as his suspicions about the youth grow, his efforts to track him down reach obsessive proportions.

Told from multiple viewpoints, this is a chilling thriller that takes us into the seamy underside of New York City. Cohen makes us care about the murder victims by showing Stefan with his hardworking and loving parents prior to their murders. And he also gives us glimpses into Quick's family life—not making excuses for his actions so much as showing why he may have become what he is, as well as depicting the tragedy of a disintegrating family life. As Stefan's obsession heightens, we see the debilitating effect it has on the man, as well as on those who care about him. Stefan is particularly well characterized, and his way of resolving his obsession with the boy rings true.

Cohen's first novel, *Taking Gary Feldman,* was nominated for an MWA Edgar in 1970. Other novels include *The Diane Game* (1973) and *330 Park* (1977).

(*M.M.*)

Coker, Carolyn. *The Other David.* New York: Dodd, Mead, 1984. (T)

In this first novel we meet Andrea Perkins, an art historian and restorer who is on leave from her teaching position at Harvard and working in Italy at Florence's Galleria dell' Academia. Andrea is a forthright, appealing young woman; at the top of her field, she has an overriding passion for her work and a devotion to the arts which is refreshing—especially in contrast to many female heroines who (very improbably) excel at their careers in spite of an overriding and tiresome preoccupation with their romantic lives. As the book opens, Andrea is given a painting by an old priest, one that he says has been in his family for hundreds of years but now should be with "the other one." The other one turns out to be Michelangelo's famed sculpture of David, which graces the great hall of the Galleria. And the painting turns out to be one of only two portraits executed by Michelangelo—a portrait of the young man who posed for the statue, given authenticity by the seal of the Medici family.

The painting cannot be completely authenticated, however, until the signature has been proved to be that of Michelangelo. And the best way to prove that is with the MC-36 computer belonging to the McCauley Museum in Houston, Texas—a computer that Andrea herself programmed the previous year. She has some hesitation about calling the McCauley's curator, Tom Daley; he is an unpleasant man who (we later find) had stolen Andrea's scholarly work while they were colleagues at the Boston Museum. And Clint McCauley, the museum's owner, is Andrea's former lover, whom she left for complex personal reasons. But Andrea's devotion to her work and excitement over this once-in-a-lifetime find overcome her qualms, and soon Daley, McCauley, and the computer are on their way to Florence.

What follows is a web of intrigue centering around the small canvas. The painting disappears, reappears, disappears again, seemingly for good. Murders are committed, people turn out not to be what they seem, and Andrea's life is in danger. The author gives us a fascinating glimpse into the art world: from the techniques of the masters to computer technology; from the formal arrangements among museums throughout the world to the hidden—and often murderous—passions of those who run them. And when the end is reached, it is not only surprising but thoroughly satisfying. A promising debut, with good characterization and plenty of action.

(*M.M.*)

Cole, G.D.H. and Margaret. *Knife in the Dark.* New York: Macmillan, 1942. (AD)

G.D.H. and Margaret Cole were extemely prolific writers between the two world wars: individually and collaboratively, they published well over two hundred books of fiction, nonfiction, and verse. G.D.H. was a prominent social and economic historian; his five-volume *A History of Social Thought* is considered a landmark work. Dame Margaret is best known for her biographies of Beatrice Webb and of her husband (*The Life of G.D.H. Cole,* 1971).

The Coles co-authored more than thirty "Golden Age" detective novels, beginning with *The Brooklyn Murders* in 1923, and six volumes of criminous short stories. *Knife in the Dark* is their next to last novel, and the only one to feature Mrs. Warrender as its protagonist. "A naturally trim and tidy old lady," Mrs. Warrender is the mother of private detective James Warrender (who affectionately calls her, among other things, "an incurably meddling old woman"). She is also solidly in the tradition of such "little old lady" sleuths as Miss Jane Marple and Hildegarde Withers, although less colorful than either of those two indefatigable crook-catchers.

Knife in the Dark takes place at a mythical ancient English university, Stamford, during the dark days of World War II. Kitty Lake—wife of Gordon Lake, a teacher of Inorganic Chemistry whose mother is a cousin of Mrs. Warrender's—is stabbed to death during an undergraduate dance which she herself arranged. Any number of people had a motive to do away with the mercurial Kitty, who had both a mean streak and a passion for other men; the suspects include her husband, an R.A.F. officer, a young anthropologist, a strange Polish refugee named Madame Zyboski (who may or may not be a Nazi spy), and a dean's wife whom James Warrender describes as "an awful old party with a face like a diseased horse and a mind like a sewer."

Like all of the Coles' mysteries, this is *very* leisurely paced; Kitty Lake's murder, the only one in the book, does not take place until page 104, and there is almost no action before or after. Coincidence plays almost as much of a role in the solution as does detection by Mrs. Warrender (who happens to be staying with the Lakes at the time of the murder); and the identity of the culprit comes as no particular surprise. For all of that, however, *Knife in the Dark* is not a bad novel. The characters are mostly interesting, the university setting is well-realized, and the narrative is spiced with some nice touches of dry wit. Undemanding fans of the Golden Age mystery should find it diverting.

Mrs. Warrender's talents are also showcased in four novelettes collected as *Mrs. Warrender's Profession* (1939). The best of the four is "The Toys of Death," in which Mrs. W. solves a baffling murder on the south coast of England.

The Coles also created three other series detectives, none of whom is as interesting an individual as Mrs. Warrender. The most notable of the trio is Superintendent Henry Wilson of Scotland Yard, for he is featured in sixteen novels, among them *The Berkshire Mystery* (1930), *End of an Ancient Mari-*

ner (1933), and *Murder at the Munition Works* (1940); and in the collection of short stories, *Superintendent Wilson's Holiday* (1928).

(*B.P.*)

Coles, Manning. *A Toast to Tomorrow.* New York: Doubleday, 1941. (E)

In Germany in March 1933, a bit of a puzzle crops up concerning a radio production called "The Radio Operator." On the surface, the show is nothing more than blatant Nazi propaganda. But to the British Foreign Office, it is much more. It seems the Morse code used as a background sound on the show is actually a code used by an undercover British agent during World War I. Why, then, is it suddenly being used again after all these years—especially since the agent who used it is now dead? A puzzle indeed.

For answers, the novel flashes back to January 1918, and we follow the life of an amnesia victim who adopts the name Klaus Lehmann. Lehmann, like most Germans, has a rough time of it in the postwar years. He meets Adolf Hitler, joins the Nazi party, and works his way up through the party ranks, all this before he remembers his true identity. He is really Hendrik Brandt. No, that isn't right. He is *really* a British intelligence agent named Tommy Hambledon, who was posing as Brandt, and who is now posing as Lehmann. And what a position for a British agent to be in!

The name Manning Coles is a pseudonym for Cyril Coles and Adelaide Manning. Under this pseudonym they produced numerous books and stories, but none of their characters was more popular than agent Hambledon. This book is the second in the Hambledon series. In the first, *Drink to Yesterday* (1941), Hambledon winds up his World War I experience and suffers the beginning of amnesia. The subsequent books—among them *Operation Manhunt* (1954), *The Man in the Green Hat* (1955), and *The House at Pluck's Gutter* (1968)—came to rely more and more on formulaic plots and stock settings, and from the Fifties on, the series lost much of its appeal.

Coles and Manning also collaborated on a series of satirical ghost stories featuring a defunct pair of cousins, James and Charles Latimer, and their equally dead pet monkey, Ulysses. Published as by Francis Gaite, these include *Brief Candles* (1954), *The Far Traveler* (1956), and *Duty Free* (1959).

(*N.D.*)

Collins, Max. *The Broker.* New York: Berkley, 1976. (O/A)

In the mid-1970s, the multitalented Max Collins (who also writes as Max Allan Collins, q.v.) produced a series of four paperback originals about a Vietnam vet turned hired killer, known only as Quarry. The Quarry series has so often been referred to as a Richard Stark (q.v.) pastiche that its own tone and morality are often overlooked.

In *The Broker,* the first in the series, we meet Quarry shooting a man in an airport men's room. Quarry's assignment is to bring what the man is holding (heroin) back to his employer, an icy sort called the Broker. Quarry complies. After complaining that he does not like to deal in drug killings, he reluctantly takes another Broker assignment, this one working with a homosexual killer named Boyd. In the rest of the novel, Collins shows us an abundantly unpleasant world peopled with all sorts of characters, from cuckolded husbands to porno-crazed geezers who look like Gabby Hayes.

What gives the Quarry books their style is the detached voice of the narrator: Quarry has no compunctions about killing people, because he feels most of them are rather foolish beings anyway. Unlike Stark's Parker, who is human only when it serves his ends, Quarry is subject to feelings other than anger—melancholy, amusement, contempt—feelings he notes, nonetheless, with the kind of removed observation one would expect from a man in his profession.

The Broker and the other three novels in the series—*The Broker's Wife* (1976), *The Dealer* (1976), *The Slasher* (1977)—are successful for another reason: They depict the waning hippie/flower-power days with a great deal of historical accuracy. The Quarry books are therefore an important part of the crime fiction of the Seventies—a quirky, idiosyncratic look at the Midwest during the Jerry Ford regime.

(*E.G.*)

Collins, Max Allan. *Kill Your Darlings.* New York: Walker, 1984. (AD)

Max Allan Collins is not merely a writer of mystery novels (and of the Dick Tracy comic strip); he is also a mystery scholar, collector, and fan. This book, third in a series featuring his detective alter ego, Mallory (like Collins, a mystery collector, fan, and writer from a small town in Iowa), is an "inside" story about mystery fans and fandom. It takes place at the Bouchercon, the annual convention for mystery fans and writers. (By a remarkable coincidence, Collins sets the story at the same Chicago hotel where the 1984 convention was actually held.)

The murder victim is Roscoe Kane, a veteran paperback mystery writer. His once-popular detective, Gat Garson, is out of fashion, and Kane is on the skids. He's at the con to receive an award from the Private Eye Writers Association, but drowns in the bathtub—an apparent accident—before the presentation. Mallory, Kane's friend and fan, isn't satisfied by the medical examiner's hasty verdict and noses around, suspecting that Kane's death might be linked to the upcoming publication of a "lost" Hammett Continental Op story.

In an introduction, Collins makes the disclaimer that his fictional Bouchercon attendees, writers and fans, are mostly composites of real characters. However, initiates will have little trouble identifying many of them, including a self-absorbed guest of honor named Keats—the creator of a sensitive-macho private-eye character. Other inside jokes and fan tributes are scattered throughout; e.g., Collins's borrowing of a gaudy metaphor from Spillane's *Vengeance Is Mine* in the climactic shooting scene.

This fast-moving and inventive novel is the newest addition to the very small subgenre of fandom mystery novels. Two others are Bill Pronzini's (q.v.) *Hoodwink* (murder at a pulp collector's convention) and Edward D. Hoch's (q.v.) *Shattered Raven* (murder at the MWA Awards Banquet).

Mallory is also featured in *The Baby Blue Rip-Off* (1983), *No Cure for Death* (1984), and *A Shroud for Aquarius* (1985).

(*A.S.*)

*Collins, Max Allan. *True Detective.* New York: St. Martin's, 1983. (PI/H)

In *True Detective,* Collins has created a brilliantly evocative period novel set in depression year 1933, Chicago. His hero, Nate Heller, is a cop who refuses to succumb to prevailing corruption on the police force. (This is a tightly woven blend of fact and fiction.) When Nate becomes involved in the shooting of gangster Frank Nitti, the corruption closes in on him. His testimony as to what happened in Nitti's office during the shoot-out is vital to several parties; and given the climate of time and place, they all assume that Nate is for sale. Nate isn't, as he explains to his pal, boxer Barney Ross. With no alternative to dishonesty other than to quit the police department, Nate goes private, working out of an office, complete with a Murphy bed, above Ross's saloon.

Nate has trouble and he has enemies, among them Chicago's corrupt Mayor Cermak, the mover and shaker of the 1933 World's Fair, and former vice president General Charles Gates Dawes, not to mention the unnamed but sufficiently dangerous Al Capone. It's a good thing that Nate also has allies like Eliot Ness, Franklin Roosevelt, and even young sportscaster Dutch Reagan.

The writing style here is hard-boiled and literate, and the novel is illustrated with black-and-white photographs of the book's true-life characters and of depression-era Chicago. So artfully are photographs matched with text that they add wonderfully to the painstakingly created atmosphere of that almost-lost time.

This novel won the Private Eye Writers of America Shamus Award as

1983's best private-eye novel, and deservedly so. A lovingly and often elegantly written novel, this is marvelous entertainment and a must read for every fan of private eye fiction.

A second Nate Heller adventure, *True Crime* (1984), involves the detective with J. Edgar Hoover and an FBI plot against the infamous John Dillinger, and is every bit as evocative and entertaining as *True Detective.* More Heller novels are planned for the future.

(*J.L.*)

*Collins, Michael. *Act of Fear.* New York: Dodd, Mead, 1967. (PI)

Dennis Lynds, using the name Michael Collins, is writing one of the very best of the contemporary private-eye series. All the novels under the Collins name feature Dan Fortune, a one-armed detective who operates out of the Chelsea district of New York City. Fortune's handicap sets him apart and makes him vulnerable; he is also introspective and compassionate, a believer in absolute truth, a man who is driven to find the answers. *Act of Fear,* Fortune's first novel-length case, won an Edgar for Best First Mystery of the year.

Act of Fear begins, like many mystery novels, with a missing person. Fortune is hired by a young man to find a missing friend. Apparently the friend has good reason to be missing, and Fortune soon discovers that he is not the only one looking. The elements of the case include the mugging of a cop, two murders, and the savage beating of Fortune's client. The plotting, as in all the Collins books, is intricate, with Fortune following all the threads to their sometimes frayed ends. His fee for the entire case is $50; he spends much more than that in solving it, but once he is involved, he has to find out the truth.

As usual in Collins's work, the book has a serious theme, in this case the difficulty of being true to oneself no matter what the consequences. It would be difficult to say that the ending is satisfying, but it is "right" in the sense that it is the only ending appropriate for the story that Collins tells.

(*B.C.*)

Collins, Michael. *Blue Death.* New York: Dodd, Mead, 1975. (PI)

Blue Death finds Dan Fortune a little less introspective than in his earlier cases, but with no less of a passion for the truth. Once more he is brought into a case for a simple $50 fee, and once more he finds himself with more than he bargained for. What appears a simple matter—locating the member of a giant corporation who has the power to sign a lease agreement for a parking lot—turns out to involve quadruple murder. Along the way Fortune is beaten, drugged, and nearly starved, but he cannot be scared off the case. He suspects that a member of the corporation is blackmailing another member for murder, and his chain of reasoning is correct. All the facts fit. Unfortunately, he finds that he has been on the wrong track entirely, and before he is able to bring things to a close, the fourth murder occurs.

The amoral world of the large corporations comes under savage attack in *Blue Death;* its members appear virtually unassailable in their complacency and power, and even in the end one cannot be sure that justice will be served. But justice is not always the point, or at least not justice under the law. Fortune is still looking for the perfect world where we are all free to run ourselves, and sometimes he gives others that chance. As in *Act of Fear,* the ending may not be entirely satisfactory, but it is appropriate. Anyone looking for the best in private-eye writing in the Chandler/Macdonald vein will appreciate any title by Michael Collins.

Other notable books in the Dan Fortune series include *The Brass Rainbow* (1969), *Walk a Black Wind* (1971), *The Nightrunners* (1978), and *Freak* (1984).

(*B.C.*)

**Collins, Wilkie. *The Moonstone.* New York: Harper, 1868. (CS)

(William) Wilkie Collins was one of the most popular and accomplished writers of the nineteenth century, and *The Moonstone* is an early classic of the suspense genre. Like Collins's other criminous works, it contains elements that later became staples of mystery writing: a purloined gemstone, carefully secreted clues, obtrusive red herrings, sinister Indians who lurk threateningly in the background, a blighted love affair, several shakily constructed alibis, numerous cliff-hanging scenes, and a mysterious suicide. Although complicated, the plot is well constructed and the reader's interest seldom flags.

The yellow diamond known as the "moonstone" was stolen from an Indian religious idol by John Herncastle, a man who chose to ignore the story of bad luck following the diamond should it be removed from the possession of the worshipers of the moon god. Upon Herncastle's death, the gem was willed to his niece, Rachel Verinder, and the young lady is about to receive it when the story opens (after a prologue and two tiresome chapters filled with background material). The diamond disappears, of course, on the night Rachel is presented it by solicitor Franklin Blake. And when Inspector Cuff of Scotland Yard appears on the scene, some clues point to Blake, while others indicate Rachel has secreted away her own diamond for some unknown and possibly unbalanced reason.

The story proceeds, divided into two periods, respectively titled "The Loss of the Diamond" and "The Discovery of the Truth" (which in itself is divided into eight narratives), plus an epilogue. In spite of these numerous sections, each broken into various chapters narrated by different characters, the reader finds himself as determined as Cuff to learn the truth. Who are the Indians? Was this caused by the curse of the moonstone? Will Rachel find happiness? Such questions are ever in the forefront. And when the end is finally reached, all clues are tied up, all questions are answered, and—yes—Rachel does find happiness.

Collins's other works are not nearly as well known as *The Moonstone,* but a number are just as engrossing and stand the test of time equally well. These include *The Woman in White* (1860), which seems to have been Collins's personal favorite; and *The Queen of Hearts* (1859), a collection that contains the cornerstone humorous detective story "The Biter Bit."

(*M.M.*)

Condon, Richard. *Mile High.* New York: Dial, 1969. (T)

In his strongest work—*The Manchurian Candidate* (1959), *Winter Kills* (1974)—Richard Condon has shown an unerring ability to find the hub throughout which the threads of American corruption, desire, insanity, politics, dread, and dreams pass, and to find that precise point of convergence which indicates that the history (and future) of the culture is as coherent and malevolent as death; in his weakest work, Condon has been a Boy Scout leader mumbling increasingly repellent horror stories around a fire to the wide-eyed troops, trying to give them a thrill at whatever cost. *Mile High* is somewhere in the middle. It is as paranoid as *The Manchurian Candidate* but lacks its purity; it runs out of plot two-thirds of the way through and has to make do with an imposed and inauthentic suspense melodrama. Condon believes his generalities here but cannot pay attention to the particulars.

The premise is audacious, wholly workable, and possibly even correct (as correct as the brainwashed-and-programmed-human-time-bomb premise of *The Manchurian Candidate,* or the presidential-assassination premise of *Winter Kills*): American Prohibition was virtually the single-handed creation of one rich and brilliant businessman who knew that it would be great for the illegal liquor business and used his modest inherited assets to build a network that, in its complexity, virtually overtook the country. When Prohibition finally collapses, Edward Courance West is worth many hundreds of billions of dollars (and it is his consolidation of widely held assets into hard cash that causes the depression).

West, however, is an unstable personality; abandoned by his mother, a dark Italian, in his childhood, he must replicate the abandonment by wreaking terrible vengeance upon his black mistresses. His psychosis leads to murder and to his removal from American society to a mile-high palace in the central Adirondacks. Here, aging, monumentally rich, safe and mad, West raves to his lifelong manservant, Willie Tobin, of the Communist peril and the rise of "the terrible black hordes" that are his alone to combat. (There is not a cause of the lunatic right to which he will not subscribe millions of dollars.)

Good enough to this point (or bad enough), and a serviceable, often terrifying *roman à clef* of several figures in midcentury American life; but there is an imposed and highly coincidental subplot dealing with the black artist wife of West's second son (the point of view character of the unnecessary middle section of the novel) who reminds West of his mother and of the black women in whose image murder was committed. Having run out its exposition and its implication, *Mile High* turns into a somewhat clumsy (and clumsily transparent) novel of menace and oversimplifies ultimately; West's "insanity" is the hole through which the book's true implication and terror drain. West becomes merely a symbol, and unfortunately, the novel "symbolic" rather than the horrifying near-documentary that *Winter Kills* is. Still, Condon's pacing, portentousness, and Clemens-like contempt for the human condition come through and sustain the narrative. At half its 160,000-word length, *Mile High* might have been a tormented, glacial vision; a century of history compressed to nightmare.

(*B.N.M.*)

*Constantine, K. C. *The Man Who Liked to Look at Himself.* New York: Dutton, 1973. (PP)

Rocksburg, Pennsylvania, police chief Mario Balzic, despite misgivings, is persuaded by the new commander of the state troopers, Lieutenant Minyon, to accompany Minyon on the first day of hunting season. Balzic isn't crazy about Minyon, and hunting (animals, that is) isn't Balzic's favorite pastime. Things go wrong. Minyon's prize Weimaraner bites him in the hand while they are in the car on the way to the hunt. Then the dog causes even more problems for Balzic by rooting around in the woods and finding a human bone. Balzic is given the task of discovering who is missing, and finding the rest of the body.

The someone missing turns out to be Frank Gallic, the partner in a discount meat business with Balzic's friend Micky Sammara. Sammara and his sister Tina have been operating the business for almost a year while waiting for Gallic to return. Minyon decides that Mickey had something to do with Gallic's disappearance and arrests him, prompting Balzic to hire feisty Mo Vulcanas, a local lawyer with a burning dislike for state troopers, to defend Sammara.

This is offbeat crime fiction, written in a readable, literate style, tightly plotted and with believable, very human characters in familiar settings. Constantine knows how to maintain suspense. He lets it unfold to a logical and satisfying conclusion.

Equally offbeat and worth reading are the other Mario Balzic novels, which include *The Rocksburg Railroad Murders* (1972), *A Fix Like This* (1975), the acclaimed *Man Who Liked Slow Tomatoes* (1982), *Always a Body to Trade* (1983), and *Upon Some Midnight Clear* (1985).

(*J.L.*)

Constiner, Merle. *Hearse of a Different Color.* New York: Phoenix Press, 1952. (AD)

In *Gun in Cheek* (1982), the undersigned reviewer's humorous study of classically *bad* crime fiction, an entire chapter is devoted to the lending-library publisher, Phoenix Press. During the Thirties and Forties, Phoenix foisted upon an unsuspecting public some of the most godawful mysteries ever penned—scores of them, in fact. Not *all* Phoenix mysteries were horrendous, however; every now and then, whether by accident or otherwise, a pretty good one seems to have slipped out. *Hearse of a Different Color* falls into that rarefied category.

Arkansas semanticist Paul Saxby comes to the backwoods town of Falksville, Tennessee, for two reasons: to study the picturesque colloquialisms of the area ("Git down and tie up, Brother Saxby; we'uns is shore hellacious proud to have you jubilating with us"), and because of a letter written to him by a local resident, Alicia Poynter, which hints at a "great and terrible crime being planned." Shortly after Saxby's arrival, at least part of that terrible crime is revealed: He finds Alicia dead of poison that may or may not have been meant for her. Saxby's investigation involves him with, among other colorful characters, a tough old lady named Cora Bob Wilkerson; the founder of the Caudry Burial Brotherhood; the owner of an abandoned sawmill (in the vicinity of which are all sorts of strange goings-on); and a dog with the magnificent moniker of Moonrise Blizzard the Second. More homicide—and the local sheriff, Masters—plagues Saxby before he finally arrives at a well-clued solution.

You should not get the impression that this is a masterpiece, however; *Hearse of Another Color* has its flaws (one of them being the title), and in places the story shows its pulp origins (it was originally published as a serial in *Short Stories* in 1946). Still, the unusual background is well depicted (Constiner was a native of southern Ohio and traveled extensively in the Deep South), the plotting is competent, and the writing is above average. Come to think of it, considering the general run of Phoenix mysteries, maybe this *is* a masterpiece—Phoenix's, anyway.

(*B.P.*)

Cory, Desmond. *Deadfall.* New York: Walker, 1965. (T)

Desmond Cory (a pseudonym of Shaun Lloyd McCarthy) has published a wide variety of suspense fiction, including espionage novels, detective novels, and thrillers. He has a firm grasp of psychological principles, and his characters show considerable depth. The details of his settings—frequently Spain—are richly evocative and suggest careful research and first-hand knowledge. He is best known for his books featuring British agent Johnny Fedora; in five of these, Fedora matches wits with Soviet spy Feramontov. There is a powerful tension in these novels—*Undertow* (1963), *Hammerhead* (1964), *Feramontov* (1966), *Timelock* (1967), and *Sunburst* (1971)—and their plots are complex and action-packed.

One of Cory's best books, however, is a nifty caper novel, *Deadfall.* Set in his favorite locale, Spain, it features an unlikely trio of characters: Michael Jeye, an acrobatic burglar; Moreau, a genius who plans jewel heists; and Moreau's wife, a beautiful and mysterious woman named Fe. As the three work together to steal a fortune in jewels, Jeye finds himself falling in love with Fe. This loss of emotional control is dangerous, both to their plans and to Jeye personally—especially since the relationship between Fe and Moreau is soon revealed to be not exactly as it seems.

Against a background of professional crime, Cory weaves a thrilling plot with deep psychological undertones. The three complex personalities are caught up in deadly motion, and themes including incest and homosexuality emerge. The pacing of *Deadfall* is more deliberate than the nonstop action of the Fedora series, and the overall effect is haunting.

Deadfall was disappointingly filmed in 1968, with Michael Caine and Giovanna Ralli. Other Cory novels notable for their psychological depth are *A Bit of a Shunt Up the River* (1974), in which a sociopath escapes from prison; and *The Circe Complex* (1975), which deals with a former prison psychologist who finds himself imprisoned for a crime he didn't commit.

(*G.K./M.M.*)

Cox, William R. *Hell to Pay.* New York: New American Library (Signet), 1958. (O/AD)

William R. Cox started in the pulp field and turned to writing paperback originals in the 1950s. He is probably better known for his westerns and juveniles than for his mysteries, but his contributions to the mystery field should not go unremarked. In fact, Cox is a very good writer, utilizing sharp characterization and a well-paced narrative, and often providing insightful comments on various topics.

Hell to Pay is the first in a series of books about Tom Kincaid, a professional gambler. Kincaid functions much like a private eye as he is unwillingly pulled into a gang war between the old members of the Syndicate and a new gang composed of Fifties-style juvenile delinquents. Even Kincaid does not understand his role in this war, but the girlfriend of a man Kincaid has hired is raped and killed, and several attempts are made on Kincaid's life. Along with his other problems, Kincaid has a longtime girl who wants him to leave New York and go west, to Vegas, so that she can work in Hollywood and still be close to him. Before the end of the book, she is involved in the war, too. In some ways, reading this book is like reading the old pulps; Cox makes fine use of Fifties slang, and the gambler's world is depicted with a good sense of realism. All the virtues of pulp fiction are present, with few exceptions. Books like this one make this reviewer wish Cox had done more mysteries.

Tom Kincaid also appears in two other very good books by Cox: *Murder in Vegas* (1960) and *Death on Location* (1962).

(*B.C.*)

Coxe, George Harmon. *Fenner*. New York: Knopf, 1971. (PI)

George Harmon Coxe was an extremely prolific writer whose early work appeared in such pulp magazines as *Black Mask, Dime Detective,* and *Detective Fiction Weekly*. His news-photographer hero, Flash Casey, first appeared in *Black Mask* in the early 1930s, and later Coxe used him in a number of novels, among them *Silent Are the Dead* (1942) and *Error in Judgment* (1961). His other news-photographer sleuth, Kent Murdock, appears in many more novels than Casey, and is a more fully realized character than the creation of Coxe's pulp-writing days. Coxe also created series characters Paul Standish (a medical examiner), Sam Crombie (a plodding detective), Max Hale (a reluctant detective), and Jack Fenner (Kent Murdock's private-eye sidekick who starred in several novels of his own).

Many consider *Fenner* the most entertaining of Coxe's later novels. Although published in 1971, it has the feel of the Forties. (Indeed, the hippie reference seems an anachronism.) Coxe has a simple formal style; he describes his characters but seldom invites the reader to identify with them. Action-oriented readers may find Coxe's work dull; there is virtually no violence, but rather a charming concern for decorum (another hint of bygone days).

In *Fenner,* Coxe begins with heiress Carol Browning's escape from a state mental institution. (Her husband committed her.) The scene shifts to Fenner's office, where the husband, George Browning, hires the detective to find his wife. Why, with all her money, did he send her to a state hospital rather than a more tolerable private one? Fenner asks. Browning's answer is unconvincing. Before Fenner can get to the bottom of this, Browning is murdered—in his wife's apartment. There's the hook; expect some good twists and a plausible conclusion. No more, no less.

Jack Fenner reappears in *The Silent Witness* (1973) and *No Place for Murder* (1975), as well as playing a role in many of the Kent Murdock novels.

(*S.D./M.M.*)

Coxe, George Harmon. *Murder with Pictures.* New York: Knopf, 1935. (AD)

This is Coxe's first novel and introduces news photographer Kent Murdock, who works for the *Boston Courier-Herald* and moves with seeming ease through the various strata of that city's society—stumbling over corpses with predictable regularity. As this first adventure opens, the jury has just delivered an acquittal in the Nate Girard murder trial. Murdock is on the job, snapping pictures; but later his concern with Girard turns personal, when he encounters his estranged wife, Hestor, with the former liquor racketeer at a celebratory party. Hestor won't give Murdock a divorce, in spite of a year's separation; Murdock wants out of the marriage, and he calls on Jack Fenner to help him. But before that situation even begins to be resolved, Girard's attorney, Mark Redfield (who is to receive a $50,000 fee for his client's acquittal), is murdered, and Murdock finds himself sheltering a girl he has noticed at the victory party—a stranger who bursts into his apartment while he is taking a shower and jumps in with him.

Quickly Murdock is back on the job at the scene of the lawyer's murder. And he soon uncovers a tangle of lies, infidelity, and intrigue that involves the dead man's wife; a "man-about-town" named Howard Archer; Archer's sister Joyce; gangster Sam Cuslik (whose brother Girard was accused of murdering); a "cheap punk" named Spike Tripp; Girard; and Hestor herself. By the time he has untangled this mess, Murdock has found the solution to more than one killing—and a unique way to resolve his marital problems.

This is a typical Coxe novel, with multiple threads that all tie together in a satisfactory manner at the end, and a love interest spiced with sex that seems oddly innocent by current standards.

Kent Murdock is also featured in, among others, *The Camera Clue* (1937), *Mrs. Murdock Takes a Case* (1941), *The Fifth Key* (1947), *Focus on Murder* (1954), and *The Reluctant Heiress* (1965).

(*M.M.*)

Coxe, George Harmon. *One Way Out.* New York: Knopf, 1960. (T)

In addition to novels featuring his various series characters, Coxe wrote a number of nonseries books. In many of these he takes his readers far from his usual Boston or Connecticut settings, utilizing such exotic locales as Guyana, Panama, Manila, Belize, and Havana.

In *One Way Out,* he takes us to New Orleans, where Rick Marsten, a newspaperman, is vacationing on his return from a two-year stint in Caracas, Venezuela. Rick has flown to the States with a fellow journalist from the fictional Republic of Maraguay, Luis Vargas, whose publication has been closed down by the current government there. And although he has trouble getting rid of the man when they reach New Orleans, he has no inkling that their acquaintance is merely the first in a series of incidents that will draw him deeply into the affairs of the troubled South American country.

A seemingly accidental meeting with an attractive woman leads to Rick being kidnapped at gunpoint from a Bourbon Street nightclub; and the kidnapping leads to an even more bizarre encounter—with a man who looks enough like Rick to be his twin brother. Before twenty-four hours have passed, Rick finds himself embroiled in the dangerous schemes of a group of strangers, trapped in a nightmare from which only he can rescue himself.

The action of this novel is played out against the rather sketchy but nonetheless colorful background scenes of New Orleans. But while there is more action in this novel than in Coxe's series books, it is truncated and lacking in punch—proving, perhaps, that the author's talents were better suited to the traditional detective story than to the thriller.

Other nonseries novels of this type are *Assignment in Guiana* (1942), *Murder in Havana* (1943), *Never Bet Your Life* (1952, set in Florida), *One Minute Past Eight* (1957, set in Caracas), *Moment of Violence* (1961, set in Barbados), and *Double Identity* (1970, set in Surinam).

(*M.M.*)

Craig, Alisa. *Murder Goes Mumming.* New York: Doubleday Crime Club, 1981. (W)

The series that Charlotte MacLeod (q.v.) writes under the pseudonym Alisa Craig features Inspector Madoc Rhys of the Royal Canadian Mounted Police. Rhys is a charming man in his late twenties, the self-described black sheep of an aristocratic British family. (His father is a famous choral director, his brother an operatic tenor, his sister a gifted clarinetist.) And indeed the family looks upon Madoc and his choice of a career as being mildly—although harmlessly—eccentric.

As this second novel in the series opens, Madoc is becoming engaged to Janet Wadman, a young woman he met and rescued from a killer in *A Pint of Murder* (1980). That is, Madoc's mother, Lady Rhys, is ordering them to become engaged before she flies to England to join the rest of the family for

Christmas. Madoc and Janet are only too happy to comply; and after the departure of mother, they also comply with her suggestion that they accept a holiday invitation to Graylings, a great estate on the coast of Bay Chaleur belonging to friends of the family. There they meet the Condryckes—a group of overfed, overjolly aristocrats.

All goes well initially, and the Christmas trappings—Yule log, wassail, mumming—are all present. But then someone steals Granny Condrycke's false teeth so she can't attend dinner, and they turn up in the mouth of the bearskin rug. Next granny turns up dead in her bed—murdered, Madoc thinks. And as a snowstorm howls around the great house and a spectral fire ship—omen of ill fortune—appears and reappears, even more terrifying events occur. Madoc finds himself on a busman's holiday as he searches out clues in an effort to prevent harm coming to any of the other Condryckes, or to his beloved Janet.

Madoc and Janet make an engaging pair, but their doting romance is a little too sticky-sweet. And the Condryckes—blond, bovine, and numerous—are very hard to differentiate. The country-house setting and the Christmas background are colorful, however, and MacLeod's wit is as sharp as ever.

MacLeod has written other (non-Rhys) novels under the Craig name: *The Grubb-and-Stakers Move a Mountain* (1981) and *The Grubb-and-Stakers Quilt-a-Bee* (1985), both of which concern a militant gardening club; and *The Terrible Tribe* (1983), which deals with a New York model transported to a New Brunswick village.

(*M.M.*)

Craig, Jonathan. *Morgue for Venus.* Greenwich, Conn.: Fawcett Gold Medal, 1956. (O/PP)

The popularity of the radio and television series "Dragnet" was responsible for the publication of several series of police procedurals in the middle 1950s. The best-known of these, and certainly the longest-lived, is Ed McBain's (q.v.) Eighty-seventh Precinct series, but another, almost equally good, came from Jonathan Craig. Craig's work has now faded into undeserved obscurity, possibly because he chose to tell his stories through a first-person narrator, Pete Selby, and thus did not develop the gallery of characters that McBain did.

All the cases handled by Selby and his partner, Stan Rayder, have strong overtones of kinky sex, and *Morgue for Venus* is no exception. The squeal begins when a body is fished from the East River. The body is that of a young woman wearing stockings and a dress, but no underwear. The case is immediately complicated by the fact that the girl has no known enemies but has apparently been associated with criminals, specifically burglars who attempted to rob the photography studio where she was working. The robbery and the murder are tied together, but just how is not clear to Rayder and Selby. Eventually, however, the crime is solved by painstaking police work. Craig has a good narrative sense; the story's pace never lags, even when Craig is working in the details of police routine and procedure that form an integral part of the novel. His dialogue is crisp, and the characters encountered by the detectives in the course of their investigation are interesting and convincing.

All the books in the Selby series are worth looking for, including *The Dead Darling* (1955), *Case of the Cold Coquette* (1957), *Case of the Beautiful Body* (1957), *Case of the Petticoat Murder* (1958), and *Case of the Nervous Nude*—"all she wore was a terrified expression" (1959).

(*B.C.*)

Craig, M. S. *To Play the Fox.* New York: Dodd, Mead, 1982. (E)

To paraphrase Machiavelli: A prince must imitate both the lion and the fox. The lion is strong enough to frighten wolves; the fox cunning enough to recognize traps.

This is the criterion that Vladimir, a Soviet spymaster, decides to apply to a perplexing problem. Two of his undercover agents in America inadvertently have become partners in the same business venture, a crop-dusting company near Sacramento, California. Vladimir is concerned that they might discover one another's covert identity, thereby endangering both agents' covers. So one of the men must be killed—better to lose one than both. The man who most closely exemplifies the strength of the lion, and yet is able to play the fox, will be spared. The other must die.

The scene shifts to California and we meet both men, plus a third partner, a man named Mac Maguire. Maguire is the founder and manager of the crop-dusting business. He runs the operation, and his two partners (although both are part-time pilots) are in it primarily as an investment and tax shelter. One of the men, however, does have visions of taking over the company and using it as a cover for flying around San Francisco and spying on shipping in and out of the Bay—it apparently not having occurred to him that a bay-view apartment and a telescope on any of San Francisco's hills (Nob, Telegraph, or, perhaps most appropriately, Russian) would serve the same purpose.

But, not to quibble. The author tells us in great detail about each man, until we feel we know them personally and become intrigued and concerned about which man will be chosen. The result is a compelling and suspenseful novel.

Craig is also the author of *Gillian's Chain* (1983) and *The Third Blonde* (1985).

(*N.D.*)

Crane, Caroline. *The Foretelling.* New York: Dodd, Mead, 1982. (PS)

The Foretelling is Caroline Crane's fourth novel. While the book is set in a small, secluded town in the Catskill Mountains of the present day, it has the feel of the 1950s. Most of the characters are united by their lack of education, lack of opportunity, and lack of realization that life could offer more than marriage, family, and steady, uninteresting work. One family runs the town, provides the jobs, and lives in a mansion—a standard Gothic setting. The heroine is a high-school girl who has been coerced into reading palms at a bazaar. Some of her predictions come true. Some of her friends are frightened, some pleased. She doesn't know what to believe, but in the tradition of the Gothic heroine, she is trusting and fails to see the dangers as quickly as the reader.

The problem with *The Foretelling* is that the author tells her story for the most part from the somewhat limited viewpoint of one character, with occasional forays into the equally limited viewpoints of a few others—thus causing it to be mostly a prosaic chronicle of events. (In contrast, the first chapter, a first-person dream sequence, is riveting.)

The plot, while standard for a Gothic, is absorbing and Crane handles the question of the occult well. She is at her best when describing the actual palm reading—what the lines mean, what the breaks in the lines foreshadow. It's hard to keep from looking at your own palm when reading.

Among Crane's other novels are *Summer Girl* (1979), *The Girls Are Missing* (1981), *Coast of Fear* (1981), *Something Evil* (1984), and *Someone at the Door* (1985).

(*S.D.*)

Crane, Frances. *Death-Wish Green.* New York: Random House, 1960. (PI/AD)

Pat and Jean Abbott, a private investigator and his wife, are returning to foggy San Francisco from a weekend in the sun. As they reach the toll plaza of the Golden Gate Bridge, they spot a familiar car being inspected by highway patrolmen and the local police. The car, which was abandoned on the bridge, belongs to Katie Spinner, daughter of friends of the Abbotts, and it appears she has jumped off the bridge. Jean Abbott, however, is not convinced the girl committed suicide; and when Pat is hired by Katie's aunt to investigate the disappearance, it becomes apparent Katie is still alive. The Abbotts, who often work as an investigative team, focus on bohemian North Beach, one of the last places Katie was seen before she started across the bridge. There they encounter an art-gallery dealer with a taste for Zen Buddhism and opium; a model who calls her favorite color "death-wish green," and dies wearing it; a mysterious stranger with a large auburn beard who was seen with the missing girl in a coffeehouse; and errant sons and daughters of some of the city's wealthiest and most respected families. For all Pat Abbott's investigative skills, in the end it is Jean who sees most of the action and carries the day.

Frances Crane's descriptive powers are considerable, and the sense of place—particularly of the fog and its effect on San Francisco—is powerful. Her secondary characters are well drawn and indeed far more vividly drawn than either Pat or Jean. Jean, the narrator/observer, remains just that, and we come away without really having gotten to know her. Pat, the detective, is merely a figure going through investigative motions.

Frances Crane has written many other novels, all of them with colors in their titles, featuring the Abbotts. Among them are *The Amethyst Spectacles* (1944), *The Buttercup Case* (1958), and *The Amber Eyes* (1962). In addition to San Francisco, they are set in such locales as Tangier (*The Coral Princess Murders,* 1954); New Mexico (*Horror on the Ruby X,* 1956); and New Orleans (*The Indigo Necklace,* 1955).

(*M.M.*)

Creasey, John. *The Insulators.* New York: Walker, 1973. (E)

One could speculate that John Creasey was really a trademark for some kind of bizarre writing machine secreted away in the English countryside. In reality, he was an individual who produced some 560 books under more than twenty pseudonyms over a forty-year period. Some writers are prolific. Creasey was incredibly so. No other mystery writer can boast of such an output.

On the other hand, if you are writing to a rigid formula, as Creasey did, you can probably put a plot together during a TV commercial. Your characters are set and good; all you have to do is imagine a catastrophe that is suitable to the talents and circumstances of one of your heroes, and off you go. That is, if you have a mind with the inventive bent of Creasey's—and more ideas per minute than most people entertain in a lifetime. That was Creasey's real forte—the number and variety of his ideas.

Under his own name—he also wrote under such pseudonyms as Gordon Ashe (q.v.), Michael Halliday, J. J. Marric (q.v.), and Jeremy Yorke—Creasey created four basic heroes. Two—Richard Rollison ("the Toff") and Superintendent Roger West—are involved with domestic crime, bringing to justice or disgrace bad boys and girls within the British borders. The other two—Dr. Palfrey and Gordon Cragie—are world travelers; they worry about international villains, the kind that alone or, usually, in gangs lust for world domination.

The Insulators features Dr. Palfrey and the men of Department Z5. From the start we know the good guys are going to win. If they don't, the world is going to blow up, and Creasey was the kind of writer who would never let *that* happen. He takes us to the brink, however, showing us the kind of absolute evil that exists in the world.

The "insulators" of this title are a gang of mad scientists/power mongers who have discovered a magic gas that can insulate humans against atomic radiation. With that as a tool, along with the requisite bombs, they try to blackmail every world government into total capitulation. Department Z5, the good guys, is a gang of international policemen headed by our hero, Dr. Palfrey—sort of a cross-cultural crime-fighting organization that pools its resources and its talents in times of world crisis. They come together in a fantastic effort to keep these scientists from erasing human misery through enslaving the world's population.

There are too many weaknesses in this plot, although it is entertaining. How many of us can believe that the bad guys could build underground nuclear arsenals all over the world without anybody noticing? And it's also hard to believe in Z5; Creasey's good guys are just too good.

Other titles about the men of Z5 include *Traitors' Doom* (1970), *The Legion of the Lost* (1974), *The Voiceless Ones* (1974), and *The Mists of Fear* (1977).

(*K.K.H.*)

Creasey, John. *No Darker Crime.* New York: Popular Library, 1976. (E)

In this novel, originally published in England in 1943, Creasey once again combats an international conspiracy, but his plot seems as if it could really happen. We feel for the good guys, instead of merely marveling at their derring-do, and we're afraid the bad guys might just pull it off.

This is a Department Z story. While the Z5-ers are the elite counterespionage fighters, up against enormous odds, which they unfailingly surmount, plain old Department Z is full of men who are simply brilliant and good, led by Scotsman Gordon Cragie. We see Cragie tired, worried, cranky—and what's worse, we see his desk get messier and messier. He is known for an untidy life but an immaculate desk, so when this happens, the case is really getting to him.

This time he can hardly keep up with reports from his agents that representatives of the British and American governments are gathering to try to figure out how to feed everyone once World War II ends. And the representatives are being assassinated. Someone, for some reason, doesn't want the grain to flow, at least not until they've driven its price sky-high and cornered the market. The British prime minister is terrified, and Department Z has only forty-eight hours to put a stop to all this before public opinion in both countries puts a wedge in negotiations, causing millions of people to die of starvation.

Cragie is a reluctant hero. Drawn into the problem, he is forced to risk his life. His moral sense and his growing love for the daughter of the major American representative compel him to match wits with the Nazi mentality. There are many close calls in this well-done thriller.

Further adventures of Cragie and Department Z are chronicled in *First Came a Murder* (1972), *Death Stands By* (1972), *The Island of Peril* (1976), and *Go Away, Death* (1976).

(*K.K.H.*)

Creasey, John. *The Toff at the Fair.* New York: Walker, 1968. (AD)

Richard Rollison, known as "the Toff," spends his leisure time, like many a topping British aristocrat, doing good deeds. He financially supports the local boxing gym, where he himself keeps in shape, and when in the course of human events someone is in distress, he hops to the rescue. He is street-wise, genius enough to be one step ahead of the bad guys. He's a lusty fellow, too, and good-looking—which means that unlike many British paragons of virtue, he's not averse to a great roll in the hay with a woman who can boil his blood.

Of course this can get him in trouble. In *The Toff at the Fair,* Rollison is almost fatally attracted to a gorgeous Gypsy woman who, it would seem, is the leader of a cocaine ring. She travels with a carnival, which her father owns, and the Toff is in the terrible position of trying to bust her and bed her at the same time.

The Toff gets into this situation because a distant cousin has sought his help. She's young, beautiful, and rich, and her boyfriend is the possible victim of blackmail. The Toff follows the boyfriend to the carnival, where the fellow starts a brutal fight with a man at one of the midway booths—three balls for a quarter and if you knock over the coconut you win a prize. The coconut never gets knocked over, but the concessionaire does, and the boyfriend pockets one of the balls and glides away into the crowd.

Dope? Blackmail? Extortion? The Toff slips up a few times in finding out, mostly in his judgment of character. He badly underestimates a number of people, including his Gypsy queen's jealous brother, who would stop at nothing to wrest the cocaine trade from his sister and his father.

The Toff at the Fair is fun, and if Creasey had only realized that cocaine wakes a person up, doesn't put a person to sleep as he has it, it would be a perfect little suspense adventure.

For more escapades of this entertaining fellow, look up *The Toff Steps Out* (1955), *The Toff Proceeds* (1968), *The Toff in New York* (1964), and *The Toff at Butlin's* (1976).

(*K.K.H.*)

Crispin, Edmund. *The Glimpses of the Moon.* New York: Walker, 1978. (AD)

Gervase Fen, Oxford professor of English language and literature, who it seems spends more time being detective than don, is the creation of Edmund Crispin, who in actual fact is Robert Bruce Montgomery. Montgomery was an organist, choral-music composer, and wrote background music for many movies. Humorous passages about the plight of composers and musicians appear in some of the Fen adventures in major and minor keys. The Fen tales are academic (with Latin quotations and private jokes) but markedly satirical, and sometimes tumble into farce. Julian Symons said that "at his weakest he is flippant, at his best he is witty." Fen is energetic, even frenetic, and when he gets going on the case, the narrative zips right along. If you like humor mixed with your crime, then all nine Gervase Fen novels will be of interest. Two collections of short stories have also been praised, but they are not as good as the novels. They are fair but flat, dependent on gimmicks, and Fen doesn't really have room to operate.

In *The Glimpses of the Moon,* Fen is on sabbatical from Oxford to write *the* book on the postwar British novel, and is not particularly interested in hearing about a two-month-old murder that the police had handily solved, getting their man. Fen's interest in the case is finally piqued when the second dismembered body is discovered and he realizes the head he has been toting about in a potato sack is the wrong one (of three). Beneath an apple tree where Fen is perched, the situation comes to a head in the pandemonious collision of a hunt, hunt saboteurs, a motorcycle scramble, a burglar's getaway, a herd of cattle driven to pasture, a scouting helicopter, and police hurrying to arrest a miscreant. The fun almost pushes the investigation into the back seat.

Crispin writes excellent set-piece scenes where the characters make exhibitions of themselves, and *Glimpses* is peopled by a superabundance of eccentrics: A retired cavalry man who loathes horses, a failed foreign correspondent, an antipopish rector in drag, a gray bureaucrat from the power board, a laconic rustic, a mad-scientist pathologist, a reclusive publican, a horror-movie-music composer, a brooding pig farmer and his nymphomaniac wife, lively and deadly policemen, even an electric power pylon come to life—all set against a background of tranquil village life in peaceful Devon.

(*T.B.*)

*Crispin, Edmund. *The Moving Toyshop.* Philadelphia: Lippincott, 1946. (AD)

The droll opening scene of *The Moving Toyshop* has Richard Cadogan in his garden in the heart of London, dickering with his publisher over advances and royalties for his latest book of poetry and absentmindedly waggling a pistol under the publisher's nose. Cadogan is "craving for adventure, for excitement: anything to stave off middle age." He soon finds it in Oxford. After lightheartedly prowling the late-night streets, he enters a dark toyshop, finds a body, and gets conked on the head. Before the first chapter is over, the body and the lethal toyshop are gone.

Cadogan consults his old friend Gervase Fen, and the investigation gets rolling (sometimes almost out of control when dashing about in Fen's sportscar, a vociferous *Lily Christine III*). The poet gets swept along, interviewing witnesses, bullying blackguards, rescuing damsels, facing death, and eventually breathlessly winding up the mystery. Along the way, the spirited duo enlists an elderly don and various clumps of students, attends chapel, puzzles out the clues in a nonsense rhyme, argues literature on the phone with the chief constable, interprets an eccentric will, and generally chases around Oxford in a boisterous fashion.

Gervase Fen is very serious and determined when being a detective, but volatile and absentminded. When in a tight spot, he plays literary games, like Unreadable Books and Awful Lines from Shakespeare, and makes up titles for the thrillers that Crispin writes. He claims that "I'm the only literary critic turned detective in the whole of fiction." The Oxford background is well realized, and the humor sustains the story. The basic plot was obviously influenced by John Dickson Carr (q.v.).

The climactic scene, revolving around the chase to catch the criminal, is so powerful, so moving, that Alfred Hitchcock borrowed it to use as the windup in his film *Strangers on a Train* (1951).

(*T.B.*)

*Crofts, Freeman Wills. *The Cask.* New York: Seltzer, 1924. (CS)

Freeman Wills Crofts's first novel, *The Cask,* is considered by many critics, including Anthony Boucher (q.v.), to be one of the best and most important books in the mystery genre. The prime virtue of this and all the Crofts novels is their tight, logical plotting, in which every detail fits solidly and smoothly. His detectives work meticulously to piece the clues together, often in order to demolish a supposedly unshakable alibi; and because they are so logical, the endings are always exceptionally satisfying. Early in his career, Crofts experimented with a number of sleuths, but in his fifth novel—*Inspector French's Greatest Case* (1925)—he introduced Inspector Joseph French, who was to appear in most of his subsequent books. Like Crofts's previous heroes, French is a bit of a plodder who slowly and carefully works his way step by step through the process of deduction to a natural conclusion.

In *The Cask,* the plot turns on alibis. When four casks fall to the deck of a ship during unloading, two of them leak wine, one is undamaged, and the last leaks sawdust. This last cask is examined more closely, and gold coins and the fingers of a human hand are found. But before the cask can be completely opened, it vanishes.

Inspector Burnley of Scotland Yard is assigned to this bizarre case. Using the few clues available to him, he is able to locate the missing cask. And when it is opened, Burnley finds the body of a young woman who has been brutally strangled. There are no clues to the victim's identity, so Burnley goes to Paris, where the cask was assembled. What follows is a detailed, complex investigation, involving timetables, a performance of Berlioz's *Les Troyens,* and a group of suspects with a multitude of motives.

(*G.K./M.M.*)

Crofts, Freeman Wills. *The Loss of the "Jane Vosper."* New York: Dodd, Mead, 1936. (CS)

Crofts was a transportation engineer and worked for railway companies for many years before retiring in 1929 to become a full-time writer. A number of his novels make use of his technical knowledge of railroading and shipping, such as *Death of a Train* (1947), in which Inspector French investigates a World War II plot to divert vital supplies being shipped to the British forces in North Africa. Similarly, *The Loss of the "Jane Vosper"* draws on Crofts's knowledge of the shipping industry.

On a dark night in the mid-Atlantic, the cargo ship *Jane Vosper* is rocked by explosion after explosion. Soon afterward, the ship sinks. An insurance investigation is launched, and it soon becomes apparent that the sinking of the ship was no accident. Inspector French enters the case and begins to piece details together—including particulars of what cargo the ship was carrying. A cargo swindle is revealed—one that leads to murder. French works with precision, ever conscious that unnecessary delay may lead to additional killings.

The background detail in this novel is particularly good, and French is in top form, always playing fair with the reader and making us privy to his private thoughts. French is likable, a pleasant, unassuming man with none of the sometimes unfortunate affectations of other popular classic sleuths. This book—and most of Crofts's others—presents no real challenge to the reader in terms of outwitting the detective and solving the case first. If anything, we feel that we are being taken by the hand and led on a genteel journey through the routine of a careful and dedicated investigator.

Other Crofts novels dealing with the shipping industry include *Mystery in the English Channel* (1931), *Crime on the Solent* (1934), *Man Overboard* (1936), and *Enemy Unseen* (1945). Books in which Crofts drew on his railroading background include *Sir John Magill's Last Journey* (1930), *Wilful and Premeditated* (1934), and *Dark Journey* (1954). A short-story collection featuring Inspector French, *Many a Slip,* was published in 1955.

(*G.K./M.M.*)

Cross, Amanda. *In the Last Analysis.* New York: Macmillan, 1964. (AD)

Amanda Cross is a pseudonym of Carolyn Heilbrun, a professor of English at Columbia University, and the play on words in the title of this novel is just what a reader might expect from one in that academic field. *In the Last Analysis* refers both to the analysis of a murder and to the fact that the murder was committed on a psychiatrist's couch.

Cross's heroine, Kate Fansler, is also an English professor, and these popular books have fostered an interest in what might be considered a subgenre: the academic mystery. Words are indeed important to the characters in the Fansler books: They consider their words; they choose them with care; they admire the skill of other speakers; they are witty; they toss in quotations from a variety of authors. Not only Kate but other characters have a quoting familiarity with literature, and these quotes and their sources can be clues. For anyone who enjoys literature and finds pleasure in the exquisite turn of phrase, the Fansler series is a treat.

Kate Fansler is described as a young woman, but she has the assurance of a more mature individual. She is the only daughter of an old New York family, in which her much older brothers did the "respectable" thing and went into business while Kate—black-sheepishly—opted for academia. In an even more rebellious manner, Kate has also opted for solving murders.

In *In the Last Analysis,* Kate refers a young woman student to psychoanalyst Emanuel Bauer, who was once Kate's lover before his marriage. The student is killed—on Bauer's couch, in his soundproof consultation room. As the doctor's office is in his home, not only he but also his family are suspect. As—for various reasons—is Kate. Her investigation includes forays into the private lives of the Bauer and Fansler families (members of the latter seem to be surrounded by a lot of heavy mahogany furniture), as well as less upstanding members of the academic establishment.

Kate's investigation—and its tidy solution—is on a par with the others in this extremely literate series, which includes *The James Joyce Murder* (1967), *Poetic Justice* (1970), and *The Question of Max* (1976).

(*S.D.*)

Crowe, John. *Bloodwater.* New York: Dodd, Mead, 1974. (PP)

John Crowe is one of Dennis Lynds's several pseudonyms—others include William Arden (q.v.), Michael Collins (q.v.), and Mark Sadler (q.v.)—and his Buena Costa County is fictional, a synthesis of many of the places and characteristics of Lynds's home state of California. That, however, is as far as unreality figures in these excellent novels. The characters are deeply and well drawn, the procedure is accurate, the plots are plausible and logical.

A prominent citizen of Monteverde, one of the county's elegant suburbs, is found dead of gunshot wounds in a seedy motel room. The gun is his own; the name he registered under is not. Detective Sergeant Harry Wood of the Monteverde Police Department has a special interest in the case, since he and the dead man, Sam Garnet, were both on the force together before Garnet climbed through the ranks of the security department to the vice-presidency of a local corporation. Wood's investigation takes him into the homes of the rich and socially prominent of the area; into the offices of powerful corporation executives; and into the past of a family that is desperately attempting to conceal a secret. The satisfying solution links diverse aspects of the case, both from the past and the immediate present.

Other titles in this series: *Another Way to Die* (1972), *A Touch of Darkness* (1972), *Crooked Shadows* (1975), *When They Kill Your Wife* (1977), and *Close to Death* (1979).

(*M.M.*)

*Crumley, James. *The Last Good Kiss.* New York: Random House, 1978. (PI)

Since the death of Ross Macdonald (q.v.) and on the basis of just three novels, James Crumley has become the foremost living writer of private-eye fiction. Carrying on the Macdonald tradition in which the PI is no longer macho but a man sensitive to human needs, torn by inner pain, and slow to use force, Crumley has moved the genre into the Vietnam and post-Vietnam era.

His principal setting is not the big city as in Hammett and Chandler (qq.v), nor the affluent suburbs as in Macdonald, but the wilderness and bleak magnificence of western Montana. His prevailing mood is a wacked-out empathy with dopers, dropouts, losers, and loonies, the human wreckage of the institutionalized butchery we call the "real world." Nobility resides in the land, in wild animals, and in a handful of outcasts—psychotic Viet vets; Indians, hippies; rumdums; and love-seekers—who can't cope with life.

Crumley's detective characters have one foot in either camp. Milodragovitch, the protagonist of *The Wrong Case* (1975) and *Dancing Bear* (1983), is a cocaine addict and boozer, the child of two suicides, a compulsive womanizer like his wealthy Hemingwayesque father; a man literally marking time until he will turn fifty-two and inherit the family fortune, which his pioneer ancestors legally stole from the Indians. Sughrue from *The Last Good Kiss* has a background as a Nam war criminal and an army spy on domestic dissidents and he's drinking himself to death by inches. Yet these are two of the purest figures in the history of detective fiction, and the most reverent toward the earth and its creatures.

Crumley has minimal interest in plot and even less in explanations, but he's so uncannily skillful with character, language, relationship, and incident that he can afford to throw structure overboard. His books are an accumulation of small, crazy encounters, full of confusion and muddle, disorder and despair, graphic violence and sweetly casual sex, coke snorting and alcohol guzzling, mountain snowscapes and roadside bars. When he does have to plot, he tends to borrow from Raymond Chandler. In *The Wrong Case,* Milodragovitch becomes obsessed by a young woman from Iowa who hires him to find her missing brother, a situation clearly taken from Chandler's *Little Sister* (1949). *The Last Good Kiss,* perhaps the best of Crumley's novels, traps Sughrue among the tormented members of the family of a hugely successful writer, somewhat as Philip Marlowe was trapped in Chandler's masterpiece *The Long Goodbye* (1954). In *Dancing Bear,* which pits Milodragovitch against a multinational corporation dumping toxic waste into the groundwater, the detective interviews a rich old client in a plant-filled solarium just like Marlowe in the first chapter of Chandler's *Big Sleep* (1939).

None of these borrowings matter in the least, for Chandler's tribute to Dashiell Hammett is no less true of Crumley: He writes scenes so that they seem never to have been written before. What one remembers from *The Last Good Kiss* is the alcoholic bulldog and the emotionally flayed women and the loneliness and guilt. What is most lasting in *Dancing Bear* is the moment when Milodragovitch finds a time bomb in his car on a wilderness road and tosses it out at the last second into a stream and weeps for the exploded fish that died for him, and dozens of other moments just as powerful.

(*F.M.N.*)

Cunningham, E. V. *Samantha.* New York: Morrow, 1967. (PP)

Samantha was a pathetic Hollywood hopeful who ended up on the casting couch with a succession of unscrupulous men. Even then, she failed to land a part. Eleven years later, the men are being murdered, apparently in revenge. Each of them is now married to a woman who just might be Samantha with a new name. Detective Sergeant Masao Masuto of the Beverly Hills Police Force has his work cut out for him.

This is the book that introduced Masuto, a Zen Buddhist like his creator, who is actually the prolific Howard Fast writing under a pseudonym. A Nisei who lives in a Culver City cottage with his wife, three children, and his beloved rose garden, Masuto is culturally about as distant from the fast-land denizens of Beverly Hills as a cop can get. Yet he declines to let them rattle him; he doesn't envy, despise, or judge them. His trademark cool—sometimes masking a very human inner turmoil—is as appealing as his sometimes acerbic wit. The Hollywood crowd, not surprisingly, is mystified by him and his Zen ways; he explains himself with a disarming simplicity that leaves them even more baffled. The contrast between the two cultures he moves between is the chief charm of this and the other Masuto mysteries, among them *The Case of the One-Penny Orange* (1977), *The Case of the Russian Diplomat* (1978), and *The Case of the Poisoned Eclairs* (1979).

Before creating Masuto, Fast published, under the Cunningham name, a number of nonseries thrillers utilizing the first names of their female protagonists as titles. Some of these have serious themes: *Sylvia* (1960), *Phyllis* (1962). Others are comedic in tone: *Penelope* (1965), *Margie* (1966). Most have rather outlandish plots that entertain despite putting a strain on the reader's credulity. Fast's first crime novel, *Fallen Angel* (1952), originally published under the pseudonym Walter Ericson, was made into the 1965 film *Mirage,* with Gregory Peck and Walter Matthau; both novel and film are taut and engrossing but suffer from that same lack of believability.

(*J.S./B.P.*)

Curtiss, Ursula. *The Noonday Devil.* New York: Dodd, Mead, 1951. (W/R)

Ursula Curtiss is a member of an impressive mystery-writing triumvirate: Her sister, Mary McMullen (q.v.), and her mother, Helen Reilly (q.v.), are also well-known suspense authors. Curtiss made her debut in 1948 with *Voice Out of Darkness,* a tale of domestic menace based on a crime of the past.

The Noonday Devil is Curtiss's third novel, and although it, too, deals with her recurring themes of past sins and drawing-room malice, it is an unusual departure for the author: While her novels usually focus on women or children, the central character of *The Noonday Devil* is a man. Andrew Sentry is still unsettled from the war, the death of his father, and the execution of his brother, Nick, in a Japanese POW camp. But Sentry discovers new purpose to life when a conversation with a stranger in a bar reveals that his brother's attempt at escape from the camp had been exposed by a fellow prisoner called Sands. Hence, the Japanese firing squad had actually been an American's instrument of murder.

Sentry resolves to track down his brother's murderer. To do so, he must reestablish contact with Nick's fiancée, who he believes to have been faithless, and various friends and acquaintances from Nick's past. The hit-and-run murder of an ex-POW and key witness from Nick's camp, and Sentry's reconstruction of Nick's last leave, convince him that he is on the right track, and that the Cabanatuan execution was Sands's cover-up for an earlier civilian crime. The question is, Who is Sands? And can he be stopped before he eliminates Andrew Sentry?

There is a tad too much coincidence in Curtiss's plot, but there is no denying her skill at creating tension and continued suspense. Sentry is a sympathetic and believable hero, and Nick's fiancée (who may represent either treachery or romance) leads the list of well-drawn support characters.

Ursula Curtiss's more than twenty suspense novels consistently entertain readers with the unsettling thought that home, family, and friends are not always a refuge, and are sometimes even the source of peril. Two of her novels, *The Forbidden Garden* (1962) and *Out of the Dark* (1964), have been made into Hollywood films. Other noteworthy novels include *The Deadly Climate* (1954), *The Face of the Tiger* (1958), and *In Cold Pursuit* (1977). A short story collection, *The House on Plymouth Street and Other Stories,* was published in 1985.

(*K.L.M.*)

Cushman, Dan. *Jewel of the Java Sea.* Greenwich, Conn.: Fawcett Gold Medal, 1951. (A/O)

Dan Cushman wrote a number of novels for Gold Medal in the 1950s, most of which were referred to by the publisher as "jungle thrillers." The books were distinguished for their exotic settings in faraway lands. *Jewel of the Java Sea,* for example, begins in Borneo, moves to Singapore, and concludes in Sumatra.

The story involves Frisco Dougherty, who has spent the last fifteen years in the tropics, hunting for a fortune in stolen diamonds. He obtains the first diamond easily because of his slightly shady reputation, and he knows there must be others. If he can find and sell them, he can return at long last to San Francisco and feel the cold fog in his face once more. The search is hampered by the presence of other hunters, including Deering, a murderous American, and his Sikh retainer. And of course, as in any good paperback of the time, there are three beautiful women of doubtful loyalties and morality. The pace is fast and the local color well done and convincing. The book is slowed somewhat by the dialogue, Dougherty being devoted to reading Boswell's *Life of Johnson* and apparently having let his reading affect his speaking, and the relationship between Dougherty and one of the women is a little too spontaneous; but there is a fine treasure story (undoubtedly influenced by *The Maltese Falcon*), and the ending is satisfactory enough to make one forgive minor quibbles.

Other Cushman "jungle books" include *Savage Interlude* (1952), *Jungle She* (1953), *Port Orient* (1955), and *The Forbidden Land* (1958).

(*B.C.*)

Dahl, Roald. *Someone Like You.* New York: Knopf, 1953. (SS)

Roald Dahl's short stories have been called—among other things—bizarre, comic, horrific, clever, and playful. Dahl depicts a world where things are a little—or sometimes a lot—skewed from the world we know, and the events he chronicles often produce wrenching horror in his reader. But he has also been known to inject a comic twist into his stories, and he toys with the reader, teasing the story line along like a mischievous child until he has us completely fooled.

Perhaps his most famous story is "Lamb to the Slaughter." It begins on a deceptively quiet note, with Mary Maloney waiting in her cozy parlor for her husband to come home from work. Mary is a devoted housewife, six months pregnant, and she takes excellent care of her policeman husband, but tonight she has neglected to take anything out of the freezer. And when she does, after her husband makes a startling announcement, a leg of lamb seems quite appropriate. . . .

"Taste" likewise deals with food. Mike Schofield, a London epicure, is giving a dinner party to which he has invited a famous gourmet. Mike is proud of his wine cellar and anxious to trip up his guest on his knowledge of fine but obscure vintages. In fact, he is so sure of his ability to do so that he makes a most dangerous wager.

These first two stories are examples of Dahl's lighter work. On the more serious side is "Man from the South," which concerns a different, more deadly wager. In "The Soldier," Dahl makes a subtle statement about the aftermath of war. And readers and writers alike will be both amused and shaken at the implications of "The Great Automatic Grammatisator."

This collection shows Dahl at his best. Other volumes of his varied and multifaceted short stories include *Kiss, Kiss* (1960), *The Best of Roald Dahl* (1978), and *Tales of the Unexpected* (1979). In addition, he has written two novels: *Sometime Never: A Fable for Supermen* (1948) and *My Uncle Oswald* (1979).

(*M.M.*)

Daly, Carroll John. *The Snarl of the Beast.* New York: Clode, 1927. (PI)

Carroll John Daly was one of the fathers of the modern hard-boiled private eye, a primary influence on such later writers as Mickey Spillane (q.v.). His style and plots seem dated today, but the presence of his name on the cover of *Black Mask* in the Twenties and Thirties could be counted on to raise sales of the magazine by fifteen percent. Daly's major contribution was Race Williams, the narrator of *Snarl of the Beast* and the first fully realized tough-guy detective (his first appearance, in the June 1, 1923, issue of *Black Mask,* preceded the debut of Hammett's Continental Op by four months). Williams was a thoroughly hard-boiled individual. As he says of one criminal he dispatches, "He got what was coming to him. If ever a lad needed one good killing, he was the boy." Williams doesn't hesitate to dole out two-gun, vigilante justice.

The Snarl of the Beast has an uncomplicated plot: Williams is asked by the police to help track down a master criminal known as "the Beast" and reputed to be "the most feared, the cunningest and cruelest creature that stalks the city streets at night." Williams is willing to take on the job and to give the police credit for ridding the city of this menace, just as long as he gets the reward. Along the way he meets a masked woman prowler, a "girl of the night," and of course the Beast himself. Daly is not known for literary niceties—his style can best be described as crude but effective—yet there is a certain fascination in his novels and his vigilante/detective. Characterization is minimal and action is everything. "Race Williams—Private Investigator—tells the whole story. Right! Let's go."

Race Williams also appears in *The Hidden Hand* (1929) and *Murder from the East* (1935), among others. Daly created two other series characters, both of them rough-and-tumble types, although not in the same class with Williams: Vee Brown, hero of *Murder Won't Wait* (1933) and *Emperor of Evil* (1937); and Satan Hall, who stars in *The Mystery of the Smoking Gun* (1936) and *Ready to Burn* (1951), the latter title having been published only in England.

(B.C./B.P.)

Daly, Elizabeth. *The Book of the Crime.* New York: Rinehart, 1951. (AD)

Elizabeth Daly was sixty-two years old when she published her first novel, *Unexpected Night,* in 1940. She wrote sixteen more over the next dozen years, all but one of them featuring a low-key, informal (and somewhat improbable) amateur sleuth named Henry Gamadge; *The Book of the Crime* is the last of her novels, although she lived another sixteen years after it was published. Daly's mysteries are fair-play whodunits concerned with murder among the upper classes, and therefore very much in the British Golden Age tradition; in fact, Agatha Christie (q.v.) once said that Daly was her favorite American detective-story writer. Many of her books have integral bibliographic elements; Gamadge is at his best in these, owing to his position as an author and consulting expert on old books, manuscripts, and disputed documents. A man "so well bred as to make Lord Peter Wimsey seem a trifle coarse" (Anthony Boucher), Gamadge works out of his fashionable home in New York's East Sixties, which he shares with his wife Clara; his young son; an assistant named Harold; and a cat named Martin that prefers petting to being petted.

In *The Book of the Crime,* Gamadge undertakes to help young Rena Austen, the bride of an odd, secretive war veteran. For a year she has been living—unhappily—with her husband, Gray, and his relatives in a musty old New York house he inherited; and for almost that long she has known that she "made a fearful mistake." That mistake turned to real fear when Gray caught her looking at two apparently harmless old books in a little-used sitting room and, in a reaction both violent and inexplicable, grabbed the books and locked her inside the room. Rena managed to escape and, with the help of a young man named Ordway, ran off to the Gamadge household, where she has been protectively installed in the guise of the family nursemaid.

To find out the truth behind her husband's strange actions, Gamadge investigates Gray and his relatives—and soon finds himself enmeshed in a tangled web of murder and larceny on a grand scale. The identity of the two old books plays an important part in the solution to the mystery, as do Gamadge's many New York connections, both social and official. Along the way there is much bookish talk, homey scenes with the Gamadges, and a new romance for Rena.

Like all of Daly's novels, this is a sedate, erudite puzzle that should please fans of Christie and fans of bibliomysteries alike.

(*E.N./B.P.*)

Daly, Elizabeth. *Murders in Volume 2.* New York: Farrar & Rinehart, 1941. (AD)

Daly's third mystery is among her best. Unmarried at this stage in his career, Gamadge is approached at home by Robina Vauregard, of an old New York family of noble English lineage. The Vauregards, it develops, are also a family with a strange ghostly legend known only to its members: In 1840 the Vauregard governess, Miss Lydia Wagoneur, went out into the arbor behind the family home in Manhattan's Traders Row, taking with her Volume II from a set of Byron's poetry—and promptly vanished, never to be seen or heard from again. Until, that is, the present year (1940), exactly 100 years from the date of her disappearance. She has apparently come back from "the fourth dimension," in the person of a young woman calling herself Lydia Smith.

The Vauregard heirs don't believe Lydia is either a ghost or a reincarnation of the vanished governess. But the family patriarch, eighty-year-old Imbrie, who is a recent convert to "New Soul" spiritualism, *does* believe. And what convinced him is the fact that Volume II has been mysteriously returned to the Byron set, evidently the very same one that had been missing for a century. Because Imbrie believes, Robina and the rest of the heirs are afraid he'll give Lydia Smith—whoever she is and whatever her game might be—a slice of the million-dollar family fortune *before* he dies.

Gamadge's investigation focuses on the heirs, among them Robina's niece, attractive Clara Dawson, with whom Gamadge finds himself smitten (and who subsequently becomes his wife); on the Chandors, a.k.a. the Zanches, founders of New Soul ("All is illusion, and the veil is lifted"); and on the surviving two members of an old Dutch family, the Dykincks, who possess a similar set of Byron's poetry, Volume II of which is missing. Murder is done, and in order to unmask its perpetrator and get to the bottom of the eerie happenings at the old Vauregard mansion, Gamadge enlists the aid of, among others, William Shakespeare, John Webster, and Martin the cat.

Well written, if excessively talky, *Murders in Volume 2* is ingeniously plotted in a way that suggests Daly reciprocated Christie's admiration and sought to emulate her. Gamadge seems more human here than in some of his other appearances, probably because he's falling in love. A few of the other characters would benefit from a swift kick in the slats, a proposal that no doubt would have horrified Daly *and* Gamadge; but the fact is, rich folks in Thirties and Forties novels could be the damnedest snobs and boors.

Notable among Daly's other mysteries are *Nothing Can Rescue Me* (1943), in which Gamadge helps out an old friend's budding-novelist aunt whose manuscript seems to have been the target of a practical joker; *The Book of the Dead* (1944), in which some cryptic jottings in an old volume of Shakespeare provide the central clue to a murderer; and such other titles as *Somewhere in the House* (1946), *The Book of the Lion* (1948), and *Death and Letters* (1950).

(*B.P.*)

Daniels, Harold R. *House on Greenapple Road.* New York: Random House, 1966. (PP)

The "Red Kitchen Murder," as it came to be known in the press, began when Marian Ord's nine-year-old daughter returned home from school to find "brown stuff . . . like paint or when you spill iodine" all over the kitchen of their tract house on Greenapple Road in the small Massachusetts town of Holburn. Marian's sister-in-law, who lived next door, called the police. But there was no body in the house or anywhere else in the vicinity. What had happened in that kitchen? Where was Marian Ord, dead *or* alive?

Dan Nalon was in charge of the investigation. Along with his fellow officers, he began probing into Marian Ord's background—and found a maze of twisted relationships that proved she was anything but an average suburban housewife. Among her "friends" were a phony minister, head of the "Church of Redemption Through Love"; a cruel and selfish ski instructor; a decent young Italian biker; an equally decent young lifeguard at the local country club; a big-shot bookie known to have Cosa Nostra connections; and a succession of men she picked up in bars. She was also guilty, Nalon discovered, of passing bad checks, welshing on gambling debts, and stealing money from her tavern conquests.

When it became apparent that her husband, George, knew of Marian's sleazy "other life," and that his alibi for the time of the Red Kitchen incident was not what it first seemed, Nalon's attention focused on him. But had Ord really killed his wife in a fit of jealous rage? Just what *had* happened that tragic afternoon in the house on Greenapple Road?

This is a taut and baffling thriller, told in a semidocumentary, *ex-post-facto* style that makes excellent use of flashbacks. The characterization, especially of Marian Ord, is of the first rank; the writing is crisp (and there is plenty of sex to spice the narrative); and the revelations at the climax are surprising, yet fairly clued. The film version, made for TV in 1970 with Janet Leigh and Christopher George, is faithful to the novel and just as suspenseful as a result.

Daniels published several other novels of merit in the Fifties and Sixties, all of them paperback originals; the best are *The Accused* (1958), *The Snatch* (1958), and *For the Asking* (1962).

(*B.P.*)

*Davidson, Lionel. *The Rose of Tibet.* New York: Harper, 1962. (A)

Like Mark McShane (q.v.), Lionel Davidson is one of those talented writers who possess a knack for seldom if ever repeating themselves from book to book. His first novel, *The Night of Wenceslas* (1960), is a tale of espionage set in Czechoslovakia (which won a CWA Golden Dagger, the first of three garnered by Davidson); *The Menorah Men* (1966) is a thriller with political overtones that takes place in Jerusalem; *Murder Games* (1978) is a whodunit laid in London's bohemian art world; and *The Rose of Tibet* is a magnificent "quest" novel of suspense and high adventure reminiscent of the work of H. Rider Haggard.

Set in 1950–51, *The Rose of Tibet* covers the perilous seventeen-month odyssey of Charles Houston. It begins in England, where Houston learns that his brother and other members of a group sent to northern India to film mountain climbing have mysteriously disappeared. At the request of the film company, he travels to India to search for information about his brother, alive or dead. In Calcutta, where his quest is apparently at an end, he hears talk of a Tibetan monastery that might hold the key—but the Chinese Communists have only recently seized control of Tibet, and no foreigners are being allowed into the country. Houston is not to be thwarted; he travels to Kalimpong and soon hires a Sherpa guide named Ringling, who leads him through Sikkim and Nepal, across the mighty Himalayas, and into the fabled Tibetan capital of Lhasa. Danger after danger plagues them en route and after they arrive at the temple of the Monkey God. But Houston survives "to enjoy the love of a goddess and to live through adventures so bizarre that almost no other man—perhaps no other man at all—has equaled them."

This is superb entertainment, utterly mesmerizing from first page to last. It is difficult to imagine any novelist more vividly evoking the awesome splendor of the Himalayas or the exotic people and landscapes of Tibet. This is high adventure as only the British can write it, and not to be missed.

(*B.P.*)

Davis, Dorothy Salisbury. *A Death in the Life.* New York: Scribner's, 1976. (AD)

The novels of Dorothy Salisbury Davis show considerable depth of characterization, both of people and of the places in which they live. She chooses a milieu—in *A Death in the Life,* it is New York's theater district—and fleshes it out with representative characters. But while these characters are typical of the locale, they are by no means stock; each in turn is developed in his own idiosyncrasies, and the resulting mix of character and place is thoroughly believable, realistic, and original.

Julie Hayes, heroine of this excellent novel, is no stranger to the theater district. The wife of a well-known and much older journalist, she is a dabbler who has moved from one interest to another, the strongest of these being the stage. At the opening of the story, Julie is seeing a psychiatrist at her husband's urging while he is overseas on assignment. The idea of the therapy is to give Julie's life some focus; but in the opening scenes, Dr. Callahan terminates the sessions, saying Julie is not attempting to help herself. Hurt and once more directionless, Julie wanders into a fortune-teller's storefront, seizes upon the idea of becoming a seeress, and in short order has set up as a fortune-teller herself.

Soon "Friend Julie," as she dubs herself, becomes immersed in the life of the neighborhood residents: Pete Mallory, a stage designer she has previously known; Goldie, an intimidating pimp who resents Julie's presence on his turf; Rita Morgan, a young hooker who would like to get out of "the life" and go home; Rose Rodriguez, the housewife upstairs who turns tricks on the side; Philip Bourke, the electrical repairman who tries to hide the fact that he's gay; Mack, Goldie's rival pimp. Her sympathies are aroused by Rita Morgan and she involves the girl with her psychiatrist—much to Dr. Callahan's dismay—in an effort to get her off the streets. But before the doctor is able to help, Pete Mallory turns up murdered in Rita's apartment, and the hooker disappears. Julie is on hand to identify Pete's body, and from then on she works with the police—sometimes a step ahead, sometimes a step behind—to find out who murdered her friend and what happened to Rita. In the process of the investigation, Julie learns quite a few things about her own strengths—things that will perhaps cause her psychiatrist to lose a client in the near future.

Julie Hayes is an extremely likable character—unpretentious, caring, and vulnerable—and the area around Broadway and Forty-fourth Street comes alive through Davis's depiction of the very real human beings who inhabit it. A first-rate novel.

Davis has written two other novels featuring Julie Hayes: *Scarlet Night* (1980) and *Lullaby of Murder* (1984).

(*M.M.*)

Davis, Dorothy Salisbury. *The Little Brothers.* New York: Scribner's, 1973. (PP)

In *The Little Brothers,* Davis takes us into what she is fond of calling her "mean streets"—in this case, Manhattan's Little Italy. The Little Brothers are a secret society of teenage boys, but not a street gang in the usual sense. They have a rigid code "based on pride and purity," the purpose of which is "to protect their own." Members must go through an "Ordeal" upon joining, and when Angie Palermo is taken into the club, he is to put the "Killing Eye" on Mr. Grossman, who runs the religious-articles shop in the neighborhood. Angie—who joins the society reluctantly—watches Grossman and realizes he is probably a heroin dealer; and when someone stabs Grossman to death one night while Angie has neglected his vigil, he begins to wonder about the power of the Killing Eye.

The homicide lieutenant assigned to the case, David Marks, is no more a typical cop than the Little Brothers are a typical gang. Intelligent, sensitive, and patient, he realizes there is more to the killing than the usual drug hit. And when he and his partner, Tommy Tomasino, a native of Little Italy, drop in on a meeting of the Little Brothers, he senses their involvement. By striking up a rapport with Angie, he extracts certain facts about what happened in the neighborhood the night Grossman died. Marks's eventual solution to the case is both surprising and poignant.

Davis has once again created a vivid in-depth portrait of a part of New York that most of us would otherwise never come to know. Her characters are real and, for the most part, likable; even the villains are people we can feel for.

Davis, who has received four Edgar nominations for her novels, has written such other memorable books as *The Judas Cat* (1949), *The Pale Betrayer* (1965), and *God Speed the Night* (1968).

(*M.M.*)

*Davis, Dorothy Salisbury. *Tales for a Stormy Night.* Woodstock, Vt.: Countryman Press (Foul Play Press), 1984. (SS)

In this collection, which spans more than thirty years, Davis draws heavily upon her country childhood, as well as the city streets of her longer fiction. Her younger years on midwestern farms provide rich material, which Davis details in her informative introduction, also acknowledging the part that youthful crisis plays in shaping a writer's work: "The soul is marked with childhood's wounds, and I am grateful for mine. As a writer, I don't know what I'd have done without them."

Those wounds, perhaps, are why these stories show such depth; the characters and settings are fully developed, and the endings, while offering clever twists, are entirely plausible. "Backward, Turn Backward," for instance, is about the investigation of a murder; only two suspects exist, and the solution must come directly from the character of one or the other of them. In "Spring Fever," Davis gives us a haunting picture of a woman on the desperate brink of middle age and shows how such restlessness as hers can indeed become deadly. "Old Friends" reminds us how little we may know of those closest to us. While these three stories are set in the country, Davis has not deserted her "mean streets" in her short fiction. "Sweet William" takes a whimsical look at what can happen to foreigners caught up in the vicissitudes of Manhattan living. And while the heroine of "The Purple Is Everything" is described as living in a "large East Coast city," one is certain the peculiar events that happen to her could occur only in New York.

This is a well-balanced, entertaining, and sometimes chilling collection that shows the best of Davis's work over her long and distinguished career. Three of the stories included here were nominated for Edgars: "Backward, Turn Backward," "Old Friends," and "The Purple Is Everything."

(*M.M.*)

Davis, Frederick C. *Deep Lay the Dead.* New York: Doubleday Crime Club, 1942. (T)

An extremely prolific contributor to the pulp magazines, where he published at least 1000 stories (among them dozens of the Operator #5 "hero pulp" adventures), Frederick C. Davis began publishing mystery novels in 1937. He produced close to forty books over the next four decades—sixteen under his own name, one as by Murdo Coombs (*A Moment of Need,* 1947), and the balance under the pseudonym Stephen Ransome (q.v.). His fiction was among the most literate and entertaining of its day (if sometimes a little too casually paced), and stands up well to the test of time.

Deep Lay the Dead is arguably his best novel. Ex–Dartmouth mathematics professor, cipher addict, and mountain climber Rigby Webb comes to an isolated corner of eastern Pennsylvania to confront a retired doctor named Chandler, whom he suspects of pulling strings to first get him fired from Dartmouth and to then keep him out of the army. His suspicions are accurate, but Chandler's reasons are noble: He is working for the State Department and General Staff, attempting to design an "indecipherable cipher" so as to win supremacy over the Axis in signal communications. Getting Rig fired was the first of several tests of Chandler's loyalty, all of which he has passed in admirable fashion. Rig agrees to work on the cipher project with the doctor, but they don't get very far with their collaborative efforts: One of the guests invited to Chandler's country estate by his wife, Claire, is an enemy agent. Murder strikes, a howling blizzard renders the house party snowbound, and tensions escalate to a fever pitch as more violence erupts. Rig eventually unmasks the traitor and saves the day, and in so doing gets to use his mountain-climbing skills (but not in the way you might think).

This is a tightly plotted, suspenseful novel built around a classic mystery situation. There is also some intriguing background information on codes and ciphers. (Another of Davis's strong suits was his ability to weave information on unusual and/or esoteric topics into his narratives.) Davis did have a tendency to truncate his action scenes, and the climax, while exciting, is much too abrupt; but the book's strengths more than make up for this and a few other minor weaknesses.

Davis created numerous series characters, for both his pulp stories and his novels. Professor Cyrus Hatch uses scientific methods and ratiocination to solve baffling crimes in several early novels, among them *Coffins for Three* (1938), *Let the Skeletons Rattle* (1944), and *Thursday's Blade* (1947). And the semihard-boiled detective team of Schyler Cole and Luke Speare, who operate out of New York, is featured in such titles as *The Deadly Miss Ashley* (1950) and *Drag the Dark* (1953). *Deep Lay the Dead* is the only nonseries novel to appear under Davis's own name; several others were published as by Stephen Ransome. Ten of his Operator #5 pulp novels were reprinted in the Sixties and Seventies under the house pen name of Curtis Steele; these carry such titles as *The Invisible Empire* and *Blood Reign of the Dictator* and provide plenty of campy fun.

(*B.P.*)

Davis, Kenn. *Words Can Kill.* New York: Fawcett Gold Medal, 1984. (O/PI)

Black San Francisco private eye Carver Bascombe just can't seem to decide what he wants to be when he grows up. On the one hand, he's merely doing detective work for the money, to get through law school and "be able to help others." On the other hand, he enjoys "the hunt." It's "something he can sink his teeth into," a deeply ingrained part of him since he was a kid in the ghetto of Detroit. So Carver carries on as a private eye, worrying about his overdue tuition and term papers—even worrying about completing his income-tax forms, for heaven's sake. And because he's a part-timer, a man sitting on the fence, he's not all that effective at his work.

In this case, Carver receives a visit from old Vietnam buddy Jackson Fayette. Fayette is now the author of the "definitive" Vietnam novel, a celebrity very much in the public eye. Fayette's mentor, Ed Colfax, was shot to death in nearby Sausalito the previous night; he wants Carver to find out why. Carver plunges into the world of Marin County writers and rare-book collecting (the latter described with dubious accuracy: One would never, for instance, display copies of rare books in a store window, where their dust jackets would fade). On the dead man's houseboat, he discovers a manuscript that indicates Colfax may have coauthored Fayette's book but received no credit for his part. Carver meets other writers, friends of Colfax's. He goes to a party, gets drunk, blurts out too much information about what he is investigating, and then almost loses his life in a fire on Colfax's houseboat. And he continues on his way, always worrying: When will he complete his overdue term paper? Does he even want to? What about his taxes? What's going *on* anyway?

Well, what's going on becomes pretty obvious to the reader, long before it becomes obvious to Carver. Still and all, there's something appealing about Carver Bascombe—something that makes this reviewer want to read more of these novels and perhaps find out the answer to that all-important question: What *will* Carver decide to be when he grows up?

Among Davis's other Carver Bascombe novels are *The Dark Side* (1976, in collaboration with John Stanley) and *The Forza Trap* (1979).

(*M.M.*)

*Davis, Norbert. *The Mouse in the Mountain.* New York: Morrow, 1943. (PI/C)

Norbert Davis was among the most talented of all the writers who specialized in pulp fiction in the Thirties and early Forties. Although he was primarily a magazine writer (he graduated from the pulps to such slicks as *The Saturday Evening Post* in 1943), he published three mystery novels featuring the detective "team" of Doan and Carstairs. Each of these is fast-paced, occasionally lyrical in a hard-edged way, and often quite funny. Davis, in fact, was one of the few writers to successfully blend the so-called hard-boiled story with farcical humor.

The Mouse in the Mountain is the first of the adventures through which Doan and Carstairs prowl and howl. (Doan is a private eye who looks fat but isn't, and who, despite a great fondness for booze, has never suffered a hangover; Carstairs is an aloof, fawn-colored Great Dane whom Doan won in a crap game and who considers Doan a low, uncouth person, not at all the sort *he* would have chosen for a master.) The scene is Mexico, where Doan has come to persuade a fugitive crook *not* to return to the United States and give himself up. At least, that is what he tells the heroine of the piece, Janet Martin, a shy (at least in the beginning) schoolteacher in the Wisteria Young Ladies' Seminary; Doan, like Sam Spade, isn't really as corrupt as he sometimes pretends.

Things begin to happen at a fast and furious pace even before Doan and Carstairs arrive in the picturesque little village of Los Altos: A famous Mexican bandit named Garcia is on the loose and causing a great deal of consternation among the local authorities. But what happens later causes considerably more consternation: the town's first earthquake in 150 years, which results in widespread destruction and chaos, and precipitates three cold-blooded murders. Doan solves the murders, of course, and restores peace and harmony to Los Altos—with not a little help from Carstairs and Janet Martin (who has also been kept busy falling in and out of love with a handsome but exasperating Mexican Army officer, Captain Emile Perona). Great fun from first page to last.

The other two Doan and Carstairs romps are *Sally's in the Alley* (1943), which has broader farcical elements and deals with Japanese spies, desert rats, and a film star named Susan Sally; and *Oh, Murderer Mine* (1946), which has a college setting and a scene in which Carstairs wreaks havoc in Heloise of Hollywood's beauty salon that will have you laughing out loud.

(*B.P.*)

Davis, Tech. *Full Fare for a Corpse.* New York: Doubleday Crime Club, 1937. (W)

The central premise of *Full Fare for a Corpse* is irresistible: Four days after Christmas, a transcontinental Union Pacific passenger train runs into a blizzard on the Wyoming Great Divide and comes up snowbound at a whistle-stop station in the middle of nowhere. Snowbound with it is a freight full of supplies, and nearby is a sheep ranch, so the 130 passengers and crew on board the ten-car train don't need to worry about provisions. What they do need to worry about is that one of their number is a murderer. (If this premise sounds familiar, it may be because you—and Tech Davis—happened to read Agatha Christie's [q.v.] *Murder on the Orient Express,* which is about murder on a snowbound train in Yugoslavia and was published three years earlier than *Full Fare for a Corpse.*)

Victim number one is an unidentified stranger who isn't even on the passenger list, but is found in his robe and slippers in one of the compartments, shot to death under very unusual circumstances. Victim number two turns up not quite dead in the baggage car, laid out next to the remains of number one. There is also a victim number three. The task of unraveling all these events falls to suave, "semiprofessional" New York sleuth Aubrey Nash, with the help of an ex–Wyoming sheriff named Sargent. And unravel them they do, but not before the murderer strikes again at an impromptu New Year's Eve celebration put on by the passengers to "ease the tension."

The handling of all this isn't bad, although the novel does have its drawbacks: Davis's prose is somewhat overblown, full of words like *parturition* and *expatiated;* Nash owes his origins (and methods) not to Hercule Poirot but to Philo Vance, though without Vance's more obnoxious qualities; and more could have been done with the howling blizzard outside the train. On the plus side, the plot is tricky enough to keep one reading and guessing, and Nash's piecing together of the puzzle is logical and well clued. There are also some good characters, some witty dialogue, and more action than you might expect in this type of whodunit. The whole thing is reminiscent of the better of those delightfully campy B-movie melodramas of the same period. A good evening's entertainment.

Davis published two other novels featuring the exploits of Aubrey Nash: *Terror at Compass Lake* (1935), which has an upstate New York setting; and *Murder on Alternate Tuesdays* (1938), set in New York City.

(*B.P.*)

Deal, Babs H. *The Walls Came Tumbling Down.* New York: Doubleday, 1968. (T)

An old sorority house is being demolished; a long-sealed air shaft is opened, and the skeleton of a baby is found inside. This event and the subsequent effect it has on the lives of seven women still living in the town where they attended college is the subject of Babs Deal's best-selling suspense novel. The author is a master at characterization, as shown by her handling not only of the women but of the men they have married and the townspeople who are rocked by the discovery. As events unfold, the present activities of the characters are skillfully interwoven with key scenes from the past. The revelation of the identity of the woman who secreted her stillborn—and illegitimate—child in the air shaft is no great surprise; it is the way the characters respond to the pressure of impending scandal that really concerns us. Mrs. Deal has a fine sense of small-town society—and what a single, shattering event can do to its fragile, interlocking structure.

The Walls Came Tumbling Down was made into an excellent movie for TV, *Friendships, Secrets, and Lies,* in 1979. This is, incidentally, a novel whose book-club edition shows up with astonishing frequency in thrift shops, garage sales, and used-book stores—attesting to its immense popularity.

Other Deal suspense titles are *Fancy's Knell* (1967), *The Crystal Mouse* (1973), and *Waiting to Hear from William* (1975). In addition, she has written such exceptional mainstream novels as *High Lonesome World* (1969).

(*M.M.*)

DeAndrea, William L. *Killed on the Ice.* New York: Doubleday Crime Club, 1984. (AD)

William L. DeAndrea's career started off with a bang when his first book, *Killed in the Ratings,* introducing sleuth Matt Cobb, won an MWA Edgar for Best First Novel of 1978. The very next year, his second book, *The Hog Murders,* won the Edgar for Best Paperback. Since then, his career has continued to blossom, with a couple of historical mysteries, a thriller, and three more Matt Cobb books. Matt is an engaging chap who works as a troubleshooter for a TV network; he's gentle with women (who don't always return the courtesy) and a good friend to his constant companion, Spot, the attack-trained Samoyed. If DeAndrea's fans are fond of Matt, they positively adore Spot, the most appealing little scene-stealer since Asta.

In *Killed on the Ice,* Dr. Paul Dinkover, "perhaps the most renowned American psychiatrist alive," is found sprawled on the ice of a Manhattan skating rink, his stomach thoroughly ventilated with a hunting knife. The ice rink is the one where Matt's network is filming a special on Olympic skater Wendy Ichimi. Wendy has a motive, and also a good start on capturing Matt's ever-vulnerable heart. When she begins to look like a potential victim herself, he has more than a professional interest in finding the murderer. Along the way, he encounters (as usual) Detective Lieutenant Cornelius Martin, Jr., the black cop from Matt's old neighborhood, and an intriguing new character—the Frying Nun, an assistant D.A. who left the convent for law school. Also offering a good dying message, interesting murder method, and a clever ruse during the climactic fight, *Killed on the Ice* is up to DeAndrea's usual high standard.

Matt Cobb's other amateur investigations include *Killed in the Act* (1981) and *Killed with a Passion* (1983).

(*J.S.*)

DeAndrea, William L. *The Hog Murders.* New York: Avon, 1979. (O/AD)

DeAndrea's second Edgar-winner is a wonderfully old-fashioned puzzle mystery complete with serial killer and a master detective reminiscent of Nero Wolfe or even the great Holmes himself. The eccentric but brilliant Professor Niccolo Benedetti is assisted by his pupil, Ron Gentry, a young private eye based in snowy Sparta, New York. Sparta is being terrorized by a homicidal maniac who, in the tradition of serial killers, writes notes to a local journalist, in this case likable Buell Tatham. He signs himself "Hog," and the cover of this paperback is a particularly arresting one, showing a stocky man's upper body topped by the monstrous head of a pig. Hog's methods are as clever as they're diabolical; his victims are random and almost invariably innocent—even a child is killed. But Benedetti, of course, is a little too quick for him.

The solution is truly unexpected, yet really as obvious as who killed Roger Ackroyd; in other words, the reader is fooled but could kick himself for it. Bonuses are the trademark DeAndrea wit and the withholding of the complete solution until the very last sentence.

In addition to his mysteries, DeAndrea has published a number of nonseries suspense novels, including *The Lunatic Fringe* (1980), which is set in New York City during the Gay Nineties; and *Cronus* (1984), a thriller about an apparent terrorist killing in the sleepy town of Draper, Pennsylvania. DeAndrea has also published one novel to date under the pseudonym Philip Degrave, *Unholy Moses* (1985).

(*J.S.*)

deFord, Miriam Allen. *The Theme Is Murder.* New York: Abelard Schuman, 1967. (SS)

Miriam Allen deFord is best known for her scholarly works on a variety of historical subjects, and for her true-crime studies—the full-length books, *The Overbury Affair* (for which she was awarded an MWA Edgar in 1961) and *Ma Barker* (1970), and the collection of short pieces, *Murderers Sane and Mad* (1965). But she was also an accomplished writer of short stories, both mysteries and science fiction (and in some cases a combination of the two); beginning in 1944, she published an aggregate of more than 100 until her death in 1975 at the age of eighty-seven.

The Theme Is Murder is her only criminous collection, and a first-rate gathering it is. There are seventeen stories here, most of which first appeared in *Ellery Queen's Mystery Magazine;* others were originally published in such diverse publications as *Shadow Mystery Magazine,* the Sixties men's periodical *Dude,* and *Windsor Quarterly.* Most are of the quiet variety, with emphasis on character and unusual backgrounds (an actual homicide case preserved on a cuneiform tablet from 1850 B.C., for instance, in "The Judgment of En-lil"; or Ancient Rome in "De Crimine"). One of her favorite themes is familial strife that builds into violence, as in such stories as "Beyond the Sea of Death," "The Oleander," and "A Death in the Family."

Each of these seventeen tales is finely crafted and thought-provoking—a single-volume legacy from a gifted spinner of mysterious webs. Recommended.

(*B.P.*)

Deighton, Len. *The Billion Dollar Brain.* New York: Putnam's, 1966. (E/T)

Len Deighton's first novel, *The Ipcress File* (1962; later filmed with Michael Caine), marked the debut of one of the major stars of espionage fiction. Since then this former photographer, illustrator, teacher, and occasional cookbook author has written a string of stylish and tightly plotted espionage novels that are thoughtful commentaries and reasoned examinations of society as well as first-rate thrillers.

One of Deighton's chief concerns is the morality of the world of espionage, but his treatment of this theme is never ponderous or heavy-handed. Instead he chooses to examine the ethics of the characters about whom he writes with an ironic wit; his prose has a lightness that further leavens this rather weighty subject. The books are also full of vivid description—of places, people, meals, natural wonders—that give the stories an air of authority; his use of documents and appendixes further convinces the reader that the espionage world is really as described. Along with John Le Carré (q.v.), Deighton is one of our foremost contemporary writers of espionage novels.

The billion-dollar brain of this novel's title is a remarkable computer owned by a Texas mogul who has assembled his own private espionage network. This wild-card covert agency poses a grave threat to just about every government on earth, and what makes it tick is the incredibly complex computer, the quintessential technical-wonder successor to man's own reason and self-asserted destiny.

Deighton's insubordinate, deceptively tough, unnamed first-person spy is given the task of neutralizing this menace, and along the way meets some fascinating characters. There is sensuous, champagne-swilling Signe Laine, a Finnish beauty who favors expensive underwear and has a knack and passion for besting males; Dawlish, the fumbling Intelligence chief who runs the show; Colonel Stok, of Red Army Intelligence; Harvey Newbegin, the neurotic American agent who is in on the chase; and the maniacal General Midwinter. The action is on an international scale, swinging from Helsinki to London, Texas, Leningrad, and New York.

This is a tightly constructed, imaginative, high-tech sort of thriller. Space Age espionage, in which Colonel Stok makes the disturbingly relevant observation "Two not very clever men will have to decide whether to extend a hand or pull a trigger."

(*J.L.*)

*Deighton, Len. *Yesterday's Spy*. New York: Harcourt Brace, 1975. (E/T)

In this novel Steve Champion, veteran of World War II espionage, symbol of the old school of "swashbuckler" agents, is matched against "the computers and the gray-faced men in Washington and London." He is a romantic figure still, if a bit long in the tooth and scarred from past battles. Champion knows what he is and prefers being it to knuckling under to the new bureaucracy. He turns maverick and poses a danger to the new order. And the new order is disturbed to discover itself incapable of coping with him. So who better to bring him to ground than another veteran of the risky and adventurous days of wartime covert action? A man who has been tamed if not totally absorbed by the new bland order, a man who can play Champion's game.

Such a man is Deighton's character Charlie, who tracks Champion to Nice, their wartime stamping grounds, where Champion is still playing at espionage his way and winning. Figures from the wartime past are still there: Serge Frankel, a Communist stamp dealer; a princess who ran a waterfront brothel; Charlie's first love, Pina. In Nice, in the 1970s, the past and future intersect for these people. The result is top-drawer entertainment.

Among Deighton's other espionage novels, all of these likewise excellent, are *Funeral in Berlin* (1965), *Spy Story* (1974), *Catch a Falling Spy* (1976), *SS-GB* (1978), and *XPD* (1981).

(*J.L.*)

de la Torre, Lillian. *The Detections of Dr. Sam: Johnson*. New York: Doubleday Crime Club, 1960. (H/SS)

At first glance, the great eighteenth-century English lexicographer Dr. Samuel Johnson seems an unlikely detective. On closer consideration, however, the idea of the man who, after years of sleuthing, published the first English dictionary (1755), and who had the original Boswell close at hand to chronicle his literary detections and adventures, seems just right. The combination of the grumpy sage Johnson and his Scottish biographer, James Boswell of Auchinleck, forms the model for the classic detective-story Holmes-Watson relationship.

The eight stories in this book are pastiches, written in Boswell's style with the fancy of the author woven into the fabric of history. The detections take place around the 1770s, mostly in London ("When a man is tired of London, he is tired of life."—S.J.), and in Bath and Stratford-on-Avon. Johnson, or "Cham," as he is sometimes called, investigates crime and chicanery, fraud and felony. His unique position enables him to mix with all classes of society and get involved in various events—from the soldiers' court-martial on the greensward of Hyde Park, to the robbery of Gothic enthusiast Horace Walpole, to the espionage exploits of the female American patriot against Gentleman Johnny Burgoyne. In "The Tontine Curse," he hears of dying children and blesses a Roman parent. The "harmless drudge" probes the pitfalls of antiquarianism and exposes forgery in "The Missing Shakespeare Manuscript." "The Triple-Lock'd Room" is a case of murder and theft at Boswell's lodgings with its weird inhabitants.

The Dr. Sam tales are scholarly and quaint and quite the best of their kind. An earlier collection is *Dr. Sam: Johnson, Detector* (1946), and there are more to come. Most of the stories originally appeared in *Ellery Queen's Mystery Magazine.*

(*T.B.*)

Delman, David. *He Who Digs a Grave.* New York: Doubleday Crime Club, 1973. (PP)

The combination of protagonists David Delman has used in this engaging novel—that of a small-town female sheriff and a male cop from New York—is an inspired one. Sheriff Helen Bly and Lieutenant Jacob Horowitz are as different on the surface as two people can be. She's a country woman with strong roots in the area around Cedarstown, an elected official who's never had to handle a murder before. He's a tough city cop who's seen more than enough violent death. And they hold opposing views about whether Horowitz's old army acquaintance Ian Kirk (who has asked Horowitz to come to town and investigate in an unofficial capacity) murdered his wife and her lover. But Bly and Horowitz are both strong, fair, and sensitive people—characteristics that allow them to work together and also allow them to fall in love.

As Bly and Horowitz piece together such facts as a missing suicide note, an unwanted pregnancy, a vanished housekeeper, and a pair of thugs who have been paid to intimidate the outsider from New York, the author skillfully depicts small-town life through his characterization of the other residents. A well-plotted novel with a realistic and satisfying conclusion.

Delman's other mysteries—*A Week to Kill* (1972), *Sudden Death* (1972), *One Man's Murder* (1975), and *The Nice Murderers* (1977)—feature Jacob Horowitz. His most recent book, *Murder in the Family,* appeared in 1985.

(*M.M.*)

*Delving, Michael. *The Devil Finds Work.* New York: Scribner's, 1969. (AD/PP)

Of the six bibliomysteries Michael Delving (Jay Williams) wrote about the adventures, in England, of the two American partners of a Connecticut-based rare-book and manuscript firm, *The Devil Finds Work* is the only one featuring both Dave Cannon and Bob Eddison. In the small town of Bartonbury, the two dealers are offered a collection of material belonging to Tristram Vail, a notorious Satanist who was once called "the wickedest man in the world." They also find themselves caught up in the investigation of the theft of a silver cup from a desecrated church. When Vail's secretary, Richard Foss, is found dead during another attempt to rob the church, Chief Inspector Codd—whom Delving introduced in the first Cannon/Eddison adventure, *Smiling the Boy Fell Dead* (1966)—is called in from Scotland Yard to investigate.

The odd activities of Vail's ambiguous friend Anthony Gaunt play a role in the mystery. As does Bob (who is a full-blooded Cherokee from Oklahoma) being challenged by the local pub's darts champion to a match in which Bob will use a bow and arrow and lined target and the other player will use a regulation dart board with appropriate adjustments made for distance. Another plot thread is Bob's romantic interest in Jill Roseblade, the niece of an eccentric woman named Miss Trout, who owns a valuable *Book of Hours* coveted by the two partners. It is Codd, with help from Dave and Bob, who finally sorts out the disparate elements and solves the mystery.

Each of the characters in *The Devil Finds Work* is fully developed (Bob is especially well drawn), and the narrative is packed with vivid descriptions of village life, the English countryside and architecture, and various works of art. Delving was also a master at conveying the differences and similarities between the English and American ways of life. (Anthony Boucher said of him: "I can't think of anyone since John Dickson Carr who has better handled England-from-an-American-viewpoint.") And his knowledge of rare books and art is that of both an expert and connoisseur.

The other five books in the series are equally fine, in particular *Die Like a Man* (1970), in which Dave, traveling in Wales, is offered an ancient wooden bowl its owner claims is the Holy Grail; and *A Shadow of Himself* (1972), which is concerned with a seventeenth-century Dutch painting and in which Delving divulges the outcome of the romance between Bob and Jill. Because of such personal elements that carry over from book to book, a sequential reading of the series is recommended.

(*E.N./B.P.*)

Deming, Richard. *Anything but Saintly.* New York: Permabooks, 1963. (O/PP)

Richard Deming wrote original mysteries and novelizations of numerous TV series, including two books based on "Dragnet." The two "Dragnet" books appeared in 1958 and 1959 and perhaps led to Deming's writing his own police-procedural series in the early 1960s. Although the series was only two books, it was competently written and entertaining. The setting of both books is the riverside city of St. Cecelia, and the first-person narrator is Sergeant Matt Rudd (real name Mateusz Rudowski), a member of the city's Vice Squad.

In *Anything but Saintly,* a businessman visiting the city is rolled by a prostitute and robbed of $500. Rudd and his partner, Carl Lincoln, set out to recover the money, only to find that the girl was murdered shortly after returning to her apartment. Being a member of the Vice Squad does not keep Rudd from getting involved in the killing, because an attempt is soon made on his own life. What looked at first like a simple case suddenly escalates into something more, with a heavily protected procurer and a big-time politico getting dragged in. The procedural details, including the peculiar workings of the St. Cecelia Police Department, are well done, and the story is terse and fast, with a good depiction of a racket-ridden city and how it is run.

Matt Rudd appears again in *Death of a Pusher* (1964). An equally good, but very different, paperback original by Deming is *Edge of the Law* (1960). He also created a one-armed private detective, Manville Moon, who appears in three novels published in the early 1950s, beginning with *The Gallows in My Garden* (1952). Other of his mysteries appeared under the pseudonym Max Franklin, notably *Justice Has No Sword* (1953).

(*B.C.*)

Dennis, Ralph. *Atlanta Deathwatch.* New York: Popular Library, 1974. (O/PI)

In 1974, Popular Library introduced a new series called "Hardman," by Ralph Dennis, by releasing the first two books in the series simultaneously. These were followed by five more that year, and another five in 1976. The series stands at twelve, and that's a shame, because although Hardman was marketed as just another men's adventure series, it was much more than that. It was a breath of fresh air in an otherwise stale subgenre that was filled with Executioner rip-offs.

Jim Hardman is a disgraced ex-cop working out of Atlanta as an unlicensed PI with an ex–football player sidekick, Hump Evans. They walk a tight legal line and will do just about anything for money that doesn't offend Hardman's morals—which are high for the kind of life he leads. In this book they are hired by a black mobster called "The Man" to find out who killed a girl he was in love with, but the plots of these novels are secondary to the actions and interactions of the main characters and the crisp writing. At its worst, Dennis's writing is well above that of the run-of-the-mill men's adventure series; and at its best, it is a fine example of PI writing that depends little on the conventions of the genre.

Other novels in the series particularly recommended are *Working for the Man* (1974), *The One Dollar Rip-Off* (1976), and *The Buy-Back Blues* (1976).

(*R.J.R.*)

Dennis, Robert C. *Conversations with a Corpse.* Indianapolis: Bobbs-Merrill, 1974. (AD/PS)

Robert C. Dennis wrote hundreds of short stories for the pulps in the 1940s and hundreds of teleplays for such popular TV series as "Dragnet," "Cannon," and "Perry Mason" from the 1950s to the early 1980s. But his output of novels, regrettably, was limited to just two—both published in the early Seventies; both narrated by architect Paul Reeder, "a psychic, a man with a freak brain capable of recovering mind pictures of past events"; and both literate and expertly constructed whodunits that even ESP skeptics can enjoy.

On a business trip to the small California wine-country town of Orofino, the "Wine Capital of the West," Reeder rents a car at the local airport and, as soon as he touches the steering wheel, has a psychometric vision telling him the man who last drove the car is now dead. Directed by his "inner mind," he embarks on a search that leads him into conflict with Sergeant Dryden of the Orofino police and with members of the Chicano community; into an abandoned winery filled with bloated rats and an equally bloated corpse; and finally to a confrontation with a homicidal madman at the Mission Santa Teresa Dolorosa. *Library Journal* called the novel "a suspenseful and menacing puzzle"; the Los Angeles *Times* praised it as "tough and furiously fast-paced . . . [with] bone-chilling situations." Both assessments are on target. The scene in which Reeder is trapped in the bankrupt winery is a minor masterpiece of its kind, guaranteed to give the most jaded reader a case of the shudders.

The first Reeder novel, *The Sweat of Fear* (1973), is also a fine piece of criminous storytelling and highly recommended.

(*B.P.*)

Dent, Lester. *Dead at the Take-Off.* New York: Doubleday Crime Club, 1946. (T)

Lester Dent is best known as the creator of Doc Savage, the Man of Bronze, who ranks with the Shadow as the most popular cult hero to come out of the pulp magazines of the 1930s. As "Kenneth Robeson," Dent wrote close to 200 full-length Doc Savage novels for Doc's own monthly magazine from 1933 to 1949. Dozens of these have been reprinted in paperback since 1964, under their original titles—*Brand of the Werewolf, The Squeaking Goblins, The Living Fire Menace,* etc. Despite hokey plots, stereotypical villains, and hurried writing, they contain some ingenious ideas and extrapolations. Dent was much more than a pulp hack; he had genuine talent and a convincing prose style that, when he took the time to polish it, matches up well with the best crime writers past and present.

Dent's best work is a pair of novelettes featuring detective Oscar Sail, which he wrote for *Black Mask* in the mid-Thirties, and *Dead at the Take-Off,* his first novel to appear under his own name. *Take-Off* is an evocative work, with postwar commercial aviation as its background. The protagonist is Chance Molloy, the owner of a small airline, AEA, who is facing financial ruin because a conspiracy headed by corrupt Senator Lord has prevented him from buying surplus military transport planes. Molloy, with the aid of two of his staff, has been trying to obtain proof of the senator's duplicity, and now believes he has found it: Lord's nephew has agreed to turn over damning evidence against his uncle at the senator's New Mexico ranch. Along with several other principal characters, including the senator's daughter, Janet, Molloy boards Flight 14 for New Mexico. En route, there is considerable intrigue, capped off when the nephew turns up dead and Janet is drugged. Later, in New Mexico, an attempt is made on Molloy's life, and the suspense continues to heighten. The violent climax takes place back on board the airliner.

There is plenty of action, but *Dead at the Take-Off* has much more than that to recommend it. The characterization is sharp, with strong psychological overtones; effective use of flashback is made; and the writing is among Dent's best. The book is jam-packed with such imagery as:

> *A double page of newspaper, snatched by the wind from the street and carried upward, went whirling past the open window, giving a flash of grayish white like a soiled ghost.*

> *The ground haze had a faint gun-metal bluish cast, not entirely transparent, but semi-transparent, like tobacco smoke after it has been blown into a bottle.*

The book has its flaws—Dent was never able to totally overcome his pulp origins and there is a good deal of melodrama here—but it is still a very good example of the mid-Forties hard-boiled crime novel. Dent's other books are somewhat less successful, although *Lady to Kill* (1946), which also features Chance Molloy, and the paperback original *Cry at Dusk* (1952) have many of the same positive qualities as *Dead at the Take-Off.*

(*B.P.*)

Dentinger, Jane. *First Hit of the Season.* New York: Doubleday Crime Club, 1984. (AD)

Critic Jason Saylin used his typewriter like a machete, hacking bits and pieces off the reputation of his least favorite actress almost daily. The lady in question, Irene Ingersoll, hated him so much she once dumped a plate of fettucini on him in a restaurant. Which was absolutely no reason to suspect her of doing him in—even though she had excellent opportunity and ample motive. Or such is the theory of Ingersoll's pal, actress and amateur sleuth Jocelyn O'Roarke. O'Roarke happens to be the girlfriend of Phillip Gerrard, the detective assigned to the case, who wants her, of course, to mind her own business. And that, luckily for Dentinger's readers, is about as likely as Sarah Bernhardt's return to the stage.

Dentinger introduced the likable O'Roarke in her first book, the very well-reviewed *Murder on Cue,* published in 1983. She's plucky, smart, and deliciously caustic: "The muscles in Maxine's face twitched as much as two face jobs would let them." Dentinger, an actress herself, writes with an insider's knowledge of Manhattan's theatrical subculture and with a literacy obviously achieved by voracious reading of books as well as plays. Fans of witty, witchy dialogue will find themselves laughing out loud.

(*J.S.*)

Derby, Mark. *Ghost Blonde.* New York: Viking, 1960. (A)

Ghost Blonde is a fine action/suspense novel. Certainly all the elements are there: an exotic location; murders and threats of more murder; blackmail, smuggling, romance, plenty of action; and as if that were not enough, the fate of an orphanage hanging in the balance.

When it is learned that the protagonist, Nicko Strang, is on his way to Singapore, he is given a letter of introduction to a woman named Lark Hamilton, only to arrive and find the same Lark Hamilton has been killed in a fire. Strang, dissatisfied with the explanations, becomes obsessed with obtaining more information about the fire and the death. It is this obsession that leads him deeper and deeper into a dangerous mystery that soon threatens his own life.

We discover an unexpected prudishness in Strang (when, for example, a woman he met aboard ship offers to move in with him). But other then that—much to Derby's credit—the story easily could pass for a current suspense novel. Strang tends to deliver rather lengthy and tedious monologues when encountering villains (this occurs three times), but *Ghost Blonde* is a book well worth the read, filled with action, intrigue, and at least one major surprise.

Mark Derby is a pseudonym of Harry Wilcox. Other of his novels, most of which take place in Singapore, Malaysia, and other exotic Far East locales, are *The Big Water* (1953), *The Sunlit Ambush* (1955), and *Sun in the Hunter's Eyes* (1958).

(*N.D.*)

Derleth, August. *"In Re: Sherlock Holmes": The Adventures of Solar Pons.* Sauk City, Wis.: Mycroft & Moran, 1945. (SS/W)

August Derleth was a literary phenomenon. In a writing career that lasted from his teens until his death at the age of sixty-two, he worked in a wide variety of genres and styles. Among his more than 150 books are contemporary novels, historical novels (both for adults and for young readers), regional history, biographies, mystery fiction, true-crime essays, pastiches, weird and supernatural fiction, children's books, personal journals, compilations of nature observations, and poetry. He edited numerous volumes of short stories and poetry, and he founded and operated Arkham House, a publishing company originally devoted to preserving the work of H. P. Lovecraft in book form; Arkham later published the first books of such writers as Ray Bradbury, Robert Bloch (q.v.), Fritz Leiber, and A. E. Van Vogt.

By his late teens, Derleth had read and reread all of the Sherlock Holmes stories, and wrote to Sir Arthur Conan Doyle (q.v.) to ask if there would ever be any more of them. Doyle's noncommittal reply spurred the nineteen-year-old Derleth to fill the gap himself. The result was "The Adventure of the Black Narcissus," the first of some seventy stories about Solar Pons of 7B Praed Street and his literary chronicler, Dr. Lyndon Parker. *"In Re: Sherlock Holmes"* gathers twelve of these stories in book form. In addition to "The Black Narcissus," the book includes "The Adventures of the Norcross Riddle," "The Retired Novelist," "The Three Red Dwarfs," "The Purloined Periapt," "The Man with the Broken Face," and others. As Vincent Starrett (q.v.) wrote in his introduction to the book, Pons "is not a caricature of Sherlock Holmes. He is, rather, a clever impersonator, with a twinkle in his eye, [who] hopes we will like him anyway for what he symbolizes." Ellery Queen's jacket blurb asked, "How many budding authors, not yet old enough to vote, could have captured the spirit and atmosphere of the Sacred Writings with so much fidelity?"

The Pons stories eventually filled seven volumes (including one novel), with an additional volume of miscellaneous commentary. The entire series was edited and revised by Basil Copper and issued as a 1306-page, two-volume set, *The Solar Pons Omnibus,* in 1982. Some diehard fans of the Pontine canon have expressed a preference for the original versions over the altered texts in the omnibus, but for the average reader the differences are hardly significant.

(*R.E.B.*)

Derleth, August. *Sentence Deferred.* New York: Scribner's, 1939. (AD)

The Sauk City–Prairie du Sac region of Wisconsin, where Derleth was born and where he lived for most of his life, was transformed into the fictional Sac Prairie and used as the background for his most ambitious literary creation. The Sac Prairie Saga was a multivolume project intended to portray life in this region from the early nineteenth century up to the present day. Derleth also used Sac Prairie as the setting for a series of ten detective novels featuring Judge Ephraim Peabody Peck.

Sentence Deferred begins as the Savings and Loan Bank in Sac Prairie closes its doors without warning. The banker, Henry Hornly, refuses telephone calls and other communication. That same night, his house is burned to the ground, and a charred and bullet-pierced body is subsequently found in the ashes. Two local men, Peter Beckit and Richard Alford, are arrested. Each had threatened to kill Hornly, and there is damning circumstantial evidence against both of them. Beckit is tried and acquitted on a technicality, whereupon Alford is tried and found guilty. At this point Judge Peck, doubting the guilt of both men, steps in. After some investigation, a brief chase and gun battle, and some interesting legal maneuvering, the truth is finally revealed.

By Derleth's own testimony, the Judge Peck novels were written in ten days each. The haste shows in some internal inconsistencies and a certain lack of polish. Most of the books use standard mystery-fiction ingredients, but there are occasional fresh and clever touches. The books also present an appealing portrait of life in a small midwestern town, and this may be their lasting virtue.

Other titles in the series include *Murder Stalks the Wakely Family* (1934), *Three Who Died* (1935), *The Narracong Riddle* (1940), *No Future for Luana* (1945), and *Fell Purpose* (1953).

(*R.E.B.*)

*Dewey, Thomas B. *Deadline.* New York: Simon & Schuster, 1966. (PI)

Thomas B. Dewey is one of detective fiction's severely underrated writers—a craftsman of no small talent whose work is among the most human and compassionate of any in the genre. Although Dewey was clearly influenced by Hammett and Chandler (qq.v.), his Chicago-based private eye, "Mac," is not one of the wisecracking, vigilante breed of fictional ops; he is intelligent, quiet, gentle, ironic, tough when he has to be, a light drinker, and a man not incapable of being hurt either physically or emotionally. All in all, a far more likable creation than the bulk of his brethren.

In *Deadline,* Mac is hired by a group of do-gooders in a last-ditch effort to save the life of a small-town youth, Peter Davidian, who has been convicted of the mutilation murder of an eighteen-year-old girl and is awaiting execution in the state prison. When Mac arrives in the rural Illinois town, Wesley, he meets considerable hostility: The crime was a particularly vicious one, and the girl's father, Jack Parrish, is an influential citizen who is convinced of Davidian's guilt. Racing against time—he has only four days before the scheduled execution, the "deadline" of the title—Mac utilizes the aid of a retarded handyman, a friend of the dead girl's named Mary Carpenter, and a schoolteacher named Caroline Adams to find out who really murdered Esther Parrish. In the process he has to overcome a conspiracy of silence, threats, and a harrowing brush with death.

This is a simple, straightforward story, told with irony, fine attention to detail, and mounting suspense. Satisfying and memorable.

(*B.P.*)

Dewey, Thomas B. *Only on Tuesdays.* New York: Dell, 1964. (PI/O)

In addition to the "Mac" series, Dewey also created another private eye, Los Angeles–based Pete Schofield, for a series of paperback originals in the Fifties and early Sixties. The Schofield novels are much lighter in tone, much sexier (as sexy as paperback mysteries could get in that era, anyhow), and lacking the depth and quality of the Mac novels. Schofield, who is married to a sultry lady named Jeannie (married private eyes never seem to work out well in fiction), is something of a bumbler and spends as much time trying to crawl into the sack with Jeannie as he does solving crimes. But things keep happening to prevent his connubial bliss—telephone calls, people showing up at highly inopportune moments, squabbles, battle wounds, and various other interventions. Dewey's technical skill and sense of humor make this sort of thing work: The Schofield books are exactly what they were intended to be—pleasant light reading—and no more.

Only on Tuesdays, perhaps the best of the series, begins when Pete comes home after a hard day and finds an unemployed actor holding a gun on Jeannie; he also finds, not irrelevantly, a new addition to the family (a dachshund, Hildy) hidden away in the bedroom closet. It ends with a frantic sailboat race to Catalina Island and another confrontation in the Schofield domicile, this time with a murderer. In between he encounters a missing wife, a wealthy yachtsman named Conway, some highly compromising photographs, and of course plenty of murder and mayhem. The sailing scenes are genuinely exciting and suspenseful, and the byplay between Pete and Jeannie, which in some of the other books becomes a bit tedious, is restrained and amusing.

All the Schofields are worth reading; along with *Only on Tuesdays,* the best of them are *Go to Sleep, Jeannie* (1959), *Too Hot for Hawaii* (1960), and *The Girl with the Sweet Plump Knees* (1963).

(*B.P.*)

*Dewey, Thomas B. *A Sad Song Singing.* New York: Simon & Schuster, 1963. (PI)

A Sad Song Singing is Mac's finest case and Dewey's masterwork. This reviewer considers it one of the ten best private-eye novels ever written—not because of its plot, which is relatively simple and straightforward, but because of its emotional depth and impact and its superb depiction of what it was like to grow up in the early 1960s. It is the only mystery novel to employ as its background the short-lived hootenanny craze of that period (hootenannies being, for those of you who might have forgotten or are too young to remember, large gatherings at which folk singers entertained with audience participation). In fact, one can't imagine *any* kind of novel more vividly or poignantly evoking that type of festival or the life-styles of its young performers.

Crescentia Fanio, twenty years old and a budding singer, hires Mac to find her missing boyfriend, Richie Darden, himself an itinerant but already well-established singer of folk songs. But it isn't just a simple case of boy losing interest in girl and leaving her behind; Cress is convinced that not only is Richie's life in danger, but so is her own. If Mac has any doubts that her fears are genuine, he quickly loses them with the appearance of two toughs who are unmistakably hunting Darden—and a mysterious suitcase he had with him when he vanished. A combination of flight, chase, and personal odyssey leads Mac and Cress from Chicago into rural Illinois and Indiana, from the world of coffeehouses and hootenannies to an isolated farm near the small agricultural community of Fairmont, Indiana—and finally to tragedy and, for Cress, rebirth.

There is plenty of action and suspense, but as in most of Dewey's novels—and even more so here—the emphasis is on mood and characterization. The father-daughter relationship between Mac and Cress is what gives the novel its emotional power: The last page is the kind of stuff that could put a tear in the eye of Mike Hammer. In all respects, *A Sad Song Singing* is a virtuoso performance.

Mac appears in a total of sixteen novels, beginning with *Draw the Curtain Close* (1947). The others are likewise first-rate, the most notable among them being *The Mean Streets* (1954), the novel in which Mac—and Dewey—realized his full potential (thus making the title, a phrase from Chandler's essay "The Simple Art of Murder," doubly appropriate); *The Brave, Bad Girls* (1956), *The Case of the Chased and the Unchaste* (1959), *Don't Cry for Long* (1964), *Portrait of a Dead Heiress* (1965), and *The King Killers* (1968).

Dewey also wrote four minor mysteries featuring a small-town hotel owner named Singer Batts, the best of which are probably *As Good as Dead* (1946) and *Handle with Fear* (1951). Of his nonseries suspense novels, two are first-rate: *How Hard to Kill* (1961), a chiller about an ex-cop's hunt for the murderer of his wife; and the paperback original *A Season for Violence* (1966), which is concerned with corruption, murder, and rape in a small California town.

(*B.P.*)

**Dickens, Charles. *The Mystery of Edwin Drood.* New York: Fields, 1870. (CS)

Charles Dickens turned to the pure mystery near the end of his life, and left us, in *The Mystery of Edwin Drood,* one of the most compelling of all literary puzzles.

Edwin Drood and Rosa Bud, both orphans, were betrothed as children by their parents. Now, as they approach their majority, this arrangement has poisoned the love between them. Edwin is fond of his uncle, John Jasper, the music director of the town cathedral, and his uncle appears fond of Edwin. But Jasper has fallen in love with Rosa, who despises him, and he is consumed by jealousy of his nephew.

Another youth, Neville Landless, admires Rosa and, goaded by Jasper, Drood and Landless quarrel. Subsequently, Edwin and Rosa agree that their marriage would not work and call off the engagement. But before they can announce their decision, Edwin disappears—apparently the victim of murder.

Evidence points to Landless, but there is no case against him because no body has been found. Landless flees in disgrace to London. Rosa, afraid of Jasper, also goes to London. A new character on the scene, known as Mr. Datchery but apparently someone else in disguise, begins dogging Jasper's footsteps.

At this point, halfway through the projected novel, Dickens died. He left evidence that Jasper was Drood's killer—but also hinted that there had been no murder. An early working title for the novel was *Edwin Drood in Hiding,* and some have speculated that Jasper failed in his murder attempt and that Datchery is really the vengeful Drood. There have been many other theories about the novel's conclusion. One, championed by the late Edmund Wilson (who hated mysteries but loved Dickens), is that Jasper was a devotee of the Indian Cult of Thugs, and that he murdered Drood as a required ritual act. Dickens's remaining notes are ambiguous, however, and he had promised that the ending would be a great surprise, even to his friends.

Dickens was a significant figure in the development of the mystery novel long before *Edwin Drood.* In 1828, when Dickens was seventeen, Robert Peel launched the modern London police force. The young writer was fascinated by the new profession, and in 1850 his magazine, *Household Words,* published four articles on police work, spawning considerable public interest in crime fighting. In *Bleak House* (1853), Dickens introduced the intrepid Inspector Bucket, a sort of nineteenth-century Columbo, who was the first fictional English police detective. Dickens was deeply influenced by his friend Wilkie Collins (q.v.), whose classic novel *The Moonstone* was serialized in Dickens's periodical *All the Year Round* in 1868.

(*M.J.*)

Dickinson, Peter. *The Last Houseparty.* New York: Pantheon, 1982. (PS/H)

Peter Dickinson is both the author of classical detective stories and a reviewer of mystery fiction for *Punch,* where he was an assistant editor for seventeen years. His early novels featured the very British Superintendent James Pibble of Scotland Yard; in many of his later books he moved into the area of psychological suspense and amateur detection. Although the structure of the majority of his stories is classic—a murder, a number of suspects, and often a closed environment such as the English country house—the settings and characters are anything but ordinary. As Dickinson himself says, "I tend to overpopulate my books with grotesques." But if he tends to the bizarre or eccentric, Dickinson also has the ability to make us believe implicitly in the existence of these people and places, and in the plausibility of the events they participate in.

The Last Houseparty is a historical mystery set in three time frames: 1937, when most of the action takes place; 1940 (briefly); and 1980, when the mystery is resolved. The author tends to skip among these without giving the reader much warning, and in the first few chapters this is very disorienting; after we become familiar with the characters, it is easier to recognize which time frame we are in.

The main action of the novel takes place at Snailwood, a grand English estate whose tower contains a fabulous clock, replete with moving figures that perform on the quarter-hour. In 1937 the estate is the domain of Lord

Snailwood and his second wife, the Countess Zena, who is famous for her weekend "dos" and "superduperdos" to which illustrious personalities are summoned. Zena's current house party is to be a political one, and various people—including an Arab prince, a professor with high connections, and Lord Snailwood's two nephews, one a publisher, the other a soldier—are to debate, in bright cocktail-party chatter, the world situation. The weekend begins successfully, with even a budding romance between Countess Zena's new secretary and the publisher nephew in the offing. But it soon degenerates and dark events take place that result in the traumatization of a young girl, the disappearance of the soldier nephew, an old man's near-fatal heart attack, the clock stopping permanently—and this being the last of Zena's famous parties.

Of course, Dickinson does not reveal all these events at once; the story builds slowly, beginning in the present, with Snailwood now a "stately home" open for public display by the financially strapped heir. He then takes us back to 1937 and the arrival of the party guests; next, forward to the African desert in World War II. We gradually realize that terrible events have destroyed the Snailwood family, and as we see what they apparently were, we also realize that there is even more under the surface. This is an intriguing novel that will keep you guessing right up to the final revelations. (*M.M.*)

Dickinson, Peter. *The Old English Peep Show.* New York: Pantheon, 1969. (PP)

The grand estate of Herryngs—now transformed into a Disneyland-like theme park called "Old England"—is one of the bizarre and fascinating settings typical of Dickinson. Owned by the war-hero Claverton brothers, one a general, the other an admiral, it is a mecca for tourists who wish to watch a fake execution, participate in a mock duel, and view the lions, which are a prime attraction of the park. The Clavertons, as well as the general's daughter and son-in-law, the Singletons, consider themselves above the law; and when the admiral's old cockswain and faithful retainer, Deakin, hangs himself, they bypass the local authorities and ask Scotland Yard to send someone who has "respect for his betters."

Superintendent Jimmy Pibble is chosen, and arrives at Old England—or "our bloody peep show," as the general privately calls it—expecting a routine case that will be over in time for him to catch the afternoon train home. But Pibble is quick to pick up on certain irregularities: off-key reactions on the part of the Clavertons and Singletons; a report of the circumstances of Deakin's hanging that does not ring true; contradictory talk from a drunken butler. Pibble's suspicions that the Clavertons have staged the situation are confirmed by a not very clever impersonation and the revelation that the admiral is missing. And a "dismayed and miserable" superintendent is forced to see the investigation—which he'd just as soon leave alone—through to its tragic conclusion.

This is a first-rate novel, humorous and well characterized and plotted, set against an intriguing and colorful background.

Superintendent Jimmy Pibble appears in such other fine novels as *The Glass-Sided Ants' Nest* (1968), in which he encounters a tribe of New Guinea aborigines who have been transplanted to London; *The Lizard in the Cup* (1972); and *One Foot in the Grave* (1979). Of Dickinson's nonseries books, possibly the most bizarre and fascinating is *The Poison Oracle* (1974), which takes place at a sheik's desert castle that has been built upside down for reasons of temperature control. By contrast, *The Lively Dead* (1975) is set in a typical London town house, yet manages to convey much the same sense of the fantastic as Dickinson's other works.

(M.M.)

*Dickson, Carter. *The Curse of the Bronze Lamp.* New York: Morrow, 1945. (CS/W)

When it became clear that John Dickson Carr's (q.v.) output of mystery novels—seven novels in less than four years—was more than his original publisher could handle, some of the books were diverted to a second publisher, to be issued under a pen name. The first of these pseudonymous works, *The Bowstring Murders* (1933), carried the by-line Carr Dickson. This was a publisher's error and was quickly corrected to the scarcely less obvious Carter Dickson. Dickson's series detective, Sir Henry Merrivale ("H. M."), was introduced in *The Plague Court Murders* in 1934 (see below). Like Carr's Dr. Gideon Fell, H.M. is fat, funny, and formidably intelligent. His appearance and mannerisms are more reminiscent of Churchill than of Chesterton, who was the model for Gideon Fell. H.M. is more overtly comic: a large, bald, vulgar, and frequently childish figure, fond of practical jokes, continually outraged at the twist of fate that put him in the House of Lords, and full of insults for the government bureaucrats with whom he must deal in his somewhat mysterious capacity as "that astute and garrulous lump who sits with his feet on the desk at the War Office."

Almost all of the H.M. stories involve locked rooms or impossible crimes. The centerpieces in *The Curse of the Bronze Lamp* are a pair of vanishings as startling as any produced by stage illusionists. Helen Loring, daughter of British archaeologist Lord Severn, has been presented by the Egyptian government with a bronze lamp taken from a Twentieth Dynasty tomb. An Egyptian fortune-teller, Alim Bey, claims that the lamp carries a curse, and that Helen will be "blown to dust as if she had never existed" if she takes the lamp out of Egypt. Helen returns to England with the lamp, having announced her intention to disprove the curse. Arriving at Severn Hall with friends, Helen gets out of the car and runs ahead of them into the entrance hallway. A few moments later, her raincoat and the bronze lamp are found lying in the middle of the hall floor, and Helen has vanished without a trace. Shortly thereafter, Lord Severn arrives from Egypt and disappears from his study in the same fashion, leaving behind his outer clothing—and the bronze lamp. H.M., whom Helen had asked for advice in Egypt (where his encounter with an Arab taxi driver provided a memorable interlude of slapstick humor), is drawn into the case.

Romantic entanglements, stolen antiquities, the activities of H.M.'s Scotland Yard nemesis, Inspector Humphrey Masters, and the continuing doom-filled prophecies of Alim Bey supply only part of the smoke screen through which H.M. must find his way, which of course he does in satisfactory fashion. As always in Carr/Dickson, the clues prove, in retrospect, to have been fairly planted, but it is a rare reader who can recognize them and put all the pieces together ahead of the detective.

(*R.E.B.*)

***Dickson, Carter. *The Department of Queer Complaints.* New York: Morrow, 1940. (SS/W)**

Its official designation is Department D-3 at New Scotland Yard, but it is commonly known as the Queer Complaints Department—the final repository for all of the cases that seem not to make any rational sense or to have any logical explanation. Colonel March, the chief of the department, likes nothing better than to add another impossible event (for which his "obvious" mind invariably supplies an explanation) to his files.

The first seven stories in this collection are Colonel March tales, each brief, polished, and ingenious. The oddities include a gun fired by a disembodied pair of gloves (". . . they hadn't got any hands inside them. Or any arms or body either, for that matter") and a bullet that passes through a pane of glass without leaving a hole; a footprint on the top of a six-foot-high hedge; a murder committed by a color-blind murderer in a nonexistent room; the loot from a robbery hidden in an invisible piece of furniture; a man stabbed to death while standing alone in the middle of a deserted street, under the eyes of an attentive witness; and a dead man who returns to life. In these stories there is just enough attention to characters and setting to provide a necessary narrative framework, but the point of each story is the working out of a clever idea. No one was better at this than John Dickson Carr/Carter Dickson. Taken at intervals rather than all at one sitting, these stories will entertain and stimulate the reader. They represent the detective-story-as-puzzle in its purest form.

The volume is fleshed out with four stories of quite a different kind.

"The Other Hangman," set in a small Pennsylvania town in the 1890s, is a classic story of a murder so perfectly executed that the murderer can confess immediately after the fact without fear of any punishment. "New Murders for Old," "Persons or Things Unknown," and "Blind Man's Hood" are chillingly effective ghost stories, each with a crime framework.

(*R.E.B.*)

*Dickson, Carter. *The Plague Court Murders.* New York: Morrow, 1934. (CS/W)

The house in Plague Court had come into the hands of the Halliday family in 1833, having earlier been associated with the horrific figure of Louis Playge, a hangman's assistant in the time of the Great Plague. For a hundred years, odd happenings, illnesses, suicides, and rumors of haunting had kept the house a white elephant that the family could neither use profitably nor get rid of. Now a group of people is invited to spend the night in the house. The group includes Ken Blake, the book's narrator; Inspector Masters of Scotland Yard; the current head of the Halliday family and his fiancée; and a psychical researcher named Darworth, who has lately gained influence over two of the Halliday women. The night is filled with unexplained incidents, but the climax comes when Masters breaks into the small stone house in the rear court and finds Darworth's dead body. The door had been double-locked, from inside and from outside; there are no other exits; and no one else is inside the house. Yet Darworth was stabbed with a dagger that once belonged to Louis Playge and was stolen the day before from a London museum.

Blake once worked for H.M. in Military Intelligence, and Masters is a friend of both men. This connection draws H.M. into his first recorded case. He is memorably eccentric, but not yet the full-blown comic figure of the later books in the series. The atmosphere of *Plague Court,* in fact, is anything but light. An air of brooding and macabre menace is set up in the early pages and expertly maintained throughout. A second grisly murder occurs before H.M. finally traps a truly surprising "least likely" murderer.

Other H.M. cases include such ingenious locked-room murders as *The Peacock Feather Murders* (1937) and *The Judas Window* (1938), both justly regarded as classics of the form. *A Graveyard to Let* (1949) is set in New York and features another miraculous disappearance, in which a man dives into a swimming pool in full view of family and friends, and never reappears. The series comes to an end in a blaze of comic glory in *The Cavalier's Cup* (1953), a substantial crime puzzle (although there is no murder) that reads like a combination of P. G. Wodehouse and Thorne Smith.

(*R.E.B.*)

Dietrich, Robert. *Murder on the Rocks.* New York: Dell First Editions, 1957. (O/PI)

Steve Bentley, series fiction's toughest tax accountant, was the creation of Robert Dietrich, better known by his more famous (or infamous) real name of E. Howard Hunt (q.v.). Because he was employed by the CIA, Hunt used pseudonyms for much of his paperback writing in the 1950s and 1960s; the Dietrich name was used first for Dell Books and later for Lancer.

In *Murder on the Rocks,* the first book in the series, Bentley is asked by the beautiful daughter of a South American ambassador to investigate the theft of an emerald worth over $1 million. Instead of the emerald, Bentley finds a corpse, and the case becomes even more complicated when the emerald is apparently returned. Another murder takes place; Bentley is threatened by gangsters; and the ambassador's other daughter, even more beautiful than her sister, practically proposes to him. Eventually Bentley, functioning much like any hard-boiled private eye, sorts things out and deals out a bit of his own kind of justice.

This is one of the better books in the Bentley series, and most of the tough narrative rings true. How tough? Here's an example: "When Cadena was a tank sergeant on Luzon he had pulled the head off a dead Jap to win a ten-cent bet." The Washington setting is described with easy familiarity and the characterization is adequate, although readers may be put off by Bentley's frequent disparaging comments about homosexuals, which are entirely unrelated to the book's plot.

Readers looking for more of Bentley's adventures should also enjoy *End of a Stripper* (1960). Perhaps Hunt's best book as Dietrich, however, is a nonseries work, *Be My Victim* (1956).

(*B.C.*)

Disney, Doris Miles. *Who Rides the Tiger.* New York: Doubleday Crime Club, 1946. (R)

Unlike so many other authors, Doris Miles Disney never wrote the same book twice, even though she frequently used Connecticut as a background and always included a romantic element. In this novel, flashbacks that sometimes catch the reader unaware create a tangled, two-layer story of a great-aunt's will, an old house filled with a lifetime accumulation of furniture and memories, and fourteen diaries that intrigue (as well as confound) the modern-day heroine, Susan. Her search for the motive behind her impoverished father's exclusion from Great-Aunt Harriet's will is aided by a recently returned Army Intelligence officer, Philip, who has a stake in the past, as well as a deep interest in Susan's future. This story could justifiably be called a Gothic, since it involves tangled family relationships, an old house, and all the other trappings; but its mounting feeling of suspense and terror transcends the form and makes *Who Rides the Tiger* a startling tale of malevolence.

Disney's skill at creating dialogue and atmosphere is also evident in her other nonseries books, including *Testimony by Silence* (1948), *No Next of Kin* (1959), *Voice from the Grave* (1968), and *Cry for Help* (1975). In addition, she created three series characters: insurance investigator Jeff DiMarco, who is featured in such titles as *Dark Road* (1946), *Method in Madness* (1957), and *The Chandler Policy* (1971); postal inspector David Madden, who appears in *Unappointed Rounds* (1956), *Black Mail* (1958), and *Mrs. Meeker's Money* (1961); and small-town Connecticut policeman Jim O'Neill, who is the hero of such early novels as *A Compound of Death* (1943) and *The Last Straw* (1954).

(*E.N.*)

Dolson, Hildegard. *Please Omit Funeral.* Philadelphia: Lippincott, 1975. (PP/AD)

It is unfortunate that Hildegard Dolson came to mystery writing so late in life, since her wit and humor add a delightful touch to the small-town police procedural. Her series characters are also delightful: former police inspector McDougal of Wingate, Connecticut, who is occasionally called in on homicide cases by the town's police chief; and McDougal's landlady and friend, Lucy Ramsdale, who is always present in the thick of things.

In *Please Omit Funeral,* a self-appointed Wingate censor named Georgina decides that there are too many "dirty" books in the high-school library, including one by town resident Lawrence Dillman. Thus, at a barbecue dinner at Dillman's home attended by Lucy, Georgina, and several other people who know and dislike the author, there is considerable tension. But it is nothing compared to the tension afterward, when Dillman is found dead of oleander poison. Suspicion points to the high-school librarian and certain members of Dillman's family. McDougal's investigation is both helped and hindered by Lucy, with her knowledge of past literary and personal relationships and her talent for being in the right place at the right time.

The relationship between McDougal and Lucy is warm, pleasant, and comfortable. Their mutual interest in cooking and gardening provides light moments throughout the series. The mystery here, as in Dolson's other novels, is well constructed and baffling. And the theme of book-banning, which is just as relevant today as it was ten years ago, gives *Please Omit Funeral* an added dimension and appeal.

Dolson, who was the second wife of mystery writer Richard Lockridge (q.v.), published three other witty novels featuring the harmonious team of

Lucy and McDougal: *To Spite Her Face* (1971), *A Dying Fall* (1973), and *Beauty Sleep* (1977).

(*E.N.*)

Dominic, R. B. *There Is No Justice.* New York: Doubleday Crime Club, 1971. (AD)

A well-kept secret for a time, but now common knowledge, is that authors of this series are Mary Jane Latsis and Martha Henissart, the collaborative team that also writes as Emma Lathen (q.v.). Quite different in tone from the world of Wall Street depicted in their John Putnam Thatcher series, the Dominic books concern the inner workings of the House of Representatives in Washington, D.C., and related activities in Newburg, Ohio, the place from which Benton Stafford (D-Ohio) is biennially elected. Stafford's legislative cohorts, Eugene Valingham Oakes (R-S.D.), Anthony Martinelli (D-R.I.), and Elsie Hollenbach (R-Calif.), serve their districts and the rest of the United States (in that order).

Coleman Ives (who was born and raised in Stafford's district) has been nominated by a Republican president to serve as a member of the Supreme Court. The hearings are being conducted by the Senate's Judiciary Committee. A member of the Senate who has opposed Ives's nomination is murdered while jogging, but Ives has a perfect alibi, since he was in New York City at the time. Stafford's involvement in the investigation deepens when another, evidently related murder takes place at a college graduation at which he is present. Intermittent conversations with his friends, usually over a couple of drinks in his office at the end of the day, make Ben and the reader aware of some gossip, rumor, and home truths about Ives, his personal activities, and the ongoing investigations, both political and police.

Each book in this series features some aspect of a congressman's job, such as hearings on educational television or applications of the Pure Food and Drug Act. The constant and varying demands on these elected officials, the way members of Congress really behave and react on a day-to-day basis, and the behind-the-scenes activities of working Washington are well depicted by Dominic. Readers who enjoy identifying a character's real-life prototype will have fun with a number of the characters.

Other novels featuring this legislative quartet are *Murder in High Places* (1970)—in which they were introduced—and *Epitaph for a Lobbyist* (1974).

(*E.N.*)

Douglas, Malcolm. *The Deadly Dames.* Greenwich, Conn.: Fawcett Gold Medal, 1956. (PI/O)

There were innumerable private-eye novels that saw print as paperback originals in the Fifties and Sixties. While many, perhaps most, were routine and forgettable, the intrepid reader will occasionally come across a real sleeper, like this book by the Canadian writer Douglas Sanderson, writing as Malcolm Douglas.

Bill Yates, easygoing Montreal private eye, takes on what looks to be a simple case of spy-on-the-straying-spouse. But before he even starts work, the client's rich aunt tries to buy him off, and she promptly goes down under the wheels of a streetcar. Not long after that, two emissaries from the local gambling czar stick him up in his office, looking for a missing will. One day and three or four corpses later, Yates is being pursued by the crooks, the cops, several double-crossing dames, and an Amazon Russian housemaid with romantic notions. The action is furious and headlong, culminating with a naked Yates being chased through the Canadian woods while being eaten alive by swarms of mosquitoes. Along the way, Yates sets the world record for the greatest number of people to get the drop on a private eye in the course of a Gold Medal paperback.

Douglas's style is classic don't-take-it-seriously private-eye material: wry, observant, and a bit gaudy—and perhaps just on the edge of parody. Radio detective fans will find it reminiscent of the marvelous scripts Richard Breen used to write for tough guy Jack Webb in *Pat Novak for Hire.* Exceptionally entertaining.

The other Malcolm Douglas Gold Medal originals—*Rain of Terror* (1956), *Pure Sweet Hell* (1957), and *Murder Comes Calling* (1958)—are less successful but still good reading. The best of Sanderson's novels under his own name is probably *Mark It for Murder* (1959).

(*A.S.*)

Douglass, Donald McNutt. *Rebecca's Pride.* New York: Harper, 1956. (PP)

Rebecca's Pride is a great home that was formerly a mill in the middle of the cane fields on an unnamed Caribbean island; and the man who must investigate the strange events that happen there is police captain Bolivar Manchenil. Manchenil is the "nasty" surname chosen by his grandfather when he was freed from slavery, and it comes from the "lovely, curiously shaped but poisonous tree." Although the captain does not understand why his grandfather would choose to call himself after a tree that has been an agent of death to many, he does not trouble himself about it; he is a man who more or less accepts the world around him at face value.

When a report comes in that there are "woolies" (ghosts) at the mill, Manchenil must investigate. The owner, a wealthy man named Fordyce ("Dice") Wales, has not been at his island retreat for many months, and the place is supposedly closed up. But there is a light on the third floor, and when Manchenil and two U.S. Treasury men who have been looking for Wales investigate, they find his maggot-infested corpse in the central supporting column where the machinery once was—a place that only a person familiar with mills of this type would have known about. Moreover, when the autopsy is performed, it turns out Wales was poisoned with the juice of the manchenil tree—a method that a native of the island is likely to have used.

The captain's inquiries begin with the Von Schook family, to whom the Pride once belonged—and in whose home, coincidentally, Manchenil was raised. There seems to have been some connection between Wales and a Von Schook daughter-in-law, Estralita (who is no paragon of virtue), and surprisingly also with Hannah, a daughter who is an actress living in New York. When Manchenil learns that Hannah not only was Wales's fiancée but also is due to inherit some $40 million now that he is dead, his loyal ties to the family who raised him are strained nearly to the breaking point. Manchenil continues his investigation, however, in his typical low-key manner, until the events set in motion by Dice Wales's death escalate to an exciting conclusion.

Rebecca's Pride, which won a deserved Edgar for Best First Novel of 1956, has recently been reissued in paperback by Carroll & Graf. Douglass wrote only two other books, both featuring the likable, contemplative police captain: *Many Brave Hearts* (1958) and *Saba's Treasure* (1961).

(*M.M.*)

Downing, Todd. *Vultures in the Sky*. New York: Doubleday Crime Club, 1935. (W/T)

Hugh Rennert, special investigator for the U.S. Customs Service, is on his way from Laredo, Texas, to Mexico City by train. One of his fellow passengers reports to him a sinister conversation overheard by his wife the night before, in Laredo, in which a threat to "blast the train" was made and there was a cryptic comment about earrings and cuffs and "don't forget the extra edition." While Rennert ponders the meaning of this, the train enters a long tunnel through El Paso de Los Muertos—and when it emerges, he finds one of the other passengers dead in his Pullman chair.

Who was the dead man and why and how was he killed? And which of the odd group of remaining passengers is responsible? Was it the drunken reporter, the badly sunburned man who hides behind dark glasses, the religious fanatic, the novelty supply salesman, the girl traveling under someone else's name, or the strange woman who seems totally devoid of emotion and who looks at life with the eyes of a spectator at a play?

Rennert's job is made all the more difficult by a strike of Pullman employees of the Mexican National Railway, soldiers sent out by the government to keep order, the kidnapping of the three-year-old son of a wealthy Anglo-American family, another murder, and an unscheduled stop deep in the Mexican desert. But matters take their deadliest turn when the Pullman containing Rennert and the suspects is mysteriously uncoupled, stranding them—with the murderer in their midst—in the middle of nowhere.

This is an expertly crafted whodunit, well-written (except for a mildly annoying overuse of commas where there should be periods) and offering a vivid, detailed portrait of Mexico in the mid-1930s. Although an American (and one-quarter Choctaw), Todd Downing lived in Mexico for many years and his work reflects not only intimate knowledge of the country but a deep love and respect for it and its people. Anyone who likes his mystery plot enlivened by frequent glimpses of another culture both old and new is certain to find Downing's work enjoyable.

All but one of his nine whodunits are set in Mexico (the one exception has a Texas border background), and all are well worth investigating. Among the best of the other six featuring Hugh Rennert and *The Cat Screams* (1934), which deals with a tide of eerie suicides in the American colony at Taxco; *The Case of the Unconquered Sisters* (1936), in which Rennert investigates a railway freight wreck and murder at an archeological dig on the edge of a huge sea of lava; and *The Last Trumpet* (1937), which has a bullfighting background. Downing's remaining two novels feature Texas sheriff Peter Bounty: *Death Under the Moonflower* (1938) and *The Lazy Lawrence Murders* (1941). The latter title, like *Vultures in the Sky,* deals with murder and mystery aboard a Mexican train.

(*B.P.*)

Downing, Warwick. *The Player.* New York: Dutton, 1974. (PI)

"The Player" is Denver private investigator Joe Reddman. He was given his Cheyenne name, "Nataq, nha-ewo-tsim-tisi," by Bluetree Woman, the Indian who raised him. It means "Man Who Plays Game"—and Reddman plays his particular game very well.

In this first recorded case, Reddman is hired by a man named Aaron Cane to clear his nephew, a rookie cop named Denny McLoughlen, of a murder charge. At the same time, he takes on another job—to look into a two-year-old, $450,000 bank robbery involving an armored car that was decked out as a stagecoach. He soon discovers the two cases are connected, but before he can uncover exactly how and why, Denny McLoughlen is murdered. That, plus his growing involvement with Denny's girlfriend, complicates his efforts, and more murder and mayhem lead up to an action-packed climax.

Downing's grasp of Denver's history recalls a rough-and-tumble past that is coated with only a thin veneer of elegance, and the Rocky Mountain scenery is used to exceptionally good effect. Joe Reddman is an interesting character, a man of great integrity, and it is a shame that he has appeared as the main character in only one other novel—intriguingly titled *The Gambler, the Minstrel, and the Dance Hall Queen* (1976), in which an old legend from the mining camps on the south slope of Pike's Peak seems to be repeating itself in present times. He also has a cameo appearance in *The Mountains West of Town* (1975), which features lawyer Nathan Tree.

These three novels comprise Downing's entire contributon to crime fiction. One hopes that others will be forthcoming.

(*R.J.R./M.M.*)

**Doyle, Arthur Conan. *The Adventures of Sherlock Holmes.* New York: Harper, 1892. (SS/C)

The most famous book of short detective stories, and one of the best, remains this collection of the first twelve short stories about Arthur Conan Doyle's immortal sleuth Sherlock Holmes. It is doubtful that the two earlier novels about Holmes would be remembered as more than curiosities today had it not been for the short stories that followed. Judged strictly as a writer of detective stories, Doyle rarely played fair with the reader: In many of the stories, key facts are withheld and we have no opportunity to match Holmes's brilliant feats of deduction. But it is not the plots so much as the characters of Holmes and Dr. Watson that have kept the stories alive for nearly a century. Doyle hit upon the perfect way to popularize the formula with which Poe and others had experimented, and his detective remains justly popular.

As many readers, both children and adults, have discovered to their pleasure, the stories in this first collection fully justify the book's enduring popularity. All twelve are worthy of note, beginning with "A Scandal in Bohemia," the least typical story in the Holmes canon. In it we meet Irene Adler and accompany Holmes on a delicate mission. It was the second story in the book, "The Red-Headed League," that really set the tone for those that followed. Here we have the client calling upon Holmes, the brilliant deductions by Holmes regarding the man's background, the statement of the problem, the investigation by Holmes, and the solution. It was a pattern that rarely varied but almost always entertained the reader.

In "The Red-Headed League," a critical and popular favorite among the Holmes stories, a man is hired because of his red hair to copy articles from the encyclopedia every day in a small office. Holmes discovers the real motive for this odd undertaking. The crime in "The Five Orange Pips" has its roots in the activities of the Ku Klux Klan, and "The Man with the Twisted Lip" takes us inside a London opium den, showing Holmes as a master of disguise. "The Blue Carbuncle," one of literature's great Christmas stories, is about a missing jewel. "The Speckled Band," about a woman frightened to death in a locked room, is a story almost everyone knows, and is probably the most popular Sherlock Holmes tale of all. "The

Copper Beeches" is about a young woman hired to carry out an odd set of instructions at a country home.

Also in the volume are "A Case of Identity," "The Bascombe Valley Mystery," "The Engineer's Thumb," "The Noble Bachelor," and "The Beryl Coronet"—all typical of the cases from Holmes's most rewarding period.

(*E.D.H.*)

****Doyle, Arthur Conan. *The Hound of the Baskervilles.* New York: McClure, 1902. (CS)**

Unlike the first two Sherlock Holmes novels, *The Hound of the Baskervilles* is successful in every way, a book that would be a classic even without the buttressing of the Holmes short stories. The legend of a gigantic hound that stalks the members of the Baskerville family on the moor near their ancestral home forms the background for the only Holmes novel to tell a complete story without recourse to a lengthy flashback following the solution.

The book opens with Holmes's deductions about Dr. James Mortimer, drawn from a walking stick he had left the night before. Mortimer himself soon returns, and tells Holmes and Watson of the legend concerning the Baskerville family. Sir Charles Baskerville has been killed recently, apparently by the gigantic hound of the legend. Holmes and Watson begin their investigation, with Holmes disappearing for a time to live in disguise on the moor itself. An escaped convict named Selden is in the area, as are a band of Gypsies. Sir Henry Baskerville seems destined to be the next victim, but the convict is killed instead, apparently by mistake. In the end Holmes and Watson face the hound themselves, and find a logical solution to the baffling case.

The Hound of the Baskervilles represents one of the few occasions in the Holmes canon when Doyle uses seemingly supernatural events to heighten the atmosphere of mystery. It is also more of a whodunit than most Holmes stories, with the sort of shifting suspicion that readers came to expect from later writers. The book can be criticized (and has been, by John Fowles and others) for its marked shortage of pure detection. But it has its clues and its red herrings—and best of all, it has Holmes and Watson, in a story that shows Doyle at the peak of his powers. Neither he nor Holmes would ever be quite so good afterward.

(*E.D.H.*)

***Doyle, Arthur Conan. *The Memoirs of Sherlock Holmes.* New York: Harper, 1894. (SS/CS)**

The second, and second-best, collection of Sherlock Holmes stories leads off with one of the two or three best Holmes adventures, "Silver

Blaze." Doyle himself admitted that his knowledge of horse racing was spotty, and others have pointed out errors in the racing background of the story, but it is a mark of the author's skill that his narrative overcomes these objections and succeeds on its own. Not only does the story offer us a clever plot and the memorable horse of the title, but it's one of Doyle's rare uses of a "least-suspected killer." It also contains the unforgettable conversation about the curious incident of the dog in the nighttime.

Though the volume lacks as many outright classics as the first collection, both "The Gloria Scott" and "The Musgrave Ritual" are important as accounts of Holmes's first two cases, before his meeting with Watson. Of the remaining eight stories, "The Greek Interpreter" is important for its introduction of Sherlock's brilliant brother, Mycroft Holmes. Also notable are "The Reigate Squires" and "The Naval Treaty," with "The Yellow Face," "The Stockbroker's Clerk," "The Crooked Man," and "The Resident Patient" only slightly less remarkable.

The best-known story in the book is certainly the closing one, "The Final Problem." It marked Doyle's first attempt to rid himself of Holmes, with a dramatic battle at Reichenbach Falls in which both Holmes and his archenemy, Professor Moriarty, apparently plunge to their deaths from a narrow Alpine ledge. Interestingly enough, most of what readers know about Moriarty comes from this single story. One of mystery fiction's most famous villains plays a part in the final novel, *The Valley of Fear,* and is mentioned in passing in a few of the stories, but his only real appearance is in "The Final Problem."

G. K. Chesterton (q.v.) considered "Silver Blaze" to be the best of all the Sherlock Holmes stories. Certainly the story, and this book, are required reading for all mystery fans.

(*E.D.H.*)

**Doyle, Arthur Conan. *A Study in Scarlet.* Philadelphia: Lippincott, 1890. (CS)

The question must be asked at once: Would *A Study in Scarlet* be remembered and read today if there had been no other Sherlock Holmes novels or stories to follow it? Certainly it would be read, to the extent that Doyle's *White Company* and *Lost World* are read, but it's doubtful the book would have anything approaching its present popularity. *A Study in Scarlet* owes its status as a cornerstone to the fact that it introduced the world to Sherlock Holmes.

However, the book is not without merit of its own. Doyle's clear achievement in creating the character of Sherlock Holmes, complete and full-blown, is nothing short of masterful. The case he investigates certainly has its points of interest, and the surprising arrest of the killer at the end of part one is a scene that would not be matched in mystery fiction until the equally surprising arrest at the conclusion of Ellery Queen's *Tragedy of X* (q.v.).

The first half of the novel deals with the meeting of Holmes and Watson, their taking rooms together in Baker Street, and Holmes's investigation of the Lauriston Garden mystery, in which two men named Drebber and Stangerson are found murdered, each with the German word for *revenge* written in blood on the wall above the bodies. Holmes traps the killer at the book's halfway point, and part two is devoted to a lengthy flashback to the early Mormon settlement of Utah, and the crimes that prompted the revenge slayings half a world away.

Though the Mormon portion of the book is interesting enough on its own, one longs to return to Holmes, and this same sort of flaw marks *The Valley of Fear* and to some extent *The Sign of the Four.* Only in *The Hound of the Baskervilles* is the narrative maintained without the final flashback. Still, no study of Holmes is complete without *A Study in Scarlet.*

Of the other novels, *The Valley of Fear* (1915) is far superior to *The Sign of the Four* (1890), in part because its flashback portion tells a fascinating story of labor unrest in the Pennsylvania coal fields of a secret society called the Scowrers, obviously patterned after the Molly Maguires. The other three short-story collections—*The Return of Sherlock Holmes* (1905), *His Last Bow* (1917), and *The Case Book of Sherlock Holmes* (1927)—all have their high spots, and all should be explored by the dedicated mystery reader.

(*E.D.H.*)

Du Maurier, Daphne. *Kiss Me Again, Stranger.* New York: Doubleday, 1953. (SS)

Daphne du Maurier is perhaps best known for her novels of romantic suspense, in which she pits a strong and sometimes evil personality against a weaker but equally interesting protagonist. Such works combine a powerful evocation of place with an effective use of the hinted-at but unrevealed fact, a pairing that results in compelling suspense. Du Maurier's career encompassed far more than these well-known novels, however; she also wrote numerous short stories, plays, biographies, and nearly a half-dozen mainstream novels.

Kiss Me Again, Stranger is a collection of eight of her best suspense short stories. What is notable about these selections is, again, the sense of place, coupled with deft characterization. The endings of the stories are fairly predictable, but the apprehension that this foreknowledge inspires in the reader is powerful, and the subtlety with which horror and suspense enter the characters' lives makes the stories truly noteworthy.

In the title story, for instance, the characters and events are mundane, but not the effect. A young London man with a middling job that fits his middling aspirations meets a young woman who is an usherette at the cinema. He is not much interested in girls, but this one fascinates him and he becomes bold enough to offer her a ride home on the bus. The events that follow build slowly to a heartrending climax, and the young man's sorrow is bound to haunt the reader for some time to come. "The Birds," which was made into the 1963 Alfred Hitchcock film of the same title, also utilizes a mundane setting, and initially even the birds are not the terrifying creatures they become, but merely restless jackdaws and gulls, small birds for whom one can feel pity after the first time the protagonist slaughters a flock of them. Similarly, "The Apple Tree" concerns a suburban Londoner's battle with a malevolent fruit tree; and while in "The Little Photographer" the protagonist (a marquise) and the setting (a luxury hotel on the Riviera) are uncommon, the other characters and the problem in which the protagonist becomes embroiled are not.

This is an excellent, well-balanced collection that effectively shows off the author's skill with the short story. Du Maurier's other collections are *The Breaking Point: Eight Stories* (1959) and *Don't Look Now* (1971).

(*M.M.*)

*Du Maurier, Daphne. *Rebecca.* New York: Doubleday, 1938. (RS)

The title character of this immensely popular novel never appears "on stage," since she is dead long before the story starts. Her persona, however, is the moving force behind the narrative, and she is so well realized that the reader comes to feel he has met her many times. The other characters, including the protagonist, fail to measure up to Rebecca, and this creates a peculiar imbalance that makes one wonder why one is reading about them when she is obviously much more fascinating.

The heroine of the story—referred to after her marriage as only "Mrs. de Winter" and before that as nothing at all—holds a position as lady's companion for an American woman who is vacationing on the Côte d'Azur. Invoking a distant connection, the old woman, Mrs. Van Hopper, strikes up an acquaintance with Maxim de Winter, owner of the grand English estate of Manderley and recent widower. When Mrs. Van Hopper becomes ill, her companion continues the acquaintance and falls in love with de Winter. They marry and return to Manderley, where the hostility of the housekeeper, who was devoted to Maxim's first wife, Rebecca, and continual reminders of the beautiful, strong-willed woman she has succeeded cast a pall over the marriage. The new Mrs. de Winter fears she can never compete with such a paragon as Rebecca, but gradually the truth about the woman emerges, and she must confront a greater, unexpected horror. There is an irony about the ending, which leaves the heroine stronger and wiser, yet immersed in a sorrow from which she will never escape.

Rebecca was made into an excellent film in 1940, directed by Alfred Hitchcock and starring Laurence Olivier, Joan Fontaine, and Judith Anderson. Du Maurier's 1951 novel *My Cousin Rachel* was also filmed (1953). In addition, she produced such popular books as *Jamaica Inn* (her first novel and also a Hitchcock film, in 1936) and *The House on the Strand* (1969).

(*M.M.*)

Dunlap, Susan. *An Equal Opportunity Death.* New York: St. Martin's, 1984. (AD)

Veronica ("Vejay") Haskell is something of a maverick, even for today's new breed of woman: She has fled a picture-perfect marriage, a well-paying executive position, and all the comforts of life in San Francisco for a cold little house and an arduous job as a Pacific Gas & Electric Company meter reader in the Russian River area of northern California. The rainy season takes its toll on Vejay, and she takes an illegal sick day; but instead of staying home, she goes to friend Frank Goulet's bar, quarrels with him, and when Frank turns up murdered, she finds herself the prime suspect.

Vejay quickly decides that local sheriff Wescott isn't going to look far for the killer; and she wonders about a number of things, including the call that Frank Goulet received at his bar while she was there—a call that prompted him to cancel the date they'd just made and thus provoked their quarrel. Carefully (at first) she sets out to question friends and residents in the area: the warm and hospitable Fortmiglio clan; Paul and Patsy Fernandez, former hippies who now own a canoe-rental business; Madge Oombs, one of the local antique dealers; Skip Bollo, a realtor; and Ned Jacobs, ranger at the nearby state park. As Vejay probes deeper, she finds herself the target of hostility, not only from the law but from these former friends and neighbors.

Vejay is forthright and refreshing, and her observations on the other denizens of the area bring them fully alive in all their peculiarities. Dunlap has a fine touch for setting, and you'll probably want to read this one curled up in front of a warm fire, since the descriptions of the biting cold and wetness of the Russian River area during flood season will chill you.

A second Vejay Haskell novel, *The Bohemian Connection,* was published in 1985; in this one, she investigates strange goings-on that center on the Bohemian Club's famous summer encampment at their Russian River grove. Dunlap is also the author of two novels about Berkeley policewoman Jill Smith—*As a Favor* (1984) and *Karma* (1984)—which skillfully capture the flavor of that offbeat and iconoclastic university town.

(*M.M.*)

Dunnett, Dorothy. *Dolly and the Bird of Paradise.* New York: Knopf, 1984.

Dorothy Dunnett's "Dolly" series is about spy Johnson Johnson, skipper of the yacht *Dolly.* Each novel is titled for the "bird" (British slang for woman) who narrates it. The "bird" in this case is Rita Geddes, a punked-out young makeup artist with blue and orange hair who is hired to travel with a client, TV personality Natalie Sheridan. In Madeira, however, Rita is severely beaten and then her friend, Kim-Jim Curtis, another makeup artist, is killed. The nefarious doings seem to involve drugs, but in fact, much, much more is going on.

As must all Dunnett's "birds," Rita becomes professionally involved with Johnson Johnson, who, in addition to being a yachtsman and sort of spy, is a famous portrait painter. Johnson enlists Rita's aid in running to ground the drug smugglers, but she really wants to avenge Kim-Jim, for reasons that she withholds from the reader. Though Rita is the narrator, Dunnett (a pseudonym of Dorothy Halliday) skillfully sees to it that she withholds any number of pertinent details—including the fact that she has a serious disability. The real mystery, locked within Rita herself, unfolds satisfyingly and amid plenty of action, including piracy on the high seas and a rip-roaring hurricane.

Dunnett, also a noted author of historical fiction, is a very deft, very literate writer; Johnson is a sardonic, quasi hero who grows on the reader as he grows on the "birds"—on whom he tends to make poor-to-awful first impressions. The other titles in this series include *Dolly and the Singing Bird* (1982; original 1968 title, *The Photogenic Soprano*); *Dolly and the Cookie Bird* (1982; original 1970 title, *Murder in the Round*); *Dolly and the Starry Bird* (1982; original 1973 title, *Murder in Focus*); and *Dolly and the Nanny Bird* (1982).

(*J.S.*)

*Durrenmatt, Friedrich. *The Judge and His Hangman.* Translated from the German by Eva H. Morreale. New York: Harper, 1955. (PS/PP)

Hans Barlach, police commissioner of Berne, Switzerland, is old, worn out, and dying of cancer. He has only a year to live.

One of his most valued officers is murdered while on an undercover assignment at a party given by a certain Herr Gastmann. Although a recent arrival in Berne, the immensely wealthy Gastmann is highly connected, and among his connections are Barlach's police superiors. Barlach, and Barlach alone, knows that Gastmann is actually a lifelong professional criminal, a cold-blooded killer who once, long ago, made Barlach himself an unwitting partner in a senseless slaying. For forty years Barlach has sought to bring

Gastmann to justice, and has always failed. Now the effort seems futile: Gastmann is at the height of his powers; and Barlach, weak and in pain, undermined and ridiculed by his own colleagues, can no longer act.

Not everything, though, is as it seems. Barlach, as he describes himself in another novel, is "a big black old tomcat who likes to catch mice." He faces his hopeless confrontation with evil incarnate in one of the most unpredictable and ingenious of all mysteries.

Durrenmatt, the Swiss novelist and playwright best known in America for his play *The Visit,* wrote four suspense novels between 1950 and 1958. *The Judge and His Hangman* was the first, followed in 1951 by *The Quarry,* another outstanding Hans Barlach story; in 1956 by *Traps,* a psychological suspense novel highly regarded in Europe; and in 1958 by *The Pledge.* All are distinguished by clear, brilliant writing and by the depth of their gaze into the basics of the human condition—goodness, evil, guilt, and death.

(*M.J.*)

Early, Jack. *A Creative Kind of Killer.* New York: Franklin Watts, 1984. (PI)

Fortune Fanelli, the first-person narrator of *A Creative Kind of Killer,* is a former cop who inherited money, made a lucky investment, and left the force. He's now a private investigator, but not exactly the usual kind. He's a single parent, trying to bring up his two teenage children and work on murder cases at the same time. His ex-wife, a soap-opera producer, has no real interest in raising children, so Fortune gets the job. He lives in New York's SoHo district, and the first murder in the book takes place right in his neighborhood. The killer is "creative," posing the corpse in the window of a boutique so artfully that Fanelli himself admits he must have passed the body six times without noticing it. His investigation of the case leads him both into the arty crowd and into the more sordid world of runaways and kiddy porn.

A Creative Kind of Killer is a promising debut. Fanelli is an interesting character, and his relationship with his children makes for a different kind of subplot. The love interest is provided by a young woman who is a dead ringer for Meryl Streep; and Father Paul, the handsome local priest, is a strong character. Early is particularly good in his descriptions of SoHo, and Fanelli's feelings about the changes in his old neighborhood are an effective commentary on one man's desire to remain involved in his community. The mystery is a good one, too, and the resolution satisfactory. It seems likely that Fanelli will appear in other cases in the near future.

Early's second novel, *Razzamatazz* (1985), is a straight thriller sans Fanelli, however.

(*B.C.*)

Eberhart, Mignon. *The Cases of Susan Dare.* New York: Doubleday Crime Club, 1934. (SS/AD)

The stories and novels of Mignon Eberhart—particularly those in her Hilda Adams (Miss Pinkerton) series—greatly reflect the influence of the work of Mary Roberts Rinehart (q.v.). In her fifty-odd-year career, Eberhart has achieved much popular success, which continues to the present day. (Her most recent novel, *Alpine Condo Crossfire,* was published in 1984.)

Eberhart specializes in presenting young women in great difficulty, through no apparent fault of their own. They often suffer the role of unpaid companion to difficult, eccentric, and wealthy relatives, or are jilted brides. The settings are often hospitals, clinics, or on board ship. Eberhart's hold on the reading public is due in no small part to the way she escalates an apparently harmless situation into one of terror, which often involves a closed group of suspects and a touch of romance-gone-wrong. Readers who expect the same flair to carry over to her historical romances will be disappointed; but in all her books, her considerable skill with geographic description is worthy of special mention, and the fashion-conscious reader will find her detailed descriptions of hairstyle and costume always accurate for the time in which the books are set.

The first story in this collection, "The Introduction of Susan Dare," is the first appearance of the young and attractive mystery-story writer who also detects on the side. Susan finds a fellow houseguest dead in a pond on the grounds of the estate where she is visiting. During the investigation she meets Jim Byrne, a reporter who is to figure prominently in both her future cases and her private life.

In "The Easter Devil," Susan returns to Chicago, where Jim and his friend, Police Lieutenant Mohrn, convince her to impersonate a nurse (nurses appear frequently in Eberhart's work) to investigate the death of an estate caretaker, as well as the suspected poisoning of the estate owner's wife. "Calico Dog" uses the now-overworked scenario of two young men who both claim to be the wealthy family's son kidnapped in early childhood; at the time this story was written, this plot was considered innovative.

The conclusions to many of Susan's cases contain more than a touch of the "Had-I-but-known," but this does not detract from the series as a whole. However, before undertaking a full-scale reading of Eberhart's works, the reader should be warned of the prevalence of such wearying names as Dodie, Monica, Serena, Eden, and Rue.

(*E.N.*)

Eberhart, Mignon. *The Patient in Cabin C.* New York: Random House, 1983. (W)

This recent Eberhart novel is typical fare. Sewall ("Sue") Gates, a young upper-class lady whom financial reverses have forced into nurse's training, is plucky, determined, and genuinely likes being a nurse; but now she is offered the opportunity to gain financial security for herself and her harmlessly alcoholic aunt Addie by marrying wealthy Monty Montgomery. Monty, an entrepreneur who describes himself as a "peddler," is only mildly alcoholic (compared to Addie) and quite well meaning, but Sue is not at all sure she wants to marry him. And she is still undecided when she and Addie board his yacht, the *Felice,* for a cruise that Addie believes is planned as a celebration of his engagement to Sue.

The yacht—a sort of seagoing version of the country estate—has a full complement of passengers: Monty's younger half sister, Lalie, a budding alcoholic herself; Sam Wiley, a man with heart trouble from whom Monty bought the yacht; Dr. Smith, head of the hospital where Sue took her training and apparently Wiley's personal physician; Lawson, Monty's attorney; Juan, the steward, who is not the deferential Chicano he seems to be; and two others, whose presence is ill-advised—Stan Brooke, Sue's former heartthrob, whom Monty hired on impulse to skipper the yacht; and Monty's former mistress, Celia Hadley. It is a ménage just made for murder—and indeed, as soon as the *Felice* sets sail in a thick fog, mysterious events begin to happen.

First Monty falls overboard, and swears he was pushed. Sue sees the steward sharpening an evil-looking hatchet. The ship's engines quit. The steward disappears, leaving a trail of bloodstains. Monty remakes his will in Sue's favor and begins talking monotonously and ominously about someone being out to get him. Addie remains foolishly drunk. A storm is brewing; Sue thinks of shipwrecks and sinkings, and Addie begins seeing things that may be more than just the product of the dt's. Finally Sue, typical Eberhart heroine that she is, begins to detect—with the usual satisfying results.

Like all of Eberhart's novels, this one is well crafted and well plotted, and her fans will feel right at home with the characters and situation. Sue Gates is not very different from Eberhart's heroines of the 1940s, and there is a curious, somewhat refreshing innocence to this seafaring tale. Perhaps the most surprising thing about *The Patient in Cabin C* is that it was written in the 1980s, rather than in those more gentle days.

(*M.M.*)

Eberhart, Mignon. *The White Dress.* New York: Random House, 1946. (RS)

Biscayne Bay, Florida, has never been as well described as in this romantic adventure of Marny Sanderson, young and attractive executive secretary to Tim Wales, owner of Wales Airlines. In the opening scene, when Marny arrives at Miami Airport with Tim, we are introduced to most of the main characters, including Tim's second wife, Judith, and his adult daughter from his first marriage, Winnie. The action proceeds to his mansion on Shadow Island—a place that itself assumes the quality of a main character.

Marny had been in love with the man Winnie is currently engaged to, and he and various other family members are at the island estate when Marny finds the murdered body of a family friend, lovely young Cecily Durrant. Suspicions and tensions arise among the members of the closely knit group at the estate, and Marny finds herself in danger when she wakes to see a man's face peering in from the balcony off her bedroom. There is another murder (of the chief suspect), and a hurricane that cuts the island off from assistance. When the crimes are finally untangled, the solution is both well motivated and satisfying. As in all of Eberhart's novels, love—long complicated by misunderstanding—is triumphant.

Other recommended nonseries novels by Eberhart are *Danger in the Dark* (1937), *Wings of Fear* (1945), *Jury of One* (1960), and *The House by the Sea* (1972). Books featuring her early investigative team of nurse Sarah Keate and detective Lance O'Leary include *The Patient in Room 18* (1929), *Murder by an Aristocrat* (1932), and *Wolf in Man's Clothing* (1942), in which Keate conducts a solo investigation.

(*E.N.*)

*Ebersohn, Wessel. *Divide the Night.* New York: Pantheon, 1981. (PP)

It must be strange to have one's books banned in one's own country, but such is the case with Wessel Ebersohn, a native and resident of South Africa who records that society as he sees it, blemishes and all. Consider his description of Johannesburg's citizens:

> *There were the super-liberals who almost felt ashamed to be white. There were the most violent and desperate racialists who would willingly kill to protect a position of privilege. There were artists and railway workers, Jews and anti-semites, nuns and whores, millionaires and the dispossessed. . . .*

Divide the Night is an intelligent and provocative novel featuring Yudel Gordon, a prison psychologist who also treats private patients. One such patient is a man named Johnny Weizman, who has the rather antisocial habit of leaving his storeroom door open all night and shooting any intruder—usually blacks, of whom he has already killed eight. As far as Yudel is concerned, Weizman is a fanatic and psychotic racist; the Special Police, however, consider him a patriotic citizen, and are much more interested in a fugitive black leader named Mantu Majola who witnessed Weizman's last murder and who just might (the security police hope) return to settle the score with the racist shopkeeper.

Caught up in the middle is Yudel, who has troubles of his own—primarily a nagging wife who feels he does not have the proper attitude toward money. Yudel is a highly sympathetic character, well drawn and very human. Similarly, Ebersohn's other characters come across as real people, which makes us care about the things that happen to them in, and as a result of, the restricted society in which they live.

The *New York Times Book Review* called *Divide the Night* "a powerful book and a well-written one that just happens to fall within the genre of the police procedural." The same could be said of the first Yudel Gordon suspense novel, *A Lonely Place to Die* (1979). Also impressive is Ebersohn's nonseries suspense novel, *Store Up the Anger* (1980).

(*N.D./B.P.*)

Egan, Lesley. *A Case for Appeal.* New York: Harper, 1961. (AD/PP)

Lesley Egan is a pseudonym for Elizabeth Linington (q.v.), who also writes under the name of Dell Shannon (q.v.). The author is well known for her three series of police procedurals done under these names, and while the procedure is very sound, it is interest in the recurring characters' lives and personal problems that seems to draw readers to these popular books.

A Case for Appeal introduces Jewish lawyer Jesse Falkenstein and his policeman friend Captain Vic Varallo. Varallo has called Jesse away from Los Angeles to the little southern California valley town of Contera to defend accused murderess Nell Varney—a woman Varallo has arrested, but whose guilt he doubts. As the story opens, Nell has just been convicted and sentenced to death for the murder of two women upon whom she supposedly performed illegal abortions. Jesse—who was called in too late to do any investigation or prepare a solid defense—intends to appeal the case. But to make a case for appeal, he must find the woman resembling Nell who really performed the abortions.

With Varallo's help, Jesse gets to know the families of the victims and the town of Contera itself—no small chore for a Jewish lawyer from the big city. And as he sifts through the testimony, it becomes apparent that deathbed statements from the aborted women can be taken in more than one way, and that someone is manipulating the interpretation of them. A nice romance between lawyer and client, plus Varallo's conflict about staying in this town—where he has come because of his family, a reason no longer valid—provide the provocative personal background that is typical of Egan. Falkenstein has an odd style of speaking that at first is confusing, but once the reader becomes familiar with it, the story—told largely through dialogue—moves along nicely.

(*M.M.*)

Egan, Lesley. *A Choice of Crimes.* New York: Doubleday Crime Club, 1980. (PP)

In the novels following *A Case for Appeal,* Vic Varallo moves to Glendale, California, and joins the police force there. A settled family man, he is now a detective and teamed with a young policewoman, Delia Riordan. In contrast to Vic, Delia is anything but sure of her personal or professional life; she has doubts about why she is in this line of work (Is it to please her father, a disabled former policeman, or is it to please herself?), as well as doubts as to whether she has ever gotten over an old love, whose memory pops into her mind all too frequently. These problems are an interesting thread running through the novel, and Delia is an interesting and likable character.

The rest of it is standard police procedure, which Egan does very well. The major case concerns an old woman who died suddenly of a heart attack; the death certificate was signed routinely, and the funeral has taken place. But a longtime friend of hers says the woman's heart was sound, and she convinces Delia and Vic that something might be amiss. This, of course, is not the only case that occupies their time: There is the abandonment of a child so deformed as not to be considered human; a series of rapes in a hospital parking lot; the stabbing of an unidentified woman at the train station; the strangulation murder of another woman; a motel stickup artist; and a third, senseless murder that could easily have been prevented. The detectives juggle cases like the pros they are, and the only difference between the novel and real life is that everything wraps up satisfactorily at the end.

Egan has a solid grasp of police procedure, and gives us a realistic portrait of what life is like for the men and women in that profession. Lively writing, good dialogue, and likable characters make this an extremely readable series. Other titles include *Detective's Due* (1965), *Malicious Mischief* (1971), *A Dream Apart* (1978), *Random Death* (1982), and *Chain of Violence* (1985).

(*M.M.*)

Elkins, Aaron. *Fellowship of Fear.* New York: Walker, 1982. (T)

The early 1980s spawned a great many new mystery writers, and Aaron Elkins is one of the best of them. This first novel introduces us to Gideon

Oliver, a young anthropology professor (Elkins himself teaches anthropology in northern California) who signed up for a summer teaching stint in Europe with the U.S. Overseas College. He's recovering from the death of his beloved wife the year before and needs a break from that reality. And he's never been to Europe.

Oliver gets a change of pace, all right. Far from the confines of academic life, he's cast as the main character in an international spy ring—but not until he's been robbed, attacked, and followed all over Europe does he take it seriously. He then teams up with John Lau, a U.S. security officer, who's not quite so naïve about these matters. After being suitably impressed by Oliver's fine investigative mind—he is a physical anthropologist, after all, and used to solving mysteries with little more than a sliver of bone and some ash for evidence—Lau teams with him and they attack the spy operation with fresh enthusiasm.

Elkins has a good sense of contemporary character, dialogue, and plot. Gideon Oliver is a good man, and Elkins is good, too. He writes sparsely, to the point, and is cagey enough to keep us wondering until the very end.

Elkins's second novel, *The Dark Place* (1983), also features Oliver and is set in the Olympic National Park in Washington State. It also has the distinction of being the first mystery to involve the ongoing hunt for Sasquatch, otherwise known as Bigfoot.

(*K.K.H.*)

*Ellin, Stanley. *The Dark Fantastic.* New York: Mysterious Press, 1983. (PI/PS)

Stanley Ellin is one of the most honored of contemporary writers of mystery fiction. Beginning with his first story in 1948, he consistently won prizes in the annual short-story contests run by *Ellery Queen's Mystery Magazine.* He is a three-time winner of the Edgar Award of the Mystery Writers of America: for Best Short Story in 1954 and 1956 and for Best Novel (*The Eighth Circle*) in 1958. Four other stories (the most recent in 1983) and one novel have appeared on the short list of nominees for the Edgar. His novel *Mirror, Mirror on the Wall* (1972) was awarded France's Grand Prix de Littérature Policière in 1975. He was elected president of the Mystery Writers of America in 1969, and in 1981 received that organization's Grand Master Award honoring his lifetime achievement in the mystery field. The point of this litany of awards is that they are all deserved. As a careful craftsman with an ear for language and a deep concern for its proper use, as an acute observer of the human condition, and as an inventive plotter with a flair for the unexpected, Ellin has maintained a consistent level of quality that makes him indeed a grand master of his art.

A string of awards and a proven track record do not, however, guarantee that publishers will jump to accept a book with potentially controversial elements. *The Dark Fantastic* was rejected by several major publishing houses before being picked up by a relatively small specialty publisher. It subsequently gathered a stack of favorable reviews in the United States, sold to a major British publisher, and has become a feather in the cap of the Mysterious Press.

The story alternates between two viewpoints: that of Charles Witter Kirwan, a retired college professor with madness eating at his brain just as cancer is eating at his body; and that of John Milano, a private detective first introduced in *Star Light, Star Bright* (1979), who specializes in the recovery of stolen works of art. Kirwan, reluctant landlord of an apartment building in a black neighborhood in Brooklyn, plans to blow up the building with himself and his black tenants inside. Among the tenants are the family of Christine Bailey, who works as a receptionist in a Manhattan art gallery currently under investigation by Milano. From this tenuous connection, the paths of Kirwan and Milano are drawn inexorably together. Ultimately, Milano is the only person who has a chance to uncover Kirwan's plot; but can he stop it in time? Ellin tightens the screws expertly, and the suspense intensifies up to the very end.

Kirwan's chapters are in the form of transcripts of a tape-recorded journal in which he attempts to explain the reasons for his destructive plan, while recounting the day-to-day progress toward its accomplishment. The transcripts are studded with racial invective—not mere ethnic name-calling, but the type of inventive viciousness that an educated mind can apply to the expression of its prejudices. These passages make uncomfortable reading, especially in view of the skill with which Ellin takes us into Kirwan's mind and makes us understand the familial and societal roots of his attitudes. Another source of discomfort for some readers lies in the explicit descriptions of Kirwan's sexual victimization of Christine's teenaged sister. But Ellin handles this highly charged material with assured skill and without a hint of sensationalism. The book is a serious psychological study, a detective story, an unusual love story, and an exercise in down-to-the-wire suspense: a worthy addition to the author's already impressive body of work.

(*R.E.B.*)

*Ellin, Stanley. *The Key to Nicholas Street.* New York: Simon & Schuster, 1952. (W/PS)

The Key to Nicholas Street was the author's second novel, and there is no better example of his ability to speak in other people's voices and to let the reader into the minds of his characters. The story is told in turn by the five inhabitants of the Ayers house on Nicholas Street in the small town of Sutton: Harry Ayers, a local hardware merchant; his chilly wife, Lucille; their two repressed and mother-dominated children; and Junie, the flighty girl-of-all-work. Figuring largely in the story are two other people: the beautiful artist Katherine Ballou, who moves in next door; and Matthew Chaves, a puzzling young friend of hers from New York.

On the same morning that Lucille tells her daughter Bettina about Harry's yearlong affair with Katherine, the latter is found at the bottom of her cellar stairs, dead of a broken neck. The death is quickly identified as murder. As the viewpoint shifts from one member to another in the Ayers household, fragmentary scenes and conversations are gradually filled in and a picture takes shape, revealing the true key to the jealousy, suspicion, and death on Nicholas Street.

The book is a formal detective story, and we do not learn which character will turn out to be the detective until almost the same moment that the murderer is revealed. It is also a study of the effect that a mean-spirited and self-seeking woman can have upon the people around her, and it is above all a work of emotional power.

(*R.E.B.*)

**Ellin, Stanley. *The Specialty of the House and Other Stories: The Complete Mystery Tales, 1948–1978.* New York: Mysterious Press, 1979. (SS)

Stanley Ellin made his first impact on the mystery field as a writer of short stories; and in spite of more than a dozen highly praised novels, it is still as a short-story writer that many readers think of him. This hefty collection contains, in chronological order, all thirty-five of the stories written during the first thirty years of his writing career. All but one of them originally appeared in *Ellery Queen's Mystery Magazine,* where the author's "annual story" is still an eagerly awaited event. The first seven stories in the collection, starting with the title story (surely one of the most impressive debuts in the field), were prizewinners in the annual *Ellery Queen* contests.

Here we have "The Betrayers," in which a young man constructs an airtight solution to the wrong crime; the Edgar-winning fantasy "The House Party"; a second Edgar winner, "The Blessington Method," with its unique approach to gerontology; "You Can't Be a Little Girl All Your Life," the story of a rape and its aftermath; "The Crime of Ezechiele Coen," with its roots going back to the German occupation of Rome in World War II; "The Twelfth Statue," a novelette of murder in a Rome film studio; "The Corruption of Officer Avakadian," concerning doctors who refuse to make house calls; and "The Question," in which the whole point of the story is compressed into a single devastating three-letter word in the final sentence. The stories vary widely in theme and setting, but exhibit the same polished craftsmanship.

In his introduction to the volume, speaking of another master of the short story, Guy de Maupassant, Ellin wrote: "Here was a writer who reduced stories to their absolute essence. And the ending of each story, however unpredictable, was, when I thought of it, as inevitable as doom." These words might have been written about Ellin's own work. When Ellin's first ten stories were issued in book form under the title *Mystery Stories* in 1956, the book was praised by Julian Symons as "the finest collection of stories in the crime form published in the past half-century." With the addition of twenty-five stories and twenty years, the judgment still stands.

(*R.E.B.*)

Ellin, Stanley. *Star Light, Star Bright.* New York: Random House, 1979. (PI)

In this novel, Ellin's New York–based series detective Johnny Milano is hired by an old flame to go to Miami to act as bodyguard for a onetime phony astrologer who has become a religious zealot. On a large south Florida estate, the zealot exercises control over Milano's old love and some of her husband's guests. The "holy man" has received notes informing him that he is to die by midnight on a certain date in the near future. Milano's task: Protect him until that fateful hour passes. The catch: The holy man doesn't want protection; he considers it part of the universal scheme of things that he should die as ordained and be reincarnated to continue his earthly mission.

Milano's job is further complicated by the other guests, all film-industry people with their own self-serving angles. There is a security force at the estate, but it isn't as competent as it should be and, like Milano, is working under a handicap.

Plenty of woman trouble here. Plenty of solid characterization, clever subplotting (which includes an intriguing speculative connection between Vincent van Gogh and Jack the Ripper), sun-washed Florida atmosphere, and a plausible, satisfying conclusion.

Several of Ellin's other novels deserve special mention. His first book, *Dreadful Summit* (1948), is a skillful study of an "adolescent mind driven by a compulsion which it does not understand and which it is unable to resist." The book was filmed by Joseph Losey in 1951 under the title *The Bio Night,* and has been reprinted under that title. Ellin collaborated with Losey on the screenplay. *Mirror, Mirror on the Wall* (1972) is a groundbreaking novel with a strong psychosexual theme. The Edgar-winning *The Eighth Circle* (1958) is both an excellent formal detective novel and a searching study of the ethics of a private detective who fights to save an accused man in whose innocence he does not believe. Ellin's most recent novel, *Very Old Money* (1985), is the disturbing story of a young professional couple's foray into the world of household service with a strange and moneyed family on Manhattan's Upper East Side.

(*J.L./R.E.B.*)

*Ely, David. *Seconds.* New York: Pantheon, 1964. (PS)

A prosperous banker leaves his New York office at noon, knowing full well he may never see it again. Following an address on a slip of paper, he takes a cab to a run-down laundry in a slum area of the city. From there, he is directed to a warehouse. From the warehouse, he is taken in the back of a truck to a large office building, and it is here the transition process begins. For the banker (soon to be a painter known as Wilson) has elected literally to change his life and be "reborn" as a new man. A surgically altered cadaver shows up in a hotel room and the banker is officially pronounced dead of a heart attack. Meanwhile, we follow Wilson through his own surgical alterations, and before you know it, he has been relocated to California and to the life of a single, moderately successful painter.

Wilson cannot relax and enjoy himself, though. His new life strikes him as shallow and meaningless, and he feels an overwhelming desire to visit his wife and daughter. This he does, going against numerous warnings from representatives of the company that gave him his new identity. The company, it seems, creates about 3000 new identities each year, so it has a stake in seeing that no one jeopardizes its operation. Obviously Wilson is one of those people who will never make the transition properly, so he is brought back for further "processing."

Few books can match the suspenseful beginning of *Seconds,* as the reader wonders what in the world is going on. The suspense tapers off when we learn what *is* going on, but increases again as we begin to wonder what the company will do with the renegade Wilson. As it turns out, Wilson is not the only man who has made an unsuccessful transition—and from a business standpoint, the company's disposition of these failures makes perfect sense.

This unusual and nightmarish novel was made into an equally suspenseful John Frankenheimer film in 1966, with Rock Hudson and Salome Jens.

David Ely has made a career of producing offbeat suspense fiction, both novels and short stories for *Ellery Queen's Mystery Magazine* and such slick magazines as *Cosmopolitan.* (One of his *Cosmo* stories, "The Sailing Club," was the recipient of the 1962 Best Short Story Edgar.) Among his other novels are *Trot* (1963), *The Tour* (1967), *Poor Devils* (1970), and the eerie *Mr. Nicholas* (1974).

(*N.D.*)

Engel, Howard. *The Suicide Murders.* New York: St. Martin's, 1984. (PI)

Until the 1980s, Canada was not known for its native detective fiction. The Benny Cooperman novels by Howard Engel—along with the work of Eric Wright and Ted Wood (q.v.)—represent the beginnings of a vital new school of crime writing in Canada.

The Suicide Murders is the first of a series of mysteries starring Benny Cooperman, private eye. Benny is a nice Jewish guy who makes his extremely modest living as a detective in his hometown of Grantham, Ontario. He still goes home to have dinner with his elderly parents at least once a week. He possesses intelligence enough, and the requisite amount of determination. Still, life or a case too often forces him to play the schlemiel.

The novel opens with the classic scene of a beautiful woman entering his office and enlisting his aid. Myrna Yates thinks her successful husband may be cheating on her. She hires Benny to trail him. This simple assignment becomes much more complicated when the seemingly faithful Mr. Yates dies of a gunshot wound to the head soon after buying himself an expensive new bike. The police say suicide. Benny disagrees. His investigation continues, as do the murders, until he brings the case to its sad, satisfying conclusion.

Benny's mean streets may be in Ontario and not L.A., but his adventures are still reminiscent of the classic American private eye. He is no tough guy, but he is strong as well as compassionate. The supporting cast of characters, including the murderer, are also nicely realized.

Benny Cooperman returns in *The Ransom Game* (1984), *Murder on Location* (1985), and *Murder Sees the Light* (1985).

(*K.L.M.*)

Erskine, Margaret. *Give Up the Ghost.* New York: Doubleday Crime Club, 1949. (PP)

Margaret Erskine wrote the same book about Scotland Yard inspector Septimus Finch twenty-one times. In each one Finch is described as having a nondescript face and a proclivity for dressing all in gray. This repetition doesn't enhance the inspector's limited charms, although it could be argued that his stolidity and matter-of-factness are positive character traits.

In *Give Up the Ghost,* crude and rather nasty drawings have been sent to the Camborough constabulary, but have been more or less ignored until the elderly housekeeper of the pompous Pleydon family is found murdered with another drawing pinned to her body. None of the Pleydons can suggest any reason for their household's being singled out, yet several days later another woman connected with them is killed, another drawing near *her* body. A band of vigilantes is formed to prowl the streets. Meanwhile Finch, in spite of the Pleydons' interference, investigates the family's history and discovers their convoluted, almost forgotten web of financial skulduggery—just in time to prevent further murders. There are moments of humor amid the gore, such as when Finch installs young Constable Roark in the Pleydon household as a butler.

Erskine—who has stated that writing thrillers was a revolt against her highbrow family—specializes in eccentric British families with long-held secrets, social pretensions, and heads of household who possess streaks of cunning. As a Scotland Yard officer, Finch solves crimes in Sussex, several seaside towns, and provincial villages. He remains as colorless through his last case, *The House on Hook Street* (1977), as he was in his first adventure, *The Limping Man* (1939). Erskine's novels are definitely an acquired taste.

(*E.N.*)

Estleman, Loren D. *Kill Zone.* New York: Mysterious Press, 1984. (A/T)

In *Kill Zone,* Loren Estleman, who is best known for his rough-and-tumble, Chandleresque private-eye novels, introduces Peter Macklin, "efficiency expert"—a euphemism for *hit man.* Macklin is the toughest character—hero or antihero—to arrive in crime fiction since Richard Stark's (q.v.) Parker; and Estleman's prose the hardest-boiled since the days of Paul Cain (q.v.) and Cap Shaw's *Black Mask.* Macklin and Estleman, in fact, would probably have been *too* grimly realistic even for the pioneering Shaw and his magazine.

A terrorist group takes control of a Lake Erie excursion boat with 800 passengers, rigging it as a floating bomb. They demand the release of three prisoners within ten days. Michael Boniface, the head of the Detroit mob, offers his assistance from his prison cell in return for parole, but it is not until the FBI discovers that one of the passengers on the boat is a cabinet member's daughter that they take him up on it. Boniface's assistance is in the form of his top "efficiency expert," Peter Macklin.

Macklin tries to concentrate on the business at hand while dealing with an alcoholic wife, the knowledge that someone close to him has betrayed him, and the fact that he is being stalked by a killer working for Charles Maggiore, acting head of the mob, who does not want Boniface to get out of prison.

Estleman takes an expertise previously displayed in PI and western novels (one of his westerns, *Aces and Eights,* won the Western Writers of America Golden Spur Award for Best Novel of 1982) and in applying it to a different type of novel has once again scored high marks. Fans of hard-boiled fiction won't want to miss it—or subsequent Peter Macklin titles: *Kill Zone* is the first of at least three.

(*R.J.R./B.P.*)

Estleman, Loren D. *Sugartown.* Boston: Houghton Mifflin, 1984. (PI)

Since the publication of *Motor City Blue* in 1980, Estleman and his tough Detroit private eye Amos Walker have been a formidable team, combining to create an average of one high-quality PI novel per year. Walker has been called "hard-edged and relentless"; Estleman has been lauded as "having put Detroit on the detective map." Both assessments are accurate; and in *Sugartown,* author and Eye carry on the tradition.

Walker is hired, first, by an elderly Polish immigrant to find her grandson, who has been missing for nineteen years: He disappeared following an ugly, tragic incident where his father shot his mother, his sister, and then himself—a scene of carnage that the boy discovered upon returning home from school. Later the old woman also asks Walter to find a family heirloom, a silver cross—a job that leads him directly into a murder case. Walker's second client is a Soviet defector and famous author who thinks a Russian spy is out to kill him. After an investigation that takes Walker through the dark underbelly of Detroit, he escapes a trap that almost takes his life and establishes a connection between the two cases.

Plenty of action and solid writing in the Chandler tradition make *Sugartown* (which won the PWA Shamus for Best Novel of 1984) the same kind of potent book as its predecessors in the Amos Walker series. The others are *Angel Eyes* (1981), *The Midnight Man* (1982), and *The Glass Highway* (1983).

The versatile Estleman has also written two novels as completely different from the hard-boiled private eye as it is possible to get: a pair of Sherlock Holmes pastiches pitting the Great Man against two legendary Victorian "monsters," *Sherlock Holmes versus Dracula* (1978) and *Dr. Jekyll and Mr. Holmes* (1979).

(*R.J.R./B.P.*)

Fair, A. A. *Owls Don't Blink.* New York: Morrow, 1942. (PI)

A. A. Fair is a pseudonym of Erle Stanley Gardner (q.v.), but don't pick up one of these novels featuring private eyes Bertha Cool and Donald Lam expecting a couple of carbon copies of Paul Drake. Cool and Lam are an amusing and endearing pair—perfect foils for one another.

Bertha Cool, at the time of this novel, is the middle-aged proprietor of an L.A. investigative firm, pared down to a mere 165 pounds but ever on the alert for a good meal. Her partner, Donald Lam, is a twerp in comparison—young, slender, and forever on the defensive for what Bertha considers excessive squandering of agency money. But there's considerable affection between the two, and with Donald doing the legwork, they crack some tough cases—and have a lot of fun while doing so.

Owls Don't Blink opens in the French Quarter of New Orleans, where Donald is occupying an apartment once rented by a missing woman he has been hired to find. He is due to meet Bertha at the airport at 7:20 the next morning and knows there will be hell to pay if he's late. Fortunately, he arrives on time, and together they meet the New York lawyer who has hired them to find Roberta Fenn, a former model. Over a number of pecan waffles—a number for Bertha, that is, who "only eats once a day"—the lawyer is evasive about why he wishes to locate Miss Fenn. But Cool and Lam proceed with the case—and Bertha proceeds with several lavish meals, still on that same day.

The discovery of the missing woman's whereabouts proves all too easy, and also too easy is the discovery of a corpse in Roberta Fenn's new apartment. But from there on out, everything's as convoluted as in the best of the Perry Mason novels. The scene moves from New Orleans to Shreveport, Louisiana, and from there to Los Angeles, where its surprising (although possibly a little out-of-left-field) conclusion takes place. And there's a nice twist in the Cool-Lam relationship that will make a reader want to read the later entries in this fine series, such as *Crows Can't Count* (1946), *Some Slips Don't Show* (1957), *Fish or Cut Bait* (1963), and *All Grass Isn't Green* (1970). Especially entertaining earlier titles are *The Bigger They Come* (1939) and *Spill the Jackpot* (1941).

(*M.M.*)

Falkirk, Richard. *Blackstone's Fancy.* New York: Stein & Day, 1973. (H)

Edmund Blackstone is a member of England's pioneering group of public law officers, the Bow Street Runners (as is another prominent fictional detective, Jeremy Sturrock, in a series written by J. G. Jeffreys, q.v.). Blackstone's adventures span a total of six novels, of which only the first four were published in this country, and are fascinating portraits of London and its environs in the 1820s.

Blackstone's Fancy, the second in the series, involves the redoubtable Blackie in the violent (and at that time illegal, owing to a 1750 act of Parliament) sport of prizefighting, and with its "fancy"—the gamblers and aficionados, many of them aristocrats, who attended the matches and otherwise involved themselves in the sport. When Blackstone is ordered to lead a campaign to stamp out prizefighting, he finds himself torn between his loyalties to the Runners and his own self-interest: On the sly, he himself has undertaken the training of a boxing protégé, a Negro youth named Ebony Joe. (Blackstone is that rarity among detective heroes, a human being with weaknesses as well as strengths.) But this is only one of Blackie's worries. Among others: Patron of pugilists and zealous reformer Sir Humphrey Cadogan is being blackmailed by one of the whores he "saved"; the man who wrote the blackmail note is brutally murdered; an attempt is made on Blackstone's own life; and Ebony Joe's father is kidnapped in an effort to force him to throw his first major bout.

The plot is cleverly worked out, but the real charm of the novel is Richard Falkirk's (a pseudonym of Derek Lambert) vivid portrait of the period, with all its social problems, strange pastimes, and criminal excesses. The narrative is also sprinkled with prizefighting history and lore, and with underworld cant, most of it (but not all, unfortunately) accompanied by translations. Falkirk's prose style is evocative, too—though it occasionally becomes too eccentric, with such dubious lines as "The girl in the bed stirred drowsily, one sleepy breast above the coverlet."

All in all, however, this is a delightful series and one wishes that new titles would be added. The other five existing Blackstone novels are *Blackstone* (1973), *Beau Blackstone* (1974), *Blackstone and the Scourge of Europe* (1974), *Blackstone Underground* (1976), and *Blackstone on Broadway* (1977). Under his own name, Lambert has also published several suspense novels, among them *The Yermakov Transfer* (1974); and an excellent biographical study of nine "masters of suspense," *The Dangerous Edge* (1976).

(*B.P.*)

Farrell, Henry. *How Awful about Allan.* New York: Holt, 1963. (PS)

Everyone in his neighborhood is saying it: "How awful about Allan!" Allan Colleigh, the rather dim bulb in an otherwise brilliant family, has had a shattering mental breakdown following his father's death in a fire from which Alan could not save him. One of the symptoms is hysterical blindness, and now that Allan has been released from the mental hospital, his admirable sister, Katherine, must shoulder the burden of caring for and supporting him in the old half-burned house where their father died. Money is short, and when Katherine suggests they take in a boarder from the university where she works, Allan tries to cooperate. But there is something about the student that disturbs him—perhaps his whispery voice, caused by a childhood accident—and Allan suffers a relapse.

At first he tries to control himself—after all, he's made so much progress with Dr. Greenough, the psychiatrist who has taken him on for Katherine's sake. But then he begins to feel he's being watched, being spied on. His friend and neighbor Olive Dearborn has never seen the student, and since Allan *can't* see him, he isn't sure *whom* he is dealing with. When he hears that Katherine's old boyfriend, Eric Walters, has returned to town, he's sure Katherine has brought Eric into the house, disguised as the mild-mannered college student. And soon he begins to believe that Eric and Katherine are trying to kill him.

The story is an exercise in mounting paranoia and terror, more frightening because Allan's fears seem to be backed up by fact. And the resolution, while it is something he has repressed all along, is more frightening than any of his paranoid imaginings. The resolution, however, is not quite the end of the story, and the ultimate climax is sure to shock you more than what has gone before.

Do read this—but don't read it while alone!

Farrell is an expert at inspiring terror in the hearts of his readers, as evidenced by his well-known *Whatever Happened to Baby Jane?* (1960), which was the basis for the chilling 1962 film starring Bette Davis and Joan Crawford. The author of numerous TV and filmscripts, Farrell has also written the novels *Death on the Sixth Day* (1961) and *Such a Gorgeous Kid like Me* (1967).

(*M.M.*)

*Faulkner, William. *Knight's Gambit.* New York: Random House, 1949. (SS/AD)

Nobel Prize–winner William Faulkner wrote six criminous short stories featuring Southern lawyer Gavin Stevens and narrated by Stevens's nephew and youthful Watson, Chick Mallison. Set in legendary Yoknapatawpha County, Mississippi, these tales are in classic Faulkner style and are peopled with characters reminiscent of his other work: Southerners who are not stereotypical but representative of Mississippi at the middle of the twentieth century. Stevens, a Phi Beta Kappa graduate of Harvard, is a quiet, contemplative man whose methods of detection are often highly unorthodox. But in spite of his erudition, he is no outsider in his native territory; he is equally at home within the confines of his study or out in the hills where moonshine is made. Chick, the nephew, is properly admiring for a Watson, but his more naive questions stem from his youth, rather than from the thick-headedness found in many a narrator of this type, thus making him all the more likable.

The stories are as slow-moving and gentle on the surface as the country in which they take place; but as in much of Faulkner's work, there is an undercurrent of raw emotion and violence held in check. In the title (and longest) story, Stevens deals with murderous jealousy within one of the county's great plantation families (whose fortune was founded on bootleg liquor); "Monk" is the story of a retarded man who commits what at first seems an inexplicable crime. And "Smoke" is about one of those feuds between family members for which the South is famous; when the murder of a judge results from his validation of a will, Stevens uses a simple but artful device to literally smoke out the killer.

In these and the three other stories—"Hand upon the Waters," "Tomorrow," and "An Error in Chemistry"—lawyer Stevens exhibits not only great deductive powers and resourcefulness but also great humanity. As he himself states, "I am more interested in justice and human beings than truth." This concern, coupled with Faulkner's deft characterization of the people he knew so well, make these stories first-rate tales of crime and detection.

Although many critics have dismissed the Gavin Stevens stories as inferior to Faulkner's other works, they are as inventive and finely crafted as the author's mainstream fiction, and in no way should be considered a departure from his high literary standards. As Ellery Queen aptly puts it in *Queen's Quorum,* "That a writer of Faulkner's now-international stature should unashamedly write detective stories proves once again—if such proof is still needed by literary snobs—that the detective story has long since come of age."

(*M.M.*)

Faust, Ron. *Tombs of Blue Ice.* Indianapolis: Bobbs-Merrill, 1974. (A/T)

During a mountain-climbing expedition in the French Alps, a sudden storm breaks and one of the two companions of American Robert Holmes is killed by a bolt of lightning; the other climber, a German named Dieter Streicher, is seriously injured. Unable to move Streicher, Holmes returns to the village of Chamonix to report the incident and request immediate help for the wounded man. A search party is sent out to the high mountain ledge where the accident occurred, but surprisingly finds no sign of Streicher, alive or dead. What could have happened to the man? Could he have managed to leave the ledge under his own power, for some unknown reason? Or has he been a victim of foul play? Streicher is the son of a vicious Nazi Occupation leader, and there are many in the little French valley who have good reason to want him dead: among them a woman named Christiane Renaud, whom Holmes desires; and her stepfather, the bitter old mountain guide Martigny.

Holmes sets out on his own to find Streicher and the truth about the man's disappearance. Most of the novel involves his determined quest, and most of it is harrowing—especially Holmes's descent into a huge crevasse, literally a tomb of blue ice. This is high-tech adventure writing, with a simple plot, strong characters, and evocative prose that includes memorable descriptive passages about mountain climbing and the glacial Alpine wilderness.

Ron Faust excels at outdoor crime/adventure fiction of all types, as his other novels prove: *The Wolf in the Clouds* (1977) which is about a pair of U.S. forest rangers and a madman on the loose in the Colorado Rockies; *The*

Burning Sky (1978), which deals with a deadly big-game hunt in a mountain valley in New Mexico (and which John D. MacDonald called "strong, tough . . . with that flavor of inevitability that seasons the good ones"); and three paperback originals with Mexican settings—*The Long Count* (1979), *Death Fires* (1980), and *Nowhere to Run* (1981).

(*B.P.*)

*Fearing, Kenneth. *The Big Clock.* New York: Harcourt Brace, 1946. (PS)

A poet of considerable stature and ability in the Twenties and Thirties, Kenneth Fearing turned to the writing of novels in 1939 and to the psychological thriller in 1941 with *Dagger of the Mind.* (This novel, set in a summer artists' colony, caused something of a stir when it was first published; Raymond Chandler, for instance, in his famous essay "The Simple Art of Murder," called it "a savage piece of intellectual double-talk.") In all, Fearing wrote five novels that can be considered criminous—by far the best of which is *The Big Clock.* This quintessential tale of psychological suspense is so good, in fact, that labeling it a small masterpiece would not be unjustified.

It is told in that most difficult of narrative techniques, multiple first-person viewpoints. Most of the story, however, is related by its chief protagonist, George Stroud, a reporter for *Crimeways,* one of a chain of magazines put out by Janoth Enterprises. Stroud is a sensitive man, a man who hates the pressures and conformity of his job, his slavery to what he calls "the big clock"; he yearns to be more like his boss, Earl Janoth. Janoth, with his "big, pink, disorderly face, permanently fixed in a faint smile he had forgotten about long ago," doesn't have to live by the dictates of the big clock. He doesn't even know there *is* a big clock, Stroud reflects.

But that is before the night Stroud happens to be in the wrong place at the wrong time, the night Earl Janoth murders his mistress, Pauline Delos: Stroud is the only person who knows his employer is guilty. This is only the beginning of his troubles, however—for Janoth knows that *somebody* saw him that night. Under the guise of performing a public service, he mobilizes his staff in an all-out campaign to find out who it is. And the man he assigns to head the task force is George Stroud himself.

The suspense that Fearing builds from this situation—through skillful intercutting of scenes told from Janoth's viewpoint and that of other members of his staff, such as Steve Hagen, Edward Orlin, and Emory Mafferson—is the kind that keeps you up into the wee hours turning pages. But *The Big Clock* is more than just a fine thriller; it is a novel of character and metaphysical insight in which the symbol of the big clock takes on more and more significance and ultimately becomes the focal point of the story.

One runs like a mouse up the old, slow pendulum of the big clock, time, scurries around and across its huge hands, strays inside through the intricate wheels and balances and springs of the inner mechanism, searching among the cobwebbed mazes of this machine with all its false exits and dangerous blind alleys and steep runways, natural traps and artificial baits, hunting for the true opening and the real prize.

Then the clock strikes one and it is time to go, to run down the pendulum, to become again a prisoner making once more the same escape.

For of course the clock that measures out the seasons, all gain and loss . . . this gigantic watch that fixes order and establishes the pattern for chaos itself, it has never changed, it will never change, or be changed.

Almost as good is the 1948 film version directed by John Farrow and featuring brilliant performances by Ray Milland as Stroud and Charles Laughton as Earl Janoth. It has been hailed, and rightly so, as one of the best *noir* films of the Forties.

Fearing's other suspense novels are worth investigating, although anyone who has read *The Big Clock* first will find them something of a letdown. The best is *Dagger of the Mind;* the others are *The Loneliest Girl in the World* (1951), *The Generous Heart* (1954), and *The Crozart Story* (1960).

(*B.P.*)

Fenisong, Ruth. *The Butler Died in Brooklyn.* New York: Doubleday Crime Club, 1943. (PP/R)

Fenisong wrote thirteen books about New York Police Sergeant (later Inspector) Gridley Nelson from 1942 to 1960. They enjoyed considerable popularity and many were reprinted in paperback. In an era of uneducated but street-wise fictional cops, Nelson has just about everything going for him. He is a Princeton graduate with a substantial private income that allows him to hire a full-time housekeeper who lives in Harlem and serves as an information pipeline through her friendships with other servants. This is of enormous value to Nelson since he is frequently assigned to investigate upper-class murders.

In *The Butler Died in Brooklyn,* tangled upper-class-family relationships are involved when Beulah Fitch Casey Danille Roberts's longtime butler, Shepard (who had just been fired without cause), is found murdered. "Booming Beulah" has just moved her entire household—including giddy granddaughter Marianne and her twin brothers—from Gramercy Park to a recently converted apartment house to be near her current husband's antique shop/warehouse. After another family murder, Nelson's housekeeper, Sammy, takes it upon herself to answer an ad for a maid in the household. Proper police procedure is followed, with long interrogation of suspects and extensive background checks, while Marianne complicates matters by trying to protect her brothers and getting herself kidnapped. It is the dogged, step-by-step investigation by Nelson, and Sammy behind the scenes, that finally solves the case just in time to prevent another murder.

Fenisong's books, even the nonseries ones like *Jenny Kissed Me* (1944), are a mixture of romance and suspense, and provide glimpses of how the other half lives. Her formula of the wealthy young police officer who "speaks the language" has been used by others, but never more successfully. Among Gridley Nelson's other successful cases are *Murder Needs a Face* (1942), *Deadlock* (1952), and *Dead Weight* (1962).

(*E.N.*)

Ferrars, E. X. *Alive and Dead.* New York: Doubleday Crime Club, 1975. (AD)

The novels of E. X. Ferrars (a pseudonym of Morna Brown, who also writes under the name of Elizabeth Ferrars) are best described as quiet and polite. The characters are usually normal middle-class British people—which is not to say they are dull; many are writers or artists or engaged in otherwise unusual professions; the women are independent and strong. But they are people to whom violence seldom happens; and when it does, they are shocked, but willingly take charge and get to the bottom of these unexpected happenings.

Martha Crayle is a typical Ferrars heroine. Middle-aged and twice divorced, she has struggled to raise two sons while caring for an invalid aunt and running a rooming house. When the aunt dies and leaves her an unexpected legacy, she moves out all her boarders except the reserved and stern Mr. Syme (who has become her confidant and, when crime strikes, a sort of Watson) and takes up volunteer work for the National Guild for the Welfare of Unmarried Mothers. It is at their offices that she meets Amanda Hassall, a young pregnant woman who claims she has been deserted by her husband and impregnated by the man she is living with. Amanda does not wish to marry the baby's father, nor does she want to put the child up for adoption as her parents have suggested. Martha takes the girl home, and a day later takes in another pregnant woman, Sandra Aspinall.

As Mr. Syme has darkly hinted, Martha should not have given refuge to these total strangers. Before Amanda has spent two nights in the house, a murdered man turns up in a local hotel, and she is reported to have been on the scene. Amanda insists the victim is her estranged husband, but her parents—who appeared shortly before the body was discovered—claim the husband died in an airplane crash the year before. In addition to the parents, the boyfriends of both young women arrive, and by the time murder is done twice, Martha thoroughly regrets her involvement and wishes she had listened to Mr. Syme. The plot twists and turns (with plenty of surprises) all the way to the very end. Ferrars writes well and creates characters that are sure to enlist her readers' sympathies. This novel is one of her best.

(*M.M.*)

Ferrars, E. X. *Frog in the Throat.* New York: Doubleday Crime Club, 1980. (AD)

Virginia Freer, heroine of *Frog in the Throat,* is staying with craftsmen friends Helen and Andrew Boscott (he's a furniture restorer, she's a weaver and tapestry worker) for a much-needed holiday. On a quiet afternoon, in walks the big mistake of Virginia's life—Felix Freer, her estranged husband. Felix is one of those charming people who have few scruples and an overwhelming capacity for lying—even when he thinks he's telling the truth. He is now lying about his reasons for dropping in at the Boscott house, and Virginia wonders why.

The events of the evening only complicate matters. At a neighbor's cocktail party, novelist Carleen Fyffe (half of a famous sister team of historical-romance writers) announces her engagement to poet Basil Deering (whom Felix has expressed an interest in meeting). Shortly after the Freers and Boscotts return home, Olivia Fyffe arrives, saying she has found her sister on the floor of their den, murdered. When they all go to the Fyffe cottage, however, there is no body. Almost everyone thinks Olivia is being dramatic for some reason of her own, or perhaps hysterical. It takes a second body and the discovery of her sister's corpse to prove otherwise, and a certain amount of detection on Virginia's part to determine Felix's connection with the murders.

The pace of this novel is slow, with good characterization of all participants except the heroine. The plot unfolds in the best tradition of the British country-house mystery, with plenty of suspicion and all ends tied up nicely at the conclusion. One wishes, however, that Virginia Freer were as well characterized as her enigmatic and complex husband and hosts. It is a little hard to care what happens to any of them when the viewpoint character is so lacking in substance.

Ferrars has been writing mysteries for over forty years; many of her tales are set in such locales as Greece, Africa, Mexico, and Australia, as well as in England. Other notable titles include *Give the Corpse a Bad Name* (1940), *Hunt the Tortoise* (1950), *The Busy Body* (1962), *The Seven Sleepers* (1970), *The Cup and the Lip* (1976), and *Crime and the Crystal* (1985).

(*M.M.*)

Fickling, G. G. *This Girl for Hire.* New York: Pyramid, 1957. (O/PI)

G. G. Fickling was the pseudonym of the writing team of Forrest E. ("Skip") Fickling and his wife, Gloria, creators of Honey West, billed on the front cover, the back cover, and even the spine of *This Girl for Hire* as "the sexiest private eye ever to pull a trigger!" Honey's sex is made much of in the course of the book: She spends as much time getting into and out of bathing suits as she does working on the case, and her measurements (38-22-36) are cited both on the back cover and in the text.

The case itself, which involves eight deaths before it ends, begins when Honey is hired by a down-and-out actor whose apparent murder leads to the other killings, all of people involved in the television industry. Despite the setting, there is little actual insight into television, unless the actors, producers, and directors really do spend most of their days and nights drinking and carousing. The book is filled with incident, even including a strip-poker game, but the plot is so confusing that the reader is unlikely to be convinced by its unraveling, which comes about more by accident than by good detective work. Still, there is a certain prefeminist charm in seeing the hard-boiled Honey at work in a man's world, despite Lieutenant Mark Storm (his real name) and his attempts to persuade her to leave the brainwork to the men.

Pyramid Books occasionally referred to Honey West as "literary history's first lady private eye," and undoubtedly the novelty of a female first-person narrator helped sell the series, but James L. Rubel's Eli Donavan was playing the same part years earlier in Gold Medal's *No Business for a Lady* (1950). Still, it was Honey who was a success, starring in eleven books and a TV series in which she was portrayed by Anne Francis.

The Ficklings produced one other short-lived series for Belmont Books, this one featuring a male private eye named Erik March, in such titles as *The Case of the Radioactive Redhead* (1963).

(B.C.)

Finney, Jack. *The House of Numbers.* New York: Dell First Edition, 1956. (O/T)

Jack Finney has the unusual ability to create edge-of-the-chair tension and sustain it throughout a long narrative. In this riveting tale, Ben Jarvis and Ruth Gehlmann conspire to help Ben's brother, Arnie, escape from San Quentin. Arnie, who was sentenced for passing bad checks while trying to raise money to buy Ruth an expensive engagement ring, has attacked a guard; there is a paroled prisoner on the way back to San Quentin to testify about the assault; and the penalty for attacking a guard is death.

Arnie appeals to Ben for help and lays out a dangerous but basically simple scheme for escape. Ben wavers, but finally he and Ruth agree to aid Arnie. The scheme unfolds bit by bit, and the reader is solidly on Ben and Ruth's side throughout, experiencing their apprehension and terror—and eventually agonizing over the same terrible decision they face. Finney knows San Quentin, although his view of it is colored by his association with then-warden Harley O. Teets, a humanitarian administrator to whom the book is dedicated. (In fact, the dialogue of the fictional warden reads a little like a public-relations release.) However, the method Finney devises for the escape is ingenious, and the characters are well drawn. The suspense, as with all Finney's works, is guaranteed to keep you turning the pages.

Although best known for his science fiction and fantasy works, such as the popular *Body Snatchers* (1955), which was twice made into a film under the title *Invasion of the Body Snatchers* (1956, 1978), Finney has also written three other suspense novels: *Five Against the House* (1954), *Assault on a Queen* (1959), and *The Night People* (1977). *Five Against the House* was made into an excellent film in 1955, starring Kim Novak and Brian Keith, and directed by Phil Karlson.

(*M.M.*)

Fischer, Bruno. *The Silent Dust.* New York: Dodd, Mead, 1950. (PI)

Bruno Fischer had a great deal of success in both the hardcover and pulp fields; and when the pulps gradually died out, he went on to sell millions of copies of his original paperback novels. In *Paperback Quarterly* (Vol. 1, No. 4), Fischer described his "usual manner" of writing as containing "movement and suspense with very little violence," and as being about "ordinary people in extraordinary situations."

The Silent Dust (one of his hardcover mysteries) is narrated by Fischer's strongest series character, private detective Ben Helm, one of the few successfully characterized married private eyes in fiction. Helm is not cast in the typical mold of the early Fifties private eye in other ways, either. He is more intellectual than physical, and the major clues in *The Silent Dust* are literary ones. The book's title is an allusion to Gray's "Elegy," and in the course of the story, other British poets are prominent. There are two offstage murders, one of an author and one of her husband, both motivated by a desire to stop publication of the author's book, entitled *A Handful of Ashes.* The author, it seems, has a nasty habit of portraying her friends and acquaintances in her works, revealing things about them that they would rather not have publicized. The suspects include a former gangster, his wife, a fifteen-year-old genius, a chauffeur with a criminal record, and a matinee idol. The writing is literate; Helm is compassionate; the story is tight and well told. And no doubt Fischer had fun writing the excerpts from the dead author's book.

Another good Ben Helm book is *More Deaths than One* (1947), in which Fischer does a fine job with the difficult multiple-first-person-point-of-view technique.

(*B.C.*)

Fischer, Bruno. *So Wicked My Love.* Greenwich, Conn.: Fawcett Gold Medal, 1954. (O/T)

Ray Whitehead, the narrator of *So Wicked My Love,* rejected by his fiancée, gives her ring to a redhead he picks up in Coney Island. He goes to the redhead's hotel room with her, discovers that she has been involved in an armored-car robbery, and watches her stab a man to death. All of this happens in the first twenty pages of the story, and the redhead continues to make life miserable for Ray Whitehead. She is one of those wonderfully amoral sexpots of paperback-original fiction that are more easily acquired than gotten rid of. Ray does manage to get rid of the $80,000 that he is stuck with (the loot from the robbery), but the girl keeps turning up at the most inopportune times. For example, when Ray's fiancée realizes that she loves him after all, who should turn up but the redhead, of course—wearing the ring. In fact, the girl becomes something of a millstone to Whitehead, involving him in all sorts of difficulties with her past and present criminal associates.

Though not as tightly plotted as some of Fischer's other work (it was expanded from a magazine story), *So Wicked My Love* is typically fast-paced. The main characters, especially Whitehead, in the role of the innocent man drawn into criminal events, are particularly well done.

Other Fischer paperbacks of interest are *Knee-Deep in Death* (1956), *Murder in the Raw* (1957), and *Second-Hand Nude* (1961).

(*B.C.*)

Fish, Robert L. *The Green Hell Treasure.* New York: Putnam's, 1971. (PP/T)

Though the Edgar-winning *Fugitive* (1962) was the first of ten mystery novels Robert Fish wrote about Jose Da Silva, *The Green Hell Treasure* is far more typical of the series. Because *The Fugitive* is about an escaped Nazi war criminal in South America, it is, of necessity, more serious than its successors. As his series progressed, Fish would make increased use of Brazil, where Da Silva, a police captain, acts as liaison between the Brazilian police and Interpol. The subject matter of his books became more exotic, and humor played a greater role.

Robert L. Fish knew Brazil intimately, having spent more than ten years there as a consulting engineer with a Brazilian vinyl plastics firm. Fish always preferred to use places in which he had lived or traveled as background for his work. Brazil, a combination of virtually impenetrable jungle and modern cities and resorts, is ideal for a man like Da Silva who is at home in any of these settings. Early books such as *Isle of the Snakes* (1963) and *The Shrunken Head* (1963) emphasize the primitive, especially the exotic and dangerous fauna and Indian headshrinkers. Though on the surface detective stories, they are as much thrillers. By the time of *The Green Hell Treasure,* the series had become a satisfying blend of sophistication and adventure.

Throughout the series, Wilson, an undercover agent at the American Embassy in Rio de Janeiro, plays "Watson" to Da Silva. If their byplay is not quite in the Wolfe-Goodwin class, it is still very witty indeed. In *The Green Hell Treasure,* they start out in Brazil, as usual, but then travel to Barbados in pursuit of half a million dollars in stolen jewels, the titular treasure. In an extremely amusing scene, the intrepid Da Silva is transformed into a nervous wreck due to his fear of flying. If the solution is somewhat obvious, the book is resolved in an exciting climax told in almost cinematic language. This is not surprising when one remembers that Fish, under his Robert Pike (q.v.) pseudonym, wrote *Mute Witness* (1963), which was adapted to the screen as the very exciting Steve McQueen film *Bullitt* (1968). Nor should the humor in *The Green Hell Treasure* amaze us when one thinks of Fish as the author of *The Incredible Schlock Homes* and, under another ichthyological pen name. A. C. Lamprey, an amusing series of comic definitions in *Ellery Queen's Mystery Magazine* called "Gumshoe Glossary."

Fish's other books under his own name are equally diverse. The novels *The Hochmann Miniatures* (1967), *Whirligig* (1970), *The Tricks of the Trade* (1972), and *The Wager* (1974), and the short-story collection *Kek Huuygens, Smuggler* (1976), feature the adventures of master smuggler Kek Huuygens. *The Murder League* (1968), *Rub-a-Dub-Dub* (1971), and *A Gross Carriage of Justice* (1979) follow the amusing exploits of three old rogues named Carruthers, Simpson, and Briggs, all of whom are ex–detective-story writers. *A Handy Death* (1973; with Henry Rothblatt) and *Pursuit* (1978) are nonseries thrillers of high caliber.

(*M.L.*)

Fish, Robert L. *The Incredible Schlock Homes.* New York: Simon & Schuster, 1966. (C/SS)

Only the most humorless Sherlockians could object to the way their hero is treated in these enormously funny parodies, all twelve of which were originally published in *Ellery Queen's Mystery Magazine.* Because Fish clearly knew the canon, these stories are also excellent pastiches of the works of Sir Arthur Conan Doyle (q.v.). He has captured Doyle's style in having a

Dr. Watson narrate the events, and the cases generally start with the same time-tested devices used to begin the Sherlock Holmes tales. A distressed potential client appears, and Homes, who has never seen him or her before, uses his best deductive methods to guess pertinent facts. He is totally wrong, but hilariously so.

Starting with a decidedly cockeyed chronology, "Watson" proceeds to refer to past successes of Homes's, and these are merely excuses for some of the most outrageous puns ever to appear in the mystery genre. For example, Homes's efforts on behalf of a Polish group are included as "The Adventure of the Danzig Men." The detective's involvement with a British lord who, because of dishonesty, had to resign from his clubs is called "The Adventure of the Dismembered Peer." Obviously, nothing is to be sacred here, including the names of the famous characters. Watson goes under the name "Watney," Mrs. Hudson becomes "Mrs. Essex," and Professor Moriarty operates as "Professor Marty." The action starts at 221B *Bagel* Street.

"The Adventure of the Ascot Tie," Fish's first published story, is probably the best in the collection, but it is only minutely superior to "The Adventure of the Stockbroker's Clark," "The Adventure of the Artist's Mottle," and "The Adventure of the Snared Drummer." Another group of stories, almost as good, was collected and published as *The Memoirs of Schlock Homes* (1974). All are delightful to read as they lovingly spoof the methods and idiosyncrasies of the most famous character in all of literature, exposing the frequently tenuous reasoning by which Sir Arthur's hero came up with his solutions. Schlock's methods are very similar—except he is always wrong, to our comic delight. It is proof of the permanent appeal of Sherlock Holmes that a talented writer like Robert L. Fish can take him apart, giving us great pleasure, and yet at the same time make us anxious to read the original stories once again.

(*M.L.*)

Fisher, Steve. *Saxon's Ghost.* Los Angeles: Sherbourne, 1969. (PS)

Steve Fisher had a long career of writing mystery fiction. He wrote for the pulps—*Black Mask, Adventure,* and *Argosy,* among many others—and for the leading slick magazines—*Esquire, Cosmopolitan,* and the *Saturday Evening Post.* Fisher also wrote more than thirty motion-picture screenplays, including *Lady in the Lake* (1946), *Johnny Angel* (1945), *The Big Frame* (1953), *I, Mobster* (1959), *Johnny Reno* (1966), and *Rogue's Gallery* (1968).

Steve Fisher's writing style can best be described as hard-boiled laced with sentimentality: His characters are prone to strong emotions; his plots are action-packed and melodramatic. But Fisher's strengths are his professional style and honest presentation of characters pushed to their limits.

The arguable best of Fisher's twenty novels is *Saxon's Ghost.* Joe

Saxon, one of the world's best stage magicians, known as the Great Saxon, finds himself involved in the occult arts when his beautiful young assistant, Ellen Hayes, disappears. Saxon has to use all his arts of legerdemain to arrive at the chilling truth: The ESP powers he and Ellen fooled audiences into believing in are real. When Saxon learns Ellen has been murdered, he uses these ESP powers to reach out to her beyond the grave to deliver a special brand of earthly justice.

Other recommended novels by Fisher include *The Night Before Murder* (1939) and his most famous novel, *I Wake Up Screaming* (1941; revised edition, 1960), which was filmed in 1942 starring Victor Mature and Betty Grable.

(*G.K.*)

*Fleming, Ian. *Casino Royale.* New York: Macmillan, 1953. (E)

The spy novels of Ian Fleming made James Bond—Agent 007 of British Intelligence—a household name and spawned a large number of films, as well as imitators both good and bad. This great escape fiction seemed just what was needed by the 1950s world—still austere after the sacrifices of World War II and newly frozen in the grip of the cold war—and the public's reaction was tremendous. Fleming gave his readers richly detailed descriptions of exotic locales, exclusive hotels and resorts, fine foods and wines, expensive cars, luxury consumer goods, and beautiful women. And for the first time, sex—illicit, hedonistic, and sophisticated—came to the forefront in the British mystery. Bond's basic character was nothing new to the genre, since he is very much in the tradition of the snobbish, urbane gentleman, but the villains *were* something new and so hideously evil and inventive in their wicked ways as to often strain the reader's credulity. The Bond novels, even with their rampant sexism and fervent anticommunism, can be great fun if read with the context of their times in mind.

As *Casino Royale* opens, we find Bond at the casino at Royale-les-Eaux, watching a powerful agent of the Opposition (SMERSH) play baccarat. Bond is acting undercover, posing as a rich client of a Jamaican import-export firm, and his mission is to see that the agent, Le Chiffre, who is reported to be on the brink of financial disaster, is "ridiculed and destroyed." Bond has been chosen for this assignment by his boss—known throughout the series only as M—because 007 is the finest gambler in the Secret Service.

Much to Bond's dismay, the Service also sends him a "Number Two": a woman named Vesper Lynd. Bond's comments are telling on this point: Although Vesper is a beautiful woman, 007 is "not amused. . . . Women were for recreation." A true professional, however, Bond eventually establishes a rapport with Vesper and comes to respect her abilities—and, inevitably, also becomes romantically involved with her.

Fleming gives his reader excellent glimpses into the operation of the grand casinos and the people who frequent them; a high-stakes baccarat game in which Bond becomes enmeshed with Le Chiffre holds even the attention of those who know or care nothing about cards. There are car chases, a literally torturous confrontation with the villain, and an ending that combines success with disillusionment in a manner characteristic of the series.

(*M.M.*)

Fleming, Ian. *Doctor No.* New York: Macmillan, 1958. (E)

Agent 007, on the road to recovery following a long convalescence after a particularly rough case (*From Russia with Love,* 1957), is sent to Kingston, Jamaica, to look into the disappearance of fellow agents Strangways and Trueblood. Both have vanished without a trace while working on a case involving a nearly extinct bird, the roseate spoonbill, which lives in a sanctuary on a private island, Crab Key. The key is owned by a half-Chinese, half-German called Dr. No, who claims to have bought the island for a guano factory. Members of the Audubon Society have become concerned about the birds' welfare, but investigators they have sent to the key have died in mysterious circumstances. Bond goes to Jamaica and arranges to be put ashore on the key, but not before he has a chilling encounter with a poisonous tropical centipede. Once ashore, he meets with a naked girl, killer dogs, hostile "Chinese Negroes," and Dr. No himself—a man whose ever-present "thin smile" disguises his truly sinister designs.

The novel proceeds to a slam-bang ending that includes a vicious torture scene, a harrowing encounter with a giant squid, and a clever coup de grace aptly labeled in the chapter heading, "A Shower of Death."

This entry in the series is a fine example of the standard plot structure Fleming employed, and ends on a more positive note than many of 007's adventures.

(*M.M.*)

Fleming, Ian. *Goldfinger.* New York: Macmillan, 1959. (E)

This is perhaps Fleming's wildest plot, involving a maniacal criminal with a lust for gold and a plan to rob Fort Knox. Bond's association with Auric Goldfinger begins in Nassau when he encounters Junius Dupont, a rich American who feels he is being cheated while playing two-handed canasta with Goldfinger. Bond agrees to watch their games and soon discovers that Goldfinger—whose desire is to sport a golden tan at all times—has a very effective method of cheating his opponent. An excellent cardplayer himself, Bond quickly extricates Dupont from the man's clutches, and considers the matter closed. Weeks later, however, Goldfinger surfaces in the files of British Intelligence as a possible international threat, and Bond finds himself once more involved with the man, this time professionally. There is the usual complement of beautiful girls, luxury clubs, and odd methods of torture and murder, but what this novel points up about the Bond series is that there is also a lot of low-key action: long, detailed card games, golf matches, and conversations. Those not interested in Fleming's passions (cards, politics, golf, and business) may find some parts of these books tedious, but the author was skillful enough to hold the reader's interest, at least minimally.

Goldfinger was made into an immensely successful film in 1964, with Sean Connery as Bond. Connery appeared as Bond in other films, notably *Dr. No* (1962), *From Russia with Love* (1964), and *Thunderball* (1965). The character of James Bond has also been portrayed by Peter Sellers (*Casino Royale,* 1967), Roger Moore (*Live and Let Die,* 1973, among others), and George Lazenby (*On Her Majesty's Secret Service,* 1969).

The novel on which this latter film is based is notable because here we see Bond at his most human—in love and planning to be married. Agent 007 also appears in two short-story collections, *For Your Eyes Only: Five Secret Occasions in the Life of James Bond* (1960), and *Octopussy, and the Living Daylights* (1966). The Bond series was continued by John Gardner (q.v.) after Fleming's death.

(*M.M.*)

Fletcher, J. S. *The Middle Temple Murder.* New York: Knopf, 1919. (AD)

Julian Symons, English author and critic, coined a good name for the multitude of middle-rank mystery writers who lacked literary skill and ingenuity—the Humdrums. J. S. Fletcher stood in the front rank of the prolific English phalanx of Humdrums. He wrote over a hundred books on a variety of subjects, and the majority were detective stories. These melodramas are extremely conventional, with the not-too-brilliant central puzzle dominating the story. They are a comfortable confirmation of decency and lawfulness for the moneyed middle class. Snobbery descends to racial prejudice (with several Chinese villains), and despicable, evil foreigners have dark complexions and comical accents. Not much scientific detection is involved, and the tenets of the Golden Age are not closely followed. There is too much reliance on coincidence, detectives missing details, failure to follow up clues, and mysterious figures who appear to wrap up the plot at the end.

It is a trifling triumph to select one of Fletcher's detective stories as his best. From *The Amaranth Club* (1926) to *The Yorkshire Moorland Murder* (1930), there is not much to choose from, except for *The Middle Temple Murder.* While the plot is fairly pedestrian, many of Fletcher's defects are absent. It is one of his earliest works, and attracted the first real notice for

Fletcher in the United States when it was championed by Woodrow Wilson. The story concerns Frank Spargo, subeditor of the *Watchman,* who happens to be present when a bludgeoned body is found in the Middle Temple. The hotshot reporter (he's as bright as any latter-day Flash Casey) teams up with Ronald Breton, barrister, to follow the clues in this devious mystery. The victim is John Marbury, from Australia, who was struck down on his first night back in London after an absence of many years. This photoprocedural novel is a case of complicated theft, legacy, parentage, and includes a suspected empty coffin. A major motif (as in many Fletcher tales) is railway travel—checking timetables; confirming alibis; zipping around to discover clues; getaways and pursuits.

Fletcher has been praised for his novels set in the English countryside, but the atmosphere in most of these is overwrought and the descriptions dull. Novels such as *The Middle Temple Murder* and *The Charing Cross Mystery* (1923) are vivid because most of the action takes place in the streets, byways, squares, stations, and buildings of London, and is reported in factual detail.

(*T.B.*)

Flora, Fletcher. *Skuldoggery.* New York: Belmont, 1967. (O/C)

A talented writer whose work received regrettably little attention during his lifetime, Fletcher Flora was one of the best producers of criminous short stories in the 1950s and 1960s. His range was remarkable: everything from hard-boiled tales for such magazines as *Manhunt* to police procedurals, to straightforward whodunits, to light whimsy, to literary stories that transcended the genre. As a novelist, however, Flora was less successful. His books are extremely well written, with engaging characters and strong suspense; but they are all short on plot, tending to be slices of life or collections of incidents rather than fully realized novels. *Skuldoggery* falls into that category, but everything else about it is so good that it ranks as Flora's best novel—though probably his least known, owing to the fact that it was published by a small paperback house and poorly distributed. (The fact that a front-line publisher failed to recognize its merits is beyond comprehension.)

When Grandfather Hunter dies, he leaves an estate of $10 million, which his greedy family—Uncle Homer; Aunt Madge; Junior; Flo; and Flo's twins, Hester and Lester—expects to inherit. Ah, but no; grandfather's will instead gives the dough to Señorita Fogarty, who happens to be a Chihuahua of questionable breeding, for her exclusive use throughout her lifetime and the lifetimes of her pups and her pups' pups ad infinitum. Of course there is a proviso that should Señorita Fogarty and all her subsequent pups expire, the inheritance then passes on to the family. And of course what the novel is all about are the bumbling attempts of Uncle Homer, Aunt Madge, Junior, Flo, and Flo's twins to dispose of Señorita Fogarty, and the determined efforts of grandfather's faithful servants, the Crumps, to thwart them.

This sort of farce is not unfamiliar, but it is nonetheless beautifully conceived and written with considerable drollery and wit. Anyone willing to spend the time and effort tracking down a copy will not be disappointed.

Most of Flora's other novels were also paperback originals; among the more notable of these are *The Hot Shot* (1956) and *Leave Her to Hell* (1958), both of which are in the tough vein. He also published three hardcovers—*Killing Cousins* (1960), another delightfully murderous farce, which won the Macmillan Cock Robin Mystery Award; *The Irrepressible Peccadillo* (1962); and *Hildegard Withers Makes the Scene* (1969), which he was commissioned to finish when Stuart Palmer (q.v.) died, and which he completed shortly before his own untimely death.

(*B.P.*)

Flynn, Jay. *A Body for McHugh.* New York: Avon, 1960. (O/A)

This is one entry in a nifty little five-book paperback series that Flynn did in the early 1960s. McHugh owns a back-street San Francisco bar, the Door, that serves as the local wateringhole for assorted spy types, ours and theirs. McHugh (no first name is supplied) is one of ours, working for one of those secret agencies tucked away in a Pentagon subbasement; he periodically takes on assignments messing around in Mexican or Caribbean revolutions, recovering Nazi war prizes, and the like. Oddly, the books were packaged as if they were typical private-eye novels; consequently, they may have failed to find the audience that would best appreciate these neatly crafted action yarns. Matt Helm fans, in particular, will find them right up their street.

In this one, a man is knifed just outside the Door, and a scared young girl, apparently there to meet him, slips out the back way before McHugh (and the FBI and CIA agents hanging around) can get a line on her. The killings that ensue (some engineered by adept assassin McHugh) have to do with a missing suitcase full of money, the loot from a double-cross-infested operation by a group of Cubans trying to get their wealth out before Castro grabbed it. The action ranges up and down the California coast, from San Francisco to L.A. to Carmel, with assorted law-enforcement agencies, intelligence agencies, and the Mafia mixed into the caper.

The other four books in the series are *McHugh* (1959), *It's Murder, McHugh* (1960), *Viva McHugh!* (1960), and *The Five Faces of Murder* (1962). Flynn also wrote a number of nonseries suspense novels, among the best of which are *Drink with the Dead* (1959), about a bootlegging operation in northern California; and *The Action Man* (1961), about a heist involving a golf tournament modeled on the one at Pebble Beach.

(*A.S.*)

Foley, Rae. *Death and Mr. Potter.* New York: Dodd, Mead, 1955. (AD)

Rae Foley is, in mystery terms, a graduate of the Mary Roberts Rinehart (q.v.) and had-I-but-known school of writing. She is known as one of the leading lights of "romantic suspense," yet in her early days Foley wrote mysteries that approximated the classic puzzler. *Death and Mr. Potter* is one of these efforts. It is the first in a series of books featuring mild-mannered Mr. Hiram Potter as amateur sleuth.

Potter is Old Money. But that money had always been in the firm grasp of his autocratic mother. As the book opens, the matriarch's funeral is concluding and the long-cowed and obedient son finds himself unexpectedly independent—both emotionally and financially. If that isn't excitement enough, a young woman plunges from a neighboring high-rise into Potter's garden. Hiram investigates out of a sense of moral outrage—and the suspicion that one of the mourners at his mother's funeral must be the murderer.

The story resembles standard murder-at-the-manor fare, except this time the manor is in Gramercy Park and not an English village. The characters are generally stock figures, from the blackmailing poor relations to the ethnic servants who (as Italians) are fat, drink too much wine, and smell of garlic.

Still, there is a certain charm to Hiram Potter and his sincere, if largely ineffectual, sleuthing. The nine Potter mysteries represent Foley's best mystery work. Although inferior in quality, Foley is better remembered for the more than twenty damsel-in-distress thrillers she produced in the Sixties and Seventies. In these, feminine but fluff-headed young women prove even more ineffectual at detecting than Hiram Potter. They are usually thoroughly bruised and battered by the time they stumble across the murderer, and into the arms of a dominant male suitor, at book's end.

Hiram Potter also appears in *Back Door to Death* (1963), *Call It Accident* (1965), and *A Calculated Risk* (1970).

(*K.L.M.*)

*Follett, Ken. *Eye of the Needle.* New York: Arbor House, 1978. (E)

Eye of the Needle is one of the best of the recent spate of World War II espionage novels. Ken Follett combines a very believable plot based on astounding historical fact with excellent pacing and—a real boon in this type of thriller—well-rounded, sympathetic characters.

The historical fact is that in 1944 the Allies created a fake army in southeastern England. To Nazi reconnaissance planes, it looked like a huge encampment set to invade France at Calais. But seen from the ground, the "barracks" had only one side and a roof; the "airplanes" were mere carcasses sunk into the ground, with no engines or wheels. It was a hoax of gigantic proportions that convinced the Nazis to concentrate their defenses at Calais instead of Normandy, and it affected the outcome of the war.

But this outcome would have been very different had there been one German spy who saw the phony encampment at ground level and reported it to Berlin. Suppose there had been such a spy, a master spy, an upper-class German, somewhat of a rebel, who refused to join the Nazi party but still had the ear of Hitler. Suppose such a spy had lived in London long enough to pass as an Englishman. . . .

This is the central premise of *Eye of the Needle.* Here Follett gives us *Die Nadel*—the Needle—who uses a stiletto to kill anyone who threatens his mission or his cover. He kills as a soldier; he doesn't enjoy it. In a moment of self-inquiry, he wonders if his personality—the ever-present wariness that keeps him at a distance from everyone else—has really not been foisted upon him by his occupation, as he likes to suppose; perhaps, he thinks, he has instead chosen his profession because it is the only type of work that can make him appear normal, even to himself. Such self-doubt (although it is a luxury the Needle rarely permits himself) has us at least nominally on his side for much (but not all) of the novel, even as the British agents—a typically tweedy ex-professor named Godliman and a former Scotland Yard man named Bloggs—match him in intelligence and quickly realize he has discovered their great hoax.

With this discovery, the chase becomes faster and more desperate. Circumstances lead Die Nadel to a storm-battered island in the North Sea, where a frustrated young woman, Lucy Rose, and her wheelchair-bound husband (he lost both of his legs in a traffic accident) live in bitter isolation and where much of the novel's action takes place. Lucy's attraction to the Needle, her fear and revulsion when she finds out what he is, and finally her desperate struggle to keep from becoming his latest victim make for some of the best edge-of-the-chair suspense writing of the past decade. (The 1981 film version starring Donald Sutherland and Kate Nelligan has its moments but unfortunately falls far short of the novel.)

Follett's success with *Eye of the Needle* led to a number of other best sellers, none of which has the same raw power and tension. Those other thrillers include *Triple* (1979), *The Key to Rebecca* (1980), *The Man from St. Petersburg* (1982), and *On the Wings of Eagles* (1983).

(*S.D./B.P.*)

Forbes, Stanton. *If Laurel Shot Hardy the World Would End.* New York: Doubleday Crime Club, 1970. (W)

During Mime Day at Shenley College, a small eastern school, students from the Classical Cinema Department all decide to dress up as Laurel and Hardy for their annual high jinks. One pair of actors takes the opportunity to murder the president of a nearby electronics corporation, Sacheville, Inc., and newly hired PR director Larry Evans is implicated in the crime. In order to save his bacon, Evans undertakes an investigation of his own, pokes around among a bunch of rather quirky (to say the least) suspects, and eventually unmasks the culprits.

This is a fine idea for a mystery, but the execution is poor. Forbes's style is a cross between eccentric and sophomoric; so is her humor. Some might find this sort of thing clever and amusing, but this reviewer isn't one of them. (The best thing about the book, in fact, is its wraparound dust jacket depicting thirteen sad-faced Laurels against an orange background—one of the niftiest jackets on any contemporary crime novel.)

Forbes is the author of numerous other novels, among them the likewise fancifully titled *Go to Thy Death Bed* (1968), *The Name's Death, Remember Me?* (1969), and *The Sad, Sudden Death of My Fair Lady* (1971). She has also written numerous mysteries under the pseudonyms Tobias Wells (q.v.) and Forbes Rydell (collaborations with Helen B. Rydell).

(B.P.)

Ford, Leslie. *Ill Met by Moonlight.* New York: Farrar & Rinehart, 1938. (AD)

Leslie Ford (a pseudonym of Zenith Brown, who also wrote as David Frome, q.v.) has often been accused of being one of the leading practitioners of the "had-I-but-known" school, and it is true that a great many of these leading and tension-spoiling statements appear in her novels. However, shortsighted critics have overlooked her carefully delineated exploration of life among people who are not too different from the average reader except in the fact that, through familial associations, political affinity, or geographic accident, they invite more than their fair share of murder and well-bred mayhem.

This is the second adventure of Colonel John T. Primrose and Sergeant Phineas Buck, one in which the unlikely but highly successful combination of retired officer and retired enlisted man is teamed with a thirty-eight-year-old widow, Grace Latham. Grace is of a distinguished Georgetown family, and her elegant home forms the backdrop for many of the books in this series. *Ill Met by Moonlight* takes place in another setting—April Harbor, Maryland, a summer playground for an inbred group of upper-crust families, where Grace and her relatives have been vacationing for years. Primrose and Buck are guests at Grace's cottage when she finds a neighbor dead of carbon-monoxide poisoning in the garage next door.

An old romance, a troubled marriage, a new love affair, and relationships with the folks in the neighboring town are all woven together in this engrossing and charming tale of love and murder.

(*E.N.*)

Ford, Leslie. *Siren in the Night.* New York: Scribner's, 1943. (AD)

Grace Latham, Colonel Primrose, and Sergeant Buck reappear in yet another locale in this wartime story. Grace is spending the spring in San Francisco because her son, a naval air cadet, is stationed there; Primrose and Buck have traveled west because of the colonel's involvement in the war effort. The city is at its charming best, except for placards indicating where the air-raid shelters are and "the sudden rising wail of the alert siren, and the lights of that Golden City fading like a million synchronized fireflies dying in the night."

A blackout, in fact, plays a key role in the discovery of the murder of Loring Kimball, popular resident of San Joaquin Terrace, where Grace has taken a house. If all the lights in the city hadn't gone out except for the one in Kimball's study, no one would have stopped in to investigate, and his body might not have been discovered for some time—thus allowing the killer to escape the scrutinizing eyes of Colonel Primrose. But the lights do go out; the body is found by neighbor Nat Donahue (who is immediately suspected of the crime); and when all residents of the small street are accounted for, it turns out that a number weren't where they should have been at the time of Kimball's death.

As Primrose probes into the lives of these residents, hidden passions and secrets come to the surface. The suspects are varied and well characterized, and the portrait Ford paints of wartime San Francisco is memorable. While as mannered as Ford's other mysteries, there is a dark side to this novel, as exemplified by the blackout and the implied threat of annihilation by the enemy.

The Primrose/Latham series is best read in order of publication, since its chief charm lies in the complexity of the relationships among the main characters. Other notable titles include *The Simple Way of Poison* (1937), *Old Lover's Ghost* (1940), and *The Woman in Black* (1947).

(*M.M.*)

*Forester, C. S. *Payment Deferred.* Boston: Little, Brown, 1942. (PS)

Payment Deferred is not a mystery. It is, rather, a stunning tour de force detailing "the perfect crime," and its devastating aftermath on a working-class British family. Everything is in the telling.

Will Marble and his family exist rather drearily on his income as a clerk at a bank. When a long-lost relative arrives from the colonies (Africa) with a fortune in cash and a sad story about having no other living relatives, Mr. Marble seizes the moment. He murders the boy, buries him in the backyard, and doubles the fortune through a series of crooked financial manipulations. He becomes a man of wealth and station. He has committed the perfect murder and has gone unpunished. All seems right with the world.

What follows is a tale of retribution visited on Mr. Marble, his wife, and ultimately his children. The family, never close, begins to fall apart. The daughter, embarrassed by her parents' common background, turns her back on the family (if not their newfound wealth) and leaves home. The son, bought off with expensive gifts and enrollment in the public school system, is both unloved and unloving. Mrs. Marble, discovering her husband's terrible secret, is forced to share his nightmare world of fear and suspicion. Mr. Marble, forever brooding, sits by an open window refusing to leave home and maintains a constant vigil on the unmarked grave. His drinking, always a problem, gets worse. A blackmailing neighbor bleeds him financially. The family seems farthest apart at those times spent together.

Forester's prose is first-rate and his characterizations haunting. And the ending is guaranteed to surprise, with just the right fanciful touch to make it a perfect ironic counterpoint to the somber tone of the rest of the novel.

C. S. Forester's fame rests on his later, noncriminous writings, in particular his series of sea adventures featuring Captain Horatio Hornblower, which remain in print to the present. Several films have been made from his novels, among them the 1942 MGM production of *Payment Deferred* (starring Charles Laughton) and the 1951 Humphrey Bogart/Katharine Hepburn film *The African Queen.* His only other crime novel, *Plain Murder,* was published as a paperback original by Dell in 1954.

(*B.T.*)

Forrest, Richard. *A Child's Garden of Death.* Indianapolis: Bobbs-Merrill, 1975. (AD)

Take one children's-book writer who is also a hot-air-ballooning enthusiast; add his fictional creations, the Wobblies, and his politician wife, plus his best friend from Korean War days, now police chief in their small Connecticut town. These staple ingredients of Richard Forrest's series about

Lyon Wentworth add up to an intriguing mix—even before the element of murder enters.

In this first entry in the series—whose titles are variations on well-known children's books—Lyon is called in by buddy Rocco Herbert to help solve an unusual type of killing: a thirty-year-old murder of a man, woman, and child whose bodies are uncovered by a bulldozer at a construction site. Rocco often relies on his friend's "unusual kind of mind," but this case is particularly painful to the writer. His own daughter was killed by a hit-and-run driver some years ago, and he and his wife have yet to come to terms with their loss. Lyon's investigation—which he frequently discusses with his imaginary friends, the Wobblies—takes him back to World War II and into a reconstruction of the life of a Jewish family who fled Hitler's Germany only to find horrors in the new world. And the resolution of the case brings a measure of peace to the Wentworths. An excellent and sensitive novel whose serious theme is leavened by a wry good humor.

Other titles featuring Lyon Wentworth: *The Wizard of Death* (1977), *Death Through the Looking Glass* (1978), *The Death in the Willows* (1979), *The Death at Yew Corner* (1980), and *Death Under the Lilacs* (1985).

(*M.M.*)

*Forsyth, Frederick. *The Day of the Jackal.* New York: Viking, 1971. (T)

As a Reuters correspondent, Frederick Forsyth reported from London, Paris, and East Berlin in the Sixties, and he brings to his fictional works the expected objectivity and thoroughness of a talented reporter. Against a background of real events and real people, he places both his fictional heroes and antiheroes: professionals in their fields who are impeccable in carrying out their jobs and are governed by unshakable commitments to their own internal standards. The heroes frequently combat established but morally corrupt government agencies, and their victories over them come about through preparation and planning. There is a great deal of motion in Forsyth's work, and the scene shifts frequently between the heroes and the antiheroes, creating a tension that is sustained until the last page.

The Day of the Jackal is Forsyth's best-known and most meticulously drawn suspense tale. Seeking the best of professional killers to take over from their own bunglers, French dissidents intent on assassinating Charles de Gaulle hire the Jackal. Working alone, the Jackal makes painstaking preparations to obtain each essential piece of equipment from the appropriate craftsmen, whom he either gives a nodding respect, views with silent contempt, or, occasionally, disposes of. In counterpoint to the Jackal's activities are scenes in which the authorities work to uncover the plot, and when Commissaire Claude Lebel, "the best detective in France," is brought in on the case, the contest becomes an even match.

Forsyth's skill is such that, despite the Jackal's morally unacceptable line of work, we feel sympathy for the character. His integrity and total commitment to his internal standards are commendable—regardless of what those standards are. And the chess game between these ultimate professionals—which takes them back and forth across Europe and the English Channel—is a joy to behold. The game grows tenser and tenser, until its climax—and *then* Forsyth gives us one more superb twist.

(*S.D.*)

Forsyth, Frederick. *No Comebacks.* New York: Viking, 1982. (SS)

The ten stories gathered here carry out the same theme as Forsyth's novels, detailing the work of competent professional men who are single-mindedly committed to achieving their goals. Forsyth details their preparations for their missions with loving thoroughness, and follows their plans through to their logical conclusions. Some of his heroes succeed; some don't. But if they don't, it is because of some strange quirk that the hero could not have foreseen. More often than not, human frailty is what produces the splendid final twists in a number of the stories.

"No Comebacks" is the cleverest example of this: The signs of what is to happen to city of London "golden-boy tycoon" Mark Sanderson are obvious all along, yet the ironic climax is still surprising and leaves us with a satisfied smile. In "There Are No Snakes in Ireland" (which won the MWA Edgar for Best Short Story of 1983), it is the bigotry of certain Irish (in this case against an Indian student named Harkishan Ram Lal) that proves to be the true villain. As in this award-winning story, Forsyth also used his experiences while living in Ireland in "Sharp Practice," a tale of a highly unusual poker game on a train. And in "A Careful Man," an individual whose meticulousness affected his family in life does so even from the grave.

These stories are more human than Forsyth's novels, the characters more memorable as people, rather than technicians, and the tension runs just as high as in the author's longer works.

(*S.D.*)

Forsyth, Frederick. *The Odessa File.* New York: Viking, 1972. (T)

In *The Odessa File,* crime reporter Peter Miller finds the diary of a survivor of the Riga Concentration Camp. Miller, an extremely able journalist and a German of the postwar generation, is stunned to discover the horrors of the camp, and he sets out to track down the camp's commandant, Eduard Roschmann (a real figure, whose story is accurately reported by Forsyth).

Roschmann is reported to be living comfortably under a new identity somewhere in Germany.

In his search for the Butcher of Riga, Miller uncovers Odessa, a secret organization of former SS members, which is supported by the gold and jewels they took from the former Jews in the concentration camps. Its aims are to aid former Nazis in returning to positions of influence in Germany and to further neo-Nazi propaganda. The anti-Nazi underground is powerful in the Germany of 1963, when this story takes place, and Miller is up against the biggest challenge of his career. German officials who are charged with prosecuting war criminals now only want to forget; Miller gets no help from them. The Israelis want to make use of him to thwart the production of an Odessa-designed guidance system that will supposedly enable Egyptian missiles to carry bubonic plague into Israel; to them, Miller is expendable.

This tense and fascinating story reads like fact, and it is with the factual that Forsyth is at his best; he can make the assembling of a bomb in a hotel room as riveting as the best chase scene. His totally fictional characters are less sure than those based on real individuals, but Miller is a sympathetic hero.

Forsyth's other thrillers are *The Dogs of War* (1974) and *The Devil's Alternative* (1979). He has also written a mainstream novel, *The Shepherd* (1974), and a nonfiction book, *The Biafra Story* (1977).

(*S.D.*)

Foxx, Jack. *Freebooty*. Indianapolis: Bobbs-Merrill, 1976. (PI/HC)

Jack Foxx is a pseudonym used by Bill Pronzini (q.v.) for four Foxx novels written in the 1970s. Two are action/adventure stories featuring Singapore bush pilot Dan Connell—*The Jade Figurine* (1972) and *Dead Run* (1975); a third, *Wildfire* (1978), is a thriller about a small California logging community menaced by both a trio of dangerous criminals and a forest fire. *Freebooty,* a historical mystery, is very different in tone from the other tautly written, action-oriented Foxx novels. This is not to say that there isn't plenty of action and suspense, but *Freebooty*'s style is gentler, evoking an earlier age, and it is spiced with frequent, delightful humor.

Fergus O'Hara and his wife, Hattie, arrive in San Francisco in 1863 en route to the port city of Stockton, where they suspect the members of a bandit gang who have been terrorizing coaches of the Adams Express Company are hiding out. As O'Hara explains, his wife is not an operative of the Pinkerton Detective Agency, as he is, but frequently assists him in his inquiries, "women being able to obtain information in places men cannot." Before the O'Haras board the steamer *Freebooty* for the inland journey, Fergus makes the acquaintance of Horace T. Goatleg, an obese man with patently suspicious motives; encounters an articulate and ribald parrot (one of the most memorable characters in a cast of outstanding ones); witnesses a near-riot on the Barbary Coast; finds a murdered man in an alley; and sustains minor injuries himself, including being half drowned by a shower of beer.

Needless to say, all of the above events tie in to further goings-on aboard the steamer. And as the O'Haras—an effective team—investigate them, their initial purposes take a series of twists and turns, leading to a final revelation that is sure to leave the reader both surprised and amused. Pronzini has a firm grasp of historical fact, and he blends it skillfully into his narrative, capturing the tenor of the times without allowing detail to slow the pace of his story. This is an entertaining novel, well plotted and full of engaging characters.

(*M.M.*)

Foy, George. *Asia Rip.* New York: Viking, 1984. (AD)

The highly evocative title of this novel comes from one of the shoal areas off the coast of Cape Cod, an area worked by the rugged men of the North Atlantic fishing industry. George Foy sets his impressive debut mystery among these men and the corrupt individuals on land who control the industry.

Lars Larsen joins the search for his friend Joe Sciacca when the latter fails to return from a fishing run. Later he is asked to continue to investigate by Sciacca's widow, Marie. When the pregnant Marie is also murdered, Larsen finds himself with a murder rap on his head, and a need for vengeance in his heart.

Foy's well-wrought plot features a lot of bloody action as Larsen traces the link between organized crime and the fishing industry. Much of the action includes feats of unbelievable derring-do by Foy's hero. Not your average fisherman, he is a former Harvard man and drug-runner. He is also the kind of central character who keeps the reader involved and believing even as he scales the beams and girders of a massive railroad bridge with an injured and infected shoulder.

George Foy has worked as a journalist covering the fishing industry. This background lends great authenticity to his first mystery/adventure novel. He is also a fine storyteller.

(*K.L.M.*)

*Francis, Dick. *Blood Sport.* New York: Harper, 1968. (T)

From the winning world of British steeplechasing (where he was Champion Jockey in 1954), Dick Francis moved effortlessly into crime fiction with his first novel, *Dead Cert,* in 1962, and continues to be a front-runner. He has written twenty-some excellent thrillers full of old-fashioned moral polarity with strains of humor. These "adventure stories" (as Francis calls them) have amazing plots of clever evilness and feature nonrecurring heroes familiar with the racing game. Flawed, uninvolved, and soulless, each central character finds the value of vulnerability and returns to the land of the living through courage and love. As a central theme, it can be compared to that of the works of Ross Macdonald (q.v.). As critic John Leonard said, "Not to read Dick Francis because you don't like horses is like not reading Dostoevski because you don't like God."

In *Blood Sport,* death lurks on a simple Sunday sail on the Thames. An American visitor is almost drowned, and his rescuer is convinced that it wasn't simply an accident. Gene Hawkins, the rescuer and hero, is an English civil servant, a "screener" who checks employees in secret-sensitive government jobs. His training permits him to spot details that make "accidents" phony, and his knowledge of guns and listening devices comes in handy. The rescued man asks for help in locating a stolen horse that has just been bought for a huge price. Hawkins is relieved to use his vacation time to hunt for missing horses, because he is despondent, filled with a "fat black slug of depression." This is the only part of his character that doesn't ring true—after all, it's only a failed love affair.

The pace picks up, and the scene changes to the U.S.A. From the farms of Kentucky, the trail is followed to Jackson, Wyoming. Along the way, Hawkins gets people together for some psychological reconditioning and exposes a bloodline scam as the scene shifts to Santa Barbara, Las Vegas, and Kingman, Arizona. The U.S. tour is fast-moving, and Francis does not dwell on local-color background, especially not to make any points. He just gives the graphic, journalistic details of a place that push the story along. (*T.B.*)

*Francis, Dick. *Odds Against.* New York: Harper, 1966. (T)

In most of his books, Dick Francis uses an ordinary man (usually connected with the racing world) as his protagonist, caught up in events that are so overwhelming and out of control that he must make heroic efforts to sort them out. But in *Odds Against,* Sid Halley has a job as a detective—the obvious choice for a tough man to right the world's wrongs. He's been doing the work for two years, and when he's shot (on page one of the story), he realizes that a bullet in the guts is his first step to liberation from being of "no use to anyone, least of all himself." He was a champion steeplechase jockey, that's what makes him tough. A racing accident lost him the use of his hand and self-respect simultaneously.

The action breaks from the starting gate and blasts over the hurdles of intrigue, menace, and crime. Halley is cadged by his shrewd and loving father-in-law into confronting Howard Kraye, "a full-blown, powerful, dangerous, big-time crook." On the track he encounters murder, mayhem, plastic bombs, and torture. But he endures, in some part to regain his self-respect, and in some part because he believes in racing, the sport, and in putting it right. A fascinating chase through an empty racecourse defies the villain. In the end, despite his tragedy, Sid Halley sees himself as a detective and as a man.

Dick Francis was so taken with the characters in this book that he went on to use them in a television series, "The Racing Game" (shown on Public Broadcasting). A second Sid Halley novel, *Whip Hand,* won the British Gold Dagger Award in 1979 and another Edgar from the Mystery Writers of America.

(*T.B.*)

*Francis, Dick. *The Danger.* New York: Putnam's, 1984. (T)

For some time after he achieved bestsellerdom in the United States, it seemed that Dick Francis (according to some critics) was not keeping up the pace. But with *The Danger,* he is back in front, writing prose as crisp and taut and lean as a racehorse. This novel runs in the really big international-thriller category, starting with "there was a God-awful cock-up in Bologna." It's about kidnapping with a touch of terrorism.

Andrew Douglas works as a partner in the firm of Liberty Market Ltd., whose credo is to "resolve a kidnap in the quietest way possible, with the lowest of profiles and minimum action." He successfully gets back the kidnap victim, Alessis Cenci, "one of the best girl jockeys in the world." They go back to England, where he engages in some psychological rehabilitation. This leads to the next hurdle, another kidnap (literally, a kid this time), and he sees a thread of connection. Douglas has the opportunity to assess his opponent—"Kidnappers are better detectives than detectives, and better spies than spies."

Then, it's a leap across the Atlantic, where the senior steward of the English Jockey Club is kidnapped in Washington, D.C.—a snatch related to the first two. Apparently Dick Francis likes the States, because he has his chief character say, "I feel liberated, as always in America, a feeling which I thought had something to do with the country's own vastness, as if the wide-apartness of everything flooded into the mind." Andrew Douglas finally comes face-to-face with his adversary genius in an exciting climax.

(*T.B.*)

*Francis, Dick. *Forfeit.* New York: Harper, 1969. (T)

Dick Francis not only uses his racing experience in his novels, but in many of them other facets of his life form the background. In *Forfeit,* his sixteen years as racing correspondent for the *London Sunday Express* is embodied in the hero, James Tyrone, journalist.

Tyrone listens to a drunken tirade from an old-time colleague who then goes back to his office and nips out the seventh-floor window onto Fleet Street. With a nose for a good story, Tyrone smells a fiddle and starts some inquiries. He knows he's on to a sure thing when he hears of blackmail and is met with unexplained violence. As a reporter, he is at great pains to protect his sources, but the dangerous headlines run by his "dreadful rag" of a paper focus the menace on him.

In typical Francis style, the fast-paced writing brings out the individuality of the hero, even though it's a typical suspense/thriller situation of a normal human being trapped in an abnormal situation. In another bit of autobiographical content, Tyrone's wife is confined to a respirator and requires constant attendance (Francis's wife once had polio). Unusual for a Francis novel, a true love story is depicted even though Tyrone feels that he lives a shadow life—full of "dust and ashes." In his pursuit of racketeers who force owners not to start their horses in a race, he faces extortion, blackmail, and "high-powered thuggery" (more violence), along with a splash of racism. He confronts the villain in the Big Cats' House in London Zoo, and comes face-to-face with an evil sociopath who's in it for the money. In the end, Tyrone saves his wife while made drunk by the villains, and then must save himself.

Forfeit won a well-deserved Edgar as Best Novel of 1969.

Francis's recent novels have all been large-scale best sellers. *The Danger* was one; others are *Reflex* (1981), *Twice Shy* (1982), *Banker* (1983), and *Proof* (1985).

(*T.B.*)

Fraser, Antonia. *Quiet as a Nun.* New York: Viking, 1977. (AD)

The heroine of this first novel by noted historian Antonia Fraser is Jemima Shore, Investigator—not a detective in the proper sense, but an investigative television reporter in London. Her show carries great influence, and it is on the strength of this that Jemima is summoned back to Blessed Eleanor's Convent in Sussex, where she attended school. Jemima was a Protestant, thrust into the convent world because of the "vagaries of her father's career," but her best friend, Rosabelle Powerstock, was a Catholic and later became a nun at the same convent. Now Sister Miriam, as Rosabelle was called, is dead under strange circumstances, having starved to death in the black tower built by the founder of the order—a structure commonly referred to by the schoolgirls as "Nelly's Nest." People give the nuns strange looks on the streets of town; a cloud hangs over the convent; the air is full of suspicion and distrust; and the Reverend Mother Ancilla turns to Jemima to find out what is amiss.

Jemima is loath to revisit the scene of her childhood, but an aborted trip to Yugoslavia with her member of Parliament—and very married—lover makes her welcome a change of scene. She settles in at Blessed Eleanor's in considerably more comfort than she enjoyed as a schoolgirl, but its charms fade when she hears strange footsteps at night, has a terrifying midnight encounter in the chapel, and discovers that politics, while very worldly, are not alien to these hallowed walls.

Jemima is an interesting character—a complex combination of a hard-driving career woman and a person who repeatedly binds herself into no-win situations with married men; she also has more than her fair share of skepticism about nuns and Catholicism. The nuns, in their diversity, are also absorbing, and it is upon their hidden motives, passions, and beliefs that the plot turns. The unusual combination of the trendy contemporary world and the Gothic old convent gives a nice look at how such a place functions in the modern world.

Subsequent Jemima Shore novels are *The Wild Island* (1978), *A Splash of Red* (1981), and *Cool Repentence* (1982).

(*M.M.*)

Frazee, Steve. *The Sky Block.* New York: Rinehart, 1953. (A)

While fishing his old vacation stream high in the Colorado Rockies, Platt Vencel is pressed into urgent service by both the U.S. Army (in the person of Colonel Julius Catron) and the FBI (agent Clement Raven). Something has gone wrong with the weather throughout the country: an unprecedented state of drought that has gone on for some months. The authorities are convinced that the cause is a hidden meteorological "doomsday device" built by an unspecified foreign power. Vencel, because of his intimate knowledge of the wilderness area, soon finds himself at the forefront of a desperate and deadly hunt for the location of the "Weather-Wrecker" and the identity of the men behind it.

Despite the novel's fantastic premise and its overtones of the anti-Communist extremism of the McCarthy era, Frazee's handling of the theme minimizes the melodramatic aspects and makes this an exciting and suspenseful chase/adventure story in the mode of Geoffrey Household and John Buchan (qq.v.). Its strong points are several: deft characterization, nicely choreographed action scenes, and superb evocation of the rugged mountain terrain. Frazee's prose style is also a plus; always terse and smoothly crafted, it takes on at times a kind of dark, rough-edged lyricism that gives the story a sense of stark reality.

Frazee was primarily a writer of first-rate western fiction. His only other criminous novels are *Running Target* (1956), expanded from the distinguished short story "My Brother Down There," which won first prize in the annual contest for 1953 sponsored by *Ellery Queen's Mystery Magazine;* and

Flight 409 (1969), a tale of survival and adventure about the search for the survivors of a plane crash in which three members of the president's cabinet were killed.

(*B.P.*)

*Freeling, Nicholas. *The Back of the North Wind.* New York: Viking, 1983. (PP)

The crime novels of Nicholas Freeling follow the giant footsteps of Georges Simenon's (q.v.) Inspector Maigret. But the more you read of Freeling, the more you realize that they follow not in but alongside those footsteps, sometimes wandering to explore at greater depth character and social relevance. Freeling writes of ordinary, unexciting policemen—Dutch police inspector Piet Van der Valk, and Inspector Henri Castang of the French National Police—who have a private eye's conscience. He presents sympathetic character studies of all the players in each of his dramas, and his detectives examine all aspects of the various crimes they are investigating, whether broad or narrow in scope.

Freeling, who was born in London and presently lives in France, began writing *romans policiers* in 1962 with *Love in Amsterdam* and followed it with nine more books featuring Van der Valk; then, in *Auprès de ma Blonde* (1972), he committed the rather shocking act of doing away with his series detective because he had grown tired of him and wanted to experiment with other types of stories and protagonists. Van der Valk's widow, Arlette, finds his murderer and concludes that particular case, among much social commentary and existential thought. She appears in two other books of her own (*The Widow,* 1979; *Arlette,* 1981)—perhaps not so successfully; at least one critic felt that widows should "wear black and smoke cigars . . . instead of solving crimes."

In 1974 Freeling published the first of his novels about Henri Castang, *Dressing of Diamond.* In contrast to Van der Valk, the veteran Castang (thirty years with the French police) possesses a sense of humor and a more dynamic wife, Vera, who is fond of quoting Conrad. Castang's relationship with his wife is a nice counterpoint to the grim realities of the murder cases he is confronted with—especially the central case in *The Back of the North Wind.*

Returning from vacation, Castang investigates the particularly heinous murder of a young woman. In a boggy part of a nature reserve in the French countryside, a forester discovers a plastic carrier bag containing a rotting mass of human flesh. A search is organized and six other plastic carrier bags are found, each containing a part of a human body. Lab analysis reveals the murder victim to have been a female of North European origin, approximately twenty years old. The dismembered parts also show human bite marks: Castang is evidently faced with a murderer who is also a cannibal.

His investigation is complicated by other pressing matters: a series of killings of ordinary citizens beaten over the head with a heavy weapon; a very strange and sinister prostitute; and political corruption within Castang's own department. Each of the interwoven plot lines is untangled neatly through procedural and psychological methods, and the result is a grim but absorbing novel packed with Gallic atmosphere.

The Henri Castang series ranks with Freeling's Van der Valk novels and with the Martin Beck series written by Maj Sjöwall and Per Wahlöö (q.v.) as the best of the European police procedurals. Other recommended titles are *The Bugles Blowing* (1976) and *Castang's City* (1980).

(*T.B./G.K.*)

Freeling, Nicholas. *The King of the Rainy Country*. New York: Harper, 1965. (PP)

Freeling received an MWA Best Novel Edgar for *The King of the Rainy Country,* one of several prizes his work has earned him (the British Golden Dagger and the French Grand Prix de Roman Policier are two others). And indeed it is probably the best of the Inspector Van der Valk novels.

In Amsterdam, strings are pulled to convince Van der Valk to undertake an unofficial missing-person investigation. Apparently a millionaire, Jean-Claude Marschal, has vanished from his luxurious home and good job, leaving behind his handsome Belgian wife, Anne-Marie. The man from Marschal's company who contacts the police, Mr. Canisius, can think of no reason for his disappearance; neither can his wife, who seems puzzled about why Canasius wants him looked for in the first place. Likewise Marschal's secretary is baffled; but something she says, coupled with a hint dropped in a discussion with the last man to see Marschal, sends Van der Valk to Cologne. The city has just celebrated its pre-Lenten carnival, and one of the beauty queens has disappeared—leaving behind all the clothing she was wearing. The man she was last seen drinking in a café with could possibly have been Marschal. Van der Valk and his German policeman friend, Heinz Stossel, trace the pair, finding a trail that includes a car purchase, the purchase of some ski equipment, and railway tickets to Innsbruck, Austria.

In Austria, Van der Valk is surprised by a visit from Anne-Marie Marschal, who tries to persuade him (in many ways, even with the offer of her body) to drop the search for Jean-Claude. But Van der Valk comes close, until the couple stages a dramatic escape from the ski slopes of Innsbruck in a stolen helicopter. He realizes that Marschal will do anything to keep the girl with him—and that he is dealing with a reckless and potentially dangerous man. The police of three countries are alerted, and for Van der

Valk the question is "Which way would the cat jump now?" When he finds the answer, he discovers a carefully concealed secret, and one tragedy is soon compounded by another.

This is an excellent novel with a tragic and haunting solution—Van der Valk at his finest. And its wonderful title is taken from a poem by Baudelaire.

Other Van der Valk adventures are chronicled in *Gun before Butter* (1963), *Double-Barrel* (1965), and *Tsing-Boom!* (1969). Freeling has also written such nonseries books as *This Is the Castle* (1968), *Gadget* (1977), and *A City Solitary* (1985).

(*T.B./M.M.*)

*Freeman, R. Austin. *Mr. Pottermack's Oversight.* New York: Dodd, Mead, 1930. (CS)

R. Austin Freeman was one of crime fiction's true innovators. He developed the "inverted" mystery story to an art; and in Dr. John Evelyn Thorndyke, he created a series detective of significant capabilities—one who has been called "the only convincing scientific investigator" in the genre. Freeman's Dr. Thorndyke novels and short stories can be said to rival Doyle's Sherlock Holmes canon in quality and cleverness of plot. Where Holmes uses deductive methods, Dr. Thorndyke draws on a wealth of scientific knowledge—everything from anatomy to zoology—to solve his cases. And although many of his plots involve technical explanations, Freeman was a master at making science and its jargon explicable to the lay reader.

Mr. Pottermack's Oversight is Dr. Thorndyke's most celebrated case. Anthony Boucher called it "a leisurely, a gentle novel, yet an acute one. . . . No other detective in fiction has ever equaled Thorndyke in the final section of explication, often so tedious in lesser hands. The scene is especially effective in this novel; and the lucid unfolding of the reasoning of John Thorndyke carries that intellectual excitement and stimulus so often attributed to the detective story so rarely found."

Marcus Pottermack is a gentleman of leisure who spends most of his time studying British *mollusca* (snails) in his garden. As the novel opens, he has realized his dream of purchasing a sundial for the garden, and in preparing the site where he intends to place it, he uncovers an old well. The discovery proves fortuitous; Mr. Pottermack receives a visit from a gambler named Lewson, who has been blackmailing him. It seems Pottermack is in reality Jeffrey Brandon, a runaway convict who is supposed dead. Lewson has had financial reverses, and once again he puts the bite on "Jeff." Pottermack lures Lewson into the garden, has a fight with him, and Lewson falls, hitting his head on the edge of the well before tumbling in. Mr. Pottermack then sets about covering up his crime.

The main problem is footsteps leading to his house in the soft earth. He can't obliterate them, and so he decides to continue them on, past his home. There is a problem, though: Lewson's shoes are on him in the well. The resourceful Mr. Pottermack decides to manufacture shoes, taking a plaster cast of the footprints and reproducing their soles. He then walks some distance in them, creating the impression that the person passed on by. Of course, there are other details to be dealt with, and Mr. Pottermack takes further steps (no pun intended) to assure his crime will never come to light. But he hasn't counted on John Thorndyke's scientific methods—methods that eventually reveal Mr. Pottermack's oversight.

Readers who enjoy the inverted detective story and/or a good intellectual puzzle will find this an absorbing novel.

(*M.M./B.P.*)

Freeman, R. Austin. *The Singing Bone*. New York: Dodd, Mead, 1923. (CS/SS)

The Singing Bone consists of five novelettes, averaging a bit over fifty pages each: "The Case of Oscar Brodski," "A Case of Premeditation," "The Echo of a Mutiny," "A Wastrel's Romance," and "The Old Lag." Though the final story is fairly routine, Freeman broke new ground with the first four and invented the "inverted" detective story. Each of the tales is told in two parts of about equal length. In part one, "The Mechanism of Crime," as it is subtitled in the first story, we actually see the crime committed and are furnished with all the facts that could be used in solving it. In part two, "The Mechanism of Detection," we follow Dr. Thorndyke as he investigates the crime, finds the clues, and finally solves it. Although the classic question "Whodunit?" is necessarily absent for the reader, there is a challenge of a sort to match wits with the detective and spot the clues in advance.

The inverted form has never been popular in fiction, although Freeman used it in three more stories and two novels, and the popular television series "Columbo" did very well by it for several seasons. Perhaps the secret was that Peter Falk's Sergeant Columbo was a far more interesting character than Dr. John Thorndyke, whose microscopic examinations lack the flair and showmanship of Sherlock Holmes. Still, the stories in *The Singing Bone* deserve rediscovery, especially "The Echo of a Mutiny," which is probably the best of them, with its atmospheric setting in a lighthouse.

Dr. Thorndyke was first introduced in the novel *The Red Thumb Mark* (1907), notable for its first use of fingerprint forgery in detective fiction. The collection *John Thorndyke's Cases* (1909) features eight conventional detective stories and is especially noteworthy for "The Blue Sequin" and "The Aluminum Dagger."

(*E.D.H.*)

Fremlin, Celia. *The Hours Before Dawn.* Philadelphia: Lippincott, 1958. (T)

Celia Fremlin has the unusual ability to take a perfectly normal, if not mundane, situation and create an atmosphere of sheer terror. *The Hours Before Dawn,* which won an Edgar for Best Novel of its year, introduces us to Louise Henderson, a sleep-starved young housewife with a fretful new infant that is causing complaints from both her family and neighbors. The only person who doesn't complain is Miss Vera Brandon, the boarder the Hendersons have recently taken in. In fact, Miss Brandon is so self-effacing and quiet that at times the Hendersons don't even know she is in the house. Soon the boarder's actions begin to arouse Louise's suspicions, and she finds herself doing all sorts of things she has never done before—attempting to search the woman's room, contacting total strangers for information about her, and finally taking the baby for a nocturnal stroll in his pram, only to fall asleep and lose him in a park.

The author skillfully weaves truly frightening events into Louise's daily routine of meals, housecleaning, and childcare, and her superb characterization has the reader thoroughly on Louise's side—and just as terrified as she is—by the time the story reaches its surprising conclusion.

Other Fremlin titles of note: *Uncle Paul* (1960), *Prisoner's Base* (1967), *The Spider-Orchid* (1978), *With No Crying* (1981).

(*M.M.*)

Friedman, Mickey. *Hurricane Season.* New York: Dutton, 1983. (W)

Set in the Fifties in the small northwest Florida town of Palmetto, *Hurricane Season* is a period piece. From the very beginning—the night the Men's Lodge puts on its *Womanless Wedding* (a wedding play in which all the characters are played by men)—we are reminded of when the story is taking place by little touches, such as the Communist Threat, Nugrape soda, and off-the-shoulder peasant blouses. These touches are used sparingly—not once do we have the sense that the author is being heavy-handed with her research. But what really makes *Hurricane Season* work is the characters, who become embroiled in murder during the sultry days of August 1952.

Events begin with the night of *The Womanless Wedding* when the swamp catches fire. Seen mainly through the eyes of Lily Trulock, a middle-aged woman who, with her husband, runs the grocery and marine supply, other unusual happenings follow: A mysterious stranger, Joshua Burns, comes to town; the daughter of the town's leading politician seduces a young religious fanatic and shortly afterward is found murdered; a book of poetry that the dead woman wrote comes into Lily's hands. And finally Lily, convinced that her son-in-law, the sheriff, is mishandling the investigation, sets out to get to the bottom of things—with surprising results.

A promising first novel that shows great sensitivity to the way small towns and the interrelationships of their residents work—be it in the Fifties or today. Friedman's second novel, *The Grail Tree,* which is set in India and California, was published in 1984.

(*M.M.*)

Frome, David. *Mr. Pinkerton Has the Clue.* New York: Farrar & Rinehart, 1936. (AD)

David Frome is a pseudonym of Zenith Brown, who also wrote under the name Leslie Ford (q.v.). As with her Ford novels, the Frome books deal with polite middle-class people to whom bloodless murder is an unwelcome but speedily dealt-with intrusion. Unlike the Ford novels, which are distinctly American, the Frome stories are distinctly British; many readers have no inkling that the author was not English but an American living in Great Britain who had great ability at adopting the English idiom.

Mr. Evan Pinkerton would be a pathetic character were it not for his deductive abilities. He is described mainly as "little" and "grey"—"little grey forehead," "little grey man," even "grey little spine." His life has been "mostly drab and often miserable," and now that he has inherited a substantial sum from his wife, he has trouble believing he really has money and continues to live parsimoniously.

As this novel opens, Mr. Pinkerton is going on a holiday to Bath, England. Before very long he has violated his parsimony by engaging a room in an expensive hotel, led there by his curiosity about Dame Ellen Crosby, a famed actress. Mr. Pinkerton observes quarrels and tensions developing among Dame Crosby's crippled brother, Major Peyton; the major's beautiful daughter, Cecily; Cecily's plain and envious sister, Gillian; Cecily's fiancé, the arrogant Vardon Crosby; Mrs. Fullaway, landlady at the hotel; and the mysterious Miss Rosa Margolious, a guest who seems always to materialize at the wrong moment. When Dame Ellen is found murdered in her bed, it is no surprise—largely due to the author's unfortunate "had-I-but-known" approach. Pinkerton, who has often assisted Scotland Yard, is called in on the case by Chief Constable Thicknesse (who investigates along with his spaniel, the macabrely named Dr. Crippen). And detect Pinkerton does, in his mild-mannered and affable way, with the usual satisfactory results.

This novel and the others in the Pinkerton series—*The Hammersmith Murders* (1930), *Mr. Pinkerton Goes to Scotland Yard* (1934), and *Mr. Pinkerton at the Old Angel* (1939), among others—will probably not suit the reader who likes his heroes larger than life. It is possible, however, to identify with Evan Pinkerton's frequent embarrassment and bumbling ways; and the plots and settings are vintage British mystery.

(*M.M.*)

Fuller, Samuel. *The Dark Page.* New York: Duell, 1944. (PS)

Film director Sam Fuller is a stylish, iconoclastic *auteur* whose movies transform tabloid trash into cinematic art. The characters in his films are larger than life, their dialogue often sounding like the copy off the back of a paperback; yet the broad strokes of his scripts are turned to poetry by fluid camera work and startling visual imagery, redeeming graces his novels tend to lack. His career as a novelist is, then, considerably less significant, although perhaps no other filmmaker of his stature has written so many novels. Prior to his filmmaking career, Fuller wrote lurid topical tales (*Burn Baby Burn,* 1935; *Test Tube Baby,* 1936), foreshadowing such "out of the headlines" Fuller films as *Pickup on South Street* (1953) and *Underworld USA* (1960). His later books are novelizations either of films he made (*The Naked Kiss,* 1963) or of films he failed to make (*144 Picadilly,* 1971). His claim to fame as a novelist, however, rests upon *The Dark Page,* a fast-moving, effective crime novel that reflects Fuller's love for Hearst-school yellow journalism, that lurid *National Enquirer* style of reporting that Fuller's movies hinge upon and transcend.

City editor Carl Chapman throws a Lonely Hearts Ball at Madison Square Garden, a cynical media event designed to boost the circulation of his paper, the *Comet.* At the party, which is attended by his wife, Rose (to whom he's happily married), he encounters Charlotte, a former wife from his former, secret life. Returning with Charlotte (whom he had never divorced) to her shabby apartment, an argument ensues and Charlotte is killed, more or less accidentally. Chapman's star reporter, Lance McCleary, latching on to the fact that the murdered woman had attended the Lonely Hearts Ball, pursues the story vigorously, not realizing he is closing in on his mentor, editor Chapman. Chapman, too, cannot resist the headline-making story, and feels just as proud as he does threatened, as Lance's muckraking tactics lead Chapman into further deceit and murder.

Fuller's style in *The Dark Page* is lively, the melodrama made palatable by the short, choppy sentences and paragraphs that are right out of his newspaper background. Well worth reading for its own merits, *The Dark Page* is a fascinating footnote in the story of a major, if offbeat, American film director.

A tidy little B movie was fashioned from *The Dark Page,* but, ironically, Fuller didn't make it: The adaptation, *Scandal Sheet* (1953), with Broderick Crawford as the city editor and John Derek as his metaphorical son, was directed by fellow B-movie magician Phil Karlson.

(*M.A.C.*)

Fuller, Timothy. *Three Thirds of a Ghost.* Boston: Little, Brown, 1941. (AD)

When his first novel, *Harvard Has a Homicide,* was published in 1936, Timothy Fuller—just twenty-two and a Harvard undergraduate—was hailed as an important mystery-story prodigy. He never quite lived up to the promise of that first book, however, either in his productivity or in the quality of his later work. It was five years before he published his second and third mysteries, another two years until his fourth, and seven more until his fifth and final book. And only *Reunion with Murder* (1941) and *This Is Murder, Mr. Jones* (1943) can be said to equal or surpass *Harvard Has a Homicide* in plotting and technique.

Despite its inherent flaws, however, *Three Thirds of a Ghost* may well be Fuller's most appealing work. One of the reasons—perhaps the main reason—is that it is set primarily in a Boston bookshop, Bromfield's, where writer Charles Newbury (who specializes in *roman à clef* novels about important Boston families, not to mention mysteries featuring an Oriental detective known as the Parrot) is shot to death while addressing 200 guests at Bromfield's 150th birthday celebration.

In *Catalogue of Crime,* Barzun and Taylor call *Three Thirds of a Ghost* "disappointing." And so it is, in terms of its rather thin plot and dubious gimmick to explain how Newbury could be killed without any of the 200 witnesses seeing who fired the shot. But Harvard Fine Arts instructor Jupiter Jones, the amateur sleuth who also stars in Fuller's other four novels, is an engaging bumbler; the cast of characters—especially Jupiter's girlfriend (later wife), Helen, Newbury's nonstereotypical Chinese secretary, Lin, and some refreshingly intelligent cops—is diverse and well drawn; and there are amusing bits of business interspersed with plenty of barbed commentary on the writing and selling of books and on pre–World War II Boston society.

If your taste runs to the humorous, sophisticated, slightly screwball type of storytelling popular in the 1930s, this bibliomystery (and any of the other Jupiter Jones romps) is definitely your sort of Boston tea party.

(*B.P.*)

Fuller, William. *Back Country.* New York: Dell First Editions, 1954. (O/A)

William Fuller, according to his publishers, was a merchant seaman, a hobo, a veteran of World War II, and a bit player in western movies. He also wrote seven novels about Brad Dolan, a big, tough drifter who travels around the south getting in and out of trouble.

In *Back Country,* the first book in the series, Dolan's car breaks down in Cartersville, a small town in central Florida. Many similar small towns turned up in the paperback originals of the 1950s, and Cartersville is filled with all the characters we love to hate—the Boss who runs the county and believes that "nigras" are all right if they stay in their place; the cruel, corrupt, pot-gutted lawmen; the redneck town bigots. Dolan enters this environment and makes all the wrong moves: He wins at gambling, insults the sheriff, makes time with the big Boss's wife. Naturally, he gets beaten and thrown in jail, but that doesn't stop him. He not only sleeps with the Boss's wife, he sleeps with the Boss's daughter. Then the wife is found in Dolan's room with her throat cut, just as the town's racial tension reaches a crisis.

These ingredients may sound familiar, but Fuller mixes them expertly, keeping the pace fast and the characters believable. Dolan's toughness (and his realization that he's not quite as hard-boiled as he thinks) is convincingly handled. There's a spectacularly vivid cockfighting sequence, and the setting is at times drawn with telling realism.

Also recommended in the Brad Dolan series: *Goat Island* (1954) and *The Girl in the Frame* (1957).

(*B.C.*)

*Futrelle, Jacques. *Best "Thinking Machine" Detective Stories.* New York: Dover, 1973. (CS/SS)

The career of Jacques Futrelle was heroically cut short by his choice of holiday transportation—he sailed aboard the *Titanic*. Before that, however, he created one of the most notable eccentric detectives in crime history, Professor Augustus S. F. X. Van Dusen (with plenty of degrees after his name), "the Thinking Machine." The professor is a famous scientist with an enormous, domelike head (he wears a hat size 8); a wilderness of straw-yellow hair; and squinty, watery blue eyes. He has thick spectacles, long white hands, and a small body. His henchman and gofer is Hutchison Hatch, a newspaper reporter. Most of the Thinking Machine's cases are brought to him by Hatch, who knows that to get a good story, one brings it to the man who can get to the bottom of an "impossible crime." The professor, in the fine tradition of armchair detectives, knows that any puzzle has a logical explanation. His sententious principle is "two and two always make four—not *some*time but *all* the time." Much of the legwork is done by Hatch off stage; the professor himself is a phone fanatic—he often goes into his little phone room and returns with the complete solution.

The *Best "Thinking Machine" Detective Stories* are a dozen collected from *The Thinking Machine* (1906), which contains seven stories, and *The Thinking Machine on the Case* (1907). Two of Futrelle's tales were shown on public television in "The Rivals of Sherlock Holmes." The Thinking Machine was introduced in a story, much anthologized, called "The Problem of Cell 13." From a simple arguing point, a challenge is proposed. The professor undertakes, on purely scientific grounds, to escape from a death cell in the penitentiary in one week. And does so. Other stories contain puzzles about dying messages, perfect alibis, buried treasure, and an occult legacy. Excellent "locked-room" variations are presented in "The Stolen Rubens," "The Phantom Motor," and "The Lost Radium." Another, "Kidnapped Baby Blake, Millionaire," where a person vanishes from footprints in a snow-filled yard, is not quite up to snuff. In "The Missing Necklace," the crook is about to give Scotland Yard the bird except for the intervention of the Thinking Machine. He is able to sum up one case thus: "The subtler murders—that is, the ones which are most attractive as problems—are nearly always the work of a cunning woman. I know nothing about women myself." Shades of Sherlock Holmes.

(*T.B.*)

Futrelle, Jacques. *Great Cases of the Thinking Machine.* New York: Dover, 1976. (CS/SS)

Editor E. F. Bleiler has selected from the almost fifty stories about the incredible brain, "The Thinking Machine," thirteen cases for this book. Only one has appeared in book form before; the others were collected from newspapers of 1906–1908. These have been called "societal stories," different from the stories in *Best "Thinking Machine" Detective Stories.* The journalistic, telegraphic writing style illuminates the American Edwardian period of the tales, which involve mostly the shenanigans of rich Back Bay Boston life. Once again the testy professor is able to recall his maxim, "Nothing is impossible. It might be improbable, but not impossible."

The stories are short—they are set up as a Problem, then the professor's explanation, or Solution. Many involve exotic suspects, impersonations, vague stock-market machinations, jewel thefts, and menagerie solutions (animals hold the crucial clue). From "The Problem of the Cross Mark," we learn to beware of drugged cigars. From "The Roswell Tiara," we learn to keep our eye on the cockatoo. And if there's an old house, there's a treasure. These tales pale in comparison to the earlier volume—science hardly enters into most of the solutions. It seems that a thoroughly bizarre situation is set up, allowing the mastermind to give an explanation and then say, "Any problem may be solved by logic." The longest story, "The Haunted Bell," was put into some editions of one of Futrelle's novels. It contains an exotic dream sequence, but the solution is straightforwardly scientific; only the ending has a surprise, even for the Thinking Machine.

(*T.B.*)

*Gaboriau, Emile. *Monsieur Lecoq.* Paris: E. Dentu, 1868. Edited version published in the U.S. by Dover, 1975. (CS)

Monsieur Lecoq, Gaboriau's twelfth book and his fifth novel in which the French detective of the title appears, is today often considered his best and most readable book. Changing reading habits, plus indifferent translations, have left the pioneer French mystery writer all but unread today, but he deserves a place in any survey of classic detective fiction.

Lecoq, introduced in his first book as a secondary character, was a minor Sûreté detective with a shady past somewhat like that of the real-life Vidocq. But he soon takes center stage in the Gaboriau novels, and in *Monsieur Lecoq* he investigates a triple murder in a poor section of Paris. The killer, apprehended at the scene, appears to be a petty criminal who calls himself May, but Lecoq suspects he might really have another identity. The duel of wits between the two men extends through the first volume of the novel. The second volume, sometimes published separately as *The Honor of the Name,* is really a separate and inferior historical novel set around the year 1815, with Lecoq and the evasive villain only reappearing in the final twenty-two pages. Though there have been numerous British and American editions of the novel, the recent Dover edition cited above (skillfully edited and introduced by E. F. Bleiler) is the first to eliminate the extraneous historical novel and jump at once from the end of volume one to the important final pages of volume two.

Gaboriau's books are not without their weaknesses, and they often suffer from cardboard characterizations and inconsistencies. Their strengths lie in plotting and background. They are not exactly the books we think of as detective novels today, but enough elements are present to argue effectively that Gaboriau deserves his title as the father of the detective novel.

Lecoq first appears as a secondary character in *The Widow Lerouge* (1866), but stars in his next two cases, *The Mystery of Orcival* (1867) and *File No. 113* (1867). He also makes a brief appearance in *The Slaves of Paris* (1868), but this is more a crime novel than a detective story.

(*E.D.H.*)

Gardiner, Dorothy. *The Seventh Mourner.* New York: Doubleday Crime Club, 1958. (PP)

Sheriff Moss Magill of Notlaw, Colorado, functions best in his beloved mountains and is reluctant to leave them. However, when local resident Harriet Farquhar Orchard dies, she makes it a condition of her will that he deliver her ashes to her home in Rowanmuir, Scotland. Moss is convinced to go only when he learns that Harriet also wanted him to investigate her sister, Lizzy, who has been released by a Scottish court with the verdict "not proven" on a charge of murder.

Wearing his customary whipcord pants, boots, and black-and-yellow striped shirt with his silver badge pinned to it, Moss evokes many stares during the trip, especially on the train from Edinburgh to Rowanmuir, which, coincidentally, all of the mourners have taken that same August morning. The assorted group is all staying at the hotel where Lizzy works as a maid. During a day trip to Glasgow, Moss hears bagpipes for the first time and, in an enchantment born of ethnic memory, falls in love with Scotland. When one of the party is pushed under a truck that same day, he puts his investigative talents to use and works with the local authorities both to discover the murderer and to fulfill Harriet's last request.

This is an unusual idea for a mystery, with excellent background and an appealing main character. Other amusing Magill adventures are *Lion in Wait* (1963), in which a toothless circus lion is accused of murder; and *What Crime Is This* (1956), in which Moss uses a hula-dancer statue with a clock embedded in her stomach to help clear up a murder.

(*E.N.*)

*Gardner, Erle Stanley. *The Case of the Fan Dancer's Horse.* New York: Morrow, 1947. (AD/PI)

In 1933, when Erle Stanley Gardner took his publisher's advice that the hero of his first novel, *The Case of the Velvet Claws,* might make a good series character, he did not know what lay in store for him—or for Perry Mason. Since then, the Los Angeles lawyer; his secretary, Della Street; and private investigator Paul Drake have become household names. And with the first airing of the immensely popular Perry Mason television series in 1957, they became household images as well, in the form of Raymond Burr, Barbara Hale, and William Hopper.

While not particularly well written or characterized, the Mason books have convoluted plots and punchy dialogue, which in the courtroom takes on the form of verbal sparring. The books are also very much alike, and perhaps this is the basis for their wide appeal. Readers know that in each one an innocent (in the legal sense) will become involved in a murder; odious Lieutenant Tragg will investigate and arrest; snide District Attorney Hamilton Burger will prosecute; and Perry Mason will vindicate his client in a dramatic courtroom revelation of the true killer.

It is these courtroom scenes that make the novels stand out from other mystery fiction. Gardner, a lawyer himself, was able to simplify courtroom procedure so even the least astute reader could understand it, while at the same time packing the scene with dramatic impact. Even those who are normally bored with legal matters can enjoy watching Perry Mason devil the D.A. in the interests of justice, and many a lawyer practicing today will admit he got his first taste of the profession through Mason's legal pyrotechnics.

The Case of the Fan Dancer's Horse begins with a hit-and-run automobile accident in California's Imperial Valley. Two cars glance off one another; Perry Mason and Della Street rush to aid the one that overturns in the ditch, and find an old Mexican woman whose car trunk contains the plumed wardrobe of a fan dancer. The woman is presumably taken away to the hospital by a passing motorist, but the accident is never reported. Mason, who has taken the fans and dancing shoes into custody, places an ad in the paper offering their return. The reply is not what he expected: The fan dancer does indeed want her property returned, but it is a horse, not a wardrobe, that she is missing.

Dancer Lois Fenton—alias Cherie Chi-Chi—is appearing in an old western town called Palomino, and Mason and Street travel there to meet with her. They return the fan-dancing paraphernalia and receive a description of the missing horse, but soon it becomes apparent that the woman they spoke with is not the real Lois Fenton. The real fan dancer—who has a complicated history—is as missing as her horse.

Approached by a young man who is in love with Miss Fenton, Mason accepts a retainer to act in her behalf, and earns it when a wealthy rancher is found murdered in an L.A. hotel room, a bloody imprint that could have been made by an ostrich feather on the wall. Lois Fenton was seen leaving the scene and quickly becomes the chief suspect.

In spite of obvious holes in logic—why, for instance, would Mason take on a client when he has seen no more of her than her ostrich plumes?—the story moves ahead at a breakneck pace. And when the real Lois Fenton finally turns up and the legal battle lines are drawn, Mason is in fine form.

(*M.M.*)

Gardner, Erle Stanley. *The Case of the Moth-Eaten Mink.* New York: Morrow, 1952. (AD/PI)

The moth-eaten mink belongs to waitress Dixie Dayton—or at least it does until the night Perry Mason and Della Street stop in for dinner at Morris Alburg's restaurant. While they are there, something—or someone—frightens Dixie and she runs out, without either her paycheck or the once-expensive coat. The restaurateur, Mason, and Street speculate about the woman's hasty disappearance, but soon find out from the police that Dayton was struck down—not fatally—outside by a passing car while fleeing a man with a gun. Mason takes charge of the mink, and in its lining finds a ticket from a Seattle pawnshop. But before Paul Drake can investigate it, the police find a second ticket in Dayton's possession; they inquire and find out it is for a diamond ring, and the pawnbroker remembers the other object left in his shop—a gun used in a cop killing one year before.

The case becomes a tangle of falsehoods, assumed identities, cryptic clues, missing witnesses, missing clients, and murder. Mason and Drake work around the clock in the interests of their clients—Morris Alburg and

Dixie Dayton, both now accused of homicide. And Lieutenant Tragg hands Mason a surprise in the last sentence.

All the Mason books are talky, relying upon dialogue rather than description, action, or deep characterization, but this one is particularly so. Tragg, in fact, holds center stage with his long-winded speeches. The plot, however, is characteristically complex, and a true Perry Mason fan will relish its twists and turns.

(*M.M.*)

Gardner, Erle Stanley. *The Case of the Sleepwalker's Niece.* New York: Morrow, 1936. (AD/PI)

Perry Mason is approached by a "peculiar" client—Edna Hammer, who seeks help for her uncle, Peter Kent. Kent has a bad habit of sleepwalking, and when he does, he heads for the carving knives and curls up in bed with one. Edna is afraid Uncle Peter will kill someone, and she wants Mason to prevent this.

Kent has other troubles: a wife who instituted divorce proceedings on account of the sleepwalking but now wants to reconcile; a fiancée whom he wishes to marry but can't unless the divorce goes through; a complicated business arrangement with a "cracked-brained inventor"; a hypochondriac half brother; and a woman tailing him in a green Packard roadster. Mason spends a night at the Kent home, and by the next morning there is a bloodstained knife under Peter Kent's pillow, a corpse in the guest room, and a client in very hot water.

The writing in this early novel is taut and lean—reflective of Gardner's hard-boiled work for such pulp magazines as *Black Mask.* The dialogue is terse and packs a good impact, and there are none of the long-winded conversations and introspections that characterize the later Perry Masons. A first-rate example of Gardner's work in the Thirties and early Forties.

Some other notable titles in the series are *The Case of the Black-Eyed Blond* (1944), *The Case of the Lazy Lover* (1947), *The Case of the Green-Eyed Sister* (1953), and *The Case of the Daring Decoy* (1957). After the late Fifties, the novels seem to lose something, possibly as a result of Gardner's work on the Perry Mason TV series. Mason is less flamboyant, and the plots are not as intricate or well tied off as in the earlier novels.

Gardner created other series characters, writing under both his own name and the pseudonym A. A. Fair (q.v.). The best of these under the Gardner name are small-town prosecutor Doug Selby (*The D.A. Calls It Murder,* 1937; *The D.A. Cooks a Goose,* 1942), whose role as a hero is a reverse of Hamilton Burger's; and Gramps Wiggins (*The Case of the Turning Tide,* 1941; *The Case of the Smoking Chimney,* 1943), an iconoclastic old prospector whose experiences reflect Gardner's childhood travels with his mining-engineer father. In addition to his novels, Gardner wrote hundreds of mystery and western stories under various names for such magazines as *Argosy, Black Mask, Sunset, West,* and *Outdoor Stories.*

(*M.M.*)

*Gardner, John. *The Garden of Weapons.* New York: McGraw-Hill, 1981. (E)

John Gardner is one of the most versatile British writers in the espionage genre. He gained early recognition for his Boysie Oakes series—*The Liquidators* (1946), *Amber Nine* (1966), and five others—which he created in the hope they would be an "amusing counterirritant to the excesses" of James Bond; these were written in the black-humor style characteristic of the Sixties. In the Seventies, Gardner scored additional critical and sales triumphs with a much different type of series—one featuring Sherlock Holmes's archenemy, Professor Moriarity, in *The Return of Moriarity* (1974) and *The Revenge of Moriarity* (1975). And in the Eighties, Gardner returned to the frantic world of Bondian spies—literally—when he began a series of new 007 adventures.

But Gardner's best book to date is not one featuring a series character; it is the realistic espionage thriller *The Garden of Weapons,* which begins when a KGB defector walks into the British Consulate in West Berlin and demands to speak with Big Herbie Kruger, a legendary figure in intelligence circles. Kruger's interrogation of the defector reveals that the greatest of Kruger's intelligence coups—a group of six informants known as the Telegraph Boys—has been penetrated by a Soviet spy. Kruger decides to go undercover and eliminate the double agent himself, without the knowledge or consent of British Intelligence.

Posing as an American tourist, Kruger enters East Berlin to carry out his deadly self-appointed mission. But the task is hardly a simple one; and Gardner's plot is full of Byzantine twists and turns involving the East Germans, the KGB, and British Intelligence. Any reader who enjoys espionage fiction will find *The Garden of Weapons* a small masterpiece of its type.

Another nonseries Gardner thriller in the same vein is *The Werewolf Trace* (1977), which has been called "a compulsively readable thriller with delicately handled paranormal undertones and a bitter ending."

(*G.K./B.P.*)

Gardner, John. *License Renewed.* New York: Marek, 1981. (E/T)

After the death of Ian Fleming (q.v.), the holders of the James Bond copyright bestowed upon John Gardner the honor and responsibility of moving the British master spy, along with his galaxy of gadgets and archvillains, into the 1980s. This established thriller writer has responded admirably.

Here Bond is assigned to infiltrate the castle of the Laird of Murcaldy, a renowned nuclear scientist who has had meetings with an international terrorist known as Franco. Bond manages to deftly extract an invitation to Gold Cup Day at Ascot. Very English. He is off to the castle in the highlands, where he meets people with names like Mary Jane Mashkins and Lavender Peacock and affects the courses of nations with names like England, France, and America.

If this novel isn't a Fleming original, it is still great fun. Everything Bond fans would expect is here: the eccentric, larger-than-life villain with his sexy and thoroughly evil female companion and preternaturally tough henchman; the seductive and seduced beautiful woman of questionable allegiance; the slyly sexual double entendre; the infusion of ultramodern technology; and the name-dropping of expensive quality brands of everything from perfume to handguns.

So artfully has Gardner penetrated and captured Fleming's style that one can only wonder if Bond's old nemesis, SPECTER, might somehow be involved. No doubt Bond's boss, the enigmatic M, could tell us; but, as usual, he is tight-lipped.

Another recommended title in the new Bond series by Gardner is *Role of Honor* (1984).

(*J.L.*)

Garfield, Brian. *Death Wish.* New York: McKay, 1972. (PS)

Brian Garfield is a highly versatile writer who excels at any number of story types and forms. He began his career in the western field, where he published dozens of novels, including at least five of outstanding quality. In 1970 he shifted his sights to the contemporary novels with criminous themes that have earned him wide acclaim in this country and best-seller status in England. These, published under his own name and the pseudonym John Ives (q.v.), cover most of the criminous spectrum: action/adventure, political intrigue, comic farce, historical suspense, espionage, and urban crime. More recently, he has published a nonfiction book on western films, written screenplays, and formed his own Hollywood production company.

Death Wish is probably Garfield's most famous (some might say infamous) novel, not so much by its own virtue but as a result of the 1974 film version with Charles Bronson. It is certainly the work that catapulted him into national prominence, at least in part because of his virulent reaction to the film.

The plot is simple and gut-wrenching. Paul Benjamin, a happily married cliff dweller on New York's Upper West Side, receives a call from his son-in-law one hot, ordinary summer afternoon. Three young hoodlums have broken into his apartment (the building was supposedly secure) and brutally beaten his wife and daughter—attacks of such violence that neither woman survives. The police are helpless; they have no clear descriptions of the youths, no way to track them down. Paul's grief, frustration, and rage finally lead him to take action himself—to buy a gun and go hunting those three kids in *their* world: the deserted alleys and streets and byways of the city after dark. But his mission of vengeance soon assumes a much larger scope: It becomes a vendetta against *all* the criminals who prey on helpless victims, a one-man vigilante committee bent on destroying as many of the enemy as possible before he himself is caught.

As the jacket blurb says, this "is the story of a society having a nervous breakdown. It is about something that causes a secret uneasiness far back in the conscious minds of many people. What would happen to a man who is unable to keep to the narrow line that stands between being a victim or executioner?" Garfield does not glorify or advocate vigilantism; his is the story of Paul Benjamin's descent into hell. The film version, however, does glorify Paul's actions. Its makers misinterpreted the novel's ambiguous ending and produced a paean to violence, an ultra-right-wing fantasy that ends with Bronson winking at the camera and silently promising more carnage to come. Garfield was so appalled at the film's distortions of his novel that he fought—unsuccessfully, for the most part—to keep it from being shown on national television.

In a sequel, *Death Sentence* (1975), Garfield completes Paul's story, reaffirms the original intent of *Death Wish,* and makes a strong antiviolence statement. This novel, however, did not have the commercial success of *Death Wish* and unfortunately seems to be one of Garfield's least-known works. This reviewer, at least, accords it considerable respect.

(*B.P.*)

*Garfield, Brian. *Hopscotch.* New York: Evans, 1975. (T)

After the debacle with the film version of *Death Wish,* Garfield produced a number of works in which there is considerable menace and *threat* of violence, but in which no one actually dies—perhaps to prove to his critics that they were distorting the intent of his work and that he certainly didn't need to shed copious fictional blood in order to tell a cracking good story. *Hopscotch* is one of those bloodless works; and testimony to the fact that it is a cracking good story is the Edgar it received for best novel of its year.

The protagonist is Miles Kendig, an ex–CIA agent forcibly retired at the age of fifty-three, who yearns to be back "in the game." Bored, traveling in Europe since his retirement, "he'd done everything to provoke his jaded sensibilities. High risks: the motor racing, skiing, flying lessons, the gambling which had been satisfying until his own capacities had defeated its purpose: he'd always been professional at whatever he did and his skills were the sort that took the risk out of it after a while." He even toys with the idea of becoming a double agent for the Russians, but decides it wouldn't be worth it: Whatever he is, he is not a traitor.

Then a mad but irresistible idea overtakes him, triggered by the thought that *The Resurrection of Miles Kendig* would be a good title for an autobiography. Why not write his autobiography? Why not put into it everything he knows, everything he learned during his long tenure as one of the best spies in the business? Why not, by doing this, set himself up as the object of an international manhunt—Miles Kendig alone against both his former employers *and* the Soviets? The ultimate exciting game played for the ultimate stakes: his own life.

Carefully, meticulously, using all the tricks he has learned over the years, he puts his mad idea into operation—a plan that includes getting himself a New York literary agent (one John Ives, a name Garfield later adopted as a pseudonym, q.v.) and holing up in a place in rural Georgia to write the book. The action literally hopscotches all over the world—Paris, Marseilles, Casablanca, Stockholm, Helsinki, London—and all over the eastern and southern United States as well. Chasing Kendig along the way (and mostly being made to look foolish) are his former CIA compatriots Myerson, Cutter, and Ross, and his former Russian adversary, Mikhail Yaskov.

Hopscotch bulges with plot and counterplot, with narrow escapes, humor, sex, suspense—all of which add up to a rousing good time for any reader, including those who don't usually care for CIA-type shenanigans. Also highly recommended is the 1981 film version (which Garfield cowrote and coproduced), starring Walter Matthau as a somewhat more lighthearted and amusing incarnation of Miles Kendig.

Garfield has also published several other novels with varying degrees of political content, among them *Line of Succession* (1972), *The Romanov Succession* (1974), and *The Paladin* (1982), the latter a thriller about Winston Churchill. *Checkpoint Charlie,* a 1981 collection of nonviolent short stories featuring a fat, old, conceited, but nonetheless engaging CIA agent named Charlie Dark, makes use of several characters from *Hopscotch*—Myerson, Cutter, Ross, and the Russian superspy Yaskov—in subordinate roles.

(*B.P.*)

*Garfield, Brian. *Relentless.* New York: World, 1972. (PP/T/A)

Much of Garfield's work is set wholly or in part in his native state of Arizona. Such early suspense novels as the Mafia chase/adventure *The*

Hit (1970), the kidnapping saga *What of Terry Conniston?* (1971), and the political thriller *Deep Cover* (1971) have vivid—and different—Arizona backgrounds. But his two best novels set in his home state are those featuring Navajo state trooper Sam Watchman, of which *Relentless* is the first.

The character of Watchman is similar in some respects to Joe Leaphorn, the Navajo tribal cop featured in three of Tony Hillerman's (q.v.) novels—a man of two cultures and two societies, a man riddled with paradoxes; and yet a man with unshakable principles who sees his duty and goes about doing it relentlessly. Watchman's duty in this case is tracking down five men, led by an ex–Green Beret major named Leo Hargit, who robbed a bank in San Miguel of $1 million and in the process shotgunned a Navajo guard. The major's escape route has been brilliantly planned to utilize a small plane; but an unforeseeable contingency—a sudden violent storm—forces the plane down in a mountain wilderness eighty miles west of San Miguel. All five bandits survive: the major, fanatical, ruthless, just as relentless as Watchman, court-martialed for atrocities in Vietnam; Walker, the pilot, who had been "good at war, but not so good at much of anything else"; Baraclough, the major's second-in-command; Eddie Burt, another ex-Special Forces officer; and Hanratty, a brutal ex-convict. All five make their way on foot to Monument Rock Ranch, a tourist outfit that runs horseback pack and hunting trips into the mountains, where they not only steal horses but kidnap the woman who lives there, Marianne Lansford, for use as a hostage.

It is Watchman's job to track them through the wilderness, to capture—or kill if necessary—all five fugitives, and to do so without harm coming to Mrs. Lansford. A seemingly insurmountable task, especially so considering that Watchman's main allies are a white cop, Buck Stevens, who calls him "kemo sabe," and a gung-ho FBI agent named Vickers who "understands Indians." What the ensuing cat-and-mouse chase boils down to is a duel between Hargit and Watchman, a professional soldier and a professional manhunter—a duel played out against the background of a savage blizzard and a landscape as relentless as the two adversaries; a duel that, in the end, proves which of them is the "better Indian."

Relentless is superb entertainment, a nail-biter of the first order. Garfield knows the Arizona wilderness and he knows men, both Indian and white, and what drives them. Almost as good is the 1978 made-for-TV film version, with Will Sampson as Watchman and *Magnum P.I.*'s John Hillerman as Major Hargit; it captures the essence and flavor of the novel, and is in fact one of the finest television suspense movies ever made.

The second Sam Watchman novel, *The Threepersons Hunt* (1974), pits the Navajo policeman against a man named Joe Threepersons, a murderer escaped from the state prison and hiding out in the hills of the White River

Reservation—an Apache fugitive on an Apache reservation. This, too, is tense, well-crafted, and expertly written entertainment.

(*B.P.*)

*Garrett, Randall. *Too Many Magicians.* New York: Doubleday, 1967. (W/H)

Any number of writers have been successful at blending crime and science fiction, but no one has done it better than Randall Garrett in his Lord Darcy series. On the one hand, the Lord Darcy stories are meticulous science-fictional extrapolations—tales of an alternate-universe Earth in the 1960s in which the Plantagenets have maintained their sway, a king sits on the throne of the Western World, and not physics but thaumaturgic science (magic, that is) is the guiding field of knowledge. On the other hand, they are pure formal mysteries of the locked-room and impossible-crime variety, ingeniously constructed and playing completely fair with the reader.

Too Many Magicians is the only Lord Darcy novel, and so delightful and baffling that a 1981 panel of experts voted it one of the fifteen all-time best locked-room mysteries. When Master Sir James Zwinge, chief forensic sorcerer for the city of London, is found stabbed to death in a hermetically sealed room at the Triennial Convention of Healers and Sorcerers, it seems no one could have committed the crime; indeed, there is no apparent way in which the crime *could* have been committed. Enter Lord Darcy, chief investigator for His Royal Highness, the duke of Normandy, and Darcy's own forensic sorcerer, Master Sean O'Lochlainn. Using a combination of clue gathering, observation, ratiocination, and magic, Darcy and Master Sean sift through a labyrinth of hidden motives and intrigues and solve the case in grand fashion.

This truly unique detective team also appears in eight novelettes, which can be found in two collections—*Murder and Magic* (1979) and *Lord Darcy Investigates* (1981). The former volume contains one of Anthony Boucher's favorite stories, the wonderfully titled "Muddle of the Woad." These, too, are clever crime puzzles; these, too, are rich in extrapolative history and the lore of magic; and these, too, are vivid and plausible portraits of a modern world that *could* exist if Richard the Lion-Hearted had died from his arrow wound in the year 1199—a world that resonates to the clip-clop of horse-drawn hansoms and carriages (for of course automobiles were never invented) and through which the shade of Sherlock Holmes happily prowls.

(*B.P.*)

Garve, Andrew. *The Ashes of Loda.* New York: Harper, 1965. (A)

Andrew Garve (a pseudonym of Paul Winterton) has produced some forty well-crafted novels of suspense. In addition to their consistent high quality, what is notable about them is their diversity, both of setting and type. Garve writes adventure, espionage, detection, and even romance with equal facility. His stories are set in such far-flung locales as the English countryside, Australia, Africa, France, and Ireland. His heroes are often policemen or quite ordinary men who rise to meet unusual circumstances with unusual fortitude, and often his villainous characters are so finely developed as to win the sympathy of his readers. Garve's readers can count on a good adventure with a tantalizing central puzzle that will keep them reading until all is resolved.

The puzzle in *The Ashes of Loda* involves the past—specifically the war record—of a Polish chemist, Dr. Stefan Raczinski. Was he, as he claims, merely a survivor of the German concentration camp at Loda, or was he guilty of war crimes in that camp? The question threatens to tear apart the relationship of the two people who care most about him: his daughter, Marya, and her fiancé, Lord Timothy Quainton. Tim, a newspaperman normally stationed in Moscow, meets Marya while on leave in London. During their courtship he discovers an old newspaper article condemning Dr. Raczinski in absentia for war crimes. Marya adamantly refuses to believe this, but there is enough doubt in Tim's mind to make him launch an investigation when he returns to Russia. It is an investigation that will leave him cut off from all official help—and eventually marked for death in the middle of a Russian winter.

Garve is well acquainted with Russia and her people, since he was a foreign correspondent for the *London News-Chronicle* in Moscow from 1942 to 1945. He puts this knowledge to good use in this exciting story, particularly in the sequence in which Tim finds himself stranded in the countryside, trying to escape the police, foraging for the essentials, and trying to survive the deadly winter weather.

Garve's other novels that make use of his knowledge of Russia include *Murder Through the Looking Glass* (1952), *The Ascent of D-13* (1969), and *The Late Bill Smith* (1971).

(*N.D./M.M.*)

Garve, Andrew. *The Lester Affair.* New York: Harper, 1974. (A)

Among Garve's other interests is a keen one in boating and the sea, and this is one of his best novels dealing with that theme. James Lester, Britain's

Progressive party candidate, seems well on his way to becoming prime minister when a strange thing happens: A young woman, Shirley Holt, claims that she and Jim Lester met during a holiday; that they bathed nude together on a deserted beach; that she went aboard his boat to spend the night; and that during the night they had a sexual relationship.

Well, all right, such things happen. And apparently no harm has been done. After all, at the time, and presently, Lester was single—a widower actually. But (and here comes the intriguing Garve puzzle) Lester himself not only denies that such a thing ever happened, he denies even knowing the woman. Needless to say, claims and counterclaims take over the election headlines. Why, Lester supporters wonder, would Jim turn his back on this woman? She *is* able to supply a very convincing account of that night, including details she seemingly would not have known otherwise, and the topaz ring she claims she lost on the boat is recovered from one of its drains. Still, Lester sticks to his story, and begins to lose his lead in the election polls.

This complex mystery is told from a number of points of view of people investigating the incident. And, as is often the case with Garve's stories, interest is sustained throughout without a single death or even the threat of death. The resolution is sure to surprise and satisfy the reader.

Garve also displays his knowledge of the sea to good effect in *The Megstone Plot* (1957) and *A Hero for Leanda* (1959). Other equally fine adventures are *The Cuckoo Line Affair* (1953), which concerns a son's fight to clear his father of a shameful accusation; *Boomerang* (1970), which is set in Australia; and *The Case of Robert Quarry* (1972), an excellent depiction of the eternal triangle.

(*N.D.*)

Gash, Jonathan. *Firefly Gadroon.* New York: St. Martin's, 1984. (AD)

Jonathan Gash's Lovejoy series is one you will either adore or viscerally dislike.

Lovejoy is immersed in the world he loves—that of antiques, legitimate or fake. (His own run heavily to the latter.) For Lovejoy, antiques are everything—well, nearly everything. His secondary passion is women. Readers who share Lovejoy's first fascination will be rewarded with descriptions of, for example, hammering a reverse silver gadroon (oval fluting) or identifying Shibayama knife handles. In auction scenes, Gash takes his fans into the English village world of off-the-wall bids, "miffs," "nerks," "groats," those who "pong" or "do a beano," and the "cack-handed," "narked," or "sussed." Lovejoy is charming and not above bending the law or the truth in the pursuit of a true antique. The romantic escapades and amours of this sprightly rogue are a delight. But for readers with no interest in or prior knowledge of antiques, the unexplained trade slang and the unabating discussion of old treasures can be overwhelming and tedious.

Firefly Gadroon is the eighth in the series. Lovejoy's trouble begins—as it often does—when he spots a luscious woman with beautiful legs at an auction. The object of his admiration "frogs" (gets) a small Japanese box he's had his eye on, and not only will she not sell it to him, she doesn't even appear to know its value. Why, then, does she insist on keeping it? That question leads Lovejoy into encounters with killers, police, international smugglers, and, of course, still more beautiful women. Lovejoy is at his roguish best in this adventure, and the background is as colorful as ever.

The first Lovejoy novel, *The Judas Pair* (1977), involves a hunt for a lost pair of sinister dueling pistols. In *The Vatican Rip* (1982), the dealer undertakes the tricky task of stealing a Chippendale table from the Vatican. And in *Pearlhanger* (1985), Lovejoy tries his hand at locating a missing person—and ends up suspected of murder.

(*S.D.*)

Gault, William Campbell. *Death in Donegal Bay*. New York: Walker, 1984. (PI)

William Campbell Gault sold his first short story to a pulp magazine in 1936; nearly half a century later, he is still writing fiction of the same high quality that has marked his long and prolific career. He has published more than 300 short stories and novelettes—mystery, fantasy, science fiction, sports—and some sixty novels, half of which are mystery/suspense and half of which are juvenile sports books.

Gault's most enduring fictional creation is ex–L.A. Rams football player turned private eye Brock Callahan, hero of eleven novels thus far. The first in the series, *Ring Around Rosa,* was published in 1955; six others followed it over the next eight years. Gault abandoned detective fiction in 1963 to concentrate on the more lucrative juvenile market, and did not return to a life of fictional crime until the early 1980s, when the juvenile vein had been played out. Callahan was given a new life as well, in a pair of paperback originals published by the short-lived Raven House; one of these, *The Cana Diversion,* was the recipient of the Private Eye Writers of America Shamus Award for the Best Paperback Original of 1982.

Death in Donegal Bay is Gault's first hardcover mystery in more than twenty years, an even better novel than *Cana Diversion* and as good as the best of the early Callahans, *Day of the Ram* (1956), *The Convertible Hearse* (1957), and *County Kill* (1962). Callahan, thanks to a substantial inheritance, is now married to his longtime girlfriend, Jan, an interior decorator, and semiretired in the beach community of San Valdesto (Santa Barbara, where Gault himself lives). But he's bored and has kept a hand in the detective business by grooming a protégé, young Corey Raleigh. When Corey is hired for a surveillance job by a con man named Alan Arthur Baker, Callahan worries that the kid has gotten in over his head and therefore sets out to do some snooping on his own. Among the people he encounters in the swanky former artists' colony of Donegal Bay are a conniving real-estate salesman, a couple of kids who run a bait shop, an ex-pug bar owner, a secretive former maid, a beautiful woman with a shady past, and an eccentric millionaire who lives in a medieval castle complete with moat and drawbridge. The murder of a vagrant opens up a Pandora's box of blackmail, narcotics, infidelity, and more homicide before Callahan, with Corey's help, untangles it all and arrives at the solution.

Rich in incident, written with wry humor and sharp observation, peopled with believable characters, this is William Campbell Gault at his best.

Callahan, Jan, and Corey return in *Dead Seed* (1985).

(*B.P.*)

*Gault, William Campbell. *Don't Cry for Me*. New York: Dutton, 1952. (T)

Don't Cry for Me is Gault's first novel, and one of several nonseries mysteries he wrote in the 1950s. His fellow crime novelist Fredric Brown (q.v.) had this to say about it: "[It] is not only a beautiful chunk of story but, refreshingly, it's about people instead of characters, people so real and vivid that you'll think you know them personally. Even more important, this boy Gault can *write,* never badly and sometimes like an angel." Gault's other peers, the members of the Mystery Writers of America, felt the same: They voted *Don't Cry for Me* a Best First Novel Edgar.

This novel (and many of Gault's subsequent books) beautifully evokes the southern California underworld of drug dealers, addicts, hoodlums, racetrack touts, second-rate boxers, and tough-minded women with larcenous and/or homicidal proclivities. Its narrator, Pete Worden, is anything but a hero; he lives a disorganized and unconventional life, walking a thin line between respectability and corruption, searching for purpose and identity. His girlfriend, Ellen, wants him to be one thing; his brother John—who controls the family purse strings—wants him to be another; and some of his "friends" want him to be a third. What finally puts an end to Worden's aimless life-style is the discovery of a murdered man in his apartment, a hood named Al Calvano whom Pete slugged at a party the night before. Hounded by police and by underworld types, Worden is not only forced into his own hunt for the killer but forced to resolve his personal ambivalence along the way.

Don't Cry for Me is first-rate—tough, uncompromising, insightful, opinionated, occasionally annoying, and altogether satisfying. An added bonus is a fascinating glimpse of the death of the pulp magazines (the primary market for Gault's fiction for the previous sixteen years), as seen through the eyes of Worden's neighbor and friend, pulp writer Tommy Lister.

Of Gault's other nonseries books, the best is probably *The Bloody Bokhara* (1952), which is set in Milwaukee and has as its background the unique world of Oriental rugs and carpets. Also noteworthy are *Blood on the Boards* (1953), which has a little-theater setting; and *Death Out of Focus* (1959), about Hollywood filmmaking and scriptwriting.

(*B.P.*)

Gault, William Campbell. *The Hundred-Dollar Girl.* New York: Dutton, 1961. (PI)

Sports—in particular football, boxing, and golf—play strong roles in many of Gault's mysteries. Ex-jock Brock Callahan solves pro-football-related crimes in *Day of the Ram* and *Dead Hero* (1963). One nonseries book, *Fair Prey* (1956), published under the pseudonym Will Duke, has a golfing background; another, *The Canvas Coffin* (1953), deals with the fight game and has a boxer protagonist. *The Hundred-Dollar Girl* likewise deals with the seedy world of professional prizefighting.

This novel is also the seventh and last to feature Gault's other series character—and second private eye—Joe Puma. Puma is tougher than Callahan, more of a loner, but imbued with the same human qualities; Anthony Boucher (q.v.) wrote of him, "He is big and muscular and can give and take punishment; he drinks and wenches and has his own ideas about professional ethics. But Gault has created him so firmly and skillfully that he is a man and not a pornographic puppet . . . an understandable and not too happy man, sometimes likable, sometimes exasperating and always real." Puma made his first appearance in a pseudonymous book—*Shakedown* (1953), as by Roney Scott—but it wasn't until 1958 that he emerged in full style; his first two major cases, *End of a Call Girl* and *Night Lady,* were published that year by Fawcett Crest, and three others followed in 1959–60. *The Hundred-Dollar Girl* is Puma's only hardcover appearance.

Hired by Terry Lopez to keep her young boxer husband from being forced by his unscrupulous manager, Gus Galbini, to throw a fight, Puma is almost immediately plunged into a murder investigation when Galbini turns up dead. Galbini's wife also hires him: She has special reasons for wanting to find out who killed her meal ticket. A variety of hoodlums and beautiful women complicate matters and lead Puma on a perilous course to the (surprising) identity of Galbini's killer. The Dutton edition's dust jacket blurb calls this "a story of violence and death at ringside, replete with action and color and full of the authentic atmosphere of life in the ring and life in the underworld." For once, a dust jacket blurb is not only accurate but justified in its praise.

Gault also brought Joe Puma back in *The Cana Diversion*—but he brought him back *dead:* The central premise of that novel is Brock Callahan's search for Puma's murderer. Those of us who liked Big Joe as well as we like Callahan, if not more so, may never quite forgive Bill Gault for so cold-bloodedly knocking him off.

(*B.P.*)

Gerrity, Dave J. *Dragon Hunt.* New York: New American Library (Signet), 1967. (O/PI)

Dave Gerrity seems unfairly destined to be a footnote in the career of Mickey Spillane (q.v.). With the phenomenal popularity of Spillane in the 1950s, a group of satellite writers sprang into orbit around him: "buddies" of the Mick's who solicited cover blurbs and contacts in the writing business to launch their own careers as hard-boiled mystery writers. Earle Baskinsky flamed out after two vivid, idiosyncratic novella-length books (*The Big Steal* and *Death Is a Cold, Keen Edge,* both 1956), as did Charlie Wells, after two readable, Spillane-imitative books (*Let the Night Cry,* 1954, and *The Last Kill,* 1955).

Only Gerrity—who sometimes published under the single-name byline Garrity (*sic*)—carved out a career of his own. His only published private-eye novel to date (several novels completed shortly before his death in 1984 may see posthumous publication) is *Dragon Hunt,* in which he unashamedly tapped into the success of Mike Hammer. Although *Dragon Hunt* is one of Gerrity's lesser works, it has been singled out for discussion because it features Mike Hammer as a *character,* making it of interest to students of Spillane, whose importance is, after all, undeniable.

With Spillane's blessing (right down to cover blurb and a photo of the Mick and Gerrity on the back cover), the novel that "introduces private eye Peter Braid" ties directly into the world of Mike Hammer in many ways. The title is a reference to "the dragon," the villain of Spillane's novel *The Girl Hunters* (1961), to which *Dragon Hunt* is vaguely a back-door sequel. Throughout the novel Braid calls Hammer on the phone for advice and help, perhaps mirroring the Gerrity/Spillane relationship. (Spillane claims not to have provided Hammer's dialogue, but one assumes he at least checked it over.) The basic plot—a dying millionaire named Adam hires the PI to protect his granddaughter from a prodigal, psychotic son named Cain—is lifted from the syndicated "Mike Hammer" comic strip in 1954, right down to the names of the characters. Spillane wrote the Sunday pages of the strip and collaborated with artist Ed Robbins on the daily scripts; in his entry in *Contemporary Authors* circa '63, Gerrity mentions as a work in progress a book that is obviously *Dragon Hunt*—then titled *Find the Man*

Called Cain—to be done in collaboration with Ed Robbins. This would explain the Hammer strip as source material for the novel, but not the lack of Robbins's name on the by-line. In any case, *Dragon Hunt* is a minor, slightly tongue-in-cheek, but likable affair, and a must for Spillane enthusiasts.

Those who wish to see Gerrity at his best, however, should seek out his Cordolini series for New American Library. In these four novels (an unpublished fifth one is known to exist), Gerrity reveals himself to be an ambitious writer, experimenting with characterization via quirky, effective dialogue; using third-person shifting viewpoints boldly; and generally avoiding the schlocky mock-"Executioner" approach of similar series of the same period. His finest hour is *The Plastic Man* (1976), which features a narrative trick so deft, so surprising, that the most seasoned mystery reader will have to give Gerrity his due.

(*M.A.C.*)

Gibson, Walter. *Norgil the Magician.* New York: Mysterious Press, 1977. (SS)

One of this century's most prolific writers, Walter Gibson was the author of 282 pulp novels featuring the most famous of all superhero crime fighters, Lamont Cranston, a.k.a. the Shadow. All 282 of those book-length works were produced between 1931 and 1949 and first appeared in *The Shadow Magazine* under such titles as "The Shadow Laughs," "The Mobsmen on the Spot," "The Creeping Death," "The Voodoo Master," and "The Shadow, The Hawk, and The Skull." Some forty of these have been reprinted over the years, most in paperback; a few of the shorter ones have appeared in pairs in such Doubleday hardcover titles as *The Shadow: The Mask of Mephisto and Murder by Magic* (1975) and in the recent Mysterious Press book *The Shadow and the Golden Master* (1984).

Gibson also created another series character for the pulps—Norgil the Magician, whose adventures appeared in the magazine *Crime Busters* in the late 1930s and early 1940s. Norgil is a stage magician: "Like Blackstone or Calvert, both headliners at the time," Gibson writes in his introduction to *Norgil the Magician,* the first of two Norgil collections, "he could switch from fifty-minute shows at movie houses to a full evening extravaganza, with an enlarged company." Norgil is an anagram of the conjurer's real name, Loring; he also can (and does) change it into Ling Ro, a name he uses "when called upon to perform wizardry in Chinese costume." Each of the Norgil stories features a well-known stage illusion as its central plot device—a version of Houdini's Hindu Needle Trick in "Norgil—Magician"; burial alive in a sealed casket in "The Glass Box"; the rising-card illusion in "Battle of Magic."

These eight stories are pulpy, to be sure (the prose is almost embarrassingly bad in places), but that shouldn't spoil most readers' enjoyment of them. The magic in each is authentic and presented with the requisite amount of mystery—Gibson was himself a practicing magician—and Norgil's melodramatic methods and illusions make for good fun. Anyone who has read and enjoyed any of the Shadow novels will certainly want to read this collection, as well as its successor, *More Tales of Prestidigitation* (1978).

(*B.P.*)

Gilbert, Anthony. *Mr. Crook Lifts the Mask.* New York: Random House, 1970. (CS)

Lucy Beatrice Malleson's mystery-writing career spanned almost fifty years and well over fifty novels. While she started her career as Anthony Gilbert with a polished and gentlemanly sleuth, Scott Egerton, Liberal M.P. and man about town, she is best known and loved for a very different kind of detective. In 1936 she introduced Arthur Crook, cockney lawyer, detective, and "The Criminal's Hope." Of course, Crook's clients are always innocent. And like Perry Mason, with whom he otherwise has very little in common, Crook always proves his client's innocence by bringing the real murderer to justice.

In this late Gilbert title, Arthur Crook plays advocate and protector for a spunky spinster named May Forbes. On her nightly sojourn to "Broomstick Common" to feed the wild cats, she stumbles upon a man (in balaclava helmet and mask) about to bury a suspiciously large bundle. While fleeing this fearsome figure, May retreats into a noisy pub, and so into the life of Mr. Crook.

The bundle turns out to be the body of a young woman of loose morals and avaricious ambition. There are plenty of men who might have wanted the victim dead. One young fellow (not surprisingly, an out-of-towner) is arrested for the crime, but since May is sure of his innocence, Crook investigates.

The puzzle of *Mr. Crook Lifts the Mask* is perhaps a little too easy to guess, but the characters, especially May (or "Sugar," as Crook calls her) and her man-hating, sharp-tongued friend, Mrs. Politi, are a delight. Arthur Crook, with his irrepressible optimism, his colorful slang, and his ancient yellow Rolls, "The Superb," is a memorable sleuth. And Gilbert is skilled at creating tidy puzzles and eccentric characters.

(*K.L.M.*)

Gilbert, Anthony. *Murder Comes Home.* New York: Random House, 1951. (CS)

Murder Comes Home finds Crook—described as a "small brown elephant" in his habitual bright brown tweed and bowler—in fine form as he deals with a nicely complex puzzle. A young couple is brought in off the street to witness a new will drawn up by a cantankerous old woman. An attending physician assures them that legal matters must be cleared up quickly because his patient may go at any time. The next day they discover that the doctor doesn't exist, and later find that all the while they were talking with the old woman about her will, the real Miss Fitzgerald must already have been dead.

Enter Mr. Crook. He and the police, who have no love lost between them, compete over clues. When two imposters are tracked down, the police are confident that the bogus doctor and patient are their murderers. Crook is not so easily convinced. He goes on to uncover a murder from the past, a blackmail plot, and various subplots and red herrings before exposing the murderer in a classic confrontation scene before the assembled suspects and witnesses.

Other Crook novels include *Murder by Experts* (1937), *The Woman in Red* (1943), and *By Hook or Crook* (1947). Readers interested in the Egerton books would do well to start with *The Tragedy at Freyne* (1927).

(*K.L.M.*)

Gilbert, Michael. *The Black Seraphim.* New York: Harper, 1984. (AD)

Michael Gilbert is one of the most versatile and prolific practitioners of the British mystery since the Golden Age. He has published over 300 short stories and over twenty mystery novels, of which *The Black Seraphim* is but the latest. He has published thrillers, novels of intrigue, police procedurals, and classic detective puzzles—and has shown himself to be competent or better at all of them.

The Black Seraphim qualifies as a classic mystery puzzle with modern flourishes. The amateur sleuth is no amateur but a professional pathologist, James Scotland, on an R-and-R visit to a British cathedral town. When the archdeacon is killed, Scotland's rest turns into a stress-filled busman's holiday.

The detection is handled along traditional lines. Gilbert, however, is interested in more than a puzzle. He enjoys examining the conflicts within the cathedral close, as well as the tensions between the secular community and their religious neighbors. With young Dr. Scotland as sleuth, there is an additional opportunity for an occasional debate over faith versus scientific inquiry.

The puzzle is worked out nicely, the characterization is excellent, and there is even a love story for them that likes 'em. Not one of Gilbert's finest novels, *The Black Seraphim* is nonetheless very fine indeed.

Outstanding among Gilbert's other nonseries books are *The Family Tomb* (1969), *The Body of a Girl* (1972; Inspector Mercer's only appearance in a novel, although he is featured in a number of short stories), and *The Night of the Twelfth* (1976).

(*K.L.M.*)

Gilbert, Michael. *Game Without Rules.* New York: Harper, 1967. (E/SS)

"The Road to Damascus," the first of the eleven stories in this collection, begins: "Everyone in Lamperdown knew that Mr. Behrens, who lived with his aunt at the Old Rectory and kept bees, and Mr. Calder, who lived in a cottage on the hilltop outside the village and was the owner of a deerhound called Rasselas, were the closest of close friends. They knew, too, that there was something out of the ordinary about both of them. Both had a habit of disappearing." What the villagers *don't* know is that Mr. Calder and Mr. Behrens are professional counterintelligence agents attached to the External Branch of the Joint Services Standing Intelligence Committee—a pair of very quiet and very deadly spies working at a job in which, as Mr. Calder has said, "there is neither right nor wrong. Only expediency."

No one is better at expedient action than Mr. Calder and Mr. Behrens. In "The Road to Damascus," they utilize the twin discoveries of a World War II hidey-hole containing the skeleton of a murdered man and the fact that a former army colonel has been selling secrets to the Russians to fashion a trap that at once explains the mystery and eliminates the spy. In "The Headmaster," it is guile and keen observation that allows them to unmask and dispose of a senior Russian agent. Most of these cleverly plotted stories are set in England; "Heilige Nacht," however, takes place in Germany, and "Cross-Over"—the most exciting of the entries—features a lengthy trek through both Germany and France.

Gilbert's style is wry, restrained, penetrating, and ironic. Reading one of these stories is like sipping a very dry martini, and the cumulative effect of two or three is also much the same—you begin to feel highly stimulated. However, there is a good deal of casual killing here, much of it done very coolly and professionally by Mr. Calder and Mr. Behrens (Rasselas, too, on occasion). The atmosphere is amoral, to say the least. (In "On Slay Down," for instance, a soldier who thinks he has accidentally killed a woman—who, in truth, was a turncoat shot down by Mr. Calder—buries the body to cover up the killing, and is rewarded by recruitment into the External Branch because he is just the sort of quick-witted fellow they want.) The result of this is also cumulative and also like guzzling dry martinis: two or three may stimulate you, but eleven in a row tend to leave you rather ossified. There is a hangover effect, too. You don't mind having hoisted (buried) a few with Mr. Calder and Mr. Behrens, but you're not so sure you'd like to go spy-killing with them on a regular basis.

Those of you who have stronger constitutions will want to consult the second collection featuring these two dignified liquidators, *Mr. Calder & Mr. Behrens* (1982).

(*B.P.*)

*Gilbert, Michael. *Smallbone Deceased.* New York: Harper, 1950. (PP/AD)

Classic Gilbert, *Smallbone Deceased* relies heavily on the legal milieu that the author knows so well: He has been an articled clerk, then a solicitor and partner with a London law firm. The action starts soon after the incredibly energetic Henry Bohun joins the firm of Horniman, Birley & Crane. Horniman Sr. has recently died of heart failure. Horniman Jr. nearly does the same when, upon opening a locked and sealed document case, he and his staff discover the decaying body of a missing trustee, Marcus Smallbone.

Smallbone's remains are reposing in the document case for the Ichabod Stokes trust, which he and Horniman Sr. had administered. And when the police are summoned and begin their meticulous routine, they find he has been strangled with a length of wire. Suspicion focuses on the deceased Horniman Sr.; they theorize the obvious—that the solicitor had been misusing the trust and killed Smallbone to cover up. But Inspector Hazelrigg of Scotland Yard isn't satisfied with this reasoning, and he approaches Henry Bohun for aid in his investigation. Bohun is a natural for this assignment because he is new with the firm and thus above suspicion; in addition, he is a victim of para-insomnia, sleeps no more than two hours a night, and has endless reserves of energy to put toward the task at hand.

As the story progresses, showing both the tireless Scotland Yard routine and Bohun's more unorthodox methods of sleuthing, the private lives of the members of the firm are revealed, as well as a number of irregularities and fanatic loyalties that have contributed to the tragedy. A second murder, committed with the same modus operandi, adds urgency to the detectives' need to solve this tangled puzzle.

Quite a bit of gentle fun is poked at the British legal profession, especially as it services so-called polite society. The end result is a well-crafted classic puzzler that, more than thirty years after its publication, still has the power to delight.

Recommended among Hazelrigg's other cases are *Close Quarters* (1947, Gilbert's first novel), *Death Has Deep Roots* (1952), and *Fear to Tread* (1953). Another memorable police detective created by Gilbert is Patrick Petrella, whose adventures can be found in the 1977 short-story collection *Petrella at Q* and the 1959 novel *Blood and Judgement.*

(*K.L.M./M.M.*)

*Gilman, Dorothy. *Mrs. Pollifax on the China Station.* New York: Doubleday Crime Club, 1984. (E)

What happens when you cross a sweet little old lady sleuth who has a "penchant for odd hats and growing geraniums" with a Bondian-style amazon spy? You get one of the most popular female mystery characters of the last twenty years, Mrs. Emily Pollifax. Dorothy Gilman had already made a name for herself as a children's author (under her married surname of Butters) when she produced her first adult novel, and Mrs. Pollifax adventure, in 1966

Mrs. Pollifax on the China Station is the sixth novel to feature the grandmotherly CIA agent, and it is a good example of the series. There is the exotic locale, this time the Silk Route in the People's Republic of China. There is a dangerous mission to perform, this time the smuggling of a man from a labor reform camp and out of the country. There is an evil, and unknown, enemy agent set to destroy the mission—and possibly our heroine. And there is, of course, the amazing Mrs. Pollifax, that gentle soul who can prove, when necessary, that her brown belt in karate is a deadly weapon.

Having researched her novel in China, Gilman provides some marvelous impressions of that mysterious land. This descriptive prose lends a level of realism to the comic-book quality of the spy story. Readers know when they pick up a Mrs. Pollifax story that evil will fail, good will prevail, and Mrs. P. will happily return to her geraniums. Gilman's gentle spy stories (with a minimum of violence) will appeal more to fans of Miss Marple than to Smiley fans.

In *The Unexpected Mrs. Pollifax* (1966), the heroine is kidnapped in Mexico and ends up in an Albanian prison. This story was filmed in 1970 as *Mrs. Pollifax, Spy,* starring Rosalind Russell. Other titles in this entertaining series include *The Amazing Mrs. Pollifax* (1970), *The Elusive Mrs. Pollifax* (1971), and *A Palm for Mrs. Pollifax* (1973).

Besides Mrs. Pollifax, Gilman has created several other intriguing women: Sister John of *A Nun in the Closet* (1975), the psychic Madame Karitska of *The Clairvoyant Countess* (1975), and the troubled yet courageous Amelia Jones in the author's most realistic mystery *The Tightrope Walker* (1979). All of whom are well worth meeting.

(*K.L.M.*)

Godey, John. *The Taking of Pelham One Two Three.* New York: Putnam's, 1973. (T)

Grand-scale-caper novels, in which millions of dollars and the lives of scores of hostages are at stake, were the vogue in the 1970s. *The Taking of Pelham One Two Three* is among the best of these, and for two reasons became a modest best seller and a reasonably good film with Robert Shaw, Walter Matthau, and Martin Balsam. The first reason is that the caper involves the hijacking of a New York City subway car (Pelham 123) full of passengers and the holding of it for a ransom of $1 million cash—an audacious sort of crime that has an appeal for people who have never even ridden the New York subways. The second reason is in the form of a neat logistical puzzle: On the surface (or rather, *under* the surface), it would seem impossible for the gang to escape with the loot, being themselves trapped underground with every tunnel exit watched by heavily armed men. So how are they planning to do it?

The head of the gang is a ruthless lunatic named Ryder, who is not above knocking off a hostage or two to make sure the city of New York complies with his demands. Or killing anybody else who might be foolish enough to get in his way. The other three gang members are a pair of toughs named Steever and Joe Welcome and an embittered ex-motorman, Wally Longman, whose technical knowledge of subway operations is at the core of the entire plan. The numerous additional characters (the novel is told in constantly shifting multiple viewpoints) include the various hostages, city policemen, subway workers, Transit Authority cops, members of the media and the Federal Reserve Bank, and the mayor himself.

Godey maintains a high level of suspense throughout, and deftly interweaves plenty of detailed information on the inner workings of the subway system. (Train buffs will find it fascinating; even casually interested readers will be impressed.) His characters are well delineated, the writing smooth and effective. And the escape plan devised for Ryder and his gang is both simple and extremely clever, utilizing a certain "foolproof" piece of equipment.

John Godey (Mort Freedgood) began his career writing Crime Club whodunits in the late Forties and early Fifties, among them such titles as *The Blue Hour* (1948) and *This Year's Death* (1953). In the late sixties he produced a pair of early-Westlake comedy/mystery pastiches, *A Thrill a Minute with Jack Albany* (1967) and *Never Put Off Till Tomorrow What You Can Kill Today* (1970). After the success of *Pelham,* he devoted himself to the production of other large-scale suspense novels; among these are *The Talisman* (1976), *The Snake* (1981), and *Fatal Beauty* (1984), the last named about a political-extremist kidnapping in Italy with far-reaching implications.

(*B.P.*)

Goldman, William. *Marathon Man.* New York: Delacorte, 1974. (T)

William Goldman, the well-known novelist and screenwriter (*Butch Cassidy and the Sundance Kid*), achieved his first major commercial fiction success with *Marathon Man*. The first half of the novel is some of the finest suspense writing committed to paper during the past three decades. Goldman weaves a complex plot involving a young budding intellectual/historian/student/marathon runner named Babe Levy, a superspy named Scylla, and Nazi war criminals on the loose in New York City. The characterization is excellent, the story line taut and fast-moving, and there are a couple of unexpected twists.

The last half of the book, however, might have been written by someone else, because the plot and everything else falls apart. The characters suddenly begin to think and act implausibly, there are several bizarre and unbelievable progressions, and the climax on the Jewish-controlled Diamond Exchange along Forty-seventh Street is unsatisfactory and filled with gratuitous and glorified violence. Goldman never seems able to make up his mind whether he wants to be funny or deadly serious; the fluctuation works surprisingly well in the first half and not at all in the second. (There *is* one nicely handled scene in the last half: a chilling interrogation by torture, simple and bloodless, that involves the use of a dental drill. This scene was likewise one of the highlights of the 1975 film of the same title, starring Dustin Hoffman.)

All in all, a potentially classic novel in the suspense field weakened and made distasteful through mishandling of its material.

Goldman's other suspense novels include *No Way to Treat a Lady* (1964; originally published as a paperback original under the pseudonym Harry Longbaugh) and *Magic* (1976).

(*B.P.*)

Goodis, David. *Down There*. Greenwich, Conn.: Fawcett Gold Medal, 1956. (O/T)

David Goodis is probably best known for the film versions of two of his books—the Bogart/Bacall *Dark Passage* and the French version of *Down There* (*Shoot the Piano Player,* directed by Francois Truffaut). Both movies are better than their sources. Goodis was a writer without real verve or flair, and he did far too much telling and too little showing in his books. He remains popular in France, however, perhaps because of the "existential" nature of his stories.

In *Down There,* Eddie Lynn is a piano player in a cheap joint called Harriett's Hut. He had once been a prominent musician, but he discovered that he owed his big break to his wife's sleeping with an impresario. She eventually confessed to Eddie and then killed herself. Eddie began his long slide to the bottom. One night Eddie's brother shows up at the Hut, being pursued by gangsters. Eddie helps him out and gets in trouble himself. Lena, a kindhearted waitress at the Hut, tries to help Eddie out, but his relationship with her leads to his killing a man. He runs to the old family home, where his brother is holed up. Lena follows him to warn him that the hoods are on his trail, and there is a final shoot-out.

The ending, like most endings in Goodis novels, is bleak and without hope, showing men at the mercy of inexplicable forces, yet still responsible for their acts. This theme runs throughout Goodis's works and is never more evident than in *Down There.*

(*B.C.*)

Goodis, David. *Street of No Return.* Greenwich, Conn.: Fawcett Gold Medal, 1954. (O/T)

Street of No Return has strong similarities of plot to *Down There,* but is a much stronger book.

Whitey, an alky once known as Edward Linden, the best singer of his generation, got involved with the wrong woman. The woman's hoodlum friends try to persuade Whitey to forget her by smashing his vocal cords, and Whitey winds up with the rest of the winos on the street of no return. One day, with a race riot in progress in the Hellhole a few blocks away from skid row, Whitey sees some familiar faces and follows them into the Hellhole, where he tries to help a dying cop. As a result, he is accused of murder, and much of the first part of the book deals with his attempts to evade the police, just as much of the first part of *Down There* deals with Eddie's attempts to evade the gangsters. Eventually the book comes to a predictable end: Whitey finds the killer and brings the riots to a stop. But as one would expect in a Goodis book, Whitey does not find the girl and live with her happily ever after. Instead, he goes back to his bottle and his friends on the street.

What sets this book apart from *Down There,* as well as a number of other Goodis novels, is the writing. The writing is not slowed down, as it often is in Goodis's works, by lengthy passages of introspection; thus the story moves along with the reader being shown, not told, and the narration is more effective than usual. One wonders why this book has never been filmed in place of other, lesser, Goodis novels.

Those with a taste for Goodis's philosophy should try *Street of the Lost* (1953) and *The Moon in the Gutter* (1954). The titles tell the story. A recent movie version of the latter was a conspicuous flop.

(*B.C.*)

Goodrum, Charles A. *Dewey Decimated.* New York: Crown, 1977. (AD)

For those who love both books and whodunits, this novel by Charles Goodrum should be required reading. It is the story of two murders, both committed and solved within the confines of Werner-Bok, one of the nation's most prestigious libraries.

Things were chaotic enough at Werner-Bok even before the murders—anonymous letters sent to the press had questioned the authenticity of two of the library's rare manuscripts. But the murder of two staff members, on top of this, threatens to destroy the library's reputation. Not that we know right away the two deaths *are* murders (one is made to seem an accident, the other a suicide). But three people begin to suspect murder: Betty Creighton Jones, the public-relations officer; Ed George, a retired librarian and friend of Werner-Bok's director; and Steve Carson, a young researcher. These three amateur detectives join forces and go about hunting clues and questioning suspects. So we have a situation in which not only the sleuths and the murder victims, but all the suspects as well, are associated with the library.

Goodrum, himself an eminent librarian, obviously knows the field as few others do. The library and rare-books information he gives us is interesting, although presented in great quantity for the sake of the information itself rather than advancing the story. But we do get caught up, along with the three amateur sleuths, in trying to puzzle out the murderer's identity.

Goodrum's other novel is *Carnage of the Realm* (1979), which has a numismatic background.

(*N.D.*)

Gordon, Richard. *A Question of Guilt.* New York: Atheneum, 1981. (H)

A Question of Guilt is a fictional account of the 1910 Dr. Crippen murder case, told mainly from the viewpoint of a couple who befriended the doctor. Set against the richly developed background of Edwardian London (with other equally good scenes in Switzerland and New York), it raises the question of whether Crippen intentionally murdered his wife.

Crippen, as true-crime buffs know, was an American doctor living in London with his wife, Belle. The marriage was a miserable one, and the doctor saw no release so he could marry his typist lover. So he poisoned Belle, dismembered her with the aid of a borrowed *Gray's Anatomy* (thus becoming one of the first do-it-yourselfers), and stupidly buried some of her remains in the basement. Crippen's clumsy cover-up led to his eventual murder trial and hanging.

But, the author asks, did Crippen *mean* to posion Belle? Gordon's hero, Dr. Eliot Beckett, thinks not. And as the story unfolds, the Crippen case becomes secondary to the story of Beckett, an idealistic and iconoclastic physician, and Nancy Grange, the high-spirited and independent American heiress Beckett eventually marries. It is a love story—from their meeting at a Swiss sanatorium where Nancy has taken her tubercular sister, through their tempestuous courtship, to Beckett's high appointment at court—but it is also the story of two people who are too idealistic for their station in life and their times, and are thus doomed to disillusionment.

Perhaps it is the disillusionment that prevents Beckett—although not Nancy—from accepting Crippen's guilt; he can face only so much erosion of his ideals. On the other hand, to this reader the question of guilt raised here seems a moot point: Even if Crippen did not intend to give his wife that fatal dose, his subsequent grisly (and thoroughly described) actions make him as culpable as if he had measured out the poison deliberately. The author has wisely left the question of guilt open at the (somewhat anticlimactic) end of the novel.

Although one could hope for a more satisfying conclusion, this is a good read, full of Edwardian lore that is skillfully woven into the story, with well-developed characters whose actions and reactions are appropriate to the times in which they live.

Gordon's previous novels, *Witness for the Crown* (1971) and *Jack the Ripper* (1980), are also fictional reconstructions of historical crimes.

(*M.M.*)

Gordons, The. *Operation Terror.* New York: Doubleday Crime Club, 1961. (PS/PP)

The successful husband-and-wife team of Mildred and Gordon Gordon produced suspense fiction for almost forty years. Their books are definitely formulaic, but they have the capacity to engage the reader's full attention. An important element in this formula is that of time running out: Something terrible is about to happen, and the hero must overcome seemingly insurmountable odds in order to save the situation. Of course the hero always succeeds, the situation is always saved, and the reader goes away thoroughly satisfied. All in all, reading such satisfying stories is not a bad way to spend one's time—especially on a cold winter's night when one would like a little manufactured terror.

In the opening scene of this novel, Kelly Sherwood is accosted in her garage by a hoodlum intent on using her as an accomplice in robbing the bank where she works. Because she is young and has no next of kin but her sister, she is a likely victim. This man threatens death to her and her sister if she does not comply with his wishes, and he hurts her just enough to show that he means it. She is angry and frightened, but not too frightened to call the FBI.

Next we meet Ripley of the FBI, and probably learn more than we'll ever need (or hope) to know about him. And we also meet Toby Sherwood, the younger sister. She is a teenager, unpredictable and fresh, and full of life and fun and a sense of fairness. She also has an undying love for and loyalty to her older sister, who has raised her since their parents died some years ago. In the ensuing action, Kelly remains the bulwark of strength that past circumstances have forced her to be, Toby grows up, and Ripley—being Ripley—perseveres.

This book is suspenseful, and has a rather well-thought-out plot and good (although in some cases overdone) character development. It is fast-paced, and even the villain has redeeming qualities. *Operation Terror* is a cut above other works by this collaborative team—finely crafted, with a realistic and contemporary setting. It was filmed in 1962 as *Experiment in Terror,* with a San Francisco setting and an ending that takes place during a Giants-Dodgers baseball game at Candlestick Park. Lee Remick and Glenn Ford had the starring roles, and Stefanie Powers portrayed the sister, but Ross Martin as an asthmatic villain steals the show.

(*T.S./M.M.*)

*Gores, Joe. *Dead Skip.* New York: Random House, 1972. (PI)

While holding down a variety of jobs, one of them a stint as a San Francisco private investigator, Joe Gores published numerous (and generally hard-boiled) short stories in the 1950s and 1960s. One of these, "Sweet Vengeance" (*Manhunt,* July 1964) became the basis for his first novel, the violent suspense thriller *A Time of Predators* (1969). *Dead Skip* is the first of three novels in the DKA File series (which also includes a dozen or so short stories)—a series Ellery Queen called "authentic as a fist in your face."

DKA stands for Daniel Kearny Associates, a San Francisco investigative firm modeled on the real agency for which Gores once worked. (It was Anthony Boucher who first suggested Gores utilize his PI background as the basis for a fictional series.) DKA operates out of an old Victorian that used to be a specialty whorehouse, and specializes in the repossessing of cars whose owners have defaulted on loans from banks and automobile dealers. Kearny, the boss, is tough, uncompromising, but fair; his operatives, each of whom plays an important role in some if not all of the novels and stories, include Larry Ballard (the nominal lead protagonist), Bart Heslip, Patrick Michael O'Bannon, Giselle Marc, and office manager Kathy Onoda.

Dead Skip begins quietly enough, with Bart Heslip (who happens to be black) repossessing a car in San Francisco's Richmond district and returning it to the DKA offices, where he files his report. But when he leaves he is struck down by an unknown assailant—and the following morning the other members of DKA are confronted with the news that Bart is in a coma in a hospital intensive-care unit, the apparent victim of an accident in a repo'd Jaguar.

Bart's girlfriend, Corinne Jones, refuses to believe in the "accident" and convinces Ballard that Bart was the victim of violence. In spite of Kearny, who seems more concerned about the cost of the wrecked Jag than about Bart's welfare (thus causing tension in the ranks), Ballard embarks on a search for Bart's assailant and an explanation for the attack. Starting with the files on Bart's recent repo jobs, he follows a twisting trail that takes him all over San Francisco and to the East Bay; involves him with a number of unusual characters, one of them a rock musician with a group calling itself Assault and Battery; and ends in a macabre confrontation that endangers not only Ballard's life but that of Giselle Marc, in a house high above the former haven of the flower children, the Haight-Ashbury.

The motivation for the attack on Bart is hardly new to crime fiction, and some of the villain's other actions are likewise questionably motivated, but these minor flaws shouldn't spoil anyone's enjoyment of what is otherwise an excellent private-eye procedural. It is, in fact, strong stuff—realistic, powerful, "a traditional American crime novel, out of *Black Mask,* Hammett and Chandler" (*New York Times*).

Even better are the other two novels in the series—*Final Notice* (1973) and *Gone, No Forwarding* (1978).

(*B.P.*)

Gores, Joe. *Hammett.* New York: Putnam's, 1975. (H/AD)

Gores is a lifelong aficionado and student of the works of Dashiell Hammett (q.v.), and Hammett's influence is clearly evident in Gores's own fiction. *Hammett* is his personal monument to the man he believes was the greatest of all crime writers—part thriller, part fictionalized history, part biography set in the San Francisco of 1928, "a corrupt city, owned by its politicians, its cops, its district attorney. A city where anything is for sale."

When an old friend from his Pinkerton days, Vic Atkinson, is murdered after Hammett refuses to help him, the former op-turned-*Black Mask* writer once again finds himself in the role of detective and man hunter. But as the dust-jacket blurb says, "During his search through the teeming alleys of Chinatown, through the cathouses and speakeasies and gambling hells of the city, Hammett discovers that the years of writing have dulled his hunter's instincts, have made him fear death—and that failure to resharpen his long-unused skills as a private detective could end . . . his life."

The blurb goes on to say, "[Gores'] dialogue crackles and sparks with the wry, tough humor of the twenties. His characters are thinly disguised portraits of the men and women who shook and shaped this most fascinating of American cities. His plot, drawn from actual events in San Francisco's corrupt political past, casts harsh light on a stark and bloody era." All of which is true enough, at least up to a point. *Hammett* is considered by some to be Gores' best book, and in many ways it is. But it also has its share of flaws, among them some overly melodramatic scenes and a disinclination on Gores' part to even mention Hammett's left-wing politics. All things considered, it is certainly a good novel—one that should be read by anyone interested in Hammett, San Francisco circa 1928, and/or fast-action mysteries of the *Black Mask* school—but it is not the great novel it has occasionally been called.

The 1982 film version produced by Francis Ford Coppola, on the other hand, is pure claptrap. Frederick Forrest is fine as Hammett, and the script by Ross Thomas (q.v.) is faithful to the novel, but the direction (Wim Wenders) is so arty and stylized that all the grittiness and power is lost. Some of the scenes, in fact, are so bad they're almost painful to watch.

Gores' other nonseries novels, *A Time of Predators* (which received an Edgar for Best First Novel of 1969) and *Interface* (1974), are also excellent. The latter is one of the toughest, most brutal novels published since the days of *Black Mask*—so hard boiled that some readers, women especially, find it upsetting. But its power is undeniable; and its surprise ending is both plausible and certain to come as a shock to most readers.

(*B.P.*)

Gosling, Paula. *The Zero Trap.* New York: Coward, McCann, 1980. (PS/T)

Paula Gosling's first novel, *Fair Game,* won critical acclaim and the 1978 John Creasey Award in England. In this, her second novel, she creates an elegant psychological thriller involving a hijacked military aircraft.

On a routine flight, the plane's nine passengers are gassed into unconsciousness. They awaken in a luxurious, isolated house stocked with the necessities for survival, and comfortable survival at that. Though they are not guarded, they cannot leave the house, because it is surrounded by snow and bone-cracking cold. And they have no idea where they are or why they are there.

These captives of cold are a diverse group. Laura Ainslie is the daughter of a U.S. Army general. Frank Dening is a federal marshall escorting accused murderer Joe Hallick to trial. There are also a sexpot entertainer who disturbs male libidos, an antagonistic army sergeant, and an outwardly mild astronomer, David Skinner, who turns out to be the toughest of the lot and becomes romantically involved with Laura Ainslee.

Obviously the unseen kidnappers want one or more of the captives for a reason. But which of the captives? And why? The bewildered hostages (and the reader) try to figure it all out as tension and isolation fray nerves and create friction.

This neatly plotted novel is full of convolutions as the hostages' plight becomes increasingly serious and the efforts to identify the extortionists keep falling short. In the confines of the house, anger, romance, fear, and lust cause problems that are almost as dire a threat to survival as are the mysterious captors.

There are plenty of plausible and fairly clued surprises, and finally everything is resolved in a twist on a twist.

Among Gosling's other novels are *Solo Blues* (1981). *The Woman in Red* (1984), and *The Monkey Puzzle* (1985).

(*J.L.*)

Goulart, Ron. *Ghosting.* Ontario, Canada: Raven House, 1980. (O/W)

A writer of very funny mysteries and science fiction, Goulart has said he likes to mix "murder, bug-eyed monsters, and satire." *Ghosting* contains no BEMs, but there *is* plenty of murder and satire. The hero, Barney Kains, is "a defrocked commercial illustrator who got dragooned into the comic-book business" as a ghost writer for the comic strip "Poor Little Pearl." It seems Archie Judd, the creator of the strip, is down with the flu for the moment. And since Archie's granddaughter, Beth, is the first woman who's been able to get Barney's mind off his ex-wife, a top model whose picture is everywhere, the job is all the more enticing. But Barney begins to have his doubts about Beth when he learns that Archie's tirades from his sickroom are on tape: There's no one in Archie's bed. What's happened to the artist? Barney has no choice but to poke around and find out.

This is a delightful piece of fluff with lots of laughs and good material about the comics biz.

Another good Goulart mystery with a comics background is *A Graveyard of My Own* (1985) which introduces Bert and Jan Kurrie, a husband-and-wife team of amateur sleuths. Goulart's other whimsical crime novels include the futuristic *Hawkshaw* (1972) and four books in the John Easy private-eye series, the best of which is *One Grave Too Many* (1974).

(*J.S.*)

*Grady, James. *Six Days of the Condor.* New York: Norton, 1974. (Also published as *Three Days of the Condor.*) (E)

Six Days of the Condor is a riveting book that subsequently became a riveting movie starring Robert Redford with the "Six" of the title halved to "Three." The story's central character is a young man named Ronald Malcolm (code name: Condor), a book-reading specialist for the CIA. He works with a small group of people in an unobtrusive building in Washington, D.C., doing just that—reading books, particularly mysteries, and passing along information (field tips, authors who seem to know too much, etc.) to

CIA headquarters. Then one day the unthinkable happens. It is Malcolm's turn to pick up lunch, and when he returns to the building he finds every one of his fellow workers massacred.

Frightening enough, certainly, but then the *real* terror begins. He phones CIA headquarters to report the killings and is instructed to meet a couple of agents at a specific location in the city. When he shows up, an attempt is made on his life, which tells him that either the CIA itself or an element within the agency ordered the killings and they are now trying to make it a clean sweep. The terror, of course, involves not knowing—not knowing why the killings took place or whom he can trust. He becomes a man truly alone, with every suspicious face in the crowd a potential threat.

This is a harrowing novel, with unsettling and far-reaching implications. No one who reads it can fail to be disturbed in one way or another.

James Grady's other novels include a sequel chronicling the further adventures of Ronald Malcolm, *Shadow of the Condor* (1975). More recent titles are *Runner in the Street* (1984) and *Razor Game* (1985).

(*N.D.*)

Grafton, C. W. *The Rat Began to Gnaw the Rope.* New York: Farrar & Rinehart, 1943. (AD)

Lawyer Gil Henry's client describes him as a young man who has "got more curiosity than an old maid and his mind is so sharp it's about to cut his ears off." Henry is this and much more—tenacious, eager, with a humorous, self-deprecating wit. Sometimes he's a bit of a bumbler, but he has the good grace to acknowledge it. And in this, his first case, his determination serves him in good stead.

Henry is hired by Ruth McClure to look into the matter of some stock she has inherited: Her father, who was recently killed in an auto accident, has left her a hundred shares in Harper Products Company, the firm where he was employed. The owner of the company, William Jasper Harper, is offering to buy the shares for much more than they are worth, and Ruth wants to know why. Henry takes her on as a client—with reservations because the senior partner in his firm is dating Harper's daughter. And when he receives an urgent summons to come to Harpersville earlier than he planned (because someone has ransacked Ruth's house), he still is hesitant. But he goes, in a car borrowed from his partner, and is involved in a near-fatal accident on the way. When the accident turns out to be due to a shot-out tire, he checks the car Ruth's father died in. There is no evidence, because there is no tire—someone has taken it from the wrecking yard.

From there on, suspicious circumstances mount up: There seems to be little love lost between Ruth McClure and her adopted brother, Tim; Ruth's father lived well beyond his means; there is a disfigured egg lady who is also living beyond her means—and indeed buys the eggs she sells to selected persons (including Mr. Harper) at the grocery store. When Henry confronts Harper personally, he is run out of town, and he must go to Louisville, Kentucky, where the company's accountants are, in search of further evidence. Before he finally gets to the bottom of this strange state of affairs, murder has been done twice—and Gil Henry is considering committing a third.

Grafton's style is easy and humorous, the plotting is good, and the characters are sure to intrigue you. Gil Henry is an extremely likable young man, and it's regrettable that he appears in only one other book, *The Rope Began to Hang the Butcher* (1944). Grafton—the father of contemporary private-eye novelist Sue Grafton (q.v.)—wrote only one other suspense novel, *Beyond a Reasonable Doubt* (1950).

(*M.M.*)

Grafton, Sue. *"A" Is for Alibi.* New York: Holt, 1982. (PI)

In this first of a series featuring female private investigator Kinsey Millhone, screenwriter Sue Grafton introduces us to a captivating character. Millhone is thirty-two, twice divorced, with no kids (after all, she can't very well ramble around California in her beat-up Volkswagen with two babes and a lonely husband waiting at home). *"A" Is for Alibi* begins with Kinsey telling us she has killed someone for the first time. The event "weighs heavily" on her mind, and in a tightly packed 274 pages we find out just how it happened.

Millhone takes us back to the beginning of the case, when she meets with the widow of a prominent attorney in Santa Teresa, a small, upper-class beach community in southern California (and Grafton's admitted tribute to Ross Macdonald, q.v.). The woman was convicted eight years ago of poisoning her philandering, abusive, and very rich husband with a capsule of oleander—a common California shrub—which she allegedly slipped into his bottle of tranquilizers so he would take it at will, when she wasn't around: "A" is for alibi.

The woman has proclaimed her innocence from the beginning. After eight years in prison for a crime she didn't commit, she wants Millhone to find her husband's real murderer. What follows is a beautifully written story of spoiled love, American-style. Ex-wives, children of divorce, ambitious girlfriends, loyal secretaries, and longtime business partners—Millhone grills all of these with the tenacity of the best hard-boiled detectives, and her female sympathies draw out the emotional reality of the characters with refreshing clarity. In the end, she has no choice but to kill someone, and we are as surprised as she is when it happens. Don't miss this one, or its sequel, *"B" Is for Burglar,* which appeared in 1985.

(*K.K.H.*)

Green, Alan. *What a Body!* New York: Simon & Schuster, 1949. (C/W)

The dust-jacket blurb calls this first mystery "the funniest, risibility-ticklingest book . . . since Wodehouse." It isn't *that* good, but it does have its moments—so many of them, in fact, that *What a Body!* was voted a Best First Novel Edgar. It is not only comical in the droll, barbed fashion of the Forties, but has an "impossible crime" plot of the sort that John Dickson Carr (q.v.) loved to befuddle *his* readers with.

When Merlin Broadstone is murdered in his fourth-floor room at the Broadstone Hotel on the island of Broadstone, Florida, millions of people cheer. Broadstone, the "Caliph of Calisthenics," the "Dictator of Diet," had made a fortune by zealously depriving people of liquor, tobacco, starchy foods, slothful behavior, and the joy of sex—all in the name of health and fitness. The Broadstone Hotel (and Broadstone Island) is a large and austere health spa, his monument to clean (if unhappy) living; it has been open only a short while, and is populated at the time of Broadstone's amazing demise by hundreds of his followers, members of his immediate family, and a number of VIPs, among them a Democratic senator, a Republican congressman, and a famous criminal lawyer.

And Broadstone's death truly *is* amazing. It seems he was shot to death inside his locked room, through a window open only a few inches, and at an angle that indicates the fatal bullet came from the swimming pool in the courtyard below. Not only that, but there is evidence that the murderer somehow entered the locked room *after* the shooting, on an inexplicable errand. According to Police Lieutenant John Hugo, the book's nominal hero (who spends more time courting Broadstone's sexy blond niece, Sandra, than he does detecting), the person responsible is someone "who can walk on the surface of a body of water six feet deep while remaining invisible. He must also be a guy who had a compulsion to put pajamas on his victim after shooting him and who would walk through the walls of a locked room to do so."

The immediate suspects include Sandra; Broadstone's brother-in-law, Arthur Hutch; and the four other members of the family, none of whom liked the tyrannical old faddist; Senator Happy Ned Dumbrow, the owner of a different island that Broadstone *didn't* buy; a hulking young man named Lovechild who has a penchant for togas; and Daniel Joyce, the plump and middle-aged family lawyer to whom the damnedest things happen. It isn't exactly love-smitten and bumbling Hugo who determines which of them is guilty and explains how the crime was accomplished (and a simple and dexterous solution it is, too); actually, one of the suspects has to do it for him.

The only real flaw in *What a Body!* is Green's determinedly author-omniscient style, which at times becomes intrusive and gets in the way of continuity. The same is true of his only other mystery, *They Died Laughing* (1952), an equally clever and amusing locked-room puzzle about the murder of a TV comedian—on and off television.

(*B.P.*)

**Green, Anna Katharine. *The Leavenworth Case.* New York: Dover, 1981. (Reprint of 1878 edition.) (PP/AD)

This is a cornerstone novel of the mystery genre—the nineteenth-century American best seller that brought the detective novel into the public eye and raised it to hitherto unknown "respectable" status. First published in 1878, it is the best known of Green's more than thirty novels and is thought by many critics to set the pattern for subsequent detective stories. As Alma E. Murch points out in *The Development of the Detective Novel* (1958), ". . . Green not only made her detective the leading figure and formulated a plan of construction that later became conventional. She also introduced characters and incidents that were new in her day, though they have since become familiar in novels of this type. . . ."

Indeed the contemporary reader will find nothing new or surprising about *The Leavenworth Case.* Mr. Leavenworth, a "retired merchant of great wealth and fine social position," is found shot to death in the library of his New York City home. The murder weapon and the key to the library door are missing; a servant girl has mysteriously disappeared; the murder could not have been perpetrated by an intruder. The cast of characters present at the scene includes Mr. Leavenworth's wards—Mary, who is his sole heir, and Eleanore, who stands to inherit nothing; Trueman Harwell, the dead man's private secretary; assorted servants, including a butler; policeman Ebenezer Gryce, "a portly, comfortable personage with an eye that never pierced, that did not even rest on *you*"; and Everett Raymond, a young lawyer from the firm that represented Leavenworth and who is the narrator of the story.

An inquest is held and suspicion falls on Eleanore Leavenworth, whose behavior is odd at best. Clues turn up in unexpected places; entranced by Eleanore, Everett Raymond allows himself to become involved in the investigation; a dark secret surfaces; and Ebenezer Gryce, proving that his eyes are more piercing than they appear, sets a clever trap for the killer.

Told in what now seems a turgid style, this predictable (by current standards) tale is nonetheless interesting for the way Green integrates the various elements into a logical, believable story. *The Leavenworth Case* is "must" reading for any serious student of the field, as well as a good choice for an evening when one is in the mood for the bloodless mayhem of a gentler age.

Green also created two other detectives, both women. Mrs. Amelia Butterworth (whom Michele Slung, in her excellent introduction to the

Dover edition of *The Leavenworth Case,* claims is "the prototype for such elderly female amateur detectives as Mary Roberts Rinehart's Miss Rachel Innes, Agatha Christie's Miss Marple, Patricia Wentworth's Miss Silver, and Stuart Palmer's Hildegarde Withers") appears with Ebenezer Gryce in such novels as *The Affair Next Door* (1897) and *The Circular Study* (1900). Violet Strange, a society-girl detective (whom Slung claims is a forerunner of Nancy Drew), appears in the 1915 short-story collection *The Golden Slipper and Other Problems for Violet Strange.*

(*M.M.*)

Green, Edith Pinero. *Rotten Apples.* New York: Dutton, 1977. (AD)

Dearborn V. Pinch is described by one of Ms. Green's publishers as "the world's oldest and cleverest detective." At well over seventy, the former at least may be true. Pinch, a charming and enterprising old gentleman who still has a sharp eye for the ladies, receives a visit from old flame Antoinette Ormach, who reveals her long-standing membership in the Rotten Apple Corps. This group of eleven, founded in the Thirties, had one characteristic in common: All had committed some sort of minor crime—from poisoning a rival's dog on the eve of a dog show to plagiarizing a poem that later won a national award. Now the remaining members of the group have begun to die in suspicious circumstances, and Antoinette is afraid she may be next. Dearborn has been known to help out friends with delicate problems they do not wish to take to the police, and Antoinette asks him to look into the matter. Dearborn declines, but when Antoinette is murdered, he undertakes an investigation out of a sense of obligation. As Dearborn probes into the lives of the Rotten Apples, he becomes convinced that one of the group wishes to see the others dead—a true rotten apple; and as he crisscrosses New York City in search of that person, he encounters more peril than any septuagenarian is entitled to. Dearborn is an endearing character and, with the exception of L. A. Morse's (q.v.) "Old Dick," the horniest old man in mystery fiction.

This entertaining elderly sleuth (who combines the best of the little-old-lady detectives with quirks of his own) reappears in *Sneaks* (1979) and *Perfect Fools* (1982).

(*M.M.*)

*Greenan, Russell H. *The Secret Life of Algernon Pendleton.* New York: Random House, 1973. (PS)

Algernon Pendleton hears voices from unexpected sources—from philodendrons, for example. But his favorite voice source is Eulalia, a Worcester porcelain pitcher, and it is only with Eulalia that he carries on long conversations. In fact, this is pretty much the essence of Algernon's existence—chatting with his pitcher and leading a quiet, contemplative life in his large old house in Brookline, Massachusetts. Of course he has to earn money occasionally, and this he does by selling, one by one, his late grandfather's collection of Egyptian artifacts (his grandfather was a famed and eccentric Egyptologist). Still, Algernon is falling farther and farther into debt, and Eulalia fears the day may come when she, too, will be sold.

Then one summer, outsiders begin to force their way into Algernon's normally quiet and isolated life. First comes an old navy friend who has left his wife, has a suitcase full of money, and has seriously considered suicide. Well, anything for a friend. At Eulalia's urging, Algernon fulfills the suicide wish by blowing his friend's brains out, helping himself to the money, and burying the body in a graveyard behind the house.

Alas, two other people discover this secret and attempt to blackmail Algernon. A Turkish antique dealer wants money; and a beautiful, but pushy, female archaeologist wants access to all the treasures and secrets of Algernon's late grandfather. The antique dealer is killed in a struggle (and also buried in the graveyard). And the beautiful archaeologist? Well, that would be telling. Suffice it to say that her fate fits in perfectly with Algernon's voices, with her obsession for Egyptian lore, and with the whole ambience of the strange old house in Brookline.

Like Russell Greenan's other novels—the highly acclaimed *It Happened in Boston?* (1968), *Nightmare* (1970), *The Queen of America* (1972), *Heart of Gold* (1975), *The Bric-a-Brac Man* (1976), and *Keepers* (1979)—this is a most unusual book with elements of black humor and underplayed horror. There is nothing else quite like a Greenan novel of suspense, as you'll see if you read this one or any of the others.

(*N.D.*)

*Greene, Graham. *The Ministry of Fear.* New York: Viking, 1943. (T)

Graham Greene has a rigid—and pretentious—habit of classifying his own work into two categories: "entertainments" and "novels." While all of his work is suspenseful and contains criminous elements, the "entertainments" are more action-oriented and their mystery elements are stronger. The "novels," on the other hand, tend to be quieter and deal with the religious thematic material that is one of Greene's preoccupations. While the author appears to want to rank his "entertainments" as secondary within his body of work, it is apparent that no less effort goes into them than into the "novels": All are well written, deeply characterized, rich in background, and highly suspenseful. In Greene's case, whatever the label, the product is bound to be superior.

As the hero of *The Ministry of Fear* states, "It all began . . . with a cake."

Arthur Rowe is at a neighborhood fete in World War II London, a fair to benefit a charitable group called the Comforts for the Mothers of the Free Nations Fund. One of the attractions is a cake—"made with real eggs"—which people are invited to guess the weight of. Rowe makes a guess, wanders off, and goes into the fortune-teller's booth. The seeress, a Mrs. Bellairs, does not tell him his future, but she does tell him the correct weight of the cake. Rowe changes his bet and wins the cake—and more trouble than he can handle.

Before he leaves the fete, several people try to get the cake back from him. The next day a mysterious gentleman moves into his rooming house and partakes of the cake with Rowe, making thinly veiled hints that Arthur should turn it over to him—and crumbling each piece offered to him. A bomb from a German plane breaks up their tea party, the cake is destroyed, the stranger seriously injured. When Rowe later inquires after him at the hospital, he finds he was spirited away by friends. And Rowe remembers something odd about the taste of the tea just before the bomb exploded. . . .

Rowe becomes obsessed with finding out who tried to kill him—and why. His efforts involve him with a private inquiry agent named Rennit and his unfortunate assistant, Jones. A trip to the offices of the Mothers of the Free Nations Fund brings him into contact with an Austrian brother and sister, refugees who will have a profound effect on the rest of his life. And a séance at the home of Mrs. Bellairs, the erstwhile fortune-teller, ends in a murder and a narrow escape. A mental hospital where patients are held virtual prisoners, more dangerous episodes, and a touchingly ironic conclusion round out this tale of wartime intrigue.

This is a gripping novel, although somewhat oddly constructed. The business about the cake makes it fairly obvious what is going on, but there are enough surprises—and Greene makes one care so much about Rowe—that you won't want to put it down. Fritz Lang filmed a highly moody version in 1944 with Ray Milland.

(*M.M.*)

Greene, Graham. *The Third Man.* New York: Viking, 1950. (T)

Rollo Martins, a somewhat drunken writer of westerns, has come to Vienna at the request of his old school friend Harry Lime. Lime has suggested he might write a piece on the postwar international refugee problem and pay his way to the divided city. But when Martins arrives, Lime is dead, having been run over by a car in front of his building, and Martins is barely in time for his funeral. There he meets Colonel Calloway of the British occupational police force; Calloway is interested in Lime, and in Martins's association with him.

Although he has little money, Martins manages to stay on in Vienna by cadging funds from a variety of people who seem extraordinarily concerned with his welfare. And soon questions about Harry Lime begin to plague him: Who was his friend, really? A harmless adult version of the boy Martins knew at school—a young rogue who played all the angles? Or a vicious racketeer, the worst Vienna has ever seen? Why did Lime really want Martins to come to Vienna? Was Lime's death merely an accident, or was it very deliberately staged? And who was the third man at the scene when he died—the third man who disappeared shortly after?

Martins becomes more and more convinced that Lime's death was no accident, and he crosses the various zones of the war-torn city searching for the mysterious third man. Set against the backdrop of postwar Vienna, and told alternately from Colonel Calloway's and Martins's viewpoints, this is an intriguing and suspenseful novel that contains a number of surprises.

The Third Man was the basis for a gem of a film of the same title, made in 1949, directed by Carol Reed, and featuring Joseph Cotten, Orson Welles, and Trevor Howard.

Other equally absorbing thrillers by Greene include *Orient Express* (1933); *This Gun for Hire* (1936), made into a tense 1942 film starring Alan Ladd in his first major role; *Brighton Rock* (1956); *The Quiet American* (1956); *Our Man in Havana* (1958), the screen version of which showcases Alec Guinness in one of his best roles; and *The Honorary Consul* (1973). (*M.M.*)

Greene, Josiah E. *Madmen Die Alone*. New York: Morrow, 1938. (PP/W)

Joseph Parisi, a homicidal inmate at the Exeter Hospital insane asylum, turns up missing one night. Circumstances are such that it is unlikely he managed to escape on his own; and it appears the only person who could have freed him is brilliant research psychiatrist Dr. Hubert Sylvester. But then Sylvester is found on the premises, brutally stabbed to death. Captain Louis Prescott of the local police is called in to investigate, and finds himself confronted with a maze of conflicting relationships among the hospital's employees, not to mention attitudes and behavior that make him wonder if perhaps some of the keepers aren't just as insane as their charges. A second murder, of a shady Italian restaurant owner named Luigi Toscarello, intensifies the hunt for Parisi; it also implicates Parisi's family, thereby opening up a whole new can of worms for Prescott to sift through. Did Parisi kill both Sylvester and Toscarello? Did someone else kill both of them? Or are there *two* murderers, one at the asylum and one outside it, each with different motives?

Despite some first-novel flaws—viewpoint lapses, too many exclamation points—and a bunch of ethnic stereotypes, *Madmen Die Alone* is a solid novel of detection, with a well-depicted background, interesting insights into psychiatry circa 1938, and a neatly clued solution. Fans of fair-play deductive puzzles should enjoy it.

Greene published one other mystery—*The Laughing Loon* (1939), set in the Minnesota lake country—before abandoning the genre to write mainstream novels.

(*B.P.*)

Greenleaf, Stephen. *Death Bed.* New York: Dial, 1980. (PI)

Stephen Greenleaf has received a great deal of critical acclaim for his novels featuring John Marshall Tanner, former lawyer turned private eye. Tanner's territory is the San Francisco Bay Area, where his cases take him into the homes of the rich and powerful, as well as into the lowest dives in the city; the author draws heavily on his knowledge of politics, business, and local events to flesh out Tanner's investigations. Greenleaf has been hailed as the successor to the Raymond Chandler/Ross Macdonald (q.v.) tradition, and it is easy to see why.

Like Philip Marlowe and Lew Archer, Tanner is less a fully developed character than an observer. Hints are thrown out about his past and private life, but they are not elaborated upon, and frankly the reader doesn't care. Greenleaf makes extensive use of simile, as Macdonald did, but with far less success; often he seems to be stretching a point, reaching for a likeness that simply doesn't come off. He is a successor to the tradition of the hard-boiled private eye developed by these writers in the sense that he is an imitator, and his work makes one wonder why we need further imitations.

Death Bed begins with a scene reminiscent of Philip Marlowe's meeting with Colonel Sternwood in *The Big Sleep.* Maximilian Kottle, dying millionaire, wishes to hire Tanner to find his estranged son, Karl. Kottle waxes philosophical about life and death—perhaps too much so for a man in such pain and close to death—and Tanner agrees to find his son for him. Karl's mother, flamboyant romance novelist Shelley Withers (!), can give few clues to her son's whereabouts, but through solid detective work—one of the strong points of this series—Tanner traces Karl, and is getting close when Belinda Kottle, beautiful young wife of Maximilian, calls to say Karl has contacted his father and is coming to see him. Shortly afterward, Maximilian dies, and Tanner considers the case closed. He is then free to undertake a search for missing investigative reporter Mark Covington, but soon discovers the Kottle case is not only still open, but also linked to the journalist's disappearance. There are a few surprising twists here, but the case builds to a rather predictable conclusion, and the primary villain (there are many, of various sorts) is introduced so late in the narrative that the solution comes a little out of left field. Chandler and Macdonald simply did it better.

Other novels featuring John Marshall Tanner are *Grave Error* (1979), *State's Evidence* (1982), and *Fatal Obsession* (1983).

(*M.M.*)

*Gresham, William Lindsay. *Nightmare Alley*. New York: Rinehart, 1946. (PS)

The underside of show business is given a brutal and yet somehow affectionate examination by William Lindsay Gresham in this justly famed novel. Carnival life is vividly, lovingly portrayed: "Swearing, steaming, sweating, scheming, bribing, bellowing, cheating, the carny went its way." Even his protagonist, Stan Carlisle, the slick, self-serving grifter, is viewed with world-weary compassion as Gresham leads him to his inevitable, much-deserved doom.

Young, ambitious Stan Carlisle has a small-time job in a traveling carnival, but by worming his way into the good graces—and bed—of mind reader Zeena, he learns the tricks of the "mentalist" trade. Along the way he accidentally causes the death of Zeena's dipsomaniac husband, giving him wood alcohol; and he turns the beautiful, virginal, father-fixated Molly into his mistress and reluctant partner in crime. Though Zeena's tarot cards have predicted Stan's eventual downfall, the Great Stanton rises to certain heights in vaudeville. But he is not satisfied, and involves himself and Molly in the even more lucrative "spook racket": The Great Stanton becomes the Reverend Stanton and begins bilking the wealthy, preying upon their lost loves and buried guilts. Then he meets and falls in love with Dr. Lilith Ritter, a psychiatrist to whom he bares his breast, and soon the seductive Lakeshore Drive psychiatrist is helping him plan one big last score.

Nightmare Alley is not a perfect book—Gresham's poetic prose at times turns a shade of purple, and his Freudian explanations for the behavior of various characters are pat and a little dated; but few tough-guy crime novels are more powerful than this, and never have "the lower depths of show business" been explored with a more knowledgeable and sadly sympathetic eye.

Gresham, whose own suicide is foreshadowed in the suicidal impulses of several of the characters in *Nightmare Alley,* was fascinated with the sleazier aspects of the entertainment world. Just as convincing as his depiction of carnival life is his inside look at the phony medium racket, which he further explored in his nonfiction work *Houdini* (1959). His only other novel, *Limbo Tower* (1949), is a hospital tale with criminal overtones.

(*M.A.C.*)

Grey, Harry. *The Hoods*. New York: Crown, 1952. (T)

This sprawling novel chronicles the career of a mob of Jewish gangsters from New York's Lower East Side, from their beginnings as a kid gang to their rise in the world of big-time organized crime. The narrator is Noodles the Shiv, whose intelligence and sensitivity outdistance his compatriots Maxie, Patsy, Dominick, and Cockeye, but whose deeds are every bit as cold-blooded.

Grey's novel is exciting, with various heists and gang-war incidents vividly portrayed, and his portraits of mobsters are believable, backing up the author's claim to be "an ex-hood himself," as Mickey Spillane's cover blurb on the 1953 Signet paperback edition puts it. But the episodic nature of the book makes *The Hoods* a fast-moving novel that lacks narrative drive.

The Hoods was a paperback best seller, going through several editions and many printings, but its latter-day claim to fame is as the source for Italian director Sergio Leone's controversial film *Once Upon A Time in America,* the screenplay of which was largely written by American mystery writer Stuart Kaminsky (q.v.). Leone's magnificent gangster epic (starring Robert DeNiro as Noodles—released in a restructured, truncated version as well as in its full 277 minutes of running time) seems destined to be the subject of discussion among film buffs for decades to come. Inexplicably, the "movie tie-in" edition published by New American Library was a novelization of the film, rather than a reissue of Grey's original novel.

Grey's other two novels, *Call Me Duke* (1955) and *Portrait of a Mobster* (1958), are also gangster tales, the latter novel a fictionalized autobiography of Dutch Schultz.

(*M.A.C.*)

*Grimes, Martha. *The Man with a Load of Mischief.* Boston: Little, Brown, 1981. (AD/PP)

An English village called Long Piddleton, an earl who prefers to be called Mr. Plant, his slightly dotty aunt (an American by birth who hasn't assimilated the British point of view even after thirty years), assorted villagers, pubs with ancient names and modern nicknames, and Inspector Richard Jury of Scotland Yard—all of these combine with an admixture of gruesome murders and eccentric antics in *The Man with a Load of Mischief.* Jury, along with his hypochondriac sergeant, arrives to investigate two unidentified murdered men whose bodies were found on consecutive nights at different Long Pid pubs. Melrose Plant, who teaches a course a year in French romantic poetry and who has given up his title, assists Jury in the investigation, but is impeded by his aunt (who has countered Plant's renunciation by assuming the title "Lady Audrey").

Among the suspects when yet another murder is discovered near yet another pub are a variety of Long Pid's inhabitants, who have moved there for reasons that require several chapters to explain. The combination of Jury's painstaking police work and Plant's background knowledge of local skeletons helps identify the victims and finally provides the killer's motives and identity. Jury is a warm and clever man, and the friendship that develops between him and Plant is just the beginning of a relationship that carries over into future novels, among them *The Anodyne Necklace* (1982), *The Dirty Duck* (1984), and *Help the Poor Smuggler* (1985).

Grimes, an American professor of English, has perfectly captured the atmosphere of the small English village, as well as created indelible and endearing characters.

(*E.N.*)

Gruber, Frank. *Brass Knuckles.* Los Angeles: Sherbourne, 1966. (AD/SS)

Frank Gruber's first novel, *The French Key* (1940), so moved critic William Lyon Phelps that he rhapsodized: "[It] is the best of 8,000 murder stories I have read." One wonders (a) what sort of godawful mysteries Phelps had been reading all his life; and (b) if he was senile at the time he made this statement. The fact is, while *The French Key* may be an entertaining novel, it falls woefully short of being a masterpiece. Like all of Gruber's novels, its prose shows the author's pulp-magazine origins, the plot has some dubious motivation and other weak elements, and the whole thing suffers (as opposed to the works of many of Gruber's counterparts) from *under*-writing—scenes chopped off short of their potential, either through haste or lack of ability.

Still and all, Gruber had a pulpster's knack for telling a lightning-fast story, and for creating oddball characters and integrating them into unusual backgrounds; for those reasons his work remains readable today. This is especially true of his short stories; his short fiction shows much more facility than his novels, as the ten novelettes in *Brass Knuckles* testify.

All ten of these stories feature Oliver Quade, the "Human Encyclopedia," hawker of the 1200-page *Compendium of Human Knowledge* (every page of which he has memorized) and accomplished amateur sleuth. The Quade adventures began in *Thrilling Detective* in 1936; the following year Gruber moved the series to *Black Mask,* where all but one of the entries in *Brass Knuckles* were first published.

Quade is an amusing character, as is his sidekick, Charlie Boston (a name Gruber borrowed for use as a pseudonym on a 1941 novel, *The Silver Jackass*). He and Charlie travel around the country looking for likely places to set up their spiel and getting into trouble as a result of their choices. In "Ask Me Another," their appearance at the Great Chicago Auditorium Poultry Show has them up to their ears in murder, mayhem, and chickens. Other creatures plague them as well—canines in "Dog Show Murder," bangtails in "Oliver Quade at the Races," and fighting cocks in "Death at the Main." In "State Fair Murder," it is the midway at the Minnesota State

Fair and Confederate colonel William Clarke Quantrill that combine to land our heroes in hot water.

These stories are lightweight and pulpy, but pleasant diversions nonetheless—and representative examples of the state of the art in such magazines as *Black Mask* in the late Thirties and early Forties. Despite factual errors and distortions, a thirty-nine-page introductory essay by Gruber entitled "The Life and Times of the Pulp Story" (which he later expanded into his 1967 memoir *The Pulp Jungle*) is compulsive reading and makes *Brass Knuckles* particularly commendable to anyone interested in the pulp era. (*B.P.*)

Gruber, Frank. *The Buffalo Box*. New York: Farrar & Rinehart, 1941. (PI)

Gruber created three other major series characters (four, actually): book salesman Johnny Fletcher and his pal Sam Cragg, heroes of *The French Key* and *The Hungry Dog* (1941), *The Mighty Blockhead* (1942), *The Scarlet Feather* (1948), and ten other adventures; private eye Otis Beagle, who stars in a trio of undistinguished mysteries; and PI Simon Lash, who likewise appears in three novels, *The Buffalo Box* being the second and best of them.

Lash is Gruber's most memorable sleuth. A bibliophile as well as a private detective, he teams with his friend and bodyguard Eddie Slocum to solve mysteries with at least some bookish element. Here, Lash is hired by an old prospector who has come riding his burro down Hollywood Boulevard and claims to be Lansford Hastings, author of *The Emigrant's Route to Oregon and California,* an extremely rare personal account of the famous Donner Party tragedy. The prospector wants Lash to find the owner of a redwood box carved in an intricate buffalo design by a wealthy member of the Donner Party named Isaac Ekert, who died in that snowbound Sierra Nevada pass in 1846. All of which is fine, except that Lash, being an astute detective, smells a rat: He happens to know that the real Lansford Hastings died in 1870.

Curiosity prods Lash into undertaking an investigation, and his interest is piqued even further when he finds a legitimate descendant of Hastings, Elizabeth Dunlap, trying to peddle a copy of *The Emigrant's Route* in Oscar Eisenschiml's secondhand bookshop. Murder complicates matters even more. Lash's investigation intensifies, leading him all over the L.A. area, to Emigrant Gap in the High Sierra, to the mountain town of Placerville, and finally back to Hollywood and both a killer and the secret of the buffalo box.

Gruber's knowledge of books and of pioneer history, and his breakneck pacing and outlandish cast of characters, make this an enjoyable book. The same is true of the other two Lash/Slocum novels—*Simon Lash, Private Detective* (1941), in which a rare Mormon pamphlet called *The Latter Day Saints' Emigrants' Guide* plays an important role; and *Murder '97* (1948), in which sinister doings revolve around a copy of an 1897 children's book by Horatio Alger called *Ralph Raymond's Heir.*

Frank Gruber's mysteries, despite their shortcomings, were quite popular in the Forties and early Fifties, as were his many western novels. Several of both types were filmed, some from his own screenplays. He also wrote the scripts for more than twenty other Hollywood B movies, among them *The Mask of Dimitrios* and the last of the Basil Rathbone/Nigel Bruce Sherlock Holmes films, *Dressed to Kill* (1946); and some 200 teleplays. Late in his life and career, he returned to the writing of novels, nearly all of them nonseries suspense stories with exotic locales. The best of these are probably *Twenty Plus Two* (1961), which was made into a film with David Janssen; *Bridge of Sand* (1963); and *The Etruscan Bull* (1969). These novels have more depth and show more craft than his earlier series mysteries, yet none of them has the appeal of the Simon Lash books, or the Oliver Quade stories, or even of the flawed Johnny Fletcher/Sam Cragg titles.

(*B.P.*)

Guthrie, A.B., Jr. *No Second Wind.* Boston: Houghton Mifflin, 1980. (PP/T)

Best known for his skillful novels of the westward expansion—among them the Pulitzer Prize–winning *Big Sky* (1948), A. B. Guthrie, Jr., is also an accomplished crime novelist. His first book, *Murders at Moon Dance* (1943), is a western mystery; so are four others written in the 1970s and 1980s, all featuring the likable detective team of Sheriff Chick Charleston and his young "Watson," Deputy Jason Beard, of the small town of Midbury, Montana.

No Second Wind is perhaps the best of the Charleston/Beard adventures. In the middle of a particularly icy winter, the town and its citizens are being heated up by a strip-mining feud between local ranchers who don't want their land destroyed and a large mining conglomerate and its transient workers. The conflict erupts into fisticuffs and then into murder at a local miner's hangout called the Chicken Shack. But murder and strip mining aren't the only things complicating the lives of Charleston and Beard; among others are what appears to be the ritual slaughtering of local cattle, an apparent influx of wolves, Jason falling in love, and one of the oddest (and funniest) justice-of-the-peace cases on record.

The sum of all these parts is a deceptively simple, easygoing, and satisfying mystery, populated by *people* instead of cardboard cutouts. If you like slam-bang action and plenty of blood and gore, this is *not* your book; but if you prefer characterization, unusual situations, and a vivid portrait of small-town western life, *No Second Wind* is definitely for you.

The other novels featuring Charleston and Beard, all of which share the same attributes as this one, are *Wild Pitch* (1973), *The Genuine Article* (1977), and *Playing Catch-Up* (1985).

(*B.P.*)

Hall, Adam. *Knight Sinister.* New York: Pyramid, 1971. (AD/T)

Before he became famous as Adam Hall with the publication of *The Quiller Memorandum,* Elleston Trevor produced five chess-oriented mystery/suspense novels; these were published in England under the pseudonym Simon Rattray, and reprinted here under the Hall name after the success of *Quiller.* They concern the adventures of wealthy Hugo Bishop, who, as a writer of books about personality under stress, investigates odd or unusual events around the world. He is assisted in this occupation by Miss Vera Gorringe, M.A., who searches out situations and people out of the ordinary.

Since his books bring him into the public eye, it isn't unusual that a married woman in love with a man who seems to have disappeared should ask Bishop for help. Although this isn't the sort of case he normally cares for, Hugo is intrigued when the missing man keeps sending the woman notes requesting assignations, which he then doesn't keep. The woman's husband, who is directing a play in which the missing man had a part, seems unaware of the triangular situation. With time out for trips in his venerable Rolls-Royce, manipulation of pieces in his everlasting chess games, intermittent consultations with Inspector Freddy Frenay (an old school friend now at Scotland Yard), and muted advice from "Gorry," Hugo engineers a confrontation scene that concludes the case but doesn't quite solve the problem.

Bishop is a combination of Peter Wimsey and Ellery Queen, with the finer points of both. The chess motif plays a definite part in the logical progression and conflict in this and the other books in the series, as indicated by the American titles: *Queen in Danger, Bishop in Check,* and *Pawn in Jeopardy,* all reprinted here in paperback by Pyramid in 1971, and *Rook's Gambit,* which appeared the following year.

Another unusual early novel by Trevor is *Heat Wave* (1958), first published under the pseudonym Caesar Smith—a harrowing psychological suspense story about a man who falls deeply in love a few short hours after murdering his wife.

(*E.N.*)

*Hall, Adam. *The Quiller Memorandum.* New York: Simon & Schuster, 1965. (E)

Originally titled *The Berlin Memorandum* in the British first edition, *The Quiller Memorandum* introduces "shadow executive" Quiller who works for an agency known only as "the Bureau"—an organization which handles such supersensitive espionage tasks that officially it does not exist and takes action only when authorized by the prime minister. Quiller's own expertise is in the area of escapes: He worked as a spy in Nazi Germany, arranging escapes from the concentration camps.

Now it is twenty years later. Quiller has finished an assignment in Berlin and is due to return to London for a well-deserved leave. Hours before departure, however, he realizes he is being followed. A man contacts him in a theater and reveals the existence of a large Berlin-based neo-Nazi organization that plans to take over Germany. One of the names the man mentions is that of a senior SS officer whom Quiller remembers from his World War II days. Slowly, Quiller is drawn into a secret and dangerous world where politics and murder come together in a sinister conspiracy.

In this and his other novels, Hall exhibits great expertise at creating and sustaining edge-of-the-chair suspense; even those who are not particularly fond of tales of international conspiracy will have difficulty putting his work down. The main problem with the Quiller books, however, is with the character of the hero himself. Quiller is a technician, expert at all the disciplines of the spy's trade and possessing a considerable knowledge of neurophysiology and psychology; his cool detachment and ability to perform well under stress are what make him so valuable to the Bureau. As a man, Quiller lacks a great deal: He has no private life, no inner torments (that we are allowed to see, at any rate), none of the faults and conflicts that make a truly interesting character. It is evidence of Hall's abilities that he is able to sustain the reader's attention in his hero's exploits.

The Quiller Memorandum was awarded the MWA Edgar for Best Novel of 1965. A film version, starring George Segal, Alec Guinness, Max Von Sydow, and Senta Berger, was made in 1966, with playwright Harold Pinter authoring the screenplay.

Some other titles in the Quiller series are *The 9th Directive* (1966), which deals with the kidnapping of a member of the British royal family in Bangkok; *The Striker Portfolio* (1969), in which Quiller returns to Germany to investigate a series of sabotages on military aircraft; *The Warsaw Document* (1970), in which he foils a Russian plot to invade Warsaw; and *The Tango Briefing* (1973), which takes place in Libya.

(*G.K./M.M.*)

*Hallahan, William H. *Catch Me: Kill Me.* Indianapolis: Bobbs-Merrill, 1977. (E/T)

A former creative director for a large New York ad agency, William Hallahan published his first novel, *The Dead of Winter,* in 1972. This chilling (in more ways than one) tale of vengeance and sudden death earned considerable praise and prompted *Publishers Weekly* to extol Hallahan as being "expert in the creation of evil atmosphere." His subsequent novels have lived up to—and surpassed—the promise of that debut. *Catch Me: Kill Me* is among his best, of such quality and merit that it was awarded a 1977 Best Novel Edgar.

Typical of Hallahan's more recent work (broad of theme and scope), it is both a novel of political intrigue and a probing character study of its three protagonists. In a men's room at Grand Central Station, a Russian Jew named Boris Kotlikoff, a minor poet who defected to the United States two years previous, is inexplicably kidnapped by Russian diplomats attached to the U.N. Inexplicably because Kotlikoff left Russia with no state secrets and is in no way a threat to his homeland. Even the most astute cold-war experts are at a loss to guess why the Soviets would perpetrate such a volatile act on U.S. soil.

Three men are involved in the search for Kotlikoff, who is apparently being held hostage somewhere in New York City. All three know each other, but only one—a CIA hatchet man named Gus Geller—has official government sanction, and that of the top-secret variety. One of the other two is working with Geller: a discredited ex–CIA agent, Charlie Brewer, whose methods can be as brutal as they are unorthodox. The third man is Ben Leary, legal counsel for the Bureau of Immigration and Naturalization, who refuses to be put off his own line of inquiry.

Suspense builds to edge-of-the-chair proportions as Geller, Brewer, and Leary battle a variety of obstacles—and each other—to find Kotlikoff and uncover the amazing truth behind his abduction. Hallahan's distinctive, clipped prose style is particularly effective here; and he once again proves himself a master of the unexpected plot twist and the surprise climax. Even readers who don't generally care for Us-versus-Them novels will find *Catch Me: Kill Me* absorbing.

(*B.P.*)

*Hallahan, William H. *The Ross Forgery.* Indianapolis: Bobbs-Merrill, 1973. (T)

The Ross Forgery, Hallahan's second novel, is an unusual bibliomystery with a compelling and ingenious premise. New York typographer Edgar Ross, one of those brilliant but unsuccessful types, is approached by tycoon

Emmett O'Kane, who wants him to create a forgery of a nineteeth-century folio by Thomas Wise. O'Kane's stated reason: to show up a fellow collector and tycoon from Texas named Thomas Long Pickett, who has the world's most complete collection of Wise pamphlets. Wise—a real person—was a famous British bibliophile who amassed one of the largest private libraries of the century; he also published, over a forty-year period, some fifty first editions of obscure works by major Victorian writers. It wasn't until just before his death that those "first editions" were revealed as forgeries and Wise was unmasked as the greatest literary forger in the English language. But what O'Kane wants isn't just a forgery; he wants a forgery of a forgery that doesn't exist—a brand-new nineteenth-century Wise pamphlet, created from scratch, that will be good enough to fool an expert and an expert's scientific equipment.

This seemingly impossible task is one that Ross, under normal circumstances, would never even have considered. But it so happens he is into the Mafia for $5000, the result of a penchant for gambling too often and not too well. So for a fee of $100,000, Ross promises O'Kane that he will somehow do the impossible. With the help of Michael Townsend, an English professor at St. David's Academy for Young Men and a bibliophile of no small expertise, Ross sets out to design a "historically accurate facsimile"—a twenty-eight-page, 1881 Peppercorn Press pamphlet of "A Lodging for the Night" by Robert Louis Stevenson.

The methods (all authentic) and machinations by which Ross and Townsend re-create the long-lost typeface and special ink and paper used in the 1880s make for fascinating reading. But that is only one aspect of this novel's considerable appeal. Ross's efforts to keep the Mafia at bay and to find out what he suspects are hidden motives on O'Kane's part are two other major plot threads; a shadowy game of deceit and deception that includes murder is yet another thread. Hallahan's construction, which utilizes constantly shifting viewpoints and the narration of seemingly unrelated events, is both straightforward and devious—a fictional sleight of hand that, when all the components finally dovetail, reveals a stunning and violent surprise ending. *The Ross Forgery* is no forgery when it comes to high-quality suspense novels: It's the real thing.

Hallahan's other thrillers have strong occult themes and fall outside the purview of crime fiction. Among these are *The Search for Joseph Tully* (1974) and *The Monk* (1983).

(*B.P.*)

Halliday, Brett. *Counterfeit Wife.* Chicago: Ziff-Davis, 1947. (PI)

Mike Shayne, the durable private eye from Miami, has hung in there for an unusually long career (in part with the aid of ghost writers—see the next entry). The appeal of the character seems rooted in the straightforward approach originally laid out by Halliday (Davis Dresser). Shayne is a tough, direct character, not tricked out with gimmicks, not given to guilt complexes or excessive philosophizing. The stories are fairly complicated, with a full complement of fights, shoot-outs, mobsters, and slinky dames. Add to that a loyal secretary (Lucy Hamilton), a wisecracking newshound (Tim Rourke), a sympathetic cop (Will Gentry), a nasty, stupid cop (Peter Painter), a lot of two-fisted drinking, and you have all the elements. Mike Shayne is the Generic Private Eye.

This crackling adventure from Shayne's middle period (after the death of his wife, while he was shuttling his home base between New Orleans and Miami) starts with the big redhead about to board a late plane to New Orleans when a nervous man, desperate to get on the flight, gives Shayne two hundred-dollar bills for his ticket. A woman claiming to be the man's wife shows up a bit too late to catch him. Curious, Shayne follows her to a roadhouse and buys her a few drinks. The bar owner pulls a gun on Shayne, demanding to know where he got one of those big bills; he and the woman try to escape in her car, which is promptly wrecked. Turns out the money is counterfeit, there's a dead kidnap victim in the trunk of the car, the cops want Shayne for the murder of the man who took his apartment . . . and the narrative barrels on from there.

Dresser's nuts-and-bolts style isn't particularly elegant, but it gets the job done. There's one terrific action sequence in which Shayne, naked, armed only with a liquor bottle, manages an escape from the counterfeiters, who were about to take him for a ride. One of the best of the Shaynes, helped considerably by the absence of simpering, kidnap-prone Lucy Hamilton.

(*A.S.*)

Halliday, Brett. *Nice Fillies Finish Last.* New York: Dell, 1966. (PI/O)

Around 1958, Davis Dresser cut back on his writing and the Halliday by-line was passed along to various ghosts. A number of mystery writers—including Dennis Lynds, Mike Avallone (q.v.), and James Reasoner—have produced the Mike Shayne novelettes in *Mike Shayne Mystery Magazine.* As to the novels, Ryerson Johnson did a couple of them, and Robert Terrall wrote two dozen. Terrall is a fine writer, a more subtle and accomplished stylist than Dresser, and his Shayne novels deserve attention. He injected new life into a rather played-out series, and came up with fresh story material. Some of the books find Shayne mixed up in international intrigue; and several have interesting gambling and sports backgrounds—this one, for instance.

Tim Rourke gets a tip from a rummy at the harness track that someone's planning to pull off a complicated multirace betting coup. Rourke's source turns up dead, apparently from accidentally swilling wood alcohol. He tries to investigate, but winds up in the hospital, courtesy of an angry jockey who didn't appreciate Rourke's questioning of the jockey's hot-pants wife. Shayne has to come in and sort it out. There's interesting development of sexual motivations and tensions among the characters—Terrall is exceptionally skilled in handling such material.

Other noteworthy Shayne novels: *Bodies Are Where You Find Them* (1941), *The Corpse Came Calling* (1942), *Blood on Biscayne Bay* (1946), *Framed in Blood* (1951), *Fit to Kill* (1958—Terrall), *At the Point of a .38* (1974—Terrall).

Testimony to Shayne's popularity in the Forties and Fifties is a series of seven B films starring Lloyd Nolan as Shayne, among them *Sleepers West* (1941), based on the novel *Sleepers East* by Frederick Nebel (q.v.), and *Time to Kill* (1942), based on Chandler's *High Window;* Hugh Beaumont (Beaver Cleaver's father) also starred as Shayne in five additional B's in the late Forties. Shayne had his own show on the radio, on and off from 1944 to 1952, with Wally Maher, Jeff Chandler, and Robert Sterling playing the detective in three different incarnations. A Michael Shayne TV series featuring Richard Denning aired in 1960–61. And after twenty-nine years, *Mike Shayne Mystery Magazine* ceased publication in 1985.

(*A.S./B.P.*)

Hamill, Pete. *Dirty Laundry*. New York: Bantam, 1978. (O/AD)

It has taken free-lance reporter Sam Briscoe all of six years to get over (if not forget) Anne Fletcher. Then one snowy night in New York she telephones to say she is in trouble. Sam, against his better judgment, agrees to meet her. But, sure enough, she *must* have been in trouble, because she is killed before she can keep the appointment.

The story is a shadowy one, but as Briscoe pieces it together, it seems to go something like this: Anne Fletcher left a rich and powerful Mexican boyfriend named Pepe. She moved from her apartment and got a job with a bank. Pepe found her and apparently bought the bank to reestablish contact with her. But Anne had incriminating papers she wanted to show Briscoe—papers alleging bank fraud, or Pepe fraud, or something of the sort. But, of course, Anne never reached Briscoe, nor did the papers. Even more puzzling is the fact that Pepe himself apparently was killed in a plane crash a few days earlier.

One thing is certain: The trail seems to lead to Mexico and to Pepe's banking connections (and this is the basis for the title, as it is discovered that a Pepe-controlled bank launders money). So it is to Mexico that Briscoe travels, and it is in Mexico that the action reaches a fever pitch. Briscoe is shot at several times, slugged, raped(!), and has a dead redhead dumped into his bathtub. Briscoe, in turn, shoots several people, slugs several more, and pursues $200 million and three culprits onto a stormy ocean.

Pete Hamill is, of course, the well-known New York newspaper columnist; he is also a talented and versatile writer, and it is a bit of a disappointment to see him employ the standard tough-guy, semi-smartass, semi-sentimental-slob narrative voice used in hundreds of such novels. Still, he does a good job of it and can certainly hold his own with anyone in the genre. Most readers of hard-boiled fiction will eagerly follow the action to an almost James Bond–like climax.

Sam Briscoe also appears in *The Deadly Piece* (1979).

(*N.D.*)

*Hamilton, Donald. *Death of a Citizen.* Greenwich, Conn.: Fawcett Gold Medal, 1960. (O/E)

Donald Hamilton has been a full-time writer and photojournalist since 1946. His first three novels were published in hardcover by Rinehart; all subsequent ones have appeared here as paperback originals. In 1953 he turned from suspense and spy fiction to westerns, and over the next several years published five superior books in this field before returning permanently to the espionage novels that form the bulk of his output.

Death of a Citizen was the first of a long-running series featuring the tough and tough-minded counterspy Matt Helm, who operates under the code name "Eric." While in the army in World War II, Helm was recruited into a supersecret counterintelligence group whose very existence is not acknowledged by other arms of the government. "What we were, never was. What we did, never happened," Helm/Eric is told by Mac, the group's chief, at the end of the war. Fifteen years pass, during which Helm acquires a family, a four-bedroom home in Santa Fe, and a profession as a photojournalist and writer of western stories. Then the girl with the code name "Tina" walks back into his life. Behind the fashionable clothes and sophisticated manner, Helm has no trouble recognizing the "fierce, bloodthirsty, shabby little waif" with whom he shared a dangerous mission in Europe and an amorous week in London afterward. She gives him the group's old recognition signal but says that without Mac's permission she cannot tell him the details of her mission. After the disposal of a body inconveniently left in Helm's bathtub, Helm and Tina flee in his truck with a varying cast of characters in pursuit. Matters come to a head in San Antonio when Mac reenters the picture and Helm begins to find out what has really been going on.

There is the usual amount of things-are-not-as-they-seem and double-dealing to keep the reader alert, but the main point of interest in this first book of the series is not the plot details; rather, it is the event referred to in the title—the death of law-abiding citizen Matthew Helm and the rebirth of the trained and deadly agent named Eric. The conversion is rapid, but convincingly done. The cool, crisp, slightly sardonic tone of the first-person narrative is perfect for the book, and remains a continuing pleasure of this series. Later books add more-complex plots, additional glimpses of Mac's agency, foreign locales, and some excellent action sequences. Assessing the Helm series in the *New York Times*, Anthony Boucher wrote: "Donald Hamilton has brought to the spy novel the authentic hard realism of Hammett; his stories are as compelling, and probably as close to the sordid truth of espionage, as any now being told." Number twenty-one in the series, *The Infiltrators,* was published in 1984.

Of Hamilton's nonseries novels, *Date with Darkness* (his first book, published in 1947) and *Line of Fire* (1955) are particularly good. *The Mona Intercept* (1980), a "big" novel of seagoing crime, received mixed reviews. As for the four Matt Helm films starring Dean Martin, they are largely James Bond parodies and do not in any way reflect the essence of Hamilton's series.

(*R.E.B.*)

Hamilton, Nan. *Killer's Rights.* New York: Walker, 1984. (PP)

Nan Hamilton (who is married to mystery novelist John Ball, q.v.) has written numerous short stories featuring this book's protagonist, Los Angeles detective Isamu ("Sam") Ohara. *Killer's Rights* is her first novel.

An established family man who is successful in his career, Nisei detective Ohara knows the traditional antipathy between Japanese and blacks; Ohara's new black partner, Ted Washington, deals not only with the possibility of that racial tension but also with the struggle to replace Ohara's old partner. The racial gangs of the prisons spread their violence outside. When a white drug dealer is stabbed, suspicion falls on the Chicano Nuestra Familia and the Black Guerrilla Family. But the investigation leads Ohara back into the part of Los Angeles he knows best—the Japanese community. Speaking Japanese and understanding the values and standards of the people so well, Ohara allows himself to slip over the line of professional detachment and become involved. And having done so, he faces the question of what to do when the justice of the courts and the police brings injustice to the Japanese victims.

Hamilton has created vivid and appealing characters against the backdrops of an Aikido *dojo,* the doll shop of a master Japanese craftsman, and a seedy-neighborhood drug raid. Sam Ohara is a very likable detective, and the deceptively simple plot gives us the illusion that we know what happened early on, then pulls us up sharply at the end.

(*S.D.*)

**Hammett, Dashiell. *The Big Knockover.* Edited and with an Introduction by Lillian Hellman. New York: Random House, 1966. (SS)

Samuel Dashiell Hammett was the father of the American "hard-boiled" or realistic school of crime fiction. As Raymond Chandler (q.v.) says in his famous essay "The Simple Art of Murder," Hammett "wrote at first (and almost to the end) for people with a sharp, aggressive attitude to life. They were not afraid of the seamy side of things; they lived there. Violence did not dismay them; it was right down their street. Hammett gave murder back to the kind of people that commit it for reasons, not just to provide a corpse; and with the means at hand, not hand-wrought dueling pistols, curare and tropical fish. He put these people down on paper as they were, and he made them talk and think in the language they customarily used for these purposes."

Hammett's first published short story, "The Road Home," appeared in the December 1922 issue of the pioneering pulp magazine *Black Mask* under the pseudonym Peter Collinson. The first "Continental Op" story was "Arson Plus," also published as by Collinson, in the October 1, 1923, issue; the October 15 number contained "Crooked Souls," another Op novelette and Hammett's first appearance in the magazine under his own name. ("Arson Plus" was not the first fully realized hard-boiled private-eye story; that distinction belongs to "Knights of the Open Palm," by Carroll John Daly [q.v.], which predated the Op's debut by four months, appearing in the June 1, 1923, issue of *Black Mask*.) Two dozen Op stories followed over the ensuing eight years; the series ended with "Death and Company" in the November 1930 issue.

The Op—fat, fortyish, and the Continental Detective Agency's toughest and shrewdest investigator—was based on a man named James Wright, assistant superintendent of the Pinkerton Detective Agency in Baltimore, for whom Hammett had worked. And his methods, if not his cases, are based on real private-investigative procedures of the period. It was in these Op stories that Hammett honed his realistic style and plotting techniques, both of which would reach their zenith in *The Maltese Falcon* (1929).

The Big Knockover contains thirteen of the best Op stories, among them such hard-boiled classics as "The Gutting of Couffignal," about an attempted hoodlum take-over of an island in San Francisco Bay, during which corpses pile up in alarming numbers and a terrific atmosphere of menace and suspense is maintained throughout; "Dead Yellow Women," which has a San Francisco Chinatown setting and colorfully if unfortunately perpetuates the myth that a rabbit warren of secret passageways exists beneath the streets of that district; "Fly Paper," in which the Op undertakes "a wandering daughter job," with startling results; "Corkscrew," a case that takes the Op to the Arizona desert in an expert blend of the detective story and the western; and "$106,000 Blood Money," a novella in which the Op sets out to find the gang that robbed the Seaman's National Bank of several million dollars, and does battle with perhaps his most ruthless antagonist.

Lillian Hellman's introduction provides some interesting but manipulated and self-serving material on Hammett and his work. This is a cornerstone book for any library of American detective fiction, and an absolute must-read for anyone interested in the origins of the hard-boiled crime story.

The Continental Op appears in several other collections, most of which were edited by Ellery Queen and published first in digest-size paperbacks by Jonathan Press and then in standard paperbacks by Dell; among these are *The Continental Op* (1945), *The Return of the Continental Op* (1945), *Hammett Homicides* (1946), *Dead Yellow Women* (1947), *Nightmare Town* (1948), *The Creeping Siamese* (1950), and *Woman in the Dark* (1951). The most recent volume of Op stories, *The Continental Op,* a companion volume to *The Big Knockover* but edited and introduced by Stephen Marcus instead of Hellman, appeared in 1974.

(*B.P.*)

*Hammett, Dashiell. *The Dain Curse.* New York: Knopf, 1928. (PI)

The Dain Curse is one of two novel-length works featuring the Continental Op. It was originally written for *Black Mask* as four separate novelettes; taken together, the four interconnected "cases" comprise a kind of criminous family saga in which Hammett all but decimates the "Black Dains" of San Francisco.

The novel begins with the Op, who has been hired by an insurance company to look into a diamond robbery at the home of Edgar Leggett (real name Dain), finding one of the missing stones: "It was a diamond all right, shining in the grass half a dozen feet from the blue brick wall." Just a few of the more than thirty characters he subsequently encounters: Leggett/Dain, a scientist working at home on a process for coloring diamonds; his daughter, Gabrielle, who feels she has bad blood and is cursed and whose drug addiction is a focal point of the story line; the family's mulatto maid, Minnie Hershey; Gabrielle's doctor, Riese; her fiancé, Eric Collinson (a puckish Hammett tribute to the pseudonym under which his first *Black Mask* stories were published); Joseph Haldorn and his wife, Aaronia, who run a religious cult called the Temple of the Holy Grail; writer Owen Fitzstephan; and a couple of other private detectives investigating Leggett/Dain's shady past.

The plot has numerous twists and turns, multiple climaxes, and plenty of atmospheric elements (the scenes enacted at the Temple of the Holy Grail, for instance). On the whole, however, it is overlong and decidedly melodramatic. As critic John Bartlow Martin wrote in *Harper's Magazine,* "In this single Hammett novel the detective shot and stabbed one man to death, helped shoot another dead, was himself attacked with dagger, gun, chloroform and bomb, fought off a ghostly manifestation barehanded, wrestled with five women, cured a girl of narcotic addiction—and . . . was obliged to deal with one seduction, eight murders, a jewel burglary, and a family curse."

The Dain Curse is more cleanly plotted and credible than the first Op novel, *Red Harvest* (1927), in which more than thirty people die, including no fewer than a dozen of the main characters. But its flaws prove that it is the novelette, not the novel, to which the Continental Op was best suited and in which his finest cases are chronicled.

(*B.P.*)

*Hammett, Dashiell. *The Glass Key.* New York: Knopf, 1931. (T)

Hammett's fourth novel is set in a nameless city modeled on Baltimore, where he grew up. Like Personville in *Red Harvest,* the city is controlled by crooked politicians in league with various mobster factions; but in *The Glass Key* Hammett gives us an insider's view of the corruption and in fact creates a corrupt political henchman as his protagonist. Ned Beaumont—tall, thin, a dandy and a compulsive gambler and tuberculosis victim like Hammett himself—is the best friend and most trusted adviser of Paul Madvig, the lower-class ethnic who controls the city. Against Beaumont's advice, Madvig has made a deal for mutual political support with upper-crust Senator Henry, hoping that the payoff for him will include Henry's lovely daughter, Janet, with whom he's infatuated. Then Senator Henry's son is murdered in circumstances that implicate Madvig. As Madvig's enemies plot to speed the politically wounded leader's fall from power, Beaumont sets out to clear his friend and patron, limit the damage to his machine, and keep the other side's crooked candidates from defeating Madvig's crooked candidates in the upcoming election. In the process he endures perhaps the most savage beating in crime fiction, and the equally painful experience of becoming involved himself with Janet Henry, his best friend's woman.

The Glass Key is one of Hammett's most powerful novels but also one of crime literature's most frustrating classics. Its third-person narrative voice, like that of *The Maltese Falcon*, is so objectively realistic and passionlessly impersonal that it seems to draw an impenetrable shield between characters and reader. As a result, generations of critics have debated all sorts of factual questions that writers less bold than Hammett would have answered unequivocally. Did Ned really intend to sell Madvig out to his rival Shad O'Rory, or is he playing double agent? For what earthly reasons did he permit Jeff, O'Rory's unforgettable moronic bonecrusher, to beat him almost to death? Is he really in love with Janet Henry or does he have a suppressed homosexual desire for Madvig? Reading the novel again and again only fuels these controversies, for Hammett refuses on principle to enter into any of his characters' thoughts and feelings, and forces us to judge from what they say and do—from inherently misleading and uncertain data. No wonder there's no consensus about *The Glass Key*! Hammett himself, and such experts as Julian Symons and Frederic Dannay (Ellery Queen), thought it was his best novel; a number of academic literary critics rank it as his worst.

Hammett's vision was one of the darkest in the history of crime fiction. He saw the world as an incomprehensible place in which no one can ever really know another, and created the world of *The Glass Key* to match. Whatever the ultimate verdict on its literary status, it's a compulsively readable, coolly sardonic portrait of an unredeemable nightworld and ambiguous relationships, and stands beside *The Maltese Falcon* as one of the earliest classics of *noir* crime fiction.

(*F.M.N.*)

**Hammett, Dashiell. *The Maltese Falcon.* New York: Knopf, 1929. (CS/PI)

The Maltese Falcon is the prototype hard-boiled private-eye novel, the finest ever written. It is also the most famous of all American detective stories, thanks in no small part to John Huston's definitive 1941 screen version. Huston remained remarkably faithful to the novel, using most of Hammett's original dialogue; and his casting was superb: Humphrey Bogart as Sam Spade; Mary Astor as Brigid O'Shaughnessy; Sydney Greenstreet as Caspar Gutman; Peter Lorre as Joel Cairo; and Elisha Cook, Jr., as the little gunsel, Wilmer. (An interesting footnote is that Warner Brothers originally wanted either Edward G. Robinson or George Raft for the lead role; it was only after both of those actors turned it down that Bogart—Huston's choice from the first—was selected. The thought of either Robinson or Raft, fine actors though they were, portraying Spade is mind-boggling.)

Sam Spade is likewise the quintessential tough detective. Other writers have altered his image, refined it; but the fact remains that without Spade, there would have been no Philip Marlowe, no Lew Archer, no uniquely American subgenre of detective fiction that has so captured the imaginations of millions that it has been elevated to the status of myth. Spade himself is a mythical figure, of course, owing in part to the fact that he is both enigmatic and misunderstood. Otherwise a Hammett admirer, Somerset Maugham called Spade "a nasty bit of goods . . . an unscrupulous rogue and heartless crook," and said that "there is little to choose between him and the criminals he is dealing with."

Maugham missed the point completely. Spade is indeed a nasty bit of goods, an unscrupulous rogue and heartless crook—*on the surface*. That is his public persona, one he wears like a suit of old clothes or the gun he sometimes needs to carry. As he says to Brigid at the end of both novel and film, words identical in both: "Don't be too sure I'm as crooked as I'm supposed to be. That kind of reputation might be good business—bringing in high-priced jobs and making it easier to deal with the enemy." Spade is hardly a saint; but in his own way, and despite his affair with his partner's wife, about which much has been made, he is an exceedingly moral man.

Similarly, don't be too sure *The Maltese Falcon* is everything it seems to be on the surface. It is hard-boiled, yes. Uncompromising, yes. Grim and brutal and even nasty in places, yes. But in its own way, it, too, is exceedingly moral.

The plot of the *Falcon* is familiar to nearly every detective-story fan and film buff. Briefly, Spade is visited by a woman calling herself Miss Wonderly; she tells him her sister ran away from New York with a man named Floyd Thursby, that the three have a date that night, and that she wants Spade to rescue the sister. Enter Miles Archer, Spade's partner, who says he'll attend to the job himself. Which he does, but not very well: He gets himself shot to death in a back alley. Also shot that foggy San Francisco night is Floyd Thursby, in front of his hotel.

Spade tracks down Miss Wonderly (in reality Brigid O'Shaughnessy); she tells him a different story and begs for his help, and he agrees. Enter Joel Cairo, who puts a gun on Spade in Spade's office and first mentions "the black figure of a bird." Enter Caspar Gutman, who eventually explains that the figure is "a glorious golden falcon encrusted from head to foot with the finest jewels," a gift to Emperor Charles V from the Order of the Hospital of St. John of Jerusalem, crusaders who persuaded the emperor to give them the islands of Malta, Gozo, and Tripoli in 1530. While en route to Spain, the falcon was stolen by the pirate Barbarossa, and over the centuries it passed through various private hands, two of those hands being Gutman's—almost. He has spent seventeen years tracking down the black bird, almost got it in Paris, almost got it in Constantinople: wants it desperately. So do Joel Cairo and Brigid O'Shaughnessy, both of whom were confederates of Gutman's at one time and both of whom have tried to double-cross him to get it for themselves. Another murder and more double-dealing lead to a grand finale in Spade's flat with all the principals present—including the falcon, which has just arrived via the ship *La Paloma* from Hong Kong. Or has it? The confrontation between Spade and the murderer of both Miles Archer and Floyd Thursby remains one of the most powerful in all of crime fiction.

The Maltese Falcon is hardly a perfect novel; such is a *rara avis* indeed, almost as rare as the Maltese falcon itself. Spade's affair with Iva Archer is never satisfactorily resolved. The character of Rhea Gutman, Gutman's daughter, seems superfluous. (John Huston thought so, too: He excised her completely from his screen version.) Bits and pieces don't quite hang together or are fused by melodrama. But this is nitpicking, really. In all ways that matter, it is truly a classic work, summed up brilliantly by Huston in the last line of the film, when he had Bogart/Spade say that the Maltese falcon is "the stuff that dreams are made of."

(*B.P.*)

Hammett, Dashiell. *The Thin Man.* New York: Knopf, 1934. (W)

The Thin Man is Hammett's last and weakest novel. By the time it was written, he had begun his affair with Lillian Hellman, been embraced and financially enriched by Hollywood, and adopted a freewheeling, alcoholic, pseudosophisticated life-style not dissimilar to the one depicted in these pages. He had, in short, lost touch with everything that had made his earlier work so innovative and powerful—his background as a Pinkerton detective, his contacts in the underworld, the lean years spent in a San Francisco flat painstakingly writing stories for *Black Mask*. Hammett could not go home again, and he knew it. Unable to write about the Op or Sam Spade, he could only write about the likes of Nick and Nora Charles. They were phonies in comparison, and he knew that, too—if not during the composition of *The Thin Man,* then not long afterward.

Nick Charles is no longer a detective, a reflection of the fact that Hammett was no longer a writer; he is an *ex*-sleuth, formerly with the Trans-American Detective Agency of San Francisco, having one last fling at his old profession. Nor is he tough any longer; he is a charming, fun-loving, *nouveau riche* alcoholic with a veneer of gentility. (His wife is just like him, the flighty type who forces him into his one last fling as a means of exorcising her own boredom—the kind of woman the Op or Sam Spade would have sneered at in the old days.)

The plot has its moments, but on the whole it is merely a standard whodunit of the period. Inventor Clyde Wynant disappears and his secretary is found murdered; Nick investigates at Nora's urging and encounters such characters as Mimi Jorgensen (his former girlfriend), Dorothy Wynant (Mimi's daughter), a crooked lawyer named Herbert Macaulay, a gangster named Shep Morelli, a nightclub owner named Studsy Burke; there is more mayhem, considerable duplicity, and enough booze consumed to float the proverbial battleship; Nick solves the case; and at the end Nora says, "Let's stick around San Francisco a while. This excitement has put us behind in our drinking." Those two lines are typical of the book's tone—light, witty, urbane. If anyone other than Hammett had written it, it would stand as an amusing piece of fluff. But compared to *The Dain Curse, The Maltese Falcon,* and *The Glass Key,* it is shallow and gutless.

Ironically, Nick and Nora Charles, thanks to the six films starring William Powell and Myrna Loy, join Sam Spade as Hammett's most famous detective characters. The films, like the novel, are witty and sophisticated; unlike the novel, they work well because Hammett *didn't* write them and because of the delightful interplay between Powell and Loy. The best are the first, *The Thin Man* (1934), based on the novel; *After the Thin Man* (1936); and *Shadow of the Thin Man* (1941). Peter Lawford starred in a popular TV series in the Fifties. It should also be noted that Hollywood is responsible for the widespread misconception that "the thin man" refers to Nick Charles. Not true. It refers to the disappearing inventor, Clyde Wynant.

(*B.P.*)

*Hansen, Joseph. *Brandstetter and Others.* Woodstock, Vt.: Countryman Press (Foul Play Press), 1984. (SS)

Joseph Hansen is best known for his novels about insurance investigator David Brandstetter. The books are notable in that the detective is a homosexual, but this is no mere gimmick: Brandstetter is a deeply characterized individual, a compassionate and caring man who is sometimes obsessively dedicated to uncovering the truth about the unusual deaths he is called in to verify. If the series has a flaw, it is that most of Brandstetter's cases have roots in the concealment of homosexuality, or involve a great number of gay witnesses—a fact that may strain the reader's credulity. On the other hand, it may be said that Brandstetter's sexual orientation makes him more aware of homosexual overtones than a straight investigator would be. And Hansen (who has stated that in creating his detective he set out to "right some wrongs. Almost all the folksay about homosexuals is false") handles his plots well and characterizes people realistically on the full range of both the gay and straight spectra. For this reader, that more than overcomes what at times seems like too great a coincidence.

There are two Brandstetter stories in this collection (Hansen's first): "Election Day" and "Surf." Both are rich in the southern California background that characterizes the detective novels; and in comparing the two, the reader can observe considerable development in Brandstetter's character—from the less developed protagonist of "Surf" (1976) to the multidimensional hero of "Election Day" (1984). In addition to these stories featuring his series sleuth, Hansen also gives us "The Anderson Boy," a haunting tale of how a man's past can catch up and threaten to destroy him; "The Tango Bear," a story set against the background of a mid-California horse ranch, with colorful scenes at a traveling carnival; and "Willow's Money," a lesbian love story that reminds us of the destructive power of *any* relationship where a weaker person feeds on the strength of a stronger one.

This is a well-balanced collection that shows the full range of Hansen's abilities, whether dealing with the gay or the straight world.

(*M.M.*)

*Hansen, Joseph. *Fadeout.* New York: Harper, 1970. (PI)

Fadeout, the first of the Brandstetter novels, opens with the detective grieving over the loss of his lover by cancer. Dave and Rod had shared a not always idyllic life for twenty years; now Dave is faced with all the attendant regrets that death brings, and only his work can relieve them.

The death claim he is investigating is of an accident where no body has been recovered. Radio star Fox Olson supposedly drowned in a flooded arroyo, but Brandstetter quickly begins to suspect that the insured has engineered his own disappearance—a theory that Olson's wife, Thorne, disputes. After a lifetime of failure, Olson had become a success; he had an up-and-coming recording career, the material possessions he'd always dreamed of, a loving and supportive wife, and a possible political career. Why, Thorne asks, would such a man want to disappear? Brandstetter doesn't know, but he begins to dig into Olson's life with the dogged patience that characterizes his investigations.

He quickly finds out that Thorne Olson has been having an affair with Hale McNeil, owner of the radio station on which Fox had his show. Mayor Chalmers of the town of Pima was Olson's political rival, and there are rumors that he planned to kidnap Fox and hold him until after the election. A houseboy named Ito, hired by Thorne as a Christmas Day surprise for Fox, was fired for no good reason after only twenty-four hours. When Brandstetter interviews Olson's daughter, Gretchen, she seems "damn cheerful for a new orphan." And from Gretchen's husband's crippled brother, Buddy, Brandstetter learns that an old friend of Fox's, known to him only as Doug, had recently returned after living in France for many years.

As Brandstetter pieces together clues from both the past and the present, he begins to come to terms with his own personal loss; and in the solution to his investigation, he also finds a key to his own future. This is an extremely strong beginning to a series, richly characterized, with memorable depictions of its southern California settings.

(*M.M.*)

Hansen, Joseph. *Nightwork.* New York: Holt, 1984. (PI)

Gifford Gardens is a decaying residential area near Los Angeles, dominated by the equally run-down Gifford mansion. Youthful gangs roam the streets, and the people feel powerless to stop them. Brandstetter shares their feelings of helplessness when he goes to the area to investigate the death claim of a trucker who lived there: While he is interviewing the dead man's family, a group of young men smash the windshield on his Jaguar; the police arrive quickly, called by DeWitt Gifford, who watches over his declining domain from his tower window, but they can merely advise Brandstetter not to drive such an expensive car into the area.

Thus Brandstetter finds the Gardens an enclave of fear: fear of the street gangs, fear of poverty, and fear in the blackened eyes of the dead man's wife. What seemed a routine accident has turned into a homicide with the sheriff's discovery of an explosive device attached to the bottom of the trucker's rig. The wife has been beaten, but she refuses to tell Brandstetter who did it or why. She does give him enough information, however, that he begins to suspect the "nightwork" (overtime trucking) her husband was doing was something out of the ordinary.

With the help of his lover and associate, Cecil Harris, Brandstetter traces the widow of another trucker who was doing nightwork before his sudden death. She is more talkative than the first widow, and she tells him that her husband took sick suddenly and refused to call his own doctor. Her information leads him to a Dr. Kretschmer, a mysterious woman known only as the Dutchess; and a houseful of unexpected guests, including three boisterous little boys. When Brandstetter finally reaches the end of his investigation, he has uncovered a number of crimes and solved a murder whose motive is at the same time socially relevant and intensely personal.

This novel says a great deal about contemporary society and contains an excellent depiction of a severely depressed area and the residents trapped within it.

(*M.M.*)

Hansen, Joseph. *Troublemaker.* New York: Harper, 1975. (PI)

In *Troublemaker* Hansen explores various aspects of the gay life in greater detail than in any other novel in the series to date. In reality there are *two* troublemakers: the killer of gay-bar owner Rick Wendell, and Kovaks, the potter who lives downstairs from Brandstetter and is trying to break in on his relationship with live-in lover Doug Sawyer. As in other novels, Hansen expertly intertwines the professional thread with the personal one, giving an in-depth depiction of his protagonist as a man as well as a detective.

Brandstetter's case begins when he interviews Rick Wendell's mother at her horse ranch in one of the canyons above Los Angeles (a setting that Hansen has used to good effect elsewhere). Heather Wendell insists that

Larry Johns, the young man arrested for her son's shooting, is Rick's murderer, but Brandstetter remains unconvinced. Johns has claimed he was in the bedroom when Rick was shot in his sitting room, and that he heard another man talking to him out there before the shot. This must be resolved before Medallion Life can pay out on Rick's policy—money his mother badly needs—because there is a slim chance Rick took his own life, and a slimmer one that his mother killed him, since Heather's prints are the only ones on the murder gun.

From the horse ranch, Brandstetter goes to the home of Ace Keegan, Rick's business partner in the Hang Ten Bar. Ace has a young boy whom he is grooming for the "Mr. Marvelous" contest (sponsored by the local bars) staying there, and he tells Brandstetter that Rick was also interested in younger men—who often took him for large sums of money. When Brandstetter asks if that could possibly account for the $1500 he has discovered is missing from Rick's personal effects, Keegan becomes reticent. Leaving Keegan, Brandstetter widens his search to include Larry Johns's friends, and before long he has uncovered a secret in Johns's past: his wife, Jomay; baby Beebee; and "Uncle" Dwayne Huncie, a "turnip-nosed old son of a bitch" lawyer who specializes in tracking down errant husbands—and then holding them up for large sums of money.

From the tangled web of these people's lives, Brandstetter begins to put together the scenario of what happened the night Rick Wendell was shot, and his case finally comes together the night of the Mr. Marvelous contest at the Big Barn, L.A.'s largest gay bar. But his case does not end there, because now he must prevent another murder.

This novel has a well-constructed plot, with plenty of red herrings and cleverly concealed clues. Hansen depicts the gay community of L.A. and vicinity—from the wealthy architect's house to Brandstetter's comfortable (albeit threatened) home to the sleazy waterfront bars in the community of Surf—with understanding and compassion, making it possible for both the gay and straight reader to empathize with his very real characters.

Another notable Brandstetter novel, *Death Claims* (1973), has a background of the rare-book business. In *Gravedigger* (1982), Brandstetter investigates a supposed murder by the guru of a sex cult. Other titles are *The Man Everybody Was Afraid Of* (1978) and *Skinflick* (1979).

(*M.M.*)

Hare, Cyril. *A Tenant for Death.* New York: Dodd, Mead, 1937. (PP)

In his twenty-year career as a mystery writer, Cyril Hare created two series characters: Inspector Mallet of Scotland Yard and Francis Pettigrew, an unsuccessful and disappointed lawyer. Mallet and Pettigrew appear in their own separate cases and also clash professionally (*Tragedy at Law,* 1943) and join forces (*With a Bare Bodkin,* 1946, and *Untimely Death,* 1958). Hare, who was not well known in America until a recent reissuing of his novels in paperback, writes well: The stories are solidly plotted; and his characters, if often unspectacular, ring true.

A Tenant for Death introduces Inspector Mallet. The book is constructed so as to hook the reader with an introductory chapter that hints at murder; we then see the principals in the case as they go about their somewhat shady business; finally the body, that of financier Lionel Ballantine, is discovered by a pair of rental agents inventorying the contents of a house where the lease has lapsed; and Mallet appears on the scene.

The circumstances of the murder are baffling: The house is in a genteelly declining section of London, not the sort of place the millionaire would frequent; the lessor, a man named Colin James, has disappeared; Ballantine's financial empire is said to have been on the verge of collapse; and a man who hated the financier was released from prison the day Ballantine disappeared.

Mallet—a self-satisfied man who takes pride in his good digestion ("No detective . . . could do his work successfully unless he were on good terms with his stomach") proceeds diligently, tracking down suspects, interviewing the principals, quietly ruminating over what he finds. And his tenacity pays off with a neatly tied-up (if not very surprising) solution. Mallet is rather colorless and not deeply characterized, but the final scene shows him to have a large heart.

The inspector's other solo adventures are *Death Is No Sportsman* (1938) and *Suicide Excepted* (1954). Pettigrew appears in *When the Wind Blows* (1950) and *That Yew Tree's Shade* (1954).

(*M.M.*)

Harper, Richard. *The Kill Factor.* New York: Fawcett Gold Medal, 1983. (O/PP)

Mimbres County, Arizona: An illegal alien is beaten to death and his body dumped into an irrigation canal. He is not the first; several others have been buried deep on the ranch where he worked. But this man has people in Mexico who care for him—including a nephew who has come to search for him. And he has also been dumped into the canal at the same time a prominent banker and his girl crash into it. The bodies are recovered together, the illegal alien hooked to the bumper of the banker's car, and Detective Sergeant Doug Roberts and his new Chicano partner, "Rabbit" Gomez, have a baffling case on their hands.

Roberts and Gomez begin their partnership with a prickly distrust, but as the case proceeds they begin to respect each other's abilities and establish a rapport. When Gomez is finally required to go undercover in order to penetrate the network of illegal aliens, Roberts is greatly concerned for his safety—and is on hand for the action-packed conclusion of their first cooperative investigation.

This is a first-rate novel, and one hopes there will be more cases featuring Roberts and Gomez. Equally good is Harper's previous paperback mystery, *Death to the Dancing Masters* (1980), which is also set in Mimbres County but features a different investigative team.

(*M.M.*)

Harrington, Joyce. *No One Knows My Name.* New York: St. Martin's, 1980. (PS)

Joyce Harrington received an MWA Edgar in 1972 for her first published short story, "The Purple Shroud," and has followed that story with dozens more of comparable quality. *No One Knows My Name* is her first novel, proving her to be equally skilled with long fiction as with the short story.

It is late spring and the summer-stock company is gathering at the Duck Creek Playhouse in a small northern Michigan resort town. It is an ill-assorted group, their backgrounds, abilities, and reasons for being there as diverse as can be: starlet Glory Hayes, beautiful, totally lacking in talent, and seething with resentment at being exiled from Hollywood to learn her craft; Tina Elliott, an obese character actress who fills her overwhelming needs with the substitute of food; Peverill Martin, an old man who dreams of a glory that will never be his; Tony Brand, a minor star who looks better than he acts; Anita Stratton, Tony's girlfriend, who came along for a vacation but now wishes herself back in New York; Hilda Kramer, a formerly famous actress with a mysterious past, who is intent on making a comeback; Larry Devine, Hilda's ex-husband, who owns the playhouse and is trying to save it from ruin as desperately as Hilda is trying to renew her career; Leo Lemming, Devine's nephew and stage manager, who handles the others with less than kid gloves.

Against a background of the Michigan woods, these characters act out a drama that is much greater than the one on stage. One of them is a psychotic killer, whose thoughts are intimately revealed to the reader in chapters where he is identified only as "I." As the others fall victim to him, the suspense mounts unbearably until the final revelation of his identity. Harrington's characterization is outstanding, especially her convincing portrayal of the deranged killer, and the interweaving of his reflections with the action is skillful.

Harrington's second novel, *Family Reunion* (1982), while of equally high quality, is very different from her first—a modern tale with Gothic overtones, telling of a young woman's reunion with her strange and often terrifying family.

(*M.M.*)

*Harris, Charlaine. *A Secret Rage*. Boston: Houghton Mifflin, 1984. (AD)

As in the bash-'n'-slash horror films of the Seventies, many of the novels that have touched on crimes of violence against women have kept those crimes detached from the real lives of the "victims." Either she deserved what she got, or she was an innocent destroyed by her victimization who could only be avenged by a male private eye/cop/vigilante/protector. In any case, the "victim" often remained a shadow figure whose entire identity was defined by the violence against her. In *A Secret Rage,* Charlaine Harris uses a completely different scenario.

A Secret Rage is the story of Nickie Callahan, a twenty-seven-year-old model who turns her back on the Big Apple to return to her southern home. She hopes to continue her education and reestablish ties to old friends and a more stable way of life, but the comfort of her homecoming is disrupted when a series of rapes and a related murder occur in her college community—and completely shattered when the violence finally strikes *her*.

Nickie is not just a victim, however. Although Harris expresses with brutal honesty the way rape can savage a woman's life, she goes beyond the horror. She shows Nickie rebuilding her life, turning from victim to survivor. Part of this process is Nickie's investigation of the crimes, together with another "victim." Her amateur sleuthing culminates in a shocking and satisfying conclusion to her own case.

Charlaine Harris writes realistically and with great sympathy about rape and revenge. She does the same for the South. Both *A Secret Rage* and Harris's first mystery, *Sweet and Deadly* (1981), are firmly rooted in their southern locale. It is a South portrayed with love and respect, without use of stock characters. The heat and the racial hatred are felt, but so is an appreciation for the land, the people, and a less manic way of life.

(*K.L.M.*)

Harris, Thomas. *Black Sunday*. New York: Putnam's, 1975. (T)

Black Sunday was among the first and best of the spate of mid-Seventies crisis/caper melodramas in which the lives of huge numbers of people are threatened by the actions of terrorists—in this case (as in some of the others), the lives of spectators at a major sporting event. Testimony to the popularity of its theme was a brief stay on the best-seller list, and an above-average 1977 film version featuring Robert Shaw, Bruce Dern, and Marthe Keller.

In retaliation for American aid to Israel, an Arab terrorist organization is plotting to blow up the Super Bowl in New Orleans, using as its prime weapon the Aldrich television blimp that will float high above the stadium.

Michael Lander, a former navy pilot whose psychotic personality has him driven to seek vengeance against a world he hates, is the man at the helm of the blimp; and in the airship's nacelle are 1200 pounds of plastic explosive.

Working with Lander, to keep him in line by protecting his fragile ego, is Dahlia Iyad, a beautiful Arabian Mata Hari. Working against the conspiracy is Major David Kabakov of the Israeli Secret Service, who knows that the guerrillas are planning an attack somewhere in the United States but has no idea what their target is or when the strike will take place. The complex machinations of both sides are set down in detail and show Harris's considerable knowledge (he is a former Associated Press reporter) of world politics, terrorism, and antiterrorist methods. A high level of tension is maintained throughout; and the climax at (and above) the Super Bowl is race-against-time suspense at its most intense. Harris's writing is good without being flashy, and his characterization, particularly of Lander and Kabakov, is excellent. All in all, this is one of the few "blockbuster" suspense novels in recent years that actually deserved its best-seller status.

Harris is also the author of the creepy thriller *Red Dragon* (1981).

(*B.P.*)

Harris, Timothy. *Good Night and Good-bye.* New York: Delacorte, 1979. (PI)

Timothy Harris's first novel about private investigator Thomas Kyd, *Kyd for Hire* (1978), was hailed as a promising debut. Kyd's second case lives up to that promise. Kyd runs a one-man operation in Hollywood. A Vietnam War veteran, he's tough when he has to be, reticent about his private life (to the point of claiming to be divorced when he's actually a widower), and can wisecrack with the best of them. Sound derivative? Yes, somewhat. But Harris has improved on the Chandler/Hammett/Macdonald tradition: Kyd is sensitive, vulnerable, and often makes mistakes. And it is his vulnerability that gets him into this case.

On page one, Kyd encounters an incredible sight: a Volkswagen driven by a beautiful woman, with a man spread-eagled on its hood. The man is naked, enraged, and when he finally gets off the car, he attempts to beat the woman. Kyd impersonates a police officer (ingeniously using his black loafer to create the illusion he has a gun) and rescues the woman. Thus begins his long and troubled association with Laura Cassidy—woman of many names, a disordered past, and a violent present. Laura periodically walks in and out of Kyd's life; he knows he should tell her to stay away (for one thing, she's a drug addict), but he is strongly—and almost fatally—drawn to her, half in love even though he uncovers lie after lie throughout their relationship. When Laura's husband, a top screenwriter, is stabbed to death and she becomes the primary suspect and a fugitive, Kyd is dragged into a messy investigation involving a bunch of nasty Hollywood characters that nearly cost him his life.

Harris knows Los Angeles, particularly the underside of Hollywood, and he draws one of the most vivid portraits of it since Chandler. This is a well-plotted novel with a deceptively leisurely pace and a hard-boiled private eye about whom it is possible to genuinely care.

(*M.M.*)

*Hart, Frances Noyes. *The Bellamy Trial.* New York: Doubleday, 1927. (PS)

Frances Noyes Hart is known primarily for this classic courtroom mystery, which was serialized in the *Saturday Evening Post* and became a successful novel, film, and play. The plot is based on the famous 1922 Hall-Mills murder case that caused public scandal among Long Island's wealthy society.

All the action in *The Bellamy Trial* takes place in the courtroom; the special strength of the book is the realism of courtroom procedure Hart uses to power her story along. Stephen Bellamy and Mrs. Susan Ives are accused of the murder of Mrs. Bellamy: The state charges that the couple were having an affair and when Mrs. Bellamy discovered them, they murdered her. Circumstantial evidence seems to support the state's contention.

The story of *The Bellamy Trial* is told through the eyes of two reporters: a young woman on her first reporting assignment and a tough, experienced professional. During the eight-day trial, they fall in love, which serves as a foil to the Bellamy-Ives relationship. The events of the trial are explosive: An important witness suddenly commits suicide; there's a surprise witness who shocks the court, and a secret letter that reveals the truth to the judge in his chambers.

Even by today's standards, *The Bellamy Trial* remains unsurpassed for suspenseful courtroom drama. No one who enjoys this type of fiction should miss it.

Frances Noyes Hart's other two suspense novels are also worth reading. These are *Hide in the Dark* (1929), which has a Halloween setting; and *The Crooked Lane* (1934), in which a young Viennese police official investigates a murder in Washington, D.C., just prior to the depression.

(*G.K.*)

Harvey, William Fryer. *The Arm of Mrs. Egan.* New York: Dutton, 1952. (SS)

Britisher W. F. Harvey is best known as the author of "August Heat," quite possibly the most disturbing supernatural story ever penned, and of numerous other tales of the macabre and occult. But he also wrote expert crime fiction, as the sixteen stories in this collection attest.

The first dozen are narrated by Nurse Wilkie, who is either an observer or personally involved in each case. Among the best of these are the title story, which deals with a woman who "to all intents and purposes was a witch" and who exacts a frightful vengeance on a doctor whom she holds responsible for the death of her only son; and "The Lake," which introduces an ingenious method of murder. The most accomplished of the nonseries stories is "Dead of Night," a chiller about a hospital patient accidentally placed in the morgue as a corpse; it compares favorably with similar nightmares penned by Poe and Woolrich. All in all, a first-rate collection that should please anyone who likes his criminous stories, in the words of the *Saturday Review,* "gracefully written, disturbingly real, delicately horrible, and quietly terrific."

Harvey also wrote one mystery novel, *The Mysterious Mr. Badman* (1934)—a bibliomystery.

(*B.P.*)

*Hayes, Joseph. *The Desperate Hours.* New York: Random House, 1954. (PS)

Joseph Hayes has had a long and successful career as a playwright and theatrical producer, and this novel—his first—shows his firm grasp of dramatic principles. The situation he presents is a gripping one: An average American family in Indianapolis finds their home invaded by three escapees from state prison. The men hold the Hilliard family—Dan; Eleanor; their daughter, Cindy; and son, Ralphie—hostage while waiting for a girlfriend to deliver some money. But there are snags, the money never materializes, and the desperate hours lengthen into days.

The Hilliards' story is told in counterpoint to the efforts to find the criminals. Jessie Webb, the deputy sheriff who sent their leader, Glenn Griffin, to prison, spearheads the investigation, sensing that the three will head for their home territory. What he doesn't realize is that *he* is the reason they have returned to Indianapolis: Griffin plans to hire someone to kill Webb once he gets the money. Matters are further complicated by Cindy Hilliard's boyfriend, lawyer Chuck Wright, who quickly realizes something is seriously amiss; Wright doesn't connect it with the escaped convicts, but he is concerned enough to take actions that force him to the most crucial decision of his life.

Hayes enlists his reader's complete sympathy for the Hilliard family, and one feels the same terror as they do, the same hatred for their captors. This is a fascinating study in family groups, the way they respond under pressure, the way they interact among themselves and with others. The Hilliards—who might be expected to be weak and ineffectual—form a cohesive unit, supporting one another and reaching inside themselves for strength they never dreamed they had. The convicts—Glenn Griffin, his brother Hank, and brother-in-crime Robish—fall to bickering and power plays, then begin to disintegrate emotionally, making the Hilliards' situation even more perilous. *The Desperate Hours* is an edge-of-the-chair read with an exceptionally satisfying conclusion.

Hayes adapted his novel into a play of the same title in 1955; in that year it also was made into an equally successful film starring Humphrey Bogart, Fredric March, Martha Scott, and Gig Young. Hayes's other fine suspense novels include *Like Any Other Fugitive* (1971), the story of two young people in a cross-country flight; and *The Long Dark Night* (1974), a novel of revenge.

(*M.M.*)

Haymon, S. T. *Stately Homicide.* New York: St. Martin's, 1984. (PP)

The British stately home (which owners have been forced by declining fortunes to place in trust and open to the public) has lately joined the somewhat outmoded country house as a setting for murder—as evidenced by recent works by Peter Dickinson (q.v.) and Elizabeth Lemarchand (q.v.). For her entry in what may become a small subgenre, S. T. Haymon has created Bullen Hall, a place with a complicated history involving Appleyard of Hungary, a fictional hero of the 1956 Hungarian uprising, and descendants of the ill-fated Anne Boleyn.

Haymon's series character, Detective Inspector Ben Jurnet, arrives at the group of artists' shops in the Coachyard of the Hall to pick up a pair of earrings a friend is making for his girlfriend. The errand is not a cheerful one, because the girlfriend has decamped to Greece and Jurnet is preoccupied with their floundering relationship. When he finds the earrings are not finished, he seeks refuge from the sweltering heat by joining a tour of the hall. There he encounters Percy Toller, a reformed burglar turned scholar, and receives an invitation to a party from the outgoing curator of the hall, Francis Coryton.

The party proves to be an interesting one: He meets everyone, and Coryton reveals his discovery of lost love letters from Anne Boleyn to her brother George Bullen and announces he intends to spend his retirement writing a book on the incestuous relationship. But before the evening is over, the new curator, Chad Shelden, has shown his ruthlessness by sequestering the letters, for "the Trust's best interests."

The next morning Shelden is found drowned in the moat—a particularly hideous corpse because he has been attacked and partially eaten by giant eels. Jurnet is called in and finds evidence that he fell from the unsafe roof of the hall to the grass below. But the autopsy results also show that Shelden was alive when he went into the moat—and his injuries were such that he could not have crawled into it on his own power. Jurnet investigates quietly and thoroughly, digging into life behind the scenes at the hall and at the coachyard. He finds tangled relationships between the artisans who live there, as well as in the distinguished Appleyard and Bullen families.

Haymon writes very well (descriptions such as that of a corpse left lying "like he was an old crisp bag, for the serfs to sweep up in the morning" remain in the reader's mind), and she has added considerable emotional depth to the hitherto "polite" British mystery. Jurnet is an extremely sympathetic protagonist, and the other characters, plus the frank sexual content of this novel, make it a thoroughly realistic look at contemporary British life.

Two of Haymon's other novels feature Ben Jurnet: *Death and the Pregnant Virgin* (1981) and *Ritual Murder* (1982); the latter won the British Crime Writers' Association's Silver Dagger Award for its year.

(*M.M.*)

Haythorne, John. *None of Us Cared for Kate.* New York: Dutton, 1968. (AD)

The big question is—who is John Haythorne? Why did he write only one book? Is Haythorne a pseudonym? No one seems to know. And more's the pity since this is a wonderfully witty book. The hero, Oliver Mandrake, is a middle-rank British diplomat beloved by his mother and both his mistresses—all of whom appear at the airport as he is about to leave suddenly for the obscure Asian nation of Talat. The British ambassador's assistant, Kate, has been stabbed in a Buddhist temple, and Mandrake has just the qualities needed to flush out the killer. What are they? A sharp intellect? A proclivity for gossip? Not exactly. They are hidden and—when revealed—quite amusing.

Once arrived in Talat, Mandrake is thrust into the life of the embassy, amid the premonsoon heat, snake worship, and a diplomatic community given to gin, peculiar passions, and the more than occasional backbite. Well intentioned, Mandrake forges ahead on his mission, but he's never quite sure his hosts aren't putting him on.

Mandrake, and the minor characters, are delightful. Talat is so clearly depicted that the reader can almost hear the mosquitoes, feel the sweat, taste the gin. And the plot includes a superb final twist.

(*S.D.*)

Head, Matthew. *The Cabinda Affair.* New York: Simon & Schuster, 1949. (AD)

During World War II, the United States agreed to buy a certain amount of mahogany timber at a rather exorbitant price, with delivery to the Portuguese West African town of Cabinda. Now that the war is over, the United States no longer needs the mahogany, and numerous extensions and delays have been granted. But no more. Either the timber will be delivered or the contract will be declared null and void.

To sort this out, Hooper Taliaferro, from the U.S. Consulate in Léopoldville, travels to Cabinda. Once there, he is a guest of the Portuguese lumber agent—a man named Falcão—and his family. The trouble is, Falcão's family consists of a beautiful but mysterious wife, a beautiful but mysterious daughter, a sex-obsessed legitimate son, and an illegitimate son who is a thief and a pimp. Add to the periphery of this group a good-looking government lawyer, a suave but dissolute Englishman, and a seedy disbarred Portuguese attorney, and *something* is almost certain to happen. Indeed, several things do happen, including murder. But it is a murder that seems to resolve itself until, back in Léopoldville at a garden party, Taliaferro tells the story to medical missionary and amateur sleuth Mary Finney. Dr. Finney is not at all convinced the murder *has* been resolved satisfactorily, and she heads for Cabinda to take charge of things herself.

It should be pointed out that Taliaferro is pronounced "Tolliver," which seems a bit of an affectation. But he makes a fine Watson and Dr. Mary Finney, the overweight mastermind behind the solutions of various baffling cases, is an astute and interesting sleuth. All these elements, combined with the colorful background, make *The Cabinda Affair* an engrossing adventure.

Matthew Head (a pseudonym for John Canaday) is an art historian and critic who has written several books dealing with the art field as well as a number of mysteries. Some of the other books featuring the investigative talents of Mary Finney are *The Devil in the Bush* (1947), which takes place in the Belgian Congo; *Murder at the Flea Club* (1957), a tale of mystery and mayhem set in Paris; and *The Congo Venus* (1976), which once again utilizes the African setting Head knows and depicts so well.

(*N.D.*)

Healy, Jeremiah F. III. *Blunt Darts.* New York: Walker, 1984. (PI)

This first book in a planned series introduces Boston investigator John Francis Cuddy, a Vietnam veteran who was in Army Intelligence and ex-insurance investigator. Cuddy has become turned off by working within the system (although he knows the "good guys" in the newspaper and police world) and lives alone, by his own standards. He is in his mid-thirties and is still mourning the death of his young wife (cause of death not known).

A schoolteacher approaches Cuddy, perplexed and concerned about a missing student whom no one seems to want to find—Stephen Kinnsington, the son of a prominent judge. The judge's mother winds up hiring Cuddy to find her grandson, with the condition that the judge know nothing about his search. Both Cuddy and the reader are puzzled by the lack of information forthcoming on Stephen, the increasingly suspicious death four years earlier of Stephen's mother, and the actively obstructive efforts of the judge and his "henchmen." Through the help of a classmate of Stephen's and the local librarian, Cuddy sets out for the Berkshires, where he deduces Stephen may have gone. Encountering great danger to himself, Cuddy finds Stephen and leads us to a shocker of an ending.

Throughout the book, which is written in a crisp descriptive style, Cuddy emerges as his own man, guided by a strong ethical sense in both his personal and professional life and possessing sensitivity and intelligence. *Blunt Darts* was named as one of the seven best mysteries of 1984 by the *New York Times.*

(*K.M.*)

Heard, H. F. *A Taste for Honey.* New York: Vanguard, 1941. (AD)

When this novel was first published in 1941, it caused something of a stir. *Newsweek* lauded it as "one of the ten best mysteries of all time." Such prominent Sherlockians and mystery fans as Vincent Starrett and Boris Karloff sang its praises, calling it "terrifying . . . perfectly done" and "a triumph of ingenuity." To this day some aficionados consider it a classic.

This reviewer wonders what all the flap is about.

In the first place, the plot is so thin that it scarcely justifies 20,000 words, let alone 50,000. The narrator, Sydney Silchester, has retired to a small English village, where he seeks only to be left alone to potter about in his garden and to indulge his taste for honey. The wife of the man from whom he gets his honey, Mrs. Heregrove, is killed by a swarm of their bees. Silchester meets an old and somewhat mysterious scientist/detective who calls himself Mr. Mycroft and who insists that Heregrove murdered his wife by breeding a new strain of "killer Italians" (bees, that is). Silchester scoffs at this idea, until he himself is attacked for no good reason by Heregrove's bees. Then he joins forces with Mycroft—or rather, wanders along in Mycroft's shadow while the old detective stalks Heregrove and metes out justice. All of this is set forth in a determinedly linear fashion, and is saved only by a surprise ending that readers and reviewers seem to have considered thunderous in 1941, but which seems pretty tame and obvious today.

On the plus side, *A Taste for Honey* offers some interesting facts about bees, and the scene in which Silchester is attacked is well done (though not particularly terrifying). On the negative side, Silchester is a twit—one of the dullest, most annoying protagonists the genre has yet produced. Worst of all, the pace is snail-slow and Heard's prose of the erudite, pontifical sort that quickly becomes tedious. Mycroft's interminable literary allusions and psychological discourses are especially recommended to insomniacs.

H. F. Heard also published two other novels featuring Mycroft, *Reply Paid* (1942) and *The Notched Hairpin* (1949); neither is very good. Much better are his short stories, the best of which may be found in *The Great Fog and Other Weird Tales* (1944).

(*B.P.*)

Hecht, Ben. *The Florentine Dagger.* New York: Boni & Liveright, 1926. (PS)

Something is wrong in Julien de Medici's life. On the surface, everything seems to be going smoothly—he has proposed marriage to Florence Ballau and the proposal has met with approval, not only from Florence but from her father, Victor, as well. But there is something beneath the surface, a certain uncharacteristic nervousness on the part of Victor Ballau and a certain unaccountable sadness on the part of Florence Ballau.

And what of Julien de Medici himself? He *is,* after all, a descendant of *the* Medici family, with its bloody history and dark secrets, and this ancestral darkness seems to haunt his mind daily.

Then, shockingly, Victor Ballau is murdered on the night the engagement is to be announced. There is a dagger in his chest, there is a false beard clutched in his hand, there is a crucifix above the wound, and there is a still-warm candle near the body.

At first, suicide is suspected; then Julien is suspected of murder; then Florence; then Victor's estranged wife. As the story unfolds, there are mysteries within mysteries, questions within questions, and explanations within explanations. The reader follows much of this through the eyes and mind of Julien de Medici, who suspects no one so much as himself—or perhaps he suspects the Medici blood flowing in his veins. Indeed, if the story has a weak point, it might be this overabundance and repetition of musing on Julien's part. But the point seems a minor one, for this is a fine novel by a master writer.

Although Ben Hecht wrote numerous novels and short stories, he is probably best remembered for such plays as *The Front Page* (coauthored with Charles MacArthur) and such screenplays as *Wuthering Heights.*

Among his other criminous works are the novel *I Hate Actors!* (1944) and the short-story collections *Actors Blood* (1936) and *Concerning a Woman of Sin and Other Stories* (1947).

(*N.D.*)

Hendryx, James B. *The Czar of Halfaday Creek.* New York: Doubleday, 1940. (SS/H)

In the Thirties and Forties, Black John Smith of Halfaday Creek was a popular series character among readers of action and adventure fiction. Dozens of novelettes featuring the giant, good-natured outlaw appeared in *Short Stories* and other pulps, and were systematically collected in some thirteen books between 1935 and 1953. Even though Hendryx primarily intended the Black John stories for the "outdoor fiction" readership, they are all nonetheless criminous in content and design—and of sufficient stature for Ellery Queen to have listed *The Czar of Halfaday Creek* and four other volumes in his 1942 reference work *The Detective Short Story: A Bibliography.*

Black John is the leader of an outlaw community in the Yukon, not far from the Alaska line, at the time of the 1898 Gold Rush. (Hendryx also wrote numerous novels with this background, most of which likewise deal with murder and mischief.) Black John, whose nickname derives from his heavy black beard—runs a tight camp. "Not favorin' the police nosin' around up here," he says, "we aim to keep the crick moral. Murder, claim jumpin', larceny in any form an' skulduggery is punished by hangin', after conviction by miners' meetin'. Other offenses is winked at." To help him in this "moral" pursuit are old Lyme Cushing, owner of the local trading post; and Black John's Mountie friend, Corporal Downey, who gets his man often enough to warrant not hassling the Halfaday boys.

As do most of the Black John collections, *The Czar of Halfaday Creek* contains five novelettes. None carries a title, however; the book is constructed of some thirty-four "chapters," apparently to give it the appearance of a novel. (All the other collections are similarly disguised.) In these stories, John saves his pal Cush from a scheming woman, unmasks a phony Secret Service agent and some other "onpeaceable" crooks, and not incidentally fattens the Halfaday treasury by a few hundred thousand dollars. These are salty tales, told with wry humor and a fine sense of what it was like in the Frozen North at the turn of the century.

Among the other Black John collections are *Outlaws of Halfaday Creek* (1935), *Black John of Halfaday Creek* (1939), *Law and Order on Halfaday Creek* (1941), and *Murder on Halfaday Creek* (1951). Novels of interest by Hendryx include *Blood on the Yukon Trail* (1930) and *The Yukon Kid* (1934), both of which feature Corporal Downey.

(*B.P.*)

*Henry, O. *The Gentle Grafter.* New York: McClure, 1908. (SS)

As almost everyone knows, O. Henry (William Sydney Porter) was the first and foremost master of the twist-ending short story. Many of his best tales have criminous themes; *The Gentle Grafter,* however, is his only collection devoted strictly to crime—the lighter side thereof—and is of such quality and historical import that Ellery Queen included it on his Queen's Quorum list.

The "gentle grafter" of the title is Jeff Peters, con man and philosopher. Together with his partner, Andy Tucker, Jeff roves the country in search of the fast buck, for "whenever he saw a dollar in another man's hands he took it as a personal grudge, if he couldn't take it any other way." His adventures are all built around the theme of separating a fool from his money. Unfortunately for Jeff, he has both a conscience and a gullibility sometimes akin to that of the "Reubs" he tries to fleece. On more than one occasion, the fool who loses his money is Jeff himself.

The fourteen stories here have a wide range of settings, characters, bunco games, and surprises. "The Octopus Marooned," for instance, takes place in a little Texas town near the Rio Grande and relates what happens when Jeff and Andy buy up all three saloons in town and attempt to establish a Thirst Monopoly. "The Hand that Riles the World" takes the duo to Washington on a mission of benign bribery for an old friend, and embroils them, to their everlasting sorrow, with a lady lobbyist. "The Ethics of Pig," a hilarious tale set "up near the spot where Kentucky and West Virginia and North Carolina corner together . . . in that neighborhood, anyway," involves Jeff with a local grafter named Rufe Tatum (whose fondest hope is "to become reckernized as the champion shoat-stealer of the world") and teaches him a lesson about pigs, circuses, and professional ethics.

Told with gusto, flair, and some of the funniest malapropisms this side of R. B. Sheridan, these wary and whimsical stories of turn-of-the-century America are enthusiastically recommended.

(*B.P.*)

Hensley, Joe L. *Minor Murders.* New York: Doubleday Crime Club, 1979. (AD)

Throughout his legal career—as a private attorney, county prosecutor, one-term state legislator, and presently as a trial judge in Indiana's Fifth Judicial Circuit—Joe L. Hensley has carried on a second career as a mystery writer. All of his nine novels reflect one or more aspects of his business-hours persona. Most are set in the Indiana riverside city of Bington, an obvious fictionalization of the community of Madison where he lives and works. Six deal with crusading criminal lawyer Donald Robak; and one of these,

Legislative Body (1972), finds Robak, like his creator, in the Indiana legislature. Two of his nonseries novels, *The Color of Hate* (1960) and *The Poison Summer* (1974), are about midwestern small-city attorneys who resemble Robak in everything but their names; and the third, *Rivertown Risk* (1977), concerns a murder trial as seen through the eyes of the judge.

Considering his background, one might expect Hensley's mysteries to feature fireworks displays of legal ingenuity in the Erle Stanley Gardner (q.v.) tradition. They don't, and in fact most of them have no courtroom action whatever. In the typical Hensley novel, his fighting liberal hero is called on to defend some out-group person accused of murder—a black ex-convict in *The Color of Hate;* a disgraced former cop in *Outcasts* (1980)—and has to cope with harassment from police, corrupt politicians, and suspects with secrets as he probes the layers of local graft and hypocrisy and tries to clear his client before trial.

Minor Murders falls squarely within this pattern. Robak takes on the defense of a ripe-bodied sixteen-year-old girl who's charged with stabbing to death the sadistic couple who ran the welfare home where she was confined by court order. She claims she can remember nothing about the murders, and there are at least three possible explanations for her memory lapse—hypnosis, LSD, and epilepsy—but the vicious and stupid local prosecutor decides that she's lying and he plans to ask for the death penalty at her trial. Investigating what really happened that bloody night at the moldering old welfare home, Robak is menaced by a brilliant young amoralist and his twin muscleboys and also by the self-anointed bishop of a fundamentalist sect.

Hensley's tone is quiet and low-key, his pace unhurried and unfrenetic, his plots rather loose and not terribly involuted. He has a nice talent for character-drawing and for describing how mid-America functions, and his sympathies are always with the underdogs. *Minor Murders* features a strong story line, a full measure of action and suspense, and much empathy with children enmeshed in the juvenile-justice bureaucracy.

The most recent Robak novel is *Robak's Cross* (1985).

(*F.M.N.*)

Heyer, Georgette. *The Unfinished Clue.* New York: Doubleday Crime Club, 1937. (PP)

Although her literary reputation is based on the more than forty Regency romances that fill the paperback racks of all English-speaking nations, Heyer also wrote twelve mysteries. All but two were published in the 1930s and all have recently been reprinted in both hardback and paperback. They depict pre–World War II house parties, resident butlers, obnoxious murder victims who control family fortunes and are always threatening to change their wills, and more ne'er-do-well relatives than anyone would care to have.

The Unfinished Clue combines many of these elements. Lady Billington-Smith's house party at the Grange turns into a murder investigation when her unpleasant husband, General Billington-Smith, is found in the study, dead of a knife wound. Among the guests are his son and the son's Mexican dancer fiancée; the general's sister-in-law; a formerly favorite nephew whom Billington-Smith had just turned down for a loan; a dilettante couple (the female half of which was flirting with the general); several neighbors who keep dropping in; and a cousin, who was in love with Lady Billington-Smith. Inspector Harding of Scotland Yard is called in when the murder is discovered; he painstakingly takes all the suspects through the activities of the fatal day and dissects their relationships with the victim and each other. The motive lies in the background of the family, and the ending, well clued, is a surprise. Unfortunately, anti-Semitic references, common in British crime novels of the Thirties, have not been changed or deleted in any of the reprints, as has been done in the works of other Golden Age authors.

Heyer created two series detectives, neither of whom is particularly memorable. Superintendent Hannasyde is featured in four of her mysteries, among them *Merely Murder* (1935) and *A Blunt Instrument* (1938). Hannasyde's subordinate, Inspector Hemingway, is the hero of four cases, including *No Wind of Blame* (1939) and *Duplicate Death* (a 1951 novel not published in the United States until 1969).

(*E.N.*)

Higgins, George V. *Kennedy for the Defense.* New York: Knopf, 1980. (T)

In his early novels—such as the best-selling *Friends of Eddie Coyle* (1972), which was filmed with Robert Mitchum in the lead—former federal prosecutor George V. Higgins portrayed the fringes of the Boston underworld with *cinéma vérité* authenticity. After a few mediocre efforts at mainstream fiction, Higgins came back to home turf, and in *Kennedy for the Defense* we see the world through the eyes of a criminal defense lawyer. Jeremiah F. Kennedy, however, is by no means Boston's Perry Mason. He's a paunchy, fortyish family man whose clients are almost invariably guilty. His function is not to defend these people in court but to make deals for them with other functionaries, getting reduced charges, probation, suspended sentences, whatever he can for his clientele of thieves, pimps, drunk drivers, and other walking lice. Highly paid for his services and unconcerned about where the money comes from, he uses his fees to finance the good life for the wife and teenage daughter he adores.

Like most Higgins novels, this one has no sustained plot but centers on a series of unrelated criminal cases that keep disrupting Kennedy's beach vacation with his family. The clients include a professional car thief who claims that a state trooper ate his license and then arrested him for driving without one; an obnoxious nabob's son who is gay and made the mistake of propositioning an undercover cop; and a hopelessly stupid young mechanic being set up for a drug bust by a corrupt FBI agent. In due course the games are played, the deals are made; credible coincidence intertwines a few of the cases; there are a couple of bloody shoot-outs, not described directly but recounted afterward by Kennedy to his wife or a neighbor; and what we laughingly call the "criminal-justice system" lurches on.

Higgins passes no overt moral judgments in this book but lets us draw our own conclusions, which may not be as complacent as those of Jeremiah F. Kennedy. But it's a compulsively readable novel, with that unique Higgins brand of dialogue combining circumlocutions and obscenities and loutish urban wit. Thanks to its background of real criminal-law practice complete with all the irritations and compromises and undeodorized smells of that milieu, *Kennedy for the Defense* ranks with *The Friends of Eddie Coyle, The Digger's Game* (1973), and *Cogan's Trade* (1974) as one of the strongest books Higgins has written.

(*F.M.N.*)

*Higgins, Jack. *Solo.* New York: Stein & Day, 1980. (E/T)

Jack Higgins is one of the pseudonyms of British author Harry Patterson (q.v.), who also writes under his own name as well as the pseudonyms Hugh Marlow, Martin Fallon, and James Graham. The prolific Patterson has given us more than forty novels since his *Sad Wind from the Sea* in 1959.

In *Solo,* a tale of an artistic genius at music and murder, Higgins is in top form. His character John Mikali is a brilliant concert pianist with a bloody past and a secretly bloody present. As he tours the world to perform in concert, he also functions as an assassin known only as "the Cretan," in the employ of Russian Intelligence in the person of secret agent "French" lawyer Jean Paul Deville.

After coolly murdering a prominent Zionist an hour before a concert in London, Mikali makes a mistake. To avoid capture by pursuing police, he deliberately runs down with his car a girl bicyclist who happens to be the fourteen-year-old daughter of Special Air Service Colonel Asa Morgan. The colonel is something of a supersoldier, an antiterrorist specialist serving in Belfast in action against the IRA. So proficient and zealous in his violent trade is Morgan that even his wife has been repelled by him and driven to divorce and remarriage to a milksop vicar. When the colonel learns the circumstances of his daughter's violent death, he vows vengeance.

With the tacit help of D15, a British intelligence service so secret that officially it does not exist, Morgan sets out to find and kill the Cretan. So we have the master hunter expertly stalking the ultimate deadly prey. And along the way, both men are loved by the same woman.

Higgins, with his smooth, succinct style, builds the suspense adroitly as the action swings from one world capital to another and to the Greek island of Hydra, where Mikali maintains a plush and secluded retreat.

Also among Higgins's novels are the World War II best seller *The Eagle Has Landed* (1975), *Storm Warning* (1976), and *Day of Judgement* (1979). Notable titles under Patterson's other pseudonyms are *The Run to Morning* (1974), as by James Graham, which is set in Libya; and *Year of the Tiger* (1964), as by Martin Fallon, an espionage tale with a Tibetan setting.

(*J.L.*)

*Highsmith, Patricia. *Ripley Underground.* New York: Doubleday, 1970. (PS)

Patricia Highsmith's fiction combines a brooding, tense atmosphere with a sense of reality that is achieved through the skillful use of carefully selected detail. This detail—color, temperature, taste, the appearance of a particularly beautiful meal—is not described at length and is never intrusive, but has the effect of making the reader feel he is present on the scene. And such a sense of reality is important in allowing the reader to believe the kinds of characters and often bizarre situations that Highsmith creates.

Her protagonists are more often antiheroes than heroes. Most are dealing with some sort of guilt; but unlike normal guilt-ridden people, they are not tormented—they view their misdeeds with a kind of detachment. The primary emotions they seem to feel are anger at injustices, both real and imagined, and fear that their evil deeds may be discovered and punishment meted out. In a number of instances, Highsmith has portrayed the curious relationship between murderers and their victims, and done it to good effect, showing it in all its complexity. Her characters are never black-and-white, but fully fleshed out individuals with all the ambiguities of real people.

Tom Ripley is one of the best of Highsmith's complex creations. In his first appearance (*The Talented Mr. Ripley,* 1955), Tom is a confused and somewhat hostile young man without much of a sense of identity. He does, however, have the makings of a con man, and when he inveigles a trip to Europe from the father of a casual acquaintance, Tom finds not ony a whole new world but a world of possibilities within himself—including the ability to kill. We are horrified when he does so, but relieved when he extricates himself from the dangerous situation he has created, because Highsmith has managed to enlist us on Tom's side from the very first.

Ripley Underground is Tom's second adventure, and he is a much different man than in the first. Years later, he is living on an estate outside of Paris with his wealthy French wife, Heloise. He dabbles at painting and likes "to garden casually," but it is a more profitable venture that plunges him once again into crime. Several years before, Tom and some friends in England perpetrated a fraud: forging the works of a dead painter and claiming the man, Derwatt, was alive and painting in Mexico. Tom supplements his income by taking a portion of the profits from this scheme, but now a rich American, a Texan called Murchison, has a theory about the paintings that may expose the forgeries. Tom already has something of an unsavory reputation—there has been talk about his previous adventures—and he knows such a scandal will cause his wife's family to turn against him and cut off the couple's generous allowance. The others involved in the scheme beg Tom to come to England; he does so, and there he hits on the plan of impersonating Derwatt.

Murchison remains unconvinced that the Derwatt painting he possesses is not a forgery, even after the painter's—actually Tom's—assurance that it is genuine. Tom invites him to France to view his own Derwatts, things get out of control, and Tom kills him. What follows is a complex series of events involving the disposal of Murchison's body (twice) and dealing with unexpected visitors and the mental breakdown of the man who has been forging the Derwatts. The police are always about, because the American has disappeared without a trace. And as Tom maneuvers through this maze, the reader is once again solidly on his side, in spite of the fact that, given the provocation, the murder was totally unjustified.

Tom Ripley appears in two other adventures: *Ripley's Game* (1974) and *The Boy Who Followed Ripley* (1980). In the former, Tom's amorality comes into full play, but there are indications that he is becoming older and wiser; in the latter, Highsmith presents Tom's most bizarre adventure, and poses some interesting questions about his sexual orientation.

(*M.M.*)

*Highsmith, Patricia. *The Snail-Watcher and Other Stories.* New York: Doubleday, 1970. (SS)

In this volume of strange and often disturbing tales, Highsmith demonstrates her consummate skill as a short-story writer. In spite of their abbreviated length, she manages to trap the reader in a frightening and oppressive world through the same use of detail that characterizes her novels. The reader finds himself totally involved in the events that unfold, and in a rapidly escalating state of tension. The world Highsmith presents often seems quite mad, but somehow we are able to accept the odd things that transpire as if they were happening to us personally.

No one who has ever encountered your garden-variety snail will ever forget the title story of this volume. A man observes two snails mating and becomes entranced with what he thinks of as their beauty. He learns all he can about snails, ceases to eat them, begins breeding them. And in the end, he learns all there is to know about them indeed.

Yet another story, "The Terrapin," concerns man's misuse of nature's creatures, as perceived through the eyes of a young boy. In "The Heroine," the protagonist's—Lucille Smith's—view of reality is so skewed that she must choose a drastic and dangerous method of achieving what others do by accident. And Highsmith creates a frightening and convincing portrait of growing madness in "The Empty Birdhouse."

This is a first-rate collection that will make you want to read more of Highsmith's short fiction, collected in *The Animal Lover's Book of Beastly Murder* (1975), *Little Tales of Mysogyny* (1977), and *Slowly, Slowly in the Wind* (1985).

(*M.M.*)

*Highsmith, Patricia. *Strangers on a Train.* New York: Harper, 1950. (PS)

This extremely accomplished first novel established Highsmith immediately as a master of psychological suspense, and the Alfred Hitchcock film of the same title (1951, starring Farley Granger and Robert Walker) brought her even greater attention. The story opens with two men—Guy Haines and Charles Bruno—sharing a compartment on a train traveling across Texas. In the way of temporary companions, they get to talking, and what emerges from their conversation is that Bruno would like to kill his father and Guy would like to kill his wife. Each man's anger feeds on the other's, and soon Bruno begins to speculate: What if he killed Guy's wife and Guy killed his father? How would they ever be detected? After all, they would be total strangers to their victims and have no detectable motives; the one with the real motive could arrange a solid alibi for the time of the slaying. Guy rejects such speculation, but the situation with his wife worsens and Bruno continues to try to enlist him in his plan. When his wife is killed, Guy knows who must have done it, and soon he finds himself drawn into a situation that is totally out of control.

This is a fascinating study in the effects of complicity upon a next-to-nonexistent relationship, and it shows how easily one person's madness may be communicated to another. As the situation continues to descend into chaos and the tension escalates unbearably, the reader hopes that some breath of sanity will save Guy from what surely seems to be inevitable.

Other equally gripping novels by Patricia Highsmith are *Deep Water* (1957), *The Two Faces of January* (1964), *The Story-Teller* (1965), and *A Dog's Ransom* (1972). In addition, she has written a nonfiction book, *Plotting and Writing Suspense Fiction* (1966), which should interest the fan of the genre as much as the writer.

(*M.M.*)

Hill, Reginald. *Who Guards the Prince?* New York: Pantheon, 1982. (T)

This is a commendable, but rather overly complex, novel. A secret society, out to gain all the wealth and power it can amass, is backing (and blackmailing) a possible American presidential candidate named Conal Connolly. But Connolly's grandfather, Pat Connolly, a supporter of the IRA, has threatened to cut *all* his grandchildren out of his will if one of them—Dree Connolly—ever marries an Englishman. Dree, it seems, has been dating Britain's Prince Arthur. Conal is afraid of losing the inheritance money he was counting on for political campaigns, and the society decides to step in and do something about the Dree-Arthur relationship.

Tracking down some of the secret society's crimes in England is Detective Inspector McHarg, a former detective and bodyguard for Prince Arthur and now a policeman in the seaside village of Sanderton. McHarg's daughter has gone to live in Boston, where she befriends Dree Connolly and has an affair with yet another Connolly—Christie. Meanwhile, McHarg has his hands full investigating a fire that killed a journalist, a human tongue found on a beach, and two very suspicious deaths. Things go from bad to worse when someone tampers with his car and he is involved in an accident that kills two teenagers. He resigns from the force and travels to America, just about the time Prince Arthur is traveling to Canada and planning a side trip to America to see Dree. And all the various elements begin to dovetail into confrontation and climax.

Despite its complexity, the story is an interesting and fast-paced one from which McHarg emerges as a stolid, menacing, but likable hero. (The secret society, if you're wondering, is the Freemasons.)

Reginald Hill (who also writes under the names Dick Morland, Patrick Ruell, and Charles Underhill) is also the author of a police-procedural series featuring Superintendent Andrew Dalziel; notable among the Dalziel titles are *A Clubbable Woman* (a 1970 title first published in the United States in 1984), *Ruling Passion* (1977), *A Pinch of Snuff* (1978), and *Exit Lines* (1985).

(*N.D.*)

*Hillerman, Tony. *Dance Hall of the Dead.* New York: Harper, 1973. (PP)

Tony Hillerman is a master storyteller, the kind who can spin you a yarn that will keep you on the edge of your chair, replete with ghosts, evil spirits, sinister happenings, legends, and all the other ingredients that make up the culture of a people. The people he writes of are the Navajo and Zuni Indians of the American Southwest. His books are full of Indian lore. (Hillerman himself went to an Indian boarding school for eight years, and knows the culture as few Anglos do.) Set against the vast and often desolate expanse of the great reservations near Four Corners (where the states of Arizona, New Mexico, Utah, and Colorado abut one another), they re-create the loneliness of the high mesas. If life is hard for those who live there, it is also hard for Hillerman's heroes—tribal policemen Joe Leaphorn and, in more recent books, Jim Chee. There are no instant backup systems on the mesas, no quick computerized information resources, indeed few methods of communication. Alone, the protagonists must rely on their own intelligence, good judgment, and instincts that have been passed down in a society almost as old as the ancient land where it sprang up.

Dance Hall of the Dead (which won the MWA Edgar for Best Novel of 1973) opens, as a number of Hillerman's books do, with a scene from the life of a resident of the reservation, in this case a Zuni. And immediately we are confronted with one of the numerous contrasts between a modern and an ancient culture that are a trademark of Hillerman's work: "Shulawitsi, the Little Fire God, member of the Council of the Gods and Deputy to the Sun, had taped his track shoes to his feet." The Little Fire God is a young Zuni man in training not for a track meet but for a religious ceremony. As he rests, thinking of many things that disturb him (but not allowing himself to become angry, because at this time in the Zuni religious calendar, anger is not permitted), a strange figure appears from behind a boulder. . . .

Now that we have been drawn into the Indian consciousness, the scene switches to Zuni tribal-police headquarters where Lieutenant Joe Leaphorn is being briefed on a jurisdictional problem. The Little Fire God, in ordinary life Ernesto Cata, and his Navajo friend, George Bowlegs, are missing, and there are indications that one of them has been knifed. While Cata's disappearance is in Zuni jurisdiction, Leaphorn is asked to find Bowlegs.

Cata is presumed dead, and the police suspect Bowlegs is his killer. But there are also rumors that a kachina—a Zuni ancestor spirit—got Cata and frightened Bowlegs. When Cata's body is found, Leaphorn's search intensifies; and as he crosses the rugged reservation, fact becomes mixed with legend, and Leaphorn, an outsider to the Zuni culture, must sort out the reality of the situation.

Dance Hall of the Dead is a fascinating study in the conflicts between two Indian cultures, as well as a fine mystery, the scenes and characters of which will haunt you for a long time after you reach its conclusion.

(*M.M.*)

Hillerman, Tony. *The Ghostway.* San Diego: Dennis McMillan, 1984. (Limited edition. Also published in a regular trade edition by Harper, 1985.) (PP)

Hillerman's second series character, Navajo tribal policeman Jim Chee, is a younger man than Joe Leaphorn and more closely tied to mainstream American society. Because of this, he is perhaps less interesting than Leaphorn, and the Chee books lack the haunting, magical quality of Hillerman's earlier work. Chee is nonetheless a complex character and the dichotomies he must face within himself are closely intertwined with the plots.

The Ghostway concerns a Los Angeles Navajo who has shot a hoodlum to death and in turn been seriously wounded in a parking lot on the reservation. The FBI is looking for the man—Albert Gorman—for some reason that they do not discuss in detail with the Navajo police, and he is traced to the hogan of a relative, Ashie Begay. But when Chee, the sheriff's deputy, and the FBI agents arrive at the hogan, they find no signs of life; the hogan's smoke hole has been plugged, its doorway boarded over, and a hole cut in one side. To Chee this means someone has died inside and the hogan—thought to be possessed by the malicious *chindi* (ghost) of the dead person—has been abandoned.

There are things that bother Chee about the situation: Ashie Begay was a wise old man, accustomed to death, and he loved his home; surely when he saw that Albert Gorman, the wounded man, was close to death, he would have moved him outside, as is the custom. And when Chee finds Gorman's body, it has been prepared as the dead are supposed to be, except Begay has neglected to wash the corpse's hair with yucca suds. Did something interrupt the preparations? And where has Ashie Begay gone?

At the time the case begins, Chee is facing a tough personal decision: Should he join the FBI and leave the reservation with his white lover, Mary Landon? Or should he stay on here where his roots are and risk losing her? Before he can resolve this, however, Ashie Begay's granddaughter, Margaret Billy Sosi, disappears from her boarding school, and Chee must track her down. Eventually he finds her in Begay's contaminated hogan—a place where even he, with his logical policeman's mind, is loath to step—but she quickly eludes him. He follows her to Los Angeles, where Navajos of the Turkey Clan, to which she belongs, live in abject poverty. Chee's investigation takes him back to the reservation again, and into its far reaches where a Ghostway (purifying ceremony) is being performed. And at the ceremony, he must confront not only a killer but also the cultural conflict within himself.

While not as powerful as the Leaphorn novels, *The Ghostway* ties its thematic matter into the plot in an extremely satisfying way, and Chee is developed to greater depth than before. Any reader will be eager to see how he resolves his conflicts in future novels.

The previous Chee books are *People of Darkness* (1980) and *The Dark Wind* (1982).

(*M.M.*)

*Hillerman, Tony. *Listening Woman.* New York: Harper, 1978. (PP)

Joe Leaphorn is assigned to a double homicide that has occurred on a remote plateau of the Navajo reservation. Hosteen Tso, an old man, had complained of illness and gone to Margaret Cigaret, known as Listening Woman, for a pollen-blessing ceremony. During a brief period when Listening Woman left him alone, both Hosteen Tso and her niece and assistant, Anna Atcitty, were bludgeoned to death.

The old man, Listening Woman reports to Leaphorn, knew something about some sand paintings that had been desecrated, but refused to discuss it, saying cryptically that he had made a promise to someone long ago. Following this rather slender lead, Leaphorn travels across the barren mesas to that part of the Indian nation where the Navajo wolves and witches are said to dwell. As in Hillerman's other novels, ancient tribal beliefs come into sharp conflict with the modern world—a conflict that is reflected in Leaphorn himself. And when he finally reaches the solution to the crimes, he sees how legend can be manipulated to suit the designs of evil men.

Hillerman has put his knowledge of Navajo custom and mysticism to good use in this novel. His stark depiction of the New Mexico landscape is particularly fine, conveying a haunting sense of how insignificant one man is against the vastness of nature, and making this a compelling and often chilling book.

Joe Leaphorn also appears in *The Blessing Way* (1970), Hillerman's first novel. A nonseries novel, *The Fly on the Wall* (1971), is a political story set in the capital of an unnamed midwestern state. In addition, Hillerman has produced a juvenile novel and various works of nonfiction, including the hilarious *The Great Taos Bank Robbery and Other Affairs of Indian Country* (1970).

(*M.M.*)

Hilton, John Buxton. *The Hobbema Prospect.* New York: St. Martin's, 1984. (PP)

This is a Superintendent Kenworthy novel, although it is another employee at Scotland Yard—a clerk named Anne Cossey—around whom the story revolves. She is marrying another employee, a man named Howard Lawson. Kenworthy attends the wedding ceremony, wishes them well, and the happy couple leaves for Spain and their honeymoon. The honeymoon, however, is less than idyllic. In the first place, Anne has her strange, recurring dream of a sandy road with tall trees on either side, reminiscent of a Hobbema painting. In the second place, she patters on and on about her childhood memories, boring Howard. In the third place, word reaches them that Anne's mother has died—an apparent suicide.

But Anne is convinced her mother was murdered, and she manages to convince others—primarily Superintendent Kenworthy—that an investigation should be launched. Then, as if the pressure of a new marriage and a murdered mother were not enough, Anne discovers she is pregnant, and it is a difficult pregnancy. And as if *that* were not enough, she is kidnapped, and the place to which she is taken has (right!) a sandy road with tall trees on either side.

The events of this story sound chaotic and confusing, and indeed they do depict a traumatic time in the life of a young woman. But basically it is a low-key, well-conceived novel, typical of the work of John Buxton Hilton.

Superintendent Kenworthy has been the author's most oft-repeated protagonist, appearing in such novels as *Death of an Alderman* (1968), *No Birds Sang* (1976), and *The Anathema Stone* (1980). Another Hilton creation, Inspector Thomas Brunt, is featured in *Rescue from the Rose* (1976), *Gamekeeper's Gallows* (1977), *Dead-Nettle* (1977), *The Green Frontier* (1981), *Surrender Value* (1981), and *Corridors of Guilt* (1984).

(*N.D.*)

*Himes, Chester. *All Shot Up*. New York: Avon, 1960. (PP/O)

Chester Himes, a black American expatriate, wrote seven wildly original novels (all but the last two paperback originals) about Coffin Ed Johnson and Grave Digger Jones, the two toughest police detectives in Harlem (and arguably the two toughest cops in all detective fiction). The stories are fast-paced, lively, and extremely violent. Himes's gaudy, exotic, funhouse-mirror vision of Harlem is at the center of all his books, as is a strong undercurrent of gallows humor.

A slow-witted merchant sailor is conned into spending his savings on a new gold Cadillac, and is taking it out on a test drive when he runs over an old woman (who turns out to be a man working a fake-accident racket). He is then pulled over by a carload of cops (who turn out to be heistmen), who steal the car. Ed and Digger are dining on "chicken feetsy" in the back room of Mammy Louise's Pork Store when they get word of the heist—$50,000 in campaign funds hijacked from Harlem's top political boss in a gun battle outside a gay bar. The "famous Harlem detectives" start busting heads looking for the money, the sailor runs amok trying to get his car back, and the bodies pile up. The Big Con and the Big Heist are Himes's favorite story ideas, and they both get a terrific workout here. The highlight of the book is a furious, bloody, stunningly kinetic car chase through Harlem's back alleys in the midst of a sleet storm, as exciting as any in fiction. Strong stuff, definitely not for body-in-the-library fanciers.

Other Coffin Ed/Grave Digger novels include *For Love of Imabelle* (1957), *The Real Cool Killers* (1959), *The Crazy Kill* (1959), and *Cotton*

Comes to Harlem (1965), the successful film version of which kicked off the wave of black-oriented action films of the early 1970s.

(*A.S.*)

Hinkemeyer, Michael T. *A Time to Reap*. New York: St. Martin's, 1984. (PP)

Emil Whippletree, the retired sheriff of Stearns County, Minnesota, is pressed back into temporary service to help the present sheriff, well-meaning but rather incompetent Corky Withers, solve the murder of one of the best-looking and loosest-living women in the county—one Trixie Miggs, floozy.

Truth be told, Emil's glad to get back into action (a man can play just so many games of solitaire), but this case is a tough one. Poor woman had her head blown right off with four or five shotgun blasts, which makes it a particularly nasty crime. Suspects abound, including an ex-husband; the woman's son; a country-and-western singer; a fanatic leader of the local right-to-life movement; and the most likely (and unlikely) of all, the parish priest. Father Creedmore's car was seen near the scene of the murder, and when he performs last rites for the victim, he manages to disturb quite a bit of evidence.

Despite the abundance of eccentrically named characters (Bawlie Wepner, Nubs Tufo, Delbert Ebenscheider, Flinch Miggs, Jiggsy Potoff, Leander Fruth, Tulip Mosey, and Florence Hockapuk) and despite one or two items that don't quite ring true (for example, could a woman really sustain four or five shotgun blasts to the head and remain sitting in a kitchen chair?), Michael Hinkemeyer has given us a human and intriguing story, a cut above the usual small-town police procedural. We follow the old, retired sheriff and the new, inexperienced sheriff as they, together and separately, go in search of a cold-blooded killer. But Christmas is coming, and nerves and tempers are on edge, and the two sheriffs disagree as to their prime suspect. Before the solution is reached, more than one red herring is dragged across the trail.

Hinkemeyer's earlier books, all nonseries suspense novels, have received high praise from critics. These include *Summer Solstice* (1976); *Fields of Eden* (1977); and a harrowing tale of politics and revenge, *Lilac Night* (1981).

(*N.D.*)

Hintze, Naomi A. *You'll Like My Mother*. New York: Putnam's, 1969. (T)

Francesca Kinsolving never met her husband Matthew's family; there wasn't time between their marriage ceremony and the day he shipped out for Vietnam. But one thing Matthew repeatedly told her has stuck in her mind: "You'll like my mother." And now, with Matthew having been killed in transit to Southeast Asia, a baby on the way, and no place else to turn, Francesca has decided to seek out Mrs. Kinsolving, Sr.

The town of Always, Ohio, is a small place on the banks of the Ohio River. Matthew's family home has the appearance of a castle, and Mrs. Kinsolving, who never answered any of Francesca's communications at the time of Matthew's death, is not the likable person her son described. Francesca is not prepared for her coldness, nor is she prepared for Matthew's feebleminded sister, Kathleen, who seems afraid of everything. Mrs. Kinsolving is not overly hospitable, but she does insist that Francesca stay the night. Francesca is reluctant, because everything about the house disturbs her; she longs to be back at the little café in town, where the bus driver has promised to look for her in case she wishes to make the return journey. But she does stay, and soon more and more frightening things are revealed about the Kinsolving family, things that pose a terrible threat to Francesca and her unborn child.

From beginning to harrowing climax, this novel is a truly terrifying experience. Hintze employs the best elements of the classic Gothic thriller, but tempers them with a modern heroine and situation in such a way that the reader is thoroughly convinced this could really happen. Don't read this while alone on a dark night!

Hintze's other novels, all of which are also commendable, are *The Stone Carnation* (1971), *Aloha Means Goodbye* (1972), *Listen, Please Listen* (1973), and *Cry Witch* (1975).

(*M.M.*)

Hirschberg, Cornelius. *Florentine Finish.* New York: Harper, 1963. (W)

Writers usually rely on research and imagination for the background material in their books. Occasionally, however, comes a writer who utilizes his or her own personal experience and expertise, and the difference is often striking—the reader *feels* the authenticity of such material. This is certainly the case with Cornelius Hirschberg, who called upon his experience in the jewelry business for the background in *Florentine Finish.*

Of course background material alone will not suffice. Interesting characters and plot are also needed. And, here too, Hirschberg does not disappoint. The book's main character is Saul Handy, an employee in a New York jewelry store, whom we join in the process of obtaining a diamond for a man named Ed Bender. The trouble is, the diamond turns out to be stolen, and Ed Bender's bodyguard turns up dead in Handy's car. So right away Saul Handy is in trouble with two sections of the New York City Police Department—Robbery and Homicide. To save his own neck and reputation, Handy (a former policeman) begins an investigation of his own, prowling the diamond markets on Forty-seventh Street, encountering two more corpses along the way, and nearly becoming a corpse himself.

This novel was awarded an MWA Edgar for Best First Novel of 1963, and indeed it is worthy of such an award. Books, however, are like diamonds—there is no such thing as an absolutely perfect one. Like other books, *Florentine Finish* has its flaws (Hirschberg relies a little too heavily on tough-guy-investigator clichés, and the murder weapon is a little too obvious). But overall it is a fine effort, and it is regrettable that this is Cornelius Hirschberg's only novel.

(*N.D.*)

*Hitchens, Bert and Dolores. *End of the Line.* New York: Doubleday Crime Club, 1957. (PP)

Dolores Hitchens was a remarkably versatile writer, having created first-rate novels in just about every category of crime fiction: whodunit, straight suspense, psychological suspense, private eye, police procedural (with her husband Bert), and neo-Gothic. (She even wrote a very good rough-and-tumble western.) Yet if she is remembered at all today, it seems to be for her series of novels as by D. B. Olsen (q.v.) about little old lady sleuth Rachel Murdock—Forties-style whodunits that are decidedly *not* her best work. This is a pity; she deserves far more attention and recognition than she received during her long career (1939 to her death in 1973).

Among Hitchens's most accomplished novels are the five she wrote with her husband, a railroad detective himself, about a fictional group of railroad cops in southern California. One of these detectives, John Farrel, appears in three books, most prominently in *End of the Line,* and is a finely drawn character: an alcoholic fighting off the pain of a wife who walked out on him, taking their child with her; struggling to keep his job and his pride while under pressure from his superiors and his junior partner, a green kid named Saunders, because he has begun to drink heavily on the job.

The case that Farrel, with Saunders's help, undertakes here is a fresh development in the six-year-old Lobo Tunnel train wreck in which sixteen people died. A conductor from the wrecked train, who vanished to Mexico with a large amount of money after the accident and subsequently spent time in a Mexican prison for manslaughter, has resurfaced in the United States. Why has he come home? And where did he get the money he took to Mexico? Was it extorted from one or more of the surviving passengers, who might have lied in their accounts of what happened that day in order to collect huge settlements from the railroad?

These questions are only a few of those that arise during the investigation. Matters are further complicated by the actions of the conductor's greedy young daughter, Peg—and by murder in a small railroad town in the desert. The procedure in this series is meticulously presented, but Hitchens doesn't allow it to rule the story; the emphasis, as in all of her work, is on character—the relationships between people, the things that motivate and obsess us all. Railroad and desert backgrounds are also vividly portrayed.

The four other books in the series are also of high quality: *FOB Murder* (1955), *One-Way Ticket* (1956), *The Man Who Followed Women* (1959), and *The Grudge* (1963). Farrel appears in the last two titles named; various other detectives—notably, Michael Kernahan in *The Man Who Followed Women*—are featured in each of the four.

(*B.P.*)

Hitchens, Dolores. *Footsteps in the Night.* New York: Doubleday Crime Club, 1961. (PP/T)

This novel, set within the confines of an exclusive southern California subdivision, is the perfect showcase for Dolores Hitchens's excellent plotting technique. It is a complex tale, depending on such complicated logistics that at the end the reader wonders how the author ever kept them straight. But the plot works, as does the characterization, and the ending might surprise the most astute fan of suspense fiction.

The subdivision of Dellwood is only partly finished when the story opens, but already the new residents have begun to move in. There are the Forrest Holdens, who were particularly eager to move in early; Miss Silvester, a sexually frustrated spinster whose house is completely filled with new possessions; the Arthurs, man and wife, with two small children and a somewhat strange grandfather; the Bartletts and their attractive teenage daughter. And there are the others: Cooper, the builder; the Dronks, father and handicapped son, who owned the original land upon which the development has been built and still live in their eyesore of a pink stucco house; the Ranalds, a young couple whose house Cooper sold out from under them.

Dellwood is attractive, with big ranch-style houses, spacious lots, stone pillars, and a gatehouse. But the lives going on inside these luxury homes are in turmoil, and one night the hidden tensions erupt into violence. When the commotion subsides, there are as many different versions of what happened as there are residents. It is the job of Lieutenant Ferguson of the local police force to sort out these stories and determine the truth, but before he does, more buried passions surface. *Footsteps in the Night* is a complex thriller, whose characters you won't easily forget.

(*M.M.*)

*Hitchens, Dolores. *Sleep with Slander.* New York: Doubleday Crime Club, 1960. (PI)

Many people seem to feel that the best hard-boiled private-eye novel written by a woman is Leigh Brackett's *No Good from a Corpse* (q.v.). But that may be because many people haven't read *Sleep with Slander.* For the undersigned reviewer's money, *this* is the best hard-boiled private-eye novel written by a woman—and one of the best written by anybody. Its protagonist, Long Beach–based Jim Sader, is a multidimensional character, much more realistic than the stereotypical tough detective; Sader uses his intelligence to accomplish his purposes. The plot, reminiscent in its complexity of both Chandler and Ross Macdonald (qq.v.), is better crafted, more compelling, and ultimately more satisfying than the Brackett.

Sader is hired by a rich old man, Hale Gibbings, whose daughter gave birth to an illegitimate child five years earlier. The child, Ricky, was given away for adoption, not through a recognized agency but to a private couple, and Gibbings has heard nothing about the boy until recently, when an anonymous letter writer tells him the child is being mentally and physically abused.

Sader undertakes the search for Ricky, following a trail that leads him to a conniving friend of Tina Champlain, the adoptive (and now presumed dead) mother; to a violent builder of boats and his drunken father; to murder, extortion, double-dealing, madness; and finally to the truth. The surprises Hitchens springs along the way are not at all easy to anticipate. A first-rate novel recommended not just for fans of the hard-boiled school but for anyone who appreciates a quality mystery.

Hitchens wrote one other novel featuring Sader: *Sleep with Strangers* (1957). This is also good reading, but marred by sentimentality and a shaky ending that reveals the wrong choice of murderer.

(*B.P.*)

Hjorstberg, William. *Falling Angel.* New York: Harcourt Brace, 1978. (PI)

William Hjorstberg is a highly unconventional writer who delights in mixing genres and breaking molds. His first novel, *Alp* (1969), blends pornography and mountain climbing; his science-fiction novel, *Gray Matters* (1971), features a Utopia run by incredible cybernetic machines dedicated to human transcendence while humans rebel against the perfect society. Other experimental works include *Symbiography* (1973) and *Toro! Toro! Toro!* (1975).

In *Falling Angel,* Hjorstberg combines 1940s private-eye fiction with the occult. PI Harry Angel, a specialist in finding missing persons, is hired to track down a famous Forties singer, Johnny Favorite. The trail leads to Central Park voodoo ceremonies, a black mass in an abandoned subway station, Coney Island fortune-tellers, and bizarre murders. Harry Angel finds he's involved in a satanic plot and he might not be able to escape alive.

Falling Angel is William Hjorstberg's most successful book; the descriptions of New York City in the post–World War II era are clever and accurate. A condensed version of *Falling Angel* was published in *Playboy* and proved very popular. In trying to describe *Falling Angel,* Stephen King said, "I've never read anything remotely like it. Trying to imagine what might have happened if Raymond Chandler had written *The Exorcist* is as close as I can come."

(*G.K.*)

Hoch, Edward D. *The Shattered Raven.* New York: Lancer, 1969. (O/W)

Edward D. Hoch is crime fiction's premier short-story writer. (He is also that *rara avis,* a writer who makes his living entirely from short fiction.) He has published more than 600 stories since his first professional sale in 1955, and has appeared in every issue of *Ellery Queen's Mystery Magazine* for the past dozen years. He also has to his credit well over 100 anthology appearances, including a score of selections for the prestigious annuals *Best Detective Stories of the Year* and *Year's Best Mystery & Suspense Stories* (which he now edits).

The Shattered Raven is Hoch's first novel and one of only four published under his own name. It is also his only contemporary mystery—the other three books are detective stories with futuristic settings—and is something of a cult novel among aficionados, owing to the fact that it deals with murder most foul at the annual MWA Edgar Awards banquet in New York and makes use of several real writers in cameo roles.

When TV commentator Ross Craigthorn is murdered on the dais while accepting MWA's Mystery Reader of the Year Award (no small honor, past recipients having included Eleanor Roosevelt and Joey Adams), it is a particularly ingenious and nasty crime: He was shot in the face by means of a slender tube attached to the microphone, "an electrified, radio-controlled zip gun." The task of finding out who killed Craigthorn falls on the unwilling shoulders of MWA's executive vice-president, Barney Hamet (no relation, of course, to the great Dashiell), and magazine writer Susan Veldt. Their search leads them to a dark secret in Craigthorn's past, one that has its origins in the little town of June, Nebraska. Unlike Barney and Susan, the reader knows the identity of the murderer from the outset—one Victor Jones. But what the reader *doesn't* know is just who Victor Jones *is,* for he is no longer using that name. Which of the suspects is really the deadly Mr.

Jones should come as no surprise to most detective-story veterans, but that won't spoil anyone's enjoyment of this solid, well-clued, "insider's" mystery.

Hoch's other three novels all feature the "Computer Cops," a team of twenty-first century government investigators led by Carl Crader and Earl Jazine. The first, *The Transvection Machine* (1971), is probably the best—an expert blend of mystery, science fiction, and social commentary. The other two titles in the series are *The Fellowship of the Hand* (1973) and *The Frankenstein Factory* (1975).

(*B.P.*)

*Hoch, Edward D. *The Thefts of Nick Velvet.* New York: Mysterious Press, 1978. (SS/AD)

The best of Edward D. Hoch's short stories are divided more or less equally among five outstanding series characters: Police Captain Leopold, whose cases are generally of the procedural variety; Rand, the retired spy, who is an expert at solving difficult codes and ciphers; Dr. Sam Hawthorne, a New England country doctor who solves "impossible" rural mysteries in the 1920s and 1930s; Simon Ark, a shadowy figure who claims to be a 2000-year-old Coptic priest and whose detections are tinged with elements of the occult; and Nick Velvet (born Velvetta, but he dropped the last two letters because the name sounded too much like a popular cheese), a master thief with a peculiar code of honor—he will risk his life and freedom to steal any object, no matter how impossible the challenge, so long as the item has no monetary value.

This quirk alone makes Nick Velvet unique among crime-fiction protagonists, and also makes for some highly unusual, even bizarre, challenges to his professional expertise. "The Theft of the Clouded Tiger," for instance, in which he is hired (he works by assignment only) to swipe a tiger from a zoo. Or "The Theft of the Silver Lake Serpent," in which a hotel owner pays him to steal a sea serpent out of a small Canadian lake. Or "The Theft from the Empty Room," in which Nick is evidently hired to steal nothing at all. Some of Nick's adventures turn into fair-play whodunits in which he is forced to play detective; in others, it is the baffling motives behind the odd things he is asked to purloin that keep the reader guessing; and in still others it is the question "How in the world can Nick possibly accomplish *that* theft?" No matter what type of story it happens to be, it is certain to be wonderfully inventive and entertaining. Hoch's mastery of the criminous short story is evident in every one of the thirteen entries in this collection.

Nick Velvet shares one other collection (with Rand, the retired spy): *The Spy and the Thief* (1971), which has seven stories featuring each character. Simon Ark appears in three collections: *The Judges of Hades and City of*

Brass, both published in 1971, and *The Quests of Simon Ark* (1985). Also published in 1985 was the first Captain Leopold collection, *Leopold's Way,* which contains nineteen stories and a useful checklist.

(*B.P.*)

Holding, Elizabeth Sanxay. *Net of Cobwebs.* New York: Simon & Schuster, 1945. (PS)

The psychological mystery, along with its first cousin, the *film noir,* became extremely popular during the mid-1940s. Elizabeth Sanxay Holding had been writing this type of book since the early 1930s, and Anthony Boucher (q.v.), one of her biggest boosters, was quick to point out her preeminence in this subgenre. Raymond Chandler (q.v.) paid her extravagant praise indeed, saying, "For my money she's the top suspense writer of them all." *Net of Cobwebs* is one of her best books.

Most of the Holding mysteries involve close family relationships. This is perhaps a carry-over from her early writing days, prior to 1930, when she primarily wrote romantic fiction. Critics like Barzun and Taylor disliked the "family wrangling" in her books, but they were in a distinct minority; most fans and critics thought otherwise. In *Net of Cobwebs* it is his family that is an apparent refuge for Malcolm Drake, a merchant seaman who is recovering from the effects of having had his ship torpedoed. He carries the additional burden of guilt regarding the death of one crew member. Plagued with nightmares and inability to remember, he suffers the further trauma of being the primary murder suspect when a relative who made him her heir is murdered with his medication.

Though women were generally her protagonists, Holding shows in this book that she has no difficulty in being equally convincing when writing from a male viewpoint, even that of a war veteran. We can accept and identify with Drake as easily as we can with the heroine of another Holding novel using World War II as its background. In *The Blank Wall* (1947), Lucia Holley seems to be a typical middle-aged housewife, concerned with writing to her husband overseas and coping with wartime shortages. When a married man "takes up" with her teenage daughter and then is found murdered, Lucia's life becomes a nightmare. The book, one of her most popular, was filmed in 1949 by Max Ophuls, with Joan Bennett and James Mason, as *The Reckless Moment.*

(*M.L.*)

Holme, Timothy. *A Funeral of Gondolas.* New York: Coward, McCann, 1982. (PP)

This is the second novel featuring Achille Peroni, "the Rudolph Valentino of the Italian Police"; the first was *Neapolitan Streak* (1980). The label would be offputting were it not for the fact that Peroni is decidedly not a glamour boy; although extremely good-looking, he is often lovelorn, frequently bumbling, and sometimes so publicity-hungry that he anonymously telephones the papers with stories of his investigative feats. In short, he is a thoroughly likable character whose public image greatly outstrips his private persona.

As the book opens, Peroni is sitting in a café near Venice's Rialto Bridge, nursing a scotch and scanning the *London Times* (which he can barely read, but which gives him nostalgic memories of a now-idealized special posting to Scotland Yard). On temporary assignment in Venice, the Neapolitan Peroni is disgruntled because crime is practically nonexistent there. His current assignment is to find out who is organizing illegal betting on the annual gondola race; the gondoliers, who often engage in relatively harmless illegal activity, are accepting bets, but someone must be behind it. Peroni accomplishes this mission in record time, but the culprit is let go because he is, of all things, a priest who is doing it for charity. Peroni then settles into dull routine, missing his native Naples and feeling out of place in this strange, crumbling city of canals and ancient palaces—but not for long. A lawyer named Bixi is found murdered in Killers' Way, an aptly named alley, and Peroni can now exhibit his expertise.

It soon becomes apparent that Bixi's killing was no random murder. As Peroni delves deeper into the matter, it also becomes apparent that the lawyer's dealings were not strictly aboveboard, and that they were closely linked with the illegal activities of various gondoliers. Peroni finds himself involved with such local characters as a retired gondolier called the Undertaker, who holds long conversations with his dead mother; the Lion—pimp and orchestrator of weird rituals; and the Hooker, a retarded old man. By the time his investigtion is completed, Peroni knows Venice—sinister secrets and all—as few natives of that city do.

This is a delightful novel, rich in Venetian background and peopled with thoroughly memorable characters.

(*M.M.*)

Holmes, H. H. *Rocket to the Morgue.* New York: Duell, 1942. (Also published as by Anthony Boucher.) (AD/PP)

Anthony Boucher (q.v.) wrote two novels under the pseudonym H. H. Holmes (an infamous nineteenth-century murderer and thus an example of Boucher's puckish sense of humor). Both feature the detective team of Sister Ursula, a nun in the convent of the Sisters of Martha of Bethany, and Lieutenant Marshall of the LAPD Homicide Squad; and both are classic fair-play, locked-room detective novels. The first, *Nine Times Nine* (1940), has the cleverest "impossible" plot and solution. But the second, *Rocket to the Morgue,* is the more interesting of the pair by virtue of its background: the southern California science-fiction community (fans and writers both) of the period. Several real people (thinly disguised) appear as characters, among them such science-fiction luminaries as Robert Heinlein, John W. Campbell, Henry Kuttner (q.v.), and C. L. Moore.

Marshall, a Rhodes Scholar as well as a cop, is introduced to the community by a friend, Matt Duncan. He is also introduced to the surviving members of the Foulkes family, whose scion, Fowler Foulkes, was the creator of Dr. Derringer, a fictional sleuth who (not coincidentally) resembles Sherlock Holmes. Fowler's son, Hilary St. John Foulkes, is the least likable member of the family; in fact, as the greedy executor of his father's literary estate, he is so widely hated as to be a sure candidate for early extinction. Which is almost but not quite what happens to him: He is stabbed in the back, not fatally, in his locked study. No one could possibly have gotten into the room, and yet neither could the wound have been self-inflicted.

Matters are further complicated by the successful murder of another man during a demonstration of rocket propulsion; and then by the death of Hilary under exactly the same circumstances as the previous attempt on his life—he is stabbed to death in his locked study. It is Sister Ursula, on the scene by virtue of her friendship with Marshall, who comes up with the right answers. The solution to the locked-room gambit is unique and plausible enough, yet somewhat unsatisfying.

There is plenty of early science-fiction lore to go along with the detecting, as well as some intriguing insights into pulp writers and writing. For these as well as for the puzzle, *Rocket to the Morgue* is well worth reading today.

(*B.P.*)

*Holt, Victoria. *The Mistress of Mellyn.* New York: Doubleday, 1960. (RS)

Victoria Holt is one of the *grandes dames* of romantic suspense, and this novel is perhaps her finest. *The Mistress of Mellyn* is well crafted, employing all the devices of a Gothic novel: the Elegant Old House, the Enigmatic Male, the Dark Secret, and the Young Woman of Breeding but Reduced Circumstances who is thrust into the midst of all this. And the particular combination of these that Holt employs works very well indeed.

Martha Leigh arrives at the TreMellyn manse on the foggy Cornish coast determined to be a good governess to Connan TreMellyn's motherless daughter, Alvean. She resolves to accept her situation and to think of the romantic-sounding TreMellyn as merely her employer. And well she should: TreMellyn is handsome but arrogant; moreover, he is carrying on a torrid love affair with the wife of a neighbor. And Alvean is a little terror whom Martha despairs of ever winning over.

The Dark Secret is that TreMellyn's wife is not dead, but ran off with another man years before. TreMellyn is arrogant because he is hiding this deep sorrow. The story proceeds, replete with the colorful details of a Cornish Christmas. Suspicions of murder intrude. Love blooms. And in the end, the Dark Secret turns out to be more sinister than anyone could have thought.

It's all very Gothicky, all very much fun, and graced with a subtle sexiness that far outclasses the blatant sex of contemporary romances. For a wintry night when you need a love story to warm you.

Victoria Holt's other novels include *The Legend of the Seventh Virgin* (1965), *The Shivering Sands* (1969), *The House of a Thousand Lanterns* (1974), and *The Mask of the Enchantress* (1980).

(*M.M.*)

*Homes, Geoffrey. *Build My Gallows High.* New York: Morrow, 1946. (T)

From 1936 to 1946, Geoffrey Homes (Daniel Mainwaring) published a dozen very good mysteries set primarily in the valleys and foothills of north-central California. *Build My Gallows High* is the last and best of the twelve, and so firmly established Mainwaring in Hollywood (he had been writing B movies since 1942) that he produced no more fiction during the last thirty-two years of his life. This novel was filmed, from Mainwaring's screenplay, as *Out of the Past* (1947), starring Robert Mitchum, Jane Greer, and Kirk Douglas—one of the half-dozen best *noir* crime films ever made.

Both novel and film are powerful studies of one man's struggle to maintain the hope of his future when his jaded past catches up with him. Red Bailey is a former New York private detective, the kind "who first looked at a client's supply of thousand-dollar bills, then at his social—and legal—status" before taking on a job; an angle player who made his big mistake when he went to work for a gambler named Whit Sterling. The job (told through flashback) was to find Sterling's ex-mistress, Mumsie McGonigle, who shot and wounded Sterling and then ran off with $56,000 of his money. Red tracked Mumsie to Mexico, met and fell in love with her; and when she claimed she'd only shot Sterling in self-defense, Red stupidly double-crossed the gambler and helped Mumsie cover her tracks from Mexico to California.

But their relationship wasn't what Red expected. When his former partner showed up at their country hideaway, murder drove the final wedge between them—and Red realized how badly he'd screwed up his life. Determined to put Mumsie and the rest of it behind him, he made his way to a small town in the foothills of the Sierra Nevada, opened a gas station, and spent most of his free time fishing. He even met a new woman, one he learned to love more than Mumsie, one he planned to marry. Now, for the first time in his life, he is content.

But then one day his past shows up in the person of a flashily dressed Greek gunman employed by Guy Parker, a crooked cop Red knew in the old days who now operates a gambling club in Reno. Red accompanies the Greek to see Parker, and finds that Mumsie is now Parker's live-in girlfriend. Parker wants Red to do a detective job for him; if he doesn't agree, then Parker will tell Whit Sterling where to find him. Red smells a setup of some kind, with himself square in the middle, but what choice does he have except to do as Parker asks? Up to a point, that is . . .

This is a taut, hard-edged thriller, powerfully told in a clipped style reminiscent of Hemingway's, with superb characterization and a hammer-blow climax. Anyone who has seen and admired *Out of the Past* will find *Build My Gallows High* every bit as memorable.

(*B.P.*)

*Homes, Geoffrey. *Forty Whacks.* New York: Morrow, 1941. (PI)

Homes/Mainwaring created three completely different series detectives for his other eleven novels, each of them with unorthodox abilities. The first was newspaperman Robin Bishop, who is featured in Homes's first five titles, among them *The Man Who Didn't Exist* (1937), which deals with the baffling suicide of a famous writer named Zenophen Zwick who seems never to have existed in the first place. The second sleuth was Humphrey Campbell, an unconventional private investigator who, with his fat, lazy, and corrupt partner, Oscar Morgan, appears in one of the Bishop novels (*Then There Were Three,* 1938) and in four of his own. And the third was Mexican cop Jose Manuel Madero, "knitter extraordinary—not only of socks but of mysterious loose ends," who stars in a pair of titles: *The Street of the Crying Woman* (1942) and *The Hill of the Terrified Monk* (1943).

Chubby Humphrey Campbell is probably the best realized of the three; certainly his cases are Homes's most intricate and satisfying detective puzzles. *Forty Whacks* involves Humphrey and Oscar in an ax-murder in the California town of Joaquin—"the second Borden case," as Campbell refers to it. Humphrey, with grumpy Oscar watching out for any illegal dollar that might be made, sets out to prove that Joe Borden wasn't responsible for the grisly remains found under the seat of an overturned rowboat floating down the San Joaquin River. Along the way he gets mixed up with a female artist's representative; a successful concert pianist who gave up his career to hunt for gold; a tough lady newspaper publisher; a couple of mayoralty candidates; and a lot more bloody murder.

The action in *Forty Whacks* is fast and furious, but there is a good deal more than that to recommend it: clever plotting, witty and remarkably good dialogue, and a lean style made lyrical in places by some of the most vivid descriptive writing to be found in all of mystery fiction. The other three Campbell-Morgan adventures—*No Hands on the Clock* (1939), *Finders Keepers* (1940), and *Six Silver Handles* (1944)—share the same qualities.

(*B.P.*)

*Hopley, George. *Night Has a Thousand Eyes.* New York: Rinehart, 1945. (PS)

Night Has a Thousand Eyes was the first of two novels published under a pseudonym made up of Cornell Woolrich's (q.v.) middle names, and of all his books it's the one most completely dominated by death and fate. A simpleminded recluse with apparently uncanny powers predicts that millionaire Harlan Reid will die in three weeks, precisely at midnight, at the jaws of a lion. The tension rises to an unbearable pitch as the apparently doomed man, his daughter, and a sympathetic young homicide detective struggle to avert a destiny that they at first suspect and soon come to hope was conceived by a merely human power. Woolrich makes us live the emotional torment and suspense of the situation until we are literally shivering in our seats.

The roots of Woolrich's longest and perhaps finest novel lie deep in his past. From the moment at the age of eleven when he knew that someday he would have to die, he "had that trapped feeling," he wrote in his unpublished autobiography, "like some sort of a poor insect that you've put inside a downturned glass, and it tries to climb up the sides, and it can't, and it can't, and it can't." Of all the recurring nightmare situations in his *noir* repertory, the most terrifying is that of the person doomed to die at a precise moment, and knowing what that moment is, and flailing out desperately against his or her fate. This is what connects the protagonists of Woolrich's strongest work, including Paul Stapp in "Three O'Clock," Robert Lamont in "Guillotine," Scott Henderson in *Phantom Lady,* and of course Reid in *Night Has a Thousand Eyes*. Only a writer torn apart by human mortality could have created these stories.

Published under a new by-line and by a firm never before associated with Woolrich, *Night Has a Thousand Eyes* seems to have been intended as a breakthrough book, to introduce the author to a wider audience, but it was too grim and unsettling for huge commercial success. The 1948 movie version, starring Edward G. Robinson as a carnival mind reader with the power to foresee disasters, had almost nothing in common with the story line of Woolrich's novel, let alone its power and terror. This book is what *noir* literature is all about, a nerve-shredding suspense classic of the highest quality and a work that once read can never be forgotten.

(*F.M.N.*)

Horler, Sydney. *The Curse of Doone.* New York: Mystery League, 1930. (E/T)

A journalist and writer of football stories (the British variety) until his early thirties, Sydney Horler began publishing "shockers" in 1925 and went on to produce upwards of a hundred over the next thirty years. He created a ménage of series characters, most of them Secret Service agents of one kind or another, including Bunny Chipstead; "The Ace"; Nighthawk; Sir Brian Fordinghame; and that animal among men, Tiger Standish. The Standish books—*Tiger Standish Steps on It* (1940) is a representative title in more ways than one—were especially popular with Horler's readership.

His greatest literary attribute was his imagination, which may be described as weedily fertile. His favorite antagonists were fanatic Germans and Fu Manchu–type megalomaniacs, many of whom were given sobriquets such as "the Disguiser," "the Colossus," "the Mutilator," "the Master of Venom," and "the Voice of Ice"; but he also contrived a number of other evildoers to match wits with his heroes—an impressive list of them that includes mad scientists, American gangsters, vampires, giant apes, ape-men from Borneo, venal dwarfs, slavering "Things," a man born with the head of a wolf (no kidding; see *Horror's Head,* 1934), and—perhaps his crowning achievement—a bloodsucking, man-eating bush ("The Red-Haired Death," a novelette in *The Destroyer, and The Red-Haired Death,* 1938).

The Curse of Doone is typical Horler, which is to say it is inspired nonsense. In London, Secret Service Agent Ian Heath meets a virgin in distress named Cicely Garrett and promptly falls in love with her. A friend of Heath's, Jerry (who worries about "the primrose path to perdition"), urges him to toddle off to his cottage in Dartmoor for a much-needed rest. Which Heath does, though not before barely surviving a mysterious poison-gas attack. And lo!—once there, he runs into Cicely, who is living at secluded and sinister Doone Hall. He also runs into a couple of incredible coincidences (another Horler stock-in-trade); monstrous vampire bats and the "Vampire of Doone Hall"; two bloody murders; hidden caves, secret panels and caches; a Prussian villain who became a homicidal maniac because he couldn't cope with his sudden baldness; and a newly invented "war machine" that can force enemy aircraft out of the air by means of wireless waves and stop a car from five miles away.

All of this is told in Horler's bombastic, idiosyncratic, and sometimes priggish style. (Horler had very definite opinions on just about everything, and was not above expressing them in his fiction, as well as in a number of nonfiction works. He once said of women: "Of how many women can it truly be said that they are worthy of their underclothes?" And of detective fiction: "I know I haven't the brains to write a proper detective novel, but there is no class of literature for which I feel a deeper personal loathing." Racism was another of his shortcomings; he didn't like *anybody* except the

English.) This and Horler's other novels are high camp by today's standards; *The Curse of Doone* is just one of several that can be considered, for their hilarious prose, pomposity, and absurd plots, as classics of their type.

Unfortunately, most of Horler's "shockers" were not reprinted in this country. Of those that were, the ones that rank with *The Curse of Doone* are *The Order of the Octopus* (1926), *Peril* (1930), *Tiger Standish* (1932), *Lord of Terror* (1937), and *Dark Danger* (1945).

(*B.P.*)

Hornig, Doug. *Foul Shot.* New York: Scribner's, 1984. (PI)

This first mystery features private eye Loren Swift, who operates not out of a large city such as New York or San Francisco but out of Charlottesville, Virginia. Hired to find Leigh Majors, a coed at the University of Virginia and daughter of a wealthy local family, Swift soon finds himself involved in much more than a simple disappearance. A fellow private detective from California, who has been prying into the Majors's affairs, is murdered; much more important, so is a black civil-rights leader named Ward Williams. Race riots resulting from Williams's death further complicate matters for Swift; as does the attempted murder of Delmos Venable, black basketball star of the Virginia Cavaliers and close friend (and probable lover) of Leigh Majors; as do hidden secrets and internecine hatreds within the Majors family.

There is some good, strong writing here. The Virginia settings are well drawn; the racial tensions and college-basketball background are adroitly handled; the narrative is fast-paced and the solution plausible; and Swift is a likable (and fallibly human) character. *Foul Shot*'s only real flaw is Swift's—or, more properly, Hornig's—penchant for that bane of the private eye, the ubiquitous wisecrack. At times his flippancies are amusing; too often they are merely intrusive. Hornig writes too well to need to resort to this device.

He does tone down the wisecracks a bit in his second Loren Swift adventure, *Hard Ball* (1985)—an excellent and even more tightly plotted mystery. If Hornig gives us more Swifts, and continues to grow with each subsequent book in the series, he will certainly become a major voice in PI fiction.

(*B.P.*)

*Hornung, E. W. *The Complete Short Stories of Raffles—the Amateur Cracksman.* New York: St. Martin's, 1984. (CS/SS)

A. J. Raffles (or simply "Raffles," as he became known to generations of mystery fans) is a gentleman, a cricketeer, and a distinguished man-about-town. He is something else, too: a notorious burglar, often preying on those wealthy people he has come to know socially.

His chronicler, former school chum Bunny Manders, records Raffles's exploits in great (and sometimes fawning) detail, much as Watson recorded the adventures of Sherlock Holmes. Perhaps this was no coincidence, since E. W. Hornung was Arthur Conan Doyle's (q.v.) friend and brother-in-law, both men creating classic literary characters—even though the characters ended up on opposite sides of the law.

Raffles's escapades were written in short-story form (twenty-six in all) and originally appeared in three volumes, the first published in 1899, the last in 1905. Now these stories have been combined in *The Complete Short Stories of Raffles—the Amateur Cracksman.*

The stories themselves record the criminal escapades of Raffles and Bunny, ranging from their first joint venture in "The Ides of March," when Bunny was tricked into aiding Raffles in a burglary, to "The Raffles Relics," in which a now white-haired Raffles actually steals relics of his own crimes from Scotland Yard's Black Museum. In these, and in the intervening stories, Raffles again and again displays his daring, his imagination, his skills as a cracksman, and on occasion his mastery of disguise—all faithfully transcribed by Bunny (although Bunny himself admits he recorded only their most fascinating adventures).

In the story "A Costume Piece," we gain an interesting insight into Raffles's motives as he chides Bunny for thinking of crime only when the wolf is at the door, then goes on to liken their criminal activity to "art for art's sake." Further, in "Gentlemen and Players," Raffles compares their secret activities to his public activity—cricket: "What's the satisfaction of taking a man's wicket when you want his spoons? Still, if you bowl a bit your low cunning won't get rusty, and always looking for the weak spot's just the kind of mental exercise one wants."

Whatever his motives, whatever his reasoning, Raffles was an almost immediate success with the public, and remains one of our best-known literary characters. (It should be noted here that some years after Hornung's death, Barry Perowne [q.v.] began a new series of Raffles stories, which continue to the present.)

Although Raffles was E. W. Hornung's most popular and enduring creation, he did write several crime novels, including *Dead Men Tell No Tales* (1899), *The Camera Fiend* (1911), and *The Thousandth Woman* (1913). (*N.D.*)

*Household, Geoffrey. *Rogue Male.* Boston: Little, Brown, 1939. (T/A)

Rogue Male caused quite a stir in both England and the United States when it was first published. It is the story of one man's private war with

Hitler and the Gestapo, although neither is mentioned by name. But it is much more than that, else its popularity would not have survived the war years: It has been almost constantly in print over the past five decades. The *Saturday Review of Literature* said, "You are not likely to find a better adventure story." And the *New York Times* called it "an overpowering tour de force . . . spare, tense, desperately alive." Those superlatives still apply today.

The novel is told in the form of a first-person journal whose author is never identified. We know only that he is a famous and well-to-do British sportsman whose name is widely known and who has been "frequently and unavoidably dishonored by the banners and praises of the penny press." In the days before full-scale war in Europe, this man set out alone on a hunting trip in Poland, and it occurred to him there that it might be his greatest challenge to stalk a different kind of game for a change—human game. Not to kill, of course; he is not a psychopath. He wants only to get close enough to a certain heavily guarded dictator to place the man in the cross hairs of his rifle's telescopic sight. And this he does, being a superb and wily outdoorsman: He comes within a finger pressure of ridding Europe of its greatest tyrant. But he doesn't fire; and because he doesn't, he is caught and brutally tortured. He tells his captors the truth, but they don't believe him. And even if they do, it doesn't matter; he must be killed to prevent the truth from leaking out and others trying the same thing.

They put him over a cliff to make his death look like an accident. Only he doesn't die; he survives the fall. And even though he is more animal than man at first, unable to use his hands (they have been mangled by his tormentors) and with his left eye a bloody horror, he still manages to make his arduous way to a seaport and stow away on board a ship bound for England. Once he arrives, however, his ordeal hasn't ended; it has only just begun. He knows that agents of the tyrant will be sent after him, knows that his only hope of survival is to disappear completely and without a trace. He makes financial arrangements with the solicitor in charge of his estate, then leaves London. But at the Aldwych train station he is accosted by an enemy agent and has no choice but to kill the man. As a result, he becomes a fugitive from the British police as well.

He flees to a remote part of Dorset, covering his tracks as he travels, and quite literally goes to ground: He digs out an undetectable burrow inside an isolated hedgerow. You might think he is safe then; so did he. But he isn't. He makes one mistake that leads the enemy agents and the police to his vicinity and forces him to live like a mole inside his burrow for days on end. And when he emerges, it is to kill again, and to vow to return to the tyrant's country and once more put the man in the cross hairs of his rifle, and this time to pull the trigger.

This is a nightmarish novel, filled with breathless chases, fascinating detailwork, and images that will haunt you for days after reading. If you like chase/adventure stories and you haven't yet read *Rogue Male,* do yourself a favor. You won't be disappointed.

(*B.P.*)

*Household, Geoffrey. *Watcher in the Shadows.* Boston: Little, Brown, 1960. (T)

While not as famous as *Rogue Male,* this too is a first-class example of that uniquely British crime novel, the thriller.

Working quietly in a sleepy English village, Charles Dennim, a zoologist, watches as the front of his home is blown apart by a letter bomb. Investigation proves the bomb was meant for him. But why? Is it because of some event in his past? Perhaps his wartime service undercover behind German lines? Information from a well-placed government friend convinces Dennim he is being stalked by a faceless killer who has struck at least three times before and always with impunity. Unwilling to risk the lives of those close to him, Dennim takes to the open fields of the English midlands and sets himself up as a Judas goat while trying to lure his would-be executioner into the open. The hunter becomes the hunted as a ruthless murderer bent on revenge stalks his prey. The final confrontation—at night in an abandoned barn on a lonely rise—will leave the reader breathless.

This is a fine novel in all respects, with a powerful and moving climax.

Recommended among Household's other thrillers are *Arabesque* (1948), *A Rough Shoot* (1951), and especially *Dance of the Dwarfs* (1968), which is in the same hunt-and-chase mold as *Rogue Male* and *Watcher in the Shadows.* Household is also an accomplished writer of short stories of adventure and suspense, some of the best of which can be found in such collections as *The Salvation of Pisco Gabar* (1940), *The Brides of Solomon* (1958), and *Sabres on the Sand* (1966).

(*B.T.*)

*Houston, Robert. *Cholo.* New York: Avon, 1981. (O/T)

Inexplicably, this stunning little paperback original seems to have passed unnoticed when it was published. It was not nominated for a Best Paperback Edgar by MWA (it should have won the award hands down), and its sales seem to have been modest. And yet in its low-key way it is probably the most powerful softcover crime novel to be published in a decade or more.

Set in modern Peru, it tells the haunting tale of twenty-year-old Andes Indian Atahaulpa Wilson Marco Polo Quispe—a *cholo,* the poorest of the poor, who now lives in a Lima slum. His only hope for the future, as he sees it, is to rob the Chinaman who owns his building and is chief bookkeeper in the Creole underworld, even though it is said that "whoever touched the Chinaman or the box he chained to his wrist when he slept was a *muerto,* a dead man." Atahaulpa compounds his mistake by killing the Chinaman, and soon finds himself fleeing not only the city police and the Chinaman's underworld friends, but government soldiers as well. Where can he go, this poor *cholo,* with all exits from the country sealed off and only a stranger, a girl named Nellie, to help him? Only one place—back home to the Andes, to the cold white mountain peaks where the condors live. There, he might have a small chance for survival, a very small chance.

There is high drama and plenty of suspense in Atahaulpa's crime and its aftermath, but *Cholo* has much more than that to recommend it. It is a sharp and bitter depiction of South American poverty, of the people who endure it and who are destroyed by it. And Houston's prose is as lean, and yet as lyrical, as Hemingway's—the novel's opening paragraph, for instance:

> *He would have to kill the Chinaman. Every time the thought came, it startled him. He lay on his mat in the straw-mat shed on the roof, watching the signs as they came on and glowed fuzzily through the thickening* garua *fog. Coca-Cola, Philips, Datsun, Nestle—all that would be left of Lima's gray skyline in a few minutes. He would have to go down to the Chinaman's office early because of the curfew. At ten the streets would become paths through a gigantic graveyard. If in the silence the Chinaman cried out . . . no, God forgive him, he'd have to kill him.*

This is a work of considerable merit, told with passion and compassion in equal amounts. Few who read *Cholo* will find themselves unmoved by it.

Robert Houston is the author of several other novels, among them the global thriller *Ararat* (1982). To date, however, *Cholo* remains his most impressive and memorable work.

(*B.P.*)

Hoyt, Richard. *30 for a Harry.* New York: Evans, 1981. (PI)

Ex-newspaperman, ex–intelligence agent John Denson is now a Seattle private eye who enjoys screw-top wine and hangs out in a pub-type bar called Pig's Alley. He is described in the dust-jacket blurb of this novel, and in that of the first novel in which he appeared, *Decoys* (1980), as a "soft-boiled" sleuth. Don't be fooled; Denson is not all that soft-boiled. He *is* one of the better PIs—and Hoyt one of the better PI writers—to come along in the Eighties.

In this, the second Denson novel, he is hired to work undercover as a journalist at the *Seattle Star* to find out who their "harry" is. "Harry" refers to an old bit of newspaper legend. Harry Karafin, after three decades on the *Philadelphia Inquirer,* was exposed as having used his position—and knowledge gained from it—to blackmail local businessmen. The owner and publisher of the *Star,* and the paper's managing editor, suspecting they have a "harry" on their payroll, hire Denson to write "30"—newspaperese for "finish"—to whoever it may be. During his search Denson becomes involved in finding the murderer of reporter Wes Haggart and two young women who were with him at the time, plus the murderer of the hit man who killed them and of the go-between who paid the hit man—a series of events that originated with the "harry."

Recent titles in the action-packed Denson series are *The Siskiyou Two-Step* (1983), which was reprinted in paperback as simply *Siskiyou,* and *Fish Story* (1985).

(*R.J.R.*)

Hudson, Jeffrey. *A Case of Need.* Cleveland: World, 1968. (AD)

Jeffrey Hudson is a pseudonym of Michael Crichton, who also writes as John Lange (q.v.) and Michael Douglas. While Crichton is well known for his thrillers, this novel is considered by many critics to be his best work. Winner of the MWA Edgar for Best Novel of its year, *A Case of Need* is a medical mystery featuring a pathologist sleuth. It was written while Crichton was a medical student at Harvard University, and makes good use of both his medical knowledge and the background of Boston and its large and distinguished medical community. The controversial issues around which the story is centered—abortion and drug abuse—are handled frankly and realistically.

Pathologist John Berry is going about his normal routine when his wife calls to tell him his friend Art Lee has been arrested. Lee, an obstetrician, has been performing illegal abortions for a number of years, not for the money but because he feels an obligation to prevent women from seeking dangerous operations from unqualified practitioners. Now Karen Randall, member of a prominent medical family, has bled to death following an abortion; according to her stepmother, Karen named Dr. Lee as the man who performed the operation. Lee has been charged with murder, but he tells Berry he didn't do it.

Berry is determined to prove his friend's innocence, and he begins to investigate, looking into the dead girl's medical records and life. He finds Karen Randall was not the upstanding young lady her family would like everyone to believe she was: She was a liar, sexually promiscuous, and this was not her first abortion. But Berry's biggest surprise comes from the autopsy results: The girl may not have been pregnant at all, and someone seems determined to cover up that fact. Berry's search for the truth—which can be likened to his search for truth in the pathology lab—takes him from the opulent Randall home to the seedy back side of Beacon Hill; into autopsy rooms and drug pads; and up against the powerful Boston medical establishment. The truth, when he finds it, is surprising and painful, something that Berry—and the reader—will not forget for a long time to come.

This well-characterized novel is a "must read" for anyone who enjoys medical mysteries.

Under his own name, Crichton has written such novels as *The Andromeda Strain* (1969), another medical suspense novel; *The Terminal Man* (1972); and *The Great Train Robbery* (1975), which has a Victorian England setting and which became a successful film starring Sean Connery and Donald Sutherland.

(*M.M.*)

Huggins, Roy. *The Double Take.* New York: Morrow, 1949. (PI)

A minor but worthwhile Raymond Chandler (q.v.) imitation, *The Double Take* is noteworthy less for itself than for the number of times its author adapted and recycled the novel during his lengthy, illustrious television-writing career. Little of the humor Huggins would display in his television work is displayed in the novel, though his Chandleresque similes only occasionally strain and the dialogue is sharp, if not Rockford-wry. The clever, convoluted plot (hinging upon an advertising executive's wife whose past holds dark secrets) would be reworked by Huggins (usually under his John Thomas James pseudonym) on various television series for over twenty-five years.

The Double Take turns up as the story source material for episodes of "77 Sunset Strip," "Maverick," "The Rockford Files" (twice), "Baretta," "City of Angels," and probably every other series with which Huggins was associated. And Huggins has been a prolific, and able, contributor to series television; among the series he created and/or produced (in addition to those already mentioned) are "Cheyenne," "The Fugitive," "The Bold Ones," "The Virginian," and "Alias Smith and Jones."

The Double Take was specifically the source material for two television series: "77 Sunset Strip" (1958), which with "Peter Gunn" launched the wave of popularity for television private eyes in the late 1950s; and "City of Angels" (1975), a 1930s period piece co-created with Stephen J. Cannell (who also co-created "Rockford"). Vaguely seedy private eye Stuart Bailey of *The Double Take* has little in common with the slick portrayal by Efrem Zimbalist, Jr., in "77 Sunset Strip" (at least until the final season of the show, which jettisoned all of the characters but Bailey, settling him in the legendary Bradbury Building, in gritty, Jack Webb–produced episodes). But in the short-lived, fondly remembered "City of Angels," Wayne Rogers—playing private eye Jake Axminster—was *The Double Take*'s Bailey to perfection; among other things, Axminster's Bradbury Building office and his police adversary, Lieutenant Quint, are directly adapted from the 1949 Huggins novel. Various episodes of "City of Angels" adapted the handful of Stuart Bailey short stories written by Huggins for the "slicks" from 1946 to 1952; three of these were collected—and linked together by Huggins as an "original suspense novel"—by Dell in 1958, using the *77 Sunset Strip* title.

Huggins also wrote two James M. Cain–influenced suspense novels: *Too Late for Tears* (1947) and *Lovely Lady, Pity Me* (1949).

(*M.A.C.*)

*Hughes, Dorothy B. *In a Lonely Place.* New York: Duell, 1947. (PS)

The novels of Dorothy B. Hughes are disturbing and haunting, conveying a fine sense of place and character. Her settings are often the American Southwest, where she makes her home, or Los Angeles, where she lived for many years; and they are depicted in such rich detail that the reader comes away with the sense of actually having visited the places. To further this effect, Hughes utilizes minor characters, natives of the various locales, in a particularly effective way; she is adept at describing a person at considerable depth in a very few words. Her major characters are very often antiheroes—flawed men who know they should be better than they are but do not have the inner resources to accomplish this; or, in the case of this novel, out-and-out psychopaths.

In a Lonely Place is one of the best portraits of a psychopathic killer in American crime fiction. Dix Steele is a young man recently released from the air corps and living in post–World War II Los Angeles. He inhabits an apartment that is not his own (and uses the real owner's possessions and charge accounts); he claims to be writing a book (which he isn't); and periodically he wanders about the city, following women.

On one of these nights after he has followed a woman from a bus to her home on Santa Monica's California Incline near the sea, Dix goes to a bar; there, something someone says reminds him of his old buddy from the service, Brub Nicolai. Dix promised Brub he would get in touch with him when settled in L.A., so he calls him and goes to his house. Brub is now a detective with the Los Angeles Police Department, and married to a lovely, quiet woman named Sylvia. Dix feels an unreasonable resentment of Sylvia, but he continues to see the Nicolais, later bringing along a would-be actress named Laurel whom he meets at his apartment building. Dix is fiercely possessive of Laurel, and when she betrays him, the series of murders of young women (which Brub has been investigating and keeping Dix informed on) steps up in pace.

Through her third-person narrative, told entirely from Dix's viewpoint, Hughes gives us real insight into the mind of a psychopath. At the same time, she withholds just enough information to keep us wondering. A masterful character study, as well as a novel of relentlessly rising suspense.

In a Lonely Place was made into a 1950 film directed by Nicholas Ray and starring Humphrey Bogart and Gloria Grahame. Unfortunately, it is a heavily altered version of the book and thus lacks its impact.

(*M.M.*)

*Hughes, Dorothy B. *Ride the Pink Horse.* New York: Duell, 1946. (PS)

This novel, set in Santa Fe, New Mexico, during Fiesta Week, is Hughes's best-known work. In it she offers an in-depth characterization of both her protagonist (Sailor, a man come to town with a mission sorely out of keeping with the festive spirit of the week) and of the nature and inhabitants of Santa Fe, a town that is an intriguing amalgam of Mexican, American, and Indian cultures.

Sailor arrives in town from Chicago, not knowing it is Fiesta Week. There are no rooms to be had, so he leaves his suitcase at one of the crowded hotels and roams the streets pondering his problem. He has been on a bus for days and is rumpled and tired, in no condition to accomplish his mission; after all, he can't go up against Senator Willis Douglass ("the Sen") looking like this. But he must see the Sen, and see him soon. There is money owing Sailor from when he was on Douglass's staff back in Chicago. And if Douglass isn't willing to make good on the debt, Sailor is willing to tell a Homicide cop named McIntyre (who has also come from Chicago to Santa Fe) what he knows about the murder of the Sen's wife.

The story unfolds amid the trappings of Fiesta—the burning of Zozobra, Old Man Gloom; the festivities in the Plaza; the candlelit Procession to the Cross of the Martyrs. We come to know Sailor, a man from the wrong side of the Chicago tracks who made it out of the gutter through the Sen's organization and is desperately afraid he may end up there again. And Sailor comes to know the people of the town—particularly "Pancho," who runs the merry-go-round called *Tio Vivo* ("Lively Uncle"), and Pila, an Indian girl who has come for Fiesta, whom Sailor buys a soda pop and a ride on *Tio Vivo*'s pink horse. Through all this, Sailor—a decent man who does not know how to better himself in decent ways—plays a dangerous cat-and-mouse game with both the Sen and the cop from Chicago.

This excellent and gripping novel was made into a film in 1947, starring Robert Montgomery and Wanda Hendrix. While essentially faithful to the book, its happy Hollywood ending makes it less powerful.

Other notable Hughes novels are *The Fallen Sparrow* (1942), *The Blackbirder* (1943, also set in New Mexico), and *The Delicate Ape* (1944). (*M.M.*)

Hugo, Richard. *Death and the Good Life.* New York: St. Martin's, 1981. (PI)

The late Richard Hugo will long be remembered as one of our finest contemporary poets, whose haunting evocations of America's wilderness and of the wilderness of the human heart will endure. For devotees of mystery fiction, however, Hugo is best known as the friend and inspiration of his fellow Montana writer James Crumley (q.v.) and the source of the title of Crumley's finest novel, *The Last Good Kiss.*

The paradox about Hugo's own single mystery novel, *Death and the Good Life,* is that it owes so little to Crumley and so much to Ross Macdonald and Ellery Queen (qq.v.). Hugo follows Macdonald in making his protagonist a contemplative, compassionate man investigating crimes of the present with deep psychological roots in the past, varying the pattern only in that Hugo's Lew Archer figure is not a private eye at all but a cop—the softest-hearted, gentlest cop in the literature.

After seventeen years on the Seattle force, Al Barnes has taken early retirement and moved to western Montana, where he becomes a small-town deputy under a fat, cigar-chomping Indian sheriff. The quiet peace of the Northwest is shattered by a series of brutal ax murders apparently committed by a six-and-a-half-foot woman maniac. Mush Heart Barnes catches this lady before page 50 of *Death and the Good Life,* and then the real story begins. For it soon becomes clear that one of the ax murders in the series was not the woman's but the work of an imitator hoping to bury his own crime in the tangle of hers. The hunt for the copycat takes Barnes to Oregon—to Portland's most exclusive suburbs, where, indistinguishable from an Archeresque PI and showing not the least familiarity with police procedure, he exposes the secret vices of the rich and reopens a twenty-year-old murder case that will shatter the lives of everyone it touches.

Hugo writes simply and unpretentiously, with a bare minimum of linguistic color, and plots like the architect of the labyrinth. In both these respects he differs hugely from James Crumley. But he shares Crumley's genius for creating softly quirky incidental characters, like the tough Portland Homicide captain and the wily criminal-defense lawyer who on the side are both published poets. If only one could believe in Hugo's detective! With his overwhelming gentleness, his optimism about human nature, his feelings of guilt for the world's woes, his sudden subliminal intuitions, his habit of telling his inmost thoughts to murder suspects, his bizarre notion of a *Miranda* warning ("I'm placing you under arrest. You know your rights because you're rich"), Al Barnes simply fails to come across as any sort of credible cop. And when it's revealed that two of the moneyed-monster suspects have been secretly flogging their black servants, Hugo's contempt for the wealthy and powerful becomes laughable.

Death and the Good Life is no classic and will not survive as Hugo's best poetry will, but it's a fascinating misfire and a historical curiosity that despite its flaws is well worth reading.

(*F.M.N.*)

*Hull, Richard. *The Murder of My Aunt.* New York: Minton Balch, 1934. (C)

After an education at Rugby and a hitch in the British military, Richard Hull joined a team of accountants, and was a mediocre accountant at best. He then read a murder mystery, quit accounting, and settled into a successful writing career. We can thank fate that he did so.

The Murder of My Aunt begins in the provincial English countryside with a delightful account by the narrator of how silly and unpronounceable the name of the village—Llwll—is, and then moves briskly along into the memoirs of Edward, a man who wants to secure his freedom from his aunt Mildred. She, it seems, controls the purse strings to the entire family fortune—such as it is.

Edward is an "intellectual" who considers himself above all the petty people of Llwll. He sees them as common shepherds and shopkeepers, and he sets his aunt among them as a common, illiterate woman. Edward conceives of the idea of murdering his aunt in a most innocent, cunning way, and at the same time attempts to lead the reader to believe that he is the victim of this quaint and earthy woman's whims. Aunt Mildred, on the other hand, constantly scoffs at Edward's foppish ways, and delights in making a fool of him. The relationship between these two and their clever and witty dialogue make for the most humorous mystery.

This book gets to the core of British wit and human silliness, and is one of the most outstanding pieces of artistic comedy you will ever come across. It is the apex of Hull's body of work, which includes *The Murderers of Monty* (1937), *My Own Murderer* (1940), and *The Unfortunate Murderer* (1942).

(*T.S.*)

Hunt, E. Howard. *The Violent Ones.* Greenwich, Conn.: Fawcett Gold Medal, 1950. (O/A)

If history remembers E. Howard Hunt at all, it will be as a convicted Watergate conspirator rather than a man who won a Guggenheim Creative

Writing Fellowship and later went on to write a great many paperback novels under several names, including his own.

In *The Violent Ones,* Paul Cameron returns home from World War II to become an assistant professor of French. When his wife takes a lover, he beats the man, crippling him for life. After serving a prison sentence, Cameron flies to France to help an old friend, who has a lead on some American gold left over from the war. The friend is murdered; Cameron meets three alluring women, one of whom he loved during the war and none of whom is to be trusted; he is savagely beaten at least three times; he administers a savage beating of his own to a homosexual who may be involved with the gold; he travels over a good part of France and into Switzerland. All of this happens in fewer than 140 pages.

If this sounds like an almost archetypal Gold Medal novel of the early 1950s, it is, and a pretty good one. It is difficult to sympathize with the burned-out Cameron, but Hunt does make the character credible. There are also some interesting experiments with second-person writing in an attempt to involve the reader in the story and put him into Cameron's situation. If Hunt doesn't quite bring these sections off, he has nevertheless tried something that few others have done.

Of interest among Hunt's other novels are *The Judas Hour* (1951) and *The Berlin Ending* (1973). He also wrote as Robert Dietrich (q.v.), Gordon Davis, John Baxter, and David St. John.

(*B.C.*)

Hunter, Alan. *Death on the Broadlands.* New York: Walker, 1983. (T)

This is a curiously compelling book. Curious because at first not a great deal happens: A woman recovering from a failed love affair travels to the East Anglia broadlands and rents a cottage for the summer. Compelling because we become interested in the woman and the people she meets, and we have a feeling *something* is about to happen, but no idea what that something will be.

Stella Rushton is the jilted woman and the book's primary character. Through her eyes we meet the other characters—mostly theater people visiting her landlord. After we are well into the story, our suspicions are confirmed and things begin to happen. There is a brief love affair with a younger man—the landlord's nephew—and soon after there is a death. The death, at first thought to be accidental, turns out to be murder, and Stella begins an amateurish investigation of her own that leads her to suspect who the murderer might be.

As do all of Hunter's novels, this one features Chief Superintendent George Gently of Scotland Yard, although the superintendent (who is vacationing in the broadlands) does not make an appearance until halfway through the book and does not become active in the story until about two-thirds of the way through. Once involved, however, he wraps up the case quickly and neatly, which follows an established pattern in the series. As Hunter himself has been quoted as saying, Gently "comes into a situation which has arisen over months, perhaps years, at its moment of crisis, and acts as a catalyst to bring it to a climax. To understand what is happening he must understand those involved and their relations during the previous development of the situation. Only then can he make a correct interpretation of circumstance and evidence."

Hunter, a Zen-Buddhist ex–poultry farmer who later turned to crime writing, has published close to thirty Gently novels, beginning with *Gently Does It* (1955). Other noteworthy titles include *Gently Floating* (1963), *Gently with the Innocents* (1974), and *Gently to a Sleep* (1978).

(*N.D./B.P.*)

Hunter, Evan. *A Horse's Head.* New York: Delacorte, 1967. (C)

Anyone who has read his 87th Precinct procedural series (as by Ed McBain, q.v.) knows that Evan Hunter has a well-developed and ofttimes ribald sense of humor. But nowhere is that sense of humor better exhibited than in *A Horse's Head*—a wacky farce that rivals anything written by Donald Westlake (q.v.) for comic invention, boffo laughs, and sheer exuberance. It also has one element that Westlake's novels generally lack (but Hunter's never do): plenty of sex, including but not limited to a seduction in the stacks of the New York City Public Library.

The hero of *A Horse's Head* is Andrew Mullaney, professional gambler, man of the world, and horse's ass. As the novel opens, Mullaney is standing on a Manhattan street corner, wondering where he can float a loan to finance a hot tip at Aqueduct, when a long black limousine pulls to the curb and a guy with a beard and a long black gun gets out and pushes Mullaney in. It's a case of mistaken identity, Mullaney thinks. But he's wrong. The people who have kidnapped him want *him,* all right—or rather, they want his corpse because they seem to have lost one of their own. They dress him up in a black suit, knock him on the head, and stuff him into a coffin.

And that's just the beginning.

What transpires after that involves the library, a cemetery in Queens, a subway train, an East Side cellar synagogue, assorted bad guys, assorted beautiful women, several madcap chases, and a "magical" black jacket that is somehow worth half a million dollars. Zany stuff, and a sure cure for the blues.

Hunter published one other comic crime novel, *Every Little Crook and*

Nanny (1972), which takes some marvelous shots at certain highly thought-of literary critics. A number of his serious novels also have criminous elements, most notably *A Matter of Conviction* (1959) and *Lizzie* (1984), an interesting "solution" to the Lizzie Borden mystery.

(*B.P.*)

Huxley, Elspeth. *The African Poison Murders.* New York: Harper, 1939. (W/H)

Elspeth Huxley, born in 1907, spent most of her childhood in Njoro, Kenya, as recounted in her well-known memoir *The Flame Trees of Thika.* She has written novels, biography, and travel books all her life, but of particular interest is a series of detective novels set in Kenya that she wrote in the 1930s.

These books feature Superintendent Vachell of the Chania CID, a young, warm-blooded fellow who learned his trade in the Royal Canadian Mounted Police. He is tall and thin with "the sandy hair and long jaw of the true Scot," a "high-cheeked, bony face, and . . . large mouth which seemed ready to expand at any moment into a friendly grin." Vachell loves Africa and police work, he loves the chase, and, as readers learn in *The African Poison Murders,* he is not above loving another man's wife.

Vachell is summoned to the farm of Dennis West because a feud between West and his neighbor, Karl Munson, has turned ugly; animals have been tortured and an African worker has been killed. The assignment suits Vachell because he has heard of this Munson, a leader in the local Nazi movement that is being closely watched by colonial police. Vachell is also very aware of Janice West, Commander West's wife, with whom he has fallen immediately—but silently—in love.

Everyone assumes that the loathsome Munson is behind the violence, but then Munson himself is poisoned in his flower-drying shed. Not long after, West is also murdered. All the evidence indicates that Janice is the killer. Vachell arrests her, but he can't believe she's guilty. If not she, though, then who? And why? Vachell finds the answers while deep in the jungle, pinned in a leopard trap while a crazed killer tries to take one more life with a poison-tipped stick.

Huxley's other Superintendent Vachell mysteries include *Murder at Government House* (1937) and *Murder on Safari* (1938). Her work is notable not only for its exotic, authentic settings, but also for her understanding of Kenya's peoples. In *The African Poison Murders,* she wrote:

"(Vachell) seemed to have run into a blind alley. Investigations in Africa often did. In Europe or America people were generally at hand to be questioned; whatever a person did, there usually turned out to be a looker-on. But here in Africa, life was lived on two levels, with a barrier between the two. Natives might see and hear and register, but to the police be blind and deaf and blank. What white men did was no affair of theirs; what they did was at all times to be hidden from the whites."

(*M.J.*)

Iles, Francis. *Malice Aforethought.* New York: Harper, 1931. (PS)

Francis Iles is a pseudonym of Anthony Berkeley (q.v.) Cox, and this novel is considered by many to be a classic of the genre. Heaven only knows why. It starts with a marvelous line: "It was not until several weeks after he had decided to murder his wife that Dr. Bickleigh took any active steps in the matter." Good! we think. Here's something to really hold our interest. And we sit down, expecting to shortly witness murder most foul. Instead we wait. And wait. And wait.

First we are treated to an exhaustive (and exhausting) description of a tennis party, complete with a large (and mainly indistinguishable) cast of characters. We view Teddy Bickleigh being pushed around by his terrible wife, Julia, and just as we are beginning to work up some sympathy for the man, we find out he is a philanderer. Then we receive a rundown on Teddy's life, which explains why he chases women but does not succeed in excusing it. The psychological profiling of both Bickleighs is probably the best thing in this book, but it goes on far too long.

If Teddy and his wife aren't likable, neither is anyone else—from prissy Gwynyfryd Rattery, whom Teddy initially imagines himself in love with, to duplicitous Madeleine Cranmere, with whom Teddy is later smitten, to the village vicar himself. And it does take Teddy an interminable time to get on with his murder—so long that when it finally happens, it's more of a relief than a shock. This book is slow going and, like its protagonist, seems to have few redeeming qualities.

The other Iles titles are *Before the Fact* (1938) and *As for the Woman* (1939).

(*M.M.*)

*Innes, Hammond. *North Star.* New York: Knopf, 1975. (A)

Hammond Innes is a giant among writers of high-adventure fiction. One reason is his passion for background detail, all of it authentic and gathered during the six months each year he spends traveling. (The other six months are spent writing, of course.) Although many of his characters seem larger than life, they are pitted against the worst that nature can deliver. The craftsmanship and realism of each Innes book carries the reader to places still exotic and often savage—places such as Saudi Arabia, Morocco, the outback of Australia, New Guinea, Antarctica, Labrador, and the Indian Ocean.

North Star features one of Innes's specialties: a story of men against the sea. Michael Randall is a man whose life is collapsing around him. His wife has abandoned him, and he himself has abandoned the elite world of his wealthy stepfather. Randall leaps at the challenge put to him by a financial whirlwind named Villiers: to help launch a desperate quest for discovery of oil beneath the treacherous waters of the North Sea. With a ragtag crew and an aging drilling platform called the *North Star,* Randall battles the sea and a series of tangled plots aimed at sabotaging the search. But the highlight of the novel is Randall's struggle to steer the drifting *North Star* to safety during a furious North Atlantic storm.

This is high adventure at its best, with a vividly drawn background, good characterization, and excitement on every page.

Another fine Innes novel of men versus the fury of the sea is *The Wreck of the Mary Deare* (1956). Also recommended are *The White South* (1950), set in Antarctica; *The Doomed Oasis* (1960), which takes place on the burning desert sands of Saudi Arabia; *Levkas Man* (1971), which transports us to the islands of Greece; and *The Golden Soak* (1973), a tale of the barren wastes of Australia.

(*G.K.*)

*Innes, Michael. *Appleby and Honeybath.* New York: Dodd, Mead, 1983. (PP)

Since 1937, Michael Innes has been delighting ever-increasing audiences with his balance of wit, humor, superior character development, and literate and precise command of the English language. His series character, John Appleby, member of Scotland Yard's Criminal Investigation Department, is a well-mannered and educated Englishman who begins his career as an inspector and ends up as superintendent of the Yard. Readers can follow Appleby throughout his career (and eventual retirement), as well as through his romance, marriage, and various other personal developments.

This case is a late entry in the series, a postretirement investigation that brings Appleby together with Charles Honeybath, a portrait artist and featured character in some of Innes's other books. Both men are weekend guests of a country squire, Terence Grinton, at his estate, Grinton Hall, Honeybath having been commissioned to paint the host in his Master of the Hunt attire. Murder intervenes, replete with a body that inexplicably disappears from a locked library. The ensuing investigation probes into the library's history, as well as the Grinton family, past and present. And it takes all of Appleby's investigative skills, plus Honeybath's insight into the art world, before they reach a joint solution.

In many of the later cases in this popular series, Appleby is accompanied by his charming wife, Judith, who is remotely related to the Grinton family. When he is talking over his cases with her, snippets of information often fall into place, and this domestic aspect greatly adds to the overall appeal of the novels.

This is one series that just keeps getting better and better.

(*E.N./M.M.*)

Innes, Michael. *A Private View.* New York: Dodd, Mead, 1953. (PP)

In this, his sixth adventure, Appleby has become Sir John and is the assistant commissioner of police, living in London. His wife, Judith, an accomplished sculptor, has asked him to accompany her to a memorial exhibition of the works of a recently murdered artist. She is looking for an abstract painting to use as a backdrop for one of her own statues—but the Applebys find much more than that.

Not long after their arrival at the Da Vinci Gallery, a painting that John has just been examining with bemused amazement is stolen. Another work—a priceless Vermeer—has also recently been stolen from the Duke of Horton. Appleby begins to suspect a tie between these two larcenies that have occurred in entirely different spheres of the art world. Also, a young woman who lived above the Da Vinci Gallery has disappeared—and she subsequently is murdered. Appleby becomes deeply involved with all three cases; and with her connections in society and the art world, Judith plays a large part in gathering information for him. There are colorful scenes with denizens of the artistic community, including a visit to the stately home of Lady Clancarron, who wants Appleby to clear up an alleged artistic vice, as well as the usual quiet domestic analysis this couple is so skilled at. And the resolution is sure to please any Innes fan.

This is a mellow exposition of the kind of high- and low-level crime that British writers excel at describing. Innes can write about anything, but he is particularly skilled when dealing with the art world—new movements, old architecture, and the foibles of eccentric and aristocratic patrons. The investigative details are well explicated without detracting from the characterization or steady, low-key movement of his plot.

(*E.N.*)

Innes, Michael. *Seven Suspects.* New York: Dodd, Mead, 1937. (PP)

Never have so many colleges and universities suffered from the sudden and curious deaths of faculty members and students than in the Innes novels. British academic life is a world of its own, seldom better described than in this novel, Appleby's debut. The reader is taken on a tour of a large university, complete with map, dotty dons, and sinister academic undercurrents.

The head of St. Anthony's College, Josiah Umpleby, has been shot to death in his residence. Because of a complicated series of locked doors, it appears that only a member of the faculty could have been responsible. The body, dressed in a dinner jacket, had a visiting professor's academic gown wrapped around its head, and a pile of aborigine bones (!) lay on the floor nearby. All faculty members who were present on the scene that night seem eager to cooperate by accusing one another and revealing to Appleby the most outrageous bits of scandal about their colleagues that he could ever hope to hear. With so many conflicting stories, it seems unlikely that the determined (if a bit plodding) inspector can sort out the truth from the distortions and petty jealousies. But he does—and admirably so.

In this series, hardly an English country mansion or academic setting has escaped its murder quota—since both Appleby and his frequent cohort Honeybath seem to have an entree to all these settings, both aristocratic and middle-class. Effective use is made of convoluted relationships and motives, and no two of Innes's books are alike (although his tendency to allow the murderer to commit suicide offstage, after confessing and explaining his crimes in considerable detail, becomes a bit tiring and unbelievable after a while).

Other especially good novels about Appleby, Honeybath, and their cohorts are *The Daffodil Affair* (1942), *Death on a Quiet Day* (1957), *The Bloody Wood* (1966), *An Awkward Lie* (1971), *The Ampersand Papers* (1979), and *Carson's Conspiracy* (1984).

(*E.N.*)

*Irish, William. *Phantom Lady*. Philadelphia: Lippincott, 1942. (PS)

A man quarrels with his wife, goes out and picks up a woman in a bar, spends the evening with her, and comes home to find his wife dead and himself accused of her murder. All the evidence is against him and his only hope is to find the woman who was with him when his wife was killed. But she seems to have vanished into thin air, and everyone in a position to know—the nameless bartender at Anselmo's, the cabdriver, the jazz drummer, the peppery Latina entertainer—swears that no such woman ever existed. The man is convicted and sentenced to die; and his secretary, who has long loved him, joins with his best friend in a desperate race against the clock, hunting through the night catacombs of New York for the phantom lady and the reason why so many witnesses couldn't see her.

This is the kind of waking nightmare that is the essence of *noir* fiction, and in his fourth suspense novel Cornell Woolrich (q.v.), writing under the pseudonym William Irish, captures superbly the emotional torment and terror of the situation. There have been dozens of crime stories about the fight to save an innocent person from the death penalty, but the race against time and mortality was a Woolrich hallmark; and unlike other writers, he never lets us forget that ultimately the race will be lost and all of us must die. Indeed, each of *Phantom Lady*'s chapter titles refers to the number of days left before the execution.

Woolrich borrowed the plot from one of his 1939 pulp stories, "Those Who Kill." What he added for *Phantom Lady* was the amalgam of elements that have become identified with him: feverish emotions, pounding suspense, and a doom-laden atmosphere. The plot is so full of Gothic involution that the final explanations require about two dozen closely printed pages, but the best feature of the book is its powerful emotional moments. Who but Woolrich could have written the scene where the morgue attendants are dragging out the body of Scott Henderson's wife and suddenly a little whiff of her perfume comes "drifting out of the empty bedroom, seeming to whisper: 'Remember? Remember when I was your love? Remember?' "

Phantom Lady was written at white heat during a period when Woolrich was creating the finest suspense novels of the time in a few months apiece. After a quarrel with editor Lee Wright, he withdrew the manuscript from Simon & Schuster, the firm that had published the so-called Black Series, and it wound up at Lippincott as the first Woolrich book under the pseudonym William Irish. Eventually the new by-line so overshadowed Woolrich that in France, where he's considered one of the great American writers, he is known almost exclusively as Irish and the name Cornell Woolrich is all but forgotten.

The novel was a huge success not only in its original edition but as a book-club selection, a paperback, and in adaptations into other media. The 1944 movie of *Phantom Lady,* starring Ella Raines and Franchot Tone and directed by *noir* specialist Robert Siodmak, is far from perfect but captures in its bizarre visual style much of the bleakness of the Woolrich universe. (*F.M.N.*)

*Irish, William. *I Wouldn't Be in Your Shoes.* Philadelphia: Lippincott, 1943. (SS)

In the years before his first suspense novel, Cornell Woolrich had written dozens of blood-chilling crime stories for the great pulp magazines of the Thirties like *Detective Fiction Weekly, Dime Detective,* and *Black Mask.* After the success of *Phantom Lady,* publishers were eager to bring out collections of these stories, and *I Wouldn't Be in Your Shoes* was the first of a long run of volumes that even today, more than fifteen years after Woolrich's death, is still continuing.

It consists of five novelettes, first published between 1935 and 1941, which rank among the finest *noir* fiction. "I Wouldn't Be in Your Shoes" (1938) is about an insignificant little man who is sentenced to die in the electric chair because one stifling hot night he threw a shoe out his open window at a yowling cat. The suspense mounts as the man's wife and an enigmatic homicide detective race the clock to find new evidence that will stop the execution. A tauntingly ambiguous climax brings this tour de force to an end.

"Last Night," a revision of "The Red Tide" (1940), belongs to a category uniquely Woolrichian, the Is-my-spouse/lover/buddy-a-murderer? story. The viewpoint character is a young woman whom we watch being torn apart by the suspicion that her desperate husband has murdered a wealthy guest at their failing dude ranch and hidden the body in some inaccessible place. Woolrich tightens the screws masterfully as evidence mounts, is explained away (or is it?), then mounts higher.

"Three O'Clock" (1938) puts us inside the mind and skin of Paul Stapp, who lies bound and gagged and immobile in his own basement while a time bomb just out of his reach ticks away toward the hour of 3:00 when he'll be blown to bits. Embodying Woolrich's terror before the specter of death and packed with unbearable suspense and anguish as the helpless everyman tries to save himself, this may well be the most powerful story Woolrich ever wrote.

The protagonist of "Nightmare" (1941) comes out of a dream in which he stabbed a total stranger to death in an octagonal mirrored room—then, to his horror, discovers more and more evidence that he wasn't dreaming but actually committed a brutal murder while out of himself.

"Papa Benjamin" (1935) deals with a jazz composer/bandleader who is put under a curse for learning too much about a New Orleans voodoo cult.

Of the five suspense classics collected in this volume, two were adapted into theatrical *films noir*—the better is *Fear in the Night* (1947), based on "Nightmare"—and two more became the bases for sixty-minute TV films. One of these, "Four O'Clock" (1957), was directed by that no less death-haunted soul-brother of Woolrich, Alfred Hitchcock.

(*F.M.N.*)

*Irish, William. *Deadline at Dawn.* Philadelphia: Lippincott, 1944. (PS)

The setting that Cornell Woolrich made peculiarly and forever his own is the New York City streetscape after dark, and the people who prowl those streets in the long and lonely hours are the protagonists of his *noir* world. In *Deadline at Dawn,* which was the second Woolrich novel to be published under his William Irish by-line, the entire action takes place on a single night in the bleak streets and man-made caves of New York, and the unique chapter heads allow us literally to see the passage of time as a man and woman are forced into a race against the clock, knowing they'll be trapped forever unless they can escape from the city before the sun rises.

Of all Woolrich's major novels, this one is the brightest and most cheerful. Usually when he employed wild coincidences (as he often did), they served as agents of people's destruction, but *Deadline* takes off from the most benevolent coincidence in the canon. On the run from a murder that he knows he'll be accused of come morning, Quinn Williams blunders into a taxi-dance joint, dazedly buys a hundred tickets, and chooses for his partner none other than a girl named Bricky who grew up one street away from his childhood home in Glen Falls, Iowa! The story line is loose and relaxed, featuring many characters and incidents without connection to the main plot. But the cliff-hanger crosscutting between Quinn's and Bricky's searches through the night streets keeps the tension high, and the two-pronged quest is punctuated by touches of pure *noir*. Bricky, for example, is an emotional basket case, a paranoid who has anthropomorphized New York City into a personal enemy out to ruin her. The only god she can pray to is a clock. "Oh, Clock on the Paramount, that I can't see from here, the night is nearly over and the bus has nearly gone. Let me go home tonight." Woolrich makes her fear so vivid that one all but forgets there will be another bus leaving for Iowa the next day.

The 1946 movie *Deadline at Dawn,* starring Susan Hayward and Bill Williams, was a curious and generally unsatisfying picture; directed by theatrical wizard Harold Clurman from a screenplay by playwright Clifford Odets, it had only remote similarities to Woolrich's novel. But a few of the film's images and haunting emotional moments capture perfectly the darkness of the Woolrich world.

(*F.M.N.*)

*Irish, William. *I Married a Dead Man.* Philadelphia: Lippincott, 1948. (PS)

A woman with nothing to live for and in flight from her sadistic husband is injured in a train wreck. She wakes up in a hospital bed surrounded by luxuries because, as she eventually realizes, she's been wrongly identified as another woman, one who had everything to live for but died in the train disaster. She grasps what seems to be a heaven-sent new life; but as time goes on—and especially as her husband invades her second identity—it turns into a gift from the malevolent god who rules the Woolrich world. At the novel's climax, she and we are confronted with only two possibilities, neither of which makes the least sense and each of which will destroy innocent lives. "I don't know what the game was," she says. "I only know we must have played it wrong, somewhere along the way. . . . We've lost. That's all I know. We've lost. And now the game is through."

This was Woolrich's last major novel and one of the finest and bleakest stories he ever wrote. The book began life as "They Call Me Patrice," a 1946 women's-magazine novelette that—thanks to a perfectly timed confession by a character who hadn't even been mentioned till that moment—ended on a deliriously happy note. What distinguishes the hardcover novel from the magazine version is its new and radically innovative climax. Either the protagonist, Helen, has been lying to us throughout (which is unthinkable), or Bill, who loves her desperately, has been lying to Helen (which is just as unthinkable). There is no third possibility—unless, as Woolrich wants us to see, logic doesn't work and the world is abandoned to darkness. This was too much for the makers of the radio version, broadcast on "Suspense," and the 1950 movie starring Barbara Stanwyck, retitled *No Man of Her Own,* both of which opted for variants on the women's-magazine happy ending.

Woolrich continued to write haphazardly for another twenty years until his death in 1968, but his golden age was the period from 1934, when he sold his first crime story to a pulp magazine, until the publication of *I Married a Dead Man* and *Rendezvous in Black* in 1948. Some of the best of his more than 200 suspense stories and novelettes are included in early collections published under his William Irish by-line, others of which are *After-Dinner Story* (1944), *The Dancing Detective* (1946), *Dead Man Blues* (1947), and *Somebody on the Phone* (1950). The hugest Woolrich story collection, published a few years after his death, is *Nightwebs* (1971). Like his novels, many of Woolrich's short stories have been adapted into movies, of which by far the most famous is Alfred Hitchcock's 1954 *Rear Window.*

(*F.M.N.*)

Irvine, R. R. *Freeze Frame.* New York: Popular Library, 1976. (O/AD)

Television is a fascinating medium, not so much for what viewers see of it (which simply isn't very interesting, stimulating, or artistic these days) but for what goes on behind the scenes. All sorts of intrigue, among other things, up to and including murder—the fictional variety, anyhow. Only a few TV-related series sleuths have appeared to date, but at least three have made their marks: Charles Larson's (q.v.) crime-show producer Nils-Frederick Blixen, William DeAndrea's (q.v.) network troubleshooter Matt Cobb, and R. R. Irvine's Action Reporter Bob Christopher.

Christopher works for Channel 3's "6 O'Clock News" in Los Angeles as "an electronic Mr. Fix-it. Welfare check late? Write the Action Reporter. Swindled out of lifelong savings? Write . . . Bob Christopher." He gets the lovelorn letters, too. And the threats. And a whole lot more. The old Apache woman, Luzita Cruz, for instance. When she first approaches him with her tale of woe, Christopher thinks somebody hired her to put him on: She says city bulldozers have leveled her house without reason or warning. But when he investigates, he finds that her story is true, and that the leveling was a "mistake" on the part of the Planning Department, owing to a new freeway that is being built close to Luzita's property. Always on the side of the underdog, Christopher campaigns publicly to get Luzita a new house. He succeeds—but not without taking his lumps from a couple of thugs dressed as the Lone Ranger and Tonto, whom he suspects are in the employ of Metric Oil, a huge conglomerate with designs on Luzita's holdings.

Matters turn even nastier after the old woman's new house is built: Christopher finds her beaten to death inside it. Determined to track down her killer, he takes on Metric Oil's western regional manager, Darrell Riggs; the former city planning officer, a nasty piece of goods named Gilson, who is now working for Metric; the Indian Power movement and its leader, Reverend Little Bear; Luzita's beautiful great-granddaughter (or is she?), Sacheme; the Lone Ranger and Tonto again; and his own network. And when he finally does see justice done, it is not without its painful personal price.

Irvine knows whereof he writes, having himself worked behind the scenes at a Los Angeles TV station, and he liberally sprinkles his narrative with informative details on news gathering and broadcasting. His style is breezy and humorous, with a good deal of wisecracking interplay among Christopher and such Channel 3 luminaries as assignment editor Wayne Gossett, news director Herb Reisner, newswriter Ralph Tomlinson, and egomaniac anchorman Lee Barnes. The plot is solid, if a little melodramatic in spots, and the wisecracking is nicely tempered with healthy doses of compassion and sentiment. All in all, a pleasant evening's entertainment—much better than watching TV.

Bob Christopher also appears in two other paperback originals: *Jump Cut* (1974) and *Horizontal Hold* (1978); his first hardcover appearance, *Ratings Are Murder,* was published in 1985. R. R. Irvine has also written one other TV mystery, *The Face Out Front* (1977), this one featuring ex-anchorman turned producer Tim Bishop.

(*B.P.*)

*Ives, John. *Fear in a Handful of Dust.* New York: Dutton, 1978. (PS/T)

John Ives is the pseudonym used by Brian Garfield (q.v.) for a pair of suspense novels published in the late 1970s. *Fear in a Handful of Dust* is the first and best of these—a book that Alfred Coppel has justifiably praised as "a remarkable tale of violence and survival. I found it unique and disturbing and a thoroughly engrossing story."

Calvin Duggai, an Indian turned psychotic by his war experiences in Vietnam, has developed an unreasoning hatred for four psychiatrists who treated him and who he believes have robbed him of his human dignity. To exact vengeance, he kidnaps the four, one of whom is a woman; takes them far into the Arizona desert; and abandons them there to die. But unbeknown to Duggai, one of the three men, Sam Mackenzie, is both a survivor and knowledgeable in the ways of the desert. Mackenzie organizes the group, teaches them survival skills, gives them hope. Even so, "Mackenzie's group has two problems to counter that go beyond the hostility of their environment," as the dust-jacket blurb puts it. "One is Duggai himself, who could return at any time to finish them off. The other is their own despair, as frustration and exhaustion chip away at their will to survive."

Despite Coppel's use of the word, there is very little violence in these pages; rather, it is the threat of violence, the aura of constant menace, that gives the novel its high level of tension. The desert background is superbly evoked. Garfield grew up in Arizona and knows its wastelands intimately; he has written of it before in several novels, but never better than in these pages. You can literally *feel* the heat, the emptiness; and the four protagonists' suffering and despair become all the more real as a result. This is suspense writing at its finest—spare, taut, and quite powerful indeed.

The second Ives novel is *The Marchand Woman* (1979), which has a Mexican setting. It has its moments, certainly, and Garfield's usual high-quality prose, but it lacks the elemental simplicity and unflagging tension of *Fear in a Handful of Dust*.

(*B.P.*)

Jacks, Jeff. *Murder on the Wild Side.* Greenwich, Conn.: Fawcett Gold Medal, 1971. (O/PI)

Nothing is known about "Jeff Jacks"; the quotation marks around his name are not necessarily intended to indicate a pseudonym. This tough, gritty, street-wise New York PI novel—and its single sequel, *Find the Don's Daughter* (1973)—is copyrighted by its publisher. The best of the two books is this one; the second, while well done, was an obvious attempt to cash in on the Mafia-book craze of the early 1970s.

Murder on the Wild Side introduces ex-cop private investigator Shep Stone, who becomes involved in the murder of a Greenwich Village handkerchief lady after he leaves Ponzo's Bar at 11:30 one night, "an early time for me to quit drinking." Also on the trail of a missing girl, Shep tangles with a tough cop; with the owner of a handkerchief boutique called Cyn-Cyn; with a fashion editor who first brought publicity to Cyn-Cyn, making a plaything of its owner, and who was heard to threaten the handkerchief lady; and with an array of New York's "characters," saloons, and shops.

The appealing thing about this novel—and its sequel—is not its plot. Rather, it is the "team" of Shep Stone and New York City. The author manages to bring to life both the sleaze and the charm of the city, elevating it to the position of a supporting character. He actually brings the streets to life, with an impact that is rare and wonderful.

In reading this book, one can't help but notice the parallels between the hard-drinking Shep Stone and Lawrence Block's (q.v.) equally hard-drinking Matt Scudder, as well as the similar styles in which their cases are narrated. Could Jeff Jacks possibly *be* Lawrence Block?

(*R.J.R.*)

Jahn, Michael. *Night Rituals.* New York: Norton, 1982. (PS/PP)

Although Michael Jahn was presented with an MWA Best Paperback Edgar for his 1977 novel *The Quark Maneuver,* his finest work to date is *Night Rituals,* a forceful combination of procedural, thriller, and psychological suspense novel.

Young women are being ritualistically killed in New York's Riverside Park. They have been bound hand and foot with palm fronds and all of the blood has been removed from their bodies. Their heads are laid on a bed of white violets, and for twenty feet around them the garbage that infests the park has been swept away.

The task of solving these grisly murders falls to Bill Donovan, commander of the West Side Major Crimes Unit. Donovan, who hangs out at Riley's Saloon—where the night barmaid, Rosie, has become his new girlfriend—begins to suspect that the killer is one of the saloon's customers. This suspicion is strengthened when Rosie's younger sister becomes a victim.

Donovan is assisted by his close friend and sergeant, Thomas Jefferson Lincoln. The black sergeant, known for hating Puerto Ricans, is nicknamed "Pancho" by Donovan. Clues alternately point to some of Manhattan's street people—American Indians, Haitian refugees, people who deal in rituals. But when Donovan's investigation becomes stonewalled, he enlists the aid of an old lover, a black undercover cop named Marcie Barnes, setting her up in the park as a decoy for the psycho killer—a move that almost gets both of them killed.

Mike Jahn's talent for vividly depicting the people and streets of New York is considerable, and makes *Night Rituals* the most riveting of his novels.

(*R.J.R.*)

Jakes, John. *Johnny Havoc and the Doll Who Had "It."* New York: Belmont, 1963. (O/PI/C)

Before John Jakes achieved considerable success with his "Kent Family Chronicles" series of historical novels, he labored for many years in the paperback-original market, turning out suspense novels, historicals, soft-core sex items, and an entertaining four-book screwball mystery series starring Johnny Havoc. Havoc is a hot-tempered, five-foot-one hustler with a penchant for getting into murder scrapes and running afoul of the law, in the person of Detective First Grade FitzHugh Goodpasture. The series was obviously intended to tap into the success enjoyed by Richard Prather's (q.v.) Shell Scott series, though the setup is more reminiscent of Frank Gruber's (q.v.) Johnny Fletcher novels.

Havoc, broke as usual, is filling in for a sick friend as a street-corner Santa Claus when a thug comes by demanding an envelope containing blackmail papers. Johnny gets bounced around by various gangsters, but, smelling money, deals himself into the operation. Along the way, he manages to incite two very funny minor riots, one in a toy-department Santa Land. There are actually *two* dolls possessing some sort of "it": One is Wednesday Wilde, a pneumatic five-foot starlet; the other is "Feend-O the Ferocious," a toy robot with the missing papers (the old "Six Napoleons" gambit).

The Johnny Havoc books are lightweight, energetic comedies, a bit silly in spots but better than many of the breed. The others are *Johnny Havoc* (1960), *Johnny Havoc Meets Zelda* (1962), and *Making It Big* (1968).

(*A.S.*)

*James, P. D. *The Black Tower.* New York: Scribner's, 1975. (PP)

The novels of P. D. James have enjoyed great popularity and critical acclaim in recent years. This is due to the fact that they resemble the better works of the Golden Age, such as those of Marsh, Sayers, and Tey; yet they are also very much in step with current times. James draws her characters in considerable psychological depth; her series characters—Commander Adam Dalgliesh of Scotland Yard and, more recently, private investigator Cordelia Gray—grow and change in response to the circumstances to which their jobs subject them. James's settings are as contemporary as her characters, and she explores such modern institutions as a forensic-science laboratory (*Death of an Expert Witness,* 1977), a psychiatric outpatient clinic (*A Mind to Murder,* 1967), and a training college for nurses (*Shroud for a Nightingale,* 1971).

Adam Dalgliesh is a well-drawn character with antecedents in Lord Peter Wimsey, Hercule Poirot, and Roderick Alleyn. A widower who has found an avocation in poetry, he has a passion for justice and a dedication to his job that, coupled with a natural intuitive talent, allow him to carry out what might seem impossible investigative feats in a thoroughly realistic way. Dalgliesh is both insightful about the people around him and introspective about his own reactions and motives.

In *The Black Tower,* the commander's sixth case, Dalgliesh is recovering from a severe bout of mononucleosis; and as one often does after a serious illness, he is having doubts about the direction his life has taken. While considering whether he should leave Scotland Yard, he receives a letter from a friend, Father Baddeley, chaplain at a private home for the disabled, Toynton Grange. The father wishes to consult him on a professional matter, and Dalgliesh, hopeful of a peaceful respite on the Dorset coast, decides to journey there. Upon his arrival, he finds that his friend has died, presumably of a heart attack, and was cremated almost a week ago. Dalgliesh quickly realizes that something is wrong at the Grange: The home's future is in doubt, and until the matter can be settled, no more patients are to be admitted. There were originally six, but one, Victor Holroyd, recently killed himself by driving his wheelchair over a cliff above the sea.

As Dalgliesh watches the situation at Toynton Grange further deteriorate, he soon becomes aware of undercurrents of intrigue and hatred. Hindered by his weakened physical condition, he nonetheless begins to look into the suspicious death of the man in the wheelchair—and into other deaths that follow.

This is an engrossing novel that gives excellent glimpses into James's primary series character. Also notable is her portrait of Ursula Hollis, a young woman with a progressively debilitating disease who has been forced to face it and come to terms with the realization that she will continue to deteriorate.

(*M.M.*)

James, P. D. *An Unsuitable Job for a Woman.* New York: Scribner's, 1973. (PI)

In *An Unsuitable Job for a Woman,* James creates the admirable private investigator Cordelia Gray. Cordelia is young and eager, yet mature enough to make sensible decisions and act in a thoroughly professional manner. As the story opens, she arrives at work at the shabby office of Pryde's Detective Agency to find the corpse of her employer, Bernie Pryde—a suicide. There is a note saying he has found out he has cancer, and is leaving the business to Cordelia. Cordelia, a very junior assistant detective, was fond of Bernie and is genuinely distressed at his death. But grief doesn't prevent her from appropriating Bernie's gun, which he would have wanted her to have, or dismissing the agency typist, who is now an unnecessary extravagance.

Hard on the heels of Bernie's death comes a request from Sir Ronald Callendar: He wants Pryde to find the cause of his nineteen-year-old son's suicide. Cordelia takes her scene-of-crime kit and sets off for Cambridge. Sir Ronald is surprised to see her—". . . it's a little disconcerting to expect a burly ex-policeman and to get you"—but Cordelia's manner is professional and he responds by hiring her. Cordelia moves into the gardener's cottage, where the young man was found hanging, and—with a sense of pleasure in being at Cambridge and vicariously sharing in the student life she herself was denied due to poverty—embarks on finding out what the last days of Mark Callendar's life were like. As she does, she finds suspicious circumstances that indicate his death was anything but suicide.

Cordelia Gray is an excellent character: grown-up, sensitive, although perhaps a bit severe. Nothing is given to her; she works for each discovery in a logical and painstaking manner. One of the first of the modern female private investigators, Cordelia is no mere gimmick but a thoroughly believable and likable human being.

In her second (and long-awaited) case, *The Skull Beneath the Skin* (1982), Cordelia undertakes a bodyguarding assignment on an isolated island off the Dorset coast.

(*S.D.*)

James, P. D. *Shroud for a Nightingale.* New York: Scribner's, 1971. (PP)

Shroud for a Nightingale is thought by many critics to be James's finest novel. Set in Nightingale, a nurses' training school, where students, teaching nurses, and the matron both work and live, the book explores the individuals in this institutional environment—those who have adapted and enjoy the politics and gossip of the school, and those who stay only because they have no other options. What little caches of individuality do they keep secreted under their conformist facades? What really matters to them? What would they kill for?

The student nurses assemble for a demonstration of tubal feeding, using one of their number as the patient. The solution, which is supposed to be of milk, turns out to be poison, and Adam Dalgliesh is called in to find the student's killer. Dalgliesh proves to be a welcome addition to the insular lives of the nurses. Using his charm, understanding, and air of command, he induces them to invite him into their suites, to reveal the intimate secrets of their colleagues, and eventually to lead him to the killer.

Dalgliesh's probing into the private lives of this varied group of characters is portrayed in a convincing manner, and both the method of murder and the motives of the killer are extremely satisfying and realistic. This may be the best of James's Dalgliesh novels.

In addition to the books about Dalgliesh and Cordelia Gray, James has written an excellent novel of psychological suspense, *Innocent Blood* (1980). (*S.D.*)

Jay, Charlotte. *A Hank of Hair*. New York: Harper, 1964. (PS)

A Hank of Hair is one of those quiet, brooding works of psychological suspense and slowly unfolding horror that seem most remarkable when composed by British writers. William Fryer Harvey (q.v.) was expert at doing them in the short-story form; based on this novel, no writer has done one better in the longer form than Charlotte Jay.

Gilbert Hand, age forty-three, is by his own admission "a silly little man," one of those nondescript, passionless types who find a small niche in life and cling to it tenaciously, and who become totally lost if something happens to wrench them out of that niche. What happened to Hand was the death of his wife, Rachel, in a freak collision between two ships off the coast of Spain (she had gone to Rome to visit her sister and was returning roundabout by boat). He hadn't even realized he loved her until she was gone; and now that she's dead, he is desolate. He sells everything except a few books and Japanese prints (such prints are his one remaining interest) and moves to London, into a room at a small, respectable hotel.

It is in this room, inside a davenport, that he finds a hank of human hair tied with green silk. And thus begins an obsession that brings Hand out of his grief and into contact with the room's former occupant, Doyle, a handsome man with odd pearly eyes, and Gladys, Doyle's plump, silly girlfriend—creating one of the strangest and most terrifying triangles imaginable. Major Sinclair, the owner of the hotel, who has an unattracive (but rich) older wife and a penchant for taking young girls to his cottage in Essex, also plays a central role in the story. As, to no small degree, do a series of brutal murders of young women, one of whom is found inside a well with a hank of her hair cut off. . . .

The novel is narrated by Hand, and it is his voice, his perceptions and fears, that create its brooding tone and its tension. The suspense builds with a kind of terrible inevitability to a climax you may see coming—or only *think* you see coming—but in any case will almost certainly give you a *frisson d'horreur*. Jay's construction is flawless (at least until the denouement) and the atmosphere of mounting terror she evokes is extraordinary. Anthony Boucher said that she "cannot write a dull or graceless sentence." Another eminent figure in the mystery field, Charlotte Armstrong (q.v.), called *A Hank of Hair* "something for connoisseurs." In fact, were it not for a mildly disappointing disinclination on Jay's part to tie off a couple of important loose ends, this could reasonably be called a small masterpiece.

Charlotte Jay won an Edgar for her first novel, *Beat Not the Bones* (1952), another hair-raising combination of mystery, psychological suspense, and natural (as opposed to supernatural) horror; that novel is set in Marapai, New Guinea, and tells the unconventional tale of Emma Warwick's search for the murderer of her anthropologist husband. Jay's seven other crime novels are set in Pakistan (*The Yellow Turban,* 1955), Lebanon (*Arms for Adonis,* 1961), New Guinea again (*The Voice of the Crab,* 1974, as by Geraldine Halls), and her native England. These, too, are of high quality and shuddersome content.

(*B.P.*)

Jeffers, H. Paul. *Murder on Mike.* New York: St. Martin's, 1984. (H/PI)

A small but persistent trend in recent years is the retrospective private-eye novel—the nostalgic adventures of PI's operating in the Thirties and Forties, contemporary re-creations of a bygone era. Andrew Bergman, Stuart Kaminsky (q.v.), and Max Allan Collins (q.v.) have each done quite well with Chandleresque heroes of this sort; judging from the two Harry McNeil novels published to date—*Rubout at the Onyx Club* (1982) and *Murder on Mike*—H. Paul Jeffers will, too. McNeil is a very likable character, "an ex-cop who's now a private investigator who'd prefer nothing better than to play clarinet with a top jazz band and leave the detective work to better guys," a shamus who uses his head and his legs and his heart in lieu of violence. Harry McNeil, "the help of the hopeless."

It is a few days before Christmas, 1939. Harry is in his office above the Onyx Club on Fifty-second Street, New York City. Enter Maggie Skeffington, a radio actress on "Detective Fitzroy's Casebook" on the Blue Network (NBC). A few days earlier, Derek Worthington, the star of the show and a man heartily disliked by his co-workers, was shot to death in Studio 6B at Radio City; and Maggie's boyfriend, announcer David Reed, has been arrested for the crime. Maggie is convinced that David is innocent, even though he is the only member of the cast and crew who does not have an airtight alibi for the time of the shooting.

Harry takes the case, of course. And meets the various suspects: J. William Richards, owner of the Mellow-Gold Coffee Company and the show's sponsor; Miles Flanagan, the producer; Veronica Blake, the head writer (with whom Harry later has an affair); Jason Patrick, Worthington's costar; Rita DeLong, an aging musician; Guff Taylor, the engineer; and Jerry Nolan, the expert sound-effects man. Any of the lot might have killed Worthington—except for those alibis. The key to cracking the case lies with young Robby Miller, a Radio City tour guide, who heard the fatal shot fired through a studio mike someone inadvertently left open and who has turned up missing. . . .

The mystery here is lightweight but entertaining—until its resolution. The final unmasking, which Harry brings about in Studio 6B on Christmas day with the aid of a self-written radio script, is farfetched and highly derivative of a famous novel by a certain popular Golden Age writer. That part of *Murder on Mike* is disappointing. Still, there is Harry. There is New York at Yuletide 1939, "a city for dreamers because it was a city that could make dreams come true," a city full of fascinating real-life characters—Winchell, Woolcott, Ed Sullivan, and comedian Fred Allen (both of whom have speaking parts), dozens more. There is an equally fine evocation of the world of dramatic radio (a subject Jeffers knows intimately: He works for a Manhattan radio station). And there is a nice, old-fashioned flavor to the narrative, a feeling that you are reading a combination of whodunit and bittersweet private-eye romance *written* in 1939.

(*B.P.*)

Jeffreys, J. G. *A Wicked Way to Die.* New York: Walker, 1973. (H/W)

Like the novels of Richard Falkirk (q.v.), those of J. G. Jeffreys (a pseudonym of Ben Healey) are set in pre-Victorian England and feature a Bow Street Runner sleuth. Of the two, Falkirk's series about Edmund Blackstone has perhaps the greater scope in depicting London and its environs at the turn of the nineteenth century; but Jeffreys's books about Jeremy Sturrock are more baffling detective stories and more vividly capture the language and feel of that fascinating period in English history. Plus they contain an abundance of bawdy and irreverent humor that at times has caused this reader to laugh out loud.

A Wicked Way to Die, Jeremy Sturrock's second case, pits the delightfully conceited Runner and his "most horrible, lecherous and bloodthirsty little rogue" of a clerk, Maggsy, against the cunning perpetrator of a locked-room murder at the Theatre Royal, Drury Lane. The victim is Robert Mytton, the son of a wealthy banker, whose death by gunshot at first seems to be suicide. Suspects include Mother Knapp, a seller of fruit and a "most notorious female pander and whoremonger"; a couple of actors, Jack Dashwood and Nicholas Lilley; a theater flunky named Boosey; Dr. Blossum, a Grub Street hack whose home turf causes Jeremy to reflect "how profoundly did the immortal Doctor Samuel Johnson observe that no place affords a more striking conviction of the vanity of human hopes than a library"; a "canonical rogue" and screever (writer of phony and/or extortionate letters and documents) called Holy Moses; and Lady Dorothea Hookham, who is "well known to have a face somewhat like a horse's arse."

On his way to the solution of this dastardly crime, Sturrock survives a number of attempts on his life, one of which takes place at the Brown Bear, a "flash house" where all manner of devilments are concocted and which is described as having "a bold eyed serving wench with her tits pretty well as open to all as her looks, a reek of fog and tobacco smoke, an assemblage of rogues sitting as dark as their own misdeeds in the candlelight . . . and timber very near as black as the Devil's fundament."

This and the other Jeremy Sturrock adventures—among them *The Thief Taker* (1972), *Suicide Most Foul* (1981), *Captain Bolton's Corpse* (1982), *The Pangersbourne Murders* (1983)—are pleasant escapist reading. It doesn't matter that the characters are sometimes difficult to keep straight or that elements of the plots sometimes don't make much sense. Their humor and backgrounds more than make up for their (relatively minor) flaws.

It should be noted that all of the Sturrock/Maggsy titles were first published in England under the pseudonym Jeremy Sturrock. Also, Ben Healey has published numerous novels under his own name, both here and in England; two of the best known are *The Vespucci Papers* (1972) and *The Stone Baby* (1973), both of which are set in modern Venice.

(*B.P.*)

Jeffries, Roderic. *Deadly Petard.* New York: St. Martin's, 1983. (PP)

The prolific Roderic Jeffries writes under several pseudonyms, including Jeffrey Ashford and Roderic Graeme. The Ashford books (among them *Investigations Are Proceeding,* 1962, and *The Double Run,* 1973) deal with the psychology of ordinary people caught up in extraordinary (and criminous) situations. As Roderic Graeme, Jeffries continued the series begun by his late father, Bruce Graeme, about gentleman thief Blackshirt; his twenty Blackshirt novels were published only in Jeffries's native England between 1952 and 1969. The early Jeffries books—*Evidence of the Accused* (1963), *An Embarrassing Death* (1965), and *Dead Against the Lawyers* (1966), among others—are lively courtroom dramas in which the accused and his attorney make a successful eleventh-hour attempt to prove innocence. In 1972 Jeffries created series character Enrique Alvarez, a Mallorcan detective whose appearance coincided with the author's move to the island of Mallorca. Set against this colorful background, these novels combine solid detection with excellent depictions of the Mallorcan people.

As *Deadly Petard* opens, it is—characteristically—hot on the island, certainly not a day for doing an excessive amount of work. That is why Inspector Alvarez is upset when his drowsy daydreams are interrupted by an order to interview an Englishwoman named Gertrude Dean. To make matters worse, the Dean woman doesn't even live in his district! Life *can* be difficult.

As the story unfolds, we learn that Gertrude Dean once provided an alibi for a suspected killer—a man whose wife was found dead with a plastic bag over her head. Now the man has turned up on Mallorca, and soon afterward Miss Dean is found dead, also with a plastic bag over her head. And because he initially interviewed her, Inspector Alvarez is ordered to take over the case. (Life continues to be difficult!)

This is a smooth-flowing, low-key novel, featuring an entertaining and likable sleuth. The plot is well constructed, although the final twist does strain one's credulity a bit. Jeffries depicts the contrast between the Mallorcans and the English residents perceptively and with considerable humor.

Other titles featuring Enrique Alvarez include *Mistakenly in Mallorca* (1974), *Troubled Deaths* (1978), *Murder Begets Murder* (1979), and *Layers of Deceit* (1985).

(*N.D./M.M.*)

Jenkins, Will F. *The Murder of the U.S.A.* New York: Crown, 1946. (PS/W)

William Fitzgerald Jenkins spent the early years of his writing career producing pulp-magazine fiction—and occasional novels—in the mystery, science-fiction, and western genres. Under his Murray Leinster pseudonym, he went on to establish a major voice in science fiction with such classic stories as "First Contact" and the Hugo Award–winning "Exploration Team."

The Murder of the U.S.A. is the best known and most successful of his mystery novels, primarily because of its unique (and rather audacious) science-fiction basis: The "murder victim" here is not a person but an entire country. When the United States is mysteriously attacked with atomic weapons, a third of the country is destroyed and the survivors don't know the identity of the attackers or their location. Hero Sam Burton and his group in Burrow 89 detect some puzzling clues and manage to piece the horror story together using a fascinating display of logic. Although this book was written within a year of the actual use of atomic weapons in World War II, Jenkins extrapolates the consequences of a mass atomic attack with startling accuracy for that era, while at the same time working within the framework of the classic fair-play whodunit. Exciting and suspenseful, it should please fans of both genres—even those who don't usually like one or the other.

The paperback edition of *Murder of the U.S.A.* (Handi-Book #62, 1947) is a particularly sought-after collector's item: Its cover depicts the Grim Reaper standing over a bombed and burning outline of the United States.

Jenkins's other criminous novels are *The Man Who Feared* (1942) and, under the Murray Leinster name, such whodunits as *Scalps* (1930) and *Murder Madness* (1931). *Scalps* is an especially interesting novel; set in Arizona, it features a successful blend of the mystery and another genre, the western, as well as an unusually sympathetic (for its time) treatment of native Americans.

(*G.K./B.P.*)

Johns, Veronica Parker. *Murder by the Day*. New York: Doubleday Crime Club, 1953. (AD)

Veronica Parker Johns created two very different series characters. The first of these is Agatha Welch, a Connecticut woman who visits her sister on a "tiny island in the West Indies" and, in the course of solving a mystery, meets and marries Judge Jack Prentiss. Agatha, who has a personal, let-me-tell-you-all-about-it style of addressing the reader, appears in two adventures: *Hush, Gabriel!* (1940) and *Shady Doings* (1941). Johns's second series character, Webster Flagg, has the distinction of being the first believable and dignified black detective in mystery fiction. (Octavus Roy Cohen, q.v., had previously created a black detective, Florian Slappey, but Slappey is little more than a stereotypical buffoon.) Flagg is the forerunner of such other notable black investigators as Ed Lacy's (q.v.) Toussaint Moore and John Ball's (q.v.) Virgil Tibbs.

Flagg is in his sixties, semiretired from the stage and the opera, and living in Harlem, where he is a property owner. One day he reports to his part-time job as butler/houseman to the wealthy Mortimer Rutherford, and finds his employer burned to death in a supposedly fireproof chair. Flagg has been let into the apartment building by one of the residents (all of whom are either employees or relatives of Rutherford), and it is only at this point that he realizes his key to the front door is missing from his key ring. Aware that, as a black man, he will be the first to be suspected of the apparent murder, Flagg sets out to investigate the residents, each of whom might have had reason to kill the dead art collector and semibenevolent despot.

The residents want to put on a lobster thermidor dinner as a sort of cheerful wake for Rutherford. Flagg arranges for it and serves, slipping off between courses to eavesdrop and to search the various suspects' apartments. Unfortunately his efforts do not bring him to any conclusion in time to prevent a second murder; but when he does realize the solution to both killings, it comes in an adroit, double-twist ending.

The second—and only other—adventure of Webster Flagg is *Servant's Problem* (1958), a lively novel with bright characters that is splendidly evocative of New York City in the 1950s.

(*E.N./M.M.*)

*Johnson, E. Richard. *Silver Street.* New York: Harper, 1968. (PP)

E. Richard Johnson was a prisoner at the Stillwater State Prison in Minnesota when he began writing crime fiction in the late 1960s. Between 1968 and 1971, working in his cell, he produced seven memorable novels about street-tough cops, cons, and criminals in unspecified midwestern locales—a literal insider's view, often bitter and angry, of the seamier side of human existence. Since 1971, Johnson has published only one novel—*The Cardinalli Contract* (1975)—and that a paperback original exploiting the popularity of Mario Puzo's Mafia best seller, *The Godfather*. The loss when Johnson stopped writing his midnight tales of urban crime and prison life was as much his as it was ours; the promise of those first seven novels was great indeed, that of a potentially major voice that, for whatever reason, unhappily appears to have been stilled.

Silver Street is Johnson's debut, and was an MWA Edgar-winner for Best First Novel of 1968. It is a deceptively simple story, set mostly along Silver Street, a.k.a. Pimps' Row, in an unnamed city—a street inhabited by pimps, whores, drug addicts and pushers, thieves, and worse, "a cop's nightmare, a festering gash on the city's face that stinks of evil when you walk it on dark nights." Death is commonplace on Silver Street, so when a pimp named Willie Mack is found stabbed on a rain-soaked night, the cop in charge of the investigation, Tony Lonto, thinks little enough of it. And Lonto knows Silver Street as well as anyone, because he was born and raised in that same slum neighborhood. He was one of the lucky ones: He got out.

But then a second pimp turns up knifed, and Lonto realizes that he's got a serial killer on his hands—a psycho with a burning hatred for pimps. The reader knows this almost from the outset; Johnson tells us who the psycho is—a young ex-soldier named Cecil—and lets us inside his head (a very nasty place to be). We know why Cecil is killing pimps: because he was once in love with a girl he didn't know was a whore; and when he got back from the jungles of Southeast Asia, he found out she'd committed suicide, learned that she'd been hooking for a living, and he blamed her pimp for her "seduction" and death. It is some time before Lonto discovers this; and when he does, it is an especially painful and personal truth, because Tony Lonto is also in love with a woman he hadn't known was a whore. . . .

Stanley Ellin (q.v.) called *Silver Street* "a savagely fascinating book from start to finish," and so it is. A few other adjectives that come to mind are *uncompromising, revealing,* and *hard as nails.* A must-read for anyone who wants the genuine goods on life on both sides of the law in a tough tenderloin neighborhood. A must-*not*-read for those who like their fictional murders bloodless and their fictional detectives polite, well educated, and witty.

Tony Lonto reappears in Johnson's third novel, *The Inside Man* (1969), about the murder of a crazy named Benjamin who carried one of those "The End Is Near" signs. *Mongo's Back in Town,* also published in 1969, is the violent tale of a hoodlum named Mongo Nash and his Christmas homecoming to help his brother out of a jam; it was filmed for TV in 1971 from a script by Johnson, with Sally Field and Joe Don Baker as Mongo. Also outstanding is *Case Load—Maximum* (1971), a prison story that portrays an idealistic parole officer who puts too much faith in a paroled con.

(*B.P.*)

Johnston, Velda. *The Phantom Cottage.* New York: Dodd, Mead, 1969. (R)

Velda Johnston's heroines are independent and plucky young women. Most have interesting careers; their work, however, is secondary to romance, and when it isn't working out with Mr. Right, they are unhappy young ladies. Fortunately, it always does work out—after some trial and tribulation on the heroine's part.

Jane Warren, the heroine of this novel, goes to the Cape Cod village of Garth with the tools of her trade—a typewriter and sketching equipment; her aging dog, Howie; and "one bruised, if not actually broken, heart." Garth is a place her friend Laura Crane—dead in a hit-and-run accident three weeks ago—once mentioned, and before Jane has been there a day she finds that Laura's real name was Laurabelle Crandall; that she was raised in Garth, not in Denver as the strange and reticent young woman had claimed; and that she left Garth suddenly a year ago, apparently taking with her a broken heart.

Jane settles in at her rented beach cottage. It is off-season, and the beach where she likes to eat her picnic suppers is deserted. There are packs of wild dogs running in the woods, and a drunken woman in town who seems to have transferred her hatred of Laura to Jane, but Jane does not allow these things to spoil her holiday. And soon she begins to receive the attentions of two young men: Gabe Harmon, who owns the town's hotel, and Bill Brockton, a marine biologist.

All seems idyllic until the night someone drugs Jane's Thermos of coffee while she is walking on the beach. She is aware of a burlap bag over her head; of being transported somewhere; of a strange, whispering voice demanding to know why she came to Garth and what Laura told her on the phone the night she died. When she comes to the next morning on the beach, Jane goes to the police, but Chief Jones—who has a suspicion of outsiders—refuses to believe her story. Jane knows now that her friend's death was no accident, but a murder whose motive has its roots in Garth. Alone, she must solve this murder.

The premise of this novel is interesting, and the Cape Cod background colorful. At times the pacing is slow; Jane finds out the secret of Laura's identity too early and too easily, and then not much happens, causing the tension to sag. But the ending is satisfying, even if it comes as no surprise that all works out with Mr. Right.

Other romantic suspense novels by Johnston include *I Came to a Castle* (1969), set in Spain; *A Room with Dark Mirrors* (1975), set in Paris; *The House on the Left Bank* (1975), also set in Paris but in the year 1870; and *A Presence in an Empty Room* (1980), which takes place in Maine.

(*M.M.*)

Jones, Cleo. *Prophet Motive.* New York: St. Martin's, 1984. (PP)

This is Cleo Jones's first mystery about Police Chief Christopher Danville of the small Mormon town of Magpie, Utah. Jones—like her hero, a lapsed Mormon—occasionally uses her story as a soapbox from which to declaim the evils of Mormon society, but this flaw is more than balanced out by the crash course she gives us in Mormon history, as well as by the insights into the stresses and strains of that society—both for the religious and for non-Mormons who must coexist with it.

The crime with which Chris Danville must deal is the murder of Bishop Manion, an "iron rod" leader of one of Magpie's twenty-one wards. The bishop has been stabbed to death in a snowy clearing, and a witness saw him struggling with a woman in a long blond wig. Footsteps in the snow lead up to and then away from the nearby home of Planned Parenthood head Naomi Green (who has long dark hair), and to the stunned family and friends of the bishop, Naomi is a convenient scapegoat. Danville, finding himself strongly attracted to the woman, is determined to prove she didn't commit the murder.

The first lead Danville receives is scratched in the ice on the windshield of his van: It tells him one of his sergeants is a fundamentalist—a strict Mormon who practices forbidden polygamy; Sergeant Wilks was about to be exposed by the bishop, and thus had a motive to kill him. Next a burglary is reported: Tapes of messages that friends and neighbors of a dying man had wanted him to deliver on "the other side of the veil" have been stolen. The dead man's wife reports that something on the tapes had bothered her husband—something he reported to Bishop Manion, and Manion agreed to look into. Finally, the son of one of the Manions' neighbors attempts suicide, leaving a note saying he killed the bishop. He didn't; it is a guilt reaction frequently occurring in the Mormon community. But a few days later, $100,000 in cash for the boy's medical expenses is delivered, supposedly from his father, who decamped the year before with a sleazy blonde and

$300,000 belonging to the new bishop, a man who made his money from a Las Vegas casino. This is the most promising lead Danville has, and convinced the missing man is close by, he begins to concentrate on finding him—a search that has shocking results.

Danville is a likable character, full of the conflicts and complexities one would expect in a divorced, lapsed Mormon still living within the Mormon community. Jones writes well, and her handling of first-person male viewpoint and action scenes is very good. The weak point in this book is her poor grasp of police procedure—often Danville's investigative methods seem less than professional. All in all, however, this is a powerful and fascinating debut.

(*M.M.*)

*Joshee, O. K. *Mr. Surie.* New York: St. Martin's, 1984. (PS)

In suspense fiction, criminals are agents of change. But there is also a powerful story in the change undergone by the criminal himself. In that respect *Mr. Surie,* a haunting novel by a native of India now living in New York City, can be seen as a sort of Hindu *Crime and Punishment*.

Balbir Surie is a Bombay businessman who has amassed a cold fortune as a principal in an international temple-robbing and smuggling operation. At the beginning of this story, he is confidently lying low after the death of his partner in crime, an Australian named Claude Scott.

In the twilight of Bombay's underworld, there is always danger. Police, politicians, and his own associates are all threats to Surie, but he is not afraid. He had decided when he was a young boy that he would never be one of the donkeys of this world, and he has survived by his wits for a long time. He is in control.

But Surie faces the gravest danger from the hell he has created within. First, he allows himself to become a party to a murder—just a simple, safe murder, and very profitable. Then begins the slow, agonizing process of realization that he has turned down a path that will never again lead toward life as he has known it. As Surie engages in complex political maneuvering to cover traces of his crimes, he finds himself unable to shake the recurring memory of a youthful friendship, probably the only unselfish friendship he has ever had, with an epileptic boy who died very young.

There is also the palpable figure of the dead Scott, whose bluff, hearty partnership had been one of the anchors of Surie's life. Now he is amazed to learn that the big adventurer had been largely a stranger to him, deeply in love with a woman and yet longing for death. First in Surie's dreams, then while awake, he sees the figure of Scott, gently mocking his love for the material world and beckoning Surie to join him.

In Surie's torment, his grip on his circumstances falters—not, as an adversary alleges, because he has lost his courage, but because "I have lost my rage." As he watches, distracted and "no longer a participant," he falls into the hands of his enemies.

Is he the loser, though? The answer lies in the song of the desecrated, dancing temple idols that rings in Surie's mind:

"Tell us if you wish
Tell us if you must
Tell us if you can:
Did you steal us?
Did we steal you?
Who is the thief?"

(*M.J.*)

Kallen, Lucille. *C.B. Greenfield: The Piano Bird.* New York: Random House, 1984. (AD)

The scene is the Gulf of Mexico island of Sanibel-Captiva. Journalist Maggie Rome has taken leave from the New England small-town paper *Sloan's Ford Reporter* in order to play nursemaid to her ailing mother. She feels a bit guilty about deserting her editor, the cantankerous C. B. Greenfield, and the guilt is exacerbated by his forlorn phone calls, but the island is lovely, the sun a welcome change from the cold northern winter. Maggie wanders the beach when not tending to her somewhat irascible but frequently delightful parent, and as she roams, she studies the other beachcombers.

At first she thinks of these people only in terms of their outstanding physical characteristics: the Tortoise, the Fox Terrier. But soon they emerge with names, and the relationships among some of them become clear. The most interesting are a group who have come to Sanibel to work on a Broadway musical: Sherman Ruskin, a writer; his rival writer on the project, Alvin Persky; Thea Quinn, a radiant blonde who is to star in the production; her lover and producer, Mitchell Grafman; Gary Webber, the composer. Then there is Sarah McChesney, an ecologist resident of the island of Captiva, who fiercely resents Grafman's intentions to build Thea a house on the beach property next to hers. And if people aren't enough to engage Maggie's lively interest, there is the bird preserve on Captiva—where Maggie last sees Thea alive and soon after that discovers her body.

Enter C. B. Greenfield, whose curiosity when Maggie tells him of the murder will not permit him to stay away. Of course he doesn't admit it. To Maggie he claims, "You *arranged* this. . . . If there were any justice, you'd be charged with two crimes. One, you're holding yourself for ransom. That's kidnapping. . . . And two, you've extorted my presence here by means of a threat. That's blackmail." The threat is that Maggie cannot return home until she is sure her mother is safe from what she thinks of as Thea's psychopathic killer; Greenfield is here merely to reclaim a member of his staff—so he says.

Greenfield's curiosity heightens as he comes into (often hilarious) contact with the denizens of the island. With Maggie doing most of the dirty work, including jumping off a ten-foot-high balcony, he investigates. And, as in previous adventures of this engaging pair, the results are unexpected.

The other lively, entertaining books in this popular series are *Introducing C.B. Greenfield* (1979), *C.B. Greenfield: The Tanglewood Murderer* (1980), and *C.B. Greenfield: No Lady in the House* (1982).

(*M.M.*)

*Kaminsky, Stuart. *Murder on the Yellow Brick Road.* New York: St. Martin's, 1977. (PI)

Stuart Kaminsky is a film writer and critic as well as a mystery novelist, and he has put his expertise to good use in his series about 1940s Hollywood private eye Toby Peters. The novels are a blend of fact and fiction—that is, of real Hollywood personalities (now deceased) and fictional characters. Peters, investigator for the stars, is wise to the ways of Hollywood; he shares an office with a dentist, Shelley Minck, who provides much of the comic relief in these books; he eats abominably—burgers, Pepsis, milk shakes; he lives in "one of a series of two-room, one story wooden structures L.A. management people called bungalows"; and he has a running feud with his brother, Homicide Lieutenant Phil Pevsner (the real family name).

Murder on the Yellow Brick Road concerns the stabbing of a munchkin—one of L.A.'s many "little people" (they prefer that label to that of midget)—on the set on which *The Wizard of Oz* was filmed. Judy Garland finds the body and calls Peters in a panic. Peters goes to MGM, where he meets Miss Garland, PR man Warren Hoff, Garland's costume designer friend Cassie James, and Louis B. Mayer himself. Mayer hires Peters to conduct an investigation and divert any adverse publicity.

What follows is an entertaining story of Hollywood in its heyday, the inner workings of the film community, and the brotherhood of the "little people." Peters meets such luminaries as Raymond Chandler, and pays a visit to Clark Gable at William Randolph Hearst's fabled San Simeon. Kaminsky does a good job of evoking both Hollywood of the Forties and the personalities of the various stars; his portrayal of the child/woman Garland is especially good.

Other Toby Peters novels include *Never Cross a Vampire* (1980), which features Bela Lugosi and William Faulkner in his screenwriting days; and

He Done Her Wrong (1983), in which Mae West calls on Peters to find her missing, sizzling autobiography; and *Down For the Count* (1985), which features fighter Joe Louis.

(*M.M.*)

Kaminsky, Stuart. *When the Dark Man Calls.* New York: St. Martin's, 1983. (PS)

This nonseries suspense novel opens with a scene set in North Carolina in 1957: A young girl named Jean lies in bed, thinking of the Pat Boone movie she plans to see the next day. Suddenly there are footsteps in the hall and horrible sounds—like a pumpkin being hurled at a wall—from her parents' bedroom. Jean knows something awful has happened—and in the morning her fears are confirmed: Her parents have been murdered in their bed with an ax.

We then move forward, to Chicago, 1983. Jean Kaiser has grown up and gotten over this childhood trauma with the aid of a psychiatrist. She herself has become a psychologist, has a daughter named Angie, is divorced, and has a nightly radio show advising people on psychological problems. Money has been tight, and the neighborhood where Jean and Angie live is dangerous and frightening, but she is about to receive an offer from CBS that will allow them to move someplace better. Everything looks to be on the rosy side until Jean receives a call while on the air—one that revives the old childhood memories and makes her wonder if her parents' killer is free from the mental institution where he has been confined for the past fourteen years. When she and Angie return home and find their pet bird killed and placed on Jean's pillow, she is terrified that the murderer, Parmenter, has found her.

Jean's suspicion turns out to be fact: She calls North Carolina and learns Parmenter has been released and is living with his sister in Chicago. The calls continue, and rather than allowing herself to be paralyzed by fear, Jean confronts the situation, first talking with Parmenter's sister and then with the man himself. Although Parmenter seems obsessed with his murders—and with Jean—the police can do nothing; nor can Jean's ex-husband, Max; nor her new lover, Roger; nor her brother, Lloyd. Then Parmenter himself turns up dead on her bed, and the *real* terror begins. . . .

This is a tension-packed novel in which fear of both the known and the unknown are placed in counterpoint to the mundane, day-to-day details of the life of a single parent in a big city. Jean and Angie are extremely likable characters, and Kaminsky portrays their excellent mother-daughter relationship with gentle humor.

A second nonseries novel by Kaminsky, *Exercise in Terror,* was published in 1985. It concerns the plight of the widow of a murdered man when her husband's psychopathic killers return eight years later to threaten her and her children.

(*M.M.*)

Kane, Frank. *Stacked Deck*. New York: Dell, 1961. (O/PI/SS)

Frank Kane had a long and varied career as a novelist and as a contract writer for radio and television. In the 1940s he wrote for such radio crime shows as "The Shadow" and "The Fat Man," and both wrote and produced "Claims Agent" and "The Lawless Twenties." His TV credits include scripts for "Mike Hammer" and "S.A. 7," and the production of "The Investigators." He published his first novel, *Death About Face,* in 1948, and followed it with thirty-four more over the next twenty years, most of them paperback originals and most featuring tough New York private eye Johnny Liddell. Liddell, who has a passion for redheads and trouble, was a popular softcover detective in the Fifties and early Sixties, appearing in twenty-eight novels and two collections. One of Kane's trademarks in the Liddell series was a pun in each title: for example, *Bare Trap* (1952), *Trigger Mortis* (1958), and *Esprit de Corpse* (1965).

Stacked Deck is one of the two collections of Liddell short stories (most of which originally appeared in such digest magazines as *Manhunt* and in the pulps); the other is *Johnny Liddell's Morgue* (1956). Not only is it representative of the Liddell series, but the Dell First Edition is representative of the cover artwork that attracted readers both to Kane's work and to that of dozens of other writers of paperback originals: The sexy Robert McGinnis cover features twin redheads with come-hither looks.

The stories are prime Johnny Liddell: action-oriented with little or no detection. In "Dead Set," Liddell is hired by erotic actress Lydia Johnson to stop whoever is blackmailing her with pornographic photos taken early in her career. Liddell manages to discover the identity of the blackmailers, but it takes a knife and a .45 to stop them in the story's violent conclusion. "Dead Reckoning" begins with Liddell chasing a stacked redhead when a gangster named Russo interrupts. Russo and Liddell duke it out until the butt of Liddell's .45 ends the argument. But later Russo is found dead and the police finger Liddell as their prime suspect.

The other six stories in the collection offer the same sort of fare—as do the various Liddell novels. Not much of a meal, really, for anyone hungry for high-quality private eye fiction.

(*G.K./B.P.*)

Kane, Henry. *The Midnight Man.* New York: Macmillan, 1965. (PI)

Henry Kane is best known as the creator of Peter Chambers, a tough but urbane New York "private richard" whose adventures were quite popular in the late Forties and throughout the Fifties. (Some of the early Chambers short stories appeared in the sophisticated men's magazine *Esquire,* which once devoted an editorial to Kane, calling him an "author, bon vivant, stoic, student, tramp, lawyer, philosopher . . . the lad who works off a hangover conceived in a Hoboken dive by swooshing down large orders of Eggs Benedict at the Waldorf on the morning after . . . the man who can use polysyllables on Third Avenue and certain ancient monosyllables on Park Avenue.") Kane wrote dozens of novels and scores of stories featuring the exploits of Peter Chambers; and yet, ironically enough, his most memorable private eye is not Chambers but a 250-pound ex-cop named McGregor. In fact, his three best mystery novels are those in which McGregor is featured—*The Midnight Man, Conceal and Disguise* (1966), and *Laughter in the Alehouse* (1968).

Like Chambers, McGregor is urbane, literate, and a connoisseur of beautiful women, gourmet food, and vintage booze. Unlike Chambers, he is prone to pithy literary quotes instead of suave wisecracks, and prefers to use wits and guile in place of guns and fists to solve his cases. He is not a career PI with an office and a secretary; he is a newly retired New York City police inspector, "pushing fifty, ramrod-straight and robustly handsome," known around headquarters as "the Old Man," who dabbles at private investigation (he has a license, of course) just to keep a hand in. He is more likable than Chambers, has more depth and sensitivity, and his three cases are less frivolous and more tightly plotted than any of the Chambers stories.

In *The Midnight Man,* McGregor has undertaken the job of closing down an illegal after-hours enterprise at a fashionable Upper East Side nightclub. The case begins as a simple one—the club's neighbors don't like the idea of drunks carousing in the wee hours—but it soon turns complicated: The after-hours operation is being run by a major New York mob figure named Frank Dinelli, whom McGregor would love to put in the slammer. When the late-night doorman, whom McGregor has bribed and who was instrumental in a successful raid on the club, is shot to death practically in McGregor's presence (he arrives just in time to grapple with the killer), the case becomes personal. Working with his pal, Detective Lieutenant Kevin Cohen, he follows leads that take him to the studio of millionaire photographer George Preston, to the offices of Park Avenue dermatologist Robert Jackson, and to a fancy loan-sharking operation that Dinelli is sponsoring. They also take him to a second murder, this one featuring an ingenious method of execution, which McGregor solves through the same combination of deduction and guile with which he wraps up the rest of the case.

Kane has a fine ear for dialogue; there is some marvelously witty repartee here, especially between McGregor and a variety of New York cabdrivers. Of course, cops don't really talk the way McGregor and Cohen do, but that's a minor flaw. As the jacket blurb says, "If high crime in high society is your cup of tea, you'll especially relish this fast, crisp, upper-echelon saga of mayhem in Manhattan." And from Anthony Boucher: "Kane has, as usual, a pretty sense of story-shape and a nice way with clues. There is a cleverly gimmicked murder, a lot of colorful night life, and much fun (and good food) for all."

(*B.P.*)

Kane, Henry. *Trinity in Violence.* New York: Avon, 1955. (O/PI/SS)

Here we have three novelettes featuring Henry Kane's long-running New York detective Peter Chambers. The Chambers stories tend to be pretty routine private-eye capers, but Kane's handling of this stock material is quite unusual. The characters deliver their lines in a peculiarly arch fashion, which veteran PI fans are equally likely to find either refreshingly novel or plain silly. Also, in the midst of typical guns-and-gangsters melees, Chambers is wont to toss off sly asides to the readers, saying, in effect, "How about this for a typical private-eye cliché?" The Chambers books can provide enjoyable light entertainment if the reader finds Kane's quirky, playful approach palatable.

Best of these tales is "Skip a Beat," with one of those once-popular story ideas you don't see anymore: A famous newspaper columnist is about to announce that a leading citizen is actually a closet Commie, but he gets knocked off before he can spill it; Chambers cleans it up. Slapdash plotting comes to the fore in "Slaughter on Sunday," in which a prominent hood hires Chambers to extricate him from a murder frame; it involves a sort of locked-room problem (a transparent one, at best), a gimmick for faking paraffin-test results, and several gaping plot holes. "Far Cry" finds Kane's durable "private richard" romancing a hood's mistress and breaking up a hot-car exporting racket.

Some of the better Chambers novels include *A Halo for Nobody* (1947); *Until You Are Dead* (1951); *Too French and Too Deadly* (1955; another locked room opus, better than the one above, but no challenge to John Dickson Carr, q.v.) and *Death of a Flack* (1961). Chambers's female counterpart, Marla Trent, appears in *Private Eyeful* (1960), and the two collaborate in *Kisses of Death* (1962). Avoid at all costs the dreadful X-rated Peter Chambers novels published by Lancer in the early 1970s!

(*A.S.*)

Kaplan, Arthur. *A Killing for Charity*. New York: Coward, McCann, 1976. (PI)

Private investigator Charity Bay is an absolute bitch. As this—her first and (fortunately) only—case opens, we find her in Hamburg, Germany, in bed with a man named Kurt who apparently has stolen money and securities from one of Charity's clients. She leaves, informs the waiting police where Kurt's guns are, and then aids them in gaining entry to his hotel room. All right—it's her job and she does it the way she sees fit. And perhaps the reader could accept that, if Charity didn't carry on her entire life in such an offensive manner.

In the first fifty pages of this novel, Charity 1) gratuitously insults an airline ticket agent who is being flirtatious with her (on Christmas Day, for heaven's sake!); 2) recalls how she "learned as much as she could" from her first employer and mentor, then "stole her first client right out from under [his] nose"; 3) reveals that she has never tipped her doorman for Christmas; 4) also reveals she has never sent her parents Christmas presents, and only twice sent cards; 5) throws away all the cards *she* has received in her absence from New York, unopened; and 6) kicks an informant in the balls.

None of these is a great sin (the informant was angry and had taken a swing at her), but they do indicate Charity is an emotional Scrooge. She carries a chip on her shoulder and takes offense at every slight, real or imagined, especially if it happens to come from a member of the male sex. Yet she is adept at slighting others, especially when they happen to be men.

Because of the general unpleasantness of the main character, the plot of the novel takes a secondary place. And this is unfortunate because, by and large, it's not bad. It concerns the kidnapping of the daughter of a diamond merchant, plus thefts and murders that have been plaguing the Forty-seventh Street diamond exchange. There is a lot of interesting background on the diamond business, some realistic police procedure, and some good writing.

Charity's character isn't all that consistent, either. There's a cop in the story—Lieutenant Jimmy Dunn—who tries what amounts to raping her. The attempt fails, not because of any extraordinary efforts on Charity's part but because one of Dunn's girlfriends shows up. And at the end of this downbeat story, even after the rape attempt, even after Dunn patronizes her in every respect, Charity *still* thinks the lieutenant's hair falls across his forehead in "a very attractive way."

This book is such an unrealistic depiction of a female private eye that it is almost a parody; and if taken as such, it's worth reading just to see how the PI novel—male *or* female—should *not* be written.

(*M.M.*)

Kavanagh, Paul. *Such Men Are Dangerous.* New York: Macmillan, 1969. (A)

Paul Kavanagh is both the name of the hero of this novel and a pseudonym of Lawrence Block (q.v.). The fictional Kavanagh is a man with a good service record in Vietnam who is now applying for a job with an organization referred to only as "the Agency," but which sounds like the CIA. As the novel opens, the Agency representative, George Dattner, is telling Kavanagh why the Agency won't hire him: He has flunked the personality tests.

Disappointed and angry at his failure, Kavanagh returns to New York City and, after a short affair that convinces him something is seriously wrong with him, converts all his assets to cash and takes off for Florida. On the plane he makes a list of rules he plans to live by, the most important of which is "When in doubt, do nothing." He finds a small, deserted island in the Keys and lives quietly by his rules, going only to a grocery store on a nearby key every six days when his supply of eggs runs out. But on returning from one of these excursions, he finds Dattner on his island. Dattner wants Kavanagh's services, not for the Agency but for himself. A supply of weapons—the "real dirty stuff"—is about to be shipped by the U.S. government to their "good guy" allies in Latin America; Dattner wants to divert it, and he is willing to split the million-dollar profit with Kavanagh.

Kavanagh abandons his rules and travels to Sprayhorn, South Dakota, where the weapons are stored on an army base. Posing as an Agency operative, he sets Dattner's plan in motion. But it is a loosely constructed plan with a great many chances of slipping up, a plan that may be easily foiled at any turn, and one of its most serious flaws turns out to be Kavanagh himself. . . .

This is an intriguing tale, full of all the double-dealing and complexities one expects from any novel involving spies and clandestine agencies. Kavanagh is a fascinating character, and Block's writing is as good as ever. The only drawback is an irritating and unnecessary bit of publisher's hype—attempting to fool the reader into thinking this is a true story and Paul Kavanagh a real person—which precedes the novel. *Such Men Are Dangerous* is good enough to stand on its own merits.

Block's other books under the Kavanagh name (in which the fictional Kavanagh does not reappear) are *The Triumph of Evil* (1972), another CIA type of adventure; and *Not Comin' Home to You* (1974), the story of a young fugitive.

(*M.M.*)

Kaye, M. M. *Death in Zanzibar.* New York: St. Martin's, 1983. (W/R)

In the 1950s, M. M. Kaye, who would much later become the best-selling author of *Trade Wind* and *The Far Pavilions,* was a young mother of two and wife of a British Army officer. "Since my husband kept being posted to all sorts of novel and entertaining places," she has said, "I wrote a 'whodunit' set in each of them."

The resultant mysteries are steeped in the most aromatic of local fragrances, and each bears as well the scent of Kaye's girlhood idols, Agatha Christie, Mignon G. Eberhart, and Mary Roberts Rinehart (qq.v.). They were not originally published in America and had been long forgotten until, following the success of her historical novels, they were revised by the author and republished in a series by St. Martin's Press. The first of this series, originally published in Great Britain as *The House of Shade,* was *Death in Zanzibar*.

Dany Ashton, savoring her independence after graduating from school, is invited for a holiday at her stepfather's house in Zanzibar (Kivulimi, which 100 years before was the house of Rory Frost in *Trade Wind*). Before Dany leaves London, she is supposed to pick up a letter from her stepfather's solicitor. Just after she has done so, the solicitor is murdered. Dany, seeing no connection between herself and the murder, takes off for Africa. But one of her fellow passengers is also murdered, and Dany realizes that somebody will do anything to lay hands on the mysterious letter. She is protected by Lash Holden, a wealthy and handsome young American publisher, but begins to wonder why it is that he seems always to be nearby when she is in danger: Is he the killer—or does someone want her to think so?

Kaye's other mysteries are *Death in Kenya* (1983; published in Britain as *Later than You Think: A Tale of 1958*); and *Death in Kashmir* and *Death in Cyprus* (both 1984). She has observed that while her settings were very up-to-date when she wrote her mysteries, a changing world has turned them into period pieces. This is true. The plots and settings alike have aged considerably, although readers of early Agatha Christie will be comfortable with these novels. Some of the less appealing aspects of the mysteries actually result from sound social observation. The racism of the central characters in *Death in Kenya,* for example, will offend many readers. But whites in Kenya during the Mau Mau scares of the 1950s could not realistically be portrayed any other way, and *Kenya* is arguably the deepest and best of Kaye's mysteries.

(*M.J.*)

Kaye, Marvin. *The Grand Ole Opry Murders.* New York: Saturday Review Press/Dutton, 1974. (PI/AD)

This is the best of Marvin Kaye's novels about publicist Hilary Quayle and her private investigator/secretary, Gene. The background is what makes this book—Nashville during the annual awards at the Grand Ole Opry, an event the author himself attended as a press representative. Kaye gives us a good look into the country-music business, cameo appearances by real-life celebrities, and one of the most disagreeable clans of music makers we could ever hope to meet.

When Hilary takes on a prospective assignment as PR woman for the singing Boulder Clan, she sends Gene to join the family on tour in Atlanta. Upon his arrival, he finds that Amanda, easily the most talented of the clan, has been called to Nashville by manager Charlie Lisle; the rest continue on tour, eventually arriving at the country-music capital, where they are confronted by an unpleasant surprise: Amanda is leaving the group to go solo, as well as marrying sister Dolly's ex-husband, Josh Mackenzie. Rivalries and resentments among the members of the clan have always been fierce; now they grow to the point of violence. Amanda dies during a rehearsal, the victim of poisoning. And Hilary Quayle—a frustrated private detective who hired Gene because of his investigator's license—arrives in town, determined to solve the murder.

Unfortunately, Hilary is not at all a likable character. Critic Michele Slung has summed up the problem very well: ". . . she is a bit high-handed and sulks when the clues don't come her way." Hilary sulks, all right—all over Nashville—and Gene comes in for more than his fair share of verbal and physical (Hilary likes to slap people) abuse. It makes one wonder why Gene, who is a pleasant if somewhat colorless fellow, puts up with her at all. And while Hilary does eventually solve the murder, it's easier to feel sympathy for the killer than for this amateur sleuth. Still, the background is colorful and the novel is worth reading for that alone.

Some other titles in the series are *A Lively Game of Death* (1972) and *Bullets for Macbeth* (1976). Kaye also writes a series about sleuth Marty Gold (*My Son, the Druggist,* 1977; *My Brother, the Druggist,* 1979).

(*M.M.*)

*Keating, H.R.F. *Inspector Ghote Caught in Meshes.* New York: Dutton, 1968. (PP)

H.R.F. Keating's books are not so much stories set in India as Indian experiences on paper. Reflecting the unhurried life in India itself, each book's pace is leisurely; the investigations appear to meander, and even the action scenes inch along. Through it all Inspector Ganesh Ghote (Ganesha, the Hindu elephant god, is said to remove obstacles) ponders the possible ramifications of his actions and weighs his conflicting responsibilities to his employer, to the victims, and, when faced with great danger, to his family. Pervading it all is the insecurity of Indian life: If Ghote is killed, his dependents will be without support; and when someone else dies, it is accepted matter-of-factly, for death is not unfamiliar in India.

Keating, like Tony Hillerman (q.v.), focuses on the importance of integrity among people in a society where the sands are always shifting. Ghote is foremost an honorable man, trying to deal truthfully with situations where honesty is not expedient.

Inspector Ghote is among the best of the non–Anglo Saxon detectives. For the most part he is convincing, though with such an in-depth treatment of a character, the question does arise: How thoroughly can a Westerner know the thoughts and self-doubts that are so personal that Ghote would not speak them aloud? There is, of course, no answer to this.

For those who delight in sharing the Indian experience, the books are a pleasure. For those who don't, they may be irritatingly slow.

In *Inspector Ghote Caught in the Meshes* (one of the earlier titles in the series), the inspector is assigned not so much to find the killer of a visiting American who took it upon himself to visit an off-limits installation outside Bombay, but primarily to protect the American's surviving brother. The authorities think the dead man may have told his brother, Professor Strongbow, about what he saw at the installation, and Ghote's orders are to find out what he knows. To Ghote's paranoiac temporary boss, the head of an FBI-like unit, Strongbow's life is clearly secondary to his knowledge. Ghote is caught between the pressure from his boss and his own desire to be candid with Strongbow; between his plans and the professor's impetuous behavior; between his sense of decency and the need to badger the professor into revealing his knowledge.

Set in Bombay and Poona, the book includes a visit to the giant statues on the island of Elephants, danger from the raging tides at Bombay's Marine Drive, and an elephant stampede in Poona. One of the nice touches is the introduction of a half-Indian character who takes it upon herself to attempt to explain the idiosyncrasies of the local life-style to Professor Strongbow.

Additional novels featuring Inspector Ghote and similarly colorful locales include *Inspector Ghote Plays a Joker* (1969), *Inspector Ghote Trusts the Heart* (1973), *Inspector Ghote Draws a Line* (1979), and *The Sheriff of Bombay* (1984).

(*S.D.*)

Keating, H.R.F. *The Murder of the Maharajah.* New York: Doubleday Crime Club, 1980. (PP/H)

This is a charming novel deliberately in the tradition of Agatha Christie (q.v.). (Many of the characters announce that they read Christie.)

The maharajah of Phopore, an uncontrolled practical joker, invites a group of British and Americans to his palace on April Fool's Day, 1930. His mischief knows no limits; he plays jokes of questionable taste on his guests and on the viceroy himself. Before the evening's banquet, his second son dies—ptomaine or poison? During the banquet he pronounces his own food poisoned, and sends his aide to the dungeons—is this another joke? But in the morning the jokes backfire.

With the maharajah's death, Detective Inspector Howard is called in. Howard is "country-born," an Englishman who has never been out of India. As the viceroy explains to his son, while Howard is "plainly a gentleman . . . he is nevertheless clearly Not One of Us." Howard has the observer's understanding of both English and Indian cultures. He knows how to deal with the new maharajah and his English floozy, with the brash American businessman and Her First Highness, whom he can interview only with an opaque screen separating them. He understands that servants hear everything, that bands of monkeys pick things up, and that his most valuable ally will be the schoolmaster for the maharajah's illegitimate sons.

As in the Ghote books, the plot is leisurely. But the setting and the characters are so delightful that the book seems to end too soon. And the very last line leaves the reader with a smile and an "Ahah!"

Additional nonseries books by Keating are *Death of a Fat God* (1966), which has a theater background; *A Remarkable Case of Burglary* (1976), which is set in England in 1871; and *A Long Walk to Wimbledon* (1978), set in contemporary England.

(*S.D.*)

Keeler, Harry Stephen. *Thieves' Nights.* New York: Dutton, 1929. (W)

Keeler was the sublime nutty genius of crime fiction. His more than seventy novels form a self-contained world of labyrinthine intrigues, combining farce, Grand Guignol, Oriental philosophy, radical social criticism, and the wildest plots ever devised by the mind of man. He invented the so-called webwork novel, in which hundreds of bizarre events explode like cigars in the white-knight hero's face but turn out in the end to be mathematically interrelated, with every absurd development making perfect sense within Keeler's frame of reference. His favorite gimmicks for tying story elements together were the loony law, the nutty religious tenet, the wacky will, the crackpot contract, and, commonest of all, the interlocking network of outrageous coincidences. He loved to have his characters talk in self-invented ethnic dialects and to throw them into quasi-science-fictional situations. He loved to attack social evils: racism, brutal cops, the military, corrupt pols, capital punishment, the maltreatment of the mentally ill—all the dark underside of an America where "Money was Emperor, and Might was Right." And most of all he loved cats, even dedicating some novels to favorite felines.

Most of Keeler's early novels are set in Chicago and feature a pseudo–Arabian Nights framework, grotesque characters and events, bitter social comment, and Victorian dialogue so as almost to suggest an American Dickens. In *Thieves' Nights,* for example, a penniless Chicago drifter named Ward Sharlow is hired to impersonate a look-alike missing heir and runs into all sorts of crazy dilemmas trying to keep up the deception in the young millionaire's household. Among the members of the household is a disfigured and suspicious-looking butler. Eventually Ward sends the butler off on a paper chase and searches his quarters, finding a long novella that the servant seems to have written in his leisure time.

In the novella, a man is sitting on a park bench telling a story to another man. In the story he tells, a young man enters the office of a crooked governor who's allergic to sunlight and starts telling him a whole series of stories, all of which revolve around a half-Jesus, half-Zorro figure known as Bayard Delancey, King of Thieves. By the time the young man has finished the last Delancey tale, he's attained his objective, namely keeping the governor so entranced that he's failed to sign certain official papers before a deadline and thus ruined himself personally and politically.

So ends the butler's manuscript, which takes up about forty percent of *Thieves' Nights,* and we return to the outer circle of the novel. Wacky complications continue to grow out of astronomical coincidences, and Sharlow runs into such typical Keeler creations as Abraham Smelzman, shyster lawyer supreme; and George Little-White-Bear, an Indian guide with a Ph.D. in psychology and an expert knowledge of Freudian dream symbolism. Finally, when Sharlow is eyeballs-deep in the stew and it seems that nothing could pull him out, into the outer circle of the book pops none other than Bayard Delancey, King of Thieves! The hero of that innermost level of the plot turns out to be as "real" as Sharlow himself or the butler, and his sudden appearance saves the day.

Keeler was quite popular in the late Twenties and Thirties, but the older he became, the wilder his flights of fancy grew, and the fewer readers flew with him. In his last years, his books weren't published in the United States or England but only in Spanish and Portuguese translations. He died in 1967, confident that someday he'd be read again—and surely he deserves to be. His mad mad world is like nothing else in fiction.

Among Keeler's other novels are *The Box from Japan* (1932), which at 765 pages is one of the longest mystery novels ever written; *The Washington Square Enigma* (1933); and *The Mysterious Mr. I* (1938) and its sequel, *The Chameleon* (1939).

(*F.M.N.*)

Keene, Day. *Notorious.* Greenwich, Conn.: Fawcett Gold Medal, 1954. (O/T)

Day Keene was a prolific writer for the pulps and later for the paperback market. He published crime, mystery, and suspense novels with Ace, Avon, Gold Medal, Graphic, Phantom, Pyramid, and Zenith, among others. Keene was an expert at the standard pulp plot in which a protagonist is put into a seemingly impossible situation, whereafter things get steadily worse.

Ed Ferron, owner of a small carnival, is just out of prison, having served three years for killing his wife's lover. His show is in financial trouble and he owes $16,000 to the bank. Arriving in the small southern town of Bay Bayou, he finds the crowds small and the newspaper printing editorials against his show. In rapid succession, he meets a beautiful blonde, gets into a fight, gets into trouble with the law, and finds himself framed for murder. And that's when things begin to get worse.

There is nothing exactly innovative in this plot, but Keene is a natural storyteller; he keeps things moving right along, and no reader is likely to get bored before reaching the end of the book. In addition, the carnival background, while not really an integral part of the plot, is put to good use. *Notorious* is one of a small group of mysteries with a carnival setting, and the cover of the first Gold Medal printing makes it a must for collectors of this theme.

(*B.C.*)

Keene, Day. *Who Has Wilma Lathrop?* Greenwich, Conn.: Fawcett Gold Medal, 1955. (O/T)

Day Keene could take a familiar story and tell it so well, and with such a well-paced combination of narrative and plot, that it would seem almost fresh. *Who Has Wilma Lathrop?* is a good example of this ability.

Jim Lathrop is a happily married schoolteacher until the night two strangers stop him to ask about his wife, give him an envelope with $5000 in it for her, and then beat him senseless. He then realizes that in his brief courtship (two months) and marriage (three months) he has really learned very little about the woman he married. But Wilma denies ever having met or heard of the two men, and Lathrop believes her. That night, however, she disappears, and things begin to get really complicated. The janitor in Lathrop's building is found beaten to death, and in the basement furnace are found a few bones, the melted heel of a high-heeled shoe, and a melted ring very much like Wilma's engagement ring. Lathrop finds himself wanted by the police for murder and by the two strangers for something else. He also finds out that his wife has a lengthy police record.

Keene's strength was not in originality of plot ideas but in the new twists he brought to them and in the way he made his characters believable, even in the oddest situations. These strengths are clearly in evidence in *Who Has Wilma Lathrop?* It's fast and satisfying.

The same is true of several of Keene's other novels, among them *Framed in Guilt* (1949), *Home Is the Sailor* (1954), *Murder on the Side* (1958), and *Too Hot to Hold* (1959).

(*B.C.*)

Kelland, Clarence Budington. *Mark of Treachery.* New York: Dodd, Mead, 1961. (W)

Some authors have a gift for idiosyncratic language and uncommon situations. One of the best of these was Clarence Budington Kelland, creator of the Scattergood Baines stories (collected in *Scattergood Baines,* 1921, *Scattergood Returns,* 1940, and *Scattergood Baines Pulls the Strings,* 1941). Kelland's male characters are tall, good-looking, intense, and very sincere; while his young women are intelligent, determined, and aggressive (with a large streak of deviousness).

In *Mark of Treachery,* Avery Truslow III accepts a challenge from his father to take over a family-owned and almost bankrupt television station in Van Buren, Pennsylvania. After picking up a young woman who claims she has missed her bus near his Long Island home and having her leave his car abruptly in Van Buren, Avery reports to work and begins to investigate why the station is in trouble. It doesn't take him long to conclude that it is being sabotaged by individuals interested in buying its license cheaply. As Avery probes further, he becomes involved with various eccentric characters: Parsifal Nebo, an urbane hippopotamus of a man; Philidor, who practices being inscrutable; and the young hitchhiking lady, who, it turns out, is visiting the local queen of society. Avery finds himself doing some courting on the side while, with the help of a young man on his staff who wants to become an announcer, he pieces together some overheard conversations and provocative situations. In a climactic scene, Avery successfuly combats creditors, sabotage, and rumor.

Kelland's quirky conversational style and bright and lively characters (all of whom are just a little larger than life) made his work a constant feature for several decades in such magazines as *The Saturday Evening Post.* (At one time he was one of the highest-paid and most popular of the *Post*'s contributors.) His novels often feature heroes who have been thrust into some unfamiliar and interesting situation, such as owning a beauty salon or cosmetic firm, or dealing with accidentally acquired counterfeit money.

Other entertaining Kelland novels include *The Great Mail Robbery* (1951), which deals with the New York postal system; *Death Keeps a Secret* (1956), whose hero is an eccentric scientist named Thomas Alva Edison Gimp; and *The Artless Heiress* (1962), whose female heroine, the improbably named Columbine Pepper Drugget, is completely out of her element when she inherits an Arizona motel.

(*E.N.*)

*Kemelman, Harry. *Friday the Rabbi Slept Late.* New York: Crown, 1964. (AD)

There is no job security for a rabbi, or at least for Rabbi David Small. According to Kemelman, Judaism is a pragmatic religion and the rabbi is well versed in the wisdom of the Talmud. He uses its lessons to judge disputes within the Jewish community, but he is not essentially different from other men; he has no supposed mystical powers like priests who turn a wafer into the body of Christ. And whenever his contract comes up for renewal, his congregation can fire him.

Rabbi David Small is in many ways the most appealing of the clergy detectives. A young and all-too-often rumpled scholar, he is committed to preserving the integrity of Judaism in the face of the growing secularism of his congregation (many of whom would like a more presentable rabbi), the chauvinism of the surrounding gentile population, and the desire of the members of the Jewish community to be well thought of by their gentile neighbors.

As a counterpoint, Kemelman has created Police Chief Hugh Lanigan a Catholic whose family has lived in the Massachusetts village of Barnard's Crossing for generations. An ethical man, Lanigan is practical where Small is unbending, and the interchanges between the two bring to light the unique and fascinating qualities of both the Jewish community (good and bad) and of New England village life.

Kemelman combines solid plotting with lively, believable characters. He has a superb ear for dialogue, particularly for that between married couples and among temple members. These converstations are crisp, idiomatic, and frequently amusing.

In *Friday the Rabbi Slept Late,* Rabbi Small finds himself suspected of killing an au pair girl whose body was found on the temple grounds and whose purse was in his car. While he searches for the reason for her murder, he must simultaneously deal with the members of the various warring factions of the temple and face the first of many attempts to vote down the renewal of his contract.

(*S.D.*)

*Kemelman, Harry. *The Nine Mile Walk.* New York: Putnam's, 1967. (SS)

Before his creation of Rabbi David Small, Harry Kemelman wrote an intermittent series of short detective stories featuring Nicholas Welt, Snowdon Professor of English Literature. All eight Nicky Welt tales, which first appeared in *Ellery Queen's Mystery Magazine* between 1947 and 1967, are collected in this volume. In his introduction Kemelman says of them, "[They] attracted attention, I think, because they were the epitome of the armchair type of detective story. The problems were solved by pure logic and the reader was given the same clues that were available to the detective hero. Furthermore, Nicky Welt was given no advantage, no special powers of intuition, no profound knowledge of criminology. In all candor, this was not so much a matter of choice as of necessity, since I myself had no such knowledge."

The best of the stories is the title piece, a small classic of ratiocination that Kemelman's peers in the Mystery Writers of America voted a "hall of fame" story in a recent poll. On a challenge from the unnamed narrator (of this and the other stories in the series), Nicky builds a logical chain of inferences from a single sentence—"A nine mile walk is no joke, especially in the rain"—that amazingly, but altogether logically, turns out to be anything but a mere mental exercise. The other tales are almost as good, with this reviewer's favorites being "The Ten O'Clock Scholar," a fascinating academic mystery; "End Play," which effectively combines chess, U.S. Army Intelligence, and murder most foul; and "The Man on a Ladder," which deals with blackmail, homicide, and a very different kind of chess game.

Any reader who enjoys fine writing, ingenious puzzles, and a cerebral sleuth in the classic mold will find this collection more than rewarding.

(*B.P.*)

Kemelman, Harry. *Tuesday the Rabbi Saw Red.* New York: Fields, 1974. (AD)

After the Edgar-winning *Friday the Rabbi Slept Late,* Kemelman went on to add the other six days of the week to the series. *Tuesday* is the least typical of the Rabbi Small novels, and in it Kemelman combines his two fields of interest—academic life and Jewish life—by having the rabbi teach a class in Jewish thought and philosophy at a local college. When the professor with whom he shares an office (and who has made anti-Semitic comments) is killed, Rabbi Small is drawn into an investigation that leads him from a campus radical group to an impecunious old New England family. He deals with both the lack of integrity in collegiate standards and the questions of gentile colleagues, which frequently begin, "You people. . . ." As always, it is by use of his knowledge of the Talmud that he discovers both the motive and the murderer.

This is a particularly good entry in the series, giving us an interesting glimpse into the academic world as well as the effects of anti-Semitism on those who suffer from it. Small is his usual likable self, and the other characters—particularly the Jewish ones, who are never stereotypical—are sure to engage the reader's interest.

On some other days of the week, the Rabbi *Went Hungry* (1966), *Took Off* (1972), and *Got Wet* (1976). And *Someday the Rabbi Will Leave* (1985).

(*S.D.*)

Kendrick, Baynard H. *The Iron Spiders.* New York: Greenberg, 1936. (CS)

Stan Rice, like his creator, knows Florida. As a deputy sheriff and deputy game and freshwater commissioner, he especially knows its wild areas. *The Iron Spiders* is the first of three novels about Rice, who also appeared in fourteen short stories published in *Black Mask* between 1937 and 1940. Like so many of the mysteries of the Golden Age, even those by a relatively hard-boiled author, it features many bizarre elements: Spiders are left at the murder scenes, and locked rooms and voodoo figure prominently in the plot.

Rice is most memorable for the gargantuan appetite that belies his tall, slim build. He claims to think of nothing else but eating, repeatedly saying of himself in the series, "I'm Miles Standish Rice, The Hungry." He clearly does dwell upon other things, primarily fishing (his great hobby since his Florida boyhood) and detection. Most of his cases combine these two interests, along with his prodigious eating. Another typical Rice quote is "I hate murder as much as I love fishing."

Clues are important in *The Iron Spiders,* but ultimately it is Stan Rice's knowledge of the local terrain, including his mobility through the swamps, that guarantees his success. Kendrick's descriptions of the Florida countryside, especially the Keys, are excellent, and his limning of a tropical storm is noteworthy. Written and set during the depression, *The Iron Spiders* is eminently successful at capturing its time as well as its place, Florida.

The other two Rice novels are *The Eleven of Diamonds* (1963) and *Death Beyond the Go-Through* (1938).

(*M.L.*)

*Kendrick, Baynard H. *Odor of Violets.* Boston: Little, Brown, 1941. (CS)

It was the creation of Captain Duncan Maclain, one of the most famous of the "disabled" detectives, that ensured Baynard Kendrick's success. Maclain lost his sight while serving as an intelligence officer during World War I, the war in which Kendrick served in the Canadian Expeditionary Forces, even prior to the involvement of the United States in the fighting. After the war Maclain became a detective, although he was wealthy enough to remain idle, enjoying his large collection of Braille books and phonograph records in the luxury apartment he maintains on the twenty-sixth floor of a building at Seventy-second Street and Riverside Drive in Manhattan. Instead, he chooses to solve crimes with his partner, Samuel ("Spud") Savage, a close friend who has even taught him to fire a gun by aiming at sounds. The "firm" includes the dogs, Schnuke and Dreist, two of the most interesting animals in mystery fiction.

Odor of Violets contains most of the elements of the classic murder story, beginning with an eccentric, wealthy family, the Tredwills of Tredwill Village, Connecticut. A beautiful young girl is killed by decapitation, and the titular odor of violets is an important clue, but, strangely enough, so is another aroma, that of gasoline. However, there is more to the book than just the tightly plotted, well resolved conclusion to a bizarre murder. The United States is on the eve of World War II, and an invention that figured in so many mystery and spy stories of the time, the improved bombsight, is involved. The head of G-2, U.S. Intelligence, on the East Coast asks Maclain's help in preventing its theft. To do that, Duncan Maclain must also capture a murderer. The action is extremely fast-paced, moving from Connecticut to New York City's Greenwich Village, and most critics consider *Odor of Violets* to be the best book in the Maclain series.

During World War II, Kendrick was very active in helping servicemen who had been blinded in combat. His well-received 1945 novel *Lights Out* tells of the rehabilitation of a sightless veteran. When Kendrick resumed his Maclain series that same year, it became obvious that he was less interested in telling the pure detective puzzle. In *Out of Control* (1945), Maclain, on his honeymoon in the Great Smokies of Tennessee, faces a murderess whose identity is never disguised. The book, especially the ending, is as exciting as most of Kendrick, but the author is now primarily interested in dealing with psychology rather than physical clues.

(*M.L.*)

Kenrick, Tony. *Stealing Lillian.* New York: McKay, 1975. (T)

At the beginning of *Stealing Lillian,* the hero, Bunny Calder, New York travel agent and head of a one-man employment bureau, runs three scams before noon. One of these is selling a young and very attractive woman on the idea of a sea cruise. Unbeknown to her, while she's sailing away, he rents out her apartment (his capture of her keys is a joy to behold) to a couple of rich midwesterners. Bunny pockets an easy thousand and no one's the wiser. . . .

Except that after a night on the town, the midwesterners and friends end up replaying the Ohio State–Michigan game, using a melon as the football. And when the young woman returns, she finds her beautiful apartment completely destroyed. Once she figures out what has happened, Bunny Calder is living on borrowed time.

Fortunately for Bunny, the lady's lawyer gets to him first. While a fine and reputable attorney in the private sector, he has over the years offered his clandestine services to the U.S. Immigration Service. Immigration has just come to him with a devil of an emergency: Middle Eastern terrorists have slipped into the country via Canada with plans of illegally securing U.S. dollars to fund their particular brand of political upheaval. The government wants to flush them out with a fake kidnap/ransom scheme. The lawyer must create a millionaire—a Howard Hughes–like individual who has decided to come out of seclusion, bringing with him a beautiful wife and adored ten-year-old daughter.

In a hilarious meeting with the lawyer and the irate young woman, Bunny is "persuaded" to play the part of the millionaire. The woman is recruited for the role of the wife—and she does an artful acting job in spite of the fact that she's ready to kill Bunny. As the daughter, Lillian, the lawyer has accepted a volunteer—a ten-year-old street-wise orphan who figures that if she survives this ordeal she can sell her story for big bucks and get out of the state-operated orphanage where a kid has to fight for mashed potatoes, let alone an occasional hug.

Lillian doesn't hug anyone—at least not in the beginning. And neither does Bunny or his "wife." They are all tough cookies, and Kenrick does a wonderful job of showing how they handle a terrifically harrowing kidnapping (two, in fact). By the end, of course, they all adore each other, and one senses there's a future for this manufactured family.

This is a very funny and lightning-paced book, highly recommended. Among Kenrick's other comedy thrillers are *A Tough One to Lose* (1972), *Two for the Price of One* (1974), *The Seven Day Soldiers* (1976), *The Night-time Guy* (1979), and *The 81st Site* (1980).

(*K.K.H.*)

Kenyon, Michael. *A Free-Range Wife.* New York: Doubleday Crime Club, 1983. (W)

Many readers demand that their mysteries contain clear-cut puzzles with numerous twists and a murderer exposed on the last page. Such readers would likely be disappointed by Michael Kenyon's novels. Other readers, especially those who enjoy humor with their murder, will be delighted.

Kenyon brings back his wacky Inspector Henry Peckover and sets him on the murder trail not in England but in France. For Peckover it is a busman's holiday with a vengeance. Accompanying his wife—a chef who takes a temporary job at the exclusive Château de Mordan—he is called in to assist an investigation of the murders and sexual mutilations of several men. Oddly enough, the one thing the men have in common is the Mordan's chatelaine, Mrs. Mercy McCluskey.

When not drinking and eating to excess, attempting to communicate with his wife, who has been stricken temporarily mute, or riding a stuffed moose through the château corridors, Peckover is hard at work tracking the killer. And there is little doubt who the killer must be. Not that Kenyon deliberately shows his hand too soon; he just plays fair in the easiest possible manner, letting the reader zero in on the obvious villain at the same time his sleuth does.

Kenyon's absurd brand of humor more than makes up for any deficiencies in the puzzle department. Peckover's chase through the shrine at Lourdes—yes, the shrine at Lourdes—is memorable, as is his bad poetry. The most entertaining aspect of the book, however, is the cockney Peckover's inability to make himself understood by the merciless French. Any English-speaking traveler in France will likely relate to Peckover's frustration as every attempt to communicate in French is met with a cold "Hng?" or *"Comment?"*

Kenyon's other delightful, light novels featuring Peckover include *The Elgar Variation* (1981) and *The Man at the Wheel* (1982). Kenyon is also the author of an earlier series of mysteries starring Superintendent O'Malley; among the best of these are *The Shooting of Dan McGrew* (1972) and *A Sorry State* (1974; set in the Philippines).

(*K.L.M.*)

Kiefer, Warren. *The Lingala Code.* New York: Random House, 1972. (AD)

This novel, winner of an MWA Edgar for Best Novel of 1972, is basically a murder mystery set in the Congo in the early 1960s. But there are so many other things going on in the newly independent and chaotic republic—riots, assassinations, political upheavals, espionage, plots and counterplots—that the murder seems to diminish in significance.

It does not diminish in the mind of the story's protagonist, Michel Vernon, however, for it was his best friend, Ted Stearns, who was murdered. Vernon and Stearns first met as fighter pilots during the Korean War and eventually both were assigned to Leopoldville in the Congo, Vernon as a CIA agent in the American Embassy and Stearns as air attaché. Then one night in 1962 Stearns is shot, and Vernon makes it his business (along with quelling various insurrections and romancing a Frenchwoman from the United Nations) to find the killer.

Few mystery novels feature such a strong and realistic background as does *The Lingala Code.* It must be said, though, that this story—perhaps because of the very scope of it, perhaps because of the early inclusion of a great deal of background material—takes a while to get into. But, once into it, the reader is sure to continue to the end, anxious to discover how the murder investigation and the various intrigues and power plays turn out.

The Pontius Pilate Papers (1976) and *The Kidnappers* (1977) are two other novels by Warren Kiefer. The latter has an Argentine setting.

(*N.D.*)

*Kienzle, William. *The Rosary Murders.* Kansas City: Andrews & McMeel, 1979. (AD)

The Rosary Murders is set in the Roman Catholic diocese of Detroit and is the first in a series of extremely popular mysteries. Its author knows both the larger community of the city and the smaller one of the church, since he is a former priest and, for fourteen years, editor of the *Michigan Catholic.* His narrator, Father Bob Koesler, occupies a similar position, as editor of the diocesan weekly paper—a position that puts him in line to find out a great many things that are less than holy.

The first murder strikes the diocese on Ash Wednesday. The victim is a nun, drowned in her bath, the crime seeming all the more horrible because of the supposed sanctity of her person. There is the suspicion that the deaths of other individuals with religious vocations—such as a priest who recently died at St. Mary's Mercy Hospital—may not have been as natural as they first seemed. The killings go on, and Detroit homicide investigators are unable to understand the murderer's motivation or the odd clues he leaves, until Father Koesler, with his knowledge of the church and its ways, uncovers a vital connection.

This and other Father Koesler novels—*Death Wears a Red Hat* (1980), *Mind Over Murder* (1981), *Assault with Intent* (1982), *Shadow of Death* (1983) and *Kill And Tell* (1984)—are full of lively and interesting characters, from Lieutenant Walter Koznicki of the Detroit Police Department to Pat Lennon and Joe Cox, rival but loving newspaper reporters. The characterization of the priests and nuns of the diocese is particularly good, revealing them in all their human strengths and weaknesses. And Kienzle's portrait of Detroit does a great deal to re-create it in the eyes of many readers, particularly those who are—like this reviewer—natives of that much-maligned city.

(*M.M.*)

*King, C. Daly. *The Curious Mr. Tarrant.* London: Collins, 1935. (First U.S. publication: New York: Dover, 1977.) (SS/AD)

Perhaps it is a reflection of American publishers' attitudes toward short-story collections that this volume, published in England in 1935 to acclaim from Dorothy L. Sayers (q.v.) and later praised by Ellery Queen (q.v.), had to wait until 1977 for its first American edition. If wealthy amateur detective Trevis Tarrant is an unremarkable sleuth, the eight cases he investigates here are remarkable indeed. The first seven are locked-room or impossible-crime stories, quite well done and brimming with atmosphere, though the last, "The Episode of the Final Bargain," leans too heavily toward the supernatural.

In the opening story, "The Episode of the Codex' Curse," an ancient Aztec codex disappears from a locked basement room in New York's Metropolitan Museum in the presence of a witness. "The Episode of the Tangible Illusion" concerns a haunted house. "The Episode of the Nail and the Requiem," a special favorite of Sayers's and Queen's, is a very good locked-room mystery. Perhaps the best story in the book, with just a touch of horror, is "The Episode of Torment IV." It recalls the "Mary Celeste" mystery with its tale of a motorboat that somehow causes its occupants to leap out and drown each time it is taken out on the lake. In "The Episode of the Headless Horrors," headless torsos are found along a populated road. "The Episode of the Vanishing Harp" concerns the disappearance of a harp from a locked room. And "The Episode of the Man with Three Eyes" is about the stabbing of a woman while in a restaurant booth with two innocent men.

King also produced six detective novels, the best of which is the extremely clever *Obelists Fly High* (1935), set aboard an early transcontinental plane. A close second is *Arrogant Alibi* (1938), about a locked-room stabbing at the time of a Connecticut flood. *Careless Corpse* (1937) is about an impossible poisoning.

(*E.D.H.*)

King, Rufus. *Malice in Wonderland.* New York: Doubleday Crime Club, 1958. (SS)

Rufus King had two distinct "careers" in crime fiction. The first was as a writer of traditional Golden Age whodunits, beginning in 1927 and continuing until 1951. He produced twenty-two novels during this period, most of which are entertaining despite some stilted prose; they are marked by clever plotting, interesting backgrounds, and touches of gentle humor. King's best work, however, is his short fiction, particularly that written during his second "career" in the 1950s and 1960s when he abandoned novels altogether and concentrated on stories for *Ellery Queen's Mystery Magazine.*

Malice in Wonderland, the second of King's four collections, was so highly regarded by the Mssrs. Queen that they included it in their Supplement Number One (1951–59) to the Queen's Quorum. The eight stories here expose the violence and corruption of the fictional town of Halcyon, Florida—after the fashion, if not in the style, of John D. MacDonald (q.v.).

Queen said that in these stories King "pungently, almost maliciously impale[s] . . . the Gold Coast, that fabulous neon strip between Miami Beach and Fort Lauderdale, with its cross section of natives and tourists, of greedy heirs and retired gangsters (alive and dead)." The best story in the collection, "The Body in the Pool," traces the strange connection between the state of Florida's electrocution of murderer Saul ("Stripe-pants") McSager and the selection of Mrs. Warburton Waverly as the county's "Most Civic-Minded Woman of the Year." Also excellent are the title story, in which a girl tries to decode a message from a long-dead playmate; and the long novelette "Let Her Kill Herself," in which an unpleasant woman makes an extremely disturbing discovery.

Some of King's early short stories are collected in *Diagnosis: Murder* (1941). Two other collections of stories about Halcyon and the Florida Gold Coast, both of which rank with *Malice in Wonderland,* are *The Steps to Murder* (1960) and *The Faces of Danger* (1964).

(*B.P./G.K.*)

King, Rufus. *Murder by Latitude.* New York: Doubleday Crime Club, 1930. (W)

Rufus King's sole series character was a New York police detective, Lieutenant Valcour. A proper gentleman detective, Valcour's only unusual characteristic is that he is a French Canadian.

Murder by Latitude is one of Valcour's more exotic cases. The *Eastern Bay* is a cheap passenger-carrying freighter making a Bermuda-to-Halifax run. Lieutenant Valcour boards the ship with the news that one of the passengers is a murderer. One of the victims is dead of strangulation, the other is in a New York City hospital; police are hoping this victim will recover to give a description of the killer. The murderer sabotages radio communication so police can not send the description of the guilty party, but Valcour has clues that indicate the murderer is aboard the *Eastern Bay* and he starts his investigation on his own among the bizarre ménage of passengers. As the degrees of latitude sail by, the murderer strikes again, leaving such cryptic clues as a lump of wax, a stolen thimble, and a pair of scissors. Valcour achieves some impressive feats of detection to tie the clues to the culprit in classic fashion.

Another recommended Valcour sea mystery is the fine *Murder on the Yacht* (1932). Valcour made an impressive debut with *Murder by the Clock* (1929) and went on to detective fame in a half-dozen novels, concluding with *Murder Masks Miami* (1939). Notable among King's nonseries novels are *A Variety of Weapons* (1943), *The Case of the Dowager's Etchings* (1944), and *Museum Piece No. 13* (1946).

(*G.K.*)

*Kirst, Hans Hellmut. *The Night of the Generals.* New York: Harper, 1962. (H)

The scene is Nazi-occupied Warsaw in 1942; a woman has been brutally murdered and sexually mutilated. The Polish police call in the German authorities because the woman was one of their collaborators, and Major Grau, head of counterespionage for the Warsaw area, begins an investigation that is to plague him for many years to come. The murder is no ordinary killing, because a witness saw the perpetrator leave—wearing the uniform of a German general. Grau knows the man is dangerous and must be apprehended: "No exceptions are to be made," he says, "even if a general's head has to roll."

There are three generals in the Warsaw area for whom Grau cannot verify an alibi: General von Seydlitz-Gabler, an old-school corps commander who has been pushed up the ladder of success by his strong and determined wife, Wilhelmine; Lieutenant General Tanz, career officer with a legendary reputation, whose "favourite hobby is arson"; and Major General Kahlenberge, a private, reticent man who is considered the "real brains of the outfit." Grau proceeds to question the men, intruding into their lives and those of their friends and families. And it is no surprise to the reader when Grau is abruptly transferred to Paris. Two years later, however, the same cast of characters is assembled there, and once again there is a brutal killing. And yet another in Dresden in 1956. . . .

This fascinating story is told from the viewpoints of the various principal characters, as well as through the device of interim investigative reports compiled in 1960 that consist of interviews with, and excerpts from letters written by, persons who knew the generals. Clues to the killer's identity—as well as a number of convincing red herrings—are carefully placed. Perhaps because any of these three finely drawn characters has the capacity for extreme brutality within him, the revelation of who the murderer is comes not so much as a surprise as a satisfying confirmation. This highly recommended novel contains all the elements to keep the reader spellbound: adventure, detection, and a completely believable love story.

A film version of *Night of the Generals* was made in 1967 starring Peter O'Toole, Omar Sharif, Joanna Pettet, and Christopher Plummer. Kirst, who is Germany's foremost suspense writer, has published such other outstanding novels as *Soldiers' Revolt* (1966), *Brothers in Arms* (1967), *Everything Has Its Price* (1976), and *The Nights of the Long Knives* (1976).

(*M.M.*)

Knickmeyer, Steve. *Straight.* New York: Random House, 1976. (PI)

Straight is a man's name—Richard Straight, to be exact. And once he *was* straight—a New York cop. Then his wife was killed by the mob, and he decided to give up, switch sides, and become a hit man. This story concerns his unlucky thirteenth hit (a man in Solano, Oklahoma) and all the things that go wrong with that hit. First another man (a man named Coady, who happens to be the person who killed Straight's wife) is assigned to work with him. Then someone witnesses the murder, necessitating yet another murder.

Then enter our protagonist, Steve Cranmer, a private detective from Oklahoma City; and his assistant, Butch Maneri. Cranmer and Maneri have been hired by the mistress of the deceased, who does not for one minute buy the popularly accepted suicide theory. At first glance, the two detectives seem physical wrecks—Cranmer is always gulping pain pills for an injured knee, and Maneri has a bad case of gastritis—but they soon prove they can take care of themselves. And it's a good thing they can, for this is an action-packed book with five killings and a couple of punch-outs.

Straight was nominated by the Mystery Writers of America for Best First Novel, and indeed it is one of those books that keeps you up, turning the pages, well past your bedtime. Oh, sure, you could say the author tries a little too hard for clever dialogue between the two detectives. You could marvel at the coincidence that brings Straight, the man who killed his wife (Coady), and a man he used to work with (Cranmer) together in a Solano, Oklahoma, motel room. But why be picky? Why not relax and enjoy a good read?

Knickmeyer's only other novel, *Cranmer* (1978), also features the Oklahoma City detective and is likewise worth reading.

(*N.D.*)

Knight, Clifford. *The Affair of the Limping Sailor.* New York: Dodd, Mead, 1942. (W)

The chief appeal of this novel is its opening situation, which parallels the famous *Mary Celeste* case. Vacationers on board the *Sea Stranger* find a fancier yacht, the *Golden Plover,* adrift in calm weather off the Baja California coast with no one on board. In her main cabin is a table set for luncheon; in the captain's cabin are bloodstains and a bullet hole; and there is evidence of a hurried exodus of passengers and crew. Among the group of vacationers is Huntoon Rogers, Knight's series sleuth. Rogers's deductive abilities are called upon immediately, and are thrown into high gear when the *Golden Plover*'s missing party is found stranded on a lonely island sans one person who has mysteriously disappeared. The missing man soon turns up dead, and it is up to Rogers to unmask his murderer and to explain the strange events that take place back on board the *Golden Plover* and later on Mexican soil.

Anyone who finds the unsolved *Mary Celeste* mystery fascinating will be engrossed by the first fifty pages. Unfortunately, the abandonment of the *Golden Plover* is all too quickly and conventionally explained, and the balance of the book is little more than a standard contrived whodunit with overtones of *Treasure Island.* Rogers is rather colorless and his deductions don't come close to plugging the holes in the plot. The sailing background is good, as are the descriptions of sea, island, and Baja California.

Knight's ability to vividly portray his wide range of settings is what makes the Huntoon Rogers mysteries worth reading. Those colorful backgrounds include the Galapagos Islands, Hawaii, Manila, the Painted Desert, Death Valley, and Yosemite National Park. Knight's first (and probably best) novel, *The Affair of the Scarlet Crab* (1937), won a Dodd, Mead prize. Other titles in the series include *The Affair of the Circus Queen* (1940), *The Affair of the Splintered Heart* (1942), and *The Affair of the Jade Monkey* (1943).

(*B.P.*)

Knight, Kathleen Moore. *Valse Macabre.* New York: Doubleday Crime Club, 1954. (AD)

The fifteen adventures of Elisha Macomber, selectman of Penberthy Island (which strongly resembles Martha's Vineyard, the author's home), are an armchair traveler's delight for their locales, dialect, diverse characters, and mystifying events. Macomber, a man of late middle years, with aquiline features and piercing blue eyes, owns and operates Macomber's Fish Market, which seems to be the unofficial headquarters of Medbury's community affairs.

Lieutenant Roger Nevens, back from an eighteen-month tour of duty in Korea, has just arrived on the ferry to pick up his wife, a dancer who has been staying and rehearsing at Holly Hill with her dance troop. He is told that she committed suicide by drowning the day before. Macomber, who had seen her dance during a demonstration of an intricate Austrian mechanical organ that was being restored for use in a nightclub, and who had heard a couple of strange conversations about her just a few days before, is convinced that she was murdered. After a second murder, this of an island native, Macomber intensifies his questioning and observations. The backgrounds of the dancers and also that of the organ repairman provide the vital clues. Macomber's solution leaves no loose ends; and justice—in its own way—is served.

A prolific writer (she published a total of thirty-five novels), Knight also wrote a series of four novels about Margot Blair, partner in a public-relations agency: The first of these is *Rendezvous with the Past* (1940); the last, *Design in Diamonds* (1944). Those of her books with no series characters are notable for their detailed descriptions of tourist locales, especially Mexico, as in *Stream Sinister* (1945) and *The Blue Horse of Taxco* (1947) and Panama (Bells for the Dead, 1942). Other Macomber titles include *Death Blew Out the Match* (1935), *The Trouble at Turkey Hill* (1946), and *Akin to Murder* (1953).

(*E.N.*)

Knox, Bill. *Rally to Kill.* New York: Doubleday Crime Club, 1975. (PP)

A prolific writer under his own name and the pseudonyms Robert MacLeod, Michael Kirk, and Noah Webster, Bill Knox writes best about his native Scotland in two successful detective series published under his own name. Both are police procedurals, one conventional and one unconventional. The conventional one, of which *Rally to Kill* is one of some twenty titles, features Glasgow Detective Chief Inspector Colin Thane and his partner, Inspector Phil Moss. The personalities of the two characters make them an excellent investigative team: Thane is married, more settled, but with a habit of letting his intuition guide his actions; Moss is a bachelor who suffers from a duodenal ulcer and limited insight, yet serves Thane as a powerful researcher. By combining their strengths, the team is able to solve the confounding cases that confront them.

One such case can be found in *Rally to Kill,* which opens with the discovery of the corpse of a young woman, savagely beaten and strangled, stuffed inside the trunk of an abandoned car. At first, Thane and Moss concentrate on locating a mysterious peeping tom who terrorized the young woman and her roommates. But they soon discover disquieting facts about the dead woman's past and a connection with a police officer whose alibi for the approximate time of her death—that he was preparing for a road rally—doesn't quite ring true. Slowly, meticulously, using authentic police procedure, Thane and Moss unravel the tangled plot; and the truth finally emerges in an exciting climax that takes place during the road rally.

This novel, like others in the series, offers a fascinating "inside" look at criminal investigation as practiced by the Glasgow CID, and a vivid portrait of contemporary Scottish life. Knox writes with a journalistic eye for detail, a result of his training and experience as a crime reporter in the 1950s.

Other recommended Thane and Moss books are *Justice on the Rocks* (1967), *The Tallyman* (1969), *Draw Batons!* (1973), *Pilot Error* (1977), and *Live Bait* (1979). The last named title is a particularly effective tale of illicit drug manufacturing linked to a network of whiskey distilleries in the remote Scottish Highlands; Knox's evocation of that part of his native country is memorable.

(*G.K./B.P.*)

*Knox, Bill. *Witchrock*. New York: Doubleday Crime Club, 1977. (PP/A)

Knox's second series of police procedurals, the unconventional one, features Webb Carrick of the Scottish Fishery Protection Service. Carrick is chief officer of the cruiser HMS *Marlin* and his beat is the remote islands of the Hebrides and the sea in which they lie—a beat he patrols with a regular cast of subordinate officers that includes Captain James Shannon and Chief Petty Officer William ("Clapper") Bell. The Carrick novels are concerned with such crimes as murder, gunrunning, smuggling, and espionage, as well as elements of native superstition and the supernatural; Knox also makes good use of his knowledge of the Hebrides fishing industry, deep-sea diving, and life on those isolated islands. As in the Thane and Moss series, the procedure followed by Carrick and his men is as authentic as the background, and gives us a rare glimpse into a way of life few of us will ever encounter firsthand.

One of the best books in the series, *Witchrock* begins with the brutal murder of a police official on Witchrock, "the most dreaded spot in the Brannan Sound"—a crime that is made to look like an accidental drowning. Carrick and his crew learn of the constable's death when they arrive at the Sound to collect ballot boxes from a clutch of offshore islands whose inhabitants are voting in a parliamentary by-election. A rash of beatings and "accidents" lead Carrick to investigate further. Among the people he meets are a lovely young woman, Shona Grant; and through her, the feared "Witch of the Isles," who is said to possess a frightening power. Carrick has to overcome the superstitions of the islanders, as well as other obstacles, before he discovers the motive behind the murder and violence—and learns the secret of the Witch of the Isles.

Striking background detail, interesting characters, and a tightly woven plot make this a first-rate mystery. The same qualities can be found in the other Carrick novels, notably *Devilweed* (1966), about the robbery of a floating branch of the Bank of Central Scotland; *The Klondyker* (1968), which combines such disparate elements as plesiosaurus sightings, cold-blooded murder, and the hunt for a sunken Spanish galleon; *Figurehead* (1968), in which Carrick and a woman scientist investigate reports of a sea serpent having attacked a fishing trawler; and *Stormtide* (1972), a tale of murder and treachery centered around a North Atlantic shark hunt.

(*B.P./G.K.*)

Knox, Ronald A. *The Footsteps at the Lock.* London: Methuen, 1928. (W)

Many people believe that Ronald A. Knox made his mark as a monsignor; some of us believe that he made hay inventing the scholarship of Sherlock Holmes; but hardly anyone recalls his six detective novels. Before he defected from detection and converted to Catholicism, Knox was one of the ringleaders of the glorious Golden Age of detective stories. As early as 1912, he was writing mock-solemn inquiries on the Sherlock Holmes stories that were satires of literary criticism. He developed "Studies in the Literature of Sherlock Holmes"—the basis for those crucial questions that still confound Sherlockians: How many times was Watson married? Which university did Holmes attend? When was the Red-Headed League dissolved?

In the 1920s, Knox promulgated definite rules for the fair-play detective story. He was also instrumental in setting up the Detection Club in England. His rules adjured against solutions using "Divine Revelation . . . Mumbo Jumbo, Coincidence . . . Death Rays, Ghosts, Hypnotism, Trap Doors . . . Mysterious Poisons Unknown to Science." And "no secret passages," which he criticized A. A. Milne for using (even though Knox himself has one in a story). Knox viewed the detective story as a game between the author and readers, with the vitally important eccentric amateur unraveling and flourishing clues, and logical deductions to reach a rational solution. In this frame he produced stories that had murder victims turn out to be suicides, accidents, the wrong victims, and mere disappearances. As he said, a detective novel "is an escape from real life," it is "deceit practiced on the reader," and "Heaven help us when the psychological crowd are let loose on it."

The Footsteps at the Lock is a typical English country-house mystery, without the butler, the male secretary, or even the country house. The locale is merely the countryside—a canoeing holiday on the reaches of the upper Thames, near Oxford. Two cousins who hate each other and are involved in complicated legacies set out on this holiday. When one disappears with evidence of foul play, the Indescribable Insurance Company calls upon its ace, Miles Bredon, to be "launched out anew upon that career of detection for which he had so remarkable an instinct, and so profound a distaste." Knox's humorous approach to detection—"I am sorry that so many characters in this story should appear only to disappear"—is exemplified by false identities and a lengthy, earnestly false confession to the sleuth's wife. The plot's languorous pace is further slowed by one entire chapter devoted to the working out of a nonsense cipher.

Although a delightful novel, its facetiousness does not hold up so well today. That's why Knox's books are almost unknown compared to more-serious practitioners of the Golden Age—Allingham, Christie, and Sayers (qq.v.).

(*T.B.*)

Koontz, Dean R. *The Vision.* New York: Putnam's, 1977. (PS)

The Vision is prolific writer Dean R. Koontz's best psychological suspense/thriller to date. The lead character is clairvoyant Mary Bergen, a real psychic who can sense murders before they happen. She and her husband, Max Bergen, assist police departments who are trying to solve serial murders committed by psychopathic killers who strike at random. Mary Bergen's powers are about the only weapon the police have to discover and stop the murders.

But the visions Mary Bergen sees lately are visions of someone murdering *her*. Is the killer one of the psychopathic murderers who fear her powers, or is it someone close to her, someone from her past? As the perpetrator moves closer and closer to the murder that Mary's visions predict, the psychic finds her power may not be enough to save her.

Dean R. Koontz is a craftsman of suspense novels; his secrets are revealed in *How to Write Best Selling Fiction* (1982). While never flashy, Koontz's work is always written at a high professional standard and always delivers believable characters in suspenseful, well-constructed plots. John D. MacDonald (q.v.) said of Koontz's work, "Good craftsmanship. The shelves fit together and the hinges work. It is all I ask of a book, and precisely what I find less and less of with each passing year." Koontz, who has also written suspense fiction under the pseudonyms David Axton, Brian Coffey (q.v.), and Anthony North, has to his credit such other recommended novels as *After the Last Race* (1974), *Night Chills* (1976), *Whispers* (1980), and *Darkfall* (1984).

(*G.K.*)

Kruger, Paul. *If the Shroud Fits.* New York: Simon & Schuster, 1969. (AD)

Roberta Elizabeth Sebenthal uses the pseudonym Paul Kruger for her series about lawyer Phil Kramer of the fictional Colorado town of Astoria. The books are written in the first person, and Sebenthal does a creditable job of creating an authentic male voice.

In this third entry in the series, Kramer's client, Barry Gibson, is arrested for the murder of his wife, Donna. Gibson insists he didn't bludgeon Donna to death, but Lieutenant Jerry Howe theorizes that Gibson—who reportedly had been having marital problems—returned from a business trip early, killed her, and then used the trip as an alibi. Both Kramer and

Donna's half sister, Ivy Carr, who arrives in town the day after the murder, believe in Gibson's innocence. And with Ivy's help, Kramer begins to dig into the dead woman's past.

Following a lead supplied by Ivy, Kramer flies to Texas, where Donna's former lover, a lawyer Ivy knew only by the first name of Orson, lived. After some difficulty, he locates Orson's brother in the little town of Perrysville and learns that Orson is dead, a hit-and-run (and probably murder) victim. Orson, his brother suspects, ran a scam with another man to bilk a wealthy client out of his entire estate, and it is possible that his accomplice killed him. Donna may have known about this scam and, had she located the missing accomplice, may have attempted to blackmail him.

Putting this together with the fact that Donna was seen with a strange man in the Astoria Airport bar the day she died, Kramer returns to Colorado and digs further. His investigation turns up a pair of local residents who are not what they seem to be; two more murders occur, and then a suicide. And at the end, Kramer is able to present Lieutenant Howe with a complicated but believable explanation of what really happened the night Donna was killed—plus a surprising final twist.

This is a satisfying, well-plotted novel, although more could have been done with both Phil Kramer's character and the Colorado background. Other titles featuring Phil Kramer are *Weep for Willow Green* (1966), *Weave a Wicked Web* (1967), *The Cold Ones* (1972), and *The Bronze Claws* (1972). (*M.M.*)

Kurland, Michael. *Death by Gaslight.* New York: New American Library (Signet), 1982. (O/H/CS/T)

Although the protagonist of this Victorian mystery/thriller is Professor James Moriarity, and none other than Sherlock Holmes plays a major role, *Death by Gaslight* is neither a parody nor a pastiche of the stories of Dr. Watson. As Michael Kurland writes in his "Author's Note," it is a novel "set in the Conan Doyle 'fantasy' world which centers on London at the end of Queen Victoria's reign; the world of hansom cabs and gas lamps, coal scuttles and gasogenes, clever disguises, secret societies, and a pea-soup fog that surrounds, envelops, and turns every passing footstep into a mystery and the sound of each passing four-wheeler into a romance."

Kurland knows that "fantasy" world well, and evokes it with the sure hand of Doyle himself. His premise is that Professor Moriarity has had something of a bad rap, owing to the fact that Holmes has been trying, and failing, to catch him at some nefarious scheme for so long he has developed "a tendency to see Moriarity under every bush and a sinister plot behind every crime." Not that Kurland does a whitewash job on the quondam professor of mathematics now living in Russell Square; he freely admits that Moriarity is a criminal, and proves it to everyone's satisfaction (Holmes's included). But he also paints Moriarity as an enigma, a not-so-diabolical genius whose quirks include Good Samaritanism and whose brilliant intellect sometimes surpasses even that of the master of 221-B Baker Street.

In *Death by Gaslight,* Moriarity and Holmes match wits to solve a baffling series of murders in 1887 London. Five members of the aristocracy have died under mysterious circumstances, each with his throat cut from clavicle to clavicle, one—Lord Walbine—in a locked room. (Connoisseurs of the locked-room mystery shouldn't expect too much of that aspect, however; the explanation of how Lord Walbine met his end will not invite comparisons to John Dickson Carr, q.v.) It is Benjamin Barnett, an American newsman whose life Moriarity saved in Constantinople and who has therefore obligated himself to the professor for two years, who persuades Moriarity to investigate; the game is already afoot for Sherlock Holmes. Working independently, the two geniuses track a vengeful killer who calls himself "the wind" through the fogbound streets of London—and it is Moriarity, with the help of his vast underworld connections, who wins the race.

Detection and the conflict between Moriarity and Holmes are just two of the plot elements. Among the others are kidnapping (of Barnett's lady love, journalist Cecily Perrine), hot-air balloons, the Great Train Robbery, a reincarnation of the infamous Hellfire Club, a cameo appearance by Jack the Ripper, and an exciting and literally explosive finale. There are also a number of references to various aspects of the Holmes canon, plus visits from Inspector Lestrade and Colonel Moran.

Sherlockians may or may not be amused at the master's occasional bumbling and the fact that he comes off second best, but it is all done with affection and in the spirit of good fun. Non-Sherlockians with a taste for mystery, historical romance (in the classic sense of that term), and rousing adventure are sure to delight in—and savor—this impeccably researched and well-crafted novel.

Likewise excellent is Kurland's first Moriarity adventure, *The Infernal Device* (1978), which was nominated for a National Book Award. It recounts how Benjamin Barnett came to meet the professor and the daring and thrilling manner in which Moriarity foils a cunning villain's dastardly plan to assassinate Queen Victoria—by exploding a prototype submarine beneath the royal yacht at the Cowes Regatta.

Kurland has also written a number of well-received science-fiction novels, and four tales of Bondian espionage and adventure featuring secret agent Peter Carthage. The best of the Carthage novels are *Mission: Third Force* (1967) and *A Plague of Spies* (1969).

(*B.P.*)

Kuttner, Henry. *Murder of a Mistress.* New York: Permabooks, 1957. (O/AD)

Henry Kuttner is best known as a science-fiction writer, both on his own and in collaboration with his wife, C. L. Moore; but Kuttner published several mysteries, including a series of books about Michael Gray, a psychoanalyst whose patients often found themselves involved in murder.

In *Murder of a Mistress,* Eileen Herrick confesses to the stabbing of her father's mistress. Gray, who has been counseling Eileen, does not believe her guilt, but he can see motives for her confession that the police cannot. Three others confess to the same murder, but this is not uncommon. One of the others, however, is murdered, and Gray discovers that the dead woman's sister was also killed some months before. Then there is an attempt on Gray's life. Obviously there is some connection among these events, but the police are not eager to find it, being certain of Eileen's guilt. Gray's investigation into the crime, based much more on psychology than on police methods, proves quite interesting, and the buried motives he uncovers lead him eventually to the real killer.

By far the most interesting aspect of the Michael Gray books is the insight that Gray, as an analyst, has into the various characters he encounters. The use of psychology, while never heavy-handed, pervades the books, unusual for their time in that they are much more closely related to the "polite" mystery than to the hard-boiled stories so popular in the 1950s. The plotting is intricate, and the major flaw is Kuttner's failure to develop the character of Gray, who remains pretty much a cipher—unlike the other characters in the story, including one who is never even seen.

Also in the Gray series are *The Murder of Ann Avery* (1956), *The Murder of Eleanor Pope* (1956), and *Murder of a Wife* (1958). Kuttner's other crime novel to appear under his own name, *Man Drowning,* was evidently ghosted by his friend and fellow science-fiction writer Cleve Cartmill. Kuttner also wrote two semihard-boiled whodunits under his Lewis Padgett pseudonym: *The Day He Died* (1947) and *Murder in Brass* (1947).

(*B.C.*)

Kyle, Duncan. *Stalking Point.* New York: St. Martin's, 1981. (A)

Duncan Kyle (a pseudonym of British author John Franklin Broxholme) is one of the newer writers of high-adventure novels to challenge Alistair MacLean and Hammond Innes (qq.v.) for thrills and suspense. Critics have called him a writer of "thinking men's thrillers"; but his novels are also thinking *women's* thrillers, because his women characters are wonderfully drawn and have important influence on and roles in the action of the plots.

Stalking Point is one of Kyle's most suspenseful books—a World War II adventure in the recent tradition of Jack Higgins and Ken Follett (qq.v.). In 1941 the Nazis suspect Churchill and Roosevelt will meet to discuss future American involvement in Britain's defense. But where? Baldur von Galen, attached to the German consul general's staff in San Francisco, and his ambitious secretary, Karen Hanzer, follow clues left by a disgraced World War I pilot named Ernst Zoll, who is in the United States illegally and pretending to be an American flier. Because of the shortage of pilots, Zoll has been recruited to test experimental planes and the new sonar devices developed to detect Nazi submarines.

The clues lead Von Galen and Hanzer to the site of the historic Churchill-Roosevelt meeting, and provide the Germans with the opportunity to kill the two major leaders—an act that would be a devastating blow to the Allies and thus win the war for Nazi Germany. But the Nazis underestimate the power of Zoll's love for his son and his passion to erase the disgrace that has haunted him for twenty years. . . .

Other recommended Duncan Kyle high-adventure thrillers are his first, *Cage of Ice* (1970), which has an Arctic setting; *Whiteout* (1976), which also has an icy background, in this case Greenland; and *Greenriver High* (1979), one of the few adventure novels to make expert use of Borneo as its background.

(*G.K.*)

*Kyle, Robert. *Ben Gates Is Hot.* New York: Dell Books, 1964. (O/PI)

There were a great many paperback private-eye series clogging the newsracks in the Fifties and Sixties. The exceptionally fine Ben Gates books deserved a better fate than to have been lost in the crowd, which they were. Robert Terrall produced some first-rate Mike Shayne thrillers, ghosting Brett Halliday (q.v.), during the same period he wrote the Gates books under the Robert Kyle by-line. The Shayne novels, however, seem like merely workmanlike contract jobs when compared with these fresh, inventive, enormously appealing stories. Ben Gates's first-person accounts could perhaps be characterized as what you might expect from Archie Goodwin working solo, were he somewhat older and rather less reticent about discussing his relations with the fair sex.

A New Jersey newspaper publisher, working on a series exposing a local gambling operator, hires Gates to protect his fourteen-year-old daughter, Elaine, the target of a kidnap threat. The gangsters almost succeed in grabbing her at her home, and again in New York when Gates tries to stash her at a girlfriend's apartment. So, for safety, the gruff, fortyish detective and his lively, sexually precocious young charge take off on an auto tour of upstate New York. Their motel odyssey is reminiscent of a famous novel, and the parallels are not lost on Elaine, who twits Gates by buying a copy of *Lolita.* Gates has to cope not only with further kidnap attempts, but with his own ambivalent feelings toward Elaine's unabashed advances. Sex is a staple of private-eye novels, of course, but very few are genuinely sexy, in the best sense of the word. This book is.

Complications ensue; Gates loses Elaine, and is nearly killed by the gangsters. The book concludes with a final confrontation at a wedding-anniversary party at the gambler's home, where Terrall pulls off a deliciously ironic twist to the old cliché of having the crooks confess into a hidden microphone.

Ben Gates Is Hot is an absolute gem of a private-eye novel. The other Gates books, equally fine, are *Blackmail, Inc.* (1958), *Model for Murder* (1959), *Kill Now, Pay Later* (1960), and *Some Like It Cool* (1962).

(*A.S.*)

*Lacy, Ed. *Breathe No More, My Lady.* New York: Avon, 1958. (O/PS)

Few writers have been able to combine compassion and sensitivity with the gutty realism of the hard-boiled story; Ed Lacy (Leonard Zinberg) made that admixture his stock-in-trade. Most of his novels are as realistic as they come, yet they are about human beings, not cardboard cutouts—people who feel deeply, whose passion and pain are so real that they become the reader's for the duration. This is especially true of his black characters, for whom Lacy, who was married to a black woman, had great sympathy and affinity. His prose is sometimes clumsy and poorly constructed, but even at its weakest it teems with life—the raw kind that fills the streets and tenements of New York City, where he lived and where much of his fiction is set. Lacy understood human suffering because he had suffered himself. And above all, he cared about people, about life, about his work.

Most of his novels were published as paperback originals, mainly because they were too earthy and offbeat for the hardcover market. *Breathe No More, My Lady* is a good example. It is probably the best and most ambitious of his softcover books; Lacy himself, in an article for *The Writer* (and with characteristic self-deprecation), called it "a somewhat serious novel proving that writers take themselves far too seriously. It's all a kind of mixed up mystery novel, but since it deals with writers and publishers, I managed to let off steam in all directions." Indeed he did, for among the novel's other virtues are any number of insightful, wry, angry, and humorous comments on publishing and professional writing—mystery writing in particular.

There are two intertwined plots here, one involving Norm Connor, the narrator and an advertising chief at Longson Publishing, and his personal and professional travails; the other concerning a Hemingwayesque writer of tough-guy mysteries, Matt Anthony, who is accused of—and subsequently tried for—willfully causing his wife's death. After news of Anthony's arrest hits the papers, Connor's boss, Bill Longson, decides to reissue one of Anthony's books; and Connor is the one who has to decide how large the advertising campaign will be, whether or not they should try to capitalize on the notoriety—a decision that could well backfire no matter which way he goes. Connor's troubles are compounded by the fact that his beautiful French wife, Michele, has left him after a heated argument; by his foolish retaliatory act of entering into a brief affair with Wilma Hunter, the wife of one of Anthony's writer acquaintances; and by Walter Kolcicki, a detective investigating the death of Francine Anthony who doesn't approve of Connor poking around in the Anthonys' personal lives.

Matt Anthony's story—a great deal of which centers around the type of fiction he writes—unfolds during his trial, which takes up the latter half of the novel. And an explosive trial it is, with a stunning final revelation to end it.

The question of Anthony's guilt is the only real mystery element here. The rest of the book's considerable suspense derives from the characters—people whose problems, weaknesses, desires, flaws, strengths are totally involving. *Breathe No More, My Lady* deserves a much wider audience than it had when it was published (it has never been reprinted).

Lacy's numerous other paperback originals are also recommended, especially the private-eye novels *Sin in Their Blood* (1952), *Strip for Violence* (1953), and *Bugged for Murder* (1961); *Go for the Body* (1954), which features an expatriate American Negro boxer living in France; *Shakedown for Murder* (1958), which has an appealing elderly, small-town Long Island cop, Matt Lund, as its protagonist; and *The Napalm Bugle* (1968), a fiery cold-war espionage/adventure tale.

(*B.P.*)

Lacy, Ed. *The Men from the Boys.* New York: Harper, 1956. (PI/PS)

The Men from the Boys is one of just five hardcover crime novels published by Lacy in this country. It may also be the best of all his criminous works, not for its mystery plot, which is minor, but for the character of Marty Bond, its narrator. In few novels of any type will you find an "I" who comes more alive, who is a more complex and fascinating individual than Marty Bond.

Marty, you see, is a self-acknowledged bastard—a tough, bigoted, fifty-four-year-old ex-cop who was thrown off the force for beating up a drug suspect; who has gone through two wives, hurting one deeply; who makes his living as a part-time house dick, part-time grifter and pimp in a sleazy Manhattan hotel; who drinks too much, sleeps with a prostitute he sometimes smacks around, and doesn't give a damn about much of anything, including himself. A wholly unlikable character, right? Wrong. Marty Bond isn't all bad; Lacy manages to infuse in him a sense of tragedy and vulnerability that makes us care for him from the outset, a difficult feat accomplished in two ways. First, Marty cares, just a little, about his stepson, Lawrence, an auxiliary cop who has aspirations of joining New York's finest. And second, he has a serious stomach disorder that he is convinced is terminal cancer.

Marty doesn't fear death—he has always been too tough for that—but he does fear cancer: "There was a horse cop I knew who died of cancer of the gut . . . He'd starved to death because the cancer squeezed his intestines tight. I spent a lot of time with him in the hospital, watching him become a bag of bones." That's not Marty's way—hospitalization, helplessness, slow death; he won't even go to the hospital for tests to confirm or deny the cancer, because he *knows* that's what it is. Instead he determines to kill himself, end his life quickly and cleanly. But when he tries, he finds that he doesn't quite have the nerve for it. His only alternative, he thinks then, is to get somebody to do the job for him. But who? Who would bother to knock off an over-the-hill house dick?

The answer comes when Lawrence is nearly beaten to death after investigating a robbery at the Lande Meat Company; the owner, Wilhelm Lande, has changed his mind and now claims that he wasn't robbed after all. The man who beat up Lawrence is "Pretty Boy" Smith—a mob enforcer who, under the right circumstances, might not be averse to knocking off an over-the-hill house dick who got in his way. So Marty sets out to find Smith by finding out what is really going on at the Lande Meat Company, partly for Lawrence's sake but mostly so he can provoke a situation in which he will be killed.

The Men from the Boys is a grim, shattering, very human novel that will linger in your memory for days after reading it. Marty Bond will linger in your memory even longer than that.

(*B.P.*)

*Lacy, Ed. *Room to Swing.* New York: Harper, 1957. (PI)

Lacy wrote several novels with black-white racial themes, and this one, featuring black private investigator Toussaint Moore, is perhaps the best. (It won an Edgar for Best Novel of 1957.) While Moore was preceded by several other black sleuths—Octavus Roy Cohen's (q.v.) Florian Slappey, who first appeared in the 1920s; and Veronica Parker Johns's (q.v.) Webster Flagg, who was created in 1953—he is the first convincing black detective in crime fiction. In fact, many would argue that Moore is more finely drawn than John Ball's (q.v.) Virgil Tibbs, the first fully realized black *series* detective. In part this is because Lacy knew his subject matter personally, having lived in New York's Harlem for many years; and in part because we are allowed access to Moore's thoughts and feelings, as we are not with Tibbs.

As *Room to Swing* opens, Toussaint Moore ("Touie" to his friends) arrives in the Ohio town of Bingston, on the Kentucky border. He is driving a Jaguar, wearing expensive clothes, and is in pursuit of a killer, hoping to clear himself of a murder for which he believes himself wanted in New York City. Immediately Touie and the Bingston white establishment clash, for the little town is more southern than northern. Moore seeks refuge, boarding with a black postman and his family, and soon enlists the daughter of the house, a lovely young woman named Frances, in his investigation.

In flashback we learn how Moore was hired by a woman named Kay Robbens to tail a Bingston native living in New York. The man, Bob Thomas, is to be the subject of a true-crime exposé by the TV station where Miss Robbens works (Thomas is wanted for rape in Bingston), and the publicity department wants him watched until the show can air. Moore follows Thomas, while dealing with such personal problems as a girlfriend who wants him to quit the detective business and go to work for the post office; but when he receives a call, supposedly from Miss Robbens, telling him to meet her at Thomas's apartment, he walks into a trap. Thomas has been murdered; the police appear on the scene; Moore hits a police officer and escapes. He can easily be identified, so he flees to Bingston in hope of turning up some lead that will clear him of Thomas's murder.

In the course of his investigation, Moore learns a great deal about life in a small southern town, intrigue in the big city—and himself. And after he solves the murder, at considerable risk of life and limb, he has a number of decisions to make that are prompted by growth in his character. This is a believable portrayal that touches on a number of sensitive themes (including homosexuality and lesbianism) and tells us a great deal about what it was like to be black in the America of the 1950s.

Other novels that reflect Ed Lacy's racial concerns are *Go for the Body* (1954), *Harlem Underground* (1965), and *In Black and Whitey* (1967). Unfortunately, Toussaint Moore appears in only one other adventure, the 1964 paperback original *Moment of Untruth*.

(*M.M.*)

Lamb, J. J. *Losers Take All.* New York: Carlyle, 1979. (O/PI)

J. J. Lamb has written three paperback originals about Zach Rolfe, a private eye who specializes in catching "the cheats, thieves, and crossroaders" who frequent Nevada's gambling casinos. Rolfe is attractive, energetic, and—like his creator—drives a Porsche and knows how to keep it in top running order. One fault of these books may be that there are just too many car parts in them for the uninitiated to comprehend, but at least the detail is authentic.

Losers Take All begins when Rolfe receives a phone call from Betti Golden, wife of Nate Golden, an old friend who owns a small weekly newspaper in Canada. It has been years since Rolfe heard from Golden, but now his wife wants Zach to drop everything and come to Canada. Nate has been writing editorials about the Canadian lotteries in his paper, and someone is threatening his life. Rolfe is hooked by the mention of gambling and agrees to go, but before he can get to the little town of Malcolm, Nate is killed in an auto accident. And before Rolfe has been in Malcolm long, he has set type so Nate's tough and determined widow can get the paper out; been hit on the head and almost killed when the newspaper building is torched; and discovered enough suspicious circumstances to warrant a full-scale investigation (aided by the gutsy Betti) into his old friend's death.

There is plenty of action in this one, as there is in the other Zach Rolfe novels—*Nickel Jackpot* and *The Chinese Straight* (both 1976)—as well as the added virtue of a nicely handled love affair.

(*M.M.*)

Lange, John. *Easy Go.* New York: New American Library (Signet), 1968. (O/A)

The protean Michael Crichton has written an Edgar-winning novel (*A Case of Need,* as by Jeffrey Hudson, q.v.), big best sellers (*The Andromeda Strain*), nonfiction about hospitals (*Five Patients*) and computers (*Electronic Life*), screenplays (*Westworld*), and directed movies (*Looker*). He began his writing career while still in Harvard Medical School with a series of crime novels with exotic settings; these books were paperback originals published under the pseudonym John Lange. The John Lange novels have gotten short shrift from the critics, but at least one of them, *Easy Go,* is solidly entertaining.

Easy Go is the story of modern tomb robbers in Egypt. Harold Barnaby, an Egyptologist, stumbles on the secret location of a Pharaoh's tomb while studying hieroglyphic manuscripts and he conceives the idea of looting the tomb. Pierce, a journalist to whom he mentions his idea, takes charge of matters, and soon the expedition gets under way. As usual with capers of this nature, however, things do not work out quite as planned.

Lange does a dandy job with the local-color aspects of his story, giving the reader a vivid sense of the flies, the heat, and the smells. His writing is extremely smooth, and his plot is straightforward until the end. Characterization is not a strong point, and the book's romantic interest is hardly developed and could easily have been eliminated, but Lange's research into tombs and tomb robbing has a certain fascination. The book succeeds quite well as light entertainment.

The John Lange by-line appears on several other books, most notably *Scratch One* (1967) and *Zero Cool* (1969).

(*B.C.*)

Langton, Jane. *Natural Enemy.* New York: Ticknor & Fields, 1982. (AD)

The novels of Jane Langton are both literate and literary; the backgrounds she utilizes are those of academia, of prose and poetry, and of the history of her native New England. Although her plots are not particularly strong, the reader is able to overlook this because of the depth in which the background material is explored. And her series detective, former Middlesex County (Massachusetts) police lieutenant Homer Kelly, now a scholar and expert on the works of Emerson and Thoreau, is one of the most likable sleuths to come along in quite some time. Langton adds further appeal to her books by the inclusion of her own pen-and-ink drawings.

Natural Enemy takes place not far from Walden Pond, on a farm belonging to Edward Heron, a widower who lives there with his daughters, Barbara and Virginia. John Hand, Homer Kelly's nephew, arrives to apply for a summer job that will help defray his college expenses for the next year. John, a budding entomologist with a large collection of spiders, is hired on the spot by the daughters; but minutes later neighbor Buddy Whipple, a man in his twenties who has rented out his home and is looking for a place to stay, appears, also applying for the position. When Barbara tells him the job is filled, Buddy goes off to complain to her father, but is soon back with the news that Edward Heron is lying dead in the old orchard, an apparent victim of an asthma attack.

We, of course, know that Edward Heron's death was not all that natural. In fact, we know that Buddy triggered the fatal asthma attack when Edward discovered him in some clandestine activity in the orchard. As events progress through the funeral and Buddy sets up housekeeping in the Herons' guest room, John Hand begins to wonder what the interloper is up to. And as he tends to his duties around the farm—and in his leisure time records the activities of a spider who is spinning a web across the door of the shed where his quarters are—John's suspicions grow, until he takes them to his uncle Homer. It is the successful combination of Homer's detective skills and John's entomological knowledge that finally brings Buddy's secret activities to light.

Langton's first novel, *The Transcendental Murder* (1964; reissued as *The Minuteman Murder* in honor of the bicentennial in 1976), deals with New England's transcendental writers. *Dark Nantucket Moon* (1975) concerns a lunar eclipse and a murder in a lighthouse on Nantucket Island. *The Memorial Hall Murder* (1978) takes place at Harvard University. And the literary subject matter of *Emily Dickinson Is Dead* (1984) is obvious from its title.

(*M.M.*)

Lanham, Edwin. *Death of a Corinthian.* New York: Harcourt Brace, 1953. (W)

Greg Matthews was a Corinthian; i.e., "he had leisure, a comfortable income, a passion for taking trifles earnestly, and, of course, a yacht. To be a Corinthian requires all that, and implies as well a gaudy isolation from workaday life, a peacock's strut for us birds of drabber plumage to admire or envy." Not everybody in the little Connecticut town of Port Lucky admires or envies Greg Matthews, however. A lot of people have good reason to dislike him, among them his wife, Kay, who has been playing around with several different men; the book's narrator, lawyer Roy Hatch, who was once in love with Kay; Tom Stearns, a real-estate agent who likes to jacklight deer and was involved with Matthews in a plan to build a yacht club in Port Lucky; and George Ashton, something of a mystery man from Florida.

When Matthews disappears from his brand-new yawl, the *Tern,* in the middle of Long Island Sound, it could have been an accident—but it could also have been murder. It could even have been a ploy on Matthews's part, for unknown reasons, since no body was found and since Kay reports seeing a man who looked like Greg *after* his disappearance. Which is it? And what exactly are the hidden motives and passions of the residents of this small New England town?

Those are the central questions asked and answered in *Death of a Corinthian,* a mystery best described as "civilized"—one of the type popular in the slick magazines of the Fifties and early Sixties. (This one was serialized in *The Saturday Evening Post* under the title *The Case of the Missing Corpse.*) Emphasis is on character and setting; the pace is leisurely, with plenty of sophisticated dialogue; and there is almost no onstage violence or unpleasantness. What lifts it above others of its ilk are Lanham's understanding of the human character and his genuine passion for sailing. The best scenes in the novel are those that take place on Long Island Sound.

Lanham wrote several other mysteries in the Forties, Fifties, and Sixties, some of these, too, serialized in *The Saturday Evening Post.* The best is *Death in the Wind* (1956), which likewise features boats and the Sound, and has a hurricane as a major antagonist. Also good are *Slug It Slay* (1946), featuring a newspaper background; *Murder on My Street* (1958); and *Six Black Camels* (1961).

(*B.P.*)

*Larson, Charles. *Matthew's Hand.* New York: Doubleday Crime Club, 1974. (AD)

The prologue and epilogue of this novel are each told from the point of view of a turtle. That being the case, you would think it the sort of bad novel that deserves to be critically shelled. But you would be wrong. *Matthew's Hand* is, in fact, a very good novel that deserves considerable praise. And it is a tribute to Charles Larson's talents that those two scenes from the turtle's viewpoint not only work but work very well indeed.

The novel's setting (not far from the pond where the turtle has observed a jettisoned sack containing a severed hand) is the small California town of Oceanport. Oceanport is a conservative town, and its residents did not particularly welcome Jesus Mary Chavez's Mexican restaurant, La Cucaracha. And since Chavez, in an argument with one of his neighbors, has proclaimed himself a Communist, the hostilities have become open—and violent. Chavez's niece, Isabel, star of the floundering TV series "Stagg at Bay," has gone to Oceanport to lend support to her uncle; and when Jesus Mary's dog is poisoned, David Sanderson, Isabel's boyfriend and the show's scriptwriter, and Nils-Frederik Blixen, the producer and an accomplished amateur sleuth, also journey to the coastal town to help their star. There they watch the troubles escalate to include a missing hardware-store owner—Jesus Mary's avowed enemy; a dismembered body in a barrel; and a charge of murder hanging over Chavez's head.

This is a lively novel, full of entertaining and believable characters. The author has an excellent grasp of the Chicano culture, and he portrays this Mexican-American family in all their warmth and emotional volatility. In addition, Larson's prose is well above average and he handles dialogue especially well. There are good insights into the world of network television as Blixen tries to solve a murder and at the same time save his poorly rated show from cancellation. And when he accomplishes the former, the solution is both startling and convincing.

Nils Blixen runs across more murder than your typical TV-studio executive; his other investigations have been chronicled in *Someone's Death* (1973), *Muir's Blood* (1976), and *The Portland Murders* (1983).

(*M.M./B.P.*)

Lathen, Emma. *Accounting for Murder.* New York: Macmillan, 1964. (AD)

Emma Lathen is called in publishers' blurbs "America's Agatha Christie." In some ways she is better. Many of the classic detective-story devices and clue-plantings are smoothly integrated into the stories; and the characters, good and bad, are generally believable. One of the delights of all the books is their chapter titles; reading them makes you want to dig into the story immediately. However, Lathen also suffers many of the defects of Christie. In particular, the formula of clues and suspects is put together in such a consistent manner that if you read many of the books (a total of twenty so far), you should be able to spot the murderer very early on, sometimes before the crime occurs.

Emma Lathen is the pseudonym of two Boston businesswomen, one a lawyer and one an economist. All of the stories have to do with business; it is wonderfully combined in character and plot and denouement. The best summation is Anthony Boucher's comment about Lathen's "extraordinary ability to clarify the most intricate financial shenanigans so that even I can understand them."

In *Accounting for Murder,* an irate stockholders' group, led by a scholarly accountant, is investigating the failing financial structure of the National Calculating Company. In the middle of an acrimonious audit, the accountant is strangled with his own adding-machine cord. Everyone in the company had a motive: Was the victim finding fraud, incompetence, a cover-up? What he ultimately found was death.

Banker John Putnam Thatcher wants to protect the investment in National Calculating of the Sloan Guaranty Trust, the third-largest bank in the world. Using his banking subordinates—Gabler, Trinkham, Bowman, and even his secretary, Miss Corsa (she has other names, to wit, Rose Theresa)—he probes the financial affairs of National Calculating, from its Wall Street office to its plant in New Jersey. The company should be making money—it has good R&D and has an electronics contract with the government. Thatcher is masterful in plucking information from tableaux of shouted "business conferences," misunderstood interviews, even party scenes. The clues always lie in corporate clichés and icons, so the police are unable to tumble to what's really going on. Thatcher's style is aloof and urbane, which lets the author bring in delicious ironic wit and keeps the emphasis on clarity of mind in the investigation. One of Thatcher's colleagues says that he is "too damn superior . . . and too virtuous." He also has a "terrible weakness for puzzles." All of which stand him in good stead as he searches for a solution and settles accounts.

(*T.B.*)

Lathen, Emma. *Banking on Death.* New York: Macmillan, 1961. (AD)

If there is room in the world of business and banking for real-life poets, politicians, and patrons of the arts, then there is certainly room for a fictional amateur detective. John Putnam Thatcher, senior vice-president of the Sloan Guaranty Trust, debuts in *Banking on Death*. In most of his cases,

Thatcher's interest lies in protecting Sloan's investments. In this case, he is prompted by his desire to protect the two young boys who are heirs to a trust.

An all-round unlikable heir to one of Sloan's "nuisance trusts" (a paltry $300,000) is murdered in midwinter Buffalo during the biggest snowstorm of the year. The suspects include various members of the victim's family, who are also beneficiaries of the trust, as well as his co-workers in Buffalo. Very carefully winnowing the clues, Thatcher listens to tales of financial folly from the malicious and self-centered suspects in a series of elaborately choreographed encounters in offices, lobbies, bars, airports, and restaurants. Along the way you learn some intricate details of trusts and something about the industrial textile business. The author makes use of an exacting timetable, cunningly disguised and prolonged, and lots of documentation—a trust, memos, letters, news articles. John Putnam Thatcher has a nose for money and murder, and in his Wall Street way elicits the clues necessary to rescue Sloan's capital.

(*T.B.*)

Lathen, Emma. *Pick Up Sticks.* New York: Simon & Schuster, 1970. (AD)

Outfitted by L. L. Bean, John Putnam Thatcher escapes from the hubbub of Wall Street to a hiking holiday on the Appalachian Trail. His minions at the Sloan Guaranty Trust are left high and dry by his disappearance into the mountains. After all, "Wall Street is, at bottom, a collection of endearingly childlike innocents, always expecting the good, the beautiful, the true, and the profitable," while in the wilderness life is real, life is earnest, and death comes as a surprise. But "a long and observant life had all but destroyed Thatcher's capacity for surprise."

He returns to his boyhood New Hampshire for a trek on part of the Appalachian Trail that marches along the crest of the White, Green, and Smoky mountains over 2000 miles from Maine to Georgia. (Keep your eye on the trail; it's a key part in the story.) Thatcher's trail companion, a local friend, Henry Morland, discovers a body, is suspected by the state police, and begins behaving like a stock New Englander, much on the order of Phoebe Atwood Taylor's (q.v.) Asey Mayo. A real-estate hustle run by a pair of Boston financiers is the focus of foul play.

As the plot flings suspicion around among the various players in this game, the author gets in some satirical bites on contemporary America. The narration is dry and disinterested—Thatcher "did not have a chance to ask if Henry was referring to [the] sales methods, or to the discovery of [the] dead body at the main lodge." After a second murder and more mystery, Thatcher decides to "opt for some hard information. . . . Hard information was to be found on Wall Street." He recruits his subordinates to take part in a crucial confrontation. The solution, as always, is all business. The final chapter, "His Last Bough," is a tent of explanations covering a knapsack of improbabilities.

(*T.B.*)

Lathen, Emma. *When in Greece.* New York: Simon & Schuster, 1969. (AD)

Emma Lathen's range is extended in *When in Greece.* The usual round of balance-sheet thrust and parry is converted here into a chase novel that looks at times like a merry romp. A most junior representative of the Sloan Guaranty Trust, Ken Nicolls, is on the spot supervising the bank's interest in a consortium erecting a Greek hydroelectric power installation. A sudden coup d'état by army officers throws a monkey wrench into the project. The undersecretary of the Ministry of Interior is reassuring, and the engineering company is slippery. Will the bank be double-crossed? Nicolls is arrested by the army, and just as John Putnam Thatcher worries over his fate, Zeus (or somesuch) provides an earthquake escape and cuts communications.

Thatcher and Everett Gabler, his crusty subordinate, arrive in Athens searching for Nicolls. But the chase is already under way. It turns out that soldiers, leftist revolutionaries, and some local assassins are turning out the villages and countryside of northern Greece for Nicolls, who doesn't know until later that he has some political microfilm. Thatcher's guile discerns the dollar-and-cents dimensions to this plot of political zealotry. He recruits two classic little old lady archaeologists, some of their friends, and assorted Greek characters because he is determined to personally unmask the miscreant who has already caused one death. Even the curmudgeonly Gabler outwits some kidnappers to join in a mirthful masquerade from Athens to Piraeus and back, through shops and a monastery, all to bring Nicolls to safety. This Keystone Kops charade squares Sloan's accounts in Greece once and for all.

(*T.B.*)

Latimer, Jonathan. *The Lady in the Morgue.* New York: Doubleday Crime Club, 1936. (PI)

Jonathan Latimer's five novels featuring private detective Bill Crane are among the most inventive and entertaining in the genre. They are the mystery equivalent of the Howard Hawks screwball film comedies of the Thirties like *Twentieth Century* and *His Girl Friday.* Oddball characters, furious pace, and snappy dialogue are hallmarks of the style; Latimer mixes in a strong element of black comedy as well.

Crane and a couple of bored reporters are hanging around the Cook County Morgue on a sweltering summer night (the morgue is the coolest place in town), waiting for someone to show up and identify a young blond woman, an apparent suicide. Instead, someone sneaks in and snatches the corpse, killing the morgue attendant in the process. Crane's client, a wealthy New York society dowager, shows up; she suspects the victim is a runaway daughter. Two rival gangsters, who think the corpse might be their girlfriend, go after Crane, thinking he engineered the corpsenapping. Crane and his agency cohorts, Doc Williams and Tom O'Malley, tear around Chicago trying to find the body, identify the body, and nail the killer. They consume heroic quantities of liquor in the process (Crane does his best detecting in a semi-stuporous condition), and crack wise at every opportunity.

Three-quarters into the book O'Malley reviews some of the action:

> *In two days we start a fight in a taxi-dance joint, find a murdered guy and don't tell the police, crash in on Braymer [a drug cult guru] and his dope mob, bust in on a party, kidnap a gal, steal a car and rob a graveyard. The only thing we ain't done is to park in a no-parking zone.*

There's more, like a second trip to the graveyard with a bulldog who cadges drinks and thinks he's a bloodhound; and a smash finale back at the morgue, with Crane under a sheet impersonating a corpse (he's well suited to the part, having inadvertently swilled a bottle of embalming fluid while looking for a drink).

A marvelously original, wild, and funny hard-boiled private-eye novel. (*A.S.*)

*Latimer, Jonathan. *Solomon's Vineyard.* London: Methuen, 1941. (PI)

This book has a curious history. Published first in England in 1941, it didn't see book publication in the United States until 1950 as a paperback titled *The Fifth Grave,* and then only in drastically expurgated form. The first line of the original is "From the way her buttocks looked under the black silk dress, I knew she'd be good in bed." The paperback version is "From the way she looked under the black silk dress, I knew she'd be a hot dame." It wasn't until a small California publisher reprinted it in 1982 that the original text saw American publication, and then only in a limited edition of 326 copies. This is most unfortunate, as *Solomon's Vineyard* is a genuine hard-boiled classic and deserves wide availability. It has *everything!* A private eye; a shoot-out at a roadhouse; necrophilia; a shoot-out in a steam bath; mobsters; a crooked police chief; a bizarre religious cult; a knife fight in a whorehouse; kidnapping; a mystery woman with a taste for kinky sex; human sacrifice; crypt-robbing—you name it, detective Karl Craven has to deal with it.

Craven, a crude but very tough investigator (very reminiscent of Hammett's Continental Op in style and physique), arrives in the small Missouri town of Paulton to help his partner get a young woman out of the cult's sanctuary, Solomon's Vineyard, which dominates the life of the town. He finds his partner's been shot dead. Soon thereafter, he finds himself a target of the local mob, who control the countrywide vice operations in concert with the elders of the cult. The cult's founder, Solomon the Prophet, has been dead for five years, embalmed under glass for viewing on Sunday; but he takes a bride every year, and the brides mysteriously disappear just after the ceremony. By "romancing" the cult's priestess (the one with the black silk dress—and a fondness for S&M), he arranges a falling-out between the mob and the cult (à la the Op in *Red Harvest*), and ultimately finishes his job.

For this book, Latimer adopted an exceptionally terse first-person narrative style (the Bill Crane novels are told in more expansive third-person prose): The average sentence length is perhaps six or seven words. The comic elements are less overt, but he indulges his taste for Grand Guignol with evident relish. *Solomon's Vineyard* is clearly Latimer's homage to the classic hard-boiled detective story, made obvious by Craven's reading *Black Mask* during a couple of brief lulls in the action (shades of Bill Pronzini's "Nameless"). As such it is a brilliant success, and deserves to be ranked with the best of Hammett, Whitfield, Cain, Davis, Chandler (qq.v.), et al.

Other fine Latimer novels, all but the last two with Bill Crane: *Murder in the Madhouse* (1935), *Headed for a Hearse* (1935), *The Dead Don't Care* (1938), *Sinners and Shrouds* (1955), and *Black Is the Fashion for Dying* (1959).

(*A.S.*)

Law, Janice. *The Big Payoff.* Boston: Houghton Mifflin, 1976. (T)

Anna Peters, the heroine of *The Big Payoff*, has been raiding the corporate power structure for years with a kind of ruthlessness that makes new-age feminists look like babes in the woods. Anna is thirty years old, was raised in poverty, and early in life realized that the career of executive secretary was her only route to financial security. For all of her adult life she's been mother/assistant to some of America's most powerful executives. And, privy to company files, she's blackmailed her way to the top.

At the time of this story, however, Anna has succeeded in beating back the temptation to take one more boss to the cleaners. She suspects that the vice-president of New World Oil, her current despised master, is responsible for the deaths of British oil technicians trying to secure the oil rights in the North Sea, off the coast of Scotland. But rather than grab a "Big Payoff" and retire to the Caribbean, she reports her suspicions to the British Embassy.

In quite a funny twist, Anna's bad karma catches up with her. This time, the British blackmail *her*. Unless she spies on her boss and New World Oil, the British agent—who has discovered Anna's former modus operandi—promises he will get her fired and tell her boyfriend she's a thief. Her usual response to possible exposure has been to leave town and live off her Swiss bank account, but now she decides it's time to pay off her debt. Her boyfriend, Harry, is more precious to her than she thought a man could be. Before the story reaches an end, Anna almost gets herself—and Harry—killed. Only her time-tested moxie and unsentimental view of the world save her from murder on both sides of the Atlantic. And in the end, Law provides us with one last, amusing surprise.

Anna is an enterprising and likable character, and *The Big Payoff* is a marvelous contemporary adventure. Also excellent are Anna Peters's other adventures—*Gemini Trip* (1977), *Under Orion* (1978), *The Shadow of the Palms* (1980), and *Death under Par* (1981).

(*K.K.H.*)

Lawrence, Hilda. *Blood Upon the Snow*. New York: Simon & Schuster, 1944. (PI/AD)

Hilda Lawrence wrote three novels featuring the odd investigative trio of private eye Mark East and spinster sleuths Bessie Petty and Beulah Pond. In addition, she published a melodramatic suspense novel, *The Pavilion* (1949), and two novellas, *Death Has Four Hands* and *The Bleeding House* (both 1950). She is best known for the East/Petty/Pond books, and for good reason: They present an interesting juxtaposition of the hard-boiled school versus the little-old-lady sleuth, between the customs and mores of Manhattan and those of a small New England village. The characters are well drawn, the setting evocative, and the interplay between Mark East and his elderly "Watsons" is entertaining.

As this first entry in the series opens, the snow is falling and Mark is arriving at the village of Crestwood. His introduction to Beulah Pond occurs when he stops to ask directions to the house where a prospective client expects him. When he eventually arrives, he is told he must wait until morning for his interview; and when he meets with Mr. Stoneman, the old man seems to think he is hiring a private secretary rather than a private detective. Mark, however, senses something is very wrong in the house; the old man seems frightened and has a hurt wrist and bruises on his face. He agrees to stay on for a few days, assuming secretarial duties, and makes it his first order of business to revisit Miss Pond, whom he perceives—rightly so—as a woman who knows a great deal about what goes on in the village. When he arrives at her home, he is introduced to Bessie Petty, and the unlikely partnership in detection is launched.

The story that follows is one of slowly rising terror. The people with whom Stoneman is staying, Laura and Jim Morey and their two children, also seem disturbed; Stoneman is reported to have been sleepwalking; the housekeeper, Mrs. Lacey, has handed in her notice and seems upset about this; strange mischief has occurred in the wine cellar; and as the black winter night closes in, Mark remembers something Mrs. Lacey said about this being "good soil for evil. . . ."

A slow-paced but absorbing chiller, as are the other two in the series—*A Time to Die* (1945) and *Death of a Doll* (1947).

(*M.M.*)

**Le Carré, John. *The Spy Who Came in from the Cold.* New York: Coward, McCann, 1964. (E)

The author of this novel that changed the direction of modern espionage fiction is an Englishman whose real name is David John Moore Cornwell, a former civil servant. After publication of *The Spy Who Came in from the Cold,* the third book in his series featuring the quietly torn and persevering George Smiley, Le Carré went on to become the dominant figure in the espionage field—yet in the view of many critics, this still is his best novel.

Le Carré's knowledge of the workings of bureaucracies contributes a great deal to the air of authenticity his novels convey. His characters are mere cogs in the interlocking wheels of enormous governmental agencies; thus the spy's human qualities come into conflict with a machinelike inhumanity, and his compassion is crushed by harsh necessity. In no book of Le Carré's is this theme better demonstrated than in *The Spy Who Came in from the Cold,* which is not so much concerned with the machinations of espionage as with the machinations of the minds of those in the profession; not so much what what they do in the course of their gray and thankless jobs as with what those jobs do to them. With this story of what happens when British agent Leamas is dispatched to entrap an enemy master spy in East Berlin, Le Carré gave the spy novel a new breath of life.

Complex in plot and lean of prose, the book generates suspense as it illustrates the demeaning forces at work in the anonymous and confusing business of espionage. Not only does Leamas encounter shades of gray, but the grays overlap; Leamas doesn't know at times whether he's standing in darkness or in light—and he begins to wonder if really there is a difference except to the people playing the dangerous bureaucratic game in which he is involved, and from which he cannot escape.

Appropriately enough, the novel ends at that most visible symbol of a segmented and saddened world, the Berlin Wall. The symbolism of the wall is matched by the symbolism of the novel's final sentence, which sums up artfully and precisely Le Carré's grim and realistic view of espionage.

George Smiley, the quintessential post–World War II spy, is also featured in *Call for the Dead* (1962), *A Murder of Quality* (1963), *Tinker, Tailor, Soldier, Spy* (1974), *The Honourable Schoolboy* (1977), and *Smiley's People* (1980).

(*J.L.*)

*Le Carré, John. *A Small Town in Germany*. New York: Coward, McCann, 1968. (E)

In this novel Le Carré abandons his continuing character, Smiley, and gives us a more ambitious book as well as a top-notch spy story. His usual theme of man against bureaucracy is here, but Smiley, who is aware of and resigned to the pitfalls in his strange profession, is replaced as a protagonist by Leo Harting and his pursuer, Alan Turner.

Harting is an aging second secretary who vanishes from the British Embassy, along with official papers whose secret contents could prove disastrous to Britain's efforts to enter the Common Market. Naturally, the British government will spare no effort to apprehend Harting and recover the papers before the damage is done.

It is Turner who is sent to find Harting; and as we accompany him on the hunt, we learn more about Harting. The picture that emerges is one of a morally bankrupt victim of the bureaucratic system. In these pages we also catch glimpses and gain insights into a British community of diplomats and their wives, playing out the last vestiges and echoes of a once dominant England, but one now at the mercy of postwar politics.

This is a thoroughly wrought and rather bitter novel, skillfully contrived to mesh suspense with serious political and social commentary. Not an easy task for the writer, but Le Carré manages to bring it off beautifully. Along with *The Looking-Glass War* (1965) and the best-selling *Little Drummer Girl* (1983), this is a non-Smiley Le Carré novel of great craft and power.

(*J.L.*)

Leffland, Ella. *Mrs. Munck*. Boston: Houghton Mifflin, 1970. (PS)

Although the majority of Ella Leffland's work has been mainstream fiction, this—her first novel—is an engrossing tale of psychological suspense.

Rose Munck is a resident of the small California town of Port Carquinez (patterned on Port Costa on the Carquinez Straits north of San Francisco). For twenty-five years she has lived there in self-imposed isolation from her neighbors. As Rose puts it, "... in this town ... there is no one whose demise could startle or pain me." It is, then, totally out of character when, after the death of her husband, she offers shelter to his crippled distant relative Patrick Leary. And as Rose goes about her preparations and greets her new boarder, the reader begins to wonder about her motives. They are certainly not altruistic; she feels no sense of duty toward Mr. Leary. Why is she so eager to open her home to him?

Rose's cruelly calculating greeting of the old man is a shock to the reader, but soon the answers to the questions it poses begin to emerge—through flashback to over twenty-five years before. We see Rose as a young woman in San Francisco: naïve, innocent, alone at a time when single women were thought to need protectors; and we see Mr. Leary as a man one could very well need a protector *against*. As Rose's present plans unfold, go awry, and take a surprising new turn, we watch, wondering if justice will be meted out—and if it is worth the terrible price it may cost.

Mrs. Munck is an exceptional study of the effects of revenge. Regrettably, it is Leffland's only suspense novel to date.

(*M.M.*)

Lemarchand, Elizabeth. *Change for the Worse.* New York: Walker, 1980. (PP)

Elizabeth Lemarchand turned to crime writing in her sixties, after a serious illness forced her to retire from her post of school headmistress. Her mysteries are of the "polite" school and pleasantly old-fashioned—employing such Golden Age devices as casts of characters and floor plans of the murder scenes—but the characters and the problems presented are thoroughly contemporary. Her series sleuths, who work in tandem in all her novels, are Scotland Yard detectives Tom Pollard and Gregory Toye; both are solid family men, and throughout the series Lemarchand provides us with glimpses into their personal lives and the progress of their careers.

Change for the Worse opens in Italy, where Julian and David Strode, neighbors of the Pollards', are vacationing. Julian has a frightening experience when she is locked inside a church where thugs are stealing cash from the alms box. The scene then shifts back to England, where the Strodes discuss the incident with the Pollards, and then the subject is dropped, seemingly irrelevant to the rest of the plot. An astute reader, however, will expect Julian's experience to later assume importance (and it does, on the final page).

Next we are taken to Fairlynch Manor, a Heritage of Britain property, where we meet Katharine Ridley, former mistress of the manor who now lives in the lodge with her granddaughter, Alix; and Francis Peck, warden of the property. In order to step up admissions to the historic site, Katharine has proposed that an art exhibit be held in the library—one that will feature paintings owned by neighboring residents. Her efforts to organize the show are disrupted, however: first by the arrival of Alix's father, Geoffrey Parr, long thought to be dead; and second by the carbon-monoxide murder of Francis Peck. Five of the pictures borrowed for the exhibit are stolen at the time of the murder, one of them an ancestral portrait belonging to the Ridleys.

Pollard and Toye arrive on the scene and begin their usual meticulous investigation. They encounter the dead man's son, Kit Peck, who is attracted to Alix and of whom Katharine vehemently disapproves; Professor Digby Chilmark, learned adviser to Heritage of Britain; George Palmer, an unlikely visitor to the manor (who we know is really Geoffrey Parr); Hugo Rossiter, a local artist; and Malcolm and Lydia Gilmore, a prosperous, entrepreneurial couple from a neighboring farm. And as the investigators probe, they begin to realize that not everyone in this cast of characters is exactly what he seems.

Readers who like their mysteries genteel and bloodless will be sure to enjoy this novel, as well as others in the series (among them *Death on Doomsday,* 1975; *Step in the Dark,* 1977; and *Suddenly while Gardening,* 1979). *Change for the Worse* is well characterized, and the English countryside setting is finely drawn. If the plot seems to hang on an unlikely coincidence, it is to Lemarchand's credit that she makes us believe it *could* happen.

(*M.M.*)

Leonard, Charles L. *The Stolen Squadron.* New York: Doubleday Crime Club, 1942. (PI/E)

Until recent years and the change in women's roles and attitudes, very few female writers adopted the hard-boiled style of Hammett and Chandler (qq.v.), no doubt because it is rooted in unpleasant violence and more suited to back alleys than to polite society. M. V. (for Mary Violet) Heberden was one of four women to appear on mystery critic James Sandoe's "personal checklist," *The Hard-Boiled Dick,* in which he listed thirty-one authors of tough-guy detective stories for "the reader who, having Hammett and Spillane to choose between, prefers the former." (The other three are Leigh Brackett, q.v.; Helen Nielsen, q.v.; and E. Baker Quinn.) Between 1939 and 1953, Heberden published thirty-three mystery novels under her own byline and that of Charles L. Leonard. All but four of the Heberdens feature a lanky, hard-bitten, fairly undistinguished New York private eye named Desmond Shannon; all twelve Leonard titles feature Paul Kilgerrin, also a private eye but a much more interesting one.

Kilgerrin, whose home base is Washington, D.C., and who specializes in espionage cases, is described as having "a powerful face, and its cold, contemptuous lines gave no indication whether its power might be used for good or evil." Indeed, Kilgerrin is a ruthless and rather amoral character: He uses any method necessary to get results, up to and including cold-blooded murder (he commits *two* of those in *The Stolen Squadron*). This quality, if it can be called that, makes him something of a forerunner of Mike Hammer, though hardly in the same league when it comes to shooting and stomping his enemies. (He doesn't like his allies too much, either. Cornered by an angry mob of factory workers, whom he has led to believe he is a fifth columnist, he thinks that "if he had a machine gun in his hands he would use it with a savage joy.")

Kilgerrin is called in by Colonel Mathewson of Army Intelligence when several small fighter planes, manufactured at the Reynoldson aircraft plant in Connecticut, are stolen during test flights—evidently by imposters who took the places of the legitimate test pilots. Mathewson and the FBI have no inkling of why enemy agents would want a squadron of fighter planes in lieu of bombers, or where those fighters mysteriously vanished to. Kilgerrin, pretending to be a German sympathizer in possession of information on undercover intelligence agents working at Reynoldson, infiltrates the nest of spies—with pyrotechnic results. Meanwhile, test pilot Gerry Cordent (one of the early "liberated" women characters in crime fiction and an associate of Kilgerrin's in this and subsequent novels) works at finding out why the wife of one of the plant's engineers has been brutally murdered in her bed—and which of the wife's circle of friends is not only the murderer but the head of the plane-stealing spy ring.

Melodramatic as it is, the plot hangs together pretty well and there is plenty of slam-bang action and excitement. The problem with this and Heberden's other novels is that she simply wasn't a very good writer. Many of her scenes seem contrived and/or truncated (except, curiously enough, her action scenes, which are lengthy and generally well choreographed); and her gangster dialogue—there are a *lot* of gangsters in *The Stolen Squadron,* all of whom have "sold out" to the enemy—is so bad it's almost painful to read. Compared to the work of Brackett, Nielsen, and Dolores Hitchens (qq.v.), Heberden's tough-guy fiction seems insignificant and interesting only as a curiosity.

Worth reading among Kilgerrin's other cases are his first, *Deadline for Destruction* (1942) and *Pursuit in Peru* (1946); the latter title contains some well-done background material on postwar Lima and the remote Peruvian jungle along the Ucayali River. The best of the Desmond Shannon novels are probably *Death on the Door Mat* (1939), *Aces, Eights and Murder* (1941), and *Murder of a Stuffed Shirt* (1944).

(*B.P.*)

*Leonard, Elmore. *LaBrava.* New York: Arbor House, 1983. (T)

This novel won an MWA Edgar for Best Novel of 1983. It deserves the honor. As does Leonard, who, before *LaBrava,* turned out a string of exceptionally high-powered suspense novels.

LaBrava is Joe LaBrava, former Secret Service agent who once drew the boring duty of guarding Bess Truman in Independence, Missouri, but who has found freedom outside the service making his living and satisfying his artistic impulses with a camera. LaBrava becomes friends with lively octogenarian Maurice Zola, who himself is a skilled photographer and owns an art-deco hotel in a seedy area of Miami. Maurice has money, a past that meshes with south Florida's past, and a good friend named Jean Shaw—*the* Jean Shaw who starred in movies with such leading men as Gig Young and Robert Mitchum. Jean is in midlife now, still beautiful, no longer a star, and has problems. Maurice and LaBrava try to help her solve her problems, which involve a crude and bullying All-American security cop named Richard Nobles and his partner, Cundo Rey, a homicidal Latin male stripper who was shipped to the United States as an undesirable from a Cuban prison.

Plenty of trouble for LaBrava as he lives and photographs at the hotel and meets such people as Franny, an attractive woman who moves into the hotel and sells the Spring Song line of rejuvenating creams to the old women in the lobby; Jill Wilkinson, a beautiful woman who works at a center for violent alcoholics; and Paco Boza, who can walk but prefers to get around in his stolen Eastern Airlines wheelchair in order to build up his arms and shoulders and be more attractive to women. The going gets tough, and LaBrava is tough enough to go right along with the flow.

This is a well-plotted novel, but its real strength is in the authentic, gritty feel of setting and characters. The dialogue here is wonderfully real and vivid, the pace breakneck, and the suspense accelerates to a clever ending with impact. Read *LaBrava,* but be warned: You'll be moved to great effort to seek out the rest of the Leonard novels. You won't be disappointed when you find them.

(*J.L.*)

*Leonard, Elmore. *Swag.* New York: Delacorte, 1976. (T)

In this novel Leonard's irrepressible but star-crossed continuing character Ernest ("Stick") Stickly, Jr., meets ambitious but unethical car salesman Frank Ryan when Stick tries to drive a car away from Ryan's employer's lot without paying for it. Ryan admires certain qualities in Stick, refuses to identify him positively in court, and buys him a drink after Stick is set free.

On some cocktail napkins, Ryan writes down his ten rules that make armed robbery in his estimation the crime with the greatest profit potential and best odds for success. He suggests that he and Stick go into the armed-robbery business together, using these ten commandments of crime as their guidelines, and Stick, though basically not the sort who likes guns, agrees.

During the following months, the two of them reap fun and profit from the merchants of Detroit, rent a luxury apartment complete with swimming pool and willing beauties from the other apartments, and get more ambitious. At least Frank gets more ambitious; Stick has better sense and some doubts. They get more deeply involved with Frank's old breaking-and-entering partner, a black kingpin of crime named Sportree who has some rough and violent friends. And Stick gets deeply involved romantically with Arlene, one of the tenants, who spends her time modeling and working on her tan.

The Leonard touch is here: fast pace, tight plot, dialogue that sings and sizzles, gritty realism, and a feel of authenticity for the seamier side of society where this novel is set. One of the best of this talented author's thrillers.

Stick also appears in the superb *Stick* (1982). Notable among Leonard's other novels are *Fifty-Two Pickup* (1974), *The Switch* (1978), *City Primeval* (1980), *Split Images* (1981), and *Glitz* (1985).

(*J.L.*)

Le Queux, William. *The Mystery of the Green Ray.* London: Hodder & Stoughton, 1915. (E/T)

William Le Queux was among the first writers of espionage fiction—a flamboyant sort who claimed that his spy stories were written to pay his expenses as a free-lancer in the British Secret Service. True or not, such self-promotion helped him become a best-selling novelist during the first quarter of this century, and to set the (less than exacting) standard for the spy genre at that time. He spent a good part of his life on the French Riviera, and many of his novels, both spy and mystery romances, are set in and around Monte Carlo, with side trips to England and the Continent. The settings appear to be authentic, as do the military and political backgrounds of his espionage stories. Unfortunately, his plots tend to be farfetched, often outrageously so, and he padded them mercilessly with description and repetitive, stilted dialogue.

A good example on all counts is *The Mystery of the Green Ray,* which is set not in Monte Carlo but in Scotland at the outbreak of World War I. The novel chronicles the adventures of a young man named Ronald Ewart, who journeys from London to Scotland to tell his betrothed, Myra McLeod, that he can't marry her as planned because he is going to enlist in the army. While Ronnie and Myra are out fishing (the one thing they most enjoy doing together), she is inexplicably struck blind. Later on, her dog, Sholto, is also struck blind and then dognapped. Why steal a blind dog? As one of the other characters says, "It seems to me that the man who steals a blind dog steals him because, for some reason or other, he wants a blind dog—that very one, probably."

With the aid of an occulist named Garnesk and a chum called Dennis, Ronnie sets out to find Sholto and to discover what "fiend of hell" made Myra blind. And of course he succeeds. As the jacket blurb puts it, he "solves the mystery of the Highland loch, recovers his girl's sight for her, captures for the British NID the wonderful installation of the Green Ray, upsets the devilish and deep-laid schemes of as cunning a pair of spies as ever Mr. Le Queux's fertile brain invented."

It is giving away nothing to tell you that the cunning spies are Germans: The villains in *most* of Le Queux's novels were Germans, both long before and long after World War I. Among other such espionage tales are *The Mystery of a Motor Car* (1905), *Spies of the Kaiser* (1909), *The Unbound Book* (1916), *The Intriguers* (1921), and *The Dangerous Game* (1926). Altogether he published more than 100 books, about half of them dealing with the dastardly deeds of foreign agents.

(*B.P.*)

**Leroux, Gaston. *The Mystery of the Yellow Room.* New York: Brentano's, 1908. (AD)

An important early cornerstone of detective fiction, and especially of locked-room stories, *The Mystery of the Yellow Room* is somewhat dated by modern standards. Still, its influence was enormous and it deserves reading by students of the genre.

The amateur detective in *The Mystery of the Yellow Room* and several later Leroux novels is Joseph Rouletabille, who has become a cub reporter for a Paris newspaper at the age of sixteen. Only two years have passed when the events of the novel take place, making him one of the youngest sleuths in adult mystery fiction. The case concerns Mademoiselle Stangerson, who had retired to bed in the room of the title. Her cries for help attract her father and a servant, who break down the locked door to find her bleeding and near death. The window is closed and barred, and she is alone in the room. A famous Sûreté detective, Frederic Larsan, investigates the case, but it is young Rouletabille who finally solves it. The solution is both clever and surprising.

This book was Leroux's first novel, and it remains today one of the masterpieces of French detective fiction. Leroux's second novel, and Rouletabille's second case, *The Perfume of the Lady in Black* (1909), is less successful but also contains a locked-room mystery. The author's most famous novel is *The Phantom of the Opera* (1911), though its fame rests primarily on the film versions.

(*E.D.H.*)

*Levin, Ira. *A Kiss Before Dying.* New York: Simon & Schuster, 1953. (PS/AD)

This MWA Edgar-winner was Ira Levin's first novel, written when he was just twenty-three, and in it he inspires the same fear and anxiety in the reader as he does in his later novels, such as *Rosemary's Baby* (1967). Told in three parts, the story is a simple one: As part of his scheme to get ahead in the world, a poor but ambitious college man becomes engaged to a rich man's daughter, Dorrie Kingship. Because her father would not approve of the relationship, they keep it secret, even from their friends at school; and this works to the young man's advantage when Dorrie becomes pregnant and refuses to have an abortion. Knowing her father would disown her if they married under these circumstances, and not wanting to be saddled with a wife who has no money, as well as an unwanted child, he kills her—rather ingeniously, and not without preliminary slip-ups.

This is the first section of the book, and it is a thoroughly convincing portrait of a psychopathic killer. The young man is never given a name, and as we begin the second section, told from the viewpoint of Dorrie's sister, Ellen, we realize we have been privy to the killer's thoughts and actions but can no more identify him than Ellen can. Ellen detects and comes close to the killer; after her section ends, a second sister, Marion, takes over; and when the identity of the killer is finally revealed, the climax, as with Levin's later work, is chilling.

This is an unusually constructed, suspenseful novel that is extremely difficult to put down—an amazing achievement for a twenty-three-year-old writer. A film of the same title, starring Robert Wagner and Joanne Woodward, was made in 1956. While reasonably faithful to the novel, of necessity it is not as intricate, but provides a nostalgic look at college students of the Fifties—and also will terrify the viewer.

Levin is well known as both a novelist—*The Stepford Wives* (1972), *The Boys from Brazil* (1976)—and a playwright—*No Time for Sergeants* (1956) and *Deathtrap* (1978). The latter title ranks with Agatha Christie's (q.v.) *Mousetrap* and Anthony Shaffer's *Sleuth* as the best and longest-running mystery play of the past several decades.

(*M.M.*)

Lewin, Michael Z. *Night Cover.* New York: Knopf, 1976. (PP/PI)

Lieutenant Leroy ("Roy") Powder, who works nights on the Indianapolis Homicide Bureau, is forty-eight years old and has only seven toes. He also has a strange arrangement with his wife whereby they never have to see one another.

In the opening chapter of *Night Cover,* another cop, Lieutenant Miller, is working on a serial-homicide case, and Powder finds himself involved after a tip on the phone from one of his informants. We soon meet Rex Funkhouser, a Taoist who comes in to tell Powder about a grade scam going on in his school and the impact it will have on his girlfriend. Powder is sorry, but he can't get involved, since no crime has been committed. Besides, there's no evidence. But this develops into a missing-person case, and Albert Samson (the private detective hero of Lewin's major series) is hired to find her.

More murders follow, as well as robberies, break-ins, etc., but the main appeal of the novel is in Lewin's portrait of Powder and of the kind of person it takes to be a dedicated cop. The events in which he is entangled act to change Powder in some major and very basic ways. Lewin's character development is stunning and insightful, and his writing style is straightforward, thought-provoking, and often humorous.

Two other novels to date feature Lieutenant Powder: *Hard Line* (1982) and *Out of Season* (1984). In the latter title, as in *Night Cover,* Powder shares the investigative duties with Albert Samson.

(*T.S.*)

*Lewin, Michael Z. *The Silent Salesman.* New York: Knopf, 1978. (PI)

An interesting thing happened to the California private-eye novel in the 1970s. It grew legs. It left California on a cross-country trip that saw it settle in the damnedest places. We now have the California private-eye novel set in Boston, Massachusetts; Detroit, Michigan; Cincinnati, Ohio; Seattle, Washington; and Missoula (a.k.a. Meriwhether), Montana. They're all fun, but the best of the lot are the Albert Samson novels by Michael Z. Lewin. Anybody who can set a PI series in Indianapolis and make it work is a genius.

Samson is cast in the mold of the true California PI. His bank account is "trying to crawl under a duck"; he's seedy, self-pitying, wisecracking, and clientless. Even a late-summer Gigantic Detective Sale hasn't helped. Things look bad.

> *I spent the first half hour after breakfast counting my money. My cash money. The two thousand dollars that made up my never-touch fund. It came to $938.00.*

Things begin to look up. A client—one Mrs. Dorothea Thomas—has a problem. It seems her brother, a pharmaceuticals salesman, was injured in an explosion at the plant and has been hospitalized. It has been several months and she hasn't been allowed to see him. Samson investigates. Samson makes waves. Samson is fired by his client. What's going on here? Before we're through, we meet up with drugs, murder, and some seriously unpleasant corporate types. We also meet "Sam," a long-lost daughter, and Mom, who owns and operates a lunch counter, and we witness a one-on-one basketball game that shows our hero up for the middle-aged fading star that he is.

Lewin never writes the same story twice (unlike some more popular authors), and he creates the kind of people we want to learn more about. There's the landlord, who barters a reduction in rent for some security work. There's a girlfriend who doesn't live in and isn't always available. There's a realistic working relationship with the rather stereotypical "friend." But mainly there's Samson.

Other Samson titles worth checking out include *Ask the Right Question* (1971) and *The Enemies Within* (1974). An interesting, if not wholly successful, nonseries novel by Lewin is *Outside In* (1980), in which a writer of private-eye mysteries, Willie Werth, decides to play detective when a casual friend is murdered—and finds himself both in and out of his element.

(*B.T.*)

*Lewis, Norman. *The Man in the Middle.* New York: Pantheon, 1984. (T)

Some suspense novels set in foreign lands are so lacking in detail that the main characters might just as well be running around Pittsburgh. Once in a while, though, an author can write a novel of intrigue and murder about a land and society you've never seen but which, when you're done reading, you'll never forget. In *The Man in the Middle,* Lewis gives us Cairo for starters, and finally an overall clear, honest, and very real picture of contemporary Egyptian society.

British journalist Ronald Kemp, aged forty-three, has left his wife and two sons in London, and probably it's just as well. She's one of those strait-laced British women and secretly hopes her rather odd husband will return one day to run daddy's country estate. British children all go away to school anyway, so Kemp sees as much of his on his visits home from journalistic adventures as he would sitting in front of a country fireplace.

He wishes it weren't so, of course. Loneliness is natural to him, as is a certain amount of cynicism—an occupational hazard in the journalism trade. Egyptian society doesn't help much, either. Fraternization with the "natives," particularly the females, can be grounds for deportation and in some cases even the death penalty. Kemp has to hide his Egyptian lover from the police—an experience so terrifying to both of them that she returns to her former nursing duties at a local hospital. Alcohol is banned except in foreign compounds. Lewis is a genius at portraying the tensions and explosiveness of a group of Westerners—oil people and engineers from the U.S.A.; journalists and diplomats from Britain—caught in a bleak country, far from home and a good hamburger. Their weekend parties at one foreign compound or another—safe places—bring out every extreme of human behavior known to man.

Those pictures are just brilliant sidelights. What's really going on here is Kemp's inadvertent stumble—while researching an article about a new tourist beach in Tripoli—into the middle of an attempted coup against the present Egyptian government. This innocent assignment places his life in danger and makes him an unwitting participant in an assassination plot. Lewis gives us a good look into Egyptian politics, international governmental meddling, and the tightwire existence of Westerners who are at the mercy of the violent and archaic cultures with which they must work.

Lewis is a world traveler and an old hand at this kind of writing. His twelve novels set all over the world—including *The Day of the Fox* (1955), *Every Man's Brother* (1968), and *The Sicilian Specialist* (1974)—show him to be a great social anthropologist as well as a fine suspense writer.

(*K.K.H.*)

Lewis, Roy. *A Gathering of Ghosts.* New York: St. Martin's, 1983. (AD).

Roy Lewis is an attorney, and he has stated that his detective novels "begin with an attempt to use my legal knowledge in a crime/fictional setting and most of my books continue to have a certain legal flavor." His legal training is apparent in more than the plots and situations of his novels; Lewis's writing style is precise (without being rigid), smooth-flowing, and frequently humorous. A number of his novels feature Scotland Yard inspector John Crow, a pleasant protagonist who works well in his more conventional mysteries.

A Gathering of Ghosts is one of his less traditional, nonprocedural novels. In it we follow the activities of Arnold Landon, a city-planning officer, as he investigates the scheduled demolition of Rampton Farm. The farm, it seems, is being purchased by Brandling Leisure Pursuits and its buildings are being razed to make way for an amusement park. But Landon discovers an old thirteenth-century barn on the property—Old Wheat Barn—and he feels it should be preserved.

The discovery, of course, stirs up great controversy among preservation-conscious and progress-conscious residents of the area. At the meeting of the planning commission, Arnold finds himself vigorously opposed by Professor Fisher, a university medievalist who swears the barn is of a common type built much later than the thirteenth century. Arnold revisits the barn for another examination—and finds that another interested party had done likewise and is still there, quite dead. Landon's subsequent private investigation leads to the solution of that and yet another murder, and lays bare the "ghostly" secret of the old barn.

This is an excellent novel, mystifying and filled with believable characters and incidents. The *New York Times Book Review* called it "an unusual book, one with a pronounced streak of poetry, that poses some problems very much in today's consciousness." In any case, a pleasant evening's entertainment.

Arnold Landon reappears in *Most Cunning Workmen* (1984), another tale of mystery and ancient secrets, this one set in the countryside of Northumberland. Recommended titles featuring Inspector Crow include *A Lover Too Many* (1971) and *Nothing but Foxes* (1979). Among Lewis's excellent nonseries novels are *A Wolf by the Ears* (1972), *An Inevitable Quality* (1978), and *Dwell in Danger* (1982); the last-named title features a likable young aspiring lawyer named Eric Ward.

(*N.D./M.M.*)

Lewis, Roy Harley. *A Cracking of Spines.* New York: St. Martin's, 1981. (AD)

Matthew Coll, late of British military intelligence, is living peacefully in a Dorset village, having realized a lifelong ambition some six months before by buying a small secondhand bookshop. Both Coll and the shop are housed in a six-bedroom Queen Anne house built in 1703; and an occasional weekend boarder, attractive Laura Cottingham, keeps him from being lonely. He is a contented man. But then he receives a call from Wilfred Frensham, owner of an old established London bookshop and an important member of the Antiquarian Booksellers Association. It seems a rash of thefts of rare books is plaguing not only members of the association but a variety of libraries and private collectors throughout southern England. Apparently responsible is a professional gang, one of whose number must be a rare-book expert, for only valuable items have been taken in each of the robberies. Frensham, who has been apprised of Coll's background, wants Coll to investigate on behalf of the association. Coll reluctantly agrees.

The early stages of his investigation take him to a college library at nearby Radford and its odd head librarian, Edward Heyman; and to the estate of the Berridges, the lord of which likes to hunt and the lady of which may or may not be a predator. A false story in the *Rare Books Newsletter* of the Libraries Association, designed to set a trap for the thieves, nets Coll his first major lead; it also nets him an unexpected swim in a river when his car is deliberately forced off the road at high speed. Much more danger awaits him as he draws closer to the gang and the identity of its leader: cold-blooded murder, an attack on him inside his own house, and the kidnapping of Laura Cottingham.

This is a lively and entertaining mystery, melodramatic in spots but with good character development and a slam-bang finale. Particularly effective is the prologue, told third-person (Coll narrates the balance of the novel), in which two gang members murder an unidentified accomplice during a robbery inside a library—by pushing him and a sack of rare books off a rope ladder, so that he cracks his spine on the floor below. The identity of the victim and the reasons for his bizarre death are not revealed until much later in the narrative, thus heightening interest and suspense.

A Cracking of Spines is also chock-full of authentic and fascinating rare-book lore: Roy Harley Lewis is himself a bibliophile and bookseller, as well as the author of a number of nonfiction works on antiquarian books. Bibliophiles will love it; so will any reader with even a casual interest in the world of rare books. Equally enjoyable are two other Matthew Coll adventures: *The Manuscript Murders* (1982), which deals with book auctions and a sixteenth-century manuscript; and *A Pension for Death* (1983), in which Coll is hired to act as a consultant buyer of valuable books for a large conglomerate. *Where Agents Fear to Tread* (1984) introduces a new and appealing Lewis hero, librarian Henry Franklin, and a new setting, Pakistan, in a mystery involving priceless, ancient Arabic manuscripts stolen from British libraries and museums and smuggled back into Pakistan.

(*B.P.*)

Lindsey, David L. *A Cold Mind.* New York: Harper, 1983. (PP)

Someone is killing the call girls of Houston, Texas—infecting them with rabies so they die a horrible, painful, and prolonged death. Homicide detective Stuart Haydon, along with several assistants, set out to do something about it, uncovering along the way a Brazilian slave-trade connection.

This is not a book for the squeamish, as scenes of death, autopsy, and laboratory animal dissection are recorded in explicit detail (the killer preserves animal eyeballs for a coffee-table centerpiece). Neither is it a book for the easily depressed, as the author chooses (perhaps because of the book's subject matter) to paint the world in general, and Houston in particular, as a rather unsavory place. Consider, for example, this fairly typical description: "The Turning Basin itself was a ballooning hernia in the intestine of Buffalo Bayou, which trailed a wormy path through the center of Houston. . . ."

Once past the realistic (or selective) harshness of the story, however, it is easy to get caught up in the crime drama that is unfolding, for the Houston police mount an all-out manhunt for this obviously mad killer. The drama is well handled by the author, who unquestionably brought a great deal of research and professional skill to the story.

David L. Lindsey is also the author of *Black Gold—Red Death* (1982).

(*N.D.*)

Linington, Elizabeth. *Crime by Chance.* Philadelphia: Lippincott, 1973. (PP)

Elizabeth Linington—who also writes as Lesley Egan and Dell Shannon (qq.v.)—has created a series of police procedurals featuring Sergeant Ivor Maddox of the Hollywood Police Department. In the first of these, *Greenmask!* (1964), we meet Maddox and his supporting cast of characters: D'Arcy, who is known for falling in love inappropriately; sophisticated and sarcastic Rodriguez; Feinman, everybody's favorite friendly cop; Rowan, contemplative and serious; Dabney, the philosopher; grandmotherly Daisy Hoffman; and competent and attractive Sue Carstairs. Later in the series, Maddox marries Carstairs, and their personal lives provide an interesting thread that links the various cases they investigate, both separately and together.

In *Crime by Chance,* the detectives at Wilcox Street are working on a variety of cases. Forged checks are being passed in the vicinity by young people with false drivers' licenses and Los Angeles City college I.D. cards. Two bodies turn up shot to death in a stolen Cadillac—one of them holding a very alive baby boy. Someone is impersonating cops by pulling over out-of-state drivers and threatening to cite them for traffic violations; when the tourists are distressed at having to stay in the area for a court date, the impersonators willingly accept cash "fines." There are the usual shoplifters, out-of-control demonstrators, and drug pushers. But the major crime running through this novel is a "mystery," something the detectives don't see often, and it intrigues Ivor Maddox.

Dorrie Mayo, a young widow with a fifteen-month-old child, has suddenly quit her job, given up her apartment, and moved back east to live with the family of her dead husband. At least that's what the typed notes she left her employer, the rental company, and a neighbor say. But Dorrie couldn't type, and she left behind two pictures that she prized highly, as well as her daughter's favorite toy. Spurred on by concern for both the mother and the child, Maddox probes into the young woman's private life and in the end discovers one of the strangest motives for a disappearance anyone at Wilcox Street has ever encountered.

This is solid procedure, as in Linington's series under both the Egan and Shannon names, and the main mystery keeps one reading right to the end. The characters of the men and women of the Hollywood force, however, are not so well developed as in the other series; Ivor and Sue Maddox in particular come off as too good to be true, too well adjusted and sane. There is something smug and unlikable about the pair, which detracts from the otherwise well-woven and interesting plots.

(*M.M.*)

Linington, Elizabeth. *Perchance of Death.* New York: Doubleday Crime Club, 1977. (PP)

It is September and Los Angeles is experiencing unseasonable rain. Sue Maddox is in a bad mood—not only about the weather but also about the fact that she can't get pregnant. In the course of the story, she complains about "all the unwed mothers, and hordes of illegitimate children just to get the welfare money, not to speak of all these obscene abortions"; about "those obnoxious Libbers"; about people in general. Her husband, Ivor, agrees: Hollywood is "a dirty, greedy town with a hell of a lot of dirty, greedy, no-good louts and bums in it." Well, perhaps the Maddoxes have good reason for their attitude toward humanity, given the kinds of cases they must deal with.

First there is Juanita, an exotic-looking woman who picks up men in high-class bars and then holds them at gunpoint. There is the battered child who dies in the hospital, and her mother who defends the boyfriend who probably killed her daughter. An old woman who was reputed to have money—but apparently didn't—has been murdered in her own home. An old man's home has been trashed, apparently by juveniles, and everything he managed to acquire in his hardworking life has been destroyed. No wonder the Maddoxes are angry.

As usual there are major cases, one for Ivor and one for Sue. Ivor is trying to unravel the puzzle of an elderly woman who disappeared after a fall that broke her hip. Relatives have traced her to a convalescent home; but when they go to visit, another woman is wearing her identification bracelet—a woman so senile she can barely speak. When the right woman turns up in another convalescent home, she is so sedated *she* can't speak. When she recovers, she claims she was hastily moved from the first convalescent hospital to the second, but the manager of the place where her relatives found her insists she was there all along. Why, Ivor puzzles, would anyone go to such lengths?

At the same time, Sue is working on the disappearance of a high-school girl. Pauline Strange vanished from her own home, seemingly without a struggle. When her body turns up, suspicion focuses on her boyfriend, but Sue isn't so sure he killed her. And when she does figure out what happened, the results are explosive.

When the novel ends, it is still raining and Sue is still complaining, but she has good cause. After being knocked down a flight of stairs, lying battered and bruised on a cot in the locker room, she says to her concerned husband, "At least . . . it was only Joe—respectable married man—who got a look at my underwear. I never realized before how very expressive that British phrase is, arse over tip."

Ivor, concerned and solicitous, replies, "Don't be vulgar."

Other books featuring the non-vulgar men and women of Wilcox Street include *Date with Death* (1966), *No Villain Need Be* (1979), *Skeletons in the Closet* (1982), and *Felony Report* (1984).

(*M.M.*)

*Linzee, David. *Discretion.* New York: Seaview, 1978. (PI)

One of the most interesting young writers to enter the mystery field in the 1970s is David Linzee, who plots deftly, writes at his best with cinematic vividness, and has a special gift for creating likable unaggressive characters. His debut novel, *Death in Connecticut* (1977), published when he was twenty-five years old, was reminiscent of *Catcher in the Rye* and *The Graduate* and Woody Allen's movies, but his second, *Discretion,* offered a merry romp across Europe in the manner of the gentler suspense films of Alfred Hitchcock.

The protagonists are Sarah Saber, bright young sophisticate and crack shot; and Chris Rockwell, a bearish and bearded young fellow who's the very antithesis of a tough guy. The couple are not only lovers but private detectives, working for Inquiries, Incorporated (Inkwink for short), a computerized agency that is part of a conglomerate of service companies. The byword at Inkwink is discretion—so much so that no one in the organization knows what anyone else is working on!

When an aristocratic French art connoisseur decides to keep for himself a priceless Fragonard that he's restored for a Rome art museum, he devises a plan that includes having an accomplice impersonate the museum's director and hire Inkwink to send an agent to Rome and test the gallery's security system by trying to steal the painting. The person assigned to this mission is Sarah and she pulls off the theft neatly. Then the real museum officials hire Inkwink to send someone to Rome to investigate the theft, and the one chosen for this job is Chris. Of course, thanks to the policy of discretion, neither detective has any idea that his/her adversary is the other.

Most of this novel is a diverting game of cat and mouse, spiced with ridicule for American corporate efficiency and Italian bureaucratic incompetence. Linzee keeps the plot under control through endless twists and turns and viewpoint shifts, but saves his biggest fireworks for the climax, which takes place in an empty French château during a *son et lumière* performance.

The tone and mood of the lighter Hitchcock films like *To Catch a Thief* are perfectly captured in *Discretion,* whose central characters and organization might have been recycled in any number of later adventures. Unfortunately Sarah and Chris returned only once, in Linzee's third and to date last novel, *Belgravia* (1979).

(*F.M.N.*)

Little, Constance and Gwenyth. *The Black-Headed Pins.* New York: Doubleday Crime Club, 1938. (R/C)

A sister team of Australian-born Americans produced some of the best screwball comedy/mysteries to grace the war years and beyond. They are the Little sisters: Connie, the concocter of plots and writer of first drafts; and Gwenyth, master of rewrite and polish.

The Black-Headed Pins is their second mystery but the first to sport their gimmick, a title with the word *black* in it. It relates the story of Leigh Smith, a savvy young woman forced to take a job as housekeeper/companion when times are bad. Leigh's boss, Mrs. Ballinger, is a pinchfisted old biddy, resolved to gather her younger relatives around her at Christmas without spending any money—even on such basics as food, drink, and heating. Mrs. Ballinger seems a good bet as victim, but instead it is her handyman nephew who perishes. As other relatives are killed or attacked, Leigh's cleaning becomes cursory and she devotes her time to detecting. By her side is an uninvited houseguest, Richard Jones, who plays cosleuth as well as Benedick to her Beatrice.

The Little novels are feverish stories of households gone haywire. The murders are absurd, and the corpses have a habit of disappearing or, as in this novel, sitting up and grinning. Clues, like the title pins, are abundant, but seem to point nowhere. Characters chase around at all hours of the day and night, heaving accusations and wisecracks at one another. They take time out for a meal, a drink, or a bit of romantic banter, and eventually track down (or stumble upon) the guilty party. All in all, a good time is had by all—especially the reader.

Silly as they are, the Little mysteries age well. Readers of modern comedy/mystery authors such as Charlotte MacLeod (q.v.) will likely enjoy the Littles' tales of madcap murder. Of the many "black" murders, *The Black Shrouds* (1941), *Great Black Kamba* (1944), and *The Black Stocking* (1946) are good examples of this sisterly collaboration in crime.

(*K.M.*)

Livingston, Jack. *A Piece of the Silence.* New York: St. Martin's, 1982. (PI)

A Piece of the Silence is the first of a series featuring Joe Binney, a New York City PI who has all the characteristics of the traditional private eye, plus one: He happens to be deaf.

Binney's deafness is not in the least a gimmick to sell the series. It's an honest attempt to depict a handicapped man as a detective, an attempt that is successful in that it offers an interesting sidelight to the cases he works on. Binney reads lips; and when his phone rings, he "sees" it because it's hooked up to a lamp that blinks. He lost his hearing in the navy, when he was with an underwater-demolition unit.

Hired by a man named Penton to dig up divorce evidence against his wife, Binney subsequently discovers the wife floating in the swimming pool at the couple's Long Island home, dead of an overdose of heroin. When Penton shows up, he lies to the police, in the person of Lieutenant Probcziewski, saying that he hired Binney to go to the house to look for a cache of drugs—which makes Binney look bad in Probcziewski's eyes. Later, Penton apologizes and persuades Binney to continue working for him, not to find his wife's killer but to make sure that she has provided for her son by a previous marriage. A new aspect is added to the case when Binney is waylaid, shot up with drugs meant to kill him, and then saved by a sharp-tongued doctor. Binney's search for the connection between his abduction and attempted murder and the death of Penton's wife leads him to a ship called the S.S. *Carlotta Perez* docked off Sandy Hook; a very unusual entertainer named Felicity ("City") Bowers; more trouble with the cops; and a rousing climax in which some homemade nitrogylcerin plays an explosive role.

Tersely written, with plenty of action and more depth of characterization and feeling than many private-eye novels, *A Piece of the Silence* is an impressive debut. Joe Binney's second case, *Die Again, MacReady* (1983), has the same qualities.

(*R.J.R./B.P.*)

Lockridge, Frances and Richard. *The Norths Meet Murder.* New York: Stokes, 1940. (AD/PP)

The husband-and-wife team of Richard and Frances Lockridge produced a long series of novels featuring Pamela and Jerry North—another husband-and-wife team, who became one of the most popular detecting duos of the Forties and Fifties. (Most readers over the age of forty will remember the 1952–54 television series "Mr. and Mrs. North," starring Richard Denning and Barbara Britton.) Jerry North is a New York publisher married to a smart young woman who probably would have been on his editorial staff in the 1980s; but back then, when men were men and women were women, Pamela is content to spend his money and keep the home fires burning. The Norths spend a lot of time together, however; maybe his publishing house just runs itself. At any rate, he doesn't want to be stuck in an office and miss things—and he would, because when his missus is on the scent, time and Pamela wait for no man.

The Norths begin their involvement in crime detection quite by accident. In *The Norths Meet Murder,* their first adventure, someone has been killed in an empty apartment upstairs in their building, and while Pam is trying to convince Jerry they should rent the place for their annual Christmas party, they discover the long-dead body in the bathtub. Pam goes through the requisite shudder/faint routine, but as soon as Lieutenant Bill Weigand of Homicide (also an ongoing character in the series) and his whiskey-loving sidekick, Mullins, appear on the scene, she tells them who the murderer is. Pam is ignored, of course. Woman's intuition has no place in crime detection.

From there on out, we follow Weigand and Mullins as they go about their customary investigative routine. Customary, that is, with one exception: Periodically they drop in on the Norths, and along with cocktails, the Norths feed them information and insight. Weigand finds himself somewhat enamored of Pam: He thinks "that it might be rather fun to be married to somebody like—well, like Mrs. North." And as he returns again and again to the North apartment, his case begins to take shape. When Pam suggests they hold a "suspect party," Weigand agrees. The party, of course, turns out to be the most interesting any of the guests has ever attended—and a most perilous one for the charming Mrs. North.

(*K.K.H.*)

Lockridge, Frances and Richard. *A Pinch of Poison.* New York: Stokes, 1941. (AD/PP)

By the time this third mystery for the Norths rolls around, Weigand has become a family friend, dropping by for a martini and conversation after going off duty. He has come to realize that his discussion of a tough case will usually elicit some off-the-wall judgment from Pam, which, if he's sharp enough to catch it, may eventually lead him to a solution. In this novel, Weigand's difficult case is the death of socialite Lois Winston, who has died after apparently having too much to drink at the roof restaurant of the exclusive Ritz-Plaza. When he is called in on the case, Weigand and his girlfriend, Dorian, are at the Norths', engaged in a nonsensical conversation about Pam's true age. All four hop into Weigand's Buick and drive across town to the murder scene.

Pam knows of the victim because she is on the committee of an adoption foundation where Lois Winston worked. There was some resentment at the foundation over the wealthy Lois taking a paying job that others badly needed, but Pam doesn't feel this was reason enough for someone to kill her. And it was definitely a killing: The woman was poisoned.

Weigand embarks on his routine. Pam attempts to investigate at the foundation, but runs across Weigand. The case seems to have something to do with one of the children the foundation has available for adoption, and as they dig into the child's background, they encounter people from a different stratum of society than that to which Lois Winston was accustomed. Their investigation is spiced with the typical humor and clever repartee that characterize all the North novels, and of course Pamela is the one to unravel a tangle of family relationships and come up with the solution.

The North novels are a lot of fun; in addition, they are tightly plotted and the characters ring true. While perhaps a little dated (in their narration, the authors refer to their characters as Mr. and Mrs. North, rather than by their first names—a convention that quickly becomes irritating), they still have plenty of sophisticated, 1940s charm.

Other recommended Pam and Jerry North novels are *Hanged for a Sheep* (1942), *Murder in a Hurry* (1950), and *The Long Skeleton* (1958). Bill Weigand appears solo in *The Tangled Cord* (1957). The Lockridges also wrote novels featuring D.A. Bernie Simmons and police detective Nathan Shapiro, characters about whom Richard Lockridge continued to write after Frances's death in 1963.

(*K.K.H.*)

Lockridge, Richard. *Dead Run.* Philadelphia: Lippincott, 1976. (PP)

Richard Lockridge was a prolific suspense novelist, the author of more than 100 books. The strong point in the Lockridge novels is his protagonists, who not only carry on their own investigations but assist in each other's cases. Lockridge's fictional world is peopled with such individuals as Nathan Shapiro, Bill Weigand, and Sergeant Mullins of New York City Homicide; New York City district attorney Bernie Simmons; and Captain Inspector Merton Heimrich of the New York State Police. These characters also appear in various earlier books authored with his first mystery-writing wife, Frances. (His second wife, Hildegarde Dolson, q.v., also wrote mysteries.) His readers can believe in the reality of this world, for each book serves to expand it.

In *Dead Run,* Heimrich's investigation is a solo one. And as a bonus we meet all the members of his family, too. Michael, his adored stepson, has gotten a ride home from college with a friend, arriving in the middle of an upstate New York blizzard. The friend happens to be a girl, and in a charming bit of old-fashioned awkwardness, Heimrich and his wife, Susan, decide to move them down the hill to the local inn for dinner and proper sleeping quarters. Home again in bed, Heimrich is awakened by a telephone call informing him that an old friend, Sam Johnson, the town's stalwart defense attorney, has been killed by a car in the inn's parking lot. Michael's girlfriend, Joan, is the only eyewitness to the hit-and-run; she saw a station wagon—but not its driver—when she was opening her window to the fresh air. Joan is now unable to continue on to New York City for Christmas with her father, but she doesn't really care; it was a duty visit—and besides, she's in love with Michael. His family welcomes her—though every morning Heimrich checks the blankets on the couch where she is now sleeping, wondering if his stepson is conducting himself honorably.

The plot progresses nicely. Michael's attachment to Joan becomes more obvious as the pages turn, and there are nice family bits. When Joan is shot at in an apparent attempt to silence her as a witness, Heimrich realizes this is a hometown job and gets on with discovering who in the small community was about to be exposed by Sam Johnson—and for what.

This is an easygoing, small-town story with good characterization and with images of the countryside that are so well drawn they will stay with you for a long time.

Other titles featuring this personable state policeman include *Murder Can't Wait* (1964), *A Risky Way to Kill* (1969), and *Not I, Said the Sparrow* (1973). Some of the Heimrich books by the team of Richard and Frances Lockridge are *Think of Death* (1947), *Stand Up and Die* (1953), and *The Distant Clue* (1963).

(*K.K.H.*)

Lockridge, Richard. *Death on the Hour.* Philadelphia: Lippincott, 1974. (W)

Death on the Hour takes us into the world of the New York media. A popular television news commentator and head of a network news department is mysteriously electrocuted by the portable television set he carried with him everywhere. A staunch liberal, Clayton Carter had resisted a move by a politically conservative conglomerate to take over the network of which he was part owner. His ex-wife stands to inherit big bucks and also stock in the corporation, and the network's president (her boyfriend) has everything to gain from Carter's death.

This is typical Lockridge fare, methodical and tightly plotted. John Stein, of New York Homicide, and Bernie Simmons, assistant district attorney, team up to perform the requisite detecting. The characterizations are memorable. The little dinners between Carter's assistant and her ex-lover, a

New York journalist come to offer his strong shoulder, are poignant reminders of the dilemma many of us know, the one where you can't quite let go of an old love. One of Lockridge's most charming characters is Carter's Siamese cat, Mau, who talks a mile a minute. As far as Lockridge (who with his wife, Frances, wrote a nonfiction book, *Cats and People,* in 1950) is concerned, a great Siamese cat is man's best friend.

Other Bernie Simmons investigations are *Squire of Death* (1965), *A Plate of Red Herrings* (1968), and *Something Up a Sleeve* (1972), among others. With his wife, Frances, Lockridge wrote of Simmons's adventures in *And Left for Dead* (1962) and *The Devious Ones* (1964).

(*K.K.H.*)

Long, Amelia Reynolds. *The Corpse at the Quill Club.* New York: Phoenix Press, 1940. (AD)

Long is a perfect example of a novelist who found her proper home with lending-library publisher Phoenix Press. Her titles were frequently the best parts of her books, except for those featuring fluttery, dithering Katherine ("Peter") Piper, an alleged writer of mystery novels who falls into a category all her own.

As a founding member of the Quill Club, a group composed of writers of anything from unreadable poetry to children's stories (one member, a retired grocer, has invented his own grammar), Peter is deeply concerned when a purple-inked and anonymous poison-pen letter is mailed to each member (except for the one whom the letter concerns). The letters put a strain on club members' relationships—which, with one exception, had been harmonious—when the group gathers at Arlea, a cottage owned by one of the members, for an intensive reading-and-writing weekend.

Peter, while out on an early-morning stroll, meets Edward Trelawney, who is connected with the district attorney's office in Philadelphia. When one of the Quill Club members dies of caffeine poisoning, Trelawney assists the local police (who admit they are in over their heads) in investigating the murder and such other matters as a missing writer's notebook/diary; a hovering husband; and the cottage cook, whose unbelievably mangled pronunciation is all phonetically spelled out for the reader. Peter goes meandering about during the night; very little writing is done; and Trelawney finally captures the culprit in a scene worthy of a Mack Sennett comedy.

Long's sentence structure tends to be choppy and her dialogue will keep any reader fully alert trying to make sense of slang, dialect, and phonetic spellings. The leftover loose ends can be disdainfully ignored by the reader, just as they were by the author. This and such other Long titles as *The Shakespeare Murders* (1939), *Murder by Magic* (1947), and *The House with the Green Shudders* (1950) are so classically bad they should be read on long winter nights, when they can be fully savored.

(*E.N.*)

Loraine, Philip. *Photographs Have Been Sent to Your Wife.* New York: Random House, 1971. (PS)

Robin Estridge's work published under his Philip Loraine pseudonym are high-quality suspense novels. Estridge has done several screenplays—*House of Darkness* (1948), *Checkpoint* (1956), *Campbell's Kingdom* (1957), *Drums of Africa* (1963), and *The Boy Cried Murder* (1966) are good examples of his screen work—and many of the Loraine novels have cinematic qualities.

Photographs Have Been Sent to Your Wife is a haunting tale of suspense. Successful television star Alan Hardy has it all: a lucrative profession he enjoys, a fine marriage to his childhood sweetheart, and the prospects of even greater achievements before him. Suddenly his world is shattered. Hardy receives a phone call saying copies of photographs showing him in bed with a fourteen-year-old girl have been sent to his wife and his employer. From that moment, Hardy's career and marriage are in ruins; all that remains for him is to find the person responsible for destroying his life. But the trail is as twisted as the bizarre desires and motives of the various other characters.

Blackmail plays a prominent role in such other Loraine works as *W.I.L. One to Curtis* (1967) and *A Mafia Kiss* (1969). A big-stakes heist of a Leonardo da Vinci painting provides the background for *The Angel of Death* (1961).

(*G.K.*)

*Lovell, Marc. *The Spy with His Head in the Clouds.* New York: Doubleday Crime Club, 1982. (E/C)

Marc Lovell is the pseudonym under which Mark McShane (q.v.) writes somewhat more restrained mysteries than those to which he signs his own name. Which is not to say that the Lovell books lack the eccentricity or farcical humor of the McShanes. These qualities are particularly in evidence in the series about six-foot-seven British spy Appleton ("Apple") Porter.

Apple is no ordinary spy and his adventures are anything but ordinary spy stories. Indeed, they are at once gentle, hilarious spoofs of James Bond and exciting chronicles full of bizarre individuals and spectacular chases. Apple is a marvelous character: bumbling, resourceful, witty, foolish, and any number of other human contradictions. Among his endearing traits are a penchant for blushing furiously at moments of emotional stress, and an eye for the ladies that more often than not lands him in a state of frustrated horniness.

In *The Spy with His Head in the Clouds,* Apple is fed a dose of a new truth serum that makes him tell all he knows about British Intelligence (which isn't much, since he is a low-level spy who specializes in the use of languages), lands him in a tiny cell, and leaves him with the taste of strawberries and a mysterious, short-term malaise called *katasak.* The person responsible is his own boss, Angus Watkin! It seems the Russians have invented this new drug, Soma-2 (Soma being the tranquilizing drug in Huxley's *Brave New World*), and have allowed it to fall into British hands. Why? What tricks do they have up their collective sleeve?

Apple, after his stint as guinea pig to test the effects of the drug, is sent to a small traveling circus to find out the truth, the circus being where Soma-2 first surfaced in England. What follows is a delightful and frenetic series of events that include a near deadly loop-the-loop ride, an encounter with a couple of gorillas (real ones, not the hoodlum variety), and a madcap climax in which Apple throws London's Paddington Station into a turmoil by means of a ploy involving the Harlem Globetrotters.

This and other Apple adventures—*The Spy Game* (1981), *Spy on the Run* (1982), *Apple Spy in the Sky* (1983), *Apple to the Core* (1983), *How Green Was My Apple* (1984), *The Only Good Apple in a Barrel of Spies* (1984), and *The Spy Who Got His Feet Wet* (1985)—are absolutely required reading for anyone who enjoys farce, nonstop action, and a truly memorable series character. They are, in fact, spy novels guaranteed to please even people who hate spy novels.

McShane's other novels published under the Lovell pseudonym are quite different from the Apple books. *The Imitation Thieves* (1971), for instance, is a darkly comic caper about four of the unlikeliest crooks you'll ever meet, reminiscent of McShane's early novels under his own name. And such titles as *The Ghost of Megan* (1968), *An Enquiry into the Existence of Vampires* (1974), *Dreamers in a Haunted House* (1975), and *Hand Over Mind* (1979) are serious-minded works that reflect the author's interest in the occult.

(*B.P.*)

*Lovesey, Peter. *A Case of Spirits.* New York: Dodd, Mead, 1975. (H)

Peter Lovesey's novels featuring Sergeant Cribb and Constable Thackeray of Scotland Yard's CID are set in England's Victorian Age (the 1880s). Each illuminates some aspect of those colorful times, such as marathon racing (*Wobble to Death,* 1970), the popular stage (*Abracadaver,* 1972), and Irish nationalist terrorism (*Invitation to a Dynamite Party,* 1974). Lovesey's historical background is accurate and used to good effect; and his plotting is highly original.

In *A Case of Spirits,* Sergeant Cribb is called in to investigate the theft of a painting from the house of a Dr. Probert while all the members of the household were out at a séance. Coincidentally, a vase was stolen from the house of a Miss Crush while *she* was at a séance at Dr. Probert's home. Cribb has been ordered to use all possible discretion in his investigation since the victims are high-society types. The medium, Peter Brand, is new on the clairvoyance scene in London, and is high on the list of Cribb's suspects.

Sergeant Cribb and Thackeray are hot on the heels of the thief at a subsequent meeting of clairvoyants when medium Brand is murdered. As they proceed to investigate this murder, they receive an education in the eccentric world of clairvoyance, as well as observe some of the more titillating morals and double standards of the times. And, of course, they cleverly solve the crimes.

A Case of Spirits is the sixth novel in the series featuring this popular investigative team. It later became a well-received PBS television series called "Sergeant Cribb," for which Lovesey and his wife adapted all of the novels as well as wrote additional episodes.

(*T.S./M.M.*)

*Lovesey, Peter. *The False Inspector Dew*. New York: Pantheon, 1982. (H/T/W)

In this wickedly funny and ingenious novel, set in 1921, we meet Alma Webster, a maiden in her late twenties who has lived her entire life through romantic fantasies. As the result of a toothache, she meets and becomes involved with a dentist named Walter Baranov. And soon finds herself a coconspirator with him in a devious scheme to murder his wife, Lydia—a scheme inspired by the real-life Dr. Crippen case.

The unfolding murder plot takes place on an ocean liner, the *Mauretania,* bound from Southampton to Cherbourg and then on to New York. Alma poses as Lydia, who is also on board—but not for long, at least not alive. Walter Baranov books passage as Walter Dew, a famous Scotland Yard investigator and the man who arrested Crippen for his crimes. When Lydia's body is dragged out of the ocean, it is not identified immediately, but foul play is suspected. So of course the captain of the ship calls on the false Inspector Dew to help solve the crime. The results are not at all what you might expect.

A subplot involves a professional gambler's attempt to fleece the son of a millionaire, and how he is foiled. Other minor plots and characters (among them the Livingstone Cordells and their beautiful daughter) enrich the substance of the novel and make it one of the most rewarding reading experiences you'll have in a long time. And you'll absolutely love the surprise ending!

Lovesey once again demonstrates his expertise at depicting the charm and flavor of a bygone era, capturing perfectly the feel of the 1920s. Yet he tells his tale in a very contemporary, sophisticated, and wryly humorous style. This may well be the finest of all his novels.

Another delightful historical mystery by Peter Lovesey is *Keystone* (1983), which is also set in the 1920s—this time in Hollywood. It features the adventures of a British vaudeville comedian named Warwick Easton who wants to be a movie cop—one of Mack Sennett's Keystone Kops, to be exact. But comedy turns to murder (on a roller coaster, among other places) and Eaton finds himself both sleuth and prime suspect. Sennett, "Fatty" Arbuckle, and Mabel Normand, among other screen personalities of that era, also play roles in this fascinating and exciting story.

(*T.S./B.P.*)

*Lowndes, Marie Belloc. *The Lodger.* New York: Scribner's, 1913. (PS)

Marie Belloc Lowndes wrote more than forty well-constructed novels with considerable psychological depth. Many of these concern ordinary women who commit murder out of passion or jealousy (among them *The Chink in the Armour,* 1912; *Letty Lynton,* 1931; and *The Chianti Flask,* 1935). In these stories, Lowndes's emphasis is on motive: What is the nature of the events and emotions that can drive a hitherto sane and civilized woman to such violence? Many of the novels incorporate courtroom scenes that are both absorbing and highly realistic. *The Lodger,* which Lowndes developed from a previous short story of the same title, concerns a series of Jack the Ripper–style murders, and it is her finest work.

The novel opens with a recounting of the sad plight of a servant couple, the Buntings, who have opened a lodging house in London's Marylebone Road, only to meet with financial ruin. In a gesture of defiance, the husband spends a badly needed penny on a newspaper so he can read about the Avenger murders: A fiend has been killing women—usually those who are inebriated—and leaving pieces of paper signed "The Avenger" pinned to their corpses. Bunting, a crime buff, is fascinated; Mrs. Bunting disapproves of his interest in such matters and refuses to listen to his talk.

On this same night, however, the financial outlook in the household improves: An odd-looking gentleman appears at the door asking for a room to let. Mrs. Bunting is so relieved that she does not mind that the man has no luggage, and when he offers to pay enough so she will not take in other lodgers, she agrees. The new lodger, Mr. Sleuth, is exceedingly odd, as the Buntings find in the days that follow: He keeps the only bag he brought with him locked in the drawer of his chiffonier; he reads the Bible constantly; he turns all the pictures of Victorian beauties that hang in his drawing room to the wall; and he leaves the house repeatedly for nocturnal prowls.

Mrs. Bunting is the first to suspect who her lodger may be. Her suspicions are strengthened when she moves the chiffonier and some "red ink"—as she convinces herself it is—spills from the drawer where the bag is locked. And one of Mr. Sleuth's suits disappears the day after one of the murders. A young policeman friend, Joe Chandler, appears from time to time, feeding Bunting tidbits on the Avenger case—and now Mrs. Bunting listens, too. But she does nothing, even when Bunting's daughter by his previous marriage, Daisy, comes to visit. And when Bunting begins to suspect what is going on, he does nothing either. And the murders continue. . . .

This is a fascinating study of unwitting complicity and of people paralyzed by their own fears and by what they perceive as a need to protect themselves—both financially and physically. The characterization is excellent; the atmosphere suitably eerie; and one of the final scenes, set in Madam Tussaud's Waxworks, is sure to chill you.

Alfred Hitchcock made a haunting, moody film adaptation of *The Lodger* in 1926. Three other versions were not nearly so successful; the 1944 attempt, starring Merle Oberon and George Sanders, is downright comic in places. Lowndes based another of her novels on a true crime case—*Lizzie Borden: A Study in Conjecture* (1940). In addition to her novels, she published seven short-story collections, seven plays, and a number of nonfiction works.

(*M.M.*)

Ludlum, Robert. *The Matlock Paper.* New York: Dial, 1973. (T)

For more than a dozen years, Robert Ludlum has consistently been one of the two or three best-selling authors in the English language. His grandiose thrillers—most of them political in nature, with strong elements of twentieth-century history—contain nonstop action, wildly imaginative (and often improbable) plots, huge casts of characters, a wealth of factual information on all sorts of topics, an abundance of flamboyant prose, and more exclamation points than any twenty other 700-page novels. Nothing is too far reaching—or too farfetched—for his fertile imagination to turn into a rousing and entertaining story; *The Gemini Contenders* (1976), for instance, postulates the existence of documents supposedly written by St. Peter that claim it was not Jesus of Nazareth but a substitute who died on the cross, thereby negating the very foundation of Christianity.

In comparison to *that* tour de force, *The Matlock Paper* is relatively tame. Why is drug traffic in the northeastern part of the United States increasing at such a rapid rate? Apparently it is because of a strong, active, and independent drug organization located at Carlyle University in Connecticut. With this in mind, the Narcotics Bureau of the Justice Department recruits one of the professors at the university to act on their behalf as an undercover agent, even passing on to him a paper that is an invitation to an important underworld meeting. The professor, a man named James Matlock, is easily motivated to accept the assignment because three years earlier his younger brother killed himself with an overdose of heroin.

The basic premise here, as in many of Ludlum's novels, is shaky at best. The government is able to supply Matlock with the names of faculty members and students who are using or pushing drugs (563 student names out of an enrollment of 1200), and yet, even though they were able to compile such an incredibly detailed list, they still seem to need Matlock's help. Once the reader is able to suspend his disbelief, however, he can settle back with a typical hard-to-put-down Ludlum story—fast-paced, informed, realistic. For Matlock tackles his assignment with a single-minded dedication that disregards the increasing danger to himself and to those around him.

Among Ludlum's other best sellers are *The Osterman Weekend* (1972), *The Chancellor Manuscript* (1977), *The Matarese Circle* (1979), *The Parsifal Mosaic* (1982), and *The Aquitane Progression* (1984). He has also written novels under the pseudonyms Jonathan Ryder and Michael Shepherd; the most notable of these pseudonymous works is *The Road to Gandolfo,* originally published under the Shepherd name in 1975 and recently reissued in paperback under Ludlum's own by-line.

(*N.D./B.P.*)

*Lutz, John. *Bonegrinder.* New York: Putnam's, 1977. (T)

One of today's best practitioners of the criminous short story, with more than 200 magazine appearances to his credit, John Lutz is also an accomplished and versatile novelist. Whether he is writing psychological suspense, police procedurals, private-eye yarns, or tales of horror with supernatural overtones such as *Bonegrinder,* his books and stories are well constructed, deftly characterized, and consistently entertaining.

On balance, *Bonegrinder* is probably his strongest suspense novel. Three factors make it stand out: its Ozark Mountains setting; its sustained tension; and its eerie sense of the unknown.

On a hot July day, at a lake near the Ozark village of Colver, a twelve-year-old boy is fatally mutilated by "something" that came out of the water and attacked him. Not long after this incident, a group of campers are frightened by strange night noises, shoot blindly into the surrounding woods, and kill a man gigging for frogs. Then, as if feelings in and around Colver aren't running high enough, Mayor Boemer, in a misguided effort to bring tourists into the area, makes a public statement hinting that a legendary Ozark lake monster, "Bonegrinder," may be on the prowl. Boemer's ploy works all too well: Soon Colver is jammed with media people, curiosity seekers, and heavily armed hunters.

Sheriff Billy Wintone is the man in charge not only of finding out the truth behind the mysterious goings-on, but of maintaining law and order among the spooked citizens and outsiders. Another mutilation slaying, this one even more brutal, makes his job twice as difficult. Better than anyone else, then, Wintone understands that if he doesn't put an end to all the craziness, and soon, much more blood will be spilled by superstitious and panicked men than ever could be by a creature "out of a late-night horror movie."

Lutz knows the beauty and mystery of the Ozarks, and brings them and their inhabitants to life in these pages. He also knows people and the effects of mass hysteria. *Bonegrinder* is Grade-A suspense, with just the right ending and just the right tone throughout.

The best of Lutz's other suspense novels are his first: *The Truth of the Matter* (1971), a paperback original that relates the self-destructive odyssey of a man named Lou Roebuck and which should have been nominated for a Best First Novel Edgar; *Jericho Man* (1980), about a madman's plan to blow up several New York City skyscrapers; and *The Shadow Man* (1981), which has a brilliant psychological premise and one of the most unusual and terrifying political assassins you're ever likely to meet.

(*B.P.*)

Lutz, John. *Buyer Beware.* New York: Putnam's, 1976. (PI)

Private eye Alo Nudger is one of the few original creations in the past two decades. What makes him unique is not where he lives, or his sexual persuasion, or any special powers he has. No, it's his monkish devotion to work and his almost neurotic fascination for detail that make him so credible and refreshing. In other words, Nudger resembles the real thing—one can imagine that real private investigators are probably not much unlike Alo, particularly in their single-minded tracking down of leads and clues.

Nudger is hired by two people to investigate the same case—first by Gordon Clark to find his missing ex-wife and daughter and to bring the daughter back; and then by Dale Carlon, who is the ex-wife's father. Carlon is rich and powerful and throughout the novel the nationwide extent of his power amazes and bemuses Nudger. What seems to be a rather simple case—a woman taking her daughter beyond the reach of her ex-husband—eventually evolves into one of the most brilliant and pitiless attacks on American business in the literature.

Though his style is understated, Lutz manages a felicity of image and an accuracy of observation rare in genre fiction. He gives us all the details we need to make his world come painfully alive. Particularly vivid is an episode with a go-go dancer whose words and edginess recall the Sixties far more precisely than do many documentaries.

In this almost everybody suffers, even people the reader is led to dislike. Also in this novel there is a real villain—the fusion of business and psychology, the whole Manson cult mentality applied to the executive offices and boardrooms of America. Without once ever editorializing, Lutz offers us a cautionary tale as well as a superlative private-eye novel.

Alo Nudger probably wouldn't be embarrassed about wearing Bermuda shorts to the supermarket. And exactly for that reason you pity and admire him. He's flesh and blood in a genre too busy with paper tigers and confections.

Nudger reappears in *Nightlines* (1985); more novels about him are planned for the future. He is also featured in the short story "What You Don't Know Can Hurt You," which won a PWA Shamus in 1982.

(*E.G.*)

Lyall, Gavin. *The Wrong Side of the Sky*. New York: Scribner's, 1961. (A)

Literate and fast-paced, Gavin Lyall's novels feature strong character development and colorfully drawn backgrounds that include Norway, Finland, the Middle East, and the Caribbean. Most also involve pilots and some aspect of flying, but even if you aren't an airplane fancier, his stories are so well plotted and gripping that you'll devour them anyway.

The hero of *The Wrong Side of the Sky* is Jack Clay, cargo pilot and surprisingly moral jewel thief. The situation into which Clay is thrust has been unfolding for some time before he comes onto the scene. Some years ago, a Nawab, in the process of fleeing from India to Pakistan, had millions of dollars' worth of jewelry stolen by a renegade pilot. Now a few of the pieces have shown up and been traced to Greece. The Nawab, along with his bodyguard and his beautiful personal secretary, has traveled to Athens in hopes of recovering the rest of the jewelry.

Meanwhile, Clay has landed at the airport in Athens for refueling and minor repairs, and has been approached by a shipping agent who wants him to take some boxes of oil-drilling equipment to Libya. But the oil-drilling equipment is really guns, which are really a cover for more of the missing jewelry. Prior to his middesert delivery, Clay figures this out, puts the plane on automatic pilot, steals the jewelry, and barely manages to escape from the desert and back to Tripoli with life and limb intact. He elects to return the jewels to the Nawab for a five-percent finder's fee, and the race is on to see who can put the clues together and track down the balance of the jewelry. Along the way there is murder, romance, and a final scene with as many turns as a corkscrew, as Clay manages to point an accusing finger at almost everyone.

Lyall's other airborne thrillers include *The Most Dangerous Game* (1963), which is a variation on the man-as-hunted-prey plot made famous by Richard Connell's short story of the same title; *Midnight Plus One* (1965), set in France and Liechtenstein; and *Shooting Script* (1966), which has as its protagonist a pilot who flies a camera plane for a film company and which deals with art smuggling in the Caribbean area.

(*N.D.*)

Lynch, Jack. *Sausalito.* New York: Warner, 1984. (O/PI)

Sausalito is a small town turned tourist trap on the north side of San Francisco Bay, and also the home of private investigator Peter Bragg. In this case, Bragg is hired by black San Francisco bookie Samuel P. Morse to find out who is trying to blackmail him about his daughter Melanie's pornographic modeling. Melanie, whom her father seldom sees, is also a legitimate model and is engaged to a wealthy white man, Duffy Anderson, who would be outraged if the explicit photos that accompany the blackmail threat are made public. Bragg's investigation takes him home from San Francisco to Sausalito, on the trail of the man who posed in the pictures with Melanie.

In the course of his investigation, Bragg encounters a lot of elements that reflect interesting contemporary concerns: the soft-core porn business (which is readying itself for a move into cable TV); a houseboat basin about to be gobbled up by an expensive hotel and convention center development; small-town politics; rich people's politics; poor people's politics. Lynch knows Sausalito well (unlike his publishers, whose cover blurb places it on an "ocean-kissed beachfront," rather than a bay), and his descriptions of the town are sharply evocative, allowing even those who know it to rediscover its charms.

Bragg, however, is yet another lone-wolf private eye, in the tradition of Hammett, in the tradition of Chandler, etc. And perhaps it is because this is such an overworked and tired tradition that Bragg's reactions seem so lifeless. Upon finding a body in the home of porno producer Cookie Poole, Bragg experiences a jolt of fear when a car backfires outside—but that's his *only* reaction. Blandly professional, he doesn't feel horror, or pity for the dead man, or even disgust at finding a body that's been dead for a couple of days. Still, for another novel "in the tradition of," this is not bad fare.

The other Bragg novels include *Pieces of Death* (1982) and *San Quentin* (1984).

(*M.M.*)

Lynn, Margaret. *To See a Stranger.* New York: Doubleday Crime Club, 1962. (PS)

It is the morning of Dorcas Mallory's wedding. She avoids opening her eyes, savoring the joy she feels upon awakening; but when she finally does, what she sees astonishes her. She is not in the London hotel room where she went to sleep; instead, she is confronted by a luxurious pink-and-white bedroom, a man in the bathroom who claims to be her husband—and a new, older face in the mirror.

In one of the few unconvincing moments in this novel, Dorcas does not scream, cry, or protest; instead, she remains strangely silent, gathering information about where she is and who she is supposed to be. The time is fifteen years after her supposed wartime wedding to Russ Winslow; the husband is not Russ but her father's stepbrother, Charles Landry; her name is not Dorcas Mallory but Lisa Landry; and it is not her wedding day but that of her daughter, Joanna.

As the story proceeds, Dorcas/Lisa begins to feel she is mad, the victim of a complex and terrifying psychosis. But there is evidence that Dorcas Mallory *did* exist: Russ, now married to another woman, is living in the village where she remembers growing up; there are records that Dorcas and her father actually stayed at the hotel she remembers; and there is Dorcas's grave in the village churchyard.

How, Lisa/Dorcas wonders, could she know such intimate and provable details of another woman's life while remembering nothing of her own? Why has she become obsessed with a dead woman? And as she probes into the past with the help of a neighborly doctor, the story that emerges is strange indeed.

This novel has a fascinating premise, and Lynn handles it well. It's a book you won't want to put down.

Margaret Lynn has written a number of other psychological suspense novels, notably *Mrs. Maitland's Affair* (1963), *A Light in the Window* (1968), and *Sweet Epitaph* (1972).

(*M.M.*)

Lyons, Arthur. *Castles Burning.* New York: Holt, 1980. (PI)

Arthur Lyons is one of the contemporary private-eye novelists whose work inevitably begs comparison with Raymond Chandler and Ross Macdonald (qq.v.) especially since his private-eye character, Jacob Asch, operates in and around southern California. Though the ironic tone and cynical patter are by now awfully familiar stuff, Lyons invests sufficient novelty in his plots and in his character, an embittered ex–newspaper reporter (and one of the few Jewish detectives around), to maintain reader interest. Lyons is one of the best of the current crop of California detective writers; his approach is stylistically closer to Chandler, not as consciously literary and portentous as late Macdonald.

A successful modern artist, specializing in garish renderings of kinky sexual images, hires Asch to find the wife and son he deserted many years ago. Asch finds the wife remarried to a prosperous Palm Springs executive, and learns that the boy was killed five years ago in an auto accident. He's about to close out what looked to be a simple investigation when the woman's stepson disappears, and then Asch's client vanishes. It gets more complicated, and quite nasty, culminating in a desperate fight in a drainage canal. There's one very observant and telling sequence in which Asch questions a spoiled, rich Palm Springs high-school girl.

Other Lyons titles worth investigating, all featuring Asch: *All God's Children* (1975), in which Asch journeys into the Word of God commune in search of a missing eighteen-year-old girl; *Hard Trade* (1982), which has a background of political corruption and big-money real-estate schemes; and *At the Hands of Another* (1983), a case that begins with Asch's investigation into the death of a man whose insurance payment is being denied because of evidence of suicide and leads into the victimization of impoverished Chicanos in a scam involving highway-accident claims.

(*A.S.*)

*McAuliffe, Frank. *For Murder I Charge More.* New York: Ballantine, 1971. (O/C/T/SS)

Augustus Mandrell, of the firm of Mandrell Ltd., is probably the oddest "hero" in all of crime fiction. He claims to have been a professional killer, a man who would murder *anyone* for a price and whose "commissions" took him all over the world before, during, and after World War II. His unrepentant and conceited accounts of his adventures are in the form of first-person "memoirs"—outrageous (and outrageously funny) mystery thrillers unlike anything else you've read. Mandrell has been compared to Dr. Strangelove, James Bond, Sherlock Holmes, the Scarlet Pimpernel, the first gravedigger of *Hamlet,* and Don Quixote (each with at least some justification). Anthony Boucher (q.v.) called him "a dazzling and devious dastard," and said that "Frank McAuliffe has hit upon just the proper detached tone for such an improper narrative; and he enjoys a fertile inventiveness that can pack an astonishing number of plot twists into one short story."

For Murder I Charge More, the third and final volume of Mandrell's memoirs—and the recipient of an MWA Edgar for Best Paperback of 1971—contains two short novelettes and two long ones. The first story, "The German Tourist Commission," opens with Mandrell in a potato field in Ireland, disguised (he is a master of disguise) as an Argentine tourist agent and waiting to kill a Nazi general named Helmut Von Ritterdorf who has recently been smuggled out of Germany. The year is 1945, just after the end of the war. With him are a French Resistance dwarf named Marcel, a wily German woman named Gretel, a Jew named Weintraub, and several members of the Irish Republican Army. Mandrell manages to kill Von Ritterdorf immediately upon the Nazi's arrival—or does he? Matters are further complicated by the presence of the *Ventura Maid,* an Oriental statue with a pair of priceless diamonds for eyes and a lethal Egyptian "curse of death" on anyone who steals them—which someone, of course, does.

"The Hawaiian Volcano Commission" continues Mandrell's adventures with Marcel, Gretel, and the IRA, plus a detective named Proferra, whom Mandrell has been murdering piecemeal—a finger here, an ear there—throughout his various commissions, and a blue-eyed German who may or may not be Adolf Hitler. Most of the action here takes place on board the ship *Haleakala* bound for U.S. soil.

"The Baseball Commission" involves Mandrell with a New York Giants baseball player named Jerry O'Sullivan, as well as the entire entourage from the previous two commissions, and has a hilarious finale at the Polo Grounds. And in "The American Apple Pie Commission," Mandrell is chased all over New York by the CIA after he disposes of a member of the United Nations.

But these brief synopses don't even begin to do justice to the stories, full as they are of weird and wonderful characters, scenes, and plot turns. Read them and you'll see. But don't expect to try just one; Augustus Mandrell is like peanuts and potato chips—one adventure just isn't enough.

The first two volumes of his memoirs, which also contain four commissions each, offer similarly compulsive reading: *Of All the Bloody Cheek* (1965) and *Rather a Vicious Gentleman* (1968).

(*B.P.*)

*McBain, Ed. *Fuzz.* New York: Doubleday, 1968. (PP)

The Eighty-seventh Precinct novels of Ed McBain (Evan Hunter, q.v.), which began in 1956 with *Cop Hater* and continue to the present, have been widely and justly acclaimed as the finest police-procedural series ever written by an American. They may in fact be the finest procedurals ever written, period. Hunter's research into actual police methods is meticulous, up-to-date, and vividly incorporated into his stories; and his understanding of the "cop mind" is acute. He doesn't write about characters, he writes about human beings who happen to be working cops; people you come to know and care about: Steve Carella, the Italian-American detective with the beautiful deaf-mute wife, Teddy; Meyer Meyer, bald and infinitely patient; young Bert Kling, who has continually tragic and painful luck with women; Cotton Hawes, possessor of a white streak in his hair where he was once knifed; Richard Genero (who once shot himself in the foot with his service revolver); Lieutenant Pete Byrnes; policewoman Eileen Burke; head of Clerical Alf Miscolo; and detectives Arthur Brown and Hal Willis.

The unnamed city McBain writes about is his native New York, thinly disguised. He has disclaimed this in the past, but not very heartily; anyone who has any knowledge of the New York metropolitan area will immediately recognize Isola as Manhattan, Calm's Point as Brooklyn, and so on through the other boroughs and districts. The city, in fact, is a character in all of the Eighty-seventh Precinct novels, and a major character in several. Through McBain's prose, you come to know the city as well as you do the characters—the good and bad sides, the decent citizens and those who make life difficult, and all too often deadly, for the men of the Eighty-seventh.

Fuzz is perhaps the best-known title in the series, thanks to the popular 1972 film version starring Burt Reynolds, Jack Weston, Raquel Welch, and Yul Brynner as the Deaf Man. Ah, the Deaf Man. He is the nemesis of the Eighty-seventh—a mysterious supercriminal who made his first appearance in *The Heckler* (1960) and keeps reappearing with some new and audacious scheme to devil both the city and the poor cops. The scheme he comes up with this time is a doozy: an extortion plot whereby either the city will pay him a huge sum of money or he will begin to systematically knock off city officials, starting with Parks Commissioner Cowper. The Deaf Man never makes idle threats, as the cops already know and the mayor and Parks Commissioner Cowper find out when the demand is ignored.

And as if the Deaf Man isn't enough for the squad to contend with, there has been a rash of muggings, rapes, and burglaries in the precinct; the squad room is being painted (apple green) by a couple of guys who fancy themselves comedians; and Carella is working undercover, disguised as a skid-row bum, to find out who is getting his kicks by setting fire to passed-out winos.

Fuzz is a marvelous book: exciting, poignant, frightening, and often quite funny. (Humor plays a strong role in all of the Eighty-seventh Precinct novels.) It also has, among its many other merits, some of the finest dialogue to be found anywhere. McBain has the best eye for dialogue of any contemporary writer—"eye," not "ear," because there is a fine distinction between dialogue written to be read and dialogue written to be spoken. Others may write better colloquy for stage and screen (Neil Simon, for instance), but when it comes to the printed page, McBain's evocation of everyday speech patterns is virtually flawless.

In addition to *Fuzz* and *The Heckler,* the Deaf Man also appears in *Let's Hear It for the Deaf Man* (1973) and *Eight Black Horses* (1985). The ploys he concocts to devil the men of the Eighty-seventh in the latter title are particularly fiendish.

(*B.P.*)

*McBain, Ed. *Jack and the Beanstalk.* New York: Holt, 1984. (AD)

With the publication of *Goldilocks* in 1978, Hunter/McBain launched a new series of mysteries featuring Florida lawyer Matthew Hope. This and each of the four subsequent novels in the series (*Jack and the Beanstalk* is the fourth) derive their titles—and the substance of their plots—from famous nursery rhymes. But the books are anything but tomes for tiny tots. They are often violent examinations of deviant crime, in more than one case motivated by the kinkier varieties of sexual experience.

Jack McKinney, son of a cattle-ranching family on Florida's west coast, is stabbed to death in his plush Calusa condominium and the $36,000 in cash he was known to have in his possession is missing. The money, which may or may not have been obtained through cattle rustling on Jack's own homestead, was to be used to finance the purchase of a bankrupt snap-bean farm. But why would a youth of lazy and greedy tendencies want a snap-bean farm in the first place?

Matthew Hope, who was handling the real-estate transaction, is further drawn into the case by his friend Morris Bloom, a detective on the Calusa police force investigating Jack McKinney's murder. Matthew soon finds himself not only more deeply involved in the dead youth's affairs but romantically involved with Jack's fifty-seven-year-old mother (who looks thirty-seven and acts twenty-seven) and personally involved in a second homicide and the disappearance of Jack's provocative sister, Sunny. To further complicate Matthew's life, he is beaten up by a couple of punks in a roadside tavern (he later gets his revenge); his steady girlfriend, Dale, walks out on him for another man (which is why he is so willing to take up with Mrs. McKinney); and he is having problems with his ex-wife and his teenage daughter, Joanna.

A strong plot with some nifty twists and turns, fine characterization, and a well-realized background make this the best book in the series so far. Two other Matthew Hope novels, *Rumpelstiltskin* (1981) and *Beauty and the Beast* (1983), are also very good. The most recent title, *Snow White and Rose Red* (1985), is less successful in that it suffers from a wholly predictable plot.

(*B.P.*)

*McBain, Ed. *Killer's Wedge.* New York: Simon & Schuster, 1959. (PP)

Killer's Wedge is perhaps the best of the early Eighty-seventh Precinct novels. It combines two distinctly different cases—the take-over of the Eighty-seventh's squad room by a mentally unbalanced and revenge-seeking woman, and, of all things, a locked-room murder—and builds such tension that it is the rare reader indeed who can put the book down unfinished.

While Steve Carella is off on a pair of errands—taking his pregnant wife, Teddy, to the doctor and then investigating the death by hanging of a rich old man inside his locked study—a woman named Virginia Dodge walks into the squad room carrying a loaded .38 and a bottle of something she claims is nitroglycerin. Her mission: to kill Carella the moment he returns, because she holds him responsible for the death of her convict husband whom Carella sent to prison. She is prepared to shoot any man who tries to disarm her—and if necessary, to blow up everyone in the squad room, including herself, with the nitro. But *is* it nitro, or just plain water? That is what Meyer Meyer and Cotton Hawes and Lieutenant Byrnes keep wondering. For they know that sooner or later they'll have to act; they can't just sit there and wait for Carella to walk in and be shot down in cold blood.

But Carella does walk in, unexpectedly. Only it is not *Steve* Carella, who is busy piecing together the solution to his baffling locked-room mystery; it is pregnant Teddy, who would do anything to save her husband's life. . . .

Killer's Wedge has enough nail-biting suspense for two novels. It also has an ingenious puzzle, marvelous characters, and wholly satisfying conclusions to both cases.

(*B.P.*)

*McBain, Ed. *Lightning*. New York: Arbor House, 1984. (PP)

Lightning is the thirty-seventh title in the Eighty-seventh Precinct series, and among the most successful. Not only does it deftly interweave two separate and bewildering cases, but it provides the boys of the Eighty-seventh Squad with two additional headaches: the intrusion of their number one cop nemesis, Fat Ollie Weeks (the slob you love to hate), and the apparent return of their number one crook nemesis, the Deaf Man.

When a young woman is found hanging from a lamppost in a deserted area of the precinct, Carella and Hawes identify her as an athlete, a runner on her college track team. Soon a second woman, also a runner, is found hanging from another lamppost—and the man dubbed the Road Runner Killer by the newspapers begins taunting the cops (after the fashion of the Deaf Man) while plotting the death of yet a third female athlete. Meanwhile, a serial rapist is plaguing the Eighty-seventh, systematically raping the same women two, three, even four times in succession, for warped reasons of his own. It is the precinct's female cops, Anne Rawles of the Rape Squad and Eileen Burke, who solve this case—but not before one of them is herself a victim of the rapist.

The suspense, as always, is considerable; the police work, as always, is fascinating; and the plotting is even above the usual high standard. McBain/Hunter also makes strong statements about the crime of rape and its effect on its victims, and offers insights into the psychology of the serial criminal. (To offset its grimmer aspects, there is plenty of humor, too: the singular affair of Meyer Meyer's brand-new toupee, for instance.) *Lightning* is compulsive reading.

Standouts among the other Eighty-seventh Precinct novels are *The Con Man* (1957); *'Til Death* (1959); *Lady, Lady, I Did It!* (1961); *Ax* (1964); *He Who Hesitates* (1965), a tour de force told entirely from the point of view of a criminal on the loose in the Eighty-seventh; *Shotgun* (1969); *Hail, Hail, the Gang's All Here!* (1971); *Bread* (1974); and *Ghosts* (1980), which successfully introduces an element of the occult into the all-too-real world of the Eight-seven.

(*B.P.*)

*McBain, Ed. *The McBain Brief.* New York: Arbor House, 1983. (SS)

During his thirty-year career, McBain/Hunter has written a large number of criminous short stories for such magazines as *Manhunt, Ellery Queen's Mystery Magazine,* and *Playboy.* Twenty of the best of these—some of which originally appeared under such pseudonyms as Richard Marsten (q.v.) and Hunt Collins—are collected here.

Police stories predominate, of course. Among these are "First Offense," the grim tale of an unrepentant teenage killer; and "The Prisoner," a powerful study of a tough, lonely, and corrupt cop who still retains a spark of human decency—two of his finest stories. Five procedurals also appear: "Chinese Puzzle," "Still Life," "Accident Report," "Small Homicide," and "Kid Kill." Written in the early 1950s, these foreshadow the Eighty-seventh Precinct series in their accurate and meticulous depiction of police work.

Hunter's first short story, "Chalk," written when he was eighteen (but not published until several years later), is also here. As are "Hot," a tale of psychological suspense that takes place aboard a navy vessel in Guantanamo Bay; "Every Morning," a short-short shocker set in the Bahamas; a pair of stories that demonstrate an ample sense of humor, "Skin Flick" and "Kiss Me Dudley" (the latter the funniest spoof of Mickey Spillane ever penned); and even a long private-eye novelette, "Death Flight," about a fatal West Coast airplane crash.

The McBain Brief is rich in the elements that have made McBain/Hunter a best-selling author for so many years: strong characterization, clever plotting, abundant humor, masterful dialogue. A must for anyone who enjoys short crime fiction at its most pungent and realistic.

Hunter has two other criminous collections to his credit, both paperback originals: *The Jungle Kids* (1956), published under Hunter's own name and focusing on juvenile delinquency; and *I Like 'Em Tough* (1958), as by Curt Cannon—hard-boiled stories about a down-and-out ex–private eye living on New York's Bowery. In addition, two of his mainstream collections—*The Last Spin* (1960) and *Happy New Year, Herbie* (1963)—each feature several stories with criminous themes.

(*B.P.*)

*McCloy, Helen. *Cue for Murder.* New York: Morrow, 1942. (W)

In his introduction to a reprint edition of *Cue for Murder,* Anthony Boucher recalled the reception of Helen McCloy's first novel, *Dance of Death* (1938): "Few first mysteries have received such generous critical praise, as the reviewers stumbled over each other to proclaim [the author] a genuine find . . . combining a civilized comedy of manners with the strictest of logical deduction." In addition to an urbane and literate style, McCloy's work is characterized by psychological insight, meticulous plotting, and the sheer ingenuity with which she handles seemingly impossible situations.

McCloy was one of the founding members of the Mystery Writers of America, and was that organization's first woman president in 1950. She was married for fifteen years to mystery writer Davis Dresser, who, as Brett Halliday (q.v.), created the popular private detective Michael Shayne. In addition to writing fiction, McCloy has been a publisher, editor, and literary agent. In 1953 she received an MWA Edgar for Mystery Criticism.

McCloy's series detective, Dr. Basil Willing, was introduced in her first book; *Cue for Murder* is his fifth appearance. Willing is a psychiatrist, once a consultant to the Manhattan district attorney's office and now, in the early months of World War II, working with the New York office of the FBI. He is in the audience at the Royalty Theater on opening night of a modern-dress revival of Sardou's Victorian melodrama *Fedora.* At the end of the first act, it is discovered that a murder has been committed on stage during the performance, but no one can identify the victim. Willing is drawn into the investigation both through his police connections and through a family friendship with the production's costume designer. The clues include a knife sharpener's canary released from its cage, the odd behavior of a housefly, a mysterious figure on a fire escape, and a script containing an underlined cue for murder.

Cue for Murder is almost a textbook example of the classic fair-play detective novel, an intricate framework in which the clues fit together like the interlocking pieces of an elaborate jigsaw puzzle. The framework is fleshed out with diverting characters, acute psychological observation, a satiric and knowledgeable rendering of the theatrical background, and a vivid portrait of wartime Manhattan, complete with blackouts and air-raid wardens. The book's strength as a novel is measured by the fact that it can be reread with pleasure even after its secrets are known.

(*R.E.B.*)

McCloy, Helen. *The Singing Diamonds and Other Stories.* New York: Dodd, Mead, 1965. (SS)

Helen McCloy wrote relatively few mystery short stories, and only four of the eight stories in this collection fall into the mystery category. All of them, however, are superior examples of the form. They all appeared in *Ellery Queen's Mystery Magazine,* and each of them was a prizewinner in the magazine's annual contests.

The book opens with what is probably the author's most famous short work, "Chinoiserie," written in Paris in 1935 but not published until 1946. It makes use of the author's art background in a tale of obsession and revenge set in nineteenth-century Peking. The title story, "The Singing Diamonds," features Basil Willing. The "diamonds" of the title are a species of flying saucer: "nine flat, elongated squares, like the pips on a nine of diamonds, flying in V-formation at 1,500 miles per hour," seen by a navy pilot and by six other eyewitnesses scattered around the country and overseas. Shortly after the sighting, the witnesses, one by one, die in unexplained ways. One of the survivors comes to Basil Willing for help. Are the deaths just an amazing coincidence, or are they murder? And how could such murders have been carried out? Willing's acute mind is equal to the task of ferreting out the truth. The story may be too fantastic for some tastes, but it is an astonishing tour de force of mystery and detection.

Another Basil Willing story, "Through a Glass, Darkly," was expanded to a full-length novel under the same title (see the following review). The remaining mystery, "The Other Side of the Curtain," is a gem of psychological suspense: A young wife, troubled by a threatening dream, visits a psychiatrist for help, but finds herself sinking deeper and deeper into the nightmare. . . .

It is difficult to believe that the other four stories in the book were written by the same author. "Number Ten Q Street," "Silence Burning," "Surprise, Surprise!" and "Windless" are science fiction of a ponderous and heavily didactic variety, minor exercises at best. But the four mystery stories make the volume worth tracking down.

(*R.E.B.*)

*McCloy, Helen. *Through a Glass, Darkly.* New York: Random House, 1950. (W)

This is the eighth Basil Willing novel, expanded from a novelette of the same title published in *EQMM* in 1948. Like many others of McCloy's works, the book has thematic and structural ties to a literary work, in this case Swinburne's lushly sinister poem *Faustine.* The book uses the legend of the *Doppelgänger* as the basis for an eerie mystery.

The central character is Faustina Crayle, mild and reserved art teacher at an exclusive girls' school. Only five weeks into her first term at the school, Faustina is abruptly asked to leave by the headmistress. The latter gives no reason for the dismissal, or for her refusal to write a reference for Faustina, but offers six months' salary as compensation. Faustina's only confidante at the school is the German instructor, Gisela von Hohenems, who happens to be Basil Willing's fiancée. When Basil delves into the case, he uncovers an amazing story. Faustina appears to have a double: Several witnesses have reported seeing *two* Faustina Crayles simultaneously in separate locations (inside a school building and elsewhere in the grounds, for example), and one of the two was always behaving in a vaguely suspicious or threatening manner. Many of the students at the school were frightened of Faustina, and several had been removed from the school by their parents. And it then appears that Faustina had been dismissed from an earlier teaching job in exactly the same circumstances. Is this a collective hallucination or hysteria, or is there a physical explanation? When a suspicious death occurs and Faustina's double is seen in the vicinity, while Faustina herself is verifiably many miles away, Basil adds another question: Is the *Doppelgänger* story merely an elaborate alibi for murder? As Basil probes into Faustina's past, unbelievable events proliferate and the threatening mood intensifies. And then there is another death. . . .

Like John Dickson Carr (q.v.), Helen McCloy has dealt with seemingly preternatural events within the compass of a fairly clued detective puzzle. The result is a fascinating book, one that many readers and critics consider McCloy's best work.

While McCloy's books were enthusiastically reviewed upon first publication, and have all been reprinted in mass-market editions, her works have not been kept in print (as have those of Ngaio Marsh and Margery Allingham [qq.v.], with whom McCloy has frequently been compared), and they are much less widely known than their quality deserves.

Thirteen of McCloy's novels feature Basil Willing. The second of them, *The Man in the Moonlight* (1940), has a university setting and is the book in which Willing first meets the beautiful Austrian refugee Gisela von Hohenems, who will later become his wife. *The Goblin Market* (1943), with a Caribbean setting, and *The One That Got Away* (1945), set in Scotland, take place during Willing's service in Naval Intelligence during World War II. The latter appeared on many "best of the year" lists and is one of McCloy's most praised novels. *Two Thirds of a Ghost* (1956) is a witty, satiric look at the New York publishing world.

In addition to her formal detective novels, McCloy has written suspense novels and psychological thrillers. Two fine examples of the former are *Do Not Disturb* (1943) and *She Walks Alone* (1948). The latter involves murder on a cruise ship to the Caribbean, and features police captain Miguel Urizar, whom Basil Willing met in *The Goblin Market.* The best of her psychological novels is probably *The Slayer and the Slain* (1957), a compelling case study with a stunning surprise ending.

(*R.E.B.*)

*McClure, James. *The Blood of an Englishman.* New York: Macmillan, 1980. (PP)

James McClure has created an exciting cross-cultural environment with his South African police team of Lieutenant Tromp Kramer, of the Trekkersburg Murder and Robbery Squad, and his assistant, Bantu Detective Sergeant Mickey Zondi. For an American fan of the crime novel, this is a subgenre of police work in an exotic locale, comparable in some ways to Arthur W. Upfield's (q.v.) Detective Inspector Napoleon Bonaparte. Critic Stanley Ellin (q.v.) has commented that one of McClure's stories is not superimposed against the cultural background but extracted from it. McClure uses his detectives and their police work to expose the rot at the core of apartheid. There are antagonisms not only between black and white but between Afrikaners and English, "coloureds" and "kaffirs." The South African system provides motives, clues, and myriad complications in all of Kramer's investigations. In spite of Kramer's friendliness and respect for the detective ability of his sidekick, he's no closet liberal. Kramer is a product of his culture and merely refrains from abusing his power too much; he quietly rescues his assistant from scrapes, and compliments him when appropriate.

In *The Blood of an Englishman,* the motivation for the shooting of an antique dealer and the murder of a visitor from England is not based on apartheid but fulminates from the past, as in a good Ross Macdonald novel. Tromp Kramer is, as usual, full of half-baked theories and, in his superior's view, works entirely on his own too often. In this investigation, he is satisfied when bullets from the two shootings prove that the cases are connected. Zondi has ideas of his own, but goes off to scrutinize a black whorehouse murder when his theories don't mesh with Kramer's. The reality of the police procedure is presented with all its comic rawness: One of the characters comments, "This *is* a white that Lt. Kramer's making all the fuss about?" By a process of tough questioning and bluff, the detectives manage to resolve this story of revenge and retribution.

(*T.B.*)

McClure, James. *Snake.* New York: Harper, 1976. (PP)

Exotic dancer Eve's sensual act features a five-foot royal python. When she is discovered in her dressing room dead of strangulation, her dancing partner turns out to be the murder weapon. And once again Tromp Kramer and Mickey Zondi are thrown into a maelstrom of violence, disorder, and duplicity.

A second case comes up involving armed robberies and murders in the black township. The detectives encounter criminal characters and cover-up caused by the South African system of apartheid. Witch doctors, nightclub owners, and Portuguese immigrants are suspected and interrogated. The culprits are finally collected by the policemen, and Zondi gets to save his white partner's life in the process. McClure creates a gripping story that shows deep insight into the lives, both high and low, of individuals living in an apartheid society. He also pays a bit of homage to crime writers Dick Francis and Ed McBain (qq.v.).

Snake continues McClure's ongoing saga of morals and malice that began with his first novel, *The Steam Pig* (1971), which is concerned with concealed racial origin and won the British Crime Writers Golden Dagger Award. The other books in the Kramer/Zondi series are *The Caterpillar Cop* (1972), *The Gooseberry Fool* (1974), *The Sunday Hangman* (1977), and *The Artful Egg* (1985). McClure's nonseries espionage thriller *Rogue Eagle* (1976), set in Lesotho (a black area surrounded by South Africa), won the CWA Silver Dagger.

(*T.B.*)

*McCoy, Horace. *Kiss Tomorrow Goodbye.* New York: Random House, 1948. (PS)

Although a veteran of *Black Mask,* Horace McCoy resented his "hard-boiled" classification, considering himself mainstream, and wrote only one genuine crime novel. Set in the Thirties during the Dillinger days, *Kiss Tomorrow Goodbye* is one of the finest gangster novels ever written.

Young hoodlum Ralph Cotter (an alias) escapes from a prison farm, killing one of his own confederates in the process, a characteristically misanthropic move for this self-described possessor of a "psychopathic superego." Helping in the jailbreak is the murdered confederate's sister, Holiday, with whom Cotter immediately shacks up. Now in a medium-size, nameless city, Cotter pulls a petty robbery, again killing a man in the process. He and his aptly named associate, Jinx, are thereafter shaken down by local corrupt police. This is an opportunity the shrewd, college-educated Cotter seizes upon, launching a scheme to blackmail the police into aiding and abetting his future crimes. His rocky relationship with Holiday—a jealous girl who nonetheless sleeps around indiscriminately on Cotter—alternates with an even stranger relationship with a spoiled society girl who has suicidal tendencies and an interest in the occult. Cotter links up with Cherokee Mandon, a slick shyster with underworld connections, and soon Cotter and his various cronies (including Mandon and the corrupt cops) are planning a reckless robbery that will require taking four lives.

The fascination of *Kiss Tomorrow Goodbye* is its stream-of-consciousness first-person narration, and its exceptionally well-realized psychotic narrator. Unlike the simplified Cotter of the James Cagney screen version (1950), McCoy's protagonist is a complex, not exactly sympathetic character, but certainly an engaging one. (Cotter prefigures similarly psychotic—and posturing—narrators in the work of Jim Thompson, q.v.). A violent deed in his past, tied to his adolescent sexual awakening, has sent Cotter into a world of crime where he feels at home. Nonetheless, it is contact with the respectable world, not the criminal one, that leads to his downfall. This is the central irony of a book that McCoy clearly intended to be his masterpiece.

Critics have seldom agreed with McCoy's estimation of *Kiss Tomorrow Goodbye;* but the critics have underestimated this work. Cotter is a deeply flawed, pretentious narrator—which has led to the writer being dismissed as deeply flawed and pretentious. Taking Cotter at face value, at his word, is dangerous; critics have tended to assume that McCoy agrees with Cotter, who says archly, "Use me not as a preachment in your literature or movies. This I have wrought, I and I alone." McCoy, of course, does not believe that Cotter is a man in control of his destiny: Cotter is a pitiful, guilt-ridden soul misshapen by childhood trauma.

Kiss Tomorrow Goodbye is a long book, but it is fast moving, deftly plotted and vividly written.

(*M.A.C.*)

*McCoy, Horace. *They Shoot Horses, Don't They?* New York: Simon & Schuster, 1935. (PS)

The basic plot of *Horses* is simple enough. In Hollywood during the early years of the depression, two young people, Robert and Gloria, meet and decide to become partners in a marathon dance contest. They need the prize money desperately. And there's always the possibility that they will be "discovered" by a talent scout in the crowd of onlookers. Robert and Gloria both have aspirations of being stars. This seems to be just one more sweaty and forlorn part of the necessary ritual.

There are other characters in the novel, of course—Rocky the emcee, the quintessential cynic; the Reverend Oscar Gilder, who manages to debase even the notion of God; and assorted doomed figures, each alive only to his or her pain, who grind in endless circles on the dance floor—but Robert and Gloria remain the indisputable focus of the book. Early on she says, "Why are these high-powered scientists always screwing around trying to prolong life instead of finding pleasant ways to end it? There must be a hell of a lot of people in the world like me—who want to die but haven't got the guts." And so we have Gloria, failed beauty, misery addict, in a life perfectly symbolized by a marathon dance: You dance till you drop, literally, in a process without dignity or meaning.

McCoy's novel is told in fragments—in effect, flash-forwards as well as flashbacks. Robert's narration is interspersed with the words of the judge who sentences Robert to death, for we know from page one that Robert killed Gloria. The burden of the book is to explain why—much as, in a similar work, Orson Welles hung the life of Citizen Kane on "Rosebud" as a way to drive the narrative.

"It was the first time I had ever seen her smile," Robert says in the first fragment. He refers to the last look on Gloria's face before he pulled the trigger. Then: "I was her very best friend. I was her only friend." That, of course, was why he killed her—because he was her friend and because she asked him to. It was perhaps the one transcendent act of his life. Not that society understands. Robert will be executed for his action.

In almost every respect—from the bitter tone of the narrative, to the complicated ethics of killing somebody out of mercy, to the curiously innocent perceptions of Robert as revealed in key scenes—*Horses* is arguably the most original novel in American literary history. Sartre and the French existentialists agreed, embracing it as one of the great novels of their movement; its success in France far exceeded its impact here.

McCoy had hoped that the novel would free him from Hollywood and studio hackwork. It didn't. Like Robert, he was doomed to a dance that would go on and on until he dropped (literally, from a heart attack). Yet *Horses* remains a "perfect" book—perfect in the way a poem can be but a novel almost never is. It is both dirge and hymn and is without peer in the language.

Horses was filmed in 1969, starring Jane Fonda, Michael Sarrazin, and Gig Young (as the master of ceremonies, a role which won him an Oscar).

McCoy's other works are tough-guy in flavor, certainly; but like *Horses* they are concerned (as critic Paul Buck puts it) with "social comment rather than crime." *I Should Have Stayed Home* (1938) deals with a naive extra coping with a Hollywood that couldn't care less about him. Somewhat neglected, this novel is worth a look; although its criminous aspects are tangential, the crisp prose and dark outlook make it read like a particularly good James M. Cain (q.v.) novel, minus the murder. *No Pockets in a Shroud* (1948) is a somewhat autobiographical crusading-reporter tale. And McCoy's posthumous *Corruption City* (1959) is, like Chandler's *Playback* published the previous year, a novelization of an unproduced screen treatment.

(*E.G./M.A.C.*)

McCutchan, Philip. *Coach North.* New York: Walker, 1974. (PP)

No, *Coach North* is not about a man named North who coaches an athletic team. It concerns a tour coach (bus) leaving London and heading north to Scotland—a coach that is about to be hijacked and its passengers held hostage.

Not that the bus driver, Frank Harkness, sees anything amiss at first. The tourists gathered aboard seem the usual assortment: three Americans, two French, one German, the rest British. But what about that sinister-looking man named Kahn, the one with the dark face and the drooping moustache? As it turns out, Kahn is the ringleader of the hijackers. He and his accomplices soon take over the bus and demand from the authorities the release of three prisoners (three spies, actually).

From that point on, our attention is switched back and forth from the bus to the police efforts to apprehend the hijackers—an effort led by a Commander Daintree. There is also the political question of whether to give in to the hijackers' demands.

The story is very British in flavor: We always know exactly which highway the bus is on; there are references to various English and Scottish songs; and phrases such as "a load of cobblers," "elevenses," and "breakdown outfit" might leave non-Britishers puzzled. The story is also taut and brutal (there are several almost casual killings).

McCutchan, who also writes under the names Robert Galway, Duncan MacNeil, and T.I.G. Wigg, has produced more than seventy-five novels since he began writing in the late 1950s. A dozen of these—among them *Bluebolt One* (1965), *Sladd's Evil* (1967), and *Sunstrike* (1979)—feature his most notable series character, Commander Esmonde Shaw, initially of British Naval Intelligence but later of the semiofficial organization known as 6D2. A more recent series chronicles the adventures of Detective Chief Superintendent Simon Shard, "seconded to the Foreign Office from Scotland Yard"; to date the Shard novels have been published only in England. Under the Duncan MacNeil by-line, McCutchan has published a number of historical thrillers set in India in the 1890s and featuring Captain James Ogilvie of the 114th Highlanders; several of these have been published in this country, among them *The Red Daniel* (1974) and *Charge of Cowardice* (1978).

(*N.D.*)

*MacDonald, John D. *The Brass Cupcake.* Greenwich, Conn.: Fawcett Gold Medal, 1950. (O/W)

The career of John D. MacDonald has been a long and varied one, beginning with the publication of this excellent first novel. His books have ranged from modest paperback originals to the immensely popular Travis McGee series, as well as fat best sellers such as *Condominium* (1977) and the recent *One More Sunday* (1984). Likewise, the quality of his work has varied, from the truly terrible *Weep for Me* (a 1951 original that MacDonald himself refuses to allow to be reprinted) and the boring small-town drama *Contrary Pleasure* (1954), to such outstanding novels of suspense as *The Damned* (1952), *Murder in the Wind* (1956), and *The Last One Left* (1967).

The recurring theme of MacDonald's work is corruption—personal, corporate, societal—and his heroes are men and women who pit themselves against it. MacDonald draws heavily upon his knowledge of finance, land development, and Florida politics in constructing intricate plots, and his novels, particularly the later ones, are filled with editorial tirades about the abuse of the environment, corporate greed, personal greed, or whatever else happens to have been bothering him at the time of writing. In the earlier novels, these statements of position seem a natural outgrowth of the narrators' personalities, but in later books they become long-winded and intrusive.

In *The Brass Cupcake,* the evil is police corruption. The hero, Cliff Bartells, now an insurance adjuster, was once on the Florence City, Florida, force, but lost his badge for not going along with the local "arrangements" between the police and gambling establishments. That badge—fancy and gold—is Bartells's brass cupcake: "Anything you got by guile . . . was called a cupcake. . . . So when they took it away from me, it wasn't even a badge any more. Just a cupcake. Something I chiseled and then got chiseled out of. A brass cupcake. Something of no importance."

The murder with which the story opens—the death of a wealthy old woman in the process of a jewel theft—pits Bartells against the police force he used to belong to. They want him to keep out of it; he wants to follow the insurance agency's usual procedure of attempting to buy back the jewels. His motives are not so pure, however—there is a fat bonus for him if he manages this. But Bartells is up against more than he bargains for: The dead woman has a lovely niece, someone Bartells can't look at in a purely professional way; the niece has a boyfriend who is little more than a gigolo; a pair of servants seem to know more about the theft than they claim to the police. By the time Bartells has sorted through the evidence—as well as his personal feelings on a number of issues—a second murder has occurred, shots have been fired at him, and he knows his future in Florence City is not promising. Unless . . .

Cliff Bartells an early version of MacDonald's later male characters: a complex man who wants to do the right thing and worries about it, because he knows he himself is not incorruptible. And in the niece, Melody Chance, we see many of the same qualities that appear in later women characters: strength, independence, and straightforwardness, a woman just a trifle weary of life who would like a good man to occasionally lean on. Mac-

Donald's depiction of secondary and even incidental characters is also excellent.

(*M.M.*)

*MacDonald, John D. *Darker than Amber*. Greenwich, Conn.: Fawcett Gold Medal, 1966. (O/CS)

The Travis McGee series, with its color-coded titles, is one of the phenomenal popular successes of the mystery genre, and it's easy to see why. McGee, who refers to himself as a "salvage consultant" (in actuality, he gets folks out of trouble the police can't help them with), has many of those larger-than-life qualities contemporary readers seem to favor. He's big, rawboned, handsome in a rugged way. A former minor pro-football player, he now lives an enviable life-style in retirement aboard his "sybaritic" houseboat, the *Busted Flush,* in Fort Lauderdale. It is a retirement from which he periodically emerges whenever the cash reserves are getting low, and he's fond of saying he likes taking it in installments rather than all at sixty-five when he won't be able to enjoy it much anyway.

But McGee's life is not all girls and glitter; there's a dark, broody side of him, a part of his mind that tells him he's capable of being a better man than he thinks he is. And he proves this, time and time again, as he fights the forces of corruption that have victimized his friends and clients. McGee is no cool professional; he takes on every case as if it were a personal crusade. And it's there that his true charm lies: He is an emotional man who realizes he's fallible and constantly strives to overcome it, knowing all the while that he never can.

McGee also has his irritating points, however. He is constantly editorializing, and in the later entries in the series these asides become overly long and predictable. (Eventually one says, "Oh, Travis, not *again!*" and skips a page.) He also has a bad habit of indulging in therapeutic sex: A woman character has been traumatized; Travis takes her on a cruise on the *Flush,* makes love to her, and she is as good as new. And the women characters, while generally likable, all talk alike—a bright, sophisticated patter that makes them fairly difficult to tell apart.

Darker than Amber begins with a unique introduction to one of these women: As Travis explains it in the classic first sentence, "We were about to give up and call it a night when somebody dropped the girl off the bridge." The girl, whom McGee narrowly rescues from drowning, is Vangie Bellemer, a "dead-eyed cookie" who has been working as a high-priced call girl. Unlike many of MacDonald's women characters, she is not very pleasant, nor is she understandable until McGee's best friend, economist Meyer, breaks through her tough shell. What he finds is a frightened woman involved in something way over her head, something that concerns money taken from "dead ones." Vangie's associates have tried to kill her once, and she knows they will try again.

They do—and succeed. And Travis, feeling guilty because he didn't prevent Vangie's death, interested because there is money involved, and curious because of the seeming magnitude of whatever is going on, starts on his crusade. He finds other high-priced call girls, a setup involving Caribbean cruises, luxury, and death. And when he and Meyer close in on the truth of the matter, through a series of elaborate machinations that are fun to watch, they find it is of even greater magnitude than they supposed.

Darker than Amber is among the best in this entertaining series.

(*M.M.*)

*MacDonald, John D. *The Executioners.* New York: Simon & Schuster, 1958. (PS/T)

Suppose you're a lawyer in a small Florida town, happily married, with an attractive fourteen-year-old daughter and two younger sons. Suppose some fifteen years ago you witnessed the brutal rape of a teenager and subsequently gave testimony that put the rapist, Max Cady, behind bars. Suppose Max Cady finally gets out of prison and comes back to your town—and suppose he begins making veiled threats and following you and your family, paying special attention to your fourteen-year-old daughter. Suppose you *know* Cady is a dangerous psychopath, that sooner or later he intends to rape your daughter and harm you and your other loved ones. What do you do?

This is the dilemma that faces Sam Bowden, and this is the stuff of one of MacDonald's finest suspense novels. The tension mounts to an almost unbearable pitch as Bowden suffers frustration after frustration and Cady moves inexorably toward explosive violence. The climax is MacDonald at his most compelling. A must-read for anyone who enjoys expertly written, beautifully plotted suspense fiction.

Surprisingly enough, considering what Hollywood has done to quality novels in the past, the film version—*Cape Fear* (1962)—is every bit as tense and powerful, and features a bravura performance by Robert Mitchum; he literally radiates evil in the role of Max Cady. Almost as good are Gregory Peck and Polly Bergen as the Bowdens. Don't miss it when it appears on the Late Show.

(*B.P.*)

*MacDonald, John D. *The Good Old Stuff.* New York: Harper, 1982. (SS)

MacDonald, like so many other writers, learned his craft in the pulps. Between 1946 and 1952, he sold hundreds of crime stories to such magazines as *Black Mask, Dime Detective, Detective Tales, New Detective, Mystery Book,* and *Doc Savage* (as well as other short fiction to science-fiction, fantasy, sports, and western pulps). A few of these criminous tales have been reprinted here and there over the years, but the greater percentage languished in (mostly undeserved) obscurity until 1981, when Martin Greenberg, Francis M. Nevins (q.v.), and Walter and Jean Shine—MacDonald aficionados all—persuaded John D. to collect the best of them. They chose thirty stories; on rereading those thirty, MacDonald considered all but three worthy of reprinting. (Minor changes were made to update certain references for the sake of clarity; otherwise he allowed them to stand as first published.) But the final total of twenty-seven was deemed too many for a single book; the result is two volumes—*The Good Old Stuff* and its companion, *More Good Old Stuff* (Knopf, 1984).

The thirteen stories in this first volume demonstrate MacDonald's considerable range within the mystery/detective format, as well as his narrative talent and power. Among them are such gems as "The Simplest Poison" (whodunit); "Death Writes the Answer" (biter-bit); "Noose for a Tigress" (pure suspense); "Death on the Pin" (character study—and the world's first and only crime story about bowling); and the novelette "Murder for Money," whose protagonist, Darrigan, is a prototype of Travis McGee. No fan of MacDonald's work should miss either this batch or the fourteen equally excellent and diverse stories in *More Good Old Stuff.*

Until these volumes, MacDonald's collected short fiction was restricted almost entirely to selections from such slick magazines as *Cosmopolitan, Collier's,* and *Playboy*—fifteen stories in *End of the Tiger* (1966) and seven in *Seven* (1971). His only previously collected pulp story was the title piece in the 1956 gathering of two novellas, *Border Town Girl.* Another two-story collection (both from the pulps), this one unauthorized, appeared in 1983 under the title *Two.*

(*B.P.*)

MacDonald, John D. *The Green Ripper.* Philadelphia: Lippincott, 1979. (AD)

This relatively recent entry is one of the *worst* in the Travis McGee series. It is bloody and violent, involving a strange paramilitary cult and all the attendant clichés, and McGee's personal vendetta against the cult seems to rob him of his more human qualities.

In a prior novel (*The Empty Copper Sea,* 1978), McGee fell in love with a woman named Gretel Howard. She lived with him aboard the *Flush* for a while, but recently has moved out to be closer to her job at Bonnie Brae, a "combination fat farm, tennis club, and real estate development." The relationship is still as warm as ever, though, and when Gretel dies suddenly of a mysterious and debilitating illness, Travis is devastated. Not so devastated, however, that he doesn't wander sideways into inquiring about the strange events that occurred at Bonnie Brae right before Gretel's death and determining that her death was somehow murder.

The rather thin story line leads McGee from Fort Lauderdale to Ukiah, California, looking for a man known as Brother Titus who heads an organization called the Church of the Apocrypha. Posing as a man looking for his daughter, Travis locates an encampment, formerly a religious commune but now as closely guarded as a top-secret military base. He is imprisoned, then recruited, and the events that transpire are too brutal and depressing to reiterate. If there is anything positive about the resolution of this novel, it is that McGee eventually recovers; unfortunately, it is a recovery that fails to recognize that vengeance seldom leaves any real satisfaction in the soul of the avenger.

Other, much better, titles in the McGee series are *The Deep Blue Goodbye* (1964), *The Quick Red Fox* (1964), *A Deadly Shade of Gold* (1965), *The Girl in the Plain Brown Wrapper* (1969), and *Dress Her in Indigo* (1969), and *The Lonely Silver Rain* (1985).

(*M.M.*)

MacDonald, Philip. *The Rasp.* New York: Dial, 1925. (CS/W)

Though Barzun and Taylor were highly critical of most of Philip MacDonald's works, including *The Rasp,* most other critics—including Queen, Boucher, and Haycraft—lauded him. It was generally agreed that while he was not an innovator, he was an excellent "polisher and improver of established techniques." A highly successful mystery writer in England, he moved to Hollywood in the early 1930s and worked on many films, including the Alfred Hitchcock classic *Rebecca* (1940).

When he is introduced in *The Rasp,* MacDonald's series detective Anthony Gethryn has graduated from Oxford, been wounded in World War I, and served as a British secret agent. His creator describes him as "something of an oddity. A man of action who dreamed while he acted; a dreamer who acted while he dreamed." Gethryn is said to be suffering from three disorders: "lack of a definite task to perform, severe war-strain, and not having met the right woman." The parallels to Philip Trent and Lord Peter Wimsey are clear. Gethryn's detective work and romantic involvement in *The Rasp* solve his problems.

In solving the murder of British finance minister John Hoode, who was killed with a heavy, coarse file, Gethryn is a witty, sophisticated sleuth who nonetheless is convincing as a man of both action and ratiocination. His love life adds depth to his character and is never intrusive. All necessary clues are presented, consistent with MacDonald's philosophy that the author of detective stories is engaged in a "competition" with the reader and must play fair.

Though *The Rasp* is primarily concerned with the solution to one murder, later MacDonald mysteries would involve the hunt for murderers who have killed a series of people. Notable among these are two non-Gethryn books: *Murder Gone Mad* (1931), in which the police are given advance warning of each murder; and *The Mystery of the Dead Police* (1933), about a killer whose victims are all police constables in London. More than a quarter of a century later, the last novel by MacDonald (and the first full-length Gethryn story in over twenty years), *The List of Adrian Messenger* (1959), would also deal in multiple murder. This novel, later the basis for a popular film with George C. Scott, concerns a list given to Scotland Yard of ten separate accident victims who might have been murdered.

(*M.L.*)

*MacDonald, Philip. *Something to Hide.* New York: Doubleday, 1952. (SS)

Quite simply one of the best collections of short stories ever written in the mystery genre, *Something to Hide* won a well-deserved MWA Edgar. Prior to book publication, four of its six stories had been prizewinners in the annual contests of *Ellery Queen's Mystery Magazine,* where they had originally appeared. It is a book of unusual variety, combining stories of classic detection with those of suspense and character.

The psychological interplay between murderer and potential victim in "Malice Domestic" is worthy of Francis Iles (q.v.) at his very best. By the time he wrote this story, MacDonald had been living in the Los Angeles area for more than a decade, and he was increasingly using it, rather than his native England, as background. Southern California is especially well realized in "Malice Domestic" and in "The Man Out of the Rain" (1954), the title story of another noteworthy MacDonald collection.

Though first published in *EQMM* in June 1947, "The-Wood-for-the-Trees" is set in the English village of Friar's Wick in the summer of 1936. It is the first and only Anthony Gethryn short story, and one wonders whether MacDonald feared that his detective might not travel well into the postwar world or across the Atlantic. Still, there is nothing old-fashioned about this perfect blend of sensationalism (there is a series of murders of the "Ripper" variety), puzzle, and background. Characterization is unusually strong and individualized considering that MacDonald had set for himself the difficult task of using twelve characters in a short story.

"The Green and Gold String" is one of only three short stories about Dr. Alcazar, whom Ellery Queen called "Sherlock Holmes and Arsene Lupin crammed simultaneously into one pair of pants." The doctor (a title to which he has no right) is a con man at a small California circus, reduced to telling the future at fifty cents a reading. He turns out to be an excellent detective, good enough to go into the investigation business with the aid of his friend, the circus weight guesser, Avvie Du Pois.

The much anthologized "Love Lies Bleeding" was a story ahead of its time. Originally published in 1950, this tale of Cyprian Morse, a playwright, and the unfortunate woman who loves him was one of the first mysteries to deal with homosexuality. It does so subtly, and the story is a jewel of character and suspense.

Many mystery readers avoid short stories, claiming they need the length of the novel in order to derive satisfaction. *Something to Hide* is proof that plot complexity, depth of characterization, and sustained suspense can be found in the shorter form if the author is as good as Philip MacDonald.

(*M.L.*)

*MacDonald, Philip. *Warrant for X.* New York: Doubleday, 1938. (CS/W)

Few classic detective novels "grab" the reader as quickly and as thoroughly as does *Warrant for X.* Sheldon Garrett, a young American playwright in London, overhears a kidnapping being planned while he is in a tea shop, but he cannot identify the plotters. (In *23 Paces to Baker Street,* the 1956 film version, the American, played by Van Johnson, is blind.) Garrett first attempts to play detective and then to interest the British police in the potential crime. He is unsuccessful on both counts. Luckily, he meets Anthony Gethryn, who, with his love of puzzles, is willing to help and to enlist the aid of Flood and Dyson, two members of the special criminal department of Gethryn's weekly publication, *The Owl.* Eventually, Gethryn is able to convince his friend Sir Egbert Lucas, head of Scotland Yard's CID, to commit his agency's resources.

A nursemaid has vanished, and she is a key to a mystery involving an efficient crime ring headed by a wraithlike leader. The pace of this book seems leisurely, but there is overwhelming excitement throughout. *Warrant for X* produces, as Christopher Morley (q.v.) described it, "frost on the spine."

Though written in Hollywood, where MacDonald had been settled for many years, this book includes the city of London as one of its main characters. The streets, the underground stations, the restaurants, and the inevitable London fog all play their roles in heightening the suspense. The use of an American viewpoint in seeing London adds to reader identification, at least in the United States. The solution is decidedly satisfying.

After he wrote *Warrant for X,* Philip MacDonald became increasingly busy as a screenwriter, working on the Mr. Moto series; *Rebecca* (1940); and a popular Humphrey Bogart film, *Sahara* (1943), among other projects. He abandoned Anthony Gethryn, though he and his creation were at their peak, except for one short story in 1947 and the atypical final Gethryn novel, *The List of Adrian Messenger. Warrant for X* remains Philip MacDonald's masterpiece, a work that readily appears on critics' lists of the ten best mysteries of all time. It even caused Alexander Woollcott to call it "the best detective story I have ever read in any language."

(*M.L.*)

*Macdonald, Ross. *Black Money*. New York: Knopf, 1966. (CS/PI)

Ross Macdonald—a pseudonym of Kenneth Millar (q.v.)—has been widely acclaimed as the most important successor to the Chandler/Hammett tradition, as well as the writer who elevated the hard-boiled private-eye novel to a "literary" form. This latter claim (and one might debate that Chandler and Hammett had already written "literature") is based partly on the fact that Macdonald's work sparkles with metaphor; his descriptions of California, his adopted state, are poetic and bring its scenes and people alive even for those who have never had occasion to visit it. However, it is the addition of deep psychological characterization and complex thematic content that is Macdonald's primary contribution to the genre.

Macdonald's depth of characterization is very much like that of his wife, suspense novelist Margaret Millar (q.v.), proving perhaps that individuals who share a long professional and personal relationship tend to approach their fiction in similar ways. Unlike Millar's protagonists, however, Macdonald's main character, private investigator Lew Archer, is more an observer than a fully fleshed-out human being. Indeed, it was the author's stated intent that Archer be a camera recording the events and people surrounding those events. However, this is a weakness of the series. MacDonald makes us care about Archer, and because we wish to know more about him, we grasp desperately at what few personal crumbs are thrown out. We know Archer was divorced by his wife, who could not abide his work as a detective; we know he was once a member of the Long Beach police force but was fired because he would not condone its corruption; we know he came close to juvenile delinquency, had a grandmother in Martinez, and worked in Intelligence during World War II. But he comes alive for us only through his professional work. As he himself states in *The Instant Enemy* (1968): "I had to admit that I lived for nights like these, moving across the city's great broken body, making connections among its millions of cells. I had a crazy wish or fantasy that some day before I died, if I made all the right neural connections, the city would come all the way alive."

Like the city of Los Angeles, Archer is not "all the way alive"—except when he is driving those freeways, tracking the truth, trying to make those connections.

Thus Archer remains the perennial observer, his emotions stirred by those around him, but in a curiously detached way. By contrast, Macdonald's other characters are richly developed and complex. The crimes Archer investigates are often outgrowths of older, concealed crimes, the revelation of which is threatened by events occurring in the present; and this threat works on the psyches of those involved, reactivating passions thought long dead or triggering emotional trauma previously held in check. The thematic content around which Macdonald weaves his complicated plots usually centers around a person's quest for identity, most often embodied in the search for a parent or one's roots. (This concern stems from the fact that Macdonald himself never really knew his father.) Although the author has been criticized for being overly concerned with one theme—in a sense writing the same book twenty-odd times—he has developed it in various imaginative ways.

In *Black Money,* Archer's client is, as usual, one of the rich. A young man named Peter Jamieson hires him to investigate the man his former fiancée, Ginny Fablon, is seeing. The man, Francis Martel, claims to be an educated Frenchman; Peter thinks he is a fortune hunter and an impostor. With the help of a local French professor, Archer concocts a test, a series of questions that any educated Frenchman could answer. When he confronts Martel and administers the test, the man passes, but Archer remains suspicious. For one thing, a seedy former used-car salesman is watching Martel's house; for another, when he attempts to take Martel's picture, the Frenchman threatens him with a gun, and later the salesman turns up beaten and locked in the trunk of his car. The salesman's aid has been enlisted by a beautiful woman with both local and underworld connections; and these connections go back many years to the time when Ginny Fablon's father committed suicide, an event that touched off the girl's emotional instability and caused her to take up with Martel. By the time murder has been committed, Archer has assembled the threads connecting several crimes that have destroyed a number of families, but connecting these only produces further explosions, which he is powerless to stop.

This is a powerful novel, set against the backdrop of a millionaires' playground in southern California and peopled with unforgettable characters. While Archer's clients in this and other books are the rich and powerful, Macdonald's characterization is perhaps at its most masterful when dealing with the little people, life's victims whose pathetic dreams are the fuel for tragedy.

(*M.M.*)

Macdonald, Ross. *The Blue Hammer.* New York: Knopf, 1976. (CS/PI)

This is Macdonald's last novel, and in it he attempts to take Archer in a new direction by providing him with an intense and ongoing personal relationship with a woman. The attempt is not wholly successful, however, and this book is one of the weaker in the series.

Archer is hired by Ruth Biemeyer, a wealthy resident of Santa Teresa (a fictional California town patterned on Santa Barbara), to find a painting that has been stolen from her home. The painting, a portrait by mysteriously vanished artist Richard Chantry, may have been taken by the Biemeyers' daughter's boyfriend, Fred Johnson, a young man of whom the girl's parents do not approve. But what starts out to be a routine case quickly becomes complicated, involving Archer with Johnson; his fiercely protective mother and alcoholic father; Richard Chantry's widow, Francine; a murdered art dealer named Paul Grimes; a possibly murdered painter named Jake Whitmore; and a thirty-year-old mystery that takes the detective into the copper-mining country of Arizona.

In the course of the investigation, Archer meets a young woman named Betty Jo Siddon, a reporter for the local paper. Betty is around thirty, a moderate feminist, independent and determined. Her character does not ring true, however; Macdonald generally characterizes women well, but they are girlish types or women well into middle age. Betty Siddon remains as shadowy as Archer, and when he quickly falls in love with her and initiates an affair, we wonder why. After all, he himself has stated that as a man gets older, if he has any sense, the women he is attracted to should also be getting older. Why, we wonder, has he so easily violated this precept—and for such a nonentity?

In spite of its flaws, however, the novel is one of Macdonald's most complex, and the background, both in California and Arizona, is well realized.

(*M.M.*)

*Macdonald, Ross. *The Ivory Grin.* New York: Knopf, 1952. (CS/PI)

While the solution of this early novel, Archer's fourth case, may seem fairly obvious, the story has a pervasive, dark atmosphere that haunts one long after the book is put down. At its beginning, the case seems a fairly routine one: A wealthy and unattractive woman who gives Archer only the first name of Una hires him to locate a black woman, Lucy Champion, who has recently left her employ. Lucy has been seen in the valley town of Bella City, and Una wants Archer to find where she is living so she can "talk to her." Archer is suspicious of Una's motives for wanting to see the young woman—she claims Lucy stole some jewelry of sentimental value from her, but Una doesn't strike him as a sentimental woman. With reservations, he travels to Bella City and has an easy time locating Lucy. But before he can report to Una, Lucy is thrown out of the house where she is rooming (for "fooling around" with the landlady's son) and goes to a motel. When he does report to Una and she visits Lucy, there is a violent scene, and later Archer finds the black woman in her motel room with her throat cut. While the police are certain the landlady's son, Alex Norris, killed her, Archer is equally certain the boy is innocent.

Archer would like to talk to Una, but she has disappeared. Following a lead from a newspaper clipping that Lucy had in her possession, he becomes involved in a missing-person case that seems to have some connection with the black woman's murder. Charles Singleton, a wealthy young man from Arroyo Beach, has disappeared and his mother is offering a $5,000 reward for information as to his whereabouts. Another investigator, a down-at-the-heels type, also has an interest in the case—as well as a lead in Bella City. And as Archer probes further, he runs across a varied cast of characters that includes a Bella City doctor and his much younger wife; a Mexican maid who has fallen into bad company; a refined young woman devoted to the memory of Charles Singleton; a chic milliner with a fondness for beer and cats; and a madman who acts out his insanity in a crazy game of death.

The Ivory Grin is rare for the early Fifties in that it deals with volatile racial issues in a sensitive and compassionate manner. Archer harbors some of the stereotypical attitudes of the times, but they are tempered by his concern for his fellow man—whatever color that man may be. This is the best of the early Lew Archer novels.

(*M.M.*)

*Macdonald, Ross. *Lew Archer, Private Investigator.* New York: Mysterious Press, 1977. (CS/PI/SS)

Macdonald's short stories featuring Lew Archer sparkle almost as brilliantly as his novels; the best of them, in fact, are miniature novels in their own right, honed to the sharpest essentials of plot, character, and incident. This volume is the definitive collection: It contains all nine of the Archer stories, the last two of which were written and published after the appearance of the first seven in book form in the 1955 paperback original *The Name Is Archer.*

The best story here is one of those two later works—"Midnight Blue," which Macdonald wrote for the regrettably short-lived (three issues) *Ed McBain's Mystery Book* in 1960. Unlike so much of Macdonald's work, it does not hinge on dark misdeeds in the past; rather, it is a deceptively straightforward account of Archer's discovery of the garroted corpse of a seventeen-year-old girl and his search for her murderer in and around a small coastal town. Its ending is one of the most tragic and emotionally intense of any criminous short story.

The seven early stories, all of which were written between 1946 and

1953 and published in *Manhunt, Ellery Queen's Mystery Magazine,* and *American Magazine,* "show my debt to other writers, especially Hammett and Chandler, and in fact did not aim at any striking originality," as Macdonald wrote in his introduction. Nevertheless, most of these are very good indeed, especially "Find the Woman," Archer's first appearance in print and a story that won a prize in a 1946 contest sponsored by Ellery Queen; "Wild Goose Chase," in which Archer is hired to prove that a man on trial for his life did not, after all, murder his wife; and "The Suicide" (originally published as "The Beat-Up Sister"), which has a twisty plot and an irresistible opening paragraph: "I picked her up on the Daylight. Or maybe she picked me up. With some of the nicest girls, you never know." Again quoting Macdonald's introduction: "It could be said that the early stories are the price I paid to become a professional writer. Short and few as they are, the writing of them altered me. I accepted a limitation of form and style which opened up a world but changed me, or a part of me, from Kenneth Millar to Ross Macdonald."

Curiously, the weakest story here is also the last of the two later works, "Sleeping Dogs," which was commissioned by *Sports Illustrated* (of all magazines!) in 1965 but published instead in *Argosy.* Its plot, which reflects Macdonald's obsession with the past and the effect of past events on the present, is a little confusing and not wholly credible. Even so, it stands well above most short stories featuring private detectives.

To an even greater extent, the same is true of *Lew Archer, Private Investigator.* It ranks with Hammett's Continental Op collections and Chandler's *Simple Art of Murder* as the finest volumes of so-called hard-boiled crime stories.

(*B.P.*)

*Macdonald, Ross. *The Wycherly Woman.* New York: Knopf, 1961. (CS/PI)

In *The Wycherly Woman,* Macdonald's theme of a young person's search for a sense of self is richly and imaginatively developed. Archer's client, oilman Homer Wycherly, hires him to find his daughter, Phoebe, who disappeared from her college in Boulder Beach nearly two months before while Wycherly was away on a cruise. Archer has little to go on except for the fact that Wycherly last saw Phoebe leaving his cruise ship in the company of her mother, Catherine. Wycherly, who was divorced from Catherine after a disturbing series of poison-pen letters, refuses to discuss the woman, claiming Phoebe would not be with her, would not have anything to do with her. But when Archer can come up with no leads in Boulder Beach or at the cruise ship in San Francisco, he violates his employer's wishes and attempts to contact Catherine.

Phoebe is not the only one missing; Catherine's house in the wealthy San Francisco suburb of Atherton stands empty, having been recently sold. And before Archer can search further, the realtor who handled the deal turns up bludgeoned in the house and Archer begins to fear Phoebe may also be dead. Investigating mainly in the San Francisco Bay Area, Archer becomes involved with the realtor's somewhat sleazy widow, Sally; Sally's twin brother, Stanley, a former disc jockey who was fired for taking payola; Stanley's girlfriend, Jessie Drake, "a startling young woman," a former go-go dancer, and would-be author who always lands on her feet "like a cat"; Carl and Helen Trevor, a prominent Woodside couple and Phoebe's uncle and aunt; and Phoebe's college boyfriend, a young man who may have more secrets than his somewhat ordinary exterior would suggest.

Archer's search takes him from San Francisco to Sacramento, back to Boulder Beach, and eventually to a small seaside resort called Medicine Stone. There is considerable motion in this excellent novel, as well as one of the most surprising and satisfying endings of all the Archer books.

(*M.M.*)

*Macdonald, Ross. *The Zebra-Striped Hearse*. New York: Knopf, 1962. (CS/PI)

Archer has an appointment with a prospective client, Colonel Blackwell; but before the man arrives, his wife, Isobel, comes to the detective's office, asking Archer not to take the case. When the colonel arrives, an argument erupts, and Archer realizes he is dealing with a divided family. When all has been smoothed over, he agrees to investigate the man Colonel Blackwell's daughter by a previous marriage is involved with—because he likes Isobel and feels Blackwell is a "sad and troubled man" heading for disaster.

The young man is a would-be artist named Burke Damis, whom Harriet Blackwell met while visiting her mother, Pauline, in Ajijic, Mexico. Archer meets Damis under a pretext and observes him with Harriet; it is obvious the rather unattractive young woman is enamored of Damis, and equally obvious that Damis does not love her. Before Archer can inform her father of this, Harriet discovers he is a detective, and she and Damis pack up and leave together, stating their intention to get married. Archer continues on the case, finds that Damis entered Mexico under the name of Quincy Ralph Simpson—and also finds that Q. R. Simpson is on the missing-persons list. By the time Archer has journeyed to the San Francisco Bay Area, where Simpson lived, and then to Ajijic, Mexico, he is convinced that Harriet Blackwell is traveling with a dangerous man, a wife killer who may be planning to repeat his crime to gain control of the Blackwell money.

A central part of this plot hinges on the presence of a hearse painted in zebra stripes that is frequently parked near the Blackwells' Malibu beach house; and Archer gains valuable information from the young surfers who virtually live in the hearse, waiting for the perfect wave. This is a good portrait of the California surfing crowd, and one of the few that neither glorifies nor vilifies it. Archer travels from place to place in the fluid motion that characterizes many of Macdonald's novels: to the Bay Area, Mexico, a small southern California town called Citrus Junction, Reno, and Lake Tahoe. And when he concludes his investigation, he uncovers a tragedy many years in the making, one in which the guilty as well as the innocent are truly victims.

This is one of Macdonald's best and most poignant novels.

The first Archer novel, *The Moving Target* (1949), was filmed as *Harper* in 1966, with Paul Newman playing the lead. While faithful to the book (except in making Archer a more lethal sort), Newman is too wisecracking and macho to depict Macdonald's hero. In 1975, Newman tried again, this time with *The Drowning Pool* (1950). While the novel gives a stunning portrait of the strains and stresses of a California valley oil town, for some reason it was relocated to Louisiana. Because Macdonald's work is so evocative of the state of California, the film version loses much of the book's power.

Two television versions of the series were also made. The first, a 1974 pilot based on *The Underground Man* (1971), starred Peter Graves as an extremely unlikely Archer. The 1975–77 series, "Archer," starring Brian Keith, was similarly unsuccessful. It is particularly unfortunate that *The Underground Man* was badly filmed, since it deals with a forest fire and—along with *The Sleeping Beauty* (1973), which concerns the consequences of an oil spill in the Pacific channel—reflects the ecological concerns which were a passion of both Macdonald and his wife.

All the novels in this series are of exceptional merit, but four others should be particularly noted: *The Galton Case* (1959), which is perhaps the best embodiment of Macdonald's identity-quest novels; *The Chill* (1964), as complex and chilling as its title, and winner of the British Crime Writers Silver Dagger Award; *The Far Side of the Dollar* (1965), which exposes the heartbreak of those who come to California expecting the answers to their dreams; and *The Instant Enemy* (1968), which is simply tragic and haunting.

(*M.M.*)

*Mcdonald, Gregory. *Fletch.* Indianapolis: Bobbs-Merrill, 1974. (AD)

Gregory Mcdonald, one of today's best-selling mystery writers, burst on the scene some ten years ago with *Fletch,* which won the MWA Edgar for Best First Novel of its year. His second mystery, *Confess, Fletch,* won the Edgar for Best Paperback of 1976.

Fletch introduced Mcdonald's fast-moving cinematic style—long on dialogue, short on description—except for *Carioca, Fletch* (1984), which is more like a travelogue of Rio than a mystery, and given more to the quick cut than the painstaking transition. Fletch is a lovable rapscallion; Mcdonald's spinoff hero, Boston policeman Flynn, is a devoted family man with a secret life. Mcdonald's fans love him more for his characters than his plots, although the plot of *Fletch* is highly original, with an ending that surely must be one of the most satisfying in the genre.

Irwin Maurice Fletcher appears at first to be a California beach bum who is singled out to make a contract hit. The proposed victim: the contractor himself, Alan Stanwyck, who says he is dying of cancer. Really, however, Fletch is a newspaper reporter working undercover on a story about drugs on the beach. Investigating Stanwyck, he learns the man is apparently in radiant health. Thus he has two professional problems to solve: Why should a healthy man want to be murdered, and who is supplying the drugs on the beach? In addition to these, Fletch has personal problems: an incompetent editor who wants to fire him, and two ex-wives who want more money.

This is a page-turner, with some of the most dazzling dialogue in contemporary fiction. In 1985 it was made into a film starring Chevy Chase. (*J.S.*)

Mcdonald, Gregory. *Flynn's In.* New York: Mysterious Press, 1984. (T)

Boston police inspector Francis Xavier Flynn isn't a cop like other cops. Even the police commissioner doesn't really know where he goes or what he does when he's suddenly called away. All he knows is that Flynn has experience in handling big matters. "You came to us from Washington, or Zürich, or someplace. You'll know how to handle this," he says when he summons Flynn in the middle of the night to a secret resort known as the Rod and Gun Club.

It develops that the members of the club are some of the most powerful men in the country who go to their secret hideaway to let their hair down. One is a judge who likes to wear evening gowns and high heels; another old geezer doesn't wear a stitch. And someone is picking them off, one by one. Flynn doesn't like the setup one little bit, but he *has* to handle it, as soon as he finds himself a prisoner at the remote club.

This is a rollicking story—thick with Flynn's deadpan wit—that's all the more difficult to pull off as there are no women characters and only the one setting. Flynn finds the murderer, of course; but by the time he does, the membership's plan to keep the crisis under control has backfired, for Flynn now knows enough to see that justice is done in a few ways the old boys didn't anticipate. Most satisfying.

Other Flynn and Fletch books include *Flynn* (1977), *Fletch's Fortune* (1978), *Fletch's Moxie* (1983), *Fletch and the Man Who* (1983), and *Fletch Won* (1985).

(*J.S.*)

*McGerr, Patricia. *Pick Your Victim.* New York: Doubleday Crime Club, 1946. (W)

While literally thousands of mysteries have been based on the attempt to discover a murderer, Patricia McGerr's is unique in disclosing the killer at the beginning and challenging detectives (and readers) to select the *victim.* Not content to rely upon an original idea, she followed through, though this was only her first book, to create a mystery that was worthy of its conception. It is small wonder that Barzun and Taylor, who labeled this book a "whodunin," also called it a masterpiece.

Pick Your Victim starts in the Aleutians in 1944, where a group of U.S. marines are fighting the "Great Battle of Boredom." Reading matter is in short supply, and the never-broken rule is that "if there was printing on it, you read it." Thus, a torn piece of newspaper discloses to Pete Robbins, former publicity agent, that his previous boss in Washington, D.C., has been arrested for murder. The name of the victim is missing, although the item states that it was an officer at SUDS (Society for the Uplift of Domestic Service), where Robbins was employed. Pete and his fellow marines agree on a sweepstakes with the prize going to the first to guess who was murdered before the news arrives from back home. Playing the role of a GI Scheherazade, Robbins tells his barracks mates about SUDS and his colleagues during his four years at that philanthropic organization.

McGerr knows Washington, D.C., and the political, economic, and social life of the nation's capital come alive in her novel. This is an unusually good blend of realism and satire, with the leading characters limned in a manner that makes them believable. The story is well plotted, with clues adroitly inserted. Unlike many books that start with splendid gimmicks, *Pick Your Victim* has an ending that is not a letdown.

Much of the authenticity in this book undoubtedly came from McGerr's employment, from 1937 to 1943, as director of public relations for the American Road Builders Association in Washington. Though never quite matching the success of *Pick Your Victim,* she has built a writing career in which originality has been the keynote. Thus, in her next book, *The Seven Deadly Sisters* (1947), she leaves the identities of *both* victim and culprit to be determined when she has her heroine learn, through a letter, that one of her seven aunts has murdered her husband.

McGerr's one series character is Selena Mead, a Washington, D.C., society woman who doubles as a counterespionage agent. In addition to appearances in two novels—*Is There a Traitor in the House?* (1964) and *Legacy of Danger* (1970)—Mead is featured in numerous short stories in *Ellery Queen's Mystery Magazine.* Some of her other nonseries mysteries are *Catch Me If You Can* (1948), *Murder Is Absurd* (1967), and *Dangerous Landing* (1975).

(*M.L.*)

McGinley, Patrick. *Bogmail.* New York: Ticknor & Fields, 1981. (PS)

Joan Kahn is one of the best-known editors in the mystery field, with a career that has spanned nearly forty years. She has specialized in publishing new and innovative authors—among them Julian Symons, Michael Gilbert, and Dick Francis (qq.v.)—and many of her discoveries (the bulk of whom are British) were the cutting edge of the movement from the old-style whodunit to the contemporary crime novel. In 1980, when Kahn moved from Harper & Row to Ticknor & Fields (she has since moved again, this time to St. Martin's Press), the first new writer she contracted with was Patrick McGinley, whose *Bogmail,* first issued in England in 1978, is a fine mainstream novel with only tenuous links to the mystery genre.

The setting is a tiny village on the wild northwest coast of Ireland, and the chief character is impotent intellectual pubkeeper Tim Roarty, who bludgeons his daughter's seducer to death with a volume of the 1911 *Encyclopaedia Britannica* and disposes of the body in the local bog. When he starts getting extortion letters from an apparent witness to the burial who signs himself Bogmailer, Roarty has the double problem of keeping his crime hidden from the police and killing whoever it is who knows where the first body was buried. At which point the frozen foot of that first body is found hanging from the door knocker of the police station. . . .

McGinley evokes magnificently the wild Donegal landscape; the look and feel and smell of the bogs and the sea; the crude and lonely village lives; the Irishman's love of talk and more talk, as if words could ease the pain of the world; the interplay of a small number of very real people in a supremely vivid environment. But the crime and suspense elements are on stage only intermittently, and at the end, when pure chance has revealed Bogmailer's identity, we never learn where in that tiny hamlet he managed to keep the corpse frozen yet unfindable by the police. What we have here is a microcosm: In *Bogmail* we can see both what was lost and what was gained in the evolution from traditional to contemporary crime fiction.

Other novels by McGinley are *Goosefoot* (1982), *Foggage* (1983), *The Trick of the Ga Bolga* (1985), and *Foxprints* (1985).

(*F.M.N.*)

*McGivern, William P. *Odds Against Tomorrow*. New York: Dodd, Mead, 1957. (PS)

The symbolism of *Odds Against Tomorrow* permits a story as powerful and tense as a mystery novel to be appreciated on another level. Four men of varied backgrounds meet in a Philadelphia hotel to plan the robbery of a bank in a small, southeastern Pennsylvania town. Three are white—one of the three, Earl Slater, a southerner who hates blacks. The fourth man, Johnny Ingram, is a young black whose presence is necessary to the success of the job. There is an immediate conflict between Slater and Ingram, and it carries into the robbery and its aftermath.

As a suspense story about a big (or at least medium-sized) caper, *Odds Against Tomorrow* compares favorably to the best work of Donald Westlake (q.v.) writing as Richard Stark (q.v.). There is the same fascination we derive from reading of the precision in planning, and the characters are far more interesting and more fully developed than Parker and his amoral gang. Not only do we get to know the perpetrators of the robbery, but we also become involved with the policemen assigned to hunt them down.

Whether or not it was William McGivern's intent, it is very easy to see the tensions involved in the bank robbery as symbolizing those in the United States in 1957. *Odds Against Tomorrow* was published the month after the riots attendant upon school integration in Little Rock, Arkansas, and the book contains enough reference to racial conflict to make it clear that McGivern was well aware of the political and social climate of the time. We know how he feels on this issue, but not because of any lectures he delivers—the story always remains primary. McGivern proves that the mystery genre is large and flexible enough to permit consideration of "serious" issues without in any way detracting from the goal of entertaining the reader.

Not surprisingly, *Odds Against Tomorrow* became a strong film (1959), albeit somewhat changed from the original novel, with Harry Belafonte and Robert Ryan playing the racial antagonists. After it, McGivern would continue to be a prolific writer of mysteries, but he never was able to match the hard-boiled writing of the novels he wrote during his first decade. The money earned from his movie sales permitted him to travel widely, and he began to set his suspense novels abroad in such places as Spain, Italy, and North Africa. They were unfailingly readable, but away from the grittiness of such locales as decaying Philadelphia, they failed to appeal to the hearts of mystery readers and critics as they had before. Whatever McGivern lost in critical acclaim, he gained in financial security as during the 1970s he became one of the leading writers of movie and television mystery films.

(*M.L.*)

McGivern, William P. *Rogue Cop*. New York: Dodd, Mead, 1954. (PP/PS)

Writing of William P. McGivern, Anthony Boucher said, "Someday McGivern will, like [Graham] Greene, be recognized as a novelist of stature and spiritual complexity; and meanwhile he will be enjoyed as one of today's ablest storytellers." *Rogue Cop* is one of the many novels McGivern wrote during the decade of his best work, 1948–57, that can be appreciated on both levels.

Sergeant Mike Carmody is an efficient Philadelphia detective, but he is beholden to the Ackerman mob, which controls city politics. "The city was their private hunting ground, created and maintained for their express pleasure. They fed on it. Like protected vultures. . . . The average citizen's indifference, cynicism and willingness to compromise was the weakness that Ackerman used as the foundation of his power." Carmody seems satisfied with his life until his younger brother, Eddie, also a policeman, but an honest one, runs afoul of the mob.

Mike Carmody is forced into questioning his values, balancing his comfort and desire for self-preservation against family and the belief in right and wrong inculcated in him by his early religious training. His family priest, Father Ahearn, becomes aware of his plight, and *Rogue Cop* contains discussions of morality not usually found in the mystery novel. Yet, so good a storyteller is McGivern (a result of his early training in the pulps) that at no time do the sheer excitement and suspense of this story flag.

The theme of the temptations facing policemen was always one that appealed to William P. McGivern and one that he wrote about very effectively. The protagonist in *Shield for Murder* (1951) is thoroughly dishonest. Dave Bannion in *The Big Heat* (1953) will not yield to corruption, and as a result his wife is murdered. We watch as this contemplative policeman, given to reading St. John, is forced into a life of vengeance. Revenge is also the motive for a police officer in *The Darkest Hour* (1955; reprinted as *Waterfront Cop*) when he is released from prison having served five years because he was framed.

Because he wrote so vividly and created characters with whom the public could identify, McGivern frequently sold his works to Hollywood. *Rogue Cop, The Big Heat,* and *The Darkest Hour* were all filmed, with Robert Taylor, Glenn Ford, and Alan Ladd respectively playing the leading roles.

(*M.L.*)

McHale, Tom. *Farragan's Retreat.* New York: Viking, 1971. (PS)

Arthur Farragan, a dowdy Irish Catholic Philadelphia businessman in his middle years, is nudged by his fascist brother and sister into a conspiracy to commit murder. After sister Anna's son is killed in Vietnam and brother Jim's boy comes home minus an arm, Jim and Anna persuade Arthur that his own son, Simon, a radical who went to Canada rather than be drafted, should himself be assassinated as a religious and patriotic act. (Or have they persuaded him? Farragan keeps telling himself that his real reason for going to Montreal is to warn Simon, not shoot him.) On the fringes of the plot are Farragan's frigid and pious wife; his nubile mistress; an alcoholic priest; a Mafia mogul; an impotent lifeguard; and a host of others. No sooner does the plan to kill Simon reach its climax than the entire Farragan clan becomes the target for a mad bomber who keeps running the Philadelphia police through hoops.

Strictly speaking, *Farragan's Retreat* isn't a mystery. It's a mainstream novel in the Joseph Heller/Kurt Vonnegut vein of black humor, but one that uses certain whodunit techniques for its own purposes; indeed, very few regular mystery writers have done as well with the least-likely suspect device as McHale does here. Of course, the book's strong suit is not crime or detection or suspense but outraged and outrageous gallows humor, aimed at what the author sees as American Nazism in all its varieties—racial, political, and religious.

McHale is much influenced by antiestablishment classics such as Heller's *Catch-22* and Vonnegut's *Slaughterhouse Five,* but every so often he commits a malapropism worthy of Michael Avallone (q.v.). On page 239 he tells us that "police . . . ranged about the house in unmarked cars," and twenty pages later that "the trailing [police] car . . . came up behind him to tell him" certain developments. It seems that the world's smallest and most talkative prowl cars are to be found on the Philadelphia force! These gaffes aside, however, *Farragan's Retreat* is not only a classic slice of nostalgia for the Big Chill generation but a fine example of how crime-fiction elements can be incorporated into novels outside the genre and can enrich such books in the process.

(*F.M.N.*)

MacHarg, William. *The Affairs of O'Malley.* New York: Dial, 1940. (Reprinted as *Smart Guy.* New York: Popular Library, 1951.) (SS)

In writing the series of thirty-three short stories collected as *The Affairs of O'Malley,* William MacHarg displayed the versatility that marked his long career. As far back as 1910 he had collaborated with Edwin Balmer on

The Achievements of Luther Trant, one of the cornerstone short-story collections in any mystery library. Written during an era when scientific detectives (e.g., Sherlock Holmes, Craig Kennedy, and Dr. Thorndyke) were popular, it used psychology as its primary means of detection. Word association and memory tests as well as the first fictional use of the lie detector were used.

Totally different are the stories that MacHarg wrote by himself during the 1930s for the "slick"magazines. Though too short to permit much authentic detail (they averaged about 2,000 words apiece), the O'Malley stories were forerunners of the police procedurals that were soon to be published. The crimes are the ordinary ones that fill police blotters, and the victims and murderers could be believable, especially if MacHarg had had the space to describe them in greater detail.

O'Malley, as a detective, is anything but extraordinary or eccentric. His grammar is poor, and he is constantly complaining. Following a rigid formula, all of the tales begin with O'Malley describing the type of case involved and why it will be difficult to solve. The stories are all narrated by a nameless, faceless "Watson" who is not a policeman and usually functions as O'Malley's driver. Though educated (he knows Latin), he puts up with verbal abuse from the detective, who often calls him "dumb," a word the detective also applies to himself.

The stories seem simple and, at first blush, appear to have been very easy to write. That is deceptive, for many of them contain misdirection that required a skilled plotter. All are readable, and several contain nice touches, indeed. "No Clues," which begins with the finding of a pretty, unidentified dead girl in a warehouse, is probably the best, but it is closely rivaled by "The Scotty Dog," which contains a variation on the Holmesian theme of the dog that didn't bark during the night. It also contains deadpan humor designed to emphasize the point frequently made that O'Malley is only a simple cop. When his narrator says, *"Cherchez la femme,"* our hero replies, "Not at all—what we got to do is look for the woman." How can we not enjoy a cop who says things like that, or, after solving a case by use of trickery, says, "Maybe instead of a cop I ought to be a crook, but I figure a crook works harder than a cop, and I ain't that fond of working"?

(*M.L.*)

*McIlvanney, William. *Laidlaw.* New York: Pantheon, 1977. (PP)

Laidlaw, the first crime novel of prizewinning Scottish author McIlvanney, was published both in England and here to considerable fanfare. Ross Macdonald (q.v.) said of it, "I have seldom been so seized by a style, or so taken by a character as I was by the angry and compassionate Glasgow detective, Laidlaw. . . . McIlvanney has broken new ground, and is to be congratulated on his talent and his daring." Maj Sjöwall (q.v.) agreed: "If

McIlvanney continues, Laidlaw's Glasgow will be to readers what Maigret's Paris, Van der Valk's Amsterdam, and Martin Beck's Stockholm are." In addition to these and other enthusiastic notices, the novel won a British Crime Writers Silver Dagger.

Almost forty, a detective inspector who has tracked down criminals everyone thought invincible, a family man and homeowner, Jack Laidlaw would seem on the surface to have every reason to celebrate life. He is, however, too sensitive and too much of an idealist for both his job and his lifestyle. Tolerating a less than perfect marriage, he enjoys his marvelous girlfriend only rarely, plagued by an almost existential guilt. And while he possesses acute instincts and abilities for crime solving, his poetic sensitivities open him to a brooding compassion for perpetrators of criminal acts. Quite unlike most policemen, in or out of books, he feels and even proclaims his disgust for a society that viciously refuses responsibility for its role in shoving some of us over the edge. Laidlaw openly sympathizes with the criminal mind, and McIlvanney makes us share his character's profound revulsion for a cruel and hopeless world. His disdain for bureaucratic police work pits him against open hostility and suspicion from most of his colleagues and all of his superiors, and we never fail to side with his rebellious outrage.

The case he must solve in *Laidlaw* is particularly depressing. A young man gripped by the guilt of closet homosexuality attempts to eradicate his unadmitted hatred of women by assaulting and murdering a teenage girl. Laidlaw follows his trail on intuition alone, and in the process we witness Glasgow's citizens at their cruelest and most desperate. It is a tale told daily in probably every big city in the Western World, yet all too seldom told as well as it is here.

This dark, bleak novel may not be for every taste. Nor may McIlvanney's style, which makes heavy use of Scottish dialect and slang. But the power of both *Laidlaw* and Laidlaw are undeniable, and the portrait of the modern Glasgow, grim though it may be, is nowhere in crime fiction—perhaps nowhere in any type of fiction—more profound.

To date McIlvanney has brought Laidlaw back for only a single encore, *The Papers of Tony Veitch* (1983), which takes the detective deep inside Glasgow's underworld. If anything, this is an even grimmer look at the Scottish city—and an even more powerful novel than its predecessor.

(*K.K.H./B.P.*)

MacInnes, Helen. *Agent in Place.* New York: Harcourt Brace, 1976. (E)

In *Agent in Place,* Helen MacInnes uses all the components that make her novels sure candidates for the best-seller list: double agents, a purloined top-secret memo, interesting and carefully researched locales, and larger-than-life characters. The story is told from multiple viewpoints, and as it unfolds, the meaning of each bit and piece of information is revealed, with all plot lines dovetailing at the end.

A classified memo from NATO is being studied at Shandon House, a New Jersey think tank. Because of the explosive nature of the memo's contents and their implications about future U.S. security planning, think-tank employee Chuck Kelso believes the American public has a right to know the contents of the first third of it. He takes the memo; copies the first section on a typewriter borrowed from his brother, journalist Tom Kelso; and, with the help of supposed friend Rich Nealey, delivers it into the hands of a reporter. Unknown to Chuck, however, Nealey has microfilmed the entire memo; Nealey, in reality a KGB agent-in-place in Washington, D.C., has orders to deliver the memo through an intermediary to his superior, Konov. Plans go awry when Konov is mugged and stabbed in Central Park following his last meeting with Nealey; Konov dies in the hospital—helped along by his comrade, Oleg, who knows the police are interested in Konov and fears he will spill state secrets. Nealey, not knowing what to do with the microfilm, transmits it to Moscow by regular channels.

Because of the peculiar typeface of the copy of the memo, suspicion of leaking it focuses quickly, first on Tom Kelso and then on his brother, Chuck. Tom's friend, NATO agent Tony Lawton (an urbane Englishman whose cover is that of a wine merchant), interests himself in the situation and discovers Neeley's identity with surprising ease. If the Kelso brothers' lives have been disrupted by this security breach, Neeley's is even more so: He has made a disastrous mistake in sending the memo on, because it has ended up on the desk of a NATO agent-in-place in Moscow, Jean Parracini, who has been operating as a KGB agent for twelve years. This advance warning allows Parracini—whose cover would have been blown by the memo—to escape Russia, and he takes up hiding at Menton, on the Riviera, where, coincidentally, a branch of the think tank, Shandon-by-the-Sea, has just been established. Lawton, visiting the NATO operatives who are protecting Parracini in Menton, becomes concerned about Jean's emotional stability and fears he may make reprisals against the think tank whose lax security caused his exposure.

The story is a tense one, played out against the background of the Riviera. There is double-dealing and triple-dealing, all of which leads to a satisfying, if bittersweet, ending. MacInnes' first novel, *Above Suspicion* (1941), was made into a 1943 film starring Joan Crawford, Fred MacMurray, and Basil Rathbone. Since this promising debut, MacInnes has gone on to produce numerous exciting espionage thrillers, among them *The Salzberg Connection* (1968), *Prelude to Terror* (1978), *Cloak of Darkness* (1982), and *Ride a Pale Horse* (1984).

(*M.M.*)

Mackay, Amanda. *Death on the Eno.* Boston: Little, Brown, 1981. (AD)

Hannah Land is a mild-mannered member of the new breed of female series sleuths introduced in the mid-1970s. She is a divorced New Yorker who, after completing her doctorate in political science, immigrates to Duke University. Besides a new life, Hannah finds murder in her new southern home.

Death on the Eno is Hannah's second case. The locale is a farm on the Eno River. The central characters are the white landed gentry of North Carolina, tied to the land by tradition and, in some cases, a deep love. Luther Turnbull is a member of this class, but is a hustler with a cruel streak. When he drowns in an apparent canoeing accident, no one is suspicious and few mourn.

But when Hannah discovers circumstantial evidence that Luther was not alone on the river the day he died, she suspects that the death was no accident. Unfortunately, when she makes her discoveries, she also undergoes her own boating accident, and spends the major part of the book in a cast to the waist. Her role, as she recuperates at the Turnbull farm, is as catalyst and observer. She is, in fact, the armchair detective whose domestic sleuthing is complemented by the professional efforts of a very likable police character, Lieutenant Bobby Gene Jenkins of the Durham police.

Death on the Eno is a mystery of atmosphere and character. The pace is slow and quiet, not unlike the natural world Mackay uses as her setting and as the mainspring for her plot.

The first Hannah Land mystery, *Death Is Academic* (1976), is more standard fare, a college mystery that serves as a good introduction to Hannah and Bobby Gene.

(*K.L.M.*)

MacLean, Alistair. *The Guns of Navarone.* New York: Doubleday, 1957. (A)

The Guns of Navarone, Alistair MacLean's second novel, was made into a hugely successful movie with David Niven in 1961 and ensured MacLean a regular spot on the best-seller lists for the next twenty or so years. Despite the fact that his writing took a decided downturn around 1968, MacLean deserved his best-selling status for his early works, most of which guarantee nail-biting, edge-of-the-seat reading. MacLean's stalwart heroes may all have been cut from the same pattern, but he was a master at putting them into complicated plots and moving them from one seemingly hopeless situation to another in a way that few other writers could match.

The Guns of Navarone is a prime example of MacLean's early work.

Keith Mallory and his small team of men are commissioned to destroy the guns of the title so that British ships can pass safely by and rescue 1200 men from the island of Kheros. Never mind the fact that the British navy and air force have been unable to silence the guns. All Mallory and his men have to do is survive storms at sea in a leaky boat, climb an unclimbable cliff, suffer through snow and bitter cold, fight off what seems like a large portion of the German army, and deal with the fact that the enemy seems to know their every move in advance. Before the mission is accomplished, MacLean generates enough suspense for two or three books by lesser writers.

(*B.C.*)

*MacLean, Alistair. *Night Without End.* New York: Doubleday, 1960. (A)

Night Without End represents Alistair MacLean at the top of his form, combining suspense with adventure, piling twist upon twist, and springing surprise after surprise, in a story that pits its protagonists against clever villains and savage nature. In fact, the Arctic setting is so well rendered and so convincing that it becomes the most powerful element in the book.

The story begins with a plane crash near the hut of an IGY scientist and his two assistants. The scientist, Dr. Peter Mason, the book's narrator, soon discovers that the crash was not accidental. The pilot and crew members were murdered by two of the seven passengers who remain alive. But he doesn't know which two. His radio is accidentally smashed, another crew member is murdered in the hut, and someone burns the wreckage of the plane. Not only does Mason need to know who and why, he needs to get the group to civilization, no easy task, since his hut sits smack in the middle of the Greenland ice cap and the outside temperature is hovering somewhere near −70° Fahrenheit. Nevertheless, the group takes off in an ancient, wood-bodied snow tractor, and things really begin to get rough. Any reader who can put this book down after reading the first few pages is a tough cookie indeed.

Equally entertaining and suspenseful are *H. M. S. Ulysses* (1956), *South by Java Head* (1958), *The Secret Ways* (1959), and *Where Eagles Dare* (1967). MacLean's work after the later date, while solidly professional, has not proved as satisfying as his early novels.

(*B.C.*)

MacLeod, Charlotte. *Family Vault.* New York: Doubleday Crime Club, 1979. (AD)

The mysteries of Charlotte MacLeod are of the "bloodless" type: While murders abound, bloodletting is never described in all its painful ugliness.

MacLeod writes with wry wit and style, and her plotting is competent. If there is any fault with the two series she has authored, it is that many of the characters are somewhat emotionless and so eccentric that the books do not seem very realistic. If, however, you are in the mood for an enjoyable, humorous, and "civilized" murder mystery, little can beat MacLeod's work.

The series featuring Sarah Kelling of the old Boston society family is probably MacLeod's best, and it is the character of Sarah herself that gives it depth. Sarah is in her twenties, and at the time of the first book, married to her fifth cousin, Alexander, a man some twenty years older than she. Sarah and Alexander live with his domineering mother, and sometimes Sarah feels she has no life of her own. Treated as an adored child by her husband, she longs for the responsibilities of adulthood that have been denied her.

As the novel begins, the Kelling family vault is being opened so Great-Uncle Frederick can be buried there. When the vault is opened, it is quickly apparent that someone other than a Kelling has been interred there—a burlesque queen named Ruby Redd, who is easily identified by the gems embedded in her teeth. Ruby Redd has been missing for thirty years, and now that her murder has been discovered, Sarah begins to wonder if Alexander—who was associated with the show girl in his wild youth—didn't kill her.

"It seemed rotten to go snooping behind her husband's back, yet one could hardly march up to him and ask point-blank, 'Did you murder Ruby Redd?' " So Sarah reasons before she begins to investigate. Her quest takes her into the Kelling family past; and before she is through, tragedy has struck twice, and Sarah's life has changed more than she could have imagined. Throughout, however, she keeps her wits and her sense of humor, and emerges the woman she has only hoped to be.

The other novels featuring Sarah Kelling are *The Withdrawing Room* (1980), *The Palace Guard* (1981), *The Bilbao Looking Glass* (1983), *The Convivial Codfish* (1984), and *The Plain Old Man* (1985).

(*M.M.*)

MacLeod, Charlotte. *Something the Cat Dragged In.* New York: Doubleday Crime Club, 1983. (AD)

The something that Mrs. Betsey Lomax's cat, Edmund, drags in is a toupee. And the toupee belongs to Mrs. Lomax's boarder of many years, Professor Ungley. But Edmund did not purloin the hairpiece from the professor's quarters, and the man himself appears not to have spent the night at home. In no time, Mrs. Lomax discovers Ungley's body behind the clubhouse of the Balaclavian Society—a group dedicated to the history of the small New England town of Balaclava Junction. And when it becomes apparent to her that Police Chief Fred Ottermole is not going to handle the case properly, she calls in amateur sleuth Professor Peter Shandy.

Shandy is on the faculty of the local agricultural college—a man who possibly knows more about turnips and rutabagas than anyone else on earth. He also knows a great deal about murder, having solved other cases in the small town, and he quickly understands what Mrs. Lomax means when she says Ungley did not trip and fatally injure himself by falling against an old harrow. Shandy, a pleasant and always hurried young man, aids the police without offending them (much), and soon enlists the expertise of a number of people at the college, turning it into a virtual crime lab.

Shandy quickly turns up a possible murder weapon, and its duplicate, the real murder weapon. He also comes across a previously unknown heir of the professor; a political scandal that threatens the college; the inexplicable disappearance of his own files; and more murder. When he is finished, he has exposed, as he puts it, "a well-laid plan that went agley," and furthered his already considerable reputation as the canniest sleuth in Balaclava Junction.

Shandy's earlier adventures are *Rest You Merry* (1978), *The Luck Runs Out* (1981), and *Wrack and Rune* (1982).

(*M.M.*)

McMullen, Mary. *But Nellie Was So Nice.* New York: Doubleday Crime Club, 1979. (W)

Mary McMullen's novels combine sharp, sophisticated dialogue with finely detailed description and a light, often humorous touch that makes them easy and entertaining reading. Many are set in New York City and environs, but others take place in such locales as England or Ireland. Her characters, like her dialogue, are generally sophisticated and witty, employed in interesting professions that provide a good backdrop for her complex and fast-moving stories.

Nellie Hand, however, is neither sophisticated nor employed in a fascinating profession. She is a middle-aged lady, a keeper of a cat, who lives in a fourth-floor walk-up on Timothy Street in Manhattan's Greenwich Village. Nellie's greatest distinction, in fact, is that she is friend to everyone, doer of favors, keeper of confidences. And when she is murdered by a person or persons unknown, these friends are aghast—after all, Nellie was so *nice.*

The friends include Enid, the owner of the dress shop where Nellie worked; Matthew Jones, a television executive who seems an unlikely companion for such an unspectacular woman; Lise Kozer, who has hinted to Nellie of vast wealth that she will one day leave to her; Lucinda Callender, a young woman in flight from shady characters; Charmian Lyle, a lovely woman trapped in a nightmarish marriage; Basil, a gallery owner and art forger; Ursula, one of Basil's artists; and finally Nellie's nephew Jeremy, who has done her proud by becoming a famous photographer. It is a lively cast of characters and a likely list of suspects—any one of the secrets they have told Nellie is sufficient reason for one of them to have killed her. In the end, it is up to nephew Jeremy—after he has stopped reeling from shock—to sort through the secrets and detect just which one triggered his aunt's unfortunate and untimely end.

(*M.M.*)

McMullen, Mary. *Death by Bequest.* New York: Doubleday Crime Club, 1977. (PS)

This novel begins with the startling announcement "It was between Trenton and Princeton Junction, on the train from Philadelphia to New York, that Waldo St. Clair conceived the idea of killing his wife."

Why? Waldo's wife, Celia, has recently inherited an old house in Philadelphia filled with rare artworks, furniture, and artifacts that could make Waldo, part owner of a Manhattan gallery, rich. And Waldo is in love with another woman, Irena Tova, who works at the gallery. Divorce is out of the question because Waldo and Irena have no money of their own. But murder . . .

Waldo makes his plans: He will take Celia away for the Christmas holidays, somewhere abroad where an "accident" can happen to her. But other factors keep intervening: Celia doesn't want to go; Waldo suspects (rightly) that she has fallen in love with his partner, Cy Hall; and a distant relative, Bernard Caldwell, surfaces, claiming he ought to share in Celia's inheritance. Waldo finally gets Celia to Dublin, supposedly on a buying trip, but he can't seem to escape from Bernard, who follows them. And just as he is about to put his plan in motion, Cy Hall appears, too. Still, Waldo persists, becoming more and more determined that Celia must die.

Like so many of McMullen's characters, Celia St. Clair is sophisticated and attractive, and it is easy to feel terror for her as Waldo goes about his murderous scheme. Even though we're pretty sure what's going on, it's difficult to put this one down until we know what the outcome will be.

McMullen, who is the daughter of mystery novelist Helen Reilly (q.v.) and sister of Ursula Curtiss (q.v.), won the Mystery Writers of America Edgar in 1951 for her first novel, *Stranglehold.* Other enjoyable books by her include *A Country Kind of Death* (1975), *Welcome to the Grave* (1979), *Better Off Dead* (1982), and *Gift Horse* (1985).

(*M.M.*)

McNamara, Joseph D. *The First Directive.* New York: Crown, 1984. (PP)

Ever since Joseph Wambaugh (q.v.) published his first novel fifteen years ago, a number of working cops have tried their hands at fiction. Joseph

D. McNamara, the chief of police of San Jose, California, is the latest. Unlike Wambaugh, McNamara does not romanticize either police work or police officers; if anything, he takes some amazing shots at the politics and attitudes of law enforcement, and also pokes fun at the police image. The book's narrator, Sergeant Fraleigh of an unnamed valley city south of San Francisco (San Jose, of course), and his two partners, Vietnam vet Paul English and a beer-guzzling hulk called The Block, sometimes act more like the bumbling cops in a novel by Donald Westlake (q.v.) than the "blue knights" in a Wambaugh epic.

Fraleigh, English, and the Block are assigned to investigate the disappearance of the daughter of a Silicon Valley bigwig named Adolph Stone. Their search leads them to a Moonie-type cult called the Moral Reaffirmation Guild (which is not very well set up or described), led by an evil type named Phillips (who never appears on stage); to the apparent double murder of Stone's daughter and a man named Don Fortune; to several attempts on their own lives (Fraleigh spends more time in the hospital than anywhere else); and finally to a nasty sex-and-blackmail racket that involves the mob and some of the state's leading politicos. Along the way Fraleigh falls in love with Don Fortune's widow, Sandra, a clinical psychologist, thereby violating the "first directive" of police work (and the title): "Don't get emotionally involved with anyone connected to a case."

McNamara has enough plot here for a 70,000-word book; unfortunately *The First Directive* is more than 100,000 words in length. The result is a story line contrived in places, rather patchily constructed, and not wholly credible. Still, as first novels go, it isn't all that bad. One of its redeeming graces is an abundance of humor (there are some laugh-out-loud passages, particularly in the first 100 pages). Another is that Fraleigh, English, and the Block are well characterized—believable, likable, human. And a third is McNamara's portrayal of the inner workings of a large-city police department, which is fascinating.

(*B.P.*)

*McShane, Mark. *The Crimson Madness of Little Doom.* New York: Doubleday Crime Club, 1966. (PS/C/T)

Little Doom is an isolated village on the Cornish coast, with a total population of fifteen of the strangest individuals gathered together anywhere, among them alcoholic Major Plate, secretive Mrs. Maroon, nasty Miss Ratchit, frivolous Tony Galleon, "dead" Peter Barlow, and horny Liz Liggit. One of these individuals is responsible for a rash of poison-pen letters mailed to the various inhabitants, each one beginning "Dear Scum" and each one bearing a local postmark. The letters are so downright nasty that one of them induced poor, unstable Ellie Barlow, Peter's wife, to take her own life. Peter has vowed to unmask and punish the letter writer, and he enlists the help of the others, especially Tony Galleon and the Major. But the letters continue to arrive, and suspicion continues to shift from one to another of the villagers—and then even stranger things begin to happen. . . .

McShane mixes equal amounts of suspense and black humor in what is a literal tour de force. Dozens of stray cats play an eerie role; there is one of the funniest seduction scenes ever committed to paper; and a drunken "gathering of the suspects" leads to a climax at the close of which, as Anthony Boucher wrote in the *New York Times,* "you have four corpses and a black sense of despair." There is also a savage twist at the very end.

If all of this makes *Crimson Madness* sound inconsistent and somewhat mad, that's because it *is.* And yet it all works beautifully. Boucher wrote further in the *Times:* "This may not be to everyone's taste, but the novel is well and, at times, brilliantly written, with some fine points and puzzle construction which a reviewer may not specify. I at least found it wholly admirable." McShane's humor is wickedly inventive, the kind with knives in it. He can turn tragedy into farce at the drop of a delightfully wacky observation or bit of business, and just as skillfully turn farce into tragedy at the drop of an unexpected corpse or two.

Other of his novels in this same vein, all carrying similarly creative titles, are *Ill Met by a Fish Shop on George Street* (1968), about the effects of a chance meeting of two old acquaintances in Sydney, Australia; *The Singular Case of the Multiple Dead* (1969), a bizarre farce about a group of nine aesthetes who decide to assassinate the chancellor of the exchequer in London because he has levied an additional one-shilling tax on all theater seats; *The Man Who Left Well Enough* (1970), another madcap mystery, in which an angel of vengeance named Dublin Gomez attempts the mass extermination of a *very* strange village of bricklayers; and *Lashed but Not Leashed* (1976), about a pair of odd criminous bedfellows named Jeremy Wood and Henry Mastin. Each of these novels is likewise recommended to readers whose taste runs to the *outré* in crime fiction.

(*B.P.*)

McShane, Mark. *Séance.* New York: Doubleday Crime Club, 1962. (PS)

Black humor is only one of McShane's fictional pursuits. He has also written several books dealing with paranormal themes, both under his own name and under his Marc Lovell (q.v.) pseudonym. Of these straightforward and often frightening tales, the best-known is *Séance,* his first novel, from which the 1964 film *Séance on a Wet Afternoon* was adapted.

London housewife Myra Savage is a medium, "a genuine one; she believed in what she did." She also believes in her husband Bill's "Plan," which will turn their lives around. The plan is to kidnap a little girl—Adriana, daughter of industrialist Charles Clayton—and then stage a mock recovery of her through Myra's paranormal powers. Myra will be honored as a gifted clairvoyant, paid handsome sums for her future services, and Bill will realize his ambitions for his wife's career.

Initially the kidnapping goes well: Ransom demands are made, and the money collected; Myra approaches the Claytons about using her powers to discover their daughter's whereabouts, and after some hesitation, a seance is arranged. But as with most kidnapping ploys, things go awry, emotions get out of hand, and the participants discover previously unsuspected facets of their own and others' personalities. One of these facets is Myra's power; she is, as she is fond of thinking, "a rarity among those in her profession." As a result, the ending is both unexpected and startling, and should please the most exacting mystery fan.

Myra Savage returns for a single encore in *Séance for Two* (1972). The prolific and diversely talented McShane is also the author of three excellent novels featuring ex-policeman turned private investigator Norman Pink—*The Girl Nobody Knows* (1965), *Night's Evil* (1966), and *The Way to Nowhere* (1967); of such other thrillers as *Untimely Ripped* (1962) and *The Hostage Game* (1979); and, as by Lovell, the hilarious "Apple" series of spy spoofs.

(*M.M./B.P.*)

Mahannah, Floyd. *The Broken Angel.* Philadelphia: Macrae Smith, 1957. (T)

Small-town newspaper editor Roy Holgren has been having a decidedly noncasual affair with his secretary, Sara Matthews. But he knows little about her; she has only been in Linville, Nevada, for a year and refuses to talk about her past. When a man named Wes Wesnick shows up in town, and Sara disappears shortly afterward, leaving Holgren an unconvincing goodbye note, Roy is half frantic. He finally tracks her down in a private sanatorium in Lodi, California, recuperating from a vicious beating. The truth about her past then comes out: She is wanted in Sacramento for the murder of the wife of her former lover, a noted plastic surgeon.

Roy arranges to hide her at an isolated slough in the Sacramento River delta, and it is there she tells him about a jewel thief named Mace Romualdo, whom the plastic surgeon operated on after a San Francisco heist; about the reward for Romualdo's capture and another reward for the return of the stolen jewelry; and about her knowledge of Romualdo's present whereabouts. This is the information Wesnick tried to beat out of her.

Roy sets out to capture Romualdo and collect the reward money, which he will use to get Sara and himself out of the country. But things do not go as planned. More complications develop, among them the reappearance of Wesnick, who claims to have a witness who can clear Sara of the murder charge. The plot continues to unfold in unexpected ways before dovetailing in an equally unexpected climax.

Taut and evocative, *The Broken Angel* also has the virtues of expert characterization and deft handling of its unconventional and complex plot. Recommended for those who like their mysteries fast, unusual, and on the tough and sexy side.

Almost as good is *The Golden Goose* (1951), another unconventional work—in this case featuring a private eye who quits the business and doesn't feel any worse about doing so "than you'd feel about getting fired off a garbage truck." Mahannah's other three mysteries are also worth seeking out: *The Yellow Hearse* (1950), *Stopover for Murder* (1953), and *The Golden Widow* (1956). One has the feeling that if Mahannah had continued to write crime fiction—his professional career lasted a scant eight years—he would have become very good indeed.

(*B.P.*)

*Maling, Arthur. *The Rheingold Route.* New York: Harper, 1979. (T)

The protagonists of Arthur Maling's novels are generally ordinary men who unwittingly become caught up in crime and must then attempt to extricate themselves. They are neither noble nor wholly good, and their crimes are often motivated by weakness or greed; but Maling develops his characters at considerable psychological depth, and in exposing them in all their foibles, he enlists the reader's sympathy for them. Maling makes us care about his people, and because we want things to work out for them, our level of interest and tension is sustained while the action unfolds.

The hero of this Edgar-winning novel is John Cochran, an American living in London and working as a smuggler of British currency. Early on we learn that there is a tragedy in his recent past, someone he loved has died; that he took his job because he could not get a work permit in England nor return to the United States; that he is lonely and wishes "there were someone he could talk things over with." And almost from the first we begin to like this man and want to know more about him.

Cochran receives a telephone call from a man claiming to have been referred to him by John's boss, David Arlen. Cochran is reasonably sure Arlen would not give his name to anyone, but he cannot check because Arlen is out of the country. He agrees to meet the caller, and soon finds himself being blackmailed into moving £350,000 to Geneva. The man behind the scheme, Arlen's lawyer, Michael Garwood, says he will have Cochran arrested the next time he tries to leave the country unless he performs this courier service, and Cochran feels he has no choice but to agree.

Garwood is not as aboveboard as he seems, however. We soon see him enlisting a second man, a psychopath named Kenneth O'Rourke, to intercept Cochran in Europe and take the money. We follow O'Rourke as he makes a trial run and goes about his preparations, and we realize what a truly dangerous adversary he is. In the meantime, Cochran is going about his everyday life, seeing friends, being "fixed up" with a visiting American woman. And it is this growing relationship with the woman, Ruth Watts, and Cochran's newfound ability to reveal his emotions and his past to someone, that in turn make him a strong, dangerous adversary himself.

The Rheingold Route is a multifaceted novel that sweeps us from London to Amsterdam to Switzerland and has a most satisfying ending. Among Maling's other engrossing suspense novels are *Decoy* (1969), *The Snowman* (1973), and *Dingdong* (1974). A series character, Wall Street research analyst Brock Potter, is featured in some of his later books, including *Ripoff* (1976) and *The Koberg Link* (1979).

(*M.M.*)

Mann, Jessica. *No Man's Island.* New York: Doubleday Crime Club, 1983. (E)

Jessica Mann has stated that she thinks of herself "not as a mystery writer, but as a novelist whose characters get involved in crime." This novel, then, is somewhat of a departure from that philosophy, since in it she presents a professional in the world of crime: Tamara Hoyland, "an archaeologist, a civil servant—and a spy." Tamara was recruited into the British Secret Service after the death in the line of duty of her lover, Ian Barnes, and now she is assigned to the bleak island of Forway, off the Cornish coast, where Barnes's widowed mother lives. Oil has been discovered on Forway, making it valuable to a number of governments and private organizations; but there are rumors that Forway is about to declare its independence from Great Britain. Tamara is to confirm or deny these rumors.

Tamara dislikes Forway, finding it "gaunt, bleak, inhospitable, and lonely." The island has a fairly unpleasant history involving piracy and slavery, and now is peopled with a few inbred families with such last names as Yetts, Aragon, Lisle, Windows, and Foggo and first names running to Godfrey, Magnus, Kirstie, and Anona. The Barnes family is represented only by Ian's mother, Freya, with whom Tamara stays. She arrives well equipped for a job of espionage, with archaeologist's gear for her cover, and devices such as a miniature camera, eavesdropping kits, and a razor-blade weapon for her real work. But she soon finds these unnecessary; the job ahead of her is one of detection.

Freya Barnes and her old friend Sir Selwyn Paull keep it no secret that they are conspiring to declare Forway's independence; and for a while this looks like some sort of whim of a couple of old people with too much time on their hands. But then the Coast Guard station burns and there are indications that someone wants to give the impression the Forway Liberation Front is responsible. Tamara and Selwyn Paull's son, Magnus, a writer, are almost killed after someone tampers with Freya's van. And finally murder is done, and Tamara must find the person responsible not only for this killing but also for a pair of old murders.

Told from both the third-person viewpoint of Tamara and the first-person viewpoint of Magnus Paull, this is a slow-paced but suspenseful tale, as moody as the atmosphere of Forway itself. Tamara is an interesting character, and it is unfortunate the author chose to introduce her as she wraps up another case—by setting off a bomb that kills two men, one of whom she has been living with. Her reactions in this first chapter are too cold and hard for the woman who emerges later in the story; it is as if Mann were trying to prove to her reader that Tamara really is a spy. And proof is what we don't need; she proves herself admirably during her adventure on Forway.

Mann is the author of a number of other suspense novels, among them *A Charitable End* (1971), which concerns a group of Edinburgh volunteer workers; *The Only Security* (1973), set in a Cornish university town; and *The Sting of Death* (1978), which deals with an ecological conflict on the south Cornish coast. She has also written a nonfiction study of women mystery writers, *Deadlier than the Male* (1981).

(*M.M.*)

Mantell, Laurie. *Murder and Chips.* New York: Walker, 1980. (PP)

This is Laurie Mantell's third novel featuring Detective Sergeant Steven Arrow and Inspector Jonas Peacock of the Lower Hutt, New Zealand, Criminal Investigation Branch. Mantell writes well, and her meticulous use of accurate police procedure gives her stories an air of authenticity. She depicts New Zealand as an old-fashioned world decades behind the United States: Women are usually found shopping or in the kitchen, and always in their place; motorcycle gangs are a serious menace; abuse of alcohol is much more prevalent than abuse of drugs; sex is still more or less a private topic.

As *Murder and Chips* opens, an inquest has brought Steven Arrow to Nelson, a town on the South Island across Cook Strait. A young man named Cody Pike has been found dead in a wood-chip pile at a lumber mill, apparently the victim of suffocation. But the death has its odd aspects: Pike was dressed in the uniform of an employee of a local hotel, although he did not work there; and someone saw a man dressed in such a fashion being grabbed by two other people in the hotel parking lot. Despite these oddities, a verdict of accidental death is declared, and although he still has his reservations, Steven's attention is momentarily diverted upon his return to Lower

Hutt by the murder of a shopkeeper. Carter Ancell was bludgeoned to death in his gift shop at the Wainui Mall; only costume jewelry was taken. Is the murderer the burglar known as Cheapskate, who takes only jewelry of low value? Or is he Ancell's nephew Luke, with whom he reportedly quarreled?

Steven and his superior, Jonas Peacock, proceed with their careful investigation—and Steven begins to wonder if this case isn't connected somehow with the death at the chip pile. There are a number of coincidences, but coincidences are common in New Zealand, a small country where rumor and innuendo travel swiftly from one outpost to another.

This is a well-plotted novel, and if there are indeed a great many coincidences, Mantell is skilled enough to make them seem reasonable. Steven Arrow; his wife, Kylie; and the others in the Criminal Investigation Branch are a likable group of characters; one wishes that Mantell would give us a more intimate look into their lives.

The previous Arrow/Peacock mysteries are *Murder in Fancy Dress* and *Murder or Three,* both published here in 1981.

(*M.M.*)

*March, William. *The Bad Seed.* New York: Holt, 1954. (PS)

A modern masterpiece of suspense, *The Bad Seed* has tended to be overshadowed by the popular play and movie it spawned. Playwright Maxwell Anderson was remarkably faithful to William March's novel, however, and those who enjoyed the adaptations will find the original novel possesses all of their virtues, and more.

Christine Penmark, her husband away on an extended business trip, is concerned when her eight-year-old daughter, Rhoda, seems to have been involved in the drowning of another child at the Fern Grammar School picnic. The dead boy had won a penmanship medal that Rhoda believed rightfully hers. Rhoda, an outwardly proper, precocious, self-sufficient little girl, has before shown a tendency toward "unending acquisitiveness"—she was in fact expelled from an earlier school for theft. Further disturbing her mother is Rhoda's apparent lack of a "capacity for affection," as a school psychiatrist put it.

Christine soon begins playing reluctant detective, exploring the drowning incident as well as previous incidents of violence to which Rhoda was connected, and, finally, most frighteningly, Christine's own beginnings, her own fears that she was adopted and that her heritage may be one of evil. At the same time, Rhoda is teased by Leroy, the janitor of their apartment building; childlike Leroy has a perverse fascination with the little girl and taunts her, accusing her of killing the little boy. Unfortunately for Leroy, Rhoda takes his teasing seriously, and soon Christine Penmark must face the reality of the "bad seed" she bore.

The Bad Seed is an exquisitely written book, its complex yet crystal-clear sentences pulling the reader down into the spiraling horror of Christine Penmark's no-win situation. March's imagery is vivid and precise ("She was a big, dull woman with the empty face of a baby," "despair and guilt were nibbling like mice at her mind") and even his minor characters are fully realized. Little violence occurs on stage, yet the very tranquillity and civility of the novel's upper-middle-class setting serves as an ironic counterpoint to the barbarity of Rhoda's deeds. March has at times been condemned for positing the notion that evil can be inherited; but the author's concern here is not the age-old question of environment versus heredity in the shaping of criminal minds: it is in the unanswerable riddle of evil itself, and its place in God's universe.

Mainstream novelist March died in 1954, the year of the publication of *The Bad Seed,* his only novel in the suspense field; he did not live to see the success of the play and movie versions of his book. March has been called (by Alistair Cooke) "the unrecognized genius of our time," and a critical re-appraisal of the body of his work seems overdue.

The movie version (1956) featured a number of players from the original Broadway cast, including Nancy Kelly, Patty McCormack, and Eileen Heckart in definitive portrayals of Christine, Rhoda, and Mrs. Daigle, the drowned boy's mother.

(M.A.C.)

Markham, Virgil. *The Devil Drives.* New York: Knopf, 1932. (W)

The Devil Drives is an offbeat and highly individual novel by a writer who, it would seem, must have had some familiarity with the work of that master American zany Harry Stephen Keeler (q.v.). It is somewhat reminiscent of Keeler's *Amazing Web* (1929), but is shorter, slighter, less ambitious, more straightforward, and, though complex enough in plot, lacks the unbelievable convolutions and ramifications of the Keeler work. The authors do share the ability to propel their narratives forward in such a manner that readers will keep turning pages breathlessly in order to discover what astounding plot development will next occur, and what outrageous coincidence will help to resolve (or amplify) the current situation.

The Markham novel concerns George Lawson Peters, the warden of Franklin Penitentiary in New Jersey, who deserts his post to seek a lost treasure left by an adventurer nicknamed "Dubrosky" for a girl named Philadelphia Boston. On his odyssey, Peters meets a gangster with a heart of garbage; a repulsive blackmailer who exacts no tribute from his victims; the blackmailer's unhappy wife; her friend the eccentric countess; and Detective Veen, who reads mysteries.

At the two-thirds point in the narrative, Peters encounters a honey of a locked-room problem. The door is locked and bolted, and the two windows are locked—all from the inside. The floor and ceiling are ungimmicked, and the fireplace and chimney show no signs of entrance or egress. The victim met his death by drowning. The author's unique solution is even more bizarre than the problem he has propounded.

The locked-room situation and many strands of the plot are finally resolved by a few well-placed Keeleresque coincidences. But Markham has still done an ingenious job of deceptive clue-planting that is worthy of Christie, Carr, or Queen; and his unexpected and grimly ironic finale is worthy of Francis Iles or Richard Hull (qq.v.).

Markham's other novels include *Death in the Dusk* (1928), *The Black Door* (1930), and *Inspector Rusby's Finale* (1933). The last-named title has an irresistable premise: A Scotland Yard inspector, spending a weekend at a crowded country house, wakes up the morning after his arrival to find that the hostess and guests have vanished and he is alone—except for the dead body of a perfect stranger. The ending, however, as Barzun and Taylor have noted, is a bit hard to swallow.

(*C.S.*)

Marlowe, Dan J. *The Name of the Game Is Death.* Greenwich, Conn.: Fawcett Gold Medal, 1962. (O/T)

The Name of the Game Is Death is Dan J. Marlowe's best book, which means that it's just about as good as original paperback writing can get. It's hard, fast, tough, and terse, with an opening scene so strong that you'll wonder if Marlowe can possibly come up with an ending to top it. But he does, and it's good enough to jolt you out of your chair.

Marlowe's narrator, Earl Drake, is a bank robber and a cold-blooded killer—they don't come any colder—who works part-time as a tree surgeon. He hates most people and loves animals. When he's wounded in a robbery in Phoenix, he sends his partner on ahead with the money and instructions to mail some of it to him each week. At first the money arrives on schedule; then it doesn't. Recovered, Drake starts for Florida to find out why. Not everyone between Arizona and Florida lives until Drake finishes his trip. In Florida, Drake gets work as a tree surgeon, makes friends with several of the locals, and even appears to be falling in love. But always in the back of his mind is his desire to find his money and his partner. He does, shortly before the (literally) explosive climax. Drake's story is strong stuff, and it moves with the speed of a bullet from his Colt Woodsman. Take a deep breath when you plunge into the story; you might not have time for another before it's finished.

Warning: Earl Drake was eventually turned into a series character, a sort of secret agent. As a result, in 1972 Fawcett issued a revised edition of *The Name of the Game Is Death* in which Drake was made a bit more socially acceptable. Find and read the original if possible.

Equally exciting books by Marlowe are *The Vengeance Man* (1966) and *Four for the Money* (1966).

(*B.C.*)

*Marlowe, Derek. *Somebody's Sister.* New York: Viking, 1974. (PI)

Somebody's Sister is an attempt by a British author to write an American hard-boiled private-eye novel—and quite a successful attempt it is. The investigator, Walter Brackett, is a fifty-three-year-old Englishman operating in San Francisco. His wife has died, his business has nearly gone to ruin, and he has an emotionally crippled partner, Harry Kemble, in a rest home. Brackett visits Kemble every Saturday; otherwise he sits in his office above Fatty's Delicatessen waiting for clients who seldom materialize. Brackett is likable and sympathetic but—in the tradition of the hard-boiled novel—he keeps his reader at a distance.

On this particular Saturday, Brackett returns from his usual visit to find the police waiting: A young girl has been killed in an auto accident on the Golden Gate Bridge, and Brackett's card was in the car; the police want him to make an identification. At the morgue, Brackett finds the girl is Mary Malewski, a prospective client who wanted him to find her father; Brackett never investigated for her, however, because she suddenly ran out of his office. Also at the morgue Brackett encounters a man named Loomis who apparently witnessed the accident. Later Loomis leaves a message asking Brackett to visit him at his Sausalito motel. Brackett goes, but before he can talk to the man, Loomis is fatally shot in the car wash across the street.

The police tell Brackett to stay out of the investigation; Loomis was a drug informer, involved in something too big for a down-at-the-heels private eye. But Brackett can't stay out of it; he senses Loomis's death and that of the girl are connected. So he digs—in the lowly dives of North Beach where the girl lived; in an expensive home in Pacific Heights where her aging lover resides—until he finally must face a personally shattering truth.

The book is well plotted, and just when the reader thinks he knows what is really going on, he encounters another unexpected twist. In fact, its only faults are minor: a clue that could have been better placed; geographical discrepancies that are more likely to bother San Franciscans than anyone else; the San Francisco police having jurisdiction over a crime which happens in Sausalito across the Bay. (The novel is dedicated to newspaper columnist Herb Caen, who is often referred to as "Mr. San Francisco"; perhaps if Marlowe had consulted Caen, these discrepancies wouldn't have happened.) Unfortunately Marlowe—who has written a number of other suspense novels, including the well-received *Dandy in Aspic* (1966)—chose not to make Brackett a series character.

(*M.M.*)

Marlowe, Stephen. *Trouble Is My Name.* Greenwich, Conn.: Fawcett Gold Medal. 1957 (O/PI)

Most of Stephen Marlowe's paperback originals feature Chester Drum, a former FBI agent turned private investigator, who operates out of Washington, D.C. Most of Drum's cases are not standard private-eye fare, however. They generally take him to some other part of the world, and they often are as much related to espionage as to other crimes.

In *Trouble Is My Name,* for example, Drum is hired to find a missing man, a man who, as it happens, is about to be nominated for the vice-presidency. The trail leads to Germany, where Drum discovers that the man was involved in the disappearance of 800,000 marks' worth of O.S.S. gold during World War II. The missing gold turns out to be a powerful lure for others as well, including Siegmund and Sieglinde, the Streicher twins, who are, as they liked to say in the Fifties, "more than brother and sister to one another." There is also the son of a Nazi war criminal and the daughter of a major who disappeared along with the gold. She does not want the money; she wants to know what happened to her father.

There is very little detection in the story, but it makes for an interesting chase across cold-war Germany. Marlowe's backgrounds are always convincing, and he tells his story very well, with just the right amount of muted violence and sex. The ending is particularly bloody, but Marlowe never overstates, and he manages to tie all the loose ends together satisfactorily.

Marlowe is a consistent and reliable writer; nearly any book in the Drum series is worth considering. Among the better ones are *Violence Is My Business* (1958), *Terror Is My Trade* (1958), *Drum Beat—Dominique* (1965), and *Francesca* (1963). And of course, no one should miss Marlowe's 1959 collaboration with Richard S. Prather (q.v.), *Double in Trouble,* featuring Drum and Shell Scott in a case that defies description.

(*B.C.*)

Marlowe, Stephen. *The Summit.* New York: Bernard Geis, 1970. (E)

Stephen Marlowe has actually had three careers. The first, under his real name, Milton Lesser, was as a well-known science-fiction writer in the early 1950s. Then he began writing mystery and detective fiction, much of it for Gold Medal Books. And in the latter part of the 1960s, he began writing hardcover suspense novels aimed at the best-seller lists. One of these is *The Summit,* which deals with high-level espionage.

The premise is that the president of the United States has gone to Switzerland to meet with the Soviet premier. The Soviet army is poised on the Yugoslavian border, prepared to invade. The Soviet leader, a man known to be sympathetic to the United States, possesses information that would be quite damaging to his country should he choose to release it. Then he disappears. The CIA wants to find him and help him defect. The KGB wants to find him and get him back to Russia so that he can be declared mentally incompetent. Failing that, the KGB is quite willing to kill him.

The ins and outs of the political situation, the chase for the premier, and the shifting loyalties of some of the characters all make this an interesting and entertaining book. It is fast-paced, and the characters are convincing. Perhaps the tone of the book is a bit optimistic for these cynical times, but the twists and turns of the plot are certain to keep you reading.

The Search for Bruno Heidler (1966) and *Come Over, Red Rover* (1968) are equally entertaining novels of suspense.

(*B.C.*)

Marquand, John P. *Mr. Moto Is So Sorry.* Boston: Little, Brown, 1938. (CS/E)

Literary snobbery is an old, sad malady, one that has infected a smallish percentage of writers ever since the first Cro-Magnon chiseled in stone what he considered to be an immortal hieroglyphic. But the gods don't seem overly tolerant of this malady; they have a way of making fools of those who contract it. Sir Arthur Conan Doyle, for instance, grew to hate Sherlock Holmes and sought to kill him off so people wouldn't keep pestering him to write more Holmes stories; he thought his historical novels and treatises on spiritualism were his true genius, and that those were what he would be remembered for.

John P. Marquand was another writer stricken with literary snobbery. He once said that his six Mr. Moto novels were his "literary disgrace," and he couldn't understand why anyone would want to read such commercial trash. What Marquand failed to realize is that Mr. I. A. Moto, the funny little Japanese with the ingratiating manner and the shrewd, shrewd brain, is *by accident* a much more interesting and enduring creation than the likes of H. M. Pulham, Esquire, or the late George Apley. Moto captured the imaginations of hundreds of thousands of readers in the Thirties, and has done likewise with the two generations of readers since. He is larger than life; like Holmes and Charlie Chan and the other Great Detectives, he has transcended his material and become a legend.

Mr. Moto Is So Sorry is arguably the best of his five adventures published between 1935 and 1942, all of which were first serialized in *The Saturday Evening Post.* It follows the formula of the others in the series: American boy of somewhat dubious character meets attractive girl in exotic foreign locale; one or both are somehow mixed up in international espionage; enter Moto, an adversary or ally or (in this particular case) both; there is adventure, peril, heroics on the American boy's part to redeem himself in the eyes of the girl and the reader; and Mr. Moto in the last analysis proves that the East is often smarter and cleverer than the West. Contrary to popular opinion (fomented by the eight Mr. Moto B films starring Peter Lorre, made between 1937 and 1939), Moto is not a detective per se; he is an agent of the Japanese government, a servant first and foremost of his country and his emperor.

The American boy in this case is Calvin Gates, who is on his way to an archaeological dig in Ghuru Nor, Mongolia. The American girl, Miss Dillaway, an artist who makes renderings of archaeological finds, is also on her way to the dig. The international espionage is Russia-versus-Japan intrigue, it being 1937, the Japanese having invaded and taken over Manchuria, and the world being on the brink of global war. At the center of this intrigue is a mysterious cigarette case with an engraving of a bunch of birds; at first Moto seems to want it, then he seems to want either Gates or Miss Dillaway to deliver it to a trader named Holtz in Mongolia. Further complications include a Russian courier; an Australian soldier of fortune named Hamby; an incident-packed train trip across Manchuria; and an Oriental despot, the prince of Ghuru Nor. The blurb on the 1977 Popular Library reprint edition says that all of this is "but part of the maze of mystery and menace that Mr. Moto had to explore with excruciating care, as corpses littered the death-dark park, and murder waited around every blood-slick turn." Marquand would have cringed if he'd been alive to read that. Mr. Moto would only have smiled inscrutably.

All in all, *Mr. Moto Is So Sorry* isn't a bad read, despite some dialogue that doesn't ring true (no doubt because it was carelessly and hurriedly written) and a vague contempt for material and audience that clouds the whole. Marquand's portrait of Manchuria and Mongolia during the late Thirties is vivid and compelling.

The other four early Moto novels are *No Hero* (1935), which has also been published as *Your Turn, Mr. Moto; Thank You, Mr. Moto* (1936); *Think Fast, Mr. Moto* (1937); and *Last Laugh, Mr. Moto* (1942). These are set, respectively, in Singapore, Peking, Honolulu, and on an obscure Caribbean island. The last, longest, and best overall of the series is *Stopover: Tokyo* (1957), in which Mr. Moto and an American Intelligence agent named Jack Rhyce join forces to break up a Communist espionage and terrorist ring operating in Tokyo. This was made into a mediocre 1957 film with Robert Wagner and Edmond O'Brien—and Mr. Moto excluded completely!

(*B.P.*)

Marric, J. J. *Gideon's Fire.* New York: Harper, 1961. (PP)

John Creasey's (q.v.) work under the J. J. Marric pseudonym is his most critically acclaimed, and this novel about Commander George Gideon of Scotland Yard won the MWA Edgar for Best Novel of 1961. Gideon is by far Creasey's most finely delineated character, and these procedurals, which follow the pattern of shifting back and forth between a number of cases, convey a clear impression of what the life of a Scotland Yard detective must really be like.

In *Gideon's Fire,* a series of slum-building fires are happening with such frequency that Gideon and his superiors suspect a dedicated arsonist, a madman who might yet burn more and more blocks of buildings. The buildings are ones that the government has been promising to renovate ever since World War II and are still standing in a state of disrepair, crammed with the poor and the derelict. They ought to be destroyed, on that everyone agrees—but not with these helpless people in them. Gideon wonders if the arsonist is trying to get a political message across—or is he just a lunatic on the loose?

This is just one of the puzzles Gideon must solve. In addition, a brutal rapist is on the prowl; a hateful husband is killing his girlfriends one by one; and a prominent businessman has run a massive stock fraud and must be prevented from fleeing the country.

Gideon and his crew perform admirably as usual, and there is a full cast of the memorable characters that Creasey—no matter what his pseudonym—creates so well. This is an excellent series, the epitome of the Scotland Yard procedural.

Other recommended books featuring George Gideon include *Gideon's Day* (his first adventure, 1955), *Gideon's Ride* (1963), and *Gideon's Fog* (1974). Creasey adapted his second novel in the series, *Gideon's Week* (1956), as a play titled *Gideon's Fear,* which was produced in 1960.

(*K.K.H.*)

*Marsh, Ngaio. *Death of a Fool.* Boston: Little, Brown, 1956. (CS/W)

Ngaio Marsh's first love in life was the theater, first as an actress in her native New Zealand in the 1920s and then as a theatrical producer and director of Pirandello and Shakespeare. She received an honorary D. Litt. degree from the University of Canterbury in New Zealand in 1956, and in

1967 the university named its new theater after her. In 1966 she was made a Dame Commander of the Order of the British Empire by Queen Elizabeth II.

It was while living in London in 1931 that Marsh decided to write a detective novel. *A Man Lay Dead* was begun that same rainy afternoon when the idea first struck, and was published three years later. It was not until her sixth novel, *Artists in Crime* (1938), that her books began to be published in the United States. By the late 1930s, Marsh's reputation was secure as one of the great names—along with Christie, Sayers, and Allingham (qq.v.)—in the Golden Age of detective fiction. The attractions of Marsh's work are well stated in a comment by the American writer Dorothy Cameron Disney: "In her ironic and witty hands the mystery novel can be civilized literature. [Her books have] style and atmosphere, humor which is never forced, characters who are fascinating and completely credible." One such character is the unobtrusively aristocratic Detective Inspector (later Superintendent) Roderick Alleyn of the CID, Scotland Yard, who appears in all of Marsh's detective novels. Combining charm, intelligence, thorough professionalism, and a talent for crime detection, Alleyn is both a commanding and an appealing figure.

In *Death of a Fool,* Alleyn and his colleagues, Inspector Fox and Sergeants Bailey and Thompson, are called to the tiny, snowbound hamlet of South Mardian and the nearby Mardian Castle. Here, every year on the Wednesday after the winter solstice, eight local inhabitants re-create *The Mardian Morris of the Five Sons,* a morris sword dance and play whose roots stretch hundreds of years into the past. ("It is probably the survival of an ancient fertility rite and combines, in one ceremony, the features of a number of other seasonal dances and mumming plays.") At dusk on a bitterly cold December evening, in the courtyard of Mardian Castle, the performance takes place before a small audience of local people. The pivotal role of the Fool is played by William Andersen, known as "the Guiser," nearing ninety but still working as the local blacksmith. His five sons dance the roles of the Five Sons in the play. Midway through the play there is a mimed execution, and the Fool ducks down behind the Mardian dolmen to await his resurrection a few minutes later. But this time there is no resurrection. Instead, the decapitated body of the Guiser is found behind the dolmen, having apparently been beheaded while his hiding place and the other performers were in full view of the audience.

There is no shortage of motives. There have been long-standing antagonisms among the brothers and between the brothers and their father. The Guiser was bitterly opposed to the romance between his granddaughter and the son of the local rector. And the old man was apparently a miser, squirreling away money in dozens of hiding places in the smithy. Alleyn must untangle these crosscurrents, and must also explain the odd behavior of Simon

Begg, operator of a nearby service station, and Mrs. Anna Bünz, an avid folklorist who has invaded South Mardian in order to watch the Mardian morris. But the biggest problem of all is to explain how the murder was committed. It takes a restaging of the sword dance before all of the pieces fall into place and the culprit is caught.

The integration of a clever mystery plot with the vivid and unusual folkloric background make this a memorable book.

(*R.E.B.*)

Marsh, Ngaio. *Light Thickens.* Boston: Little, Brown, 1982. (CS/W)

It is no surprise that many of Ngaio Marsh's detective novels have theatrical settings. In *Killer Dolphin* (1966), director Peregrine Jay reopened the long-abandoned Dolphin Theatre in London to present a play based on the life of Shakespeare. The production was dogged by ill luck, culminating in theft and murder, both of which were solved by Roderick Alleyn.

Now, in *Light Thickens,* we are present at another of Peregrine Jay's productions at the Dolphin. This time it is a staging of *Macbeth.* The normal difficulties of such an undertaking are augmented by the special attention being given to the sword fights and to the scenes involving the three witches. The antics of a touchy and eccentric cast, the usual superstitions associated with "the Scots play," and the attentions of a malicious and macabre practical joker add to the problems. In the first half of the book we are taken through the four weeks of rehearsals and through opening night. A couple of weeks later, Jay has brought his sons to see the play. By coincidence, Chief Superintendent Roderick Alleyn is also in the audience that evening. When, at the conclusion of the play, Macduff comes on stage followed by an attendant bearing the head of Macbeth impaled on a claymore, Jay and Alleyn are the first to realize that it is not an artificial head. It is a real one.

Alleyn must, as usual, untangle the romantic involvements and emotional crosscurrents among the cast and crew, weed through alibis, and interpret the physical evidence before closing in on the murderer.

From the detective-story point of view, the book is not among Marsh's best. The detection is weak, the coincidences too numerous, the motivation unconvincing. But the book is beautifully written. Marsh's deep knowledge of, and feeling for, the theater, and for Shakespeare's works in particular, shine through the text. The progress of the production, from first reading to final ensemble, is lovingly described, and the account of the performance itself is so vivid that you would swear it was taking place before your eyes. As the summing-up of a combined life in mystery fiction and the theater, this last of Ngaio Marsh's thirty-two detective novels is a worthy testament.

(*R.E.B.*)

*Marsh, Ngaio. *Overture to Death.* New York: Furman, 1939. (CS/W)

Trouble is brewing in the tiny Vale of Pen Cuckoo in the Dorset countryside. The Vale boasts not one but two frustrated, middle-aged spinsters, Miss Eleanor Prentice and Miss Idris Campanula. Miss Prentice, a relatively recent arrival and the cousin of widowed Squire Jernigham, is long-suffering and viper-tongued. Miss Campanula is an overbearing Tartar. The two women are uneasy friends, united in "good works" and spreading gossip, but rivals for the attention of the local rector, Mr. Copeland. Both women disapprove of the attachment between the squire's son, Henry, and the rector's daughter, Dinah. And everyone disapproves of the affair between the local medical man, Dr. Templett, and the exquisite but questionable Mrs. Ross, another recent arrival. It is precisely this group of eight people who get together to put on an amateur theatrical production to raise funds for the local parish house.

It seems impossible that the group could work together long enough to prepare the entertainment, and indeed there are storms and tantrums aplenty along the way, but at last the evening of the performance arrives. One of the spinsters has volunteered to play Ethelbert Nevin's *Venetian Suite* on the piano as an overture, but at the last minute an infected finger prevents her from playing. Her friend and rival steps in, offering Rachmaninoff's Prelude in C-Sharp Minor. The first three ominous chords of the prelude are followed by a sharp explosion, and the pianist "fell forward. Her face slid down the sheet of music, which stuck to it. Very slowly and stealthily she slipped sideways to the keys of the piano, striking a final discord in the bass. She remained there, quite still, in a posture that seemed to parody the antics of an affected virtuoso. She was dead."

As soon as it becomes clear that murder is involved, and that the local police surgeon (Dr. Templett) and the acting chief constable of the county (Squire Jernigham) are among the suspects, Scotland Yard is called in. Detective Inspector Alleyn and his team arrive that same night. Among the first things they must decide is which of the two women was the intended victim. The movements of all the suspects must be tracked, and reluctant witnesses must be persuaded to talk. Finally, such disparate clues as a squeaking gate, an anonymous letter, a child's water pistol, five potted aspidistras, and half a Spanish onion must find their places in the pattern.

The characters are amusing, or amusingly awful, and presented in fully rounded portraits. The clues are fairly planted so that an attentive reader can anticipate the reasoning of Alleyn and his colleagues. This is a superior example of the literate whodunit.

Other aspects of Marsh's talents, and of Alleyn's as well, are displayed in other novels. *Death in a White Tie* (1938) shows Alleyn at work in London society. *Death of a Peer* (1940) introduces the Lampreys, a memorable family of eccentrics who reappear in later books. In *Died in the Wool* (1945), Alleyn is in New Zealand during World War II. In *Final Curtain* (1947), Alleyn's wife, the painter Agatha Troy, takes center stage, as she is commissioned to paint a portrait of the Shakespearean actor Sir Henry Tancred, and runs into a particularly nasty murder. Troy (as Alleyn calls her) is also very much present in *Clutch of Constables* (1969).

Incidentally, the fact that two of the three books reviewed here involve beheading is sheer coincidence. Marsh was known for her gruesome murder methods, but she seldom repeated herself.

(*R.E.B.*)

*Marshall, William. *Sci Fi.* New York: Holt, 1981. (PP/C)

William Marshall's "Yellowthread Street" mysteries—Yellowthread Street being a police precinct station in the mythical Hong Bay section of Hong Kong—are the weirdest, the wildest, and the funniest police procedurals ever written. What makes the series so unique are Marshall's thoroughly off-the-wall sense of humor, offbeat writing style (lots of italicized and capitalized words, among other eccentricities), pyrotechnic plots, and any number of thrill-a-minute scenes.

Sci Fi has all of these in abundance, the result being a sort of updated and R-rated *Marx Brothers in the Orient* in which a ray-gun-wielding individual known as the Spaceman begins incinerating people and property in and around the Empress of India Hotel, the site of the All-Asia Science Fiction and Horror Movie Congress. The ray gun is really a flamethrower and there is plenty of method to the Spaceman's apparent madness: He is after $1 million in cash on display as a publicity stunt in the hotel's lobby. Or is he? Some of the plot and counterplot involves a character called the Green Slime; some of it involves horror movies, science-fiction movies, big-job movies, psycho movies, godfather movies, and just about every other kind of movie you've ever seen; and all of it is cleverly and effectively worked out, with a couple of genuine surprises along the way. There is even a nifty subplot about a mysteriously appearing and disappearing Volkswagen van at a downtown carpark.

Marshall's protagonists, the men of the Yellowthread Street station—Detective Chief Inspector Harry Feiffer, Senior Detective Inspector Christopher O'Yee, and Detective Inspectors Spencer and Auden—are delightful and utterly zany characters. There are plenty of action, bodies galore, and a spectacular sock finish. Great crime fiction this may not be, but it sure is fun while it lasts. Sort of like *The Brain Eaters* or one of the other sf/horror films it pays homage to.

Just as wild and wonderful are the other books in the series, especially

The Hatchet Man (1975), about which *Publishers Weekly* said, "If the Monty Python gang decide to do a Kojak episode and set it in Hong Kong, the working script might read something like this novel"; *Thin Air* (1977), which begins with the wholesale murder of fifty-seven passengers on board a Tokyo charter flight, the work of a mad extortionist calling himself the Principal; *Skulduggery* (1979), which asks the question "What do you do when you come across a raft bearing a man's skeleton, ankles roped together; one dead fish; a mound of sweet potatoes; a set of false teeth; and a ten-inch length of blue-painted drainpipe?"; *Perfect End* (1982), which is probably the most dazzling Yellowthread Street novel, dealing as it does with a raging typhoon, the gruesome murders of six officers from a nearby precinct, a maze of Chinese mythological symbolism, and O'Yee's obsession with emulating the great American pioneer spirit; and *The Far Away Man* (1984), which involves the hunt for an apparent psychotic killer and Spencer and Auden's efforts to track down the source of agonized screams that start at the top of a high-rise apartment building and plummet—disembodied—to the bottom.

(*B.P.*)

Marsten, Richard. *Even the Wicked.* New York: Permabooks, 1958. (Also published as by Ed McBain.) (O/T)

Evan Hunter (q.v.) published several paperback-original suspense novels in the 1950s as by Richard Marsten, all of which have since been reprinted under his much better-known pseudonym Ed McBain (q.v.). Although none of these early works lives up to the highest standards of his later work in the field, all are entertaining and hold up well. Readers looking for an hour or two of pleasant escapist reading of the realistic softcover-original style of the period won't be disappointed.

Even the Wicked is one of the best of the Marsten titles (and also the shortest at not much more than novella length). With his young daughter, Penny, widower Zachary Blake returns to the island of Martha's Vineyard where his wife, Mary, drowned the previous summer in an apparent swimming accident. But a vacation isn't Zach's purpose this time; he is convinced Mary was murdered for some unknown reason, even though an investigation following the incident appeared to rule out the possibility of foul play, and he wants to see what he can stir up now, a year after the fact. What he does stir up is another murder (this one with an Indian tomahawk) and a kidnapping, among other things that propel him into a deadly offshore confrontation with a group of desperate men. And the truth about Mary's death sets him free to pursue a new relationship with local newspaper reporter Enid Murphy.

This is a simple story, suspensefully told, with Hunter's usual fine characterization and peerless dialogue. The Martha's Vineyard background is also well evoked.

Noteworthy among the other Marsten titles are *Runaway Black* (1954), a strong tale of a Harlem youth on the run from a murder he didn't commit; *Vanishing Ladies* (1957), about a vacationing cop and his mysteriously missing fiancée; and *Big Man* (1959), the story of the rise and fall of a small-time hoodlum. Another notable softcover original by Hunter is *Don't Crowd Me* (1953), published under his own name; this one takes place in upstate New York (Lake George) and features sex and murder in an idyllic vacation setting.

(*B.P.*)

Martin, Robert. *To Have and to Kill.* New York: Dodd, Mead, 1960. (PI)

Jim Bennett, Robert Martin's Cleveland-based private eye, was born in the pulp magazines of the early 1940s; dozens of long novelettes featuring Bennett (and many more starring Martin's two other series characters, Dr. Clinton Shannon and a second PI, Lee Fiske) appeared in *Dime Detective* until that magazine's demise in 1953. Martin later revised and expanded several of these into novels published in the Fifties and Sixties—one such revision/expansion being *To Have and to Kill,* from a novelette called "A Shroud in Her Trousseau" (*Dime Detective,* June 1949).

In one sense the Jim Bennett series was typical pulp fare, in that it featured plenty of rough-and-tumble action; but in another sense it was atypical because it also placed strong emphasis on detection and on character development, especially that of Bennett himself. In an era when first-person private eyes were usually little more than boozing, wenching ciphers, Bennett comes off as a real human being: a man tough when he has to be, yet gentle, likable, and vulnerable—an earlier version of Thomas B. Dewey's (q.v.) "Mac."

The setting of *To Have and to Kill* is a fancy Lake Erie estate owned by Max Daney, heir to a soft-drink fortune and a pal of Bennett's. Bennett is on hand to act as best man at Daney's marriage to a scheming woman named Laura Reynolds. But a gunshot at the crack of dawn, and Bennett's discovery of a dead woman sprawled on Daney's private beach, puts an end to the wedding plans. With the help of his amenuensis and ladylove, Sandy Hollis, Bennett sorts through a maze of jealousy, hatred, and infidelity to get to the bottom of things.

This low-key novel is well-written and well-plotted, with Martin's usual excellent characterization, some nicely choreographed scenes, good suspense, and twice as much emotional content as ninety-five percent of the private-eye novels of its day. Well worth your time.

The best of Bennett's other full-length cases are *Tears for the Bride* (1954), *The Widow and the Web* (1954), *A Key to the Morgue* (1959), and *Bargain for Death* (a 1972 U.S. paperback reprint of a novel originally published in England in 1962). Dr. Clint Shannon is featured in a handful of books published under Martin's pseudonym of Lee Roberts; notable among these are *If the Shoe Fits* (1959) and *Death of a Ladies' Man* (1960). And Lee Fiske takes up the detecting cudgels in *Little Sister* (1952) and *The Case of the Missing Lovers* (1957), also published as by Lee Roberts.

(*B.P.*)

*Mason, A.E.W. *At the Villa Rose*. New York: Scribner's, 1910. (CS)

A.E.W. Mason was a fine and prolific writer whose career spanned the first half of the twentieth century. His experiences as civilian head of British Naval Intelligence during World War I provided rich material for his exciting novels of intrigue, and he traveled throughout the world gathering the background detail that makes his settings come so vividly alive. Mason's novels are well characterized, and he placed considerable emphasis on psychological motivations. *At the Villa Rose* is Mason's third novel and was quite innovative for its time—so much so that it has remained a minor classic in the field.

As the novel opens, there has been a murder in the French village of Aix-les-Bains. A wealthy older woman has been killed for her extensive collection of jewelry, and a younger woman—her companion—has disappeared and is suspected of complicity in the murder. It so happens that one Julius Ricardo is spending his annual vacation in Aix-les-Bains, and for a rather pompous, self-centered man, Ricardo has a wide circle of acquaintances. One such acquaintance is the young English scientist Harry Wethermill, fiancé of the suspected woman. Another is Inspector Hanaud, a well-known detective of the French Sûreté. As chance would have it, Hanaud is also vacationing in the area, and Wethermill implores Ricardo to approach him about the murder case.

Hanaud reluctantly agrees to become involved, and all three men travel to the Villa Rose to inspect the scene of the murder. It is here Hanaud discovers there is more to the case than meets the eye, and he launches an investigation that will take him as far afield as Geneva, Switzerland. Soon, however, the proper culprits are brought to justice. In fact, it happens so soon that we are only two-thirds of the way through the book. (The remaining one-third deals with details, motives, and methods of the crime.)

There is a Holmes-Watson feeling about the Hanaud-Ricardo relationship—one the competent professional, often keeping his own counsel; the other self-important, but often completely mystified by the goings-on. Hanaud himself is an intriguing character. Stout and good-humored, he frequently reacts to Ricardo's ill-advised comments with bursts of comedic sarcasm.

Other well-crafted books include *The House of the Arrow* (1928); *The Prisoner in the Opal* (1928), Mason's second-best-known novel; and *They Wouldn't Be Chessmen* (1935). Some of Mason's most accomplished Secret Service stories can be found in the 1935 collection *Dilemmas.*

(*N.D.*)

Mason, F. Van Wyck. *Himalayan Assignment.* New York: Doubleday, 1952. (A)

A prolific producer of mystery and adventure stories, F. Van Wyck Mason wrote numerous novels (quite popular in their time) featuring Hugh North, an Army Intelligence officer who travels the globe solving various mysteries, delivering various secrets, enduring various hardships, and engaging in various romantic interludes, all in the name of democracy and the American way of life. Mason's standard plot includes a number of murders and a puzzle that North must unravel. The two earliest North novels included a Watson-like character, Dr. Walter Allan, who was the narrator. Later (beginning with *The Fort Terror Murders,* 1931) Mason dropped this approach and began relying on straightforward third-person narration, mostly from North's viewpoint.

In *Himalayan Assignment,* the time is around 1950, and Tibet has recently been occupied by the Chinese. North's mission is to join a scientific expedition traveling to the Himalayan kingdom of Jonkhar. Once there, he will endeavor to persuade the powers that be to hold fast against the Communist tide, knowing full well the Communists would love to use Jonkhar as a stepping-stone into Nepal and India. The assignment is dangerously complicated by the time of year (the snows could start anytime), and by the fact that North's predecessor was killed on these same mountain passes.

After a treacherous and costly journey, North arrives in Jonkhar only to find two Communist contingents—one from China and one from Russia—also vying for control of the country. These contingents, like North, have mercenaries, of which the two most outstanding are a silver-haired but sensuous huntress and a General Sam Steel (an old, tough, resilient adversary of North's).

Many of Mason's other novels take place in the Orient, among the more interesting of which are *The Shanghai Bund Murders* (1933), *The Hongkong Airbase Murders* (1937), *The Singapore Exile Murders* (1939), and *Saigon Singer* (1946). Others have European, Middle Eastern, African, and Balkan settings. The Hugh North stories are definitely dated (both the writing style and dramatic content are overdone), but the sheer adventure and strong, detailed background material make them worth reading. Most of them, anyway. A few are hilariously awful; one is *The Cairo Garter Murders* (1938), which overflows with such lines as: "Thereupon North released a small mental spring which tilted gallons of cold caution over this young woman's appeal."

(*N.D./B.P.*)

Masterson, Whit. *The Gravy Train*. New York: Dodd, Mead, 1971. (Also published as *The Great Train Hijack*. New York: Pinnacle, 1976.) (T)

Whit Masterson was originally the pseudonym of Robert Wade and Bill Miller, a pair of San Diego writers who began collaborating in 1946 and over the next fifteen years turned out more than thirty novels as by Masterson, Wade Miller (q.v.), Dale Wilmer, and Will Daemer. Much of their output was in the tough vein—the Max Thursday private-eye novels as by Wade Miller, for instance—but they also wrote straight suspense fiction, offbeat crime novels, adventure stories, and humorous mysteries. When Miller died suddenly in 1961, Robert Wade continued to produce suspense novels under the Masterson name (and on two occasions under his own name). *The Gravy Train* is typical of Wade's solo fiction over the subsequent two decades: fast-moving, intricately plotted, with an unusual and well-realized background.

It begins with the escape of a professional guerrilla and former army colonel named Anthony Heaston from a Colombian prison, where he is serving a life sentence for his part in an attempted insurrection. Heaston and his small band of commandos, known as Heaston's Hellions, had fought valiantly in Vietnam, only to be court-martialed for executing a Vietnamese official—even though Heaston claimed he was acting under orders. The charges were eventually dropped, but Heaston's career was ruined, leading him to resign and take the mercenary route. His second-in-command, Bronko Shaman, is one of those who helped break him out of prison; another is a mystery man who calls himself Mr. Zeus.

Certain parties in Washington get wind of Heaston's escape and the additional facts that he has returned to the United States and disappeared. The job of finding out what he's up to falls to FBI agent Jake Duffy, one of the Bureau's new young whizzes with an unorthodox method of operation. By tracking Bronko Shaman, who has also disappeared, Duffy learns that Heaston and his six surviving Hellions have reunited in the purchase of an abandoned ranch in the California desert. The ranch, Tres Muertos, is an old Hollywood film site for westerns and still has several miles of connected railroad track, a steam locomotive, and some rolling stock. It soon becomes apparent to Duffy that Heaston and his men are training for a commando raid on a train—an old-fashioned Jesse James–style train robbery. But Duffy can't make his superiors believe it, at least not at first. What kind of super-valuable cargo travels by train these days? And who would bankroll such an audacious scheme? And why?

The answers to those questions are on the fantastic side—the Hollywood type of fantastic. (The loot is worth $50 million, for one thing.) Some of the characters are Hollywood types, too, including Duffy; he comes across more as a cavalier private eye or Bondian secret agent than an FBI operative (seduction count: two, and two others passed up, one because he has a headache). Much of the dialogue reads like a film script, and a number of scenes seem choreographed for cinematic effect. Despite all of that, however, *The Gravy Train* is a model of construction and jam-packed with suspense. And it has a whiplash climax with a nifty stinger in the end of the whip.

Also worth investigating are the collaborative Mastersons: *Badge of Evil* (1958; the basis for the classic Orson Welles film *Touch of Evil*) and *The Dark Fantastic* (1959); and such Masterson thrillers by Wade alone as *Play Like You're Dead* (1967) and *The Slow Gallows* (1979).

(*B.P.*)

Masur, Harold Q. *Bury Me Deep*. New York: Simon & Schuster, 1947.

Like most of Harold Q. Masur's mysteries, *Bury Me Deep* is narrated by lawyer Scott Jordan, a character Masur says in *Twentieth Century Crime and Mystery Writers* was "first conceived to fall somewhere between Perry Mason and Archie Goodwin." The author wanted to cross the complex plots of Gardner (q.v.) with the wry wit of Rex Stout (q.v.), and in many ways he succeeded.

Bury Me Deep has an opening typical of post–World War II hard-boiled novels: The narrator walks into his apartment to discover a beautiful blonde clad only in black panties and bra. A couple of hours later she is dead, and Jordan is drawn into a complicated case involving the legal technicalities of inheritance and divorce. There are enough motives and suspects to make the reader's head spin, but all the clues are present if one knows how and where to look for them. The story is well told and moves fast, and if Jordan is not quite Archie Goodwin, he can hold his own in most company. The ending is cleverly worked out and surprising.

Most of the Scott Jordan books hold up well when read at present, as recent reprints in the Raven House series demonstrate. Masur is an entertaining writer whose following would no doubt be larger had he produced a larger body of work. Other good books in the Jordan series include *So Rich, So Lovely, and So Dead* (1952), *The Big Money* (1954), *Send Another Hearse* (1960), and *The Name Is Jordan* (1962), the latter being a collection of very good short stories.

(*B.C.*)

Matheson, Richard. *Someone Is Bleeding*. New York: Lion, 1953. (O/PS)

While Richard Matheson would go on to become a major figure in the fields of fantasy and science fiction with such distinguished works as *I Am Legend* and his *Shock!* series of short-story collections, his first novel was solidly criminous—a book whose influences ran heavily to James M. Cain (q.v.) and Hemingway.

Someone Is Bleeding is the somewhat overwrought tale of writer David Newton who meets a lovely but deeply disturbed young woman named Peggy Lister and falls into tormented love with her. Peggy, icon that she is, is surrounded by men whose overwhelming desire in life is to possess her. Because of her psychological problems, possession means keeping her physically around them—since it is unlikely that anyone will ever have her heart or mind, given her pathological distrust of men, which seems to stem from having been raped by her father.

For its era, *Bleeding* was a surprisingly complex psychosexual tale. Peggy, a dark goddess who literally rules the lives of her men, is all the more chilling a woman for the sympathetic way in which David sees her for most of the book. She is the helpless, beautiful woman-child that many men fantasize about and long to protect as proof of their own masculinity.

As the novel rushes to its truly terrifying climax (it is an ending that must rank, for pure horror, with the best of Fredric Brown and Cornell Woolrich, qq.v.), we see how much Peggy comes to represent the pawn in a quest. Her men are willing to scheme, lie, and die to have her.

Despite its foreshortened structure, which gives it the singular tone of a short story, and despite the fact that the prose occasionally becomes overheated—one wishes for a flash of humor once in a while—*Someone Is Bleeding* is a satisfyingly complex, evocative study of loneliness, dreams, and pathology. Matheson also gives us an exceptionally good look at the Fifties and its snake-pit moral code, its demeaning view of women, its defeated view of men. He packs an icy poetry, a bittersweet love song, and moments of real terror into this debut.

(*E.G.*)

Maugham, W. Somerset. *Ashenden: or The British Agent*. New York: Doubleday, 1928. (E/SS)

Ashenden, a writer by profession, is in reality a British agent living in Switzerland during World War I. Recruited in a rather casual manner by "R." of British Intelligence (they met at a party one night), Ashenden accepts the assignment, thinking it might furnish material for his writing.

In fact, however, the work proves fairly mundane, consisting mostly of channeling messages to and from England. But occasionally there is a more hazardous assignment; and Switzerland itself is a nesting place for spies, providing many varied and colorful characters. There is, for example, the hostile elderly expatriate Englishwoman, governess to two Egyptian princesses, but a woman whose heart ultimately belongs to England, as she professes in a dying word to Ashenden. There is the Hairless Mexican, a general in exile from his own country, a comic figure, but an extremely dangerous man. In one episode, Ashenden and the Hairless Mexican travel to Italy in hopes of intercepting some valuable papers carried by a Greek courier, but the trip ends in disaster. There is the Baroness von Higgins, a beautiful but hard woman, Ashenden's occasional bridge partner, and almost certainly a spy for the Central Powers. And the cast of characters goes on.

The Ashenden adventures were originally published as short stories, but were put together in this one volume under the guise of a novel (an annoying publishing habit of the day). As a result, although a few of the characters endure throughout various episodes, the book will seem rather disjointed if approached as a legitimate novel.

Ashenden is hardly Somerset Maugham's best work, for this is the author who gave us such classics as *Of Human Bondage* (1915), *The Moon and Sixpence* (1919), and *The Razor's Edge* (1944). But it is an entertaining book that provides a nostalgic glimpse into an intrigue-filled, but somehow more innocent, time.

(*N.D.*)

*Melville, James. *The Chrysanthemum Chain*. New York: St. Martin's, 1982. (PP)

Superintendent Tetsuo Otani is the foremost of the current crop of foreign detectives. The reason is that James Melville (who is British) shows us not only what Otani does, but why, as a traditional Japanese, he does it. He tells us how Japanese society has shaped Otani—a fact that is fully displayed in Otani's actions. And all this is done with wry humor. There are wonderful scenes in which the British, dealing with the formalities following the death in Japan of one of their nationals, try to rush through the seemingly endless offers of tea from every official they meet, and the Japanese, seeing this, despair at the British lack of common courtesy.

Besides Otani, Melville gives us a diametrically opposed policeman, Jiro Kimura, who speaks fluent English and is fascinated by the West and especially by European secretaries. He also gives us the traditional conservative, Noguchi, known as "Ninja"; and Mrs. Otani, outwardly a traditional subservient Japanese wife, inwardly warm and competent—and not about to miss out on anything she wants to know.

When David Morrow, a British teacher of English, is stabbed to death, the case falls to Jiro Kimura, head of the Foreign Affairs Section of the Hyogo Prefectural Police Force. But it quickly becomes apparent that this is too important an investigation to be handled by an underling, and Otani himself must take charge. For a teacher of English, David Morrow had some unusual arrangements: He had a male student living in as attendant and sometimes lover; he had connections in the higher ranks of Japanese and foreign society; and he had file cards of 3000 acquaintances with comments too cryptic for even Kimura, with his excellent English, to decipher. David Morrow also had a lot of money for a teacher. All of which adds up to an interesting problem. Otani's investigation takes him into the foreign business and film world, into the government of his own country, and eventually imperils not only himself but also his family.

Melville's plotting is sharp and the action is suspenseful. The novel is a true escape into the exotic and well-described world of contemporary Japan. Otani and company also appear in *A Sort of Samurai* (1981), *The Ninth Netsuke* (1983), *Death of a Daimyo* (1984), and *Sayonara, Sweet Amaryllis* (1984).

(*S.D.*)

Meredith, D. R. *The Sheriff and the Panhandle Murders*. New York: Walker, 1984. (PP)

What in tarnation is going on in Crawford County, Texas? Four murder attempts—two of them successful—in just a few days' time. The homicide rate per capita is higher than Houston's!

It all began with the murder of a pretty Mexican teenager named Maria Martinez. She had her head bashed open and then was stuffed, still alive, into a huge barbecue pit, where she burned to death. Then came Billy Joe Williams. An airplane dumped a load of parathion insect spray on his pickup truck, causing a wreck that knocked him unconscious. The killer then held Billy Joe's nose and mouth shut so he suffocated. You would think the circumstances of Maria's death might cast a pall over the Frontier Days Barbecue, but it didn't. The good citizens of Crawford County were standing around, chomping down barbecue, when two of them were shot from the courthouse. Obviously a madman was loose in their midst.

The man who has to bring this wave of murder under control is Sheriff Charles Matthews, a recent immigrant from Dallas, and his crew of not terribly competent deputies. The woman who brings us this story is D. R. Meredith, a third-generation native of the Southwest. Her knowledge of the region soon becomes apparent, for not only is it an interesting and suspenseful story, but we are almost able to smell the dust, beer, and sweat of the Texas Panhandle.

An avid reader of mysteries probably will pick out the killer halfway through the book. But that's all right—you still have to read to the end to be sure you picked the right person. Then some might complain that Meredith wraps up the story in too rosy a manner. But that, too, is all right—the rosy haze of a dusty Texas sunset is a fine sight.

Meredith's second novel, *The Sheriff and the Branding Iron Murders,* was published in 1985.

(*N.D.*)

Merwin, Sam, Jr. *Murder in Miniatures*. New York: Doubleday Crime Club, 1940. (W)

Michael Troop is co-owner of a small, two-person advertising agency in New York City. He is also Michael Peter Igor Vassilov Tropanoff, a half–White Russian prince whose father, Prince Serge Alexis Tropanoff, was a "biggie under Tsar"; but Michael has kept his heritage a secret because he's not uppity and because his father is a nasty bastard who deserted his mother, a Manhattan debutante, shortly after their marriage was consummated. *Was* a nasty bastard, that is: Serge was murdered by his lover, a Russian Communist secret agent, in Shanghai in the novel's prologue; it seems Serge had something valuable the commies wanted, which, the secret agent learned before she bumped him off, is in Michael's possession in New York (only Michael doesn't know he has it). Then Michael's cousin, Prince Alexis Chavadze, who is next in line for the title and is also a rich perfume maker and a client of Michael's ad agency, has his throat slit at a gala party announcing his engagement to a model who is really in love with Michael. Then it turns out that what Michael has that old Serge had that the commies want are a bunch of fancy toy cossacks that seem to be made out of solid lead. . . .

Oh, never mind. The plot defies a decent synopsis because it is hopelessly (but rather pleasurably) silly and confused. Which is just one of the book's charms, along with cops who use the word *pixilated;* a rich industrialist whose "grasping vitality . . . almost seeped through his big pores"; a Russian villain who has "an erratic series of teeth, ranging from black to gold," and speaks English with a Bronx accent; a bunch of rich guys who get their kicks playing war games with toy soldiers; and a bevy of sexy females, including a "debutramp" who gets *her* kicks by looking at corpses with slashed throats. But the main fascination of *Murder in Miniatures* is Merwin's garbled prose style. The novel bulges with such passages as:

> *A butler, thin and redheaded, who moved like well-oiled machinery in slow-motion, took his coat and hat beneath an oval chandelier that had once served as a footpath for Roman maidens and hung from the ceiling like an inverted crab, its dull, poorly reflected glow barely bringing the marble-walled foyer out of dusk.*

His voice was slow, deliberate, unaccented like that of a Frenchman, though his accent, even in those few words, suggested the streets of Canarsie.

There was silence, and Michael felt desperation separate his ribs.

He felt crumby, like a dinner napkin after a meal.

A prolific pulp writer who later became the editor of several different magazines (one of them being *Mike Shayne Mystery Magazine* in the late Seventies), Merwin published seven other mystery novels of comparable stylistic ingenuity. Three of these—*Knife in My Back* (1945), *Message from a Corpse* (1945), and *A Matter of Policy* (1946)—feature a 300-pound, cigar-smoking female sleuth named Amy Brewster. The "pixilated" cop in *Murder in Miniatures,* Sergeant Jim Lanning, also appears in the Amy Brewster adventures.

(B.P.)

Meyer, Nicholas. *The Seven Percent Solution: Being a Reprint from the Reminiscences of John H. Watson, M.D.* New York: Dutton, 1974. (CS)

The scenario of this novel is that Dr. John H. Watson, chronicler of the exploits of Sherlock Holmes, dictated his last Holmes adventure while on his deathbed in 1940. It was a tale almost forty years old that he had sworn to suppress while the major characters were still alive. Watson died before he polished the manuscript and without heirs. His secretary, not knowing what to do with the rough draft, simply stored it in her attic, and it was not until 1970, when she died and her bereaved husband sold the house, that it came to light. What we have here purports to be the "edited" version of perhaps the most sensational Sherlock Holmes tale yet.

In this final episode, Holmes must fight the most dangerous of enemies: himself. For too many years he has fed his brain with cocaine, and—as anyone familiar with the effects of the glamour drug of the Eighties would expect—it has finally and inevitably taken a devastating toll on him. As the story opens, Holmes is in the extremes of paranoia, opening his door to his old friend Watson—whom he is convinced is his old nemesis, Dr. Moriarty, in disguise—only after Watson's most impassioned pleading. Of course, this state of mind has been brought on solely by the abuse of the drug, and Watson is in the odd position of having to save his own hero. The first third of the book is spent on his efforts to seduce the great detective into traveling to Vienna, where, Watson hopes, Sigmund Freud, the only medical scientist vaguely familiar with cocaine addiction, will cure him.

This is a fascinating tale, exposing cocaine's power over even the smartest of men, and a tale, too, that reveals the skeletons in Holmes's own closet. Dr. Moriarty may be a fantasy enemy at this point, but we soon find he has a deeper connection with the detective's past than even Holmes has realized.

Sherlockians and non-Sherlockians alike are sure to enjoy this supposed last adventure, which was made into a film in 1976 starring Laurence Olivier, Vanessa Redgrave, Joel Grey, and Robert Duvall. Meyer's second Holmes novel, *The West End Horror* (1976), is set in 1895 and features the Marquess of Queensbury, Bernard Shaw, Oscar Wilde, Gilbert and Sullivan, Frank Harris, and Bram Stoker.

(*K.K.H.*)

Miles, John. *The Silver Bullet Gang*. Indianapolis: Bobbs-Merrill, 1974. (C)

Aldred Timberscombe's day begins like any other day: He walks out of his suburban home, trips over his son's minibike, and has a fight with his wife. But hours later he is in the employee lounge of the computer firm where he works, plotting a bank robbery. For Aldred, the robbery starts out as a game, just idle conversation with co-worker Moose Simpson. But the pressures of a less-than-idyllic homelife, stupid memos from the president of the company, and his office mate's announcement that he is throwing over the daily grind and going back to school in sunny California are more than Aldred can bear. Frustrated and fast approaching forty, Aldred senses life is passing him by; his solution is to attend a meeting at Moose's home—the first meeting of the Silver Bullet Gang.

There are five of them: Aldred, "plodding and phlegmatic" Moose, attorney Ed Jernigan, flamboyant Caree Flynn, and "resident revolutionary" B. J. Pansza. The first meeting—at which they pretend to be playing poker—seems a lark to Aldred; after all, he reasons, he can always back out. But them B.J. announces, "When we commit to this, we *commit.*" And Moose asks, "Anyone want out?" And Aldred thinks he "could be as crazy as the next man."

The next few weeks are crazy indeed. It turns out Moose has given much more thought to this plan than any of them initially supposed. The bank is chosen, the target date is a football Saturday, and the gang sets to work casing First Security Bank—with hilarious results. Almost immediately they are spotted by Sergeant Henry Toole of the local police force, who has come in to see about a boat loan. Unaware that they are being observed, the gang proceeds with their preparations, which not only pave the way to a bona-fide robbery but also plunge the innocent and bumbling Aldred into a lunatic time that includes near-adultery, sexual depletion, and the biggest, most unexpected score of his lifetime.

This is a very funny book, and the suspense is in no way diluted by its comic qualities. One sympathizes with poor embattled Aldred from first page to last. Other, more serious-minded suspense novels by John Miles (a pseudonym of Jack Bickham, an accomplished mainstream and western novelist) are *The Night Hunters* (1973), *The Blackmailer* (1974), and *Operation Nightfall* (with Tom Morris, 1976).

(*M.M.*)

Millar, Kenneth. *The Dark Tunnel.* New York: Dodd, Mead, 1944. (E/T)

Prior to the publication of the first Lew Archer novel, *The Moving Target,* in 1949, Kenneth Millar (Ross Macdonald, q.v.) published four excellent if not highly successful suspense novels under his own name. *The Dark Tunnel* was the first of these, written when Millar was twenty-eight years old and in pursuit of a doctorate in English at the University of Michigan, where much of the action takes place.

Alec Judd, head of the War Board at "Midwestern University" in Arbana, confides to his friend, Dr. Robert Branch (the narrator), an English professor, that he suspects one of the board members of being a Nazi spy. The man he suspects is Dr. Herman Schneider, head of the school's German department for the past several years, who ostensibly fled the Hitler regime in 1935. Schneider's son, Peter, also comes under suspicion; as does Ruth Von Esch, an actress whom Branch met and fell in love with during a trip to Germany in 1937, and who comes to Arbana after a mysterious six-year disappearance. An alleged suicide, two attempts on his own life, and a savage murder for which he is framed plunge Branch into a series of nightmarish chases that lead from Arbana to Detroit and finally to a harrowing climax in a remote section of Canada.

Despite its melodramatic components, this is a novel of ambition and complexity. Among many virtues are a pair of ingenious murder methods, one of which succeeds and one of which doesn't; a well-portrayed academic background enhanced by a variety of erudite references; and an expert blending of disparate thematic material, in particular certain social and psychological issues of the period. The style is hard-boiled in that it utilizes the kind of detached realism that Joseph T. Shaw pioneered in the pages of *Black Mask* and that Hammett and Chandler refined and made famous. But Millar also refined it in his own way, beginning with this first novel, by adding elements of the literary, the scholarly, the lyrical. *The Dark Tunnel* even includes a liberal seasoning of similes and metaphors of the type that would later stud the Lew Archer novels like raisins in a series of bread puddings. For instance: "Now I could see only the dim outlines of the room . . . the dark roses beside the window. I lay and watched the black mass of the roses, red in the sun and black at night like blood, rich and delicate to the touch like a loved woman, drowsy and dark like sleep and death."

The other three novels first published under Millar's own name are

Trouble Follows Me (1946), *Blue City* (1947), and *The Three Roads* (1948). The last two are better and more ambitious than *The Dark Tunnel,* certainly, but it is still the firstborn that demands the closest scrutiny.

(*B.P.*)

Millar, Margaret. *Banshee.* New York: Morrow, 1983. (PS)

One of Margaret Millar's early series characters is Paul Prye, a psychiatrist/detective. Although she has long abandoned him (as well as Inspector Sands of the Toronto Police Department), her novels still show her considerable grasp of psychological principles. Her characters are developed at great depth, and the worlds they populate are recognizable yet odd, matters always being slightly skewed from reality as we know it. Her narratives often hinge upon a single, critical plot element that is withheld from the reader until the very end; and there are sometimes tangled past relationships, as in the work of her husband, Kenneth Millar/Ross Macdonald (q.v.), whose career her early successes inspired. Many critics feel that Millar is a better writer than her acclaimed husband was; in fact, their approach to fiction is strikingly similar. Those who prefer their mystery fiction hard-boiled will tend to favor Macdonald; those who prefer a gentler touch will turn to Millar.

Banshee explores the effect an eight-year-old child's death has upon her family and those close to her. Annamay Hyatt—whom we come to know through periodic flashbacks—disappears, and later her decomposing body is found in a wooded area near her home. The funeral is held, and Millar introduces the principals of the story: the Hyatts themselves, Kay and Howard; Ben York, the architect who designed not only the Hyatts' house but Annamay's playhouse; Peter Cunningham, devoted son, and his alcoholic mother; the Reverend Michael Dunlop and his critical wife, Lorna; Mrs. Chisholm, known as "Chizzy," the Hyatts' housekeeper; Annamay's cousin Dru, who is stricken by her death; Dru's mother, Vicki, and her current husband, John Campbell. These people have suffered intensely during the weeks between Annamay's disappearance and the time her body was found, but now the emotional upheaval is only beginning, as the search for her killer commences.

Millar portrays the effects of the bizarre events following Annamay's funeral and the erosion caused by suspicion with skill and sensitivity. She is particularly good at characterizing children; Annamay and Dru are fully drawn as people, without the condescension or cuteness so many writers employ when dealing with young people. And the solution to the baffling disappearance and subsequent events is both surprising and poignant.

(*M.M.*)

*Millar, Margaret. *Beast in View*. New York: Random House, 1955. (PS)

Helen Clarvoe is a wealthy but emotionally stunted woman, estranged from her mother and brother and living alone in a Hollywood hotel. As the story opens, Helen receives a call from a woman named Evelyn Merrick, who claims to be an old friend. Evelyn begins pleasantly enough, but soon the conversation degenerates into a threat. Badly frightened, Helen has no one to turn to, because she has no friends. Finally she contacts her late father's financial adviser, Paul Blackshear. Blackshear advises her to get out of town for a while, away from the woman; probably, like most disturbed people, she will tire of calling when she receives no answer. Helen can't imagine leaving—what would she do all alone in a strange place? She begs Blackshear to locate the woman and find out what she wants.

Finally Blackshear agrees—he is about to retire and needs a pursuit more interesting than collecting stamps. He traces Evelyn through a modeling agency, to a photographer whom she has posed for, and then to an artist whom she asked for a job. While he is with the artist, a disturbing incident occurs that makes him realize Evelyn is as unstable as her call to Helen has indicated. And by the time he has tracked her down and gotten to the roots of Evelyn's terrible problem, two persons are dead and many more have been emotionally destroyed.

This is an excellent novel, considered by many critics to be Millar's finest, and a winner of the MWA Edgar. For new readers of Millar's work, the central plot point may be obvious, due to the fact that many other—and often lesser—writers have imitated it. Nonetheless, it is suspenseful reading, right up to the last subtle metaphor.

(*M.M.*)

*Millar, Margaret. *Beyond This Point Are Monsters*. New York: Random House, 1970. (PS)

As a boy, Robert Osborne playfully placed a sign on the door of his room that read, "Beyond this point are monsters." Osborne has since grown up, married, and disappeared—an apparent murder victim in the mess hall of his ranch near San Diego. A year has passed, and his wife, Devon, has accepted the evidence of the murder—which includes a large quantity of blood on the mess-hall floor and a knife with bloodstains on it—and is petitioning the court to have Robert declared legally dead. His mother, however, has never given up hope that her son, or at least his body, will turn up. She sits in court listening to the testimony of those who saw Robert during his last hours, still trying to reject this ultimate truth.

Testimony is given by Devon: Her husband went out after dinner looking for his dog and never returned. By Dulzura, the cook: He had a great deal of cash in his wallet. By Estivar, the ranch foreman: Osborne had once been a good friend to the Chicano laborers, but had changed when he went away to school; since then, all was business between them. Testimony is also given by Lum Wing, the mess-hall cook; by Ernest Valenzuela, the former policeman who handled the case; by Leo Bishop, a neighbor; by Carla Lopez, a young woman who feels she is "jinxed"; by Estivar's son, who found the knife. And behind the facts, other, less easily defined elements lurk: the fact that Osborne's parents had a shaky marriage; that Osborne's father died in a drunken fall from a tractor at ten in the morning; that Osborne had an affair with Leo Bishop's wife; that Mrs. Bishop was killed in a flash flood while apparently attempting to run away with Robert.

In addition to characterizing all the principals, Millar brings the missing man to life for us, both by what the others say and by the skillful use of flashback. And when the end comes in a single, brilliant revelation, the reader is convinced that indeed beyond that point there are monsters.

Millar's series novels featuring the wonderfully named Paul Prye are *The Invisible Worm* (1941), *The Weak-Eyed Bat* (1942), and *The Devil Loves Me* (1942). Inspector Sands appears in *Wall of Eyes* (1943) and *The Iron Gates* (1945). Other excellent novels of psychological suspense include *Rose's Last Summer* (1952), *An Air that Kills* (1957), *The Listening Walls* (1959), and *Stranger in My Grave* (1960).

(*M.M.*)

Miller, Wade. *Guilty Bystander*. New York: Farrar, 1947. (PI)

The collaborative team of Bob Wade and Bill Miller—writing as Wade Miller, Whit Masterson (q.v.), Dale Wilmer, and Will Daemer—was a reliable producer of hard-boiled fiction in both hardcover and paperback. Their one series character was San Diego private eye Max Thursday, who made his debut in this book.

As introduced, Thursday is about as far down the social scale as private eyes ever get: He's an alcoholic, living in a fleabag hotel, getting by on the charity of the hotel's proprietor, a former whorehouse madame. Then Thursday's ex-wife appears, begging for help; their young son has been abducted and the kidnappers are demanding some unspecified ransom, not money. Max has to pull himself together, stay sober, and regenerate his detecting skills in order to save his son. He soon finds himself contending with a couple of free-lance gunmen, the cops, a double-crossing hooker, and a pair of Italian fishing magnates who run the local rackets. It all has to do with a bag of pearls.

This is a tough, fast-moving private-eye novel; it has much the same feel as *I, the Jury,* published the same year, though a bit less violent, and with scant sex. (It's interesting that Spillane's later *The Girl Hunters* starts out with a setup that's almost identical to the one in this book, with Mike Hammer having to pull himself out of the gutter to save his partner, Velda.) There are flaws: The off-the-bottle theme gets lost when the plot complications take over, and the final confrontation scene with the surprise mastermind is weak. Still, a satisfying yarn; and it made a slick 1950 movie with Zachary Scott as Thursday.

Some other Miller titles of note: *Deadly Weapon* (1946), featuring Thursday's cop friend Lieutenant Austin Clapp; *Uneasy Street* (1948) and *Calamity Fair* (1950), with Thursday; and *Kitten with a Whip* (1959).

(*A.S.*)

Milne, A. A. *The Red House Mystery*. London: Methuen, 1922. (AD)

A. A. Milne is justifiably famous for his House at Pooh Corner children's books. He is almost as renowned, in some circles, for being attacked by Raymond Chandler (q.v.) in "The Simple Art of Murder." Curiously, Chandler's 1944 diatribe against "The Triple Petunia Murder Case" and "Death Wears Yellow Garters" school of classic detective story seems almost out-of-date today. In fact, an apologist for the hard-boiled school might find it difficult to defend today's crime writing in Chandler's terms—"It was second-grade literature because it was not about the things that could make first-grade literature." There must be hundreds of current tough-guy stories where characters "do unreal things in order to form the artificial pattern required by the plot." Chandler praises Dashiell Hammett because he wrote in the American language. (Is it possible to criticize English writers for failing to do this?) Though Chandler states, "I like the English style better . . . they are incomparably the best dull writers," he chooses to shoot detailed jabs at Milne's ultra-English *Red House Mystery*. Most of the defects he finds in this book have to do with identification of the body, and half have to do with the inquest. Not all of these criticisms are justified. Perhaps *The Red House Mystery* was singled out because critic Alexander Woollcott praised it as "one of the three best mystery stories of all time" (which it's not).

A. A. Milne came out of the nursery to write this one novel of classic detection. Julian Symons, English critic, puts Milne in the group of Golden Age authors, including Ronald A. Knox (q.v.), that he calls "Farceurs." This book is important because it was the first to inject such levity into investigation and to present the story as a humorous game. In the story, the master of the Red House is expecting his long-lost ne'er-do-well brother to return bringing a cloud of menace after fifteen years in Australia. The brother appears, is admitted to the house, and a shot rings out. Antony Gillingham arrives in time to hear the shot and decides to turn sleuth when it develops that the master of the house has disappeared. He teams up with his friend and fellow houseguest Bill Beverley, and they look into the lake, sift the library, survey timetables, and interview witnesses to the absolutely classic conclusion.

If you want to have a good time, this is a book that makes easy fun of murder, dexterously shifts suspicion, and is not so tediously serious. Rex Stout (q.v.) called it "charming."

(*T.B.*)

Mitchell, Gladys. *Laurels Are Poison*. London: Joseph, 1942. (CS)

Anthony Boucher observed that "there are no moderate attitudes on the work of Gladys Mitchell; either you love her . . . or you plain can't read her." That judgment continues to hold true today. Like Dorothy L. Sayers (q.v.), Gladys Mitchell is idiosyncratic in the extreme. Her mysteries are *very* British—full of arcane folklore, difficult country dialects, and more than a touch of the supernatural. They also feature one of the more memorable sleuths of mystery fiction, Dame Beatrice Lestrange Bradley.

Besides a highly prolific career as a novelist under her own name as well as the pseudonyms Stephen Hockaby and Malcolm Torrie, Gladys Mitchell also had a forty-year career as a teacher. It is not surprising, therefore, that several of her best novels deal with school environments. *Laurels Are Poison* is one of these.

The setting is Cartaret [teachers] Training College for women. Mrs. Bradley is called in as temporary warden (i.e., housemother) at a residence hall when the original warden, a Miss Murchan, disappears after a school dance. With Mrs. Bradley's arrival, the sleuthing begins, as does a series of sometimes malicious pranks. It is up to "Mrs. Croc" (as she is nicknamed) to sort out past crimes from present offenses, and innocent student rags from the more vicious attacks of a campus "ghost."

Laurels Are Poison is a well-crafted mystery, and Mitchell handles the school milieu and the characterization of students and staff exceedingly well. But the book's greatest claim to fame is probably the introduction of a character named Laura Menzies. Laura is a student at Cartaret, an enthusiastic if mischievous jock who goes by the nickname "Dog." She is brave and inquisitive. Mrs. Bradley concludes, "I like that child. She is intelligent."

Laura later becomes Dame Beatrice's secretary and Watson. And, conveniently, she ensures the cooperation of Scotland Yard by eventually marrying Detective Inspector Robert Gavin of the CID.

(*K.L.M.*)

Mitchell, Gladys. *The Rising of the Moon*. London: Joseph, 1945. (CS)

While not set in a school, *The Rising of the Moon* also focuses on young people. This haunting tale of Ripper-style murders in a "little artery of a town" is narrated by thirteen-year-old Simon Innes. The murders are seen through the intelligent yet innocent eyes of Simon and his eleven-year-old brother, Keith.

Mitchell never makes a false move with her narrative. Simon is utterly believable and quite endearing. He is also the perfect Watson. He has curiosity combined with a childish lack of tact. He relates events and his impressions of them well, but although adults often betray themselves before him, Simon isn't yet able to analyze fully what he has heard and seen. That is where Mrs. Bradley comes in. As a "consulting psychiatrist for the Home Office," she can analyze Simon's data and solve the gruesome case.

The Rising of the Moon is above all atmospheric, evoking time, place, and character extremely well. Mitchell's portrait of the British working poor is richly drawn without being either romanticized or condescending. The same could be said of her portraits of children, in the form of Simon and Keith. The details of domestic existence (from the jealous turmoil between a husband and wife to the ingredients of a pot of soup) become even more important than the latest murder victim. Murder and day-to-day life become inevitably linked to one another under the waxing and waning moon.

(*K.L.M.*)

Mitchell, Gladys. *Speedy Death*. New York: Dial, 1929. (CS)

Mrs. (not yet Dame) Bradley is introduced in *Speedy Death,* in a manner few readers will forget. The book starts out like a classic country-house puzzle. Numerous guests gather for the weekend at Chayning Court, the estate of a cantankerous but wealthy old gentleman named Alastair Bing.

Surprisingly, perhaps, it is not Bing who becomes the first corpse; Mitchell does nothing that ordinary. Instead, the victim is a world-famous explorer named Everard Mountjoy. It shocks everyone when Mr. Mountjoy is found drowned in his bath. It shocks them more when the drowning turns out to be murder. But the *real* shocker is that Mountjoy's corpse (complete with the distinctive two missing fingers) is undoubtedly that of a woman.

A guest named Carstairs seems to be taking the role of amateur sleuth, with a little professional competition from an Inspector Boring. But it is the yellow, cronelike Mrs. Bradley (compared variously to a pterodactyl and an alligator) who makes the key discoveries and predicts, and frustrates, murderous attacks on two other guests.

Nevertheless, when a second corpse is discovered in the bath, Mrs.

Bradley isn't consulted as mastermind, but rather arrested and later tried as murderer. Suffice it to say, the book is full of surprises, and Mrs. Bradley enters the world of detection as a highly original sleuth.

Oddly, most of Gladys Mitchell's work has never been published in the United States. Two that have are the Sherlockian tale *Watson's Choice* (1955; published in the United States in 1976) and a strange mystery entitled *Winking at the Brim*, featuring a Loch Ness–like monster (1974; U.S. edition, 1977).

(*K.L.M.*)

Moore, Barbara. *The Doberman Wore Black*. New York: St. Martin's, 1983. (AD)

Gordon Christy has an aversion to chameleons, but he's taking care of one that's gotten chilled, so he puts it in his shirt to warm it up. Who could resist such a James Herriott of a sleuth? Anyone with even the slightest soft spot for animals will enjoy *The Doberman Wore Black*. Christy's a veterinarian on his way to Vail, Colorado, to baby-sit the practice of a fellow vet on vacation. He's traveling with the chameleon and a couple of cockatoos when a black MGB runs him off the road. Next to the driver sits a grinning black Doberman.

When he gets to Vail, things start happening fast—he's dispatched immediately to subdue a dog found in the apartment of a murdered man. As he arrives at the building, the pushy MGB is just leaving. Inside the apartment the same Doberman is baring her teeth. Needless to say, Christy does the practical thing and makes friends with the dog. But someone has killed young Philip Schumacher, and before long there's an attempt on the dog's life. Then someone ransacks Christy's condo. And Philip's brother, Peter, is killed.

Christy's in deep, but he has a trusty canine ally. He and Gala the Doberman rout the villains with a great flying of fur. Along the way, Christy can't be at all sure who his friends are. Particularly questionable is Cletus Knight, an extremely rich and colorful Doberman fancier with no visible means of support.

There's as much veterinary lore as plot in this book, an element that will charm some readers, perhaps annoy others. But even the irritated won't stay mad for long—this is too good-humored a book to resist.

(*J.S.*)

Morgan, Michael. *Decoy*. New York: Ace, 1953. (O/AD/T)

The undersigned reviewer once went on record as calling *Decoy* "the worst mystery novel ever written." Subsequent discoveries have perhaps invalidated that statement—but not by much. *Decoy* is still one of the giants (midgets?), a novel so deliciously bad that it must be read again and again to be fully savored and appreciated. Its authors—Michael Morgan is the pseudonym of a pair of Hollywood publicity agents named C. E. ("Teet") Carle and Dean M. Dorn—were true poet laureates of the absurd.

The plot of *Decoy* does not lend itself well to simple summary. It has to do with an unofficial Lonely-Hearts Club/gigolo/blackmail racket in Hollywood operated by a villainess called "the Duchess"; but another gang from the East Coast, led by a mysterious "Mr. Upstairs" who goes by the name of King Lazarr, is trying to muscle in on her crowd. In the middle of this mob warfare is one Bill Ryan, hero and narrator, who is a Hollywood stuntman. He is also a dumb cluck, by his own testimony on at least a dozen occasions throughout the book. Also involved are several hard-boiled types colorfully named Joe Salka, Belmont Spur, Geoffrey Dare, Russell Orth, and Mr. Yegg and Mr. Thug. Plus several soft-boiled and sexy ladies. There is quite a bit of exciting action, most of it choreographed so Bill Ryan can use his stuntman's wiles to escape the jaws of death. Quite a few interesting murders as well, including one in which a minor baddie is impaled on the spine of a huge (*very* huge) cactus.

To give you an idea of the complexity of the plot—and of the inimitable Morgan style—here is a passage of dialogue spoken to Bill Ryan, who is masquerading under the alias of Reynolds at the time, by the wicked Duchess:

> *"I didn't find out your name just today, Reynolds. I knew it last Friday when you busted into the picture, claimin' you was a friend of Russell Orth's, wantin' a setup with the Andrews dame. I could of cooked your act that day. I said let you have plenty of rope. I wondered how come you said you was a friend of a guy who was already croaked. Russ was one of my pets, brother. I know about your playin' games through the Traxton halls so's you could make contact in the men's room with Salka and Spur. Right after that you tied onto Frank's tail an' followed him outside the hotel. You never came back, an' early this ayem, another of my best boys was found on the lawn—dead as a poop. Today you show up here with that dreamy-eyed blond, Judith Monroe, actin' like you was a real gee-gee. That give you an idea of what I know?"*

Some other samples of the Morgan genius:

> *She laid a hand on my arm and I knew I really had her in the palm of my hand because her face was contorted.*
>
> *I wanted to see the murderer of that beautiful creature seated in the gas chamber. I wanted it so bad my saliva glands throbbed.*

> *I sat beside her in the Traxton's Parisian Room and let the edges of my eyes siphon up the pleasure of her tall, slender figure in a blue evening gown which made a low-bridged criss-cross right above where the meat on a chicken is the whitest.*

There is more—much, much more. A chuckle on every page, in fact, and a belly-laugh in every chapter. *Plus* a mind-boggler of a climax in which Bill leaps out of a moving car onto the tail of a small plane, grabs the rudder, and rides the tail into the ground "like a cowboy bulldozing [*sic*] a steer."

Almost as bad/good/wonderful is the first Michael Morgan novel, *Nine More Lives* (1946), which also features Bill Ryan and such lines as "Inspiration splattered me in the face like a custard pie."

(*B.P.*)

Morice, Anne. *Murder in Mimicry*. New York: St. Martin's, 1977. (AD)

Tessa Crichton is not your usual bubble-headed ingenue actress. She is a professional who works at her craft and is most at home on stage, rather than in a TV studio or on a movie sound stage. In *Murder in Mimicry,* her cousin Toby's play, after a successful run in England, is to open in Washington, D.C., with Tessa playing the second lead, a part written for her. Robin Price, her husband of five years, a Scotland Yard detective, has to remain in England when Tessa leaves for Washington, where she plans to stay with a friend in her Georgetown house close to the Kennedy Center.

The play's leading man is nicknamed "the Daemon King," and he thoroughly lives up to his reputation—rehearsals are littered with the victims of his caustic tongue. As if that isn't enough, there is blackmail backstage; Tessa's housemate is found unconscious from a knock on the head in the foyer of her house (evidently someone mistook her for Tessa); and shortly afterward a member of the cast is discovered dead after apparently being mugged during a midnight walk. Tessa gets to know the investigator assigned to the case, Detective Monk of the Metropolitan Police, and he conscripts her into his investigation of behind-the-curtain life.

Other than husband Robin, the one recurring male character in Morice's Tessa Crichton novels is her cousin, Toby Crichton, owner of a well-run country house where Tessa frequently visits between roles. Toby's vast acquaintanceship among theater people and his country neighbors has more than once figured in Tessa's other adventures. The life of an actress, with its varied theatrical locales, is an excellent backdrop for crime stories, and Morice has yet to exhaust its possibilities.

A 1979 Tessa Crichton adventure, *Murder in Outline,* shows Tessa returning to her former school as a drama critic and judge; *Death in the Round*

(1980) exploits the activities of a Rotunda Theatre. *Dead on Cue* (1985) concerns the Alibi Club, a group of mystery writers.

(*E.N.*)

Morley, Christopher. *The Haunted Bookshop*. New York: Doubleday, 1919. (T/E)

The Haunted Bookshop is a book lover's paradise. Located in Brooklyn in "one of the comfortable old brownstone dwellings which have been the joy of several generations of plumbers and cockroaches . . . there is no secondhand bookshop in the world more worthy of respect." The shop is owned by Roger Mifflin and his wife, Helen. Roger considers himself an expert in "bibliotherapy"; it is his pleasure "to prescribe books for such patients as drop in here and are willing to tell me their symptoms. . . . There is no one so grateful as the man to whom you have given just the book his soul needed and he never knew it." A wise man, Roger Mifflin, in addition to being a quintessential bibliophile and bookseller; only a wise man could lament the fact that "the world has been printing books for 450 years [over 500 years now] and yet gunpowder still has a wider circulation."

Roger knows just about everything there is to know about books, and so the Haunted Bookshop ("haunted by the ghosts of all great literature") has an extremely varied and sometimes unusual clientele. The young advertising executive Aubrey Gilbert, for instance, a man who comes to Roger to sell him on the idea of advertising and winds up succumbing to bibliotherapy. And Titania Chapman, whose father wants her to work with Roger for a while to "get some of her finishing school nonsense out of her head." She, too, loves books, so it is only natural, not to mention fitting and proper, that she and Aubrey should meet and fall in love in the Haunted Bookshop.

And then there are the spies. Bolsheviks and Huns, who surreptitiously come to the shop not because they are interested in books but because they are using a particular book—Carlyle's *Oliver Cromwell*—as part of a nefarious scheme involving incendiary bombs and a plot to assassinate President Woodrow Wilson. But never mind about them. This novel isn't really about post–World War I spies or incendiary bombs or assassination plots. It isn't really about young love, either.

It is about books. Selling them, buying them, reading them, enjoying them. Loving and understanding them. It is a tale for bibliophiles, for booksellers (especially for booksellers, who are treated herein with a reverence second only to books themselves); for anyone to whom books are so much more than doorstops, dust-catchers, and quick reads on a plane flight or a commute run. Christopher Morley was himself a bookseller and dedicated bibliophile, as well as an editor, essayist, poet, Sherlockian, detective-fiction aficionado, and the founder of the *Saturday Review of Literature*. No man loved books more than he, not even Vincent Starrett or Roger Mifflin.

The Haunted Bookshop is Morley's only bibliomystery (bibliospy-story?), a fact that, as Howard Haycraft says in *Murder for Pleasure,* "only sharpens every reader's regret that he . . . never turned his hand to bona fide detection." Roger Mifflin does appear in one other bookish novel, *Parnassus on Wheels* (1917). That, too, is a charming and delightful glimpse into both the world of books and a far more hopeful and innocent age.

(*B.P.*)

*Morrell, David. *First Blood.* New York: M. Evans, 1972. (PS)

First Blood was David Morrell's first novel, and an impressive debut it was and is. Its protagonist, Rambo, is an extraordinary character: an ex–Green Beret veteran of the Vietnam War, one of the young men the military trained to kill but never taught how to stop killing. As the book opens, Rambo is hitchhiking his way across the country, sleeping at night in the woods and the fields. When he arrives in Madison, Kentucky, he is picked up by Sheriff Will Teasle, who immediately senses there is something not quite right about this drifter, something more than just his long hair and beard. Teasle escorts Rambo out of town; Rambo returns; Teasle drives him to the city limits again; Rambo comes back. Finally Teasle arrests and books him. But Rambo doesn't remain in jail for long. After killing one of Teasle's guards, he escapes into the countryside.

What follows is a desperate contest between the hunted and the hunter. In alternating chapters we see Rambo as he eludes Teasle and the National Guard, and Teasle as he directs the manhunt. On his side Rambo has the Special Forces training that allowed him to survive in the jungles of Vietnam and in a Viet Cong prison camp. Teasle has manpower and all the resources of law-enforcement agencies—plus his own determination to bring the man in. Soon we realize that this is not merely a contest between the law and the lawless but between two men who are diametric opposites: Teasle, the veteran of Korea, where he earned a Distinguished Service Cross, a respected and integrated member of society; and Rambo, also a veteran, also the possessor of a medal, but deeply scarred by his experiences and cast out by a society that is ashamed of the men who fought what is now considered a dirty war. As the search intensifies and the contrasts between the two men—in philosophy as well as methods of fighting—become more pronounced, it turns into a personal confrontation during which each man must face his most basic fears and incapabilities.

First Blood is a violent book; by the time we reach the end, the body count is depressingly high. But the characterization is excellent, the suspense unrelenting, and the story has great relevance for today's society (unlike the current "Rambo" craze generated by the Sylvester Stallone motion picture adaptation, which emphasizes macho behavior and mindless brutality). This classic confrontation between opposites is not to be missed.

Other recommended novels by Morrell are *Testament* (1975), *The Totem* (1979), *Blood Oath* (1982), and *The Brotherhood of the Rose* (1984), which also concerns the effects of the "trained killer school" on those who have learned their lessons too well.

(*G.K./M.M.*)

Morrison, Arthur. *Martin Hewitt, Investigator*. New York: Harper, 1894. (CS/SS)

Of all the rivals of Sir Arthur Conan Doyle (q.v.), Arthur Morrison was far and away the most successful during the period 1890 to 1905. Like Doyle, he deprecated his mystery writing, preferring his authentic fiction about the slums of London, *Tales of Mean Streets* (1894), and his monumental, two volume *Painters of Japan* (1911), a reference work based upon his lifelong interest in Oriental art.

Martin Hewitt, Investigator contains other similarities to Doyle and his Sherlock Holmes canon. Both the Holmes and the Hewitt stories first appeared in *The Strand,* and they were each illustrated by Sidney Paget. Although Hewitt's methods are very similar to those of Holmes, he is a far different character. He has few of the Sherlockian eccentricities, tending more toward blandness in personality. Though he is well read in science, especially hypnotism, he is less likely to lecture on the subject. Occasionally, though, his ego will come to the fore and he will make pronouncements such as "I am often able to discover tracks in grass that are invisible to others." The Morrison equivalent of Doyle's Watson is a journalist, Brett, who narrates the Hewitt tales and is generally treated in a good-natured, albeit condescending, manner.

Though it is the first and best known of the Martin Hewitt stories, "The Lenton Croft Robberies" is somewhat overrated. It is most notable for its introduction of Hewitt, a highly successful criminal investigator for attorneys who decides to open his own business as a detective. The story also, on its first page, has Hewitt saying to his chronicler, "I consider you, Brett . . . the most remarkable journalist alive. Not because you're particularly clever, you know; because, between ourselves, I hope you'll admit you're not. . . ." More representative of Morrison's strong plotting and storytelling ability are "The Case of the Dixon Torpedo" and "The Loss of Sammy Crockett." The former recounts the theft of plans for the deadly, secret weapon so beloved of many writers. It's a lively tale with an interesting Russian suspect, named Mirksy, whom Paget paints as the archetypal bomb-throwing anarchist. "Sammy Crockett" is one of the best mysteries with a sports background, in this case the annual Padfield 135-Yard Handicap. It's not as amateurish as it sounds, for there is heavy betting on the result, and Hewitt is called in when the title character, the favorite, disappears.

If Arthur Morrison added nothing especially new to the development of the mystery in his Martin Hewitt stories, he helped advance their popularity. A seemingly insatiable market had been created by Doyle, and in Hewitt Morrison created the best of the Sherlock Holmes deduct-alikes.

(*M.L.*)

Morse, L. A. *The Big Enchilada*. New York: Avon, 1982. (O/PI)

Response to L. A. Morse's *Big Enchilada* has been widely (and wildly) varied. Some see the book simply as an excellent novel of the hard-boiled school. Others see it as a parody of the hard-boiled novel as practiced by Mickey Spillane (q.v.). Still others, including this reviewer, find it a failure either as a hard-boiled novel or as a parody. Here is a sample of the writing: "I would shoot fire into their bellies and make them puke and squirm on the floor. I would splatter the walls with their brains. Vengeance! I could taste it in my mouth." This is the narrator, Sam Hunter, speaking, in reaction to his secretary's murder. It's not that he objects to her murder, as such, though. It's because "She had been okay—as a woman and a secretary—and there weren't too many of that kind around."

If this is parody, it doesn't work. If it is serious, then it *really* doesn't work. The book abounds with similar examples. The plot involves blackmail, sex, and heroin; it also involves the tying together of several seemingly separate cases. Chandler could sometimes pull this sort of thing off, but *The Big Enchilada* seems to be nothing more than a farrago of incredible coincidences. The character of Sam Hunter represents the ultimate in sexism. He refers to one female character as having "the hollow cheeks and the wide mouth of the inveterate cocksucker," a comment which would probably make even Mike Hammer blanch, not to mention your maiden aunt. Parody? Maybe, but when the guy who says it has raped his secretary only a few pages previously, you have to wonder. At least Morse has succeeded in one thing—he has written a book that no one remains neutral about.

Sam Hunter reappears in *Sleaze* (1985), a case in which he's hired to protect the editor of a porno magazine; the title says it all. An earlier Morse novel, *The Old Dick* (1981), received an MWA Best Paperback Edgar.

(*B.C.*)

*Motley, Willard. *Knock on Any Door*. New York: Appleton-Century, 1947. (PS)

This epic crime novel by one of our few black writers has retained its power, and stands as the definitive, in-depth portrait of the life of a slum-bred hoodlum. Motley's "hero," Nick Romano, is a complex, flawed but sympathetic character, always more than just a symbol of juvenile delinquency, never romanticized into a tragic figure—rather, a pitiful soul who might have been *any* boy subjected to poverty and a brutal upbringing.

The 240,000-word narrative follows Nick from Denver, as an altar boy of twelve, to a courtroom in Chicago, where at age twenty-one he will stand trial for murder. When his father's business fails and poverty comes to the middle-class family, Nick falls in with a bad crowd and, before long, is in reform school for a crime he didn't commit. There he is taught to hate authority and begins his schooling in the ways of crime. When he is released and joins his family in Chicago, he quickly drifts to skid row, where he and other misspent youths underwrite their drinking and whoring by gambling and "jackrolling" (mugging). Handsome teenage Nick also plays the "phoneys," homosexuals who pay for his sexual favors. In and out of jail for various robberies, Nick's hatred for the corrupt, brutal police grows, centering on Officer Riley, who proudly wears three notches on his belt for the men he's killed. But a spark of sensitivity remains in Nick, and he falls genuinely, deeply in love with Emma Schultz, a fine, gentle girl whose own life is marred by an alcoholic mother. When the fragile marriage tragically shatters, Nick spirals further into a life of crime.

Motley's social conscience is undeniably present in the narrative, but he does not cop out: Nick's environment plays a large part in guiding him down a twisted path, but Nick is also shown to be weak, to pass up opportunities to reform and grow. Grant Holloway, a writer who seems to be Motley's voice, takes the boy under his wing, but Nick stubbornly refuses to cooperate. Only in the harrowing final chapters does Motley's compassionate view turn into a social message, as the author's anti-capital-punishment stand flows eloquently, unashamedly forward.

Motley's often poetic prose provides an emotional counterpoint for the stark, unpleasant drama he stages; and the climactic murder trial is a masterpiece of courtroom suspense. The film version (1949), directed by Nicholas Ray and starring Humphrey Bogart in a composite of the Grant Holloway and attorney Andrew Morton characters, simplifies and romanticizes Nick's story; nonetheless, it is a worthwhile adaptation, with a surprisingly effective portrayal by John Derek (his film debut) as Nick Romano.

A first-rate sequel, *Let No Man Write My Epitaph* (1958), deals with Nick Romano, Jr.'s battle with drug addiction; Motley's other two novels were not crime-oriented. Motley has never been granted his rightful place among major black American writers, perhaps because his novels did not focus on black protagonists, even though the social problems his novels dealt with were common to blacks. His work, however, transcends racial considerations.

(*M.A.C.*)

*Moyes, Patricia. *A Six-Letter Word for Death.* New York: Holt, 1983. (CS)

In the late Fifties, as many of the Golden Age masters of the British mystery were retiring or expiring, new blood (so to speak) entered the field. Many of the younger generation turned their hands to more realistic mystery forms, but a few novices stayed with the old ways and true. Such a writer is Patricia Moyes, whose dedication to the classic British puzzle has been a comfort to cozy fans since *Dead Men Don't Ski* (1959).

A Six-Letter Word for Death is but the latest in a long-running series featuring Chief Superintendent Henry Tibbett of Scotland Yard and his wife, Emmy. It is a classic country-house mystery set on the Isle of Wight. A nobleman publisher invites a group of pseudonymous mystery authors called the Guess Who for a weekend house party. Meanwhile, Henry (invited as guest expert and lecturer) has received a series of clues by mail—crossword-puzzle sections indicating that the party guests may all have skeletons in their closets. When murder follows, Tibbett's investigation intensifies to a classic, if overly melodramatic, confrontation with suspects and murderer.

Moyes manages to poke a bit of affectionate fun at mystery fiction and its creators. She also creates a traditional tale much more satisfying than some of her recent work set in the West Indies. Moyes takes a touch of the police procedural, a dash of the husband-and-wife mystery/adventure, and creates a very pleasing product in the style of the Golden Age.

A Six-Letter Word for Death is one of Moyes's best mysteries of the last ten years. Other notable Tibbett cases are *Murder a la Mode* (1963), *Johnny Under Ground* (1965), and *Seasons of Snows and Sins* (1971).

(*K.L.M.*)

Muller, Marcia. *Leave a Message for Willie.* New York: St. Martin's, 1984. (PI)

The female private eye has been a part of crime fiction for a long time; but the female private eye who is depicted by a woman writer, and is a woman first and a detective second, and is an *integral* part of crime fiction, has been around only since 1977—the year Marcia Muller introduced Sharon McCone in *Edwin of the Iron Shoes.* Up to that time, the few licensed women ops were (a) hard-boiled caricatures of their male counterparts, created wholly or at least in part by males; (b) slinky sex objects with a rod or a knife strapped to one curve or another; (c) both of the above. Honey West, for instance, she of the smutty jokes and the kick-'em-in-the-balls disposition. Muller and McCone were the harbingers that changed all that. They brought realism and humanity to the female private investigator—and just as important, they brought dignity. Since their arrival on the mystery scene, several other women have created female detectives, some of whom have achieved greater success and critical acclaim. But no one does it any better than Muller.

Admittedly, *Edwin* and two other titles in the McCone series—*Ask the Cards a Question* and *The Cheshire Cat's Eye,* both written in the late 1970s but not published until 1982 and 1983, respectively—are rough-edged works, good but flawed. But in the long run, that is a positive rather than a negative fact. The writer (and the detective) who makes his or her debut working at optimum ability has little or no room to grow. Both Muller and McCone just keep getting better with each book, tackling more complex cases, dealing with Sharon's eccentric San Diego-based family, buying Sharon a house, giving up one romantic interest for a more positive one. (No woman with any self-respect could have a lasting relationship with a cop, Greg Marcus, who persists in calling her "papoose" because she is one-eighth Cherokee Indian.)

In *Leave a Message for Willie,* Sharon's new love interest, disc jockey Don del Boccio, has accepted a job in San Francisco (he used to work in the coastal town of Port San Marco, where she met him in *Games to Keep the Dark Away,* 1984) and has moved in with her in her new house. A temporary arrangement—or is it? Coping with Don *and* refurbishing her new home are small difficulties, though, compared with Willie Whalen. Willie, an acquaintance of Sharon's boss, Hank Zahn of All Souls Legal Cooperative, is an apparent junk dealer who maintains a stall at the Saltflats Flea Market south of San Francisco; his main business, however, is that of fence for stolen merchandise. His problem, which McCone reluctantly agrees to help him with as a favor to Hank, is a young man wearing a yarmulke who keeps hanging around the stall and Willie's house. Willie wants to know why.

When Sharon traces the man, Jerry Levin, he claims to work for a group that recovers stolen Torahs, the sacred Hebrew scrolls. Willie denies knowing anything about any Torahs. But then Sharon finds Levin shot to death in Willie's garage—and not long after that, Willie's girlfriend, Aida, is also murdered. The police tab Willie for the crimes, and he disappears. Convinced of his innocence, McCone begins a search that leads her from San Francisco to a remote part of the Santa Cruz Mountains; from a rabbi named Halpert to a weapons dealer named Fat Herman; from an illegal Mexican alien to an alcoholic Vietnam vet; and from the bright world of flea markets to the shadowy one of paramilitary survival games.

This is a solidly plotted novel with a unique and colorful background and some convincing action scenes. But its emphasis, as in all of Muller's novels, is on people—ordinary people, all different kinds. Believable people. And that, of course, is what good fiction is all about.

Muller's most recent McCone novel is *There's Nothing to Be Afraid Of*

(1985), which is set in San Francisco's Vietnamese refugee community. Predictably, it's even better than *Willie*—the best book in the series so far.

(*B.P.*)

Muller, Marcia. *The Tree of Death.* New York: Walker, 1983. (AD)

Muller's second series is wholly different from the McCone books. Her heroine is neither Caucasian nor a private (or professional) detective; rather, she is a Hispanic curator of a Mexican arts museum and amateur sleuth named Elena Oliverez. And the novels take place not in San Francisco but in Santa Barbara, which has a substantial Mexican heritage. There are a number of Chican*o* detectives in crime fiction, among them Dell Shannon's Luis Mendoza and Rex Burns's Gabriel Wager (qq.v.); but to date Elena Oliverez is the only Chican*a* sleuth. And a very good one she is—sharply drawn, with emphasis on her human qualities as well as her deductive abilities. Her cases are not only expertly constructed mysteries but realistic depictions of museum operation, the world of Mexican art, and the Mexican-American community in general.

The Tree of Death, Elena's first case, focuses on the internal workings of the Museum of Mexican Arts, which are anything but smooth. Among its other problems is a greedy and much-disliked director, Frank De Palma, who knows how to curry favor and raise funds but knows next to nothing about art, Mexican or otherwise. He thinks the symbolic *arbol de la vida* (Tree of Life) donated by Isabel Cunningham, a descendant of one of the Spanish land-grant families, is a magnificent work of art, when in fact it is one of the most hideous objects Elena has ever seen: eight feet tall, over four feet wide, painted in numerous garish colors, its ceramic branches containing the Virgin Mary, Adam and Eve clutching bright green fig leaves, angels with banjos and horns, a serpent munching a blue and yellow apple, and a great deal more. Frank wants the *arbol* in place in time for the Cinco de Mayo celebration the next day. Elena puts up a vehement argument, loses her patience, and in front of witnesses says, "Somebody ought to kill you!"

That night, somebody *does* kill "Tio Taco"—although at first his death seems to be an accident, for Frank is found lying beneath the Tree of Life, his skull crushed. But when the police, in the person of Lieutenant Dave Kirk, discover that Frank's death was indeed murder, Elena becomes the primary suspect. In order to clear herself, she embarks on her own investigation—one that is fraught with peril, involves a clever variation on the locked-room gambit, turns up some other surprising facts, and culminates in a deadly confrontation in the museum's basement.

Elena is an engaging sleuth, all the more so for her warm and often humorous relationship with her mother, Gabriela, and Gabriela's geriatric boyfriend, Nick, both of whom lived in a Goleta trailer park. (Elena's second adventure, *The Legend of the Slain Soldiers,* 1985, focuses on murder and intrigue at the trailer park, as well as on elements of Mexican-American history.) *The Tree of Death* is a mystery-for-fun, more lightweight than the McCone books, but equally enjoyable Elena is someone you'll like as soon as you meet her, someone you'll want to get to know better.

(*B.P.*)

*Murphy, Warren. *The Ceiling of Hell.* New York: Fawcett Gold Medal, 1984. (O/PI/T)

Warren Murphy is the author of more than eighty novels, including sixty titles in the popular and long-running *Destroyer* series that he cocreated and coauthors with Richard Sapir. But Murphy is a versatile writer who enjoys doing other types of crime and adventure fiction, including serious novels like *The Ceiling of Hell*—a combination of thriller and private-eye mystery that was awarded a PWA Best Paperback Shamus.

In the first chapter, Secret Service agent Steve Hooks takes a bullet in the knee while saving the president of the United States from an assassin's bullet. With some help from a grateful chief executive, Hooks, complete with cane and a brace on his leg, opens his own agency.

His first job, a referral from the Secret Service, is to guard the life of a German professor, an anti-Nazi who is in the United States to lecture. In turn, the professor wants to hire Hooks to track down a woman named Anna Mueller. When the professor is killed while in Hooks's care, he takes it on himself to continue the search for the woman, feeling it might lead to the professor's killer. What it leads to is a threat of the rise of a fourth reich—in the United States!

There are twists and turns galore, and Hooks must also deal with a wife who has been in a coma ever since she was shot at the same time and place he was, and the growing attraction between himself and her sister. All of it is expertly handled—as Warren Murphy's work usually is.

Noteworthy among Murphy's other nonseries novels—and further testimony to his versatility—are a locked-room mystery, *Leonardo's Law* (1978); an excellent political thriller, *The Red Moon* (1982); and a tour de force about a confrontation between good and evil in the world of chess, *Grandmaster* (1984). The last-named title was coauthored with his wife, Molly Cochran, and won an Edgar for Best Paperback of its year; it is especially recommended for its blending of the thriller, the novel of espionage, and the story of psychological suspense.

(*R.J.R.*)

Murphy, Warren. *Trace and 47 Miles of Rope.* New York: New American Library (Signet), 1984. (O/PI)

This is the second novel in Murphy's new and popular PI series about insurance investigator Devlin Tracy, known as "Trace." Trace lives in Las Vegas with his Japanese girlfriend, Chico, a part-time blackjack dealer and part-time hooker.

Trace's cases for Garrison Fidelity Insurance Company usually take him away from his home in Las Vegas, but in this book the case comes to him. The safe in the home of the Countess Felicia Fallaci is broken into and her manservant is killed. The public at large doesn't know whether or not anything is missing, but the insurance company does and they hire Trace to try to find what amounts to a fortune in jewels before they pay off on her insurance policy. In the course of his investigation, he encounters "characters" like the amorous countess herself, a German baron, a porno bombshell with a limited vocabulary, and a sleazy PI named R. J. Roberts, who was "twenty pounds too heavy and two days too dirty."

The Trace books depend heavily on characterization, most specifically the off-the-wall character of Trace himself. He's an on-again, off-again boozer; he has the sharpest tongue of any PI in history, and possibly the quickest mind—though not necessarily "detective" quick; and he has opinions about everything and is not afraid to voice them. Other recurring characters are, of course, Chico, who is more than a match for him; Walter Marks, vice-president of Garrison Fidelity, whom Trace takes great pleasure in teasing; and Bob Swenson, president of Garrison, who is sometimes as off-the-wall as Trace, to Marks's exasperation. Murphy is in perfect control of his characters and material because he himself is a lot like Trace—and only someone with a mind like his could write a series like this one.

The Trace books are quick, pleasurable reads, falling somewhere between the *Destroyer* series and Murphy's "serious" thrillers. The first in the series was *Trace* (1983); others are *When Elephants Forget* (1984) and *Pigs Get Fat* (1985). Still more are planned for the future, which is good news for anyone who likes his PI fiction fast, funny, and unconventional.

(*R.J.R.*)

Nebel, Frederick. *Six Deadly Dames.* Boston: Gregg Press, 1980. (Reprint of paperback original published in 1950 by Avon.) (SS/PI)

Of all the private eyes who battled their way through the pages of the pulp magazines in the Thirties and Forties in pursuit of truth, justice, and the American Way, one of the toughest and most vividly drawn is Frederick Nebel's slightly jaded, slightly shady "Tough Dick" Donahue. Donahue made his debut in the November 1930 issue of *Black Mask* in a story called "Rough Justice," and appeared in fourteen more cases until his "retirement" in 1935. A former New York City cop who was fired for raiding the wrong gambling joint, he works for the Inter-State Detective Agency and is not above using illegal methods to achieve his goals. "I've been up against crooks, guns, and I've double-crossed them to get what I wanted," he says in one story. "That's what my game is. It's not a polite business of question-and-answer bunk. You work against crooks and you've got to beat them at their own game."

Toughness is only one of the elements that make the Donahue stories memorable. They are also vivid portraits of the New York underworld at the end of Prohibition, rich in the street slang of the period and spiced with an underplayed sense of gallows humor. The best of the six novelettes included in *Six Deadly Dames* are probably the first two, "The Red Hots" and "Get a Load of This," which are complete stories but can also be read as a two-part novella; they deal with the theft of a valuable necklace, Donahue's blood-spattered search for it, and a couple of decidedly lethal sisters. Also good are "Death's Not Enough," in which Donahue finds himself doing battle with a female "torpedo" named Beryl Mercine; and "Save Your Tears," in which boxing, gangsters, and a flame-haired Jezebel named Token Moore combine to give Donnie all the trouble he can handle.

Nebel wrote two other excellent pulp series: one featuring another private eye, Cardigan, for *Dime Detective;* the other, for *Black Mask,* starring Captain Steve MacBride of the Richmond City police and Kennedy of the *Free Press.* Neither series has been collected—yet. Nebel also wrote two first-rate crime novels: *Sleepers East* (1933), which deals with intrigue aboard a fast-moving train and was filmed three times, once as *Sleepers West;* and *Fifty Roads to Town* (1936), a study of the explosive passions of several people snowbound in a small upstate Maine village.

(*B.P.*)

Neely, Richard. *The Walter Syndrome.* New York: McCall, 1970. (PS)

Lambert Post is a mild-mannered classified-advertising phone solicitor for the *New York Journal;* his association with the silver-tongued Charles Walter begins quite innocently, as he listens to Walter flatter landladies into placing "rooms to let" ads in the paper. Walter, whose upper-class background and ease with people impresses Post, finds a "most fascinated and sympathetic audience" in him, and soon he progresses from boasting of his exploits to enlisting Post's participation in a little game: Walter gets the names of recent widows and divorcées from the paper, then calls them up and makes a date; but Post is the man who shows up, explaining Walter has been called out of town. Quickly the encounters turn ugly. One woman humiliates him in front of a roomful of guests; another has her boyfriend beat him up. Angry at the women's treatment of Post, Walter embarks on a plan of revenge.

The first woman, Jennifer Hartwick, is knocked unconscious, raped, and left in a room at a hotel; because of an anonymous call, the police think she is a prostitute. The second woman, Diane Summers, and her boyfriend, Edward Cranston, are found shot to death. At first the police suspect a murder/suicide, but then they find that a third party purchased the gun; and Walter—ever protective of Post—realizes that Lambert can be identified not only as the man who bought the weapon but also as someone with a grudge against Jennifer Hartwick. Thus, he reasons, Jennifer must die, too. Soon the papers are carrying stories about the Executioner, a man who punishes women for their wickedness. And as investigative reporter Maury Ryan of the *Journal* delves into the case, the Executioner begins to contact him by phone, throwing out teasers and taunting him.

Told from the viewpoints of Post, Walter, and Ryan, this is a truly frightening tale. By the time a fourth woman is murdered and we realize the Executioner's plans for a fifth, it is impossible to put the book down. While the astute reader may pick up on what is going on fairly early, the outcome is nonetheless chilling—and the ultimate revelation is a total surprise.

Neely has written other tales of psychological suspense, among them *Death to My Beloved* (1969), *The Japanese Mistress* (1972), *Lies* (1978), *The Obligation* (1979), and *Shadows from the Past* (1983).

(*M.M.*)

Nelson, Hugh Lawrence. *The Season for Murder.* New York: Rinehart, 1952. (PI/A)

Denver private investigators Zebulion Buck and Jim Dunn, posing as avalanche-control experts, arrive in the small Colorado mountain town of Geneva in May, the time of the spring thaws. Their Pine Detective Agency has been retained by a Washington agency (Buck has contacts in Washington) to search the wilderness around Geneva for the wreckage of a small plane that crashed during a storm the previous January—a plane carrying an important government official who in turn was carrying a large sum of money. They put up at Tom Cook's posh, Swiss-style Alpine Lodge and get to know the local residents; and as they do, they realize there are undercurrents of tension flowing beneath the town's placid surface.

When the plane is finally found, not only is the money missing but in the vicinity is the corpse of a prospector, Old Joe, who appears to have died under suspicious circumstances. The investigation takes other unexpected and deadly turns: Buck is almost killed by a sudden rockslide of the sort that did in Old Joe (and as if that weren't enough, he contracts a case of Rocky Mountain spotted fever); more local intrigue develops; Dunn has a run-in with a bearded oddball named Kermit the Hermit; and a second death, this one definitely murder, occurs. All of which sweeps Buck and Dunn into a tense climax in which they are forced to do battle with both a murderer *and* a raging forest fire.

The Colorado setting is vividly depicted, and the medium-to-soft-boiled Buck (who is part Indian) and Dunn (an ex-Texan) are engaging if not especially pithy or illustrious characters. As in Nelson's other mysteries, the puzzle and its unraveling is adequately handled. The action and outdoor scenes are the high spots, in particular those involving the forest fire, and generate considerable suspense.

Most of the other novels featuring Buck and Dunn, all with Colorado settings, are also worth investigating. The standouts are *Ring the Bell at Zero* (1949), in which Buck and Dunn find themselves snowbound with a murderer in an old mining town that has been turned into a summer resort; *Murder Comes High* (1950), in which death stalks a uranium-mining party camped in the high-mountain wilderness; and *Gold in Every Grave* (1951), wherein Dunn takes part in a Vigilante Days celebration that features a mock lynching—except that this year the victim is shot to death as he is being strung up. Nelson also wrote a series of novels featuring a San Francisco cop named Steve Johnson, but with the exception of the first—*The Title Is Murder* (1947), a bibliomystery—these are undistinguished and rather dull.

(*B.P.*)

Nevins, Francis M. *Corrupt and Ensnare.* New York: Putnam's, 1978. (AD/S)

Francis M. Nevins, professor of law at St. Louis University, knows his subject when he writes about his series character Loren Mensing, also a professor of law. His other well-known continuing character is con artist Milo Turner. So Nevins works opposite sides of the street in his fiction, and does it very well. He also writes excellent nonfiction, having won an Edgar for his 1974 *Royal Bloodline,* an incisive analysis of the works of Ellery Queen (q.v.).

In this novel, detective/professor Mensing is drawn into a case involving the death of a state supreme court justice when the judge's widow discovers in his closet a shoebox containing $50,000. A quiet investigation is called for, by someone not only skilled at his job but having knowledge of the law. Mensing possesses these qualities, and having been a protégé of the judge, he will be sympathetic as well as knowledgeable.

The investigation leads Mensing to the Bennell Foundation, the philanthropic division of Benneco, a multinational oil company. The judge had cast the swing vote in favor of Benneco in the most controversial case during his tenure on the court. Before giving up on the judge's integrity, Mensing probes deeper and uncovers CIA involvement and a Benneco family heir with plans of his own for the company's holdings in Latin America.

This is a flawlessly plotted, adroitly written thinking man's mystery. Corrupt you it won't, ensnare you it will.

Francis M. Nevins's other novel featuring Loren Mensing is the entertaining *Publish and Perish* (1975). The multitalented professor has also edited several anthologies, among them a book of "lost" Cornell Woolrich (q.v.) stories, *Nightwebs* (1971), the foreword to which gives testimony to Nevins's expertise in matters Woolrichian and passion for his subject's life and work.

(*J.L.*)

Nichols, Fan. *The Loner.* New York: Simon & Schuster, 1956. (PS)

This novel opens with a deceptively simple scene: A young man who apparently is visiting a patient at a mental hospital manages to get a lift back to New York City with two women who are also visitors. He has them fooled, and for a moment he almost fools us. But then we realize that the man is a patient bent on escape. The scene is a deft bit of characterization of the man, Gilbert Gray, and it lends credibility to the manner in which he is able to fool others throughout the course of this suspenseful tale.

Gilbert reaches Manhattan and contacts his sister, Sheila, a prostitute. At first she insists he return to the hospital, but finally she backs down—an old pattern, because she feels responsible for his mental problems—and gives him money. Alone in a big city, a disturbed man can get into trouble, even if he has only $20. . . .

The next day, a B-girl from the Club Monterrey is found strangled, and reporter Barry Kimball of the *Daily Courier* is on the scene. Barry is on better terms with the police than many reporters, and soon he finds himself drawn into the case as protection for a photographer named Joan Markham, who may have taken the murderer's picture with the dead woman at the nightclub. Barry, an embittered divorced man, initially resists his attraction to Joan; but as he becomes more involved, her safety becomes vitally important to him. The man who murdered the B-girl has made no overt effort to contact Joan, but Barry worries about her anyway; he doesn't like the fiercely possessive young man down the hall, nor does he care for Joan's roommate, Cindy, a would-be actress.

Events proceed—including another murder—and we view them through the eyes of Barry, Joan, and the sister, Sheila, as well as from Gilbert's warped vantage point. From the subtle beginning to the action-packed conclusion, Nichols gives us a rare and convincing glimpse into the mind of a psychotic killer, made all the more bizarre for the rationality of the other viewpoint characters.

Other suspense novels by Fan Nichols (who also wrote erotic novels) include *Ask for Linda* (1953), *He Walks by Night* (1957), and *Be Silent, Love* (1960).

(*M.M.*)

*Nielsen, Helen. *Detour.* New York: Washburn, 1953. (W)

Helen Nielsen was one of the few women to write for such male-oriented magazines as *Manhunt* in the early Fifties, and the influence of this early training ground shows in her crisp prose and skillful handling of action scenes. Nielsen herself has commented that she is "old-fashioned enough to believe that characters still make a story, and that every story, especially a mystery, must have a beginning, a middle, and an ending." This concern is reflected in the careful construction of her plots; Nielsen always plays fair with her reader, placing the necessary clues cleverly. Her characters are well delineated and experience considerable change as a result of the violent events that happen to them.

An early novel, *Detour* is the story of two men: Danny Ross, an eighteen-year-old who is fleeing the United States for Mexico, not "running away from life . . . running toward it"; and Trace Cooper, dispossessed scion of the once-wealthy family for which his town—Cooperton—is named, sometime lawyer, and (recently) full-time drunk. The novel opens just after Danny's jalopy has given out on a desert road. He thumbs a ride with an old man, Dr. Gaynor, who buys him a soda at a café outside Cooperton. But before they can continue their trip into town, the doctor, who has just received a $200 payment from one of his patients, is brutally beaten to death. And Danny, who has $200 (his life savings) in his pocket, becomes the chief suspect.

No one in Cooperton is willing to believe Danny's protests of innocence, except perhaps for Sheriff Virgil Keep's peculiar wife Ada. But then Alexander Laurent, a celebrated criminal lawyer living in retirement with *his* peculiar son on the former Cooper ranch, takes an interest. Laurent asks Trace Cooper to look into the case; Trace gets started by busting up the bar in which he has been drinking and being thrown into the cell next to Danny's. Before Trace's investigation is concluded, a second murder has taken place; Dr. Gaynor's death is linked with the death of the local "bad girl," Francy Allen; suspicion has fallen on nearly everyone in the town; and Ada Keep has made a stand for the first time in her life. Both Danny and Trace are men who have a lot of growing up to do, and in the course of this tautly written, suspenseful novel, they both accomplish that.

(*M.M.*)

*Nielsen, Helen. *Sing Me a Murder.* New York: Morrow, 1960. (PS)

Playwright Ty Leander lost his wife, singer Julie San Martin, when fire swept their southern California canyon home. Ty, who had quarreled with Julie and left town to work in solitude on his latest play, is consumed with guilt over her death. So consumed, in fact, that he attempts to hang himself in a rooming house—in the exact room where a woman named Mary Brownlee was murdered when her boyfriend allegedly threw acid in her face the day Ty last saw Julie. Coincidence—or *is* it? Ty's friends—designer Alex Draeger, lawyer Cole Riley (who is defending Mary Brownlee's boyfriend), and producer Marcus Anatole—don't think so. Ty called Cole before his obviously fake suicide attempt, and immediately after his "rescue" he announced that he was tired of living and would try to convince the police *he* murdered Miss Brownlee, thus sparing the life of the boyfriend, who possibly is not guilty.

The friends agree to keep tabs on Ty, and are alarmed when he shows up at the murder trial. Although initially he refused to believe his wife was dead, now Ty seems obsessed with finding out the details of her last days: who she saw, where she had the oil of her Ferrari changed, what dress she wore to a cocktail party at Alex's. And when Ty knocks out Alex's protégé, a textile designer, and takes a bottle of nitric acid from his studio, the friends are seriously alarmed. His behavior becomes even more erratic when he finds out that the murder victim looked enough like Julie to have been her twin. His friends are convinced he is about to go off the deep end. Regardless of his mental state, when a second murder occurs, Ty's game becomes a dangerous, nearly fatal one.

This is a richly complex novel, about which Anthony Boucher said, "Substantial as a novel of character in the modern vein of suspense, it is as inventive and deceptive as any strict classic puzzle—a meaty book, opulent with unpredictable pleasures." This reviewer is in total agreement.

Other highly recommended novels by Nielsen are *The Fifth Caller* (1959), which concerns the murder of an odd and unorthodox female physician; *After Midnight* (1967), featuring series character lawyer Simon Drake; and *A Killer in the Street* (1967), which tells of a couple's cross-country flight from a brutal killer.

(*M.M.*)

O'Cork, Shannon. *End of the Line.* New York: St. Martin's, 1981. (AD)

T. T. Baldwin, the heroine of *End of the Line,* tells this story in the first person. She is a self-contained, often smug young woman in her early twenties who has made a career for herself in sports photography, and she narrates her tale as if she either wished she were Hemingway or were sleeping with him.

The story takes us to a shark-fishing festival in a small town outside New York City. T.T. and Floyd Beesom, her chauvinist partner on the *New York Graphic,* have been asked by managing editor Barkley to investigate the disappearance of a very valuable diamond necklace belonging to Barkley's old Harvard classmate Gordon Kittredge, and to try to find the well-known gemsmith who vanished with it. Avram Stein is presumed to be either dead or on the run with the jewels.

But meanwhile, out on the shark-fishing boat, Jeremy Yunker, the man who insured the necklace, has been killed, apparently as the result of an accident. And his is not the only corpse to show up. The story leads us to a littered beach, an old family mansion, and all over New York, then finally takes us back out to sea for more fun and adventure. The climax is exciting if rather confusing, but the formidable T. T. Baldwin unscrambles most of it for us.

O'Cork, who is married to mystery writer Hillary Waugh (q.v.), is an entertaining storyteller with good timing and skill in her action scenes. Her main characters come fully alive, although some of the minor ones fail to ring true. In all, this novel has more strong points than weak ones, and T.T.—who first appeared in *Sports Freak* (1980) and returns in *Hell Bent for Heaven* (1983)—is an engaging young woman.

(*T.S.*)

O'Dell, J. W. *Loan Shark.* New York: Belmont Tower, 1975. (O/T)

Terry Southern once claimed that real gold can be found by mining the muddy waters of American commercial fiction. *Loan Shark* is a good example of Southern's contention—a raw, indisputably minor book that nonetheless has the power to move and is blessed with a crude kind of poetry.

Ex-con Joey must be saved by his policeman brother, Frank Cassidy, from the wrath of a mobster to whom Joey owes not only money but also an apology for insulting a family member. Much of the New York Mafia pursues Joey while Frank does all he can to forestall the inevitable.

While there's nothing new in the story, and while much of the writing suffers from haste and a penchant for pulpiness, O'Dell (if that is indeed his/her name) presents the brothers in surprisingly persuasive detail. Joey is the sort of loser for whom death is a mercy. Loud, frantic, alternately beseeching and abusive, he is a man fate earmarked for a bad end many years ago. O'Dell presents him just sympathetically enough that we hope he can somehow escape his own mistakes, knowing all the while that he can't.

Frank is more complex, a decent man compromised by a certain bitterness. O'Dell gives us a portrait of a widower who, while missing his wife, nonetheless clearly recalls her faults—just as, while he has affection for his brother, he is also disgusted by the man for being the tortured weakling that he is.

A bleak world is sketched in here—from the scuzzy movie theaters where Joey hides from the mob to the warehouse where the climax is played out. What gives the story its reach is O'Dell's ability to infuse his people, even the sluglike hoods, with real hope—and then to crush that hope utterly. A nasty and numbing performance, altogether, with all the faults of quick-buck fiction, but also with moments of real insight and compassion.

While *Loan Shark* does not deserve a huge audience or even a resurrection, its cunning, energy, and seedy beauty are worth the hunt for a used copy.

(*E.G.*)

O'Donnell, Lillian. *The Children's Zoo.* New York: Putnam's, 1981. (PP)

Perhaps it is her experience as an actress and director in the theater that has given Lillian O'Donnell such a good sense of timing. Whatever the reason, the novels in both her New York policewoman Norah Mulcahaney and special investigator Mici Anhalt series are page-turners. O'Donnell began her career with a number of traditional domestic mysteries. She has also written two mainstream novels. However, it is primarily for the Norah Mulcahaney series that she became known.

The Phone Calls (1972) was one of the first serious novels about a woman police officer. In it Noah emerges as a likable and competent professional. As the series progresses, Norah marries a police detective, tries to become pregnant, adopts a child, loses the child, and deals with such demands of domestic life as in-laws. Her domestic life so colors her professional life that it is essential for the reader to share her interest in pregnancy, children, and extended family life in order to truly enjoy the books.

The first murders in *The Children's Zoo* are of defenseless animals and a guard. They lead Norah to a posh private high school and into the lives of Manhattan's rich and not-so-rich adolescents and their parents. She must deal with the callousness of overindulged youths as well as submerged class conflicts, and there is a subplot concerning the Coke-bottle rape of Norah's visiting niece. This book is typical of the Mulcahaney series—timely premise, crisp and exciting plot, and considerable domestic concern.

Some other titles in the series are *Don't Wear Your Wedding Ring* (1973), *Leisure Dying* (1976), *Cop Without a Shield* (1983), and *Ladykiller* (1984).

(*S.D.*)

O'Donnell, Lillian. *Wicked Designs.* New York: Putnam's, 1980. (AD)

For those of O'Donnell's readers who don't care for domestic entanglements, there is the Mici Anhalt series. Mici is, in many ways, the next generation after Norah Mulcahaney. She is single, independent, and has a job—with the Bureau of Victims of Crime in New York City—which allows her to investigate both as an amateur and as a professional. She can use her title when it will help, but she is not restrained by police regulations. And she can make mistakes that a trained police officer could not—as well as laugh at herself for making them. Because she does not carry a gun and has not had police training, Mici relies on her wits to solve her cases. She is an enthusiastic and appealing heroine.

In *Wicked Designs,* Mici is thrust into investigating the murder of a dowager whose body was found at the bottom of the subway steps next to a locked entrance. There were drugs in her system and needle marks on her arms, but her nephew refuses to believe she was an addict. He and his pregnant wife alternately complain and goad Mici into continuing her investigation—which includes trips to the morgue, the D.A.'s office, a fortune-teller's digs, and the office of a candidate for governor. To lighten the seriousness of the investigation, O'Donnell uses the domestic problems of the nephew and the subsequent annoyances they cause Mici. (He passes out on her couch; his *wife* passes out on her couch; and she barely knows these people!) None of these elements are extraneous, however. The plot is well constructed, the characters are interesting and believable, and the solution includes a twist that is sure to delight O'Donnell's fans.

Other Mici Anhalt titles are *Aftershock* (1977) and *Falling Star* (1979).

(*S.D.*)

O'Donnell, Peter. *Pieces of Modesty.* London: Pan, 1972. (O/E/SS)

Modesty Blaise first appeared as a comic-strip character in 1962, and the first novelization of her exploits was published in 1965. She is often thought of as a female James Bond, but her wildly entertaining adventures certainly entitle her to stand alone as a fascinating fictional character.

A good way to make Modesty's acquaintance is to read the stories collected in *Pieces of Modesty,* each of which reveals something of her background and philosophy. At the age of eighteen, Modesty commanded the Network, the most successful crime organization outside the United States. After dismantling the Network, she occasionally found herself working for the intelligence section of the British Foreign Office, as she does in "The Giggle-wrecker," in which a very reluctant defector is transferred from East to West Berlin. A better story is "I Had a Date with Lady Janet," narrated in the first person by Modesty's formidable associate Willie Garvin, who comes to Modesty's rescue when she is held captive by an old enemy ensconced in a Scottish castle. "A Better Day to Die" and "Salamander Four" might be read as companion pieces. In the former, Modesty finds herself captured by guerrillas, along with the other passengers on a bus. One of the passengers, a minister who believes strongly in nonviolence, sees the results of brutality and is changed by them. In "Salamander Four," a sculptor given to noninvolvement finds himself involved against his will when Modesty helps a wounded man, but the ending is less predictable. "The Soo Girl Charity" features Modesty and Willie in a robbery for charity and has an amusing twist at the end.

For colorful writing and nonstop action, the books about Modesty Blaise are hard to beat, especially such titles as *Modesty Blaise* (1965), *Sabre-Tooth* (1966), *I, Lucifer* (1967), and two titles published for the first time in the United States in 1984—*The Silver Mistress* (1973) and *The Xanadu Talisman* (1981).

(*B.C.*)

Offord, Lenore Glen. *The Glass Mask.* New York: Duell, 1944. (AD)

Lenore Glen Offord is one of the truly underrated writers of the World War II and postwar periods. Her characters are engaging and true to their times and environments. Her heroine, Georgine Wyeth, is the forerunner of today's feminists—a single mother supporting her daughter with short-term jobs, forcing herself to deal with her fears, to stand up for herself, insisting all the time that she's tired of being saved. Most of Offord's books are set in Berkeley or other areas of northern California. She excels in portraying the uniqueness of the university town and the wartime atmosphere—the paranoia as well as the desperate excitement. Although she deals more with innocent romantic situations than is stylish now, every seeming digression into a character's personal life is relevant to the plot.

In *The Glass Mask,* the chief responsibility for detection shifts from Georgine Wyeth to pulp writer Todd McKinnon, though the story is told from Georgine's viewpoint. Todd, Georgine, and Georgine's eight-year-old daughter stop off in a Sacramento Valley town to satisfy his curiosity about a family mystery: Did Gilbert Peabody hasten the death of his ailing grandmother in order to inherit her house and thus be able to afford to marry? There is no proof, only verdict by rumor. Unable to face the innuendo, Gilbert has enlisted in the army and gone, leaving his wife to deal with the townsfolk and the more unpleasant relatives. By varying means, she tricks and inveigles the McKinnon-Wyeth ménage into staying on day after day to investigate the nocturnal footsteps in the attic, the family patriarch who rants and feigns seizures, and the mystery of what the old lady got from the bank the day she died and where she hid it.

This is an entertaining tale, and one of Offord's best. Georgine Wyeth is also at her most appealing in *Skeleton Key* (1943), in which she investigates the murder of a wartime air-raid warden during an unexpected blackout. Unfortunately, Offord's output was not great: merely eight mysteries, four other adult books, and a juvenile. Especially good among the other mysteries are *Murder on Russian Hill* (1938), *The 9 Dark Hours* (1941), and *The Smiling Tiger* (1951).

(*S.D.*)

O'Hanlon, James. *Murder at Horsethief.* New York: Phoenix Press, 1941. (AD)

This novel, like Michael Morgan's *Decoy* (q.v.), is of such hilarious awfulness that it deserves cult status. The "heroes" here (as in O'Hanlon's other novels) are Jason and Pat Cordry, a couple of wisecracking amateur sleuths who were once Hollywood film extras—a sort of lowbrow Mr. and Mrs. North. The setting is a neo–Wild West town, Horsethief, Arizona, near which gold has been rediscovered. The Cordrys, lost in the desert, stumble on a Horsethief lynch mob that is about to hang a Mexican for the murder of a popular local doctor. Jason intervenes and manages to save the Mexican's life by announcing that the man is innocent and that he, Jason, will find the real culprit; the mob is so awed by this bravado that it backs down and agrees to let Jason go sleuthing—with the proviso that if he *doesn't* reveal someone else as the murderer within two weeks, they will hang him and the Mexican both.

Jason and Pat soon find themselves playing cat and mouse with an impressive and improbable array of individuals, among them a crooked saloon owner who was once an L.A. mobster; a group of entertainers calling themselves Frankie Sparrow and his Seven Swinging Canaries; a tribe of Malooga (*sic*) Indians who live in the nearby mountains and say clever things like "How" and "Ugh"; and a group of vigilantes who wear flour-sack hoods and operate as the Haunts of Horsethief. Jason finds the villain responsible for the doctor's death and other nefarious deeds, of course, but not before he and Pat suffer a series of narrow escapes reminiscent of one of the old Republic film serials.

Indeed, O'Hanlon probably *wrote* a film serial or two, during his other "literary" pursuit as a Hollywood scriptwriter. He fancied himself a humorist, with special emphasis on wisecracking repartee; but his real genius was not so much in terrible B-movie dialogue, as in creative butchery of the English language through phonetic spellings and some of the weirdest idioms ever committed to paper. Just two examples, as spoken by an Indian and a preacher, respectively:

> *"Come catchum smoke. Chetterfiel ceegret. Come back byeumbye aftah braves makeum pow-wow wit' Lomitaha."*
>
> *"Brethern . . . and sistern . . . we are gathered heah t' give decent burial t' our departed friend an' brothah, Doc Thayah. Y'all knowed Doc t' be a mighty good man, which is more'n we kin say fer the murderin' skunk what plugged him! The Good Book sez 'Fergive us our trespissis like we fergives them what trespissis ag'in us. By the way, lambs o' the flock," the gentleman deviated, "come Sunday, Ah'm preachin' a powerful pregnant sermon on that subjeck of trespissin', in the Hossthief Theater, an' Ah wan's y'all t' be theah! Brothah Herman's Happy Harbor is mah new name fer the place, an' in it Ah inten's t' do a lotta soul-patchin'!"*

If the sublimely ridiculous and the ridiculously funny tickle your fancy, then *Murder at Horsethief* is the book for you. As are O'Hanlon's other zany efforts: *Murder at Malibu* (1937); *Murder at 300 to 1* (1938), featuring a racehorse named Disaster that eats potted geraniums; *Murder at Coney Island* (1939); and *As Good as Murdered* (1940), in which Jason attempts to emulate his creator by becoming a Hollywood scriptwriter, only to find himself enmeshed in a screwball real-life adventure identical to one he creates for the screen.

(*B.P.*)

Olden, Marc. *Dai-Sho.* New York: Arbor House, 1983. (T/A)

Much of Marc Olden's work reflects the fact that he is a martial-arts expert, but none more so than this novel, a blend of ancient and contemporary Japan. Literally translated, the title means "big sword, little sword," those carried by the samurai of old Japan.

Frank DiPalma, an ex-cop turned famous television crime reporter, returns to Japan to find out who killed the woman Frank loved and left eleven years before, Katherine Hansard. She has left behind a son, Todd Hansard—Frank DiPalma's son, although the boy doesn't know it. DiPalma himself is an expert martial artist, specifically the art of Filipino stick fighting. In Japan he encounters an old enemy, Kon Kenpachi, ostensibly a Japanese film director, but in reality much, much more. Kenpachi, a believer in Bushido and all that goes with it, awakes in Todd Hansard the spirit of a long-dead samurai, and DiPalma becomes embroiled not only in murder but in trying to save his son before Kenpachi and the warrior spirit can take the boy beyond his—or anyone's—reach.

Filled with interesting characters, subplots and counterplots, and detailed depictions of ancient and contemporary Japan, this is a powerful novel, expertly written by a man who knows his subject, and his craft.

Marc Olden's "Black Samurai" series—*Black Samurai* (1974) and *The Deadly Pearl* (1974) are just two of the titles—was filmed with Jim Kelly. He has also written more than twenty other novels, among them *Poe Must Die* (1978), which utilizes Edgar Allan Poe as a detective.

(*R.J.R.*)

Olsen, D. B. *The Cat Wears a Noose.* New York: Doubleday Crime Club, 1944. (AD)

Early in her career, Dolores Hitchens (q.v.) published most of her novels under her (then) married name, D. B. Olsen—standard mysteries of the Thirties and Forties that feature a pair of series sleuths and lack the quality and insight of her later work. One of her series detectives is A. Pennyfeather, professor of English literature at Clarendon College; the other, much better known, is the quintessential spinster snoop, Miss Rachel Murdock, who—with the help of her sister, Miss Jennifer; her cat, Samantha; and occasionally police detective Stephen Mayhew—solves all sorts of sinister goings-on in southern California, Oregon, and the Southwest.

The Cat Wears a Noose (all of the Miss Rachel novels have the word *cat* in the title and generally involve a cat in some way or other) is typical of the series. Miss Rachel is asked by young Shirley Melissa Grant to investigate some unpleasantness in the home of her uncle, John Terrice, which is nearby; it seems she is being harassed for unknown reasons, the latest indignity being the death of her pet canary. Meanwhile, unbeknown to Miss Rachel, Miss Jennifer has witnessed a murder on the front steps of the Terrice house.

Miss Rachel soon embarks on her investigation (by taking a job as the Terrice's cook)—"the affair she decided eventually to call the Case of the Sliver of Doubt, in which she played a game of wits with Murder over such trivialities as a cologne bottle, a red robe, a wedding ring in a nest of cotton, a werewolf, and a woman who wore garlic. . . . As to the werewolf, Miss Rachel prefers not to think. There are deeps in the human soul like the chasm in the western Pacific, where strange things swim, where old terrors peer from their medieval darkness, where long shapes coil and seem asleep, where the unbelieved comes to life." Etc. It will come as a surprise to no one that, deeps in the human soul notwithstanding, the werewolf in these pages isn't real.

This and the other Miss Rachel novels are mildly diverting but seem dated and contrived by today's standards, full as they are of melodramatic plot components and writing of the sort quoted above. Others of interest, for their backgrounds if nothing else, are *Cats Have Tall Shadows* (1948), set at an inn on the Oregon coast; and *The Cat Wears a Mask* (1949), set in New Mexico and involving Kachina Indian legends. The Pennyfeather series is more interesting, although the professor is somewhat colorless and pedantic in his approach to crime solving. His best case is probably *Enrollment Cancelled* (1952), in which he solves the murder of a student on the Clarendon campus; this has some neat plot twists and a well-realized academic background.

(*B.P.*)

O'Malley, Patrick. *The Affair of the Blue Pig.* New York: M.S. Mill, 1965. (C/W/A)

This is the seventh novel by Patrick O'Malley (a pseudonym of Frank O'Rourke, who is better known for his western and off-beat mainstream fiction) featuring the amusing duo, Harrigan and Hoeffler. The two are agents for an unnamed intelligence organization headed by a benevolent individual known only as the Old Man. In this adventure, they take leave—with the agency's blessing and aid—to help an old friend, Andrew Volker, solve a murder for which a friend of his has been framed.

Twelve years before, Harrigan and Hoeffler provided Volker, a man whose "lean old parrot" facade is deceiving, with a new identity after failing to clear him of a murder his wife had framed him for. Now Volker leads a sedate, if unsatisfying, life as a retiree, wintering in Florida and summering at Swan Lake, Minnesota. It is on his final day at the lake that a woman he has met once, Maureen Whittleby, is murdered. A second acquaintance, Alex Ganzbrook, is accused of the killing and flees to Volker's cottage. Because he sees the parallel to his situation of twelve years ago, and because he instinctively likes and trusts the younger man, Volker helps Alex escape from the Swan Lake area and takes him to California, where both the family members of the dead woman and Harrigan and Hoeffler live. The agents happen to be in Switzerland now, but they quickly return in response to Andrew's request for help.

Employing all the resources of their organization, Harrigan and Hoeffler enlist Volker and Alex Ganzbrook in their investigation of the members of Mrs. Whittleby's family, who reportedly hated her because she controlled the family purse strings. And through their clever and amusing machinations (one of which is posing as researchers inquiring into the sex lives of residents of Marin County), the case is brought to a surprising and satisfying conclusion.

Harrigan and Hoeffler are an engaging team, and their low-key, humorous interchanges are delightful. Neither man is characterized to any great depth, but the nonseries characters—notably Andrew Volker and Alex

Ganzbrook—are developed with sensitivity and understanding. This series is highly recommended for the reader who likes comedy mixed with good detection and a variety of settings.

Some other titles featuring Harrigan and Hoeffler are *The Affair of the Red Mosaic* (1961), *The Affair of Chief Strongheart* (1964), and *The Affair of the Bumbling Briton* (1965). Under the name Frank O'Malley, O'Rourke wrote a very good private eye novel, *The Best Go First* (1950). And under his own name, he has published such novels of suspense as *High Dive* (1954) and the amusing *The Abduction of Virginia Lee* (1970).

(*M.M.*)

Oppenheim, E. Phillips. *The Great Impersonation.* Boston: Little, Brown, 1920. (E)

The author of some 150 novels, as well as numerous short stories, E. Phillips Oppenheim was one of the major producers of popular fiction in the early part of the twentieth century. Dubbed "The Prince of Storytellers," he set most of his thrillers in his native England, or on the Riviera (his second home), although various other European and exotic locations make an appearance from time to time.

The Great Impersonation begins in Africa, of all places, and with the unlikely meeting of two old Eton schoolmates—one English and one German—who, while hardly twins, do happen to look alike. Their paths, however, have led in different directions since Eton. The Englishman, Sir Everard Dominey, after making a muddle of his personal and financial life in England, has spent a decade roaming around Africa. The German, Baron Leopold von Ragastein, is in the German Army and is at present recruiting and drilling an army in German East Africa.

World War I is drawing near, and the Germans would like very much to have a cleverly placed agent in the so-called ruling class of England. With this in mind, von Ragastein decides to kill Dominey and take his place. Dominey has, after all, been away from home for ten years; and von Ragastein has, after all, spent enough time in England to be able to adapt to the life. During the major part of the book, the reader watches this adaptation as the alleged Dominey, aided by a German agent, returns to prewar England and to the Dominey country estate.

Obviously, having been published in 1920, some of the story's language is dated. But the plot is a strong one, featuring conflicting romantic interests; an insight into the German war plans and into the political division in England over the coming war; a ghostly creature who haunts the Dominey estate; and a fine surprise ending.

As mentioned, Oppenheim (who also wrote under the name Anthony Partridge) created a great many novels. Just a few of his crime and espionage titles are *The Mysterious Mr. Sabin* (1905), *Havoc* (1911), *The Double Traitor* (1915), and *The Stranger's Gate* (1939). His best work was probably done in the short-story form, however; the most accomplished of his shorter work can be found in such collections as *The Seven Conundrums* (1923), *Crooks in Sunshine* (1933), and *General Besserley's Puzzle Box* (1935). Oppenheim is largely ignored today—not altogether fairly. His books offer an interesting and accurate look at the times in which they were written, as well as some entertaining escapist reading.

(*N.D.*)

**Orczy, Baroness. *The Old Man in the Corner.* New York: Dodd, Mead, 1909. (SS/CS)

Though she was born Hungarian and spoke no English until she was fifteen, Baroness Emmuska Orczy did all her writing in the latter language. Her adventure novel *The Scarlet Pimpernel* (1905) was such a popular success in England that the detective short stories she had written for *The Royal Magazine* from 1901 to 1904 were collected and published. Strangely, a *second* series of stories about "The Old Man" were published *first,* in *The Case of Miss Elliott* (1905). Four years later her first twelve stories finally saw print as *The Old Man in the Corner.*

Almost exclusively an armchair detective, the title character spends his time in an ABC teashop in London, subsisting on a diet of milk and cheesecake, while his "Watson," Polly Burton, brings him cases that are apparently insoluble. Endlessly tying and untying intricate knots in a piece of string, he solves her cases without ever visiting the scenes of the crimes or questioning any suspects. There is internal evidence in the stories, however, that raises questions about his sedentary role (e.g., his habit of turning up with photographs that relate to the crimes and are unavailable to Burton) and these elements provide an interesting mystery within the mystery.

The old man's motto is "There is no such thing as a mystery in connection with any crime, provided intelligence is brought to bear upon its investigation." A mystery interests him only "when it resembles a clever game of chess, with many intricate moves which all tend to one solution." With this as his philosophy, it is not surprising that he does not really care whether justice is served, and he actually favors the criminal, considering the police to be invariably stupid.

There is scarcely a weak story in this remarkably consistent collection, but three stand out. In "The Mysterious Death on the Underground Railway," the unusual setting is well conveyed to the old man as well as to the reader. "The Regent's Park Murder" is one of the best plotted, and it makes fine use of London's inevitable fog. After arriving at a plausible solution, the old man seems pleased that the criminal has "escaped human justice and . . .

deserved the full and ungrudging admiration of yours very sincerely." "The Mysterious Death in Percy Street" is probably Orczy's most famous detective story, and justifiably so, with its surprise element. Though written more than three-quarters of a century ago, these stories have not lost their appeal with the passage of time.

(*M.L.*)

Ormerod, Roger. *The Hanging Doll Murder.* New York: Scribner's, 1983. (PP)

Detective Inspector Richard Patton of a small northern England town has three days till retirement. His replacement, who will come at a higher rank, is on his way. Patton, never a favorite of his boss, is being eased out—until he becomes involved in the case of a body whose face and fingers have been blown off by a shotgun blast. Is this the corpse of a local child-rapist/murderer? Has he been killed by the uncles of the victim? Or is this the husband that Amelia Trowbridge reported missing? As the investigation evolves, Patton finds himself falling in love with Amelia, falling even further out of favor with his superior, and offending even his friends on the force.

The wary attraction between Patton and Amelia Trowbridge is sensitively shown, and the superficial, meaningless, and all-for-expedience interchanges of the police bureaucracy are well depicted. One wonderfully understated touch here deals with Patton's eating habits. Amelia feeds him while they discuss their feelings and her missing husband. When Patton looks at the faceless body of the deceased, he does so with a sandwich in his hand. Virtually the only place free of food is the morgue.

The plot is well done. All the clues are fairly presented, sometimes more than once (though some key items are not so familiar to American readers as to the British), and when the final superb twist comes, the reader is left feeling that he should have seen it coming all along.

The Hanging Doll Murder is Roger Ormerod's eighteenth novel, but the first to be published in the United States. (A second novel, *Seeing Red,* was published here in 1985.) Among his other titles, several of which feature a detective named David Mallin, are *The Silence of the Night* (1974), *The Bright Face of Danger* (1979), and *Cart Before the Hearse* (1980).

(*S.D.*)

Ozaki, Milton K. *The Dummy Murder Case.* New York: Graphic Books, 1951. (O/AD)

Milton K. Ozaki wrote a number of books under his own name, as well as under the name Robert O. Saber. His first books featured Professor Caldwell (a professor of psychology) and his assistant, Bendy Brinks (the

"Watson" of the series), who aided Homicide Lieutenant Phelan in his more interesting cases. Later he published series private-eye tales with such detectives as Carl Good and Max Keene (or Carl Guard and Phil Keene, depending on the publisher). Finally, he wrote a series of interesting crime novels for Gold Medal Books, the best of which is probably *Inquest* (1960).

The Dummy Murder Case features Caldwell and Brinks. The latter has set up a fake murder as part of a demonstration for one of Caldwell's lectures on "visual responses." Lieutenant Phelan arrives to investigate the fake murder, and a very real body is discovered. The plot is complicated by such elements as the fact that the dead girl seems to have made her living by gift-wrapping empty boxes and that her former employer (a suspect in the case) is involved in some very complex maneuvers in the wheat market. Throw in a beautiful cartoonist with an illegitimate son who isn't really hers, a department-store heiress and her beautiful mother, and other assorted red herrings and the result is a fairly entertaining mystery. Caldwell is no Nero Wolfe, and Brinks is no Archie, but the story certainly has its moments. The book is surprisingly different in its approach from most of the earlier paperback originals with which it is likely to be lumped, and worth seeking out as a curiosity if for no other reason.

The other Caldwell/Brinks adventures were both originally published in hardcover—*The Cuckoo Clock* (1946; reprinted as *Too Many Women*) and *A Fiend in Need* (1947).

(B.C.)

Page, Marco. *Fast Company.* New York: Dodd, Mead, 1938. (W)

Harry Kurnitz (a.k.a. Marco Page) will be remembered, if at all, as a screenwriter. He penned the weakest of the Thin Man films—*The Thin Man Goes Home* (1944)—but partially redeemed himself in 1957 with his excellent script for the screen adaptation of Christie's *Witness for the Prosecution.* His novels, including the bibliomystery *Fast Company,* have sunk into a more or less deserved obscurity.

In this novel, rare-book dealer and part-time sleuth Joel Glass teams up with his wife, Garda, to solve the murder (referred to as "the blessed event") of a much hated fellow New York book dealer. It seems there are two main suspects in the killing of Abe Selig. The prime suspect is Ned Morgan, a former assistant of Selig's, who happens to be a convicted book thief recently paroled from prison. Suspect number two is everybody else who ever met Abe Selig. There are several other murders, and rare books keep disappearing and reappearing, but it's all rather ordinary. There are some interesting glimpses into the world of rare books and book forgery. There is even an occasional good line: "[He] had an alibi tighter than a Scotch auditor. . . ."

But the parts add up to less than the whole. The plot is predictable and doesn't begin to live up to the "hard-boiled" promise of the dust jacket.

Fast Company was the winner of the 1938 Red Badge Best First Mystery Prize, which says something about the quality of the competition that year. It was made into a movie called *Fast and Loose* that same year (screenplay by the author)—an obvious attempt to capitalize on the success of the Thin Man series. The movie version isn't very good either.

The other Marco Page novels are *The Shadowy Third* (1946), which also has a New York setting; and *Reclining Figure* (1952), which takes place in California.

(*B.T.*)

Page, Martin. *The Man Who Stole the Mona Lisa.* New York: Pantheon, 1984. (T/H)

John Pierpont Morgan was one of the most ruthless capitalists ever let loose on nineteenth-century America, and if we can believe Martin Page's graphic description, the most physically repulsive. People literally fled from his hideousness, and he responded by using human beings as puppets in his money game, useful only as they served his psychopathic greed.

In this exceptional novel of adventure and suspense, Morgan has set his sights on the *Mona Lisa.* She might be the only woman who ever really smiled at him, and if he has to blow up half of France to get her, she will be his.

The man who actually has the nerve to steal the world's most famous priceless painting will charge Morgan $1 million to do it. He's a fascinating individual, Adam Worth (a temporary identity), and smart enough to know that even the richest of men can be seduced by their own greed. Actually he's probably a genius; who else could be so confident that there is a crack in the Louvre somewhere, just big enough to let Leonardo's masterpiece slip through? It's not long before Page has us believing it, too—hoping Worth gets away with his big heist.

Page's first novel, *The Pilate Plot* (1979), was selected Best First Novel of the Year by the British Arts Council, and though the author has been an international journalist most of his life, we can only hope that he continues his adventures in mystery fiction.

(*K.K.H.*)

*Palmer, Stuart. *Cold Poison.* New York: Mill, 1954. (CS)

Miss Hildegarde Withers is the definitive little-old-lady sleuth upon whom many future spinster, schoolmarm, and librarian sleuths were based. Her prominence on the mystery scene was ensured by a 1932 film based on her first adventure, *The Penguin Pool Murder,* starring Edna May Oliver; and the ensuing fourteen novels and short-story collections in which she is featured brought her even greater recognition. Five other films, with a variety of female stars, reinforced the much-loved image of a snoopy, highly intelligent, eccentric woman who helps the police in their investigations.

In *Cold Poison,* Miss Withers has semiretired (from her teaching position) to California, but old habits die hard—especially when the production manager of Miracle-Paradox Studios asks her to investigate the four uncomic, Penguin-decorated valentines promising death that have been received in the cartoon department where *Peter Penguin's Barn Dance* is being animated. Using the subterfuge of chaperoning Tallyrand, her French poodle who is modeling for the artists, Hildegarde starts by going to see the one practical joker among the suspects. She finds him dead of what turns out to be poison-ivy poison.

When she calls her old policeman friend, Inspector Oscar Piper, in New York, Oscar realizes that this case could very well tie in with one he couldn't solve in New York four years before, so he flies to the Coast to assist. He and Hildegarde become familiar with the world of cartooning and the various characters and their jobs—which takes up a good part of the book. When all clues are assembled, Hildegarde sets up a final confrontation in the screening room at the studio, even though she lacks the final clue necessary to confirm her suspicions. During this showing of the valentines and Hildegarde's attempt to compare them to sketches by members of the cartooning staff, an attempt is made to poison her coffee—and a little-known fact arises that helps her solve the case.

This entertaining case was Hildegarde's next to last; her final appearance was in *Miss Withers Makes the Scene* (1969), which was begun by Palmer and completed by Fletcher Flora (q.v.) after Palmer's death.

(*E.N.*)

Palmer, Stuart. *The Penguin Pool Murder.* New York: Brentano's, 1931. (CS)

In this novel, which introduced Hildegarde Withers to the mystery-reading public, Miss Withers takes her grade-school class to the New York Aquarium, where one of her students sees a body floating in the penguin pool. As soon as the police arrive, Hildegarde begins making suggestions; and after having another teacher take the students back to school, she insists on helping Inspector Oscar Piper by taking notes in shorthand (which she has studied as part of her hoped-for avocation as police assistant). Hildegarde takes time off from teaching to run around New York with Oscar until, with her guidance, the baffling case is solved.

This is a low-key introduction to one of the genre's more likable investigative pairs. Hildegarde is presented as your typical old-maid schoolteacher: austere, sensible, and entirely out of patience with what she considers the police's inefficient and bumbling ways. Oscar, on the other hand, is your typical cigar-smoking cop: tough on the outside but thoroughly cowed by what he would never admit is a formidable woman. The friendship and affection that develops while they are investigating the strange death among the penguins—with Oscar doing the legwork and Hildegarde supplying insight—is one that continues throughout the thirteen-book series and numerous short stories. (Hildegarde acts on the theory that years of dealing with children in the classroom make her an expert on devious behavior patterns in adults, too—and Oscar is eventually forced to admit she is right.) At the end of this first adventure, Hildegarde and Oscar go off hand in hand to the marriage-license bureau; however, they must have changed their minds on the way, because they remain platonic—albeit fond—friends throughout the rest of the series.

Outstanding among the other Hildegarde Withers novels are *The Puzzle of the Red Stallion* (1936), *Miss Withers Regrets* (1947), and *The Green Ace* (1950). Hildegarde's shorter cases can be found in such collections as *The Riddles of Hildegarde Withers* (1947) and *The Monkey Murder, and Other Hildegarde Withers Stories* (1950), both of which are digest-size paperback originals published by Mercury Press.

A later series character, Howie Rock, is an obese, middle-aged former newspaperman who appears in *Unhappy Hooligan* (1956) and *Rook Takes Knight* (1968). The first of these novels makes use of Palmer's unusual background as a circus clown for Ringling Brothers.

(*E.N./M.M.*)

*Palmer, Stuart, and Craig Rice. *People vs. Withers and Malone.* New York: Simon & Schuster, 1963. (CS/SS)

Intermittently from the late Forties into the early Sixties, Palmer and his good friend and fellow mystery writer Craig Rice (q.v.), with whom he had worked on the scripting of the 1942 film *The Falcon's Brother,* collaborated on half a dozen novelettes for *Ellery Queen's Mystery Magazine.* Each story teams the crusty Miss Withers, that "tall, angular person who somehow suggested a fairly well-dressed scarecrow," with Rice's hard-drinking, womanizing Chicago lawyer, John J. Malone. And all six are collected in this volume.

Working in tandem, Withers and Malone solve what the dust-jacket blurb describes as "hectic, hilarious homicides." A fair assessment: Both Palmer and Rice wrote cleverly constructed, fair-play whodunits flavored with (sometimes wacky) humor, and the blending of their talents produced some memorable stories. One is the title novelette, in which Hildegarde and

John J. hunt for a missing witness in the murder trial of a Malone client and wind up pulling off some courtroom pyrotechnics to rival any in the Perry Mason canon. In "Cherchez la Frame," the two sleuths travel to Hollywood to look for the missing wife of a Chicago gangster and find her strangled with Malone's tie in his hotel bathroom. But the best of the stories is probably the first Withers and Malone collaboration, "Once Upon a Train" (original title: "Loco Motive"). This spoof of the intrigue-on-the-Orient-Express genre takes place on the Super-Century en route from Chicago to New York and features a dead man lurking sans clothing in Miss Withers's compartment, the murder weapon conveniently planted in Malone's adjoining compartment, and a combination of quick thinking by the little lawyer and a bizarre dream by the angular spinster that unmasks the culprit. "Once Upon a Train" was one of two Withers and Malone stories sold to MGM—"resulting finally," Stuart Palmer writes in his preface, "in *Mrs. O'Malley and Mr. Malone,* a starring vehicle for James Whitmore, in which Miss Withers mysteriously changed into Ma Kettle." Palmer and Rice were two of the scriptwriters on that (perhaps deservedly) obscure 1951 film.

Each of these six stories is enjoyable light reading and should appeal not only to fans of either or both series, but to anyone who enjoys what Ellery Queen refers to in the book's introduction as "madcap capers . . . full o' fun."

(*B.P./G.K.*)

Papazoglou, Oriana. *Sweet, Savage Death.* New York: Doubleday Crime Club, 1984. (AD)

Oriana Papazoglou is married to William L. DeAndrea (q.v.), and with this first novel she joins her husband as an accomplished mystery writer. Interestingly enough, *Sweet, Savage Death* deals amusingly and knowledgeably with another genre—that of the romance.

Patience Campbell McKenna ("Pay," to her friends) is an engaging new sleuth: a skinny six-footer who fasts neurotically to maintain her scant 125 pounds. At heart, she's a hard-hitting free-lance journalist, but serious journalism doesn't pay the rent, so she makes ends meet by writing category romances. A tame enough life, it would seem; but then her friend, Myrra Agenworth, America's most famous romance writer, is found dead in Riverside Park. Returning home from the funeral, Pay finds her door locked—bolted from the inside. Police are summoned and a body is found—that of Myrra's literary agent. Of course Pay can't stay there after this, but that's all right because she's expected elsewhere anyway—at the Third Annual Conference of the American Writers of Romance, where most of the action takes place. Who would think the sweet ladies who write those things could be so murderous? Being the number one suspect, Pay has to sort it all out.

Sweet, Savage Death is a lively yarn that offers a nice locked-room puzzle and lives up to its amusing title.

Papazoglou's second novel is *Wicked, Loving Murder* (1985).

(*J.S.*)

Paretsky, Sara. *Deadlock.* New York: Dial, 1984. (PI)

V. I. Warshawski is one of the most interesting of the Young Women Detectives—a title she would probably not find amusing.

Warshawski, a Chicagoan all the way, is the daughter of a half Italian, half Jewish mother and a Polish father. She is no amateur detective. She was an attorney for the Cook County public defender's office, but decided that she could effect more justice by investigating on her own. Now she's a private eye specializing in financial cases—insurance, banking, white-collar crime. Many of these cases seem to lead to murder. Warshawski is hardly an unfeeling person, but when she's working, she's tough. Her love life appears normal enough, but it's rarely presented in any detail. She's got a first name—Vicki—to go with the initials, but the only person she allows to use it is an old friend of her father's from the Chicago Police Department.

In *Deadlock,* Warshawski is drawn into a complex shipping and insurance racket when her cousin, a former hockey star working for a grain company, is pushed under the screw of a Great Lakes freighter. Boom Boom (the cousin) had wanted to see her before he died. He'd found something going on that wasn't on the level. It involved shipping invoices, and it must have been important enough to cost Boom Boom his life.

Warshawski wants to avenge her cousin. In doing so, she not only has to watch her step, she has to learn the grain-shipping business from bow to stern before she can thresh out a surprising and very dangerous criminal.

The first V. I. Warshawski novel was *Indemnity Only* (1982); a third, *Killing Orders,* appeared in 1985.

(*M.J.*)

Parker, Percy Spurlark. *Good Girls Don't Get Murdered.* New York: Scribner's, 1974. (PI)

There have been few black writers of crime fiction. (There *have* been several black fictional detectives, of course—Virgil Tibbs, John Shaft, Toussaint Moore, and Pharaoh Love are among the best known—but those four and most of the rest were created by Caucasians.) And of the few, only three have done a significant body of work in the field: Chester Himes (q.v.), with his series of novels about a pair of black Harlem cops, Coffin Ed Johnson and Grave Digger Jones; John B. West (q.v.), a Liberian doctor who, rather ironically, wrote a number of hard-boiled paperback mysteries featuring a *white* private eye; and Percy Spurlark Parker, who has published only one novel to date but has numerous short stories to his credit and is a regular contributor to *Alfred Hitchcock's Mystery Magazine* and other publications.

Good Girls Don't Get Murdered, like many of Parker's shorter works, stars Big Bull Benson, full-time owner of a Chicago hotel and its adjoining bar (both of which he won in a poker game), and part-time private eye. The murder of a young woman named Alicia whom he befriended, and the eventual harassment by a white cop, D. R. Ryan, forces Bull into his own hunt for Alicia's killer. His investigations lead him from one end of the black community to the other—from its underworld figures and its street gangs to an influential black newspaper and a middle-class suburban family. Violence dogs him every step of the way, and finally explodes in a climactic confrontation on the roof of a tenement in Bull's own neighborhood.

Tough, tense, sharply realistic, *Good Girls Don't Get Murdered* is at once an entertaining mystery and a microcosmic portrait of black urban America as only a black man can paint it.

(*B.P.*)

Parker, Robert B. *Promised Land.* Boston: Houghton Mifflin, 1976. (PI)

A former professor of English at Northeastern University, Robert B. Parker decided at the age of forty to forego his academic career and pursue a new one as a writer of hard-boiled detective novels. (He wrote his Ph.D. dissertation on Hammett, Chandler, and Macdonald.) Since the publication of his first novel featuring ultramacho Boston private eye Spenser, *The Godwulf Manuscript* (1973), Parker's career has been meteoric. Critics have been profuse in their praise, hailing Parker as a kind of hardboiled messiah, the "true" successor to Chandler and Macdonald; calling Spenser an "archetype like John Wayne and Travis McGee" (*New York Times Book Review*). They have raved about Parker's plots consistently demonstrating that people are more important than money or the law. They have lauded the warm, often funny relationship between Spenser and his girlfriend, Susan Silverman, a high-school guidance counselor. They have praised Spenser's love of good food and good drink (there is a lot of eating and drinking in Parker's novels). They have rhapsodized over his ability to toss off flip, barbed wisecracks with machine-gun rapidity. And they have pontificated on his "moral code" and how noble he is for adhering to it no matter what the consequences in his own life and the lives of others.

But not everyone agrees with either the superlatives or the specifics. There are those who find Parker's novels underplotted, pretentiously literary, talky, excessively (and sometimes gratuitously) violent, fundamentally immoral, and populated by an array of unpleasant characters; who find Spenser an overbearing tough with psychotic tendencies who dislikes most of his clients, manipulates them and events to suit his "moral code," and stands far too ready and willing to commit coldblooded murder; who feel that Spenser is not the romantic many claim him to be, but rather of the same ilk as the black thug and murderer, Hawk, with whom he shares a rapport and with whom he sometimes plots and carries out a variety of unlawful acts (indeed, that Spenser is worse than Hawk because Hawk at least admits his criminality, while Spenser operates under a pretense of siding with the angels). There is a telling passage of dialogue in *Promised Land,* in fact, spoken by Hawk to Susan Silverman after Spenser has roughed up another hoodlum: "Just don't be so sure me and old Spenser are so damn different, Susan."

Promised Land is the fourth Spenser novel and one of the better entries in the series (primarily because Spenser doesn't murder anyone in it). He is hired by Harvey Shepherd, a real-estate developer from Hyannis, out on Cape Cod, to find Harvey's missing wife, Pam. Which Spenser does, in the company of two ultramilitant feminists in New Bedford. But instead of bringing her home, or at least telling his client where she can be found, he indulges in a lengthy metaphysical discussion with her, determines that she is an unhappy person looking for some meaning in life through casual affairs with macho men, and decides she ought to be left to her own devices. A short while later, he receives a call from her asking his help: It seems she stupidly allowed herself to take part in a bank robbery engineered by the two feminists to get money to buy guns so they can start a paramilitary group—a robbery in which a bank guard was gunned down. (Shades of Patty Hearst.) But Pam Shepherd isn't Spenser's only problem; her husband is another. It seems Harvey has got in deep with a loan shark named King Powers, for whom Hawk works as an enforcer, as a result of one of his real-estate deals crumbling.

Spenser undertakes to get both Shepherds off the hook at once by arranging a set-up deal with the local authorities that snares the bank-robbing feminists and King Powers (not Hawk, though; Spenser lets *him* escape). However, he doesn't foresee an obvious final confrontation in which not only he but Susan *and* the Shepherds are almost killed.

There is more plot here than usual, though not much more, and fewer of the annoying wisecracks that permeate the later books. And Spenser's relationship with Susan Silverman—the best part of any of the novels—is explored at quite some emotional depth. (That is what *Promised Land* is really about: the seldom-achieved true and honest relationship between men and women.) There are some good descriptions of Cape Cod and its way of life. On the negative side, Spenser doesn't do very much detecting, beats up on people on three separate occasions (one of them a woman, though he does have provocation in that case), and imbibes enormous amounts of beer and wine without having to visit the men's room. (He must have a bladder the size of Rhode Island.) And the only likable, sympathetic character in the entire book is Susan Silverman.

How a private-eye novel like this one could win a Best Novel Edgar (beating out some pretty good competition to do so), when neither Chandler's *The Long Goodbye* nor any of Ross Macdonald's superb middle-period Lew Archer titles were even *nominated* for that award, is beyond this reviewer's powers of comprehension.

(*B.P.*)

Parker, Robert B. *The Widening Gyre.* New York: Delacorte/Seymour Lawrence, 1983. (PI)

Parker's recent novels have even less plot than the early ones, just as much violence, and a lot more wisecracks. They are, in fact, almost self-parodies. But the worst thing about them is their heavy-handed literary pretension—the kind that says to the reader, "I don't give a damn if you don't think this is a good detective story; I'm not interested in writing a detective story, I'm interested in writing Literature." Readers and some critics have already begun to complain; they want a story as well as a message and clever one-liners and they're not getting it in books like *The Widening Gyre.*

The crime plot here is negligible. Spenser is on the trail of a blackmailer who is attempting to force candidate Meade Alexander out of the Massachusetts senatorial race by threatening to release videotapes of Alexander's wife, Ronni, in hot pursuit of sexual freedom with a man young enough to be her son. Spenser has no trouble discovering the rather tenuous link between a local rackets boss and Meade Alexander, nor in finding the blackmailer and meting out his usual brand of justice. But all of this takes a back seat to what amounts to a metaphysical probing of "the mysteries of existence." For it seems that Susan Silverman has left Boston to attend medical school in Washington, D.C., and Spenser keeps trying to convince himself that she isn't running away from *him* at the same time. That is the central issue of the novel: the uncertain future of his relationship with Susan. "The widening gyre," in fact, is a phrase from William Butler Yeats's "The Second Coming," a poem that foresees the end of one era and expresses fear at what the new age will bring.

This is all very compelling; Spenser's love for Susan, and for his surrogate son Paul Giacomin (rescued by Spenser from a terrible fate in *Early Autumn,* 1981), is the major positive aspect of the series: It deepens his humanity, makes us care for him at least a little. But it is not enough to carry the novel, much less an entire series. When Susan puts an end to their relationship and moves to San Francisco in *Valediction* (1984), we do not feel sorry for Spenser; we feel relieved for Susan. Until, that is, *The Catskill Eagle* (1985), Parker's worst novel to date, in which Spenser and Hawk coldbloodedly murder several people en route to the rescue of *Susan* from a terrible fate. When she gratefully re-establishes her relationship with Spenser as a result, we no longer care for either of them.

Parker's other Spenser novels include *God Save the Child* (1974); *The Judas Goat* (1978); *Looking for Rachel Wallace* (1980), in which can be found the immortal line "the sun was shining its ass off"; and *Ceremony* (1981).

(*B.P./J.L.T.*)

*Parrish, Frank. *Snare in the Dark.* New York: Dodd, Mead, 1981. (A/AD)

When friends who normally do not read mysteries ask me to recommend a mystery writer, I invariably suggest Dick Francis (q.v.). They inevitably become "hooked" on him, read all of his books, and then turn to me for another suggestion. Frank Parrish is the writer I next advise them to read. Like Dick Francis, he has the knack of grabbing readers on page one and never releasing his grip on their attention. His villains, like those of Francis, are unspeakably nasty, and we develop a real rooting interest for Frank Parrish's protagonist, Dan Mallett.

Our identification with Mallett is a bit surprising since his "occupation" is that of poacher and he is essentially an amoral character. But he is as different as the way he earns his living, and there is a part of us that likes this modern-day Robin Hood who never really hurts anyone not deserving to be hurt. Mallett is a dropout from a promising banking career who wants to be beholden to no one and wishes to live his life outdoors as much as possible. However, he has a mother who needs hip-replacement surgery and refuses to submit to what she considers the humiliation of being hospitalized under the British national health system.

At the beginning of *Snare in the Dark,* we meet Mallett setting his usual illegal snares as a way of earning some of the money he needs for her operation. He is not averse, in this and other books, to a bit of burglary also when the victims are obnoxious and can afford the loss. He witnesses the murder of his sworn enemy, gamekeeper Edgar Bland, and because he is the logical suspect, he can't inform the police. Hunted by them, he lives off the countryside, trying to find the murderer in order to clear himself. He is helped by a beautiful young nurse, one of many females in the series who are attracted to this unconventional hero who can be sophisticated or act the country bumpkin, depending on his need. The police in his district in the west of England believe the worst of him. When he tries to help them, finally, by disclosing the murderer, it has "the effect of establishing, to the police, not his innocence but his impertinence." For Dan Mallett, poacher/detective, discovering a murderer never quite ends his trouble with the law.

There is an authenticity about the Mallett series that is tremendously appealing, especially to those of us who spend most of our time behind desks and/or typewriters. We walk with him over dry leaves, trying our damnedest not to make a sound. Though we know the very early hours of the morning are the best time for poaching, we feel the chill as we wait in a cramped position for our prey, our arms and legs growing numb. We are out in the rain, as often as not. Are we sorry that Frank Parrish had Dan Mallett give up the more comfortable life inside a bank for the much more precarious existence as a poacher? Not likely.

The other Dan Mallett adventures are *Fire in the Barley* (1977), *Sting of the Honeybee* (1979), *Bait on the Hook* (1983), and *Death in the Rain* (1984).

(*M.L.*)

Patterson, Harry. *To Catch a King.* New York: Stein & Day, 1979. (E)

Harry Patterson's first best seller was *The Eagle Has Landed* (1975), published under his well-known pseudonym Jack Higgins (q.v.)—a story about a German plan to kidnap Winston Churchill during World War II. In *To Catch a King,* the plot is similar, but this time the target is the duke of Windsor. The idea is to persuade the duke to take over the throne of England after the German invasion and serve as titular head of the Nazi-controlled country. Failing persuasion, the Germans will kidnap him (rushing him from Portugal, where he is staying, across the border to Spain) and eventually force him to accept the English throne.

The man assigned to this task is Brigadeführer Walter Schellenberg, major general in the SS, master of counterintelligence, and adviser to Heydrich, Himmler, and Hitler himself. Even with all these credentials, Schellenberg turns out to be a rather odd sort of person. He does not really consider himself a Nazi, is not in sympathy with many Nazi ideas and goals, has no real hope of completing the task he is assigned, and further complicates the assignment by falling in love with and aiding the escape of a Jewish woman whose mission it is to warn the duke of Windsor.

As with many novels about World War II, the hint is dropped that this episode may have been the turning point in the war. Despite this ostentatious claim, the book is a typical Harry Patterson thriller that holds the reader's interest and prolongs the suspense until the very end.

Another best seller published under the Harry Patterson name is *The Valhalla Exchange* (1976).

(*N.D.*)

Paul, Elliot. *Mayhem in B-Flat.* New York: Random House, 1940. (AD)

Elliot Paul wrote nine books featuring Homer Evans, bon vivant and male chauvinist of the first water. *Mayhem in B-Flat* is the third, and continues the saga of an incredible coterie of French and American eccentrics first introduced in *The Mysterious Mickey Finn; or Murder at the Café du Dôme* (1939). Paul, who was first a foreign correspondent and then literary editor for the Paris edition of the *New York Herald,* uses the French background, argot, and even restaurant menus to good effect in this series.

Homer Evans is a young, rich Boston dilettante who, in this adventure, learns that a world-famous Guarnerius violin has been stolen during a concert in Paris. Determined to recover it, he enlists the aid of his piano-playing, sharpshooting American girlfriend, Miriam; the commissioner of police; assorted members of the Parisian underworld (who are often too busy shooting at each other to be of any real help); and a love-sick Boston maiden who wants the violinist more than the violin. Before the Guarnerius is found and rescued in a three-day skirmish that eventually involves a cast of hundreds, we are treated to a number of truly hilarious scenes, as well as frequent digressions for indulgence in gourmet meals, fine wines, fistfights, and a bit of nautical arson.

It has been claimed that the creation of Evans was a literary reaction to S. S. Van Dine's (q.v.) effete sleuth Philo Vance. Certainly Evans outdoes Vance in all his idiosyncrasies. And it is evident that Paul became so involved with his own satirical humor that his pastiche became a parody of itself. The early books are set in the pre–World War II days; with the fall of Paris, Paul transported Evans and his companions to the United States—specifically, the lower Yellowstone Valley of Montana, from which Miriam hailed. Unfortunately, the combination of Montana reservation Indians and cosmopolitan Parisians presented in *Fracas in the Foothills* (1940) was more ludicrous than literary. Homer Evans's other adventures—among them, *Waylaid in Boston* (1953) and *The Black and the Red* (1956)—don't stand up well as detective stories, although their colorful backgrounds almost make up for the lack of plot.

(*E.N.*)

Pendleton, Don. *The Executioner.* New York: Pinnacle, 1969. (O/A)

Sergeant Mack Bolan, the ideal sniper in Vietnam, is called home on compassionate leave when his father shoots the other members of the family and then takes his own life. Bolan learns that his father was in debt to a Mafia-controlled loan company and was unable to pay off the debt; as a result, in an attempt to save her father from the loan sharks' reprisals, Bolan's young sister, Cindy, had been forced into prostitution. After burying his family, Bolan decides to get revenge, having been perfectly trained to do so and being psychologically suited for the job. He begins simply, with a .444 Marlin lever-action rifle, but by the end of the book he is using flares and rockets, leveling houses as well as killing men. (The book's apt subtitle, on the jacket though not the title page, is "War Against the Mafia!") Before his battle is well begun, Bolan realizes that he does not hate his enemy, that vengeance is not the issue, that there is nothing personal involved. It is simply the good guys against the bad guys, and he is the good guy. He isn't interested in philosophical discussions of good and evil. The Mafia is the enemy, and he will destroy them or die in the attempt.

When Don Pendleton created the Executioner, he probably didn't know that he had altered the direction of paperback series fiction. His hero caught the imagination of so many readers that imitations soon flooded the stands (the Butcher, the Marksman, the Sharpshooter, the Assassin, etc.). But Mack Bolan was the first, and his simple, hard-boiled philosophy was carefully worked out as the books progressed. To read this series is to watch the development of a real American phenomenon.

There have been some fifty books in the series to date, all bearing such titles as *Miami Massacre* (1970), *New Orleans Knockout* (1974), and *Colorado Kill-Zone* (1976).

(*B.C.*)

*Pentecost, Hugh. *The Cannibal Who Overate.* New York: Dodd, Mead, 1962. (AD/W)

In a remarkable literary career that has spanned some sixty years, Judson Philips (q.v.) has published more than 100 novels and hundreds of short stories under his own name and his prominent pseudonym, Hugh Pentecost. Philips began writing for the pulp magazines in the 1920s, and published his first novel, *Red War* (a collaboration with Thomas M. Johnson), in 1936. His first book as by Pentecost, *Cancelled in Red* (1939), a mystery puzzle with a stamp-collecting motif, won a Dodd, Mead "Red Badge" prize. The reason for Philips's literary longevity lies in his ability to skillfully blend solid plotting with well-drawn settings, both urban (New York City) and rural (New England), and to create characters—in particular his many different and highly individual protagonists—who are believable and sympathetic human beings. "The name of the game is people," he has said. "They are endlessly rewarding, never uninteresting, and where everything begins and ends."

Over his long career, Philips has created dozens of series detectives, amateur and professional. One of the most popular in recent years is Pierre Chambrun, resident manager of the ultra-exclusive Hotel Beaumont in

Manhattan. Chambrun's *raison d'être* is the smooth and sedate operation of the swank hotel. When crime—usually murder—threatens the Beaumont's grand reputation, he uses his wits and the skills he learned as part of the French Underground in World War II to bring about a rapid solution to the problem.

In *The Cannibal Who Overate,* the first of a score of novels in the Chambrun series, the problem is a world-famous author named Aubrey Moon—a seventy-five-year-old super-rich sensualist and sadist, the "cannibal" of the title, whose "chief delight in life . . . was finding the weak spots in people and exposing them without pity, cruelly." Moon, living in luxury in one of the Beaumont's cooperative penthouses, has obviously made a host of enemies during his jaded climb to fame and fortune; now it seems a plot is afoot to entice one or more of those enemies into killing him. The list includes Pamela Prym, a beautiful call girl whom Moon had degraded; an equally beautiful secretary, Sandy Stewart, whom he used mercilessly; an aristocratic old lady, Mrs. Haven, whose life he turned into a nightmare; and a young flier named John Wills who may have the best reason of all to hate the old man. Moon enlists Chambrun's aid in finding the would-be killer; and it's a race against time for the hotel manager, who finds himself in the uncomfortable position of protecting a man he personally loathes—a position that becomes more and more untenable as corpses begin to pile up in the Beaumont's hallowed confines. . . .

This, like the other Pierre Chambrun novels—which include *The Shape of Fear* (1964), *The Golden Trap* (1967), *Time of Terror* (1975), *Random Killer* (1979), and *Remember to Kill Me* (1983)—is entertaining reading with a number of surprises. And in the bargain it offers a vivid inside look at the operation of a large metropolitan hotel.

(G.K./B.P.)

Pentecost, Hugh. *The Day the Children Vanished.* New York: Pocket Books, 1976. (O/T)

In July 1976, a busload of children vanished in Chowchilla, California. Alert mystery fans contacted the media about the resemblance between this shocking mystery and a Hugh Pentecost short story called "The Day the Children Vanished," which appeared in *Ellery Queen's Mystery Magazine* in 1958. The real-life children were found unharmed, their kidnappers were eventually arrested, and no connection between the plot of the story and the planning of the actual crime was found. But the media had brought a measure of fame to the Pentecost story, and Pocket Books asked Philips if he would do a novel-length expansion. The result, published in October 1976, is a fine novel—an improvement over the short-story version—and shows Philips's skill at handling fictional children realistically and sympathetically.

On a winter morning, the school bus that regularly carries nine children from Clayton (Connecticut) to the regional school in Lakeview each school day vanishes, and along with it all nine kids and the driver. The fears and anxieties of parents and authorities are suspensefully depicted as hours pass and a massive search fails to find any trace of the missing children. It takes the skill of Clyde Haviland, a tall, stoop-shouldered, scholarly-looking investigator from the attorney general's office—and a lot of help from other sources—to uncover the astonishing truth behind the disappearance.

The book's similarity to the events in the Chowchilla kidnapping is slight; *The Day the Children Vanished* has a unique identity of its own, even though the novel version would not have been written without the notoriety the short story received during the Chowchilla case.

(*G.K.*)

Pentecost, Hugh. *The Price of Silence.* New York: Dodd, Mead, 1984. (AD)

Perhaps the most human of all of Philips's series sleuths is Uncle George Crowder, a former county attorney who once prosecuted a man for murder, got a conviction that led to the man's execution, and later found out to his horror that the man was innocent. Crowder resigned from his post and disappeared from the New England village of Lakeview for ten years; when he returned, he built himself a cabin in the woods and lived there alone with his dog, Timmy. Now he is the constant companion of his twelve-year-old nephew, Joey Trimble, teaching the boy woodsman's skills and introducing him to the exploits of Sherlock Holmes and the Knights of the Round Table. Joey worships Uncle George and often helps out when the local authorities can persuade George to join in this or that criminal investigation. Uncle George and Joey appear in three novels, of which *The Price of Silence* is the most recent, and in numerous short stories, some of which can be found in the excellent 1970 collection *Around Dark Corners.* In the introduction to that collection, Philips/Pentecost writes, "I have tried [in these stories] to mirror some of the wonders of growing up along with the standards of decency and compassion and understanding as represented by Uncle George. I have always called them the Uncle George stories. My younger readers call them the Joey stories. Perhaps I have managed a minor miracle and appealed to both young and old." Indeed he has.

The Price of Silence, however, is *not* for young readers: It deals with grisly murder, disembowelment, other acts of brutal violence, kinky sex, and drugs—a *very* modern novel, one might say. Which is one of the reasons it doesn't quite work. Both Uncle George and Joey seem out of place involved with such ugly crimes.

It is summer in Lakeview, the time of the County Fair. Boy Scouts, cleaning up after a Lion's Club picnic, find in an equipment shed the disemboweled corpse of a man murdered and further mutilated by a shotgun blast to the head. Uncle George is called in by Captain Purdy of the state police, and his first contribution is to correctly identify a stray dog—a springer spaniel that won't leave the vicinity of the shed—as the victim's pet. At the fair, with the dog in tow, Uncle George learns that the animal belongs to Stan Chard, a former carny magician and sword swallower who seems to have struck it rich and is traveling in style with a former hooker named Stormy Knight. After managing to identify the corpse as Chard, Stormy disappears. Uncle George, while hunting for her (she is later found savagely beaten and near death), formulates the theory that Chard was gutted because he either swallowed something or pretended to swallow something that his killer desperately wants. But what? Drugs? Precious gems? Blackmail evidence of some kind? Uncle George doesn't know—but someone thinks he does. An attempt is made on his life that claims another victim instead, his home is ransacked, and there are other deadly happenings before a final confrontation is reached in the home of one of Lakeview's leading citizens.

There is good suspense here, and the relationship between Uncle George and Joey is as warm and appealing as ever. But the identity of the murderer(s) and the motive behind the various homicides and attempted homicides strains the reader's credulity. The novel is worth reading, certainly—but *Around Dark Corners* is a much better introduction to Uncle George and Joey. So, too, are the other novels in the series—*Choice of Violence* (1961) and *The Copycat Killers* (1983).

Writing under the Pentecost name, Philips has created a number of other series sleuths, notable among these the huge, red-bearded artist John Jericho, who is featured in such novels as *Sniper* (1965), *The Girl with Six Fingers* (1969), and *A Plague of Violence* (1970); and public-relations expert Julian Quist, hero of such adventures as *Don't Drop Dead Tomorrow* (1971), *The Judas Freak* (1974), *The Homicidal Horse* (1979), *Death Mask* (1980), and *Substitute Victim* (1984).

(*B.P.*)

Perowne, Barry. *Raffles of the Albany*. New York: St. Martin's, 1976. (SS)

When E. W. Hornung (q.v.) died at the early age of fifty-four, he left behind one of the more popular characters in crime literature: Raffles, the amateur cracksman.

In 1932, over a decade after Hornung's death, Barry Perowne was asked to continue the Raffles series. This he did, not only with short stories, as Hornung had done, but with novels as well. This book, *Raffles of the Albany*, contains eleven of these Raffles short stories.

The stories are entertaining, certainly. But the Perowne Raffles is quite different from the Hornung Raffles. While the Hornung Raffles advocated art for art's sake (and, by extension, crime for crime's sake), Perowne seems almost embarrassed about his character's criminal background. True, the stories usually contain an obligatory break-in of some sort, but in fact precious little is actually stolen, and the theft often seems to have a redeeming social value. What's more, the break-ins themselves are covered quickly and are usually of secondary importance to the story.

In truth, Perowne has elected to make his character more an adventurer than a criminal—and in doing so, has become an almost shameless name-dropper. Consider: In "The Victory March," Raffles and Bunny Manders, his "Watson," observe the queen and meet Arthur Conan Doyle. In "John L. Sullivan Obliges," Raffles is introduced to the prizefighter and to the Prince of Wales. He also champions the cause of women's rights in Britain. In "Tusitala and the Money-Belt," Raffles and Bunny meet Robert Louis Stevenson and help restore a just government to Samoa. In "The Baffling of Oom Paul," they enlist to fight in the Boer War and, while so engaged, help Winston Churchill escape from South Africa.

Again, it should be emphasized that the stories *are* entertaining. But one wonders how Hornung—or, for that matter, the original Raffles—would view this metamorphosis.

Barry Perowne is a pseudonym of Philip Atkey (who also has used the pseudonym Pat Merriman). All the Raffles novels and collections were published under the Perowne name and include *The Return of Raffles* (1933), *Raffles and the Key Man* (1940), and *Raffles Revisited* (1974). Perowne has also published numerous other novels, among them the historical mystery *A Singular Conspiracy* (1974).

(*N.D.*)

*Perry, Anne. *Callander Square.* New York: St. Martin's, 1980. (H/PP)

Anne Perry's books featuring London police inspector Thomas Pitt are called "Victorian mysteries." One look at the covers of the paperback editions would lead the reader to believe they are just more of what has been called the "Gasp in the Grass" genre—the kind of stories that find the virginal heroine crawling at least once across the grassy slopes of a Victorian mansion in the moonlight.

Not so. Perry has very cleverly portrayed British Victorian society with a sharp eye for its particular brand of social deceit. She is especially skilled at making the reader realize the almost unbelievable subjugation of women in those days, and if one ever wonders why women began to rebel against social constriction at the turn of the twentieth century, these books will clear up that mystery, too.

Detective Thomas Pitt is a working-class hero in the extraordinary position of being called upon periodically to blow the cover of the English aristocracy. Being a policeman, he can exercise certain influence; if any blustering old gent attempts to order him out of the Morning Room, Pitt can threaten a search warrant. He rarely needs to resort to such tactics, however, because he gets inside help from his charming wife, Charlotte, who stepped out of her upper-class world to marry him. She is an honest and enthusiastic woman whose family despairs of her insistence on following her own inclinations (although most of the women she grew up with admire her courage). And she is invaluable to Pitt, since most of his cases involve his exposing the passion beneath the icy breast of the upper classes. Pitt analyzes the facts with cool logic, while Charlotte uses her family connections to pick up pertinent gossip over tea and crumpets.

In *Callander Square,* gardeners have inadvertently dug up the corpses of two newborn babies in the square of one of the most affluent suburbs of London. The neighborhood residents, while forced to admit the monstrosity of the deaths, simply chalk them up to the immorality of some servant girl who "let herself" be molested—probably by a footman, perhaps the master of the house; gentlemen always dally with the servant girls "just for a spot of fun." It is too bad, they concede, that the girl was stupid enough to get herself into such a mess—but then, what can one expect from the working class anyway?

Of course, those babies never belonged to a servant girl, and it is Pitt's job to expose the enormous hypocrisy of the self-righteous elite—as well as two murderers, a blackmailer, and a gentleman drunk. This is an excellent novel that says a great deal about social pretension and the harm it can do.

Other highly recommended books in this series are *The Cater Street Hangman* (1979), *Paragon Walk* (1981), *Resurrection Row* (1981), *Rutland Place* (1983), and *Bluegate Fields* (1984).

(*K.K.H.*)

Perry, Ritchie. *Fool's Mate.* New York: Pantheon, 1981. (E)

Over a decade ago, Ritchie Perry created a roguish secret agent called Philis. Philis is sometimes blackmailed into assignments by his bureaucratic superior, Pawson, head of the vaguely defined Section SR 2 of British Intelligence, a department that apparently specializes in missions no one else wants. Philis and Pawson are very sympathetic characters, and the relationship between them is spiced with dry humor. Philis's adventures are tales of sharply escalating tension, the appeal of which is best explained in the words of Perry himself (who confesses to writing as much for his own entertainment as anyone else's): ". . . it must be very difficult for a reader to guess how a book will finish when [initially] the author isn't sure himself."

Fool's Mate is the best Philis adventure to date. Pawson has Philis assigned to bodyguard a VIP; the mission is to bring her safely across France to England. But Philis discovers the VIP is a sexy Ugandan named Kudlip—who happened to be one of Idi Amin's favorite mistresses. Philis, who is never paid enough, senses money in the situation and cuts his own deal with financier Sir Keith Tenby, who would like Kudlip as *his* favorite mistress. But before Philis can deliver her, he finds they are hunted by a band of Amin's assassins, a vengeance-crazed Ugandan, and various underworld thugs. There are bang-up action scenes in Marseille as the pair fight to get free of their pursuers and push on across France.

Fool's Mate is great fun, and it is entertaining to watch Philis make fun of the political absurdities of a number of contemporary alliances. Other adventures of this amusing character include *The Fall Guy* (1972), *Your Money and Your Wife* (1976), *Dutch Courage* (1978), and *Grand Slam* (1980).

(*G.K.*)

Perry, Thomas. *Metzger's Dog.* New York: Scribner's, 1983. (C/T)

This is a joyous romp of a thriller featuring the funniest band of brigands since Donald E. Westlake's (q.v.) Dortmunder gang. While pulling a routine caper—a small matter involving a million dollars' worth of cocaine—the gang inadvertently comes into possession of a Toyota-size dog and a worthless-looking manuscript. Immelmann, Kepler, Chinese Gordon, and Margaret the moll keep the surly canine only because Gordon's cat, Dr. Henry Metzger, takes a fancy to it. The manuscript is more promising—it's about psychological warfare, and they figure the CIA will pay plenty to get it back.

A deal is struck, but the public servants of this great nation prove untrustworthy. Double-crossed, the tiny gang of four decides to teach the mighty CIA a lesson it'll never forget. And then the real fun begins. Besides having one of the smartest mouths in the West, Chinese Gordon can think of dazzling plans on a moment's notice. His revenge plot is a dandy; even the CIA's ruthless Ben Porterfield, "a man who had eaten armadillo. That said it all.") can't keep up with him. In fact, he can seemingly be outsmarted by only one being on earth—his own cat, Dr. Henry Metzger.

A dynamite read—the plot is ingenious, the dialogue terrific, and the comedy wild and wacky.

Perry's previous book, *The Butcher's Boy,* is totally different from this one—a tense thriller about an assassin and the government worker who must apprehend him; it won the MWA Edgar for Best First Novel of 1982. His latest title is *Big Fish* (1985).

(*J.S.*)

*Peters, Elizabeth. *Crocodile on the Sandbank.* New York: Dodd, Mead, 1975. (H)

Crododile on the Sandbank is a wonderfully amusing romp in Egypt in the 1880s with all the trimmings—*dahabeeyahs* (houseboats), royal tombs, and mummies, both dead and walking. Into the world of archaeology blunders a self-proclaimed "middle-aged spinster" (age thirty-two) who has used her newly inherited fortune to leave England and her avaricious relatives. Sensing herself to be plain, Miss Amelia Peabody has decided against marriage, saying, "Why should any independent, intelligent female choose to subject herself to the whims and tyrannies of a husband? I assure you, I have yet to meet any man as sensible as myself." But then she meets Radcliff Emerson, a voluble and single-minded sociologist. A Tracy-Hepburn relationship immediately develops.

Where she meets Radcliff is at an archaeological dig he and his brother share on the Nile. Amelia and her companion, a young woman she befriended in Rome, have stopped there for a brief visit, but the short stay they envisioned is lengthened by a series of threatening events, endangering the artifacts and finally the lives of the four protagonists.

The story is told from Amelia's viewpoint. She is exceptionally well educated, full of endurance, and never, never forgoes her principles. Peters's skill is in keeping the friction inherent in this situation amusing, yet making the characters just realistic enough to be credible and immensely likable. And though the reader realizes the outcome of the plot before Amelia does, it doesn't matter; it is the interchange between the characters that is the delight of the book.

In further adventures, presented in the form of Amelia's memoirs—*The Curse of the Pharaohs* (1981) and *The Mummy Case* (1985)—she marries Emerson and returns to the Nile with an expanded cast of characters, including her precocious son, Ramses, and an Egyptian cat, Bastet. Peters (whose real name is Barbara Mertz, and who also writes as Barbara Michaels) has written such other entertaining novels as *The Jackal's Head* (1968), *Borrower of the Night* (1973), *The Copenhagen Connection* (1982), and *Die for Love* (1984).

(*S.D.*)

Petersen, Herman. *Old Bones.* New York: Duell, 1943. (AD)

Herman Petersen was a prolific contributor to the aviation, adventure, and detective pulps of the Twenties and Thirties; one of his stories appears in the famous "Ku Klux Klan Number" of *Black Mask* (June 1, 1923). Between 1940 and 1943, he published four crime novels advertised by the publisher of three of them, Duell, Sloan & Pearce, as "quietly sinister mysteries with a rural background." All four are set in an unnamed county in an unspecified part of the country (presumably upstate New York, Petersen's home base). Three feature a team of more or less amateur sleuths: old Doc Miller, the county coroner; Paul Burns, the D.A.; and the narrator, Ben Wayne, a gentleman farmer. Miller does most of the sleuthing, Burns most of the worrying, and Wayne most of the leg work.

Old Bones, the last and nominally best of the Doc Miller books, begins with the discovery—by Wayne's wife, Marian—of a jumble of old bones wedged into the bottom of a standpipe at an abandoned gristmill. Before the authorities can remove them, someone else gets there first and tries unsuccessfully to hide them. Doc Miller's eventual examination and investigation reveal that the bones are those of Nathaniel Wight, a black-sheep member of the district's leading family; that he died of a crushed skull; and that he has evidently been dead for five years—ever since the night he was banished by old Aunt She, eldest and most imperious of the Wights, who believed he had seduced his cousin Amelia. It soon becomes apparent that someone in the Wight family, or someone close to it—perhaps more than one person—is willing to go to any lengths to keep the truth about Nate's death from surfacing along with his bones.

Much of the action takes place at or near the mill, and in the swamp that separates it from the Waynes' farm, known as Dark House. In one harrowing episode, Wayne nearly drowns inside the standpipe; in another he is attacked in the mill loft and superficially stabbed. A second murder, the actions of a transient who has been bothering women in the area, a nightmarish stormy-night chase through the swamp on the trail of a kidnapped girl, and a tense and fiery conclusion are some of the other highlights.

Old Bones drips atmosphere and understated menace. Its mystery is well constructed, with some legitimate detection on Doc Miller's part; there is a nice sense of realism in the characters; and the touches of folksy humor are adroitly handled. The novel does have its flaws: We are told almost nothing about the backgrounds and private lives of the protagonists, people we *want* to know better; the solution to the mystery comes a little too easily and quickly; and more could have been done with the final confrontation. But the pluses here far outweigh the minuses. This and Petersen's other servings of fictional Americana are well worth tracking down.

Doc Miller, Paul Burns, and the Waynes are also featured in *Murder in the Making* (1940) and *Murder R.F.D.* (1942). *The D.A.'s Daughter* (1943) also has a rural setting and emphasizes comedy along with murder and mischief. Petersen's only other mystery novel, "The House in the Wilderness," was published serially in 1957 and did not see book publication.

(*B.P.*)

Petievich, Gerald. *Money Men* and *One-Shot Deal.* New York: Harcourt Brace, 1981. (PP)

These two short novels are printed in one volume and are Petievich's first published fiction. He is a former member of the U.S. Army Intelligence Corps, and later was a special agent of the U.S. Secret Service assigned to counterfeit investigations. He knows intimately the subject he's chosen for fiction, and that's what makes these novels work so well.

Both novels feature Treasury agent Charles Carr. In *Money Men* he is after the man who shot to death another agent in a motel room that Carr had bugged. Not only do Carr and his partner, Jack Kelly, suffer the agony of listening to their fellow agent being murdered while they are too far away to help, they also must bear the brunt of the responsibility for the tragic operation. Carr is going to be transferred, most likely to a desk job, but he talks his superior into giving him a few weeks before the move and he uses that time to stalk the agent's killer.

Carr and Kelly work against the clock as they slowly close in on a con man named Red Diamond and his young cohort Ronnie Boyce. The setting is Los Angeles, the action fast, the plot tight, all written in a style that smacks hard of realism.

Washington, D.C., as well as Los Angeles is the setting for *One-Shot Deal.* This novel is the more ambitious of the two, and probably the best. Here Carr is set on the trail of someone who has engineered the theft of government security paper from the U.S. Bureau of Engraving and Printing, the special kind of paper used to print money. The someone is a fascinating villain named Larry Phillips, an ex-con who is a skilled hypnotist and runs with beautiful blond prostitute Melba, a woman who is literally under his spell. The story is intricately plotted and builds in suspense to a satisfying conclusion.

Both novels are written in a direct, uncompromising style that establishes a tough authenticity. The dialogue is hard-edged and street-wise, and the knowing attention to detail lends a stark reality that only an insider can bring to this kind of fiction. *Money Men* and *One-Shot Deal* are both lean, mean, and entertaining.

Other Petievich novels are *To Live and Die in Beverly Hills* (1983), *To Live and Die in L.A.* (1984), and *The Quality of the Informant* (1985).

(*J.L.*)

Philbrick, W. R. *Slow Dancer.* New York: St. Martin's, 1984. (PI)

Mystery fiction has seen more women detectives hang out their shingles in the last five years than in its entire history. Naturally, most of these characters are written by women, fueled by a personal understanding of the modern woman's changing role. W. R. Philbrick is one of the few men who can write a modern female detective and make us believe her.

Connie Kale has no one to rely upon but herself. Her dad's still alive, but a massive stroke has taken his speech and his mobility. A golf pro for thirty years, he can only remind Connie that she's not the Women's Golf Champion of the World, a title for which he prepared her since childhood. Her first year on the circuit cracked her nerve—something about being a very small fish in a very big pond—and she's returned to her small New England hometown to start a new career as a private investigator. Her clients value her knowledge of the community and her graceful sense of discretion. She cleans up the messes in their lives with no one the wiser—no small talent in a small town.

In *Slow Dancer,* though, it looks like she might not pull it off. Mandy O'Hare has gotten herself killed in a sleazy motel room after one of those dives into decadence only the rich can afford. Mandy's daddy and grampa have always bought her out of trouble before, but this time all they can manage is to keep the sordid details hushed up. Daddy, you see, is running for governor, about to realize grampa's greatest and last ambition for him. This is grampa's last gasp, and Mandy's death, allegedly at the hands of a local male stripper, is not going to stop him.

This family of aristocrats is being eaten away from within, and grampa wants to know who is rotten and who is not. Connie's father was the old man's golf pro, and Connie is practically a member of the family herself. (She and Mandy used to play on the estate together when baby girls.) Old man O'Hare figures if anybody can find out what's going on and keep her mouth shut about it, Connie can.

Connie, however, has her doubts. Mandy was a brat, and the family is already tainted by suicide, infidelity, and insanity. Besides, murder is hard to cover up anyway, no matter who you are. It's a Pandora's box, and by the time Connie lets all the contents out, this great and powerful family is exposed for the cesspool it is, and Connie barely escapes with her life.

Philbrick writes exceptionally well; his prose sparkles. And he writes Connie well, although women readers might wish to see more of her softer edges than Philbrick shows. Philbrick's other novels are *Shooting Star* (1982) and *Shadow Kills* (1985). The latter will be of particular interest to mystery buffs, as its hero is a mystery writer who is confined to a wheelchair.

(*K.K.H.*)

Philips, Judson. *The Laughter Trap.* New York: Dodd, Mead, 1964. (PS/AD)

Although his work as Hugh Pentecost (q.v.) is better known, Judson Philips has published some excellent novels of suspense and detection under his own name, and created one notable series character—Peter Styles, a national columnist for *Newsview* magazine who specializes in human-interest stories. *The Laughter Trap* is the first of many novels featuring Styles and dramatizes the tragic events that irrevocably altered the shape of his life and career.

While on their way home from the Darlbrook Lodge in the Green Mountains of Vermont, Styles and his elderly father, Herbert, a successful but alcoholic advertising executive, are forced off the road by two thrill killers. Herbert Styles dies in the fiery wreck; Peter is thrown free, but sustains a serious injury that forces doctors to amputate his right leg halfway between the ankle and the knee. He recovers with the help of a former lover, Liz Connors, whose husband is a doctor specializing in prosthetic devices. His new artificial leg allows him to move around with only the slightest limp, and once he has recovered, he devotes his life to an ongoing search for the men who cost him his father and his leg. His only clue is the "hideous high giggling laugh" he heard before the crash.

All of this is told in flashback and through conversations with others as Styles returns a year later to Darlbrook Lodge. He has wired for private accommodations, but ends up sharing a room with the lodge's publicity man, Jim Tranter, through whose eyes we view the rest of the story. Styles's first evening at the lodge is without unusual incident—until he awakens Tranter in the middle of the night, claiming he has again heard the hideous laughter. In the morning, a much more disturbing event is revealed: Two young women staying in one of the cabins—Jane Pritchard and Martha Towers—have been brutally stabbed to death. Jane Pritchard's father appears on the scene, accompanied by his other daughter, Laura, and offers a reward for the apprehension of the slayer. Styles interests himself in the investigation, believing the killings and the laughter he heard have a connection. By the time he solves the grisly double homicide, the usually peaceful atmosphere of the mountain lodge has been disrupted by yet another killing, an attempted murder, a melee in the bar, and dangerous undercurrents of hatred and suspicion. But while Styles finds satisfaction in the resolution of the case, he finds only frustration in his search for the driver of the car who took his father's life.

Styles continues his quest in such other novels as *The Twisted People* (1965), *Nightmare at Dawn* (1970), *Walk a Crooked Mile* (1975), and *Why Murder* (1979). Of the other series characters created by Philips under his own name, the most interesting are Carole Trevor of the Old Town Detective Agency and her ex-husband, wealthy man-about-town Maxwell Blythe, who appear in two early mysteries: *The Death Syndicate* (1938) and *Death Delivers a Postcard* (1939).

(*M.M./B.P.*)

*Philips, Judson. *Whisper Town.* New York: Dodd, Mead, 1960. (T)

Judge Sayre Woodling of the New England community of Rock City was once one of the town's most eminent men. Now—because of a series of tragic events and serious mistakes—he has been removed from his judgeship, disbarred, and has become a pathetic alcoholic. It is his custom to drink at the Rock City Club until he develops double vision, then drive up Cobb's Hill to Timothy's Bar and Grill, where he rounds out his evening's imbibing. But on the night this novel opens, Woodling doesn't make it over the hill without incident; a car full of teenagers gets in his way and he forces them off the road. Two boys and a girl are burned to death in the crash; a second girl survives—barely. Woodling doesn't realize how serious the accident is at the time, and drunk as he is, he covers up, creating an alibi for himself, and then attempts to aid the police in their investigation.

It is later at the police barracks that Woodling's old classmate Avery Hatch unwittingly hands him an idea of how to further deflect suspicion. Hatch, in a stunning burst of illogic, states that the police ought to be after "the real criminals responsible for this disaster." These criminals, he goes on to propound, are the people who are responsible for the town's young people "running around town in fast cars with nothing on their minds but sex." In short, they are the people who support the teaching of a section on reproduction in the high-school biology class.

Woodling soon has mounted a full-scale campaign against such evil; it suits his purposes even more perfectly that one of the champions of this rather mild (by today's standards) form of sex education is Annabelle Winters, the young woman whose inherited trust he milked years ago, resulting in his disbarment. The campaign gathers heat when Woodling enlists the support of such citizens as Harriet Caldwell, the spinsterish domestic-science teacher; Bradley Connors, a former itinerant preacher who now leads the Rock City Tabernacle; and sinister Sergeant Teliski of the police. Arrayed firmly on the other side of the issue are such voices of reason as Annabelle Winters, retired schoolteacher Sarah Marshall, and school-board chairman Marc Swanson. And the one man who initially sees the damage that can be done by this conflict, newspaper editor Bill Jason, is powerless to persuade people to call a halt to it before the town is torn apart. Before votes on the issue can even be cast, that is exactly what happens: Hostilities boil to the surface, resulting in a near-riot, the burning of a cross on Annabelle Winters's lawn, the severing of long-standing friendships, and murder.

This is a gripping story of a small town caught in the vise of unreasoning hatred and prejudice. The character of Sayre Woodling is drawn with understanding and complexity, and the internal story—of the events that turned him into the man who caused this tragedy—explains (but does not attempt to excuse) his actions.

Other engrossing nonseries novels by Philips include *Killer on the Catwalk* (1959), *Murder Clear, Track Fast* (1961), and *The Dead Can't Love* (1962).

(*M.M.*)

Pickard, Nancy. *Generous Death.* New York: Avon, 1984. (O/R)

Romantic suspense of the had-I-but-known variety currently enjoys the bad reputation it often richly deserves. Still, there are plenty of writers who put these elements to good use in their mysteries, and in a completely honorable and entertaining manner. Nancy Pickard is such a writer and *Generous Death* is such a mystery.

The lovely Jennifer Cain may sometimes blunder into danger, like a typical HIBK heroine, but she spends most of her time as the successful director of her local civic foundation. She cajoles money out of Port Frederick's rich, philanthropic class with a clear conscience, but becomes concerned when wealthy citizens start dying off in an unnatural manner. Her concern shifts to personal alarm when an anonymous note indicates that she may be the next victim.

As damsel in distress, Jennifer does do dim-witted things like obeying an anonymous summons to rush into the cold night, as well as predictable things like falling for the detective in charge of the case. But Jennifer is also brave and resourceful enough to confront and subdue a murderer using an item of her intimate apparel as a temporary restraint.

Pickard nicely balances realism, romance, and comedy in her novel and even utilizes a bit of high-tech abracadabra for her murderer's false alibi. Proof that Pickard is just as resourceful as her modern-day heroine/sleuth. Her second novel, *Say No to Murder,* appeared in 1985.

(*K.L.M.*)

Pike, Robert L. *Bank Job.* New York: Doubleday Crime Club, 1974. (PP)

Robert L. Pike is the amusing pseudonym used by Robert L. Fish (q.v.) for two series of police procedurals. The books, too, reflect Fish's sense of humor, with plenty of good-natured repartee among his policemen; but the crimes are serious in nature, and the police procedure is very learned. The first of the series features Lieutenant Clancy of New York's Fifty-second

Precinct; the second features Lieutenant Jim Reardon of the San Francisco force. Ironically, the first novel about Clancy, *Mute Witness* (1963), was the basis for the 1968 Steve McQueen movie *Bullitt,* which was filmed in San Francisco.

In *Bank Job,* four men hold up the Bay View branch of the Farmers & Mercantile Bank in San Francisco, shooting a patrolman to death as they make their getaway. Lieutenant Reardon is aware that a cop killing must be cleared up quickly, and he takes personal responsibility for the investigation. The first thing he picks up on when viewing videotapes of the crime is the smooth way the four worked together; it seems as if they have been a team many times before. And when one of them was wounded by a discharge from the dying officer's gun, there was a cool, professional quality to the way they picked him up and put him in the getaway car. Could they perhaps have worked together in the military? Reardon wonders.

Soon the death toll is up to two: The robbers hijack an ambulance to get medical help for their wounded comrade; the man is already dead, but the ambulance driver is killed by the robbers' stupid actions, and the other medic lives to tell the tale. Reardon steps up the search for the remaining three killers; and when the body of their dead comrade turns up in highly unusual circumstances, he devotes his efforts to making an identification that will, he hopes, lead to the others. The plot twists and turns, continually surprising the reader, and seeming impossibilities are explained only when Reardon pinpoints a crucial and overlooked fact.

Fish, who lived on the East Coast, spent considerable time in San Francisco researching for this series, and he puts his background material to good use in such action-packed scenes as a helicopter search over the San Bruno Mountains and in moody, descriptive passages at an old pier where a derelict freighter is docked. The repartee between Reardon and his subordinates is highly entertaining, and there is a nice subplot about Reardon's lady friend who has staunchly been refusing to marry a cop.

The other novels featuring Jim Reardon are *Reardon* (1970) and *The Gremlin's Grampa* (1972). In addition to *Mute Witness,* Lieutenant Clancy and company appear in *The Quarry* (1964) and *Police Blotter* (1965). Under the Pike name, Fish also wrote one nonseries novel, *Deadline 2 A.M.* (1976). (*M.M.*)

** Poe, Edgar Allan. *Complete Stories and Poems of Edgar Allan Poe.* New York: Doubleday, 1966. (SS)

A book such as *1001 Midnights* would hardly be complete without the inclusion of Edgar Allan Poe, the founding father of the mystery and detective story as we know it today. Poe created the first important series sleuth, C. Auguste Dupin—a character very much modeled on Francois Eugène

Vidocq, the reformed thief and forger who became the first chief of the Sûreté in 1811 and later wrote a highly glamorized autobiography. And in just five famous short stories, the tormented master of the macabre anticipated almost every possible type of criminous tale: the sensational thriller and the locked-room "miracle problem" in "The Murders in the Rue Morgue" (1841); the analytic exercise and the fictional extrapolation of a real-life crime in "The Mystery of Marie Rogêt" (1842); the puzzle story in general and the code-and-cipher tale in particular in "The Gold Bug" (1843); the secret-agent adventure and the classic tale of ratiocination (a word Poe himself invented) in "The Purloined Letter" (1844); and the solving of a small-town murder mystery by the narrator in " 'Thou Art the Man' " (1845).

Those five stories are included in this definitive volume, of course, in the first of five sections, *Tales of Mystery and Horror.* As are such other classic works as "The Black Cat," "The Tell-tale Heart," "William Wilson," "Berenice," "The Cask of Amontillado" (one of the most chilling murder stories ever written), "The Pit and the Pendulum," and sixteen others. The remainder of the volume is comprised of Poe's stories of humor and satire (a side of his literary canon that has not often been emphasized), his "flights and fantasies," the complete text of the seldom-found novella *The Narrative of A. Gordon Pym of Nantucket,* and all fifty-five of his mostly dark and melancholy poems.

Some of Poe's fiction may seem turgid, verbose, and overly pedantic by today's standards; but even his weakest stories are worth whatever effort it might take to read them. This is where it all began; these are the very roots. Every serious student, aficionado, and collector of crime fiction should have this or a comparable volume of Poe's works in his permanent library.

(*B.P.*)

Porter, Joyce. *The Chinks in the Curtain.* New York: Scribner's, 1967. (E/C)

Edmund Brown is a reluctant spy. First recruited into the espionage business by sheer coincidence—he spoke Russian and resembled a Russian agent—he was sent to Russia on an ill-fated mission detailed in *Sour Cream with Everything* (1966). Now he has no sooner returned to London (after a year of hiding in the British Embassy in Moscow) than he is sent out again, this time to Paris.

In *The Chinks in the Curtain,* Brown's assignment for SOD (Special Overseas Directorate) is to discover why an industrial espionage source has dried up. The source—an exiled Russian prince—lives in a huge château in a rather shabby area of Paris. Along with the prince, the château is inhabited by his wife, his wife's lover, their niece, and occasionally a sinister Russian priest. Brown befriends and beds the niece, thereby gaining entrance to the household. What follows for Brown is a comedy of creeping and spying and fending off amorous advances from practically everyone as the story escalates to an action-filled, if somewhat disastrous, conclusion.

Brown is an inept, self-centered, and cowardly agent. He apparently is Joyce Porter's attempt to bring a Dover-like character to the international spy scene. In that sense, the attempt fails—Dover is in a class by himself. But the Edmund Brown stories are amusing and entertaining in their own right.

Edmund Brown reappears in *Only with a Barge Pole* (1974).

(*N.D.*)

* Porter, Joyce. *Dover Goes to Pott.* New York: Scribner's, 1968. (PP/C)

Chief Inspector Wilfred Dover is the most odious of British policemen. He is fat and sloppy, he is self-centered and spiteful, he is lazy yet boastful. On a list of people you would hate to see arrive on your doorstep, he might rank right behind Attila the Hun. Why, then, have the Dover books become so popular? Curiously, the answer might be that Dover is so unlikable as to be likable.

Dover and his much-abused assistant, Sergeant MacGregor, are sent to the town of Pott Winckle on a murder case. (It is Scotland Yard's practice to send Dover as far away as possible.) The daughter of the town's richest and most powerful citizen has been murdered, and this citizen—one Daniel Wibbley—is so convinced his son-in-law is the killer, he offers Dover a bribe to prove it. Dover is deeply touched and, in order to earn the bribe, temporarily puts aside his habitual four daily meals and twelve hours of sleep and actually bestirs himself to visit the scene of the crime. After this feat, he wanders sullenly around the neighborhood, offending and browbeating possible witnesses, while at the same time helping himself to their food.

The next morning finds Dover, worn out from this unusual effort, more typically ensconced in the hotel while MacGregor does the legwork. MacGregor has recognized Dover's myopic obsession with proving the son-in-law's guilt and and he becomes just as obsessed with proving someone else guilty. Naturally, Dover will not tolerate this. He has the son-in-law arrested on insufficient evidence and attempts to beat the truth out of him—a serious mistake on Dover's part; for the son-in-law, although outweighed by a hundred pounds, manages to thrash Dover in self-defense.

Amazingly enough, after this horrendous beginning, things eventually do sort themselves out and the case is solved, with "the oaf of Scotland Yard" chalking up another to his credit.

One is struck, throughout the Dover series, with the almost loving detail with which Joyce Porter describes Dover's physical and behavioral blemishes: the beady, malevolent eyes; the huge, sagging, unshaven jowels; the hippolike body clothed in cheap, ill-fitting suits; his abominable and gluttonous mannerisms; and his innate ability to offend almost anyone. Yet it should be noted that Joyce Porter is a fine writer of detective novels. Although the Dover character she has created is so powerful it threatens to take over many of the stories, Porter proves herself the ultimate master and keeps the reader in suspense (as well as hysterics) until book's end.

Other books in the Dover series are *Dover One* (1964), *Dover Two* (1965), *Dover Three* (1966), and *Dover and the Unkindest Cut of All* (1967). Another pair of Joyce Porter's novels features sleuth Constance Morrison-Burke: *Rather a Common Sort of Crime* (1970) and *The Package Included Murder* (1976).

(*N.D.*)

* Post, Melville Davisson. *The Strange Schemes of Randolph Mason.* New York: Putnam's, 1896. (SS)

This collection of seven short stories was published in the same year that the younger Oliver Wendell Holmes, then a justice of the Supreme Judicial Court of Massachusetts, published his classic essay "The Path of the Law." The hallmark of law as a discipline, Holmes contended, is that it adopts the viewpoint of "the bad man," the totally amoral person who will do whatever he pleases, no matter how harmful to others, unless he knows that civil or criminal liability will fall upon him for certain acts. The function of the lawyer is to advise "the bad man" so that he can stay just this side of the line separating lawful and unlawful conduct—which is by no means the same as the line between decent and outrageous conduct. What seems to follow is that if there's a way within the rules of the game for a lawyer to save his client from liability, he must take it. This conception of law and lawyers, born in the age of social Darwinism and devil-take-the-hindmost business ethics, is still accepted in theory and practice by most American lawyers today. It also informs most of the Randolph Mason stories.

The creation of aristocratic West Virginia attorney Melville Davisson Post, Mason is a sardonic, cynical lawyer who specializes in advising people how to commit crimes and, thanks to loopholes in the system, get away scot-free. He's at his best when his client is tried for some crime and he makes his argument to the judge that technically what the client did was not a crime at all so that he must be released at once. Invariably, at least in the first two Mason collections, our legal eagle prevails and a furious but checkmated jurist is compelled to turn loose an obviously guilty defendant.

Most of the Mason stories revolve around fine points of 1890s jurisprudence: partnership law in "Woodford's Partner," contract law in "The Error of William Van Broom," the law of embezzlement in "The Sheriff of Gullmore." These tales are only of historical interest today. But in the first and longest story in the collection, "The Corpus Delicti," the crime the bad man gets away with by following Mason's advice is nothing less than murder. By dissolving the flesh and bones of his ex-mistress in sulfuric acid, Samuel Walcott denies the authorities what under New York law at the time was an absolute prerequisite for a murder conviction, namely a body. Mason triumphantly expounds the law at Walcott's trial; and metaphorically if not literally gnashing his teeth, the judge directs the jury to find Walcott not guilty.

Post took a lot of heat for writing stories like these. His defense was that he pointed out loopholes in the law so that courts and legislatures could close them up, and the Mason tales have indeed been credited with inspiring some reforms. The second collection about this scoundrel, *The Man of Last Resort* (1897), was in the same vein as the first. But then Post underwent a change of heart, and in the final book of the Mason trilogy, *The Corrector of Destinies* (1908), our protagonist uses the technical rules of law as a weapon not to flout simple justice but to secure it.

(*F.M.N.*)

** Post, Melville Davisson. *Uncle Abner, Master of Mysteries.* New York: Appleton, 1918. (SS)

In his finest series of tales, which began appearing in *The Saturday Evening Post* and other magazines in 1911, Post transcended human law altogether and, with the power of a man born again, wrote of the divine law that stands above man's puny systems of (in)justice. These stories are set in rural West Virginia in the mid–nineteenth century and center around Abner, a huge, bearded, grimly austere, and supremely righteous countryman who smites wrongdoers and mends destinies like a biblical prophet transplanted to the New World. In every respect—plotting, characterizations, narrative, and dialogue—Post imbued these eighteen stories with a power and majesty comparable to (and of course derived from) the King James version of the Bible. They capture the essence of evangelical Protestantism and integrate it into detective fiction with the same supreme skill that G. K. Chesterton (q.v.) was simultaneously lavishing upon his Father Brown stories in the service of rationalist Catholicism. And they're as compulsively readable today as they were seventy years ago.

There is hardly a weak story in the collection, and even the titles—"The Angel of the Lord," "The Tenth Commandment," "An Act of God," "The Age of Miracles," "The Devil's Tools," "The Hidden Law"—reflect the harsh Calvinistic atmosphere of Abner's world. The most famous of the eighteen is "The Doomdorf Mystery," in which Abner and the local justice of the peace, Squire Randolph, probe the locked-room shooting of a hideously wicked farmer. The perfectly constructed climax is one of the most powerful in any mystery short story. But a number of less-known tales in the collection are just as good, among them "The Tenth Commandment" with its Socratic dialogue on human law and divine justice, "The Straw Man" with its rich mixture of theology and deduction, and "Naboth's Vineyard" with its thunderous courtroom denouement. The characteristic Post themes of bloodlines, succession to land, and the nature of justice reappear a few decades later in William Faulkner's (q.v.) stories about lawyer Gavin Stevens, who despite his mild manner and tolerant cosmopolitanism qualifies as the closest spiritual descendant of Uncle Abner.

Uncle Abner is by no means the only series character Post created after Randolph Mason. His short stories about British detective Sir Henry Marquis are collected in *The Sleuth of St. James's Square* (1920); and those about Colonel Braxton, a contemporary southern lawyer, are to be found in *The Silent Witness* (1929). The exploits of two other Post detectives were brought together in hardcover in *Monsieur Jonquelle, Prefect of Police of Paris* (1923) and *Walker of the Secret Service* (1924). Few of the stories he wrote about other characters have survived the generations as well as the Abner series.

Near the end of his life, Post wrote four final tales about his most enduring creation, and the entire cycle of twenty-two stories, rearranged in the order of their composition, was published as *The Complete Uncle Abner* (1977), a volume in the University of California's sadly short-lived Mystery Library series. It's primarily on the basis of these tales that Post is universally regarded as the finest American writer of detective/crime short stories between Edgar Allan Poe and Dashiell Hammett.

(*F.M.N.*)

Potts, Jean. *Go, Lovely Rose.* New York: Scribner's, 1954. (W)

Welcome to the small town of Coreyville. Coreyville is like small towns everywhere—extended families, really. Everyone knows everything that's going on, and minds everybody's business but his or her own. Take the trouble over at the old Doc Buckmaster place, for example. The doctor himself has been dead for years, leaving the housekeeper, Mrs. Henshaw, to raise the kids. Rachael, the older of the two, is off working in Chicago now, which means nineteen-year-old Hartley is there alone with the Henshaw woman. And it's no secret they don't get along, especially lately, after Mrs. Henshaw burned all his drawings. So when Mrs. Henshaw is found at the bottom of the cellar stairs, dead of a broken neck, and young Hartley doesn't even remember what he was doing that day . . . well, there's bound to be talk.

Rachael comes home from Chicago, which is probably the last thing in the world she wanted to do—come home to relive all the childhood anxieties she thought she had left behind. (Mrs. Henshaw wasn't exactly the most understanding parent substitute, you see—nor the most popular woman in town, by a long shot.) Anyway, Rachael comes home to find the evidence against Hartley mounting at an alarming rate. Soon, in fact, he is arrested for murder. But friends and neighbors close ranks behind Rachael and, with the assistance of a detective named Mr. Pigeon, go about unearthing more physical evidence—a candlestick, a strongbox, a scarf, etc. In the process, they also dig deeply into Coreyville's secrets, and eventually manage to solve the case. The friends and neighbors are fine people. It's too bad one of them has to be the murderer.

This is a realistic and engaging small-town drama, well deserving of the MWA Best First Novel Edgar it received. Jean Potts's subsequent novels are less whodunits than suspense stories with mystery elements; noteworthy among them are *The Diehard* (1956), which also has a nicely realized small-town background; *The Evil Wish* (1962); *The Trash Stealer* (1968); and *My Brother's Killer* (1975).

(*N.D.*)

Powell, Talmage. *The Girl's Number Doesn't Answer.* New York: Pocket Books, 1960. (O/PI)

Talmage Powell made his first professional sale in 1943, of a mystery novelette that was cover-featured in a pulp magazine, and followed it with some 500 additional short stories and novelettes over the past forty-two years. Of his twenty novels, most of which are criminous, five paperback originals published between 1959 and 1964 feature Tampa private investigator Ed Rivers—a far more realistic creation than the bulk of softcover private eyes who appeared and disappeared in the Fifties and Sixties.

In *The Girl's Number Doesn't Answer,* Rivers comes to the aid of an old friend, former marine Nick Martin, who stands accused of using a samurai sword to brutally murder three Japanese during a drunken blackout. Motive: fifteen years of crippling pain that has had him in and out of hospitals, the result of wounds suffered on Iwo Jima. Nick's wife, Helen, believes he is innocent; so does Rivers, whose search for the real killer of the Yamashita family involves him with Nick's business partner; a Japanese wrestler named Prince Kuriacha; a sleazy fellow private eye; and a cultured madame who calls herself Tillie Rollo.

There is plenty of action here, the racial overtones are handled with aplomb, and the Tampa scene is vividly evoked—in particular Ybor City, the Cuban barrio on the edge of which Rivers lives. But it is the character of Rivers that stands out and gives the novel its depth and solidity. Tough but human, a man with feelings and problems, he generates a good deal of empathy in the reader; when he sweats in the muggy Tampa heat we sweat right along with him, and share his desire for a cold beer or a cooling swim.

The other four Rivers adventures are also above average: *The Killer Is Mine* (1959), *With a Madman Behind Me* (1961), *Start Screaming Murder* (1962), and the unfortunately titled *Corpus Delectable* (1964), in which Gasparilla Week, Tampa's annual Mardi Gras celebration, is strikingly portrayed. Notable among Powell's other crime novels is his first, *The Smasher* (1959), the tense story of a man named Steve Griffin and his relentless hunt for the deliberate hit-and-run murderer of his wife.

(*B.P.*)

Prather, Richard S. *The Cockeyed Corpse.* Greenwich, Conn.: Fawcett Gold Medal, 1964. (PI/C/O)

Richard S. Prather had extraordinary success in the Fifties and Sixties with his Shell Scott private-eye novels, selling over 40 million copies. But he failed to update the character, and Shell Scott is now out of fashion and out of print. He is, however, remembered fondly by thousands of private-eye fanciers who started with Shell Scott in adolescence (principally because of the sexy parts) and only later graduated to the "serious" stuff like Hammett and Chandler (qq.v.). Moreover, the books are still marvelously entertaining, lively and funny, a uniquely successful hybrid of tough-guy fiction and knockabout low comedy.

Shell Scott is an experienced, thoroughly hard-boiled private eye who works the L.A.–Hollywood territory. He is also, well, not exactly supremely competent sometimes. He does much of his detecting in a semiaddled state brought on by (a) glandular overload in the presence of the voluptuous babes that figure prominently in his cases, or (b) a bit too much to drink, usually consumed whilst attempting seduction of the aforementioned babes, or (c) being hit on the head a few too many times, or (d) all of the above. This gets him into some of the damnedest scrapes!

In this one, a movie producer sends him to a dude ranch in Arizona where they're doing location shooting for a "nudie" entitled *The WILD West,* and where a starlet has been killed in somewhat suspicious circumstances. Immediately upon arrival, he's shot at by a hoodlum on horseback. It seems that the ranch is crawling with hoods, the remnants of a gang whose now deceased boss Shell put away a year ago. He has precious few opportunities to cultivate the acquaintance of the four surviving starlets, since they're getting shot at during the lulls when he's not getting sapped, beaten up, or shot at again.

Finally, Shell manages to deduce the explanation for all this hostile activity, and effects a rescue of the girls by the obvious stratagem of arming himself with a tranquilizer gun and stalking the hoods disguised as a rock. This climactic scene gives rise to that memorable line "You won't believe this, but that rock just shot me in the ass!"

(*A.S.*)

Prather, Richard S. *Gat Heat.* New York: Trident, 1967. (PI/C)

Shell Scott goes out to meet a prospective client at his house during a party. Quite a party—all the guests are drunk and naked, and having a helluva good time, except the client, who is reposing behind a bush with his head bashed in. The case involves a blackmail ring that is putting the squeeze on a group of wealthy suburban "swingers." The blackmailers are tied into the mob, whose gunmen make several determined attempts to put Shell out of the picture. During one such attempt, our hero manages to film the action. He shows the celluloid evidence to his pals down at the police department, forgetting that the film also features candid footage of one Tootsie, cavorting at the beach.

Mortified, the laughter of the cops still ringing in his ears (also extra ringing caused by several blows to the head sustained in earlier action), Shell sets out to salvage his reputation by mounting a blitzkrieg assault on the hoods' fortress, armed with a crossbow and an experimental rocket pistol swiped from the police armory.

A typically wild case with a slam-bang finale, though the epilogue is a bit unusual in that Shell winds up in jail and sans the company of a pliant tomato (they are all either married or crooks in this one).

(*A.S.*)

*Prather, Richard S. *Strip for Murder.* Greenwich, Conn.: Fawcett Gold Medal, 1955. (PI/C/O)

This early novel marks a turning point in Prather's work. Though comic elements were present in the books from the first, they were basically straight post-Spillane private-eye stuff, albeit with a light touch. With this book, broad farce became the essential ingredient, and Shell Scott became a private eye like no other (though his antecedents are clear: Jonathan Latimer's [q.v.] Bill Crane, and Robert Leslie Bellem's [q.v.] Dan Turner).

Shell is hired to check on the background of a possible fortune hunter recently married to the daughter of a very wealthy woman. Another private investigator working on the case has been murdered, and another daughter has had a couple of attempts on her life. Shell has to protect her, but complicating matters somewhat is the fact that she lives in a nudist colony. Shell very reluctantly signs on as athletic director. The case also ties into a mob-run nightclub, done up as a medieval castle, which Shell is forced to invade at one point, dressed in a suit of armor (jousting is not his strong suit). The book concludes with a wild shooting scrape, fire, and riot at the nudist colony. Shell escapes the bullets by latching on to some gas-filled balloons, which unfortunately drift right over the heart of Los Angeles (he's coming direct from a nudist colony, remember).

This novel, surely one of the classic Shell Scott capers, was cruelly dismissed by Barzun and Taylor in *A Catalog of Crime;* they evidently didn't get the joke. Prather reportedly considers it his best book. It was written while he was suffering from a severe case of boils, an unfortunate side effect of a health-food diet that included raw calves' brains. Intense focus on the typewriter masked the pain—and helped to produce a wonderfully loony private-eye novel.

Other antic Shell Scott novels include *Slab Happy* (1958); *Kill the Clown* (1962); *The Trojan Hearse* (1964); and *Double in Trouble* (1959), a collaboration between Prather and Stephen Marlowe (q.v.), in which Shell Scott teams up with Marlowe's private-eye character Chester Drum.

(*A.S.*)

Price, Anthony. *The Old Vengeful.* New York: Doubleday Crime Club, 1983. (E)

Anthony Price is one of the modern breed of spy novelists, but his stories are invariably tied to the past. Price's particular forte is creating a basic plot of good-guy Britons struggling against the powers of darkness and the KGB, and doing so against the backdrop of a historical, often military, event. *The Old Vengeful* is a recent offering that is representative of Price's work.

Historian and British agent Dr. Paul Mitchell is assigned an investigation by his superior, mentor, and series protagonist David Audley. It seems that the CIA has given Britain a tip about an upcoming KGB mission in England called "Project Vengeful." All the British have to do is figure out what the mission *is* and how to thwart it.

A long line of British warships were all named the *Vengeful.* Since they are unsure whether the ships are clues or red herrings, Mitchell is told to research them all as well as keep an eye on the daughter of a recently deceased *Vengeful* veteran and naval historian. So, amid research into the Napoleonic wars and an increasing involvement with the plain but intelligent daughter, Mitchell must try to sort out what the Russians are up to.

Those uninterested in military history may well wonder what Price is up to, muddying his Eighties spy thriller with the dead past. Those who are familiar with military history will think otherwise. They will admire Price's considerable talents for lacing past with present, and the Great Wars with the cold war.

Among Price's other espionage novels are his first, *The Labyrinth Makers* (1971), *Other Paths to Glory* (1975), and *Sion Crossing* (1985).

(*K.L.M.*)

Proctor, Maurice. *The Pub Crawler.* New York: Harper, 1957. (PP)

Maurice Proctor wrote more than a score of English police-procedural novels, many of them featuring Detective Chief Inspector Harry Martineau, a character who has been favorably compared to John Creasey's (q.v.) George Gideon. All of his novels are set in imaginary cities in the north of England—*The Pub Crawler* takes place in the industrial town of Airechester—and the best of them have a sense of gritty realism reminiscent of the Eighty-seventh Precinct series of Ed McBain (q.v.). They do not have McBain's depth, however, nor his sense of humor; and little emphasis is placed on the personal lives of the detective characters, or on their on-the-job interaction. Proctor's appeal, therefore, is somewhat limited, although he does tell a strong story and his police methods are authentic, his characters and settings well drawn.

The "pub crawler" of the title of this nonseries novel is Bill Knight, a twenty-three-year-old recent graduate of the police academy whose first assignment is an undercover one: to establish himself as a laborer in the Champion Road district of Airechester and to gather information on illegal betting at the area's many pubs. Knight doesn't like the idea of being a spy and goes about the task grudgingly. But his job turns into something much more—an undercover murder investigation—when the owner of the Starving Rascal pub, Sam Gilmour, is bludgeoned to death on the premises and his collection of valuable gold coins stolen. Suspects in the case include Gunnar Byles, the unpleasant young son of Knight's Champion Road landlady; and a retired lawyer, John Harper, the putative father of Gay Gilmour, who worked for her real father at the Starving Rascal. Knight finds himself drawn to Gay, and at the same time pursued by Gunnar's eighteen-year-old sister, Junie—a situation that forms a which-girl-will-he-choose subplot.

There are no real surprises in *The Pub Crawler;* the story line is straightforward, with Knight's undercover activities taking up two-thirds of the narrative. (The other third is procedural, involving Detective Inspector Robert Fairbrother, who is in charge of the homicide investigation.) But Proctor writes well, sprinkling his narrative with evocative lower-class British slang, and the various motives of the characters are realistic and believable.

Proctor's novels featuring "gentleman policeman" Harry Martineau include *Somewhere in This City* (1954), *The Devil Was Handsome* (1961), and *Homicide Blonde* (1965). Other notable nonseries procedurals are *Hurry the Darkness* (1951) and *Three at the Angel* (1958).

(*B.P.*)

Pronzini, Bill. *Games.* New York: Putnam's, 1976. (T)

Games is not dissimilar in its fundamental shocking premise to Pronzini's later novel, *Masques* (1981): In both, the protagonist is enmeshed in a situation of inexplicable, mounting evil and physical threat, while the woman with whom he is involved becomes an early target; in both, the central plot twist is similar in design. But *Games* is the more disturbing of the two because it has elements of *roman à clef* and an overlay of genuine political implication.

David Jackman, the fortyish protagonist who views all of life in terms of games, is an influential United States senator haunted by the persona of his powerful, deceased, domineering father, trapped in a dead marriage, and involved in an adulterous affair built upon role-playing and intimations of perversity. He takes his mistress, Tracy, to a small island owned by his family, off the Maine coast, for what is planned as a brief retreat over Memorial Day weekend. But it soon becomes apparent that they are not alone on the island; unseen forces begin a devilish cat-and-mouse game with them that builds inexorably in both menace and horror. When Tracy is abducted and evidently murdered in terrible fashion, and the stalking forces close in on him, Jackman loses his trained game-player's instincts and is driven to the brink of madness.

Like so many Pronzini protagonists, Jackman finds the resilience to finally confront his tormentors and to understand the awful truth behind their actions. His unraveling and the way in which, having touched bottom, he recovers himself is the focal point of the novel. Phantasmagoric, surreal, and hallucinatory scenes here are among the strongest set pieces in Pronzini's writing outside of the "Nameless Detective" series, and while this is not as precise or as colorful a novel as *Masques,* it has a wider range of implication.

It is, perhaps, this implication that functions as a deleterious factor. Jackman the politician and the resemblances he bears to a certain real-life model are more interesting than anything that is done to him; the novel seems to have a very large subject placed in narrow terrain (this is essentially a two-character novel) and, disappointingly, it resolves itself upon the plot level while leaving the conceptualization untouched. There is both more and less to *Games* than meets the eye. But it is consistently readable, and as well paced as either of Pronzini's prior noncollaborative suspense novels: *Panic!*

(1972), which has a southwestern desert setting; and *Snowbound* (1974), which takes place in an isolated village in the High Sierra.

(*B.N.M.*)

*Pronzini, Bill. *Quicksilver*. New York: St. Martin's, 1984. (PI)

Bill Pronzini's "Nameless Detective" series is the ongoing story of an ordinary man who happens to be a private investigator. "Nameless" (he is without an appellation simply because neither Pronzini nor his original editor could think of a suitable one) is a big Italian in his fifties, fond of beer, garlic olive-and-anchovy pizza, and women—whom he readily admits he doesn't understand. His apartment in San Francisco's Pacific Heights houses his collection of some 6500 pulp magazines from the Thirties and Forties, and he also readily admits that his fascination with the pulps is probably the reason he became a cop and then a private eye. A low-key but emotional man, often melancholy, "Nameless" would have been better off back in the days of the pulps than in our present-day high-tech society. In spite of his calling, he is a peaceable, law-abiding man who abhors the violence and death he encounters. While death is by necessity a common occurrence in the series, it is always taken with utmost seriousness. It can be said that any of today's private eye novelists is the inheritor of the literary tradition of Chandler and Hammett, and Pronzini has enlarged upon that tradition, taking it in a new direction by creating a character who is unique, rather than a pale copy of Marlowe or Spade.

The early "Nameless" novels—notably *The Snatch* (1971) and *The Vanished* (1973)—portray the detective as a gloomy man, obsessed with his health but unable to stop smoking. He has terrible trouble with women—due partly to his work and partly to the fact that his relationships are intense and humorless. This all begins to change, however, when he develops a possibly malignant lesion on one lung and is forced to confront his own mortality (*Blowback,* 1977). As he explains it in *Twospot* (1978, with Collin Wilcox):

> *. . . the specter of death had changed me in a lot of ways over these past five months. . . . I had made peace with myself and the world around me. I was no longer inclined to view certain things and certain people with cynical eyes. I was no longer inclined to care too much and too deeply about the lives and the suffering of others. . . . Not that I have stopped caring; it is just that human pain and human folly do not hurt me so much any more.*

The new "Nameless" is free to give full rein to his wry sense of humor; and what's more, he now has a decent relationship with a woman, Kerry

Wade—although he doesn't understand her any more than he did his past lovers.

As *Quicksilver,* the eleventh entry in the series, opens, the detective is inspecting an office with his new partner, Eberhardt, formerly of the San Francisco Police Department. He has reservations about the office (which contains a light fixture that looks like a "grappling hook surrounded by clusters of brass testicles"), about the partnership, and about the diet on which Kerry has recently placed him. And he is glad to escape, to see a client about what may be his last solo case. Haruko Gage—a domineering Japanese woman married to a self-effacing Caucasian—has been receiving expensive presents in the mail, pieces of jewelry, and they disturb her; she wants to find out who is sending them. The detective starts with her former boyfriends: Edgar Ogada, a hardworking young landscape nursery employee; Kinji Shimata, who owns an art gallery in nearby Japantown; Nelson ("Nellie") Mixer, a professor who specializes in seducing his female students; and Ken Yamasaki, a Japanese bathhouse employee. While trying to contact Yamasaki, "Nameless" stumbles onto the murder of the bathhouse owner, a man rumored to be a member of the Yakuza (Japanese Mafia); and soon he must contend not only with Yakuza thugs but with connections that go back to World War II and the Japanese internment camps.

Quicksilver is a well-plotted novel with a haunting resolution that will have special meaning for readers who are alarmed by the political and social trends of contemporary society. The background on the Japanese in present-day San Francisco, as well as in northern California during the war years, is particularly well handled.

(*M.M.*)

Pronzini, Bill. *Undercurrent.* New York: Random House, 1973. (PI)

One of the interesting things about the early "Nameless" novels (before the present publisher began billing each in the series as "A 'Nameless Detective' Mystery") is that the uninitiated reader can get through most of a book before realizing the detective has no name—a tribute to Pronzini's excellent characterization of his hero. *Undercurrent* is the third in the series, and self-admittedly the author's "Ross Macdonald pastiche"; but in spite of its Macdonaldesque metaphors, which occasionally stretch a point too far, it stands on its own as an exceptionally good piece of writing, sharply evocative of its coastal California setting.

"Nameless" is hired by a lovely young woman, Judith Paige ("the kind of girl they used to call 'sweet' and 'wholesome' without sniggering about it") to investigate what her husband, Walter, has been doing on weekends. (She thinks he is seeing another woman.) The detective tails Paige to the picturesque oceanside town of Cypress Bay and takes a room in the same motel. Paige emerges once and has a conference on the beach with a heavy-set balding man, then returns to his room. "Nameless" watches for some time more before he remembers the room's beachside entrance—and when he goes to investigate, he finds Paige has been stabbed to death.

The detective cooperates fully with Cypress Bay police chief Ned Quartermain, and when he goes to sign his statement, he asks Quartermain about the one odd thing he observed in Paige's room—a paperback novel from the early Fifties by an old pulp writer, Russell Dancer. It was odd for Paige to have a book that is nearly a collector's item, especially since his wife says he wasn't a reader.

Quartermain is interested, but not very, and lets "Nameless" have the book. And later, unable to leave town and feeling restless, "Nameless" tracks down Dancer at his beachfront shack. Dancer admits to having known Paige back in the Sixties when they both ran with a hard-drinking crowd in Cypress Bay, and gives him a list of the others in the group. While talking to them, "Nameless" finds that Paige had recently expressed an interest in buying a newsstand in town; that the mention of Paige's name severely distresses one couple; and that the balding man Paige talked with on the beach is familiar with at least one member of the now-defunct crowd. Before he is able to piece together these facts and figure out the significance of Dancer's novel, however, arson and a second murder occur, and the copy of the paperback mysteriously disappears.

Undercurrent is the best of the early "Nameless" novels, fully revealing the detective as a compassionate and uncommonly humane individual. Its ingenious resolution—which is cleverly set up with well-concealed clues—is sure to delight the reader.

Trivia question for "Nameless" fans: we all know *he* doesn't carry a label, but what make is his car? Clue: the detective and the car have a lot in common.

Other entries in this ongoing "biography of a detective" are *Labyrinth* (1980); *Hoodwink* (1981), which takes place at a pulp writers' convention and won a Private Eye Writers of America Shamus as Best Novel of 1981; *Scattershot* (1982); *Dragonfire* (1982), set primarily in San Francisco's Chinese community; *Bindlestiff* (1983); *Nightshades* (1984); *Double* (1984, in collaboration with this reviewer); and *Bones* (1985). A collection of "Nameless" short stories, *Casefile,* was published in 1983.

(*M.M.*)

*Pronzini, Bill, and Barry N. Malzberg. *The Running of Beasts.* New York: Putnam's, 1976. (PS)

More than any other contemporary mystery writer, Bill Pronzini has the knack for joint authorship with all sorts of collaborators, including John

Lutz, Marcia Muller, Collin Wilcox and investigative reporter Jack Anderson. But rooted as Pronzini is in the uncluttered tale-spinning tradition of the pulps and the fair-play detection games of Christie and Queen, one might have predicted disaster if he were to co-author books with a master of plotless, characterless stream-of-consciousness interior monologues like the *noir* science-fiction writer Barry N. Malzberg. Surprise! *The Running of Beasts* turned out to be the finest suspense novel since the death of Cornell Woolrich (q.v.).

The union of Pronzini's gifts for plotting and tight structure with Malzberg's obsessional style and motifs gave birth to a spine-freezing variation on the old number about the mad killer terrorizing a city. After several women have been slashed to death Ripper-fashion in the Adirondack resort community of Bloodstone, a psychiatrist theorizes that the murderer is a schizophrenic, someone whose everyday personality is totally unaware of its murderous dark persona. The novel is divided into more than 150 brief segments told from the alternating viewpoints of six central characters: the tortured state-police official in charge of the case; the brutal and guilt-wracked local constable; a New York journalist who returns to her hated hometown to cover the crimes; an alcoholic ex-actor and horseplayer with whom the journalist falls in love; a mother-ridden local reporter with dreams of writing a best seller about the murders; and the Ripper. We know that one of the first five is the Ripper's daylight personality, but Pronzini and Malzberg have structured the book so skillfully that at the end of each segment we are convinced beyond doubt that *that* viewpoint character is the killer. The frenzy of oscillating suspicion and mounting suspense is sustained over more than 300 pages of a gigantic shell game, challenging us to guess which shell the P (for psychosis) is under.

The second Pronzini-Malzberg collaborative novel, *Acts of Mercy* (1977), was a disappointing political thriller about a paranoid president. But their third and to date final book in tandem, *Night Screams* (1979), once again blended the authors' disparate talents into an excellent suspenser about a maniac systematically killing off members of a group of psychics—one of whom comes to believe (although she can't convince outsiders) that the murderer is part of the group. Like *The Running of Beasts,* it's a sharply written tour de force of terror that defies the reader to lay it down unfinished.

(*F.M.N.*)

Propper, Milton. *The Family Burial Murders.* New York: Harper, 1934. (PP)

Milton Propper was born in 1906, graduated from the University of Pennsylvania Law School with honors in 1929, and saw his first detective novel published the same year. He never practiced law but went to work in the mid-1930s for the Social Security Administration and continued mystery-writing on the side. His fourteen whodunits are usually set in Philadelphia and its suburbs and feature young Tommy Rankin, the homicide specialist on that city's police force.

Propper was far from a paragon of all the literary virtues. He wrote dull prose, peopled his books with nonentities, flaunted like a badge of honor his belief that the police and the powerful are above the law, and refused to play fair with the reader. Yet paradoxically his best books hold some of the intellectual excitement of the early novels of Ellery Queen (q.v.). Propper generally begins with the discovery of a body under bizarre circumstances: on an amusement park's scenic railway in *The Strange Disappearance of Mary Young* (1929); during a college-fraternity initiation in *The Student Fraternity Murder* (1932); in a voting booth in *The Election Booth Murder* (1935). Then he scatters suspicion among several characters with much to hide, all the while juggling clues and counterplots with dazzling nimbleness. His detectives are gifted with some extraordinary powers—for example, they can make startlingly accurate deductions from a glance at a person's face—and have no qualms about committing burglary and other crimes while searching for evidence. Propper novels often involve various forms of mass transportation and complex legal questions over the succession to a large estate. Near the end, having proved all the known suspects innocent, Rankin invariably puts together some as yet unexplained pieces of the puzzle, concludes that the murderer was an avenger from the past who infiltrated the victim's life in disguise, and launches a breakneck chase to collar the killer before he or she escapes.

Such is the Propper pattern. One of the books in which it shows to best advantage is *The Family Burial Murders,* whose opening is reminiscent of Ellery Queen's (q.v.) 1932 classic *The Greek Coffin Mystery:* Rankin is summoned to one of Philadelphia's stately mansions after one body too many turns up at the gravesite during the funeral of a wealthy dowager. The old lady clearly died of natural causes, but her nephew, who also lies in her coffin, was just as clearly murdered, and Rankin's investigation turns up an assortment of suspects with motive and opportunity. Propper juggles the legal tangles surrounding the dead woman's estate with an array of trains, trolleys, elevated lines, and interurban electric trams that give him the crown as mystery fiction's number one transportation buff.

Unlike his novels, Propper's life became ever more wretched and messy. He alienated his family, lived in squalor, was picked up for homosexual activity by the police whose lawbreaking he had glorified, eventually lost all markets for his writing and, in 1962, killed himself.

(*F.M.N.*)

Quarry, Nick. *The Hoods Come Calling.* Greenwich, Conn.: Fawcett Gold Medal, 1958. (O/PI)

Nick Quarry (a great pseudonym) was one of the names used by prolific paperbacker Marvin H. Albert, who also wrote entertaining books as Al Conroy and Tony Rome. Most of the Quarry novels are part of the series featuring Jake Barrow, a tough private eye in the Spillane tradition. *The Hoods Come Calling* is the first book in the series.

Barrow returns to New York after two years in Chicago, where he has been trying to forget his wife's infidelities. All he wants from her is the $1600 he left in their joint account, which he plans to use to buy into a private detective agency. He goes to her apartment to pick up the money, and she shows up drunk. He carries her upstairs and is seen by the neighbors. When he leaves for a minute, she is murdered. Barrow conceals the body, but he is soon being hunted by the police, as well as by his wife's hoodlum friends. He must prove his innocence by finding the guilty party. Along the way, there is a bit of 1950s sex (not too graphic) and a considerable amount of violence (which Quarry handles very well).

The familiar story has just the right mixture of action and detection to keep things moving along at a rapid clip, and Barrow makes a credible hard guy, though his character seems a bit inconsistent at times. There is at least one nice surprise in store for the reader; and the ending, in which Barrow proves to be not quite as dishonest as the hoods believe him to be, is quite satisfactory.

Other lively Nick Quarry novels include *No Chance in Hell* (1960), *Till It Hurts* (1960), and *Some Die Hard* (1961).

(*B.C.*)

*Queen, Ellery. *The Greek Coffin Mystery.* New York: Stokes, 1932. (CS)

With one inspired stroke—using the same name, Ellery Queen, for their detective character and their own joint pseudonym—the Brooklyn-born cousins Frederic Dannay and Manfred B. Lee launched their common literary career, and the excellence of their output from 1929 until Lee's death in 1971 made the Queen by-line a guaranty of the best in American detective fiction. One key to their success was their capacity to modify the character of Ellery and the kind of books they wrote so as to keep up with changing times and tastes, and their work can thus be divided into four diverse periods.

The most popular American detective character of the late 1920s was S. S. Van Dine's (q.v.) impossibly intellectual aesthete/sleuth Philo Vance. The early Queen novels, with their patterned titles and their portrait of Ellery as a scholarly dilettante and walking encyclopedia, were very much in the tradition of Van Dine's best sellers although superior in plotting, characterization, and style. A professional mystery writer himself, Ellery leaves his typewriter to play amateur sleuth whenever his father, Inspector Richard Queen of the NYPD, encounters a case too complex for ordinary procedure. The first-period Queen novels, from *The Roman Hat Mystery* (1929) through *The Spanish Cape Mystery* (1935), are richly plotted specimens of the Golden Age deductive puzzle, full of bizarre circumstances, conflicting testimony, enigmatic clues, alternative solutions, fireworks displays of virtuoso reasoning, and formal challenges to the reader to identify the murderer ahead of Ellery.

Each of the nine first-period novels about Ellery is a gem, but the fourth, *The Greek Coffin Mystery,* has long been a personal favorite. It begins with the death (by natural causes) of blind art dealer Georg Khalkis and his burial in the church graveyard next door to his West Fifty-fourth Street brownstone. When the funeral party returns to the house, it's discovered that the steel box containing Khalkis's will is missing from his wall safe. The police are called, but the box is still unrecovered two days later. Invited to attend a conference on the case, Ellery deduces that the box can be in only one place, namely Khalkis's coffin. An exhumation order is obtained, the coffin is opened, and inside is found not the will but the decaying corpse of a second man, strangled to death and lying on top of Khalkis's body. Thus begins what is probably the most labyrinthine brain-crusher of a pure deductive novel ever published in the United States.

About a third of the way through the book, Ellery offers a devilishly ingenious solution to the murder, based on the amount of tea water in a percolator and the color of a dead man's tie. But this is just the first of four analyses Ellery propounds during the novel, with each solution radiating outward from its forerunners and accounting for more of the total picture. The fourth and final explanation embraces the entire network of plot and counterplot and reveals, with complete fairness to the reader, a "player on the other side" whose identity is a stunner of epic dimensions. *The Greek Coffin Mystery* is a top-of-the-line deductive puzzle, as fresh and intellectually stimulating today as it was more than half a century ago.

(*F.M.N.*)

*Queen, Ellery. *The New Adventures of Ellery Queen.* New York: Stokes, 1940. (CS/SS)

In addition to writing nine Ellery Queen novels and four Drury Lane books during their first period, Dannay and Lee also launched a series of Ellery Queen short stories, eleven of which were collected as *The Adventures of Ellery Queen* (1934). That volume includes Queen's earliest dying-message tales, "The Bearded Lady" and "The Glass Domed Clock," and closes with "The Mad Tea Party," which was clearly inspired by Lewis Carroll's

Alice in Wonderland books and which Fred Dannay always considered his favorite among the early Queen stories. Six years later came *The New Adventures of Ellery Queen,* bringing together the balance of the cousins' short stories from Period One plus the tales from their relatively weak and Hollywood-influenced second phase. Like their first collection, it was a mixed bag, but its best tales are among the finest Queen ever wrote.

The book opens with what is probably the finest detective novelette of all time, "The Lamp of God" (1935), in which Ellery visits a nightmarish Long Island mansion during the dead of winter to help find a fortune in gold for the long-lost daughter of a maniacal family. After a raw-nerved evening of encounters with enigmatic treasure hunters, Ellery and the rest of the search party go to bed, and wake up to an event that convinces them the world has gone mad. The entire huge mansion has disappeared during the night.

"The Lamp of God" is a superb piece of atmospheric writing, chilling the reader's bones both literally and existentially, summoning up the fear that the world has been abandoned to the demonic, then exorcising the chaos through the strict exercise of reason. With its symbolism of light against darkness and sun against cold integrated completely into the plot, the story is a near-perfect example of what detective fiction is all about.

The best of the Period One short stories in *New Adventures* is "The House of Darkness" (1935), in which Ellery solves a murder committed under pitch-black conditions in a surrealistic amusement park. The gimmick whereby the killer carried out his scheme in total darkness so appealed to Dannay and Lee that they recycled it several times in their scripts for the long-running (1939–48) "Ellery Queen" radio series. Even better as stories are two of the four sports tales that make up the final section of *New Adventures.* "Man Bites Dog" (1939) is set in the Polo Grounds during a World Series game, and Ellery and his father investigate the death of a baseball superstar of the past who dropped dead in his box after mistakenly picking up and eating a hot dog meant for his estranged wife. In "Mind Over Matter" (1939), Ellery attends a world-heavyweight-championship boxing match, later discovers the dethroned champ's corpse in a parking lot, but seems much more anxious to find his missing camel's hair coat than to catch the killer—because he knows that when he's gotten the one, he'll have the other. These are the best stories Dannay and Lee wrote during their second period.

(*F.M.N.*)

*Queen, Ellery. *Calamity Town.* Boston: Little, Brown, 1942. (CS)

Queen's second period ran from 1936 to 1940 and was marked by the strong influence of the slick magazine and Hollywood. But in 1942 Dannay and Lee began their third and richest period of creativity, which lasted until 1958 and embraced twelve Queen novels and two short-story collections. In their third period, the cousins fused complex deductive puzzles with in-depth characterization, finely detailed evocations of place and mood, occasional ventures into a topsy-turvy *Alice in Wonderland* otherworld (as in *There Was an Old Woman,* 1943), and explorations into history, psychiatry, and religion.

The first book of this period and one of the best is *Calamity Town,* which is subtitled "a novel" rather than "a problem in deduction" like the first-period Queen exploits. Ellery is no longer a Philo Vance clone detached from the terrible events around him but a human being involved in horrors and torn by them. On August 6, 1940, Ellery steps off a train at Wrightsville, a tight-knit "typical American community" that with the outbreak of World War II has become a boomtown. Needing a place to stay where he can write a novel, he rents a house from Wrightsville's first family, a house that is reputed to be a jinx, and becomes entangled in the emotional problems of the Wrights and their daughter's erratic new husband. Then comes murder: At the family's New Year's Eve party, one of the drinks with which the birth of 1941 is toasted has been laced with poison. The crime tears apart the family and the town; and subsequent events—the police investigation, a sensational trial, and more deaths—are treated not as pieces of a puzzle (though a neat plot is hidden among them) but as nightmares happening to real people, with Ellery powerless to help and contributing nothing until the last chapter.

Dannay and Lee took infinite pains in creating Wrightsville and dozens of its inhabitants, many of whom reappear in later novels such as *The Murderer Is a Fox* (1945), *Ten Days' Wonder* (1948), and *Double, Double* (1950), which are also set in this superficially idyllic community. Wrightsville is as real a place and as vivid a character as the literature of crime has produced, and *Calamity Town* as compelling a novel.

(*F.M.N.*)

*Queen, Ellery. *Cat of Many Tails.* Boston: Little, Brown, 1949. (CS)

Midway through Queen's third period came what many rank as the finest book Dannay and Lee ever wrote, *Cat of Many Tails,* which opens during a summer heat wave a few years after the end of World War II. The atmosphere quivers with threats of holocaust, with references to Hiroshima, the Nazi death camps, the cold war, the partition of Vienna, the first Arab-Israeli conflict, the anti-Communist witch-hunts, and the shadow of nuclear annihilation. But the international news that daily reminds New Yorkers of their mortality has been dwarfed by local headlines conveying the same message. A mass murderer is loose in the city. He has strangled six victims in less than three months, and in every possible respect—ethnically, economically, socially, geographically—each victim is unconnected to the others. The faceless Gramercy Park bachelor, the aging prostitute from Times Square, the struggling shoe salesman from Chelsea, the madcap heiress who loved the subways, the bitter paralytic of East 102nd Street, the black girl from Harlem, and all the later victims of "the Cat" share only the cords of Indian tussah silk that are found around their necks.

Shattered by the events in *Ten Days' Wonder* (1948), Ellery has dropped out, refusing to intervene in others' lives, but the bait of involvement, with all its pain and risk, is dangled before him again, and he snaps at it, joining in the city-wide hunt for the Cat, taking part in strategy conferences, writing press releases and radio speeches, coordinating with countless police agencies and psychiatrists, trying to keep the lid on the seething city, reviewing endless files, and plodding up countless blind alleys until, suddenly and beyond expectation, the obvious yet subtle link connecting the victims and their murderers leaps into sight. And the truth once again shatters Ellery as it did in *Ten Days' Wonder.*

Almost every character in the huge cast of *Cat of Many Tails*—even the many victims, who are never shown alive but only described by survivors—emerges as a vividly portrayed individual; and from the interweaving of the lives of almost a hundred people, Queen brings New York City itself to life as a breathing entity. In this book Dannay and Lee evoke all sorts of aspects of life in the city, from racial turmoil to oppressive heat, from the chaos of a full-scale riot to the simple pleasures of radio series like "The Shadow" and "Stella Dallas." Combining a stunning plot with dozens of fine character sketches and a variety of symbolic levels, *Cat of Many Tails* stands at the pinnacle of the Queen canon and offers permanent testimony to what can be done within the framework of a mystery.

(*F.M.N.*)

*Queen, Ellery. *Glass Village.* Boston: Little, Brown, 1954. (AD)

The witch-hunting reign of terror that Senator Joe McCarthy and the House Un-American Activities Committee and their ilk unleashed on their fellow citizens in the early 1950s ruined the lives of thousands without even the semblance of constitutional safeguards. The paranoia of those Red Menace years inspired *The Glass Village,* the first of the two Ellery Queen novels in which Ellery does not appear. (The other is the negligible *Cop Out,* 1969.)

The setting is the withered New England village of Shinn Corners, a paradigm of the country at large in that all but a few of its citizens are embittered puritanical bigots. The single part-time resident and thus the only one with ties to the more enlightened outside world is Judge Lewis Shinn. Visiting the judge for a week is his nephew Johnny Shinn, an ex-military man who witnessed Hiroshima, was sexually mutilated in Korea, and has lost all belief and hope and capacity to love. A main focus of this novel is on Johnny's slow journey back to the human race.

What precipitates his return is a brutal murder. Aunt Fanny Adams, the famous ninety-one-year-old primitive painter, is bludgeoned to death in the studio of her Shinn Corners home one rainy afternoon. A foreign-looking tramp had been seen in the village before the murder, and the outraged citizens of the town hunt this man down, beat him, almost lynch him, refuse to turn him over to the state police, and insist on trying him themselves. To avert a gun battle between his neighbors and the authorities, Judge Shinn agrees to hold a mock trial in Shinn Corners—a trial deliberately full of legal absurdities, designed to placate the mob now and be reversed by an appeals court later. Among the jurors is Johnny Shinn.

The trial is the centerpiece of the book, and a fine farrago of black humor it is. Before the first witness is called, ten jurors swear that they're already certain the tramp is guilty. The bailiff, the court reporter, most of the jurors, and the judge take turns testifying against the poor wretch. Judge Shinn takes over as prosecutor while the prosecutor testifies against the defendant. The tramp's lawyer is silent about gross violations of his client's rights but fights like a tiger over the admissibility of trivia. Judge Shinn solemnly bangs the darning egg he uses as a gavel and hands down legal rulings he knows to be dead wrong. So much for due process in the McCarthy era, or on the other side of Alice's rabbit hole. But *The Glass Village* is also a first-class detective novel, with bizarre clues and a quasi dying message and all sorts of inspired misdirection.

As usual in third-period Queen, the detective puzzle is fused with some unusually bleak moods. Near the end of the novel, when Johnny thinks about the vicious boobs who are his fellow jurors and fellow Americans and reflects that "man was a chaos without rhyme or reason; that he blundered about like a maddened animal in the delicate balance of the world, smashing and disrupting, eager only for his own destruction," it's clear that this *noir* view is shared by Queen.

Dannay and Lee retired as writers between 1958 and 1963, but then came a fourth and final period that ended with Lee's death in 1971. Most of the Period Four output relies on heavily stylized plots and characterizations and the recycling of countless motifs from the earlier periods.

(*F.M.N.*)

Quentin, Patrick. *A Puzzle for Fools.* New York: Simon & Schuster, 1936. (AD)

Patrick Quentin is a pseudonym of the collaborative team of Hugh Wheeler and Richard Wilson Webb—who also wrote as Quentin Patrick. From 1936 to 1952, the pair produced a series of successful novels featuring

Peter Duluth, a former Broadway producer and recovering alcoholic, and his wife, Iris. After 1952, Wheeler went on alone to write seven more novels under the Quentin name, four of them featuring a New York police detective, Lieutenant Timothy Trant (who also appears in novels by Wheeler and Webb under the Quentin Patrick—or, in the original editions, Q. Patrick—pseudonym). The novels are well written and well characterized, and frequently the plots are as baffling as the pseudonyms under which they were created. The endings of these novels, be they as by Patrick Quentin or vice versa, are sure to both surprise and satisfy the fan of traditional mysteries.

A Puzzle for Fools opens in the expensive sanatorium where Peter Duluth has gone to dry out. Bad enough to be in a mental hospital, doubting your own sanity and the sanity of those about you, but what if you also begin hearing a voice whispering to you at night? And what if that voice sounds remarkably like your own? And what if that voice warns you to get away, for there will be murder?

This is Duluth's plight. However, instead of doubting him, the director of the clinic believes every word and asks for his help in solving not only this particular puzzle but also several other strange goings-on around the clinic. Thus does Duluth become a sort of Sherlock Holmes at work in a mental institution.

Certainly Duluth, and the police, have their work cut out for them, because soon the whispering prophecy comes true and one of the staff members is murdered, only to be followed by the murder of one of the patients. This, of course, is a rich and fertile field for the whodunit, and Quentin handles it well; not only must all the patients be considered suspects, but all the staff members as well. And there are secrets to be discovered on both sides.

Other complex "puzzle" mysteries starring Peter Duluth include *Puzzle for Players* (1938), *Puzzle for Puppets* (1944), and *Puzzle for Fiends* (1946). Among the novels featuring Lieutenant Timothy Trant are *Death for Dear Clara* (1937) and *Death and the Maiden* (1939), both as by Q. Patrick; and *My Son, the Murderer* (1954) and *Family Skeletons* (1965). Wheeler and Webb also wrote a series of mysteries under the pseudonym Jonathan Stagge (q.v.).

(*N.D./M.M.*)

*Quentin, Patrick. *The Ordeal of Mrs. Snow and Other Stories.* New York: Random House, 1961. (SS)

Writing with his various partners and alone, Hugh Wheeler also produced a large number of first-rate short stories published under both the Patrick Quentin and Q. Patrick names. The best of them—the title novella and eleven shorter pieces—appear in this collection (the only one under either pseudonym). Testimony to the quality of these twelve stories is the Special Edgar the collection received in 1962.

In the short form, at least, Quentin is at his best writing about children, which is why several of the entries here feature child protagonists. "Little Boy Lost" gives us a glimpse inside an English girls' school, as seen through the eyes of the headmistress's son, Branny, a rather strange and secretive youth. "A Boy's Will" tells the tale of a young Italian lad who victimizes a generous American patron. Other children "who perpetrate hideous crimes without the slightest sense of guilt or remorse," as the dust jacket blurb states it, can be found in "Portrait of a Murderer" and "Witness for the Prosecution." And while the protagonist of "Mother, May I Go Out to Swim?" is thirty-six years old, he is really just a little boy at heart—a very deadly little boy. . . .

The stories that feature adults are no less convincing. "The Ordeal of Mrs. Snow" is pure, chilling suspense about a woman kept prisoner inside her own home. "This Will Kill You" relates the events leading to the unhappy end of a mild-mannered druggist named Harry Lund. "Thou Lord Seest Me" tells the sad story of an office drudge who is a failure at life and just as much of a failure when he decides to alter his humdrum existence by committing murder.

These are low-key stories, evocatively written, populated by believable human beings both good and bad (and some a combination of both). A nice sharp irony extrudes from most of them, some of it so sharp and subtle that it might take a while before you feel the sting. A satisfying, mordant, and sometimes quietly vicious gathering that should be included in the library of any fan of the criminous short story.

(*B.P.*)

Rabe, Peter. *Dig My Grave Deep.* Greenwich, Conn.: Fawcett Gold Medal, 1956. (O/T)

Contemporary reviewers compared Peter Rabe favorably with both Chandler and Hammett, and with some justification. Rabe's best work achieves a harsh objectivity that is typical of Hammett in such books as *The Glass Key.* Rabe's specialty was the hard-boiled gangster novel, though he also published a series of comic spy novels in the 1960s, a fine "mad avenger" book, and a truly offbeat novel about an American gangster in a foreign environment, as well as a series of novels about a "retired" gangster named Daniel Port, beginning with *Dig My Grave Deep.*

In theory, of course, no one retires from the rackets and lives to tell the tale, but Port is intelligent as well as tough; he has a plan that will allow him to leave alive. But first, out of loyalty to his old boss, Port decides to help fight off the challenge of the so-called Reform party, a group that is trying to achieve political as well as criminal power in Port's city. He does so with brains as well as violence, though there is certainly violence in this book.

Rabe's matter-of-fact, understated style is particularly well adapted to describing violent encounters, including violent sexual encounters, and he does a quietly effective job of doing so in *Dig My Grave Deep.* What is unexpected in the book is its humor, of both the tongue-in-cheek variety (Rabe's character names are always worth a second look) and off-the-wall variety (Port's bodyguard is involved in several hilarious incidents). The successful mixture of violence, humor, and effective storytelling makes one realize that Rabe's works are worthy of more attention than has been accorded them in recent years.

Other books in the Daniel Port series, all worth seeking out, are *The Out Is Death* (1957), *It's My Funeral* (1957), *The Cut of the Whip* (1958), *Bring Me Another Corpse* (1959), and *Time Enough to Die* (1959).

(*B.C.*)

Rabe, Peter. *Kill the Boss Good-By.* Greenwich, Conn.: Fawcett Gold Medal, 1956. (O/PS)

Kill the Boss Good-By is typical of Peter Rabe's best work. Fell, boss of the San Pietro rackets, has mysteriously dropped from sight. In his absence, his number two man, Pander, decides to take over and run the show. Naturally, Fell returns, but he returns from a place where racket bosses seldom go—a sanatorium where he has been under treatment for manic psychosis. The rest of the novel, although it contains the necessary paperback-original action and scenes of sharp, effective violence, is really a psychological study of Fell's gradual decline into genuine madness. As he begins to lose his tenuous hold on reality, becoming more and more confident of success as his mental powers decline, he destroys himself and most of those around him.

Like many of Rabe's novels, this one builds to an emotionally shattering climax. Rabe is one writer who always delivers where it matters most—on the last page.

Notable among Rabe's other nonseries softcover originals are *Benny Muscles In* (1955), *A Shroud for Jesso* (1955), *Journey into Terror* (1957), *Mission for Vengeance* (1958), *Girl in a Big Brass Bed* (1965), and *Black Mafia* (1974). Also excellent is his only hardcover, *Anatomy of a Killer* (1960), a tale of unflagging tension and psychological suspense about a "jinxed" hit man named Sam Jordan.

(*B.C.*)

Radley, Sheila. *A Talent for Destruction.* New York: Scribner's, 1982. (PP)

Sheila Radley's first novel, *Death in the Morning,* was published in 1978 (in the United States in 1979); since then she has attracted an enthusiastic following on both sides of the Atlantic. Her prose style is highly descriptive; the opening of this novel, for example, tells of the coming of the first snow to East Anglia and is sure to arouse strong feelings of nostalgia in any reader who was a child in a snowy clime. Series character Detective Chief Inspector Douglas Quantrill is a pleasant, low-key family man who is capable of being "envious as hell" of his younger, unmarried colleague, Inspector Martin Tait. And Radley's portrayal of the nuances of contemporary English village life is highly evocative.

This third novel in the series opens with the discovery of a skeleton in Parson's Close, a meadow adjoining the Saint Botolph's rectory in Breckham Market. Quantrill, who has been summoned to the manse to discuss his son's possible involvement in vandalism at the church hall, is on the scene immediately and soon ascertains that the skeleton, which has suffered the ravages of animals, has probably lain there no longer than this winter. A tentative identification is made through the efforts of Detective Constable Wigby (who does most of his investigating in pubs): The skeleton may be Athol Garrity, an Australian whom Rector Ainger allowed to pitch a tent in the Close the previous summer. Although the rector readily admits the former presence of Garrity, Quantrill is uneasy because Ainger did not mention the Australian when he first viewed the skeleton; and soon the inspector's inquiries center upon the rector; his wife, Gillian; and Gillian's senile father. A young Australian woman who lived with the Aingers for a while that summer, a church organist who killed himself, and a second murder all figure prominently in the complex case.

Radley handles her explanation of the crimes in an interesting way: As Quantrill is about to wrap up his case, she shifts into flashback, showing what actually happened in and around the rectory the previous summer. This long section dovetails nicely into the novel's climax and resolves the potential problem of long-winded explanatory chapters. Inspector Quantrill also appears in *The Chief Inspector's Statement* (1980).

(*M.M.*)

Randisi, Robert J. *Full Contact.* New York: St. Martin's, 1984. (PI)

Manhattan private investigator Miles Jacoby is somewhat of a novice at his profession; a former boxer, he retired and went to work for veteran private eye Eddie Waters. But through a streak of violent bad luck, "Jack" is now without a mentor, a kid brother, or an apartment. He is not without friends, however: Two of them, Billy and Karen Palmer, who are modeled on the real-life proprietors of Bogie's in Manhattan, allow him to live in the office/apartment behind their restaurant. And when his Chinese bookie friend, "Knock Wood" Lee, is arrested for the murder of a client who owed him a great deal of money, Jacoby goes to bat for him.

The case is intertwined with another that Jacoby has recently taken on—a missing-person investigation that centers around a karate school—and he juggles both, making mistakes that betray his tyro status, but correcting them in time to bring each to a surprising conclusion. Even though he bumbles a bit too much, Jacoby is a likable character who enjoys spending a great deal of his time in restaurants. (The book, in fact, provides a culinary tour of both fictional and nonfictional New York eating establishments, and one wonders why Jacoby doesn't weigh 500 pounds.)

Randisi (who is the founding father of Private Eye Writers of America) has written two previous paperback originals featuring this character: *Eye in the Ring* (1982) and *The Steinway Collection* (1983). A fourth novel, *The Disappearance of Penny* (1980), features Henry Po, investigator for the New York Racing Commission. Po doesn't hang out in restaurants, but he may hold the private eye (fictional or otherwise) world's record for time spent in bed with women met in the course of an investigation.

(*M.M.*)

Ransome, Stephen. *The Unspeakable.* New York: Doubleday Crime Club, 1960. (PS)

Frederick C. Davis (q.v.) published some of his best books under the name Stephen Ransome, a pseudonym he reserved for his nonseries suspense novels. (At least that was his methodology for most of his career. After 1955, when he abandoned his Cole and Speare series, he published only one pulp-novella reprint, *High-Heel Homicide* [1961], under his own name, and his last fourteen novels as by Ransome; four of those last fourteen, beginning with *One-Man Jury* in 1964, feature a Florida cop, Lee Barcello.) A strong case can be made for *The Unspeakable* as the most accomplished of all of Davis's novels. Its multiple levels of tension, its probing dissection of life in small-town America, and its quiet but uncompromising treatment of one of the most heinous of crimes make it a work of some distinction.

When five-year-old Chrissie Alonzo disappears from her home in the Pennsylvania village of Pennswick one hot August night, everyone is at a loss to explain what might have happened to her. There is hardly any crime in Pennswick, no reason to suspect anyone of deviant behavior. And yet, when a massive search of the area fails to turn up the little girl, the townspeople begin to fear the worst. One of the local cops, young Russ Burnett, focuses his suspicion on John Kirk, a professional news photographer and former Pennswick resident who has returned to his hometown for a period of rest following a nervous breakdown. Ostensibly Burnett does so because Kirk lied to him about his whereabouts on the night of Chrissie's disappearance; but the fact that Kirk and Burnett's wife, Laury, were once engaged to be married is a major issue in what soon develops into a case of persecution. Only Pennswick's police chief, Dan Gurland, a friend of Kirk's, prevents Burnett from arresting the photographer.

This is just one of the tensions Davis effectively builds here. Others involve Chrissie's drunken father and distraught mother, and their neighbors—weak-willed Garv Harker and his drudge of a wife; secretive Titus Michaels; and Mona Warren, the nicest girl in town. And yet another concerns Kirk and Laury, whose love for each other was accidentally but irrevocably rekindled the night Chrissie vanished. That is why Kirk has lied to Burnett; he *can't* tell him the truth, he thinks, when Burnett confronts him, for "the truth as an answer had been and would always be worse than impossible. *I was over in the park, in the dark, with Laury. I was making love to your wife.*"

Chief Gurland reflects at one point, "Before this case was finished it would leave its lasting mark in some degree, slight or bone-deep, on everyone it touched." He couldn't have been more right. *The Unspeakable* is quality suspense writing that pulls no punches, yet avoids sensationalism and delivers its considerable impact through character development and skillful storytelling.

Other notable Ransome novels include *Death Checks In* (1937), a Woolrichian tale of mounting suspense told in a total of ninety-one cinematic scene-shifts; *A Shroud for Shylock* (1939), one of the first mysteries to feature a female private detective; and *Some Must Watch* (1961), an edge-of-the-chair tale about a mysterious man in black stalking a woman who "had no enemies in the world."

(*B.P.*)

Rathbone, Julian. *Watching the Detectives.* New York: Pantheon, 1983. (PP)

It is easy to like this story's protagonist, Police Commissioner Jan Argand of the fictional country of Bralot, because he is human (he is middle-aged, rather homely, and his wife is in a mental institution), and because he is honest (his honesty is sometimes embarrassing to the police department).

This is not the first of Julian Rathbone's well-written Jan Argand novels (nor is Argand his only recurring protagonist), but in this story Commissioner Argand has a new job. He has just been appointed head of the Bureau of Advice and Investigation—a newly formed bureau set up to investigate complaints against the police.

Two of the first complaints to come his way involve overzealousness on the part of the police, both resulting in beatings. A group of marijuana-smoking nudists and a couple of male homosexuals were the targets. There is also a report or two concerning racism on the part of the police. But—and this is what disturbs Commissioner Argand—of the first forty-eight complaints referred to his department, nineteen are subsequently dropped or withdrawn.

Then mob action begins, such as an antinuclear demonstration that is met with brutal reprisal. During one such demonstration, an officer from Argand's new department is killed.

And at the center of it all, trying to sort things out and bring some measure of order, is Commissioner Argand, who at one point is threatened by an attempt on his own life.

Jan Argand also appears in *Base Case* (1981). A second likable series character, Turkish policeman Nur Bey, appears in such novels as *Diamonds Bid* (1967), *Hand Out* (1968), and *Trip Trap* (1972).

(*N.D.*)

*Rawson, Clayton. *Death from a Top Hat.* New York: Putnam's, 1938. (CS)

Magician detectives were popular in the pulps and on radio, even more so in the comics. Few made it into hardcover, however, and only one became a true classic detective character—Clayton Rawson's Great Merlini. The crimes are outré and fantastic, locked-room puzzles and "impossible crimes," appropriate to the theatrical atmosphere that Merlini brings to the proceedings. Yet at the same time they are down-to-earth and even slightly plausible (well, as plausible as anything of this sort is ever likely to get).

The major supporting characters, journalist-narrator Ross Harte and harried police inspector Homer Gavigan, are more deftly drawn than the cardboard caricatures typical of pure puzzle stories. Merlini himself comes across as a genuinely believable character, a fairly ordinary guy when he's not—literally—pulling rabbits out of hats. This sets Merlini apart from the pulpish aura that surrounded other magician detectives, including Rawson's own Don Diavolo (who appeared in pulp stories under his Stuart Towne [q.v.] pseudonym).

Death from a Top Hat marked Merlini's debut. A reclusive occultist is found murdered in a sealed room, his body stretched out on a pentagram drawn on the floor, all the trappings requisite for summoning demons scattered about. The suspects are his thaumaturgical associates: a master escape artist; a sleight-of-hand specialist (who slips a police tail by vanishing from a constantly watched taxi); a ventriloquist; a psychic researcher; a spirit medium (who conveniently goes into trances when the police questioning becomes too intense); and a husband and wife mind-reading team. Merlini is brought into the case as a consultant to the police, who have, as you might expect, more than a little difficulty coping with conjurers and demonologists.

Just as Merlini has the mechanics of the locked-room killing figured out, a second murder takes place, this time with the killer apparently levitating himself out of a second-story window, leaving no footprints in the surrounding snow. Ultimately, Merlini unmasks the killer at a magicians' society performance, while one of the suspects is catching a bullet between his teeth.

This is an impossible-crime classic, preposterous fun in the grand manner. Rawson did overuse one rather transparent device: Nearly every time Merlini is about to explain something, or a suspect is about to blurt out an important clue, the phone rings, or someone bursts into the room. This uncharacteristically clumsy bit of business is readily forgiven. Rawson was himself an accomplished conjurer, and much fascinating magician's lore is worked into the narrative. There are also some amusing cross-references to detective fiction; John Dickson Carr's (q.v.) famous "Locked Room Lecture" from *The Three Coffins* gets another workout. And speaking of Carr—those readers (this reviewer among them) who find Fell and Merrivale awfully hard to put up with in order to get through the puzzle will have no such difficulty with the Great Merlini.

(*A.S.*)

*Rawson, Clayton. *The Great Merlini.* Boston: Gregg Press, 1979. (CS/SS)

This long-overdue book collects all twelve Great Merlini short stories. They originally appeared in *Ellery Queen's Mystery Magazine,* where Rawson was managing editor for many years. Nine are lightweight, one-gimmick short-shorts, most of which were *EQMM* contest stories (the magazine's readers were invited to supply the omitted solution). Three, however, are of considerable length, and can be thought of as Merlini novels in miniature; as such, they maintain Rawson's high standard of invention, novelty, and puzzlement.

"From Another World" concerns the stabbing of a psychic researcher in an absolutely sealed room. The chief suspect is an apport medium who claims to be capable of transporting distant objects by mental power. Merlini has to explain how the murder weapon got into the room, if not by psychokinesis.

In "Off the Face of the Earth," a crooked judge one-ups Judge Crater by vanishing from a Grand Central telephone booth being closely watched by the cops. One of the suspects in this one is a mind reader named Zyyzk who says he's from Anatares.

In "Nothing Is Impossible," a UFO specialist is shot in another locked room. There's a live suspect in the room (mysteriously stripped of all his clothes), but there's no gun to be found, and the only apparent clue is a strange footprint, perhaps left by a small saucer pilot!

The other Great Merlini novels, all wonderful, are *The Footprints on the Ceiling* (1939); *The Headless Lady* (1940), which has a circus background; and *No Coffin for the Corpse* (1942).

(*A.S.*)

Reese, John. *The Looters.* New York: Random House, 1968. (Also published as *Charley Varrick.*) (T)

When sixty-two-year-old ex-con Charley Varrick embarks on the robbery of a bank in the small central California town of Tres Cruces, he figures that it will go off without a hitch, and that he and his three partners will gross maybe $30,000. He is wrong on both counts. A rookie cop named Stainless Steele spots the getaway car idling in front of the bank and calls in about it; and then the old guard inside decides to get heroic and shoots one of Charley's accomplices before Charley blows *him* away. The shoot-out continues outside, with Charley's girlfriend and getaway driver, Nadine, getting hit in the knee, Stainless Steele being wounded, and another cop dying with a bullet in his throat. Charley and the other accomplice escape with the money. It is only later, after they dispose of both the car and the wounded Nadine, that they stop to count the take—and find the staggering sum of $357,000.

How did a little country bank come to have that much money in its vault? The FBI, in the person of Agent Murray, and the local chief of police, Bob Horton, both wonder the same thing. And what they find out is that the Tres Cruces National Bank is controlled by a San Francisco–based management corporation that is in turn controlled by the Mafia: The bank is a clearinghouse for Mafia money being channeled into legitimate businesses so it can come out of hiding with a minimum of taxation. But can anything be proved against either the bank's president, Harold Young, or the head of the management firm, J. J. Schirmer? Can the FBI bust the entire network wide open?

The dust-jacket blurb calls this "a realistic, compelling story of a bank robbery and its aftermath," but that doesn't quite do it justice. It is also a fascinating account of illegal and quasi-legal banking practices and of some of the ways in which the Mafia launders its money. And above all it is a story of people, some good, some bad, all realistically drawn: Stainless Steele, a mama's boy and something of a coward who finally grows up; Murray and Schirmer, who hate each other because they are Jews on opposite sides of the law; Horton, who has an unusual sexual hang-up; Molly Edwards, a sadistic Mafia "button man" (hit man) who winds up with the

$357,000; and poor Charley Varrick, the one who started it all but isn't around to see the finish. (Charley has a relatively small role in the novel, but was made the central figure in *Charley Varrick,* the 1973 film version starring Walter Matthau and Joe Don Baker.)

John Reese's other crime novels are equally good: *Pity Us All* (1969), the grim and provocative story of the murder of an infant; and *Omar, Fats and Trixie* (1976), an offbeat comic mystery set on a dude ranch outside Las Vegas. A much-underrated and versatile writer, Reese produced hundreds of pulp western stories, dozens of slick-magazine stories and articles, several acclaimed juvenile novels, and some thirty of the finest western novels published during the past two decades. A third of those thirty westerns comprise a series featuring a roving 1880s private detective named Jefferson Hewitt and are crime novels as well. Among the best are *Texas Gold* (1975), which deals with counterfeiting in Texas; *Sequoia Shootout* (1977), about murder and the white slave trade in the High Sierra; and *Dead Eye* (1978), about a huge land swindle in Canada. These and the other Hewitts are reminiscent of such fine old TV series as "Maverick" and are highly recommended.

(*B.P.*)

*Reeve, Arthur B. *The Silent Bullet.* New York: Dodd, Mead, 1912. (CS/SS)

So popular in his time that his detective, Craig Kennedy, was known as "the American Sherlock Holmes," Arthur B. Reeve was clearly the best known American detective-story writer during the decade 1910–20. Kennedy bears many resemblances to Holmes, including his use of science in detection and his "Watson," the often confused Walter Jameson, with whom he shares an apartment near Columbia University, where Kennedy teaches chemistry but also acts as consulting detective. Their cases often start in a way remarkably similar to Doyle's—with a client arriving at their apartment, or with New York police inspector Barney O'Connor (the Inspector Lestrade of the series) coming to pose a problem.

Kennedy has raised Holmes's knowledge of science to the nth degree, updating the Sherlockian monographs (Kennedy has a complete file of automobile tire tracks) and making use of every possible invention of the time—and some not yet in use. In *The Silent Bullet,* a collection of twelve short stories originally published in *Cosmopolitan* (a far different magazine then than it is today), Reeve makes use of such devices as the electromechanograph, the dynamometer, the telantograph, and the gyroscope. In "The Silent Cracksman," Reeve applies Freudian psychology, including a word-association test. "The Seismograph Adventure" involves poison and spiritualism and sees Kennedy using his new improved seismograph, one patterned after "a very recent model by Prince Galitzin of the Imperial

Academy of St. Petersburg." With it Kennedy can not only tell the size and direction of earthquakes, he can also record rappings at a séance.

In "The Black Hand," Kennedy battles the Mafia and displays a Holmes-like love of music while helping an opera singer recover his kidnapped child. Holmes's cocaine habit was famous, and in "The Artificial Paradise" Craig Kennedy surprisingly takes mescal, though not for recreational use but rather to help him solve a case. "The Terror in the Air" is probably the best tale in the collection, with Kennedy trying to prove that a series of airplane accidents involving the application of the new Norton gyroscope are not the fault of the inventor. The dialogue at the end when Kennedy catches the villain is wonderfully evocative of its time: ". . . one motion of your hand and you are a dead man. Stand still—where you are. You are caught red-handed."

The Craig Kennedy stories and their creator now reside in the limbo of detective fiction, resurrected for nostalgia, if at all, rather than for their quality. Yet while it is true that they are fixed in an earlier, simpler time, many of them are still quite readable. Reeve told a story well and was quite adept at holding a reader's attention. These are strong traits in any era.

(*M.L.*)

Reeves, Robert. *Cellini Smith: Detective.* Boston: Houghton Mifflin, 1943. (PI)

In just three novels and nine *Black Mask* novelettes, Robert Reeves produced some of the most entertaining and offbeat hard-boiled crime fiction of the late Thirties and early Forties. (The bulk of these were written while *he* was in his twenties; his promising career was cut tragically short by a military jeep accident during World War II.) All three novels and seven of the nine novelettes feature Cellini Smith, a detective who begins his career in the employ of New York gangsters—*Dead and Done For* (1939)—and who then moves to Los Angeles to free-lance. It has accurately been said about Cellini that he is something of a screwball and vaguely incompetent; he has a great fondness for liquor, for instance, and a penchant for getting himself "under the weather" at odd moments during his investigations. Most of Reeves's other characters are of the screwball variety as well. Likewise his plots. There is a good deal of wry, wacky humor sprinkled throughout his rough-and-tumble narratives, and even the wisecracks are on the eccentric side.

Cellini Smith: Detective, the last of the three novels, begins when a young hobo named Danny Meade is found shot to death—with a slingshot and a couple of round, sharpened metal slugs—in a hobo jungle just outside L.A. called the Luxembourg Gardens. The denizens of the Gardens, having no faith in Detective Sergeant Ira Haenigson and the other local cops, pool their meager resources and set out to hire a detective; they settle on Cellini because he is the only one hungry enough and nutty enough to take on a murder case for the munificent retainer of $26.94. And what a case it is! Danny, Cellini learns, wasn't really a tramp; the odds are that his murder has something to do with the eighteen hidden pockets sewn inside his clothing, and the expensive gold talisman he hocked shortly before his death, and the amazing fact that he had been trying to panhandle $20,000.

Among the suspects are Monk, a Bible-spouting ex–tent preacher who hates sin, except when he's the one doing the sinning; Mr. Rapoport, owner of the Paree Burlesque House; Danny's girlfriend, Chloe, that "past mistress of the G-string"; Alex Bornaman, "munitions salesman for the mobsters," who regards violence with distaste; and a pair of ex-vaudevillians turned thugs, Dado and Vanzy, who still like to do comedy routines while busting people's heads. (Dado, patting his shoulder holster: "This is my religion." Vanzy: "In rod we trust.") Add grave robbing, a disappearing corpse, and a tungsten mine, and you have a detective novel with just about everything.

The first Cellini Smith novel, *Dead and Done For,* is more violent and less amusing than its successors; Cellini is much more suited to the rarefied (and loonified) atmosphere of southern California. The second novel, *No Love Lost* (1941; serialized in *Black Mask* as "Dog Eat Dog," September/October/November 1940), involves Cellini with the habitués of the Hangover bar, a wrestler named the Terrible Turk, and a drunken ex-pug named Duck-Eye Ryan who reappears as Cellini's sidekick in some of the *Black Mask* stories.

(*B.P.*)

Reilly, Helen. *Compartment K.* New York: Random House, 1955. (PP/R)

During the Thirties, Forties, and Fifties, Helen Reilly was one of the more popular writers of police mysteries set for the most part in New York City and environs. Unlike many women crime novelists of that period, she wrote straightforward stories about the Manhattan Homicide Squad that were firmly rooted in correct police procedure. One of her early books, *The File on Rufus Ray* (1937), has in fact been called the "ultimate in police procedurals"; after the fashion of the "Crime Dossiers" of Dennis Wheatley (q.v.), published around the same time in England, *Rufus Ray* contained facsimiles of the evidence gathered by the police and even included glossy suspect photos and cigarette ashes in a tiny glassine envelope.

In all, Reilly published thirty-five novels under her own name and three under the pseudonym Kieran Abbey. Thirty-one of that total, beginning with *The Diamond Feather* (1930) and culminating with *The Day She Died* (1962), feature dour, dedicated Inspector Christopher McKee, head of the

Manhattan Homicide Squad, who has a "fatal gift of being too often in the right." The McKee novels of the Thirties and early Forties are constructed as fair-play whodunits, with clues well placed throughout. From the late Forties onward, suspense rather than detection became the keynote of Reilly's work, and a variety of heroines were used as main-viewpoint characters.

One such heroine is *Compartment K*'s Rose O'Hara. Most of the events of the novel are seen through her eyes; McKee does his detecting at a distance here—the story is set in Canada—and Reilly allows the inspector's subordinate, Detective Todhunter, who is on the scene, to play a more important role than usual.

As the book opens, Rose is on her way via the Canadian Pacific *Commonwealth* (a crack express train) from Montreal to Vancouver and thence to the Canadian Rockies for a visit with her widowed cousin, Elizabeth Questing, who has a lodge at Amethyst Lake. Also on the train are Nils Gantry, a writer and Rose's fiancé; Daniel Font, the man who jilted Rose less than a year ago for another woman; Font's wife, Candy; Candy's mother, Loretta Pilgrim, whose brother was Elizabeth Questing's husband; Harry Belding, Elizabeth's "man of business," and his wife, Gertrude; Colonel Robert Hugh Eden, who appears to be a friend of Elizabeth; and Gil Davidson, an Englishman who tells Rose he is going to the lodge as an uninvited guest.

It soon becomes obvious to Rose that they are *all* going to the lodge—much to her dismay and confusion. As far as she knows, there is little love lost between Elizabeth and her late husband's family. While she is puzzling about this, fiancé Nils also has a surprise encounter: Todhunter, whom he knows from New York, tells him a story in confidence. It seems Todhunter is on the train because he suspects one of the party may be the murderer of an unidentified woman who was killed in the courtyard of Elizabeth's Manhattan house three nights earlier. Todhunter asks Nils to keep quiet about this: "I'm in textiles, gray goods, we just met, and you don't know me from Adam."

Before the train arrives at its destination, however, a second murder occurs. And when the party finally arrives at the lodge, events unfold—occasionally aided by Inspector McKee's long-distance information from New York—that prove the solution to murder lies in crimes of the past.

This is a tightly plotted novel, with more than a touch of romance. The scenes on the train and of the Canadian Rockies are particularly memorable.

(*M.M./B.P.*)

Reilly, Helen. *Murder in Shinbone Alley*. New York: Doubleday Crime Club, 1940. (PP)

Shinbone Alley is a stone's throw from Manhattan's Greenwich Village. At night the streets of this largely industrial area are dark and deserted, and Patrolman Grim has little to keep himself occupied. But on this night, as he is passing the mouth of the alley, a sound comes from above and a white shape hurtles downward. When Grim reaches the point where the body has hit the ground, he sees it is a young woman dressed in a bridal gown.

Inspector Christopher McKee arrives at the scene. The woman has been identified as Barbara Baron, one of the previous year's most popular debutantes. It appears she has fallen fourteen stories from the smoking balcony of the International School of Design, where she was modeling the wedding gown she had created in a fashion show. McKee goes to the school, informs the people gathered there of the young woman's death, then inspects the premises. Barbara's fur coat is spread on the balcony wall; there are indications she had sat down to smoke a cigarette; and to McKee's practiced eye, it is obvious she was pushed.

The first third of the story is concerned with McKee's routine at the school. It turns out that Barbara Baron was heartily disliked by almost everyone there: The young woman was snobbish, rude, untruthful, and "had never been taught the difference between *meum* and *tuum*" when it came to other women's men. Various possible motives for her murder emerge: Was it the obvious one—money? The school is staffed by various relatives of the future heiress, some of whom would be sure to gain by her death. Or did one of the painting instructors, Philip Mountain, push her off the balcony because she resisted his amorous advances and threatened to have him fired? Or did someone take exception because she intended to marry the school's director, Jorden Fairchild, the next day? McKee sorts through the evidence, aided by the dogged Detective Todhunter. A second murder occurs, another is attempted, and eventually meticulous procedure and McKee's gift for detection bring the case to its unexpected conclusion.

This is a compelling novel from start to finish. To her considerable grasp of police procedure, Reilly adds believable characters and a depth of emotion that makes this a cut above the typical procedural. Her policemen think and feel, and are capable of empathizing with both the victim and the suspects.

Reilly—the mother of suspense writers Ursula Curtiss and Mary McMullen (qq.v.)—wrote thirty-one novels featuring McKee and his cohorts. Of these, the earlier ones tend to have more depth and complexity; among them are *The Diamond Feather* (1930), *McKee of Centre Street*

(1934), *Dead for a Ducat* (1939), *Mourned on Sunday* (1941), and *Three Women in Black* (1941).

(*M.M.*)

Rendell, Ruth. *The Fever Tree.* New York: Pantheon, 1982. (SS)

One of the most impressive qualities of Ruth Rendell's work is her grasp of the dark side of the human character and her ability to portray it in a dramatic and convincing fashion. Whether she is writing a short story, one of her compelling novels of psychological suspense, or an entry in her popular series featuring Chief Inspector Wexford of the British village of Kingsmarkham, she depicts fully fleshed-out characters in all their complexity. The plots work, not so much because of neatly placed clues or clever twists (although these are present, too), but because the underlying motivations are logical and true to the participants' inner natures.

The Fever Tree is Rendell's third short-story collection. (The others are *The Fallen Curtain and Other Stories,* 1976; and *Means of Evil and Other Stories,* 1979.) The stories are varied, but all carry the Rendell trademark of evil lying just below the surface of ordinary, even mundane, events. In the title story, a man and his wife are on vacation in an African game preserve, a vacation that is also a reconciliation. The man has been unfaithful and only recently returned to his wife. And as the wife, a childlike woman who insists on breaking the preserve rules, gets out of the car time and time again to look at the animals, terrible thoughts begin to form in both of their minds—thoughts that do not lead to a predictable conclusion.

Likewise, "Thornapple" is a plant, but nothing so exotic as Africa's fever tree—merely the jimsonweed that appears in many English gardens. James, a young boy, is a bit of an amateur botanist, and poisonous plants particularly interest him. "Not that James had the least intention of putting these poisons of his to use." But then the accepted order in James's family is disrupted, causing a great many things to get out of hand.

Things get out of hand quite frequently in the life of the protagonist of "A Needle for the Devil." As a child, Alice Gibson's personal devil often "led her to violence." She learned to control her impulses by practicing handicrafts, but when she goes into nurse's training, circumstances force her to abandon most of them, and knitting becomes her salvation. Knitting, with all those lovely sharp needles . . .

This is a well-balanced collection, and the stories included are among Rendell's best short fiction. (One of her short stories, "The Fallen Curtain," won the Mystery Writers of America Edgar in 1974.)

(*M.M.*)

*Rendell, Ruth. *Master of the Moor.* New York: Pantheon, 1982. (PS)

The English moors, with their stark, eerie loneliness, have long fascinated writers of suspense fiction. In this excellent novel of psychological suspense, Rendell utilizes this setting as the scene for a series of murders of women, and the combination of the oppressive atmosphere and the killings takes a horrible emotional toll on those living nearby.

Until he finds the first body, Stephen Walby thinks he knows Vangmoor—considers himself, in fact, "master of the moor." Daily he traverses its crinkle-crankle paths, up the foins (hills) and past the abandoned soughs (mine shafts). But on the day he finds the strangled girl's body, his life changes. The moor, once a popular place, becomes deserted—"known not as somewhere unique and beautiful but as the place where a young girl had been killed." Not altogether displeased by this, Stephen begins to visit the moor more frequently. The murders continue, and Stephen often returns from his walks in a feverish state. Occasionally he is as low as his chronically depressed father; and his already stressed marriage begins to fall apart. On top of this, other events begin to make Stephen wonder about his parentage; at times he isn't sure who he is—or *what.*

This is one of Rendell's best novels, and even if the reader begins to suspect what is going on, he can never be sure, up to the last terrifying revelation.

Other equally gripping tales are *One Across, Two Down* (1971), *The Face of Trespass* (1974), and *A Demon in My View* (1976).

(*M.M.*)

*Rendell, Ruth. *Speaker of Mandarin.* New York: Pantheon, 1983. (PP)

This is the twelfth novel featuring Detective Chief Inspector Reginald Wexford and his subordinate, Mike Burden, of the English village of Kingsmarkham. By now they have developed into a competent, professional, and thoughtful pair who work comfortably together. It is their very decency and stability that give them the ability to spot the aberrations of the guilty. People trust the middle-aged, overweight Wexford, but frequently they underrate him. Wexford notes and makes use of this. The reader, too, can trust Wexford, accept his judgments, and enjoy the sense of immediacy that creates.

In *Speaker of Mandarin,* we see Wexford away from the village that provides a closed environment for many of the books in this series. He is in China, where he has completed a police-related mission and joined a British tour group. In the few days he spends with them, he is haunted by an aged

Chinese woman hobbling on her tiny bound feet, seemingly desperate to speak with him. She appears and disappears and turns up at the next stop, the next city, only to vanish again. Is she real, or is Wexford hallucinating? The inspector wonders and worries. The tour group takes a trip down the Li River, and a man—" 'Not one of us. A Chinese' "—drowns and is forgotten. But months later, back in Kingsmarkham, one of the group is shot in the head, and the plot turns and turns again as Rendell teases the reader into thinking he has the solution—only to surprise him anew.

Other enjoyable titles in this popular series are *From Doon with Death* (1965), *Wolf to the Slaughter* (1968), *A Guilty Thing Surprised* (1970), *Shake Hands Forever* (1975), and *An Unkindness of Ravens* (1985).

(*S.D.*)

Resnicow, Herbert. *The Gold Deadline.* New York: St. Martin's, 1984. (AD)

Norma and Alexander Gold could easily become two of your favorite people. They are certainly among the most charming of detecting couples in recent American mystery literature. Resnicow's first novel about them, *The Gold Solution* (1983), gained him instant fans, and this second makes us hope for more.

Alex Gold is a retired engineer with a Nero Wolfe–like mind, the sort of genius who gathers all the facts in a murder case; lapses into deep meditation; and when he returns to consciousness, explains it cogently to the rest of us. Unlike Wolfe, however, Alex has a wife, and she's as valuable to him as Archie Goodwin was to his boss. Alex is recovering from a heart attack that has forced him to retire from his engineering profession and most other strenuous activities; his mind is not idle, however, and he puts it to good use as a consultant. As with Nero, when he runs out of money he takes on a tough task; and as with Archie, Norma does the dirty work.

Resnicow's cast of supporting characters is splendidly drawn. Norma is a rare portrait—a six-foot woman living in a society that has never quite accepted the woman being a head taller than the man. But Norma thinks of her man as a giant, and it's been years since she considered the height difference. (A wonderful thread in this story is her determination to change the self-image of a younger woman of her size whose tall, gorgeous body is concealed by rounded shoulders and baggy clothes.) The Golds' neighbors and good friends Pearl and Burton Hanslik are finely drawn—he is a prominent New York lawyer, and she is Norma's best friend and part of the team when Alex is working on what would seem to most mortals to be an insoluble case.

The Gold Deadline takes us into the world of ballet, revealing its seamier side and—with the murder of one of its most tyrannical and hated directors—its most sinister aspects. The action begins at a gala farewell performance to the Boguslov Ballet Russe, which the Golds and Hansliks attend as guests of billionaire Max Baron—a performance that ends with the killing. The Golds apply their talents to the question of which of director Viktor Boguslov's many enemies killed him in a theater full of ballet lovers, and a strong portrait of the world of dance emerges. A marvelous romp with some of the smartest, nicest people in New York.

The Golds return in another adventure, *The Gold Frame* (1984). Resnicow is also the author of two paperback crossword-puzzle mysteries, *Murder Across and Down* and *The Seventh Crossword,* both published in 1985.

(*K.K.H.*)

Reynolds, William J. *The Nebraska Quotient.* New York: St. Martin's, 1984. (PI)

The adage that there is nothing new under the sun would certainly apply to the classic private-eye novel (as well as the classic cozy mystery). Luckily, readers don't turn to new PI novelists looking for revolutionary, totally inventive prose. What they want is an agreeable affirmation of their favorite formula. This is precisely what *The Nebraska Quotient,* a first novel, represents.

Reynolds's hero sports the same name as the state used as the locale. Nebraska—a private eye turned free-lance writer—wants nothing more than a cool breeze and a chance to finish his novel when the hot night and his screen door are shattered by the body of a man collapsing into his apartment. The man is his crooked ex-partner, a PI named Morris Copel. Copel is battered, shot, and soaking wet, but he manages to pull an envelope of porn pictures from his crotch before dying.

When Nebraska recognizes the woman in the photos as the daughter of a respected politician, he is drawn back into a private investigation of corruption and sexual betrayal. Right down to the heartland Mafia and the seductive woman, this story is in the classic (some might say cliché) hard-boiled vein.

There may be little new here, but Reynolds handles it all with a good bit of style. Nebraska's sardonic voice keeps us entertained and leaves us hopeful of even more impressive adventures to come.

(*K.L.M.*)

Rhode, John. *The Claverton Affair.* New York: Dodd, Mead, 1933. (CS)

As a mystery novelist, John Rhode (Cecil Street) was neither an entertainer nor a great prose stylist; but at his best he created dexterous plots and was extremely adept at juggling clues before an unwary reader. His approach to his work was sober and his stress always on detection. His series character, Dr. Lancelot Priestley, is of considerable importance in the genre—an erudite, rather humorless detective who uses his extensive scientific knowledge and a ratiocinative mind to solve his cases. Assisting him in such matters as the gathering of physical evidence are various subordinates, the most notable of whom is Scotland Yard inspector (later superintendent) Jimmy Waghorn, who made his debut in *Hendon's First Case* (1935) and was a constant sleuthing companion of Dr. Priestley's thereafter.

The Claverton Affair is something of a departure for Dr. Priestley in that here he does more legwork than Archie Goodwin at his most peripatetic. The story is told entirely from the good doctor's point of view, and the appearances of recurring characters Superintendent Hanslet and Harold Merefield are kept to an absolute minimum. The novel is also notable because Dr. Priestley's biographical details are at variance with those presented in previous and subsequent adventures. If this material is to be taken seriously, there is grave doubt that the detective is entitled to be addressed as "Professor."

Claverton begins when Dr. Priestley is summoned to visit his old friend Sir John Claverton, who is ill. The detective finds himself distinctly uncomfortable in the presence of various relatives at his friend's house, and the interview is unsatisfactory. He promises to return in a few days, and as he leaves he learns from another old friend, Dr. Oldland, the sick man's physician, that Sir John had been poisoned by arsenic during the course of his illness.

When Priestley returns, he discovers that Sir John has unexpectedly died in his absence. He leaps to the conclusion that his friend was the victim of poison and alerts the authorities, but a thorough postmortem fails to detect foul play. Tests for poison—carefully checked by Dr. Priestley—fail to reveal traces of arsenic or any other known poison. Yet the remorseless logician, with all the evidence against him, still harbors the deepest suspicions.

This is not the best Priestley, but it certainly is one of the better novels; written less than a decade after Rhode created his most famous sleuth, it still retains a freshness and vigor that will not be found in the (much) later work, which became strictly formularized and exceedingly dull. The people are well defined and not the expected "cardboard"; Dr. Priestley is a more human and fully rounded (but no less irritable) sleuth than usual. (At one point he actually utters a slight chuckle!) The plot and puzzle—usually Rhode's strong points—are good, and even with a too-casually dropped vital clue, most readers will be unable to spot the exact method of murder.

(*C.S./B.P.*)

*Rhode, John. *Death in Harley Street.* New York: Dodd, Mead, 1946. (CS)

After dinner one Saturday night at Dr. Priestley's Westbourne Terrace home, a guest who knows of his host's insatiable desire to solve crime puzzles offers to tell him about a puzzling death. It seems that the prominent gland specialist Dr. Richard Mawsley has suddenly died from an injection of strychnine. Careful investigation indicates it was not murder, and suicide is unlikely because the dead man had so much to live for. An inquest decides that it is accidental death, but it seems inconceivable that Dr. Mawsley could have made such a stupid blunder.

This problem strongly arouses Dr. Priestley's interest, and he "suggests" to his friend Jimmy Waghorn that further investigation might be in order. Much later, when many of the facts are in, Dr. Priestley states that Mawsley's death was neither accident, murder, nor suicide—even though appearances suggest that he died by his own hand—but that a *fourth* alternative is possible. Dr. Priestley is soon able to gather enough evidence to prove his point.

Death in Harley Street is one of John Rhode's best novels, and certainly a high point of his work during the Forties. It is distinguished by its steadily engrossing narrative and its subtly conceived and baffling puzzle. Armchair detectives will find it a battle of wits they will be hard-pressed to win.

Rhode wrote a phenomenal total of seventy Dr. Priestley novels, beginning with *The Paddington Mystery* in 1925 and ending with *The Vanishing Diary* in 1961. Other notable titles among them include *The Murders in Praed Street* (1928), *Dr. Priestley Lays a Trap* (1933), *Murder at the Motor Show* (1936), *Invisible Weapons* (1938; a clever locked-room mystery), *Death on the Boat Train* (1940), and *Shadow of an Alibi* (1949). A wartime adventure sans Priestley, *Dead of the Night* (1942), is interesting for its portrait of England under siege (as is the 1941 Priestley investigation *Signal for Death*). Cecil Street also published numerous novels of detection under a second well-known pseudonym, Miles Burton (q.v.).

(*C.S./B.P.*)

*Rhode, John, and Carter Dickson. *Fatal Descent.* New York: Dodd, Mead, 1939. (W)

Although John Rhode's name appears first on the by-line of this Golden Age collaboration, there is considerable internal evidence (e.g., prose style, characterization, a good deal of humor) to suggest that Carter Dickson (John Dickson Carr, q.v.) did most if not all of the writing. Rhode's principal contribution was probably some of the mechanics of the plot, perhaps the central "impossible" gambit upon which the story turns—and a dandy one it is, too, no matter which author was responsible for it.

The bulk of the novel takes place at the Temple—the six-story building in St. Martin's Lane, London, that houses Tallant Publications Ltd., an influential and "morally uplifting" publishing firm founded by Sir Ernest Tallant. Things have not been so moral at Tallant Publications in recent days, however. There have been a series of seemingly petty thefts around the offices, of such items as a little traveling clock, a toy airplane, a valuable bound volume of Addison's *Spectator* papers, and a .45-caliber Webley revolver. But the situation doesn't remain petty for long. In the presence of witnesses, one of whom is police surgeon Horatio Glass, Sir Ernest is shot to death inside his private elevator as it descends from his fifth-floor sanctum. The fatal bullet was fired from above the car, smashing its glass skylight in its top, yet it is shown to be impossible that (a) any of the elevator doors on any of the floors could have been opened while the car was in motion; (b) that anyone could have stood on top of the car and fired the shot; and (c) that anyone could have rigged an "infernal device" inside the shaft that utilized either a timing or remote-control mechanism to fire the weapon.

The task of getting to the bottom of the mystery falls to the imaginative Dr. Glass (who once supplied the police with sixteen separate explanations of a murder case—none of which were right); and to Chief Inspector Hornbeam, an unimaginative and methodical policeman who believes in facts, not theories, and whom Glass constantly exasperates. Among their suspects are Patricia Tallant, Sir Ernest's headstrong niece; William Lester, Pat's lover and editorial head of Tallant's Death Circle of Detective Novels; G. P. O'Reilly, who runs Tallant's Six-Gun Westerns even though he knows nothing about the Old West; Grey Haviland, cynic and tippler, who is in charge of Tallant's Allied Magazines; Helen Lake, Sir Ernest's secretary; and the firm's second-in-command, Stephen Corinth. One of these people apparently murdered Sir Ernest. But why? And above all, how? It takes an attempt on the lives of Glass and Hornbeam and a second murder, among other factors, before the two sleuths, working in tandem and independently, arrive at the solution.

Some aficionados—of Carr's work in particular—seem not to hold this novel in very high regard. But this reviewer persists in finding it a delight from start to finish. The "impossible" gimmick is cleverly worked out (so cleverly that Glass is able to provide two complete alternate solutions that are proven wrong); British publishing circa 1938 provides an intriguing background; the characters are all well developed; and the good-natured bickering between Glass and Hornbeam contributes quite a few chuckles. *Fatal Descent* isn't either author's best novel, certainly, but it *is* an enjoyable baffler that outshines a good many others of its ilk and time period.

(*B.P.*)

Rhodes, Vivian. *Groomed for Murder.* New York: Ballantine, 1984. (O/AD)

The tradition of Nick and Nora, Pam and Jerry, Jeff and Haila, and the countless husband-and-wife sleuth teams of the Thirties and Forties lives on in *Groomed for Murder.* This maiden mystery introduces us to two transplanted New Yorkers, Susan Finkelstein and Nick Comici, who experience culture shock and the thrill of amateur sleuthing in the wilds of Los Angeles.

As the novel opens, Susan is having some doubts about her longtime relationship with a self-centered jerk whose greatest affection seems to be for Mallomars. So when her handsome, randy hairdresser dies suspiciously, Susan takes her mind off her discontent by investigating. To this end a gay pal introduces her to Nick, an investigative reporter from the Big Apple. Romance develops, as does a multimurder mystery. It seems the hairdresser spent as much time blackmailing as he did creating coiffures. Suspects include a sex goddess ex-wife, a sleazy talent agent, a fanatic whale fancier, and a grandmotherly yenta.

Rhodes has great fun sending Susan and Nick to Tupperware rallies and orgy clubs, and that fun is definitely communicated to the reader. In the great amateur-couple tradition, there is plenty of comedy and no police procedure in *Groomed for Murder.*

Fans of hard-hitting realism may look elsewhere. Those who like their mysteries laced with laughs and lovemaking will be fully satisfied. The kinky sex and strong language might have shocked Mr. and Mrs. North, but Nick and Susan are products of their times as well as of a classic mystery tradition.

(*K.L.M.*)

*Rice, Craig. *The Fourth Postman.* New York: Simon & Schuster, 1948. (CS/C)

Craig Rice (Georgiana Ann Randolph) had several successful literary careers in the Thirties, Forties, and Fifties: journalist, radio writer and producer, author of both fictional and true crime stories, Hollywood scriptwriter, publicist for Gypsy Rose Lee, and ghostwriter for Lee and actor George Sanders. She was one of the few mystery writers to be profiled in—and featured on the cover of—*Time* magazine. Her mystery novels, most of which offer a nicely balanced blend of fast action, detection, and screwball comedy, were extremely popular in the Forties and early Fifties—especially those featuring Chicago lawyer John J. Malone, a hard-drinking, womanizing parody of the hard-boiled detective. Rice was adept not only at plotting and at infusing her stories with unusual and well-defined background detail, but at creating memorable characters. Two of these are Jake and Helene Justus, who play important roles in most of Malone's adventures; Jake is a press agent just scraping by who, fortunately for him, happens to be married to Helene, a beautiful blond heiress. The Justuses frequently find themselves involved in a murder case and call in Malone to help them. After prodigious amounts of alcohol are consumed, and some rather adroit sleuthing is nonetheless done, Malone arrives at the proper solution—much to the dismay, on more than one occasion, of another recurring character: Daniel von Flanagan, an Irish homicide cop who has legally added the "von" to his name to avoid stereotyping.

The Fourth Postman is among the oddest of the novels featuring Malone and the Justuses. The central mystery here is who murdered three postmen in the same alleyway in an exclusive Chicago suburb, each by a blow to the head. Why would anyone want to murder *one* postman, let alone *three?* The police think wealthy and slightly cracked Rodney Fairfaxx had a reason, even if it is a screwy one: He has been waiting thirty-five years for a letter from his girlfriend, whom he thinks is still alive but who in fact went down with the *Titanic* in 1912, and he could have believed the postmen were holding out on him. Malone, while investigating, gets hit over the head and nailed to the wall of a cellar in a deserted house; a fourth postman, who *isn't* a postman, is struck down but survives; and Jake Justus contracts a bizarre case of the chicken pox. In the end it is Malone, with the help of a beer-drinking dog, who deduces the real motive in the case, clears old Rodney Fairfaxx, and brings a not-so-clever murderer to justice.

One reviewer of the period called this "a beguiling blend of rib-tickling humor and spine-curling terror." The words may be a bit hyperbolic, but the judgment is valid. Baffling, exciting, and fun.

The same is true of the other entries in the series, among them *The Right Murder* (1941), in which a dead man pays a visit to Malone in Joe the Angel's Bar, his favorite wateringhole, on New Year's Eve; *The Big Midget Murders* (1942), in which a brutal mimic known as the Big Midget is murdered by eleven unmatched silk stockings tied into a noose, and Jake Justus, in the wrong place at the wrong time, is forced to stuff the corpse into a bass-fiddle case; *The Lucky Stiff* (1947), wherein Malone is plagued by the apparition of a woman wrongfully executed in the electric chair; and *My Kingdom for a Hearse* (1957), which involves the little lawyer with several women who claim to be a model named Delora Deanne and who keep disappearing, only to turn up again in bits and pieces.

(*G.K./B.P.*)

*Rice, Craig. *The Thursday Turkey Murders.* New York: Simon & Schuster, 1943. (AD/C)

Rice's second major series is likewise enjoyable—more so if your taste runs to even broader mystery farce than that engaged in by Malone and the Justuses. The adventures of Bingo Riggs and Handsome Kusak, a pair of gullible city slickers and reluctant amateur detectives, are gems of "whimsy and wickedness" (*Saturday Review of Literature*) so packed with screwball characters and plot components that you may feel a little wacky yourself after reading one.

In *The Thursday Turkey Murders,* Bingo and Handsome are driving from New York to Hollywood, where they plan to establish the International Foto, Motion Picture, and Television Corporation of America (they're street photographers, you see). In their possession is $1200, what remains—after the purchase of such necessities as their maroon roadster—of the $10,000 they earned by dint of having solved four murders and the kidnapping of a Pigeon in *The Sunday Pigeon Murders* (1942). On their way through the little backwater town of Thursday, Iowa, they accidentally run over a turkey. A local farmer demands $10 for the dead bird; but after some shrewd bargaining, Bingo instead gives him $1000 for 500 *live* turkeys and his ramshackle house. (Simple mathematics: 500 turkeys *x* $10 each = $5000 come Thanksgiving. And then they can continue to Hollywood in even grander style.)

The only problem is, there are only 200 turkeys, worth $2 each, and the long-gone farmer didn't really own them *or* the house. The man who does own them is willing to let our intrepid heroes stay in the house temporarily, but this is anything but a godsend: That night Bingo and Handsome find a dead man on the premises whom nobody seems to know. Then the 200 turkeys mysteriously disappear. (They get blamed for that, too.) Then a gang of four escaped convicts descends on the house in the middle of the night and there is a terrific fight. Then a beautiful woman shows up with a gun, tells the boys a cockamamie story (or is it?) about a fortune in stolen gold that her father helped heist from a bank many years ago and buried somewhere in the vicinity. Then, come morning, *she* disappears with their last $172—and the 200 turkeys mysteriously *re*appear, as if they'd never been gone in the first place.

There is more, of course—much more. (All of the above happens in less than 100 pages of a 300-page book.) But you get the idea. Do Bingo and Handsome solve the murder(s)? Of course. They're a good team of sleuths when they set their minds to it. For one thing, Handsome has a photographic memory, which comes in handy on more than one occasion. (He also has implicit faith in Bingo's judgment which *doesn't* come in handy and makes for some funny bits of business.) Do the boys get any of their money back? Do they find the buried gold? Read the book and find out.

The only other Bingo and Handsome novel is *The April Robin Murders* (1958), which Rice had three-quarters finished at the time of her death; it was completed by Ed McBain (q.v.) and was published under their joint bylines. This one is a Hollywood romp (it only took the boys fifteen years to get there) and revolves around a Charles Addams–type mansion that once belonged to silent-screen star April Robin.

Craig Rice also had her serious moments as a crime novelist—all of them under pseudonyms. As Michael Venning, she wrote three mysteries in the early Forties featuring a gentlemanly detective named Melville Fairr; the best of these is probably *Murder Through the Looking Glass* (1943), a psychological puzzler about a man named Jeffrey Bruno who is also a man named John Blake, and vice versa. As Daphne Sanders, she published one suspense novel, *To Catch a Thief* (1943). She also ghosted both of the burlesque-based mysteries ostensibly written by Gypsy Rose Lee: *The G-String Murders* (1941) and *Mother Finds a Body* (1942); and with science-fiction writer Cleve Cartmill, ghosted the first of two novels published as by actor George Sanders, *Crime on My Hands* (1944). One other humorous Rice novel of note, published under her own name, is *Home Sweet Homicide* (1944), a semiautobiographical mystery in which the three children of a mystery writer solve a neighbor's murder. This was made into an entertaining 1946 film with Lynn Bari, Randolph Scott, Peggy Ann Garner, and Dean Stockwell.

(*B.P.*)

Rich, Virginia. *The Cooking School Murders.* New York: Dutton, 1982. (AD)

The Cooking School Murders is a first novel that has received a great deal of attention. Love of food and mysteries seem, for some reason, to go together. And not only does the book deal with the art of cooking, but the various characters' recipes are included.

Mrs. Eugenia Potter returns to her childhood home in the small lakeside Iowa town of Harrington (population 4785) to dispose of the family homestead. While there, she organizes an adult-education class at her former high school—a cooking class, to be taught by famous chef James Redmond. She has promised the chef twelve students, and she fears she will not meet her quota. She does, however, and as they gather for the first class, the group (including herself) consists of Gregory Andrews, Eugenia's emotionally unstable nephew who is recovering under her care from an attack of hepatitis; debonaire European MacKay Moore, who has been Eugenia's friend for many a year; Ralph and Dottie DeWitt, born-again Christians; Jack Vanderpool, a well-off business-and-insurance man; Julie Hofmeyer, who has barely mastered the art of heating a TV dinner; Lynette Dorrance, competent and controlled community leader; John Edward Cassaday, houseman and cook for a family of summer residents; Miss Varlene Varstaag, prim home-economics teacher at the high school; Roger Hofmeyer II, Julie's son and, at thirty, the town's newest millionaire; Roger's date, the strikingly beautiful Jacquelyn Moresback, whose arrival seems to create a subtle disturbance within the group; and Charlene ("Charlie") Ragsdale, a young, bohemian designer of greeting cards.

The first cooking-class session involves the uses of kitchen knives, and by the next morning one of the students has turned up carved. Jacquelyn Moresback is found stabbed in the parking lot behind her apartment building, and next MacKay Moore is discovered in his garage, the victim of carbon-monoxide poisoning. Eugenia accompanies Chief of Police Pete Felderkamp on a search through Moore's house, and they find a suicide note, addressed to Eugenia, confessing to killing Jacquelyn. Eugenia doesn't believe this of her old friend, and she sets out to prove that MacKay, too, was murdered. Her quest takes her into the secret lives and passions—both past and present—of the Harrington residents she used to know so well, and to the unveiling of a particular passion that has proved fatal.

Rich has captured well the emotions of a sixties-ish woman returning home for the first time in many years; Eugenia's memories of the past, and of people as they were as opposed to as they are now, are depicted in detail. In addition to her grasp of cooking, Rich has a good feel for the idiosyncrasies of small-town living; and the pace of the narrative is like the pace of a small-town summer evening before it settles into full night.

Rich's second venture into culinary crime is *The Baked Bean Supper Murders* (1983); and her third is *The Nantucket Diet Murders* (1985).

(*S.D.*)

*Rinehart, Mary Roberts. *The Circular Staircase.* Indianapolis: Bobbs-Merrill, 1908. (R)

Mary Roberts Rinehart is best known today—and often unjustly ridiculed—for being the founder of the had-I-but-known school of detection. (For the uninitiated, this is the type of story in which the heroine, fully knowing that a troll resides in the fruit cellar, nonetheless ventures down there, gets bopped on the head, and upon recovery announces, "Oh, had I but known the troll was in residence, I would never have gone down there!") This somewhat condescending judgment of a vastly popular body of work that spans nearly fifty years is unfortunate, because if one looks at Rinehart's novels within the context of their time, there is much to be admired about them. A great deal happens in a Rinehart book; the suspense is always high; and even if they venture forth ill-advisedly, at least her heroines have the gumption to get up and do it, rather than sitting back with their embroidery and waiting for some male to do it for them.

The Circular Staircase, Rinehart's first novel, is a good example of these action-packed tales. Within the first six chapters, the heroine, Rachel Innes, arrives at a New England country house she has rented for the summer and the servants all quit; she is terrorized by strange sounds in the night; the sounds prove to have root in fact; a strange cuff link appears in an unlikely place; her nephew and niece arrive with a man she has never heard of, who later turns out to be the niece's fiancé; the two young men disappear in the middle of the night; a stranger is shot to death in the house; Rachel finds her nephew's revolver half buried in the flower bed and hides it from the police; the young men remain missing; and the police detective chases someone down a laundry chute. Rachel, feisty maiden lady that she is, sleuths with fierce determination, dealing with eerie happenings in the night and further disappearances and reappearances, until she apprehends a ghost who is altogether too real.

Melodrama? Well, yes, but considering when it was written, this is pretty good stuff. And if you think *this* is farfetched, consider the play that Rinehart (with Avery Hopwood) based on the story, and its subsequent novelization. (Since the play strayed far afield from *The Circular Staircase,* Rinehart felt immune from charges of self-plagiarism—and rightly so.) *The Bat* (1926) is about a supercrook, replete with sinister batlike shadow, who roams an old country house, terrorizing its inhabitants for his own bad reasons. Apparently there is money hidden within, although we are never sure how the Bat knows this. Moreover, we are never told who he really is, where he came from, or why he has a penchant for Bat suits. Perhaps every author is allowed one journey into the outer stratosphere of imagination; if so, this is Rinehart's. In fact, *The Bat* is so bad that Bill Pronzini (q.v.) gave it a lengthy and hilarious treatment in his 1982 study of "alternative classics," *Gun in Cheek.*

The Circular Staircase was reissued in 1985 by Carroll & Graf in a paperback reprint of the original edition, complete with illustrations; reading it in such form provides a better feel for Rinehart's work within the context of the times. Should the reader discover a taste for this sort of genteel melodrama, other recommended Rinehart titles are *The Man in Lower Ten* (1909), *The Red Lamp* (1925), and *The Yellow Room* (1945).

(*M.M.*)

*Ritchie, Jack. *A New Leaf and Other Stories.* New York: Dell Books, 1971. (O/SS)

For more than thirty years, Jack Ritchie was one of the two or three best writers of the criminous short story. He published several hundred stories between 1953 and 1983, including at least one minor classic ("For All the Rude People"). Anthony Boucher said of him, "What I like most about Jack Ritchie's work is its exemplary neatness. No word is wasted, and many words serve more than one purpose. Exposition disappears; all needed facts are deftly inserted as the narrative flows forward. Ritchie can write a long short story that is virtually the equivalent of a full suspense novel; and his very short stories sparkle as lapidary art." Donald E. Westlake (q.v.), in his introduction to this volume (Ritchie's only collection and only book), agrees. He quotes a line from one of Ritchie's own stories—"I had the feeling the boy could have written *War and Peace* on the back of a postcard"—and adds with Ritchian succinctness, "Exactly."

The eighteen stories in *A New Leaf* are among Ritchie's finest, of course. Sixteen of them first appeared in *Alfred Hitchcock's Mystery Magazine,* his primary market throughout his career; one first appeared in *Manhunt* and one ("Living by Degrees") is an original story. Included are "For All the Rude People," Ritchie's best-known and perhaps best story overall—a gem about a quiet, intelligent man who is suffering from a terminal illness and uses the time he has left to do something drastic about the lack of common courtesy in modern society; "Remains to Be Seen," another gem, about a man who may or may not have murdered his wife; "The Crime Machine," which deals with murder-for-hire and a marvelous invention that may or may not be capable of transporting a person through time; such delightful and pungent short-shorts as "Package Deal," "Queasy Does It Not," and "Shatterproof"; and the title story, which concerns itself with a man who marries for money, plans to murder his wife in order to collect it, and then runs into an unexpected snag: He finds himself falling in love with her. "A New Leaf" was filmed in 1971, an excellent production starring Elaine May and Walter Matthau that remained faithful to the tone if not the substance of Ritchie's story.

This is a superb collection and should be required reading for anyone interested in writing the criminous short story.

(*B.P.*)

Roberts, Willo Davis. *Didn't Anybody Know My Wife?* New York: Putnam's, 1974. (T)

Dr. Herbert Scott knew little enough about his young wife, Alison, when they were married—just that she was beautiful and that she made a terrific bed partner. He had no idea that she was lazy and too willing to pick fights, or that she coveted clothes and money. Now, two months later, he understands how mismatched they are, for he has a small practice in an area of the (unnamed) city called Little Ghetto and is perfectly content to forsake the good life for the satisfaction of helping people in need. He also has an attractive secretary, Maggie Marchetti, who is much more sympathetic and whom he finds himself smitten with. Divorce from Alison seems imminent, even desirable.

But it isn't divorce that ends his marriage to her; it is murder most foul. Arriving home one hot summer night, he finds Alison viciously beaten and hacked to death with a cleaver, her blood spattered throughout the kitchen. Scott has no alibi, and when no other suspects surface, the police turn their attention to him. Alison, it seems, was three months pregnant, a longer period of time than Scott has known her; this, coupled with Maggie's presence, could be construed as a motive. Then a pair of bloodstained overalls is found, with a letter in the pocket containing Scott's fingerprints. The police come to arrest him, but he panics and manages to escape. Thus begins a nightmarish struggle to elude a city-wide police dragnet and, with Maggie's help, to find Alison's killer—no easy task in either case. Who was Alison? Who made the anonymous phone call that sent the police to his house moments after he discovered her body? Why did she clean the house before she was murdered? Why was he framed with those bloody overalls?

This is a deftly plotted suspense novel with a dazzling (if somewhat melodramatic) twist at the end that should catch most readers unaware. Roberts writes extremely well from the first-person male viewpoint—so well, in fact, that Newgate Callendar, in his *New York Times* review of *Didn't Anybody Know My Wife?,* referred to Mrs. Roberts as "he" throughout. Fast-paced and gripping.

Before turning to other types of crime fiction, Willo Davis Roberts was one of the best practitioners of the paperback Gothic mystery popular in the Sixties and early Seventies. Over the past dozen years, she has alternated among juvenile mysteries, neo-Gothic suspense novels of high caliber such as *White Jade* (1975) and *The Sniper* (1984), and such well-crafted thrillers as *Expendable* (1976; also expertly written from the first-person male viewpoint) and *A Long Time to Hate* (1982).

(*B.P.*)

Roeburt, John. *The Lunatic Time.* New York: Simon & Schuster, 1956. (W)

The title of this novel is a perfect reflection of the events depicted in it and the feeling they engender in the reader. The terse style and short, slice-of-life chapters create a mood of unreality and lunacy that closely matches the protagonist's mental state and enables the reader to empathize with him as the strange story unfolds.

Harry Jonas is a writer for *The New Era,* a Manhattan magazine that emerged in the days of the New Deal and now limps along on a stipend from a wealthy benefactress. Jonas is also a psychiatric patient and a drinker who spends much of his time in a tavern on the Bowery called Chino's. It is there that he meets Paula Adano, a newcomer who sits at the bar night after night, drinking martinis and giving away her "amateur" status by "making faces, like a kid with distaste for medicine." Paula and Harry keep crossing paths: First she rescues him when he pulls a terrible drunk; then he rescues her after she has been attacked on the street. Before long, Harry has been dragged into Paula's one-woman crusade—to prove her twin brother, Frank, didn't kill a high-priced hustler named Mona Leeds.

Harry and Paula go to the building where Mona Leeds lived; they find out she had an address book, now in the possession of the janitor's sister. The sister finally surrenders the book—after a weird scene involving prayer in a home chapel—and Harry starts investigating the men listed there. He is constantly at odds with a Homicide captain named Del Robbia; he drops in from time to time for sessions with his psychiatrist that do him no good; he and Paula become lovers; and the craziness escalates and escalates.

Most mystery fans will guess what is really going on in *The Lunatic Time* from the beginning, but that doesn't at all detract from the strange puzzle. With his characterization of Harry Jonas, Roeburt has accomplished a very difficult thing: portraying a man on the verge of madness from a first-person viewpoint and doing it convincingly and sympathetically.

Roeburt wrote a number of other suspense novels, but none comes close to the excellence of this one. (He also wrote numerous radio scripts for such shows as "Gangbusters.") His series character, police officer Johnny Devereaux, appears in such titles as *The Hollow Man* (1954) and *Tough Cop* (1949). Jigger Moran, a disbarred attorney turned New York City cabdriver, is featured in (among others) *Jigger Moran* (1944) and *There Are Dead Men in Manhattan* (1946).

(*M.M.*)

*Rogers, Joel Townsley. *The Red Right Hand.* New York: Simon & Schuster, 1945. (PS/W)

This classic suspense novel has the quality of a hallucination. From the opening paragraph, we are drawn into a strange world where eerie and seemingly impossible events are happening; and as we view them through the eyes of the narrator, Dr. Harry Riddle, we begin, as he does, to believe in their reality and to search desperately for some rational explanation for them.

The story begins after most of the events have taken place, with Riddle trying desperately to puzzle them out as he sits in the study of Adam MacComereau, a professor emeritus of psychiatry at Harvard. The *late* Adam MacComereau, we learn: Murder has been done more than once. Various shadowy and frightening events are described, without their chronology or connections being given. There is a woman asleep on a nearby sofa toward whom Riddle feels protective, while also holding back fear of his own insanity. And as he sits there, thinking about the events that have passed, he begins to reconstruct what they really signify.

While driving from Vermont to New York City, Riddle had car trouble on a back road; when he finally got under way, he encountered the woman, Elinor Darrie, lost and fleeing through the underbrush. As Riddle tells us, "It was a simple enough incident." Elinor and her fiancé, Inis St. Erme, were driving to Vermont to be married. On the road they picked up a tramp—a little, twisted man whom Riddle comes to think of as Corkscrew—and when they stopped for a picnic, there was a fight between the tramp and St. Erme. Elinor heard a terrifying scream and fled. Riddle and Elinor investigated the spot and found a quantity of blood, but nothing else.

As Riddle says, "It was such a damned ordinary and commonplace crime, on the face of it." But other aspects surface—such as St. Erme's missing right hand; a mutilated blue hat that Riddle found on the road before he met with Elinor; the noise "like a great frog croaking in the weedy ditch" near where Riddle's car broke down; and the ugly little man, Corkscrew—who is he and how has he gotten away after apparently doing murder?

This is a dizzying and confusing novel, but pleasurably so. And when the action has been unraveled, its apparent solution explained, confusion is initiated again, and more action occurs. And when *that* has been unraveled, its solution stands alone, and the result is stunning indeed. In thinking over the wonderful experience of reading *The Red Right Hand,* the reader can only marvel at how the author constructed such a baffling and complex plot without leaving a thread untied. And—corollary to that—how he did so without driving himself as mad as his narrator fears he is becoming.

Rogers, however, *did* remain sane and capable of writing other memorable novels: *Lady with the Dice* (1946) and *The Stopped Clock* (1958). In addition, he wrote reams of fiction for both the pulp and slick magazines, and a first (but less memorable) novel, *Once in a Red Moon* (1923).

(*M.M.*)

Rogers, Samuel. *Don't Look Behind You!* New York: Harper, 1944. (PS)

A small Wisconsin college town, sweltering and edgy under a brutal summer heat wave. The sadistic knife-slaying of a young woman whose body was found in the nearby woods. A second attack, thwarted at the last second, so that the perpetrator's bloodlust is left unfulfilled. A small group of men—three college professors and a doctor—who are fascinated by the psychology of blood rites and mass murder. And a young, attractive Nurse's Aide named Daphne Gray, who has every reason to believe that she will be the next victim.

These are the primary ingredients of *Don't Look Behind You!* Familiar ingredients, perhaps, but in the hands of Samuel Rogers they evolve into something extraordinary: a waking nightmare of the sort Cornell Woolrich (q.v.) specialized in, and at the same time a serious study of homicidal psychosis and of the effects of obsession and the power of suggestion on the "normal" human mind. Early on, one of the characters states the novel's theme this way:

> *"There is no real difference in kind, one might say, between the most innocent and natural behavior and a series of the most brutal murders: it's rather a difference of emphasis of degree. The criminal violence involved is not something utterly new and strange: it's just the gross, the pathological distortion of something normal, something already there, in all of us. Most of the time we move along complacently, and take our sanity for granted. But haven't you sometimes felt, when you've been sick or tired or worried, that sanity was like a tightrope strung across a great gulf, that you have to walk over it and if the slightest little adjustment should go wrong you'd topple off and never stop falling . . . that if you let yourself even look down you might grow dizzy and have the devil of a time keeping your balance? You're mighty lucky if you haven't."*

Rogers writes extremely well; his powers of description are so acute, in fact, that you literally *feel* the oppressive heat, the omnipresent fear. The depth of his characterization is considerable, particularly of Daphne and her fiance, Harold. And even though there are no real surprises in the plot, Rogers (like Woolrich) builds the suspense so intensely and inexorably that you won't care. If you like the old-fashioned kind of psychological horror novel in which the author achieves his effects subtly, rather than through lavish descriptions of blood and gore, don't miss this one.

Rogers's other two suspense novels, *You'll Be Sorry!* (1945) and *You Leave Me Cold!* (1946), also reflect his interest in abnormal psychology. But these two are detective stories as well; both feature the deductive abilities of Paul Hatfield, a chemistry professor and amateur ornithologist who has a minor role in *Don't Look Behind You!* Especially good is *You'll Be Sorry!*, which contains two plot twists that caught this somewhat jaded reader unawares.

(*B.P.*)

Rohmer, Sax. *Bat Wing.* New York: Doubleday, Page, 1921. (W)

Sax Rohmer was the by-line used by the British writer Arthur Henry Ward on more than fifty books of crime, mystery, and the supernatural. For a number of years, he made a precarious living writing songs and comedy sketches for British music-hall performers. With the creation of that epitome of Oriental villainy Dr. Fu Manchu in 1912, Rohmer's reputation was quickly established. During the World War I period and again in the late 1920s and 1930s, he was one of the most widely read (and most highly paid) writers of popular fiction in the English language. In the United States, more than 200 issues of *Collier's* magazine carried his stories, which were also adapted for radio and the movies.

Among the exotic thrillers on which Rohmer's popularity was based, there are only a few books that qualify as detective novels in any strict sense. The first of these was *Bat Wing,* featuring private investigator and ex–Secret Service agent Paul Harley. Harley also appeared in one other novel (*Fire-Tongue,* 1922), a number of short stories, and a stage play. He was quite clearly intended to be a "great detective" in the Sherlock Holmes tradition, and his admiring journalist friend Malcolm Knox fills the Dr. Watson role. (The models actually mentioned in the book are Poe's Chevalier Dupin and his unnamed companion.)

Harley and Knox are invited to Cray's Folly, a manor house in the Surrey hills, by its new owner, Colonel Don Juan Sarmiento Menendez. There have been attempts on the colonel's life, and as a threat or warning, the severed wing of a bat has been nailed to the door of his house. During his first interview with Harley, the colonel spins an unlikely tale of an encounter with a voodoo cult in the West Indies, and of the cult's presumed desire to avenge an injury done to the cult leader. Thereafter, the colonel unaccountably refuses to discuss his fears and suspicions, and it is left to Harley to discover that there are sources of antagonism much closer at hand. A neighbor, Colin Camber, has repeatedly and openly expressed his hatred for the man he calls "Devil Menendez."

When murder finally strikes, Camber is immediately arrested. Harley doubts Camber's guilt, but can get no cooperation from the local police inspector, "a large person bearing a really interesting resemblance to a walrus, but lacking that creature's intelligence." (Harley is almost comically offended to find that the inspector has never heard of him. He pulls some strings in order to have a much more cooperative Scotland Yard officer assigned to the case.) By a clever device, Harley demonstrates how the murder was committed, but there remain further clues to be followed before the murderer is revealed. The solution to the crime was more novel in 1921 (though not original with Rohmer even then) than it seems today, when so many other authors have used it.

Many modern readers will find Rohmer's prose awkward and his style ponderous. The casual ethnocentrism and even sexism (the colonel's beautiful cousin, Madame de Stämer, is repeatedly praised for her "masculine intelligence") cannot be denied. Still, it is possible to suspend the critical faculties and enjoy Rohmer's vivid evocation of setting and his talent for creating a menacing atmosphere out of familiar things.

(*R.E.B.*)

*Rohmer, Sax. *The Dream Detective.* New York: Doubleday, Page, 1925. (SS/AD)

In 1913, only a few months after the introduction of Dr. Fu Manchu, Rohmer published in *The New Magazine* in England a series of stories under the general title "The Methods of Moris Klaw." It was not until twelve years later that the stories were collected in book form in the United States. Moris Klaw belongs to that subcategory of fictional sleuth called "psychic detectives." The crimes that he encounters often seem to have occult or supernatural aspects, and Klaw himself sometimes uses psychic methods in his investigations. He also functions as a more traditional amateur criminologist and detective. Klaw, having appeared suddenly in London with his beautiful daughter, Isis, and with no traceable previous history, is the proprietor of a very odd curio shop in Wapping Old Stairs, guarded by a parrot who announces visitors with the cry "Moris Klaw! Moris Klaw! The devil's come for you!"

In "Case of the Tragedies in the Greek Room," Klaw uses his method of "odic photography" to solve a pair of mysterious deaths in a London museum. (He visits the scene of the crime and goes to sleep upon an "odically sterilized" pillow that he carries with him. When he awakes, he finds that his sleeping mind has "photographed" past events that provide clues to the mystery.) In other cases, Klaw solves thefts of stolen artworks or historical relics (and in one case, he and his daughter carry out such a theft themselves). In the cases of "The Whispering Poplars" and "The Haunting of Grange," Klaw explains the mechanisms of elaborate murder plots. In the amusing case of "The Headless Mummies," he encounters a man with an entirely rational reason for beheading a series of Egyptian mummies. And in "The Chord in G," he finds that a musical chord is the crucial clue to a brutal murder. The book concludes with the "Case of the Veil of Isis," the only overtly supernatural story in the collection, and (for those readers whose tastes lie in this direction) one of the best.

The Moris Klaw stories are cleverly plotted and crisply told, and they have dated very little over the years. Klaw himself is a fascinating creation. The book has been reprinted several times, most recently in 1977, but deserves to be more widely known.

(*R.E.B.*)

*Rohmer, Sax. *The Trail of Fu Manchu.* New York: Doubleday Crime Club, 1934. (T)

Most of Sax Rohmer's early works were in a form popular with magazine editors: a series of connected stories, each complete in itself, but with enough continuity to keep readers coming back for the next episode (and, not incidentally, to make it easy to package the series as a "novel" for publication in book form). The first three Fu Manchu books (beginning with *The Insidious Dr. Fu Manchu* in 1913) were really a single extended series of thirty stories, published in magazines over a five-year period. The stories were narrated by a London physician, Dr. Petrie (no first name was ever given), drawn into the battle against Fu Manchu by friendship with the ex–colonial administrator and government agent Nayland Smith. Smith and Petrie were aided by one of Fu Manchu's agents, the slave girl Kâramanèh, who had fallen in love with Petrie. At the end of the series, Fu Manchu has apparently been defeated. Petrie and Kâramanèh marry and settle in Cairo. The stories are set in a sort of perpetual 1912, with no intrusion from real-world events of the period. Fourteen years later, Fu Manchu's organization is revived by his daughter, Fah Lo Suee (*Daughter of Fu Manchu,* 1931), and Fu Manchu himself becomes active again. The stories have now reentered "real time" and the setting has shifted from England to the Near East. In *Fu Manchu's Bride* (1933), set on the French Riviera, Dr. Petrie reappears. It is revealed that his and Kâramanèh's baby daughter, Fleurette, was stolen from them, and has been raised as a member of Fu Manchu's household. She is rescued with the help of an American botanist, Alan Sterling.

As *The Trail of Fu Manchu* opens, we learn that the rescue was only temporary: Fleurette is once more in Fu Manchu's power, and Fu Manchu is again operating in England. Settings and characters from the early stories reappear, but Fu Manchu has a new hideout in a system of abandoned tunnels beneath the Thames, where he is carrying out a particularly devilish alchemical process for manufacturing gold. The central portion of the book, in which Smith, Sterling, and Fah Lo Suee are held captive in the caverns beneath the Thames and threatened with an agonizing death, is a set piece of sustained action and suspense, with a literally explosive conclusion. And in the surprising climax to the book, Dr. Petrie plays a part that will have fateful consequences for everyone concerned.

Because of the reappearance of so many characters and locales from the early stories, the book has an almost nostalgic air. Whether consciously intended or not, the book serves as a summing-up of the earlier episodes, clearing the way for the new adventures to follow. And it stands by itself as a fast-paced and ingenious thriller, well worth your attention.

Fu Manchu reappears in six additional novels: *President Fu Manchu* (1936), *The Drums of Fu Manchu* (1939), *The Island of Fu Manchu* (1941), *Shadow of Fu Manchu* (1948), *Re-Enter Fu Manchu* (1957), and *Emperor Fu Manchu* (1959).

(*R.E.B.*)

Roos, Kelley. *Murder on Martha's Vineyard.* New York: Walker, 1981. (PI/T)

Kelley Roos is in reality the husband-and-wife collaborative team of William and Audrey (née Kelley) Roos. Like another successful husband-and-wife team, Richard and Frances Lockridge (q.v.), they began writing in

1940; and like Pam and Jerry North, their sleuths were a happily married couple, Haila and Jeff Troy. The Troy novels were typical of that era, combining sophisticated humor, bloodless murder, and climaxes in which the wife is imperiled and quickly rescued. Unlike many novelists who hit on a successful formula, however, the Roos team was willing to experiment: first by introducing another married detecting duo, Connie and Steve Barton—who appear in only one novel, *The Blonde Died Dancing* (1956)—and then by moving into novels of psychological suspense and intrigue. They were even willing to experiment with their first sleuthing couple's relationship: In their swan song—*One False Move* (1966)—Jeff and Haila Troy have been divorced (although they reconcile at the successful conclusion of their case). Perhaps this willingness to grow and change with the times—along with solid plotting and characterization—is the reason the Rooses have remained so popular over a more than forty-year span.

Murder on Martha's Vineyard (where the authors live during the summers) is one of their more recent titles, and combines psychological suspense with some good detection by a private eye. A young, newly married woman, Nancy Webster, is returning with her husband David to take up residence on Martha's Vineyard, where they both grew up. But this is no ordinary move for Nancy: Three years ago, on the Vineyard, she was tried for her first husband's murder. Nancy was acquitted, but she wants to clear her name, so she hires private investigator Timothy O'Hara to look into this three-year-old killing.

O'Hara—a broken-down man in his sixties whom his agency has sent because they consider the case hopeless and don't want to spare a better operative—arrives at the Vineyard, begins looking around, and is soon convinced there is something to Nancy's side of the story. But then Nancy is kidnapped, and her husband foolishly withholds the fact from both the police and O'Hara. With no way of learning this because David doesn't know Nancy has hired him, O'Hara quickly closes in on a ruthless killer, unaware of the danger. . . .

The story is told from various viewpoints, including that of the unidentified murderer, and from the first we know someone is planning to kidnap and kill Nancy. The identity of the villain becomes obvious quite early, and as the search for Nancy and a young girl who vanished at about the same time mounts, it is also fairly obvious how it will be resolved. Nonetheless, the tension remains high; Nancy is an admirable character, as are O'Hara and other residents of the Vineyard; and the background of old frame houses, sand beaches, and cottages closed for the winter is appealing.

Another of Roos's nonseries novels that takes place in New England is *Requiem for a Blonde* (1958). Others are set in New York City, among them *Necessary Evil* (1965) and *What Did Hattie See?* (1970). Spain is another setting that the team uses to good effect, as evidenced by *A Few Days in Madrid* (published in 1965 under the names Audrey and William Roos) and *Scent of Mystery* (a 1969 novelization of the film version of their 1947 novel *Ghost of a Chance,* which—believe it or not—was originally set in New York City).

(*M.M.*)

Roos, Kelley. *Sailor, Take Warning!* New York: Dodd, Mead, 1944. (AD)

Jeff and Haila Troy are an attractive couple: He works in a New York photography studio; she's a former aspiring actress who now struggles to keep the family budget balanced. They have a nice, bantering way of talking to each other and a keen ability to find a mystery almost anywhere. This one begins at a lake in Central Park, where a young friend introduces them to the members of the Knickerbocker Model Yachting Club. These builders and sailors of model boats are an oddly assorted group: "Commodore" Austin Marshall, a rich but parsimonious man; Tony Gilbert, a handsome actor currently appearing in a Broadway hit; Bernard Marshall, Austin's jolly, chubby brother; William Phillips, a dour man whose only pleasure seems to be sailing his model ship; George Mead, a wheelchair detective, and his lively daughter, Penny. But the Troys are not destined to know the "Commodore" for long: Within fifteen minutes of the time they meet him, he is murdered—stabbed to death with a piece of steel the size of a nail while sitting on one of the park benches in sight of all the others.

Jeff is first on the scene, and he quickly dispatches Haila and their young charge. Shortly after Haila (who narrates all their adventures) returns to their Greenwich Village apartment, Jeff arrives with some police friends who are eager to discuss the case. No conclusions are reached, but once the police depart, an envelope is slipped under the Troys' door containing $1000 in cash and a note asking him to find out who killed Austin Marshall. Jeff and Haila set off immediately on the trail of a murderer—and quite a trail it is.

It leads them into the private lives of the remaining members of the Knickerbocker Model Yachting Club, and they find that not all is ideal. Further violence follows: Phillips's wife is attacked in her own home; the Troys' apartment is ransacked and the $1000 (which Haila has stolen from Jeff and hidden in her tea canister) is taken. Jeff's client finally admits to having hired him—and why. And that revelation leads to a chance encounter with a stranger and a mission that at first seems like a crazy side trip and turns out to be anything but.

This is a lively adventure in which secrets are revealed at every turn.

The Troys are a delightful duo whose detecting abilities can also be appreciated in *Made Up to Kill* (1940), *There Was a Crooked Man* (1945), *Murder in Any Language* (1948), and *Beauty Marks the Spot* (1951).

(*M.M.*)

Roscoe, Mike. *One Tear for My Grave.* New York: Crown, 1955. (PI)

Mike Roscoe's tough Kansas City private eye Johnny April appeared in five novels between 1952 and 1958. Although the first four went through various printings and editions, neither Roscoe nor April is much remembered today. Both are due for revival and reassessment, as the handful of Johnny April stories are among the best produced in the wave of hard-hitting PI fiction that followed the big splash made by Mickey Spillane's (q.v.) Mike Hammer.

One Tear for my Grave finds April in the presence of millionaire Avery J. Castleman and a corpse. This prologue ("The 23rd Hour") is followed by a flashback ("The First 22 Hours") that comprises the bulk of the book. The lure of a fat retainer coaxes April out of bed at two in the morning to aid bookie Eddie Norris and his moll, Nicky, who have a corpse on their hands—or, actually, in their back seat. Norris claims innocence—somebody dumped this stiff in his car, says the bookie. From the cops April learns the corpse is a society type named David Matthews.

Over the coming hours, various bookies—all of them owed money by Matthews—begin to die, and not of natural causes. Among them is Norris. April bumps heads with one particularly nasty bookie named Carbone, who trashes April's office to convince him to "lay off" this case, which only serves to enrage the detective. April then meets with Ginny Castleman, the delicate, sympathy-arousing society girl engaged to the late Matthews; he also meets her mysterious Oriental servant, whose quiet concern for his mistress seems strangely obsessive. While bobbing and weaving between bookies and their thugs, April encounters Carbone's moll, Lola, and a love/hate relationship blossoms. Eventually he finds that Matthews had paid off all the bookies before their deaths; and at the Castleman mansion, April has a final confrontation with Carbone as the convoluted, ultimately tragic mystery unravels. An epilogue ("The 24th Hour") brings the book full circle.

What sets such Roscoe mysteries as *One Tear for My Grave* apart from the crowd of would-be Spillanes is a studiously spare style. The novel is stripped for speed, consisting mostly of crisp dialogue and one- and two-sentence paragraphs. Despite this, the language is often vivid and evocative; witness the four opening lines (and four opening paragraphs) of the novel:

There are two times when a man will lie very still.
When he is finished making love with a woman.
When he is finished with life.
The man on the floor lay still with death.

Roscoe was two men—Michael Ruso and John Roscoe—who were real private eyes, employed by Hargrave's Detective Agency in Kansas City. The team's first three books—*Death Is a Round Black Ball* (1952), *Riddle Me This (1953), and Slice of Hell* (1954)—are also excellent. The final Johnny April novel, *The Midnight Eye,* did not appear till 1958, half an Ace Double. While some of the poetic touches were still present, this marked a dropping off in quality over the first four, and a near absence of the dialogue/short-paragraph approach. Perhaps the team had broken up and only one of them recorded this final Johnny April case.

(*M.A.C.*)

Rosen, R. D. *Strike Three, You're Dead.* New York: Walker, 1984. (AD)

Harvey Blissberg, the hero of *Strike Three, You're Dead,* is a baseball player recently traded from the Boston Red Sox to a new American League expansion team, the Providence Jewels. Called "Professor" by his younger teammates for his reading habits and off-diamond attire, Blissberg is stumped for a motive to the murder of his roommate, Rudy, and begins looking for the murderer out of a combination of curiosity and guilt. Discouraged by management, teammates, and police, Blissberg gets support from his girlfriend, a local TV sportscaster, and his brother, a baseball fanatic, as he tries to determine why his best friend on the team wound up drowned in the team whirlpool. His quest for the murderer takes on a new urgency when he, too, becomes a target.

Baseball statisticians will have a very slight edge in solving the murder, but such avidity is not needed. Rosen's clever plotting, quick wit, and subtle understatement makes this book both entertaining and easy to read. In the second book in this series, *Fadeaway* (1985), Blissberg has retired to become a professional detective and is called in to solve the murder of two NBA basketball stars.

Strike Three, You're Dead was named one of the seven best mysteries of the year by the *New York Times,* and won a Best First Novel Edgar. Rosen is also the author of two nonfiction books and numerous essays, criticisms, and articles on sports and humor.

(*K.M.*)

Rosenberger, Joseph. *Death Merchant: Hell in Hindu Land.* New York: Pinnacle, 1976. (O/A/E)

The remarkable success of Don Pendleton's (q.v.) Executioner series (several million copies sold) naturally spawned the usual bunch of imitators, some of whom enjoyed no small success of their own. The most literate of these is Mike Barry's (q.v.) Lone Wolf saga; the least literate (and funniest) is Joseph Rosenberger's ongoing adventures of Richard Camellion (a.k.a. the Death Merchant). Camellion is a sort of lunatic James Bond in that he is primarily occupied in eradicating threats to the free world arranged by Communist forces or members of a SMERSH-like organization called Spider. He, too, travels all over the world; the main difference between him and Bond is that 007 accomplishes his missions with wit and intelligence as well as violence, while the Death Merchant displays as much wit and intelligence as a "Goju-Ryu karate ball-of-the-foot *koga geri* groin kick," which he uses whenever he is engaged in hand-to-hand (or hand-to-foot) combat. Rosenberger takes the same jovial pleasure in describing breaking bones and teeth (spurting blood, too) as Camellion does in knocking off foreign "boobs."

There are plenty of broken bones and teeth, and oceans of blood, in *Hell in Hindu Land,* number twenty in the series. It seems the CIA has been receiving reports that a mysterious secret room in a Buddhist monastery in India contains "secrets from the stars"—e.g., plans for a "bio-plasm" force that can defy gravity and a "psychotronic generator" that can harness the energy of the human mind—which were allegedly brought to earth by ancient astronauts from another planet. Camellion is dispatched to India to check out this bizarre report and, if there is any truth in it, to gain control of the plans before his old KGB nemesis, Major Kondrashev, can claim them for Mother Russia. All of which is pure nonsense, of course—but no more so than Camellion's antics on Indian soil, which are principally comprised of feverish battles with the Russians and/or the deadly tribesmen of Rajmahal.

What makes such as this worth reading (marginally so and in small doses) is Rosenberger's inimitable style. (It has been said that he possesses unappreciated comic talents and that the Death Merchant series is not pastiche but parody; there is no evidence, however, to support such a claim.) The following representative snippet should serve as an indicator of whether or not you would like to become better acquainted with Rosenberger and Camellion:

> *Vende looked sicker than a Bible salesman on a cheap shot to nowhere when he found himself staring into the big blackness of an Auto Mag muzzle. The Indian's face twisted like a pretzel! Camellion could see that he was sorting through the mental junkpile of his mind, desperately searching for the right answers.*

"Drop the HK and pretend you're trying to grab a couple of clouds from the sky," Camellion said lazily. "NOW!"

Surprise and confusion flickered over the faces of the other men. Dr. Panduhabaya looked as depressed as a sailor who had hoped for love but had been forced to settle for a pint of cheap booze and mechanical sex with a cheap slut.

Other titles in the series include *The Albanian Connection* (1973), *The Mato Grosso Horror* (1975), *Armageddon, USA!* (1976), and *Blueprint Invisibility* (1980).

(*B.P.*)

*Ross, Barnaby. *The Tragedy of X.* New York: Viking, 1932. (CS)

After selling their third Ellery Queen novel, Fred Dannay and Manny Lee took their literary agent's advice and quit their jobs in the advertising and publicity business to make it as full-time writers or go broke. As professionals the cousins found that they could complete a 90,000-word detective novel every three months. But instead of glutting the market with four Queen exploits a year, they restricted Ellery to two annual adventures and launched a new series character under a second pseudonym for the balance of their output.

For their new by-line, they chose Barnaby Ross; and as their new detective, they created actor/sleuth Drury Lane, a world-famous interpreter of Shakespearean roles who has been forced into retirement by the onset of total deafness. Lane has built his own Elizabethan village on his estate above the Hudson, a village dominated by Lane's private castle and populated by down-and-out theatrical folk who wear Shakespearean costumes and use Shakespearean names in return for Lane's bounty. But the re-creation of the master's physical world doesn't satisfy Lane, and since he can't create dramatic worlds like the Bard, he turns to intervening in—and so in a sense rewriting—the dramas of real life. We are left in no doubt that the mainspring of his existence is his drive for power. During the Golden Age of the detective novel, it was radical indeed to identify the detective's impulse to rummage through others' lives with the dark side of human nature, and in this respect the Drury Lane quartet anticipates films like Hitchcock's *Rear Window* and plays like Shaffer's *Sleuth.* Yet despite their implicit rebuke to the authoritarian tendency in the genre, the Lane novels provide richly plotted, complexly clued specimens of fair-play detection on a par with the best early Ellery Queen books.

First and perhaps best of the four is *The Tragedy of X,* in which Lane joins with the NYPD's Inspector Thumm to investigate the murder of the much-despised stockbroker Harley Longstreet on a passenger-jammed crosstown trolley by means of a ball of cork riddled with poison-tipped needles. This is followed by a second murder, with one of the Longstreet suspects thrown from the upper deck of the Weehawken ferry and crushed to pulp as the boat pulls into its slip; and then by a third killing, carried out aboard a New Jersey commuter train within a few feet of Lane himself.

What enables Lane to solve the chain of crimes is the last act of this third victim. During a night train ride that one passenger will not live to complete, Lane delivers a classic lecture about the final moments of existence, setting the rationale for dozens of subsequent Ellery Queen dying-message stories when he asserts, "There are no limits to which the human mind cannot soar in that unique, godlike instant before the end of life."

The Tragedy of X is not only a brilliant detective novel and a disturbing study of power hunger, it's also a superb portrait of its time and place, when the depression racked the economy and ruthless businessmen lived by the dog-eat-dog ethos of pure capitalism, and when cities and suburbs were connected by streetcars, ferries, electric interurban lines, short-line passenger trains—in short, by a mass-transit system that worked. All this Dannay and Lee bring to life in the first of the four Drury Lane novels. Lane's second case, *The Tragedy of Y* (1932), is equally powerful and spellbinding. The series came to an irrevocable end with the fourth Barnaby Ross title, *Drury Lane's Last Case* (1933).

(*F.M.N.*)

Ross, Ivan T. *Requiem for a Schoolgirl.* New York: Simon & Schuster, 1961. (AD)

Although there have been numerous academic mysteries over the past fifty years, relatively few of them have dealt with the high-school scene. In the 1950s, the success of Evan Hunter's (q.v.) *Blackboard Jungle* inspired a prolific if short-lived subgenre of crime fiction about street gangs and teenage delinquents; but most of the stories in such magazines as *Guilty* and *Trapped,* and most of the novels of the period, dealt with violence outside the schools, or violence within them that bore little relation to the learning process at that level. Teachers as protagonists were also few and far between; the focus was on kids, *bad* kids, and on shivs, zip guns, rumbles, and other forms of bloodletting.

During the Fifties and in subsequent decades, only a handful of traditional mysteries appeared in which the high-school scene was presented in a positive and accurate fashion, and in which a teacher served as a compassionate sleuth. And only one such teacher/sleuth appeared in more than one novel: Ben Gordon, an English instructor at Mark Hopkins High School in an unnamed, fictional eastern city. The creation of Ivan T. Ross (Robert

Rossner), Gordon is featured in four novels published between 1960 and 1964, of which *Requiem for a Schoolgirl* is the second.

The schoolgirl of the title is seventeen-year-old Laurie Mitchell, the daughter of upper-middle-class parents who is nonetheless teetering on the edge between bad and good. Gordon, who is more tolerant of her less-than-exemplary behavior than are her other teachers, finds Laurie bright and witty, with a passion for books and considerable talent as a writer, which is the profession she hopes to enter when she's older. But she doesn't *get* any older: One morning Gordon receives a note from Laurie's mother informing him that Laurie has "passed away suddenly." When Gordon investigates, he finds that she apparently committed suicide by taking an overdose of sleeping pills, and that she left a note saying, "Ask Monty—he knows why." But no one seems to know who Monty is.

A chance encounter at a local bar gives Gordon the startling information that Laurie was working as a part-time B-girl, and that other teenage girls are similarly employed around the city. Even more startling news awaits him: Laurie was also hooked on heroin, and was therefore more deeply mixed up with the local criminal element, headed by a "prominent citizen" named Alex Bodine, than anyone could have imagined. Working with the local police, Gordon sets out to find the truth behind Laurie's death. But before he does, and before he helps to expose a vicious exploitation racket, he has to survive a statutory-rape frame-up, assaults, and an attempt on his life.

Though it may seem tame in comparison to the sort of depravity we read about in today's newspapers, this was volatile material for its time, reminiscent in theme of Thomas B. Dewey's *The Mean Streets* (q.v.). Ross handles it well, if sometimes a little too melodramatically, and his characters and settings come alive; a former high-school teacher himself, he was particularly adept at evoking life inside a large urban high school in the Fifties and Sixties.

Also recommended are the other three Ben Gordon mysteries: *Murder Out of School* (1960), *Old Students Never Die* (1962), and *Teacher's Blood* (1964).

(*B.P.*)

Roth, Holly. *Shadow of a Lady.* New York: Simon & Schuster, 1957. (PS)

Holly Roth tried a variety of occupations before turning to mystery fiction in her mid-thirties. Her short, brilliant career, resulting in over a dozen spy thrillers and mysteries under three names, was tragically ended by her mysterious death in the waters off Morocco in 1964.

Her first mystery was the excellent spy story *The Content Assignment,* published in 1954. *Shadow of a Lady* is her fifth novel, and a fine example of her craft. It opens with Laura Selby starting a solo drive through France to Geneva filled with a rebellious spirit and a touch too much chablis. She is rebelling against the ghosts of her past life and most especially against her devoted, mild-mannered, well-organized (and still married) fiancé, John Seton-Smith.

When Laura fails to make it to Geneva, Seton-Smith starts an investigation. And when the decomposed body of a woman very similar to Laura is found in a railway trunk resembling one purchased by Seton-Smith in Paris, her lover is charged with murder.

The sleuthing is performed by a private eye named Monte Gordon, and by Inspector Richard Medford of the CID. The plot is a real page-turner, culminating in a dramatic courtroom climax. But it is the characterization that sets *Shadow of a Lady* apart as a superlative mystery. Roth's understanding of the complexities of human relations, and how the burdens of the past haunt those relations, is impressive—all the more so for the way she is able to tightly weave the intricacies of heart and mind into the plot of her mystery story.

Roth's Inspector Medford returns in *Too Many Doctors* (1963). Other recommended titles include *The Content Assignment* (1954) and *The Crimson in the Purple* (1956).

(*K.L.M.*)

Royce, Kenneth. *The XYY Man.* New York: McKay, 1970. (A)

Who is that shadowy figure scaling the wall of the Chinese Legation? Can it be Spider Scott, newly released from Wormwood Scrubs? Doesn't he know another conviction will land him right back in prison, this time for ten years? But what if he was persuaded by British Intelligence to use his talents for Queen and country (and money)? Of course, if the Chinese catch him at it, he might well wish he *were* back in prison. For that matter, can British Intelligence be trusted? Won't they simply hand him over to the police once the job is completed? And what is the job anyway—what secret is inside the tin box he is to steal?

In this, the first of the "XYY man" series, Kenneth Royce introduces us to Spider Scott. It seems the two sex chromosomes that make up male cells are labeled X and Y. A few men, such as Spider, have an extra Y chromosome. Such men are "all more than six feet tall and predisposed to crimes against property rather than violence." In Spider's case, he dearly loves to break and enter and, of course, steal. In fact, he already has served two prison terms for doing just that. And now he is forced into a situation where he has to do it again.

These are set apart from most suspense novels by the detail Royce employs to describe the planning as well as the actual illegal entry. We can vicariously (and nervously) climb drainpipes and tiptoe through darkened houses right along with Spider.

More of Spider Scott's adventures are told in *The Concrete Boot* (1971), *The Masterpiece Affair* (1973), *The Woodcutter Operation* (1975), and *The Crypto Man* (1984). A nonseries thriller dealing with Middle Eastern oil is *10,000 Days* (1981).

(*N.D.*)

Russell, John. *The Red Mark and Other Stories.* New York: Knopf, 1919. (Also published as *Where the Pavement Ends.*) (SS)

John Russell was a master of the wry, suspenseful, and unusual tale of adventure and mystery. The best of his staggering total of 1600 published short stories, many of which are set in the South Seas, have been favorably compared to the work of Kipling and O. Henry (q.v.). No less a personage than Sir Arthur Conan Doyle called *The Red Mark,* Russell's first collection, "the best book of short tales by any debutant since Kipling's *Plain Tales";* and Ellery Queen included it on his prestigious Queen's Quorum list.

The fourteen stories here are set in such locales as New Caledonia, Borneo, Tahiti, the China Sea, New Guinea, and the Polynesian island of Fufuti. The title story tells of an ironic and grisly vengeance exacted against a cruel island convict master named M. de Nou. "The Slanted Beam" is also a revenge story, one that asks—and answers—the question "Can a dead man commit murder?" A strange and tragic triangle comprised of a missionary's daughter, a white trader, and a Polynesian "who looked most distractingly like a young woodland god" is the central theme of "The Passion-Vine." And in "The Price of the Head," probably Russell's best-known short story, the devotion of a native Melanesian named Karaki to a drunken trader, Christopher Alexander Pellett, leads to an amazing climax that involves the strange bedfellows of poetry and headshrinking.

These are marvelous tales of a vanished way of life, rich in the sights and sounds and smells of exotic ports of call of seventy-five years ago. Their clever plots, their high-quality prose, their passion, and their sympathetic treatment of "men of color" make them every bit as vital today as when they were written.

A second Russell collection, *Cops 'n Robbers* (1930), is also recommended. This one gathers thirteen crime stories with American settings, among them Russell's own favorite among all his stories, "The Man Who Was Dead," a tale of eerie horror reminiscent of W. W. Jacobs's classic "The Monkey's Paw."

(*B.P.*)

*Sadler, Mark. *The Falling Man.* New York: Random House, 1970. (PI)

No private-eye novels capture the nightmare America of the Vietnam and Nixon years like the four that Dennis Lynds wrote under the by-line Mark Sadler during the early 1970s. Hippies, environmental crusaders, heroic black militants, parents angry and bewildered at the revolt of their children, student revolutionaries, brutal cops (and a few gentle ones), corrupt politicians, rapacious capitalists, endangered trees—Sadler evokes all these figures of the Big Chill with fierce power as they are encountered by his protagonist, New York PI and ex-actor Paul Shaw.

First and best of the series is *The Falling Man,* in which Shaw unexpectedly drops in at his office late one night and surprises a young man searching his files. During their struggle, the youth falls out the window to his death, and Shaw then begins a grim hunt for the reason behind the burglary. That the boy turns out to be named Jon Calvin is sufficient tip-off that the ultimate villain will be the success-at-any-price ethic of Big Business. Murders and savage beatings punctuate the story line, and Shaw himself winds up credibly closer to death, and reacting less heroically and more humanly, than almost any other fictional PI in the same spot. Events grind to a halt all too often so that some white hat dissident can orate about the ills of our society, but few mysteries succeed so well at combining tight plot control and strong characterizations with such a shattering evocation of how the system works.

In *Here to Die* (1971), Shaw revisits his own past as a struggling young actor and steps into a caldron of racism, sexism, sadism, guerrilla theater, black power, student protest, police lawlessness, and murder in the seething California college town of San Perdido. The story line is packed with clutter, coincidence, and propaganda speeches, not to mention beatings and killings. But the scenes where hundreds of cops club and stomp peacefully protesting students, and later conduct a bloody unprovoked raid on Black Panther headquarters, are immensely powerful. Sadler has no peers at integrating the foul underside of that period into the traditional PI novel.

In *Mirror Image* (1972), Shaw messes with old-line political corruption in a New Jersey seaside resort, but this time Sadler loses control of his labyrinthine plot and the result is a chaotic mishmash redeemed in part by some fine characterizations and vivid writing. *Circle of Fire* (1973) sends Shaw back to California, into a hypocrisy-riddled lumber and tourism community in the sparsely settled north of the state, where the political hacks are in a donnybrook with environmentalists, and two people have been blown to bits with a homemade bomb. The absence of compulsive speechifying by every character in sight is delightful, but the unfair and abrupt solution leaves chunks of story line as murky as before. The vivid Sadler images of ecological concern ("The giant trees towered in the afternoon sun to the left of the highway, the light shafts soft among their straight trunks like the muted pillars of light inside some temple") are as evocative as those in the late novels of Ross Macdonald (q.v.). Paul Shaw's most recent appearance is in an elusive Raven House paperback, *Touch of Death* (1981).

(*F.M.N.*)

*Salas, Floyd. *Tattoo the Wicked Cross.* New York: Second Chance, 1981. (PS/T)

This excellent prison novel was originally published in 1967 by Grove Press and was given another round in the marketplace by Second Chance. It is a remarkable account of homosexual rape and revenge on a California juvenile prison farm. Its hero is fifteen-year-old, four-foot-ten Aaron D'Aragon, who enters the institution to find that his friend Barneyway, similarly small and vulnerable, has been reduced by a brutal homosexual named Buzzer to an object of shame, fear, and derision.

Aaron has courage and dignity, and no small amount of fighting ability, and he tries to protect his friend and talk him into trying to fend off Buzzer. Aaron scoffs at Barneyway's assertion that to struggle is useless and perhaps even suicidal, but it is only the presence of larger protectors, who admire Aaron for his gameness and boxing ability, that keeps Buzzer and his cohorts away from Aaron. Eventually Aaron loses his protectors, and finds himself almost as vulnerable as Barneyway. Except that Aaron has arranged for the means to defend himself.

Friends and family on the outside naïvely urge Aaron to stay out of trouble; events on the inside force him toward trouble and a longer prison sentence. Pressure builds. Neither of his alternatives is pleasant.

Salas doesn't sensationalize his subject, but neither does he back away from it. This is a savage novel and a work of art, a powerful, ugly, poetic, and compassionate rendering that even the squeamish should read. One of the best prison novels ever written.

(*J.L.*)

Sale, Richard. *Passing Strange.* New York: Simon & Schuster, 1942. (AD)

Richard Sale moved from a promising career in the pulps into movie work, which is a shame, because when he did write an occasional mystery novel, the result was usually quite interesting. *Passing Strange,* narrated by Dr. Peter Merritt, may be the first bicoastal mystery. The first third of the book is set in Hollywood; the setting then moves to New York for the rest of the story.

Merritt goes to the West Coast because he receives a telegram asking him to come help with his sister-in-law's difficult pregnancy. While he is there, performing a cesarean on a famous actress whose doctor is incompetent, the incompetent is shot three times while standing in the delivery room watching the operation. The killer, dressed in hospital gown and mask, escapes easily. When Merritt returns to New York, there is an attempt on his own life, and two more people connected with the case are murdered.

Some of the medical details may be dated, but *Passing Strange* remains fine entertainment. The pace is brisk, the humor often clicks, and the show-business characters are just as "right" today as they were forty years ago. Besides, how often do you read a book in which Spanish fly is a major plot device?

Sale also wrote *Lazarus #7* (1942), set entirely in Hollywood, which is as light and fast as *Passing Strange,* and which may be the only mystery novel featuring leprosy. *For the President's Eyes Only* (1971) is a rousing spy novel.

(*B.C.*)

Samson, Joan. *The Auctioneer.* New York: Simon & Schuster, 1975. (PS)

What would happen if one very powerful and charismatic personality were to take over a small country town? What if he enlisted some of the town's most influential personalities in a devious plan for his own profit? Would people resist? And if they did, what would be the result?

This is the premise of Joan Sampson's only novel, written with the help of a grant from the Radcliffe Institute (she died shortly after its publication, in 1976), and it is an intriguing and promising one. The book is well written and proceeds logically from the first frightening inklings of what is taking place to the violent denouement. But somehow it doesn't quite come off, and the failure seems to be in the characterization.

Harlowe, New Hampshire, is a picture-book town, unspoiled by the great exodus of city dwellers, simple and full of community spirit. We see the town through the eyes of a nearby farm family—John and Mim Moore; their daughter, Hildie; and John's aging mother. The Moores are people who belong to the land, who live almost Spartanly. And they are generous people: When Bob Gore, the only town cop, comes to tell them of the auctioneer who has offered to raise money for deputies by selling cast-off items collected from local residents, the Moores donate gladly; and when the demands for more and more items for more and more auctions escalate, they accede with good grace. But soon they realize that Perly Dunsmore, the auctioneer, has their friends and neighbors in a grip of terror—such a strong grip that they will give until they have no more possessions, no more livelihood. Not to give in to Perly is sure to invite disaster, they find—if not death.

All this is interesting, but the reader quickly begins to wonder about the passivity of the townspeople, particularly of the Moores, who have been characterized as strong country folks. Perhaps a few people would have knuckled under to Perly Dunsmore's demands, but an entire town? There is too little resistance; and when resistance does come, it is still too little, and much too late. There is a flatness about this novel that robs even the most dramatic scenes of what could have been raw, explosive emotion.

Nonetheless, it *is* a fascinating premise, and the portrait of the Moores and the town of Harlowe is well drawn. These are people we can care about; it is too bad they seem to care so little for themselves.

(*M.M.*)

*Sanders, Lawrence. *The First Deadly Sin.* New York: Putnam's, 1973. (PP)

The contemporary blockbuster suspense novel comes in several patterns, but one of the most popular is the urban thriller pitting a decent big-city cop with personal problems against a psychotic perpetrator who kills at random. The many recent books in this vein stem from *The First Deadly Sin.*

Brooklyn-born Lawrence Sanders was almost fifty when he gave up his career editing magazines like *Mechanix Illustrated* and *Science and Mechanics* and began writing fiction for a living. His first novel, *The Anderson Tapes* (1970), was both a best seller and a tour de force of technique, with its big-caper-gone-wrong story line presented entirely through the transcripts of illegal electronic eavesdropping by a numbing variety of police agencies. Three years later came *The First Deadly Sin,* an even bigger best seller whose success launched a subgenre of crime fiction.

One of the most imitated of the devices Sanders employed in this novel is the alternation between the viewpoints of the psycho and the cop. The random killer is Daniel Blank, well-paid junior executive for a corporation publishing *Mechanix Illustrated*-like magazines, who butchers strangers with a mountaineer's ice ax in pursuit of his passion to become a "saint of evil." His nemesis is Captain Edward X. Delaney, commander of the NYPD's 251st Precinct, a man tormented by the moral monstrosities in his city and by the incurable illness of his wife, a man as committed to simple decency as his antagonist is to existential evil. The long-drawn-out duel between the two is told in a simple but vivid style, combining strong narrative drive and characterizations with close procedural detail and occasional scenes of graphic sex and violence. Running well over 500 pages, and sagging somewhat at its Adirondack mountaintop climax, *The First Deadly Sin* paved the way for many an overblown procedural lacking the cumulative power of Sanders's style.

In *The Second Deadly Sin* (1977), Delaney comes out of retirement to handle the murder of a prominent artist whose world seems to have been full of enemies. Structured around the theme of greed as *The First* had been around the motif of pride, this sequel was more of a straightforward whodunit, as long and leisurely as its predecessor but lacking the smell of evil. *The Third Deadly Sin* (1981) is lust, or rather the sexual exploitation of women, and Delaney once again returns to active duty to hunt a woman who periodically dresses as a hooker and ritually stabs her customer to death during sex. *The Fourth Deadly Sin* (1985) deals with anger, of course, and is probably the least successful entry in the series. Only time will tell if Sanders will write a Delaney novel around each of the remaining three deadly sins—and if a 500-page thriller can be built around such vices as gluttony and sloth.

(*F.M.N.*)

Sauter, Eric. *Hunter.* New York: Avon, 1983. (O/AD)

Hunter—Robert E. Lee Hunter, to those who don't know any better—is a writer of some reputation who lives alone on an island in New Jersey with his dog, Jules. A former journalist who wrote a book on the Sixties "not so much to chronicle the age but to get it all away from me," he has bought the island in the Delaware River with his proceeds from the "terribly relevant" movie version, and now wants only peace and the chance to rebuild the porch on his house. As the novel opens, Hunter is beginning to realize he isn't about to get either.

Three weeks before, a sort of friend named Billy Rye came to see Hunter, sounding troubled. Hunter didn't pay much attention to Billy, a small-time criminal who "drifted between crime and the straight world with manic abandon." But now Billy's sometime girlfriend, Di, tells Hunter that Rye is missing and asks him to look into the disappearance. Spurred by the demands of friendship—as well as by the fact that two men have ransacked Di's apartment and beaten her in an attempt to learn Billy's whereabouts—Hunter begins his search.

It takes him to Jamie Hale, Billy's attractive female lawyer; and then to a prostitute whose address Rye has been using. Finally it leads him to Ironline, New Jersey, a strange and hostile little town where Billy was raised. And there Hunter must contend with an inimical police chief who seems intent on covering up what really happened when Billy's mother, Rose Culley, burned to death while passed out on her sofa. Before Hunter is finished, he has exposed more than one of the secrets of Ironline, a town that, he finds, takes care of its own.

Hunter is an extremely appealing character, a child of the Sixties grown up; his low-key manner masks both the cynicism and wisdom that come from leaving off outmoded ideals. Sauter plots well, and the ending of his hero's first adventure is both believable and poignant.

Subsequent Hunter novels are *Hunter and the Ikon* and *Hunter and Raven* (both 1984).

(*M.M.*)

*Sayers, Dorothy L. *Clouds of Witness.* New York: Dial Press, 1927. (CS)

One has to look to Margery Allingham and Agatha Christie (qq.v.) to find a Golden Age mystery writer comparable to Dorothy L. Sayers (she insisted on the "L"). She wrote well within the conventions of the fair-play detection story and yet achieved with her style and ingenuity an intellectually respectable novel of high literary standards. One of her greatest contributions over the course of eleven novels and many short stories was the creation of that outstanding detective Lord Peter Wimsey. Although today some view him as snobbish and frivolous, he is certainly a singular character, with all the intellectual powers and necessary eccentricities of a Great Detective. But Sayers did not merely create one fascinating character; she invented an entire world for him, peopled with such notables as his manservant Bunter, mystery writer Harriet Vane, the efficient Miss Climpson, and, of course, the Wimsey family. Each of these characters is well developed, and throughout the series of Wimsey novels we see considerable change and growth in a number of them.

The setting of *Clouds of Witness* is perfect for the aristocratic sleuth. In the North Riding of Yorkshire lies Riddlesdale, the shooting lodge of the duke of Denver. One night Lord Peter's brother, the duke, finds the body of their sister's fiancé just outside the house (a real country house). Lord Peter, with his well-bred mannerisms and gentleman's monocle, has wide range for investigation and deduction among the moors and country accents of Yorkshire. He sees his sleuthing as great fun, but at one point he faces a "choice between hanging either my brother or my sister." Of course, he opts for Truth and Right. Assisted by Detective Inspector Charles Parker (who is later promoted and eventually marries the sister, Lady Mary), Lord Peter uses his impeccable language credentials to find information in France. In his effort to save his brother, who is jailed for the murder, Lord Peter's life is endangered three times in smashing scenes of bullet, bog, and storm.

For the Golden Age, this book has a sensational sizzle of sex, nobility, danger, airplanes, bolshevism, and a stunning trial in the House of Lords (the duke must be judged by his peers).

(*T.B.*)

Sayers, Dorothy L. *Have His Carcase.* New York: Brewer Warren & Putnam, 1932. (CS)

Next to Lord Peter Wimsey, mystery writer Harriet Vane is Sayers's most interesting and complex character; and in two of the eleven Wimsey novels, this independent young woman assumes much more than a supporting role. At the beginning of *Have His Carcase,* we join Harriet on a walking trip along the southwestern coast of England. She has undertaken this journey as a sort of therapy after her murder acquittal (*Strong Poison,* 1930) and feels it to be more beneficial than leaning on Lord Peter for solace—a remedy he has repeatedly offered. (Harriet's attitude toward Wimsey is rather skeptical and rejecting at this point in the series; the gradual development of their relationship is interesting in light of the characterological change that precedes it.)

Some eight miles north of her destination at Wilvercombe, Harriet stops for lunch. While eating, she spies a solitary rock on the beach, and a man lying on it. Further investigation shows the man to be dead of a cut throat. Harriet goes for help, but also cannot resist phoning in the story to the *London Star.* The publicity brings Wimsey to her hotel at Wilvercombe; and the conflicting physical evidence in the case, plus the local police's failure to interpret it, cause Vane and Wimsey to join forces in this first mutual—although not always harmonious—investigation. This is a well-plotted mystery with a nice interplay between the two major characters.

Harriet Vane reappears as the major sleuth in *Gaudy Night* (1936), set at an Oxford college that closely resembles Sayers's alma mater, Somerville. (*M.M.*)

*Sayers, Dorothy L. *In the Teeth of the Evidence and Other Stories.* New York: Harcourt Brace, 1940. (SS/AD)

In addition to the eleven Wimsey novels, Sayers produced twenty-one short stories about the nobleman detective, two of which are reprinted in this volume. Also included are five stories about wine merchant Montague Egg, a lesser creation who fails to engage the reader's attention as Wimsey does. The other ten stories in the collection are nonseries suspense, and these are perhaps the most interesting, revealing the author's wide knowledge of various subjects and her great imaginative powers.

The best of the nonseries stories is a tale of horror, "The Cyprian Cat." A man journeys to Little Hexam in Somerset for a holiday meeting with an old friend and the friend's new wife. The man has a severe cat phobia, and on the way down, in the railroad compartment he unknowingly shares with his friend's wife, he senses the presence of a feline. At the country inn where they are staying, there also are cats, including one great striped gray-and-black tabby, a Cyprian, that slowly begins to terrorize him—until he takes extreme measures.

Commercial traveler Montague Egg, on the other hand, seldom relies on extreme measures. A bit of a plodder, it isn't his fault that unusual things occur as he is making his rounds with his wine samples. In "Falseweight," Egg arrives at the Royal Oak Inn in time to identify a corpse—a fellow salesman—and his careful attention to detail aids the police with more than just an identification. "Bitter Almonds" shows off both Egg's investigative powers and Sayers's considerable knowledge of poisons—one of her favorite murder methods. The Egg stories, while well plotted, for the most part seem to be mere exercises at the craft.

In contrast to Egg's careful logic, Wimsey's deductions shine in the title story, "In the Teeth of the Evidence," which very appropriately involves Lord Peter's dentist. And in "Absolutely Elsewhere," Wimsey assists his brother-in-law, Chief Inspector Parker of the CID, in a short but intriguing case in which all the suspects claim to have been elsewhere at the time of a wealthy bachelor's murder.

This is an excellent collection that shows the full range of Sayers's short stories, from the rather thin Egg tales to the classic sleuthing of Wimsey to expert horror stories. The Wimsey stories have been brought together in *Lord Peter: A Collection of All the Lord Peter Wimsey Stories* (1972). Other Sayers collections are *Lord Peter Views the Body* (1929), *Hangman's Holiday* (1933), *A Treasury of Sayers Stories* (1958), and *Striding Folly* (1972).

(*M.M.*)

*Sayers, Dorothy L. *Murder Must Advertise.* New York: Harcourt Brace, 1933. (CS)

Sayers herself worked in advertising for ten years, and she drew upon that background to create this fascinating and richly detailed novel of Lord Peter's undercover investigation of murder in a London ad agency. Going by the colorful alias of "Death Bredon," Wimsey joins Pym's Publicity as a copywriter, replacing an employee who died in a suspicious fall down the firm's staircase. Apparently the copywriter, Victor Dean, had noticed that there was more wrong within the firm than the usual tensions and rivalries of a creative enterprise, and soon Wimsey senses the same.

Wimsey's job is aided by the fact that he has "never in his life encountered a set of people with such active tongues and such apparent leisure for gossip" as those at Pym's. One thing he learns is that Victor Dean used to run with a fast crowd, led by the beautiful but unsavory Dian de Momerie. This group of "Bright Young People" seem far out of Dean's league, and Wimsey wonders what he was doing with them. While maintaining his false identity against the curiosity of his colleagues, Wimsey infiltrates the de

Momerie crowd by assuming a second disguise—that of a harlequin who appears unexpectedly in strange places (a tree among them). And as he comes to know this corrupt world, he begins to make a connection between the drugs they use with abandon and the strange goings-on at Pym's. But before he can ascertain what this connection is, murder is done, and a masked harlequin, widely suspected to be a man called Bredon, is the chief suspect. . . .

This is a sparkling novel in which Wimsey's chameleon personality and ability to move easily from one level of society to another are shown off to excellent advantage. Sayers's depiction of a dubious fringe of London society is particularly good, and it makes for a refreshing change from Lord Peter's usual coterie of high-toned associates.

(*M.M.*)

*Sayers, Dorothy L. *The Nine Tailors.* New York: Harcourt Brace, 1934. (CS)

Tailor Paul is one of the bells in the 128-foot tower at the parish church of Fenchurch St. Paul in the Fens of East Anglia. Tailor Paul tolls nine times for the death of a man, hence *The Nine Tailors* of Dorothy L. Sayers's tale of detection that breaks the bonds of the puzzle story to become a novel of manners. This is one of her later works that transform Lord Peter Wimsey into a real human being facing human dilemmas. The story confronts some problems of between-the-wars England and injects the randomness of real life into the plot. Lord Peter, in earlier works, was a silly-ass-sounding, foolish-looking lord, but has developed sophistication of interest and intellect. Sayers particularly developed this in the four "Harriet Vane" novels, where Lord Peter loves, woos, wins, and weds his heart's desire, all while saving her from the gallows and suspicion and spite.

Even though Sayers grew up in this corner of England, she did not use the setting of Fenchurch St. Paul for mere picturesqueness—the atmosphere is integral to both plot and theme. The campanology begins as the story opens when the traveler, Lord Peter Wimsey, is roped into nine hours of change-ringing Kent Treble Bob Majors at the church. Later the body of an unknown man with his hands cut off is found in a fresh grave in the churchyard. Lord Peter gets involved in the corpse's identity crisis, an emerald robbery of many years before, a double-cross, and a formidable cipher that furnishes indications about the loot and the death. His man Bunter, except for extracting a couple of significant clues, plays a smaller part than in some other stories. God's wrath visits a natural disaster on the Fens' drains, dykes, and sluices and provides a resolution not quite as comfortable in human terms as usual in detective stories.

This is one of the five Lord Peter dramas that the BBC televised and which were shown on Public Broadcasting's "Masterpiece Theater" in the mid-1970s.

(*T.B.*)

Scherf, Margaret. *The Beaded Banana.* New York: Doubleday Crime Club, 1978. (AD)

In tone and approach, Margaret Scherf's novels are reminiscent of a more recent trio of mysteries set in a small Montana town: those written by A. B. Guthrie, Jr. (q.v.), featuring Chick Charleston and Jason Beard. Peopled with eccentric and generally likable characters, and spiced with a wry humor, Scherf's books are competently—if a bit predictably—plotted. Scherf has created three series, two of them set against the well-detailed background of her native state of Montana. They are entertaining tales of relatively bloodless murder (even her pathologist heroine, Grace Severance, is retired, so we don't have to witness her making butterfly incisions on corpses); and they are extremely satisfying because, as Scherf herself has stated, "the central problem is soluble, unlike most of the problems in the real world." There is not a mean bone in any of her mysteries, which is no doubt one of the main reasons for their popularity, past and present.

The problem with which Dr. Grace Severance concerns herself in *The Beaded Banana* centers around the old Wooding house in the small town of Summerhill. A monstrosity in extremely bad repair, it has been donated to the town with the idea that it will be restored as a museum. The town is sharply divided on the issue, and when the body of Roscoe Moss, a former Las Vegas casino owner who has returned to his hometown to retire, turns up in a trunk at the mayor's open house at the mansion, the conflict escalates. Grace, who has attended the opening reluctantly, is determined to stay out of the matter; but as usual her curiosity gets the best of her, and soon she is sleuthing in her low-key but effective manner.

The case is complicated by the presence in town of a movie company that is filming "a very bad picture in a beautiful setting"; by continual appearances—both at Grace's house and in the attic of the town's weird lady—of a member of the company, a black man in a white fur hat; and by a missing bullet and murder weapon. One of the local state legislators claims he received a call from the murdered man warning him that the legislator and three other people were in danger—a call that was interrupted before Moss could explain why. Someone tries to run Grace off the road—in a car bearing the mayor's stolen license plate. Arson is committed. And the large beaded banana created by the black man in the fur hat ("In Hollywood this is very big. Any kind of fruit covered in beads," he explains) figures somewhere in all this. But where? And why?

Grace Severance, with her sharp wit and wry observations, is a totally likable character as well as a very able sleuth. Some other entertaining novels featuring the retired pathologist are *The Banker's Bones* (1968), *The Beautiful Birthday Cake* (1971), and *To Cache a Millionaire* (1972).

(*M.M.*)

Scherf, Margaret. *The Cautious Overshoes*. New York: Doubleday Crime Club, 1956. (AD)

The Reverend Martin Buell of the Episcopalian Christ Church in Farrington, Montana, is probably Margaret Scherf's most popular sleuth. The crusty, likable little cleric with a nose for homicide appears in six mysteries whose accent is on folksy humor and on detection of a sort that puts few demands on either Father Buell or the reader.

Set in icy February, *The Cautious Overshoes* begins with Diana Castlemain asking the reverend, who is about to leave for a bishops' meeting in Helena, to make inquiries about the whereabouts of her brother, Dean, who has mysteriously disappeared. Dean, it seems, has been in trouble in the past and Diana is afraid that he has again got himself mixed up with the wrong people. It is Buell who first makes the connection between the missing Dean and the unidentified corpse of a young man found inside a freight car, dead of gas fumes from a charcoal burner used to keep produce from perishing at subzero temperatures. The man's features have been burned beyond recognition, but fingerprints identify him as Dean Castlemain.

Buell pokes around in his quiet way and uncovers some odd relationships among such principals as politically powerful Pink Kelly; Pink's wife, Amy, who is "devoted to slot machines and twenty-one," and who also likes to "get up at five in the morning and do a washing, and then tell people all day long that she had got up at five and done a washing"; Harvey McLaren, owner of the local general store, who looks like a wistful robin; Sam Gorham, a young lawyer addicted to ties with trout painted on them; and Diana's fiancé and Farrington's leading entrepreneur, the unfortunately named Gregory Snade. Eventually Buell also uncovers a large-scale swindle and, with the aid of a pair of overshoes, the identity of the person behind both the swindle and the murder of Dean Castlemain.

The central appeal here is the interplay among the characters, which at times overshadows the mystery elements. Most of them are nice country folk; even the villains aren't such bad people at heart. Father Buell, whose occasional uncharitable comments and attitudes make him very human indeed, is especially appealing, both as a person and as a detective.

Other novels featuring Martin Buell are *Gilbert's Last Toothache* (1949), *The Curious Custard Pie* (1950), *The Elk and the Evidence* (1952), *Never Turn Your Back* (1959), and *The Corpse in the Flannel Nightgown* (1965). Scherf's third series is not set in her home state, but in New York City, where she worked for several years; this one features a husband-and-wife team of decorators and amateur sleuths, Emily and Henry Bryce, who star in five books, among them *The Gun in Daniel Webster's Bust* (1949) and *The Diplomat and the Gold Piano* (1963). Scherf has also published a number of nonseries mysteries, notably *The Corpse Grows a Beard* (1940), *The Case of the Kippered Corpse* (1941), *Dead: Senate Office Building* (1953), and *Don't Wake Me Up While I'm Driving* (1977), the last being an all-out boozy farce set in North Dakota during Prohibition.

(*B.P.*)

Schorr, Mark. *Red Diamond: Private Eye.* New York: St. Martin's, 1983. (PI)

Simon Jaffe is a New York cabby. And as is natural with anyone who contends daily with the traffic on Manhattan's streets, he teeters on the edge of sanity. The only thing reinforcing those tenuous links with reality, in fact, is his hobby—a collection of pulp magazines that he reads and rereads in the basement of his home. *Black Mask, Spicy Detective, Dime Detective*—these are Simon's safety valves. That is, until the day his wife sells them, receiving $2300 "for all that crap."

Simon doesn't go around the bend all at once; but as he cruises the city streets, he slips more and more into the persona of his favorite fictional private eye, Red Diamond. And the more time he spends as Red, the more important it becomes to find the object of Red's affection—the gorgeous Fifi LaRoche, who is on the run from the evil Rocco Rico. . . .

Mark Schorr has painted a convincing and satiric portrait of a man sinking into madness, through skillful interweaving of scenes from reality and scenes from Simon's life as Red. And it is not the reader's fault if, after fifty pages or so of this delightful novel, he himself begins to wonder what is real and what is not. Those who manage to keep some of their wits about them will wonder how on earth the author is going to extricate his hero from this dreadful mess. Without giving that neat trick away, suffice it to say that Red Diamond appears unscathed in *Ace of Diamonds* (1984) and *Diamond Rock* (1985).

(*M.M.*)

Scott, Jack S. *The Poor Old Lady's Dead.* New York: Harper, 1976. (PP)

This first novel by Jack S. Scott (a pseudonym of Jonathan Escott) presents an old folks' home of rather macabre proportions and introduces the likable detective team of Sergeant Howes and his superior, Detective Inspector Rosher. When the poor lady of the book's title, a Mrs. Baddow, dies at the Haven from an apparent fall down some stairs, it seems at first to be an accidental death. But the investigation of Howes and Rosher alters from routine to probing when a check of police files reveals that "two other old girls have snuffed it up there. One five years ago. Found dead, gas fire on. Bedroom. Verdict: Accidental death. One two years ago—fall downstairs. Same stairs. Verdict: Accidental death."

If the deaths of the three old women constitute some sort of murder conspiracy, who is responsible? And why? Trying to get answers out of the suspicious and frightened elderly residents of the Haven is no easy task, as Howes finds out.

The Poor Old Lady's Dead is a suspenseful and unusual procedural whodunit, marked by excellent characterization (though some of the characters are vile) and a soundly constructed plot with a nice surprise at its climax. Howes and Rosher are a compelling pair of detectives—Howes in particular; the sergeant's personal problems—he is a happily married man with a pregnant girlfriend—make him intensely human, if not wholly sympathetic.

The two detectives reappear in several other novels, among them *The Shallow Grave* (1977), *A Clutch of Vipers* (1979), *The Gospel Lamb* (1980), *The Local Lads* (1983), and *A Death in Irish Town* (1985).

(*G.K./B.P.*)

Scott, Justin. *The Shipkiller*. New York: Dial, 1978. (A/T)

Justin Scott, the son of western pulp writer Bradford Scott, began his career by writing humorous caper novels such as *Treasure for Treasure* (1974) under his own name, and a pair featuring "retired" (at age twenty-seven) hash dealer Donald Bracken under the pseudonym J. S. Blazer, *Deal Me Out* (1973) and *Lend a Hand* (1975), which are so imitative of the work of Donald Westlake (q.v.) that they can be termed pastiche. Later, however, he developed his own style and approach and applied them to the large-scale novel of suspense and adventure. *The Shipkiller* was his first book of this type, and so well done that it became a modest best seller.

This powerful story of vengeance begins when Carolyn and Peter Hardin are sailing their ketch *Siren* off the coast of Normandy. A squall brings disaster: Out of the rain comes a monstrous Liberian supertanker, *Leviathan,* which collides with the *Siren* and sinks it. Peter manages to survive both the collision and his ordeal in the raging seas; Carolyn doesn't. His life shattered, Peter Hardin now exists for only one purpose: to wreak vengeance on the *Leviathan* and her master—symbols of the gigantic, mindless forces that can blithely crush the individual and escape unpunished. Hardin's quest for justice against overwhelming odds leads him from England to the South Atlantic to the Persian Gulf, and makes for fascinating reading. The various backgrounds are decribed in exquisite detail, with numerous glimpses and insights into oil politics and supertanker logistics.

Also recommended is Justin Scott's second major novel, *A Pride of Royals* (1983)—a World War I espionage thriller featuring an expert blend of historical and fictional characters and incidents.

(*G.K/B.P.*)

Seeley, Mabel. *The Listening House.* New York: Doubleday Crime Club, 1938. (R)

Mystery historian Howard Haycraft once called Mabel Seeley the "White Hope" of the "American-feminine detective story." For good reason. It was Minnesota-born Seeley who brought a gritty realism to the generally reviled "had-I-but-known" school long associated with Mary Roberts Rinehart (q.v.). Seeley accomplished this by presenting believable working women as protagonists and by basing horrific mysteries in the reality of everyday life.

The Listening House, Seeley's first novel, well represents her fresh approach to traditional material. Divorcée Gwynne Dacres, unjustly fired from her advertising job, is forced to economize by taking furnished rooms in a slightly seedy mansion. Strange things seem to happen in and around this creaking boardinghouse owned by a malevolent old crone. When this old woman disappears and is eventually discovered murdered (in a scene that will curl the toes of many a reader), the danger turns on Gwynne.

While Seeley utilized themes and plot elements associated with Gothic and horror fiction, *The Listening House* is also a play-fair mystery novel with the detecting handled by the heroine and a wiseacre fellow tenant, as well as the police. The murder is linked, not surprisingly, with the secrets and corruption of the past. And what a past! Seeley touches on everything from blackmail to white slavery, with a secret treasure thrown in for good measure. And she somehow manages to make it all believable.

Seeley's intelligent and gutsy career women sometimes walk into danger, but never with the kind of ditsy abandon found in most had-I-but-known fiction. They may find romance by book's end, but never through mindless surrender. Seeley's characters and stories, like *The Chuckling Fingers* (1941) and *The Beckoning Door* (1950), remain as "modern" and suspenseful today as when they were written.

(*K.L.M.*)

Sela, Owen. *An Exchange of Eagles.* New York: Pantheon, 1977. (A)

An Exchange of Eagles is Owen Sela's best book. It features a fantastic political conspiracy called Double Eagle that takes place in 1940, shortly after Roosevelt's reelection.

Two men, Paul van Osten of Germany's secret Abwehr and Max Schroeder of U.S. Army Intelligence G2 (C), meet to propose an incredible agreement for peace: the double assassination of Hitler and Roosevelt to halt the momentum toward World War II. As the plans for the double assassination go forward, American agent David Stannard is smuggled into Nazi Germany to observe the preparations for Hitler's death. But elements in the German and British intelligence services already are investigating Double Eagle, and Stannard finds himself an active participant in the attempt to assassinate Hitler. The twin plots twist and turn until the novel's explosive conclusion. *An Exchange of Eagles* is a top-notch thriller.

Owen Sela has written several high-quality thrillers. His first novel, *The Bearer Plot* (1972), reflects his knowledge of international finance. (Sela is a chartered accountant with a London accounting firm; originally from Ceylon, he now divides his time between writing and his accounting practice in London.) His latest novel, *The Kremlin Control* (1984), features a KGB officer who investigates the strange death of a Russian general and a secret plot that could lead to World War III.

(*G.K.*)

Serafin, David. *Madrid Underground.* New York: St. Martin's, 1984. (PP)

Police-procedural novels about American cities like Los Angeles and New York are fairly common. Police stories about foreign capitals are not. The wife-and-husband team of Sjöwall and Wahlöö (q.v.) created an important series of police mysteries focusing on changes in Swedish society, as well as in the life of their police protagonist. It could be said that David Serafin is creating a similar series about Spain and his Superintendent Luis Bernal of Madrid's Brigada Criminal.

Madrid Underground is the third Bernal mystery. Ostensibly, it is a mystery about a serial killer who leaves his victims (whole or in parts) on subway trains. Bernal and his group must stop the psychopath before the whole city panics. The novel recounts their careful and methodical investigation of the sensational killings in a highly unsensational, almost reportorial style.

Beyond this, Serafin also observes the emotional and political climate of Spain in 1977 as the country struggled toward democracy after the death of Generalissimo Franco. He does this with quiet care and some insight. Serafin's novels go beyond the basic police mystery, and Luis Bernal is a more complex figure than your run-of-the-mill police detective. The two earlier Bernal novels are *Saturday of Glory* (1981) and *Christmas Rising* (1982). The fourth in the series is *The Body in Cadiz Bay* (1985).

(*K.L.M.*)

Shannon, Dell. *No Holiday for Crime.* New York: Morrow, 1973. (PP)

Dell Shannon—a pseudonym of Elizabeth Linington (q.v.), who also writes as Lesley Egan (q.v.)—has been referred to in all three incarnations as "the Queen of the Procedurals." Rightly so: The Shannon books about Lieutenant Luis Mendoza of the Los Angeles Police Department are one of three series of procedurals the author has created. They are also the most popular, and this is directly owing to the characters of Mendoza and his colleagues at Parker Center. Shannon spices her tales of police routine with intimate details about the lives of her policemen, and these details keep her readers coming back book after book.

In *No Holiday for Crime* we encounter Mendoza on Christmas Eve. The lieutenant is definitely not your average Chicano (nor your average policeman); he is a dapper man who drives a Ferrari and has a wife, twin children, a faithful housekeeper, an assortment of cats (including one who drinks whiskey), and an old English sheepdog named Cedric. On this night he is concerned with the usual variety of cases. Central Headquarters of the LAPD has just merged Robbery and Homicide; thus, the detectives must deal with a series of liquor-truck hijackings, a rash of burglaries, a teenage drug overdose, a hit-and-run fatality, and a couple of service-station holdups. Crime, Mendoza reminds himself, takes no holidays, and neither do the detectives on his squad.

Shannon does manage to give us a glimpse into their personal holidays, however: On Christmas Eve we go home with all the principals and learn about their lives and families. Then it's business as usual: the baffling case of a young Mormon girl who was strangled while waiting for a bus in Los Angeles.

Lila Askell had been living in Santa Barbara, but had decided to return to her close-knit family in Salt Lake City. She knew no one in L.A., but the morally upright and reserved girl apparently got into a car with someone, who strangled her and dumped her body. Mendoza and colleagues dig into her past and begin to wonder if she *did* know someone local after all; if not, why is her roommate's boyfriend in Santa Barbara so nervous? Then there is the black man who raped a wealthy woman and shot her husband. It seems an isolated incident, but soon he seems to strike again. . . .

Marred only by an excess of dialogue, too little action, and what some readers may find to be an extremely elitist and conservative view of contemporary society, these procedurals are nevertheless accurate and fully engage one's interest.

(*M.M.*)

Shannon, Dell. *Streets of Death.* New York: Morrow, 1976. (PP)

The chief problem facing the LAPD Robbery and Homicide Squad in this novel is an intriguing one: Edwin Fleming, paralyzed and confined to a wheelchair, has disappeared from his second-floor apartment while his wife was at work. Or so Marta, the wife and a homesick German national, claims. Luis Mendoza and his colleague Nick Galleano wonder about the story; it seems an impossible disappearance, and surely the overworked, lonely young wife had reason to want to be rid of her burdensome husband. With no leads, they set out to prove Marta has a boyfriend who assisted her in doing away with Edwin. But no boyfriend materializes, and Nick Galleano—up until now a confirmed bachelor—finds himself drawn to Marta.

Of course, there are the routine cases—if anything the LAPD Robbery/Homicide Squad handles can be called routine. Three young men—referred to as "pretty boys"—have been attacking senior citizens. A rapist is on the loose; and from all descriptions, he can't be more than fifteen. A young runaway is murdered, and the friend she ran away with got a good look at the probable killer. A young girl is a suicide, apparently after an overdose—not of drugs but of reading material about spiritualism, which convinced her to join relatives in the next world. A priest has been murdered, his crucifix stolen. And then there is the old man who claims he overheard a tenant of his building conspiring with a girlfriend to murder his own mother. The old man claims he heard this when they were talking with the apartment door open, but no one on the squad believes *that.* People don't plot murder so anyone in the hall can hear; the old man must be making it up—or is he?

Again, Shannon deftly interweaves personal information with this mélange of cases: Mendoza's wife, Alison, is expecting another child; morning sickness is taking a toll on their happy home. And at the end, she employs a clever device (which is also used in the other Mendoza novels): throwing out a teaser about a case that has just come up, the squad's next "offbeat one."

Shannon has been praised for her solid depiction of modern police work, and this praise is well deserved. The personal vignettes are a sort of glue that binds the various cases together, and the major crimes keep the reader turning the pages until the last arrest is made. A major problem with this series is that the men and women of the Robbery/Homicide Squad are too idealized; none has a drinking problem or suffers from ulcers or emotional ailments (all of which are common with real working cops, as shown in the extremely realistic work of Joseph Wambaugh, q.v.); the biggest problem any of them has, in fact, is making time for the family or a date.

Nevertheless, this is a good series, which, if the cops had typical human flaws, might rank with the Eighty-seventh Precinct series of Ed McBain (q.v.). Other representational titles include *Case Pending* (1960), *Root of All Evil* (1966), *Appearances of Death* (1978), *Exploit of Death* (1983), *Destiny of Death* (1984), and *Chaos of Crime* (1985).

(*M.M.*)

* Shattuck, Richard. *The Wedding Guest Sat on a Stone.* New York: Morrow, 1940. (C/W)

What a wedding night! Sue and Ty Grant have been married at La Cucaracha (!), a desert resort belonging to a friend, and after numerous delays, are about to partake of connubial bliss when Sue blunders into the wrong room, whips off her frothy white negligee—and crawls into bed with a corpse.

The corpse is Macy Turner, nobody's favorite man; he has been killed with a bayonet and is lying in his wife's brother's bed. Nobody wants to believe that Whitney Blake killed his brother-in-law (in fact, nobody would blame him very much if he *had*), so Sue and Ty conspire with others who appear on the scene to get rid of the body. Resort owner Millie Westover is pressed into removing the evidence from the scene, while two of the regulars, Beppo and Butterball, aid Ty in removing the corpse. At first they plan to dump it behind "the half breed's saloon" in nearby Alkili Junction, where a lot of bodies end up. But when they deposit Macy's remains there, White Skin, the saloon owner, catches them and orders its removal. (He later posts a sign reading, "No Dumping of Dead Bodies Allowed Here.") The trio now have a real problem on their hands, until they remember the walk-in freezer at La Cucaracha.

With Macy on ice, the conspirators devote their time to investigating who really did kill him. Suspects abound: Macy's wife, Enid, who reportedly married him for his money; Duncan, known familiarly as "Dunk," a Scotsman who was raised in England ("My father hated the British, so he moved to London so he could hate them harder") and has never gotten the hang of a Scotch burr; Jack Smith, masseuse at the hotel, who has a "vocabulary dirtier than the Augean stables"; Cedric Jones, a dude-ranch operator who can "find nothing in common with a horse"; and Jessup James, a rich former actor "too bad for Hollywood even fifteen years ago, when it was pretty rank itself." With such material to work with, the conspirators sneak around and snoop, formulating theories that are sometimes hilarious, dragging poor Macy's corpse all over so they can "accuse" the suspects with it, and in general bumbling and bungling—until, surprisingly, they nab their murderer.

This is a wonderfully amusing book, with rich, bawdy (for its time) humor and unforgettable characters. A must for anyone who likes humor mixed with his homicide.

Shattuck (whose real name is Dora Richards Shattuck) is the author of three other entertaining and amusing novels: *The Snark Was a Boojum*

(1941), *Said the Spider to the Fly* (1944), and *The Half-Haunted Saloon* (1945). Under her own name, she published a Gothic mystery, *The Wailing Woman,* in 1973.

(*M.M.*)

Sheldon, Walter J. *Rites of Murder.* New York: St. Martin's, 1984. (AD)

This novel introduces Bishop Paul Burdock of the Catholic archdiocese of Washington, D.C. Burdock is the latest in a spate of clerical sleuths—a subgenre that has its roots in G. K. Chesterton's (q.v.) Father Brown stories, and whose more recent members include Harry Kemelman's Rabbi David Small, William X. Kienzle's Father Robert Koesler, Margaret Scherf's Reverend Martin Buell, and Charles Merrill Smith's Reverend Randollph (qq.v.). A talented fundraiser, Bishop Burdock has been brought to the nation's capital because of his ability to wring contributions from the tight fists of the rich and powerful. He enjoys his work and the famous people he meets, but that doesn't keep him from caring equally for the most lowly or sinful of his parishioners. And it is the death of one of these sinners—high-priced call girl Laureen Triplett—that involves him in his first adventure.

Laureen is found garroted in a park in a seedy section of the city. When Bishop Burdock hears of the murder, he remembers her as the parishioner who asked him to help her get her daughter into a convent school where the girl had been rejected because of Laureen's profession. Now Burdock wonders about the little girl, Alicia; as an orphan, she will be forced to leave the school and go to an orphanage. The ideal solution, Burdock thinks, is to have the child adopted, perhaps by her natural father. So, after conferring with her, he sets out to locate someone willing to take Alicia in.

His quest puts him in contact with men at opposite ends of the political spectrum: Alicia's "uncle," Major General Harry Dillard, the head of a paramilitary organization known as the Freedom Militia, which assists the local police forces in times of emergency; and lawyer Sam Cable, who is affiliated with the Federation for American Institutional Reform, a liberal organization similar to the ACLU. Both men deny paternity of Alicia, and neither is particularly interested in helping her out. And as Burdock sandwiches his attempts to do something for the child between his fund-raising activities, two more women are killed in much the same fashion as Laureen Triplett. To the surprise of no one—including the archbishop of Washington, who decries Burdock's methods as "unorthodox, unconventional"—he is soon deep into a most unholy investigation, which leads to a final confrontation in which there is no way he can turn the other cheek.

Burdock is one of the more appealing clerical detectives to come along in recent years. He is a gentle man who collects mystery novels, books on true crime, and jazz records, and treasures the spare moments when he can play his beloved piano; but he is also capable of relentless pursuit of the truth.

Sheldon is a veteran author of such paperback originals as *The Blue Kimono Kill* (1965), set in Tokyo; *The Red Flower Kill* (1971), set in Thailand; *Gold Bait* (1973), set in Korea; and *The Yellow Music Kill* (1974), which takes place in China.

(*M.M.*)

Sherburne, James. *Death's Clenched Fist.* Boston: Houghton Mifflin, 1982. (H/AD)

Death's Clenched Fist is (evidently) the last of three madcap mysteries by historical novelist James Sherburne, all of which are set in the Gay Nineties and all of which feature Paddy Moretti, a half Irish, half Italian reporter for the New York sporting newspaper the *Spirit of the Times.*

Paddy is forever getting into trouble of the damnedest sort. In this case it starts when he gets thrown out of McSorley's Saloon for the heinous crime of smuggling a woman into that all-male bastion. Barred from his favorite wateringhole for six weeks, Paddy drifts to a Bowery bar called Zum Groben Michel (Tough Mike's, to the local cops), where he gets mixed up with a bunch of anarchist revolutionaries led by zealous (and sexy) Marya Perlman. Marya's crowd is adept with bombs; so when Tammany Hall politician Tim Kanady, an avowed antiradical, is blown up in his office by a box of booby-trapped cigars, the anarchists are the chief suspects. But Paddy isn't so sure. He thinks Kanady's death may be connected to the strange circumstances surrounding a racehorse named Bonnycastle, owned by rich sportsman Harrison Cobb. Not to mention a luxurious, anything-goes whorehouse called "The Circus," the domain of a sinister sort named Axel Klepp.

Paddy's wild adventures include a decidedly unromantic affair with Marya, fun and games at a May Day rally in Union Square, some lifesaving assistance from his uncle Paolo (who happens to be a Mafia don), a visit to the Velvet Room at Crapaud's (a "velvet room" being a dark, quiet place where a drunk can "finish off the night" with a bowl of straight alcohol for a quarter—if he isn't mugged and murdered first), and a most harrowing experience in the depths of The Circus.

The mystery here is fairly predictable, but that doesn't matter a whit. The novel's appeal is in its delightful characters, its sophisticated and amusing prose, and especially in its minutely detailed look at life, lust, and corruption in the Big Apple in the 1890s. Recommended to anyone who enjoys historical mysteries and/or mysteries that are just plain fun.

Likewise recommended are the other two Paddy Moretti adventures—*Death's Pale Horse* (1980), in which he solves a horse-racing/crooked gambling/confidence game/spiritualism conundrum at Saratoga Springs; and

Death's Gray Angel (1981), in which our intrepid hero travels to Cogswell, Kansas, to cover a boxing match and finds himself involved with, among other characters, Sidewinder Sam Sallee and Warren Quarles, the Confederate Angel of Death.

(*B.P.*)

Sheridan, Juanita. *The Chinese Chop.* New York: Doubleday Crime Club, 1949. (AD)

Except for Charlie Chan and Mr. Moto, Asian detectives are unusual. "Yellow menace" stories of Chinese as thugs or villainous masterminds are much more common. An Asian *woman* sleuth is rare in the extreme. This is Juanita Sheridan's accomplishment in her entertaining series following the exploits of Lily Wu and her "Watson," roommate, and "foster sister," Janice Cameron.

As *The Chinese Chop* opens, Janice, the narrator, has just moved to New York from her native Hawaii to start a new life. The postwar housing crisis frustrates her ambitious plans until a young Chinese woman she had known slightly in Honolulu offers to share a room she has just found in a Greenwich Village mansion turned rooming house.

Mysterious attacks made against members of the household culminate in the torture and murder of the new building super. The plodding police investigate, but it is Lily who does the most successful detecting. Lily plays the fragile and obsequious China doll only for effect; Janice recognizes early on that her petite roommate is as "strong as steel" and possesses an indomitable spirit.

Sheridan portrayed people of various ethnic groups in an amazingly unstereotypical and believable fashion, and managed to take a few subtle jabs at prejudice against Asians and Italians in this readable mystery of past crimes and family honor.

Lily and Janice solved their later cases in Hawaii—a locale with which Sheridan was obviously familiar. They appear in *The Kahuna Killer* (1951), *The Mamo Murders* (1952), and *The Waikiki Widow* (1953). An earlier novel coauthored with Dorothy Dudley, *What Dark Secret* (1943), features a prototype of Lily, a Chinese-Hawaiian reporter with the Anglo name of Angie Tudor.

(*K.L.M.*)

Shimer, R. S. *Squaw Point.* New York: Harper, 1972. (T/W/R)

There have been remarkably few crime novels set in Alaska, no doubt because few crime novelists have had the opportunity to visit America's last (and still remote) frontier. (A large number of outdoor adventure novels, on the other hand, have Alaska settings, notably those by Jack London, Rex Beach, and an undeservedly obscure writer, Robert Ormond Case, whose books about a flier named Ravenhill are vivid depictions of the Alaska wilderness in the 1930s.) Of the few mysteries based there, the only ones of note are a trio of whodunits by Eunice Mays Boyd—*Murder Breaks Trail* (1943), *Doom in the Midnight Sun* (1944), and *Murder Wears Mukluks* (1945)—set in Fairbanks and environs and featuring storekeeper and amateur sleuth F. Willard Smyth; Alistair MacLean's (q.v.) 1980 tale of intrigue involving the Alaska pipeline, *Athabasca;* and R. S. Shimer's first and only novel, *Squaw Point.*

The recipient of a Best First Novel Edgar, *Squaw Point* is remarkable for its portrait of Alaskan island life. If you have a penchant for mysteries with strong local color, this evocative portrayal of the stark, powerful beauty of the Aleutian Islands (where Shimer and her husband once taught school) is worth searching out. It is not a typical whodunit; indeed, its mystery elements are secondary to the setting and seem unimportant compared to the terror and awe provoked by a dirty Alaskan "blow" that forms the centerpiece of the book, an event introduced by this passage: "The sea was what the people on Nuga called 'flat cum.' There wasn't a ripple. The water was a sheet of slate, a smooth mill pond, a glass promise, an Alaskan deception. Seamen worried about that kind of sea." With the arrival of the black-striped clouds and shrieking winds, the death on Nuga Island of Skookum Jack, partner of the (locally) legendary smuggler Miro Tokin, and the murder on Squaw Point of a greedy victimizing missionary become relatively small matters.

In the eye of both natural and human tempests is Gusti Lundt, a schoolteacher transplanted from a working-class neighborhood in Seattle. She came to Nuga Island to teach and learned to love this world where children use anemone blossoms for fish lures and a woman "could be single and unashamed of the fact." Now Gusti is being forced to leave Nuga because there are no longer enough schoolchildren to justify the government's paying her salary. She hitches a final ride off the island on a fishing boat, and inadvertently aids the Coast Guard's discovery of stolen seal pelts on board Miro Tokin's boat. What follows is the storm, wreaking havoc on Marshal Walter Loman's hunt for the murderer and Miro's game with the Coast Guard, yet also helping to bring romance into Gusti's life, in the person of Coast Guard ensign Nels Borgeson.

Yet the plot never stops taking a back seat to the islands and their way of life: blueberries and smoked salmon; gossipy schoolteachers and earnest archaeologists; women as prizes and prostitutes; sailors and cannery workers; rollicking dances and crackling radio telephones; loneliness and beauty and the awesome forces of nature. *Squaw Point* is an elegy of Alaska caught in a seine of smuggling and murder.

(*B.F./B.P.*)

Short, Christopher. *The Big Cat.* New York: Dodd, Mead, 1965. (C/T)

The Big Cat is a malevolent deity who has singled out blocked writer Bill Grant "as a particularly desirable prey." It is thoroughly evil, capable of assuming any one of an infinite number of disguises, and so powerful it is certain to get him in the end. This reasoning allows Grant to work seriously on drinking himself to death, since if the Big Cat is going to win, nothing really matters—does it?

One sweltering Sunday Grant is sitting in his Manhattan apartment drinking rye when he spots a girl in a hotel room opposite taking her clothes off. He continues to watch because "There is obviously only one reason for being a Peeping Tom and spying on a girl while she is undressing. The reason is, of course, sex, which, the Puritans notwithstanding, is a pleasant thing." What he witnesses is not so pleasant or sexy, however; a man with a gun enters the room, forces the girl to dress, and abducts her. Soon Grant is lurching down the sidewalk to pull off a successful rescue that only a drunk could manage.

Later, in one of his favorite bars, he learns that the girl, Marcia Fontaine (which Grant rightly assumes is a false name), has been a witness to a gang murder in a barbershop where she has been working as a manicurist. She is to testify at the trial of the hood who has been set up to take the rap for the killing—but she intends to testify that he didn't do it. The mob knows this, hence the abduction. Grant tries to get her police protection, but the cops don't believe either of them. And later, at his apartment, the rest of the story comes out: She is really Marcia Denfield; her father, Paul, is attorney general of Massachusetts, and he has disappeared while working on an investigation of the self-same mob; she has come to New York to find him. Grant decides to help her and lurches forth once more (while Marcia remains in his apartment, finding booze everywhere, including in the Listerine bottle).

Grant's forays take him to a tonsorial parlor full of cocaine-addicted barbers; to an apartment where a bovine hood is playing gin rummy with a naked girl; and to a murderous encounter with this same gangster, who proves to be "really a very stupid man." And finally Grant ends up in proper Boston, where he discovers some very improper things indeed. Grant's tale has a "story-book ending which . . . would appeal to the most moralizing fairy-tale spinners"—but not until he has a final confrontation with his old nemesis, the Big Cat.

This is a very funny book that utilizes an unusual and successful combination of wry humor and psychological depth. Short, an Englishman, has done an excellent job of capturing the atmosphere in both Boston and New York in a blistering late-summer heat wave. Among his other novels are

Dark Lantern (1961), which is set in Germany; *The Black Room* (1966), a historical that takes place in Germany in 1892; and *The Blue-Eyed Boy* (1966), a thriller based in a small southern town. Short also ghostwrote the Leslie Charteris (q.v.) novel *The Saint and the Hapsburg Necklace* (1976).

(*M.M.*)

Silver, Victoria. *Death of a Harvard Freshman.* New York: Bantam, 1984. (O/AD)

How easy can it be to write a literate, very adult murder mystery in which none of the major characters is even old enough to drink? Not very, surely—and yet Victoria Silver pulls it off in fine style, without the slightest hint of Nancy Drewism. Her sleuth, Lauren Adler, is completely believable as a freshman—youthful in her outlook, frequently frivolous in her thoughts, but intelligent and resourceful rather than silly and girlish.

When Lauren gets bored in her seminar on the Russian Revolution, she amuses herself by ranking her professor and fellow students as to personal attractiveness. Black, brilliant Russell Bernard is also most beautiful, Lauren decides; she's understandably delighted when he asks her for a date and disappointed when he apparently stands her up.

Dejected, she goes back to her dorm and learns the reason he didn't show up—he's been murdered. The police suspect a common mugger; yet Russell's death is so similar to that of Rasputin, recently covered in her seminar, that Lauren is convinced the murderer is one of her classmates. Recruiting her gay friend Michael Hunt, she sets out to investigate. The solution is just right—and so, for that matter, is every sentence and every word of this thoroughly satisfying book.

(*J.S.*)

*Simenon, Georges. *The Strange Case of Peter the Lett.* New York: Covici Friede, 1931. (Current translation: *Maigret and the Enigmatic Lett.* London and New York: Penguin pb, 1963.) (CS)

Commissaire Jules Maigret is to French crime fiction what Sherlock Holmes is to British: *the* detective, the immortal. He has appeared in more than seventy novels and countless short stories and novelettes, translated into dozens of languages and turning their author, Belgian-born Georges Simenon, into not only the most famous of European novelists but the wealthiest.

In a very real sense, however, the Maigrets aren't mystery fiction at all.

They contain no clues and deductions and usually only the barest minimum of plot. The great-hearted bear of an inspector does not reason from data; instead, he enters a milieu, walks around in the rain, patiently sucks on his pipe, stops in the local brasserie for a beer or calvados, mingles with the people and absorbs atmosphere until he is so much at one with his environment that the truth is clear to him. Simenon's great strengths as a writer lie in the domains of character and setting.

Already wealthy from the hundreds of books he wrote in the Twenties, Simenon created Maigret in 1929 while his bark *Ostrogoth* on which he was touring the canals of Europe was laid up for repairs at the Dutch port of Delfzijl. The town has since erected a statue of Maigret to commemorate the occasion. He wrote a Maigret a month for the next year and a half.

Those first eighteen Maigrets are ranked by many connoisseurs as the finest Simenon ever wrote, although the first two are in some ways untypical. In *The Strange Case of Peter the Lett,* the first Maigret to be written, Simenon borrows from contemporary British thrillers to such an extent that his first London publishers promoted him as the Edgar Wallace of France. Maigret's adversary in this debut novel is a chameleonlike mastermind with several identities and a wild scheme to organize the international gangster community. But Simenon uses this plot as he uses the domestic intrigues in his more typical Maigrets—as a screen on which to project the shadow play of character and atmosphere. And even in his first Maigret, he draws people and milieu with breathtaking skill—from a tormented Latvian intellectual to a passionate female derelict, and from a snobbish Paris luxury hotel to a squalid fishing village.

More in the Maigret mainstream is *M. Gallet Décédé* (1931). (Its first English translation was as *The Death of Monsieur Gallet,* Covici Friede, 1932, and Penguin has kept it in print for more than twenty years as *Maigret Stonewalled.*) Here as usual the inspector probes a crime of private nature, the strange death and even stranger life of a *petit bourgeois* jewelry salesman who seems—like many of Simenon's most compelling characters—to have had at least two identities. Unlike most Maigrets, this one is modeled on the British deductive puzzles of the Golden Age, with a beautifully dovetailed plot, genuine clues, and a noble surprise ending.

Though filtered through translations that are sometimes terrible, Simenon's evocations of sight and sound and smell and feel bring places to life with such immediacy that readers who have never been to Europe are ready to swear they've seen the milieus he describes. The same skills vivify the shorter Maigrets that Simenon wrote for French magazines in the middle and late 1930s. Two generous selections of these stories and novelettes are available in the collections *Maigret's Christmas* (1977) and *Maigret's Pipe* (1968).

(*F.M.N.*)

Simenon, Georges. *Maigret's Boyhood Friend.* New York: Harcourt Brace, 1970. (CS)

Between 1933 and the end of World War II, Simenon all but abandoned Maigret and devoted himself to writing the grim social and psychological novels on which rests much of his critical reputation as a serious author. After moving to the United States in 1946, he revived his immortal character; and until ill health forced him to stop writing fiction in 1972, he turned out from two to four books a year about the great inspector. Like the earlier cycle of Maigrets, these, too, stress character and milieu over plot. What lingers in the memory is the sense of place: the sunny island of Porquerolles in *The Methods of Maigret* (1957); the seedy nightclubs of *Inspector Maigret and the Strangled Stripper* (1954); the world of young Nouvelle Vague filmmakers in *Maigret's Pickpocket* (1968) and of dissaffected Sorbonne students in *Maigret and the Killer* (1971).

Typical of the late Maigrets and better than many is *Maigret Hesitates* (1970), in which an anonymous letter warning of a future murder brings the inspector into the household of a brilliant Paris maritime lawyer who is haunted by the legal concept of criminal insanity. The plot is simple as ever, but the sense of place is so vivid and the characterizations so rich (especially the haunted Parendon and his monstrous wife, a domestic pair that reflect the shattering of Simenon's second marriage) that the book simply runs rings around most conventional detective novels.

That novel was followed both in France and the English-speaking world by *Maigret's Boyhood Friend.* The boyhood friend of the title is Florentin, a small-time hustler and habitual liar, who runs sniveling to Maigret for help when the woman who had been supporting him while being financed by four other lovers is shot to death in her apartment. Declining to arrest the dissolute and insufferable Florentin even though all the evidence points in his direction, Maigret probes the lives of the dead woman's lovers and the nature of her relationship to each. The characterizations and Parisian atmosphere are as fine as anything in late Simenon.

With *Maigret and Monsieur Charles* (1973), both the foremost European detective series and Simenon's half-century of writing fiction came to an end. Since then he has written several books of autobiographical reminiscence, culminating in the huge and overpowering *Intimate Memoirs* (1984). However many years Simenon has left before he returns to his beloved earth, Maigret, we can be sure, will survive as long as people read.

(*F.M.N.*)

*Simenon, Georges. *The Blue Room and The Accomplices.* New York: Harcourt Brace, 1964. (PS)

While Simenon is best known for his Maigret novels, his nonseries works of psychological suspense are equally compelling. They express a kind of dark inevitability, a sense of events unwittingly set in motion by one's actions and then gathering an uncontrollable momentum of their own. This volume presents two of the best of these novels.

In *The Blue Room,* Simenon explores the erotic—and ultimately disastrous—relationship of an innocent man and a woman who is as ruthless as she is passionate. Tony's main interest in life is making love with his mistress, Andree. Naïve and trusting, he remains unaware of her evil nature until his wife and her husband are found dead of strychnine poisoning. Tony is arrested for the crimes, and the story of what went before is told in flashback as he is questioned by the police. Even though we already know where the events are leading, we nevertheless fear for Tony as we watch Andree's corruption overwhelm him; and the final encounter of the lovers at the trial is one of the more chilling in mystery fiction.

The Accomplices is completely different in tone and theme from *The Blue Room,* but equally haunting. Joseph Lambert is married, the father of six children, and has another on the way. A fairly successful businessman, Lambert feels everything is going his way. But then the unexpected happens: While Lambert is driving wildly down the road, engaged in an amorous dalliance with his secretary, he loses control of his car. A school bus filled with children swerves to avoid him, but crashes into a wall and bursts into flame; dozens of little children die in the accident. Lambert moves quickly to cover up his guilt, but his unconscious proves to be his own prosecutor, judge, and jury. This is a fascinating novel of psychological torment and pressure, and has grave implications for modern society.

(*G.K./M.M.*)

*Simenon, Georges. *The Venice Train.* New York: Harcourt Brace, 1974. (PS)

Justin Calmar is an ordinary man; everything in his life seems well ordered and complacent. Then he takes his family on a vacation to Europe, and on the train from Venice to Paris a stranger approaches and asks him to deliver an attaché case. Calmar agrees. But when he enters the Paris apartment where he is supposed to make the delivery, he finds a murdered woman. Panicked, he flees—and his life is forever altered.

Fear and paranoia take control of Calmar. He becomes obsessed with the attaché case and the events surrounding the bizarre affair. He hungrily reads newspapers looking for clues to the stranger's identity, and finds that the man, too, has been murdered. Will he be next?

When Calmar finally opens the attaché case, he finds bundles of American hundred-dollar bills, English fifty-pound notes, and Swiss francs: a literal fortune. But this only deepens his fear: Someone will surely come to take the money away from him. He embarks on a frantic routine to keep the case hidden, continually shifting it from train-station lockers to bus-station lockers and back again. His existence degenerates into a nightmare of anxiety, depression, and continued paranoid behavior—he is a man at the breaking point long before anything happens to substantiate his terror.

Few writers can match Simenon when it comes to the novel of psychological suspense, and this is one of his finest books of this type. Justin Calmar is a memorable and tragic character; and Simenon's theme is powerfully stated. Relentless though it may be, *The Venice Train* is a novel for our time, with implications that transcend its simple plot and a message for us all.

Outstanding among Simenon's many other novels of psychological suspense are *The Man Who Watched the Trains Go By* (1946), *Act of Passion* (1953), *In Case of Emergency* (1958; made into an excellent French film with Brigitte Bardot and Jean Gabin), and *The Innocents* (1974).

(*G.K./B.P.*)

Simon, Roger L. *Wild Turkey*. San Francisco: Straight Arrow, 1974. (PI)

Wild Turkey is concerned with liberated sex and freewheeling drug use in southern California, but it isn't very sexy or much of a turn-on. In fact, the only thing that keeps it from falling into the category of a tired cliché is its protagonist, private eye Moses Wine—a former hippie who now has taken on the responsibilities of earning a living and single fatherhood. (His ex-wife has left their young boys with him in order to go to Europe and "find herself.") Bemused by the often bizarre world around him—particularly by its women, whom he admits he is incapable of understanding—Wine views its eccentric people and strange institutions with a sort of wondering acceptance and presses on with his case, sandwiching investigative forays between pickups at the baby-sitter's and deliveries to the grade school. The relationship between Wine and his two kids is one of the best things about this book: As he says, ". . . they're friends of mine. We like to hang out, prefer each other's company."

As *Wild Turkey* opens, Wine is visited by guerrilla journalist Dr. Gunther Thomas (any relationship to gonzo journalist Hunter Thompson is purely intentional), who wants to do a piece on Moses Wine in action for *Rolling Stone.* He has a photographer in tow—Anthony Streeter-Best—and the perfect case lined up: Deborah Frank, daughter of a movie mogul and ABC News anchorwoman, has been stabbed to death in her suite at the Beverly Wilshire; Jock Hecht, formerly prominent novelist turned writer of sensational nonfiction tomes (the latest is to be on sex), is suspected of the killing.

Soon the three are on the way to the Chateau Marmont, where Hecht is staying, toking on a joint, with youngest son, Simon, in the back seat since the baby-sitter isn't available. Wine takes the case; Hecht quickly turns up dead, an apparent suicide; and Hecht's wife retains Wine to prove her husband didn't kill himself. Right away he becomes embroiled with such institutions as the Kama Sutra Sexual Phrontistery, the Sexual Liberation League and its subsidiary Liberation Institute, and the House of Dominance; and along the way he meets such individuals as a "distinguished gentleman" and "model prisoner" at Terminal Island (reputedly a member of the Jewish Mafia); a therapist who is the "most important person in the sex business" in Topanga Canyon; a luxury car full of Cuban refugee thugs; and assorted porn-movie personnel.

Wine's reaction to all of this is dryly humorous, and he detects with the best of them, but unfortunately it all boils down to an overused and predictable solution. Still, it's easy to forgive Moses Wine for being hired for a run-of-the-mill case like this. Wine's first case was *The Big Fix* (1973), which was made into a film starring Richard Dreyfuss as Wine. A third Wine novel, *Peking Duck,* appeared in 1979, and his latest adventure is *California Roll* (1985).

(*M.M.*)

Singer, Loren. *The Parallax View.* New York: Doubleday, 1970. (PS/T)

Free-lance journalist Malcolm Graham is summoned by longtime colleague William Tucker to view the familiar newsreel of the John Kennedy assassination. On the film are several press photographers and journalists, including Graham and Tucker, witnessing the president reacting to the impact of the bullets. A frightened Tucker points out to Graham that an impossibly high number of these colleagues have since died untimely and presumably accidental deaths. Except that Tucker doesn't believe their deaths were accidental; he thinks someone is going down the list, murdering them. Four are still alive, and Tucker and Graham are among them.

They contact the other two surviving members of the press appearing in the brief filmstrip: a hard-bitten female journalist with whom Graham was sexually involved; and a homosexual reporter who doubts that any of them are actually in danger.

As Graham and Tucker delve more deeply into the question of who might be stalking them, the novel builds in suspense and action, and the fascinating premise on which it is based is gradually revealed. This is more than a simple thriller; it is a clever comment on the possible grotesqueries inherent in a massive bureaucracy.

A unique concept, airtight plotting, and a terse, evocative style blend to create a masterly suspense novel. It was reissued in 1981 by Second Chance Press, in both hard- and softcover, as one of the books they decided was of high enough quality to merit another round in the marketplace. It was also released as a movie in 1974 starring Warren Beatty; the movie version is considered by critics and film buffs to be something of a classic in its genre. The book is better.

This was Loren Singer's first novel. Later novels include *That's the House, There* (1973) and *Boca Grande* (1974).

(*J.L.*)

Singer, Shelley. *Free Draw*. New York: St. Martin's, 1984. (AD)

This is Shelley Singer's second novel featuring the detecting duo of Jake Samson and Rosie Vicente. (The first was *Samson's Deal,* 1982.) Jake is a former Chicago cop who "had his trial by fire in the summer of 1968" and quit the force to move to California; there he bummed around for a while and finally settled down in the flatlands of the East Bay. Now he undertakes occasional unofficial investigative jobs, usually in the guise of a journalist for friend Artie Perrine's investigative magazine, *Probe.* Rosie is Jake's tenant, a lesbian carpenter with a flair for detecting. Together they are an appealing pair: affectionate but respectful of one another's privacy and different sexual orientations, smoothly efficient when chasing down clues. And the rapport between them—bantering and humorous, yet solidly supportive—strikes just the right note.

At the beginning of *Free Draw,* Artie Perrine calls Jake in a panic: His nephew, Alan, found a body that morning in the drainage ditch in front of Artie's house in a wooded Marin County canyon. Stupidly Alan panicked, ran, and later lied to the police about knowing the dead man. *Did* Alan know him? Jake asks. Yes, Artie says, the man is David Smith, head of a correspondence school that *Probe* had hired Alan to investigate; what's worse, recently Alan had quarreled with Smith in front of witnesses. Artie wants Jake to look into the case, and soon he has persuaded him to move into a neighbor's home in the canyon while pursuing his investigation. When Jake returns to the East Bay and tells Rosie about the case, she insists on joining forces with him.

Their investigation brings them into contact with the residents of Artie's canyon, including a lesbian couple, one of whom has designs on Rosie; a gay male whose house is filled with pictures of naked men; and a fellow who periodically gets drunk and shoots at the redwood trees—his explanation being that "they're too big." When they attend a neighborhood meeting—held naked in a hot tub—they find that all of the residents of the canyon had reason to kill the victim. And when the murder weapon turns out to belong to Alan, Jake steps up his efforts, which include a foray into the Bright Future Correspondence School, where a number of things seem amiss, and a trip up the coast to a quaint little inn in Mendocino.

Singer's characters work well together, and she has a nice feel for both the northern California settings and eccentrics she portrays.

(*M.M.*)

*Sjöwall, Maj, and Per Wahlöö. *The Laughing Policeman.* New York: Pantheon, 1970. (PP)

The wife-and-husband team of Maj Sjöwall and Per Wahlöö are considered by many to be Sweden's foremost mystery writers. Their series of ten police procedurals set in Stockholm is notable for its lean, journalistic style; careful attention to the details of procedure; and realistic, often grim, outlook on society. The authors, both Communists, attempted to make a political statement in these novels, and to a varying degree each book does. It is not a strident statement, however, but an outgrowth of the characters and the way they live. The characters are well drawn and fully fleshed out, and as the series progresses, they grow and change. The subplots concerning the personal lives of the men on Stockholm's Homicide Squad—Superintendent Martin Beck and his colleagues Lennart Kollberg, Gunvald Larsson, Einar Ronn, and the comic patrolmen Kristiansson and Kvant—are well integrated with the main story and are part of this series's great appeal. When reading these novels, one cannot help but be reminded of Ed McBain's (q.v.) excellent Eighty-seventh Precinct series, although the Sjöwall/Wahlöö books lack the leavening effect of humor that is present in the McBains.

The Laughing Policeman—which won the Mystery Writers of America Edgar for Best Novel of 1970—begins quietly with Martin Beck and Lennart Kollberg playing chess on a rainy night. But the peaceful mood does not last long; eight people have been shot to death on a bus near the end of its route, and one of them is Detective Subinspector Ake Stenstrom of the homicide squad. There was no reason for Stenstrom to have been on that particular bus, and there is something odd about the vehicle, too—it is not the type generally used on that route.

There is one survivor, a man named Schwerin, who remains unconscious in the hospital. When he is finally able to answer questions, Schwerin gives the name "Koleson" and dies. And as the men of the Homicide Squad try to decipher this last utterance, plus dig into the life of their dead colleague, public outcry over the lack of a quick solution escalates, making their job all the more difficult.

This engrossing novel was made into a 1973 film of the same title, starring Walter Matthau and Bruce Dern. Unfortunately it loses a great deal of the appeal of the novel, since its setting inexplicably moved to San Francisco.

(*M.M.*)

Sjöwall, Maj, and Per Wahlöö. *The Man on the Balcony.* New York: Pantheon, 1968. (PP)

A man on a balcony observes the quiet Stockholm street below as the sun comes up at a quarter to three in the morning. He watches for hours, until he spots a schoolgirl with a red-checked satchel of books. Just before Martin Beck leaves for a trip south to Motala to help out a fellow police officer, there is a call from a woman complaining about a man on a balcony; but before Gunvald Larsson can get the details, the woman hangs up. The call doesn't seem important at the time. After all, the police are overworked, what with the muggings in Vanadis Park.

It is in the park that, shortly before Beck returns to Stockholm, the body of a little girl is found, raped and strangled. Eva Carlsson had been accosted by child molesters twice in the past, and the police check out that lead. But before they can check it thoroughly, a second little girl is found dead in yet another park. And soon it appears that the only adult witness to the crimes may have been a person who has good reason to avoid the police: the mugger who has been terrorizing the parks of the city. A suspect is arrested, but he is stubbornly uncooperative, and it seems the police will be forced to decipher the unreliable and sometimes garbled accounts given them by their child witnesses. It is a long time before anyone connects the murders with the man on the balcony, and even then there is not much to go on. This is a tension-packed story that personally involves the reader in the efforts to end these hideous crimes.

(*M.M.*)

Sjöwall, Maj, and Per Wahlöö. *Roseanna.* New York: Pantheon, 1967. (PP)

This is the first in the Martin Beck series, and begins with the discovery of the body of a young woman in a canal south of Stockholm. She has been strangled and sexually assaulted, and the police's job is made all the more difficult because they must first establish her identity before they can try to find her killer. Martin Beck and his colleagues Kollberg and Melander journey south to the town of Motala, where they join forces with a local officer, Gunnar Ahlberg.

The case appears to be nearly insoluble. There are no missing women in the vicinity, and no one recognizes the photos of the victim that the police circulate. The search extends to missing persons from all over Sweden, and then to those of foreign countries, and finally focuses on the unlikely town of Lincoln, Nebraska. The men of the Homicide Squad are not too hopeful—after all, their last communication with the United States (from Astoria, New York) looked promising until the police there admitted their error in neglecting to mention that their missing person was a Negro.

But eventually it is confirmed that the dead woman in the canal is a librarian from the American Midwest, Roseanna McGraw. It is now up to the Homicide Squad to reconstruct Roseanna's life from the time she left Lincoln until her body surfaced in the canal. And as they probe deeper, they find her life was far different from what one would normally expect of a librarian from Nebraska.

Other especially good novels in this series are *Murder at the Savoy* (1971), *The Fire Engine that Disappeared* (1971), and *The Terrorists* (1977).

(*M.M.*)

*Sladek, John. *Black Aura.* New York: Walker, 1979. (AD)

In 1972 John Sladek won a short-story contest sponsored by the *London Times* and the publisher Jonathan Cape. First prize was the guaranteed publication of a first mystery novel; *Black Aura* is that novel. (It was first published in England in 1974 but not in this country until 1979.) We owe the contest judges—Lord Butler, playwright Tom Stoppard, and Dame Agatha Christie (q.v.)—and of course John Sladek a debt of gratitude, for this is a wonderful book, one of the finest (and funniest) "impossible crime" novels to be published since the halcyon days of John Dickson Carr (q.v.).

The hero of *Black Aura*—and of the prizewinning short story, "By an Unknown Hand"—is Thackeray Phin, an American "dropout from a think tank, professional logician and amateur sleuth" now living in London. His ongoing advertisement in the *Times,* outlining his credentials and requesting a challenge—"anything irrational considered"—doesn't seem to be getting results. However, over tea one afternoon, a discussion between Phin and his friend Beeker results in a challenge to Phin to penetrate the secrets of Viola Webb, London's most famous medium. Phin therefore joins Mrs. Webb's Aetheric Mandala Society, where he is welcomed with open arms, a fact that puzzles him greatly until he learns that his hostess knows all about his amateur sleuthing and wants him to find out who is altering the society's ledgers and supposedly raking off the till.

Phin discovers that one David Lauderdale died in Mrs. Webb's house of an alleged drug overdose, and that David's father has subsequently joined the society to investigate his son's death; the father suspects foul play. A short while later, Doc Lauderdale disappears from inside a locked bathroom, a room with no means of escape—unless, of course, you believe in "astral projection," as some members of the society do.

At that point, Phin, with the aid of Beeker, draws up a list of suspects that include Mrs. Webb, who can see "the black aura of impending death"; retired wing-commander Dank, a man with an ardent belief in a different kind of spirit; Reverend Stonehouse, who has an odd connection with the chapel at the local funeral parlor; and Professor Hackel, a psychologist who doesn't believe in ghosts or black auras. Is one of them responsible for David Lauderdale's death and his father's disappearance? Or is it someone—or something—else?

To quote the dust-jacket blurb: "The curse of an Egyptian amulet, strange doings in a dark séance parlor, lurking death in an orgone box, psychic poison and live burial [and an "impossible act of levitation"]—John Sladek's taut brainteaser fairly creeps with fiendish happenings. It is superb entertainment." It certainly is.

Also superb is the only other Thackeray Phin novel, *Invisible Green* (which followed the publication of *Black Aura* in England but was published here *before* that title, in 1977). This one also contains an ingenious locked-room mystery. Sladek, like Phin a transplanted American living in London, has recently—and unfortunately for mystery readers—been devoting himself solely to the writing of science fiction.

(*B.T./B.P.*)

Slesar, Henry. *The Thing at the Door.* New York: Random House, 1974. (PS)

The Thing at the Door opens in 1955, showing Gail Gunnarson as a lonely six-year-old who has just lost her mother, a suicide—and who is about to begin a twenty-year battle against insanity. The scene quickly shifts to the present: Gail is a grown woman, an art student with more than her share of problems—she has difficulty sleeping, thinks men are following her, suffers from terrifying nightmares. In desperation she turns to a psychiatrist, Dr. Vanner, who has helped a friend from school. But the therapy only seems to intensify the terrors, and Gail feels very alone in the world; her only relatives, Uncle Gilbert Swann and his son, Piers, have lived far away in Europe for twenty-one years.

Gail's birthday approaches, her twenty-first, when she is to take control of the fortune left to her. The bank that has managed her funds is concerned about her mental stability, and arranges for a young man, Steve Tyner, to investigate her. Tyner is tenacious and realistic—as well as attracted to Gail. He soon becomes convinced she isn't crazy, but events happen that would push any normal person to the brink of insanity: Her relatives are reported killed in a landslide; her friend Helen, who referred her to Dr. Vanner, kills herself; and she is haunted by the image of the "thing" that appeared at her door over twenty years before.

Slesar writes well, and he has woven a suspenseful story that is resolved in a satisfactory manner. The reader is always a little ahead of Steve Tyner, and the solution comes as no great surprise, but the author enlists so much sympathy for his characters that it's hard to put this one down until you know for sure that everything will be all right.

A partner in an advertising agency as well as a fiction writer, Slesar has published over 500 short stories and novelettes, as well as novels, motion-picture scripts, and radio and television plays. His first novel, *The Gray Flannel Shroud,* won the MWA Edgar in 1959. In addition, he has published two collections of short stories: *A Bouquet of Clean Crimes and Neat Murders* (1960) and *A Crime for Mothers and Others* (1962).

(*M.M.*)

Smith, Alison. *Someone Else's Grave.* New York: St. Martin's, 1984. (PP)

This first novel introduces Police Chief Judd Springfield of Coolridge Corners, Vermont. He is an introspective man of early middle age with a devotion to self-education (he takes up a new subject every year), and is eminently satisfied with his place and situation in life. Judd finds his skills tested when Miss Adams, sixty-ish resident of the town, finds a fresh body buried just below the surface of one of the graves she has been decorating for Memorial Day. (Between her discovery and her report at the police station, she is also attacked in her kitchen and almost killed.)

Judd learns that the body is that of a young woman who was employed in a local office as an accountant, who lived in a boardinghouse, and whose hobby was jogging. Then two other women are murdered within the week, all three seemingly by the same person, for no apparent reason and with no discernible relationship to each other. It takes skill and talents that he didn't know he had for Judd to set a final trap and catch the killer.

Dateline headings, as from a police blotter, make the time frames clear and add to the tension. Smith's crisp conversational style and low-key characterizations are definite assets. Small-town cop stories abound, but this one stands out. A very promising first novel. Smith's second novel is *A Trap of Gold* (1985).

(*E.N.*)

Smith, Charles Merrill. *Reverend Randollph and the Unholy Bible.* New York: Putnam's, 1983. (AD)

C. P. Randollph is unique in the subgenre of the clerical detective. A former professional quarterback, he is used to good living, and he finds it as a minister of the Church of the Good Shepherd. The church building is located within an office-hotel high-rise in downtown Chicago, and the "manse" is its luxurious penthouse. By this fifth book in the series, Randollph has acquired a wife—Samantha ("Sammy") Stack, a glamorous talk-show hostess—and an English chef, Clarence, who describes the preparations of each entree with such care that readers can almost cook it themselves.

Aficionados of the clerical suspense novel who delight in displays of pious hypocrisy will be disappointed with these books. The characters in the series are, for the most part, quite likable and civilized. Even the gangsters are appealing. Randollph knows his church history and discusses religion knowledgeably with his affable bishop, Freddie, and Lieutenant Michael Casey, the Roman Catholic police inspector. But because his ministry is unique, Randollph is more an administrator than a pastor; his problems come not so much in consoling the bereaved as in finding time to perform this duty in between paper work and board meetings. And it is when he is bemoaning this unsuspected aspect of the job that Randollph comes most alive and seems most human. In his exercise of the shrewdness and tact that is necessary to run a prestigious, well-endowed church, Randollph is more like Emma Lathen's (q.v.) banker hero, John Putnam Thatcher, than Harry Kemelman's (q.v.) embattled Rabbi Small.

In *Reverend Randollph and the Unholy Bible,* Randollph has managed to make one of his infrequent calls, to a wealthy parishioner, Johannes Humbrecht—and he is confronted by a shocking sight: Humbrecht has been bludgeoned to death. Randollph has "never seen a freshly slaughtered human carcass before," but before long he is in the thick of the investigatory fray. It seems the killer took Humbrecht's Gutenberg Bible—a valuable enough item, but this particular one is more so because it was one of the last ones Gutenberg printed, for his own personal use. Because of his knowledge of things religious, Randollph assists Lieutenant Casey in his attempts to track the killer down; these take him into the art world; into contact with biblical scholars, diverse members of the clergy, and threatening gangsters—and finally into an audience with the pope himself (who turns out to be a football fan).

There is little real tension or threat in this story, but the plot is solid, and the unveiling of the culprit is a very satisfying surprise.

The Reverend Randollph has appeared in four other adventures: *Wages of Sin* (1974), *Avenging Angel* (1977), *Fall from Grace* (1978), and *Holy Terror* (1980).

(*S.D.*)

Smith, David. *Timbuktu.* New York: Dodd, Mead, 1983. (AD/A)

Timbuktu is the second book in a series featuring James Stevens, an American lawyer; and Muntaka, the Nigerian judge he met while working as a consultant in Africa (*The Leo Conversion,* 1980). Their relationship developed as they followed the sixteenth-century journey of Leo Africanus in search of a precious manuscript stolen from a Nigerian museum.

In *Timbuktu,* Stevens has returned from Africa and has been working for three years with the law firm of Winslow, Wallace, Wilson & White in New York City. Slightly bored by the routine, Stevens convinces the firm he should go to Dakar to research gold investments for clients when he receives a cryptic cable from a nun, Sister Monique (whom he met in *The Leo Conversion*), asking for his help. The trip is not simple. Because of an air strike, he gets cramped space on a freighter that obviously is carrying illegal cargo. He meets a British man who winds up killed by a dart last touched by Stevens; agrees to take a sealed envelope to a dealer in Dakar in exchange for his life; finds the dealer dead and takes refuge in a funeral procession to avoid a gunman. There he meets Muntaka, and they head to Timbuktu, where they find that Sister Monique is concerned about missing boys and girls who are presumably being sold into slavery.

Their search for the slavery ring is complicated by the discovery of illegal traffic in ivory tusks and rhinoceros bone, as well as by the realization that the sealed envelope in Stevens's possession contains half of a page from a missing journal written by one of the first white men to reach Timbuktu. (He was killed when he tried to leave—a fate Stevens and Muntaka would prefer not to share.) The suspense is heightened as they find themselves pursued by many people who are trying to stymie their investigations and the pair aren't always sure *which* investigation. Gradually the people and their interests are sorted out and the answers to both past and present mysteries are resolved.

David Smith, currently vice-dean of the Harvard Law School, served as a consultant to the customary courts in West Africa and has traveled there extensively. His descriptions of the country—both its physical beauty and its life-styles—make for fascinating and informative reading; and the development of the relationship between Stevens, an impulsive, somewhat brash American, and Muntaka, a reflective, wily Nigerian, demonstrates their radical cultural differences in a human, often funny, and very touching manner. Both books contain historical information in the immediate context of a contemporary mystery, which adds to the suspense and to the appreciation of the development of African nations and traditions. While it is best to read these books in order, each can stand alone in its clever plotting, rich description, and appealing character.

(*K.M.*)

Smith, Julie. *Death Turns a Trick.* New York: Walker, 1982. (AD)

Rebecca Schwartz describes herself (perhaps a bit too frequently) as a Jewish feminist lawyer and (tongue-in-cheek) as an uptight middle-class spinster of twenty-eight. In one of her distinctly nonfeminist moments, she dons a silver lamé low-cut blouse, a slinky black skirt with a slit, and "wicked woman shoes" for a blind date—but then decides she looks too ridiculous to be seen in public. On the other hand, Rebecca also agrees to play ragtime piano at a client's bordello, finds herself in the middle of a phony police raid, discovers a senator who is literally hiding nothing in the basement, is arrested for drunk driving—in the madam's car—and comes home to find a dead hooker on her living-room floor. None of it is designed to enhance her stature as a lawyer or a nice Jewish girl.

Rebecca is a delightful character who may be humble when talking about herself but has plenty of chutzpah when trying to solve the murder. And Smith has a witty, let-me-tell-you-all-about-it style and gives the reader fascinating glimpses into the various life-styles of San Francisco.

Schwartz's second adventure, *The Sourdough Wars* (1984), chronicles a life-or-death battle over a valuable sourdough starter within the bakery establishment of San Francisco. A third nonseries Smith novel, *True Life Adventure* (1985), tells of former reporter and would-be-mystery writer Paul MacDonald's experiences when he takes a job writing client reports for a detective agency and stumbles into a murder case. For this one, Smith needed to do little research: She is a former reporter, knows what it is like to be a would-be mystery writer, and once held a job writing client reports for a detective agency.

(*S.D.*)

Smith, Martin. *Canto for a Gypsy*. New York: Putnam's, 1972. (T)

This story centers around Saint Stephen's Crown (the Holy Crown of Hungary). In the year 1000, Pope Sylvester II sent the crown to Saint Stephen when he became the first Christian king of Hungary, and the crown began its revered, but hazardous, existence. During World War II, it ended up in American hands, and is now being returned to Hungary. But first it will be displayed in Saint Patrick's Cathedral for five days. And here we are asked to believe, despite the presence of a Hungarian security force and members of the New York Police Department, that the person really needed to take care of the crown for these five days is our protagonist, a Gypsy antique dealer named Roman Grey.

All right. A little hard to accept, perhaps, but Grey does have some of the needed attributes: He speaks Hungarian and has a knowledge of crown jewelry. Besides, the reader should not let a little stretching of credibility get in the way of a good story. For a good story is exactly what develops when Grey decides to accept the assignment, not knowing that a notorious art thief is already planning to steal the crown. Grey, as it turns out, is a good choice, for he brings to the job Gypsy cunning and a jeweler's expertise, and manages not only to help protect the crown but to unearth its long-hidden secret.

This is the same Roman Grey who made his literary debut in Martin Smith's acclaimed previous book, *A Gypsy in Amber* (1971). In that novel, too, the reader is immersed in excitement and intrigue, plus a generous helping of Gypsy lore.

(*N.D.*)

Smith, Martin Cruz. *Gorky Park.* New York: Random House, 1981. (PP)

Martin Cruz Smith is the Martin Smith (q.v.) who authored the two "Gypsy" novels; he adds his middle name to what he considers his more ambitious and commercial work. And *Gorky Park* is certainly both ambitious and commercial, a best seller that also achieved wide critical acclaim for its well-researched glimpse inside modern Russia.

The snow can conceal many things, especially in a place like Russia. But spring is setting in, the thaw is beginning, and three corpses are discovered in Moscow's Gorky Park. How long have they been there? Maybe two weeks, maybe six months. Their frozen condition makes a more exact estimate impossible. But the odd thing about the bodies is the mutilation: faces cut away, eyes removed, fingers (and therefore fingerprints) cut off.

The case belongs to Arkady Renko, chief homicide investigator of the MVD, even though the KGB is sniffing around also to see if any matters of security are involved. Murders in Russia are usually straightforward—someone getting drunk and killing someone else (frequently a drunk husband killing his wife). This case is especially puzzling, not only because of the grotesque mutilation but because of the subsequent interest and involvement of a couple of Americans.

This is a well-written, interesting book, but it must be said that an air of dismal hopelessness pervades it. However, this, too, can be credited to the author and his ability to capture the mood of the weather, the Russian lifestyle, widespread distrust, and omnipresent bureaucracy. All in all, Smith has given us a fascinating portrait of a Russian murder investigation.

Another modest best seller published under the Martin Cruz Smith byline is *Nightwing* (1979), which has a New Mexico setting and a good deal of eerie Indian lore.

(*N.D.*)

Snow, Kathleen. *Night Walking.* New York: Simon & Schuster, 1978. (PS)

Night Walking is a multiple-viewpoint novel about a psychotic killer who stalks three roommates in New York City. The plot, shifting between the viewpoints of the heroines, the police, and the killer, is typical of this type of novel. What makes Snow's book unusual is her thorough understanding of the young women who come to New York, find entry-level jobs, and share apartments. Anyone who has had a number of roommates will recognize the characters.

Snow's theme is that rape and the threat thereof are used by male society consciously and unconsciously to keep women dependent—whether it be the rapist, the police, or the fathers or boyfriends who warn the women not to go out alone.

When beautiful Alexandra Baskin is found raped and murdered, her surviving roommates decide not to tell the police that she had slept with so many men, was gone so many nights that when she didn't come home they were not alarmed. If the police knew that, they figure, they would conclude that Alex was "asking for it" and make only a superficial effort to find her killer. But the decision also comes from their own unsettled feelings about Alex. Less attractive, less sexually free, they are caught between their anger at her various abuses of their friendship and their unvoiced wonder at and jealousy of her popularity. But having decided to withhold what may be key information, they can't be sure how much they have hampered the police, and, in doing so, endangered themselves.

We watch anxiously as the anonymous psychopathic killer stalks his next victim; and we begin to realize—at the same time his potential victims do—that this is no random slayer, but someone known to them, someone who, in fact, may be very close to a resident of the apartment. As time passes and the threat increases, they—and we—begin to scrutinize each of their friends and acquaintances, trying to see clues as to which one might possibly be a psychopath masquerading behind a familiar facade.

Snow clearly has done a lot of psychological research, plus made a study of police procedure, and she writes very well. This is a disturbing novel that any reader will have difficulty putting down.

(*S.D.*)

*Spicer, Bart. *The Dark Light.* New York: Dodd, Mead, 1949. (PI)

Anyone with a list of private-eye writers who are "almost as good as Raymond Chandler" probably has the name Bart Spicer somewhere near the top. His novels featuring Philadelphia PI Carney Wilde are among the best of their kind.

In *The Dark Light,* the first in the series, Wilde is hired by Deacon Andrew Jackson, a black man, to find out what has happened to the Reverend Matthew Kimball, minister of the Shining Light Church. Kimball was to appear on a New York radio show, but disappeared the day before air time.

Before Wilde gets too far into the case, however, Jackson is murdered, and shortly thereafter Kimball's wife is killed. Then there is the little matter of a missing diamond earring worth $7000. In making the right connections among these events, Wilde has to deal with the church's wealthy sponsor, her beautiful daughter, and a hard-nosed cop, among other assorted characters, all of whom are carefully delineated.

Spicer's prose is tough but literate, and his plot is complicated but tight. His narrator, Wilde, strikes just the right notes of toughness and compassion throughout. Everything adds up to a first-rate job of writing and storytelling, making the current neglect of Spicer's work as big a mystery as anything in his books.

The other six Wilde novels are uniformly fine. They are *Blues for the Prince* (1950), *Black Sheep, Run* (1951), *The Golden Door* (1951), *The Long Green* (1952), *The Taming of Carney Wilde* (1954), and *Exit, Running* (1959). (*B.C.*)

Spillane, Mickey. *Day of the Guns.* New York: Dutton, 1964. (E/T)

Properly overshadowed by Mike Hammer, espionage agent Tiger Mann is the hero of Mickey Spillane's only other series of mystery novels. Mann remains a pale shadow of the mighty Mike, a Bond-era reworking of the Hammer formula; but the first entry in the series, *Day of the Guns,* has considered merit.

Tiger Mann is employed by an espionage organization funded by ultraright-wing billionaire Martin Grady, for self-professed altruistic, patriotic purposes. Chatting with a Broadway columnist in a nightclub, Tiger spots a beautiful woman who strikingly resembles a Nazi spy named Rondine who attempted to kill him years before. Though he loved Rondine, Tiger has sworn to kill her should he encounter her again. The woman, Edith Caine, professes not to be Rondine, but Tiger refuses to believe her and sets out to learn what she is up to. Soon he is battling a Communist conspiracy, and in a striptease finale that purposely evokes and invokes the classic conclusion of *I, the Jury,* Tiger must face the naked truth about Rondine.

Day of the Guns is a fast-moving and fine example of Spillane's mature craftsmanship; he has great fun doing twists on himself, as the conclusion of the novel shows. But this book—and, particularly, later Tiger Mann entries—lacks the conviction of the Hammer novels. Tiger Mann is Mike Hammer in secret-agent drag: His style and world are Hammer's; despite mentions of faraway places, the action is confined to New York. But while Hammer is an antiorganization man, Tiger, for all his lone-wolf posturing, is a company man. This goes against the Spillane grain.

The three other Tiger Mann novels are *Bloody Sunrise* (1965), *The*

Death Dealers (1965), and *The By-Pass Control* (1966). Each declines in quality.

(*M.A.C./J.L.T.*)

*Spillane, Mickey. *I, the Jury*. New York: Dutton, 1947. (PI)

When Mickey Spillane published *I, the Jury* in 1947, Hammett's first novel had been in print nearly twenty years and Carroll John Daly and Raymond Chandler (qq.v.) were still writing. Yet there is little doubt that Spillane's book was a seminal work of tough-guy fiction, inspiring hundreds of imitators in the booming paperback market of the 1950s. No one, however, was quite able to match Spillane's unique combination of action, sex, and right-wing vengeance.

The main character of *I, the Jury* is Spillane's most famous creation, Mike Hammer—tough, implacable, and prone to violence, with perhaps even a touch of madness. When his war buddy is murdered, Hammer swears to get revenge: "And by Christ, I'm not letting the killer go through the tedious process of the law." Hammer smashes his way through the suspects ("My fist went in up to the wrist in his stomach") until he determines the guilty party, whom he has sworn to kill in exactly the same way his friend was murdered. Along the way, he meets the nymphomaniac Bellemy sisters, one of whom has a strategically located strawberry birthmark; Charlotte Manning, a beautiful psychiatrist; Hal Kines, the improbable white slaver; and of course he fends off the advances of Velda, his sexy, loyal secretary. He finally confronts the killer in a slam-bang ending never to be forgotten by anyone who has read it, concluding with perhaps the best last line in all of Spillane's books, most of which have memorable, melodramatic climaxes.

Spillane's novels have been attacked for their violence and their vigilante spirit, and no doubt these things are present in the books. But Spillane is first and foremost a storyteller, and his stories, no matter how improbable, always work, pulling the reader along willingly or unwillingly into Mike Hammer's violent world.

I, the Jury was brought to the screen in 1949, with Biff Elliott in the starring role. Like the novel, it emphasizes violence and has an ending to enrage the sensibilities of any feminist who happens to watch it.

(*B.C.*)

Spillane, Mickey. *The Long Wait*. New York: Dutton, 1951. (T)

The Long Wait, Mickey Spillane's first nonseries novel, is the author's variation on the one-man-against-municipal-corruption theme as found in such novels as Dashiell Hammett's (q.v.) *Red Harvest.* The Mike Hammer–like narrator/hero, whose name is either Johnny McBride or George Wilson (even *he* isn't sure), returns to the town of Lyncastle to clear up a robbery-and-murder charge against McBride. His motive, as usual in Spillane's work, is revenge: One man is to get his arms broken, and one man is to die. Actually, a lot of people die before the narrator accomplishes his lofty goal, but not before he absorbs more physical abuse than seems even remotely possible.

And speaking frankly of credibility, it must be admitted that *The Long Wait* contains enough coincidence and enough improbable, even downright incredible, plot devices for four or five books. There is violence galore, too, and a lot of voyeuristic sex (the final scene is a rewrite of the striptease that concludes *I, the Jury*). None of this affects the story adversely, however. Typically, Spillane pulls it off. The pacing and the fierce conviction of the narrative voice grab the reader and carry him relentlessly along. Spillane seems to have had a high old time writing *The Long Wait,* and the reader who is willing to grin, plant his tongue in his cheek, and go along with him is in for a hell of a ride.

Other nonseries books by Spillane with more or less Hammer-like heroes are *The Deep* (1961) and *The Delta Factor* (1967). *The Erection Set* (1972) and *The Last Cop Out* (1973) are Spillane's only books with third-person narration.

(*B.C.*)

Spillane, Mickey. *One Lonely Night.* New York: Dutton, 1951. (PI)

It's Mike Hammer versus the Red Menace, and it's no contest. When Mike discovers that there are actual Commies living and operating in the United States, he goes berserk, the kill music singing in his head. When they capture Velda to force Mike to give them the secret documents he has found, he takes a tommy gun and blows so many of them away that he doesn't even bother to count.

So much for the plot. What most readers fail to consider about *One Lonely Night* is the amount of introspection in the book, which begins and ends with Hammer seriously questioning both his methods and his sanity. The fact that he is a killer has finally been brought home to him by a judge who says that Hammer enjoys killing, that he is just as bad as those he kills, if not worse. The judge's remarks haunt Hammer throughout the book, and at one point he even finds himself agreeing that the judge is correct: "So I *was* mad. I *was* a killer, and I was looking forward to killing again. I wanted every one of them from bottom to top. . . ." Of course in the context of the story, as the reader sees, Mike is not actually quite as bad as he seems, and he eventually realizes that he isn't. If he is evil, at least he is "evil for the good." He kills only those who deserve killing, the "cancerous Commies" in this case.

One Lonely Night is melodramatic in the extreme and appears so far right that it comes out of left field, but in the red-scare Fifties it found a sympathetic audience. It is of interest today chiefly for the insight it provides into Hammer's character.

Mike Hammer is also in top form in *Vengeance Is Mine!* (1950), *My Gun Is Quick* (1950), *The Big Kill* (1951), *Kiss Me Deadly* (1952), *The Girl Hunters* (1962), and *The Twisted Thing* (1966). *The Girl Hunters* was filmed in 1963 with Spillane himself playing Mike Hammer (and doing a fairly creditable job).

(*B.C.*)

Stagge, Jonathan. *The Dogs Do Bark.* New York: Doubleday Crime Club, 1937. (AD)

Writing as Patrick Quentin (q.v.) and Q. Patrick, the collaborative team of Hugh Wheeler and Richard Wilson Webb has received a considerable amount of acclaim from such eminent critics as Anthony Boucher, much of which is certainly deserved. When they donned the guise of Jonathan Stagge, however, as they did for nine novels in the 1930s and 1940s, it might be said that they went from the sublime to the ridiculous.

The Dogs Do Bark (the title comes from a line in a nursery rhyme: "Hark, hark, the dogs do bark") is the first of the Stagge novels, all of which feature the first-person narration of a country doctor named Hugh Westlake and all of which more or less take place in the village of Kenmore. (Kenmore's location is not stated here; in subsequent novels we learn that it is in Pennsylvania.) The book opens with a crisp November outing for members of the Kenmore Hunt Club, a jolly bunch who think nothing of trespassing on land posted by an anti-hunting farmer and who get their jollies watching a pack of hounds tear a fox to pieces. On this particular outing, they stumble on a "fox's earth" which contains the nude body of a woman sans both her arms and her head. A short while later, Westlake discovers that the arms have been disposed of by tossing them into the kennel where the hounds are kept—the reason the voracious barking of the dogs disturbed his sleep the night before. A grisly situation, to be sure, but one tinged with horror and menace and plenty of suspense in the unanswered question: What happened to the victim's head?

But from this point on, the novel degenerates into a silly farce replete with much pointless running around, numerous red herrings, the murder of a second woman, the murder of a horse named Sir Basil, mass burglaries, mass disappearances, and an unintentionally hilarious scene in which our hero, trapped in a burning barn, spends more time worrying about his dignity than he does in trying to escape. ("It is a curious point of human psychology that even in a moment of life and death one hesitates to make oneself ludicrous." And he's alone at the time!) The entire plot hinges on a false assumption that everyone, including Westlake and a county cop, Inspector Cobb, makes without once considering a glaringly obvious alternative possibility.

But the basic ludicrousness of the novel lies in its characters. None of them—again including Westlake and Cobb—is very likable; they are all self-righteous, priggish, condescending, vaguely bigoted, and contemptuous of anyone who does not approve of murdering small animals for sport. They are also far more upset at the carbon monoxide poisoning of Sir Basil, "the fastest and most beloved horse in Colenso County," than they are at the mutilation murder of the young woman. In fact, the Hunt Club holds an elaborate funeral for the horse, in which all of them dress royally in their riding habits and stand around solemnly while Sir Basil is buried in his owners' front lawn.

In fairness it should be noted that none of the other Jonathan Stagge novels is as awful as *The Dogs Do Bark,* although Dr. Westlake and his precocious and brattish young daughter Dawn *do* manage to remain rather unlikable throughout the series. Other titles include *The Stars Spell Death* (1939), *Death My Darling Daughters* (1945), and *Death's Old Sweet Song* (1946).

(*B.P.*)

*Stark, Richard. *Butcher's Moon.* New York: Random House, 1974. (A)

To date there have been sixteen novels about hard-bitten professional thief Parker, and *Butcher's Moon* is the sixteenth. Nearly twice as long as any single previous entry in the series, it represents a culmination of themes and a summation of events, but leaves the eager reader afraid that Richard Stark (Donald E. Westlake, q.v.) may have nothing left to say about his enigmatic antihero. Since at this writing it has been ten years since the publication of *Butcher's Moon,* that conclusion seems warranted.

Parker and his sometime partner, actor Alan Grofield, return to Tyler, the scene of a botched armored-car robbery of several years previous, the take of which was abandoned out of necessity. At the time Parker had said, "I know where it is. Someday I'll go back and get it." That day is now, and Parker sets out to retrieve the money from Lonzini, the mobster Parker figures found the money. When Lonzini fails to cooperate, Parker and Grofield begin pulling jobs—hitting a gambling casino, drug dealer, numbers operation, etc. Much like the Continental Op in Hammett's *Red Harvest,* Parker's activities trigger power plays within the local mob, while the level of violence escalates. When Grofield is captured, Parker assembles a string of thieves (characters from previous Stark novels) to pull a simultaneous series of capers he has carefully worked out. From the grand haul these jobs will realize, Parker plans to take no share—he merely asks his fellow thieves to repay him for his work by helping him afterward: "I want Grofield back, and I want my money. And I want those people dead." The twelve men are to hit the mob "safe house" where Grofield is being held, and kill all his captors. Stark builds climax upon climax as the various capers play out and as bullets fly and bodies pile up.

Butcher's Moon brings Parker full circle: Taking on the mob in order to retrieve "his" money (never mind that it was stolen from somebody else to begin with) was where Parker began in the trilogy of *The Hunter* (1962), *The Man with the Getaway Face* (1963), and *The Outfit* (1963). Significantly, *Butcher's Moon* reveals Parker a changed man. While neither he nor Stark would likely admit it, Parker has "mellowed"—he gathers his friends together to rescue a friend. And as one of those friends, father figure Handy McKay, tells him, "That's not like you . . . going to all this trouble for somebody else. . . ." Handy also questions Parker's seeking revenge: "I've never seen you do anything but play the hand you were dealt."

Parker's association with Grofield and his attachment to his live-in love, Claire (begun in *The Rare Coin Score,* 1967), have ever so subtly humanized him. This seems to make him, and Stark, uneasy. And that may explain the long silence from Stark since *Butcher's Moon.*

If *Butcher's Moon* is indeed the final Parker, crime fiction's greatest antihero certainly goes out with a bang, with all the cast brought back on stage for one last supercaper. And while he may indeed be turning into a human being, Parker is no less capable of his usual cold-blooded violence. Nor is Stark shy about depicting such shocking scenes as the one in which Parker is delivered a severed finger that once belonged to Grofield (not only a continuing character in this series but the hero of four of his own Stark novels). When the mob bearer of these bloody tidings says "I'm only the messenger," Parker shoots and kills him, saying, "Now you're the message."

(*M.A.C.*)

*Stark, Richard. *The Hunter.* New York: Pocket Books, 1962. (A/O)

Although one of the most influential series of the Sixties and Seventies, the Parker novels have never really been a huge popular success in the United States. They have shuttled from one publisher to another, while gaining critical acclaim and cult status, selling handsomely in foreign editions, and generating six motion pictures—the income from which no doubt justified the effort put into the books by an author who is finally coming to be viewed as one of the major figures of the twentieth-century mystery. The impact Parker has had on the tough crime novel can be gauged by a subgenre Stark has virtually invented: the so-called crook book. Prior to Stark, only Robin Hood thieves like Raffles or the Saint had taken center stage in series fiction; and W. R. Burnett (q.v.)—in whose path Stark most clearly treads—did not write series fiction about his amoral antiheroes.

Parker's recorded adventures begin in *The Hunter* (sometimes republished as *Point Blank,* the title of the stylish 1967 John Boorman–directed movie version with Lee Marvin and Angie Dickinson). Betrayed and left for dead on a heist by his wife, Lynn, and his friend Mal Resnick, Parker returns with a single-minded mission: to get the $45,000 due him. He first contacts his remorseful wife (who describes herself as a "Judas ewe") and, without really intending to, intimidates her into suicide. When he finally corners Resnick, now employed by the mob, he finds Resnick has turned the money over to his "Outfit" bosses. With a sense of logic unique to him, Parker forces Mal to tell him the names and whereabouts of the various mob bosses, then strangles him and sets about getting his money back from the mob.

What begins as a personal vendetta—which Parker cloaks in the practical consideration of getting his money back (it is characteristic of him to bury his emotions, his humanity)—turns into a darkly humorous tale of one man battling an organization. Parker is a self-sufficient, single-minded loner out of an earlier, wilder America; the soft, big-business boys don't stand a chance against him.

Richard Stark's prose is as straightforward and matter-of-fact effective as Parker himself. His narrative structure, here and in the other Parker novels, is not so straightforward: Working in the third person, it is Stark's method to follow the initial Parker-point-of-view section of the book with a section that shifts to Parker's antagonist's point of view (or, in later novels, the points of view of various characters, including antagonists), and then, finally, shift back to Parker's viewpoint. Events are often seen more than once, from varying perspectives, moving back and forth in time, creating a sense of inevitability where Parker's Frankenstein-monster forward momentum is concerned.

The Parker series is one of the most evenly written in crime fiction; the sixteen novels are consistently well done and readable. If forced, one might point out *Plunder Squad* (1972) as a somewhat perfunctory Parker, and *Deadly Edge* (1971) as a particularly fine example. Offbeat entries include *The Jugger* (1965), in which Parker plays detective: and *Slayground* (1971), a set piece in which Parker hides from and does battle with mob interlopers in an amusement park.

Parker has inspired two spin-offs: Grofield by Stark, and Dortmunder by Westlake. Actor Alan Grofield, whose first appearance was in the Parker novel *The Score* (1964), has appeared in four novels of his own: *The Damsel* (1967), *The Dame* (1969), *The Blackbird* (1969), and *Lemons Never Lie* (1971). The first three resemble slightly straighter versions of Westlake's famed comic crime novels and, in their foreign locales, prefigure his massive *Kahawa* (1982). Grofield seems a slightly different character in his solo novels, struggling to perform the role of protagonist and not sidekick; but the two personas converge in the Parker-like *Lemons Never Lie. Butcher's Moon* is a sequel to both the Parker entry, *Slayground,* and the Grofield entry, *The Blackbird,* which share nearly the same first chapters (detailing a botched armored-car job).

The Dortmunder books are deadpan comedy versions of Parker capers: The first, *The Hot Rock* (1970), is a specific reworking (of *The Black Ice Score*), and Grofield has a leading role. Later, in *Jimmy the Kid* (1974), Dortmunder's gang read and follow as a blueprint a nonexistent Parker novel entitled *Child Heist;* this nicely counterpoints the differences between the cute absurd world of Westlake/Dortmunder and the grim absurd one of Stark/Parker.

(*M.A.C.*)

Starrett, Vincent. *The Case Book of Jimmie Lavender.* New York: Gold Label, 1944. (PI/SS)

Comprising about a fourth of the published cases of Jimmie Lavender, the only sleuth in mystery fiction named for a major-league baseball player, these twelve tales from the Twenties and Thirties are representative examples of the now mostly forgotten detective short stories of Vincent Starrett, better known today as the biographer of Lavender's inspiration, Sherlock Holmes. By modern standards, none is of the first rank, but most are well-plotted puzzles cast in the classic mold, with a nice blend of cerebral deduction and physical action, and even fifty years and more later they have their attractions.

Several of the victims in the ten episodes concerned with murder are dispatched in picturesque ways and in a variety of interesting settings. Among the latter: a nightclub, a cruise ship, a golf course, a hospital, a university campus not far from the grounds of the 1933 Chicago World's Fair, and even an airplane cockpit. In one of the tales, a house "vanishes"; in another, the scene of the crime itself disappears; in a third—a locked-room homicide—the case is solved twenty years *before* it occurs. And every so often the proceedings are enlivened with some typical Chicago-style gunplay.

Though not as fully realized or memorably limned as some of his more celebrated Golden Age contemporaries, Lavender himself is an engaging protagonist, warm and whimsical throughout, though perhaps a bit too omniscient at times. He is aided in his investigations by his equally likable companion and chronicler, "Gilly" Gilruth, a refreshingly able Watson. Taken in small doses, their adventures are still fun to read, both for their own sake and as pleasantly nostalgic reminders of a more innocent era in the history of the crime-fiction genre.

Starrett also published a number of mystery novels, none of which is particularly distinguished. Three of these feature a detective with the unlikely name of Walter Ghost: *Murder on "B" Deck* (1929), *Dead Man Inside* (1931), and *The End of Mr. Garment* (1932). Starrett's best novel, however, is probably *Murder in Peking* (1946), which has a nicely evoked Chinese background. Other of Starrett's criminous short stories can be found in *Coffins for Two* (1924) and *The Blue Door* (1930); two of the stories in the later volume feature Jimmie Lavender.

(*E.N.*)

Stein, Aaron Marc. *The Cheating Butcher.* New York: Doubleday Crime Club, 1980. (AD)

Since he began his career in 1940, Aaron Marc Stein has published almost a book a year, as well as numerous novels under his George Bagby (q.v.) and Hampton Stone pseudonyms. Typical of Stein's books under his own name are lively, interesting characters, exotic foreign locales, and light humor that in no way detracts from the mystery. Stein has stated that he favors the mystery story because its audience is interested in the author's technique, and he has polished this technique carefully; although the two series published under his own name (as well as those he has created under his pseudonyms) are quite different in character and type, one thing the reader can rely on is a consistently entertaining and well-crafted story.

The Cheating Butcher features a sleuth whom Stein introduced in 1958 in *Sitting Up Dead.* Matt Erridge is a consulting engineer who travels the world from one job to another, usually to places that are, as he puts it, "the backsides of nowhere—places where there's nothing but sand and flies and the problems that go with handling a crew of hardbitten roughnecks who react to isolation and boredom by going mean." Fortunately, Matt also has a mother and a basset hound, Mathilda, who both miss him. And as this adventure opens, Mom has gotten Matt a consulting job in Venice, where she and Mathilda are staying. Matt is to advise a committee headed by the Principessa Mary Calvacanti-Ruffo (née Mary Poffenheim of the New Jersey plumbing-fixtures fortune) on how to save the decaying city from crumbling into its canals.

When Matt arrives in Venice, he is met by Mom, Mathilda, and the principessa's son, Jack. Before they have reached their hotel on the island of Torcello, someone fires at Jack's launch. Jack shrugs it off, attributing it to some of the ever-active terrorists who plague Italy. Matt isn't so sure. And when he finds a funeral wreath on his bed with a note reading "Ioncchi go home" (which he interprets to mean "Yankee go home"), he is even more convinced he was the target of the shot. A visit to the florist who made up the wreath indicates it was stolen from the Basilica San Marco; a visit to the basilica reveals it to be full of police, since a valuable jewel-encrusted book cover has also been stolen. And to top it off, when Matt returns to his hotel, his mother complains of finding a drunk passed out in her bed. Matt investigates, finds no one in her bed, but a corpse in *his.* It's all very confusing, and it seems up to him to figure out why anyone should be taking such exception to his presence in Venice—which he does, with great aplomb.

This is a breezy adventure set against the background of one of the world's most fascinating cities. Mom and Mathilda, as well as numerous Italians encountered along the way, are amusing characters. And Matt has a confidential, easy way of conversing with the reader that makes us feel we're being let in on something terrific (as well as occasionally setting us up for the awful events in store).

Some of Matt Erridge's other adventures are *Blood on the Stars* (1964), set in Texas and Mexico; *The Finger* (1973), set in Czechoslovakia; *Lend Me Your Ears* (1977), another Italian adventure; and *The Rolling Heads* (1979), which takes place in France.

(*M.M.*)

Stein, Aaron Marc. *The Dead Thing in the Pool.* New York: Doubleday Crime Club, 1952. (AD)

The heroes of Stein's first series—eighteen novels from 1940 to 1955—are a pair of archaeologist sleuths, Tim Mulligan and Elsie Mae Hunt. As with Stein's later creation, Matt Erridge, their profession enables him to set the novels anywhere in the world; and the vocation of archaeology adds a further dimension, that of being able to explore the history and nuances of the cultures they encounter. Stein has a knack for realistically depicting the natives of his various settings, and their views of Americans—whom they often find inexplicable—are particularly amusing. That and the interplay between Mulligan and Hunt, colleagues and platonic friends, make this a most enjoyable series.

As this novel opens, Elsie and Tim are in Mexico, staying in an expensive housing development on a *pedregal* (ancient lava field) near Mexico City where a national university is being built; their job is to study and catalog whatever archaeological finds may surface during the construction. Through the error of a servant, Elsie and Tim are suddenly summoned one night to the rented home of actress Dolores Conway, who has found a "dead thing in the pool" in her garden. Dolores wanted the police; what she gets is this learned pair of sleuths. And the "dead thing"—a bloody human arm that she observed sticking up from a supposedly bottomless lava pit—appears to be no joke. But before the police can be summoned, Eulogios, the servant who has been given the seemingly undemanding task of guarding the pool, is knocked senseless, and the arm vanishes.

Even as the police search the "bottomless" pool for the body, guests for what Dolores Conway calls a "completely knocked-out party" are arriving: Pico de San Juan, an actor who plays all the "village idiot" parts in Mexican films; Manolo, a famed jai alai star; Bob Jeffrey, Dolores's next-door neighbor from Beverly Hills; Carmella Flores, the actress known as the Cuban Bombshell. While these people socialize, Garcia of the local police force searches the pool and soon concludes there is no body. Garcia joins the party, the party becomes wilder, and when Garcia leaves he takes the servant, Eulogios, in for questioning. The next morning Tim awakes with a hangover to find two young men from the party, Pete and Mike Rocsznocszewcszki ("We can't pronounce it ourselves unless we're sober," Pete says) on his couch. Elsie Mae, Tim, and the unpronounceable brothers form an odd investigative quartet as the question of what happened to the dead thing in the pool becomes more complicated—and as usual "Mooyihan" and "Oont," as the Mexicans call them, come up with surprising results.

This is typical of the entertaining adventures of this likable pair, and the background on the *pedregal* is particularly good. Some other Mulligan and Hunt mysteries are *The Sun Is a Witness* (1940), set in the American Southwest; *Only the Guilty* (1942), which takes place in Colombia; *Shoot Me Dacent* (1951), a Dublin mystery; and *Moonmilk and Murder* (1955), the pair's last adventure to date, which is set in France.

(*M.M.*)

Stephens, Reed. *The Man Who Killed His Brother.* New York: Ballantine, 1980. (O/PI)

The man who killed his brother is Mick ("Brew") Axbrewder. The killing happened when Brew, a private investigator in the California town of Puerta del Sol, intervened in what he thought was a bank robbery and accidentally shot the cop who was chasing the robber—his brother, Rick. Since then nobody calls him Mick anymore (it's a reminder that he's the only living half of the Rick-and-Mick equation), and since then Brew has been drinking heavily. His partner, Ginny Fistoulari, head of Fistoulari Investigations, tries to bring him out of it, and sometimes for a limited period she does. But it takes the disappearance of his niece, Anthea, daughter of Rick's widow, Lona, to make him care about a case again.

When Anthea vanishes, Brew sobers up. He and Ginny begin to question authorities at the girl's school, where she was last seen. Soon they find that other girls of her age have disappeared from their schools, and that they have later turned up dead, bearing evidence of heroin addiction. A recent missing-girl case is that of the daughter of fellow private eye Tred Hangst; she has not yet been found. Brew, Ginny, and Tred join forces, and soon a pattern emerges, one that indicates someone connected with the school system is responsible for the deaths and disappearances.

This is grim stuff, full of harrowing circumstances and events. Brew teeters on the edge of sobriety, pushed to his emotional limits, always on the verge of seeking solace in the bottle. And when a solution is reached, it is not without its terrible cost.

This is a riveting read, recommended for those who like their private-eye fiction hard-boiled. The book is made all the more interesting by the fact that Reed Stephens is a pseudonym for Stephen R. Donaldson, the best-selling writer of Tolkienesque fantasy novels—a type of fiction as diametrically opposed to that of realism and the mean streets as it is possible to get.

A second Brew Axbrewder/Ginny Fistoulari novel, *The Man Who Risked His Partner,* was published in trade paperback by Ballantine in 1984. (*M.M.*)

*Stout, Rex. *Fer-de-Lance.* New York: Farrar & Rinehart, 1934. (CS)

After a successful business career and indifferent success as a writer of psychological novels, Rex Stout found his place in literature by creating two of the most memorable characters in detective fiction, Nero Wolfe and Archie Goodwin. There has been conjecture that Wolfe and Goodwin represent the two diverse elements in their creator's personality. That is plausible, though speculative. What is beyond dispute is that they are a perfect amalgam of the classic and hard-boiled detectives, in the words of Wolfe scholar Art Scott, "a unique hybrid of both schools."

Fer-de-Lance, the book that introduces Nero and Archie, is a long one for several reasons. The readers of the time expected complicated plots, preferably on the bizarre side. This book, with one foot firmly planted in the Golden Age of detection, certainly provided this. A college president dies on the golf course, and only Wolfe is sure his death was not due to natural causes. Following exhumation of the body, Wolfe is able to prove it indeed was murder, and the weapon was certainly exotic—a rigged golf club complete with a deadly snake. If the murder method is a bit hard to accept, the motives, with their roots in the past, do ring true. However, the murderer is disclosed well before book's end, thus reducing some of the suspense in what follows.

What made this book such a notable first detective story were the main characters, whom Stout so carefully (and, perhaps, lovingly) limns. Wolfe is the eccentric near-genius whose mental quirks would fill a Freudian index. He is a misogynist, an agoraphobic, and an obsessive-compulsive who lives his life according to a schedule from which there must be no deviation. He is also massively obese, gorging himself on vast amounts of gourmet food and beer. And he is a language scholar who will go into a rage if English is misused. Archie, on the other hand, is a colloquial-speaking all-American boy from Ohio, though he is as hard-boiled as his contemporaries, the private eyes of the pulp magazines. He is tough enough that he does not have to consume much alcohol and sticks to milk, his beverage of choice. Women are strongly attracted to him.

Fer-de-Lance is written in a deceptively simple manner with its emphasis on dialogue and its limited use of description. The pictures we get are all through the eyes of Archie, the narrator, and they tell us all we need to know, with scarcely a wasted word. Rex Stout here began a series by exhibiting what Howard Haycraft has correctly called "an exceptional literary talent."

(*M.L.*)

* Stout, Rex. *Too Many Cooks.* New York: Farrar & Rinehart, 1938. (CS)

The most memorable Nero Wolfe books are those in which he leaves his home. Frequently, he ventures out only under duress, but it is by free choice, albeit with great foreboding, that he boards a railroad in *Too Many Cooks.* He is distrustful of all moving vehicles and even lectures Archie on the "two thousand three hundred and nine moving parts" of the train engine. Still, as a gourmand, he cannot pass up the opportunity to attend a meeting of the great chefs of the world. It is especially his hope that he will be able to obtain the secret recipe for *saucisse minuit* from the famous Jerome Berin. Murder occurs at the meeting site, and since Berin is the prime suspect, Wolfe sets out to prove him innocent, thus incurring his gratitude and securing the desired recipe.

Food means a great deal to Nero Wolfe, and no book in his canon deals more effectively with the subject. Stout, no mean trencherman himself, even provides an epilogue in the form of eighteen mouth-watering recipes from Wolfe's files. However, do not be deceived into thinking that it was due to the cuisine described that Barzun and Taylor labeled this book a "masterpiece." It earned their praise and that of other Wolfian scholars (it is the selection that appears most often on lists of the best Nero Wolfe novels) because of its value as a mystery and as a novel.

The plotting in *Too Many Cooks* is tight, and the suspects interesting and varied. Physical action is not avoided; Wolfe even faces a murderer's bullet while dressed in his famous yellow pajamas. The Kanawha Spa and its locale in Marlin County, West Virginia, are well realized. However, as in all of the series, it is the byplay between Wolfe and Goodwin that makes this book excel. Archie is funny as ever, though a bit testy, even with his employer, expressing his displeasure at Wolfe's complaints about having to leave home. Archie is also given to frequent racial slurs in this book. Wolfe, however, delivers a superb talk on the subject of the elimination of racial prejudice. Wolfe's motive could have been to secure information from a group of Negro waiters, but we know enough about Stout's own liberal beliefs to assume it was heartfelt. *Too Many Cooks* is at once a mystery of its age and a book ahead of its time.

(*M.L.*)

*Stout, Rex. *Some Buried Caesar.* New York: Farrar & Rinehart, 1939. (CS)

Rex Stout went from strength to strength, following *Too Many Cooks* with *Some Buried Caesar,* another book frequently mentioned among the very best Nero Wolfe novels. Once again, Stout is at his best when he takes Wolfe away from the security of West Thirty-fifth Street. This time it is the chance to show some of his albino orchids at a fair in upstate New York that makes him travel about 250 miles by car. When he and Archie are near their destination, their car has a blowout, and they walk across a field to a nearby house. In one of the best scenes in any Wolfe book, he and Archie are chased by a gigantic bull. (The paperback version of this book was called *The Red Bull.*) The visual image of the usually sedentary detective fleeing for his life on a remote farm remains with the reader many years after having read this novel.

Rescued and given lodgings for the night, Nero and Archie become involved in a feud over the valuable prize bull, which leads to murder. Wolfe eventually solves it, but he is clearly not very anxious to do so. In fact, it is in this book that he admits, "My only serious fault is lethargy, and I tolerate Mr. Goodwin, and even pay him, to help me circumvent it." To a large extent, *Caesar* is Archie's case, the type of book that inspired Howard Haycraft to call Archie "the one example in history . . . of a Watson who steals the play from his Holmes, and a first-rate HOLMES to boot." After all, this is the book in which Archie meets the wealthy Lily Rowan, one of the many distinctive minor characters who have turned Nero Wolfe's world into such an interesting and believable universe. She dubs him "Escamillo" because of the incident with the bull. When Archie is thrown into the local jail on suspicion of withholding evidence, she acts as his go-between to Wolfe, at one point pretending to be Archie's mother, Mrs. Titus Goodwin. Meanwhile, in another highly amusing bit of action, Archie is busy trying to organize the prisoners in the jail (located in Crowfield, New York) into a union.

The above description implies that *Some Buried Caesar* is somehow atypical of the entire series, an experiment in slapstick. Not at all. The humorous scenes are perfectly integrated into a tightly plotted mystery, one with more surprises than most. When Wolfe appears to be making headway, there is an outbreak of anthrax among the livestock. Later, the person who has key evidence becomes a second murder victim. Archie's imprisonment adds to his employer's problems, but Wolfe proves surprisingly flexible, albeit a slow starter, and equal to the task.

Only a handful of mystery writers were really successful at combining detection and humor. Subtle humor and dialogue were always Stout strong points, and while the humor is a bit more physical in *Caesar,* it makes for a very funny and enjoyable mystery.

(*M.L.*)

*Stout, Rex. *And Be a Villain.* New York: Viking, 1948. (CS)

It is almost routine for science-fiction writers to publish trilogies, but the three-novel concept is rare in the mystery. The Arnold Zeck novels that Stout began with *And Be a Villain* were never publicized as a trilogy, but nonetheless they constitute a separate portion of the Nero Wolfe opera. Zeck is a modern "Napoleon of Crime," and his confrontation with Wolfe can be compared to Sherlock Holmes versus Professor Moriarty. Elements of melodrama are present in the Zeck trilogy, and they are not out of place when two such formidable adversaries clash.

Even without Zeck, *And Be a Villain* can stand by itself as one of the stronger mysteries in the series. Wolfe, in temporary financial embarrassment, is goaded by Archie to take the unusual step of soliciting business. He offers to solve the murder of a guest who was poisoned on an extremely popular radio program as he drank the sponsor's own product while millions of Americans listened. Two more murders will occur, though by less unusual means, before Wolfe solves the case and collects his fee. During the course of his investigation, he discovers that he is intruding upon Zeck's network of blackmail and political corruption. Wolfe shows uncharacteristic awe of Zeck, telling Archie, "If ever in the course of my business I find that I am committed against him and must destroy him, I shall leave this house, find a place where I can work—and sleep and eat if there is time for it—and stay there until I have finished. I don't want to do that, and therefore I hope I'll never have to."

A temporary period of detente with Zeck enables Wolfe to solve the case, disclosing the murderer during one of the gatherings of all suspects in his office that his fans have come to anticipate and love.

In the next Wolfe novel, *The Second Confession* (1949), the case on which Wolfe is working causes his path again to cross the empire of Arnold

Zeck, who expresses his displeasure by attacking Wolfe where he is most vulnerable. However, once more Wolfe solves a murder without an all-out battle with Zeck. This book is also notable for the opportunity it presents Stout, to include politics for one of the few times in a detective story. He expresses, through Wolfe, his contempt for the American Communist party.

The Zeck-Wolfe war, for which Stout had been preparing his readers, breaks out in full force during *In the Best Families* (1950), a book Guy M. Townsend has accurately called "the most unusual episode of the entire Wolfe saga." It is the book in which Wolfe announces his retirement, and that is only one of the surprises in the final volume of the series-within-a-series that begins so auspiciously with *And Be a Villain.*

(*M.L.*)

* Stout, Rex. *The Black Mountain.* New York: Viking, 1954. (CS/A)

There has been endless speculation regarding Nero Wolfe's origins. With his tongue planted firmly in his cheek, Wolfe's biographer, William S. Baring-Gould, pronounced him the illegitimate child of Sherlock Holmes and Irene Adler. No book by Stout tells more about Wolfe's past life than *The Black Mountain,* which even has the detective return home to his native Montenegro, now part of Communist Yugoslavia. We learn about his antifascist activities during the 1920s and that he speaks eight languages.

Two characters who have appeared previously are important to this book. One is Marko Vukcic, his fellow countryman as well as his oldest and closest friend. We know Vukcic as one of the chefs in *Too Many Cooks* and as owner of Rusterman's Restaurant, the only eating establishment for which Wolfe will leave his home and his own chef, Fritz Brenner. In *The Black Mountain,* the reader who is convinced that Wolfe hates all women will be surprised to meet Wolfe's daughter, Carla. She is adopted and had appeared in a previous book, *Over My Dead Body* (1939).

Surprise—that too-frequently neglected element in mystery fiction—seizes us in *The Black Mountain* and prevents us from being distracted too greatly by one of Stout's least likely plots. We willingly suspend disbelief as Wolfe and Archie travel throughout Europe, even behind the Iron Curtain. Because Wolfe remembers so much of his native terrain, he is less dependent upon Archie than in other books. In fact, Archie, not knowing foreign languages, requires Wolfe as an interpreter, even for the translations that permit his first-person narration of this book.

There is more physical action in *The Black Mountain* than elsewhere in the series, and Archie more than holds his own, even earning a rare commendation of "Very satisfactory," the highest praise Wolfe bestows. There is also a great deal of political discussion, but all of it is appropriate, considering the times and the locales. We learn that though Wolfe abhors communism, he hates the tactics of Senator Joseph McCarthy. We are also treated to Wolfe lumping fascism and communism (including Hitler and Stalin) together as Wolfe condemns both ideologies.

Too often the adventures of recurring characters in popular detective series are predictable. That was less true of Nero Wolfe than of almost any other major detective, and *The Black Mountain* stands as a monument to the pleasures to be derived when an imaginative author is willing to throw his readers off their guard.

(*M.L.*)

*Stout, Rex. *Trouble in Triplicate.* New York: Viking, 1949. (SS/CS)

After eight successful full-length Nero Wolfe novels, Rex Stout began to experiment. *Black Orchids* (1942) and *Not Quite Dead Enough* (1944) each contain two short novels. Beginning in the immediate post–World War II years, Stout would frequently publish novelettes in the "slick" magazines, and these formed the basis for eleven additional collections, ten of which had three novelettes. *And Four to Go* (1958) has four.

Trouble in Triplicate was the first of the ten collections, all of whose titles contain the word *three* or some variation of it. It is also a strong collection, with all three novelettes of excellent quality. "Help Wanted, Male" is set in 1944. Archie, though an army major, is residing at West Thirty-fifth Street, having been assigned by the military to Wolfe. Is it any wonder that his employer displays great conceit, even hiring a double for himself when he receives a death threat? Wolfe claims this action was not due to cowardice, saying, "Should I be killed, I doubt if the murderer would ever be caught." During the course of the novelette, Archie says that about twenty people have threatened Wolfe's life during the last decade. Wolfe's reply is "Pfui. At least a hundred."

"Before I Die" is wonderfully evocative of its time, the days of the war-caused meat shortage in the United States. Wolfe is suffering more than most Americans, sounding like an addict as he says, "I want slices of beef and pork. I want some meat to eat. Lamb. Veal." He is even willing to undertake a job for a gangster to get his hands on black-market meat. It is an atypical but thoroughly lively case.

"Instead of Evidence" is narrated by Archie one week after his return to civilian status. Wolfe appears to have regained his principles: Refusing an offer to be paid his $5,000 fee in cash so he need not report it on his tax return, he declares that he would not cheat "a hundred and forty million of my fellow citizens." Once again, in this amusing tale, the practical Archie convinces the reluctant Nero that he should take a case for the good of the household bank account. Archie says, ". . . he can't fire me because then he would never do any work at all and would eventually starve to death."

The novelette collections were especially successful because in a shorter format the increasingly simple plots Stout was using were less noticeable. Therefore, Stout for the remainder of his career would continue his experiment in a shorter length but would abandon all other changes in format. After 1941, every novel would be about Wolfe. Previously, Stout had tried out a variety of detectives, but none of them could compare in popularity with Wolfe and Goodwin. Still, it is worthwhile for the fan to seek out such items as *Double for Death* (1939) featuring Tecumseh Fox; *Red Threads* (1939), Inspector Cramer's only solo appearance; and *The Hand in The Glove* (1937), about a female private eye, ahead of her time, named Theodolinda ("Dol") Bonner. Bonner would occasionally reappear in Wolfe books and was apparently one of the few women he would tolerate.

Outstanding among the later Wolfe novels is *The Doorbell Rang* (1965), in which Wolfe takes on J. Edgar Hoover and the FBI. It was a rather daring assault for its time and, in light of subsequent revelations about Hoover and the Bureau, remains both relevant and thought-provoking. Also entertaining are Wolfe's involvement with the publishing industry in *Plot It Yourself* (1959) and with dude-ranching in Montana in *Death of a Dude* (1969).

(*M.L.*)

Strange, John Stephen. *Look Your Last.* New York: Doubleday Crime Club, 1943. (AD)

The mystery-writing career of John Stephen Strange (a pseudonym of Dorothy Stockbridge Tillett) spanned nearly fifty years, from the 1920s to the 1970s. During those years Strange produced a varied body of work utilizing a variety of sleuths. She began with a gentleman detective, Van Dusen Ormsberry, in *The Man Who Killed Fortesque* (1928), in which the victim is killed on top of a double-decker bus, and went on to feature a police-detective protagonist, George Honegger, in such novels as *Murder Gives a Lovely Light* (1941). But her best-known sleuth is newsman and photographer Barney Gantt.

Look Your Last is Strange at midcareer and is not only a highly readable mystery but also a good example of the incorporation of war themes into the mystery novel. The year is 1941, and Barney Gantt has just received the Pulitzer Prize for his investigation into conditions in New York's public schools. But like everyone else, Barney is more interested in the political news of Europe as the United States poises on the edge of World War II.

While the novel does contain a murder mystery, it is more concerned with the intrigues of war. Many of the issues raised remain timely: We are shown, for example, the questionable loyalties of the American oil conglomerates, dirty tricks, and international corporate and political intrigue; we are even shown First Amendment strife between the press and the legal system.

We have no doubt that Barney will solve the murder case and expose at least part of the corruption. But *Look Your Last* retains a feeling of melancholy and uncertainty that even the romantic resolution between Barney and his ladylove of eight years, Muriel, cannot completely dispel. Strange's vivid expression of the time is even more effective than her mystery plot.

Although not widely read today, Strange's novels are worth reading, especially for their depiction of bygone days. Noteworthy are *The Strangler Fig* (1930), which was considered one of the best detective stories of the period 1928–33 by critic William Lyon Phelps; *Black Hawthorn* (1933), which deals with the opium trade; and *For the Hangman* (1934), in which a scandal-sheet columnist is murdered.

(*K.L.M.*)

*Stribling, T. S. *Clues of the Caribees: Being Certain Criminal Investigations of Henry Poggioli, Ph.D.* New York: Doubleday, 1929. (SS/CS)

A cornerstone of the Haycraft-Queen Definitive Library of Detective-Crime-Mystery Fiction, *Clues of the Caribees* is the best-known work in that genre by Thomas Sigismund Stribling, a Pulitzer Prize–winning novelist. It collects five tales about Professor Poggioli, psychologist/criminologist at Ohio State University, which were originally published in *Adventure* magazine during 1925 and 1926. Poggioli is on sabbatical, and the stories all take place during his travels in the Caribbean.

Despite his profession, Poggioli is far from memorable as either a psychologist or a detective. In the former capacity, he is content to throw out the most glittering generalizations about groups—e.g., ". . . she is of Venezuelan blood, fiery and rash," and another person is described as having the "conservative temperament of the brunette type." The professor tends to be impressed by glowing, albeit false, accounts of his alleged exploits. In reality he bungles into solutions, and though he is often very nervous, he rashly places himself in positions of peril.

If neither the detection nor the psychology justifies the fame of this book, there are still reasons why it should be read. Few writers have caught the West Indies so accurately and with so wry a sense of humor. In the story "Cricket," the title sport is used ironically as metaphor. The stories contain some devastating portrayals of tourists, especially those from the United States. One staying at a Curaçao hotel in "The Refugees" complains when a murder site is placed off limits, "It's a shame we can't go in and look at the body. I paid my three bucks a day here, and they told me it included everything."

"The Governor of Cap Haitien" is the best and longest story, taking up almost one-third of the book's more than 300 pages. Though voodooism is a strong element in it, the struggle between dictator and rebels makes it still timely, more than half a century after it was written. Its climactic battle demonstrates Stribling's ability to write action scenes: ". . . men crushed together like an enormous steel-tipped football scrimmage." "A Passage to Benares" is the most famous story in the book for many reasons, including its references to the Loeb-Leopold case so famous in the United States during the 1920s; its surprise ending has been justifiably described as "positively thunderous."

In *Clues of the Caribees,* T. S. Stribling showed that Poggioli (and he) were interested in the philosophic aspects of crime. Though he tended to generalize regarding the races, he also clearly exemplified an abhorrence for racial prejudice that was also to mark his later work. After putting Poggioli temporarily on the shelf, he won a Pulitzer Prize in 1932 for *The Store,* second novel in his trilogy about a southern family. He also wrote some powerful short stories about crime and racial violence in the U.S. South, most notably "Judge Lynch," a 1934 story reprinted in *Ellery Queen's Mystery Magazine* in September 1950. During the late Forties and Fifties, Stribling revived Poggioli in stories written for digest-size magazines and set mainly in Mexico, Florida, and the author's native Tennessee. They were collected in 1975 by Dover in *Best Dr. Poggioli Detective Stories.*

(*M.L.*)

Stuart, William L. *Night Cry.* New York: Dial, 1948. (PP/PS)

Lieutenant Mark Deglin of the New York Police Department is a tough cop. He hates criminals and he doesn't mind knocking them around when the situation calls for it. The young football hero Kendall Paine, for instance. It is obvious to Deglin that Paine is both a drunken punk and the murderer of a man knifed during a fight at a posh gambling club; he deserves to get himself roughed up when he tries to resist arrest at his apartment. Besides, Deglin is in a foul temper: He has just been passed over in the civil-service advances; and another cop, one he doesn't like, named Knight, has been promoted to the captaincy Deglin feels is rightfully his.

But Deglin hits Paine *too* hard, and the kid dies. He doesn't think much of it at first—not until he calls Knight to check in and is told that Paine was innocent, the real killer has confessed. Deglin has no choice, then—not the way he sees things. He arranges matters to make it look as if Paine has skipped and then gets rid of the body—becomes a criminal himself. The cover-up might have worked out all right for him, too, if it weren't for two things: One, Paine's corpse washes up out of the river, alerting Knight to the fact that he's been murdered; and two, Deglin falls in love with Paine's fiancée, the beautiful Morgan Taylor. . . .

This hard-hitting, tersely written novel of a good cop gone bad, of a man "walking in the night, [knowing] what it was to have the soul cry out for understanding and find none," is one of the best of its kind and should not be missed by anyone who enjoys the hard-boiled school of crime fiction. It was filmed as *Where the Sidewalk Ends* (1950), with Dana Andrews (one of his best performances) and Gene Tierney in the starring roles.

William L. Stuart wrote only two novels before being swallowed by the insatiable maw of Hollywood: this one and the equally tough and excellent *The Dead Lie Still* (1945). One wonders what he might have accomplished if he had opted for a career as a novelist instead of one as a screenwriter.

(*B.P.*)

Swanton, Scott. *Sweetheart.* New York: Bantam, 1980. (O/PP/AD)

Cissy Tagliano is the sweetheart of the California coastal town of Half Moon Bay, but her life isn't ideal in spite of such honors as being crowned queen of the Summer Festival. Her mother is dead; her father, Frank, is overly protective; her brother is estranged from the family. And on the night of the Summer Festival, Frank picks a fight with Gordon Wolfe, a young photographer who he thinks has been bothering Cissy. Frank apologizes, but later Cissy turns up missing. Friends say she's probably taken off to think things over. Gordon Wolfe claims she wasn't upset the last time he saw her, shortly before she disappeared. But Frank Tagliano has a bad feeling and, much as he'd like to deny it, so does Acting Chief of Police Claude Decker.

Convinced Decker isn't doing his job, Frank begins investigating Cissy's disappearance on his own, concentrating on Gordon Wolfe. Decker has his hands full controlling Frank, who seems obsessed with the idea that the boy knows more than he is telling. The girl's brother, Paul, returns from San Francisco to help; local teenagers who knew Cissy get in on the act; and Decker has an investigative circus on his hands—one that finally produces results.

The ending of this novel is not a surprise, nor is it meant to be. Scott Swanton gives us a good depiction of small-town life—a side of California we seldom see in fiction—and excellent characterization, both of the obsessed and grief-stricken father and of a cold, emotionless killer. This is one of those books that makes you care what happens to the people, so much so that you won't want to put it down until the final resolution is reached. A promising first novel by the coauthor of *My Search for Patty Hearst* (with Steven Weed).

(*M.M.*)

Swarthout, Glendon. *Skeletons.* New York: Doubleday, 1979. (T)

B. James Butters is a writer of children's books (notably the "Frisby the Fly" series), and very successful he is at it, too: He has a swanky New York apartment, a 1958 Rolls-Royce Silver Wraith, and a wardrobe that would have impressed Beau Brummell himself. One of the reasons he is so successful is that he is really a little boy at heart: "I LOVE good and HATE evil." He also loves his ex-wife, Tyler Vaught, in spite of the fact that she ran off with another writer, Max Sansom, a manufacturer of best sellers, after only three months of marriage. So when Tyler calls him and says that Max is dead, the victim of a hit-and-run driver in Tyler's hometown of Harding, New Mexico, Jimmie is ecstatic—even more so when Tyler offers to move back in with him, remarry him, if he'll do her one small favor. To wit: go to Harding himself, find out who killed Max (she thinks he was murdered), and, even more important to her, try to lift the shroud of mystery that covers two separate events in the town's—and her personal—history.

Jimmie doesn't want to go; he is a self-confessed coward and city boy. But he loves Tyler (even more so after a night in bed), so he gets into his Rolls and drives west to Harding. Where he runs smack into hostility, deceit, more murder, and a rather horrible secret conspiracy that stretches all the way back to two historical events, one in 1910 and one in 1916. The first concerns one of Tyler's grandfathers, a lawyer named Buell Wood, who shot and killed three cowboys after their hoorawing caused the death of his young wife; he was subsequently acquitted of murder, besting an old adversary, Charles Vaught, who happens to be Tyler's *other* grandpa. The second incident concerns the capture of four members of Pancho Villa's army after a bloody raid on a nearby town; the four were tried for murder, with Charles Vaught prosecuting, Buell Wood defending, and a jury on which were four citizens who had also sat on the Buell Wood jury six years earlier. The four Villistas were acquitted after an impassioned speech by Wood; the enraged townspeople began to talk lynching; the four Mexicans were finally freed in a "Texas horse race" (given an hour's headstart, on foot, to try to flee 13 miles to the border). Their actual fate has never been determined, although it is assumed they were run down and killed. Likewise undetermined is the fate of Buell Wood, who disappeared that same night, mysteriously.

But what does all of this have to do with events in Harding more than sixty years later? Why was Max Sansom killed? Why has Tyler's mother been institutionalized for thirty years? What is the hold sheriff Pingo Chavez has over the descendants of Vaught and the four jurymen? And what is the significance of the numerals "11:14," which, in various typographical arrangements, begin each of the novel's chapters?

These are only a few of the questions that Jimmie Butters must answer, while at the same time attempting to preserve his skin (some of which he loses, in fact, when he is tied beneath a car and dragged through the desert). Never mind that Jimmie is one of the unlikeliest heroes in all of crime fiction. Never mind that some elements of the complex plot don't ring true or hang together or make a great deal of logical sense. Just settle back, take a firm grip on your suspension of disbelief, and enjoy the ride—one full of thrills, chills, effective flashbacks to 1910 and 1916, and plenty of humor and surprises.

Glendon Swarthout is the best-selling author of such diverse novels as *They Came to Cordura, Where the Boys Are, The Shootist,* and *Bless the Beasts and Children,* all of which were made into films. *Skeletons* is his first suspense novel.

(*B.P.*)

*Symons, Julian. *The Detling Secret.* New York: Viking, 1983. (H/PS)

Julian Symons is widely considered to be one of the foremost authorities on mystery and detective fiction, as well as one of its leading practitioners. He is the author of what is thus far the definitive history of crime fiction, *Mortal Consequences* (1972), a book that earned him a richly deserved Best Critical/Biographical Edgar. He has also won numerous other awards from the Mystery Writers of America, the British Crime Writers Association, and the Swedish Academy of Detection, for both his criticism and his fiction.

Symons's novels and short stories are psychological character studies rather than conventional mysteries. They are accurate reflections of life in that they are played out against authentic backgrounds and do not always neatly tie off loose ends, do not always resolve in a way that is wholly satisfying to his characters or his readers. Writing in *Twentieth Century Crime & Mystery Writers,* critic George Woodcock says that "Symons is concerned with how the crimes he portrays reflect the decay of society, with the pretenses of the world of culture, and with politics and power as corrupting elements. The world he has peculiarly made his own is that Bohemian half-world where failed writers and hack artists encourage the emergence of a crime; this is a world where the murderer and the victim seem to attract each other." Symons himself has written that what "absorbs me most in our age is the violence behind respectable faces," and asks, "What better vehicle can you have [to show that] than the crime novel?"

His theme works equally well in the Victorian period piece, a type of novel at which Symons is particularly adept. His ability to re-create the way of life in England before the turn of the century is second to none; reading *The Detling Secret,* for instance, is like reading Conan Doyle, only at much greater depth. The story revolves around the political turmoil of the 1890s: The question of home rule for Ireland is a hotly debated issue; special departments of the Home Office and the CID have been established to keep watch on such political criminals as anarchists and Fenians (members of an Irish-American revolutionary society that has fomented terrorism in Ireland). Against the background of these turbulent times, Symons spins a tale of love and murder, and depicts not one but two families with dangerous secrets.

Young and ambitious Liberal M.P. Bernard Ross has fallen in love with Dolly Detling, daughter of Tory leader Sir Arthur Detling. Sir Arthur objects strenuously to the match, and not only on grounds of their differing politics. For one thing, Ross's antecedents are hazy, and even when the younger man explains them, Sir Arthur is not sure he is telling the whole truth. But Dolly's wishes prevail, and she weds Ross. And soon she begins to feel something is not right with her marriage; Ross has too casual an attitude toward his political work and the issue of home rule, which his party supports; he refuses to discuss politics with her, and she feels he is hiding something. When a failed artist, Eustace Settleby, is bludgeoned to death in his studio, he has a piece of paper in his pocket on which Ross's name has been written. And there are rumors that Ross has links with two Fenians who have recently been tried for murder and acquitted.

Dolly must put her fears and suspicions aside when the Detling family gathers at Chadderley, their country house in Kent, for the Christmas holidays. It is an ill-assorted group consisting of Sir Arthur and Lady Detling; Dolly and Ross; her sister, Nelly, and Nelly's artist lover, Charlie Bangs; her brother, Roderick, and his family; Roderick's friend from the Irish Section of the Home Office, Paul Patterwick; Josiah Blader, a company promoter variously thought to be either a genius or a crook; and Duncan ("Lucky") Hatherley, an American investor who arrives in the country on a strange mission. It is there at Chadderley that a second murder occurs and the secrets of both Ross and the Detlings are forced into the open.

Symons has published one other superb Victorian mystery, *The Blackheath Poisonings* (1979). Like *The Detling Secret,* it is rich in period detail and atmosphere.

(*B.P./M.M.*)

Symons, Julian. *A Three-Pipe Problem.* New York: Harper & Row, 1975. (AD)

Fans of Sherlock Holmes and of the modern detective novel alike will enjoy this story of how a television actor who feels an obsessive identification with the character he plays sets out to solve a series of crimes.

Sheridan Haynes first achieved fame by playing the great detective on the stage, and then went on to portray him in a TV series, which, at the opening of this novel, is beginning to receive poorer and poorer ratings. Two murders have recently occurred in London—that of a public-opinion researcher and of a member of Parliament from West Dorset—and because of the nature of the killing blows, the press has dubbed them the "Karate Killings." In an interview with Haynes, a journalist asks him if he feels Sherlock Holmes could solve the murders were he alive today. Yes, Haynes replies—and then begins to wonder if maybe *he* can solve them.

"Sherlock Could Solve Karate Killings, Says TV's Sherlock Holmes," the newspaper headline reads. Soon Haynes is prowling London in his raglan overcoat. It isn't the first time the actor has showed signs of overidentification with Holmes; he lives in Baker Street in rooms that re-create the detective's digs. But that was mainly for publicity's sake, and his detecting is something that the TV station management has warned him against, in spite of the flagging ratings. A third killing, of a pornographic-book seller, only makes the bogus Sherlock more determined. As we watch Haynes's efforts, we are also privy to the parallel investigation of Scotland Yard's Chief Superintendent Roger Devinish, and by the time their paths finally intersect, Haynes has found that his life is changed in more ways than he would have imagined.

Among Symons's other outstanding novels of suspense are *The Narrowing Circle* (1954), *The Colour of Murder* (1957), *The Players and the Game* (1972), and *Sweet Adelaide* (1981).

(*M.M.*)

*Symons, Julian. *The Tigers of Subtopia and Other Stories.* New York: Viking, 1983. (SS)

Symons's short stories are every bit as accomplished as his novels, and make use of the same thematic material—as can be seen in this collection of eleven of his best and most mordant shorter works written over the past twenty years. The "tigers" of the title, as the dust-jacket blurb says, are metaphoric, "standing for the mindless violence that can erupt even in the calmest suburbia—the terror they induce is no less real than that of the jungle."

In "A Theme for Hyacinth," for example, an elderly man is manipulated by an exotic young woman into arranging the death of her husband, with tragically ironic results. Both "The Flaw" and "The Best Chess Player in the World" are stories of the not-so-perfect elimination of an unwanted wife; in the former it is an actor who conceives what he believes is a flawless method of murder, in the latter a printer with the grand name of George Bernard Shaw. The bureaucrat in "The Murderer" comes home one evening to find the police waiting: His wife has been killed in an auto accident that also claimed the life of her employer. When the bureaucrat sorts through his wife's private papers, he finds love letters from the man she died with—and he then undergoes an amazing transformation: His prudish attitude toward sex changes into something much more deadly. And in "The Flowers that Bloom in the Spring," a retired civil servant becomes obsessed with the idea that his neighbors are murderers when they dig a grave in their garden and their visiting cousin disappears.

The *London Times* said that these eleven tales are "artfully flecked with unease, in which the smothered passions of suburbia, the henpecking of husbands and a good deal of bad sex are feelingly delineated. Madness often hovers in the wings." Provocative and unsettling as they are, fans of the criminous short story will want to savor them in measured doses.

More of Symons's fine short fiction can be found in *How to Trap a Crook and Twelve Other Mysteries* (1977) and in two collections featuring one of his series characters, private investigator Francis Quarles: *Murder! Murder!* (1961) and *Francis Quarles Investigates* (1965). The last two titles were published only in England.

(*G.K./B.P.*)

*Talbot, Hake. *Rim of the Pit.* New York: Simon & Schuster, 1944. (T/W)

In 1981 a panel of experts on the "impossible crime" story selected *Rim of the Pit* as second only to John Dickson Carr's (q.v.) *The Three Coffins* among the finest novels of this type. It is an honor well deserved; even Carr at his most inventive could not have crammed more baffling and uncanny elements into one novel, convinced the reader that at least some of them *must* be of supernatural origin, and then proceeded to explain each rationally and plausibly.

Set in the dead of winter at Cabrioun, an isolated hunting lodge near the Canadian border, the novel utilizes the classic situation of a group of people trapped together by the elements, at least one of the group a cold-blooded murderer. Among the group are the Ogdens—unpleasant Frank, his wife, Irene, who dabbles in spiritualism, and his stepdaughter, Sherry; Luke Latham, a shrewd businessman whose purpose in coming to Cabrioun is "to make a dead man change his mind"; Svetozar Vok, a Czech refugee magician with a face like a reincarnated mummy; Professor Ambler, a secretive anthropological expert; Madore Troudeau, a half-breed guide who believes that the restless souls of the dead return to haunt the living; and gambler Rogan Kincaid, the amateur sleuth who uses observation, logic, and deduction to explain the fearful series of events that plague the snowbound lodge. Events such as the magical appearance and disappearance of an apparition during one of Irene Ogden's séances. And the footprints in the snow that begin and end so far away from anything that it seems they could only have been made by a supernatural flying creature, a windigo whose touch can strip a man of his very soul. And murder in a sealed room, and a dead man's voice floating on the wind across a frozen lake, and an encased accordion that plays a murder victim's favorite song, and a corpse that flies through the air as if on invisible wings.

These and other things strange and wonderful are the stuff of *Rim of the Pit,* a web of "complicated and brilliant plots," as Robert Adey says in his definitive 1979 study *Locked Room Murders.* A vividly described background, good characterization, a nice understated prose style, and some genuinely eerie scenes are other pluses. Prediction: If you read the first page, you won't put this novel down unfinished.

Talbot wrote one other complex "impossible" featuring Rogan Kincaid: *The Hangman's Handyman* (1942), which is set in an ancient, storm-lashed house on an island off the Carolina coast and, among its other mysteries, deals with a man who is killed by a spoken curse and whose body immediately begins to decompose. This one isn't quite in the class of *Rim of the Pit,* but it's pretty good just the same.

(*B.P.*)

Tapply, William G. *The Dutch Blue Error.* New York: Scribner's, 1984. (AD)

The Dutch Blue Error is the second book in the Brady Coyne series. Coyne, a lawyer to Boston Brahmins, finds detective work is often what his clients want. Since Coyne is divorced, has an apartment overlooking Boston Harbor and loves to fish and play golf, he likes the money he gets from his clients and usually obliges them. In his second book, we meet Xerxes ("Zerk") Garret, a young black law graduate who substitutes for Coyne's pregnant secretary while studying for the bar exams.

Oliver Hazard Perry Weston summons Coyne to help him quietly buy a duplicate of the Dutch Blue Error, a stamp owned by Weston and thought to be one of a kind. Weston takes great pride in his stamp collection, especially since being confined to his house in a wheelchair. Tormented by the thought that his stamp might not be unique (Weston is not an attractive person, treating his adoring son badly), he asks Coyne to act as "his legs" and locate the stamp, validate it, and then negotiate payment. Coyne reluctantly agrees, and these chores lead him to some unusual characters as he keeps appointments in the Combat Zone, Harvard Square and the Peabody Museum, where he and Zerk have a body on their hands. The police quickly settle on Zerk as the likely murderer, and suddenly Coyne has an increased desire to straighten out the question of the Dutch Blue Error and clear Zerk. The book is well plotted and the ending is both unpredictable and realistic.

Death at Charity's Point, the first in the Coyne series and winner of the 1984 Scribner's Crime Novel Award, features Coyne's investigation of the apparent suicide of a wealthy client's son at a liberal boarding school. While this is an intriguing case, Coyne's politics and sensitivities are vague. In *The Dutch Blue Error,* he is more clearly defined and likable.

Brady Coyne also makes a cameo appearance in *The Penny Ferry* by Rick Boyer (q.v.).

(*K.M.*)

Taylor, Andrew. *Waiting for the End of the World.* New York: Dodd, Mead, 1984. (T)

This is a tough novel to classify. It features one William Dougal, who was also the protagonist of Taylor's 1982 novel *Caroline Minuscule,* which won the Crime Writers Association award for best crime novel of that year. Dougal's adversary is the same in this book, too—the enthusiastically villainous Hanbury. Hanbury lures Dougal and his muscular friend Malcolm to a meeting of the British Apocalyptic Society, where they are forced to sit through a lecture concerning the environment, UFOs, and biblical prophecy. This pretty much sets the tone of the novel, which is madcap, adroit, and intriguing.

Hanbury has blackmail in mind this time around, and Dougal has his hands full. Sometimes they are full of Zelda, a beautiful black woman who is kidnapped by Hanbury. Blackmail and kidnapping aren't all that are involved here; Hanbury is also active in gun-running, drug smuggling, and various other illegal pursuits.

The undersigned reader can't help but think it's a shame Hanbury never met Professor Moriarty, that arch villain of the Sherlock Holmes stories. If the two of them ever teamed up, they could set crime forward and society backward at least a hundred years.

This is an offbeat, on-target novel, fast and entertaining.

(*J.L.*)

Taylor, Elizabeth Atwood. *The Cable Car Murder.* New York: St. Martin's, 1981. (AD)

Elizabeth Atwood Taylor's first mystery novel may keep us all away from cable cars for a good while. Here we get an intimate look into top-drawer San Francisco society—and, really, it's the same as everywhere else: Neurotic socialites hung up on social pretense create just as many sham marriages and messed-up teenagers in enlightened San Francisco as they do in St. Louis; and murder abounds, too, even though they claim "that kind of thing never happens to people like us."

The matron of this particular upper-class clan has not come home from braving the last-minute Christmas crowds in Union Square; neither has she kept her date at the psychiatrist's, where she and her college-student daughter were scheduled for their annual "heart-to-heart." The daughter calls around, discreetly inquiring if her mother is there, and by the time she's hysterical she's reached her mother's estranged elder half sister, Margaret. Years ago Margaret opted out of high society for a more real and personally significant life—and it's been *real.* Her husband has been dead for five years, killed in a motorcycle accident, and Margaret is just coming out of a five-year drunk (three months and seventeen days since she has had a martini at teatime). On the way up, but still shaky, she is suddenly the only family member willing to take on the mystery of her half sister's disappearance and, as it turns out, death in an apparent cable-car accident.

With the help of Richard Patrick O'Reagan—a fifty-ish retired cop who'd like to paint pictures all day but can't quite get the cop thing out of his blood (he still wears a police whistle around his neck)—Margaret blasts through the facade of the upper class, exposing the greed, deceit, and psychic paralysis that is there no matter how much money the rich spend to hide it. And we get a great dose of San Francisco in the bargain. Taylor writes especially well, with just enough contemporary philosophizing to juice up the usual whodunit action.

(*K.K.H.*)

*Taylor, Phoebe Atwood. *The Cape Cod Mystery.* Indianapolis: Bobbs-Merrill, 1931. (AD)

Back in the days when America had character, Phoebe Atwood Taylor created a sleuth with a regional background that made him as American as any detective before or since. She took a New England caricature and fleshed it into a believable Cape Cod Yankee. For twenty years, through twenty-four books, Asey Mayo, the "Codfish Sherlock," appears in flannel and cords, with his Stetson or yachting cap, sometimes sporting a "single-action Army forty-five," and pursues criminals from Orleans to Provincetown in his fancy Porter roadster. Asey is salty—he shipped on the last of the clippers; he sailed the seven seas as a cook's helper, an able seaman, and a mate. He has an almost unintelligible accent, and when he's on a case his voice ranges from a quarterdeck roar to a smooth, dangerous purr. This surly old investigator bases his detecting on "common sense" as he shrewdly sorts out disappearing witnesses; moving bodies; and stealthy, suspicious characters. Taylor has been credited with making murder fun and putting humor into homicide, but sometimes the gears don't mesh and it becomes mechanical. The plots slip into similarities of development, and the action becomes manic, with dashes through the woods, bashes on the head, and headlong drives down country lanes. In a couple of the books, the clues aren't quite fair.

" 'Millionaire son of automobile pioneer kills famous scribe in cabin.'—radio report." The "Homespun Sleuth" in his debut, *The Cape Cod Mystery,* clears up the mess that his boss, Bill Porter, has gotten himself into. Asey Mayo is his handyman and mechanic (in fact, in later stories we find that Asey helped in the design and testing of the Porter automobile—and during the war, tanks—and later rises to chairman of the board of the company). The victim is the oily novelist Dale Sanborn. He had plenty of enemies, both among the picturesque yokels and among the summer people from the city. The scene is Asey's hometown, 300-year-old Wellfleet, where at one point Porter is confined in the old pillory. In his rustic way, Asey gets his teeth into this mystery (as well as his "chewn" tobacco) and delves into anarchism, socialism, sardines, contemporary literature, long-lost relatives, and the Lucy Stone League.

The pace of the story is slow, unlike most of the later books. As in the first several titles in the series, the narrator is a refined spinster, who brings with her another instance of the absolutely superfluous cat that haunts many otherwise fine mystery stories—in this case called Ginger. The author provides an unusual murder weapon but an unbelievable and unsatisfying finish (for the murderer). At the end, Asey nonchalantly accepts accolades as "mere baggy-tell."

(*T.B.*)

Taylor, Phoebe Atwood. *Octagon House.* New York: Norton, 1937. (AD)

Octagon House is a real barn-burner of a mystery novel. (Well, it's really only one of the suspects in the book who is a barn-burner. He does it to cover up some clues.) Once again the "Hayseed Sherlock," Asey Mayo, is confronted with a foul deed and thrust headlong and breathless into the mystery. The town of Quanomet is up in arms over the new WPA mural in the post office. It's terribly indescribable; and in addition, the arrogant painter has included caricatures of leading citizens. The townsfolk want to tar and feather him, and when his wife is found murdered, there are plenty of suspects. But is this really an art critic's revenge? Why is the victim's sister accused and on the run? Is the ambergris that keeps disappearing (it's worth $50,000) a motive? Did the rich playboy, whom the victim was unfaithful with, have the opportunity? The sensation roils the summer folk, turns the natives into a mob, and brings in outlanders who think quahoggin' is the same as clammin'.

Asey Mayo has to stir this chowder of complications and sort out the clues. Someone paints over the mural to cover evidence; and after a spectacular plane crash, another murder occurs. Asey looks with suspicion at a blackmailer and at skulkers in the woods. To disguise himself, he merely dresses like everyone else, instead of in his expected hick Cape Codder attire, and he gets close to the action to investigate. He has some help from Jennie, his cousin Syl's wife, and her party-line listening service. Asey pulls in all his nets in time to let the state troopers take over and wrap up the case so he can get back to his sailboat for a little time away from all the hustle and tussle.

(*T.B.*)

Taylor, Phoebe Atwood. *Proof of the Pudding.* New York: Norton, 1945. (AD)

Asey Mayo had only a few post–World War II adventures. In *Proof of the Pudding,* after his stint of war work, he arrives back on Cape Cod driving a red jeep and finding no welcome committee. Not even his housekeeper, Jennie, cousin Syl's wife, is glad to see him. She sends him out to help with the cleanup after the recent hurricane, which devastated everything around Wellfleet and Pogue Inlet. While wandering in disaster's aftermath, the "Codfish Sherlock" finds a well-dressed corpse near the beach. The victim turns out to be the daughter of a man Asey had a fight with thirty years ago, and he figures that local gossip will accuse him of the murder. (By the way, the pudding of the title belongs to the victim—she never got to eat it.)

He's right about the accusations because his lobster-pot buoy is the blunt instrument that dispatched the victim. State trooper Hanson chases him as "the only logical suspect," and Asey's regular helper, Dr. Cummings, doesn't appear until near the end of the story. The case is complicated by looters picking up valuable antiques, rosebud plates wrapped in cod line, and a needless Siamese cat. The hero buzzes around in beachwagons, endures a long spell of eavesdropping, and suffers a bonk on the head. With a little help from Jennie, Asey cleans up the mess, and accepts the congratulations of all who believed he was the murderer just the day before. What the story lacks in plot plausibility, it makes up for in harum-scarum action.

Asey's other cases include *The Mystery of the Cape Cod Players* (1933), *Banbury Bog* (1938), *The Perennial Boarder* (1941), *Punch with Care* (1946), and two collections of three novelettes each—*Three Plots for Asey Mayo* (1942) and *The Asey Mayo Trio* (1946). For something even more reliable in the comedy/detection vein, Taylor also wrote several books using the pseudonym Alice Tilton (q.v.).

(*T.B.*)

*Taylor, Samuel W. *The Man with My Face.* New York: Wyn, 1948. (AD/T)

This compelling story begins with an ordinary man arriving at the suburban Redwood City train station after an ordinary day at his accounting office in San Francisco. Chick Graham doesn't have a care in the world—he has even remembered to bring the butter and pork chops his wife, Cora, requested. But Cora isn't there to pick him up, and when he phones home, she doesn't seem to recognize his voice. Finally she puts a man on the line, who claims to be Chick Graham! The real Chick takes this as some sort of dubious practical joke, but when he arrives home he finds Cora, her brother, Buster (who is also Chick's business partner), and Buster's wife, Ethelene, playing bridge—with a man who is his mirror image.

The four treat him as an intruder, so Chick leaves in search of the police. But when he returns with an officer, who is mystified by his strange complaint, the quartet in the house convince the cop that the man at the bridge table is the real Chick Graham—and Chick's dog backs them up by attacking him. Within hours Chick finds himself a fugitive, wanted for a murder committed by a bank messenger named Albert Rand who shot a guard and disappeared with $2 million in government bonds that morning in Los Angeles—and who turns out to be Chick's look-alike.

It doesn't take Chick long to figure out what is happening from clues in his past: It is a carefully laid plan that has been years in the making, ever since Chick and Buster were in the army together, and it involves Rand, Cora, Buster, and Ethelene. Betrayed by his wife and closest friends, Chick goes underground. Calling on an old girlfriend, who has also been victimized by the plan, for help, he begins to play a dangerous cat-and-mouse game with both the criminals and the police. You won't be able to put this one down.

Samuel W. Taylor's only other suspense novel is *The Grinning Gismo* (1951), also set in the San Francisco area. Unfortunately, it doesn't come close to measuring up to his first one.

(*M.M.*)

Teilhet, Darwin and Hildegarde. *The Crimson Hair Murders.* New York: Doubleday Crime Club, 1936. (W)

Baron Franz Maximilian Karagôz und von Kaz is the kind of fictional sleuth that could only have been created in the 1930s. Penniless, proud, prickly, and parlous, the Baron is a former head of the special investigation department of the city of Vienna, who resigned as the result of a calamitous political error and "escaped from a firing squad to the barbaric states of America to seek his fortune." Once arrived in the barbaric state of California, the baron manages to get himself mixed up in all sorts of nefarious goings-on, as chronicled in four unconventional mysteries published between 1935 and 1940.

The Crimson Hair Murders is Baron von Kaz's third adventure. It opens with him on his way to San Francisco by ship from Austria, where he had returned on borrowed money to claim the Karagôz fortune left him by his uncle. Unfortunately, said fortune consisted of nothing more than a two-headed krone piece depicting the benign countenance of Emperor Francis Joseph, so the Baron is still penniless. And despondent. Now how can he afford to marry his ladylove, Caryl Miquet?

Greater troubles commence for the baron in Acapulco, where his ship docks for a brief stay. In a cantina he overhears part of a sinister telephone conversation about an heiress, spoken by a man who looks like a Botticelli angel; the man immediately tries to poison him—and winds up dead himself when the wily Baron switches brandy glasses. After the ship leaves its next port, Manzanillo, the Baron is drugged and wakes up in his stateroom with the nearly nude body of a girl with hair "of such a violent red it could be considered crimson," stabbed to death with his umbrella sword. And once the ship docks in San Francisco, he runs afoul of the owner of a steamship company, a cat, a bald-headed giant, a locked cellar, and the business end of a mallet. All of which lead him to a confrontation with a murderer "hundreds of feet above San Francisco Bay on the fog-washed roadway of the great new [this is 1936, remember] Golden Gate Bridge."

This and the other Baron von Kaz mysteries—*The Ticking Terror Murders* (1935, by Darwin Teilhet alone), which takes place in San Francisco and Carmel and features a clever magician's illusion; *The Feather Cloak Murders* (1936), set partially in Hawaii; and *The Broken Face Murders* (1940), set in the South Bay (California) wine country—are a curious mixture of Machiavellian plotting, overripe prose, tongue-in-cheek humor, and surprisingly brutal violence. The Baron himself is not averse to knocking off adversaries, with or without his umbrella sword; and even when nonviolent, his methods are decidedly unorthodox. Still, for all his faults, he is an engaging character. And his adventures, if taken with a grain of salt, are great fun when you're in the mood for this sort of pure Thirties bombast.

Darwin Teilhet wrote several other criminous (and espionage) novels, among them an "impossible" mystery, *Murder in the Air* (1931), and the well-received *The Fear Makers* (1945). Hildegarde Teilhet was also an accomplished crime and espionage novelist; to her credit are such tales of intrigue as *The Assassins* (1946) and *A Private Undertaking* (1952). The Teilhets also wrote two nonseries collaborative novels: *The Double Agent* (1945) and *The Rim of Terror* (1950).

(*B.P.*)

*Tevis, Walter. *The Hustler.* New York: Harper, 1959. (PS)

Before his death at fifty-seven in 1984, Walter Tevis published three suspense novels rooted in gambling, and four science-fiction books. This relatively small *oeuvre* has a promising overture, the highlight of which is his most famous work, *The Hustler;* and a satisfying coda, the masterpiece of which is a sequel to the early famous work. Between the brilliant initial and final bursts was, sadly, silence—the result of a decades-long writer's block and Tevis's admitted retreat into academia and alcoholism.

The Hustler charts Fast Eddie Felson's growth of character as he moves from talented amateur to full-fledged pro. Arriving with his small-time mentor, Charlie, at Bennington's Poolroom in Chicago, cocky Eddie challenges the legendary Minnesota Fats to a game. A marathon two-man tournament ensues, and Eddie's skill with a cue stick is proven again and again, but, finally, the consummate professionalism of Fats wears him down. Nearly broke, Eddie retreats into a relationship with a sad alcoholic woman, a physical and emotional cripple, and they lean on each other. He begins small-time poolroom hustling again, but so exults in his first major post-Fats victory that the losers take revenge, breaking his thumbs. A physical and emotional healing is needed before any rematch with Fats; and the enigmatic gambler Bert, his new, big-time mentor, teaches Eddie the meaning of being a winner, a true professional: "If you want the glory and the money, you got to be hard," you have to commit to the life you've chosen.

The Hustler is a fine suspense novel, with its milieu of smoky, seedy, sometimes violent poolrooms, its world of gambling in which organized crime lurks in the wings. Tevis's style is tough-guy spare, but subtly shades, with the deceptively casual grace of Fast Eddie on a roll; the poolroom action is riveting even for readers unfamiliar with pool. The initial set piece of Eddie and Fats's encounter is such a tour de force, however, that all else seems anticlimax, until the second, ultimate showdown.

The Color of Money (1984), Tevis's final novel, is that rare sequel that surpasses its predecessor. Fast Eddie comes out of self-imposed retirement to find himself an old man in a young man's game, and a changed game at that. A longer, richer book, *The Color of Money* is the metaphorical story of Tevis's own successful comeback—just as *The Hustler* metaphorically chronicled the start of his writing career.

The Hustler was turned into a celebrated 1961 Robert Rossen–directed film, starring Paul Newman as Eddie and Jackie Gleason as Fats. Incidentally, Tevis insisted that he invented Minnesota Fats, and that only after the success of his novel did a small-time hustler (a heavyweight in weight only) appropriate the name.

(*M.A.C.*)

*Tey, Josephine. *The Daughter of Time.* New York: Macmillan, 1951. (CS)

One of the foremost writers of the Golden Age of detective fiction, Josephine Tey created characters of greater complexity than those of many of her contemporaries. They are at once true to their times and, in many cases, transcend them. Tey's carefully honed plots are of the classic puzzle category and her solutions are always believable. Series detective CID investigator Alan Grant is a gentleman who has opted for police work. Unlike Dorothy Sayers's (q.v.) Lord Peter Wimsey, Grant is a professional police officer who uses his social training as an effective aid in his work. His low-key, businesslike behavior keeps the reader's attention focused primarily on the suspects and the progress of his investigation. Besides the Alan Grant series, Tey created several other amateur detectives who appear in various nonseries novels.

The Daughter of Time is one of the classics of the mystery field, and is all the more fascinating because the subjects are real historical figures and the mystery involves a 500-year-old secret. Hospitalized after a particularly ignominious fall through a trapdoor, Inspector Grant is given a folder of pictures to divert him from his injuries. Among them is one of King Richard III. "What do you know about Richard the Third?" Grant asks his visitors. The invariable answer is that Richard killed the little princes—his nephews—in the Tower of London so he could become king. That is the interpretation of Sir Thomas More, of the historian Holinshed, and of Shakespeare. But in looking at Richard's picture, Grant sees not the murderer of his innocent wards but a man with the face of a judge—anguished, troubled perhaps, but not evil. And so with the help of friends who will get him books or do library research, Grant sets about finding out what made this man, who was "by all accounts an abnormally civilized and well-living creature . . . a good administrator . . . a good staff officer and good soldier," change suddenly and smother his young nephews in the Tower.

The research presented in this book is considerable and clearly set forth so that even those of us who bog down in the bevy of royal Richards, Henrys, Elizabeths, and Annes can follow it. The story moves quickly. Grant is at his best as he deals grumpily with the limitations of hospital routine while enthusiastically pursuing the mystery of Richard III.

Tey's other novels featuring Alan Grant are *The Man in the Queue* (1929, as by Gordon Daviot), *To Love and Be Wise* (1951), *The Singing Sands* (1953), and *A Shilling for Candles* (1954).

(*S.D.*)

Tey, Josephine. *Miss Pym Disposes.* New York: Macmillan, 1948. (W)

Miss Lucy Pym is a former French teacher who has written a book on psychology, never dreaming it would become a best seller or that she would become famous. But now requests for her to deliver lectures are pouring in, and one of them comes from her old school chum Henrietta, who is headmistress at Leys Physical Training College in the English countryside. Miss

Pym plans to stay only for the day, but allows herself to be talked into remaining for graduation.

Initially the students seem a normal group—just the sort of wholesome young women who would want to become physical-education teachers. When Miss Pym hears talk of the "college crime," she is surprised and questions Henrietta about it. It turns out to be nothing more villainous than food-pilfering—not an unusual transgression in such active young people. But as Miss Pym continues to observe them, she realizes that emotional problems are hidden under some of the healthiest exteriors. And when a real crime happens and a student named Barbara Rouse dies of a skull fracture shortly before graduation, at first it seems like an accident—to everyone but Lucy Pym.

Barbara Rouse was not well liked—an indifferent student who suddenly had begun taking first-class honors in almost every subject. Miss Pym has reason to suspect she cheated on her exams—but surely that wasn't reason enough for someone to kill her. In searching for a motive, she examines the characters of the various young women at the school. There is Pamela Nash, the intelligent and beautiful head senior; exuberant and comical Joan Dakers; Fröken Gustavson, a homesick Swede; Teresa Desterro, a sexually aware South American nicknamed the "Nut Tart"; intense and brooding Mary Innes; frankly unambitious Miss Thomas; and Miss Morris, who when first sighted is abducting a skeleton named George. As Lucy Pym uses her knowledge of psychology to sort through the hidden passions and interlocking relationships among the students and staff, she becomes aware of what really has happened—and must grapple with deciding what her responsibility in this affair should be.

Miss Pym Disposes is a top-notch example of Tey's ability to characterize an individual in very few words. Each of the students and staff of the college is sharply differentiated from the others—no small task with such a large cast—and many are developed in considerable psychological complexity. Lucy Pym herself is an admirable and unassuming character, and her observations on the young women and the college itself are sure to hold a reader's interest. It is a shame that Tey did not choose to make Miss Pym a series character.

Tey published two other nonseries novels: *The Franchise Affair* (1949) and *Brat Farrar* (1950; also issued in the United States as *Come and Kill Me* in 1951).

(*M.M.*)

Thayer, Lee. *Out, Brief Candle!* New York: Dodd, Mead, 1948. (AD)

The life of Emma Redington Lee Thayer is more fascinating than any of her novels. Born in 1874, she quickly established herself as a painter of murals on the walls of private homes, and some of her work in this field was displayed in 1893 at the Chicago World's Fair. Later she specialized in doing the designs for stamped bookbindings, and countless early-twentieth-century titles were made visually more appealing thanks to her skill. It was only after World War I that she started writing books herself, turning out a total of sixty mystery novels, for all but the last three of which she also designed the dust jackets. Apparently she holds the record for both professional and personal longevity in the mystery field, for her last book, *Dusty Death* (1966), came out when she was ninety-two, and she lived to be ninety-nine. She seems to have been a nice, refined, well-to-do old lady. Unfortunately she wrote her novels for an audience she thought of as exactly like herself, with no attempt to widen her appeal.

Fifty-nine of Thayer's sixty books deal with redheaded gentleman detective Peter Clancy, a dinosaur among sleuths if ever there was one. Imagine a stick figure from Edwardian times adrift in the decades of depression, war, angst, and civil rights, and trying desperately to pretend that nothing has happened, and you have something of the flavor of a Peter Clancy exploit. Thayer's novels move with the speed of an arthritic snail trying to cross a piece of flypaper. Her plotting is abysmal, her style unbearable, her characters impossible. In most of his adventures, Clancy is attended by an ever-deferential valet named Wiggar, a Jeeves clone without a drop of humor, who is constantly getting off *bons mots* like "Oh, Mr. Peter, sir!" Her favorite device for bringing a book to climax was to have God Almighty himself strike down the killer from on high, while Mother Nature whipped up a furious storm and the rhetoric swirled and squalled. Those who might think this description is exaggerated are referred to *Accessory after the Fact* (1943) and *Still No Answer* (1958), as well as to our main entry.

Out, Brief Candle! takes its title from *Macbeth* and its kickoff situation from Agatha Christie (q.v.): Like Poirot in *Death in the Air* (1935), Clancy investigates a murder aboard an airliner on which he was a passenger. Like all Thayer novels, this one is twice as long as necessary; but a slightly ingenious solution, combined with a truly grisly encounter between a little girl and a body in a coffin, lifts it to the ranks of Thayer's best, whatever that means.

Lee Thayer is a highly specialized taste, but if for no other reasons than her industry and longevity, she deserves better than to be totally forgotten.

(*F.M.N.*)

*Thomas, Ross. *The Cold War Swap.* New York: Morrow, 1966. (E)

Mac's Place is a bar located in Bonn, West Germany. It is run by McCorkle and Padillo, two expatriate Americans. The only trouble is that

Padillo, from time to time, has to assume his other role as an undercover agent, take a leave of absence from the bar business, and travel to some country or another on some mission or another. Padillo never tells McCorkle where he's going or what he's up to, and that's the way they both want it.

However, in this story, that arrangement begins to come unraveled. Padillo is off on another trip (nothing new there), but just as he is leaving, there is a killing in the bar that seems somehow related to his departure. And just as the furor over the killing is beginning to die down, there is an urgent message for McCorkle—a message from Padillo, trapped in East Germany and asking for Mac's help.

This is the first of several fine international adventure/espionage novels from Ross Thomas, and with each successive book he has established himself more and more firmly as a master of the genre. His stories, moving at a fast and intricate pace, are peopled with an amazing array—some critics might say an almost distracting array—of characters. A typical Thomas protagonist is seldom young; rather, he is flirting with middle age, is a little world-weary but still able to take care of himself, and should know better than to get involved in the situation that confronts him. But, for personal and/or professional reasons, he does become involved.

And indeed, McCorkle does become involved. He travels to East Germany to be met by betrayal, a certain amount of failure, and a certain amount of success. The scenes that take place during his stay behind the Iron Curtain are especially palpable and nerve-racking.

Other novels featuring McCorkle and Padillo are *Cast a Yellow Shadow* (1967) and *The Backup Man* (1971).

(*N.D.*)

*Thomas, Ross. *The Mordida Man.* Simon & Schuster, 1981. (A/E)

Sometimes it seems the CIA gets blamed for everything. For example, when the Venezuelan Gustavo Berrio-Brito (more commonly known as "Felix") disappears, it is assumed the CIA kidnapped him. Felix is a hero to the Third World countries, and these countries in particular are sure the CIA must be behind his disappearance. So sure, in fact, that a delegation from Libya kidnaps the U.S. president's brother in retaliation and threatens to send him back "piece by piece" until Felix is released. To back up this threat, the first note from Libya is accompanied by an ear.

Alas, this is not the only amputation going on. Felix, it seems, was actually kidnapped by a man named Leland Timble. Timble, an expatriate bank robber, had hoped to use Felix as his reentry ticket to the United States, but unfortunately Felix dies shortly after his kidnapping. To maintain the illusion that Felix is still alive, Timble's men amputate two of his fingers before dumping him into the ocean. Felix, it is decided, will be ransomed, via his fingers, to both Libya and Israel for $10 million each.

A sticky situation, made stickier still by the fact that the aforementioned CIA is surreptitiously at work on the case, as are the Israelis. The person working directly for the president is a man named Chubb Dunjee, ex-congressman and the so-called Mordida Man (a title he acquired in Mexico, where he used bribes and extortion to keep people out of jail—the Mexican derivation of the word *mordida* means payoff). Dunjee is the book's main character and we follow his activity throughout. But he is supported, and often hampered, by a veritable United Nations cast of characters.

(*N.D.*)

*Thomas, Ross. *The Singapore Wink*. New York: Morrow, 1969. (A)

Edward Cauthorne, an ex–Hollywood stunt man presently dealing in restored used cars, is the hero of this particular Ross Thomas novel.

Two years ago, Cauthorne felt he was responsible for the death of a fellow stunt man Angelo Sacchetti. During the shooting of a pirate film in Singapore harbor, Cauthorne and Sacchetti had been aboard a Chinese junk, dueling with swords, when Sacchetti fell overboard and never came up. The odd thing about the fall was the slow, deliberate, almost obscene wink he gave Cauthorne just before he hit the water. Practically every day of his life since then, Cauthorne's mind conjures up the fall and the wink and he breaks out in a cold sweat, accompanied by a severe case of the shakes, until the hallucination is over. This, in fact, is the reason he had to quit the stunt business and go into the used-car business.

But now word (delivered by two Mafia-like hoods) comes to Cauthorne that Sacchetti is alive and well, living in Singapore, and blackmailing his godfather, Charles Cole. Cole, a power behind the scenes in Washington, D.C., sends for Cauthorne and asks him to go to Singapore, find Sacchetti, and retrieve certain sensitive documents.

And so we are off, traveling through another Ross Thomas international thriller, accompanied, as usual, by a varied cast of characters: Carla Lozupone, the beautiful but dangerous daughter of a Mafia don and Sacchetti's former fiancée; Sam Dangerfield, the seedy, aging FBI agent who wants to nail Lozupone; Lim Pang Sam, businessman and head of Singapore's Secret Service; Captain Nash, adventurer and smuggler; Richard K. E. Trippet, formerly of British Intelligence, now Cauthorne's partner in the used-car business; and of course the ever-elusive Angelo Sacchetti himself.

Appropriately enough, the story ends as it began—in a battle aboard a boat in Singapore harbor.

Among Thomas's other nonseries novels are *Yellow-Dog Contract* (1969), *Chinaman's Chance* (1978), *The Eighth Dwarf* (1979), and *Briarpatch,* a story of political intrigue and personal vengeance which won the Edgar for Best Novel of 1984.

(*N.D.*)

*Thompson, Jim. *The Killer Inside Me.* New York: Lion, 1952. (O/PS)

The back cover of this paperback original has the following statement from the publishers: "We believe that this work of American fiction is the most authentically original novel of the year. *The Killer Inside Me* is Lion Books' nomination for the National Book Award of 1952." Lion was not a major publisher, even in the paperback field, and their novel had little chance to win. But there are those who believe it should have, because Thompson's book is one of the most powerful and frightening looks into a madman's mind that has ever been written.

Lou Ford, the narrator, is a deputy sheriff in a small west Texas town. He is a "good old boy," well liked by everyone. He is also a psychopathic killer. Two men in one body, trapped by "the sickness," he is set off on his trail of murder by a prostitute. Before he is done, he has killed or caused the death of everyone he cares for. It takes a tough mind and a strong stomach to read this book, but the amazing thing about it is that Thompson manages to make his monster sympathetic, and that the sympathy comes from understanding. The reader is made to feel what it must be like to be Lou Ford, and the tortured violence of the book clearly reflects the tortured nature of Ford's soul.

One thing that can be said about few books can be said with certainty about *The Killer Inside Me:* No one who reads it will ever forget it.

(*B.C.*)

Thompson, Jim. *Pop. 1280.* New York: Gold Medal, 1964. (O/C/PS)

The psychopaths of Jim Thompson's novels—and his best novels invariably feature psychopathic protagonists—have much in common, but each is distinct. The closest Thompson comes to repeating himself is in *Pop. 1280,* where protagonist Nick Corey bears a great resemblance to Lou Ford of the better-known *Killer Inside Me.* Like Ford, Corey is a law officer (a sheriff), and like Ford, he feigns folksy stupidity while committing cunning, vile, and often pointless murders—using his position as sheriff to cover them up. The setting is a small southern river town before the turn of the century, and the flavor is at once reminiscent of Erskine Caldwell and Mark Twain;

the latter influence is such that Corey at times seems a psychopathic Huck Finn.

Thompson is at his best here—on familiar ground, he seems almost to be having fun, not trying as hard to be an artist as he did in the sometimes uneven telling of Lou Ford's story. *Pop. 1280,* a reworking of his most famous book, may well be his best. This is partially because *Pop. 1280* is a black comedy; *The Killer Inside Me* is far too bleak for Lou Ford's absurd behavior to approach the black humor that pervades the later novel. Corey seems so picked on and put upon (by his shrewish wife Myra, among others) that the reader begins to root for this combination Li'l Abner/William Heirens. Also, Corey's shrewdness—and sickness—dawns so gradually that the reader initially underestimates Corey—just as other characters in the novel have done. By the end, Corey has come to the conclusion that he is Jesus Christ, but concludes also that being Christ doesn't seem to be of any particular advantage.

Behind Thompson's black humor is the notion that the human condition is so unpleasant as to drive each of us mad, at least a little. And perhaps, after identifying with or at least allowing ourselves to be confined within the point of view of a madman, we will understand the madness of, say, a Richard Speck—and the madness in ourselves—a little better.

An award-winning French film, *Coup de Torchon* (1981), directed by Bertran Tavernier, transplants Thompson's tale to Equatorial Africa, 1936, but captures the spirit of the work to perfection. Tavernier's film has helped draw attention to Thompson and *Pop. 1280,* and Black Lizard Books brought this minor masterpiece back into print in 1984, as one of a trio of Thompsons published in self-consciously old-fashioned "paperback" format, with covers evoking old pinball-machine art.

(*M.A.C.*)

Thompson, Jim. *Savage Night.* New York: Lion, 1953. (O/PS)

Although *Savage Night* has never attained the cult status of Jim Thompson's *The Killer Inside Me,* it is an equally unnerving book, one that still has the power to shock despite the more than thirty years that have elapsed since its original publication. Carl ("Little") Bigger (a.k.a. Carl Bigelow), a tubercular professional killer who is all of five feet tall, is sent to murder a key witness in an upcoming trial. His plan is to do so by enlisting the help of his victim's wife, but he hasn't counted on the complications that arise, including the distrust of the local sheriff and his own feelings for Ruth, the deformed girl who works for his victim. Like Lou Ford in *The Killer Inside Me,* Bigger is oddly sympathetic. He is a cold-blooded killer, but he is at the same time a human being. He coldly seduces the wife, but his affair with Ruth is quite different. He has decent impulses, and even acts on them.

The book has a number of unexpected twists in the plot, but what really interests the reader are Bigger and his inner conflicts. The climax comes in a crescendo of violence and madness unsurpassed in the work of any other writer of paperback fiction, and perhaps even in Thompson's other work. The chapters become shorter as the madness and violence grow, with the last six chapters occupying only three pages of text. The final chapter is one sentence long, but it is as devastating as any conclusion you are ever likely to read.

Thompson wrote several other powerfully unique novels that should not be missed, including *A Hell of a Woman* (1954), *Wild Town* (1957; in which Lou Ford has a cameo appearance), *The Getaway* (1959), *Pop. 1280* (1964), and *Texas by the Tail* (1965).

(*B.C.*)

Thomson, June. *A Question of Identity.* New York: Doubleday Crime Club, 1977. (PP)

If the reader has ever wondered what British police work is all about, this story—and others by June Thomson—will bring it to life. Thomson writes quiet, meticulously plotted mysteries set in the English countryside or small towns. Her hero, Inspector Rudd (Inspector Finch in the British editions), is a low-key sort whose personal life seems limited to his sister and pet dog, which he rescued from abandonment in his first case (*Not One of Us,* 1971). The settings are well described, and the procedure lends the stories an air of authenticity.

In *A Question of Identity,* an archaeological expedition working through the summer in the Midland farm country digs up a few bones one afternoon. Before anyone can start claiming a major historical find, someone notices the corpse's boots are still intact. In fact, the body has been in the ground for only a couple of years. Better to alert the police than the Royal Academy.

Now it is up to Detective Inspector Rudd to figure out who the almost unidentifiable corpse is and who put him there, so neatly laid out—complete with burial shroud (albeit an old wool blanket held together with safety pins). What manner of murderer would take such care of the object of his sacrilege? Rudd has little to go on, but his methodical pestering of the neighboring farmers turns up a missing man, the brother of Geoff Lovell who owns the adjoining farm. And when that lead comes to nothing, he is forced to reconstruct his theory and start all over again. There are no big surprises, just a reshuffling of possibilities—and all, of course, falls into place during the last ten pages.

Good characterizations, a believable plot, and an informative depiction of lower-middle-class Englishmen still hanging onto their land make this an enjoyable novel. The same is true of the other Inspector Rudd novels, among them *The Long Revenge* (1974), *Deadly Relations* (1979), *Shadow of Doubt* (1981), and *Sound Evidence* (1985).

(*K.K.H.*)

*Tilton, Alice. *The Left Leg.* New York: Norton, 1940. (AD/C)

Take a character who is the spitting image of William Shakespeare, make him a former professor at—and subsequent owner of—a suburban Boston boys' academy, further make him the author (under the pseudonym Murgatroyd Jones and unbeknown to his intimates) of a series of pulpy, best-selling thrillers about a character named Haseltine, and you have a unique fictional detective. Leonidas Witherall, surrounded by a changing cast of scatterbrains who all end up calling him either Bill or Bill Shakespeare, is the perfect nucleus for the series of comedy/mysteries created by Phoebe Atwood Taylor (q.v.), writing as Alice Tilton. Witherall is more defined as an individual, not so stereotypically "Yankee" as Asey Mayo, her other series detective. His wild escapades feature lots of action—chases on buses and trucks; games of hide-and-seek from cruising carloads of police; planted clues and suspicious lurkings; witnesses appearing and disappearing. Other mirth and mystification is provided by bizarre getups and disguises, mistaken identities, spying in slush and snow, and some incredible disgressions on literary and other matters. And at the end of each, swinging his pince-nez, Witherall solves the puzzle and plans conclusive action using Haseltine's tactics.

Fans of humor with their gore will get a kick out of *The Left Leg.* The Scarlet Wimpernel, a devastating blonde wearing a scarlet wimple, gets Bill, er, Leonidas, thrown off a local bus. He is chased by the police, who are trying to recover her stolen purse. Hiding in a hardware store, he enlists the aid of the owner, Link Potter. Together they find the only man who can provide Witherall with an alibi, Marcus Meredith, the present owner of the boys' academy, dead in his study—and all the evidence points to Leonidas. Not only is Meredith's artificial leg missing, but while searching for clues and hiding from the law, Witherall's helper becomes the missing Link.

Tangled in the "tentacles of the octopus of fate," Witherall gets assistance from the chairwoman of all the town's committees, a hardened world traveler; her secretary, who is really a radio actress; Frenchy, an ex-gangster friend; and a photography fanatic. Through some improbable impersonations at an earnest rector's colossal rummage sale, the final melodramatic scene is set up to unmask the murderer and extort a confession.

Leonidas Witherall is the hero of a total of eight madcap adventures, the first of which is aptly titled *Beginning with a Bash* (1937, but not published in the United States until 1972). The other six titles are *The Cut Direct*

(1938), *Cold Steal* (1939), *The Hollow Chest* (1941), *File for Record* (1943), *Dead Ernest* (1944), and *The Iron Clew* (1947).

(*T.B.*)

Towne, Stuart. *Death Out of Thin Air.* New York: Coward, McCann, 1941. (AD/SS)

The Great Merlini was not Clayton Rawson's (q.v.) only magician/detective specializing in "impossible" crimes. In 1940 Rawson took a week apiece to write four long novelettes about illusionist/sleuth Don Diavolo, which were published in the short-lived *Red Star Mystery Magazine* under the by-line Stuart Towne. Although zippy-paced and full of crude storytelling drive, the Diavolos suffer from careless plot details, pulpy hokum, unfairness to the reader, and such an overabundance of miracle crimes that one soon stops caring how the gimmicks were pulled off.

In 1941 the first two Diavolo exploits were retitled and issued in hardcover as *Death out of Thin Air.* In "Death from the Past" (published in *Red Star* as "Ghost of the Undead"), a frightened female medium is murdered, apparently by a vampire bat, in a locked room whose only other occupant was Diavolo himself. Accused of the killing by mutton-witted Inspector Church, the don escapes from custody, disguises himself as a maharaja, and goes after a bat-faced vampire man who claims to be a reincarnated medieval Satanist. After 30,000 words of blistering action and wheezy plot elements—the séance, the secret passage, the sardonic Middle-European count, the vampire, and the king of cliché alibis—Diavolo stops to decipher the murder victim's dying message and accuses a killer who's been obvious almost from page one.

"Death from the Unseen" (published in *Red Star* as "Death out of Thin Air") begins with the disappearance of a crackpot who claims to have invented an invisibility machine. Then someone apparently uses the machine to commit a murder right in police headquarters. The invisible killer boasts to Inspector Church about certain jewels he will steal no matter what precautions the police take. Church brings Diavolo into the case, but the thefts are miraculously pulled off anyway. The plot turns out to be unfair, incredible, and so cluttered with feats of legerdemain as to deaden the sensibilities, but the raw(son) inventiveness keeps one turning pages breathlessly as the pyramid of idiocies piles up.

The third and fourth Diavolo novelettes—"Claws of Satan" and "The Enchanted Dagger"—were collected during World War II as one of the rarest paperback originals of all time, *Death from Nowhere* (Wiegers Publishing Co., no date).

(*F.M.N.*)

Tracy, Don. *Naked She Died.* New York: Pocket Books, 1962. (O)

Don Tracy wrote historical novels and mysteries, several of the latter featuring Master Sergeant Giff Speer, an undercover agent for the U.S. Army's Military Police. Speer's organization is the type that is "so hush-hush that most ranking generals in the Pentagon [have] no knowledge of its existence." Speer's cases often involve hints of espionage, but they are usually cast as straight mystery plots. A good example is *Naked She Died* in which the daughter of a noncom who is working with the space program is murdered. Speer is called in to find out whether the murder is connected with an organization known as "America Before the Moon," a Communist front devoted to slowing if not stopping the placement of an American on the moon.

It soon becomes clear to Speer that there is more going on at Fort Beauregard than normal army life, and in fact there is another murder soon after he arrives. The murders are connected—indeed, they are committed by the same person—but Tracy provides so many suspects and so many possible motives that the reader is not likely to arrive at the answer before Speer.

As in several of the Speer stories, the army-base setting is well drawn, and Tracy clearly knows the characters he is dealing with. These things set the story apart from the usual mystery and make it interesting reading.

Another entertaining Speer novel is *Look Down on Her Dying* (1968), and a nonseries book of interest (but with a terrible title) is *A Corpse Can Sure Louse Up a Weekend!* (1973).

(*B.C.*)

*Tracy, Margaret. *Mrs. White.* New York: Dell Books, 1983. (O/PS)

Mrs. White, which was awarded the MWA Edgar for Best Paperback of 1983, evokes an overpowering sense of terror by juxtaposing chilling events with the mundane routine of an everyday wife and mother. In the opening chapter, we see a woman, Mrs. Porter, who is about to prepare chicken cacciatore. She goes on a routine shopping trip, returns home—and is brutally murdered. The identity of the killer—Paul White, devoted husband of Joan—is no secret from the reader. And it slowly becomes apparent to Mrs. White that something is terribly amiss.

Joan White's first inkling of this occurs when her husband claims to have been working at a time when he was not. The third "Housewife Murder," as the press has dubbed them, is committed that same day, but Joan does not connect the two events. Instead, she jumps to the obvious conclusion: Paul must be having an affair. Joan discusses the possibility with her landlord, Jonathan Cornell, in one of those conversations about a "friend" who is afraid her husband has strayed. Cornell says, "A man can't live a lie," and points out that "Somewhere, there's always a clue."

As Joan ponders this, images from the early days of her relationship with Paul rise up—disturbing images that she does her best to push into the background. And when she finally searches for the clue, what she finds is more horrifying than mere evidence of another woman. Terrified for herself and her two young children, Joan feels paralyzed initially, coming to loathe her once-adored husband. Her increasing panic—as viewed by Joan herself, the police, Jonathan Cornell, and Paul White—spurs the action of the story to a gripping conclusion. The story is intercut with scenes from Paul's viewpoint before and after he commits his murders, and these serve to heighten the tension to an amost unbearable level.

This is an edge-of-the-chair novel you'll read in one nervous sitting. (*M.M.*)

*Train, Arthur. *Mr. Tutt's Case Book.* New York: Scribner's, 1936. (SS)

Arthur Train's most memorable character was undoubtedly Ephraim Tutt, a shrewd old lawyer with a Lincolnesque appearance and manner, who appeared in a dozen short-story collections gathered from the pages of *The Saturday Evening Post,* as well as in one novel. In many mays Tutt was a forerunner of Erle Stanley Gardner's (q.v.) Perry Mason and John Mortimer's Horace Rumpole, often using loopholes in the law and legal technicalities in the service of justice.

The first magazine appearance of Mr. Tutt came in 1919, with the first book collection following just one year later. An earlier lawyer of fiction, Melville Davisson Post's (q.v.) Randolph Mason, had also used legal loopholes, and it's interesting to note how often the name Mason figures in courtroom fiction. In addition to Randolph Mason and Perry Mason, there is Hezekiah Mason, a prosecutor who is the frequent adversary of Mr. Tutt.

Mr. Tutt's Case Book is an omnibus volume containing twenty-six stories drawn from previous collections. The book is unique in that it is bound to resemble a legal textbook and contains notes and citations of actual cases following each story. There is also a comprehensive index of subjects covered in the stories.

Among the stories in the book, special note should be taken of "The Human Element" and "The Dog Andrew," two of the best in the series, which deal respectively with a murder trial and a boundary dispute between neighbors. Unfortunately a few of the stories betray racist elements common at the time, as in "Mock Hen and Mock Turtle," set in New York's Chinatown, and "The Kid and the Camel," about a murder in the city's Syrian community. Some of the most entertaining stories take place during Tutt's side trips to the upstate town of Pottsville. One of these, "Mr. Tutt Takes a Chance," about fraud involving a will, is more of a detective story than most of the series.

The first collection of stories, *Tutt and Mr. Tutt* (1920), was followed by a somewhat padded Tutt novel, *The Hermit of Turkey Hollow* (1921). The best collection is probably the third, *Tut, Tut! Mr. Tutt* (1923), though a late collection, *Mr. Tutt Comes Home* (1941), has more stories that qualify as real detection.

(*E.D.H.*)

Treat, Lawrence. *V as in Victim.* New York: Duell, 1945. (PP)

Lawrence Treat is generally recognized as one of the first proponents of the modern police procedural. In such early novels as *B as in Banshee* (1940) and *D as in Dead* (1941), Treat featured a clever criminologist named Carl Wayward; these books were conventional mysteries, entertaining but without much innovation. *V as in Victim,* however, was Treat's "breakthrough" book. In this novel he gave mystery readers a new look at the police—a realistic detailing of their methods of investigating crime, as well as insight into the politics and personal lives of various individual policemen.

Mitch Taylor is the veteran cop with family problems who sees bribes as society's natural lubricant and is not above accepting certain kinds. Jub Freeman is a new-style policeman: He is skilled in forensic science, and his laboratory knowledge provides the means by which many of the pair's cases are broken. In their debut in *V as in Victim,* Taylor and Freeman investigate a routine hit-and-run accident that ties in with a homicide at a local hotel. Mitch Taylor uses his no-nonsense approach of legwork, interrogation, and information gleaned from informants, while Jub Freeman puts the clues to scientific analysis—a combination that eventually solves the case. Treat's low-key, straightforward narrative style and plotting technique add to the sense of realism.

Taylor and Freeman, along with Homicide Lieutenant Bill Decker, are featured in several of Treat's novels—among them *Q as in Quicksand* (1947), *Weep for a Wanton* (1956), and *Lady, Drop Dead* (1960)—as well as many short stories. "H as in Homicide," perhaps their finest short case, was the recipient of a 1964 Best Short Story Edgar; this and several others were collected in *P as in Police* (1970).

Treat has also published two highly successful puzzle books, *Crime and Punishment* (1981) and *More Crime and Punishment* (1983), each of which contains twenty-four picture mysteries.

(*G.K.*)

Trevanian. *The Eiger Sanction.* New York: Crown, 1972. (E/A)

Trevanian (a pseudonym used by three different authors) is a writer of unusual powers: He writes spy farces, police procedurals, and love stories with equal skill. Each of his books is an adventure because he doesn't repeat himself; the only constant is that his novels have a wide appeal for very different audiences.

The Eiger Sanction, which was a runaway best seller in 1972, introduces Jonathan Hemlock, a college professor of art history who doubles as a freelance assassin for a secret U.S. intelligence agency, CII, headed by a bizarre albino named Yurasis Dragon (pun very definitely intended). Hemlock's passions in life are his house (a converted church on Long Island), collecting stolen impressionist paintings, and grand-scale mountain climbing. Such passions are extremely expensive, more than a mere college professor could afford; therefore Hemlock charges a fee of $10,000 for each "sanction" or counterassassination of an enemy agent who has assassinated one of ours.

His sanction in this case is to "demote maximally" (another euphemism, this one meaning to purge by killing) the man responsible for the murder of a CII agent known as Wormwood. His quest takes him from Montreal, where Wormwood was done in, to Arizona and finally to Switzerland. He knows that his quarry is one of three men, all world-class mountain climbers, but he doesn't know which one: Jean-Paul Bidet, a forty-two-year-old wealthy French manufacturer; Karl Freytag, twenty-six and sole heir to a German industrial complex; or Anderl Meyer, twenty-five and Viennese, a former medical student now a Tyrolean guide. And it isn't until the four men set out to climb the awesome Eigerwand in the Swiss Alps that he finally learns who his adversary is.

Many of the trappings of the novel are deliberately outrageous, but when Hemlock gets down to the business of investigating which of his fellow climbers is his target, Trevanian allows farce to take a back seat to serious adventure; and his descriptions of the Eigerwand climb and its outcome generate considerable suspense. These climbing scenes were also the highlight of the 1975 film version starring Clint Eastwood and George Kennedy.

Jonathan Hemlock reappears in *The Loo Sanction* (1973), another best-selling blend of spy spoof and globe-trotting adventure. Trevanian's other novels are *The Main* (1976), a Montreal-based police procedural both tense and powerful; *Shibumi* (1979), a tale of Oriental revenge; and *The Summer of Katya* (1983), a haunting love story.

(*G.K./B.P.*)

Trott, Susan. *The Housewife and the Assassin.* New York: St. Martin's, 1979. (T)

Susan Trott's first novel is set in Marin County, California, and is rich in all the trappings of that much-maligned and parodied locale. The heroine, Augusta Gray, is a devoted wife and mother who has a crippling phobia about going anywhere alone—one that she does her best to conceal. It is on a grocery-shopping trip, among the "flamboyant fresh fruits" and "beautiful produce," that she conceives of writing an international jogging book, a project she hopes will put life back into her flagging marriage. When husband Duke ridicules the idea, Augusta begins her researches on her own, thus becoming a runner, a more self-sufficient woman, and—inadvertently—the target of an assassin.

The story is told in switching viewpoint by three people whose lives are on a collision course: Augusta; Ephraim, the assassin; and his client, Evalyn. When Augusta begins her running, Ephraim and Evalyn have met but have no professional relationship. But then Augusta sets a series of events in motion, all of which are rooted in her newfound pride in having become a runner. First she receives an inheritance from an aunt, and rather than turn it over to Duke, as she would have in the past, she keeps it for herself. With it she buys a Japanese print she has always wanted and a sports car (which she keeps garaged where Duke won't find out about it). Her morbid fear of going out alone has abruptly vanished, and the sports car permits her to range far and wide—eventually to San Francisco, where she bumps into an old friend, Daniel Swanson. Daniel and Augusta begin an affair. Evalyn, a wealthy woman who is in love with Daniel, begins to suspect; and since she never does anything on a less than grand scale, she hires Ephraim to find out whom Daniel is sleeping with and kill her. Thus comes the collision toward which the housewife and the assassin have been speeding.

The parts of the story told from Augusta's viewpoint have a natural and sprightly style, and the reader is immediately in sympathy with this warm and irrepressible woman. Those parts told from the viewpoints of Ephraim and Evalyn, however, are somewhat coy and off-putting. The character of Ephraim never really rings true, and thus the unusual ending is not quite believable. Still, Augusta is well worth knowing, and her character more than overcomes these other flaws.

This is Trott's only suspense novel to date. Her second novel, a mainstream story also set in Marin County, is *When Your Lover Leaves . . .* (1980); it was made into a TV movie in 1983.

(*M.M.*)

Troy, Simon. *Waiting for Oliver.* New York: Macmillan, 1963. (PS)

The work of Simon Troy (a pseudonym of Thurman Warriner) is distinguished for the eccentricity of its plotting, characters, and construction. Most people in a Troy novel aren't "normal"; they are obsessed, perverse, secretive, profoundly different. So, too, the situations in which they find themselves. This is true whether Troy is writing tales of psychological suspense and horror, like *Waiting for Oliver,* or what might be termed "psychological procedurals" featuring his sensitive Cornish policeman, Inspector Smith. All of Troy's novels—even the few that don't quite work—are quietly disquieting and absorbing from start to finish.

Waiting for Oliver is probably his oddest book. It is the story of a frightening, almost symbiotic relationship between two men who have known each other since boyhood: Oliver Townside and the narrator, Alex Monro. Oliver is the dominant personality, a personification of evil, a kind of modern vampire who, spongelike, absorbs the personas of those around him, corrupting or destroying them. Alex has always been terrified of Oliver, has always hated and pitied him, and yet has always responded to Oliver's hynoptic power and done his bidding. When they were children, he could not bring himself to expose his friend/enemy as the perpetrator of unspeakable acts of violence. Nor could he bring himself to seek personal vengeance as an adult, when Oliver maliciously seduced Alex's sweetheart, Margery, married her, and later coldbloodedly murdered her.

When the book opens, two years have passed since Margery's "accidental" fall from a cliff near Petit Sant, Oliver's home in the Channel Islands. Alex, a teacher in a small secondary school in England, has had no contact with Oliver since then and prefers to keep it that way. But when he receives a telegram announcing Oliver's intention to take a second wife—Frances, another woman Alex knows—he is drawn back to the islands. It is then, while once more waiting for Oliver, that he realizes he cannot let the man marry Frances, for surely he will murder her too. He sets out to do what the local police have not been able to do—prove that Oliver killed Margery—and also to free himself from Oliver's thrall, if necessary to destroy the evil before it destroys him.

The suspense here builds slowly, inexorably, to a terrifying climax on one of the smaller islands. And as a bonus, Troy portrays the Channel Islands (as he does all his settings) with a sharp eye for detail. The novel does have its flaws: its eccentric construction makes things seem confusing at times, especially in the early pages; Troy withholds vital information about Oliver's and Alex's boyhood until much too late in the book; and there are minor points that seem a bit *too* quirky, that don't quite ring true. Still, this is a powerful and unsettling work.

Also well-worth investigating is Troy's only other nonseries psychological suspense novel, *Drunkard's Walk* (1961), and his ten mysteries featuring Inspector Smith. Among the best of the Smith novels are *Second Cousin Removed* (1961), *Don't Play with the Rough Boys* (1963), and *Cease Upon the Midnight* (1964). The last-named title also has a Channel Islands setting. Under his own name, Troy/Warriner also published a series of novels featuring an outspoken private detective named Mr. Scotter, none of which has been published in this country.

(*B.P.*)

Truman, Margaret. *Murder in the White House.* New York: Arbor House, 1980. (AD)

Both Harry and Bess Truman were mystery fans, so it's fitting that their daughter Margaret took up writing novels in this genre during the 1980s, beginning with *Murder in the White House,* a feeble effort but one that made use of elements most appropriate to Truman's background, with the presidential living quarters as the murder scene and the members and closest associates of a fictional first family as prime suspects. Secretary of State Lansard Blaine, a brilliant and egotistical ex-professor of diplomatic history, is garroted to death with a piece of thin wire in the Lincoln Sitting Room on the second floor of the White House. Ron Fairbanks, a young Washington lawyer serving as special counsel to President Robert Lang Webster, is appointed by his chief to head the murder investigation, which stretches over most of the book and reveals the dead man to have been an insatiable womanizer, a taker of financial and sexual bribes, a blackmailer—in short, one whose death might have been devoutly wished by countless persons, perhaps even by the President himself.

Murder in the White House is not a study of character or scene, for the sleuths and suspects are uniformly dull and the official background routinely sketched in. It's not a police procedural, for the police never lift a finger to solve the murder. It's not a fair-play detective story, for there are no clues; the murderer simply confesses at the climax, at least one loose plot end is left untidily dangling, and as for how the killer made that bloody loop of wire vanish from a White House ringed by investigators, the character in question cavalierly tells us that "I disposed of it." Perhaps the book is best described as a TV movie in prose, amiable, unchallenging, easy to read.

Despite its flaws, *Murder in the White House* was enormously successful, as have been Truman's subsequent books: *Murder on Capitol Hill* (1981), *Murder in the Supreme Court* (1982), *Murder at the Smithsonian* (1983), and *Murder on Embassy Row* (1984). These later titles show much improvement, with more convincing plots, stronger characterization, and a more realistic depiction of the Washington scene.

(*F.M.N.*)

Turnbull, Peter. *Big Money.* New York: St. Martin's, 1984. (PP)

At the beginning, this promises to be one of those sparse, gritty police procedurals featuring a disinterested recitation of events and a minimum of characterization; the only thing of a personal nature we know about any of the people in the first chapter is that a cleaning woman left breakfast behind for her husband. Thankfully, however, as the story develops, we start to gain a greater and fuller insight into the characters—especially the policemen of P Division CID, Glasgow, Scotland.

It is this particular police unit that is investigating the quarter-of-a-million-pound robbery at the post office, a robbery perpetrated by six masked, armed, and well-disciplined men who left behind little trace of themselves. But gradually a few clues come to light: an elderly eyewitness, a couple of fingerprints in the abandoned getaway car, traces of a rare sea-cabbage plant in the car, and an apparent tie-in between the robbery and a two-year-old missing-persons case. Curiously, the men of P Division—who supposedly work together every day—seem to know very little about each other personally. But they get the job done. From the bits and pieces of information they are given, they put together an efficient investigation.

Big Money is an interesting and readable police procedural, with a feeling of authenticity about it. Peter Turnbull also wrote three previous novels about the men in P Division: *Deep and Crisp and Even* (1982), *Dead Knock* (1983), and *Fair Friday* (1983).

(*N.D.*)

Tyre, Nedra. *Twice So Fair.* New York: Random House, 1971. (W)

Nedra Tyre was born in Georgia, and she has drawn on her background as a southerner to produce a number of suspenseful and deftly characterized mystery novels. She portrays small towns like the one where this novel takes place in all their insularity, incestuousness, and pettiness, but with a certain compassion. And her characters, while what you might expect of that milieu, are never stereotypical.

Why was Rosalind Wells's devoted husband, Matthew, visiting one of his English-literature students at her artist's studio in the middle of the night, when he was supposed to be at the office grading papers? Rosalind took him away from his first wife, and now she supposes he might have been seduced again—an occupational hazard for college professors. Not many of them, however, end up dying for it. Matthew is dead of asphyxiation, apparently a victim of a faulty gas heater, as is his girlfriend, Jeanette Sloan. Or was she his girlfriend? And was it an accident? Is there murder about?

Terrified to face her husband's possible infidelity, but knowing instinctively that her life cannot continue until she learns the truth, Rosalind proceeds to bring the skeletons out of the closet. Not an aggressive person at all, she tiptoes through this conventional college town where it is a sin to hang one's laundry on Sunday, much less entertain gentlemen callers in the middle of the night. Rosalind has such a caller; he appears out of the dark and remains in the dark, sitting in her living room and telling a story only a lunatic could conjure up. Or *is* it so insane? Rosalind believes him enough to risk her ladylike reputation—and her life. What she finds sets this stodgy old southern town on its ear.

Among Tyre's other novels are *Mouse in Eternity* (1952), which features a social worker in Atlanta; *Death of an Intruder* (1953), which deals with the plight of the elderly; and *Hall of Death* (1960), set in a southern girls' reformatory.

(*K.K.H.*)

*Uhnak, Dorothy. *The Bait.* New York: Simon & Schuster, 1968. (PP)

One strength of Dorothy Uhnak's work is the considerable accuracy of her police procedure, owing to her fourteen years' experience as a police officer. This accuracy, however, goes beyond attention to detail, creating an uncompromising portrayal of the unpleasant and often shocking realities of police work. Her characterization ranges from superficial to excellent, and many of her best characters are the criminal and underprivileged. *The Bait,* first in Uhnak's series about Christie Opara, detective first class on the New York City D.A.'s Special Investigations Squad, won the Mystery Writers of America Edgar for Best First Novel of 1968.

Christie Opara, herself the widow of a policeman, is working on an important drug case but circumstances force her into arresting a man for indecent exposure on the subway while she is en route to a critical meeting. The delay causes her to miss it; and before she can resume the investigation, she is pulled off the case and placed on another. As days pass and we follow Christie through her daily routine, she begins to receive disturbing phone calls; and as she doggedly investigates the details of three grisly murders, a pattern emerges—a pattern that points to the perpetrator of the phone calls. In order to apprehend the killer, Christie herself must be the bait in a trap of her own devising, and the suspense heightens rapidly as the time approaches for the trap to be sprung.

Good procedure interwoven with scenes from the viewpoint of the killer, as well as nice glimpses into Christie's personal life. Christie is an engaging heroine who faces the world on her own terms and puts up with nonsense from no one.

The other novels in this series are *The Witness* (1969), in which Christie is the only person who can identify the murderer of an organizer at a student political demonstration; and *The Ledger* (1971), in which she must try to extract information about a narcotics ring from a high-priced Puerto Rican call girl.

(*M.M.*)

Uhnak, Dorothy. *False Witness.* New York: Simon & Schuster, 1981. (T)

This novel is Uhnak's most hard-boiled to date, definitely not for the squeamish. Its heroine is New York Assistant District Attorney Lynne Jacobi, bureau chief of the Violent Sex Crimes Division. Jacobi is thirty-eight, politically wise, and determined; she has been on every bureau in the D.A.'s office and is a natural contender for the head job itself when the present D.A., Jameson Whitney Hale, declares his candidacy for the U.S. Senate. But Jacobi is not without humor or vulnerability, and those qualities, combined with her toughness, make her Uhnak's best heroine yet.

The story opens when Jacobi is called to a crime scene in the middle of the night. A TV talk-show hostess, Sanderalee Dawson, has been raped and savagely mutilated in her luxury apartment near Carnegie Hall (the details of this are recounted graphically, and you won't want to read this too close to mealtime); the woman, a black and a former model, is alive, but just barely. Because of her celebrity, the D.A.'s office must immediately begin to work with the police in building a case that will stand up in court. It is a case that can make or break Jacobi's career, ruining her if she mishandles it, making her a certainty for the D.A.'s job if she prosecutes successfully. Jacobi, however, is a dedicated lawyer and a dogged investigator; her main commitment is to the truth.

There are few clues to the identity of the attacker, except that he was white, dressed in jogging clothes, and there was something peculiar about his running shoes. Dawson is in a coma and may not be able to identify the man even if she pulls through. Jacobi and her staff—among them Bobby Jones, who is also her lover, and former nun Lucy Capella—interview Dawson's friends and associates, but their break doesn't come until the woman regains consciousness and names her attacker. And when she does, it barely seems possible that he could be the man.

Jacobi works against pressures from the D.A., who very much wants her to be his successor; from various political factions in the city; from a newswoman who is trying to make her part of a documentary on women in powerful positions; and from her lover, who thinks she is on the wrong track. And just when she goes to court and gets her indictment, things fall apart on all fronts.

Told in a straightforward, often humorous style, this is an intriguing and well-plotted story. Uhnak allows us into Jacobi's professional and personal life, and we come away shaken by both the events that happen and their resolution.

(*M.M.*)

Uhnak, Dorothy. *The Investigation.* New York: Simon & Schuster, 1977. (PP/T)

In this nonseries novel, Sergeant Joe Peters of the District Attorney's Investigating Squad in an unnamed Queens community goes out on what appears to be a routine missing-child call. The father of the two missing boys is the sort one would expect in this solid middle-class neighborhood; but the mother, Kitty Keeler, frequents exclusive clubs, owns more expensive clothes than her estranged husband could possibly have provided, and has an address book containing the names of more than a hundred men—many of them high-placed in politics or with underworld connections. The small boys are soon found murdered, and Kitty's actions make her the obvious suspect. In time, however, Joe Peters begins to doubt Kitty's guilt and sets out to prove she did not kill her sons. As he is drawn further into the case, a romance develops between the two of them, and Joe's obsession with Kitty is resolved only by his discovery of the truth about what happened the night her boys disappeared.

Unfortunately, in spite of all its sensational trappings, the story comes off flat; and its obvious parallels to the Alice Crimmins case are intrusive to a reader who is familiar with that true crime. It is difficult to imagine the protagonist as really having an obsession, and it is likewise difficult to care about Kitty or the resolution of her plight.

Uhnak's other nonseries novel, *Law and Order* (1973), is the saga of three generations of a family of Irish Catholic cops. Her nonfiction book *Policewoman: A Young Woman's Initiation into the Realities of Justice* (1964) deals with her experiences during fourteen years with the New York City Transit Police.

(*M.M.*)

Underwood, Michael. *A Party to Murder.* New York: St. Martin's, 1984. (AD)

Writing under the name Michael Underwood, John Michael Evelyn has been publishing some of the finest in British legal mysteries for over thirty years. Called to the bar in1939, Underwood has had a varied career in public prosecution and government legal service. He has drawn on this first-hand knowledge to produce detailed and realistic courtroom suspense.

A Party to Murder is a recent offering and features Underwood's latest series sleuth, Rosa Epton. The "elfin-like" Rosa, a solicitor and partner in the London firm of Epton & Snaith, is called to the country town of Grainfield when an old friend, also a woman solicitor, is accused of murder. The friend, Caroline Allard, works out of the chief prosecuting solicitor's office and is the major suspect when the office gossip is murdered at the end of the office Christmas party.

Underwood sets up his situation well. The conflicting ambitions and intrigues within a legal office provide plenty of suspects; and if Ms. Allard acts in a particularly foolish manner for a legal professional, Ms. Epton is sharp enough for both of them. When Rosa is unable to prove her case against the individual she identifies as the real murderer, she coaches her barrister colleague to perform a dramatic Perry Mason–style courtroom confrontation.

Underwood's fiction is seldom action-packed, but it can provide genuine enjoyment for fans of mannered British mysteries who wish an authentic legal milieu. Other Underwood titles include *Murder on Trial* (1958), *The Crime of Colin Wise* (1964), *A Pinch of Snuff* (1974), *Death in Camera* (1984), and *The Hidden Man* (1985).

(*K.L.M.*)

*Upfield, Arthur W. *The Bone Is Pointed.* New York: Doubleday Crime Club, 1947. (CS/A)

One of the absolutely original detectives in the genre was created by Arthur W. Upfield, an Englishman who lived most of his life in Australia. Upfield worked at a fascinating succession of jobs (which he drew upon for his stories) before establishing himself as a writer. After publishing a few romantic thrillers, he settled down to the chronicles of his renowned series character, half-caste Detective Inspector Napoleon Bonaparte. Bony, as he insists everyone call him, uses aboriginal skills inherited from his mother for tracking and reading signs in the "Book of the Bush." From his father he inherited white man's reasoning and patience and, most important for his success, the ego to sustain him on seemingly hopeless investigations.

In twenty-nine Bony books over nearly three decades—beginning with *The Barrakee Mystery* (1928), which was a best seller in Australia and England but was not published in the United States until 1965, as *The Lure of the Bush*—Upfield explored the small towns and stations of the Outback, stretching over millions of acres and populated with jackeroos, squatters, prospectors, swagmen, and more or less civilized aborigines. A couple of the later books do not measure up to the high standard of the early ones, and a few are merely conventional thrillers with Nazi spies and the like; but even these are rich in both background description and atmosphere. In the Sixties, Anthony Boucher spoke for thousands of readers when he said, "The complex half-caste Bony is my favorite fictional detective of the past twenty years."

The Bone Is Pointed is one of Bony's finest and most dangerous investigations. Five months after a white stockman disappears in suspicious circumstances, Bony is called into the case. As he says, "Once I begin an investigation I stick with it until it is finished." In this one he confronts the secrets and silence of the residents of Karwir Station in western Queensland. More menacing are the local blacks who had a grudge against the missing man. A cause for alarm in many quarters is Bony's tenaciousness and patience in unraveling a case; at one point he spends an hour examining a tree to find a significant clue (shades of Sherlock). The danger becomes acute when the aborigines "point the bone" at Bony. They intend to remove him from the case by magic, a mental willing to death that depends on the executioners' mental power of thought transference: The evil magic is "sung" into the victim. This leaves Bony with a deadline of a few weeks to complete his investigation before the boning is agonizingly fatal. Another complication is Bony's racial pride, which will not permit failure for fear of reverting to his aboriginal roots and returning permanently to the bush.

In this book Upfield utilizes the full panoply of aboriginal lore—myths, beliefs, superstitions of the blacks; their communication by "mulga wire" (telepathy); walkabouts, medicine men, invisible shadowing; and all the other elements of the "Book of the Bush." Another theme that Upfield explores here and in many of his other novels is meteorological catastrophe and elemental events, such as flood, drought, windstorm, and, in this instance, an exciting rabbit migration. In the bush, Bony is an emperor, and in this case he triumphs even more royally than usual.

(*T.B./M.M.*)

*Upfield, Arthur W. *The New Shoe.* New York: Doubleday Crime Club, 1951. (CW/W)

Once again Inspector Napoleon Bonaparte is on a trail months cold (two months, to be exact). And once again he appears on the scene in disguise, this time as a vacationing pastoralist, a sheep-station owner. But the case of *The New Shoe* offers a new setting for Bony: the beautiful summer resort of Split Point on the southern coast of Australia, in the state of Victoria, where he is admittedly somewhat out of his element.

A nude corpse found entombed inside Split Point Lighthouse is what brings Bony there. Despite the effort to hide the body and obscure its identity, murder will out. Bony is convinced that there is a local connection. When his "assistant," the tavernkeeper's dog, Stug, turns up a piece of footwear of recent origin, Bony knows he is on the right path. He delves into the close-knit, conspiratorial relationships of the small coastal community, and what he uncovers—another murder, for one thing—leads him to say that "greed and loyalty, bitterness and love, viciousness and altruism, are some of the ingredients of this mystery." Surrounded by suspicious country people, some of whom think *he* might be a villain, Bony must use his wits and his bushcraft to make a proper pattern of these elements and bring a murderer to justice.

As always, Upfield makes excellent use of background, creates memorable characters, and provides expert detection. One especially impressive creation is old Ed Penwarden, the master woodworker, who provides Bony with a custom-made coffin as a memento of this case.

(*T.B.*)

*Upfield, Arthur W. *No Footprints in the Bush.* New York: Doubleday Crime Club, 1944. (CS/A)

No Footprints in the Bush is more violent and more of an adventure/thriller than most of the Bony books. In the Land of Burning Water, a south Australia valley filled with mirage "water," the detective encounters two warring tribes of blacks, a warring family, and a criminal with internal warring influences. A megalomaniac is threatening the peace of the McPhersons' homestead at the far end of the Outback. Bony must use white man's reasoning and loyalty to battle the menace; and with the assistance of a flying doctor and a World War ace, he fights back. The theme of a family split is used in many of Upfield's books, and in this one Bony must vie with white man's morality to conclude the investigation.

Before he does, the detective is snake-bitten and, because of his weakened state, captured by the villain. An ally, Burning Water, chief of the Wantella, embarks on an exhaustive pursuit to the sacred repository of another tribe (the sanctuary carries the taboo of death) to rescue yet another captive. And in the end, Burning Water makes a supreme sacrifice to save Bony's life.

Upfield presents vivid geography with exciting descriptions of Bony's beloved bush as the detective uses his aboriginal skills and senses to finalize the case. "In many things it is the aboriginal who is the highly developed civilized being and the white man who is the savage." The action is nonstop, with ruthless white man's torture; armed clashes with wild aborigines; black man's medicine; feats of flying skill; and the stealth of cunning bushcraft. In some ways the Bonaparte books may be compared to the works of Tony Hillerman (q.v.) about the Indians of the American Southwest. Both authors rely on ethnographic detail to flesh out their stories, and their characters are products of two conflicting cultures.

(*T.B.*)

Upfield, Arthur W. *The Sands of Windee.* London: Hutchinson, 1931. (CS/A)

This is the first of several cases in the career of Napoleon Bonaparte that he does not bring to an official conclusion. His sentimentality stands in his way, and in this respect he operates like many fictional private eyes or amateur detectives. Bony sees himself as a detective, not a policeman. His pride and his success are in finding the solution to the mystery, not in meting out official "justice," and the only crime that interests him is the perfect murder—others are too banal.

The sands of Windee have covered the tracks, traces, and clues relating a man's disappearance some two months previous. Marks was a visitor to Windee Station in New South Wales, and after he left the homestead he was not seen again. The missing man was a bent (crooked) policeman on the run. His car is found abandoned, and an official photo of the crime site gives Bony the clue (an aboriginal sign) that he was murdered. (It later develops the body was disposed of in a unique and perfect fashion.) However, the lack of other clues and corpse does not slow down Bony's investigation. He gets hired on at the station in the disguise of a swagman, and it is a combination of his black man's knowledge of bushcraft and passion for the chase and his white's man's imagination that enables him to arrive at the truth. Bony also faces one of the toughest personal conflicts of any of his cases, one between his cultural orientation and his professional obligations. The climax involves the vast upheaval of a bushfire, in which Bony brings the miscreant to a fiery end.

Recommended among Bony's other adventures are *Murder Down Under* (1943), his first to be published in the United States; *Wings above the Claypan* (1943), which makes use of a baffling "impossible" disappearance; *Death of a Swagman* (1945); *The Mountains Have a Secret* (1948); and *The Man of Two Tribes* (1956).

(*T.B.*)

Upton, Robert. *Fade Out.* New York: Viking, 1984. (PI)

You could love private eye Amos McGuffin for his name alone—but he also has a wry way about him. After McGuffin crashes two cars, Ronald Worthy, the president of Executive Rent-A-Car, denies him any more vehicles. "Isn't that just like Ron," says our hero to the clerk. "As if I were the only guy sleeping with his wife."

McGuffin lives in San Francisco, where he hangs out at Goody's bar, putting away Paddy's when he isn't on a case—which is just about all the time of late. In fact, he's just bending an elbow when Nat Volpersky tracks him down at Goody's. It seems Volpersky's son, Ben Volper, a Hollywood producer, is thought to have committed suicide by wading out into the Pacific Ocean after leaving an unsigned note on his typewriter. But Volpersky doesn't believe it; and Izzy Schwartz the deli man, his only friend in California, has recommended McGuffin to find his son. That means McGuffin has to go to Los Angeles, where he encounters the Bronx Social Club—a group of Ben's childhood friends who've made it big in show biz. "Who else can you trust?" Volpersky asks.

But McGuffin isn't so sure the old neighborhood pals are trustworthy. He's even less inclined to put his faith in Aba Ben Mahoud, a wealthy Arab who financed Ben's last picture. And he has serious doubts about Pedro Chan, the six-foot-six cop assigned to the case.

After pursuing a single-minded inquiry throughout most of the book, he suddenly sees the light and pulls the solution out of a hat. Upton didn't really play fair on this one, McGuffin's latest case. (He made his debut in 1977 in *Who'd Want to Kill Old George?*) But no matter. Even though we can't see it coming, the denouement is ingenious. And McGuffin is a delight.

(*J.S.*)

Valin, Jonathan. *Natural Causes.* New York: Congdon & Weed, 1983. (PI)

Since the appearance of his Harry Stoner novel, *The Lime Pit* (1980), Jonathan Valin has been hailed as among the best of the present-day private-eye writers. Of the first Stoner adventure, *Publishers Weekly* said, "Wow! One of the roughest, toughest and most completely convincing private eye novels in a long time." Other critics have praised Valin as the second coming of Chandler. That may not be fair, since Valin is a good writer and storyteller in his own right, and Stoner, a PI who works out of Cincinnati, is a fully individuated character.

In this, the fifth Stoner novel, the PI is hired by United American Productions to go to California and find out who killed the head writer of their biggest soap opera, one Quentin Dover. In describing Stoner's investigation, Valin also vividly depicts the world of a big-time soap opera—of which he knows much. He spent a year as a story consultant on a popular daytime soap.

Stoner runs the gamut of Hollywood personae: directors, actors, agents, not to mention the victim's beautiful alcoholic wife. Add drugs and murder and a jaunt south of the border and you've got the story of how and why a man with a half-a-million-dollar-a-year job would get himself involved with something that could—and did—get him killed.

Valin may indeed be one of the best of the present-day PI writers, but to compare him to Chandler is to do him a disservice—one that critics all too frequently perform.

Harry Stoner also appears in *Final Notice* (1980), *Dead Letter* (1981), and *Day of Wrath* (1982).

(*R.J.R.*)

Vance, John Holbrook. *The Fox Valley Murders.* Indianapolis: Bobbs-Merrill, 1966. (PP)

John Holbrook Vance is one of a handful of writers who have won major awards in two different genres. In the science-fiction field, where he writes as Jack Vance, he received a Hugo for his 1963 novel *The Dragon Masters;* and in the mystery field, he received a Best First Novel Edgar for his 1960 tale of intrigue in Tangier, *The Man in the Cage.* Vance has published a dozen mysteries, most of the formal variety. The two best feature Sheriff Joe Bain of the fictional central California county of San Rodrigo; *The Fox Valley Murders* is the first of these.

A smallish agricultural county south of San Jose, San Rodrigo is loosely modeled on the one in which Vance spent his childhood. He portrays it with a great deal of feeling and clarity, utilizing a variety of towns and rural settings much as Dennis Lynds, writing as John Crowe (q.v.), would do a few years later in his "Buena Costa County" series. People and places are so strikingly depicted, and county history, social problems, and politics so well integrated into the narrative, that San Rodrigo and its inhabitants seem utterly real.

In *The Fox Valley Murders,* Bain—a wild youth who has settled down to become a very good lawman—has been appointed acting sheriff after the recent death of old Ernest Cucchinello, the incumbent for many years and a man not above a little corruption. The county elections are not far off; Bain wants the sheriff's job permanently, campaigns hard for it, but is facing stiff competition from a well-backed progress-and-reform group. He is also facing a volatile situation centered around Ausley Wyett, a native of the town of Marblestone, who was convicted sixteen years before—despite his protestations of innocence—of the brutal rape/murder of a thirteen-year-old girl. Now out of San Quentin on parole and back home, Wyett has written the same letter to each of the five men whose testimony sent him to prison, asking: "How do you plan to make this up to me?"

It isn't long before the five recipients begin to die one by one in apparent accidents. Is Ausley responsible? And if not, then who is? And why? And, just as important, *how?* How do you make a man die of a heart attack in front of a witness (Bain himself)? How do you cause a man who has been picking mushrooms all his life to eat a poisonous toadstool? How do you make someone fall off a ladder and break his neck in full view of his wife, with no one else around? Bain is hard-pressed to find the answers before local citizens decide to take the law into their own hands and/or the election sweeps him right out of office.

Brimming with suspense, evocatively written, ingeniously constructed (with a number of dovetailing subplots and plenty of clues for the armchair detective), this is a first-rate novel that "fills the bill for real entertainment in the true sense of the word" (King Features Syndicate). Almost as good is Joe

Bain's second case, *The Pleasant Grove Murders* (1967), in which the likable and very human sheriff once again faces political problems and a baffling multiple homicide (three brutal hammer murders).

Notable among Vance's other mysteries are a pair under pseudonyms, both published in 1957—*Isle of Peril,* as by Alan Wade, and *Take My Face,* as by Peter Held; *The Deadly Isles* (1969), a tale of murder in Tahiti and the Marquesas; and *Bad Ronald* (1973), a psychological thriller.

(*B.P.*)

van de Wetering, Janwillem. *The Blond Baboon.* Boston: Houghton Mifflin, 1978. (PP)

It is not unusual for an author to create a fictional village, county, or even a nation, but Janwillem van de Wetering has established his own world view within everyday Dutch society. He shows us the basic decency of the Dutch people and their evenhanded concentration on means rather than ends. His books contain all the standard elements of police procedurals, but their attraction is not so much the discovery of the murderer as the depiction of the relationships that evolve in the course of an investigation and the antagonisms that must be worked out. As in life, none of van de Wetering's characters is wholly good or bad, and this perhaps accounts for much of the realism of the series.

One of van de Wetering's primary interests is Zen Buddhism (his Buddhist experiences are recounted insightfully and amusingly in two excellent nonfiction books—*The Empty Mirror,* 1973; and *A Glimpse of Nothingness,* 1975), and the relationship between his primary detectives exemplifies relationships inherent in that discipline. The Commissaris—aging, rheumatic, and wise—is the secular equivalent of the Zen Master, guiding both the investigations and the development of his sergeant. Sergeant Rinus de Gier is the disciple, experiencing an awakening born of the tragedies he must deal with that brings him to a state of detachment, fearlessness, and emptiness.

In *The Blond Baboon,* a small dog is poisoned and then his owner is murdered. Are these random crimes, or is there a connection between them? The detectives of the Amsterdam Municipal Police do not jump to conclusions: Possibly, they say, but possibly not. The murdered woman, Elaine Carnet, was a semiretired furniture importer. She could have been killed by her business partner, who is so nervous when questioned by the police that he appears to be having a stroke; or by Gabrielle Carnet, her daughter and heir; or by the man known as the blond baboon, Elaine's former business manager and former lover, from whom the police learn to expect the unexpected. During the course of the investigation, we come to know the suspects well as they not only present their alibis but also discuss their unique philosophies of life.

This is perhaps the best of the van de Wetering books set wholly in

Amsterdam. He captures the feel of the city as gale winds blow through and men rush to reinforce the dikes. He takes us inside those tall, narrow houses along the canals, aboard the boats of both the Water Police and their prey, and into (yes, *into*) a canal itself. If the series has a failing, it is in van de Wetering's characterization of women: As he presents them, they—at best—do not have lofty thoughts and—at worst—are mere sex objects.

(*S.D.*)

*van de Wetering, Janwillem. *The Japanese Corpse.* Boston: Houghton Mifflin, 1977. (PP)

In this novel van de Wetering puts to good use his knowledge of Japan, acquired while he was a student in a Zen Buddhist monastery in Kyoto. In addition, he draws heavily on his experience both as a businessman and as a member of the Amsterdam Municipal Police Force. The knowledge he has gleaned from these varied pursuits is skillfully blended to produce an exciting and intriguing tale.

The Japanese Corpse begins in Amsterdam with the discovery of a murdered Yakuza. The Yakuza, members of a Mafia-like organization, are highly disciplined and very secret; they are reputed to control all sorts of illegal operations—drugs, prostitution, extortion, and pornography—as well as an unknown number of legitimate businesses. The investigation of this particular gang member's killing takes the detectives into the Japanese underworld of the city, and they soon find that both heroin and Japanese temple art are being smuggled into the country and sold there. After picking up a few leads from their informants, the Commissaris and de Gier decide to follow up the case in Japan. Adopting the identity of businessmen who are anxious to cut into the Yakuza trade, they journey to Kyoto—into the heart or the Yakuza organization and, not coincidentally, into great danger.

Van de Wetering's use of Japanese settings and his familiarity with the structure of Japanese society and the nuances of its behavior lends an air of authority to the story. There is a delightful scene in a Yakuza-run nightclub, where de Gier picks up a hostess; an action-packed powerboat chase; and a visit to a Yakuza chief's island castle. The descriptions are excellent, and the novel rewards the reader with not just a good story but a fascinating view of Japan and its people.

Other highly recommended books in this excellent series are *Outsider in Amsterdam* (1976), *The Corpse on the Dike* (1976), *The Maine Massacre* (1979), and *The Streetbird* (1983). Van de Wetering is also the author of *Inspector Saito's Small Satori* (1985), a collection of short stories featuring a Japanese policeman, some of which were originally published in magazines under the pseudonym Seiko Legru.

(*S.D.*)

*Van Dine, S. S. *The Bishop Murder Case.* New York: Scribner's, 1929. (CS)

In 1923, a combination of overwork, emotional strain, and drug abuse brought about the collapse of a little-known art critic named Willard Huntington Wright. During his long convalescence, he began reading detective stories for amusement. After devouring several hundred, he decided that he could write better whodunits than those he'd read, prepared synopses for three murder puzzles, and was offered a contract by Maxwell Perkins, the legendary Scribner's editor. Thus was born Philo Vance, the first important character in the history of novel-length American detective fiction.

With his mandarin affectations and speech patterns, Vance comes across as the most insufferable of prigs. A wealthy intellectual aesthete with an encyclopedic knowledge of every abstruse topic under the sun, he plays amateur sleuth out of sheer boredom and a desire to prove one of his pet theories. Just as the world-renowned art connoisseur Bernard Berenson (on whom Vance was apparently modeled) could examine a centuries-old painting and identify the artist purely from clues like brushstroke technique, Vance claims that a Berenson of criminology could identify the creator of a murder after examining the circumstances, clues, and suspects. In *The Benson Murder Case* (1926), Vance's friend Markham, district attorney of New York County, gives him a chance to test his theory. It is a rather routine book, much indebted to the real-life murder of bridge expert Joseph Elwell, and with a perfect-alibi gimmick that the reader penetrates long before Vance; but its huge commercial success launched S. S. Van Dine, Wright's mystery-writing pseudonym, as the new superstar of the whodunit.

The format of the typical Philo Vance novel is as rigid as the movement of the tides. Each book is titled *The* [Six-Letter-Word] *Murder Case* and narrated by Vance's secretary, Van Dine, a cipher of a character if ever there was one. The police are total dolts, and at the first sign of the bizarre in a case, Markham summons Vance. All the suspects are impossibly rich and cultivated. Their dialogue sounds like a Ph.D. dissertation, complete with footnotes. Each investigation centers on a theme—Egyptology in *The Scarab Murder Case* (1930), dog shows in *The Kennel Murder Case* (1933), tropical fish in *The Dragon Murder Case* (1934)—which permits Van Dine to incorporate all sorts of scholarly disquisitions into the story line. One or several follow-up murders enliven (if that's the word) the latter half of each book. Finally, and with total unfairness to the reader, Vance expounds his masterly solution and lays bare a murder scheme of a charmingly ridiculous nature.

The best of Van Dine's dozen novels are the second, third, and fourth. *The Canary Murder Case* (1927) has to do with the strangulation of a Broadway show girl with a habit of blackmailing her wealthy lovers. Vance determines certain personality traits the murderer must have possessed on the basis of how the crime was carried out, then invites all the suspects to play poker with him. The way each man plays his cards convinces Vance that one and only one could have killed the woman. Readers unfamiliar with poker tend to solve this one far ahead of Vance because the murderer has rigged up another of those alibi gimmicks that stand out like a black eye.

In *The Greene Murder Case* (1928), Vance looks into a series of murders that is decimating a wealthy and degenerate family. Despite the constant presence of police, the crimes go on till there are almost no suspects left.

And in Van Dine's finest novel, *The Bishop Murder Case* (1929), Vance is called in on a series of murders, each modeled on a Mother Goose rhyme—so that Mr. Joseph Cochrane Robin, for example, is killed by a bow and arrow. The environment of the crimes is the most heavily intellectual in any Van Dine novel, but all the talk about Einstein and Bertrand Russell and the intersecting worlds of physics and mathematics and philosophy is in the book for a reason; and on all counts—memorable plot, *outré* characters, powerful climax (in which Vance executes the mad killer in front of his friend Markham and then dares the D.A. to arrest him), integration of high metaphysics into the story line—*Bishop* is Van Dine's masterpiece.

Though today's readers tend to find him intolerably stilted, Van Dine is of crucial historical importance as the creator of the skeletal structure for the classic American detective novel and of the first great American Sherlock Holmes figure. The structure was perfected in the early 1930s by Ellery Queen (q.v.), and both Queen and Rex Stout (q.v.) created more durable American Holmeses, but Van Dine was the pioneer, and it's most unlikely that Ellery Queen and Nero Wolfe would have come into existence without him.

(*F.M.N.*)

*van Gulik, Robert. *The Haunted Monastery and The Chinese Maze Murders.* New York: Dover, 1977. (H/AD)

Robert van Gulik was a Dutch diplomat who was stationed in the Far East for much of his career. During his tours in the Dutch Foreign Service, van Gulik studied Oriental history, literature, and art. He became expert in these areas and began a second career as a translator; some examples of the scholarly works van Gulik translated and edited are *Erotic Colour Prints of the Ming Period* (1951), *Chinese Pictorial Art as Viewed by the Connoisseur* (1958), and *Sexual Life in Ancient China* (1961).

In 1940 van Gulik discovered *Dee Goong An,* a Chinese story of detection during the T'ang dynasty—originally written in the late seventeenth or early eighteenth century. Van Gulik translated the work and had it privately published in Tokyo and London in limited edition. The reception of the work, and van Gulik's own fascination with ancient China, led him to write seventeen books about Judge Dee Jen-djieh, the seventh-century magistrate whose celebrated cases have been called "the finest ethnographic detective [stories] in English."

The Judge Dee novels and novelettes are classic puzzles, exercises in ratiocination and deduction in which Dee works strictly within the historical parameters of Chinese administrative and criminal law. But they are also superb historical set pieces, offering graphic portraits of daily life in medieval China.

Two fine examples are *The Haunted Monastery* and *The Chinese Maze Murders,* a pair of early works (the former was first published in 1961, the latter in 1957) that feature a trio of interrelated novelettes. *The Haunted Monastery*—which was filmed for TV in 1974 as "Judge Dee and the Monastery Murders," with Khigh Dhiegh in the leading role—takes place in the ancient Taoist Monastery of the Morning Cloud, where Judge Dee and his wives have gone to seek refuge from a mountain storm. Three women have been murdered there; also dead is the Abbot Jade Mirror, who collapsed in the presence of fifteen monks after delivering a mystical sermon and whose death Judge Dee also suspects is murder. Elements of the supernatural play a strong role in the story, as does the Taoist Hell—a hall filled with statuary depicting the various torments of the netherworld. The eerie atmosphere of the monastery, the ongoing series of bizarre happenings, and some of the magistrate's best detective work make this one of the two or three best books in the series.

Also superb is *The Chinese Maze Murders,* which has as its setting the northwest border town-district of Lan-fang and which begins with Judge Dee being attacked by forces of a local gangster who wants the district magistrate dead. Next, Dee is faced with finding a hidden testament in a scroll painting that has important implications. And finally, he must discover the identity of a murderer who tortures women and cuts off their heads, before the madman can strike again. All three cases have their clues and solutions in a mysterious garden maze where Judge Dee must go to find the truth.

This Dover edition is enhanced by van Gulik's introductory and postscript material to *The Chinese Maze Murders,* in which he discusses the origins of both that novel and the Judge Dee series; and by twenty-seven of his evocative black-and-white illustrations.

(*G.K./B.P.*)

van Gulik, Robert. *Judge Dee at Work.* New York: Scribner's, 1973. (H/AD/SS)

Judge Dee at Work contains eight of the honorable magistrate's shorter cases, each set in a different time period. "Five Auspicious Clouds," for instance, takes place in A.D. 663 in Peng-Lai, a remote district on the northeast coast of the Chinese Empire, and deals with the apparent suicide of the wife of a minor district official. "The Murder on the Lotus Pond" occurs in A.D. 667 in Han-Yuan, an ancient little town built on the shore of a lake; Judge Dee must solve the curious case of the poet who was murdered "while peacefully contemplating the moon in his garden pavilion." In "The Coffins of the Emperor" it is A.D. 672, the setting is an isolated district on the western frontier of the mighty T'ang Empire, and there are two distinct problems for Dee to solve with his usual élan—"one affecting the fate of the nation, the other the fate of two humble people."

These and the other five stories here are carefully plotted and richly detailed. As the *Los Angeles Times* said of the collection, "If you have not yet discovered Judge Dee, I envy you that initial pleasure . . . the discovery of a great detective story. For the magistrate of Poo-yan belongs in that select group headed by Sherlock Holmes." Indeed he does.

All of the other Judge Dee books are excellent. Especially notable among them are *The Chinese Lake Murders* (1960), *The Chinese Nail Murders* (1962), *The Willow Pattern* (1965), *The Phantom of the Temple* (1966; a particularly complex tale in which a haunted Buddhist monastery and ancient religious rites play vital roles), *The Red Pavilion* (1968), and *Necklace and Calabash* (1971).

(*B.P.*)

*Vickers, Roy. *The Department of Dead Ends.* New York: Spivak, 1947. (O/SS)

Roy Vickers's early novels, while competent, are highly derivative of the work of his more popular contemporaries, such as Eric Ambler, E. Phillips Oppenheim, Sax Rohmer, and Edgar Wallace (qq.v.). But in 1935, Vickers sold a short story, "The Rubber Trumpet," to the British magazine *Fiction Parade,* the first in an excellent series of tales about Scotland Yard's Department of Dead Ends—a series that established him as a major writer of crime fiction. This imaginary department is the place where the evidence from unsolved crimes is stored; and in the stories, solutions to many of these emerge through chance, fate, or serendipity. There are thirty-eight stories in all, each of them a fine example of the inverted detective story pioneered by R. Austin Freeman (q.v.): The department's personnel use a seemingly meaningless clue to unravel this or that mystery, and the reader is in the enviable position of both observing and trying to anticipate their methods while knowing the solution toward which they are moving.

In "The Case of the Social Climber," a historic snuffbox once belonging to King George IV is the key to the explanation of an apparently motiveless murder. In "The Yellow Jumper," a frustrated maternal instinct leads to a murder that the department solves a year later through analysis of perfume and ladies' fashions. "The Man Who Murdered in Public" features a killer who marries young women, insures their lives, then drowns them in bogus boating accidents; only a bracelet belonging to his first victim holds the clue that can convict this multiple murderer.

The Department of Dead Ends series is renowned not only for Vickers's meticulous plotting and use of the inverted form, but also for his insights into the social classes of his characters. In story after story, the various motives for murder reside in the demands of this or that character's status.

Other excellent short-story collections by this prolific author include *Eight Murders in the Suburbs* (1954) and *Best Detective Stories of Roy Vickers* (1965).

(*G.K./M.M.*)

Vickers, Roy. *The Sole Survivor and The Kynsard Affair.* New York: Dover, 1983. (O/PS)

This republication of Vickers's two 1952 novellas, "The Sole Survivor" and "The Kynsard Affair," offers contemporary readers two of his best longer stories and a pair of ingeniously worked out mystery plots.

"The Sole Survivor" provides a puzzle reminiscent of Agatha Christie's *And Then There Were None* (q.v.). When the ship *Marigonda* founders during a storm, six men are shipwrecked on a desert island. Five of them are murdered one by one; the sole survivor, Clovering, is rescued and returned to England. The events that took place on the island are narrated by "Clobbers" in a court deposition—a strange tale of paranoia and bad blood tinged with elements of the supernatural. Did Clovering murder his five fellow maroons? Was there another person on the island all along, unbeknown to the six? Was one of the five dead men a schizophrenic Jekyll-and-Hyde who committed the murders while in his homicidal alter ego? Or was a supernatural agency somehow responsible for the deaths? Vickers's sure hand with plot and character, plus plenty of desert-island atmosphere, lends this story considerable tension and makes it compulsive reading throughout.

"The Kynsard Affair" calls to mind the best of the Department of Dead Ends stories, expanded to short-novel length through complexity of plot and character development. After a murderer named Gibbern is legally hanged, a woman is found beaten to death in an abandoned car near the gallows site—a murder devilishly similar to the one for which Gibbern was executed. But just who was the victim in this case? Was it Barbara Kynsard, the emotionally unstable wife of a prominent barrister? Or was it Betsy Trotwood, the "friend" of a successful greengrocer? It seems to Scotland Yard that it must be one or the other—but then what happened to the one it *isn't?* Vickers springs a nice surprise at the end of this twisty tour de force, a tale that, as the publisher's blurb says, "provide[s] the reader with the best in intrigue and entertainment."

Recommended among Vickers's more than thirty full-length mystery novels are *A Date with Danger* (1944), *Maid to Murder* (1950), and *Gold and Wine* (1961).

(*B.P./G.K.*)

Von Elsner, Don. *How to Succeed at Murder without Really Trying.* New York: New American Library (Signet), 1963. (Also published as *The Jake of Diamonds.* New York: Award, 1967.) (O/AD)

If you are interested in bridge as well as mysteries, you will certainly enjoy the adventures of both Jake Winkman and David Danning. The author, himself a bridge professional and columnist, has set eleven paperback originals against the background of one of America's favorite indoor sports. The books about Jake Winkman will take you behind the scenes at major bridge tournaments, with diagrams of bridge hands and a lucid explanation of each, as well as a bit of name-dropping. Winkman makes his living as a paid bridge partner for players who want to earn master points, and once in a while he discovers a body, forcing him to find out why he was set up to take the rap for murder.

In *How to Succeed at Murder without Really Trying,* Hawaii is the setting for the Mid-Pacific Regionals. Jake is all set with paying partners for the ten-day schedule when a police officer tries to arrest him just an hour after his arrival for a jewel theft that took place the night before. A lieutenant follows him around and is present when Jake discovers a corpse in his hotel-room closet. From then on, the action, mixed with a rigid playing schedule, moves even faster, as Jake realizes that the only way to keep out of jail is to find the missing diamonds and the killer. The in-and-out-of-bed activities and conversations provide possible motives, as do the various players' compulsions to win the Regionals. But as in all of Von Elsner's novels, the mystery is secondary to the principal attractions of the bridge background, the exotic locale, and plenty of good, crisp dialogue.

Jake Winkman's other adventures are *The Ace of Spies* (1966) and *The Jack of Hearts* (1968).

David Danning, Von Elsner's other bridge-playing series character, is the younger half of a look-alike father-and-son spy team, both lawyers. Notable among the Danning novels—all of which have truly awful titles—are *Those Who Prey Together Slay Together* (1961), *Who Says a Corpse Has to Be Dull* (1962), *Don't Just Stand There, Do Someone* (1962), and *A Bullet for Your Dreams* (1968), which introduced an appealing new character, a beautiful female professor named Greta.

(*E.N.*)

Wade, Henry. *A Dying Fall.* New York: Macmillan, 1955. (W)

Henry Wade (Henry Lancelot Aubrey-Fletcher) was a highly regarded Golden Age writer of formal detective and police stories. Most of his output appeared between 1926 and 1940—fourteen novels (including a contribution to the 1932 round-robin Detective Club mystery, *The Floating Admiral*) and the Queen's Quorum collection *Policeman's Lot* (1933); he published nothing during the war years and only seven more novels during the period 1947–57. A number of his books are procedurals featuring Chief Inspector Poole, a series that Howard Haycraft in *Murder for Pleasure* calls "quietly pleasant" and places "somewhere between the conventional detective story and the livelier naturalistic method according to the gospel of Bentley and Berkeley." Wade was also a master of the inverted detective story and, late in his career, of the novel that combines the suspense story with elements of detection, police procedure, and the inverted mystery. *A Dying Fall,* Wade's next to last book, falls into that last category.

After his best horse loses the 1952 Royal Cup to one owned by wealthy widow Kate Waygold, a race on which he bet heavily to win, hunter and racing sportsman Charles Rathlyn faces ruin. But Mrs. Waygold, who is some years his senior, takes a liking to him and saves his bacon by offering him a job as her racing manager. Their relationship soon escalates into one much more personal, and they are eventually married. Rathlyn, it seems, now has everything he could possibly want: money, freedom, a major stable of horses, and a marriage he findes comfortable if loveless. But it isn't that simple, of course. Kate has a drinking problem and becomes overbearing in her affections; and Rathlyn finds himself falling in love for the first time in his life, with a neighbor's much younger daughter, Anne Faery.

Not long after Rathlyn discovers that his wife walks in her sleep, a problem few people in the household know about, Kate topples over a second-floor balustrade and breaks her neck on the marble floor below. But did she really fall while sleepwalking or was she given a push by Charles? Kate's devious-minded secretary, Isabel Wey, claims it was a push and tries to blackmail Charles—and is soon found dead of an apparently self-inflicted overdose of sleeping medicine. Detective Superintendent Hant of the Barryshire CID passionately believes Rathlyn is guilty of murder in both cases; his superior, Colonel John Netterly, isn't so sure. Neither is the reader, for we are privy to some but not all of Charles's thoughts, and to just enough other information to make us think first one thing, then another.

The cat-and-mouse game Wade plays with both his characters and the reader is gripping and nicely resolved. (Anthony Boucher said that *A Dying Fall* "culminates in one of the most effective whipsnap endings of recent years." True enough, although the veteran mystery addict may see it coming.) There is a good deal about fox-hunting here, which may be off-putting to those readers who, like this one, find that their sympathies lie more with the fox than with hunters or hounds. Nevertheless, this is a strong novel with considerable depth of characterization, and should please fans of the British mystery.

Wade's other nonseries books include *The Dying Alderman* (1930), *Heir Presumptive* (1953; originally published in England in 1935), and *The Litmore Snatch* (1957). Chief Inspector Poole's prowess can be found in such titles as *No Friendly Drop* (1932), *Constable, Guard Thyself!* (1935), and *Too Soon to Die* (1954).

(*B.P.*)

Wager, Walter. *Blue Murder.* New York: Arbor House, 1981. (PI/T)

This is Walter Wager's third novel featuring private investigator A. B. (Alison) Gordon. Gordon is self-described as "the best looking thirty-five-year-old woman she knew, and she knew half the major actresses and sex symbols in Hollywood." A former CIA operative, she runs her own agency in Beverly Hills; it is a fair-size, expensive operation, and most of Gordon's clients are affiliated with the entertainment business. Gordon herself is cool, controlled, and thoroughly professional, with high-placed connections throughout the state and the country. All this perfection may initially be off-putting to many readers, but only until they get to know Gordon.

As *Blue Murder* opens, we observe the shocking machine-gun slaughter of nine people in a small factory not far from Disneyland. We then join Alison Gordon as she pays a call on a new client, entertainer Lauri Adams, otherwise known as the Bitch. Adams wants Gordon to locate her missing brother, Sidney—a routine-enough case, which Gordon agrees to take on. But then the viewpoint shifts back to one of the perpetrators of the slaughter at the factory, and we realize these cold-blooded killers are cops. And Sidney turns out to be one of the people killed in the massacre. And the FBI claims the mob perpetrated it, but the mob says no. Meanwhile Gordon agrees to continue working for Lauri Adams, to find out what Sidney's life had been like in the weeks before he died. "We're not touching the murder," Gordon insists to her close associate Andrew Agajanian. "Sure," he says.

As the story progresses, we become aware of a plot of monstrous scale, of which the murders at the factory are only a small component. A right-wing group, code-named Lexington, is planning to take over America and place its own people in the White House and Pentagon. But Gordon's investigation into Sidney Adams's last days threatens to destroy their carefully laid plans, and although she has as yet no inkling of their existence, they are very aware of her every move. . . .

This is a well-plotted thriller with plenty of action, and Gordon is an appealing character. We quickly find that she is a woman who has seen many dead bodies in her day, but is still capable of feeling for the victims; while she is thoroughly professional, she is able to become caught up in a case out of compassion for a man who died too young. And Wager also allows us to see Gordon's vulnerability: While beautiful, well off, and sophisticated, she is often lonely and is "also old-fashioned enough to believe that there was *one* special man out there for her."

Gordon's other adventures are *Blue Leader* (1979) and *Blue Moon* (1980). In addition, Wager has written such suspense novels as *Viper Three* (1971), which was filmed as *Twilight's Last Gleaming* (starring Burt Lancaster and Richard Widmark) in 1977; and *Telefon* (1975), which became a less-than-successful movie starring Charles Bronson in 1977.

(*M.M.*)

*Wainwright, John. *An Urge for Justice.* New York: St. Martin's, 1982. (PP)

John Wainwright has published more than a hundred crime novels over the past twenty years and is considered by many critics to be one of the best writers of the British police procedural. Wainwright's novels differ from the typical procedural format—that used by his favorite American crime novelist, Ed McBain (q.v.), for example—in that they concentrate on one major case, rather than a number of cases; as in the McBain books, however, heavy emphasis is placed on the actions and motives of the perpetrators. *An Urge for Justice* is among Wainwright's best books to date because it brings together all of the author's strengths: tight plotting, realistic characterizations, and convincing backgrounds.

When an old woman is murdered by hanging with piano wire, the police find they have more than just a brutal killing on their hands. There are hidden connections between the woman and the Nazi concentration camps of World War II, and the police must follow a trail of clues stretching decades into the past, as well as deal with a rough type of justice that has been meted out in contemporary England. As usual, Wainwright displays great skill at depicting teams of police working together, sifting through marginal evidence and cryptic clues as they attempt to fashion an accurate picture of both the old woman and her killer.

Highly recommended older titles by Wainwright are *The Hard Hit* (1975), *Death of a Big Man* (1975), and *Landscape with Violence* (1976). Outstanding among his recent works are *Clouds of Guilt* (1985), which starkly chronicles a respected banker's descent into a hellish life of crime, and *All Through the Night* (1985), in which Wainwright takes us inside a small-town police station on a typical night filled with both usual and unusual crimes.

(*G.K./M.M.*)

Wallace, Edgar. *The Four Just Men.* Boston: Small, Maynard, 1920. (T)

Edgar Wallace wasn't just prolific, he was a fiction factory. He turned out a prodigious amount of work in the Twenties and Thirties, and in England during that era the "King of the Thrillers" was the author of one out of every four books sold. He started as a journalist, and before his untimely death in Hollywood in 1934, just after he completed the screenplay for *King Kong,* he wrote and dictated a couple of hundred novels, short stories, stage dramas, and screenplays. Movies and television producers have made hundreds of films using his stories. He was the highest-paid writer of his time, and he lived well above his means. His talent was in turning out exciting stories that are rapidly paced, with lots of action and quick changes of scene. Most of his criminous fiction was set in London, particularly the West End, with its snobs and swells, its slick, rich-living crooks and policemen of independent means. Some of his plots are shoddily put together, and some depend on such trappings as disguises, mistaken identity, and coincidence. His command of underworld slang of the period was excellent; but many characters are mere stereotypes, and some stories read like reruns of previous ones.

Perhaps Wallace's best-known novel is *The Four Just Men,* his first book. While most of his work is definitely an acquired taste, you can see in this tale why it had such popular appeal. The Just Men—who are identified only by the first names of Manfred, Gonsalez, Poiccart, and Thery—believe they are instruments of a divine providence, especially for those who are above or outside the law. In this case, they plot against the English foreign secretary, who is bent on committing what they perceive as a political injustice. They send threats and promise a date and hour of death. This melodrama uses dramatic confrontations, masked murderers, and the power of the press. All London is thrown into a tizzy, and the police are mustered to protect the government minister.

Rather mild by today's thriller standards, the story still has its convoluted moments. It was originally published by Wallace himself in 1905, and a reward was offered for correct solutions to the mystery. This made the book an instant best seller, and caused financial losses when several readers answered correctly.

Later there were five sequels featuring the Just Men—only *three* of them henceforth, because Thery loses his life in this first adventure. Those five are *The Council of Justice* (1908), *The Just Men of Cordova* (1917), *The Three Just Men* (1930), *The Law of the Three Just Men* (1931), and *Again the Three Just Men* (1931).

(*T.B.*)

*Wallace, Edgar. *The Murder Book of J. G. Reeder.* New York: Doubleday Crime Club, 1929. (AD/SS)

Edgar Wallace's best collection of crime short stories was issued in England with the title *The Mind of Mr. J. G. Reeder* (1925). Critic Julian Symons said that "the most clearly realized of his detective is the absent-minded, spinsterish Mr. J. G. Reeder." Certainly this sleuth—with his long-faced look of wistful helplessness, his slither of side whiskers, his pince-nez constantly drooping on his nose, wearing a disreputable hat, a frock coat, and square-toed boots, and carrying a constantly furled umbrella—does not look like England's outstanding agent of the public prosecutor's office.

In these eight stories, Mr. Reeder's assets are a "criminal mind," an encyclopedic memory of the underworld, and a playful ruthlessness. His lugubrious demeanor permeates the stories and exposes him as a diffident sentimentalist. Bank crimes are a hobby of his, and he suddenly appears when forgers are passing their "snide." "The Poetical Policeman" inadvertently provides poetic justice for a bank robber. "The Treasure Hunt" proves that crooks can be useful to the forces of law. Reeder has a little fun with a visiting yegg who's running a con game in "The Troupe." A mad criminal consigns victims to a horrible death in "The Stealer of Marble." "Sheer Melodrama" in the theater is just Mr. Reeder's style; he doesn't believe it's as farfetched as real-life criminality with bent coppers and forged foreign banknotes. In "The Green Mamba," the uncrowned emperor of the underworld misbelieves Reeder to be the rabbit, but the detective strikes back, like the snake.

The compression of the short-story form enabled Wallace to compose tight little tales with touches of wit and to overcome clichés, faulty plots, and trite characterizations. These are by far the best the author had to offer.

Also good are the four other books in the Reeder saga: *Room 13* (1924) and *Terror Keep* (1927), both novels; and two additional collections—*Red Aces* (1930), which contains three novelettes, and *Mr. Reeder Returns* (1932), which contains four novelettes.

Still readable among Wallace's prodigious output of nonseries criminous novels are *Captains of Souls* (1922), *The Green Archer* (1924), *The Terrible People* (1926), *The Feathered Serpent* (1928), *The Silver Key* (1930) and *The Frightened Lady* (1933). His only other notable series character is the melancholy and mordant Inspector Elk, who appears in such novels as *The Fellowship of the Frog* (1928) and *The India-Rubber Man* (1930).

(*T.B.*)

Walling, R.A.J. *Marooned with Murder.* New York: Morrow, 1937. (PI/W)

R.A.J. Walling, a British journalist and newspaper editor who began writing mysteries as a hobby in his late fifties, received a good deal of acclaim during his time. (His first book was published in 1927, his last posthumously in 1949.) The *New York Times* stated in 1936 that Walling had considerable skill in weaving mystery plots; the *Saturday Review of Literature* decided that he wrote suavely baffling stories; the eminent critic Will Cuppy said of one of his early novels that it was "absolutely required reading."

This reviewer couldn't agree less.

In the first place, Walling wrote some of the dullest mysteries ever committed to paper; it may even be said that he elevated dullness to a fine art. And in the second place, his series sleuth, private inquiry agent Philip Tolefree, is a twit. He says things like, "You're a vandal, Pierce. You've feloniously broken into my ivory tower. Never mind. I'd have been bored in another half hour. How'd you find me out? Sit down, my dear fellow. Cigarette? Pipe? Well, carry on. What's the trouble now? Or did you come for the sake of my beautiful eyes?" He is also fond of quoting obscure Latin phrases, treating his sometime-Watson, Farrar, as if he were an idiot, and withholding information from everyone including the reader.

Although Tolefree operates out of a London apartment, most of his cases seem to take him into the countryside. He solves them in the accepted Sherlockian manner of detection and deduction, using an inexhaustible fund of knowledge both esoteric and ephemeral. Another reason he is so successful at unmasking murderers is his familiarity with such matters and motives as skeletons in closets, hidden relationships, peculiar wills, strange disappearances, and Nazi infiltrators, since nearly all his investigations seem to uncover one or any combination of these.

Marooned with Murder is no exception; its central plot points are hidden relationships and a strange disappearance. It begins well enough, with a dandy premise: Tolefree and Farrar, on a holiday in the Scottish Highlands, decide to rent a boat and sail her out of one of the fjordlike lochs into the Atlantic. A sudden storm shipwrecks them on the tiny island of Eilean Rona, where they are rescued by the lord of the isle, Martin Gregg; artist Bill Parracombe; and two odd and fiercely loyal Scotsmen, Fergus and Jamie. Also staying at the island's ancient castle for the summer are Gregg's wife and small son, and the boy's governess. The storm continues to batter Rona, preventing any of them from leaving. A chance remark by Farrar, about a retired sea captain he knows named Strachan who lives over on the mainland, for some reason seems to frighten everyone; so does the remark that Tolefree is a detective. It soon becomes clear that Strachan had been hunting lost treasure on the island and disappeared one foggy Sunday three months before, along with his boat and a mysterious companion; and that the inhabitants of Rona know something about that disappearance and are desperate to protect their guilty knowledge.

So far, so good. But Walling spoils the stew by interminable passages of cat-and-mouse dialogue, annoying cryptic remarks from Tolefree, and a lot of rather silly running around. He also lets the reader know early on that Tolefree and Farrar do not fear for their lives; they think their hosts are all swell people, even though one of them may be a murderer. The result is plenty of mystery but no menace and therefore no tension. And the mystery isn't satisfying, either, when its rather predictable solution is revealed.

Walling has been called (by his publishers) "the foremost exponent of the seemingly 'quiet' mystery, the civilized story with . . . excitement and drama seething below the surface." Readers who *don't* find that a euphemism for *dull,* and would like to examine Walling's work for themselves, should try *The Corpse in the Coppice* (1935), *The Corpse with the Floating Foot* (1936), *The Corpse with the Eerie Eye* (1942), and *A Corpse by Any Other Name* (1943). The last-named title has some effective descriptions of Londoners coping with the wartime blackout and blitz.

(*B.P.*)

Wallmann, Jeffrey M. *Judas Cross.* New York: Random House, 1974. (PP)

Dan Brashear is a New Jersey cop. A good cop for the most part, although like many of his peers he isn't above taking a little "sensible graft, a small bite that kept the wheels greased and the mobs out and the local boys fat and sassy." You had to take a little, Brashear rationalized; otherwise, you'd wind up like Turnbeau, his partner, who was honest and who was always passed over for promotion.

But then Brashear's careful fence-straddling comes to an abrupt end. First, there is heavy pressure from the reformist Wilcox Committee to clean up the city. And then Turnbeau is brutally murdered while Brashear is out collecting a little of his sensible graft. Turnbeau's murder is quickly "solved," but Brashear knows the real killer is still at large and suspects who it must be. His sense of guilt and his cop's instincts force him to seek justice for Turnbeau, thereby alienating himself from his fellow officers and endangering his job, his marriage, and his own life.

This is a taut, suspenseful novel—"the ageless tale of man's progression through revelation, resolution and redemption," as the dust-jacket blurb puts it. Its one notable flaw is some unabashedly purplish writing: "An opacus moon crossed Sanponset River with the crisp, chewing breeze, leaped above Steuben Hill and poured down among the inner suburbs, coasting along wide, tree-lined Frenchtown Avenue to wash the intersection with Wiletta Lane in a pale milky bath." Brashear's story would have been better served, perhaps, if the straightforward approach of most of the narrative had been maintained throughout.

Wallmann is the author of three other suspense novels: *The Spiral Web* (1969), a paperback original of dubious merit; *Clean Sweep* (1978), the amusing and clever tale of a group that sets out to literally break the bank at Monte Carlo; and, in collaboration with Bill Pronzini (q.v.), under the joint pseudonym William Jeffrey, *Day of the Moon* (1983), an action mystery published only in England.

(*B.P.*)

Walsh, Thomas. *Nightmare in Manhattan.* Boston: Little, Brown, 1950. (PP)

A six-year-old boy has been kidnapped—and, amazingly, Frances Kennedy, secretary to the boy's father, saw two of the kidnappers on a train and reported them as suspicious characters to the police even before anyone officially knew of the kidnapping. This enabled the police to get a jump on the case, and soon three of the four kidnappers were either taken into custody or killed. This left one, the ringleader and most dangerous of the lot, a man named Vincent Coniff. Coniff's nemesis turns out to be a man equally rugged, determined, and dangerous, but on the right side of the law. This man—a member of the railroad police—is William Patrick Calhoun, or "Tough Willie," as he is known around Manhattan Depot.

"Manhattan Depot" is almost certainly New York's Grand Central Station, and it is here that most of the action takes place. Few people know it like Calhoun, who works there, and Coniff, who has explored it thoroughly with the idea of using the station at rush hour for the exchange of the ransom money. As the tension mounts, the reader is taken into almost every nook and cranny of Manhattan Depot. The money is in the station. So are the kidnapper and the kidnapped boy. So, also, are a number of disguised policemen. But the kidnapper has outwitted and eluded them before. Can he do it again?

This tense novel, which emphasizes mood, character, and setting, won a Best First Novel Edgar. Although the relationship between Willie Calhoun and Frances Kennedy is a bit awkwardly developed, and there are other minor flaws, *Nightmare in Manhattan* stands up well to the test of time and still provides suspenseful reading.

Walsh's other novels are also worth investigating; among them *The Night Watch* (1952); *Dangerous Passenger* (1959), which has a New York cabby as its protagonist; *A Thief in the Night* (1962); and *The Action of the Tiger* (1968). Walsh was also an accomplished writer of short stories, for such slicks as *Collier's* early in his career and for *Ellery Queen's Mystery Magazine* for more than thirty years. One of his *EQMM* stories, "Chance after Chance," the moving tale of a defrocked Catholic priest, won a 1978 Best Short Story Edgar.

(*N.D.*)

*Wambaugh, Joseph. *The Blue Knight.* Boston: Little, Brown, 1972. (PP)

As a member of the Los Angeles Police Department, Joseph Wambaugh observed the streets and alleys of that city for fourteen years before he turned to writing fiction full-time. His first novel, *The New Centurions* (1970), was an instant success, and he has followed it up with a number of other best sellers. Wambaugh's novels are gritty and realistic, and in them he explores at some depth the psychological effects that the law-enforcement profession has on the men and women who work in it.

Bumper Morgan is a twenty-year veteran of the force, a beat officer patrolling the seedy section around L.A.'s Main Street. Recently forced into a black-and-white by an old injury, Morgan regrets not being out on the streets and has elected to retire, marry, and move to San Francisco, where his fiancée has received a job offer. The story opens three days before he is to leave the force.

Telling his story in first person, with numerous flashbacks that recapitulate a lifetime as a cop, Bumper takes us along on his beat. We see the warm Jewish merchants of Main Street; the drug addicts and homosexuals who hang out at Bumper's old nemesis, the Pink Dragon bar; the aging burlesque queen and informant whom he pays for information with the stipulation the money will go in trust for her daughter; the bookmakers and loan sharks and alcoholics; the people of Japan town, the Arab community, and Chicano Olvera Street. And we see Bumper's relationships: with Cassie, the woman he plans to marry; with Cruz Segovia, his longtime sergeant and closest friend. In the space of three days, Bumper gives us a crash course in what it's like to be a cop—from petty arrests, to court testimony, to trying to stop an unruly student demonstration. And at the end he shows us what police work can do to a man, how it can rob his life of warmth and happiness.

In this novel (which was filmed in 1975, starring George Kennedy and Alex Rocco), Wambaugh has painted a powerful portrait of a cop who could be any cop on the beat, a "comic blue policeman" who thinks himself "disgusting and pathetic"—and who in reality is none of those things.

(*M.M.*)

*Wambaugh, Joseph. *The Choirboys.* New York: Delacorte, 1975. (PP)

The powerful opening of this novel takes place in a cave in Vietnam in 1967. Two unnamed marines have taken shelter there from the enemy, and one of them suffers a severe emotional break. Although we do not learn their identities until much later in the book, we can surmise that this incident provides the fuel for future tragedy.

The scene then shifts to Los Angeles nearly ten years later. The "choirboys" are a group of policemen who attend "choir practice"—otherwise known as drinking binges—in MacArthur Park after going off night duty. We are told that a tragedy has taken place during one of these sessions and that a young man has been shot to death. Wambaugh then goes into flashback and takes us through the months prior to this final choir practice, introducing us to the participants, allowing us to glimpse their routine—and not-so-routine—tours of duty. We come to know intimately such characters as Roscoe Rules, the meanest and probably most despicable man in the precinct; Aaron Mobley, a twenty-five-year-old alcoholic who somehow still manages to function on the job; Francis Tanaguchi, a Nisei who feels more Mexican than Japanese; Spermwhale Whalen, a veteran cop who has a big stake in making it to his twenty-year retirement date; Sam Niles and Howard Bloomguard, physical opposites who nonetheless complement one another as partners; Spencer Van Moot, who can wangle a "freebie" out of any merchant he meets; Baxter Slate, whose "different" quality is hard for his fellow cops to pin down.

With frequent black humor, Wambaugh shows us both the strengths and weaknesses of his characters, as well as the daily strains, sordidness, and departmental hypocrisy with which they must cope. And when tragedy finally befalls them, the only surprise is that is hasn't happened sooner.

This is a first-rate novel that goes several steps beyond the standard police procedural. It was filmed in 1977, starring Charles Durning and Perry King. Among Wambaugh's other novels of the police world are *The Black Marble* (1978) and *The Secrets of Harry Bright* (1985).

(*M.M.*)

Watson, Clarissa. *The Fourth Stage of Gainsborough Brown.* New York: McKay, 1977. (AD)

Clarissa Watson is co-owner and director of an art gallery on Long Island, and she puts her knowledge of the art world to good use in her three novels about artist and gallery assistant Persis Willum. Her depiction of the art world—its trendiness, petty jealousies, passions, and intrigues—is sure, and fleshed out with memorable characters. While many of the eccentrics

Watson portrays are representative of real types who frequent museum openings and galleries, they are never stereotypical; and Persis herself, an independent but vulnerable thirty-six-year-old widow, is a delight.

The title character of this first novel, Gainsborough Brown, is an artist of flamboyant reputation—and definitely *not* a delight. Painters go through many "stages" in their work; at the time the book opens, "Gains" is in his third major stage; before he reaches his fourth, he is dead. After Gains drowns in the swimming pool at a birthday party that Persis's aunt Lydie (an art patron and another extremely appealing character) has thrown for herself, Persis decides his death was no accident. And as an employee of Long Island's North Shore Gallery, which handled the artist's work, she feels compelled to find out who killed him and why. Armed with an unusual detective's tool—a sketch pad—Persis moves in what she hopes is an unobtrusive manner through the chic art world, from Manhattan to Paris, from elegant galleries to a studio full of cruelly satiric sculpture. Unfortunately, her investigative efforts have not gone unobserved, and she comes upon the solution to her first case at considerable danger to herself.

Watson's writing, like her heroine, is witty and stylish, and her plot is full of surprises. The other Persis Willum novels are *The Bishop in the Back Seat* (1980) and *Runaway* (1985).

(*M.M.*)

*Watson, Colin. *Just What the Doctor Ordered.* New York: Putnam's, 1969. (PP)

One measure of accomplishment for any writer of fiction is how successfully he or she transports us to his/her own individual world of imagination. Certainly one of the more successful in this regard is Colin Watson and his fictional town of Flaxborough. Much to our delight, and to the chagrin of Inspector Purbright of the Flaxborough Police Department, an amazing amount of crime seems to occur in this English village.

Just What the Doctor Ordered begins with a number of sexual assaults on the women of the town. Miss Butters is accosted in Gorry Wood; Miss Sweeting on Heston Lane; Miss Pollock by the reservoir; and at St. Hilda's a man threatens to "pollinate" Mrs. Pasquith. The fact that the attacks are perpetrated by elderly gentlemen, who make their escape by running sideways, only adds to the puzzlement. Inspector Purbright at first suspects an herbal concoction that promises amazing renewed virility. But few cases are quite so simple, as any Colin Watson fan will tell you, and this one takes several additional turns, including murder, before a solution is found.

Inspector Purbright—flanked by his superior, Chief Constable Chubb; his subordinate, Sergeant Love; and his perpetual thorn-in-the-side, Miss Lucilla Teatime—is at the center of the Flaxborough novels, but the real stars are the amusing and eccentric townspeople themselves. This and the other novels in the series are recommended without reservation. Those other novels include *Hopjoy Was Here* (1963), *Charity Ends at Home* (1968), *Six Nuns and a Shotgun* (1975), *Plaster Sinners* (1981), and *Whatever Happened at Mumblesby?* (1983).

Colin Watson is also the author of an excellent sociological study of the British crime novel between the two world wars, *Snobbery with Violence* (1971; revised edition, 1979).

(*N.D.*)

Waugh, Hillary. *The Con Game.* New York: Doubleday Crime Club, 1968. (PP)

The novels of Hillary Waugh are characterized by tight plot lines that contain no superfluous action or complications. Each of his stories is lean, tense, and to the point, and it was this streamlined approach and good sense of structure that made Julian Symons select the 1952 novel *Last Seen Wearing . . .* for his list of the 100 greatest crime stories written up to 1959. Over the past thirty-some years, Waugh—who is married to fellow suspense writer Shannon O'Cork (q.v.)—has created several series characters: private eyes Sheridan Wesley and Philip Macadam, who are both highly derivative of the Chandler/Hammett tradition; Lieutenant Frank Sessions of Manhattan's Homicide North; and Police Chief Fred Fellows of Stockford, Connecticut. Fellows, a down-to-earth, overweight cop and severe taskmaster, is probably the most appealing of these; and the small-town milieu is one Waugh knows well, since Stockford is very much like the Connecticut setting where Waugh grew up (although life there is definitely more fraught with peril than in New Haven).

The Con Game, Fellows's eleventh case, is sharply evocative of the suburbs of the Sixties. Four couples have conspired to bribe elected officials in a land deal; now the $60,000 they have amassed to do so is missing, as are two of the conspirators, George and Dierdre Demarest. Fellows's job is to find them—and the money. His investigation reveals affairs, hopes of affairs, suspicions of affairs, revenge after affairs, and divorce because of affairs—in short, almost every kind of sexual misconduct in Stockford. And those citizens who are not motivated sexually are sure to be moved by greed. Fellows treads carefully through this social minefield, trying to determine what each devious-minded person is hiding, but of course he cannot tread carefully enough. And before the case is over, he must use a creative method to determine the whereabouts of his quarry.

Fellows is an able police officer and a sympathetic character who employs not only good procedural methods but also the logical processes of classical detectives to get his woman or his man. Some of Waugh's other books in this series are *Sleep Long, My Love* (1959), *Born Victim* (1962), and *End of a Party* (1965). Among the Manhattan North novels are *"30" Manhattan East* (1968) and *Finish Me Off* (1970).

(*M.M.*)

Webb, Jack. *One for My Dame.* New York: Holt, 1961. (T)

Jack Webb the mystery writer is not Jack Webb the actor. Jack Webb the mystery writer never played Sergeant Joe Friday, and he never wore badge 714. Instead, Jack Webb the mystery writer produced a number of entertaining books featuring a priest, Father Joseph Shanley, and a detective, Sammy Golden, as well as two exceptional thrillers.

One for My Dame is a thriller that Hitchcock should have filmed. It has all the elements: an innocent man, for over two years a prisoner of war in Korea and now the owner of a pet shop, who has information that Mafia killers want; a beautiful girl on the run; a great supporting cast, including a character actor who lives in model homes, a Great Dane, a hill monkey, and a myna bird who shouts things like "Watson, the needle!"; and even a lovely blonde. The pace is brisk, the style is literate, and there's enough action to satisfy nearly anyone. This is the kind of book that one reads in a single sitting, looking up surprised to discover how fast the time has gone by. The resolution seems a bit drawn out, but the rest of the book more than compensates.

Webb's other thoroughly entertaining thriller is *Make My Bed Soon* (1963), a little bit tougher but every bit as much fun. The best of the Shanley and Golden mysteries are probably *The Big Sin* (1952), *The Brass Halo* (1957), and *The Deadly Sex* (1959). Webb also wrote several novels under the pseudonym John Farr; two of these—*Don't Feed the Animals* (1955) and *The Lady and the Snake* (1957)—feature well-realized zoo backgrounds. Another good Farr novel is *The Deadly Combo* (1958), whose chief appeal is an expert depiction of the world of jazz music.

(*B.C.*)

Wells, Carolyn. *The Wooden Indian.* Philadelphia: Lippincott, 1935. (PI)

During the first four decades of this century, Carolyn Wells wrote more than eighty mystery novels—most of them to a strict (and decidedly outmoded) formula she herself devised. She has been called, with some justification, an expert at the construction of the formal mystery, and she has also been credited with popularizing the locked-room/impossible-crime type of story, of which she wrote more than a score. Her other claim to fame is that she was the author of the genre's first nonfiction work, a combination of how-to and historical overview called *The Technique of the Mystery Story* (1913). Unfortunately, that book is far more readable today than her novels, which are riddled with stilted prose, weak characterization, and flaws in logic and common sense.

The Wooden Indian, one of her later titles, is a good example. It features her most popular series sleuth, Fleming Stone, a type she describes in *The Technique of the Mystery Story* as a "transcendant detective"—that is, a detective larger than life, omniscient, a creature of fiction rather than fact. And indeed, Fleming Stone is as fictitious as they come: colorless and two-dimensional, a virtual cipher whose activities are somewhat less interesting to watch than an ant making its way across a sheet of blank paper. The same is true of most of her other characters. None of them come alive; and if you can't care about a novel's characters, how can you care about its plot?

The plot in this instance is a dilly. An obnoxious collector of Indian artifacts, David Corbin, keeps a huge wooden Indian, a Pequot chief named Opodeldoc, in a room full of relics at his home in "a tiny village in Connecticut which rejoiced in the name of Greentree." One of the accouterments of this wooden Indian is a bow and arrow, fitted and ready to fire. And fire it does, of course, killing Corbin in what would seem to be an accident (or the fulfillment of an old Pequot curse against the Corbin family), since he was alone in the room at the time and there was no way anyone could have gotten in or out. Several guests are on hand at the time, one of them Fleming Stone. Stone sorts out the various motives and clues, determines that Corbin was murdered, identifies the culprit, and explains the mystery—an explanation that is not only silly (as were many of Wells's solutions) but implausible, perhaps even as impossible as the crime itself was purported to be.

Fleming Stone is featured in such other titles as *The Clue* (1909), *The Mystery of the Sycamore* (1921), and *The Tapestry Room Murder* (1929). Wells also created several other series detectives—Pennington ("Penny") Wise, Kenneth Carlisle, Alan Ford, Lorimer Lane—all of whom are as "transcendant" as Fleming Stone. Her novels are important from a historical point of view, certainly; but the casual reader looking for entertaining, well-written, believable mysteries would do well to look elsewhere.

(*B.P.*)

Wells, Tobias. *Have Mercy on Us.* New York: Doubleday Crime Club, 1974. (W)

Best known for her fourteen novels about the adventures of Boston police officer Knute Severson, Tobias Wells (Deloris Forbes, who also writes as Stanton Forbes, q.v.) has enjoyed a twenty-year career as a mystery author. In her more recent books, she has allowed amateur detectives to supplant Knute as the principal focus of the story, but—as in *Have Mercy on Us*—he still plays a small but important part.

Mercy Bird is a sixty-ish, single mystery writer who lives next door to Knute in Wellesley, Massachusetts. Her work on her current book is not going well, and her bank account is getting low when she sees an ad offering free room and board to aspiring songwriters. The would-be patron is Countess Marianne von Hohoken of the neighboring town of Dover. Mercy makes up a lyric and sends it along and, much to her surprise, is invited to move into a guesthouse on the countess's estate, Ravenscroft. Not long after arriving with her Saint Bernard dog, Algernon, one of her fellow scribes dies; and yet another is found dead a couple of days later.

Highly suspicious of what is going on on the great estate, Mercy asks Knute, who is just getting ready for a vacation trip to Florida, to look into things; the police chief in Dover, she feels, is not cooperative. He agrees to monitor the situation through long-distance calls. Mercy then takes her housemate, Frances Porter—whom she is convinced will be the next to die—to stay at her house in Wellesley, but they are quickly lured back to Ravenscroft. Fortunately for them, Knute has kept his promise to telephone regularly, and it is his final call that triggers the solution to the puzzle.

Good humor, fine characterization, and careful attention to detail make even the more improbable of Wells's novels readable. What might have been simply a routine police-procedural series is instead a warm, well-crafted, and suspenseful ongoing story about people who grow and develop in response to the strange situations in which they find themselves.

Some other novels in the Knute Severson series are *A Matter of Love and Death* (1966), *Die Quickly, Dear Mother* (1969), *The Foo Dog* (1971), and *A Creature Was Stirring* (1977).

(*E.N.*)

Wentworth, Patricia. *The Gazebo.* Philadelphia: Lippincott, 1956. (CS)

Patricia Wentworth's series detective, Miss Maud Silver, has been likened favorably to other little-old-lady sleuths, notably Christie's (q.v.) Miss Jane Marple. Miss Silver, however, takes the detection business several steps further than Miss Marple; she is a professional private inquiry agent and often receives quite lucrative remuneration for her services. Miss Silver possesses many of what we have come to think of as accouterments of the spinster sleuth: rather outmoded hats, a benign appearance, and the ever-present bag of knitting. These serve as an effective camouflage for her keen observation of the world; as her friend Scotland Yard detective inspector Frank Abbot often says, ". . . as far as she was concerned the human race was glass-fronted. She looked not so much at them as through them, and . . . saw whatever there was to see." Miss Silver combines this discerning observational power with a thoroughly professional manner and a compassionate approach to her clients.

The Gazebo is one of Wentworth's best novels. Miss Silver puts in a delayed appearance (in chapter 9, after we have already become acquainted with the problems of her future client) at a cocktail party given by a friend in the English suburban community of Grove Hill. There she meets Althea Graham, a young woman who is a friend of a former client (in these novels, almost everyone in the world seems connected by virtue of having been aided by Miss Silver at one time or another), and discusses a problem Althea has been having. Two parties have been trying to buy the Graham home: a Mr. Blount, who says his wife cannot do without it, even though Mrs. Blount's reactions to the house are tepid; and Fred Worple, a sharp dresser whom one "wouldn't expect to meet in society." Both men have made offers of far more than the house is worth and are pressuring for a sale, as is Althea's ailing and selfish mother, who wants to take the money and go on a cruise. Althea is the real owner of the house (her father didn't trust leaving it in her mother's name) and she doesn't want to sell because her former fiancé, Nicholas Carey, has returned to town and wishes to resume the romance.

Althea later consults Miss Silver again; the detective counsels her to marry Nicholas and arranges for a companion for Mrs. Graham. But before the companion can assume her duties, Mrs. Graham turns up strangled in the gazebo behind the house after having quarreled with her daughter and Nicholas. Miss Silver appears immediately when Althea summons her, and aids Detective Inspector Abbot in sorting through the nuances of small-town life, clues that lead to a motive rooted deep in the past, and chicanery that is going on in the present.

Maud Silver is at her charming best in this novel, and the portrait of Grove Hill's residents—particularly a trio of nosy spinster sisters—is most entertaining. Unfortunately, the film that was made of *The Gazebo* (1959, with Glenn Ford and Debbie Reynolds) bears very little resemblance to the book.

(*M.M.*)

Wentworth, Patricia. *Poison in the Pen.* Philadelphia: Lippincott, 1955. (CS)

The village of Tilling Green is normally a tranquil place, but recently a series of poison-pen letters have been sent to various residents. One of the recipients is Joyce Rodney, a stepcousin of Detective Inspector Frank Abbot, and he is concerned enough to discuss the problem with Maud Silver. Abbot says, "It will probably all fizzle out"; but ten days later Doris Pell, a young resident of the Green, drowns herself, apparently because she received one of the distressing letters. Miss Silver agrees to travel down there, taking up residence at the guesthouse of Miss Irene Wayne, where Abbot's cousin also makes her home.

There is great excitement in the village because nearby Repton Manor is about to celebrate the wedding of heiress Valentine Grey to Gilbert Earle, a penurious young man who is heir to a title. Miss Silver listens to all the gossip—they say, among other things, that Valentine is not really in love with Gilbert—and attends the wedding rehearsal, where she senses something is amiss. The next morning, one of the bridesmaids, Connie Brooke, is found dead of an overdose of sleeping pills. While many think her another suicide, Miss Silver and local Chief Constable March suspect murder, since the dead girl had told the vicar she thought she knew who had written the anonymous letters.

Other events occur to disturb the tranquillity of the little community: Jason Leigh—the vicar's nephew and Valentine's former love—returns after a long absence; Valentine finds her fiancé has been having an affair with her guardian's wife and calls off the wedding; more poison-pen letters are received; another person dies of poisoning, and this time it is certainly murder. With this latest killing, Constable March and Miss Silver step up their investigation, and she makes skillful use of the village grapevine to uncover evidence leading to the letter writer and killer. Her discovery leaves her in considerable peril, and in fear for more than just her own life.

Other entertaining and well-plotted Maud Silver adventures include *Grey Mask* (1929, her first), *The Case Is Closed* (1937), *The Key* (1944), *Through the Wall* (1950), and *The Girl in the Cellar* (1961, her last). Wentworth created one other series character, the somewhat inept Inspector Ernest Lamb, who appears in some of the Silver books as well as alone in such titles as *The Blind Side* (1939) and *Pursuit of a Parcel* (1942).

(*M.M.*)

West, John B. *An Eye for an Eye.* New York: New American Library (Signet), 1959. (O/PI)

John B. West was a man of many talents and achievements: A doctor, he was both a general practitioner and a specialist in tropical diseases; he was also the owner of a broadcasting company, manufacturing firm, and hotel/restaurant corporation. He lived in Liberia, was black, and late in his life—as a pastime, apparently—wrote novels about white private eye Rocky Steele, of New York City.

West appears to have been used by Signet Books as an attempt to fill the gap when their star seller, Mickey Spillane (q.v.), stubbornly refused to write any more novels (until *The Deep* in 1960, that is). While the Rocky Steele novels were never any real competition for Mike Hammer (or anyone else), the six titles in the series did go through various printings and editions.

An Eye for an Eye, the first Rocky Steele adventure—in which for no particular reason the private eye avenges the death of the blond, beautiful, and wealthy Norma Carteret—is singled out here arbitrarily, as all of the books seem to be of a similar "quality." (One book, the posthumously published *Death on the Rocks,* 1961, does have an African setting to distinguish it.) While unquestionably lower-rung Spillane imitations (like Mike Hammer, Rocky Steele smokes Luckies, packs a .45, refuses the advances of his lovely secretary, has a loyal police contact, etc.), the West novels are goofily readable, as Rocky Steele teeters between the violence and revenge of Hammer, and the broads and campiness of Shell Scott. The world West creates (actually, re-creates) is pure pulp fantasy, and makes the work of Carroll John Daly (q.v.) read like documentaries. The energetic pulpiness of the plots, and West's confident, tin-ear, tough-guy dialogue (" 'Mercy! That rat didn't know what the word meant, and I wasn't gonna teach him' ") gives his private-eye stories the same sort of appeal as Robert Leslie Bellem's (q.v.) Dan Turner tales and Michael Avallone's (q.v.) later Ed Noon novels. (*M.A.C.*)

*Westlake, Donald E. *Dancing Aztecs.* New York: Evans, 1976. (C)

The marvel of Donald E. Westlake is his amazing versatility. With equal facility he has written light comedy, pure farce, private-eye stories, police procedurals, straight suspense, caper novels, mainstream fiction, science fiction, and nonfiction under his own name and pseudonyms; mysteries of penetrating psychological insight under the name Tucker Coe (q.v.); and, as by Richard Stark (q.v.), a series of antihero stories harder than any of the hard-boiled stories published in *Black Mask.* Which just about covers the entire literary spectrum, except for westerns, romantic historicals, and haiku poetry—and don't be surprised if Westlake decides to write one or all of *those* someday, just for the hell of it.

He began his novelistic career with five good but derivative hard-edged novels, among them *The Mercenaries* (1960), a private-eye adventure; and *Killy* (1963), a story of detection and psychological suspense in a small town. No, make that *four* good but derivative hard-edged novels; *Pity Him Afterwards* (1964), the tale of a madman on the loose, isn't really very good at all. Which perhaps helped Westlake decide to try his hand at something different: *The Fugitive Pigeon* (1965), the first of his marvelously comic mysteries. It was with that book, his sixth, that he found his true métier, and ever since he has moved this type of novel onward and upward to new heights of hilarity.

Dancing Aztecs is the best of Westlake's crime farces from his middle period (1970s). It tells the tale of Jerry Manelli, a New York City hustler with a hot tip on a priest—a thousand-year-old, two-foot-tall, ugly, misshapen dancing Aztec priest made out of solid gold, with emeralds for eyes, worth approximately $1 million. It seems this priest was stolen from a museum in the South American nation of Descalzo and subsequently smuggled through American Customs in a shipment of imitation priests made out of plaster; but somebody fouled up along the way and one of the copies got delivered instead to the million-dollar priest's New York destination, while the authentic priest was mixed up with fifteen other copies, all of which were delivered to various people in the city and its environs. Jerry's task: Find the real priest, and fast, before whoever has it realizes what it is and/or the original band of thieves get to it first.

Jerry's odyssey (and a dizzying one it turns out to be) leads him all over Manhattan, and to Connecticut, Long Island, and Jersey. It involves him with hoodlums, con men, "a yam-fed Descalzan beauty," union thugs, street thugs, a Harlem mortician, a Wall Street financier, a drunken activist, a college professor, "a visitor from another planet," and dozens more. Will Jerry pull off the greatest scam of his career, find the golden Dancing Aztec (not to mention True Love), and live happily ever after? Read the book and find out.

The dust-jacket blurb calls *Dancing Aztecs* "a silly city symphony of raucous laughter and sudden realities, running to the ragged rhythm of New York *now.*" Which is not good writing but nonetheless apt. It isn't Westlake's funniest novel, but some of its bits of business rank right up there with his most hilarious—his interpretation of black street dialect, for instance. A silly city symphony, indeed.

(*B.P.*)

*Westlake, Donald E. *God Save the Mark.* New York: Random House, 1967. (C)

God Save the Mark, for which Westlake received a much-deserved MWA Best Novel Edgar in 1968, is a comedy whodunit with barely restrained elements of slapstick—a type of book no one in the world has done better than Westlake. Its narrator and bumbling hero is Fred Fitch, a mark among marks; i.e., an easy victim, a ready subject for the practices of confidence men; i.e., the perfect sucker. Fred Fitch has more fake receipts, phony bills of sale, and counterfeit sweepstakes tickets than any man alive. He has even purchased a "money machine," which is on a par with shelling out good hard cash for a piece of the Brooklyn Bridge. As the jacket blurb says, "Every itinerant grifter, hypster, bunk artist, short-conner, amuser, shearer, short-changer, green-goods worker, pennyweighter, ring-dropper and yentzer to hit New York considers his trip incomplete until he's also hit Fred Fitch. He's sort of the con-man's version of *Go;* pass Fred Fitch, collect two hundred dollars, and move on."

But Fred's earlier problems seem minor compared to those he encounters after a relative he didn't know he had, the mysterious Uncle Matt, is killed (murdered, in fact) and he is willed $300,000. First of all, every grifter, hypster, bunk artist, etc., seems bent on relieving Fred of some or all of that hefty bequest; second and by no means least of all, the person or persons unknown who bumped off Uncle Matt is or are now trying to bump off Fred. The characters he meets as he tries to find out what is going on include a stripper named Gertie Divine, the Body Secular; a lawyer named Goodkind; an elusive crook named Gus Ricovic; a couple of cops called Steve and Ralph; a needle-happy doctor named Osbertson; and a former partner of Uncle Matt's named Professor Kilroy. Add to them the wackiest chase sequences this side of a Mel Brooks movie, and you have—or will have—any number of chuckles, laughs, and guffaws. Anybody who doesn't find this novel at least semihilarious probably wouldn't crack a smile at a politician's wake.

Two of Westlake's other novels in this same vein are likewise fast, funny, and fun: *The Busy Body* (1966) and *The Spy in the Ointment* (1966). Two more—*Who Stole Sassi Manoon?* (1969) and *Somebody Owes Me Money* (1969)—are less successful (*Sassi Manoon,* in fact, may be Westlake's worst novel), which is no doubt the reason he turned to other types of comic suspense.

(*B.P.*)

*Westlake, Donald E. *The Hot Rock*. New York: Simon & Schuster, 1970. (C)

Donald Westlake tells the story that he had an idea for a Parker novel (Parker is the grim, ruthless heistman featured in a series of very hard-boiled books published under Westlake's pseudonym Richard Stark, q.v.) in which Parker had to keep stealing the same object again and again. It just wouldn't work as a Parker novel—the idea was inherently too funny—so Westlake created the Dortmunder gang and launched a series of very successful comic caper novels with this book.

The African nation of Talabwo wants to obtain custody of the massive Balabomo emerald, currently in the hands of a rival country and on display in a museum exhibit. Their U.N. ambassador contracts with an odd assemblage of heistmen, led by master planner John Dortmunder, for the theft and delivery of the stone. Dortmunder, Kelp, Chetwick, Greenwood, and Murch pull off a very slick job, almost, but Greenwood gets nabbed by the cops, and he was the one holding the emerald. So they have to bust Greenwood out of jail, which they do, only to learn that he hid it in a police-station holding cell. So they have to break into the cop shop, which they do, only to learn that the stone isn't there anymore, which necessitates yet another, even more elaborate caper, and so it goes. . . .

Westlake doesn't depend on blatant farce to generate laughs; his approach to the comic caper is rather subtle. Initially, the setup isn't very different from what one might find in a straight Parker novel, but the crooks are just a bit odd, and the caper just a tad outlandish. As things proceed, the gang's exceptional bad luck escalates and the situation gets quite out of hand, becomes increasingly ludicrous, and increasingly funny.

The Hot Rock was made into a very successful film, which, atypically, follows the book rather closely (though the casting of Robert Redford as Dortmunder is pretty far off the mark). The movie, alas, did omit the wildest caper in the book, the kidnapping of Greenwood's lawyer from a sanatorium using a locomotive. Two other Dortmunder books have made it to the screen, both badly botched: *Bank Shot* (1972), in which the gang steals an entire bank on wheels; and *Jimmy the Kid* (1974), wherein Dortmunder and company use a (nonexistent) Richard Stark Parker novel as the blueprint for a kidnapping, with predictably disastrous results.

The most recent entry in the series, *Why Me?* (1983), is also one of the best and funniest. This one involves Dortmunder and his gang with a Turkish national treasure stolen by a band of Greeks; and with the FBI, the New York City Police Department, and no less than three terrorist groups from three different countries.

(*A.S.*)

*Westlake, Donald E. *Levine.* New York: Mysterious Press, 1984. (PP/SS)

In the late Fifties and early Sixties, Westlake was a frequent contributor to the digest-size mystery magazines. Included among his output were five novelettes—four published in *Alfred Hitchcock's Mystery Magazine* between 1959 and 1962 and one in *Mike Shayne Mystery Magazine* in 1965—about Abraham Levine, a detective with Brooklyn's Forty-third Precinct. Levine is no ordinary cop; he is fifty-three years old and lives on the edge of his emotions, constantly worrying about his aged heart, constantly taking his pulse; a man who is "so tensely aware of his own inevitable death that he wound up hating people who took the idea of death frivolously," as Westlake writes in his introduction to this collection of the five early Levine stories plus one brand-new novelette.

Each of Levine's cases ties in with his relationship with death, "his virtual romance with death," for "death fascinated Levine, it summoned him and yet repelled him." "The Best-Friend Murder" involves him in a complicated psychological case of murder and suicide whose principals are both young, healthy males. In " 'Come Back, Come Back . . .' " it is Levine versus a man on a ledge, a man who wants to take his own life. In "The Feel of the Trigger," perhaps the best of the four *AHMM* novelettes, it is Levine versus Levine when he is forced into a kill-or-be-killed showdown with a teenage murderer. "The Sound of Murder" takes Levine "farther down the same road, and when I finished it," Westlake says, "I wondered if I hadn't gone too far . . . made him someone no longer relevant to his theme." Not so. He brought Levine back for one more appearance, albeit three years later, in "Death of a Bum"—a story that was rejected by *AHMM* and other markets because it has no resolution, because it has instead one of the most painfully emotional endings of any story in the genre. It was and is the ultimate Levine story; Westlake knew it and retired the character.

Until 1984, that is, when the idea for this collection was broached to him. The early stories weren't sufficient to make a complete book; he would have to write a sixth Levine novelette for that purpose. On the one hand, it is fortunate he agreed to do so, for now the early stories have been made available in book form. On the other hand, it is unfortunate that Westlake chose to write "After I'm Gone." Not because it is a bad story; it isn't—it is Westlake at his most facile, with an up-to-the-minute plot involving high-tech gangsters and a perfectly fitting and proper resolution, both of the story and of the miniseries. No, the problem is that the intense feeling that makes the early works so poignant—the very core of the Levine series—is missing here. There is a detachment, a truncation of emotional content—as if Westlake, after twenty long years, has lost touch with the essence of his character.

That one slick, somewhat superficial (and therefore frivolous) story keeps this collection from being what it should be: a wholly suitable monument to a man named Abraham Levine, a man who hated people who take the idea of death frivolously.

(*B.P.*)

Weston, Carolyn. *Poor, Poor Ophelia.* New York: Random House, 1972. (PP)

Carolyn Weston's three novels featuring the Santa Monica Police investigative team of Casey Kellog and Al Krug are not as well known as the popular television series they served as the basis for—"The Streets of San Francisco," starring Karl Malden and Michael Douglas. They are, however, excellent procedurals, with plenty of action and fine characterization of southern California and its denizens. The relationship between Kellog and Krug—the former a college graduate with liberal ideas about society and police work; the latter a hard-bitten veteran of the force—is well portrayed in all its tensions. (This is practically the only thing about the novels that the television series accurately reflects.) And Weston utilizes an interesting device of telling part of the story from the viewpoint of an innocent person who has inadvertently become involved in a murder and finds himself suspected of it.

In this first book, Kellog and Krug are assigned to the case of an unidentified young woman whose body has been fished out of the bay. She has been killed by a blow to the head rather than by drowning, and the only clue is the laminated card of a lawyer, David Farr, that hangs on a cheap chain around her neck. There are also indications that she was a drug addict. Farr, an up-and-coming young professional, admits to knowing the woman, but not well; he claims he cannot imagine how his card came to be on her body. But as the story emerges, told both from Casey Kellog's and David Farr's viewpoint, it seems that the attorney's relationship with the dead woman was more complex than he has indicated, and soon Farr finds himself on the brink of arrest.

Weston's portrayal of Farr as a frightened and hunted man is excellent, and the reader finds himself strongly on his side as the story moves to an action-packed conclusion. The pilot film for the TV series, also titled "The Streets of San Francisco" (1972), was a faithful adaptation of this novel and starred Malden and Douglas in the roles they later played in the series, as well as Robert Wagner as a somewhat dissipated and bewildered David Farr.

Kellog and Krug appear in only two other cases: *Susannah Screaming* (1975), in which they investigate the apparent suicide of an actress who hours before reported a hit-and-run attempt on her life; and *Rouse the Demon* (1976), in which a therapist who has been treating youthful drug addicts is murdered under strange circumstances. A nonseries novel, *Danju Gig* (1969), takes place in West Africa.

(*M.M.*)

Wheat, Carolyn. *Dead Man's Thoughts.* New York: St. Martin's, 1983. (AD)

Cassandra Jameson was a student at Kent State University the day four of her friends were shot down by the National Guard. Ten years later she is a public defender in New York City. Easing the burden of the poor wretches caught in a merciless judicial system, she carries out the ideals born so tragically that day in Ohio. The fight has taken its toll, however. Bordering on burnout, Cassandra harbors a hatred for a judiciary that seems to enjoy sacrificing eighteen-year-old Puerto Rican girls to the jail cells of Manhattan. It eats away at her day after day. A photographer in her spare time, she thinks she could turn that into a profession if she had the guts. Maybe *next* year . . .

She's a great lawyer, too, it turns out. But it takes the murder of her current lover—Nathan Wasserstein, also a public defender—at the hands of what would seem to be a vicious homosexual lover, to convince her just how good an attorney she is. In her efforts to prove that Nathan was not the kind of man to get his sexual jollies by being tied up, beaten, and assaulted, Cassandra blows the lid on some of New York's "finest" people. And in the process, she regains her commitment to public defense.

Kids of the Sixties are now beginning to tell their stories, and Wheat tells it better than most. This first novel—which *Library Journal* called "literate, witty, with . . . characters who have real depth and honest emotions"—is an extremely promising debut.

(*K.K.H.*)

Wheatley, Dennis. *Gunmen, Gallants, and Ghosts.* London: Hutchinson, 1943. (Revised edition, London: Arrow, 1963.) (SS)

Dennis Wheatley was a prolific writer who produced over sixty books in such various genres and subgenres as mystery, black magic, adventure, and historical romance. The four series he created are each very different from the others, and thus it may be said that in Wheatley's work there is something for practically every type of reader. The first of these—fast-moving adventure stories loosely based on Alexandre Dumas's *Three Musketeers*—features the duke de Richleau in such titles as *The Forbidden Territory* (1933), *The Golden Spaniard* (1938), and *The Prisoner of the Mask* (1957). A British espionage agent, Gregory Sallust, stars in, among others, *Black August* (1934), *The Scarlet Imposter* (1942), and *Traitor's Gate* (1958). Historical espionage novels featuring Roger Brook include *The Launching of Roger Brook* (1947), *The Sultan's Daughter* (1963), and *Desperate Measures* (1974), set in the period 1783–1815 in such locations as the Americas, Asia, and Europe. Finally, Wheatley created a series of three revenge novels featuring Julian Day: *The Quest of Julian Day* (1939), *The Sword of Fate* (1944), and *Bill for the Use of a Body* (1964).

The best sampler of Wheatley's varied output is his excellent short-story collection *Gunmen, Gallants and Ghosts.* This volume offers the best of his work, divided into categories: ghost stories; other stories of the occult; stories of crooks and war; and other, mostly historical, writings. The best ghost story is "The Case of the Thing that Whimpered," featuring Neils Orsen, a man who can foretell the future. In the occult section, "In the Fog" brings a man's haunting past face-to-face with his present. The crooks-and-war section features the classic "When the Reds Seized the City of Gold," with the Johannesburg Insurrection of 1922 as its backdrop.

Wheatley is also known for the "Crime Dossiers" series of detective games (created with Joe Links). These feature folders containing evidence of a crime—photographs, letters, bloodstained fabrics, reports—which supply the reader with the same clues the police would use to solve the case. Among these are *Murder off Miami* (1936; originally published in the United States as *File on Bolitho Blane*) and *Who Killed Robert Prentice?* (1937; originally published in the states as *File on Robert Prentice*).

(*M.M./G.K.*)

White, Lionel. *The Big Caper.* Greenwich, Conn.: Fawcett Gold Medal, 1955. (O/T)

Lionel White specialized in the caper novel, the plot of which usually centers on some crime of large dimensions that a gang decides to commit. In *The Big Caper,* the crime is bank robbery. Flood, the mastermind behind the robbery, assembles a team for the job—an old safecracker, an arsonist to create a diversion, two men to disable the power plant, two tough guys for the strong-arm work, and a man and a woman to pose as husband and wife while casing the bank and establishing a base of operations.

As in most caper stories, small things go wrong, things that no amount of planning can take into account. Flood's major problem, however, is that the man and woman decide that they like being husband and wife. In fact, they fall in love, and they discover that the life they really want is the one they are pretending to live in the small town where the bank is located. White doesn't cheat, however. The robbery does occur, and the scenes depicting it are almost cinematic in the way that the various activities of the characters are intercut. (Indeed, the book was made into a movie, though not a very good one, with Rory Calhoun in the leading role.)

The first part of the book is carried along by White's skill as manipulating a large cast of characters and by proper injections of the vivid violence he describes so well in many of his books. The style is appropriately terse, and White deals with his subject matter in an extremely convincing manner.

(*B.C.*)

White, Lionel. *The Money Trap.* New York: Dutton, 1963. (PS)

The Money Trap may be the last major White novel, and as such it holds a special place in a career that was never adequately appreciated by aficionados of the crime genre.

Joe Baron is a detective, as is his friend and partner Pete Delanos. But the men share much more than a police vehicle—they also find their lives defined by an increasing sense of dread and boredom. When the opportunity comes along to take a million dollars from a crooked doctor named Parnell who worked out an incredible scheme with a sad junkie Parnell later kills, the opportunity is too exciting for either man to refuse. And so they set about stealing the doctor's million dollars from him.

Literary wisdom at the time was that White was a better plotter than a writer. While his style is stolid and only rarely graceful, here he shows an earnest and occasionally brilliant interest in human psychology. His portrait of Baron, particularly how the man deals with his failing marriage, is a much truer and less theatrical look at divorce than some of the more literary crime writers would later depict it.

This is a brooding book—Baron is never quite satisfied with anything that happens—but as usual, White provides enough plot twists to fill a whole shelf of lesser novels, and enough suspense to show himself the major-minor figure he is.

White's other page-turning capers include *The Snatchers* (1953), *Clean Break* (1955), *Operation—Murder* (1956), *Hostage for a Hood* (1957), and *Steal Big* (1960). *Clean Break* was the basis for one of the classic *film noir* gangster epics, *The Killing* (1956), which starred Sterling Hayden in one of his best roles.

White, Teri. *Bleeding Hearts.* New York: Mysterious Press, 1984. (PS)

Tom Hitchcock breaks out of a mental hospital, meets his brother Jody, and leads him on a nightmarish murder spree through Los Angeles. The victims, like Tom and Jody, are young homosexuals. The two cops assigned to the case are Spaceman Kowalski and Blue Maguire, an unlikely pair, as Spaceman is a reverse snob and Blue is a rich kid who works as a cop because he likes it. Spaceman has a son about the age of many of the murder victims, and his son happens to be missing.

In a sense, the story is a chase played out as the two cops close in. But it's also very much a story of relationships—the one between Tom and Jody; the other between Spaceman and Blue. It's brutal, bloody, and so compelling that the book seems to stick to the reader's fingers, causing one to miss meals. White is that rare writer who can mesmerize her reader like the ancient mariner, holding him in a horrified trance until her story is done. She seems to know more about the seamy side than an ex-con and as much about the human mind as Krafft-Ebing, and she writes beautifully. Thus, *Bleeding Hearts,* despite its violence, will appeal to a good many more readers than those simply seeking thrills.

Triangle, White's first novel, won an Edgar for Best Paperback of 1982.
(*J.S.*)

Whitechurch, Victor L. *Stories of the Railway.* London: Routledge & Kegan Paul, 1977. (Reprint of collection first published in England in 1912 as *Thrilling Stories of the Railway.*) (SS)

This Queen's Quorum title, one of the scarcest collections of short crime fiction in its original edition, is of historical significance in that the protagonist of eight of its fifteen stories, health faddist and railway enthusiast Thorpe Hazell, is the genre's first "specialty detective"—a character greatly admired by Dorothy Sayers and of course Ellery Queen (qq.v.). All fifteen stories are also notable for their clever plots and for their authenticity, not only of their railway backgrounds but of the various procedural methods employed in each: Whitechurch, himself a railway enthusiast (and a canon in the Anglican church), was one of the first writers to make a proper study of police procedure.

Hazell is a particularly appealing character, for his eccentric (and wryly amusing) exercise routines and dietetic opinions, and for his compassion in dealing with the various criminals he encounters. He owes his origins to Sherlock Holmes, but his methods tend to be much more straightforward and realistic, even in the most baffling of cases. "Sir Gilbert Murrell's Picture," for instance, which has a highly ingenious impossible-crime ploy: the plausibly explained disappearance of a loaded boxcar *from the middle of a moving train.* (It is so ingenious and so workable, in fact, that it was used as the basis for an episode of the "Banacek" TV series.) Hazell's talents are also at their best in unraveling the mysteries of "Peter Crane's Cigars," which deals with railway smuggling, and "The Adventure of the Pilot Engine," which is concerned with early-1900s politics and a runaway locomotive. Emphasis in the nonseries stories is on the various technical aspects of railroading, as well as on crime; the best of these are "The Mystery of the Boat Express" and "A Case of Signalling."

These stories are for the most part free of the flowery prose of much turn-of-the-century fiction, which makes them even more appealing to the modern reader. Anyone interested in early crime fiction, Holmesian plotting, and/or railroad mysteries will find *Stories of the Railway* a surprising treat.

Canon Whitechurch also published several criminous novels, among them *The Templeton Case* (1924), *Murder at the Pageant* (1931), and *Murder at Exbridge* (1932); and contributed a segment to the round-robin London Detection Club mystery *The Floating Admiral* (1932).

(*B.P.*)

Whitfield, Raoul. *Green Ice.* New York: Knopf, 1930. (A/T)

Raoul Whitfield was a prolific contributor to *Black Mask* during the early glory years, publishing almost 100 stories between 1926 and 1934. Along with Hammett, Daly, Gardner, and Nebel (qq.v.), Whitfield appeared in almost every issue during that eight-year span. Under the pen name Ramon Decolta, he wrote stories about Jo Gar, the Manila police detective.

In the early 1930s, he produced three hard-boiled novels: *Green Ice*

(1930), *Death in a Bowl* (1931), and *The Virgin Kills* (1932). *Green Ice* is a tough first-person narrative of Mal Ourney, a newspaperman recently released from a two-year stay in Sing Sing, where he was serving a stretch for manslaughter actually committed by ex-girlfriend Dot Ellis. She had been drinking Ourney's liquor and killed two men in a car accident. Out of a false sense of compassion, Ourney took the "two-spot" for her. While in prison he decided to wage a one-man vendetta against the brains behind organized crime who trap the little guys into criminal activity. He calls them the Crime Breeders.

Green Ice is filled with fast, violent action in the classic *Black Mask* style (the story appeared there in five parts between December 1929 and April 1930) and with Mal Ourney's reflective mode toward life in America during the end of the jazz age, which was controlled by mobster guns. The plot is convoluted in the extreme: At least twelve characters are killed trying to locate five fabulous missing emeralds, the "green ice" of the title, each worth $50,000; all the mobsters, molls, and cops (crooked and otherwise) Ourney meets are after the stones; and all of them—even the good cops—are willing to kill for them.

After several murders, Ourney finally determines that two rival mobs, led by "Tip" Christenson and Virginia ("Virgie") Beers, are after the stones. Both names are cruelly ironic: Christenson is certainly no son of Christ—he's a cold-blooded killer—and Virgie Beers isn't virginal in any sense. There is a final bloody confrontation in the steel-mill town of Duquesne, close to Pittsburgh, with the "noble soul" Ourney caught in the cross fire.

Green Ice is evocative of an era of hard men living hard lives. That world is cruel and unforgiving; Mal Ourney's very name roughly translates as "bad trip." His is a world controlled by the power brokers—his hated Crime Breeders—evil men and women searching for an elusive, easy fortune but finding only death.

Whitfield's novel does not have the raw power of Paul Cain's (q.v.) *Fast One;* neither is it as unrelentingly sordid. It does, however, have a protagonist who is altogether more likable than Cain's bad guy Kells. Ourney is a white knight with a sense of decency that puts the sordidness of the mobsters into perspective. Whitfield's novelistic style is fluid and not overly clipped, contributing greatly to the speed of the action and to reader enjoyment. The novel is quite representative of the best of the hard-boiled novels.

(*J.L.T.*)

Whitney, Phyllis A. *Blue Fire.* New York: Appleton, 1961. (R)

The romantic suspense novels of Phyllis A. Whitney are set in well-researched exotic locales or historical eras, and Whitney displays considerable skill in interweaving her background material with her plots. Her heroines are strong young women, usually with careers, who are forced to confront some secret in their family past; often this confrontation involves a conflict with a parent of either sex. The protagonists show a great deal of independence, and while the resolution of the mystery always involves a commitment to a strong male figure, it is implied that by no means will the heroine give up her independent ways.

In *Blue Fire,* Susan van Pelt, a newspaper photographer, is summoned back to South Africa by her estranged father. She is reluctant to go—her mother divorced her father and fled South Africa when he committed some mysterious crime and went to prison. But Susan falls in love with Dirk Hohenfield, her father's ward and the man he has sent to persuade her to return, and goes to Cape Town as his bride. Once there, Susan learns that her father's alleged crime involved diamond smuggling and that he is most likely innocent of it. Suspicion focuses upon Susan's dead mother, something Susan cannot accept. It becomes apparent to her that if she is to clear her mother, she must probe her memory for some clue not only to the diamond smuggling but also to the disappearance, at about the same time, of a legendary stone—the Kimberly Royal. As Susan delves into the past, she must also confront the present: racial tensions, apartheid, and a woman who claims she is the one Dirk really loves.

Excellent background on South Africa and the diamond industry. The ending is quite predictable but nonetheless satisfying.

(*M.M.*)

Whitney, Phyllis A. *Domino.* New York: Doubleday, 1979. (R)

Laurie Morgan was banished from her grandmother's house in Jasper, Colorado, in childhood, after apparently committing some act that was so terrible to Persis Morgan that she felt the child had destroyed her entire life. The adult Laurie, a widow and a successful New York editor, has no recollection of the incident and has put her unhappy childhood behind her. Her life is not without difficulty, however: She is subject to strange spells in which she sees disturbing silver light flashes, attacks that she has come to think of as her "aberration."

Suddenly Persis Morgan, in her typical high-handed fashion, contacts Laurie by telegram, demanding she return to Jasper and help her with an unnamed problem. Laurie, knowing the spells she has been experiencing must somehow be tied to the forgotten childhood trauma, agrees to journey to Colorado in the hope that confronting the past will cure her. There, in a mansion near the famed Domino ghost town, Laurie finds her grandmother—a strong-willed but frightened woman who demands that Laurie help her defeat her enemy, a developer who is threatening to destroy the area. Laurie is willing, but wants to know what happened when she was a child. Persis refuses to tell her, stating that any attempt to recover her money of the events preceding her banishment will only harm both of them. Laurie, however, is determined to confront the events she has repressed. As the story progresses, Laurie begins to realize there is good basis for what at first seemed unreasoning fear and panic on her grandmother's part; and as she probes deeper into both past and present-day problems, she comes into great danger.

Set against the vivid background of a ghost town and a played-out silver mine, this is one of Whitney's faster-paced and more engrossing novels. The author skillfully uses the one withheld fact—why Laurie was banished—to keep the reader turning the pages. And the answer, when it finally comes, is most satisfying.

(*M.M.*)

Whitney, Phyllis A. *Listen for the Whisperer.* New York: Doubleday, 1972. (R)

Journalist Leigh Hollins was abandoned at birth by her mother, Laura Worth, a famous actress who bore her illegitimately and gave her up to her father. Now Leigh's father—also a writer, who met Laura Worth while working in Hollywood—has died, and his last request is that she seek out her mother in the Norwegian town of Bergen, where Laura has been living for some years. A tragedy on the set of *Listen for the Whisperer,* Laura's last picture, prompted her to go into retirement, and she has been little more than a recluse ever since.

Leigh views Laura's abandonment of her as an unnatural crime, and at first she is reluctant to have anything to do with the woman whose beautiful face stares down at her from the screen at a Laura Worth revival. But then she conceives of going to Norway and making her mother pay for the desertion. She approaches Laura with the idea of interviewing her for a book on the Hollywood stars, and after some difficulty, she is admitted to the house where Laura lives with her husband. Once there, she realizes that all is far from well: An old murder—the tragedy that occurred on the set of Laura's last film—still haunts the former actress; and there are actual whispering voices in the house. As Leigh contends with a budding romance and reluctantly aids her mother in resurrecting the past, she is forced to come to terms with her deep resentment of a woman whom she cannot help but admire. And the resolution of what really happened that night in Hollywood so many years before is sure to satisfy the reader.

This is a strongly plotted novel, and the background material on Norway is excellent. Whitney has the ability to make her reader see the scenery, feel the crispness of the air, taste the national foods; this wonderfully titled book makes the reader feel he has really been there.

Other equally good Whitney titles are *Red Is for Murder* (1943; also published as *Red Carnelian* in 1968), *Silverhill* (1967), *Spindrift* (1975), *Poinciana* (1980), and *Dream of Orchids* (1984).

(*M.M.*)

*Whittington, Harry. *Brute in Brass.* Greenwich, Conn.: Fawcett Gold Medal, 1956. (O/T)

For thirty-five years, Harry Whittington has produced consistently outstanding paperback fiction. He has won a Spur Award from the Western Writers of America, as well as two "Porgies" (for a mainstream novel and a historical novel) presented by the *West Coast Review of Books.* In France he has been honored by the *Maison de la Culture* of Reims at the annual *polar* festival. Other writers so honored include Bill Pronzini, Evan Hunter, Donald Westlake, Robert Bloch, and Julian Symons (qq.v.). All the latter names are probably much more familiar to American readers than Whittington's, which is too bad since his crime novels can easily stand with the best in the field.

Brute in Brass is a good example. Mike Ballard, the title character, is a tough cop on the take, a man who cares for himself. When a condemned man calls on him for help because Ballard was the only cop who treated him decently, Ballard tells him that he treated him only with indifference, that he mattered so little that he had already forgotten him. Naturally Ballard refuses to help, but he changes his mind when the man's wife visits him. Ballard wants the wife on his own terms, and he agrees to reopen the investigation. At the same time, Ballard himself is being investigated for blatantly ignoring criminal activity. The two cases collide in a way that is not surprising, but Whittington does surprise the reader by the way he handles Ballard's character. Ballard is a thoroughly despicable man at the beginning, but Whittington slowly reveals the causes of Ballard's attitude, while at the same time allowing Ballard to discover a small core of decency within himself. It's a very small core indeed, but it does exist, and it makes the climax of the story intense and satisfying.

As in most Whittington books, the pace of *Brute in Brass* is faster than a speeding bullet. No one who reads the first chapter is likely to put the book down until the last page is turned.

(*B.C.*)

Whittington, Harry. *Web of Murder.* Greenwich, Conn.: Fawcett Gold Medal, 1958. (O/T)

Web of Murder may be Harry Whittington's most cleverly plotted book. It's the story of a lawyer, his beautiful secretary, and their plot to murder the lawyer's wealthy wife. There's also a hard-nosed cop who hates killers and has never failed to get his man. The situation may be familiar to readers of James M. Cain (q.v.), but the working out of the story is pure Whittington. The lawyer considers his plan carefully and finally puts it into motion. It seems perfect, but of course things begin to come unraveled—though not necessarily in ways that the reader would expect. It's one little thing after another, and each one is slightly worse than the last, each one putting the lawyer in a slightly weaker position, and each one giving the story an unexpected twist. (Although the twists may not be expected, they are beautifully set up.)

It would not be fair to the reader to detail the plot further, but perhaps it would be fair to say that the book leaves the reader with something to ponder: Is there a fate worse than imprisonment and/or death? There probably is, and one can be sure that justice, if not the law, is served. As always with Whittington, the dialogue is crisp, the action is fast, and the storytelling is first-rate.

Among other satisfying originals by Whittington are *Call Me Killer* (1951), *Mourn the Hangman* (1952), *The Woman Is Mine* (1954), *The Humming Box* (1956), *A Night for Screaming* (1960), and *Hell Can Wait* (1960). The last-named title is a particularly good example of Whittington's expertise at depicting characters pushed to the limits of their physical and mental resources. The best of his three hardcover mysteries is probably *Strangers on Friday* (1959), a taut suspense tale about a man named Mac Rivers who accidentally finds himself caught up in the corruption of a "little sewer of a town" called Roxmount.

(*B.C.*)

*Wilcox, Collin. *Aftershock*. New York: Random House, 1975. (PP)

Collin Wilcox began his mystery-writing career with two novels featuring a San Francisco reporter, Stephen Drake, who was possessed of extrasensory perception—*The Black Door* (1967) and *The Third Figure* (1968). While this attribute was extremely useful in solving crimes, readers apparently found it less than believable. In 1969, Wilcox abandoned Drake in favor of San Francisco police lieutenant Frank Hastings (first case, *The Lonely Hunter*), and since then his cleanly written procedurals have brought him a loyal and enthusiastic audience.

The Hastings novels combine straightforward procedure with interesting personal details about the life of the hero. Hastings is a former football player, former PR man and husband of a rich woman, and former alcoholic. Now he is a dedicated cop with a solid relationship with a nice woman and a growing relationship with her two sons. He becomes deeply involved with his cases, is not afraid to engage in hand-to-hand combat with the villains, and is not above a little philosophical commentary on a society that he views with a fairly jaundiced eye. Hastings works several cases at once—two of them major—and Wilcox's portrayal of the unique people and places of San Francisco characterizes the city, making it a living force with which his hero must contend as he goes about his investigations.

In *Aftershock,* Hastings is dealing with the homicide of a wealthy seventy-year-old woman. Suspects abound, including her much younger husband and a pair of children—one a gay male, the other a society matron—who do not seem above murder-for-profit. But the lieutenant also has a personal threat to contend with: A young psychopath, James Biggs, has a grudge against him, and is taking it out by terrorizing Hastings's girlfriend, Ann Haywood. Biggs is the son of a woman who was inadvertently wounded in a police shoot-out; the shot paralyzed her and she later took her own life. Now a civil suit is pending against the department, and Biggs has gotten it into his head—even though Hastings did not fire his own gun in the shoot-out—that the lieutenant is personally responsible for his mother's death. Hastings doesn't dare take action against Biggs, for fear it will bring a charge of police harassment, but how much more of Biggs's terror tactics can he withstand?

The two plot lines are skillfully woven together, and after Hastings solves the rich woman's murder, the tension created by Biggs's ongoing campaign of terrorism escalates into a dramatic climax.

(*M.M.*)

Wilcox, Collin. *Doctor, Lawyer. . . .* New York: Random House, 1977. (PP)

Lieutenant Hastings is called to the scene of the murder of an affluent Pacific Heights doctor, Gordon Ainsley; and from the extortion note left under the body, it becomes clear that other killings—of a lawyer, merchant, and chief—will occur unless the city of San Francisco pays $100,000 to the murderer. The note has earmarks of being from the People's Army of Liberation, an urban revolutionary group similar to the Symbionese Liberation Army; but the murder weapon, an army-issue .45, proves difficult to trace. When a lawyer, Jonathan Bates, is killed two days later and a second note is found with his body, Hastings realizes the killer is choosing his victims in alphabetical order, by the first letter of their last names. While he cannot guess which merchant the murderer intends as his third victim, he *can* guess that the "chief" is his boss, Police Chief Dwyer.

A Browning .380 handgun is found near the scene of the lawyer's killing and proves to be the murder weapon. Hastings and his men step up their search for ownership of both the Browning and the gun that killed Ainsley.

It takes them to the seedy Tenderloin district and a dramatic and near-fatal confrontation on a construction site, and finally to a totally unexpected and surprising location. As the investigation continues, political and departmental pressures mount, and Hastings must attempt to deal with them and keep his personal life under control, as well as extract information from a hostile witness who also happens to be his former—and embittered—girlfriend. There is a nice tension in this race to prevent a murder about which everything is known except when and where the killer will strike. *Doctor, Lawyer* . . . is one of Wilcox's best novels.

Other titles in this popular series are *Dead Aim* (1971), *Long Way Down* (1974), *Power Plays* (1979), *Stalking Horse* (1982), and *Victims* (1985). Wilcox also teamed Hastings with Bill Pronzini's (q.v.) "Nameless Detective" in *Twospot* (1978). He has written two excellent nonseries suspense novels: *The Faceless Man* (1975, as by Carter Wick) and *The Third Victim* (1976).

(*M.M.*)

Wilde, Percival. *P. Moran, Operative.* New York: Random House, 1947. (AD/C/SS)

P. (for Peter) Moran is not really a private operative, not yet; he is studying to be one with the Acme International Detective Correspondence School of South Kingston, New York—much to their chagrin. The problem is that Pete, who works as a chauffeur for a Wall Street tycoon living in a Connecticut village, isn't very competent. Or very compos mentis, for that matter. While he has a knack for stumbling into crime—and then reporting same via letters to Acme's chief inspector—he also has a knack for never making the right "deduct," no matter how simple a case may be; for in fact converting confusion into utter chaos. And yet he always manages to come out on top of things, sometimes even heroically so. Which of course stands him in good stead with members of the "opposite sect" who therefore aren't averse to demonstrations of his "sensual driving" ability.

"The 'gorjous' Pete," as Ellery Queen called him, "stands alone as the Mail Order Master Manhunter, the Correspondence School Sleuth Supreme, the Defective Detective De Luxe." *P. Moran, Operative* collects seven of his adventures (five of which were first published in *Ellery Queen's Mystery Magazine* in the early to mid-Forties). The best of the stories is "P. Moran, Diamond-Hunter," in which our hero is "hired" by a friend of his boss's, a rich "ameba" named Findlay, to discover what happened to eleven valuable rose diamonds that disappeared during a party. It isn't Pete who solves the case, though; that honor goes to his boss's new maid, Marrylin, who once took a "cause" in the Art and Craft of the Detective Story at a girls' college, and who deducts the whereabouts of the missing diamonds by enlisting the aid of Conan Doyle, Carr, Chesterton, Sayers, Queen, Christie, and Edgar Wallace (qq.v.)—but not before Pete uses a hammer to break up a roomful of valuable works of art and is almost shot with an elephant gun as a result.

Also very good are "P. Moran, Shadow," in which Pete accidentally busts up a marijuana-peddling ring run by a bunch of "Italians" who are really American gangsters led by a German; "P. Moran, Deductor," in which he learns the art of occupational deduction and foils a holdup with a "violin" unlike any Stradivarius ever made; and "P. Moran, Fire-Fighter," which finds him hiring out to prevent arson, committing it instead, and coincidentally foiling a bank robbery.

The sobersided Barzun and Taylor refer to these stories as "supposedly comic" and being of "indifferent quality." Nonsense. They are uniformly well done and uniformly funny, sometimes hilariously so, and stand up well to the test of time. Ellery Queen considered Pete Moran the best comic detective of his era.

Percival Wilde was primarily a playwright who wrote plays for children as well as adults (and for the vaudeville stage early in his career). His first book of detective fiction, *Rogues in Clover* (1929), a Queen's Quorum title, features the adventures of a rascally detective named Bill Parmalee who specializes in solving cardplaying and other gambling mysteries. Wilde also wrote four entertaining mystery novels, the best of which are *Inquest* (1940) and *Tinsley's Bones* (1942).

(*B.P.*)

*Williams, Charles. *Aground.* New York: Viking, 1960. (A/T)

Like Harry Whittington (q.v.), Charles Williams wrote a number of exceptionally good action/adventure paperback originals in the 1950s and 1960s, most of them set in Florida and other parts of the South. But it was in his handful of hardcover novels involving the sea that Williams produced his finest work. Few writers have been able to capture the true essence of the symbiosis between a born sailor and the ocean on which he sails; no crime-fiction writer did it better than Williams, himself a former radio operator on U.S. Merchant Marine vessels.

Aground is among his best work—a simple, straightforward tale that rushes headlong to a tremendously exciting climax. When a Miami-based yacht, the *Dragoon,* vanishes under mysterious circumstances, charter captain John Ingram finds himself suspected of a marine swindle. Joined by the woman who owns the *Dragoon,* Rae Osborne, he undertakes to find the missing vessel. What they don't know is that the yacht contains a deadly cargo, and that a group of criminals, led by an implacable type named Morrison, is also on the hunt. Ingram's and Rae's search for the yacht comprises the first third of the book; the last two-thirds chronicles what happens after they find it, aground on a sandbar in a remote section of the Bahama archipelago, and is suspense writing at its most intense and inventive. Once begun, the final 100 pages *must* be read uninterrupted.

But there is more to this and other Williams books than action and suspense. His characterization is sharp and complex, his settings are richly developed, and his descriptions of the sea and his characters' relationships to it often reach lyrical proportions. A Grade-A novel on all counts.

The same is true of *Dead Calm* (1963), which also features Ingram and Rae—now married and honeymooning aboard their new yacht, *Saracen,* in the Pacific—in a tantalizing thriller about madness and murder at sea.

(*B.P.*)

Williams, Charles. *Talk of the Town.* New York: Dell First Editions, 1958. (Also published as *Stain of Suspicion.*) (O/T)

Of Williams's many paperback originals for Fawcett Gold Medal and Dell, *Talk of the Town* ranks at or near the top. Bill Chatham, an ex–San Francisco cop busted for brutality against a dope pusher, is passing through the small northern Florida town of Galicia on his aimless way to St. Petersburg when a minor traffic accident damages his car, forcing him to lay over. The place in which he chooses to stay is the Magnolia Lodge, a run-down motel owned by Georgia Langston. The Langston woman is sickly, wasting away without hope or prospects, ostracized by the townspeople, who believe she murdered her husband, a popular native son. They also believe that a man named Strader—shot to death the same night Langston died, for resisting arrest after being caught disposing of Langston's car—was her lover and accomplice in the crime.

Attracted to Mrs. Langston, sympathetic to her plight, Chatham begins asking questions about that night and about the individuals involved. The more questions he asks, the more unwelcome he becomes in Galicia; and a stranger's destruction by acid of one of the motel rooms convinces him that Georgia Langston is not only innocent but the victim of a deadly local conspiracy. Hounded by the local law on one hand and the conspirators on the other, Chatham gradually pieces the truth together. But not before he is almost killed himself, in a scene of such sudden and savage violence that the reader is not likely to forget it.

Williams's usual excellent characterization and ability to create a mood of mounting suspense, plus a tightly knit plot, lift *Talk of the Town* well above the average paperback original of the Fifties.

Another of Williams's first-rate originals is *Man on the Run* (1958), a chase novel in the purest sense of that term: The entire book is comprised of Russell Foley's harrowing efforts to avoid capture in a statewide manhunt, so he can prove his innocence of murder. Also very good are *Hill Girl* (1951),

Hell Hath No Fury (1953), *A Touch of Death* (1954), *The Big Bite* (1956), and *All the Way* (1958).

(*B.P.*)

*Williams, Charles. *Scorpion Reef.* New York: Macmillan, 1955. (Also published as *Gulf Coast Girl.* New York: Dell, 1956.) (T/A)

Scorpion Reef was Williams's first sea thriller, and is probably his magnum opus—a novel of remarkable complexity and power, reminiscent of Joseph Conrad in its evocation of man's affinity for the ocean. It begins with the discovery (by the crew of an American tanker) of an abandoned sloop in the Gulf of Mexico—a sloop well provisioned, with no sign of violence or sickness aboard, floating derelict on a calm sea after the fashion of the *Mary Celeste.* The only clue to what happened to its passengers is a logbook, whose lengthy first-person narrative ends with an entry like none that the tanker's master has read in forty years: "*. . . the blue, and that last, haunting flash of silver, gesturing as it died. It was beckoning. Toward the rapture. The rapture . . .*"

The logbook's first-person narrative explains the events leading to the abandonment of the sloop. The narrator, Bill Manning, a former writer turned Florida sailor and salvage diver, was hired by attractive Shannon Wayne, ostensibly to recover a valuable shotgun from the botton of a lake. He soon found himself emotionally involved with the woman—and in the midst of a complex plot involving her pilot husband, a fortune in sunken treasure, two cold-blooded killers, and a salvage operation on board the sloop *Ballerina.*

The suspense mounts inexorably, and the plot twists are both unexpected and effectively staged. The scenes aboard the sloop in the open Gulf, particularly in the last fifty pages, contain some of Williams's most stirring prose. And if that isn't enough to satisfy the most demanding reader, there is a beautifully set up surprise ending.

Williams's other two oceanic mysteries, *The Sailcloth Shroud* (1960) and *And the Deep Blue Sea* (1971), are also good. His last novel, *Man on a Leash* (1973), forsakes the sea for a much drier milieu—the Mojave desert; it is the grim story of a man's relentless search for the brutal murderers of his father, and has an ending of considerable impact. This one, too, is unreservedly recommended.

(*B.P.*)

Williams, David. *Unholy Writ.* New York: St. Martin's, 1976. (AD)

In *Unholy Writ,* David Williams presents the first of a series of adventures about Mark Treasure, a not quite middle-aged British merchant banker. Treasure has been billed as England's answer to Emma Lathen's (q.v.) John Putnam Thatcher, but the coincidence of their occupation is their only similarity. Treasure, happily married to a well-known actress, gets involved in many of his cases as a result of tying up loose financial ends away from his place of business, and in this first book he is spending the weekend in the village of Mitchell Stroke, with a relative and her husband, General Sir Arthur Moonlight.

Moonlight, who has almost closed the sale on Mitchell Hall, his ancestors' home for 300 years, wants Treasure to help him get out of the deal. The new owner, George Scarbuck, is a building contractor and he has already begun extensive remodeling on the place, including putting in a swimming pool, which is being dug by Filipino workers. Scarbuck is the leader of the reactionary Forward Britain movement and plans to make Mitchell Hall its headquarters.

The book opens with a letter written in 1644 by the original builder of the house, James Moonlight, to his wife. In it he mentions that he had buried all of her jewels and a manuscript "of the Will." This letter and the buried properties play a prominent part in the weekend Treasure spends at the hall—a weekend that sees two people murdered; the local vicar getting into a fight; a Shakespearean scholar searching for evidence of early play performances in the area; the death of the local gravedigger; and a bit of golf on the side. Treasure also participates in a breathtaking late-night car and motorcycle chase.

Further adventures of Mark Treasure involve another historic house in *Treasure Preserved* (1982), a multi-million-pound company's attempted take-over of a small firm in *Advertise for Treasure* (1984), and a murder at a wedding at an English country house in *Wedding Treasure* (1985).

(*E.N.*)

Williams, Gordon M. *The Siege of Trencher's Farm.* New York: Morrow, 1969. (PS)

The most interesting thing about this novel is its setting: a rural part of West Anglia where time has virtually stood still for thousands of years. Superficial progress—in the form of automobiles and tractors and television sets—has come to the parishes of Dando and Compton Wakley, but essentially the old traditions and ideas live on. As Williams describes the area in his first chapter, it is possible to envision the past in this countryside, "to think . . . of the men who have lived here before, of rough-clad armies coming over the bare brows of these same hills, of the savage fair-haired men who came from the sea, of kings and nobles on panoplied horses . . . there was a dark side to this corner of England."

And it is to this place that his protagonists—George and Louise Magruder and their daughter, Karen—come: George to finish a book he is writing; Louise because she is English and, after years of living in the United States with her American husband and daughter, wishes to return home for a time. Their stay at Trencher's Farm, however, is far from idyllic, from the moment they find their pet cat strangled and tossed into the newly fallen snow. The Magruders have not been getting along anyway: He does not care for the isolation of the place, nor the unfriendliness of the natives, which borders on hostility; she is constantly on edge, critical of her husband, and doesn't know why; and the daughter simply wishes she were home with the friends and the things she knows.

When a Christmas party is given at the Dando village church, Louis and Karen attend. Before the party is over, a retarded child has disappeared into the snowstorm. There is additional cause for alarm because a child-murderer has escaped after an ambulance accident while being transported between a hospital and the nearby Two Waters Institution for the Criminally Insane.

The Magruders start for home, but on the road they hit a man with their car; and it is not until they have taken him into their home that they realize he is the criminal—a pitiful, wasted little man with the intellect of a child. They attempt to contact the local police, but word gets out in the village, and a band of local men, their brutality aggravated by drink, come to the farm, demanding that the Magruders turn the criminal over to them. At this point, Magruder, who has long considered himself a weak man, refuses to go along with what he perceives as mindless violence. But can he hold off the men, with no weapons and little support from his wife or daughter?

Williams's description of the West Country parishes and their deprived (and sometimes depraved) inhabitants is haunting and evocative, and the prolonged siege of the family at Trencher's Farm is suspenseful; but the Magruders are less than likable characters, and a great deal of reader sympathy for them gets lost because of their superficial bickering. Still, the novel is worth reading for the background alone.

Williams, who was born in Scotland, has written such other suspense novels as *The Last Day of Lincoln Charles* (1965) and *From Scenes Like These* (1969).

(*M.M.*)

Willie, Ennis. *And Some Were Evil.* Chicago: Merit, 1964. (A/O)

In the early to mid-1960s, Camerarts Publishing Company of Chicago published an infamous line of soft-porn books, earning them a place of honor among aficionados or paperback ephemera. Their "Novel Books" line promised much, delivered less, but any publisher that could publish the likes of *Dammit—Don't Touch My Broad, My Wild Nights with Nine Nudists,* and *Sensual Stenos,* plus *two* autobiographies by Mamie Van Doren, can't be all bad.

Camerarts also published Merit Books—and a line bringing up the rear (no pun intended) behind Novel Books is an unlikely place to look for a "cult" tough-guy writer. But there he is: Ennis Willie, creator of Sand—"the man nobody walks on," a strangely effective combination of Richard Stark's (q.v.) Parker and Mickey Spillane's (q.v.) Mike Hammer. Since Novel Books (and Merit Books) seemed devoted to churning out mediocre Spillane imitations, it comes as a shock to find that perhaps the best of Spillane's many imitators is the mysterious Willie, who seems to have disappeared (at least under that by-line) after his run of twenty Merit books, published between 1961 and 1965. (Willie published one non-Camerarts novel, *Vice Town,* 1962, for the even more obscure Vega line.)

Willie's heroes invariably have unlikely, macho names (Gard Hogan, Birch Sunday, Cord Mando, Cruss Ballard, Tripp Fortune) in books with unlikely, lurid titles (*Incredibly Seductive, So Naked! So Dead!, Politician's Playgirl, Modern Gigolo, Luscious, Teasing Body!*). The books themselves are wild melodrama played deadpan, yet there is little or no intentional parody here: Willie shares with Spillane an utter belief in his larger-than-life heroes, the most notable of whom (and Willie's only series character) is Sand, the mob's former fair-haired boy who quit only to be continually pursued by hit men.

In *And Some Were Evil,* Sand is driving over a "hard-baked Mexican road," using the Sierra Nevada at his left as his guide. He does "not think about the man he had killed five hours ago in Guadalajara," nor of the contract killers pursuing him. As dusk falls, a small American child in white runs in front of his headlights, and to avoid hitting her, he runs his car off the road. Before he has had a chance to get his car out of the ditch and help the child—inexplicably named Zita—he is sapped.

He wakes up among villagers who seem frightened when he mentions one of the child's cryptic remarks: that she is someone's "goat without horns." He then encounters several rich Americans, among them Lorna Wallace, a woman from his past (specifically, his love interest from *Haven for the Damned,* 1963, the action of which took place five years before that of this novel). In a wild coincidence typical of Willie, the little girl turns out to be Sand's child by Lorna.

Sand sets out to rescue the kidnapped child, who is being held by a voodoo sect (!) led by the Grand Zombi (!!), earmarked for human sacrifice (their "goat without horns"). Along the way Sand makes love to both Lorna and her sister, Phyllis; and has a Sergio Leone–style balletic gunfight with three hit men who have tracked him down. He ends up rescuing his daughter in a grand finale inside a mountain cave full of religious fanatics—a scene that plays like *Indiana Jones and the Temple of Doom* by Mickey Spillane.

Despite Willie's working in third person, he very nearly equals Spillane's famed first-person narrative drive; and echoes of the Mick ring out in the vivid scenes of violence, purple-prose sex passages, frequent italicized stretches, and "socko" surprise endings. Several of the eight Sand novels have Lovecraftian horror overtones, including the first, *Scarlet Goddess* (1963), and the haunting *Haven for the Damned.*

(*M.A.C.*)

Wilson, Barbara. *Murder in the Collective.* Seattle, Wash.: Seal, 1984. (AD)

There have been many attempts at political mystery fiction since the late Sixties. These efforts were often published by small presses, and often the book design was clumsy, a fitting complement to the writing within. Politics can easily overpower a mystery, the puzzle getting lost in the polemic. This is easier to hide in the law-and-order police procedural (e.g., by Elizabeth Linington, q.v.) than in mysteries at the opposite end of the political spectrum.

One of the most successful examples of the small-press (left-leaning) mystery is *Murder in the Collective* by Barbara Wilson. The author wishes to educate her readers about U.S. involvement in the Philippines and our support of the Marcos regime, as well as say something about feminist politics and gay life. She somehow manages to do all this without losing sight of her murder mystery.

When the sole lesbian member of a small Seattle printshop collective suggests a merger with a struggling lesbian typesetting firm called B. Violet, the casual bickering of the weekly meeting turns to tense confrontation. The confrontation escalates when the two groups meet. B. Violet's shop is later trashed in the night. That same night, a member of the Best Printing collective is murdered.

Narrator Pam Nilson, of Best Printing, plays amateur sleuth. (The police make few appearances in Wilson's mystery.) The author keeps her narrative eye on the members of the two collectives; on how they deal with each other, before and after murder. Pam also delves into the past and inner life of the victim, who turns out to be much more than a spacey guy who loved his Walkman.

Survivors of the Sixties may well enjoy this unusual mystery. Those offended by leftist politics or a lesbian love story will probably wish to avoid *Murder in the Collective* and the rest of the Pam Nilson mysteries planned by Barbara Wilson.

(*K.L.M.*)

Wilson, Colin. *The Schoolgirl Murder Case.* New York: Crown, 1974. (PP)

Colin Wilson's output over the past three decades has been extremely varied; in addition to crime and mainstream novels, he has produced biographies, essays, plays, and various nonfiction studies on such subjects as the occult, sexuality, writing, crime, and psychology. Wilson has described his aim in his work as developing a type of "new existentialism," and while *The Schoolgirl Murder Case,* the latest of his five crime novels, is a good example of the contemporary British police procedural, it also reflects the attitudes and ideas displayed in his more unconventional works.

Chief Superintendent Gregory Saltfleet of Scotland Yard is called to a crime scene in a Hampstead garden, where a schoolgirl has been raped and strangled with a telephone cord. Upon examination of the body, it becomes apparent she has been moved to the site from wherever the murder occurred. Saltfleet wonders about the nearby Victorian house belonging to a Lady Edgton, who is away in Ireland, but there is no legal means of gaining access. Investigation of the premises must wait, he decides, until the owner can be contacted.

Saltfleet goes about his careful routine, attempting to identify the dead girl; but when the results of the postmortem are reported, it seems his efforts have been in the wrong direction: The victim is no schoolgirl, but a woman in her mid-twenties, in all likelihood a prostitute who specialized in dressing up for her clients. The line of inquiry now leads to Lady Edgton's nephew, writer Manfred Lytton, who periodically uses the library in the house near the crime scene. Lytton has been away for some days, and the woman at his home, who claims to be his housekeeper but is probably also a call girl, is nervous about something.

When the police finally gain access to the Edgton house, they find she has good reason for her disquiet: Lytton is lying dead in a bedroom, and the clothing that the dead prostitute probably wore to the house is in another room. The postmortem confirms that Lytton was murdered, and Saltfleet theorizes that the woman was killed to cover up this fact. His investigation now takes him into the world of high-priced (and not so high-priced) call girls; of black magic (which Lytton was mixed up in) and pornographic books. And by the time he is finished, he has seen a dark underside of London that few citizens or policemen ever encounter.

Wilson plots well, his procedure is solid, and Gregory Saltfleet is a pleasant, low-key character whose occasional philosophic reflections give this novel quite some depth. Wilson's other crime stories are very different from this one: *Ritual in the Dark* (1960), *Necessary Doubt* (1964), *The Glass Cage: An Unconventional Detective Story* (1967), and *The Killer* (1970).

(*M.M.*)

Wilson, Dana. *Make with the Brains, Pierre.* New York: Julian Messner, 1946. (PS)

Despite having one of crime fiction's worst and most misleading titles, *Make with the Brains, Pierre* is neither a bad nor a whimsical nor a detective novel. Rather, it is a grim tale of psychological suspense, reminiscent of the work of Cornell Woolrich (q.v.) in its incisive examination of a man destroyed by love, hate, and the dark side of his own soul.

The narrator, Pierre Bernet, is a French film cutter who came to Hollywood before the Nazi take-over of his country and who is now, five years later, out of work, disillusioned, and trapped between two cultures. As the book opens, he waits to be shot down by two unidentified men lurking outside his apartment building; we are not told why—only that he accepts his fate, in fact welcomes it, and that he has apparently committed some frightful act that warrants it. Through flashback, we gradually learn about his relationships with Eleanor, the young film extra he worships; Jerry, his best friend; Joe Sherman, the married film technician whom Eleanor desperately loves; Sherman's blowsy French wife; Fred Marshall, a rich man with strange and evil hobbies; and the box-office stars Roger Niven and Marjorie Dean, who are in the midst of a messy divorce action. But it is not externals so much as Pierre's complex internal makeup that leads him along the twisting pathway to murder and self-destruction.

This is Wilson's only novel—a surprising accomplishment in its evocation of the Gallic character, the postwar Hollywood life-style, and the elements of human tragedy. (And if that isn't enough to convince you to seek it out, perhaps the following jacket quote by Dorothy Kilgallen will suffice: "I could not put it down. I *had* to know what that thing in the bathtub was!")

(*B.P.*)

*Wodehouse, P. G. *Wodehouse on Crime.* New York: Ticknor & Fields, 1981. (C/SS)

P. G. Wodehouse, who wrote almost 100 novels and hundreds of short stories, was once called "the best living writer of English." True or not, he was certainly one of the foremost humorists in any language. The world he created in a career spanning seventy-some years was one entirely his own, where his genius allowed time to advance only until about 1927 and froze it there in crystalline tranquillity, even in his last book, which he was working on when he died in 1975 at the age of ninety-three. His is a large and friendly world, full of joy and wit, inviting constant visits and always rewarding. There would seem to be no place for crime in this idyllic public-schoolboy realm—and indeed, although Wodehouse was a lifelong mystery fan, he seldom wrote of matters criminous. Only a few of his short stories can be classified as mysteries, and none of his novels (though some of them do have mild criminous elements).

The stories in *Wodehouse on Crime* (edited by D. R. Bensen) are, then, rarities—and first-rate rarities at that. These "Dozen Tales of Fiendish Cunning" feature the various members of the Wodehouse ménage—Bertie and Jeeves; Mr. Mulliner's nephews; the ineffable Ukridge; the inmates of Blandings Castle; and the negligible intelligences of the Drones Club. "Strychnine in the Soup" concerns a missing mystery novel and the lengths to which a mystery-story addict will go to finish reading a book. The lawlessness in "Crime Wave at Blandings" has to do with a niece who resembles a dewy rose and boys with air guns. Bertie Wooster and Jeeves rally round the unfortunate mutt, Bingo Little, in "The Purity of the Turf" as a "ferret-faced egg with not a few pimples" attempts to nobble the favorites in the Choir Boys Handicap and the Egg and Spoon Race. One of the few detectives in Wodehouse's world is found in "The Smile that Wins": Adrian Mulliner, who thwarts villains and snaffles an overfed old bohunkus by following his doctor's prescription.

As good as these selections are, perhaps a couple of other stories should have been included. Wodehouse's only true mystery, "Death at the Excelsior," is one; although it's a very early tale (1914) and not one of his best, it does have a clever locked-room-murder gimmick, with a unique weapon. Another omission is "The Amazing Hat Mystery." But why quibble? *Wodehouse on Crime* is a nostalgic delight as is, a book—like all of Wodehouse's work—to make you smile and to lift your spirits. Medicine for melancholy. (*T.B./B.P.*)

*Wood, Ted. *Dead in the Water.* New York: Scribner's, 1983. (PP/T)

Reid Bennett is a Vietnam veteran who knows how to take care of himself. He has a trained German shepherd named Sam who is not only good company but as good as any man when there's trouble. The burghers of the village of Murphy's Harbour, Ontario, thought Bennett—who had left the Toronto police force because he couldn't stand the publicity after he killed two rapists with his bare hands—had the makings of a good one-man police force, and Bennett was ready for some rest. Reasoning that "nothing violent ever happens here," he took the job.

But he was wrong. In two tough, exciting novels (so far), Murphy's Harbour has become something like the murder capital of North America, and Reid Bennett has faced a bloodcurdling array of villains without a bit of competent human help. He's got Sam, though, and man and dog are among the most memorable characters in current suspense fiction.

In *Dead in the Water,* a Murphy's Harbour man has taken two visitors from Manhattan out in his small boat. The boat is found empty. Two of the men are dead, and the third is missing.

Bennett learns that the missing man, Dr. Derek Pardoe, is a top chemist who had engaged the boat for some sort of clandestine meeting. The dead Manhattanite was his bodyguard. Bennett doesn't think that reputable chemists hire bodyguards who get killed, and he is convinced that narcotics are at the heart of this case. But he doesn't know anything else. Is Pardoe a killer, or another victim? Who was the chemist supposed to meet, and about what?

Bennett finds himself in a struggle for his life, but he doesn't know who he's fighting or what the stakes are until the end. The only friends he has are Sam and Murphy, a crippled World War II veteran who helps Bennett at the office and whose chief talent seems to be delivering bad news.

Ted Wood is a former Toronto police officer who knows police procedure and combat techniques, but who also has a keen feeling for the loneliness and the pressure of a policeman's life. *Dead in the Water* is a polished, entertaining first novel. It was the 1983 winner of the Scribner Crime Novel Award, and was followed in 1984 by *Murder on Ice,* which deals with the kidnapping of a winter-carnival beauty queen. The second book is as intense and absorbing as the first, but contains much more graphic violence and may not appeal to everyone who enjoys the earlier work. The same is true of the third book in the series, *Live Bait* (1985).

(*M.J.*)

Woods, Sara. *The Bloody Book of Law.* New York: St. Martin's, 1984. (AD)

Sara Woods is considered Canada's foremost detective novelist, even though her books are set in England and strongly influenced by the British mystery tradition. Her plots are tightly constructed and always play fair with the reader, allowing him to detect along with her lawyer hero, Antony Maitland. Her courtroom scenes are particularly good and more firmly grounded in reality than those of Erle Stanley Gardner (q.v.), whose Perry Mason engaged in stunning (and hardly believable) legal pyrotechnics. Woods's legal knowledge was acquired during World War II, when she worked in a London solicitor's office.

The one factor that keeps her numerous fans returning for each successive novel is probably Antony Maitland himself, and his warm, domestic circle of supporting characters—wife Jenny; uncle Sir Nicholas Harding, who owns the house where the Maitlands lie in London's Kempenfeldt Square and occupies the downstairs flat; and in later titles, Uncle Nick's wife, fellow barrister Vera Langhorne, whom the confirmed bachelor has finally married. Antony is in chambers with his uncle (meaning he works for Harding's law firm), and the older man provides a perfect foil for him, always questioning his nephew's rash actions and sudden intuitions, counseling caution at every turn—usually with very few results. Add to this family group close friends Meg and Roger Farrell and Chief Inspector Sykes, and Antony has a large and sympathetic sounding board for his ruminations on the puzzling legal problems he runs across.

The problem this time is a young free-lance journalist, Vince Gilchrist, who has been accused of burglarizing the home of family friends while they were away dining with Vince's mother. Valuable jewelry has been taken, and Vince has been picked out of an "identification parade" (lineup) as having been outside their home at the time of the crime. The police have a strong case because Vince was convicted of a similar burglary, also of family friends while they were dining with his older brother and sister-in-law. But Vince has a large number of explanations for how he came to be arrested twice for crimes he didn't commit—and Antony thinks they might be true, so he goes around and interviews the burglary victims and members of the Gilchrist family.

It is not until a "retired" burglar named Ned Bates owns up to the crime that Antony has any success with his investigation. But once the case against Vince is dismissed, Bates recants his story; Antony's old nemesis, Chief Superintendent Briggs (the mere mention of Briggs's name is enough to make Antony stutter, as he habitually does when angry), is talking about filing charges of interfering with a witness and bribery. Then Vince Gilchrist is shot to death, Briggs begins to talk about adding murder charges to the list, and Anthony must use all his investigative acumen to get himself out of one of the biggest fixes of his career.

This is a slow-moving book, in which very little seems to happen for quite a while; but the cast of characters at Kempenfeldt Square are in top form, and fans of courtroom mysteries will relish watching Antony extricate himself from this particular problem.

(*M.M.*)

Woods, Sara. *Though I Know She Lies.* New York: Holt, 1965. (AD)

The trial of a beautiful woman, Barbara Wentworth, who is accused of murdering her older sister, has put Sir Nicholas Harding on the spot. Barbara looks guilty; Harding's associate, Derek Stringer, is very unprofessionally falling in love with the accused woman; and Uncle Nick, although he hates to admit it, is very much in need of nephew Antony Maitland's special investigative talents. "You're inviting me to meddle?" Antony asks, employing with no small satisfaction his uncle's favorite word for his detecting. "I'm *asking* you to interfere," Uncle Nick replies.

With such official sanction, Antony begins to probe into Barbara Wentworth's life and the circumstances surrounding the murder of her sister, Laura Canning. The prosecution claims Barbara gave Laura an overdose of a sedative; her motive allegedly was money, a dispute over their father's estate. The circumstantial case is strong, and Antony has very little time. He begins with Barbara herself, finding her stunningly attractive, direct, and given to sudden mood shifts. The information she gives him leads to the exclusive Knightsbridge fashion salon where she worked; to her flat and her two roommates; and—indirectly—to being attacked by a pair of assailants armed with sand-filled cardboard tubes.

Between investigative forays, Antony sits in on the court proceedings. The case for the prosecution looks strong, but as the Crown attempts to prove her guilt, a letter comes to Sir Nicholas, written in a childish hand: "she didn't she didn't she didn't." *Someone* has faith in Barbara's innocence, and Antony is certain it is Clare Canning, Laura's daughter, now living with her father and his new wife in Wood Green. If he can talk to Clare, perhaps he will discover a new lead. But Clare's father and his wife won't allow that. Clare has been deeply disturbed by the murder, and the Cannings only want what's best for her. . . .

This is one of the more engrossing novels in the Maitland series, full of interesting characters, multiple secrets, and the usual charm of the Maitland ménage (although one of the more appealing members, Vera, has yet to join it, this being before she and Uncle Nick tie the knot). Although talky and containing scant action (as in all of Woods's novels), the characters and tight plotting go a long way to make up for those deficiencies.

Other recommended novels about Maitland and family are *Let's Choose Executors* (1967), *Yet She Must Die* (1974), *Exit Murderer* (1978), *Dearest Enemy* (1981), and *An Obscure Grave* (1985).

(*M.M.*)

*Woolrich, Cornell. *The Bride Wore Black*. New York: Simon & Schuster, 1940. (PS)

Woolrich was the greatest writer of pure suspense fiction who ever lived. He was the Poe of the twentieth century and the poet of its shadows, carving out of his wretched, doom-haunted, solitary life a body of work so grotesquely powerful that a category had to be invented to describe it. That category is *noir,* and Woolrich's novels and short stories of suspense, almost all of them written in a fifteen-year burst of creativity between 1934 and 1948, form the cornerstones of *noir* literature and its cinematic offshoot, *film noir.*

At the end of the 1930s, after several years of writing shorter crime fiction for the pulp magazines, Woolrich made the transition to hardcover crime novels. If one doesn't count the *noir* classic *Manhattan Love Song* (1932), which was published as a mainstream title but would be called suspense fiction today, *The Bride Wore Black* was Woolrich's first full-length work in the crime field. Its leitmotif is the avenging angel: Julie Killeen's husband is killed on the church steps moments after their marriage; and in a ritual substitution of deathmaking for lovemaking, she devotes the rest of her life to tracking down and systematically murdering the drunk driver and his four cronies whom she holds responsible.

Woolrich divides the book into five free-standing episodes, each built around a three-step dance. First a chapter showing Julie, each time in a new persona, preparing the trap for her current target; then the execution, with each victim being ensnared in his own romantic image of the perfect woman; finally a segment dealing with Wanger, the homicide detective who's stalking the huntress through the years. At last in part 5 they meet, and Julie learns that, like the men she killed, she too has been victimized by a perverse, malignant, and unknowable power; that a bizarre tangle of coincidence has ruined her precisely as she in turn ruined her prey, for no reason whatsoever.

Woolrich's style in *The Bride Wore Black* is unusually objective and emotionless, and the book lacks the great heart-in-the-throat set pieces of later novels. What makes it stand out is its perfect balance of sympathy among its characters. No one surpasses Woolrich at portraying how the death of a loved one affects the survivor and at making us empathize with the atrocities the survivor commits after the love dies. Multiple murderess and psychotic though Julie is, we are forced to see the world as she sees it. But likewise Woolrich is unbeatable at making us empathize with people whose lives are torn apart by malign forces they can't comprehend, and so we must also stand in the shoes of each of Julie's targets. In the Wanger chapters, we get to understand how things look to the one who's hunting the hunter. And at the climax we see how Woolrich himself views the world and the dark powers above the world that crush us at their whim.

(*F.M.N.*)

*Woolrich, Cornell. *The Black Curtain.* New York: Simon & Schuster, 1941. (PS)

Woolrich's second suspense novel opens on May 10, 1941, as part of a moldering building falls on a man as he walks along a crowded city street. And like the beam that fell on Mr. Flitcraft in the parable Dashiell Hammett's (q.v.) Sam Spade tells in *The Maltese Falcon,* this act of blind chance alters the man's life forever. The blow restores Frank Townsend's memory after three and a half years' amnesia, and he begins the slow process of getting to know his wife again and picking up the threads of his former existence. For most writers that would have been the end of a story, but for Woolrich it was the beginning. There's a phantom from Townsend's interim identity that is out to destroy him, and soon Townsend becomes obsessed with finding out who and what he was during the lost years. He finds love, hate, and a murder charge waiting for him behind the curtain.

The premise of *The Black Curtain* is tailor-made for Woolrich, and in the first two sections of the novel he evokes with desperate *noir* urgency the feeling of being without an identity and hunted by unseen forces. Woolrich plunges us so deeply into his protagonist's anguish that we ignore the absurd prerequisites of the plot (for example, that Townsend was carrying not a scrap of identification at the time of either the first or the second blow). In the novel's third section, when he has to resolve the nightmare, Woolrich loses his way and rigs a complicated hair's-breadth cliff-hanger climax with roots in his pulp fast-action whizbangs of the 1930s. The closing chapters lack the intensity of the earlier parts of the book and leave all sorts of questions naggingly unanswered; but like almost everything Woolrich wrote, these pages, too, are all but impossible to lay down unread.

Faulty it may be, but *The Black Curtain* is surely one of the best suspense novels ever written on the overworked theme of amnesia. It was filmed in 1942 as *Street of Chance,* with Burgess Meredith as the man searching for his past, but by far the best adaptation of the novel was the half-hour radio version broadcast on "Suspense" in 1943 with Cary Grant as Townsend. The radio play drastically altered and improved Woolrich's story line but kept true to its bleak spirit, and the result was a *noir* classic of the first order.

(*F.M.N.*)

*Woolrich, Cornell. *The Black Angel.* New York: Doubleday Crime Club, 1943. (PS)

Woolrich's fourth novel in the so-called Black series is one of the most wrenching and bizarre works in the canon. Written in first person from the viewpoint of a woman, *The Black Angel* deals with a terrified young wife's race against time to prove that her husband, convicted and sentenced to die for the murder of his mistress, is innocent and that one of the several other men in the dead woman's life is guilty. Her strategy is much like that of Julie in *The Bride Wore Black:* Adopting a new persona for each operation, she invades the lives of a number of emotionally vulnerable men—a Bowery derelict, a drug-pushing doctor, a Park Avenue socialite, and a gangster—and destroys each of them, innocent and culpable alike. Woolrich makes us feel her love and anguish, her terror and desperation, the obsessions that grow to madness inside her as she ruins others and herself to get her man back from Mr. Death.

The roots of *The Black Angel* extend deep into Woolrich's past as a writer and a man. The basic story line is a kind of extension from his early *noir* novel *Manhattan Love Song* (1932), with further borrowings from his pulp stories "Murder in Wax" (1935) and "Face Work" (1937). The destroying-angel motif was one of Woolrich's favorites, but instead of the calm objective style of *The Bride Wore Black,* this time his approach was subjective and extremely emotional. And since in *The Black Angel* we know from the first chapter what forces are driving the woman protagonist, we can both empathize with her and shudder at what she's doing throughout the length of the book.

It was an immensely successful novel, quickly adapted into a radio play for "Suspense" and then a few years later into a movie. *Black Angel* (1946), starring June Vincent, Dan Duryea, Broderick Crawford, and Peter Lorre, changed much of Woolrich's plot but stayed true to his spirit. This classic *film noir* was directed by British-born Roy William Neill, who had also made most of the great Sherlock Holmes pictures with Basil Rathbone and Nigel Bruce.

Woolrich's other novels under his own name include *Black Alibi* (1943), *The Black Path of Fear* (1944), *Rendezvous in Black* (1948), and the paperback originals *Savage Bride* (1950) and *Death Is My Dancing Partner* (1959). He also wrote as William Irish (q.v.).

(*F.M.N.*)

Wormser, Richard. *The Invader.* Greenwich, Conn.: Fawcett Gold Medal. 1972. (O/T)

Richard Wormser is known both for his westerns—he won a WWA Spur Award for *Ride a Northbound Horse* (1964)—and for an impressive group of mystery and suspense novels, most of them paperback originals. The best of his criminous works is *The Invader,* which blends facets of the two genres expertly into an unusual combination of contemporary western, suspense novel, and Mafia novel, and earned an MWA Edgar for Best Paperback of 1972.

Ken Craigie is sheriff of New Mexico's Santa Ynez County, a rugged rural area patrolled by Craigie's four deputies, who put a thousand miles a day on the three cruisers and jeep that comprise the county fleet. When Mafia front man Dan Dominick buys land holdings in Santa Ynez and starts to turn the old Angel Ranch into a fortress, Craigie finds himself challenged for control of the county. Wormser draws the two opposing forces in stark detail: the slick, urbane Mafia leader and his group of enforcers pitted against the dedicated, savvy western sheriff and his deputies. The result is a suspenseful, violent novel distinguished by strong characterization and plot and a vividly portrayed background.

Among Wormser's other novels are *The Man with the Wax Face* (1934) and *The Communist's Corpse* (1935), two early mysteries featuring the off-beat detective team of New York police sergeant Joe Dixon and a tall, ungainly, and very radical Swedish fireball named Erika Strindberg; a tale of suspense, *The Hanging Heiress* (1949); two softcover mysteries narrated by a not-very-likable small-town California cop named Andy Bastian—*Drive East on 66* (1961) and *A Nice Girl Like You* (1965); and another Mafia novel, *The Takeover* (1971).

(*G.K./B.P.*)

Wren, M. K. *Nothing's Certain but Death.* New York: Doubleday Crime Club, 1978. (W)

M. K. Wren must really hate the Internal Revenue Service, and it is her prejudice that makes this novel really satisfying. The victim is a tax auditor, Eliot Nye. Before his murder, Nye claimed that restaurateur Brian Talley of the seaside town of Holliday Beach, Oregon, owed some $50,000 in back taxes. Talley is the logical suspect, but before he is even arrested he gets in his licks against the IRS: "They take your money *before* you owe it—and that's just out-and-out confiscation—and never pay a damn cent of interest. . . . They don't pay any interest on *your* money, but they damn sure collect it when they think it's *their* money."

Right on, Mr. Talley. From that moment to the very last turn of the page, the reader is rooting for you, even if you should turn out to be guilty as sin!

The person who witnesses Talley's tirade is Conan Flagg, bookstore owner and sometimes private investigator. And at Talley's insistence, he accepts a valuable ring as retainer to hunt down the person who knocked the tax collector unconscious and framed Talley by freezing Nye to death in the restaurant's food locker. The problem is a thorny one, because before Nye died he traced Talley's initials in his own blood on the freezer door. And though there are suspects aplenty—a down-at-the-heels real-estate broker, a dope-dealer janitor, two temperamental chefs, and the mysterious individual who tipped the IRS to audit Talley—there is no getting around those bloody letters.

Flagg investigates, leaving his bookshop in the capable hands of his assistant, Miss Dobie, and the bookstore cat, Meg. He is abetted in his efforts by friend Steve Travers of the state police, and hindered by Holliday Beach police chief Earl Kleber. And as the plot unfolds, so do the characters of the principal suspects—as well as the charming personality of this small seaside village.

Unfortunately, there's not much plot to unfold. It's a very predictable solution; and the clues, while well-placed, are pretty old-hat. *However*—in spite of the fact that an astute reader will figure out the murderer's identity before page 50—the characters are well drawn and the setting attractive.

Other titles in the appealing Conan Flagg series include *Curiosity Didn't Kill the Cat,* (1973); *A Multitude of Sins,* (1975); *Oh, Bury Me Not,* (1976); and *Seasons of Death,* (1981).

(*M.M.*)

Wylie, Philip. *The Murderer Invisible.* New York: Farrar & Rinehart, 1931. (T)

Drawing upon H. G. Wells's classic *The Invisible Man,* but adding touches of his own, Philip Wylie wrote a book that anticipated many of the most popular elements of pulp fiction of the 1930s and 1940s. Supervillains of magazines like *Doctor Death* owe much to Professor William Carpenter, self-proclaimed possessor of "the greatest mind in the world today, one of the greatest since civilization began." This scientific genius hates mankind because all of his life his ungainly appearance has drawn derision. When he is cheated in the stock market, he becomes a recluse and uses a quarter of a million dollars (at 1930 prices) of his remaining fortune to set up a laboratory that is equipped "for every conceivable type of work in chemistry, biology, physics, metallurgy, and surgery." His object: to make himself invisible and gain revenge on society.

The Murderer Invisible opens as a Gothic, with the appearance of the professor's lovely, penniless foster niece. He offers her work and gradually comes to love her in a Beauty and the Beast relationship. On hand to try to thwart Carpenter's efforts is the prototype of the pulp hero, Bromwell Baxter, who was a football star, war hero, and mountain climber, besides being a superb scientist. Baxter has the money, physical prowess, and daring of his successors—the Shadow, Doc Savage, and the Spider.

The rural New Jersey location of Carpenter's laboratory and mansion, where he frightens his unsophisticated neighbors, proves an effective setting as Carpenter completes his experiments. From there he launches a campaign to murder those who bilked him in the market, and bring the world under his dominion. Explosions, blackouts, floods, and robberies are easy when one cannot be seen. New York is in an uproar, and Carpenter is delivering ultimatums to the president and the entire world. Only his niece and Baxter, as his former employees, know enough about his method to hope to stop him.

Anthony Boucher, the preeminent critic, invented the category he called the "great bad book," one such as *The Insidious Dr. Fu Manchu,* which is so outrageous in its plot, characters and purple prose that it proves to be a joy to read. Philip Wylie's blend of mystery and science fiction is just such a book. We love its anachronisms (a heroine who curses by saying "Apple sauce!" and a hero who apologizes when he says "Damn"). The pace is lightning-fast, and the melodramatic plot draws us on in spite of its improbabilities. This is truly one of the greatest of all the bad books.

Wylie's other mysteries are much more conventional, but still entertaining. *Corpses at Indian Stones* (1943) is a nicely done whodunit about intrigue and buried treasure at an upstate New York resort, and features an engaging amateur sleuth named Agamemnon Telemachus Plum. *Three to Be Read* (1951) contains a trio of interesting novellas, two of which—"Experiment in Crime," a mystery about a pedantic young college professor given to stuffy lectures on the stupidity of criminals; and "The Smuggled Atom Bomb," a spy story—were published separately as full-length books by both Avon and Lancer.

(*M.L.*)

Wyllie, John. *The Long Dark Night of Baron Samedi.* New York: Doubleday Crime Club, 1981. (AD)

John Wyllie has written several novels featuring black African doctor Samuel Quarshie and his wife, Prudence. Quarshie, who took his medical degree at McGill University in Canada, has a considerable reputation as an investigator in his home country of Akhana; and it is this talent that causes him great difficulty while on holiday on the Ile de Sintra off southwest Africa's Ebony Coast. It is an unpleasant place for a holiday, a former slave depot where the "aura left behind by hundreds of years of human torture and degradation . . . had soured the island itself." Quarshie is there only as a favor to his friend Judge Kwame Oturu, who is writing a book on slavery and needs Quarshie's fluency in English, plus his medical knowledge, to complete the project. But when the head of GES (les Gardiens de l'Etat Souverain), President Darapa's personal police, is found murdered in the old barracoon (the building used to house the slaves prior to transit), the doctor's investigative skills are demanded by the president himself.

Quarshie dislikes the Ile de Sintra, and he loathes President Darapa and Gambion, the capital city, seeing "the whole place as a monstrous example of hypocrisy, with [Darapa] on the top of the heap, where he was kept in place by French investment, French military power, and French advisors." But he agrees to aid in the investigation because Darapa threatens his wife and friend if he doesn't.

The investigation proceeds slowly, with Quarshie gathering facts during long conversations over beers. The dead man, Kofi Akasaydoo, was found butchered on the flogging block in the barracoon; beneath him was a voodoo symbol. He had been with a woman shortly before his death, and was seen leaving the house where he was staying on the island around three in the morning, presumably for a rendezvous with his killer. Akasaydoo is rumored to have been on the outs with Darapa; and from the evidence at his apartment, he appears to have had exotic sexual preferences. Among his effects at the barracoon are a piece of paper with notes on the mineral corundum (aluminum oxide) and a doctor's prescription. A torn cloakroom ticket seems to have some importance; someone has searched Akasaydoo's apartment, perhaps looking for what was secreted in the unknown cloakroom. Among the scores of people who would want to harm him is a young woman who openly admits she was living with Akasaydoo with the intention of killing him.

Before Quarshie can put all these facts into any logical order, the judge is kidnapped and brought to the barracoon. When Quarshie attempts to rescue him, he is confronted by a cold-blooded killer who warns of dire consequences if Quarshie does not solve the case. But before he accomplishes this, tragedy strikes and Quarshie is afraid he and his wife will never see their homeland again.

This is a slow-paced but well-plotted story that incorporates fascinating background material on racial and political issues in Africa, as well as on African voodoo. Other adventures of the likable Dr. Quarshie include *Skull Still Bone* (1975), *Death Is a Drum . . . Beating Forever* (1977), and *A Tiger in Red Weather* (1980).

(*M.M.*)

Wynne, Anthony. *The Case of the Gold Coins.* Philadelphia: Lippincott, 1934. (AD)

Anthony Wynne (Robert McNair Wilson) was one of the lesser Golden Age writers—the creator of Dr. Eustace Hailey, a Harley Street specialist in mental disease who once offered the following opinion: "The really interesting crimes are those . . . in which the method employed, as well as the motive, constitutes a puzzle." Method is indeed the most interesting element in Wynne's mysteries: No less than sixteen of his twenty-eight novels feature an "impossible crime" of one type or another (most often the use of an "invisible agency" to murder someone in closed or guarded surroundings). Some of his "impossibles" are quite ingenious—*The Case of the Gold Coins,* for instance.

In this case Hailey's assistance is solicited by Captain Jack Ainger of the CID to investigate the strange death of Lord Wallace in a remote section of Northumberland. Wallace's body was found in the middle of a wide expanse of beach near his home, badly battered and bruised, with a knife driven into his back. The location of the wound and bloodstains found under the corpse prove that he died on the spot. Yet there are no footprints in the sand for many yards in any direction and no way either the murderer or the sea could have erased any. A thrown knife is out; that still wouldn't explain the absence of footprints. Also out are the possibilities of the body having been dropped from an airplane or hurled by a catapult or by bodily force.

Dr. Hailey sets about questioning the suspects: Lady Wallace, the sister-in-law of the murdered man; Ruth Wallace, the lord's niece; Colonel Bolton, a neighbor and old enemy of Wallace's; the colonel's daughter, Pamela; Wallace's solicitor, Giles; and one of the local squires, Peter Ingram, who was engaged to Ruth but is now in love with Pamela. Don't be misled, though: This is no actionless house-party drama; there is a good deal of skulking around in the night, two more murders, a couple of close shaves for Dr. Hailey (one of which involves sailboats and an unexpected predawn swim), eerie doings on a little offshore island, more intrigue centered on an old flour mill near the Wallace estate, and a hidden treasure of gold sovereigns.

All the elements are here for a dandy novel. Unfortunately, Wynne's handling of them results in "rather heavy melodrama," as Howard Haycraft termed his work. Wynne wrote well, but in a solemn, reserved, curiously detached manner, as if he were unable to involve himself in his narrative. And Hailey is something of a colorless and plodding sleuth, whose only distinct character traits are taking snuff and "drawing his hand across his brow," both of which he does constantly.

Still, the explanation of how Lord Wallace was murdered is worthy of John Dickson Carr (q.v.)—although one facet of it is a little hard to swallow—and alone makes the novel worth reading. The same is true of such other Hailey investigations as *The Green Knife* (1932), in which there are three locked-room murders by stabbing; *The Toll House Mystery* (1935), in which a murdered man is found shut up alone in a closed car surrounded by untrodden snow; and *Emergency Exit* (1941), about a stabbing in an air-raid shelter surrounded by unmarked snow. Also interesting is the lone Dr. Hailey short-story collection, *Sinners Go Secretly* (1928), which contains two "impossibles." If you enjoy this type of mystery, don't pass these up. Despite their flaws, Wynne's puzzles will keep you guessing and absorbed throughout.

(*B.P.*)

Yarbro, Chelsea Quinn. *Ogilvie, Tallant & Moon.* New York: Putnam's, 1976. (AD)

Chelsea Quinn Yarbro is best known for her work in the horror and science-fiction genres, but she has published two mysteries about San Francisco lawyer Charles Spotted Moon, an Ojibwa Indian. In this first case, Moon is hired by a friend, physician Miranda Trobridge, who is being sued for malpractice. One of Miranda's patients, a young boy with Parkinson's disease, has died; his parents suspect a mercy killing. There are rumors that Miranda aided another patient in ending prolonged suffering, and the clinic where she works offers no support, eventually trying to fire her in spite of an ironclad contract.

Attention focuses on the clinic when Charlie finds a dead man in its parking lot. The victim, a drug salesman, has taken a massive dose of anticoagulants and died a particularly horrible and grotesque death. The situation continues to deteriorate when it is publicly revealed that Miranda did indeed aid in the first mercy killing. Amid pressures from his law partners, who regard this as a hopeless and unpopular case, as well as pressures from the clinic and his client (who is falling apart under the strain), Charlie doggedly investigates. And when he begins to suspect that the death of the drug salesman and the death of Miranda's young patient are somehow linked, he employs a unique method to get to the bottom of it.

Charlie Moon is an interesting character, but there is a curious flatness to him; often we feel we are looking *at* him rather than through his eyes. Yarbro does use his Indian background to good effect in her plot, and the novel is well written; but the murderer is introduced to the reader far too late in the story, thus making the ending less believable than it otherwise might have been.

Yarbro's second Moon novel, the wonderfully titled *Music when Sweet Voices Die* (1979), has an opera background—a milieu that the author, who is also a composer, knows well.

(*M.M.*)

Yates, Dornford. *Blind Corner.* New York: Minton, 1927. (A/T)

The so-called clubland heroes of British crime fiction flourished between the wars, offering the reading public a steady stream of adventures in which a young man sets out with a group of wealthy friends (always male) to right wrongs and bring villains to justice. The major examples of this type of hero were probably H. C. McNeile's Bulldog Drummond, John Buchan's (q.v.) Richard Hannay, and Dornford Yates's Jonah Mansel and Richard Chandos, though each used other characters as well.

Yates's best novel, *Blind Corner,* told in the first person by young Chandos, opens with his coming upon a murder while motoring back from a French holiday. The dying man entrusts his pet dog to Chandos's care, and hidden inside the dog's collar is the secret of a great treasure worth almost a million pounds. Accompanied by his friends Jonah Mansel and George Hanbury (and their three manservants), he sets off for the Castle of Wagensburg in Austria to find the treasure and steal it from "Rose" Noble and his sinister gang.

In a sequel, *Perishable Goods* (1928), Noble gets his revenge by kidnapping the wife of Jonah's cousin. Both books are good examples of British upper-class reading between the wars, and it's a mark of Yates's skill that they still have the ability to entertain. Attention should also be called to a later Yates novel, *She Fell Among Thieves* (1935), which is preferred by some critics.

(*E.D.H.*)

Yorke, Margaret. *Devil's Work.* New York: St. Martin's, 1982. (T)

Margaret Yorke spent the early years of her career writing what she calls "problem novels"—stories of crisis and conflict within a family group. In 1970, however, she turned to crime writing with *Dead in the Morning,* a novel of conventional detection featuring Patrick Grant, a "literary don" who bears great similarity to other erudite detectives prevalent in the suspense field. It was not until she broke away from this series character and published her first novel of psychological suspense—*No Medals for the Major* (1974)—that Yorke found her métier, and since then she has produced a number of finely crafted stories of ordinary people caught up in extraordinary situations. Yorke plots well, but her primary emphasis is on character, and in *Devil's Work* she is in top form.

As the book opens, we meet Alan Parker, an out-of-work salesman nearing fifty, the kind of man who "tried every day to make some other road user happy by yielding way when it was not mandatory." Alan has been unemployed for some weeks now, but has not as yet gotten up the courage to tell his wife, Daphne, about his dismissal. With time on his hands, he prowls the streets of the small city of Berbridge, England, and eventually befriends a little girl, Tessa Waring. Their friendship leads to a friendship with Tessa's mother, Louise, a widow subject to nervous attacks. Alan attempts to lighten Louise's burden, as does Tessa, a spunky kid who at the tender age of seven takes a kind of responsibility for her mother that most children don't face until their teens. But Tessa is vulnerable, too, and her trust in a seemingly harmless neighbor leads to her kidnapping. And Alan, who is fast falling in love with Louise, finds himself caught up in a web of lies of his own making.

Yorke's characters are developed in great complexity, and the plot is nicely multileveled, too. On the surface is the kidnapping, but just below is the disintegration of a decades-old marriage, the feelings of failure of an out-of-work professional man, and the insecurities of an overburdened and psychologically abused young mother. Add to that the psychotic neighbor who wants to pull off this snatch for twisted reasons of her own and you have an exciting thriller.

Some of Yorke's other engrossing novels of psychological suspense are

The Small Hours in the Morning (1975), *The Scent of Fear* (1980), *The Hand of Death* (1981), *The Smooth Face of Evil* (1984), and *Intimate Kill* (1985). (*K.K.H.*)

Zackel, Fred. *Cocaine and Blue Eyes.* New York: Coward, McCann, 1978. (PI)

San Francisco PI Michael Brennan meets Joey Crawford in a truck stop over a Christmas Eve breakfast and agrees to give the young man a ride home. Along the way Crawford finds out that Brennan is a PI and hires him to find his "old lady," who left him. At first Brennan refuses, but when Crawford shows up dead by New Year's Eve, and Brennan receives a note—"Find Dani for me,"—and a thousand dollars from the dead man in the mail, he decides to look into the matter.

The case leads him to Pacific Heights and a wealthy family that made its money in fish and is less than anxious for the missing girl to turn up. The girl's huge blue eyes and her ultimate involvement with Crawford and cocaine provided the title, which is probably one of the best PI titles in recent years. Unfortunately, the book is not one of the best PI novels in recent years, although it is well written—in a style very much reminiscent of Ross Macdonald's (q.v.) early work. Macdonald, in fact, praised *Cocaine and Blue Eyes* highly in a dust-jacket quote, perhaps because it is such a conscious pastiche.

Zackel, who apparently has a flair for titles, followed this debut with a second Brennan novel, *Cinderella after Midnight* (1980). *Cocaine and Blue Eyes* was filmed for TV in 1982 with O. J. Simpson, curiously enough, playing Brennan, who in the novels is white.

(*R.J.R.*)

**Zangwill, Israel. *The Big Bow Mystery.* New York: Rand McNally, 1895. (CS/W)

British novelist and playwright Israel Zangwill made only one excursion into the mystery field, at the age of twenty-seven, when he was invited by the *London Star* to write a "more original piece of fiction" for them. The result, which ran serially in the newspaper during 1891, was certainly original—the first locked-room mystery novella.

There had been locked-room mysteries before, in the works of Edgar Allan Poe (q.v.) and Joseph Sheridan LeFanu, but both had involved elementary trickery with windows and the reader had no real opportunity to solve the puzzle. *The Big Bow Mystery,* written partly as a parody of detective stories, is a classic whodunit that still reads quite well today. Whether or not retired police inspector Grodman can really qualify as a Classic Sleuth may be open to question, but from the moment he is summoned by Mrs. Drabdumb to break down the locked door of Arthur Constant's bedroom, it is clear we are witnessing the birth of a classic mystery situation.

John Dickson Carr (q.v.) once observed that Israel Zangwill invented a fictional device that has since been used in many forms, "on a ship, in a ruined house, in a conservatory, in an attic, and even in the open air." But Zangwill's first version still remains one of the best, and rightly established him as the father of the locked-room mystery. Scores of later mystery writers were intrigued by the plot possibilities suggested by Zangwill's work, and went on to create endless variations on the locked room and the impossible crime.

Running just over 30,000 words in length, about half as long as the average mystery novel today, *The Big Bow Mystery* has rarely been published as a separate volume in this century. It appears in Zangwill's 1903 collection *The Grey Wig*. More recently it was included in Hans Stefan Santesson's 1968 anthology *The Locked Room Reader* (Random House) and David Willis McCullough's 1984 anthology *Great Detectives* (Pantheon).

(*E.D.H.*)

Zaremba, Eve. *A Reason to Kill.* Markham, Ontario: PaperJacks, 1978. (O/PI)

Even Zaremba's first mystery surely represents one of the more unusual experiments with the female hard-boiled private eye. First of all, her heroine, Helen Keremos, is a Canadian. Second, she is a lesbian. But if the locale of Zaremba's mystery is obvious, the sexual identification of her sleuth is not. Since Zaremba refrains from chronicling the amorous adventures of her detective, it is only her empathy with male gay characters and occasional name-calling by disgruntled straight men that give her sexual identity away.

Keremos, who operates out of a second-floor walk-up in Vancouver's Chinatown, is called in by an academic to trace his missing son, last seen in Toronto. With the help of a researcher friend named Alex, Keremos checks out the young man's past as well as his friends and family—all suspects. These include his sculptor mother and her drunken lover; a boyhood friend and his masculinity-obsessed father; and an appealing bisexual hood on the edge of Toronto's entertainment biz. Keremos concludes that Martin Milwell's disappearance is somehow linked to his recent acknowledgment of his homosexuality, but she must still discover the how and why of his disappearance.

The plot, which seems to be building to an obvious solution, has several twists to deliver before its unusual conclusion—one that turns the classic reenactment of the crime into an exercise in collective decision-making.

Keremos's cross-Canada trek tells us much about the country and its people as well.

Tough, a navy veteran with plenty of street smarts, Keremos is nonetheless a sympathetic figure. When she takes on two thugs (after a few too many drinks), we may question the realism in the portrayal, but Keremos's macho antics are mild compared to most of her male fictional counterparts.

The politics of Zaremba's novel, sexual and otherwise, is clearly recognizable as part of the Seventies. For her portrayal of a believable PI, hard-boiled and female, Zaremba should be recognized as an early entry in a mystery trend of the Eighties—and very probably beyond.

(*K.L.M.*)

Zochert, Donald. *Murder in the Hellfire Club.* New York: Holt, 1978. (H/AD)

It has been the vogue in recent years for writers to use genuine historical figures as characters in their novels. Detective-story writers are no exception; numerous mysteries have appeared in which real people now deceased have played roles from the cameo walk-on to major speaking parts to the wearing of the hero's mantle. But only one such historical figure (so far) has twice been made the detective hero by two different authors—and in both cases, challenged to solve a locked-room murder. That figure is Benjamin Franklin—"printer, postmaster, diplomat, scientist, inventor, wit, raconteur, editor, spy, philosopher"—and the two novels, published nearly twenty years apart, are Theodore Mathieson's *The Devil and Ben Franklin* (1961), set in Philadelphia in 1734; and *Murder in the Hellfire Club,* which takes place in London in 1757. Zochert's novel is by far the better of the two, by virtue of historical accuracy, erudition, style ("The morning light was tinged with ocher, such as aborigines use to coat the eyelids of the dead"), wit, and—yes—a much better locked-room gambit.

Franklin, accompanied by his son, Peter, has come to London to "bring the light of reason to the brothers Penn in their management of the Pennsylvania proprietorship." While enjoying an evening of slumming and good wine with two of his old cronies in the Vulture Tavern, Franklin is approached by Francis Dashwood, "a jolly dog . . . [who] thinks to call himself a priest of learning [but] surrounds himself with women who pray with their knees upwards." Dashwood is the leader of a private club of sybarites, which he calls the Society of St. Francis but which others refer to as a reestablishment of the outlawed Hellfire Club. In any case, someone appears to be so offended by the Franciscans, as Dashwood tells Franklin in a private audience the following morning, that he has sent an anonymous verse threatening to dispatch all thirteen "souls unsaved."

This is no idle threat, for the first victim has already been claimed: John

Raleigh, poet and pornographer, who has been found dead in a sealed room at the Vulture Tavern, with no apparent marks of violence upon his body. Dashwood wants Franklin, whose great reputation has preceded him to England, to investigate. Which "Dr. Fatsides" does, pronouncing Raleigh's death, when he has viewed the scene, "a very pretty puzzle." Other murders follow, one of them equally as ingenious as Raleigh's, and Franklin has a devil of a time (pun intended) before his wits, keen observation, and knowledge of certain scientific principles of the period bring about the surprising solution to the crimes. (Hint for connoisseurs: The answer to the locked-room puzzle has to do with a mousehole.)

This is a beautifully crafted novel, rich in the language and atmosphere of the period, spiced with sly and bawdy humor—a cerebral mystery that should delight armchair detectives, locked-room aficionados (John Dickson Carr [q.v.] would have heartily approved of Zochert's ingenuity), and anyone who likes his sleuthing done in a period setting.

Donald Zochert's subsequent crime novels have been about as different from *Murder at the Hellfire Club* as it is possible to get: a pair of hard-boiled thrillers featuring complex private eye Nick Caine—*Another Weeping Woman* (1980) and *The Man of Glass* (1981). These are smoothly written stories, but one can't help wishing for an encore performance by "Dr. Fatsides"—or at least some other challenging period "impossible."

(*B.P.*)

BIBLIOGRAPHY

REFERENCE BOOKS

Adey, Robert. *Locked Room Murders.* London: Ferrett, 1979.

Barzun, Jacques, and Wendell Hertig Taylor. *A Catalogue of Crime.* New York: Harper, 1971.

Brooks, Tim, and Erle Marsh. *The Complete Directory to Prime Time Network TV Shows, 1946–Present.* New York: Ballantine, 1979.

Burack, A. S., ed. *Writing Detective and Mystery Fiction.* Boston: The Writer, 1967.

Dunning, John. *Tune in Yesterday: The Ultimate Encyclopedia of Old-Time Radio,* 1925–1976. Englewood Cliffs, N.J.: Prentice-Hall, 1976.

Everson, William K. *The Detective in Film.* Secaucus, N.J.: Citadel, 1972.

Halliwell, Leslie. *Halliwell's Film Guide.* 2d ed. New York: Scribner's, 1979.

Haycraft, Howard. *Murder for Pleasure: The Life and Times of the Detective Story.* New York: Appleton, 1941.

Hubin, Allen J. *The Bibliography of Crime Fiction, 1749–1980.* New York: Garland, 1984.

McCormick, Donald. *Who's Who in Spy Fiction.* New York: Taplinger, 1977.

Nieminski, John. *EQMM 350: Author/Title Index to Ellery Queen's Mystery Magazine, Fall 1941 through January 1973.* White Bear Lake, Minn.: The Armchair Detective Press, 1974.

Nolan, William F. *Hammett: A Life at the Edge.* New York: Congdon & Weed, 1983.

Pronzini, Bill, ed. *The Arbor House Treasury of Detective and Mystery Stories from the Great Pulps.* New York: Arbor House, 1983.

———. *Gun in Cheek.* New York: Coward, McCann, 1983.

Queen, Ellery. *The Detective Short Story*. Boston: Little, Brown, 1942.

Reilly, John M., ed. *Twentieth Century Crime and Mystery Writers*. New York: St. Martin's, 1980.

Scheuer, Steven. *Movies on TV* (various editions). New York: Bantam, 1973–83.

Steinbrunner, Chris, and Otto Penzler. *Encyclopedia of Mystery and Detection*. New York: McGraw-Hill, 1976.

Symons, Julian. *Mortal Consequences: A History from the Detective Story to the Crime Novel*. New York: Harper, 1972.

Wells, Carolyn. *The Technique of the Mystery Story*. Springfield, Mass.: The Home Correspondence School, 1913.

Zinman, David. *Saturday Afternoon at the Bijou*. New York: Arlington House, 1973.

MAGAZINES

The Armchair Detective. Various issues, 1967–84.

Ellery Queen's Mystery Magazine. Various issues, 1941–84.
Manhunt. April 1953.

CONTRIBUTORS

BRINEY, ROBERT E. Professor and Department Chairman, Computer Science Department, Salem State College, Salem, Mass. Editor: *Master of Villainy: A Biography of Sax Rohmer* (1972). Contributing Editor: *Encyclopedia of Mystery and Detection* (1976), *Encyclopedia of Frontier and Western Fiction* (1983). Contributor to *Twentieth Century Crime and Mystery Writers, Twentieth Century Science Fiction Writers, Twentieth Century Western Writers.* Member of Editorial Board, "The Collection of Mystery Classics," Bantam Books (1985).

BAIRD, THOMAS. Pseudonym of professional writer of numerous nonfiction books and articles. Member of Baker Street Irregulars. Aficionado of detective and mystery fiction.

COLLINS, MAX ALLAN. Author of sixteen novels in the mystery/suspense field. Author (with James L. Traylor) of *One Lonely Knight:* Mickey Spillane's Mike Hammer (1984), a critical study of the work of Mickey Spillane. Editor of *Tomorrow I Die* (1984), a collection of Spillane's shorter works. Since 1977, sole writer of the internationally syndicated "Dick Tracy" comic strip. Creator (with artist Terry Beatty) of the "Ms. Tree" comics feature.

CRIDER, BILL. Chairman of Department of English, Alvin Community College, Alvin, Tex. Author of one mystery novel. Coauthor (with Jack Davis) of *The Coyote Connection* (Nick Carter series). Contributor to *The Dictionary of Literary Biography, Twentieth Century Crime and Mystery Writers, The Armchair Detective,* and other periodicals. Collector and aficionado of old paperback crime novels.

DUNLAP, NEWELL. Free-lance writer and book reviewer. Former editor of a business newsletter; has also worked in the fields of photography, filmmaking, and cartooning.

DUNLAP, SUSAN. Author of six mystery/suspense novels. Member of Mystery Writers of America. Aficionado of contemporary American crime fiction.

FRANCIS, BETTY. Business executive, armchair detective, and collector of crime fiction.

GORMAN, ED. President of midwestern advertising agency. Author of 200 articles and short stories, and four novels (1985–86). Aficionado and collector of crime fiction.

HOCH, EDWARD D. Author of more than 650 short stories and five novels. Editor of *Best Detective Stories of the Year* and *The Year's Best Mystery and Suspense Stories.* Past president of Mystery Writers of America.

HOPE, KAROL KAY. Free-lance writer and reviewer. Author of the nonfiction works *MOMMA, The Sourcebook for Single Mothers* (1976) and *Out of the Frying Pan: A Decade of Change in Women's Lives* (1979).

JOHNSON, MARK. Journalist and reviewer of crime fiction for the San Jose *Mercury-News.*

KELLEY, GEORGE. Professor of Business, Erie County Community College, Erie County, New York. Contributor to *Twentieth Century Crime and Mystery Writers, Twentieth Century Science Fiction Writers, Twentieth Century Western Writers.*

LACHMAN, MARVIN. Coauthor and Senior Editor of *Encyclopedia of Mystery and Detection* (1976; MWA Edgar-winner). Coauthor and coeditor of *Detectionary* (1971). Author of numerous articles and book reviews for *The Armchair Detective* and other periodicals, including his own magazine devoted to mystery and detective fiction, *Just in Crime.* Contributor to *Twentieth Century Crime and Mystery Writers.*

LUTZ, JOHN. Author of eleven suspense and detective novels, and 150 criminous short stories. Book reviewer for *St. Louis Globe-Democrat.*

MAIO, KATHLEEN L. Librarian and free-lance writer. Reviewer for "Murder in Print" column of *Wilson Library Bulletin.* Book editor and mystery critic for *Sojourner: A Women's Forum.* Contributor to *Twentieth Century Crime and Mystery Writers* and *American Women Writers: A Critical Reference Guide.*

MALZBERG, BARRY N. Author of more than seventy-five novels, a score of them in the suspense field. Coeditor of fifteen anthologies of crime, fantasy, and science fiction. Recipient of the John W. Campbell Memorial Award for the Best Science Fiction Novel of 1972, *Beyond Apollo.* Contributor of numerous articles, essays, and book reviews to various magazines.

MATTES, KATE. Owner of Murder Under Cover (also known as Kate's Mystery Books), Cambridge, Mass. Book reviewer for *Boston Observer.*

NEHR, ELLEN. Aficionado and collector of crime fiction. Contributor to *Twentieth Century Crime and Mystery Writers* (revised edition).

NEVINS, FRANCIS M., JR. Professor of Law at St. Louis University. Author of two mystery novels and forty short stories and novelettes of crime and suspense. Author of *Royal Bloodline: Ellery Queen, Author and Detective* (1974; MWA Edgar-winner). Author of dozens of articles and book reviews dealing with crime fiction for the *New Republic, The Armchair Detective, Journal of Popular Culture,* the *St. Louis Globe-Democrat,* and other publications.

RANDISI, ROBERT J. Author of six criminous novels, scores of western novels, and numerous short stories, articles, and book reviews. Founder of the Private Eye Writers of America (PWA). Editor of *The Eyes Have It* (1984), the first annual PWA anthology.

SCOTT, ART. Research chemist. Aficionado and collector of crime fiction. Editor of *Elementary, My Dear APA,* bimonthly collection of mystery-fan magazines, and publisher of his own magazine, *Shot Scott's Rap Sheet,* for the series. Contributor to *Twentieth Century Crime and Mystery Writers.*

SHIBUK, CHARLES. Coauthor and Senior Editor of *Encyclopedia of Mystery and Detective* (1976; MWA Edgar-winner). Coauthor and coeditor of *Detectionary* (1971). Contributor to *Twentieth Century Crime and Mystery Writers.* Contributor of numerous columns and book reviews to *The Armchair Detective* and other publications.

SMITH, JULIE. Author of three mystery/suspense novels and numerous short stories. Book reviewer for the *San Francisco Chronicle* and *San Jose Mercury-News.* Regional Vice-President of Mystery Writers of America.

SYMONS, TONI. Bookseller and aficionado of crime fiction.

TAYLOR, BRUCE. Owner of San Francisco Mystery Books. Aficionado and collector of crime fiction.

TRAYLOR, JAMES L. Coauthor (with Max Allan Collins) of *One Lonely Knight: Mickey Spillane's Mike Hammer* (1984). Editor of *Hollywood Troubleshooter: W. T. Ballard's Bill Lennox Stories* (1985). Contributor of articles on crime fiction to *The Armchair Detective* and other publications, and of book reviews to the *Atlanta Constitution.*